Encyclopedia of
COMMUNITY

Encyclopedia of COMMUNITY

From the Village to the Virtual World

Karen Christensen & David Levinson
general editors

VOLUME
1

A Sage Reference Publication

SAGE Publications
International Educational and Professional Publisher
Thousand Oaks ▪ London ▪ New Delhi

Cover image: Barn raising at Gould Farm in Monterey, Massachusetts.
© Robert Lazzarini; used by permission.

For information:

Sage Publications, Inc.
2455 Teller Road
Thousand Oaks, California 91320
E-mail: order@sagepub.com

Sage Publications Ltd.
6 Bonhill Street
London EC2A 4PU
United Kingdom

Sage Publications India Pvt. Ltd.
B-42 Panchsheel Enclave
Post Box 4109
New Delhi 110017
India

Printed in the United States of America

Library of Congress Cataloging-in-Publication Data

Main entry under title:

The encyclopedia of community: From the village to the virtual world / Karen Christensen and David Levinson, editors.
p. cm.
A Sage reference publication.
Includes bibliographical references and index.
ISBN 0–7619–2598–8

1. Community-Encyclopedias. I. Christensen, Karen, 1957- II. Levinson, David, 1947-

HM756.E53 2003
307.'03—dc21

2003009119

03 04 05 06 07 10 9 8 7 6 5 4 3 2 1

Berkshire Publishing Staff

Project Directors	Karen Christensen and David Levinson
Project Coordinator	George Woodward
Associate Editor	Marcy Ross
Senior Copy Editor	Francesca Forrest
Copy Editors	Ann Farkas, Mindy Keskinen, Frank Mann, Mike Nichols, Suzanne Noel, Glenn Perkins, Mark Siemens
Information Management and Programming	Cathy Fracasse, Deborah Dillon, Trevor Young
Editorial Assistance	Sarah Conrick, Emily Cotton, Elizabeth Eno, Junhee Kim

Sage Publications Staff

Acquiring Editor:	Rolf A. Janke
Editorial Assistant:	Sara Tauber
Production Assistant:	Patricia Zeman
Permissions Editor:	Karen Wiley
Typesetter:	Tim Giesen/Straight Line Design
Indexer:	Mary Mortensen
Cover Designer:	Ravi Balasuriya
Production Artists:	Michelle Lee, Sandra Ng Sauvajot

Contents

List of Entries, *vii*

List of Sidebars, *xiii*

Reader's Guide, *xix*

Contributors, *xxv*

Introduction, *xxxi*

Acknowledgments, *xliii*

About the Editors, *xlvii*

Entries

VOLUME I: A-D
1–420

VOLUME II: E-L
421–888

VOLUME III: M-S
889–1368

VOLUME IV: T-Z
1369–1833

Appendix 1: Resource Guides, *1497*

Appendix 2: Libraries Build Community, *1533*

Appendix 3: Community in Popular Culture, *1553*

Appendix 4: Master Bibliography of Community, *1611*

Index, *1735*

GENERAL EDITORS

Karen Christensen
David Levinson
Berkshire Publishing Group

EDITORS FOR SPECIFIC TOPICS

Robin Jarrett (Human Development)
University of Illinois at Urbana–Champaign

Dennis Judd (Urban Studies)
University of Illinois at Chicago

William Metcalf (Intentional Communities)
Griffith University

Roberta Moudry (Community Design)
Cornell University

Ray Oldenburg (Social Life)
University of West Florida

Sonya Salamon (Rural Studies)
University of Illinois at Urbana–Champaign

Thomas Sander (Social Capital)
Saguaro Seminar, Harvard University

Michael Shuman (Community Economics)
Green Policy Institute

Barry Wellman (Internet and Communities)
University of Toronto

Michael Zuckerman (Historical Communities)
University of Pennsylvania

List of Entries

Activist Communities
Adolescence
Adolescents and Landscape
African American Communities
African Americans in Suburbia
Age Integration
Age Stratification and the Elderly
Agoras
Agrarian Communities
Agrarian Myth
Agricultural Scale and Community Quality
Alienation
Alinsky, Saul
Altruism
Amana
Amish
Anarchism
Apartheid
Appalachia
Architecture, Vernacular. *See* Vernacular Architecture
Arcosanti
Aristotle
Artists' Colonies
Arts. *See* Community Arts
Ashrams
Asian American Communities
Asset-Based Community Development
Assimilation
Asylum
Attachment. *See* Community Attachment
Auroville
Avatar Communities

Bankruptcy
Bars and Pubs
Barter
Bedroom Communities
Beguine Communities
Birth
Black Economy
Blockbusting
Blogs
Book Clubs and Reading Groups
Boomtowns
Boosterism
Boundaries
Bruderhof
Buddhism
Burgess, Ernest Watson
Burning Man

Calvin, John
Caste
Cattle Towns
Celebration, Florida
Chain Stores
Charisma
Chautauqua
Chernobyl
Child Care
Children
Chinatowns
Christianity
Citation Communities
Cities
Cities, Inner
Cities, Medieval
Citizen Participation and Training
Citizenship
Civic Agriculture
Civic Engagement. *See* Community Building; Community Organizing; Collective Action; Local Politics; Social Capital; Town Meetings
Civic Innovation
Civic Journalism
Civic Life
Civic Structure
Civil Disobedience
Civil Society
Civility. *See* Incivilities Thesis
Class, Social
Cocooning
Cohousing
Collective Action
Collective Consumption
Collective Efficacy
Colleges
Colonialism
Columbia, Maryland
Common Law
Communications Technologies
Communism and Socialism
Communitarianism
Communities of Opposition
Communities of Practice
Community. *See* Introduction; Civic Life; Communitarianism; Social Capital
Community, Sense of
Community Action
Community Arts
Community Attachment
Community Building
Community Colleges
Community Currencies
Community Development Corporations
Community Development in Europe
Community Empowerment
Community Garden Movement
Community Health Systems

Community in Disaster
Community Indicators
Community Informatics and Development
Community Justice
Community Land Trust
Community Mental Health Centers
Community Organizing
Community Ownership
Community Policing
Community Psychology
Community Satisfaction
Community Schools
Community Service. *See* National and Community Service
Community Studies
Community Supported Agriculture
Computers and Knowledge Sharing
Condominiums
Conflict Resolution
Conflict Theory
Conformity
Confucianism
Congregations, Religious
Congrès Internationaux d'Architecture Moderne
Consumer Culture
Conviviality. *See* Bars and Pubs; Festivals
Cooperative Extension System
Cooperative Parish Ministries
Cooperatives. *See* Community Currencies; Community Ownership; Student Housing Cooperatives
Corporate Social Responsibility
Counterfeit Communities
County Fairs
Crime
Crowds
Cults
Cultural Ecology
Culture of Poverty
Currencies. *See* Community Currencies
Cybercafes
Cyberdating
Cybersocieties
Cyborg Communities

Damanhur
Dance and Drill
Death
Decentralization
Declining Communities
Democracy
Development. *See* Economic Planning; Environmental Planning; Sustainable Development
Deviance
Diasporas
Digital Divide
Disabled in Communities
Displaced Populations
Durkheim, Émile

Economic Planning
Ecovillages
Edge Cities
Education. *See* Colleges; Communities of Practice; Community Colleges; Home Schooling; Intentional Communities and Children; Online Communities of Learning; School Consolidation; Schools
Elder Care and Housing
Elderly in Communities
Electronic Democracy
Electronic Government and Civics
E-Mail
Emissaries of Divine Light
Empathy
Enclosure
English Parishes
Entrepreneurship
Environmental Justice
Environmental Planning
Ephrata
Ethnicity and Ethnic Relations
Eugenics
European Community
Export-Led Development in Regional Economies

Faith Communities
Family, The
Family and Work
Family Violence
Farm, The
Fascism
Feminism
Festivals
Films. *See* Appendix 3: Community in Popular Culture
Findhorn Foundation Community
Food
Food Systems
Fourierism
Fraternities and Sororities
Free Rider
Friendship

Gangs
Garden Cities
Gated Communities
Gay Communities
Geddes, Patrick
Gemeinschaft and Gesellschaft
Gender Roles
Genocide
Gentrification
Gentrification, Stalled
Ghettos
Ghost Towns
Global Cities
Globalization and Globalization Theory
Glocalization
Goffman, Erving
Good Society
Grassroots Leadership
Greenbelt Towns
Greenwich Village
Growth Machine
Guanxi

Hare Krishnas
Harlem
Harmony Society
Hate
Healing
Healthy Communities
Hierarchy of Needs
Hinduism
Hollywood
Home Schooling
Homelessness
Homesteading
HOPE VI
Horticultural Societies
Hospices
Household Structure
Housing
Housing, Affordable
Howard, Ebenezer
Human Development
Human Rights
Hutterites

Immigrant Communities
Imperialism
Import-Replacing Development
Incivilities Thesis
Indicators. *See* Community Indicators
Individualism
Industrial Revolution
Informal Economy
Information Communities
Information Overload
Initiation Rites
Instant Messaging
Institutionalization
Intentional Communities
Intentional Communities and Children
Intentional Communities and Communal Economics
Intentional Communities and Daily Life
Intentional Communities and Environmental Sustainability
Intentional Communities and Governance
Intentional Communities and Mainstream Politics
Intentional Communities and New Religious Movements
Intentional Communities and Their Survival
Intentional Communities in Australia and New Zealand
Intentional Communities in Eastern Europe and Russia
Intentional Communities in France
Intentional Communities in Germany, Austria, and Switzerland
Intentional Communities in India
Intentional Communities in Israel—Current Movement
Intentional Communities in Israel—History
Intentional Communities in Italy, Spain, and Portugal
Intentional Communities in Japan
Intentional Communities in Latin America
Intentional Communities in Scandinavia and the Low Countries
Intentional Communities in the United Kingdom and Ireland
Intentional Communities in the United States and Canada—Current Movement
Intentional Communities in the United States and Canada—History
Interest Groups
Internet, Domestic Life and
Internet, Effects of
Internet, Social Psychology of
Internet, Survey Research About
Internet, Teen Use of
Internet, Time Use and
Internet in Developing Countries
Internet in East Asia
Internet in Europe
Islam
Island Communities

Jacobs, Jane
Jealousy
Jerusalem
Judaism
Justice. *See* Community Justice; Environmental Justice; Social Justice

Kinship

Labor Markets
Labor Unions
Land Use and Zoning
Las Vegas
Latino Communities
Le Bon, Gustave
Leadership
Left Bank
Levittown
Liberalism
Libertarianism
Liminality
Literature. *See* Appendix 3: Community in Popular Culture
Little Italies
Local Manufacturing
Local Politics
Loneliness
Love
Lower East Side
Luddism
Lynd, Helen Merrell and Robert Staughton
Main Street
Malls. *See* Shopping Centers and Malls
Manufacturing. *See* Globalization and Globalization Theory; Local Manufacturing
Markets, Street
Marriage
Mass Society
McDonaldization
Mead, George Herbert
Men's Groups
Merchant Communities
Migrant Worker Communities
Military Communities
Mill Towns
Millenarianism
Mining Towns
Mobile Home Communities
Model Cities
Modernity. *See* Globalization and Globalization Theory
Monastic Communities
Moravians
Morgan, Arthur E.
Mormons
Moses, Robert
Multiculturalism
Multiplier
Mumford, Lewis
Music

National and Community Service
National Community
Native American Communities
Natural Law
Neighborhood Unit Concept
Neighborhood Watch
Neighborhoods
Neighboring
Network Communities
New Harmony
New Towns
New Urbanism
Newsgroups and E-Mail Lists
Nonmonetary Economy
Nonprofit Organizations

Olmsted, Frederick Law
Olmsted Brothers
Oneida
Online Communities, African American
Online Communities, Communication in
Online Communities, Computerized Tools for

Online Communities, Diasporic
Online Communities, Game-Playing
Online Communities, History of
Online Communities, Religious
Online Communities, Scholarly
Online Communities, Youth
Online Communities of Learning
Organizational Culture
Organized Crime
Osho
Out-Migration of Youth
Owen, Robert

Park, Robert Ezra
Pastoral Societies
Patriotism
Peer Groups
Personalization and Technology
Pilgrimages
Place Identity
Plant Closures
Plantations
Pluralism
Polis
Political Economy
Popular Culture. *See* Appendix 3: Community in Popular Culture
Populism
Poverty. *See* Social Capital, Impact in Wealthy and Poor Communities; Rural Poverty and Family Well-Being
Pressure Groups
Prisons
Privacy
Progressive Era
Public Aid
Public Goods
Public Harassment
Public Health. *See* Community Health Systems; Community Mental Health Systems; Healthy Communities; Social Services
Public Libraries
Public Opinion
Puritans

Quakers

Race and Racism
Radburn, New Jersey
Railroad Towns
Ranching Communities
Rebellions and Revolutions
Recreation
Redfield, Robert
Refugee Communities
Regional Planning Association of America
Regionalism
Regulation
Religion. *See* Buddhism; Christianity; Cults; Faith Communities; Hinduism; Islam; Judaism; Mormons; Pilgrimages; Quakers; Sikhism
Religion and Civil Society
Resettlement
Residential Mobility
Resource-Dependent Communities
Revolution. *See* Rebellions and Revolutions
Rituals
Riverside Community
Rural Community Development
Rural Poverty and Family Well-Being

Sacred Places
Salons
Schmalenbach, Herman
School Consolidation
Schools
Scientology
Seasonal Homes
Secret Societies
Sectarianism
Semiotics
Service Learning
Shakers
Shantytowns
Shared Work
Shopping Centers and Malls
Shtetls
Siedlung
Sikhism
Silicon Valley
Simmel, Georg
Six Degrees of Separation. *See* Small World Phenomenon; Ties, Weak and Strong
Small Towns
Small World Phenomenon
Smart Growth
Social Capital
Social Capital, Benefits of
Social Capital, Downside of
Social Capital, Impact in Wealthy and Poor Communities
Social Capital, Trends in
Social Capital, Types of
Social Capital and Economic Development
Social Capital and Human Capital
Social Capital and Media
Social Capital in the Workplace
Social Control
Social Darwinism
Social Distance
Social Justice
Social Movements
Social Movements Online
Social Network Analysis
Social Services
Socialism. *See* Communism and Socialism
Sociolinguistics
Sport
Sprawl
Stakeholder
State, The
Stein, Clarence S.
Street Life
Student Housing Cooperatives
Subsidies
Suburbanization
Suburbia
Sustainable Development
Systems Theory

Technology. *See* Communications Technologies
Telecommuting
Theme Parks
Third Places
Ties, Weak and Strong
Tocqueville, Alexis de
Tönnies, Ferdinand
Total Institutions
Tourist Communities
Town and Gown
Town and Hinterland Conflicts
Town Meetings
Tragedy of the Commons
Transcendentalism
Transnational Communities
Transportation, Rural
Transportation, Urban
Trust

Twelve Step Groups
Twin Oaks

Urban Homesteading
Urban Renewal
Urbanism
Urbanization
Utopia

Veblen, Thorstein
Vernacular Architecture
Vigilantism
Villages
Violence. *See* Conflict Resolution; Family Violence; Genocide
Virtual Communities
Virtual Communities, Building
Voluntary Associations
Volunteerism

Warsaw Ghetto
Waste Facility Siting
Watersheds
Wealth. *See* Class, Social; Gated Communities; Social Capital, Impact in Wealthy and Poor Communities
Weber, Max
Whyte, William Hollingsworth
Wired Communities
Wirth, Louis
Work. *See* Family and Work; Labor Markets; Migrant Worker Communities; Mill Towns; Mining Towns; Shared Work; Social Capital in the Workplace; Telecommuting
World War II

Xenophobia

Yamagishi Toyosato
Youth. *See* Gangs; Internet, Teens Use of; Out-migration of Youth
Youth Groups

ZEGG
Zoar
Zoning. *See* Land Use and Zoning

Appendix 1, Resource Guides, appears at the end of this volume as well as in Volume 4.

List of Sidebars

Activist Communities
Issues in the Twenty-First Century
Adolescence
An African Girl's Initiation Ceremony
African Americans in Suburbia
Modern Research Tools Help African Americans Trace Their Roots
Age Stratification and the Elderly
Age Grades
Agrarian Communities
Carloway Village, an Agrarian Community on the Isle of Lewis and Harris, Scotland
Sheep Keep Power Lines Clear of Vegetation
Agrarian Myth
Our Neighbors Gossip About Us—How Can We Stop This?
Agricultural Scale
Impact of Larger Farms
Alienation
What Does Alienation Mean?
Altruism
The Parable of the Good Samaritan (Luke 10:25–37, New King James Version)
Anarchism
Selection From Emma Goldman's Address to the Jury at her Anti-Conscription Trial, July 9, 1917
Apartheid
Preamble to the Constitution of South Africa (Adopted: May 8, 1996 / In Force: February 7, 1997)
Asian American Communities
Hmong in Minneapolis
Asset-Based Community Development
Combining Assets From Different Sources
Assimilation
English as a Second Language
Asylum
The Charter House
Auroville
Ram Dass on Auroville
Bankruptcy
The Ten Largest Bankruptcies in U.S. History (as of January 1, 2003)
Barter
Valuing Trade Goods
Black Economy
The Mafia and the Black Economy
Book Clubs and Reading Groups
The Popularity of Online Book Clubs
Boosterism
Boosterism in the Twenty-First Century
Buddhism
Punishment for Damaging the Sangha

Calvin, John
Selections From the *Ecclesiastical Ordinances*, by John Calvin (1541)
Caste
Caste in Indian Society
Chain Stores
Retail Pricing Matched to Community Income
Child Care
Child Care in West Africa
Children
Children at Play
Chinatowns
To Help Their Children
Christianity
The Biblical Basis for Community (From the King James Version)
Cities
Seattle Matches Citizen Effort With City Dollars
Cities, Inner
Financial Skills for Minority Residents
Citizen Participation and Training
A Definition of Citizenship
Citizenship
W. E. B. Du Bois on the Town Meeting and Democracy

Civic Agriculture
City Farming
Civic Life
Citizens Versus Industrial "Progress"
Civics "Boot Camp"
Civic Structure
Watershed Communities
Class, Social
The Hired Help
Cohousing
Saving Money Through Cohousing
Cohousing—The Ethnic Mix
Collective Action
Citizens Define a "Living Wage"
Colleges
Eton College
Colonialism
Indigenous and Colonial Forms of Administration
Communism and Socialism
Mao Zedong on Dealing with Counterrevolutionaries
Selection From *The Communist Manifesto* (1848), by Karl Marx and Friedrich Engels
Communitarianism
Democratic Communitarianism
Community, Sense of
The Need to Keep It Small
Community Action
A River Comes Clean
Community Arts
Arts Spark Downtown Revival
Community Building
Characteristics of a Healthy Community
Community Currencies
The Kula Ring
Community Development in Europe
Creating Social Cohesion in Europe
Community Empowerment
Selection From *The Quest for Community*
Community Garden Movement
Turning Vacant Lots Into Community Gardens
Community Health Systems
The Peckham Experiment
Community Justice
Communities Help Determine Justice
Community Organizing
Contract or Community, by Robert N. Bellah
Community Ownership
The Seikatsu Club Consumer's Co-Operative Union
Community Policing
Breaking Down Barriers Between Youth and Police
Community Satisfaction
The Church Supper
Community Schools
The Coalition for Community School's Key Principles of Community Schools
Conflict Theory
Feuding
Conformity
Adolescent Conformity
Congregations, Religious
Church and Friends
Consumer Culture
A World Without Money
Corporate Social Responsibility
Businesses Band Together to Aid in Child Care
Corporate Accountability as an International Issue
County Fairs
The Great Barrington, Massachusetts, Agricultural Fair in 1903
Crime
Laws of Old
Cults
The Cult of the Leader
Cultural Ecology
Using the Cultural Ecology Model to Explain Cultural Change
Culture of Poverty
Selection From Oscar Lewis's *La Vida* (1966)
Cybersocieties
Symptoms of Pathological Internet Use (PIU)

Death
Funerals and Social Status
Decentralization
The Fourteenth Amendment
Democracy
Jean-Jacques Rousseau on Democracy
Deviance
Correcting Deviant Behavior
Diasporas
Armenian American Political Issues and Parties
Digital Divide
The Digital Divide in the United States
Disabled in Communities
Special Help for Deaf Women and Children Who Are Abused

Economic Planning
Economic Goals
Elder Care and Housing
Community Support Helps Elderly Avoid Nursing Homes
Emissaries of Divine Light
EmNet—The Emissaries Online
English Parishes
The English Parish in George Eliot's *Middlemarch* (1871)
Entrepreneurship
The Ashanti Entrepreneur in Eighteenth-Century West Africa

The Rural Entrepreneur in Central Thailand
Environmental Planning
Berkshire Grown
Ethnicity and Ethnic Relations
Ethnic Identity in the Cuban American Community in West New York, New Jersey
Eugenics
Selection From Sir Francis Galton's *Hereditary Genius*

Fascism
Adolf Hitler Speaks
Extracts From the Manifesto of the National-European Communitarian Party
Festivals
New Year's Celebrations
Festivals and Work
Food
Cementing Social Ties
Food Systems
The Bear Hunt
Friendship
Encouraging Friendships Through Building Design

Gangs
Mark Twain on Gangs
Gangs in Chicago
Globalizing Gangs
Garden Cities
The Unexpected Results of the Vision for Garden Cities
Gay Communities
Group Helps Gay and Lesbian Retirement Issues
Geddes, Patrick
The Talents of Patrick Geddes
Gender Roles
Women Are Women and Men Are Men
Genocide
The Destruction of Indigenous Peoples
Ghettos
The Haitian-American Ghetto in Brooklyn, New York
Guanxi
English Manners, as Viewed by Jane Austen
Technology and Guanxi

Healing
Personal Growth Through Community
Healthy Communities
Horsens, Denmark—An Example of a Healthy Community Project
Hollywood
A Year in Hollywood
Home Schooling
Home Versus Public Schooling
Homesteading
Cooperative Homesteading in Laura Ingalls Wilder's *Little House on the Prairie*
Horticultural Societies
The Value of Land
Hospices
Hospices—In Life and Death
Household Structure
Forms of Marriage Arrangement
Housing
The Rewards of Building Affordable Housing
Human Development
Aggression Training on Taiwan
Hopi Chores

Immigrant Communities
Character Loans and the Establishment of the Cuban American Community in Miami
Imperialism
Imperialism and Religious Conversion
Individualism
Balancing Individual and Community Responsibilities
The Individual Reconsidered, by Robert N. Bellah
Informal Economy
Food Stamp Holders Shop at Farmers Markets
Information Overload
Community Newspapers Still Appeal to Readers
Initiation Rites
The Caco Chatiar Ceremony
Intentional Communities
Intentional Communities Organizations
Intentional Community Journals and Magazines
Intentional Communities and Children
Social Contexts of Nuclear Versus Communal Families
Intentional Communities and Communal Economics
Collective Cooking Returns to Neighborhoods in Canada
Living the Good Life
Intentional Communities and Environmental Sustainability
A Case Study in Sustainable Communal Living
Intentional Communities and Governance
Dealing With Power Issues
Intentional Communities in Eastern Europe and Russia
Virtual Visits to Intentional Communities in Russia and Eastern Europe
Intentional Communities in Germany, Austria, and Switzerland
Web Sites for Intentional Communities in Germany, Austria, and Switzerland
Intentional Communities in Japan
The Spirit of Atarashiki Mura
The Light of Oneness
Intentional Communities in the United Kingdom and Ireland
Songs of the Diggers

Intentional Communities in the United States and Canada—History
The Constitution of the Celo Community, Established in North Carolina in 1937
Internet, Effects of
Health Care Resources Reach Native Americans Via the Web
Internet, Social Psychology of
The HomeNet Study
Internet, Teen Use of
Providing Low-Cost Internet Access to Communities
Internet in Developing Countries
The Internet Creates a World Market for Recycled Goods
Internet in Europe
Arabianranta—A Virtual Village and Design Oasis
Island Communities
Tristan da Cunha

Judaism
The Tower of Babel

Kinship
Kin Ties in Highland Scotland
Kinship and Small-Town Life

Labor Markets
Saving Jobs
Labor Unions
Unions Open Door to Minorities
Land Use and Zoning
Burlington, Vermont Zoning Ordinance
Latino Communities
Latinas Working to Clean Up Environment
Liberalism
Selection From *A Letter Concerning Toleration,* by John Locke (1689)
Libertarianism
Libertarian Response to Communitarianism
Liminality
Liminality in Mexico
Little Italies
Italian Americans and Baseball
Local Manufacturing
Plant Recycles New York's Wastepaper Blizzard
Local Politics
The Town Hall as Community Territory
Loneliness
Isolation and Loneliness in Small Town America, by Edith Wharton
Love
Love, Sex, Marriage, Family and Community on Okinawa
Lower East Side
Selections from *The New York Pushcart: Recommendations of the Mayor's Commission*
Luddism
The Luddites in English Literature, by Charlotte Bronte

Marriage
The Ideal Wife
Three Ways of Making a Marriage
Men's Groups
Military Societies
Migrant Worker Communities
Migrant Laborers Seize the American Dream
Mill Towns
Renewal Out of the Ravages of a Steel Mill
Millenarianism
The Second Coming
Mining Towns
The Ugliness of Mining Communities
Monastic Communities
The Status of the Monk
Moravians
Moravian Missionaries Depart
Morgan, Arthur E.
Arthur Morgan on Why "Community Is Like Gold"
Mormons
Doctrine and Covenants, Section 59
Multiculturalism
What Do We Call Them?
Mumford, Lewis
Selection From Lewis Mumford's *The City in History*

National and Community Service
Selection From William James's "The Moral Equivalent of War"
National Community
Characters of Five Nations—Germany, England, France, Italy, and Spain
Neighborhood Watch
A Different Sort of Neighborhood Watch
Neighborhoods
American and British Ideas of Being Neighborly
New Towns
Selection From Ebenezer Howard's *Garden Cities of To-Morrow* (1902)
Nonprofit Organizations
IRS Classification of Tax-Exempt Organizations (1986 Tax Code)

Online Communities, African American
Online Community of Black Mathematicians
Online Communities, Youth
GenerationNet: Online Voice for Young People
Online Communities of Learning
Online Bidding System for College Courses
Out-Migration of Youth
Selection from *Sister Carrie* (1900), by Theodore Dreiser

Owen, Robert
Robert Owen on Community

Pastoral Societies
The Social Significance of Herd Animals in East Africa
Peer Groups
Teen Court
Pilgrimages
The Hajj (Muslim Pilgrimage to Mecca)
Place Identity
Place Identity, Ethnic Identity, and Assimilation
Pluralism
How to Limit Pluralism
Political Economy
Markets in Niger
Populism
Selection From the People's Party Platform of 1896
Privacy
Privacy, Strangers, and Life in Public
Progressive Era
Selection From *The Jungle,* by Upton Sinclair (1906)
Public Harassment
The Street Harassment Project
Public Libraries
A Place That Feels Like Home
Excerpt From the American Library Association's *Freedom to Read Statement*
Public Opinion
Ad Watches: Media Responsibility in Covering Ads
Puritans
A Nineteenth-Century View of the Puritans

Quakers
Persecution of the Quakers

Race and Racism
Canadian Prime Minister Mackenzie King on Asian Immigration in 1947
Ranching Communities
Ranching Families Return to Their Roots
Recreation
The Community Dance
Redfield, Robert
Robert Redfield on Community
Refugee Communities
Change Over Time and Generation in a Refugee Community
Religion and Civil Society
Selection from John Donne's "Devotions Upon Emergent Occasions" (1623)
Rituals
Hopi Ceremonial Rituals
Rural Community Development
Economic Woes of the Rural South

Salons
The Salon of Elizabeth at Urbino
School Consolidation
Community Schools Build Better Citizens
Schools
Community Involvement With Public Schools
Schools Reflect Community Values
Scientology
Selection From *The Founding Church of Scientology Washington, D.C., et al., v. United States of America*
Secret Societies
The Mani Society of the Azande of the Sudan
Sectarianism
Revelation 20 (King James Version)
Shakers
A British View of Shakers
Shared Work
An American Barn Raising: The Epitome of Social Capital
Shopping Centers and Malls
The Islamic Bazaar
Shtetls
Wealth and Poverty in the Shtetl
Sikhism
The Sikh Community in the United States After September 11th
Small Towns
A Gently Satirical Story of Life in a Sleepy Provincial English Town
Small World Phenomenon
The Small World Research Project
Social Capital
Walking the Civic Talk After September 11th
Social Capital, Benefits of
A Sad Day for the "Regulars"
Self-Sufficiency and Social Capital
Social Capital, Downside of
When Social Capital and Personal Development Collide
Social Capital, Trends in
Global Concepts of Modernity
Social Capital, Types of
Social Capital and Public Capital
The Women's Institute: A Model for Building Community
Social Capital and Economic Development
Bonding and Bridging in the Korean Community in Hawaii
Social Capital and Human Capital
Predictors of Academic Success
Social Capital in the Workplace
An Army of One
Social Control
Social Control in an Okinawan Village

Social Darwinism
Herbert Spencer on Progress
Social Distance
Durkheim on the Social Causes of Suicide
Social Justice
Social Justice in Early Twentieth-Century America
Social Services
Social Services in a Multicultural World
Sociolinguistics
The Cajuns as a Linguistic Community
Sprawl
Spawl and Nature
State, The
Selection From *The Quest for Community*
Suburbanization
The Mall as Suburbia's Version of City Streets
Suburbia
One Urbanite's Opinion of Suburbia
Sustainable Development
Sustainability and GNP

Telecommuting
Working Productively at Home
Theme Parks
Smithsonian Theme Park
Third Places
Where Everybody Knows Your Name
Ties, Weak and Strong
Maintaining a Sense of Ethnic Identity in Multicultural America
Tocqueville, Alexis de
Selection From Tocqueville's *Democracy in America*
Total Institutions
Social Distance and Hierarchy in Total Institutions
Town Meetings
Rules and Regulations for Better Maintaining Order in Town Meetings
Tragedy of the Commons
Individual Property and Community Blight
Transcendentalism
Selection from "New England Reformers," by Ralph Waldo Emerson (1844)
Selection from Henry David Thoreau's *Wild Fruits* (1860)
Transnational Communities
What the Basques Say About Maintaining Ties to the Homeland
Transportation, Rural
Rural Transportation Program Matches Drivers and Riders
Transportation, Urban
Using Home Zones to Control Traffic
Twelve Step Groups
The Twelve Steps of Alcoholics Anonymous

Urbanism
The West Bow Lawnmarket, Edinburgh

Veblen, Thorstein
Thorstein Veblen on the Leisure Class
Villages
Selection From Mark Twain's *The Adventures of Tom Sawyer* (1876)
Kingsthorpe in Northamptonshire, England
Virtual Communities
What Is The WELL?
Voluntary Associations
Men, Women, and Voluntary Associations
Volunteerism
Employer-Sponsored Volunteering

World War II
Mrs. Miniver

Reader's Guide

This list is provided to assist readers in locating entries on related topics. It classifies articles into twenty general categories: Activism and Social Transformation; Biographies; Communities, Affinity; Communities: Case Studies; Communities, Instrumental; Communities, Intentional; Communities, Primordial; Communities, Proximate; Community Design; Economics; Global Studies; Human Development; Internet and Communities; Politics and Law; Processes and Institutions; Religion; Rural Life; Social Capital; Social Life; and Urban and Suburban Life. Some entry titles appear in more than one category.

ACTIVISM AND SOCIAL TRANSFORMATION

Activist Communities
Alinsky, Saul
Altruism
Appendix 1—Resource Guides: Community Organizing and Activism
Appendix 1—Resource Guides: Volunteerism
Appendix 2—Libraries: Community Organizations and Action Groups
Appendix 2—Libraries: Voting and Elections
Blockbusting
Civic Agriculture
Civic Innovation
Civic Journalism
Civil Disobedience
Collective Action
Communities of Opposition
Community Action
Community Building
Community Development Corporations
Community Development in Europe
Community Empowerment
Community Garden Movement
Community Organizing
Community Studies
Feminism
Gay Communities
Grassroots Leadership
Healthy Communities
Interest Groups
National and Community Service
Populism
Pressure Groups
Public Opinion
Smart Growth
Social Movements
Social Movements Online
Stakeholder
Voluntary Associations
Volunteerism

BIOGRAPHIES

Alinsky, Saul
Aristotle
Burgess, Ernest Watson
Calvin, John
Durkheim, Émile
Geddes, Patrick
Goffman, Erving
Howard, Ebenezer
Jacobs, Jane
Le Bon, Gustave
Lynd, Helen Merrell and Robert Staughton
Mead, George Herbert
Morgan, Arthur E.
Moses, Robert
Mumford, Lewis
Olmsted, Frederick Law
Olmsted Brothers
Osho
Owen, Robert
Park, Robert Ezra
Redfield, Robert
Schmalenbach, Herman
Simmel, Georg
Stein, Clarence S.
Tocqueville, Alexis de
Tönnies, Ferdinand
Veblen, Thorstein
Weber, Max
Whyte, William Hollingsworth
Wirth, Louis

COMMUNITIES, AFFINITY

Activist Communities
Appendix 2—Libraries: Book Clubs and Reading Groups
Artists' Colonies
Book Clubs and Reading Groups
Chautauqua
Citation Communities
Fraternities and Sororities
Gangs
Men's Groups
Public Libraries
Salons

Twelve Step Groups

COMMUNITIES: CASE STUDIES

Amana
Amish
Appalachia
Arcosanti
Auroville
Beguine Communities
Bruderhof
Burning Man
Celebration, Florida
Chautauqua
Chernobyl
Chinatowns
Columbia, Maryland
Damanhur
Emissaries of Divine Light
Ephrata
Family, The
Farm, The
Findhorn Foundation Community
Greenwich Village
Hare Krishnas
Harlem
Harmony Society
Hollywood
Hutterites
Jerusalem
Las Vegas
Left Bank
Levittown
Little Italies
Lower East Side
New Harmony
Oneida
Puritans
Quakers
Radburn, New Jersey
Riverside Community
Shakers
Silicon Valley
Twin Oaks
Warsaw Ghetto
Yamagishi Toyosato
ZEGG
Zoar

COMMUNITIES, INSTRUMENTAL

Activist Communities
Agoras
Appendix 2—Libraries: Self-Help and Support Groups
Asylum
Boomtowns
Cattle Towns
Colleges
Communities of Opposition
Communities of Practice
Community Colleges
Community Development Corporations
Community Schools
Elder Care and Housing
Gangs
Ghost Towns
Homesteading
Hospices
Information Communities
Markets, Street
Merchant Communities
Migrant Worker Communities
Military Communities
Mill Towns
Mining Towns
Prisons
Public Libraries
Resource-Dependent Communities
Schools
Shopping Centers and Malls
Student Housing Cooperatives
Total Institutions
Twelve Step Groups

COMMUNITIES, INTENTIONAL

Amana
Amish
Appendix 1—Resource Guides: Intentional Communities
Arcosanti
Ashrams
Auroville
Bruderhof
Cohousing
Damanhur
Ecovillages
Emissaries of Divine Light
Ephrata
Family, The
Farm, The
Findhorn Community Foundation
Fourierism
Hare Krishnas
Harmony Society
Hutterites
Intentional Communities
Intentional Communities and Children
Intentional Communities and Communal Economics
Intentional Communities and Daily Life
Intentional Communities and Environmental Sustainability
Intentional Communities and Governance
Intentional Communities and Mainstream Politics
Intentional Communities and New Religious Movements
Intentional Communities and Their Survival
Intentional Communities in Australia and New Zealand
Intentional Communities in Eastern Europe and Russia
Intentional Communities in France
Intentional Communities in Germany, Austria, and Switzerland
Intentional Communities in India
Intentional Communities in Israel—Current Movement
Intentional Communities in Israel—History
Intentional Communities in Italy, Spain, and Portugal
Intentional Communities in Japan
Intentional Communities in Latin America
Intentional Communities in Scandinavia and the Low Countries
Intentional Communities in the United Kingdom and Ireland
Intentional Communities in the United States and Canada—Current Movement
Intentional Communities in the United States and Canada—History
Monastic Communities
Moravians
Mormons
New Harmony
Oneida
Osho
Riverside Community
Shakers
Twin Oaks
Utopia
Zoar

COMMUNITIES, PRIMORDIAL

African American Communities
African Americans in Suburbia

Amish
Appendix 1—Resource Guides: Community Studies
Appendix 1—Resource Guides: Race and Ethnicity
Appendix 1—Resource Guides: Religion
Asian American Communities
Beguine Communities
Chinatowns
Congregations, Religious
Cults
Cyborg Communities
Disabled in Communities
English Parishes
Faith Communities
Gangs
Gay Communities
Immigrant Communities
Latino Communities
Little Italies
Monastic Communities
Moravians
Mormons
Native American Communities
Puritans
Quakers
Refugee Communities
Sacred Places
Scientology
Shakers
Shtetls
Transcendentalism
Transnational Communities

COMMUNITIES, PROXIMATE

Appalachia
Appendix 1—Resource Guides: Community Studies
Appendix 1—Resource Guides: Housing and Homelessness
Chinatowns
Condominiums
Edge Cities
Elder Care and Housing
Hollywood
Homelessness
Little Italies
Lower East Side
Mobile Home Communities
Neighborhoods
Seasonal Homes
Shantytowns
Silicon Valley
Small Towns
Villages

COMMUNITY DESIGN

Arcosanti
Appendix 1—Resource Guides: Community Planning and Development
Celebration, Florida
Cohousing
Columbia, Maryland
Congrès Internationaux d'Architecture Moderne
Ecovillages
Environmental Planning
Fourierism
Garden Cities
Gated Communities
Gentrification
Gentrification, Stalled
Greenbelt Towns
HOPE VI
Howard, Ebenezer
Jacobs, Jane
Levittown
Morgan, Arthur E.
Mumford, Lewis
Neighborhood Unit Concept
New Towns
New Urbanism
Olmsted, Frederick Law
Olmsted Brothers
Owen, Robert
Radburn, New Jersey
Regional Planning Association of America
Siedlung
Smart Growth
Sprawl
Stein, Clarence S.
Urban Homesteading
Utopia
Vernacular Architecture

ECONOMICS

Appendix 1—Resource Guides: Community Economics
Appendix 1—Resource Guides: Housing and Homelessness
Appendix 2—Libraries: Business, Economic, and Employment Resources
Appendix 2—Libraries: Community Health
Asset-Based Community Development
Bankruptcy
Barter
Black Economy
Chain Stores
Collective Consumption
Community Currencies
Community Health Systems
Community Land Trust
Community Ownership
Consumer Culture
Corporate Social Responsibility
Economic Planning
Entrepreneurship
Export-Led Development in Regional Economies
Food Systems
Free Rider
Housing
Housing, Affordable
Import-Replacing Development
Informal Economy
Labor Markets
Land Use and Zoning
Local Manufacturing
Multiplier
Nonmonetary Economy
Plant Closures
Public Goods
Regulation
Resource-Dependent Communities
Shared Work
Social Services
Subsidies
Sustainable Development
Tourist Communities
Tragedy of the Commons
Transportation, Rural
Transportation, Urban
Waste Facility Siting

GLOBAL STUDIES

Apartheid
Appendix 1—Resource Guides: Global and International
Appendix 1—Resource Guides: Race and Ethnicity
Appendix 1—Resource Guides: Religion
Appendix 2—Libraries: Libraries and International Partnerships
Artists' Colonies
Ashrams

Assimilation
Birth
Boundaries
Buddhism
Christianity
Cities
Cities, Medieval
Civil Disobedience
Colonialism
Communism and Socialism
Communities of Opposition
Community Currencies
Community Development in Europe
Confucianism
Cultural Ecology
Culture of Poverty
Dance and Drill
Death
Democracy
Diasporas
Displaced Populations
Ecovillages
Environmental Justice
Ethnicity and Ethnic Relations
Fascism
Feminism
Festivals
Food
Food Systems
Gay Communities
Genocide
Global Cities
Globalization and Globalization Theory
Glocalization
Hinduism
Horticultural Societies
Human Rights
Immigrant Communities
Imperialism
Internet in Developing Countries
Islam
Island Communities
Judaism
McDonaldization
Migrant Worker Communities
Millenarianism
Multiculturalism
Music
Pastoral Societies
Pilgrimages
Plantations
Political Economy
Race and Racism
Rebellions and Revolutions
Refugee Communities
Regionalism
Resettlement
Sikhism
Social Capital and Economic Development
Sociolinguistics
State, The
Sustainable Development
Tourist Communities
Transnational Communities
Villages
Waste Facility Siting
World War II

HUMAN DEVELOPMENT

Adolescence
Adolescents and Landscape
Age Integration
Age Stratification and the Elderly
Appendix 1—Resource Guides: Childhood and Adolescence
Appendix 2—Libraries: Historical and Genealogical Research
Appendix 2—Libraries: Literacy
Birth
Child Care
Children
Community Health Systems
Community Mental Health Centers
Community Schools
Death
Disabled in Communities
Elder Care and Housing
Elderly in Communities
Family and Work
Family Violence
Gender Roles
Healing
Home Schooling
Household Structure
Human Development
Initiation Rites
Liminality
Marriage
Peer Groups
Recreation
Schools
Youth Groups

INTERNET AND COMMUNITIES

Appendix 1—Resource Guides: Internet and Communities
Appendix 2—Libraries: Community Bulletin Boards
Avatar Communities
Blogs
Citation Communities
Communications Technologies
Community Informatics and Development
Computers and Knowledge Sharing
Cybercafes
Cyberdating
Cybersocieties
Digital Divide
Electronic Democracy
Electronic Government and Civics
E-Mail
Glocalization
Information Communities
Instant Messaging
Internet, Domestic Life and
Internet, Social Psychology of
Internet, Survey Research About
Internet, Teen Use of
Internet, Time Use and
Internet in Developing Countries
Internet in East Asia
Internet in Europe
Internet, Effects of
Newsgroups and E-Mail Lists
Online Communities, African American
Online Communities, Communication in
Online Communities, Computerized Tools for
Online Communities, Diasporic
Online Communities, Game-Playing
Online Communities, History of
Online Communities, Religious
Online Communities, Scholarly
Online Communities, Youth
Online Communities of Learning
Personalization and Technology
Social Movements Online
Telecommuting
Virtual Communities
Virtual Communities, Building
Wired Communities

POLITICS AND LAW

Anarchism
Apartheid
Appendix 1—Resource Guides: Conflict and Justice

Appendix 1—Resource Guides: Politics and Government
Appendix 2—Libraries: Voting and Elections
Boosterism
Citizenship
Civic Structure
Common Law
Communism and Socialism
Communitarianism
Communities of Opposition
Community Justice
Community Policing
Conflict Resolution
Conflict Theory
Crime
Decentralization
Democracy
Deviance
European Community
Fascism
Grassroots Leadership
Incivilities Thesis
Interest Groups
Leadership
Liberalism
Libertarianism
Local Politics
National and Community Service
National Community
Neighborhood Watch
Organized Crime
Patriotism
Polis
Populism
Pressure Groups
Public Opinion
Regulation
Social Control
Social Darwinism
Social Justice
Stakeholder
State, The
Town Meetings
Vigilantism

PROCESSES AND INSTITUTIONS

Appendix 1—Resource Guides: Connection to Place
Cocooning
Collective Consumption
Community, Sense of
Community Arts
Community Attachment
Community Colleges
Community Indicators
Community Organizing
Community Psychology
Community Satisfaction
Conformity
Counterfeit Communities
Decentralization
Declining Communities
Economic Planning
Enclosure
Environmental Planning
Eugenics
Fourierism
Gentrification
Globalization and Globalization Theory
Glocalization
Guanxi
Hierarchy of Needs
Institutionalization
Luddism
Mass Society
McDonaldization
Millenarianism
Natural Law
Organizational Culture
Place Identity
Pluralism
Political Economy
Residential Mobility
School Consolidation
Sectarianism
Small World Phenomenon
Social Network Analysis
Suburbanization
Sustainable Development
Systems Theory
Ties, Weak and Strong
Urbanism
Urbanization
Xenophobia

RELIGION

Amana
Amish
Appendix 1—Resource Guides: Religion
Arcosanti
Ashrams
Auroville
Beguine Communities
Bruderhof
Buddhism
Calvin, John
Christianity
Confucianism
Congregations, Religious
Cooperative Parish Ministries
Cults
Damanhur
Emissaries of Divine Light
Faith Communities
Hare Krishnas
Harmony Society
Hinduism
Hutterites
Initiation Rites
Intentional Communities and New Religious Movements
Islam
Jerusalem
Judaism
Millenarianism
Monastic Communities
Moravians
Mormons
Oneida
Online Communities, Religious
Pilgrimages
Puritans
Quakers
Religion and Civil Society
Rituals
Sacred Places
Scientology
Shakers
Shtetls
Sikhism
Zoar

RURAL LIFE

Agrarian Communities
Agrarian Myth
Agricultural Scale and Community Quality
Amish
Appalachia
Appendix 1—Resource Guides: Rural Life and Studies
Cattle Towns
Civic Agriculture
Community Land Trust
Community Supported Agriculture
Cooperative Extension System
Cooperative Parish Ministries
County Fairs
Ecovillages

English Parishes
Ghost Towns
Homesteading
Horticultural Societies
Main Street
Out-Migration of Youth
Pastoral Societies
Ranching Communities
Rural Community Development
Rural Poverty and Family Well-Being
Town and Hinterland Conflicts
Transportation, Rural
Watersheds

SOCIAL CAPITAL

Altruism
Appendix 1—Resource Guides: Social Capital
Citizen Participation and Training
Civic Agriculture
Civic Innovation
Civic Life
Civil Society
Collective Efficacy
Community Development Corporations
Community Garden Movement
Community in Disaster
Good Society
Network Communities
Nonprofit Organizations
Progressive Era
Religion and Civil Society
Service Learning
Social Capital
Social Capital, Benefits of
Social Capital, Downside of
Social Capital, Impact in Wealthy and Poor Communities
Social Capital, Trends in
Social Capital, Types of
Social Capital and Economic Development
Social Capital and Human Capital
Social Capital and Media
Social Capital in the Workplace
Social Network Analysis
Ties, Weak and Strong
Trust
Voluntary Associations
Volunteerism
World War II
Youth Groups

SOCIAL LIFE

Age Integration
Age Stratification and the Elderly
Alienation
Altruism
Appendix1—Resource Guides: Social and Public Life
Bars and Pubs
Caste
Charisma
Civil Society
Class, Social
Community Psychology
Conflict Resolution
Conformity
Crowds
Cybercafes
Cyberdating
Dance and Drill
Elderly in Communities
Empathy
Festivals
Food
Friendship
Gated Communities
Gemeinschaft and Gesellschaft
Gender Roles
Guanxi
Hate
Healing
Hierarchy of Needs
Homelessness
Household Structure
Individualism
Intentional Communities and Daily Life
Internet, Domestic Life and
Jealousy
Kinship
Loneliness
Love
Marriage
Men's Groups
Neighborhoods
Neighboring
Peer Groups
Privacy
Public Aid
Public Harassment
Recreation
Secret Societies
Small World Phenomenon
Social Distance
Social Network Analysis
Sport
Street Life
Theme Parks
Third Places
Ties, Weak and Strong
Town and Gown

URBAN AND SUBURBAN LIFE

African Americans in Suburbia
Appendix 1—Resource Guides: Small Towns and Village Life
Appendix 1—Resource Guides: Urban and Suburban Studies
Bedroom Communities
Blockbusting
Chinatowns
Cities
Cities, Inner
Cities, Medieval
Columbia, Maryland
Community Land Trust
Edge Cities
Garden Cities
Geddes, Patrick
Gentrification
Gentrification, Stalled
Ghettos
Global Cities
Greenbelt Towns
Greenwich Village
Growth Machine
Harlem
Housing
Jacobs, Jane
Las Vegas
Left Bank
Levittown
Little Italies
Lower East Side
Model Cities
Mumford, Lewis
New Towns
New Urbanism
Radburn, New Jersey
Smart Growth
Sprawl
Suburbanization
Suburbia
Transportation, Urban
Urban Homesteading
Urban Renewal
Urbanism
Urbanization

Contributors

Ainsworth, Scott
University of Georgia

Alkalimat, Abdul
University of Toledo

Allan, Graham
Keele University

Altus, Deborah
Washburn University

Andelson, Jonathan G.
Grinnell College

Andersen, Lisa
University of Technology, Sydney

Anderson, Ben
University of Essex

Anderson, Elijah
University of Pennsylvania

Ardashev, Gregory
University of Louisville

Ashton, Paul
University of Technology, Sydney

Badcock, Christopher
London School of Economics

Bahr, Howard M.
Brigham Young University

Bainbridge, William Sims,
National Science Foundation

Baker, Andrea J.
Ohio University

Bakker, Peter
Eindhoven, Netherlands

Bang, Jan Martin
Solborg Camphill Community

Bannister, Robert C.
Swarthmore College

Bates, Albert K.
Global Village Institute for Appropriate Technology

Bauman, John F.
University of Southern Maine

Baym, Nancy K.
University of Kansas

Bazemore, Gordon
Florida Atlantic University

Bendik-Keymer, Jeremy
Colorado College

Bendiner-Viani, Gabrielle
City University of New York

Benson, Lee
University of Pennsylvania

Bernard, H. Russell
University of Florida

Bershady, Harold J.
University of Pennsylvania

Birx, H. James
Canisius College and University of Montana, Western

Blakely, Edward
New School University

Blandy, Doug
University of Oregon

Blank, Martin J.
Institute for Educational Leadership

Block, Walter
Loyola University of New Orleans

Boase, Jeffrey
University of Toronto

Boggs, George R.
American Association of Community Colleges

Borio, Lucilla
Global Ecovillage Network

Borner, Katy
Indiana University

Bowman, Sally
Oregon State University

Brazill, Timothy J.
California State University, Fullerton

Briggs, Xavier de Souza
Harvard University

Broude, Gwen J.
Vassar College

Brown, David
McGill University

Brown, Ralph B.
Brigham Young University

Brown, Richard Maxwell
University of Oregon

Bruckman, Amy
Georgia Institute of Technology

Brumann, Christoph
University of Cologne

Bryant, M. Darrol
University of Waterloo

Bumpus, Matthew F.
California State University, Chico

Bunz, Ulla
Rutgers University

Burgess, Norma J Bond
Syracuse University

Burton, J. Bryan
West Chester University

Butcher, A. Allen
Fourth World Services

Cahn, Edgar S.
University of the District of Columbia

Campbell, Colin
University of York

Campbell, Heidi
University of Edinburgh

Cannon, Brian Q.
Brigham Young University

Carruthers, John I.
University of Arizona

Caulkins, D. Douglas
Grinnell College

Cernea, Michael
George Washington University

Champlin, Dell P.
Eastern Illinois University

Chandler, Mittie Olion
Cleveland State University

Checkoway, Barry
University of Michigan

Chen, Wenhong
University of Toronto

Cheng, Joseph
City University of Hong Kong

Cho, Jaeho
University of Wisconsin, Madison

Christensen, Karen
Berkshire Publishing Group

Christensen, Michael
Drew University

Christian, Diana Leafe
Communities Magazine

Chrosniak, Patricia N.
Canisius College

Clarke-Ekong, Sheilah F.
University of Missouri, St. Louis

Clavel, Pierre
Cornell University

Clendenning, Greg
University of Wisconsin, Madison

Coates, Richard J.
Findhorn Foundation

Coates, Richard J.
Diggers & Dreamers

Coenen, Craig R.
Mercer County Community College

Congdon, Kristin G.
University of Central Florida

Cook, Daniel
University of Illinois, Urbana-Champaign

Crano, William
Claremont Graduate University

Cummings, Michael S.
University of Colorado, Denver

Damer, Bruce F.
Contact Consortium

Daniels, Bruce C.
Texas Tech University

Darling, David L.
Kansas State University

Darrah, Charles N.
San Jose State University

De Pillis, Sr., Mario S.
University of Massachusetts, Amherst

Deely, John
University of St. Thomas, Houston

DeMarco, C. Wesley
Oklahoma City University

Dennis, Michael Robert,
University of Kansas

DiDuca, Deborah
University of Essex

Diner, Hasia
New York University

Donlon, Jon Griffin
Center for Cultural Resources

Donnelly, Andrew J.
Tufts University

Douthwaite, Richard
Westport, County Mayo, Ireland

Dowsett, Gary W.
Columbia University

Drakulich, Kevin M.
University of Washington

Drucker, Susan J.
Hofstra University

Duguid, Paul
Copenhagen Business School

Durnbaugh, Donald F.
Juniata College

Durrance, Joan C.
University of Michigan

Durrett, Charles
The Cohousing Company

Dykstra, Robert R.
State University of New York, Albany

Edgley, Charles,
Oklahoma State University

Endres, Danielle
University of Washington

England, Lynn
Brigham Young University

Erickson, Patricia E.
Canisius College

Erickson, Victoria Lee
Drew University

Ersing, Robin L.
University of Kentucky

Etzioni, Amitai
George Washington University

Farrell, Susan A.
Kingsborough Community College, City University of New York

Fehr, Beverley
University of Winnipeg

Fernandez, Kathleen M.
Zoar Village State Memorial, The Ohio Historical Society

Fernandez-Maldonaldo, Ana Maria
Delft University of Technology

Fieldman, Glenn E.
San Francisco State University

Finholt, Thomas A.
University of Michigan

Fisher, Danyel
University of California, Irvine

Fisher, Karen E.
University of Washington

Fisher, Stephen
Emory and Henry College

Flinn, Frank K.
Washington University in St. Louis

Fogarty, Robert S.
Antioch College

Forrest, Beth Marie
Boston University

Forster, Peter M.
University of the South Pacific

Forsyth, Ann
University of Minnesota

Fountain, Jane E.
Harvard University

Fowler, Jerry
United States Holocaust Memorial Museum

Fox, Judith
East Dennis, Massachusetts

Francaviglia, Richard
University of Texas, Arlington

Frank, Katie
University of Toronto

Frederick, Kimberly
Brandeis University

Freie, John F.
LeMoyne College

Freudenburg, William R.
University of California, Santa Barbara

Friedland, Lewis A.
University of Wisconsin, Madison

Friedland, William H.
University of California, Santa Cruz

Friedman, Jonathan
Ecole des Hautes Etudes en Sciences Sociales and Lund University

Frumkin, Peter
Harvard University

Furia, Pete
Wake Forest University

Gamarnikow, Eva
University of London

Gardner, Carol Brooks
Indiana University, Indianapolis

Garlough, Christine Lynn
University of Minnesota

Gavron, Daniel
Motza Elite, Israel

Gelles, Richard J.
University of Pennsylvania

Gering, Ralf
Kusterdingen, Germany

Gilles, Jere L.
University of Missouri, Columbia

Gladstone, David L.
University of New Orleans

Glover, Troy D.
University of Illinois, Urbana–Champaign

Goldsmith, William W.
Cornell University

Gonzales, Angela A.
Cornell University

Goreham, Gary A.
North Dakota State University

Gorman, Margo
Combined European Bureau for Social Development

Goss, Kristin A.
Harvard University

Gough, Robert J.
University of Wisconsin, Eau Claire

Gray, Tom,
Pinetel

Green, Gary Paul
University of Wisconsin - Madison

Greenberg, Daniel
Living Routes – Ecovillage Education

Grierson, David
University of Strathclyde

Griffin, Liza
Oxford Brookes University

Griffin, Roger
Oxford Brookes University

Grimm, Jr., Robert T.
Corporation for National and Community Service

Groce, Nora
Yale University

Guest, Avery M.
University of Washington

Gumpert, Gary
Communication Landscapers

Gunn, Christopher
Hobart and William Smith Colleges

Hagedorn, John M.
University of Illinois, Chicago

Hampton, Keith N.
Massachusetts Institute of Technology

Hansen, David M.
University of Illinois, Urbana–Champaign

Hansen, Gary L.
University of Kentucky

Hardy, Dennis
Middlesex University

Harkavy, Ira
University of Pennsylvania

Hartley, Laura C.,
Lesley University

Hays, R. Allen
University of Northern Iowa

Haythornthwaite, Caroline
University of Illinois, Urbana–Champaign

Henderson, Elizabeth
Peacework Organic Farm

Herring, Horace
Open University

Hirschhorn, Larry
Center for Applied Research, Philadelphia

Hodgett, Susan L.
Queen's University Belfast and Dalhousie University

Hove, Thomas,
University of Wisconsin, Madison

Hudson, John
University of Bath

Humphreys, Keith
Veterans Affairs Health Care System and Stanford University

Hunter, Albert
Northwestern University

Husbands, Christopher T.
London School of Economics and Political Science

Immergluck, Daniel,
Grand Valley State University

Introvigne, Massimo
Center for Studies on New Religions (CESNUR)

Ishida, Toru
Kyoto University

Jackson, Jr., John L.
Duke University

Jobes, Patrick C.
University of New England

Johnson, Sharon
Oregon State University

Johnston, William M.
Melbourne College of Divinity

Jones, Anthea
Cheltenham Ladies' College

Jones, James
North American Students of Cooperation

Jones, Quentin
New Jersey Institute of Technology

Judd, Dennis R.
University of Illinois, Chicago

Kaplan, Jeffrey
University of Wisconsin, Oshkosh

Kawasaki, Leslie Tkach
University of Tsukuba

Kearney, Michael
University of California, Riverside

Kelly, Barbara M.
Hofstra University

Kendall, Lori
State University of New York, Purchase College

Kestnbaum, Meyer
University of Maryland

Ketels, Christian H.M.
Harvard University

Kim, Amy Jo
There, Inc.

Kin, Lau
City University of Hong Kong

King, Loren A.
Brown University

Kirchner, David
Millikin University

Kishi, Ikuo
Yamagishi Toyosato

Klaw, Elena
San Jose State University

Klemanski, John S.
Oakland University

Klemek, Christopher
University of Pennsylvania

Kneedler, Richard
Franklin & Marshall College

Komoch, Agnieszka
Community of Lebensgarten, Germany

Korsching, Peter
Iowa State University

Kozeny, Geoph
Community Catalyst Project

Krannich, Richard S.
Utah State University

Krase, Jerome
Brooklyn College

Kraybill, Donald B.
Elizabethtown College

Kretzmann, John
Northwestern University

Kumar, M. Satish
Queen's University Belfast

Lai, David Chuenyan
University of Victoria

Langman, Lauren
Loyola University of Chicago

Lauer, Sean R.
University of British Columbia

Lavenda, Robert H.
St. Cloud State University

Lea, Martin
University of Manchester

Leigh, Andrew
Harvard University

Leigh, Nancey Green
Georgia Institute of Technology

Lenhart, Amanda B.
Pew Internet & American Life Project

Levin, Jack
Northeastern University

Levinson, David
Berkshire Publishing Group

Levy, Barry
University of Massachusetts, Amherst

Lewis, David
London School of Economics

Lietaer, Bernard
Munich, Germany

Loader, Brian D.
Community Informatics Research & Applications Unit

Long, Thomas L.
Thomas Nelson Community College

Loomis, David
University of North Carolina, Chapel Hill

Low, Setha
City University of New York

Lyson, Thomas A.
Cornell University

Machacek, David W.
University of California, Santa Barbara

MacKenzie, John M.
University of Aberdeen

MacTavish, Katherine
Oregon State University

Madsen, Richard
University of California, San Diego

Malina, Anna
e-Society Research, Scotland

Maloney-Krichmar, Diane
University of Maryland, Baltimore County

Mancebo, François
Université Paris 4 Sorbonne

Mann, Gurinder Singh
University of California, Santa Barbara

Mann, Ralph
University of Colorado

Mann, Steve
University of Toronto

Marcuse, Peter
Columbia University

Martin, Mimi
New York University

Mazzone, Jason
Yale University

McCarty, Christopher
University of Florida

McClure, Peggy
Drexel University

McClure, Wendy R.
University of Idaho

McCook, Kathleen de la Peña
University of South Florida

McInerney, Jeremy
University of Pennsylvania

McNeil, Sue
University of Illinois, Chicago

McNeill, William H.
University of Chicago

Meidinger, Nicole J.
University of Notre Dame

Melton, J. Gordon
Institute for the Study of American Religion

Menkel-Meadow, Carrie
Georgetown University Law Center

Metcalf, William,
Griffith University

Mettler, Suzanne
Syracuse University

Metts, Jr., Wallis C.
Spring Arbor University

Michelson, William
University of Toronto

Miller, Timothy
University of Kansas

Mitchell, Stacy
Institute for Local Self-Reliance

Mitra, Ananda
Wake Forest University

Mohammed, Asad
University of the West Indies

Mohanty, Bindu
Auroville Universal Township

Moris, Jon R.
Utah State University

Morton, Lois Wright
Iowa State University

Mott, Wesley T.
Worcester Polytechnic Institute

Moudry, Roberta
Cornell University

Mueller, Elizabeth J.
University of Texas, Austin

Murdock, Steve H.
Texas A&M University

Murero, Monica
International Institute of Infonomics, University of Maastricht

Musolf, Gil Richard
Central Michigan University

Nash, Victoria
University of Oxford

Near, Henry
Regional College, Safed

Neustadtl, Alan
University of Maryland

Nevarez, Leonard
Vassar College

Ngok, King-lun
City University of Hong Kong

Nirenberg, John
Shinawatra University

Nolan, Jason
University of Toronto

Nomura, Saeko
Kyoto University

Norris, Tyler
Community Initiatives LLC

Norton, Sydney J.
St. Louis Art Museum

Oden, Michael D.
University of Texas, Austin

O'Flanagan, Patrick
University College, Cork

Oldenburg, Ray
University of West Florida

Oliver, J. Eric
Princeton University

Oliver, Pamela E.
University of Wisconsin, Madison

Oliver, Paul
Oxford Brookes University

Orum, Anthony M.
University of Illinois, Chicago

O'Sullivan, Robin K.
University of Southern Maine

Otto, Christian F.
Cornell University

Owens, Patsy Eubanks
University of California, Davis

Palen, J. John
Virginia Commonwealth University

Paulsen, Krista E.
University of North Florida

Pendall, Rolf
Cornell University

Penney, Robert A.
George Washington University

Pepper, David
Oxford Brookes University

Perry, Joseph B.
Bowling Green State University

Pfeffer, Max J.
Cornell University

Piazza, James A.
Meredith College

Pitzer, Donald E.
University of Southern Indiana

Pochat, Jean-Michel
Global Ecovillage Network–Europe

Porter, Karen A.
University of Puget Sound

Preece, Jennifer
University of Maryland, Baltimore County

Prono, Luca
University of Nottingham

Puentes, Robert
Brookings Institution

Rabrenovic, Gordana
Northeastern University

Redensek, Jeannette
City University of New York

Reichel, Philip L.
University of Northern Colorado

Reidhead, Van A.
University of Missouri, St. Louis

Reingold, David A.
Corporation for National and Community Service

Reisch, Michael
Children Now and University of Michigan

Reisner, Ann
University of Illinois, Urbana-Champaign

Ritzer, George
University of Maryland, College Park

Roach Anleu, Sharyn L.
Flinders University

Roba, William
Scott Community College

Robinson, John P.
University of Maryland

Robinson, Tony
University of Colorado, Denver

Rogers, Lawrence E.
South Dakota State University

Rojas, Hernando
University of Wisconsin, Madison

Rojas, James
Latino Urban Forum

Rosenbaum, Dennis P.
University of Illinois, Chicago

Rosenthal, Rob
Wesleyan University

Ross, Andrew
New York University

Ross, Marcy
Berkshire Publishing Group

Rotkin, Michael
University of California, Santa Cruz

Royle, Edward
University of York

Royle, Stephen A.
Queen's University Belfast

Said, Abdul Aziz
American University

Salamon, Sonya
University of Illinois, Urbana–Champaign

Salamone, Frank A.
Iona College

Sampson, Robert J.
Harvard University

Sandhu, Amandeep
University of California, Santa Barbara

Sandstrom, Kent L.
University of Northern Iowa

Sargisson, Lucy
University of Nottingham

Satterthwaite, Ann
Planning Consultant

Schaub, Laird
Fellowship for Intentional Community

Schildkraut, Deborah
Oberlin College

Schimmel, Kimberly S.
Kent State University

Schneider, Stephen
Ryerson University

Schneiderman, Howard G.
Lafayette College

Schulenburg, Alexander Hugo
Corporation of London

Sedo, DeNel Rehberg
Mount Saint Vincent University

Shah, Dhavan V.
University of Wisconsin, Madison

Shapiro, Gabriel
McKendree College

Shepherd, William G.
University of Massachusetts, Amherst

Shuman, Michael H.
Green Policy Institute

Silverman, Robert Mark
Wayne State University

Simon, Karl-Heinz
University of Kassel

Sirianni, Carmen
Brandeis University

Smith, Marc A.
Microsoft Research

Smith, Martin J.
University of Sheffield

Smith, Robert C.
Barnard College and Columbia University

Sonnad, Subhash R.
Western Michigan University

Spears, Russell
University of Amsterdam

Squires, Gregory D.
George Washington University

Stald, Gitte
University of Copenhagen

Stameshkin, David M.
Franklin & Marshall College

Stanton, Max E.
Brigham Young University, Hawaii

Stevens, Charles
Miami University

Stillman, Todd
University of Maryland

Straus, Emily
Brandeis University

Sturmer, Stefan
Christian-Albrechts-Universität zu Kiel

Sullivan, Bill
Santa Rosa, California

Sullivan, Daniel Monroe
Portland State University

Sweeney, Donald A.
Texas A & M University

Taylor, Ralph B.
Temple University

Tepper, Steven J.
Princeton University

Thomas, Alexander R.
State University of New York, College at Oneonta

Thomson, Irene Taviss
Fairleigh Dickinson University

Thurman, Quint C.
Southwest Texas State University

Tickamyer, Ann R.
Ohio University

Tomasek, Kathryn
Wheaton College

Toth Jr., John F.
West Virginia Wesleyan College

Tsai, Gloria
Nazareth College of Rochester

Ubertaccio, Peter
Stonehill College

Uhlenberg, Peter
University of North Carolina, Chapel Hill

Upton, Dell
University of Virginia

Valentine, Mary
California Federation of Teachers

Vogt, Peter
Moravian Church

Walsh, Margaret
Keene State College

Washington, Sylvia Hood
Northwestern University

Weinstein, Judith L.
Barnert Hospital

Wellman, Barry
University of Toronto

West, Thomas R.
Catholic University of America

White, Douglas
University of California, Irvine

White, Howard D.
Drexel University

Williams, Brett
American University

Williams, Brian Glyn
University of Massachusetts, Dartmouth

Wilson, Janelle L.
University of Minnesota, Duluth

Wilson, John
Duke University

Wojtowicz, Robert
Old Dominion University

Woolcock, Michael
World Bank and Harvard University

Worden, Nigel A.
University of Cape Town

Wunsch, James L.
Empire State College

Xanthopoulos, John
University of Montana, Western

Yodanis, Carrie L.
University of British Columbia

Zakai, Avihu
Hebrew University of Jerusalem

Zetter, Roger
Oxford Brookes University

Zhou, Min
University of California, Los Angeles

Ziebarth, Ann C.
University of Minnesota

Introduction

Community is a concept, an experience, and a central part of being human. It is a subject that touches every one of us, a subject so complex and interdisciplinary that it takes a work like this to provide the depth and breadth of information that students, scholars, information specialists, and professionals in both public and private sectors need if they are to understand the nature of community fully.

We need *The Encyclopedia of Community* because we live at a time when our desire for community seems to grow in proportion to our sense that it is declining. Yet there have never been so many efforts under way to build, restore, find, and study community as there are today. Some of these efforts reflect a longing for an earlier era when, we imagine, we could find common values. Many images of community—trick-or-treating in handmade costumes, World War II victory gardens, the Queen's Jubilee street parties—are nostalgic. But there is a huge array of contemporary efforts to be explored—community health networks, online support groups, local currencies, or cohousing developments. The *Encyclopedia* is not, however, an unthinking celebration of community. Community is something we run from, as well as toward. Community has its downsides. Readers will find that the contradictions of community are examined in dozens of articles as well as later in this Introduction.

We explore hundreds of different communities, the human webs that provide essential feelings of connectedness, belonging, and meaning. Communities are indeed the core and essence of humanity, around which everything else is woven or spun. They provide emotional and practical security and a sense of continuity through shared memory. They give us a sense of purpose. They sustain us throughout our lives, in neighborhoods, schools, workplaces, and apartment buildings, as well as in more extended networks of friendship and common purpose. These human webs are generally intimate enough to allow face-to-face contact. They depend on personal knowledge and trust. They are a primary source of happiness in good times, and essential sources of support and solace during bad times.

Community is widely studied. The disciplines of history, sociology, anthropology, psychology, economics, public administration, town planning, and religious studies all examine aspects of community, and for all these disciplines, the *Encyclopedia of Community* should prove an indispensable resource. For scholars and students at the college level, the encyclopedia is a state-of-the-art review. For people outside the academic world, it is a unique resource tool. Many health professionals, government officials, social workers, and clergy are focused on community issues and community development. They will be able turn to the encyclopedia for inspiration and illumination, for stories and strategies.

The *Encyclopedia of Community* gives us, at last, a vantage point from which we can examine these vital human webs and explore a vital aspect of individual and social experience. In hundreds of entries, leading scholars address what may be the most perplexing and challenging questions facing us in the twenty-first century: How and why do humans maintain their connections to one another, to particular geographic places, and to shared social, religious, and ethnic traditions?

For most of history the community has been indispensable. Pioneers and settlers in countries such as the United States, Canada, Australia, and New Zealand, for example, spoke pridefully of themselves as individualists when they were dependent on their neighbors for every sort of survival. They could not put a roof over their heads without the cooperation of others. They could not get in their harvests without the help of others. They could not deliver their children or doctor their sick without good relations with others. They had no savings system except investments in goodwill with others. They had no welfare or old age protection but the assistance of others. They had no public safety or defense against human enemies and natural disaster but the collaboration of others. To deprive a person of social interaction within his or her community—through banishment, shunning, or excommunication—was a fairly common, and extreme, form of punishment.

In the latter half of the twentieth century, for the first time in human history, at least some people—in the urban, developed world—could truly get along without cordial relations with their neighbors. Hospitals, trust funds, Social Security, supermarkets, contractors, banks, and the panoply of modern institutions make it possible to make money among people with whom one does not live and to secure essential services by paying fees to other strangers or specialist acquaintances who can be replaced, if necessary, by strangers.

Consequently, communities—in industrialized, Westernized nations, at any rate—become more elective than imperative. In the United States, people are no longer Italian, or Republican, or Seventh-Day Adventist because their parents were or because they have to be. They can embrace their Native American, or Norwegian, or Jewish heritage because they choose to celebrate that aspect of their repertoire of identities. Further, they can style it according to their own preferences and predilections. Contemporary Protestants, Catholics, and Jews alike customize their religions to suit themselves, and so do contemporary ethnic groups. We improvise our sexuality and abandon our old political partisan allegiances for an unprecedented independence.

But the absence of sustaining primary communities is no minor thing. Humans need to be connected, and without adequate communities we suffer from personal and social ills that include depression, poor health, and crime. At its most extreme, an absence of human ties leads to violence and extreme social disorders—one has only to think of the stereotypical description of a serial killer as a loner.

The world's most eminent living world historian, William H. McNeill, author of the National Book Award winner *The Rise of the West: A History of the Human Community,* concludes in the recent book *The Human Web: A Bird's Eye View of World History* (published by Norton, 2003) that our future depends on finding new kinds of communities to replace those of the past:

> Either the gap between cities and villages will somehow be bridged by renegotiating the terms of symbiosis, and/or differently constructed primary communities will arise to counteract the tangled anonymity of urban life. Religious sects and congregations are the principal candidates for this role. But communities of belief must somehow insulate themselves from unbelievers, and that introduces frictions, or active hostilities, into the cosmopolitan web. How then sustain the web and also make room for life-sustaining primary communities?
>
> Ironically, therefore, to preserve what we have, we and our successors must change our ways by learning to live simultaneously in a cosmopolitan web and in various and diverse primary communities. How to reconcile such opposites is the capital question for our time and probably will be for a long time to come. (William H. McNeill & J. R. McNeill 2003, pp. 326–327).

WHY COMMUNITY?

Over the past century and a half, especially in the United States, there have been many expressions of concern about the breakdown of community. There have been influential books on community throughout the twentieth century, from *The Quest for Community* by the conservative political scientist Robert Nisbet (1953) to Paul Goodman's *Communitas* (first published in 1947 and reprinted in 1960), which was influential in the back-to-the-land hippie movement in the 1960s and early 1970s.

In *Community and Social Change in America* (1978), historian Thomas Bender linked this concern to such social stresses as industrialization and immigration and the social problems associated with them. Since Bender's book was published, concern about community has reached a new peak, for two reasons. First, many fear that the forces of globalization will overwhelm local communities. Local businesses are being displaced by enterprises with a global reach, such as Wal-Mart. People all over the world are more mobile, and thus less likely to know their neighbors or be involved in local organizations and local government. Second, a variety of social problems—violent crime, gangs, poor-quality schools, even lack of civility—have been connected to the breakdown of community. The communitarian movement was organized by the sociologist Amitai Etzioni (a contributor to the *Encyclopedia of Community*) to encourage adherence to social norms through the revival of community.

Influential books of the 1990s were the sociologist Ray Oldenburg's *The Great Good Place* and the writer Howard Rheingold's *The Virtual Community.* These make an interesting pair. Oldenburg explores real, physical places—bars, cafes, barbershops, beauty parlors—where people hang out. Rheingold's focus is the World Wide Web and the relationships we form and communities we find online.

In the last few years of the twentieth century, community received considerable popular attention thanks to the work of political scientist Robert Putnam, of Harvard University. Putnam's research, set out first in a journal article and then in the 2000 book *Bowling Alone,* examines the ways in which the U.S. social fabric is fraying. He warns that people are disconnected from friends, family, neighbors, and their fellow citizens, and that the United States is in danger of becoming a nation of strangers. Putnam's work has spurred considerable interest in the idea of social capital, and initiatives to renew our civic life have been taken up by the Saguaro Seminar on Civic Engagement at Harvard University's Kennedy School of Government, as well as by foundations, civic organizations, and governmental bodies in the United States and elsewhere, especially in the United Kingdom.

Social fragmentation has many causes, and there is considerable debate about what really causes the breakdown of community. Some claim that new but still satisfactory forms of community are replacing the old ones. Factors discussed in the encyclopedia include work patterns, family structure, age demographics, suburbanization, television and computers, and women's roles.

One of the most important facts about modern life may be that we have more connections and fewer dependencies. As a result, many people seem to think of community as an amenity, not a necessary state of being or a reciprocal commitment, and in fact the term seems to mean simply "home and comfort" to some. Ironically, some writers present community in a way that seems positively individualistic, focused purely on the benefits to the individual. These approaches present a fresh set of challenges, which the *Encyclopedia of Community* can prepare us to address. Consider the problem of community development in rural areas. Newcomers seek out bucolic, arcadian surroundings—but then want all the amenities of the cities they have left behind while being less interested in those unique characteristics of the area that make it special to natives: the public spaces that confer a unique place identity; strong ties that form overlapping, supportive social networks; and taken-for-granted relationships that cross generations. Housing developments encroach on the natural environment while urban attitudes—and rising housing prices—can make local people feel that their community is being altered in ways they cannot control. Small towns have been portrayed by novelists and social scientists as having solid, even rigid, social structures, but to some scholars they now seem amorphous and fragile.

For many, the violent events of September 11, 2001, were a powerful reminder that even in modern, individualistic societies we are still dependent on one another in times of crisis. Community was the buzzword in the months immediately after the terrorist attacks of September 11, 2001. Tony Blair, the United Kingdom's prime minister, gave what was dubbed the "power of community" speech, emphasizing the need for a just, equitable, compassionate world community, noting that "our self-interest and our mutual interests are today inextricably woven together." Since that time, world events have made a truly united global community seem increasingly remote, but it remains an important concept. And while there is little evidence that September 11 has fostered long-term social connectedness, it certainly underscored the importance of both planned and organized communities, such as the community of firefighters and rescue workers, and spontaneous communities, such as the one comprising the passengers of United Airlines flight 93, who appear to have come together to fight the hijackers of their plane.

Traditionally, human community has had a geographic base: To be a community, people have needed to be physically near one another. Today, however, many people find the strongest sense of community within groups that are not geographically based. That is possible because community is a cultural construct that can be conceived in an almost infinite variety of ways. Even hermits, we are told, like to think that they belong to the Community of Eremites. There is a dynamic relationship between the need for people to belong to community and the extraordinarily varied ways in which that need is met.

HOW TO USE THE ENCYCLOPEDIA OF COMMUNITY

The *Encyclopedia of Community: From the Village to the Virtual World,* in four volumes, draws together the work of 399 contributors from eighteen countries. It contains a total of 1.25 million words: one million words in 500 entries; an additional 100,000 words in 266 extensive primary-text sidebars drawn from letters, diaries, society records, memoirs, novels, newspaper accounts, and community plans; and appendices of 150,000 words. Entries range in length from 500 to 6,000 words, and there are more than 100 visuals, including photographs, tables, and charts.

While many encyclopedias are written by a handful of nonexperts who simply assemble information from other reference works, the *Encyclopedia of Community* is the work of highly visible scholars at dozens of major institutions. The contributions here represent fresh, original thinking at the cutting edge of a variety of disciplines. Among our hundreds of authors are Ray Oldenburg, writing on bars and pubs and on "third places"; Hasia Diner (author of *Jewish Americans*), writing on the Lower East Side; Paul Duguid (coauthor of *Social Life of Information*), writing on communities of practice; Charles Durrett (coauthor of *Cohousing*), writing on cohousing; Amitai Etzioni, writing on communitarianism; Amy Jo Kim (author of *Community Building on the Web*), writing on building virtual communities; Jack Levin (author of *Will to Kill*), writing on hate; William McNeill, writing on villages and on dance and drill; George Ritzer (author of *McDonaldization of Society*), writing on McDonaldization; Dell Upton (author of *Architecture in the United States*) writing on New Urbanism, and Min Zhou (coeditor of *Contemporary Asian America: A Multidisciplinary Reader*), writing on Asian American communities.

The *Encyclopedia of Community* addresses these and many other questions:

- How have people experienced community, throughout history and around the world?
- How are communities different from other kinds of groups and associations?
- Are we really "bowling alone," or have we found new forms of community thanks to widespread mobility and the Internet?
- Have cars and television destroyed our sense of community?

In the four appendices in Volume 4, readers will find a wide variety of resources to help them find solutions to such questions as these:

- How can I build, or find, community?
- How can community help my family, my school, or my business?

We have made great efforts to ensure that our coverage of community from a theoretical perspective does not obscure the fact that community is the experience of real people. We have found a variety of ways to make real-life stories part of the encyclopedia, often by using sidebars of primary text to show the human dimension of ideas and beliefs about community. More than half the enties are accompanied by sidebars drawn from fiction and nonfiction, including excerpts from ethnographic reports (eyewitness accounts written by anthropologists). By kind permission of Frances Moore Lappé, we also present extracts from the archives of the American News Service, a project of the Center for Living Democracy, founded by Frances Moore Lappé and Paul Martin DuBois in 1995. The full archives are being made available to researchers by Berkshire Publishing Group and Ms. Lappé at www.berkshirepublishing.com/ans.

Nor have we forgotten that community features prominently in popular culture, whether popular books such as *Clan of the Cave Bear* and the Harry Potter series; well-known literary works, such as *Pride and Prejudice;* or television programs, such as *Mayberry R.F.D.* and *Ed*—not to mention films. Our Community in Popular Culture appendix includes 200 novels, 141 nonfiction books, 47 stage productions, 229 movies, 28 documentaries, 64 television programs, and 63 songs that embody some aspect of the theme of community. Scholars and practitioners will find it thought provoking, and teachers will be able to use it to encourage analysis and discussion. Besides that, it's just plain fun.

Finally, skeptics who wonder whether community is a topic large enough to merit an encyclopedia of this scale will be convinced not only by the 500 entries written by experts but also by the Master Bibliography of Community, which includes 4,800 citations to books and journal articles. The literature on community is vast because the topic is at the core of the human experience. The *Encyclopedia of Community*'s Master Bibliography is the first comprehensive, interdisciplinary, and international bibliography for the study of community, and we trust that it will be of great value to researchers.

Encyclopedias should always be organized for the convenience of the reader. We have divided the entries in the *Encyclopedia of Community* by category, based on the editors' widely varied interests and expertise, but they've been presented here in A-to-Z order. This means the reader will find Apartheid next to Appalachia, Schools next to Scientology. But we recognize that readers will want to be able to move from entry to entry, tracing an idea or exploring a particular aspect of community, so there are four navigational tools.

The first two are standard: a comprehensive topical index at the end of Volume 4 and detailed cross-referencing at the end of individual entries. We wanted to do more, though, because many readers will come to the *Encyclopedia of Community* looking for answers to specific questions. Therefore, although we chose not to include articles on community-oriented organizations (simply because it would have been impossible to decide where to draw the line), we do list a wide variety of them from around the world in the Resource Guides appendix, which is divided into twenty-one topical sections with such headings as community economics, rural studies, and volunteerism.

With the help of two leaders within the U.S. library community, Sarah Ann Long and Nancy Kranich (both past presidents of the American Library Association), we also developed a resource section specifically for librarians. Libraries have a unique role in the world because they are both knowledge centers and public places. They are more valuable now than ever, the one place in every community where everyone—no matter what their age, income, or ethnic background—is welcome. The library resource appendix is full of practical ideas for creating community, for supporting civic engagement, and for building social capital. Sections are cross-referenced to the wide range of relevant articles on these topics, providing a unique way of connecting information within the encyclopedia to many other resources, most important, those in the library.

COVERAGE

The *Encyclopedia of Community* covers hundreds of efforts to change, revitalize, and maintain communities; it presents varied and often conflicting perspectives on what community is and what it means. Its entries explore types of community (intentional communities, ethnic communities, and community colleges, for example), famous communities, issues and trends in community building, institutions that influence and sustain communities, and a wide variety of concepts and theories. Important terms such as *social capital, civic engagement, sense of community,* and *communitarianism* are explained. In terms of historical reach, the encyclopedia reaches back to the earliest days of human settlements, continues through the centuries to eighteenth-century utopian societies, covers the communes of the 1960s, and probes today's cybercommunities.

The following list outlines the areas of community research that have been brought together for the first time in the *Encyclopedia of Community* and credits the editor who reviewed the entries in each category.

Community Design (Roberta Moudry)

Ways in which the planning and design of a community can affect its development, and how its physical development can affect the lives of its inhabitants.

Community Economics (Michael Shuman)

Key concepts involved in the ability of a community to allocate resources and provide goods and services to all its residents.

Human Development (Robin Jarrett)

Community contexts influencing human and family development across the life cycle from childhood to old age.

Intentional Communities (William Metcalf)

Historic and contemporary full-time, residential communities in which members have deliberately come together to live.

Internet and Communities (Barry Wellman)

Changes that have been wrought on world society and on our understanding of the nature of community with the advent of new technologies.

Rural Life (Sonya Salamon)

Distinguishing features of rural people and places, as well as contemporary issues related to rural poverty and community development.

Social Capital (Thomas Sander)

Key concepts and definitions related to the idea of social capital—that is, that social networks have value stemming from trust, reciprocity, and information flows between individuals.

Social Life (Ray Oldenburg)

Basic concepts of social structure, social organization, social institutions, social differentiation, and social processes that influence daily interactions.

Urban Studies (Dennis Judd)

Understanding urban areas and urban issues through the study of community and of neighborhoods in particular.

Historical and Contemporary Communities (David Levinson and Michael Zuckerman)

Entries on specific communities, some place-based, such as Appalachia and Silicon Valley, and others more diffuse, such as the Hutterites and the Shakers. Also provided is a selection of short case studies of influential communities such as New York City's Lower East Side and Harlem, Poland's Warsaw Ghetto, and Auroville in India.

In our Reader's Guide, we have classified these communities using a set of criteria unique to the *Encyclopedia of Community.* While the classifications do not absolutely or uniquely define the communities (some communities fit into more than one category), we feel that this system provides a useful way to explore the essence and impact of different types of human groups and networks.

Affinity Communities

Communities or categories of communities in which membership is based on common interest, such as book clubs, reading groups, and artists' colonies.

Instrumental Communities

Communities or categories of communities in which membership is based on the shared desire to achieve specific goals, whether political, economic, or other. Examples include activist communities and hospices.

Primordial Communities

Communities or categories of communities in which membership is based on ties of blood, kinship, race, ethnicity, or deeply held shared beliefs, such as Asian American communities and monastic communities.

Proximate Communities

Communities or categories of communities in which membership is based on residence in a particular place, such as shantytowns or condominiums.

Global Studies (Karen Christensen and David Levinson)

The *Encyclopedia of Community* gives considerable attention to global topics such as participatory democracy, consumerism, cultural identity, and individualism that are viewed differently and have differing impacts in various parts of the world. Throughout the encyclopedia, we show diverse political, cultural, and religious perspectives toward private obligation, civic engagement, and how best to live together. Authors come from around the world and a total of eighteen nations, and the editors have made a determined effort to go beyond the distinctly U.S. focus of much community research. One of our goals in creating this publication is to increase the internationality of community scholarship.

Early in the twentieth century, the Chinese Nationalist leader Sun Yat-sen said that the "Chinese people are like a sheet of loose sand." Discussion of community in China and elsewhere in Asia has been very much tied to the idea of a sense of community based on national identity. In contrast with Europe and the United States, a powerful, modern state has been considered essential to social cohesion, even as family ties to a home village, where ancestors are buried, continues to be central to an individual sense of identity. In fact, a 1991 report from a medical research society ascribed the long lifespan of Chinese intellectuals to the fact that they had devoted their lives to the struggle for collective interests. Among scholars in Asia today, there is considerable interest in the concept of a civil society and the maintenance of national and regional culture in the face of globalization and modernization.

Europeans tend not to use the word *community* as much as Americans, concentrating instead on concepts such as active citizenship, the third sector, and social inclusion. There is also confusion in Europe over the term *social capital,* which is sometimes used, by the World Bank and others, in the way it is used in the United States, but is used in a completely different way by the European Union. The term *community* has different resonance in different parts of Europe. In essence, according to Gabriel Chanan of the Community Development Foundation in London, the Anglo-Saxon countries and a few northern European countries, specifically Holland, Belgium, and Scandinavia—more or less historically Protestant countries—share a similar understanding of community, but that understanding is not shared by the rest of Europe. In Germany, *community* intimates Nazism to some, while in ex-Communist countries it suggests Communism. In France, it sounds statist; that is, it suggests centralized government control.

It is therefore important to recognize that when we use the word *community* in this work we often mean what is elsewhere called, variously, active citizenship, local partnership, third sector, nongovernmental organizations (the pan-European term for community and voluntary organizations, which are central to the concept of social capital in the United States), civil society, local autonomy, or social inclusion.

Biographies

In order to fully cover these themes, we have chosen to include only a very limited number of biographical entries, and, like many other publications, we have largely excluded living people. However hundreds of people, both past and present, who have been or are influential in the development of communities or our thinking about community are discussed in context in the relevant entries.

WHAT IS COMMUNITY?

Community is a diffuse concept, and what is meant by community varies widely from one culture to another. The word itself derives from the same Latin root as the word *common: communis,* meaning, according to the *Oxford English Dictionary*, "fellowship, community of relations or feelings." Medieval Latin used *communis* to mean "a body of fellows or fellow-townsmen," and today community has both an abstract and a concrete meaning: in the abstract, a sense of commonality and, in the concrete, actual, specific groups of people who have certain circumstances or interests in common.

It sometimes seems that anything can be called a community. Our goal in the encyclopedia is not to eliminate some definitions and elevate others but to take the broadest possible look at the multitude of human webs —groups, networks, ties, and bonds—that we call community.

Some people imagine that community came after family, beginning when humans started living in bands. But world historians such as David Christian explain that bands, both pre-human and pre-chimpanzee, came first. Both humans and chimpanzees are, as Aristotle suggested more than 2,000 years ago, social rather than individual creatures. These earliest of communities served for defense and coordinated action against predators, made possible the intensive care needed by human infants, and also provided opportunities to exchange information—not so different, really, from some of the things that bring communities together today.

And while foraging societies spent most of the year in family groups, rules of exogamy (that is, prohibiting people from mating with close kin) exist in all human societies. Recent research suggests that given sufficient resources, foraging people routinely come together for special events (for example, the aboriginal Australian festivals called corroborees), and have done so for as long as human culture has existed, some 250,000 years.

In the distant past, a vivacious sense of community helped proto-humans survive by diffusing information and making them more effectively cooperative. While sociality is a characteristic of many (but not all) animals, community is the defining characteristic of humans alone. Only humans form social groups, or webs, that can exchange and share attitudes, ideas, beliefs, and identity. The flow of human history, in fact, depends on the ways these human webs expanded and gathered power across the millennia, thanks to competition that rewarded more effectual cooperation among ever-larger numbers of individuals.

Another important concept that has—like community—struggled for a clear, authoritative definition is culture, the core concept in the field of anthropology. The debate about what culture is went on for several decades until in the early 1950s the profession asked anthropologist Alfred Kroeber at the University of California, Berkeley, to sort it out. Kroeber wrote a reasonably terse volume listing some 250 different definitions he had culled from the literature and then added several new possibilities, finally recommending just one. The profession was duly grateful, and went on to ignore what he suggested. In his work *Social Structure* (published by Macmillan, 1949), ethnographer George Peter Murdock remarked:

> The community and the nuclear family are the only social groups that are genuinely universal. They occur in every known human society, and both are also found in germinal form on a subhuman level. Nowhere on earth do people live regularly in isolated families. Everywhere territorial propinquity, supported by divers other bonds, unites at least a few neighboring families into a larger social group all of whose members maintain face-to-face relationships with one another. (Murdock 1949, pp. 79–80)

The lesson here is that absolute definitions are not necessary; it may be the fluidity of a core concept that makes it so useful. Community may be thought of as a geographic place, shared hobbies or interests, a warm sense of togetherness, interaction in a common space such as a chat room, and so forth. The encyclopedia brings together many views of community, not eliminating any definition but providing a forum in which they can be compared and understood. Whatever definition the reader has in mind, we are confident that all major aspects of it will be covered.

THE CONTRADICTIONS OF COMMUNITY

> The proposition is that many of our social ills would vanish if we would all begin to experience one another (once again) as members of a community, a goal that can

> be facilitated by small-scale settlement patterns that encourage face-to face interactions among diverse neighbors. But what happens when one's neighbors want to party until 2 a.m., or wash their cars and play loud rap music on the village green, or let their lawns grow wild? (Dell Upton [1994], "Just Architectural Business as Usual." *Places, 13*(2), p. 66)

The problem of community is not simply its decline (if indeed it is declining). While community values are invoked to justify civility, tolerance, and the best of human nature, community is also essential to fundamentalism, violent antisocial groups, religious and racial intolerance, and other human ills. Community can both support humanistic, civil life and destroy it. Robert Bellah, coauthor of *Habits of the Heart* (published by University of California Press, 1985), put it this way: "The word 'community' leads a double life. It makes most people feel good, associated as it is with warmth, friendship, and acceptance. But among academics the word arouses suspicion. Doesn't community imply the abandonment of ethical universalism and the withdrawal into closed particularistic loyalties?" (Bellah (1995/1996, Winter, "Community Properly Understood: A Defense of 'Democratic Communitarianism'" *The Responsive Community, 6*(1). http://www.gwu.edu/~icps/bellah.html).

Humans have a fundamental need to belong, to be part of a community, while at the same time wanting to be valued as unique. Depending on the period in history and the culture, the balance may weigh more heavily to one side or another, or the conflict between the two desires may be more or less intense. There are times when this conflict is particularly poignant. One example, eloquently documented in Abraham Verghese's *My Own Country* (published by Simon & Schuster, 1994), is the early days of the AIDS epidemic in the United States, when gay men who had fled their rural small-town homes—and the families and communities that would not accept them—were forced by illness to return to these communities to die. The way their families and towns responded is a fascinating example of the challenges and complexities of community and of human relationships. There can be diametrically opposed views on something as routine as the opening of a new Starbucks cafe. One person may consider this an exciting community development, the creation of a place where community members can meet and mingle. Others see the arrival of Starbucks as a sign of the end times, when true community and friendly local faces are replaced by the standardized anonymity of a global chain.

Some progressives think community is an extension of democracy, that in community everyone is equal, everyone gets something. This is a far cry from community as traditionally experienced. Communities are often hierarchical, and their stability comes from the fact that everyone knows his or her place. A popular view among progressives, especially in the United States, is that everyone likes community:

> Community is a concept, like humanity or peace, that virtually no one has taken the trouble to quarrel with; even its worst enemies praise it. . . . In fact, however, neither our economy, nor our government, nor our educational system runs on the assumption that community has a value—a value, that is, that *counts* in any practical or powerful way. The values that are assigned to community are emotional and spiritual—"cultural"—which makes it the subject of pieties that are merely vocal. (Wendell Berry [1987], *The Landscape of Harmony.* Five Seasons Press, p. 57)

This is not, in fact, true. Many conservatives love the idea of small communities. W. H. Regnery, the wealthy, conservative businessman who funded Celo Community in North Carolina in the 1930s (as well as the right-wing publishing company with his name), believed that self-sufficient farming rather than urban public housing and industrial jobs would revive the pioneer spirit of the United States. But there have been some who see community and any communitarian tendency as a threat to capitalism, free enterprise, and individual rights. Similarly, there are many political liberals who are strongly committed to individual rights, and who have vehemently combated the rights-and-responsibilities agenda of the communitarian scholars led by Amitai Etzioni. The idea of community does presuppose that the group, people together, has a value and rights. There are times when what is good for the community as a whole is in direct conflict with what is good for a given individual. In recognizing the often harsh realities of community—lack of opportunity and privacy, pressure to conform—we have attempted to go beyond the popular views of community that see it as little more than a pleasant amenity to be sought and consumed at will.

THE STUDY OF COMMUNITY

Currently, thousands of scholars, activists, writers, government officials, students, and others around the world are studying efforts to change, revitalize, and maintain communities. There are hundreds of community studies programs and centers at colleges in the North America and Europe, and community is also covered in such diverse disciplines as sociology, anthropology, geography, political science, history, psychology, environmental studies, economics, public health, education, management, leadership, urban and rural studies, architecture and planning, American studies, medicine, and social work.

With so many people from so many fields interested in community, it is no surprise that numerous paradigms, rationales, theories, and research methods have been applied to the study of community. Broadly speaking, these myriad approaches can be divided into two general and somewhat overlapping categories. The first, and more traditional, approach stresses the study of community and community life through description, analysis, comparison, and explanation. The second, more recent, approach is an activist one: It seeks to change communities and sees communities as a force for social change. Since the turbulent 1960s, many university community studies programs have trained young people to utilize the community as an agent of social transformation.

Numerous private and nonprofit community development organizations take the second approach, and many scholars see community as an organizing principle for social action in areas as various as economic development and environmental activism. For example, the architecture movement known as the New Urbanism aims to create developments that will encourage community life. Similarly, environmentalists are forming communities called ecovillages, where they can develop and practice sustainable living techniques in the company of like-minded people.

The study of community by social and behavioral scientists continues to be informed by the seminal work of the German sociologist Ferdinand Tönnies (1855–1936) and the French sociologist Émile Durkheim (1858–1917). Tönnies set forth the basic dichotomy between community (gemeinschaft) and society (gesellschaft), while Durkheim articulated the basic nature of emerging urban settlements.

Until 1970, U.S. history was for all practical purposes the history of the nation as a whole. Those who studied U.S. communities were dismissed as antiquarians, chauvinists, and ancestor worshipers. Since the 1970s, there has been an abrupt about-face, and now the most admired and sophisticated work in the profession is community studies. This field has won the lion's share of prestigious prizes, and students of communities have garnered the most admiring and thoughtful reviews, the most attractive jobs, the best fellowships. The study of communities marked the new direction of the field, the "new social history," as it was called for many years. In more recent years, the same impulse flourishes in a new guise—microhistory—which seeks to tell resonant stories in a thickly described local setting.

Why this turn to community concerns? Why this allocation of attention and prestige to those who have made the turn, and why at this time? Some of it is surely the recognition that narrow professional specialization is itself a dead end. The world isn't divided as the disciplines of the university are. Religion is relevant to politics, psychology is relevant to religion, sociology to psychology, economics to sociology, and on and on. History in particular has moved forcefully from a self-imposed insularity to a dazzling—even excessive—disciplinary cosmopolitanism, in two ways, both of which have brought historians to an unprecedented concern for community.

First, historians have enlarged their horizons has been by borrowing from other disciplines. The extent of this borrowing has been almost immeasurable, and sociology, literary studies, economics, and a host of others have all had fashionable followings. But the single steadiest source of inspiration over the past three decades has been anthropology, with its abiding tradition—its veritable defining dimension—of fieldwork in a bounded community. Insofar as anthropology has helped form the paradigm for the historical turn to the social sciences, it has ineluctably afforded historians models of analysis based in small societies more than in vast national ones.

Second, historians have turned their attention from subjects (for example, the New Deal, or the Civil War) to problems. Since the 1960s, an increasing number of historians have sought not just to describe the world but also to change it. In the process, they discovered that the things they sought to change did not yield neatly to the ministrations of specialists. Like academics in other disciplines who have hoped to touch the world, historians found that they had to develop multidisciplinary means to address multidimensional problems and achieve multifaceted ends. They began thinking of new arenas in which they could collaborate with their new partners, and the community was one of the most obvious new arenas. Just as the fruit fly became part of the defining paradigm of early genetics, or the laboratory rat of behavioral psychology, the community became a conditioning focus of historical endeavor.

There were developments internal to the discipline of history that encouraged this change in focus. History relies on primary sources, so it mattered mightily that the primary sources on the nation seemed very nearly exhausted while those on the mill town, the reform school, the insane asylum, the ethnic enclave, and hundreds of other communities were virtually untapped. And historians' shift in interest reflected a shift in the interest of the American public as a whole: For historians—as for the general public—the national perspective was losing appeal; historians were intrigued by larger or smaller frameworks. In the age of the Internet and the global economy, in a time of cheap travel and with the emergence of English as the language of the world, many began thinking in terms of world history, Atlantic history, and other transnational frameworks. In an age when the immensity of things discouraged people, many others began to care more about groupings closer to home, where they felt they could still matter. When university scholars turned to the study of communities, they could scarcely help noticing that communities had been central to human existence all along. In a similar way, developments in other fields are bringing scholarly subjects closer to people's real-life experience and providing guidance on how to deal with pressing social challenges.

Family

We are familiar with what has become a common political adage, that it takes a village to raise a child, meaning that child rearing should be a community effort. In intentional communities, child rearing has often been considered of particular importance, and in some communities child rearing is deliberately taken over by the community as a whole.

Recently, urban sociology researchers have concentrated on low-resourced, inner-city neighborhoods, and have demonstrated that these contexts have a negative "community effect" on youth. This urban research highlights the question of what to do when collective child-rearing customs become (or are) problematic. Youth function as do the canaries in the mine shaft (or, as sociologist Ralph Brown suggests, canaries in the gemeinschaft): How youth fare developmentally is an indicator of a community's well-being.

Social Capital

Social capital shows that in every act of giving or reciprocity, there is an act of short-term altruism and long-term self-interest (since these networks, norms, and behaviors ultimately improve the community, which means a better life for the giver). The term *social capital* also stands in strong contrast to the warmer, looser, fuzzy *sense of community* popular in everyday parlance. *Social capital* clearly appeals to hard-nosed economists, but some wonder whether the phenomena of human networks and reciprocity should be reduced to transaction-based economic terms.

Technology

Technology has made possible the formation of new communities that are very different from earlier communities—but one has to remember that simply calling something a community does not mean that it provides its members with the same benefits that earlier, less technological forms of community have provided. In *Bowling Alone,* Robert Putnam provides useful observations about the fact that even if users of a chatroom call something a community it doesn't mean that they can easily mobilize other members of the chatroom, or get social support, or job leads from their fellow community members. Other scholars have pointed out that technology often reinforces our existing ways of relating to one another rather than creating new ways.

Nevertheless, the notion of virtual communities has excited the world of community scholarship, and the worlds of learning, information management, and scholarship generally. John Seely Brown, Director of the Xerox Palo Alto Business Center, and Paul Duguid (an *Encyclopedia of Community* contributor) write about the community-forming character of the Internet and in the *Social Life of Information* about how communities form around fields of knowledge and their key documents.

Business

The study of community has also been of much interest in the business world. Perhaps the key work remains that of German social theorist Max Weber (1864–1920), who set forth the basic model of the modern bureaucracy. In the twentieth century, much effort has been devoted to applying the findings of social and behavioral research to corporations. The goal is to use empirical research to help build and maintain more effective work units and foster communication between people at different levels, and the word *community* is used, in a variety of ways, throughout the literature on corporate human resources and organizational development. In the *Encyclopedia of Community,* we have expanded this focus by giving a great deal attention to community economics as well, and to social capital in the workplace.

COMMUNITY IN PRIVATE LIFE

Many, perhaps most, of the entries in the *Encyclopedia of Community* have something to say about the impact of community in our daily lives. For the many readers who not only are trying to understand human ties in an academic way but also are curious about how to experience, personally, a richer sense of community, the encyclopedia provides many perspectives and possible solutions, from cohousing to intentional communities.

The communities in which we live have direct impact on our private lives in several ways. First, communities provide us with a sense of identity. This can be something as basic as what we call roots—which, naturally, extend beyond family to place and culture—to the idea of a hometown. There are many people today who simply have no single place they think of as home, whose family ties are weaker than anything imaginable to our ancestors, and who, not surprisingly, spend time trying to create new communities to fill that void. But the majority of people in the world continue to be rooted in ways that are hard for mobile, urbanized, individualistic Westernized people to imagine; as a result, both the experience of and ideas about community vary enormously from country to country.

Second, communities frequently provide us with a sense of meaning and purpose. This is certainly true of religious communities, in which shared meaning (specific spiritual or theological beliefs) might be described as the primary unifier. But the need to find a sense of meaning and purpose is at the core of human groups as diverse as social activists and Trekkies—and the encyclopedia explores the shared meanings that link people in communities.

Third, communities provide conviviality. At its most basic community is, as the popular television program *Cheers* put it, the place "where everybody knows your name." Ray Oldenburg called such spots "third places" (third, because they are neither the workplace nor the home); they are all the places where people hang out, exchange news, and connect. The encyclopedia touches on this theme in a number of articles, but conviviality—the pleasures of community—is a topic that merits further exploration.

Finally, civility—how we behave toward strangers in the public sphere—is an important feature of community. A particularly diffuse concept, civility is beginning to get attention from civic leaders, scholars, and even political pundits. Civility extends to how we treat public property and facilities, how we park, and how we address and interact with those who are not part of our community. Increased travel and tourism, which brings strangers into even remote small towns, mean that we continually come into contact with people we will never see again. All cultures have had social norms for dealing with strangers, and many cultures have had strong requirements for hospitality. But what we see today in many places is a breakdown of basic civility. As a result, civic and school leaders, among others, are pressing for more attention to this aspect of living together.

WHAT HAVE WE LEARNED?

An encyclopedia creates a community—a virtual think tank—of scholars. Although our mission was not to produce findings, the process of putting together the *Encyclopedia of Community* broadened our horizons and increased our understanding of our human community. As the encyclopedia is used by students, scholars, and professionals throughout the world, we expect it to generate further research, international collaborations, and the testing of ideas and theories.

During the eighteen months it took to create the encyclopedia, we made a variety of observations that may be of interest to readers. First, the thorough research and countless case studies our contributors supplied have confirmed the importance of community in our lives. Community, we discovered, is related to family and friendship, but it has dimensions of its own that are vital to individual health and to the health of societies.

We found that much of the study of community has often been remote from the daily lives and concerns of the people studied. It needs to be broadened to address a number of pressing topics in definitive ways. These include child rearing, social support and inclusion, face-to-face communities after urbanization, the survival of traditional communities, and bridging or integration between different communities.

We also hope that gender will be examined more closely. It is striking that the best-known writers on community are, even today, men. While we have many women contributors, there is a preponderance of men, especially in public policy and economics. This is true in other emerging fields, usually because male scholars are in a position to take more career risks with new topics. Community is a human story, a human need, and we look forward to seeing more work done to bring gendered perspectives into every area of community studies.

Some topics that we wanted to include had not yet been studied broadly enough in terms of their relationship to community. These include sex and sexuality (that is, intimate relationships in community context) and shared work (both historically and in modern times, in the workplace and among neighbors and friends).

Environmentalists often propose that living in small

communities—with local food and energy supplies and little dependence on cars—is the key to solving global environmental problems. While there are many efforts in this direction, from mass transit systems to community supported agriculture, we need a deeper understanding of the challenges involved in using community to solve environmental problems. The relationship between community and consumerism needs further attention, and we also need more study, especially internationally, of the connection between community and modernity. Comprehensive, cross-cultural coverage of these topics will be of great value.

We would also like to see more knowledge drawn from archaeology and evolutionary history. Why has community been around for so many millennia, and how has our need for community evolved as the species (and, later, various cultures) evolved? In prehistoric days, living in community increased each individual's chances of survival, because together they could protect one another and work together to develop and manage a consistent food supply. More research into the sociobiology of community would be invaluable, as there are likely to be considerable debates over whether we are hard-wired to cooperate and what the implications and consequences are if it turns out we are.

We expect to see continued and increasing interest in the effects of development on community, in rich and poor nations, in urban, rural, and suburban areas. In Westernized countries, newer suburban subdivisions lack shared public space, yet without vibrant public spaces the community identity of a town erodes. What will that mean for the future of the suburban subdivisions? We are learning that for small towns as much as for big cities, it is important to preserve mixed socioeconomic classes, mixed uses of space, and public spaces in general. As in a city, the combination of commercial and residential activities in a small town makes it resilient by providing a more textured, vital life. Despite having been liberated from place, people in the twenty-first century still long for some idealized place to live equivalent to an agrarian community, a place where they can be known and nurtured, a place to which they can be attached and where one can sustain a coherent identity.

It is striking that humans are inclined to value something more when it becomes elusive, hard to obtain, perhaps even less essential. Cervantes wrote *Don Quixote,* his satire of chivalry, when chivalry was waning. Max Weber describes the Protestant ethic as the Protestant ethic ceases to make a difference in the economy or even to differentiate between Protestants and Catholics. Similarly, if the community is now coming into view as never before, the implication may be that community is not rising in cultural centrality and power, but declining.

Elective identity has increasingly become a human aspiration. It is at once our glory and our agony. Immigrants came to the New World, for example, to be free to make something more of themselves than they thought they could at home. Pioneers went west for the same reason. With globalization and Americanization, the idea of elective identity is reaching many other parts of the globe.

But as the historian Alexis de Tocqueville (1805–1859) saw so long ago, our freedom doesn't fulfill us. We yearn to belong, to be anchored, to be embedded, to be in a place and to have a place. We will always crave community and the sense of belonging it confers, even while we see its dangers (community can, in the extreme, lead to ethnic cleansing, to the Ku Klux Klan). Community remains a figment of our fondest imaginings as well as a necessity of our existence whose claims on us we ceaselessly struggle to defeat. The *Encyclopedia of Community* captures the fullness of our deep and contradictory responses to community.

To conclude, consider two types of social capital: bonding and bridging. Bonding social capital creates stronger ties within a group; bridging social capital builds stronger ties between groups—across social class or ethnic lines, for example. In publishing, we can compare bonding knowledge and bridging knowledge. Most academic books and journals, and most encyclopedias, increase bonding knowledge—the knowledge developed within a particular discipline, by people who already know one another. Interdisciplinary efforts like this, however, are designed to create bridging knowledge, something bigger than the sum of its parts. This is where a major encyclopedia can play a role that simply isn't possible for smaller, specialized publications. This is the mission encyclopedias must embrace in the future.

—The Editors

Berkshire Publishing Group LLC
Great Barrington, Massachusetts

Acknowledgments

Although the *Encyclopedia of Community* was completed in record time for a scholarly encyclopedia—less than eighteen months to design the project, develop the list, commission contributions from renowned scholars, and have them ready for typesetting—its conceptual gestation took considerably longer. And although it was completed in a small town in New England, it began in London more than ten years ago, as my environmental writing led me into research on community.

My coeditor David Levinson is a cultural anthropologist who, always curious, began to look at the various books and journals I had assembled on community. He realized how much scholarship there was on community in other fields he had worked in, and we soon saw the potential for a major encyclopedia.

Acknowledgments for this project range far beyond that for most encyclopedias. The *Encyclopedia of Community* is not only ambitious but perhaps also audacious, and David Levinson and I could not have pulled it off without an extraordinary and widely varied team—or community—both within and without Berkshire Publishing Group.

Our first thanks must go to Rolf Janke at Sage Reference, who immediately grasped the importance and relevance of this topic when we first explained it over lunch in San Francisco in November 2000. He took our proposal to his colleagues at Sage Publications, in Thousand Oaks, California, and he was able to inspire VP Blaise Simqu and CEO Michael Melody, who saw the project's potential and the interesting fit it made with Sage's acclaimed book and journal program in sociology and urban studies. We are thrilled to have this opportunity again to collaborate with Sage on a groundbreaking scholarly project.

The small editorial team at Berkshire Publishing began this project during the final months of development on our even larger *Encyclopedia of Modern Asia.* As a result, we often thought of the Chinese concept *guanxi. Guanxi* is akin to what we call networks or relationships. *Guanxi* is the greatest reward of huge multiauthored projects, and we turned to many people we already knew when we began the *Encyclopedia of Community.* And the new connections we have made are already leading to further work on human relationships of various kinds, such as the more hierarchical relationship of leaders and followers.

Putting together an editorial board can be a considerable challenge, especially for a project as interdisciplinary and innovative as this one. While David Levinson and I came up with the project concept and served as general editors, we received invaluable assistance from the project's editors—a distinguished group of scholars who have devoted their careers to the investigation of different aspects of community. They have our warmest thanks for an exceptional editorial effort and have become dear colleagues and friends.

In developing the editorial board, my first call was to Ray Oldenburg, a sociologist at the University of West Florida and author of *The Great Good Place.* I had corresponded with Ray about community since the early 1990s, and it was a pleasure to work with him.

Sonya Salamon, an anthropologist who works in rural sociology, joined the board and provided a broad and truly up-to-date look at community in rural life. She also encouraged us to expand our coverage of family and community. Her colleague at the University of Illinois at Urbana-Champaign, Robin Jarrett, helped us in this area.

Two of our editors came to us through architectural historian Dell Upton, thanks to a piece of community serendipity that merits notice. I was active in a campaign to save the neighborhood elementary schools in the Berkshire Hills Regional School District, and one of my comrades in the effort, James Mullen, passed along various articles and magazines related to New Urbanism, because we felt that many of the arguments for New Urbanism could also be made for preserving town-centered schools. One of those magazines contained an article by Dell Upton that struck a chord, and when I contacted him he suggested that we ask Roberta Moudry to serve as editor for our architecture and planning entries and Michael Zuckerman to serve as editor for history. Mike provided entry reviews of exceptional precision, and he did a great deal to improve and expand our coverage.

One of the special pleasures of this project has been picking a favorite book off my shelf and contacting its author about helping with the project. We did this many times, but perhaps first with Michael Shuman, author of *Going Local: Creating Self-Reliant Communities in a Global Age,* who provided guidance on a wide range of community economics topics.

Dennis Judd came to us through Sage, as longstanding but newly retired editor of their *Journal of Urban Studies.* His perspective was a perfect fit, and we especially enjoyed meeting him in Chicago because his love for that city was so evident. It has been wonderful to work with editors who are so committed to their subjects.

William Metcalf was the ideal editor for the entries on intentional communities. Bill is past president of the Intentional Community Studies Association and author of numerous publications on intentional communities around the world. In addition, he is based outside the United States—adding to our global perspective.

To move to the most recent developments in the study of community, editor Barry Wellman—coeditor of *The Internet in Everyday Life*—not only provided extensive coverage of online and virtual communities, but he also was an extraordinary contributor to the Community in Popular Culture database. (Readers will find the Popular Culture entries in Appendix 3 of Volume 4, and with ongoing contributions, at our Web site, www.berkshirepublishing.com/cpc.)

Amitai Etzioni was another obvious candidate for editorship. He was unable to join the board but contributed an important entry on communitarianism, which also sets out the history of how sociologists have looked at community. Robert Putnam, too, became an important supporter of the project, and his colleague at the Kennedy School of Government's Saguaro Seminar, Tom Sander, joined our board. Tom and his wife were expecting a baby when we first talked, and he made it clear that his time was limited, but over the course of the project he went above and beyond what we expected, and provided contacts and guidance that helped to keep us on course.

This is a case when I wish I could acknowledge every contributor with a special comment, because their response to the project was so heart-warming, especially in early days when we wondered just what we had taken on. Community is a huge subject and very hard to get hold of—something like a jellyfish, I sometimes thought—so the phone calls saying, "I don't usually write for encyclopedias, but this project is really special and I want to do it" meant more than certain people realized. Our warmest thanks to all of the people whose thoughtful work is now available in the *Encyclopedia of Community.*

I would especially like to thank those who went above and beyond, pitching in either by making numerous suggestions of authors to contact, giving us valuable advice on coverage, or writing additional entries, sometimes under very tight deadlines: Jan Bang; Deborah DiDuca, Monica Murero, and Victoria Nash; Charles Edgley; Anna Malina; Tyler Norris; Larry Reynolds; Frank Salamone, Alexander Thomas, and Duncan Watts.

Robert Putnam and Robert Bellah provided thoughtful comments, and we value their encouragement for a project that draws in so many ways from their pioneering efforts. Throughout the course of the project, encouragement came from many quarters. We were honored to have comments from Daniel Bell of City University of Hong Kong, who was helpful about Asian thinking on community, and our thanks also go to Chaibong Hahm of Yonsei University in Seoul, Korea, who put us in contact with Daniel and other Asian colleagues working on civil society and related topics.

A longstanding contact, Gabriel Chanan, director of Policy and Research at the Community Development Foundation in London, deserves special thanks for his interest in the project, the contacts he put us in touch with, and his consistently thoughtful advice on European perspectives.

For contributions to and thought-provoking comments on the introduction, I particularly want to thank coeditor Michael Zuckerman, as well as David Christian, William McNeill, and Paul Duguid.

We also had the pleasure of getting to know several librarians who have been astonishingly active in promoting the concept of community and democratic participation within the library world. Kathleen de la Peña McCook of the University of South Florida contributed the entry on public libraries and also provided useful suggestions for the appendices and suggested further contacts. Kathleen first made us aware of how much is being done to build on the public library's unique role as community center. Sarah Ann Long, past president of the American Library Association (ALA) and director of the North Suburban Library System, responded to the project with terrific enthusiasm and a real understanding of what we were trying to achieve, as did fellow former ALA president Nancy Kranich and Deb Robertson, director of the ALA Public Programs Office. Their suggestions and guidance were invaluable as we put together the Libraries Building Community appendix, and we're especially glad to have been able to include some extracts from speeches given by Sarah and Nancy because these pieces so clearly show their passion for making libraries places that build community—and democracy.

The encyclopedia's sidebars include a selection drawn from the archives of the American News Service (ANS), founded by Frances Moore Lappé and Paul Martin DuBois in 1995. We are grateful to Ms. Lappé for her kind permission to use this fascinating material, which adds a human dimension to the discussion in a variety of articles, from environmental action to food pantries, and to editor Tom Sander for reminding us of this wealth of community-based stories. The ANS was a project of the Center for Living Democracy. Over five years, its stories covering "America's search for solutions" appeared in over 300 newspapers and in almost half of the top 100 newspapers by circulation. Subscribers included the *Boston Globe* and *USA Today Weekend.* ANS was supported by the Robert Wood Johnson Foundation, the William and Flora Hewlett Foundation, the MacArthur Foundation, and the Lilly Endowment, among others. Berkshire Publishing is making the full archives available online, free of charge, to researchers on a wide range of community issues, at http://www.berkshire.com/ans.

An effort like this draws on the talents of virtually everyone within a small company like Berkshire. Project coordinator George Woodward took charge of a particularly complex project with poise and consistent good humor. He developed great rapport with editors and authors, and he played a key role in shaping our Community in Popular Culture database. Associate editor Marcy Ross was also a lively contributor to the Resource Guides and Popular Culture database, and she managed the copyediting process and our team of freelance copy editors with characteristic warmth and skill. The key member and senior editor of the copyediting team was Francesca Forrest, who has an exceptional ability to work collaboratively with scholars to ensure that their ideas are presented in language that will be accessible and engaging to all. Entries came from many authors whose first language is not English, and from many unused to writing for a general audience, so the work of Marcy, Francesca, and our entire copyediting team is an invaluable feature of this Berkshire Reference work.

The *Encyclopedia of Community* provoked a great deal of discussion in the office, especially as all the other project coordinators—Sarah Conrick, Elizabeth Eno, and June Kim—were involved in final manuscript checking, and then as the Resource Guides and Popular Culture database were compiled. Our technology department—Debbie Dillon, Cathy Fracasse, and Trevor Young—stepped in with practical assistance at every stage, and also provided an amazing variety of book, movie, and music suggestions. Thomas Christensen, Rachel Christensen, and Emily Cotton also lent valuable administrative support to the project.

The production department at Sage Reference also deserves hearty thanks for their enthusiasm, professionalism, and timeliness in handling a project of this scale. It's been a pleasure to work, once again, with Diana Axelsen, Ravi Balasuriya, Steve Martin, Kate Peterson, Sandra Ng Sauvajot, Sara Tauber, Olivia Weber, Karen Wiley, and Patricia Zeman.

I began thinking about these acknowledgments while in a place—and a situation—at the heart of community. I was at Town Hall, observing the weekly meeting of our Board of Selectmen, and I was there because I was trying to decide whether to run for office again. While politics is by no means the only aspect of community covered in these volumes, the relationship between community building at a personal level and community building in public life is a recurrent theme. Democracy depends, our contributors explain, on the many connections, ties, and common understandings that are the stuff of community at many levels. Our thanks, therefore, go to one particular community, that of Great Barrington, Massachusetts, where we have learned so much about both the upsides and downsides of community life.

—Karen Christensen

About the Editors

GENERAL EDITORS

Karen Christensen is an editor and author who has focused for more than ten years on community and environmental issues. She is CEO of Berkshire Publishing Group.

In response to a suburban childhood, she became fascinated by Japan and China, and then, at age ten, by farming. At fourteen she ran away to a commune, and at sixteen she made a solo trip by bus deep into Mexico. After college, she lived in London for more than ten years, where she worked with Valerie Eliot on the T. S. Eliot *Letters*. Her book, *Eco Living*, now in its third U.K. edition, and a children's picture book, *Rachel's Roses*, have been published in France, Germany, Taiwan, and China, and she has taught seminars at the College of Creative Studies at the University of California, Santa Barbara, and at the City Institute in London.

In addition to serving as senior editor and shepherd of the *Encyclopedia of Community*, she was project director of the *Encyclopedia of World Environmental History* (Routledge, 2003), and coeditor of the *Encyclopedia of Modern Asia* (Scribners, 2002), *International Encyclopedia of Women & Sports* (Macmillan, 2001) and *Encyclopedia of World Sport* (ABC-Clio/Oxford, 1999).

In Britain, she helped found the Women's Environmental Network and the Ecological Design Association, and she was briefly the U.K. Green Party's speaker on women's issues. Karen has been active in community affairs and local politics, both in her London neighborhood and in the Berkshires. She is currently working on a book about the search for community, *A Smaller Circle*.

David Levinson is a cultural anthropologist specializing in contemporary social issues and well-known editor of major print reference publications. For twenty-one years, he was on the staff, and latterly vice-president, of the Human Relations Area Files (HRAF) at Yale University.

His first work, a study of the Bowery in New York, was published when he was still an undergraduate. He has written widely on ethnicity, social problems, and human relationships, covering such topics as international ethnic relations, multiculturalism, substance abuse, homelessness, and violence against women and children, as well as management and cross-cultural research methods.

In 1992, he was a visiting scholar at the National Museum of Ethnology in Kyoto, Japan, and he has received research grants from the Connecticut Humanities Council and the National Institutes of Mental Health.

Levinson currently serves as Berkshire's president and editorial director. He was general editor of the *Encyclopedia of Crime and Punishment* and the *Encyclopedia of Modern Asia.* Among his recent publications are the first volumes in the *Religion & Society* series (Routledge), *Ethnic Groups Worldwide* (Oryx Press 1998), *Religion: A Cross-Cultural Dictionary* (trade paperback, Oxford University Press 1998), and the *Encyclopedia of Human Emotions* (Macmillan 1999). Other publications include the *Encyclopedia of World Cultures, American Immigrant Cultures: Builders of a Nation,* the *Encyclopedia of Cultural Anthropology,* the *Encyclopedia of Marriage and the Family,* and the *Encyclopedia of World Sport.*

He is currently writing a history of African American

church community in Great Barrington, where Berkshire Publishing is based and where leading intellectual W. E. B. DuBois was born and raised.

EDITORS

Robin L. Jarrett is Associate Professor of Family Studies in the Department of Human and Community Development, University of Illinois at Urbana-Champaign. Her research interests include child and adolescent development, African American families, family functioning and resilience, urban poverty, and qualitative research methods.

Dennis R. Judd is Professor of Political Science at the University of Illinois at Chicago. For several years he has been a major contributor to the literature on urban political economy, urban economic development, national urban policy, and urban revitalization. He also has published extensively on urban regeneration in Europe and the United States.

William Metcalf is a self-employed researcher and author, as well as an Adjunct Lecturer at Griffith University in Australia. He specializes in the study of intentional communities and has previously served as president of the International Communal Studies Association, which is headquartered in Israel. During thirty years of research, he has visited well over 100 intentional communities worldwide. He is working on two books, the *Findhorn Book of Community Living* and the *Encyclopedia of Australian Utopian Communalism.*

Roberta Moudry is an architectural and urban historian. She received her M.A. and Ph.D. from Cornell University, where she conducted studies of early-twentieth-century American planned communities and the architectural and business culture of life insurance. She has taught courses in American urban and planning history and architectural theory.

Ray Oldenburg has held positions in the state university systems of Minnesota, Wisconsin, Nevada, and Florida. His areas of specialization are community and public life, and he is known internationally for his book *The Great Good Place*, which appeared in 1989 and is presently in its third edition. The idea of "third places," a term he coined, has inspired projects including the Milestone community in Pensacola, Florida. and he now advises such cities as San Jose, Stockholm, and Osaka on community development.

Sonya Salamon is Professor of Community Studies in the Department of Human and Community Development at the University of Illinois at Urbana-Champaign. She has studied Illinois rural communities, as well as families and communities, for some thirty years, and is past president of the Rural Sociological Society. Her most recent book is *Newcomers to Old Towns: Suburbanization of the Heartland.*

Thomas Sander is Executive Director of the Saguaro Seminar on Civic Engagement in America at Harvard University's John F. Kennedy School of Government. He managed the Social Capital Community Benchmark Survey, the largest survey of social capital to-date, measuring levels of social capital in forty communities nationwide.

Michael Shuman is a Stanford-trained attorney and economist. He currently runs two institutions: Bay Friendly Chicken Inc., a community-owned poultry company in Maryland; and the Green Policy Institute, which undertakes public policy research and writing related to sustainable communities. He is author of *Going Local: Creating Self-Reliant Communities in a Global Age.*

Barry Wellman is Professor of Sociology at the University of Toronto and Director of the NetLab at the university's Centre for Urban and Community Studies. He is also Chair Emeritus of the Community and Urban Sociology section of the American Sociological Association. He is the coeditor of three books, including *The Internet in Everyday Life* (Blackwell 2002). He found community in the 1950s on the streets of New York City and found the Internet in science fiction novels at the same time. He has been immersed in some form of the Internet since 1976.

Michael Zuckerman is Professor of History at the University of Pennsylvania. He has been studying American communities all his scholarly life. His first book, *Peaceable Kingdoms*, was an interpretation of the New England town in the eighteenth century that helped establish the "new social history." In subsequent books and articles, he has wrestled with the plight of children in suburbia, the writings of Lewis Mumford, the decay of the cities, the uses of community service in teaching, and the place of religion in community studies.

A

ACTIVIST COMMUNITIES

Activist communities are those that seek some sort of structural change in existing social, political, or economic systems, or in some combination of those arenas. They are often distinguished from mutual-aid or self-help organizations that tend to avoid seeking political or social change. Activist movements are often categorized by the type of community in which they organize. These include communities delineated by geography (which may become involved in, for instance, neighborhood organizing), issue (typical issues being civil rights, labor, and health care), and identity (with people coming together for social activism based on their shared gender, race, ethnicity, religion, age, or disability).

Among geographically based activists in the United States, the most common type of activist community is the neighborhood organizing group. Neighborhood activists are often distinguished from neighborhood associations, which generally are not interested in structural social change. These latter groups are often focused on socialization or neighborhood preservation, including the maintenance of property values and, often, the exclusion of "undesirable elements" from the area. Neighborhood activists are more likely to be working for more equitable access to resources, such as financial capital, public services, or health care. They tend to operate in lower-income neighborhoods or neighborhoods of color. Neighborhood organizing continues to be a substantial area of activism in the United States. Geographically based activists—and neighborhood activists—are present not only in the United States but also in other nations. Just as segregation—often by class or ethnicity as much as by race—persists in other countries, geographic activism is also present. In some countries, such as the United Kingdom, neighborhood-based activists might be considered to have had more success in contributing to public policy and action.

Issue-based activists are perhaps the most common in the United States. They attempt to form communities of interest on a policy issue or set of related issues. These often are national in scope, although statewide and even citywide communities are often formed, sometimes as chapters of larger national organizations (examples include local chapters of the Sierra Club or Common Cause). In modern U.S. history, some of the most important activist communities have been issue based. These include communities that campaigned for workers' rights and that helped organize unions, the feminist movements of the nineteenth and twentieth centuries, the civil rights movement, and the antiwar movement of the 1960s. Similar movements are present in the twenty-first century. Some of the newer issue-based activist communities include the antiglobalization movement, the living wage movement, and the movement in support of campaign finance reform. Similar issue-based activists exist across the globe. Antiglobalization activists, for example, are quite active in Europe, gaining particular attention for protesting against American cultural and agricultural importation, an activity perhaps epitomized by the general rejection of Euro Disney.

While not entirely new, identity-based activist communities are currently perhaps the most controversial. Identity-based activists believe that the common history, circumstances, and legacies of individuals that share a certain key trait—such as race, gender, ethnicity, or disability—require that their activism be based in such identities. Individuals of the same or similar identities or experiences, the argument goes, need to band together to work for change on behalf of their community. Advocates of this school of activism often argue that other approaches are too often dominated by white male leadership and perspectives. While older identity-based activist communities, such as, for example, the National Association for the Advancement of Colored People (NAACP), often permitted and even encouraged the support of those not sharing the identity, many modern proponents of this approach do not seek such external support.

DIFFERENT METHODS, DIFFERENT STYLES

Activist communities can also be distinguished by the methods and mechanisms they use to pursue change. These include direct service, research, advocacy, and direct action. Direct-service organizations, which some do not consider activist, focus on the development of resources and services for people in a community. They might, for example, organize a soup kitchen or a housing program.

Groups employing research as a principal method typically conduct applied research on problems and issues to stimulate public discussion and promote solutions to the problems. Many U.S. public interest organizations publish reports and studies aimed at particular issues and problems. Examples include the Center on Budget and Policy Priorities, which focuses on welfare, tax, and budget issues, and the Economic Policy Institute, which focuses on employment and economic growth issues. In the United Kingdom, the New Economics Foundation produces research on economic disparities and employment-related problems.

Advocacy movements tend to focus on political action. They employ a variety of methods, including research, education, media campaigns, and lobbying, to gain changes in public policy. Advocates may be representative organizations (e.g., membership groups such as the NAACP), or they may be independent organizations without a membership base. While volunteers or members may be involved with lobbying and advocacy efforts, such participation is a means to an end rather than an end in itself. Advocacy organizations tend to be issue based, but may also be identity based, or even geographically based.

The last type of activist community is the direct action group. Like advocacy groups, direct action groups tend to seek changes in policy. They also use some of the same tools as advocacy groups—including research and education. However, a main goal of direct action movements is direct involvement of members of the community in the activism and in the development of political relationships. Indigenous leadership is important in the philosophy of direct action groups, who aim to develop the political power of community members and to make them aware of this power. Many U.S. direct action activists trace their methods to the work of Saul Alinsky (1909–1972) in the 1930s and later. Alinsky developed a model of direct action neighborhood organizing that involved both self-help and social action. His in-your-face confrontational style began with the formation of the Back of the Yards Neighborhood Council (BYNC) in Chicago in the late 1930s. BYNC successfully developed relationships with unions and the Catholic Church, which made it a formidable force in Chicago, even able to stand up to the political machine. Alinsky went on to train organizers all over the country and wrote important books on activism and organizing.

In addition to the different methods of organizing, there is a large variation in how militant or aggressive activist communities operate. Many activists are fairly moderate in their methods and objectives. They may seek structural change, but they tend to seek modest levels of change. They also tend to use mainstream methods—including policy analysis, research, and education—as their primary methods. Many of the larger environmental groups, for example, fit this description, and this may account for much of their success. On the other hand, there are activist organizations and movements that seek highly controversial and radical changes to policy. Some of these groups also employ highly confrontational methods—including picketing and visible protests. Many tend to accept conflict as a fundamental principle of their operations.

HISTORICAL FOUNDATIONS OF ACTIVISM

Activist communities do not have a single genesis. The sixteenth-century Protestant Reformation, which grew out of dissatisfaction with abuses and corruption in the Catholic Church, is an early example of European activism, and one can point to many uprisings of people against tyrannical governments as a form of activism. In that vein, the heroes of the American Revolution might be considered the earliest U.S. activists; Thomas Paine, the populist writer of that era, has certainly been a model for many activists, even up to the present. However, modern activism is generally tied to a few historical developments in the nineteenth and twentieth centuries. First, the women's suffrage movement certainly created a model for many activists to follow. Similarly, workers' rights and unionism formed the basis for activism and advocacy work through the mid-twentieth century. The social reform movement in the early twentieth century, including efforts to regulate working and living conditions and to increase business regulation, created a new paradigm. In that new paradigm, government came to be viewed by many as a key force for improving important aspects of citizens' quality of life, especially for the poor and less advantaged.

Until at least the 1920s, however, activism in the United States was a fairly narrow arena of public activity. Generally dominated by socially responsible members of the elite segments of society, only union activism had provided for much participation by lower-income groups. Neighborhood organizations were largely preservationist and conservative in nature. By joining economic justice issues and direct action methods, Alinsky helped democratize activism. He provided a blueprint for local communities all over the country to organize for political and economic power. Yet he also realized the importance of tying local organizations together to achieve change on a larger scale.

An example of Alinsky-style organizing that developed from a neighborhood-based effort to activism on a national scale started in Alinsky's hometown, Chicago. Alinsky worked closely with a former businessman named Tom Gaudette, who through his Catholic Church activism became interested in neighborhood organizing. Gaudette helped form an Alinsky-based neighborhood group on the far west side of Chicago called Organization for a Better Austin. OBA was concerned with poor schools and neighborhood decline. One local resident who became active in OBA was Gale Cincotta, who went on to lead the national fight for the federal Community Reinvestment Act (CRA). The CRA requires banks and savings and loans to offer credit throughout their entire market areas and prohibits them from targeting only wealthier neighborhoods with their lending and services.

COLLABORATION AND CONFLICT AMONG ACTIVISTS

In the twentieth century, the increasing role of the federal government was both a cause and a result of the growth of social activism. Union activity and support helped make possible President Franklin D. Roosevelt's New Deal. Similarly, the civil rights movement and activism on poverty issues helped spur the Great Society programs of the 1960s. At the same time, the increasing importance of the federal government in issues of social and economic justice increased the need for activists to expand beyond their local horizons to form national networks and coalitions and to build political power at the federal level.

In the neighborhood-organizing and community development arenas, for example, a number of nationwide organizations developed in the latter half of the twentieth century to support local efforts and to work for federal policy changes. These include such national networks as Citizen Action, National People's Action (founded by Gale Cincotta), and the Association of Community Organizations for Reform Now (ACORN).

In the very late twentieth and early twenty-first century, a growing number of activists—especially in the environmental and worker-rights arenas—have recognized that the globalization of the economy has constrained what can be done even at the federal level. Thus, a new breed of activism has arisen that is seeking to address global issues and policies. Chief among the targets of these movements are international financial institutions, including the World Bank and the International Monetary Fund. These new coalitions seek to collaborate across international boundaries to develop multinational activism strategies.

However, with activism also comes occasional conflict among activists. Variations in the types, methods, and militancy of different activist movements, together with their propensity to intersect on many different issues, can lead to discord among activists. More aggressive activists sometimes accuse more pragmatic groups of "copping out." Alinsky-style direct action groups may resent the less indigenous approach of advocacy groups. And the advocacy groups—especially those that are specialized and have developed a large amount of expertise on an issue—may decry the lack of expertise on the part of the direct action activists.

DID YOU KNOW...

Major activist issues in the twenty-first century include the following:

Worker Rights	Women's Rights	Environment
Human Rights	World Peace	Globalization

There are a few areas in which activists frequently come into conflict with one another. First, direct action advocates, while often aggressive in style, frequently seek concrete objectives that they feel are achievable over the fairly short term. This is key to Alinsky-style organizing. If people are to be encouraged to become engaged and use their power, they must see that direct action works. They need victories. Thus, the community-building nature of direct action activism may necessitate being pragmatic and reaching compromises that are far from ideal. Issue-based advocates, on the other hand, may be willing to invest years of work to achieve a more desirable policy outcome. So there is a tension between pragmatism and idealism as well as a conflict between shorter- and longer-term time horizons.

Conflicts can also arise over the importance of relationships. Some activists value relationships so highly that they will compromise to a great degree on an issue in order to sustain an important relationship. For example, some organizers view relationships with public officials and others as key to building community power. If necessary, they are willing to compromise on an issue primarily for the sake of developing that relationship. Other activists do not value such relationships so highly and are willing instead to alienate officials who stand in their way.

ACTIVISM IN THE TWENTY-FIRST CENTURY

By many measures, activist communities remain strong, both in the United States and in many other parts of the world. The recent surge in activism on issues of global economic change and environmentalism suggests that there may be a continued growth in activism in less developed countries. In the United States, the shift to conservative politics and policies in the 1990s almost certainly reinvigorated activism in many respects. Funding organizations and others saw an increased need for such work. Although many people imagine activist communities as primarily on the left of the political spectrum, in fact activism exists on both the left and the right. Few can claim to be more dedicated activists that those fighting gun control or abortion rights in the United States—both issues associated with the political right. Whatever the politics, activist communities will continue to evolve and may, as in the twentieth century, find new techniques and new philosophies to guide them.

—Dan Immergluck

See also Alinsky, Saul; Civil Disobedience; Community Action; Community Empowerment; Gay Communities; Grassroots Leadership; Local Politics; Social Justice

Further Reading

Bobo, K., Kendall, J., & Max, S. (2001). *Organizing for social change: Midwest Academy manual for activists.* Santa Ana, CA: Seven Locks Press.

Boris, E. T., & Steuerle, C. E. (1999). *Nonprofits and government: Collaboration and conflict.* Washington, DC: Urban Institute Press.

Delgado, G. (1997). *Beyond the politics of place: New directions in community organizing in the 1990s.* Oakland, CA: Applied Research Center.

Fisher, R. (1994). *Let the people decide: Neighborhood organizing in America.* New York: Twayne Publishers.

The Midwest Academy. (2002). *The Midwest Academy direct action organizing process.* Retrieved November 8, 2002, from http://www.mindspring.com/~midwestacademy/Organize/page5.html

Walls, D. (1993). *The activist's almanac: The concerned citizen's guide to the leading advocacy organizations in America.* New York: Fireside Books.

ADOLESCENCE

Many past societies, even those in ancient times, had language that referred to a period between childhood and adulthood—what we call adolescence. In modern society, adolescence has been shaped by broad social and economic changes associated with the rise of industrialization, as well as prolonged time spent in formal education. This specific life stage called adolescence can be observed around the world. However, how it is understood and how it impacts self and others vary considerably depending on the community and society in which it occurs.

THE AGES OF ADOLESCENCE

While adolescence can be observed around the globe, there is no specific, universally accepted age range that defines the beginning or end of this period for every community or society. In modern society, the typical ages associated with adolescence range from ten to eighteen. However, as educational demands have increased in the face of a rapidly changing integrated world economy, the period associated with adolescence has lengthened and can include ages up through the mid-twenties. In the absence of clearly defined age boundaries of adolescence, social factors, such as marriage, help define this period for communities and societies.

Thus, the ages of adolescence can vary for different communities and societies.

THREE MARKERS OF ADOLESCENCE

Despite the fluctuation in the age range of adolescence, the developmental task of the period essentially remains the same: a successful transition to becoming a fully functioning productive member of adult society. The relative success of this transitional period hinges on the interaction of three markers of adolescent development.

Biological Changes

Throughout childhood, physical growth is steady and relatively predictable, but with the onset of puberty dramatic changes begin to occur to the body. Rapid acceleration of growth, development of primary and secondary sex characteristics (the former being changes to the reproductive organs themselves and the latter being outward signs of maturity, such as growth of pubic hair), increases in muscle and fat, and increased circulatory and respiratory capacities all occur during puberty. Remarkably, when the adolescent is growing most rapidly, he or she gains in height at a rate equal to that of a toddler. These changes are arguably the one universal aspect of adolescence around the world. However, the impact of these changes is not universal and depends on the context—the environment—in which they occur. For example, some cultures have formal initiation rituals associated with puberty, signifying to the community that the individual is now an adult and receives adult status and responsibilities. In the United States, the responses to pubertal changes are often less pronounced and more private, with few, if any, initiation rituals (responses are often limited to joking or teasing). These varied responses to puberty in different communities help contribute to the adolescent's self-concept.

An African Girl's Initiation Ceremony

In many societies around the world, the transition from childhood to adolescence or adulthood is marked by a formal ceremony. The following text extract provides an introduction to the chisungu *rite of the Bemba people of Zambia.*

The chisungu of the Bemba is usually described either as a puberty rite for girls or as a female initiation ceremony. It consists of a long and rather elaborate succession of ritual acts which includes miming, singing, dancing and the handling of sacred emblems. In the old days the chisungu invariably preceded the marriage of a young girl, and was an integral part of the series of ceremonies by which a bridegroom was united to the family group of his bride, in a tribe in which descent is reckoned through the woman and not through the man, and in which a man comes to live with his wife's relatives at marriage rather than a woman with her husband's. . . .

The Bemba chisungu is an individual nubility rite practised for each girl, or for two or three girls together and it is preceded by a short puberty ceremony proper. When a girl knows that her first period has come she tells older women and they must "bring her to the hearth" again (ukumufishyo peshiko), or "show her the fire" (ukumulanga umulilo) since her condition has made her "cold." This is done by rites which vary slightly from locality to locality. The ukusolwela ceremony is one in which doctored seeds are cooked on a fire and the girl must pull them out and eat them burning hot. In another rite she is washed with medicine cooked in a special pot and she drinks this medicine too. She is then isolated indoors for a day or more and fed with a small ball of millet porridge cooked in new fire so that she may be made free to eat again without harming herself or others. This is the usual Bemba way of returning to the community a person who has passed through an unusual or dangerous state.

The girl then waits till it is convenient for her chisungu ceremony to be danced. I call this latter a nubility rite since it is clearly considered as a preliminary to the marriage ceremony; indeed, Bemba accounts frequently confuse the two. Formerly the girl came to her chisungu already betrothed, and this is usually the case today. The bridegroom plays a part in the rite in his own person, or is represented by his sister. He contributes to the cost of the rite by paying the mistress of the ceremonies. The chisungu protects the young couple against the magic dangers of first intercourse and gives the bridegroom the right to perform this act, which is thought to be entirely different from all that follow it.

Source: Richards, Audrey I. (1956). *Chisungu: A Girl's Initiation Ceremony Among the Bemba of Northern Rhodesia*. London: Faber and Faber, 1956, pp. 17, 54.

Cognitive Changes

Paralleling the biological changes of adolescence, there are significant cognitive changes, that is, changes in ways of thinking, that occur at the same time. Some of the key cognitive changes occurring during adolescence include the ability to think more abstractly and engage in more complex thought processes, and an increased awareness of one's own thinking processes. For example, adolescents are able to solve the following problem because of increased abstract thinking: If A is less than B and B is less than C, is A less than or greater than C? Most adolescents can solve this problem, but the prepubescent child finds it difficult or impossible to solve. An important by-product of these newly developed abilities is the capacity to understand complex language devices, such as metaphors, satire, and sarcasm.

One of the most influential theories of cognitive development during adolescence came from the Swiss psychologist Jean Piaget (1896–1980). His theory holds that thinking develops in predictable stages from childhood through adolescence and into adulthood. According to Piaget, the "formal operations" stage begins at adolescence at approximately eleven years and is completed at around eighteen years, although the upper age range can vary considerable (from approximately fifteen to twenty-one). In this stage, unlike the previous stage (concrete operations), adolescents develop the capacity to reason about a problem using formal abstract logic—the type necessary to solve the problem given above.

Other important theories of adolescent cognitive development have also been developed. Information-processing theories aim to identify changes in adolescents' thinking, such as increases in long- or short-term memory, that allow them to solve more complex problems. Another theory, social cognitive theory, aims to understand how adolescents learn from other people and from the community (their social environment).

Social Changes

In addition to the biological and cognitive changes occurring during adolescence, important changes also occur between the individual adolescent and society during this period. Some of these include changes in legal, political, economic, and interpersonal status. In the United States, at sixteen a person can legally drive a vehicle, at eighteen one can vote, and many delay career decisions until their mid-twenties. Adolescents in other countries experience similar changes, although the age at which these changes occur varies. For example, in Germany adolescents decide relatively early (between ages fifteen and sixteen) to pursue vocational education or higher education. Significant interpersonal changes also occur. There is an increase in intimacy between friends as well as increased interest in romantic relationships.

As might be expected, the timing and recognition of these social changes vary considerably depending on what particular community or culture the adolescent is in. Some societies clearly separate the boundaries between childhood, adolescence, and adulthood, marking the transitions with ceremonies and rites of passage to signify the change in the individual's status. For example, bar mitzvah and bat mitzvah (male and female, respectively) ceremonies are often held in Jewish communities and signify that the individual has attained adult status. With this event, the individual has conferred on him or her the religious rights and responsibilities associated with adult status. Other societies or cultural groups demarcate the boundaries between childhood, adolescence, and adulthood less clearly, with few, if any, formal events to signify a change.

ADOLESCENTS WITHIN COMMUNITIES

The biological, cognitive, and social changes associated with adolescence do not occur in isolation; their impact on development interacts with the communities in which adolescents are situated. Research continues to document community assets (for example, community and school support) as crucial ingredients in healthy adolescent development, although not all communities surround adolescents with a similar set or number of assets. Those communities that provide youth with opportunities to contribute to their society and learn important skills (such as goal setting, decision making, and communicating) are better prepared to assist their adolescents in the transition from adolescence to adulthood. In turn, these adolescents often become active and productive members of their communities in adulthood.

—David M. Hansen

See also Fraternities and Sororities; Gangs; Human Development; Internet, Teen Use of; Online Communities, Youth

Further Reading

Arnett, J. J. (2001). *Adolescence and emerging adulthood: A cultural approach.* Upper Saddle River, NJ: Prentice Hall.

Benson, P. L. (1997). *All kids are our kids: What communities must do to raise caring and responsible children and adolescents.* San Francisco: Jossey-Bass.

Eccles, J., & Gootman, J. (Eds.). (2002). *Community programs to promote youth development.* Washington, DC: National Academies Press.

Feldman, S. S., & Elliot, G. R. (Eds.). (1990). *At the threshold: The developing adolescent.* Cambridge, MA: Harvard University Press.

Mortimer, J. T., & Finch, M. D. (Eds.). (1996). *Adolescents, work,*

and family: An intergenerational developmental analysis. London: Sage.
Muuss, R. E. (1996). *Theories of adolescence* (6th ed.). New York: McGraw-Hill.
Steinberg, L. (1996). *Adolescence* (4th ed.). New York: McGraw-Hill.

ADOLESCENTS AND LANDSCAPE

Adolescents use and value many types of landscapes. These landscapes are the settings for many of the activities teens engage in, and the activities are often the means by which the teens complete important developmental tasks. The study of the relationships between adolescents and place is relatively recent, with the earliest studies undertaken in the 1970s. In fact, the concept of adolescence itself is relatively new. With the enactment of child labor laws and the school reform movement around the beginning of the twentieth century, adolescence was first identified as a distinct stage in life. During the 1950s, the influence of the mass media helped to further crystallize adolescence by promoting common values and attitudes among members of this age group. The research on adolescents and place has identified landscapes that are important to adolescents, the things they do there, and the reasons adolescents think those landscapes are important.

THEORETICAL FOUNDATIONS

Research on people-place interactions has its foundations in ecology and humanistic psychology. Ecology gives us the basic premise that people and the environment are interdependent. Humanistic psychology, an approach that emerged in the late 1950s, provides a foundation for understanding people's experiences and their responses to external factors.

In exploring the relationships between adolescents and physical environments, there are two avenues we may pursue. First, we can examine how youth interact with their environments; second, we can determine what youth think about their environments.

How Do Youth Interact With Their Environment?

The interaction with physical environments can take many forms. Individuals or groups can use it, they can change it, they can adapt to it, and they can destroy it. Adolescents' interactions with their environment have been documented and analyzed through behavior observations, behavior trace mapping, and photography. Behavior observations include documenting the activities occurring in a particular environment and are typically conducted at various times over several weeks or months. Information such as when the persons arrive, how long they stay, who they come with, and what they do is recorded. Behavior trace mapping involves looking for clues as to the past use of the environment. These clues can include worn paths in the grass, an opening cut into a fence, or fast-food wrappers on the ground. Photography and video recordings are used to record activities at various times or seasons. These images are analyzed for use patterns.

What Do Youth Think of Their Environments?

Three areas of study address the question of what youth think of their environment: place preferences, environmental cognition, and place affordances. Place preference studies seek to determine what places adolescents prefer and to identify the characteristics that make those places appealing. Researchers have sought to understand many parameters of adolescents' preferences, including types of places (e.g., park, commercial area, school grounds); type and extent of nature (e.g., indoor potted plants, manicured lawn, unmanaged forest); and the absence or presence of others. Methods used to conduct preference studies range from large-scale group surveys with two-dimensional images (actual and simulated) to individual interviews at actual locations. Environmental cognition studies seek to identify how the individual perceives a particular environment. Cognition studies ask individuals or groups to describe the environments in question. These descriptions are recorded as drawings, often referred to as "mental maps"; as collage drawings using pre-existing images; or through words. Place affordance studies examine how successful particular environments are in allowing individuals to undertake their desired activities and often employ individual questionnaires.

LANDSCAPES THAT ARE IMPORTANT TO ADOLESCENTS

Parks, schools, commercial areas, places around home, and undeveloped open spaces all have been identified as places important to adolescents. These places are where teens go to be with their friends, to play sports, to have fun, and to be by themselves. These places also provide physical settings for the completion of several develop-

Two high school students mix technology and nature when they do their schoolwork beside a baseball field.
Source: Steve Prezent/Corbis; used with permission.

mental tasks that are undertaken during adolescence, including the development of self-esteem, self-identity, a sense of belonging, social competence, social responsibility, and the ability to manage free time.

Talking, in particular talking with their peers, provides adolescents with opportunities to experiment with various behaviors and opinions and to explore taboo topics. This activity is an important step in developing satisfying social relationships and in developing adolescents' self-identity and self-esteem. Getting together with their friends also helps adolescents develop social competence; they have to plan their meeting time, location, and activity, and decide who will attend. The places that seem to be best suited for this activity are parks, schools, and malls or other commercial areas. In several studies, the neighborhood park was selected by teens as a place where they like to go because they can get together with their friends. Female teens are more likely than male teens to go to parks simply to hang out with their friends, whereas male teens may go to play ball or to engage in other activities. School also provides an important place for engaging with their peers. Although adolescents often do not like or value school highly, it is a place where they enjoy seeing their friends. Lastly, commercial areas, particularly those in suburban and urban areas, provide opportunities for adolescents to interact with their friends and with other adolescents they may not know. Opportunities to "try on" new identities and to have some anonymity is important.

Recreation provides a mechanism for teens to develop social competence and social responsibility. Whether engaged in individually or as part of a team, sports activities provide guidance for adolescents in establishing and accomplishing goals, an important lifelong skill. When trying to perfect a new pitch, jump, or hit, adolescents develop patience and learn the discipline of practice, two traits valued in adult workers. Team sports require working with others and following rules. For their part, individual sports, such as skateboarding, have unwritten rules such as waiting your turn. Sports fields and sport-specific courts or parks, such as tennis courts, basketball courts, and skateboard parks, provide locations for these activities. In addition, many adolescent recreational activities are conducted in undesignated areas such as parking lots, neighborhood streets and alleys, and urban plazas.

Landscapes that provide adolescents with an opportunity to be alone or with close friends are also important to their development. Adolescents need places where they can think about who they are and who they want to be, sort through problems, and be rejuvenated. Teens, particularly females, often find places at home or close to home for this purpose. A quiet place in the backyard, down the street, or in their own room can be used as a retreat. In many communities, adolescents also find undeveloped lands such as hillsides, cliffs, waterfalls, lakes, and agricultural fields good places to go to be alone. These places are often valued because they are places where the youth can look out but feel like they cannot be seen. These places, termed "prospect refuges" by British geographer Jay Appleton, have been found to be particularly important to adolescents.

PLACE USE: CONFLICTS AND RESPONSE

Adults often view adolescents' use of these various landscapes in a negative light. At worst, they feel threatened by groups of teens who are "hanging out"; at best, they find it an unproductive use of time. Adults are uncomfortable with teens being alone because of the possibility of illicit or inappropriate activities. Also, some recreational activities, such as skateboarding, are viewed negatively because of the property damage they can cause and because such activities—for instance, in a parking lot—can often interfere with others' use of the area.

In addition, places are typically designed or set aside with specific anticipated uses in mind. The designers, managers, property owners, and others expect the place to be used in that manner. Using such a place in a different way is seen as a violation of it.

This is the underlying cause of many of the conflicts between adolescents and others in the landscape. Places are not typically designed with the adolescents' desired uses in mind; therefore, when they engage in these activities, they are seen as violators of the place. The responses to these violations are often curfew, loitering, and skateboarding ordinances that prohibit certain behaviors, and the application of design practices, such as the removal of seating areas or the addition of skate stops along walls, that discourage the undesired behaviors. Conversely, efforts to provide places for adolescents include the creation of youth centers and skateboard parks in some communities. Approaches such as these, which incorporate the likely activities of teens into public areas, result in fewer conflicts between adolescents and other users and provide adolescents with supportive environments.

—Eubanks Owens

Further Reading

Appleton, J. (1975). *The experience of the landscape.* New York: John Wiley & Sons.

Hester, R. T., McNally, M., Hale, S., Lancaster, Mi., Hester, N., and Lancaster, Ma. (1988). "We'd like to tell you . . ." Children's views of life in Westport, California. *Small Town, 18*(4), 19–24.

Kaplan, R., & Kaplan, S. (Eds.). (1978). *Humanscape: Environments for people.* North Scituate, MA: Duxbury Press.

Klein, H. (1990). Adolescence, youth, and young adulthood: Rethinking current conceptualizations of life stage. *Youth & Society, 21*(4), 446–471.

Korpela, K. M. (1992). Adolescents' favourite places and environmental regulation. *Journal of Environmental Psychology, 12*(3), 249-258.

Lieberg, M. (1995). Teenagers and public space. *Communication Research, 22*(6), 720–744.

Lynch, K. (Ed.). (1977). *Growing up in cities: Studies of the spatial environment of adolescence in Cracow, Melbourne, Mexico City, Salta, Toluca, and Warszawa.* Cambridge, MA: MIT Press.

Owens, P. E. (2001). Recreation and restrictions: Community skateboard parks in the United States. *Urban Geography, 22*(6), 782–797.

Owens, P. E. (1997). Adolescence and the cultural landscape: Public policy, design decisions, and popular press reporting. *Landscape and Urban Planning, 39*(2–3), 153–166.

Owens, P. E. (1994). Teen places in Sunshine, Australia: Then and now. *Children's Environments, 11*(4), 292–299.

Owens, P. E. (1988). Natural landscapes, gathering places, and prospect refuges: Characteristics of outdoor places valued by teens. *Children's Environments Quarterly, 5*(2), 17–24.

Silbereisen, R., & Noack, P. (1988). Adolescence and environment. In D. Canter, M. Krampen, & D. Stea (Eds.), *Ethnoscapes: Vol. 2. Environmental Policy, Assessment and Communication* (pp. 19–34). Brookfield, VT: Avebury.

Silbereisen, R. K., & Todt, E. (Eds.). (1994). *Adolescence in context: The interplay of family, school, peers, and work in adjustment.* New York: Springer-Verlag.

Sommer, R. (1983). *Social design.* Englewood Cliffs, NJ: Prentice Hall.

Valentine, G., & Skelton, T. (Eds.). (1998). *Cool places: Geographies of youth.* New York: Routledge.

Zeisel, J. (1981). *Inquiry by design.* New York: Cambridge University Press.

AFRICAN AMERICAN COMMUNITIES

Communities primarily occupied by African Americans are often referred to as black communities, and in much of the contemporary literature, as inner-city communities or neighborhoods, urban communities, or ghetto communities. The term *ghetto* was originally a reference to sections within European cities where Jews were required to live; today it is often applied to any slum area where minorities live because of because of social discrimination or economic pressures. In many urban communities, there is also a relationship between ethnicity, race, and socioeconomic status. According to data from the 2000 U.S. census, blacks or African Americans make up 12.3 percent of the total U.S. population; the Northeast is the region with the highest percentage of Africans; and the District of Columbia has the greatest percentage of African Americans (61 percent). Black segregation in 2000 was higher in the Midwest (74.5 percent) and the Northeast (69.9 percent) than in the South (59.1 percent) and the West (54.7 percent). A comparison of cities and urban areas throughout the United States reveals considerable variation in the levels of discrimination African Americans face and the quality of life they experience. Variation between and among African American communities may be considered the norm, rather than the exception. However, as late as the 1960s and 1970s the "enduring ghetto" model still represented much of the sociological research focusing on African American communities.

IDENTIFYING AFRICAN AMERICAN COMMUNITIES

The persistence of discrimination and the ongoing struggle against its consequences are also evident in immigrant communities' attempts to disassociate themselves from African Americans, as with West Indians living in the San Francisco Bay Area, who feel that "foreign blacks" are more acceptable to the white majority. Discrimination, especially when based on skin color, tends to lump together Afro-Latino culture groups, Caribbean blacks, and black Puerto Ricans when referring to black communities, a fact that makes it all the more necessary to contextualize any discussion of African American history and community development.

When attempting to properly represent any community, we are wise not to minimize the existence of multiple identities. How people self-identify and what leads them to speak in terms of "we" are critically important to our understanding of their socially constructed reality. Those who may be referred to here and in other texts as African Americans may actually self-identify as black American, colored, Afro American, African, or simply American. Significant in this complex situation is the existence of a "shifting nature and hybridity of cultural identities" (Mattingly, Lawlor, & Jacobs-Huey 2002, p. 744). African Americans are constantly stereotyped in both popular representations and scholarly work; to avoid stereotyping it is important to recognize diversity as well as commonality.

According to the scholar Michael Williams, "The African American community is distinctive partly because it is maintained as a social unit by power structures external to it" (Williams 1993, p. 360). However, to the extent that a community is an association of people who share a common identity, are located within a specific geographic location, and share a common language and cultural heritage, there are a number of very viable and identifiable African American communities in the United States. For some, racial affinity is the predominant characteristic; for others, it is class mobility or occupational niche. In some cases, African American communities have been born as a result of "white flight." Evidence suggests that families and churches have been the most important sources of support and resources in black communities. Participation in churches is often an integral part of the upbringing of children and is an important means of creating a sense of group solidarity. Churches provide both social and spiritual functions; they are known to provide a venue in which personal identity can be developed and group culture expressed.

AFRICAN AMERICAN COMMUNITIES IN THE ANTEBELLUM AND POST–CIVIL WAR SOUTH

Africans were originally brought to North America in the seventeenth century to work in cities as laborers or house servants. During the latter part of that century and into the next, the number of blacks in the emerging cities grew because workers were needed and European immigrants were fewer in number and less willing to do some of the labor needed. By the late 1600s, Africans were also being imported in large numbers to serve the needs of tobacco and cotton plantation owners.

African American communities in the South experienced long-term gradual changes rather than abrupt ones. Historian John W. Blassingame gives a detailed account of slave narratives that expressly show the importance of the family and community relations among slaves. In addition to the fact that "the Southern plantation was unique in the New World because it permitted the development of a monogamous slave family" (Blassingame 1972, p. 77)—despite the many obstacles put in the way of keeping the family together—other social and religious avenues (e.g., clubs, creating and performing music) existed to ensure that blacks engaged in communal activities. Historian Eugene Genovese characterized the old South as a "historically unique kind of paternalistic society" (Genovese 1976, p. 4).

After the Civil War, the Thirteenth Amendment (outlawing slavery), the Fourteenth Amendment (providing for black citizenship), and the Fifteenth Amendment (instituting universal suffrage for men), gave a new energy to African American communities. The immediate consequence was a sanctioning of black political rights and opportunities. During Reconstruction, southern blacks represented their communities by holding positions locally and nationally, as city mayors, state legislators, and members of the U.S. Congress. Unfortunately, these new freedoms were short-lived, and they were often challenged by a number of external factors, such as being denied the right to vote and the inability to secure well-paid union jobs. By the close of the nineteenth century, the Jim Crow laws had been established. These denied many southern blacks the right to vote, and office holders became mostly white. In the first half of the twentieth century, African American communities in the South faced the dilemma of having constitutional rights on paper but no way of affirming and enjoying those rights in practice.

MIGRATION TO THE NORTH AND WEST

African Americans began leaving the South in the years following the Civil War, a pattern that became increasingly significant after 1900. The "Great Migration" of 1916–1919 reshaped both newly formed African American communities in the North and West and the communities from which the exodus occurred in the South. Economic changes, such as the declining need for farm labor, encouraged African Americans to leave the South for the factories of more industrialized parts of the country. By 1920 there were more than one million African Americans living in New York City, which at that time had a larger black population than any other urban area in the United States.

Migrants to northern cities faced the challenge of creating new communities. In *AlabamaNorth* (1999), historian Kimberley Phillips examined African American migration from the South to Cleveland, Ohio, between 1915 and 1945, as well as the community the migrants developed. According to Phillips, Cleveland's African Americans developed an associational life that "retained religious values and an expressive culture rooted in their experiences as migrants from the South" (Phillips 1999, p. 188). This associational life in turn provided the necessary foundation for self-organization. Drawing on their experiences in the South, Cleveland's African American migrants started their own churches and fraternal organizations and developed their own social clubs. As the number of migrants increased, southern ways permeated Cleveland's black culture, as evidenced in the increase in storefront churches and ecstatic worship practices and in the popularization of gospel quartets. Cleveland's new migrants arrived in the city in search of better economic opportunity, but they quickly set about creating a culture that was both familiar and supportive.

Although the Great Depression of the 1930s shattered the confidence of the African American urban middle class and their dream of racial advancement through economic self-help, the prosperous years of the 1920s showed what the new urban African American communities were capable of, even in the face of unremitting racism. New York's Harlem Renaissance of the 1920s is famous for its literary output, and African Americans in other cities flourished as well. *Black Metropolis* (1945), an important sociological study by St. Clair Drake and Horace R. Cayton, characterized the period from 1924 through early 1929 as one of growth and expansion within the Chicago African American community and specifically among its middle class. Businesses owned by blacks flourished, employment opportunities for black workers were good, and there was a general sense of optimism and well-being. The notion of creating a "black metropolis"—a city within a city—held great promise for many but unfortunately was never fully realized.

The early 1990s saw the beginnings of a reverse migration (from North to South) among upwardly mobile African Americans. In addition, what some have referred to as black gentrification is occurring, both in northern cities such as Pittsburgh, Cleveland, and New York, and in the south, especially in Atlanta and Dallas, as a growing number of upper-middle-class African American professionals return to their roots. The black communities associated with those cities often hold an important piece of history and heritage for the returnees. Many early black artists, athletes, and politicians came from those communities, which were abandoned in a wave of urban renewal projects in the 1950s and 1960s.

Sign for the Apollo Theater in Harlem. The theater is probably the best-known symbol of African American life in New York City.
Source: Alan Schein Photography/Corbis; used with permission.

COMMUNITY VIABILITY

The cases of the African American community of Greenwood, Oklahoma, and Annapolis, Maryland, demonstrate two extremes in the fate of black communities. Greenwood, near Tulsa, is remembered for the tragedy of its demise. In the early 1900s, Greenwood was probably one of the most prosperous African American communities found anywhere. It was sometimes referred to as the "Black Wall Street." In 1921, a black man was accused of holding onto a white woman and causing her to flee in a panic. An incident that should have been easily handled got out of control when the story got out to the white community. In the end, it is estimated that most of the community was burned to the ground, and perhaps as many as 300 people died.

The middle-class African community of Annapolis, which dates back to 1832, represents a very different reality. This community was apparently able to ward off the racial hatred and associated hostilities of the times. Archaeologists have unearthed this autonomous black community established by free blacks, who later bought the freedom of their enslaved relatives. The community reportedly had a sufficient number of people with a diverse enough set of skills to be self-sufficient, a rare phenomenon among minority communities, then and now. In the twenty-first century, there still exists a very active African American community in Annapolis.

Black communities—especially upwardly mobile ones—have been thought to provide buffer zones from the onslaught of racism. These communities also serve as insulation for preserving cherished values in the midst of changing mores. Currently, researchers are interested in how African American communities address the needs of their youth. Examinations of the impact of poverty on African American communities have attempted to present a more specific account of how neighborhoods, work, and family relationships influence individuals' lives. The studies also illustrate how parents, neighbors, and adolescents develop mechanisms for coping with poverty that include strategies motivated by parental concerns, obligations towards family members and neighbors, peer relationships, and concern for self-respect.

Black community institutions, particularly religious institutions, serve to reinforce the role of the family in personal identity development. For those families involved, the church provides opportunities for cultural expression and individual growth and development unmatched by other settings.

THOUGHTS FOR THE FUTURE

African Americans will continue to be motivated by universally shared desires for family and fellowship. National and local demographics, political interests, and socioeconomic opportunity will also most definitely influence choice and access. Understanding the variables at work will be important for understanding the reality of our society.

—Sheilah F. Clarke-Ekong

Further Reading

Blassingame, J. (1999). *The slave community: Plantation life in the antebellum South.* Oxford, UK: Oxford University Press.

Canaan, G. (2001). Part of the loaf: Economic conditions of Chicago's African-American working class during the 1920's. *Journal of Social History, 35*(1), 147–174.

Danziger, S., & Lin, A. C. (Eds.). (2000). *Coping with poverty: The social contexts of neighborhood, work, and family in the African-American community.* Ann Arbor: University of Michigan Press.

Drake, S. C., & Cayton, H. (1993 [1945]). *Black metropolis: A study of Negro life in a northern city.* Chicago: University of Chicago Press.

DuBois, W. E. B. (1899). *The Philadelphia Negro.* New York: Lippincott.

Farley, R. (1991). The urbanization of Negroes in the United States. In K. Kusmer (Ed.), *Black communities and urban development in America, 1720–1990* (Vol. 8, pp. 1–18). New York: Garland. (Originally published 1968 in *Journal of Social History, 1*(3), 241–258)

Gerber, D. (1977). *Black Ohio and the color line, 1865–1915.* Urbana: University of Illinois Press.

Grossman, J. R. (1989). *Land of hope: Chicago, Black southerners, and the great migration.* Chicago: University of Chicago Press

Hall, S., & P. DuGay (Eds.). (1996). *Questions of cultural identity* (pp. 1–18). London: Sage.

Harmston, F. K. (1983). *The community as an economic system.* Ames: Iowa State University Press.

Hartigan, J. (1999). *Racial situations: Class predicaments of whiteness in Detroit.* Princeton, NJ: Princeton University Press

Henri, F. (1975). *Black migration: Movement north, 1900–1920.* Garden City, NY: Anchor Press.

Hine, D. C. (Ed.). (1986). *The state of Afro-American history: Past, present, and future.* Baton Rouge: Louisiana State University Press.

Hintzen, P. C. (2001). *West Indian in the West: Self-representations in an immigrant community.* New York: New York University Press.

Jackson, F. M. (1983). Black families, children and their churches. In G. McWorter (Ed.), *Studies on black children and their families: Proceedings of the 6th annual conference of the National Council for Black Studies* (pp. 1–14). Urbana: University of Illinois Afro-American Studies and Research Program.

Katzman, D. (1980). *Race relations in the urban South, 1865–1890.* Chicago: University of Illinois Press.

Kolchin, P. (1994). *American slavery: 1619–1877.* New York: Hill & Wang.

Kusmer, K. (1976). *Ghetto takes shape: Black Cleveland, 1870–1930.* Chicago: University of Illinois Press.

Kusmer, K. (Ed.). (1991). *Black communities and urban development in America, 1720–1990* (Vol. 8). New York: Garland.

Madigan, T. (2001). *The burning: The massacre and destruction of*

a place called Greenwood. New York: St. Martin's Press.
Mattingly, C., Lawlor, M., & Jacobs-Huey, L. (2002). Narrating September 11: Race, gender, and the play of cultural identities. *American Anthropologist, 104*(3), 743–753.
Osotsky, G. (1968). The enduring ghetto. *Journal of American History, 55*(2), 243–255.
Phillips, K. (1999). *AlabamaNorth: African-American migrants, community and working-class activism in Cleveland, 1915–45.* Champaign: University of Illinois Press.
Smallwood, A., & Elliot, J. M. (1988). *The atlas of African-American history and politics: From the slave trade to modern times.* Boston: McGraw-Hill.
Spear, A. (1967). *Black Chicago: The making of a Negro ghetto, 1890–1920.* Chicago: University of Chicago Press.
Stack, C. (1974). *All our kin: Strategies for black survival in a black community.* New York: Harper and Row.
Strickland, A. (1966). *History of the Chicago Urban League.* Urbana: University of Illinois Press.
Tatum, B. D. (1999). *Assimilation blues: Black families in white communities: Who succeeds and why?* New York: Basic Books.
Thomas, P. (1967). *Down these mean streets.* New York: Knopf.
Williams, L. S. (1999). *Strangers in the land of paradise: The creation of an African American community, Buffalo, New York, 1900–1940.* Bloomington and Indianapolis: Indiana University Press.
Williams, M. (1993). *The African-American encyclopedia.* New York: Marshall Cavendish Corporation.
Wright, G. (1985). *Life behind a veil: Blacks in Louisville, Kentucky, 1865–1930.* Baton Rouge: Louisiana State University Press.

AFRICAN AMERICANS IN SUBURBIA

For African Americans and other minority groups, where to live is an issue with multiple considerations. Although the 1968 Fair Housing Act explicitly outlawed redlining (discriminatory practices in real estate), there are still reports of real estate agents purposefully steering minorities into specific and often racially segregated neighborhoods. Race, followed by economic class, is still very much a part of suburban community identity.

The literature on suburbanization in the United States is interesting in its narrow scope and focus. Since the 1960s, there has been an active research agenda on the development of suburbs, but much of this has addressed Caucasian populations. With a few exceptions, historians have focused on suburbs of elite and middle-class whites, and they have defined suburbs according to the standards of these communities. Sociologist Kenneth Jackson, for example, argues that the United States' distinctive landscape can be summarized as follows: "Affluent and middle-class Americans live in suburban areas that are far from their workplace, in homes that they own, and in the center of yards that by urban standards elsewhere are enormous" (Jackson 1987, p. 6). For Jackson, homeownership, low population density, and commuting from dormitory neighborhoods are essential to the definition of suburbia. Middle-class suburbia is not merely a physical landscape, however. As sociologist Robert Fishman explains, "suburbia. . . expresses values so deeply embedded in bourgeois culture that it might also be called the bourgeois utopia" (Fishman 1987, p. 4). At the root of the physical pattern of middle-class suburbia, then, is a cultural landscape, a set of ideas including an idealization of family life, leisure, feminine domesticity, and union with nature that are deeply rooted in Anglo American culture. Given this characterization of American suburbs as middle-class in essence, it is not surprising that working-class black suburbs have received little attention. But failure to consider them results in an incomplete picture of U.S. suburbanization in the early twentieth century.

BROADENING THE PICTURE OF SUBURBS

Many early black suburbanites, like many working-class whites, settled at the outskirts of town as a means of adapting to urban industrial life. Faced with low incomes and unstable employment, blue-collar workers used suburban property in similar ways, regardless of race. Before the advent of the welfare state, they sought economic security through various forms of domestic production and sacrifice. They grew extensive gardens, took in work, kept livestock, rented rooms to newcomers, and delayed obtaining costly services such as water and electricity. Many even built their own homes. Racism, too, contributed to these patterns by limiting black access to credit and skilled labor. While working-class white suburbs moved closer to middle-class norms over time, early black suburbs lagged behind in income, housing quality, and public improvements. In these ways, class as well as race shaped the process of African American suburbanization before 1950.

Early black suburbs are important to the history of U.S. suburbanization. Although African Americans never constituted more than 5 percent of the United States suburban population before 1960, they were part of a much larger (and equally neglected) group of blue-collar suburbanites who formed the majority in many suburbs before 1940. Indeed, the suburbs appear to have been as attractive to working-class workers as they were to middle-class Americans. However, the precise fea-

Modern Research Tools Help African Americans Trace Their Roots

RICHMOND, Va. (ANS)—Like many African Americans, Elvatrice Parker Belsches' search for her ancestry was inspired by the "Roots" miniseries of the late 1970s.

Belsches, a pharmacist who began her family search five years ago, has an advantage "Roots" author Alex Haley could only have dreamed of: Web sites to help African Americans research their ancestry and to link up descendants of African slaves and their slave owners.

One such Web site, AfriGeneas, boasts an ambitious goal: to find and document for each family the last slave-holder and the first African on American soil.

Valencia King Nelson, a genealogist who created the site, which averages about 1,000 visits a day, said that while that is AfriGeneas' goal, the chances of success are remote. "That's almost impossible to do. The hope is that people can find out just something about where they came from," she said. "Any progress toward connecting families is okay."

Belsches couldn't agree more: What she has uncovered about her family ancestry, with the help of AfriGeneas, has led her to leave her pharmacist position and devote her time to writing a book and creating a documentary.

Belsches traced her family line to a great-great-grand-mother, Winnie Debro Webb, who worked for a white family in New York before returning to her native North Carolina around the turn of the century to build a home on five acres she had purchased.

Through a marriage license Belsches discovered that Winnie's maiden name was not Debro but Devereux and established the link between her family and the Devereux family, a prominent North Carolina clan that owned up to 1,600 slaves.

To date, using the archives of various universities, she has uncovered 1,300 of the slave names along with a wealth of information about their health, social and religious lives. "I wanted at this point to contact other descendants so that I could share my findings and plan for a grand reunion much like the one done by Dorothy Redford at Somerset Plantation in North Carolina," she said. Belsches put a query out on AfriGeneas and hooked up with another women who also traced her roots to the same Devereux plantation.

This past March, Belsches, with two of the descendants she met through AfriGeneas and five of the white Devereux descendants she traced through a genealogical surname database (www.rootsweb.com), made a pilgrimage back to the last standing plantation of the Devereux family near Scotland Neck, N.C.

"It was an emotional day, to say the least," said Belsches. "We reconnected with our ancestors and spoke with gratitude about how far God had brought us. I now seek to unite as many descendants as possible with their Devereux slave ancestors."

As she toured the plantation, Belsches said, "I felt it was an honor and a privilege to walk those hallowed grounds that our ancestors walked."

Making the trip along with the descendants were various historians and videographers recording the event for the documentary. They had breakfast in town together, then spent the morning and afternoon touring the plantation which is now a private hunting club.

Belsches said the most evocative moment for her and the other slave descendants was coming upon dikes along the Roanoke River that the slaves had built: "That was very emotional," she said. Another highlight of the trip was when a Devereux family member produced a picture of an actual slave cabin on the plantation: "I can't tell you how long I've been looking for a photo like that," she said.

Belsches's story confirms what Nelson, who runs the AfriGeneas Web site, stresses: It is critical to have descendants of slave owners participate. "Our biggest need is to have descendants of slave owners. They are the key to the curtain that is between the years 1610 and 1870," she said. "Only through these slave owner descendants can African slave descendants get through to these years."

Belsches said, "Doing slave genealogy is a daunting thing. Most slaves are recorded by their first names only. I'm blessed to have uncovered a list like that for the betterment of everyone. I feel truly blessed."

Belches is still in search of other Devereux slave descendants and is using AfriGeneas to find them: "That's the best way to find them. My goal is to unite as many descendants as possible," she said.

In addition to the work underway on the documentary, Belsches recently made a presentation of her findings to the National Genealogical Society.

Source: "Modern Research Tools Help African Americans Trace Their Roots." American News Service, August 19, 1999.

tures of suburban landscape and lifestyle differed with class. The presence of several hundred thousand African American suburbanites in northern suburbs, as well as millions of other working-class suburbanites, challenges urban historians to write suburban histories that include the full range of Americans who lived on the city's edge. It suggests that *suburbanization* should mean the whole expansion of U.S. cities beyond their bounds, not just the celebrated decentralization of the white middle class.

AFRICAN AMERICANS IN THE SUBURBS TODAY

During the 1970s, the United States became a suburban nation, with more people living around central cities (37.6 percent) than in them (31.4 percent) or in rural areas (31 percent). Notable black suburbs included East Cleveland, Ohio; Compton, California; Blackjack, Missouri; and Warren, Michigan. In a recent interview, Blackjack residents revealed that they continue to feel that their community provides a "safe sanctuary" for them. Looking specifically at African American residential patterns outside of major cities also requires reviewing some more inclusive demographic data. In the midst of the nation's growing diversity—in which about 69 percent of the population is white, 12.3 percent African American, 12.5 percent Hispanic, and about 4 percent Asian—African Americans remain the most racially isolated group, according to U.S. census data for 2000.

The percentage of African Americans living in suburbs grew from 34 percent in 1990 to 39 percent in 2000, while Hispanics went from 46 percent to 49 percent and Asians from 53 percent to 58 percent. Though whites (non-Hispanic) accounted for 82.1 percent of U.S. suburbia in 1990, census data indicate that almost one in four suburban residents is now African American, Hispanic, or Asian. Contrary to the theories of some academics, blacks who move out of the city are adopting more affluent suburban lifestyles. Blacks who move to suburbia tend to experience a steeper jump in income than do people of other races. Today, more blacks can afford to move to the suburbs because they are rapidly becoming more educated and affluent. The 2000 Current Population Survey reported that 17 percent of African Americans now have college degrees, up from 15 percent in just one year. Blacks also registered a record-high median income, which gave them the opportunity to move into middle- and upper-middle-class residential areas removed from the inner cities. Like whites, affluent blacks head to the suburbs with their good fortunes. Today, 10 percent of suburban blacks have incomes of $100,000 or more, compared with less than 5 percent of blacks in the city.

—Sheilah F. Clarke-Ekong

Further Reading

Fishman, R. (1987). *Bourgeois utopias: Visions of suburbia.* New York: Basic Books.

Harrison, R. (2001, September/October). Residential segregation persists as Afro-Americans Move to Suburbs. *The New Crisis, 108*(5).

Jackson, K. T. (1987). *Crabgrass frontier: The suburbanization of the United States.* New York: Oxford University Press.

AGE INTEGRATION

Age integration, like race integration, involves two distinct but related issues. The first is the use of age to restrict involvement in social organizations or social activities; the second is the lack of social interaction between individuals at different stages in life. Clearly, age barriers may limit opportunities for cross-age interaction, but it also is possible for age segregation to occur even when no explicit age barriers exist. Hypothetically, a fully age-integrated community would place no formal or informal age restrictions on participation in any activity, and age would not be a predictor of who interacted with whom. A wholly age-segregated community would be just the opposite: Individuals would interact only with others in the same age category. Neither extreme is found in the real world, of course, so meaningful questions involve the degree of age integration or segregation. For example, how much age segregation is there in different social settings? What determines the level of age integration in a community? What are the consequences of particular levels of age integration for individuals and social organizations?

SOCIAL SETTINGS

Degree of age segregation varies considerably across social organizations and communities. The examples discussed here illustrate areas in which age integration or segregation is a relevant issue in industrialized societies.

Education

Many children experience substantial age segregation very early in their lives, when they are left at childcare centers populated by other infants. Almost all experience age segregation by the time they begin school around age five. Strict age grading in most schools begins with kindergarten, after which educators expect "normal" students to march lockstep with their age peers through the years of compulsory schooling. One can imagine a more age-integrated approach to education in which students would have opportunities to teach and learn from students of different ages (as was common in the United States during the nineteenth century), but contemporary examples of this are rare. Colleges and universities, including graduate and professional schools, report an increase in recent decades in the percentage of students who are older than "traditional" students. This change may reflect some loosening of age norms and lessening of institutional barriers encountered by older students who seek formal higher education. Educators increasingly write about lifelong education, although this in not yet a common experience for people in later life. Further, older people who engage in structured learning often do so in age-segregated settings (Bible studies for older people, discussion groups at senior centers, and so forth).

Work

Neither children nor older people are generally present in work settings. Work options for the young are restricted by child labor laws and by the virtual disappearance of apprenticeships, which were once common mechanisms facilitating age integration. Age discrimination in hiring, although generally against the law, continues to restrict work opportunities for older people. Equally important, pension incentives and normative pressures encourage workers to exit the workforce as they approach old age.

Although people below and above certain normative ages are excluded from work settings, potentially there could be substantial age heterogeneity among adults who work together. Further study is needed to examine how much age diversity exists in various work settings, whether cross-age interactions in work settings are common, and under what conditions mentoring relationships—in which older workers help younger ones to develop skills and confidence—develop.

Religious Institutions

Many people of all ages are involved in religious communities, and churches, synagogues, mosques, and so forth provide a context for substantial potential age integration. However, the presence of diverse ages within a house of worship does not guarantee that cross-age interactions are encouraged or occur frequently. Indeed, it is common for many religious institutions to promote age segregation by using age as the criterion for structuring their classes and programs.

Neighborhood

Little attention has been given to the age composition of neighborhoods, except for research on the intentional age segregation of older people in retirement communities and research on the transmission of poverty that includes adult-child ratios as a variable. After retirement, most people age in place; that is, they stay in the same neighborhoods they were living in before reaching old age. But some do move from age-integrated neighborhoods to retirement communities in later life, and this is an interesting phenomenon. Older people generally report high satisfaction with age-segregated living, where they feel safer, have access to more social activities, and enjoy the support of others with similar life experiences. Critics of retirement communities are concerned that age-segregated living may promote negative stereotypes of older people and encourage older people to disengage from the larger society.

Long-Term Care

Most nursing homes and other long-term care facilities are highly age segregated, providing few opportunities for their older residents to develop friendships with children and young people. However, some deliberate efforts to promote interaction between young people and nursing home residents have demonstrated that cross-age friendships can improve the emotional and physical well-being of the older people. These friendships also can help reduce ageism among children and promote an ethic of responsibility.

Politics

In the United States, one must reach a certain age to be entitled to the Old Age Insurance component of Social Security (the federal pension program) and to Medicare (the federal medical program for the elderly), so age is a barrier that keeps the young from having access to these income maintenance and health care programs. A "gray lobby," sponsored by AARP and other age-restricted organizations, has emerged with the goal of protecting and expanding the special benefits targeted toward older people. Other, less well-known organizations (for example, Generations United) work to reduce age barriers and to promote intergenerational programs. In several European nations (Germany, the Netherlands, and the Czech Republic), "gray parties" have formed to represent the interests of older people in parliaments. Similarly, grassroots movements have emerged to advocate the interests of older people, such as Aging Differently in the Netherlands and National Pensioners Convention in the United Kingdom.

ANALYSIS

Age segregation has not yet become as salient a social and political issue as race or sex segregation. Nevertheless, it is a pervasive feature of many communities and has potentially significant implications. Age barriers restrict flexibility over the course of one's life and limit opportunities for individuals to integrate education, work, and leisure activities throughout life. Age barriers especially limit opportunities for younger and older persons to be productive members of society. Like other types of segregation, age segregation reduces interactions that might dispel stereotypes of those who are not in the same group. In general, greater age integration could be a force promoting a more civil society, in which people of diverse ages recognize a common purpose and have a sense of responsibility for one another. However, those who consider age segregation natural and those who gain privileges from age segregation are likely to oppose removing age barriers to participation in communities.

—Peter Uhlenberg

Further Reading

Foner, A. (1974). Age stratification and age conflict in political life. *American Sociological Review, 39*(2), 187–196.

Newman, S., Ward, C. R., Smith, T. B., Wilson, J. O., & McCrea, J. M. (1997). *Intergenerational programs: Past, present, and future.* London: Taylor & Francis.

Riley, M. W., & Riley Jr., J. W. (1994). Age integration and the lives of older people. *The Gerontologist, 34*(1), 110–115.

Streib, G. F. (2002). An introduction to retirement communities. *Research on Aging, 24*(1), 3–9.

Uhlenberg, P. (2000). Integration of old and young. *The Gerontologist, 40*(3), 276–279.

Uhlenberg, P. (2000). Why study age integration? *The Gerontologist, 40*(3), 261–266.

Uhlenberg, P., & Hamil-Luker, J. (2001). Age integration in long-term care. *Geriatrics and Aging, 4*(6), 1, 30–31.

AGE STRATIFICATION AND THE ELDERLY

Age stratification is a principle of social organization in which groups are formed on the basis of age rather than other criteria such as work status or gender. Age is often a criterion for membership in social groups. These groups may be differentiated by age into strata, or layers. In industrialized societies, time and age are important. Individuals define themselves, in part, according to their age. Age norms are socially defined expectations about behavior based on age. According to age norms, individuals are expected to attend school and become eligible to drive, drink alcohol, vote, and retire at set times in their lives. Certain life events may be on time or off time in relation to age norms. For example, very early or late parenthood and very early or late retirement are off-time events. And what is "age-appropriate" changes over time.

Sociologist Matilda W. Riley and her colleagues developed the age stratification approach in the 1970s to link the importance of age in social structures to the aging of individuals and cohorts (individuals who are all born during a certain time period, usually five- or ten-year intervals) over the life course. A population has an age structure, which is composed of age strata, and associated roles. Individuals move through age strata, from infancy to old age, in roles and statuses related to that age. Age stratification is sometimes referred to as "aging and society" to emphasize that individual lives and social structures interact throughout the lifespan.

GENERAL CHARACTERISTICS OF AGE STRATIFICATION

Aging is a universal experience. Each age stratum, however, is also divided by race, class, and gender differences. The presence of these divisions decreases the likelihood that conflicts based on age alone will disrupt a society. Age strata are also interdependent. As changes occur in one age stratum, other strata are affected. As individuals in an age stratum move through time, the surrounding society is affected and simultaneously affects the individuals.

The situation is similar for age cohorts. Age cohorts move through their life course together and are replaced by subsequent cohorts. Cohorts differ from one another because each cohort experiences some common life events at about the same age, such as wars or economic depressions. There is, however, also great variation within cohorts, caused by such factors as differing occupations, marital status, and levels of education. Furthermore, individuals in a cohort may enter life stages, such as parenthood or retirement, at different times.

Sociologist Leonard Cain differentiates age status

Age Grades

While all societies use age as a criterion to sort members into groups, some societies do this in formal ways and organize some of their members into age-based groupings called age grades or age sets. Members of the each age grade are expected to behave in certain ways and have life-long obligations to one another. Age grades established for Iroquois boys are an example of this custom.

At the age at which sex differentiation [between boys and girls] entered the socializing process, boys formed age-grade groups which mimicked the hunting and warlike occupations of the men. These groups initiated the process of weaning the males away from the control of the family of orientation [origin]. Whereas the training of girls bound them more closely to the family group, the association of the boys with their age mates in the village freed them from kin associations and laid the foundation for future hunting and war parties. When a boy was about fourteen and able to accompany the men on hunting trips, his father and other men of the hunting party took an interest in training him in the use of the bow and arrow and other manly weapons. The men of the tribe recounted, for the benefit of the growing generation, their exploits on the warpath in order to instill in the youth ideals of courage and patriotism. The game of lacrosse also provided valuable training for the warpath.

Source: Noon, John A. (1949). *Law and Government of the Grand River Iroquois*. New York: Viking Fund Publications in Anthropology, No. 12., p. 33.

from age stratification. Cain maintains that age status focuses on justice and equity issues, whereas age stratification emphasizes conflict and tension between age strata. Age status is institutionalized in societies in that individuals and cohorts are accorded the rights and duties that are associated with their age, regardless of whether they move through age statuses on or off time.

Age integration is a characteristic of families and households, where individuals of varying ages are mutually dependent. Age segregation is common in Western societies in the spheres of work, education, and leisure. Age segregation has been called the "institutionalization of the life course" (Kohli 2000, p. 279), meaning that outside family life, individuals are mostly engaged with their age peers. Social and economic policies tend to reinforce age segregation. Riley and Riley argued in a 1994 article in *The Gerontologist* that age integration would improve the quality of life for all ages and that age should be less pivotal in determining roles.

It may be argued that age integration is beneficial for all social groups because it promotes intergenerational activities, particularly between children and older adults. Intergenerational programs among non-kin have multiplied in recent years, and the proportion of coresiding grandparents and grandchildren has increased. Older adults are a potential source of assistance in child care and education of children, while children can learn the value of community service by contributing to the lives of older adults (by teaching computer technology, for example). Attitudes of children toward older adults and toward aging are more positive if the children have had positive personal experiences interacting with older individuals.

In general, home care for older adults is age integrated, but most group care is age segregated. Age segregation is common in retirement communities, where groups of individuals and families of similar ages cluster together. There are advantages in designing housing specifically for older adults: It can be designed to enrich social interactions and opportunities, or to minimize fear of crime. Although older adults are not disproportionately the victims of crime, studies have shown that their levels of fear and anxiety are higher than other age groups, which can result in limiting social activities.

POPULATIONS OF OLDER ADULTS

Globally, declining fertility and increased longevity mean that the world's population is continuing to age; by 2025 there will be higher proportions of older adults and lower proportions of children. One measure of aging is the dependency ratio of older adults to working-age populations, reflecting the number of older adults that must be supported by working adults. In the United States and other more developed countries that have traditionally maintained the highest dependency ratios for the elderly, these ratios are predicted to increase from a range of 19 to 22 elderly per 100 working people to 30 to 34 elderly per 100 working people by the year 2025.

Within counties or communities in the United States, the proportion of older adults in the total population varies greatly. For the 381 counties in which the older population represents 20 percent or more of the total population, or for communities with similarly high proportions, this demographic indicator has social, economic, and political consequences for social relationships in communities.

SOCIAL INTERACTION AMONG OLDER ADULTS

Glen Elder and Monica Johnson have delineated five principles that shape a typical life course (2003):

1. "The principle of lifelong development and aging" (p. 57): human development and aging are lifelong processes;
2. "The principle of human agency" (p. 58): individuals make choices throughout their lives within social contexts;
3. "The principle of historical time and place" (p. 62): historical location shapes the life course of individuals;
4. "The principle of timing" (p. 64): timing affects life stages, transitions, and events; and
5. "The principle of linked lives" (p. 68): lives are linked through social relationships.

This last principle, the principle of linked lives, describes social networks and community ties. For older adults, social relationships are formed and maintained with family members, neighbors, friends, and associates from work and organizations. Some older adults form personal relationships with service providers. Although many studies of older adults have focused on types of formal and informal social support that provide assistance to elders, older adults are themselves sources of support for family members, friends, and neighbors.

The major family relationships for most adults are with spouse or partner, parents, children, and other relatives. The relationship with the spouse or partner is the major social relationship for many older adults. In terms of mutual assistance and interaction between generations, older women and female adult children tend to interact more and provide more varied help than men. Income levels also affect exchanges; more affluent family members, whether older or younger, may provide greater assistance. Black families engage in mutual aid more than other ethnic groups. A large majority of older adults have relationships with siblings. Relationships with other kin, including grandchildren, vary by individual.

Most of the research on social interaction among older adults has focused on families, but there has been some work on friendships, particularly in relation to residential settings. Friendship ties are important because they are based on reciprocity and common interests, and may be particularly significant for elders who live alone. Lower levels of social interaction among older adults are associated with older age, poorer health, lower socioeconomic status, and widowhood (particularly among men).

In 1992, psychologist Laura Carstensen advanced a theory of socioemotional selectivity in later life that maintains that as adults grow older, they become increasingly more selective in their choice of social partners. They choose emotionally close social partners and ignore more peripheral social partners. These choices are based on individual perceptions of time left to live. The same pattern of choices has been found among young adults who were nearing death. Social interactions to gain new skills or knowledge are discontinued.

SOCIAL RELATIONSHIPS AND LIVING ENVIRONMENTS

Social relationships occur within houses, neighborhoods, and communities. Because older adults spend a considerably greater proportion of time in their living environments than do younger adults, these environments have a significant impact on the nature of social relationships. In the United States, as in other countries, older adults prefer to "age in place," that is, remain in the homes and neighborhoods where much of their life histories have occurred. While a certain percentage of the older American population migrates to warmer climates or alternates between their life-long home and a vacation home, the majority of older adults choose to stay in their family home as long as their health and finances permit. Attachment to "home" among older adults in small towns may mean attachment to a house, to land, or to a community.

About 90 percent of older adults live in conventional housing, such as single-family houses or apartments. Home ownership rates in 2000 were highest among the 65- to 74-year-old age group (81.3 percent), decreasing slightly to 77.3 percent among 75- to 84-year-olds, and decreasing sharply among householders aged 85 and over, to a rate of 66.1 percent. Out of the top ten cities with the highest proportion of one-person households in 2000, the percentage of older adults who reported living alone ranged from 15.7 percent to 34.9 percent.

Supportive living environments in late life should provide enough challenge to encourage growth, but not be so demanding that they cause stress. The person-environment fit framework developed by M. Powell Lawton and Lucille Nahemow suggests that living environments need to match the individual competencies of older adults. Further, the less competent the individual, the greater the impact of the immediate living environment. Competence refers to a variety of types of functioning, such as self-care and social skills. If an individual experiences personal disability, lacks adequate income, or is socially isolated, for example, he or she is more susceptible to the influence of immediate environmental situations.

Some older adults migrate to urban areas, rural areas, and group living arrangements. Age-segregated housing provides an opportunity to observe the formation of community. In her 1973 book *The Unexpected Community,* sociologist Arlie Hochschild found a great deal of social interaction and engagement among retired low-income widows who were residents of an apartment building. In *Fun City*, a study of a large retirement community by Jerry Jacobs (1974), residents were not engaged with each other and were withdrawing from social activity. Irving Rosow (1967) studied longtime residents of apartment buildings, controlling by age density, and found that the presence of more older residents was positively associated with social interaction with neighbors. These studies show that the relationship of age-segregated housing to the development of community is very complex and depends on a wide variety of factors, such as age, income, health status, and the extent to which residents share common values and attitudes.

Moving into a nursing home may mean leaving a familiar living environment and giving up social relationships. In the early 1980s, Renee Shield studied a nursing home in which there was a noticeable lack of community formation. Shield concluded that this lack was caused by the ambivalent relationship between the facility and the community setting and also by the fact that the facility fostered dependency on, rather than reciprocity in, the facility, so that residents were not contributing to each other or to the institution. This lack of community was present despite the facts that the facility was considered by objective measures to be better than others, residents were of similar ethnicity, and they often knew each other before they were admitted.

Why are some elders able to achieve a sense of community in a nursing home? It appears that elders who are able to maintain their family and social relationships and a sense of continuity fare better in long-term care settings. Other factors include having a voice in the placement choice, having prior knowledge of the facility, the length of stay, and the quality of the facility.

COMMUNITY RELATIONS AND LATE LIFE

Studies of participation patterns over the life course show that even in late life, people tend to continue to engage in community activities, including religious activities, and to participate in informal discussions. One form of community social organization, the neighborhood, is an especially important source of social interaction and social support for older adults. More "neighboring" activity is associated with such structural characteristics as higher education and income and such personal characteristics as extroversion and good physical health. Neighbors are perceived as sources of emergency assistance, and specific individuals are identified as good friends and reliable helpers.

Senior centers may serve as the hub of a community, providing programs and services to older adults, family caregivers, and other community members. They may be particularly important in rural areas. There is some evidence that older adults are drawn to senior centers for the social interaction and sense of community. Senior centers may also be linked to community agencies and community-based services.

Studies of the older adults who attend specific senior centers indicate that the centers tend to serve one or two types of elder populations, but not many types simultaneously. The elder population is diverse in several key ways: socioeconomic status, minority status, and mental and physical health status. Individuals who differ greatly on these statuses do not interact with each other as age peers.

Studies have shown that older adults participate more in religious organizations and activities than in any other type of community activity. Churches and synagogues are age-integrated settings, but they often provide opportunities for age-peer activities that are tied to religious fellowship.

Older adults are involved in grassroots community organizations, in service organizations, in professional organizations tied to their former work lives, and in advisory boards or committees for human-service agencies. Local volunteer organizations are particularly active in rural areas, contributing to a sense of community. Some older adults have embraced lifelong learning and have returned to the classroom for extended learning. Because adults are living longer, healthier lives, adults over the age of sixty-five represent a potential source of volunteers in all communities.

—Sally Bowman and Sharon Johnson

See also Elderly in Communities

Further Reading

Brown, A. S. (1996). *The social processes of aging and old age.* Englewood Cliffs, NJ: Prentice Hall.

Cain, L. D. (1987). Alternative perspectives on the phenomena of human aging: Age stratification and age status. *Journal of Applied Behavioral Science, 23*(2), 277–294.

Carstensen, L. L. (1992). Social and emotional patterns in adulthood: Support for socioemotional selectivity theory. *Psychology and Aging, 7*(3), 331–338.

Cavanaugh, J. C., & Blanchard-Fields, F. (2002). *Adult development and aging* (4th ed.). Belmont, CA: Wadsworth.

Connidis, I. A. (2001). *Family ties and aging*. Thousand Oaks, CA: Sage.

Elder, G. H., & Johnson, M. K. (2003). The life course and aging: Challenges, lessons, and new directions. In Settersten, R. A. (Ed.), *Invitation to the life course: Toward new understandings of later life* (pp. 49–81). Amityville, NY: Baywood Publishing Company.

Frye, C. L. (1996). Comparative and cross-cultural studies. In Birren, J. E. (Ed.), *Encyclopedia of gerontology* (Vol. 1, pp. 311–318). New York: Academic Press.

Groger, L. (1995). A nursing home can be a home. *Journal of Aging Studies, 9*(2), 137–153.

Hochschild, A. R. (1973). *The unexpected community.* Englewood Cliffs, NJ: Prentice Hall.

Jacobs, J. (1974). *Fun City: An ethnographic study of a retirement community.* New York: Holt, Rinehart and Winston.

Jerrome, D. (1992). *Good company: An anthropological study of old people in groups*. Edinburgh, UK: Edinburgh University Press.

Kohli, M. (2000). Age integration through interest mediation: Political parties and unions. *The Gerontologist, 40*(3), 279–281.

Krout, J. A. (1988). Community size differences in service awareness among elderly adults. *Journal of Gerontology, 43*(1), 528–530.

Lawton, M. P., & Nahemow, L. (1973). Ecology of the aging process. In C. Eisdorfer & M. P. Lawton (Eds.), *The psychology of adult development and aging* (pp. 619–674). Washington, DC: American Psychological Association.

Moody, H. R. (2002). *Aging: Concepts and controversies* (4th ed.). Thousand Oaks, CA: Pine Forge.

Pillemer, K., Moen, P., Wethington, E., & Glasgow, N. (2000). *Social integration in the second half of life*. Baltimore, MD: The Johns Hopkins University Press.

Riley, M. W. (2001). Age stratification. In Maddox, G. (Ed.), *The encyclopedia of aging* (3rd ed., pp. 46-49). New York: Springer Publishing Company.

Riley, M. W., Johnson, M. E., & Foner, A. (Eds.). (1972). *Aging and society: Vol. 3. A sociology of age stratification.* New York: Russell Sage Foundation.

Riley, M. W., & Riley, J. W., Jr. (1994). Age integration and the lives of older people. *The Gerontologist, 34*(1), 110–115.

Rosow, I. (1967). *Social integration of the aged.* New York: Free Press.

Rossi, A. S., & Rossi, P. H. (1990). *Of human bonding: Parent-child relations across the life course*. New York: Aldine de Gruyter.

Settersten, R. A. (Ed.). (2003). *Invitation to the life course: Toward new understandings of later life*. Amityville, NY: Baywood.

Shield, R. R. (1990). Liminality in an American nursing home: The endless transition. In J. Sokolovsky (Ed.), *The cultural context of aging: Worldwide perspectives* (pp. 331–352). New York: Bergin & Garvey.

Simmons, R., & O'Neill, G. (2001). *Households and families 2000: Census 2000 brief.* Retrieved May 1, 2002, from http://www.census.gov/prod/2001pubs/c2kbr01-8.pdf

Uhlenberg, P. (2000). Integration of old and young. *The Gerontologist, 40*(3), 276–279.

Wethington, E., & Kavey, A. (2000). Neighboring as a form of social integration and support. In K. Pillemer, P. Moen, E. Wethington, & N. Glasgow (Eds.), *Social integration in the second half of life* (pp. 190–210). Baltimore: The Johns Hopkins University Press.

Woodward, J., & Damon, B. (2001). *Housing characteristics 2000: Census 2000 brief.* Retrieved May 1, 2002, from http://www.census.gov/prod/2001pubs/c2kbr01-13.pdf

AGORAS

The agora lay at the heart of the ancient Greek city. It was centrally located, served as a communal meeting place, and witnessed a variety of public activities, including economic transactions, judicial and administrative proceedings, and religious practices.

The term *agora* derives from the verb *ageiro*, meaning "to gather together." In the *Odyssey,* when Telemachus assembles the men of Ithaca to announce his plans to go in search of his father, Odysseus, Homer uses both the noun *agora* and the verb *ageiro* to describe the assembly. As the Greek city-states took shape during the period from 800 to 600 B.C.E., a public place of assembly became a necessary feature of the city's layout. In Athens and other mainland cities, this area often lay below an earlier citadel, the acropolis, but in the colonial cities of Ionia, Sicily, and southern Italy, the agora was often purposefully laid down at the center of an orthogonal grid.

The agora was a religious space. Its boundaries might be marked by monumental gateways or inscribed stones, as at Athens. Within the boundaries of the agora, altars, small sanctuaries, and even temples were dedicated to the various gods who oversaw the welfare of the state. The Athenian agora, for example, housed an altar to the twelve Olympian gods and was ringed by temples such as the famous Hephaisteion, still standing, and the temple of Apollo Patroos, where a statue was dedicated to the god by Athenians seeking his protection against the terrible plague of 431 B.C.E.. Each year in August, the entire citizen body assembled for a procession that crossed the agora before heading up to the Acropolis. This celebration was the Panathenaea, a festival in honor of Athens' patron goddess, Athena. The route of the procession through the middle of the agora and past the principal buildings of the democracy shows that the agora brought the Athenian community together as both a religious and a civic body.

As a civic space, the agora was often fitted out with law courts, council chambers, and state archives. It was in these buildings that the official versions of the city's laws were put on public display and here that magistrates were examined both before taking and leaving office. Preliminary judicial inquiries were conducted in the agora, as for example when Socrates had to present himself before a magistrate on the charges of corruption and impiety. Law courts for full trials, which might involve juries of more than 1,000, were built on the edge of the agora.

Major buildings, whether temples, stoas (covered porticoes), or civic buildings, tended to be placed along the sides of the agora, leaving the central space open. In this space, hundreds of stalls were set up, and the range of economic activities taking place suggests that the agora was like a huge bazaar. Sausage sellers, money lenders, candle makers, metal workers, perfumiers, shoemakers, and potters all congregated in parts of the agora. Watching over everything were state officials, who ensured that fair weights and measures were used and that grain was sold at fair prices. Thus in the economic activities of daily life as much as in civic and religious functions, the agora was central to the ancient Greek community.

—Jeremy McInerney

Further Reading

Camp, J. M. (1986). *The Athenian agora: Excavations in the heart of classical Athens.* New York: Thames and Hudson.

Lang, M. (1978). *Socrates in the agora.* Princeton, NJ: American School of Classical Studies at Athens.

Martin, R. (1951). *Recherches sur l'agora grecque: Études d'histoire et d'architecture urbaines* [Research on the Greek agora: Studies in history and urban architecture]. Paris: E. de Boccard.

Thompson, H. A., & Wycherley, R. E. (1972). *The agora of Athens: The history, shape and uses of an ancient city center.* Princeton, NJ: American School of Classical Studies at Athens.

Wycherley, R. E. (1978). *The stones of Athens.* Princeton, NJ: Princeton University Press.

AGRARIAN COMMUNITIES

Agrarian communities evolve from small, land-based rural populations that are directly or indirectly dependent on agriculture. A classic study of how agrarian communities work was conducted in the nineteenth century by the German sociologist Ferdinand Julius Tönnies (1855–1936), who studied gemeinschaft (versus gesellschaft) societies. Tönnies described gemeinschaft communities (communities based on kinship and other common bonds) as rooted in a place, with inhabitants living close together and depending on farming. Gesellschaft communities (communities with mechanistic and impersonal ties among people), in contrast, were characteristic of modern urbanism.

Even in the nineteenth century, however, Tönnies's ideas were unrealistic and expressed his nostalgia for an idealized village of peasantry and others, with little differentiation on the basis of class, social standing, or other distinctions. Because ownership tied people to particular land holdings, Tönnies's gemeinschaft communities had stable kin groups and tightly knit neighborhoods. Because the kin group was also the productive-work group, kinship ties were the arena of social action, with family goals taking precedence over those of the individual. Such agrarian communities, although strongly integrated, might not always agree on all matters, but Tönnies ignored the social costs of their lack of privacy, autonomy, and individualism. Yet he assumed that an agrarian community was morally and socially superior to an urban community, believing, as had Thomas Jefferson, that yeoman farmers who worked their own land were the bulwark of a democratic society.

In nineteenth-century America, such beliefs motivated the great transfer of public land wealth from the U.S. government to family farmers in the homesteading movement. Homesteaders were expected to live on and work their farms, thereby earning ownership of the land. The Homestead Act of 1862 transferred 270 million acres of public land. To gain ownership after registering a land claim, the homesteader had to build a home and prove the land was farmed at the end of five years to gain ownership. These farmers were expected to have a vested interest in the well-being of their communities, and such communities were viewed as fundamental to sustaining a democratic society.

Scholars are now learning that some cultural attributes of agrarian places are correlated with positive social outcomes, such as vital communities with supportive environments for family life and child rearing.

A rural community today, however, may be agrarian culturally, but few community members may actually be engaged in agriculture; historical processes in the United States and, to a lesser extent, in Western Europe have concentrated farm operations, resulting in fewer farm families than in earlier years.

NINETEENTH-CENTURY AGRARIAN COMMUNITY FORMATION

The motive underlying the founding of a particular place affects the extent to which members share a set of cultural traits that characterize an agrarian community. Historian Page Smith identifies two distinct types of U.S. nineteenth-century rural communities according to their formation processes: "covenant" towns founded on the basis of a philosophical agreement of purpose by a relatively homogeneous ethnic or religious group, and "cumulative" towns, which grew without a plan through gradual settling by individuals impelled by economic motives. People established covenant communities to perpetuate a way of life typically based on an agrarian vision, as described in the Bible. Cumulative towns were committed to boosterism; growth, progress, commercial achievements, and making money were indicative of community well-being. Covenant towns tended to remain small, true to the covenant of origin, and predominantly agrarian culturally and economically. Cumulative towns, shaped by individual entrepreneurial vision, were not as agrarian in orientation, and either successfully boomed into commercial centers or eroded.

Rural towns west of the original thirteen colonies of the United States developed according to these two types. In one pattern, railroad company agents and religious or social promoters recruited immigrants to the villages established along their rail lines. First-comers in turn recruited other families from their area of origin. Eventually chain migration formed settlements of relatively homogeneous ethnic or religious groups.

In another pattern, a community developed when individual households independently chose to concentrate in one locale, where railroad towns were established. This cumulative process created ethnic and religious diversity, even if most settlers were farmers.

Before World War I, covenant communities were ideal contexts for the perpetuation of agrarian cultural practices. They possessed a critical mass of homogeneous families linked by occupation and kinship, contributing to cohesive communities that reinforced shared cultural attributes such as ethnicity. Given the relative isolation of rural agricultural communities, pressures for conformity to behavioral norms were strong, but correspondingly support was strong among members and against a foreign, potentially hostile outside world. The clustering of like families similarly promoted the development of communal associations and religious activities that easily reinforced community integration around agrarian norms for farming and citizenship. Norms in cumulative com-

Carloway Village, an Agrarian Community on the Isle of Lewis and Harris, Scotland

One approaches the village along a sometimes single-track road which switches around sharp curves, over low hills and through peat-filled hollows. The sea is visible intermittently between the hummocky, rock crowned hills. Black peat-cuttings slash the level ground near the road and the slopes of nearby hill-sides. The moor is an ever shifting pattern of black, bronze, grey and green rock, heather and mosses.

As one enters the village a first impression is of straggling, dun-colored stucco houses set more or less at random at or near the road, or glimpsed disappearing along a side road over a nearby hill or into a distant hollow. Large black-brown stacks of dry peat stand near every house. The ruins of traditional black houses, some lying in tumbled disarray, others converted into byres, loomsheds or sheep-dips, are scattered among the newer houses. Long, narrow strips of fenced in bye land slant up across the hillsides, occasionally smooth from regular mowing or grazing, but more often rush-infested and apparently untended. An occasional cow grazes in a drainage ditch alongside the road, or on the brighter green of the fertilized and fenced grazing schemes on the nearby moor. At certain seasons of the year sheep wander at will along the roads, over hills, or huddle in the lee of rock outcroppings or buildings to keep out of the wind. On a rare, still winter morning, or a quiet summer evening, peat smoke rises straight up from a score of chimneys, or pools in the hollows like mist. It is very quiet, except for the wind and the nearby sea. Few people are normally to be seen. The bleating of sheep, the occasional bark of a dog or rattle of a motor, sometimes the clickety-slap of a loom from a hillside or roadside loomshed, are all the sounds to be heard.

Source: Coleman, Jack David. (1976). *Language Shift in a Bilingual Hebridean Crofting Community.* Ann Arbor, MI.: Xerox University Microfilms, pp. 50–51.

munities, which were less based on ethnicity, tended to be more diverse and economically driven.

Certain religious denominations have supported the maintenance of agrarian communities and practices. In particular, the church hierarchy and the organizational philosophy of mainstream denominations, such as Roman Catholics or Lutherans, aimed at developing stable agrarian communities anchored by the church, where immigrant congregations shared an ethnocultural as well as religious heritage. Over time, these denominations maintained congregations whose religiosity overlapped with a sense of community; church membership equaled membership in an agrarian community.

In contrast, churches founded by New World Protestant denominations such as Methodists, Baptists, or Disciples of Christ were more concerned with individual salvation than with the advancement of the community where the church was located. Because these denominations did not regard community stability as a high priority, church resources were invested primarily in cementing their members' religious commitment. In time, these churches divided rural communities into hierarchical, competitive subsets; characteristics such as socioeconomic status took precedence over factors such as ethnic heritage and agrarian practices. These churches developed community norms that over the long term subordinated agrarian cultural and community goals to entrepreneurial or capitalistic ones.

Agrarian communities were also maintained by the life-course pattern of elderly farmers. At retirement, farm couples moved into the nearby villages, after the chosen successor married and took over the family farm. Farmers saved to buy a house in town, or, alternatively, children had to purchase the family farm to finance the parental retirement move. The move to town made it easier for older people to attend church, shop, receive medical care, and visit with friends. In turn, retirees volunteered in civic affairs and contributed a general level of watchfulness that provided a community with security and well-being. This pattern, however, began to fade as roads improved, farms were concentrated, and agrarian villages lost doctors and other amenities to larger, central places. As farm family numbers declined in the late twentieth century, ties to the land were weakened, ties that had symbolized that the local community identity was agrarian.

AGRICULTURE IN AGRARIAN COMMUNITIES

Although farming practices may change dramatically over time, agrarian communities are sustained by a stable core of families who have farmed their land for several generations. The basis for community stability is that much of the land farmed by local families is also owned by them. According to American sociologist Robert Netting, smallholder agrarian communities around the world share common features associated with sustainable farming systems and agrarian community vitality: small-scale, intensively worked, diversified farms on land owned or to which permanent tenure rights are held by the operator. Tenure to or ownership of land assures such farmers that they have long-term and even heritable rights to the land. Farmers in these communities, be they in Africa, Asia, Europe, or the Americas, do not maintain the environment for its own sake, although they believe in the good of stewardship. They practice stewardship of the land so that their succeeding kin can farm good soils and maintain the agrarian way of life treasured by their forebears. Frequently, property is owned in common by an agrarian community. If so, institutions allow community members to share, monitor, and protect these resources against exploitation. Finally, although economic inequality might be present in such communities, Netting found that persistent class stratification is not present, and socioeconomic mobility is possible and does occur.

In the United States, agrarian communities tend to be populated by more farm families working farms that are smaller in size than other farms that are typical of a particular region, such as the Midwest. Such communities have many members who attend church, engage in civic activities, and produce children, thus ensuring the persistence of the small town. In these communities, children are socialized to respect the superiority of life in an agrarian community. Even when the farm operation or a child's goals rule out his or her becoming a farmer, children from communities with an agrarian culture make life decisions that allow them to live, if not work, in the community. Part-time farming is one accommodation that farm families make for continuity of the agrarian way of life while supporting a family. Farmers and their heirs resist selling family land, for local land ownership (as opposed to absentee- or rented-land tenure) is the key force in maintaining the way of life.

COMMUNITY LIFE AND AGRARIAN PRACTICES

Today, U.S. rural communities are often only culturally agrarian, because farming employs a declining number of local people, due to concentration pressures in the agricultural sector. Residents struggle to keep their communities agrarian by not accepting that town growth is inevitably a good thing. But in reality, there is little to attract upscale newcomers to agrarian towns in, for example, the U.S. Midwest. These towns were never grand places; their modest houses clustered densely along the tree-lined streets laid out in the historic railroad-town grid pattern. A few stores line the main street, and perhaps a café is open for breakfast and lunch. Some farmers still retire into town and are involved in civic activities. Such towns retain some young families who are strongly attached and thus willing to commute for work.

What is culturally agrarian about such a community? Status differences among people are downplayed, although everyone knows differences exist. People work hard at sustaining the community; in the process, they generate large stores of social resources that allow them to mobilize easily to accomplish other cooperative activities, whether rituals, festivals, school support, or managing in a disaster. For example, an agrarian community uses all sorts of strategies to sustain institutions such as a café, because people recognize that public arenas are critical in forming and maintaining a place attachment, through the regular, taken-for-granted interactions that generate connections linking people and allowing norms to be shared.

Sheep Keep Power Lines Clear of Vegetation

NOTTINGHAM, N.H. (ANS)–It's 5 a.m. and a flock of 1,000 sheep quietly munch a breakfast of maple, birch, oak, cherry and poplar saplings. They will eat for 5 hours, take a break, then go back and eat until 9:30 p.m.

The pastoral scene has an additional feature. High above the flock are giant transmission lines, and the sheep are on an environmental mission, clearing the lines of vegetation that most power authorities banish with herbicides.

"They're a self-propelled mowing machine, each with inch-wide cutters in the front," says D. Dickinson Henry Jr., president of Bellwether Solutions, a vegetation management company based in Concord, N.H. that uses sheep to control unwanted vegetation.

Henry's sheep are in New Hampshire from May to September eating vegetation under power lines. They winter in the South dining on kudzu, a pervasive weed in Florida. While both projects are in experimental phases, Henry is confident that sheep, rather than herbicides or mowing machines, can be both environmentally friendly and a cost-effective way to get rid of unwanted vegetation.

The sheep's assignment this summer is to eat up 30 miles of vegetation underneath power lines owned by Public Service of New Hampshire, the state's largest electric utility, with transmission lines that extend 1800 miles throughout the state.

The Grazing Power Project, which began last summer, is an experiment to see if sheep can control the growth of trees in the power company's transmission line rights-of-way better and more economically than using expensive and noisy mowing machines, which cost about $200 to $800 per acre to use. In the past, PSNH had contracted a mowing company to mow 5,000 acres per year at $1.5 million.

While it is too early in the project to tell if the sheep are more cost-efficient than mowers, PSNH's spokesperson said the company was pleased with the way the sheep performed last summer. So was the U.S. Environmental Protection Agency, which granted the utility company an EPA Environmental Merit Award this spring for the project.

"We first thought it was a silly idea," admitted Martin Murray, spokesperson at PSNH. While sheep have been used to control vegetation for Canadian lumber companies and Vermont ski areas and have been used for centuries in Ireland to munch on roadside vegetation, sheep have never been used underneath power lines. Henry, a commercial sheep farmer and former president of the Audubon Society of New Hampshire, convinced PSNH that it could work and was contracted for 3 years to prove it.

–Marcia Passos Duffy

Source: "Sheep Keep Power Lines Clear of Vegetation." American News Service. July 1, 1999.

It would be wrong to assume that everyday life in agrarian communities is always happy, tolerant, or without conflict. People who live in such towns say that everybody knows what everyone else is doing, but nonetheless a democratic consensus characteristically emerges: "I don't think anybody makes decisions. I think it just happens. . . . But don't get me wrong, people stand behind our leaders," was a comment by an agrarian community member in Illinois. A view of the local interactional process by a farmer in an agrarian community is: "We're smaller than most towns so we get madder at each other. But we work together too" (Salamon 2003, pp. 67–68).Trust in the basic goodwill of one's neighbor, despite conflicts, is evidenced in these descriptions of community decision making in an agrarian town.

CHILD REARING IN AGRARIAN COMMUNITIES

It is a common political adage that it takes a village to raise a child—child rearing should be a community effort. According to popular belief, small towns are good places to raise children. Treatment of youth is indicative of how a community thinks about itself, its image, its priorities, and the part youth play in its future. A critical hallmark of an agrarian town is the tolerance and nurture of youth, who are understood to determine whether a beloved community has a future. Because a sentiment prevails that children belong to the agrarian community (not just to their families), child rearing is a responsibility assumed by the entire town. The downside is that people are nosy, and when young people get into trouble (for example, by lying about their age to buy cigarettes or skipping school), parents know about it at once. But the watchfulness of neighbors is viewed as a positive attribute of community by developmental researchers. When adults other than parents are watchful, children develop in an adult-centered context in contrast to the peer-centered context present in suburban places. According to sociologists Glen Elder and Rand Conger, who studied agrarian communities in Iowa, a peer-centered environment is less favorable to successful youth development. Children raised in adult-centered communities learn a place attachment that pulls them back as adults to raise their children in a supportive community, even if they have to commute distances to manage it. The social cost of living there means that everyone knows everyone else, and all must cooperate to ensure the community's vitality.

For most of the twentieth century, small towns, according to conventional U.S. wisdom, were places that the best and brightest left. This exodus led sociologist E. A. Ross to declare famously in 1915 that in Illinois, Indiana, Missouri, and Michigan lie "communities which remind one of fished-out ponds populated chiefly by bullheads and suckers [two types of rather undesirable fish]" (Ross 1915, p. 157). Defying the insinuations of conventional wisdom, however, those "bullheads and suckers" left behind in rural communities spawn some smart and capable youth generation after generation. In an agrarian community, the entire population has an effect on youth that is greater than the sum of its parts.

By the 1980s and 1990s, what should have been "fished-out ponds" in rural Iowa, after a seventy-five-year exodus of the best and brightest, were found by Elder and Conger to be rich and resourceful agrarian communities providing opportunities that maximize experiences allowing youth to gain mastery of life skills. A community's involvement in the shared task of raising its children is a social resource that allows agrarian communities to mobilize for other enterprises that benefit the greater good, whether the activities are environmental, economic, educational, or political. The cooperation and trust inherent to agrarian community social relationships can be traced to the survival strategies developed by the community's first settlers. These traits are consistently renewed through joint acts aimed at raising youth or otherwise benefiting a town.

In the U.S. Midwest, strong bonds that made people cherish agrarian hometowns as special places emerged as an unintended consequence of people's caring enough to pull the community through changes wrought by the ups and downs of the wider society. Change is managed so as to retain what people valued about the town, and the community forged in turn sustains the inhabitants. Youth, the products of these agrarian communities, reflect the trust and commitment that exists—they are trained to be good citizens, to be engaged. Although these observations typify Midwestern agrarian communities, given the work of ethnologist Robert Netting in Switzerland and Africa (and other researchers), such characteristics could well be found in other regions of the world.

—Sonya Salamon

See also Agrarian Myth; Agricultural Scale and Community Quality; Rural Community Development; Rural Poverty and Family Well-Being; Small Towns

Further Reading

Barlett, P. F. (1986). Part-time farming: Saving the farm or saving the lifestyle? *Rural Sociology, 51*(3), 289–313.

Booth, A., & Crouter, A. C. (Eds.). (2001). *Does it take a village: Community effects on children, adolescents, and families.* Mahwah, NJ: Lawrence Erlbaum.

Elder, G. H., Jr., & Conger, R. (2000). *Children of the land: Adversity and success at century's end.* Chicago: University of Chicago Press.

Freudenburg, W. R. (1986). The density of acquaintanceship: An overlooked variable in community research. *American Journal of Sociology, 92*(1), 27–63.

Goldschmidt, W. R. (1978). *As you sow: Three studies in the social consequences of agribusiness.* Montclair, NJ: Allanheld, Osumun. (Original work published 1942)

Hollingshead, A. B. (1937). The life cycle of Nebraska rural churches. *Rural Sociology, 2*(2), 180–191.

Netting, R. M. (1993). *Smallholders, householders: Farm families and the ecology of intensive, sustainable agriculture.* Stanford, CA: Stanford University Press.

Oldenburg, R. (1999). *The great good place: Cafes, coffee shops, bookstores, bars, hair salons and other hangouts at the heart of community* (3d ed.). New York: Marlowe & Company.

Putnam, R. (2000). *Bowling alone: The collapse and revival of American community*. New York: Simon & Schuster.

Ross, E. A. (1915). *Changing America: Studies in contemporary society.* Chautauqua, NY: Chautauqua Press.

Salamon, S. (1992). *Prairie patrimony: Family, farm and community in the Midwest.* Chapel Hill: University of North Carolina Press.

Salamon, S. (2003). *Newcomers to old towns: Suburbanization of the heartland.* Chicago: University of Chicago Press.

Schwartz, G. (1987). *Beyond conformity or rebellion: Youth and authority in America.* Chicago: University of Chicago Press.

Smith, P. (1966). *As a city upon a hill: The town in American history.* New York: Knopf.

Tönnies, F. (1940). *Fundamental concepts of sociology (Gemeinschaft und Gesellschaft)* (C. P. Loomis, Trans. and Supplements). New York: American Book Company. (Original work published 1887)

Williams, B. (1988). *Upscaling downtown: Stalled gentrification in Washington, D.C.* Ithaca, NY: Cornell University Press.

AGRARIAN MYTH

The agrarian myth is the belief that the most desirable form of community is found in rural, specifically agrarian, village life. In the agrarian village, fundamental Western values such as a strong work ethic, independence, and integrity are supposedly fostered and passed from one generation to the next. Consequently, declines in the value of agrarian life and agrarian villages are seen as signals of an even larger decline of society itself. For those who believe in the agrarian myth, community type and morality become inseparably connected in the rural agricultural village. All other contemporary manifestations of community are incomplete or counterfeit.

The agrarian myth is primarily a Western phenomenon. Historian Richard Hofstadter argues that the myth becomes prominent when it becomes less and less of a reality. Consequently the myth is most advanced in the more technologically developed and urbanized countries, and cases outside of the West are limited. According to Hofstadter, "in origin the agrarian myth was not a popular but a literary idea, a preoccupation of the upper classes, of those who enjoyed a classical education, read pastoral poetry, experimented with breeding stock, and owned plantations or country estates. It was clearly formulated and almost universally accepted in America during the last half of the eighteenth century" (Hofstadter 1955, p. 25).

THE MEANING OF MYTH

Myth does not refer to stories of fantasy or patent untruths. Rather, "myths express the collective mentality of any given age and provide patterns for human action" (Peterson 1990, p. 9). They are part of a people's historical self-identity. Hofstadter adds the proposition that myths become more pronounced the further they are removed from everyday reality. People like to cling to the identities they have created for themselves even if those identities no longer seem to fit. This is true for the agrarian myth.

THE ORIGINS OF THE AGRARIAN MYTH

The origins of the agrarian myth in Western society are at least twofold: They include the Judeo-Christian tradition on the one hand and Roman philosophers and poets on the other.

In the Biblical book of Genesis, Adam and Eve were expelled from paradise in Eden and told that they would now have to work for their food. They would have to raise it. Farming came to be associated with God's solution to humans' fall from grace. Paradise lost and the quest to regain it became part of Western culture and its perpetual quest for perfection. It centered on the perfectability of human beings through the perfecting of their institutions, most notably, their communities. Humans would regain their Eden in agricultural villages through farming.

After the end of the Punic wars (between Rome and Carthage) in 146 B.C.E., Roman agriculture began to shift from small to large holdings. Prominent war veterans were rewarded for their service with land. Small-scale farming had been viewed as a moral activity because Rome, though large and urban, was still predicated on agrarianism. Roman intellectuals constantly reminded people of this, typically making the connection on a moral basis, and as a result, the "gentleman farmer" became the rhetorical ideal. As many veterans began accumulating large amounts of land, requiring hired labor, farming became more connected with business. Small farmers were increasingly squeezed out. Roman poets decried the loss of the small farm and predicted ruinous results for Rome. Cato (234–149 B.C.E.) argued that "a well tended farm is a sign of good character" (Wolf 1987, p. 67). Varro (116–27 B.C.E.) was convinced that a simple rural life had made Rome great. The Augustinian poets (34 B.C.E.–17 CE) picked up the theme as well. Virgil (70–19 B.C.E.) credited

Our Neighbors Gossip About Us—How Can We Stop This?

There is an old joke about rural communities that "your neighbors know your business before you do." The question above, posed in a British advice manual, suggests that lack of privacy is a real problem for many peoples in agrarian communities.

Question

My husband and I live in a small cottage, one of many in a little country town. Most of the people around us are aged too. We have not a great deal of money, but our children send us as much as they can, and with our old age pension we manage to live moderately comfortable. Unfortunately all this is spoiled by the continual gossip of our neighbours. My husband says that they are always talking about us, and from the hush that comes over their conversations when I pass I am inclined to think this is the case.

For some time this gossip has been preying on my husband's mind and he threatens to tell the neighbours exactly what he thinks of them. In fact, he did tackle one man, who told him that it was "all his own stupid imagination." But I know they do talk about us, and it hurts me to think that we are constantly discussed by ill-informed people with little education. What do you suggest we can do about it?

Answer

Perhaps you have given the key to the whole situation when you say that your neighbours are "ill-informed people with little education." They may not be this at all—indeed it is more likely that the fault is in yourselves. Villages are always hotbeds of gossip, but it is improbable that the whole community would be in the wrong and only you right.

This is the rub and in short probably the root of the trouble lies in the fact that you have been—without meaning it—a little "upstage" and have shown your neighbours too plainly that you consider yourselves vastly their superiors in education and general intelligence. Even if this were true they would not relish being shown so, and the more you showed this feeling, the more they would resent it.

You do not mention ever having been on friendly terms with your neighbours. This is important, for if you keep yourselves to yourselves and stand conspicuously aloof from the rest of the community, it is hardly surprising if they gossip about you, for human nature is insatiably curious and when it does not know it is not slow to invent.

Under the circumstances the best thing you can do is to go out and make friends with your neighbours. This may be difficult at first, both for you and for them, for you will have barriers in yourselves to break at first, particularly as you have shown your contempt for them so clearly. Gradually, however, when they see your genuinely friendly motives, they will thaw and, little by little, you will be admitted to the community.

In short the best advice here is to drop your assumption of superiority, calm your suspicions of your neighbours, and make yourselves part of their society. They will soon stop their gossiping—which may, in any case, be part of your own imagination and suspicions—and you will be happier than you have been for many a year.

Source: Edynbry, R. (n.d.). *Real Life Problems and Their Solution.* London: Odhams Press Limited, pp. 305–306.

Jove, the god of agriculture, with making farming hard, but he believed that therein was its virtue. And Horace (65–8 B.C.E.) compared country and city life, extolling the virtues of the former and arguing that "the rebirth of Rome and Roman citizens is at stake, and with it the hope of mankind" (Wolf 1987, p. 70).

AMERICA'S VERSION OF THE AGRARIAN MYTH

The idea that agriculture was virtuous was widely accepted as a focus of the emerging American experiment of the eighteenth and nineteenth centuries. Writers and social thinkers such as Crèvecoeur, Benjamin Franklin (who believed that agriculture was the only honest way for a nation to acquire wealth), and William Jennings Bryan all gave the agrarian myth a uniquely American tone. Most notable, however, was Thomas Jefferson, who opposed Alexander Hamilton's support for industrialization. Jefferson wrote, "The small land holders are the most precious part of a state" (Hofstadter 1955, p. 25), and "Those who labor in the earth are the chosen people of God, if ever He had a chosen people, whose breasts He has made His particular deposit for substantial and genuine virtue" (Peterson 1990, p. 13). This Jeffersonian agrarianism became one of the primary ingredients in the emerging American sense of identity. The yeoman farmer became the symbolic moral backbone of U.S. society.

The notion that the United States' rural agriculturalists uphold the nation's morality has become so pervasive in the collective U.S. consciousness that rarely has there been a serious U.S. presidential candidate who has not evoked some element of it. Most refer to small-town virtues, and those who can speak of their small-town roots. Parents still threaten to send their problem children off to the countryside to learn proper values.

THE AGRARIAN MYTH IN THE UNITED STATES TODAY

The agrarian myth has shaped the way contemporary Americans conceive of the good community. It will be small enough to know one's neighbors by name; if it becomes too large, then formal or legalistic relationships will pervade daily life, to society's detriment. Morality must be forged through honest face-to-face interaction, not legalistic mistrust. The good community will be agriculturally based, which will make it beholden to no one for the essentials of life. This theme of self-sufficiency is one of the hallmarks of the agrarian myth. Yet contemporary agrarian villages are perhaps the least self-sufficient communities in the United States today. They are highly subsidized. But the romance remains. Postmodern critics of contemporary life, such as the writer and social critic (and farmer) Wendell Berry, keep alive the clarion call of the Roman poets to return to the small farm or face cultural ruin. Elements of the theme have also been championed by the communitarian movement and similar movements. For those social movements, modern life has been betrayed by overt individualism and its associated individual rights. To counter this, the communitarians and others argue, society must be more local, more civil, and more oriented toward the group. Elements of the agrarian myth play well into this perspective. It has been repackaged in more modern clothes. Thus, the myth not only has indelibly imprinted on the American psyche the image of an ideal rural agricultural community, but also it has remanifested itself in even larger debates over contemporary morality and civility. In many respects, it is Jefferson and Hamilton all over again. Much of the contemporary sense of community in the United States is still predicated on the belief that agrarian life is the foundation of American morality, and even though most Americans no longer live in agricultural villages, that is where they believe they *should* live.

—Ralph B. Brown

Further Reading

Berry, W. (1977). *The unsettling of America: Culture and agriculture.* San Francisco: Sierra Club Books.

Hofstadter, R. (1955). *The age of reform.* New York: Vintage Books.

Peterson, T. R. (1990). Jefferson's yeoman farmer as frontier hero: A self-defeating mythic structure. *Agriculture and Human Values, 7*(1), 9–19.

Redfield, R. (1955). *The little community.* Chicago: University of Chicago Press.

Simmel, G. (1983). The metropolis and mental life. In R. L. Warren & L. Lyon (Eds.), *New perspectives on the American community* (pp. 18–27). Homewood, IL: The Dorsey Press.

Tönnies, F. (1963). *Community and society.* (C. F. Loomis, Ed.). New York: Harper Torchbook Editions.

Wirth, L. (1938). Urbanism as a way of life. *American Journal of Sociology, 44*(1), 1–24.

Wolf, A. (1987). Saving the small farm: Agriculture in Roman literature. *Agriculture and Human Values, 4*(2/3), 65–75.

Zimmerman, C. C. (1938). *The changing community.* New York: Harper and Row.

AGRICULTURAL SCALE AND COMMUNITY QUALITY

The relationship of agricultural scale to community well-being has been the subject of scores of social science studies. The guiding hypothesis in almost all of this work is that agricultural communities that are dominated by a small handful of very large farms will have a significantly lower quality of life than will agricultural communities in which farming is organized around smaller-scale family operations.

EARLY STUDIES

One of the earliest studies that tested this hypothesis was undertaken by the rural sociologist E. D. Tetreau, who examined the relationship between farm scale and community well-being in Arizona in the 1930s. Tetreau advocated a "balanced agriculture" that included enough smaller, resident family farmers to ensure community viability. According to Tetreau, "In a given area a balanced agriculture should support a sufficient proportion of farmowners' families to maintain local government and public education according to accepted standards. Any excessive reduction in the numbers of resident owner families will tend to weaken local initiative and deliberations without which popular government is an empty shell" (Tetreau 1940, p. 204).

In what has become the touchstone for social scien-

DID YOU KNOW...

In rural areas, as large farms replace smaller farms, the quality of community life declines–with lower salaries, weaker government, declining educational standards, fewer community organizations, and more environmental pollution.

tists interested in this topic, anthropologist Walter Goldschmidt contrasted communities of large and small farms in California in the 1940s. Goldschmidt's findings were originally published as a report to the U.S. Senate in 1946 titled *Small Business and the Community*. The report was later republished in 1978 as a book, *As You Sow*.

Arvin, the community of large farms in Goldschmidt's study, was dominated by farms that were considerably bigger than those found in Dinuba, the community of smaller farms. According to Goldschmidt, "The differences between average farm size are great—in the neighborhood of 9 to 1 when taken on an acreage basis, 5 to 1 in value of products, and 3 to 1 if adjusted for intensity of operations. Nine-tenths of all farm land is operated in units of 160 acres of more in Arvin as against one-fourth in Dinuba" (Goldschmidt 1978, p. 393). However, both Arvin and Dinuba were similar in population size, shared value systems and social customs, and were "part of a common system of agricultural production, best understood as industrialized" (p. 393).

Goldschmidt sought to relate the scale of farm operations to social and economic factors reflecting the two communities' quality of society. He found that residents in the community dominated by large-scale, corporately controlled farming experienced lower standards of living and quality of life than residents in the community where production was dispersed among a large number of smaller farms. Goldschmidt concluded that "the reported differences in communities may properly be assigned confidently and overwhelmingly to the scale of farming factor" (p. 284). In his conclusions, he noted that Arvin's large-scale farming operations led to the majority of the population's having to work as wage labor for others. That in turn had a direct effect on social conditions in the community.

In the 1980s, rural sociologist Dean MacCannell compared social and economic conditions in counties in California, Arizona, Texas, and Florida in which agriculture was highly industrialized to conditions in counties in which agriculture was the dominant industry, but was not highly industrialized. MacCannell found that communities surrounded by industrial farms showed income extremes, with a few wealthy families, many poor ones, and almost no middle class. The absence of a middle class, he noted, had a serious negative effect on the commercial life of the communities and on their social services, public education, and local government. He concluded that as agricultural industrialization increases, farm size increases and social conditions in rural communities become worse.

RECENT STUDIES

In one of the first nationwide studies to examine the relationship of farm structure to community well-being, sociologist Linda Lobao used all U.S. counties as her units of analysis. Her findings, published in 1990, were consistent with those reported in earlier studies. She found that a system of family-operated, commercially oriented farms was associated with better socioeconomic conditions for communities, including higher and more evenly distributed incomes, lower unemployment, and lower infant mortality.

A 2001 study by sociologist Thomas Lyson and his colleagues confirmed the relationship between farm scale and community well-being. However, they noted that the effect of scale and organization of agriculture on community life is mediated by other factors, such as levels and type of citizen involvement in civic affairs. Their study showed that communities in agriculturally dependent counties in the United States tended to have more favorable social and economic conditions when their residents were engaged in civic affairs or there was a high percentage of residents who were self-employed or who operated small independent businesses. While large-scale industrial-style farms can have negative impacts on community welfare, their impact is muted by the presence of an active citizenry and an economically independent middle class.

ENVIRONMENTAL CONSEQUENCES OF LARGE-SCALE FARMING

Farm scale has also been shown to be related to community structure and the environment. Large-scale industrial agriculture, which is more mechanized than smaller-scale agriculture, often leads to a depopulation of rural communities, which in turn threatens the viability of rural schools, churches, small businesses, and the provision of social services. Further, there is evidence that large-scale farming generally degrades the land and depletes water supplies to a greater degree than does smaller-scale farming, as agribusiness corporations seek rapid profits while ignoring the environmental consequences of their practices.

The relationship between agricultural scale and community quality has been documented in numerous studies since at least the 1930s. The overwhelming empirical evidence from these studies suggests that community well-being is negatively associated with farm scale. Simply put, as farm scale increases, community well-being and vitality decrease.

—Thomas A. Lyson

Further Reading

Bible, A. (1974). Impact of corporation farming on small business. In R. D. Rodefeld, J. Flora, D. Voth, I. Fujimoto, & J. Converse (Eds.), *Change in rural America* (pp. 205–216). St. Louis, MO: The C. V. Mosby Co.

Goldschmidt, W. (1978). *As you sow*. Montclair, NJ: Allanheld, Osmun.

Lobao, L. (1990). *Locality and inequality*. Albany, NY: SUNY Press.

Lyson, T. A., Torres, R., Torres, & Welsh, R. (2001). Scale of agricultural production, civic engagement and community welfare. *Social Forces, 80*(1), 311–327.

MacCannell, D. (1988). Industrial agriculture and rural community degradation. In L. E. Swanson (Ed.), *Agriculture and community change in the U.S.* (pp. 15–75). Boulder, CO: Westview Press.

Tetreau, E. D. (1940, June). Social organization in Arizona's irrigated areas. *Rural Sociology, 5*, 192–205.

ALIENATION

Alienation, which generally denotes a separation from the mainstream of society, is a very old concept in human thought, and the term has been used to describe everything from rebellious adolescent music to heroin addiction to religious fundamentalism. According to the Dutch sociologist Felix Geyer, alienation is an umbrella term describing an objective condition—the fragmented nature of modern society; a widely shared subjective feeling of loneliness and discontent; or separation from, if not rejection by, society and its values.

CLASSICAL SOCIAL THEORY

Within a few generations after the rapid urbanization of the eighteenth century, urban dwellers forgot the cultural and social ways of rural community, instead having adopted the methodical, rational outlook demanded by the world of commerce. Not remembering the poverty, long hours of toil, and stifling conformity of rural life, people came to see modern life as alienating and inauthentic. The fragmented, transitory nature of modern social relationships and their instrumental, calculating qualities were seen as "unnatural" compared to the more inclusive and genuine, authentic nature of rural communities. At the same time, various philosophies such as romanticism and transcendentalism extolled spirituality, a simple way of life, and reestablishment of a closeness to nature, with a goal of restoring the lost past that had been consumed by Reason.

Sociology emerged in the nineteenth century as people began to reflect on the nature of the new capitalist social order. French philosopher Auguste Comte (1798–1857), the father of sociology, gave his new science the name *sociologie* and hoped it would discover the laws governing human society, just as the laws of nature governed physics. In his six-volume *Course of Positive Philosophy* (1830–1842), Comte described the three stages that each science passed through, from the theological stage in which God was the explanation, to the metaphysical stage in which philosophy was used to explain the world, and finally to the scientific stage, in which observations allowed the formation of theories that in turn were verified by observation. This stage, Comte believed, should see the establishment of a society governed by scientists who would solve all social problems by scientific methods. Like most French intellectuals, Comte was not religious, but nevertheless he thought that religion served an important social function in maintaining communities. While Comte did not use the term alienation, he understood how religion, as a communal experience, was the social glue that held communities together. His insight would inform de Tocqueville, who would later note the importance of America's voluntary church membership in sustaining communities in the new and growing America—and indeed, 180 years later, religion remains an important part of American life.

By the end of the nineteenth century, sociologists were concerned with ideas proposed by the German theorist Ferdinand Julius Tönnies (1855–1936): the change from gemeinschaft (society based on kinship and close personal ties) to gesellschaft (impersonal modern society), from human relations based on status to those based on contract. In this transition, the individual flourished at the cost of attenuated social bonds.

In *The Communist Manifesto* (1848), by the German philosophers Karl Marx (1818–1883) and Friedrich Engels (1820–1895), and in other writings, Marx made

What Does Alienation Mean?

Alienation is a concept that is difficult to define, but certain words do convey the core elements of alienation:

Anomie	Meaninglessness
Discontent	Powerlessness
Fragmentation	Rejection
Isolation	Separation
Loneliness	Withdrawal
Marginality	

the concept of alienation central to his critique of capitalism. On the one hand, capitalism ended the feudal system whereby people were subservient to their social betters. and it destroyed the "idiocy of rural life." On the other hand, capitalism led to the exploitation of workers, to their poverty and alienation. As peasants became factory workers, as they sold their labor as a commodity, they became commodities themselves, little more than animals—they forgot their humanity and their potential for freedom and creativity. The workers created an economic system that stood outside them, rendered them powerless, and engendered the breakdown of communities. Marx saw humans as inherently social creatures who needed social ties and commitments for self-fulfillment. But the historical conditions of industrialization, the grueling demands of factory work—often more than twelve hours a day—and the anonymous nature of city life left people without social ties, communities, or the time to create and maintain them. Marx predicted that the inherent contradictions of capitalism would lead to its demise through violent revolution.

Like a number of nineteenth-century visions of utopian communities, some of which were religiously based, socialism—collective ownership of the means of production—and communism—the political party and agenda aimed at realizing and directing a socialist state based on collective ownership of the means of production—promised to overcome alienation, to allow people to move from the realm of necessity to that of freedom and thereby to create the kinds of communities destroyed by capitalism. While this did not happen after the Russian Revolution in 1917, such ideas had inspired a number of East European Jews to emigrate to what was then Palestine and to establish kibbutzim, small agricultural collectives; this movement, called Zionism, was founded by the Hungarian organizer Theodor Herzl (1860–1904). With the passage of time, the kibbutzim became victims of their own success. As more people came to Israel, they moved to the dynamic, growing cities, while the kibbutzim were often transformed from isolated communal agricultural communities to bedroom communities for urban workers. While Zionism, as an attempt to establish egalitarian communities in Palestine, had a strong appeal to Russian Jews, and many others as well who were alienated from the mainstream of a then highly anti-Semitic European society, today fewer than 4% of the Israelis live on kibbutzim, most preferring to live in the urban centers.

Perhaps more than any other classical sociologist, the French theorist Émile Durkheim (1858–1917) was concerned with the demise of traditional communities and the attenuation of social ties in the face of the modern division of labor, urbanization, and rapid social changes. Durkheim gave the name "anomie" to the social instability and fragmentation of communities created by industrialization. In his study of criminal codes, *The Division of Labor in Society* (1893), he noted that traditional communities were held together by harsh, repressive codes of justice in which gruesome public torture was a celebration of collective outrage that maintained social solidarity. In *Suicide* (1897), he found that those with the weakest community ties and the fewest constraints were more likely to commit "egoistic" suicide than were others more entrenched in their communities. Conversely, certain powerful communities might command self-sacrifice or "altruistic suicide." Finally, much like Auguste Comte, Durkheim considered religion important for holding communities together. While Durkheim did not use the term "alienation," he did understand how religious beliefs and practices (or legal codes and civic or political events) provided collective rituals that fostered solidarity and cohesion among participants, affirmed a common identity, and reinforced their shared value system. This was as true for a religious service as a military parade or a spectator sporting event.

German sociologist Max Weber (1864–1920) thought that modernity was based on "rationalization of the world." As everything became quantified in the name of efficiency, people lost their humanity, trapped by the "iron cage" of Reason. Whereas for Marx alienation was the condition of the factory worker who owned neither the means nor the products of labor and was rendered alienated, powerless, and condemned to live in fragmented communities, for Weber, this state of alienation was the general condition for most people, whether in factories, offices, or stores. German philosopher Georg Simmel (1858–1918) saw the metropolis as the seat of the rational, monetary economy, with heightened individualism and blasé indifference as defenses against overstimulation. His poignant analyses clearly showed how the extreme occupational differentiation and rational nature of modern urban life led to social fragmentation that allowed fuller development of the individual, but provided for weaker, more superficial ties between individuals. The loneliness of modernity has been noted by many social critics. Simmel's insights influenced the growth of urban sociology as a distinct specialty.

In the 1920s and 1930s, with Robert Park and Ernst Burgess, the Chicago School of sociology, and Louis Wirth's reformulation of Georg Simmel, small-scale neighborhood communities with distinct moral norms were seen as integral aspects of modern cities—and bulwarks against alienation. In a number of ethnographic studies of Depression-era Boston and Chicago communities, studies of postwar suburban communities, and recent studies of the urban poor, the dialectic of alienation and community has become a crucial aspect of social science.

ALIENATION AND COMMUNITY

A number of sociologists have attempted to use the concept of alienation, as a breakdown of community ties, to explain other social phenomena, from the appeal of nationalism in the late 1800s to the rise of Fascism in Germany in the 1920s to the proliferation of delinquent gangs in the 1950s. With modernity and the demise of aristocratic power came the rise of republicanism, which implied that government represented the will of the people. This viewpoint served as much to make people into political communities as it did to legitimate modern forms of representative government. So powerful were the ties of nationhood that people would give their lives for the sake of their country. But national communities also held the potential for becoming reactionary.

American psychiatrist Erich Fromm (1900–1980) argued that the erosion of stable communities and the weakened social ties led to alienation in the form of social isolation and powerlessness. To overcome this condition, Fromm thought that people sought to "escape from freedom" through submission to authoritarian leaders and membership in cohesive communities. In the sixteenth century, Protestantism had provided such communities with meaningful values, and in the early twentieth century, after World War I, many people embraced Fascism to find a sense of community through a larger social movement. Fascism not only provided a powerful sense of community based on the nation, but designated others, such as Jews and Communists, as despicable enemies, which in turn led to war and genocide.

While the concept of alienation may have helped researchers to understand large-scale social transformations, it has also been applied to particular institutions such as work. In one classical study, Robert Blauner found that workers who lived in small factory towns or were members of strong unions were less alienated and more satisfied than other workers. Finally, alienation has been seen as a social psychological dimension of normlessness, powerlessness, meaninglessness, social isolation, and self-estrangment.

CRITIQUES OF ALIENATION

Many scholars discard the notion of alienation as vague, not clearly defined or easily measured. Perhaps more important, some dismiss it as a "romantic" notion, if not an illusion, that evokes the small town or village community where people knew one another, enjoyed warm, supportive relationships, and felt tied to their communities. But such a view masks the lack of privacy, the squelching of creativity, and the typically harsh authoritarianism and intolerance in these communities. Such communities are typically distrustful of, if not hostile to, outsiders. Others question whether alienation can be measured by surveys, or whether alienation exists in the mind of the self-privileged observer.

VARIETIES OF ALIENATION

Nevertheless, many scholars contend that alienation remains a useful concept; indeed, the very fuzziness of the term helps in making sense of a variety of social conditions and problems. Different societies, subcultures, and age groups seem to vary in the extent to which members are alienated.

Adolescent Peer Groups

Adolescence, a transitional stage in the life cycle, is a period between childhood and adulthood in which young people attempt to establish their autonomy from parents and their own identities and to explore their newly emergent sexuality. Young people typically constitute themselves through membership in various subcultures or countercultures, which provide secure, accepting communities where they "fit in." As such, adolescence is often a period of separation from the larger society and a time of membership in age-based subcultures typically distinct from—and often rejecting and resisting—mainstream society. While many youth belong to church groups, student governments, debating clubs, and science clubs, many others join gangs and participate in such activities as raves (late-night gatherings where music, drugs, and sex freely mix). Much of the popular culture marketed to young people, from shock-rock concerts (e.g., Marilyn Manson) to professional wrestling, creates communities of fandom or audienceship, in which large numbers of people join together and, through common celebrations of the vile, vulgar, and grotesque, find a sense of community, identity, and meaning. Indeed, for many criminologists, the intersection of adolescence, marginal status, and poverty fosters an alienation from dominant norms and adult communities, which leads to the formation of adolescent gangs and juvenile delinquency.

Poverty and Deviance

A long tradition of urban sociology has suggested that poor communities are socially and culturally alienated, isolated from the norms and lifestyles of the larger society. William Wilson has argued that the loss of industrial jobs has left inner-city inhabitants alienated from the world of legitimate work and isolated from those involved in work and community. Instead, young people are prone to join gangs that may provide innovative, if not legal, avenues of work, such as drug selling or theft. Many poor people are prone to drug addiction.

Fundamentalism

In a rapidly changing world, where masses of people move from villages to cities and where traditional values have been challenged, one major response has been the resurgence of religious orthodoxy. Religion, as Durkheim noted, is a way of overcoming the fragmentation of society and the anomie or valuelessness of transitional eras, when the old values wane and new values are not clearly established. While often equated with the Christian right, fundamentalism has been growing among Jews, Muslims, and Hindus as well. Although fundamentalism has a variety of appeals, one of its central lures is the establishment of strong communities and support networks that ostensibly work together for various social causes and virtues. In the United States, the pro-life movement exemplifies people working together to create a community; although they are unlikely to overthrow existing abortion laws, these people can influence the behavior of doctors who offer abortions and women who seek them.

The question of fundamentalism moves alienation from a sociological plane to a current political reality—religious fundamentalism often moves from communities of belief to justifications for political conflict and terrorism. Much of the conflict in Northern Ireland and in the former South Africa was sustained by intolerant fundamentalisms that preached hatred to others. In the Muslim world, many people have embraced fundamentalism as a response to rapid social change, uncertainty, attenuated communities, and exposure to Western values. For a very small number of extremists, fundamentalism has shaded into terrorism as a way of addressing grievances against the United States, other Western powers, and Israel.

Many experts on Islamic fundamentalism note that its greatest appeal is to recent immigrants to cities, where social ties tend to be much weaker than in villages, and where people are exposed to modern, threatening values such as secularism, hedonism, and gender equality. Fundamentalism provides cohesive communities and affirms traditional values. But at the same time, as young people grow up in cities, go to school, and gain exposure to wide ranges of information, the appeal of fundamentalism wanes. Finally, homegrown American terrorists such as Timothy McVeigh and John Muhammad had not only become alienated, but had embraced fundamentalist religions. McVeigh had been a Christian fundamentalist, although at the time of the Oklahoma City bombing, he was not in a religious community. Similarly, Muhammad had converted to fundamentalist Islam. The impacts of globalization and changes in domestic economies in the last decades have made it increasingly difficult for people with limited skills to find the meaningful jobs that enable them to establish stable marriages and become members of stable communities. Such alienated people can become dangerous.

Virtual Communities

One of the most widely noted changes of recent years has been the proliferation of Internet use, seen by many as promoting isolation and alienation as people withdraw from society and remain fixed to computers. But this is only partly the case; the Internet has also enabled the formation of virtual communities that are just as real as any other community. The Internet has become a major means for progressive activists to form online communities that are now formidable actors protesting neoliberal globalization and formulating humanistic alternative globalizations.

POSTMODERN IDENTITIES

Thus many people have attempted to overcome alienation and isolation through the formation of alternative communities. In the modern or postmodern world, a dominant social concern has been finding meaningful associations to sustain those marginal, alienated members of society who seek comfort, solace, and attachment in alternative communities. Such communities, typically in modern cities or mediated through the Internet, now include gays, transvestites, transsexuals, skinheads, and the modern primitives who embrace extreme body modifications—vast numbers of tattoos and body piercings. These are seen as initiation rites marking the transition from mainstream society to more authentic primitive community that disdains the superficiality of modernity and its alienated social life.

The nature of alienation, especially in relation to the erosion of community ties, is thus a vast and complex field. Although alienation can be associated with many social and political problems and may well be inherent to the nature of the postmodern world, it can also, as the German philosopher G. W. F. Hegel (1770–1831) claimed, inspire freedom, progressive social change, artistic creativity, and humanistic values. One of the ways people can overcome alienation is through love and attachment to one another, to their communities, and in the new global era, even to humanity itself.

—*Lauren Langman*

See also Hate; Loneliness; Social Distance

Further Reading

Bellah, R. (1985). *Habits of the heart.* Berkeley & Los Angeles: University of California Press.
Blauner, R. (1964). *Alienation and freedom: The factory worker and his industry.* Chicago: University of Chicago Press.
Durkheim, É. (1951). *Suicide: A study in sociology.* Glencoe, IL: Free Press. (Original work published 1897)
Durkheim, É. (1964). *The division of labor in society.* Glencoe, IL: Free Press. (Original work published 1893)
Fromm, E. (1941). *Escape from freedom.* New York: Farrar & Rinehart.
Geyer, F. (Ed.). (1996). *Alienation, ethnicity and postmodernism.* Westport, CT: Greenwood Press.
Israel, J. (1971). *Alienation: From Marx to modern sociology: A macrosociological analysis.* Boston: Allyn & Bacon.
Langman, L., Morris, D., & Zalewski, J. (2003). Cyberactivism and alternative globalization movements. In W. A. Dunaway (Ed.), *Emerging issues in the 21st century world-system* (pp. 218–235). Westport, CT: Greenwood.
Durkheim, E. (1964). *The Division of Labor in Society.* New York: Free Press. (Original work published 1893)
Marx, K. (1998). The economic and philosophical manuscripts. In R. Tucker (Ed.), *Marx-Engels reader* (pp. 66–126). New York: Norton.
Ollman, B. (1971). *Alienation: Marx's concept of man in capitalist society.* Cambridge, UK: Cambridge University Press.
Putnam, R. (2000). *Bowling alone: The collapse and revival of American community.* New York: Simon & Schuster.
Torrance, J. (1977). *Estrangement, alienation, and exploitation: A sociological approach to historical materialism.* New York: Columbia University Press.
Walliman, I. (1981). *Estrangement: Marx's conception of human nature and the division of labor.* Westport, CT: Greenwood Press.
Wilson, W. J. (1987). *The truly disadvantaged: The inner city, the underclass, and public policy.* Chicago: University of Chicago Press.

ALINSKY, SAUL (1909–1972)

U.S. founder of community organizations

Born and raised in Chicago, Illinois, Saul Alinsky did undergraduate and graduate work in sociology at the University of Chicago. He studied with Robert Park and E. W. Burgess, two founders of the Chicago School of sociology, and did field work with Clifford Shaw, who ran the Institute for Juvenile Research on the city's Near West Side. In his fieldwork, Alinsky interacted with the likes of Al Capone's gang. After working in the state penitentiary in Joliet, Illinois, Alinsky was assigned to help facilitate a community organization in the Back of the Yards, a lower-income neighborhood south of Chicago's stockyards. In building that organization, which became the Back of the Yards Neighborhood Council (BYNC), Alinsky was clearly influenced by Shaw, who believed community organizations ought to be built primarily through empowering local residents. Shaw and Alinsky offered an alternative to the settlement house model of community organization dominated by professional social workers and outsiders. Shaw favored stimulating a "by-the-bootstraps" self-help approach.

While following the indigenous organizing approach, Alinsky added larger structural economic issues to his model of organizing. He also used "action"—a form of visible protest against powerful individuals and institutions—to maximize media attention and embarrass his targets, who included some of the most powerful businesses and government officials of the day. He was heavily influenced by labor leaders, in particular the charismatic leader of the early Committee for Industrial Organization (CIO), John L. Lewis (1880–1969). Lewis's CIO worked to organize the meatpacking workers in the stockyards just as Alinsky was helping establish the BYNC. Alinsky's interactions with the local CIO clearly influenced his continual interest in economic justice issues. Another key ingredient Alinsky brought to organizing was his ability to collaborate with the Catholic Church. In particular, his relationships with Bishop Bernard Sheil and Father Jack Egan proved to be instrumental in much of his work in Chicago and elsewhere.

While Alinsky's politics were always somewhat enigmatic, they were generally left of center. He sympathized with Communists and socialists, but never joined their organizations. Moreover, he was always opportunistic. An example was his assisting Lewis in supporting Wendell Wilkie, the Republican presidential nominee, against Franklin Roosevelt in the 1940 presidential election. Alinsky probably did not support Wilkie personally, but he wanted to cement his good relationship with Lewis, who was perhaps the most powerful labor leader in modern history.

In 1945, Alinsky published *Reveille for Radicals.* The book was an attack on liberal politics that called for a new set of "people's organizations" around the country as the vehicle for a new populism. Such groups were intended to fill a void left by overly self-interested labor unions.

Alinsky established the Industrial Area Foundations (IAF) in the 1940s to support the establishment of people's organizations around the country. The IAF helped establish organizations in Kansas City, Missouri; St. Paul, Minnesota; Rochester, New York; and elsewhere. In Chicago, Alinsky helped establish the Organization for the Southwest Community (OSC) during the late 1950s and early 1960s. Alinsky encouraged—somewhat unsuccessfully—many of the organizations he helped establish, including BYNC and OSC, to adopt modest pro-integrative policies that he argued would slow racial transition. The issue of race and housing proved a key weakness in Alinsky's organizing strategy. In fact, BYNC became somewhat known as an anti-integrationist organization, and OSC became bitterly divided over the issue.

Alinsky went on to publish *Rules for Radicals* in 1971, shortly before his death. Overall, his theories and practices can still be seen—perhaps in modified forms—in a wide variety of community organizations around the country. The IAF still exists and continues its work in a number of places.

—Dan Immergluck

Further Reading

Alinsky, S. (1945). *Reveille for radicals.* Chicago: University of Chicago Press.

Alinsky, S. (1971). *Rules for radicals.* New York: Random House.

Horwitt, S. D. (1989). *Let them call me rebel: Saul Alinsky—his life and legacy.* New York: Alfred A. Knopf.

Sanders, M. K. (1970). *The professional radical: Conversations with Saul Alinsky.* New York: Harper & Row.

Silberman, C. E. (1964). *Crisis in black and white.* New York: Vintage.

ALTRUISM

Merriam-Webster's Collegiate Dictionary defines altruism as "unselfish regard for or devotion to the welfare of others." The term is derived from the French *autre* and the Latin *alter*, both meaning "other." French sociologist Auguste Comte is credited with coining the term around 1850, though scholarly interest in what we now call altruism dates back at least to the ancient Greek philosophers. In moral philosophy, the major exponent was the eighteenth-century British writer and philosopher David Hume, who saw in human beings a natural ability to sympathize with others and to act on such sympathy through "benevolence and generosity" (Batson 1991, p. 30).

As described by the scholars C. Daniel Batson (1991) and Kristen Renwick Monroe (1996), altruism, in common usage, has at least three components. First, altruism implies either a motivation or an intent to enhance another's well-being. Thus, if a person enhances another's well-being without meaning to do so, that is not altruism; on the other hand, if a person intends to enhance another's welfare, but unintentionally diminishes it, he or she would still be considered altruistic. Second, altruism implies action; merely wishing someone well is not altruism. Third, altruism carries the risk of diminishing one's own welfare in the process of enhancing another's.

Although altruistic motivations cannot be directly observed, they can be inferred from observable acts. Such acts include returning a lost wallet to its owner, donating blood, volunteering for a charity, and helping a stranger in distress. Altruism can be planned or spontaneous; individual or group-based; episodic or sustained; public or anonymous. Because it is presumed to be rare but desirable, most societies try to reinforce altruistic behavior, for example by providing "volunteer of the year" proclamations, tax deductions for charitable donations, and heroes' medals to those who risk their lives to save others.

BACKGROUND

There is an important distinction between normative and positive theories of altruism. Normative theories are concerned with why people should (or should not) engage in good works; such theories are associated with philosophy and religion. Positive theories are interested in the causes and consequences of altruism; these theories are associated with the social and biological sciences.

The call to good works is a central tenet of most major world religions. The Bible tells Christians to "love thy neighbor as thyself" and teaches altruism through parables such as the Good Samaritan and Jesus' tending to the sick and downtrodden. In Judaism, performing good deeds and acts of charity *(tzdakah)* is one of three core obligations of the faith, and caring for parents is likewise obligatory. In Islam, almsgiving to aid the poor is one of the five pillars of the faith. Buddhism teaches that compassion helps one to achieve inner peace.

Although altruism is a cornerstone of religious thought, moral philosophers and other scientists of human nature have long debated whether true altruism exists. Philosophers going back to Plato and Aristotle have argued that people are fundamentally driven by self-love and self-interest and that we act "altruistically" to help ourselves, not others. In psychology this principle is called egoism. A leading scholar of altruism, C. Daniel Batson, argues that "the assumption of universal egoism is so fundamental and widespread in our culture that it is hard to recognize, like water for a fish" (Batson 1991, p. 3). The view of humans as fundamentally self-oriented runs through western philoso-

The Parable of the Good Samaritan

(Luke 10:25-37, New King James Version)

25 And behold, a certain lawyer stood up and tested Him, saying, "Teacher, what shall I do to inherit eternal life?"

26 He said to him, "What is written in the law? What is your reading of it?"

27 So he answered and said, "You shall love the LORD your God with all your heart, with all your soul, with all your strength, and with all your mind, and your neighbor as yourself.

28 And He said to him, "You have answered rightly; do this and you will live."

29 But he, wanting to justify himself, said to Jesus, "And who is my neighbor?"

30 Then Jesus answered and said: "A certain man went down from Jerusalem to Jericho, and fell among thieves, who stripped him of his clothing, wounded him, and departed, leaving him half dead.

31 Now by chance a certain priest came down that road. And when he saw him, he passed by on the other side.

32 Likewise a Levite, when he arrived at the place, came and looked, and passed by on the other side.

33 But a certain Samaritan, as he journeyed, came where he was. And when he saw him, he had compassion.

34 So he went to him and bandaged his wounds, pouring on oil and wine; and he set him on his own animal, brought him to an inn, and took care of him.

35 On the next day, when he departed, he took out two denarii, gave them to the innkeeper, and said to him, "Take care of him; and whatever more you spend, when I come again, I will repay you."

36 So which of these three do you think was neighbor to him who fell among the thieves?"

37 And he said, "He who showed mercy on him." Then Jesus said to him, "Go and do likewise."

Source: Bible Gateway. Retrieved January 3, 2003, from http://bible.gospelcom.net.

phy and can be found in the works of such philosophers as St. Thomas Aquinas, Jeremy Bentham, Thomas Hobbes, Friedrich Nietzsche, and others, as well as in psychology (in the theories of Sigmund Freud) and neoclassical economics.

Social philosophers and scientists have sought to reconcile the assumption that people are self-interested with the observation that they often act contrary to self-interest. For example, why did seemingly unexceptional individuals risk their lives to hide Jews from their Nazi persecutors during World War II? The answers generally revolve around the notion that prosocial behavior increases the altruist's psychic, social, biological, or economic welfare.

For example, psychology holds that altruism allows individuals to relieve distress or guilt at seeing another suffer; alternatively, individuals may act altruistically to feel good about themselves or to satisfy a social expectation. Economists, meanwhile, have reconciled altruism with their model of people as self-interested "utility maximizers" by stretching the concept of utility to include a sense of duty and psychic gratification. Other economists believe that altruism is actually a rational investment in one's long-term welfare, since collectivities are likely to protect altruists in order to sustain their welfare-enhancing contributions. Sociobiologists, who have observed higher levels of altruism within families than between them, believe that helping behavior has evolved through kin selection, the process by which altruists single out family members for assistance and thereby propagate their altruistic genes. A variant, the theory of reciprocal altruism, holds that natural selection favors helpers because they are more likely to receive help when they need it and thus to survive. In recent years, many scholars have begun to believe that altruism is part of human biological makeup.

The motivational puzzle notwithstanding, prosocial behavior is quite widespread in human populations. For decades, social scientists have sought to understand the extent, nature, causes, and consequences of such behavior. One major thread of research, that on good Samaritans, was largely inspired by an episode in which altruism was lacking: the 1964 murder of Kitty Genovese, who was stabbed on a New York City street in front of three dozen onlookers who did not call the police. More recently, political scientist Robert Putnam has argued that altruism is an important barometer of social capital, or the strength of community ties, and by extension an important contributor to healthy democracy.

MAJOR TRENDS IN ALTRUISM

For centuries, altruistic behavior has been inspired by, and organized through, houses of worship and religious associations. By the late nineteenth century, however, a growing chorus of Western secular authorities argued that altruism was a civic obligation, particularly for the prosperous (Putnam 2000, p. 117). Organized altruism, in the form of charities, service associations, and philanthropic foundations, spread throughout the late nineteenth and twentieth centuries. In 2002 there were roughly 866,000 charitable organizations, including roughly 88,000 grant-making foundations, in the United States alone.

Research shows that altruistic behavior is quite prevalent. In most studies of spontaneous helping, for example, half or more of people came to the aid of strangers, particularly in low-risk situations and when they were asked directly to help. In terms of planned altruism, surveys have shown that in the United States, nearly half the adult population volunteers in any given year; estimates recently have ranged from 44 percent to 49 percent. By comparison, a 1995 survey of eight European countries found that the average was far lower (27 percent). The volunteering rate ranged from 12 percent in Slovenia to 43 percent in the Netherlands (Anheier & Salamon 2001, p. 9).

When compared to volunteer rates in the United States, charitable giving rates are far higher than volunteer rates: 89 percent of U.S. households gave something in 2000. Overall, about 2 percent of the United States' gross domestic product goes to charities and houses of worship each year; in 1999 that amounted to more than $190 billion.

Although most people are altruistic, at least some of the time, there is indirect evidence that U.S. society has become less altruistic in recent decades. The cause is a decrease in many of the individual and situational factors that encourage helping behavior, together with an increase in factors that inhibit altruism. Inhibiting factors include urban residence, cultural diversity, disengagement from community life, and individual malaise. Volunteering has increased over the past generation, but only because of the exceptional efforts of older and young people; volunteering among middle-aged adults has declined markedly. The decline among middle-aged adults is attributed to several factors, including the increase in middle-aged women who work full-time and generational differences in civic-mindedness. Likewise, while the total amount of money given to charity has increased over time, the fraction of personal income contributed has stagnated or even fallen. Surveys in the United Kingdom suggest that generosity may be flat there as well. The fraction of British households that give to charity declined slightly between the mid-1970s and mid-1990s, though the average donation rose slightly in inflation-adjusted terms (Institute for Fiscal Studies 2002).

DETERMINANTS OF ALTRUISM

Studies of altruism have revolved around a core question: Is giving behavior caused by nature, nurture, circumstance, or some combination of the three? Research conducted in the 1970s tended to focus on situational determinants, such as the gender or race of the victim (in cases of altruism involving aid to a person in distress) and the number of other people around. In the 1980s, researchers began to examine the biological (evolutionary) and psychological (developmental) roots of altruism. Increasingly, researchers believe that these explanations are complementary rather than mutually exclusive.

At least nine factors have been consistently linked to people's willingness to help others. These factors may be categorized as either individual determinants—those inherent to the altruist, or situational determinants—the circumstances surrounding the need for aid.

Individual Determinants

The individual factors that correlate with helping behavior are gender, upbringing, innate personality, mood, and social network.

First, in terms of gender, studies have found that men are more likely to assist strangers than are women. As of 1986, of the nearly 200 tests of gender differences in helping behavior, a significant majority (more than 60 percent) found men to be more helpful than women. However, gender effects appear to be sensitive to the way in which altruism is measured. Men are more likely to provide "chivalrous" aid to strangers in distress, but women are more likely to nurture members of their social network.

Second, the nature of one's upbringing is believed to influence altruism. In their literature review published in 1990, Jane Piliavin and Hong-Wen Charng cite four studies that have found an intergenerational component to helping. In these studies, altruists either have reported that they were inspired by parental role models or were found to have closer than average relationships with inspiring parents or other authority figures.

Third, there is some evidence that one's personality is tied to helping behavior. Although early researchers believed that altruism (or lack of it) was largely determined by circumstance, scholars are beginning to think that some people have an altruistic personality, the cornerstone of which is the ability to empathize with others. In turn, studies have found a small but statistically meaningful relationship between an individual's empathy and his or her helping behavior. Another review of the research concluded that people who feel a strong moral obligation toward others are more likely to behave altruistically (for example, to donate blood) than are people who feel less obligated.

Fourth, people who are generally in a good mood are more helpful than people who tend to be somber. For example, in one well-known experiment, one group of people was shown a sad movie, and another group saw an emotionally neutral movie. After the movies, subjects in both groups were approached for a charitable donation; viewers of the sad movie had lower donation rates than those who viewed the neutral movie. A review of thirty-four mood studies found strong support for the proposition that feeling good leads to doing good, although the size of the effect varied substantially across studies.

Finally, there is consistent support for the notion that the size of one's social network powerfully affects the likelihood of altruistic behavior. As sociologist Paul Amato has noted, "The more social roles individuals play—including that of friend, parent, spouse, neighbor, co-worker, club member, and church member—the greater the demands that are placed on them to provide assistance, and, consequently, the more helping behavior they are likely to exhibit" (Amato 1990, p. 32). Interestingly, helping behavior appears to build on itself: The more assistance one receives from friends and family members, the more one helps others, in terms of both planned and spontaneous acts of altruism.

Situational Determinants

Studies find that, broadly speaking, three situational factors affect the likelihood that an individual will behave altruistically: whether he or she is asked to help, the number of others around when the request is made, and the degree to which the would-be altruist can identify with the person who needs assistance.

First, the most consistent finding is that people tend

to help when they are asked to do so. For example, nearly two-thirds of adults who are asked to volunteer do so, compared to only one-quarter of adults who have not been asked. In addition, 81 percent of households that were asked to give did so, compared to just 50 percent of households that were not solicited (Independent Sector 1999, p. 96). Donors were just as likely to give because they were asked by someone they knew as they were to give out of feelings of moral duty or altruism (Independent Sector 1999, p. 107).

Another important factor is the number of other people who are around to help. After the Genovese murder, researchers coined the term "bystander effect" to refer to the observation that passersby are more likely to help a stranger when they are alone than when in a group. The vast majority of bystander studies (nearly nine out of ten) have found this effect (Latané, Nida, and Wilson 1981). Social psychologists have offered several explanations for the bystander effect. First, the diffusion-of-responsibility hypothesis suggests that people in crowds justify inaction on the grounds that someone else will step in and help. A second explanation concerns the would-be helper's fear of embarrassment if the situation is not really an emergency. The third (and related) explanation is pluralistic ignorance: each person figures that because no one else is intervening, nothing is amiss.

Finally, people are more likely to help those with whom they have some affinity or identification, such as people of the same race or political ideology. Studies also have found that when the would-be helper has had prior contact with the person in need, even if only in passing, assistance is more likely to be offered. Finally, people are more likely to help victims considered deserving according to social norms. These findings from experimental psychology dovetail with Hume's observation that altruism is rooted in humans' sympathy for others.

—Kristin A. Goss

Further Reading

AAFRC Trust for Philanthropy. (2000; 1998). *Giving USA*. New York: Author.

Amato, P. R. (1990). Personality and social network involvement as predictors of helping behavior in everyday life. *Social Psychology Quarterly, 53*(1), 31–43.

Batson, C. D. (1991). *The altruism question: Toward a social-psychological answer*. Hillsdale, NJ: Lawrence Erlbaum.

Becker, G. (1976). *The economic approach to human behavior*. Chicago: University of Chicago Press.

Carlson, M., Charlin, V., & Miller, N. (1988). Positive mood and helping behavior: A test of six hypotheses. *Journal of Personality and Social Psychology, 55*(2), 211–229.

Eagly, A. H., & Crowley, M. (1986). Gender and helping behavior: A meta-analytic review of the social psychological literature. *Psychological Bulletin, (100)*3, 283–308.

Eisenberg, N., & Miller, P. A. (1987). The relation of empathy to prosocial and related behaviors. *Psychological Bulletin, 101*(1), 91–119.

Frank, R. H. (1988). *Passions within reason: The strategic role of emotions*. New York: W. W. Norton.

Goss, K. A. (1999). Volunteering and long civic generation. *Nonprofit and Voluntary Sector Quarterly, (28)*4, 378–415.

Hornstein, H. A. (1976). *Cruelty and kindness: A new look at aggression and altruism*. Englewood Cliffs, NJ: Prentice Hall.

Hume, D. (1902). *An enquiry concerning the principles of morals*. (L. A. Selby-Bigge, Ed.). Oxford, U.K.: Oxford University Press. (Original work published 1851)

Independent Sector. (2001; 1995). *Giving and volunteering in the United States*. Washington, DC: Author.

Latané, B., & Darley, J. M. (1970). *The unresponsive bystander: Why doesn't he help?* Englewood Cliffs, NJ: Prentice Hall.

Latané, B., Nida, S. A., & Wilson, D. W. (1981). The effects of group size on helping behavior. In J. P. Rushton & R. M. Sorrentino (Eds.), *Altruism and helping behavior: Social, personality, and developmental perspectives* (pp. 287–313). Hillsdale, NJ: Lawrence Erlbaum Associates.

Monroe, K. R. (1996). *The heart of altruism: Perceptions of a common humanity*. Princeton, NJ: Princeton University Press.

Piliavin, J. A., & Charng, H. (1990). Altruism: A review of recent theory and research. *American Review of Sociology, 16*, 27–65.

Putnam, R. D. (1993). *Making democracy work*. Princeton, NJ: Princeton University Press.

Putnam, R. D. (2000). *Bowling alone: The collapse and revival of American community*. New York: Simon & Schuster.

Rushton, J. P. (1980). *Altruism, socialization, and society*. Englewood Cliffs, NJ: Prentice Hall.

Rushton, J. P., & Sorrentino, R. M. (Eds.). (1981). *Altruism and helping behavior*. Hillsdale, NJ: Lawrence Erlbaum Associates.

Trivers, R. L. (1971). The evolution of reciprocal altruism. *Quarterly Review of Biology, 46*, 35–57.

Underwood, B., Berenson, J. F., Cheng, K., Wilson, D., & Kulik, J., et al. (1977). Attention, negative affect, and altruism: An ecological validation. *Personality and social psychology bulletin, 3*(1), 54–58.

Wilson, E. O. (1978). *On human nature*. Cambridge, MA: Harvard University Press.

AMANA

Also known as the Amana Colonies, and in some contexts as the Amana Society, Amana was a settlement established in 1855 by German and Swiss Pietists in Iowa County, Iowa. The name "Amana" was taken from a hill referred to in the Song of Solomon (4:8). Within a decade of its founding, Amana had grown to seven villages on approximately 25,700 contiguous acres. From 1855 to 1932, the members of the church-dominated Amana Society held all property collectively and labored without pay for the common good, receiving from the Society food, clothing, housing, a modest spending allowance, medical and dental care, and burial. Amana reached its peak population of 1,800 in the 1880s. In 1932, the members voted to reorganize the community, ending communal living and separating the business and religious functions. The former retained the designation Amana Society; the latter took the name Amana Church Society. Especially since the mid-1960s, Amana has been a major tourist destination in Iowa.

ORIGINS

Amana's origins lie in Pietism, a seventeenth-century Protestant reform movement in Germany. The doctrinal ancestors of the founders of Amana came from the branch known as Radical Pietism, which held that reform of the state-supported Lutheran church from within was impossible and that only by separation from it could the individual attain salvation. In 1714, a number of separatists gathered at the home of Eberhard Ludwig Gruber (1665–1728), a defrocked member of the clergy, to pray and discuss scripture. This marked the beginning of the Community of True Inspiration, so called because of the members' belief that God inspires specially chosen human "instruments" (German: *Werkzeuge*) to convey his will to people.

In the first five years, fourteen *Werkzeuge* associated with the group delivered hundreds of testimonies in Germany, Alsace, and Switzerland, hoping to stimulate a spiritual awakening among the people. Gruber himself never became inspired, but he had the ability to distinguish true from false inspiration on the basis of both the outward features of testimonies and his own esoteric intuition. By 1718, Johann Friedrich Rock (1678–1749) emerged as the sole *Werkzeug* in the community, and he and Gruber worked to establish congregations of "Inspirationists." Most converts came from the artisan and merchant classes in small towns or villages, though the professions were also represented.

The Inspirationists aroused hostility among civil and religious authorities. The church condemned the group's separatism and rejection of infant baptism and viewed the phenomenon of inspiration as fundamentally subversive; civil authorities distrusted their pacifism, refusal to swear oaths, and desire for separate schools. Inspirationist leaders were regularly summoned to appear before clerical committees, magistrates, and town councils to answer charges, and occasionally they were fined or imprisoned.

DECLINE AND REVIVAL

After Rock's death, no new *Werkzeug* appeared to take his place, and lay elders managed the spiritual affairs of the group. For a time the Inspirationists continued to thrive, but by 1780 signs of decline were unmistakable, and by 1815 only a handful of congregations remained active. The group seemed headed for extinction when a revival occurred in 1817 with the appearance of three new *Werkzeuge*: Michael Krausert (flourished c. 1817–c. 1823), Barbara Heinemann (1795–1883), and Christian Metz (1794–1867), only the last of whom had been raised in the community. The three visited the old Inspirationist congregations and presented testimonies calling for a reawakening, arousing enmity from some but sympathy from others. Their followers became the core of the new Community of True Inspiration. By 1823, Krausert and Heinemann had lost their inspiration, and Metz emerged as an especially gifted leader.

EMIGRATION TO THE UNITED STATES

The Inspirationist revival led to a new wave of persecution. Beginning in the 1820s, secular rulers banished the group from several districts in Germany, leading Metz and the elders to gather the displaced members on leased estates in the more tolerant principality of Hesse. The Inspirationists who moved to the estates lived in closer proximity to one another and with more economic ties than those who remained in their home districts. When the rents on the estates became too high and the space too limited, and intolerance in the wider society continued, Metz called for all Inspirationists to emigrate to the United States and establish a religious colony. In 1842, agents purchased a suitable tract near Buffalo, New York, and registered the community under law as a charitable religious association called the Ebenezer Society, named after a monument stone mentioned in I Samuel. More than 700 Inspirationists came from Europe to settle Ebenezer in the first year, and others followed.

AMANA IN THE TWENTIETH CENTURY

The establishment of the Ebenezer Society was possible because the wealthier members placed a down payment on the land and helped pay passage for the poorer ones.

The Amana Colony Church and bell tower in Homestead, Iowa, in 1995.

Source: Philip Gould/Corbis; used with permission.

In 1945, Metz fashioned a religiously sanctioned system of common property out of this pragmatic arrangement. The Inspirationists erected four villages at Ebenezer, engaged in agriculture, and manufactured wool and a variety of handicrafts. They had their own physicians and dentists and operated their own schools. Women worked mostly in the community gardens and kitchen houses, where the members ate meals communally. Ebenezer was substantially self-sufficient and avoided unnecessary contact with the world outside the community, though they successfully marketed agricultural produce and woolens and hired some non-member workers. As additional members continued to arrive from Europe and a few new members joined from the vicinity of Ebenezer, the need for more land became pressing and prompted a phased relocation to Iowa between 1855 and 1862, after which the Ebenezer property was sold.

The communal system continued to operate successfully in Amana, and the community prospered. Although Metz died in 1867, inspiration had returned to Heinemann in 1849, and she assumed spiritual leadership while the elders ran the community's economy. After Heinemann's death in 1883, the elders experienced increasing difficulty maintaining the community's separation from the wider society. The automobile, mail-order catalogues, young members curious about the world, excursionists curious about Amana, and the draft and anti-German sentiment during World War I exacerbated the situation. Finally, in the 1920s, economic downturns and a massive fire in the woolen mill convinced an increasing number of members that the communal system, with its strict regulations and religious control, could no longer work. A substantial majority voted to reorganize Amana in 1932 as a for-profit, joint-stock company, with members of the old Society receiving shares in the new corporation. The communal kitchens and gardens and many of the small craft businesses were disbanded. The new Amana Society offered wage-earning jobs to most members, who in turn purchased homes from the Society and began to live much more like other Americans.

Amana remains a thriving community today with a distinct identity. The corporation has been successful (a highly lucrative appliance business, developed after the reorganization, grew so large it had to be sold); many privately owned businesses also operate in the area. The church is active, a historical museum preserves and presents the story of the past, an arts guild promotes the arts, and hundreds of thousands of tourists visit Amana each year to shop, dine, and learn about the community. In 2014, Amana will observe the 300th anniversary of the community's founding.

—Jonathan G. Andelson

Further Reading

Shambaugh, B. H. M. (1932). *Amana that was and Amana that is.* Iowa City: The State Historical Society of Iowa.

Barthel, D. L. (1984). *Amana: From Pietist sect to American community.* Lincoln: University of Nebraska Press.

AMISH

The Amish are a Christian subculture that traces its origin to the Anabaptist movement, sometimes called the Radical Reformation, of 1525 in Zurich, Switzerland. In 1693, the Amish developed their own identity under the leadership of Jacob Ammann (c. 1644–c. 1730) when they separated from other Anabaptist churches in Switzerland and France. No longer present in Europe, the Amish now live in twenty-five U.S. states and the Canadian province of Ontario. At the beginning of the twentieth century, they numbered about 5,000. Today, counting children and adults, the Amish claim some 180,000 adherents. Although they do not evangelize or proselytize, the Amish population doubles about every twenty years, due to their large families and their ability to retain more than 85 percent of their offspring in the community.

An important way in which the Amish build community is by championing communal rather than individualistic values. Individuals in Amish society are valued and accorded dignity, but they are expected to yield to the cooperate guidelines established by the elders of the church. The community supersedes the interests and freedoms of the individual. In this sense the Amish stand apart from the individualistic culture of U.S. society.

In a broad sense, community consists of a network of social relationships, affective attachments, and a sense of identity. The Amish community mirrors these broad contours of community but also buttresses their solidarity along the dimensions of geography, family, symbols, rituals, and technology.

In a mix of the modern and traditional, an Amish horse-drawn carriage parked in front of a Wal-Mart in Ethridge, Tennessee.

Source: Dave Bartruff/Corbis, used with permsission.

GEOGRAPHY

The Amish community is organized into some 1,300 local church districts with specific geographical boundaries. About twenty-five to thirty-five families live in each district. Beyond daily interaction within their district, members gather for worship services every other week in the home of a family. Districts divide as they grow, so that in all districts a single home can accommodate all the district's members for worship. Amish life is orally based and locally organized, intensifying face-to-face interaction. Even the rules and discipline of the church are unwritten. Multiple social relationships are multiplex, as family, neighborhood, religion, education, work, and recreation crisscross within the local church district.

FAMILY

The Amish community is knit together by sizable families. On the average, families have seven children, and more traditional Amish subgroups may have ten to fifteen offspring. The average Amish person has at least seventy-five first cousins, many of whom live nearby. This thick web of family ties intersects across church districts and helps to bind the community together.

Endogamy (marriage within a group) is also an important practice that helps the Amish build and sustain their community. An Amish bishop will marry a couple only if both bride and groom are members of the Amish church. This helps to retain young people who otherwise might leave, and it also limits the influence of other religious and ethnic traditions. A few outsiders occasionally join the Amish church.

SYMBOLS

Several public symbols of ethnic identity set the Amish apart as a distinctive community. Their special clothing (which varies somewhat from region to region) provides a public badge of identity that reinforces both their membership in an ethnic community and their separation from the larger U.S. culture. In addition, the Amish speak a German dialect and learn English as a second language in school. Their use of this dialect in everyday life creates a distinctive worldview because it gives them a different perspective, a sharp sense of separation from the outside "English" world, and a connection to their past. Finally, the use of horse and buggy for transportation provides another public symbol of their rejection of modern ways.

RITUALS

Several distinctive practices help to establish social fences around the Amish community. Young people typically join the church between the ages of eighteen and twenty-one, when they are baptized. This is a voluntary decision, but it has pivotal consequences. Baptismal candidates not only confess their Christian faith but also promise to obey the practices of the church for the rest of their life. If they transgress by buying a car or flying in an airplane, they are expected to make a public confession in church. Those who refuse are excommunicated and are subject to rituals of shaming designed to bring them back to the flock. Upon confession of their faults, the wayward can be restored to full fellowship. Twice a year, prior to their communion service, members renew their promise to uphold the teachings of the church.

TECHNOLOGY

A distinctive feature of Amish life is their rejection of some forms of modern technology. The Amish view some technology as a threat to the well-being of their communities, so they screen new technologies to make sure that they will support, not disrupt, the Amish way of life. The car, for example, threatened to fragment their community, which is best sustained through face-to-face relationships. Horse and buggy transportation helps to hold the community close together. Thus Amish communities forbid owning and operating motor vehicles. They do, however, permit members to ride in cars.

Telephones installed in the home, electricity from public utility lines, computers, and television are other forms of modern technology that the Amish forbid. All of those tools would tie them closer to the outside world and erode the solidarity of their ethnic community. The church often makes a distinction between using technology and owning it. Thus the Amish are permitted to use public telephones and sometimes install them in businesses or in a community phone booth at the edge of their property. The Amish prohibit the ownership of computers, televisions, radios, and compact-disc players. The Amish emphasize organic reality, not virtual reality.

The Amish permit the use of electric batteries for flashlights and small power tools. The degree to which particular technologies are permitted or forbidden varies considerably from region to region, but all Amish groups are cautious about adopting forms of technology that in the long run would weaken the social bonds of their community.

There is no central office, national leader, national annual meeting, or centralized bureaucratic structure that holds the Amish community together. Although there is no centralized authority above the dozen or more subgroups, and although congregations maintain local autonomy, the Amish have maintained a loosely linked federation of some 1,300 congregations. By anchoring congregations in a local base of social interaction, developing distinctive symbols and rituals, and warding off the corrosive effects of technology, they have developed thriving communities that give members a distinct sense of meaning, identity, and belonging—scarce commodities in a postmodern world.

—Donald B. Kraybill

Further Reading

Kraybill, D. B. (2001). *The riddle of Amish culture* (Rev. ed.). Baltimore: Johns Hopkins University Press.

Kraybill, D. B., & Bowman, C. D. (2001). *On the backroad to heaven: Old order Hutterites, Mennonites, Amish, and Brethren*. Baltimore: Johns Hopkins University Press.

Kraybill, D. B., & Nolt, S. M. (1995). *Amish enterprise: From plows to profits*. Baltimore: Johns Hopkins University Press

Scott, S. (1986). *Why do they dress that way?* Intercourse, PA: Good Books.

Scott, S. (1981). *Plain buggies: Amish, Mennonite and Brethren horse-drawn transportation*. Intercourse, PA: Good Books.

Weaver-Zercher, D. (2001). *The Amish in the American imagination*. Baltimore: Johns Hopkins University Press.

ANARCHISM

In the minds of the general public, anarchism stands for an endorsement of anarchy, which is thought by many to mean a state of chaotic lawlessness. It would therefore seem to be diametrically opposed to the affirmation of community. In fact, anarchism refers to two absolute, apparently contradictory but complementary virtues toward which a good life must strive: the integrity of the individual human conscience, resistant to the dictates of both institutional power and the mob; and the dedication of the individual to the general good. Some anarchists have stressed only the individualist half of that formula, but a full anarchism looks to a community of workers and citizens who freely give themselves to the common well-being. A perfect communal anarchist is no more possible than a perfect exemplar of the Beatitudes of the Sermon on the Mount, but like the Beatitudes, communal anarchism offers an ideal toward which society and its members in all their fallibility can aim. This entry examines several of the ideas and problems associated with anarchism as they have presented themselves in the last two centuries, when anarchism became identifiable as a political ideology.

ANARCHISM AS AN IDEOLOGY

When not used as a term connoting chaos and violence, anarchism is often narrowed to mean only the rejection of government. Insofar as the Greek word *archos* ("ruler") suggests a monarch or a parliament and the prefix *an* means "no," the definition of anarchism as repudiation only of government makes sense. But for anarchists from the nineteenth century onward, denunciation of government has been a mere subsection of their proposition that no institution and no collectivity can have an inherent right to power and command over any other—even if it be the will of the entire human race, save one, against that single one. The temporary power to restrain a particular wrongdoer is another matter, but that must not be confused with assigning the restrainer an inalienable authority to control. For instance, the domination that the white majority in the United States has exercised over its black minority, especially in the days of slavery, is as repulsive to the anarchist ethos as is rule by a czar. Nothing less than a civil war brought the white majority to end slavery, nearly ninety years after proclaiming an ideology of freedom. So in rejecting the majority as a guarantor of liberty, anarchists show good judgment.

Of all the institutions that anarchists have opposed, probably the most encompassing is not the state but property. Property (defined and supported by the state, to be sure) is deeply embedded in the popular mind—especially in majority-run republics—as possessing some sort of right of its own. The power of property to impose its will on the powerless—the power of landowners, for example, to set the terms on which they will allow tenants to work, or of corporations to determine where their employees will invest their future—is far greater than the petty authority of monarchs, parliaments, and armies. It is a further complication of the anarchist ideal that some anarchists have supported private property in moderate amounts as enhancing the independence of the individual, and collective property (in, for instance, a factory) as vital to the self-direction of the people who are to be its owners.

Anarchists have differed with Marxists in their concept of how progress and freedom are to come about. It is generally thought that the anarchist opposition to Marx-

Selection From Emma Goldman's Address to the Jury at Her Anti-Conscription Trial, New York City, July 9, 1917

In their zeal to save the country from the trouble-makers, the Marshal and his helpers did not even consider it necessary to produce a search warrant. After all, what matters a mere scrap of paper when one is called upon to raid the offices of Anarchists! Of what consequence is the sanctity of property, the right of privacy, to officials in their dealings with Anarchists! In our day of military training for battle, an Anarchist office is an appropriate camping ground. Would the gentlemen who came with Marshal McCarthy have dared to go into the offices of Morgan, or Rockefeller, or of any of those men without a search warrant? They never showed us the search warrant, although we asked them for it. Nevertheless, they turned our office into a battlefield, so that when they were through with it, it looked like invaded Belgium, with the only difference that the invaders were not Prussian barbarians but good American patriots bent on making New York safe for democracy.

The stage having been appropriately set for the three-act comedy, and the first act successfully played by carrying off the villains in a madly dashing automobile—which broke every traffic regulation and barely escaped crushing every one in its way—the second act proved even more ludicrous. Fifty thousand dollars bail was demanded, and real estate refused when offered by a man whose property is rated at three hundred thousand dollars, and that after the District Attorney had considered and, in fact, promised to accept the property for one of the defendants, Alexander Berkman, thus breaking every right guaranteed even to the most heinous criminal.

Finally the third act, played by the Government in this court during the last week. The pity of it is that the prosecution knows so little of dramatic construction, else it would have equipped itself with better dramatic material to sustain the continuity of the play. As it was, the third act fell flat, utterly, and presents the question, Why such a tempest in a teapot? Gentlemen of the jury, my comrade and co-defendant having carefully and thoroughly gone into the evidence presented by the prosecution, and having demonstrated its entire failure to prove the charge of conspiracy or any overt acts to carry out that conspiracy, I shall not impose upon your patience by going over the same ground, except to emphasize a few points. To charge people with having conspired to do something which they have been engaged in doing most of their lives, namely their campaign against war, militarism and conscription as contrary to the best interests of humanity, is an insult to human intelligence.

Source: The Emma Goldman Papers. Berkeley Digital LibrarySunSITE. Retrieved January 28, 2003, from sunsite.berkeley.edu/Goldman.

ism fixes on Marx's embrace of socialist government as a temporary instrument of progress on the part of the proletariat, but the widest gulf between Marxism and anarchism is in imagination and temperament, and it centers on the concept of history. Marxists see history as a dialectic of class struggle, and they are tempted to present that dialectic as setting its own terms, making human beings no more than its vehicle. Anarchists, to the contrary, assume that a just and liberated future, if such a future is to be, will come when the people decide to create it. That position creates a paradox for anarchism. Every human being must be free and independent; whoever is coerced into right conduct by history or the state is not acting from motives of virtue, and the community that results will not be a true community, because it comes into being through the oppression of some of its members. But freedom includes the freedom to be selfish, and even the freedom to surrender your freedom to a government or public opinion or the mob. Yet a genuine community, its members acting out of motives beyond self-interest, may become a reality. What mechanism will bring this about?

ANARCHISM AND ETERNAL STRUGGLE

For some anarchists, the answer is simple: There is no such mechanism. The reconciliation, the identity, of individual self-possession with a generous commitment to the common good is an ideal, the only ideal worth holding; but since it must be freely chosen, it cannot be inevitable.

Pierre-Joseph Proudhon (1809–1865), a leading mid-nineteenth-century French anarchist theorist, suggested that the good society will be an unendingly difficult achievement. War of a kind, Proudhon explained in his two-volume 1861 work *La guerre et la paix,* is inherent to humanity, and virtuously so. But the argument moves from the principle of war to a principle of antagonism that is the essence of action, material, mental, or moral. Proudhon held that action requires as a prerequisite a *non-moi* ("not-me") that resists and contradicts the actor. This holds equally, whether the struggle is a political one among individuals equally sincere in belief, or an internal struggle within a single person. Proudhon's anarchism, then, demands a life of watchful austerity, an end to war as military venture but the continuation of combat both within the self and with outer circumstances. And that is a life of virtue, better than a life of effortless free community.

The twentieth-century French Algerian existentialist philosopher Albert Camus (1913–1960), deeply anarchist in thought and sensibility if not in politics, defined the rebel, in effect, as every individual in rebellion against imperfection and injustice. To affirm your own life and freedom is a free act; and your free affirmation of both requires you, so Camus concluded, to affirm the life and freedom of every other human being. In the name of justice and freedom, you may have to kill an oppressor, because not to do so is to deny the right to freedom and life of the oppressor's victims. But to kill an oppressor is to negate the life and freedom in him, and therefore to contradict the universal community of life and freedom for which the rebel is fighting. And the dilemma will not go away: no historical dialectic of a Marxist sort will ever of its own momentum eliminate the contradiction. If it were to do so, there would be no freedom to choose wrongly and thereby freedom to choose rightly. The revolutionist of Marxist or other persuasion aims at a future perfect and thereby eliminates the purpose of rebellion. Camus's rebel faces a world that, because it will never be clear of injustice, vice, or misery, provides the occasion for the continuing act of rebellion that affirms life and freedom. It would be stretching Camus's view only slightly to make all good work and art a rebellion—an effort to perfect some thing (a table or machine or the fictional life in a novel) that will forever resist full perfection—and an embrace on the part of the worker or artist of a self-discipline that no human being will ever fully achieve.

ANARCHISM AND COMMUNITY

The complement to anarchist freedom is the anarchist community. In the late nineteenth century, Mikhail Bakunin (1814–1876), a Russian aristocrat turned radical, caught the paradox. Bakunin believed that freedom depended on a consciousness of the humanity of other individuals. Fail to see the capacity for freedom and right to it in others, he argued, and you will not see an image of that right and that capacity in yourself. So freedom depends on society, in which individuals can be present and visible to one another, revealing their right to freedom and therefore yours. Society, however, also has the power to control the individual. Less brutal than the state, society controls by the constant insinuating presence of its conventions, customs, and beliefs. So the free individual must also be in some way a rebel against society; and insofar as society has implanted itself in all its members, free individuals must also be rebels against a part of their very selves. Bakunin left unresolved, as it must be, the dilemma of reconciling freedom and community.

Among all anarchists, it was another dissident member of the Russian aristocracy who spoke most extensively of nature as the foundation of a stateless society. In the course of a lifetime that brought him imprisonment in both Russia and France as well as a long residence in Britain, Pyotr Kropotkin (1842–1921) became the beloved theorist of an anarchism that concentrates not on violence even as means to the good society but on the exaltation of mutual aid; *Mutual Aid* is the English-language title of a study he published in 1902. In a puzzling deviation, he supported Russia's participation in World War I. But his condemnation of the Bolshevik rule that followed was in the best anarchist tradition. Emma Goldman (1869–1940), the Russian Jewish immigrant to the United States whose anarchism drew decades of fire from the U.S. authorities, committed herself in her later years to opposing, like Kropotkin, the Bolshevik travesty of revolution.

Kropotkin was a student of biology and evolution. He accepted much of the Darwinist explanation of evolutionary progress: that nature selects among genetic characteristics, allowing only some of them to survive through generations of struggle for survival. But he attacked the notion, popular among some social and economic commentators, that the struggle in nature that has produced such an excellent thing as the human species must continue within economics if the thinning out of the unfit and the perfection of fitness are to continue. His concept of the real process of evolutionary improvement formed the theoretical basis of his hopes for a future stateless human community.

Kropotkin did not deny the fact of natural selection, but he insisted that the struggle for survival is not among individuals of the same species. Rather, it is rather a struggle on the part of the individual to stay alive in the face of all the challenges that the environment presents. The winners, the individuals whose genetic makeup gives them the greater capacity to adapt and the ability to pass on that capacity to offspring, have fought no battles with the losers. They have survived simply because they were equipped to survive under the circumstances at hand: to draw nourishment, for example, from a food supply that their sisters and cousins could not digest. That understanding of natural selection does not at all conflict with the Darwinism of Charles Darwin; it clashes only with the Darwinism of many of his admirers, whether scientists or capitalist ideologues.

So far, Kropotkin's argument merely does away with the proposition that nature actually cheers on the aggressive and competitive. The rest of his thesis offers an exactly opposite proposition: that nature bestows her benefits on species within which dwells an impulse toward mutual aid. Mutual aid is a drive in itself, a sense of solidarity with others, at least of one's own species. Species possessing it flourish. It may be seen in deer that band together to fend off some encircling predators; it has been seen in peasants who offered food to bedraggled and hungry prisoners of war from an enemy nation as the prisoners were marched through the streets.

Kropotkin's proposal can mean either or both of two things. It could imply simply that mutual aid is useful to species, and to individuals within them, so we should find it a good plan to work with. Or it could be employed to argue that we are equipped to enter into community uncoerced by government or anything else. We must have mutual aid genetically programmed in our minds and our procreative faculties; otherwise, our ancestors would not have survived to produce us. But if mutual aid is the way of human nature, how is it that government and war and economic exploitation come about at all? The best answer may come from Kropotkin's acknowledgment that human beings are also strongly endowed with a press toward individual self-development. Perhaps, then, government and wealth and capitalism express that impulse, corrupted into an appetite for power.

For models of mutual aid or means of attaining it, anarchists have had diverse sources to draw on. Proudhon, who despite his famous pronouncement that "property is theft" accepted some degree of property, hoped that among differing workers' communes goods could be exchanged that represented equal amounts of labor. Kropotkin rejected the idea that a product can be evaluated according to the quantity of work that has gone into producing it. He looked to a future in which workers would freely produce and their production would go freely to whoever needed it. The Industrial Workers of the World (IWW), formed in the United States early in the twentieth century, hoped that what they called One Big Union, embracing the whole of the working class worldwide, would embody the new social order. Within labor as the IWW envisioned the future, free organization for the purpose of resisting capitalism and the state is to transform itself into organization for the sake of the daily life of the future. In their country's village past, Russian radicals thought they had discovered a model of free community in the periodical agreement by the local peasantry over the use of its lands. Then the revolution of 1917 presented them with yet another possible commune system. The way of the future might lie in the *soviets*, or committees, that sprang up in the military, the factories, and elsewhere in Russia to provide means of decision making upon the crumbling of the czarist state and aristocracy. When in 1921 the Bolsheviks crushed the soviets at the naval base of Kronstadt, anarchists lost faith in the new *archos* that were insolently appropriating the good old radical term *communism*.

But since anarchism is ultimately not a system but an ethos, the best answer to the question of how it can realize itself is that it is already present in everyone who at the command of conscience defies an unjust law or sacrifices self-interest to a peace movement or a commune. Anarchism has lived, for a moment and very imperfectly, in the *soviets* of the Russian revolution, in the radical wing of the Spanish Civil War, in the draft resisters of the Vietnam era, in the Catholic Worker communities in U.S. cities. Ultimately it can live nowhere except within the individuals who choose it. Otherwise it will be one more system: and then it will not be anarchism.

—*Thomas R. West*

Further Reading

Bakunin, M. (1974). *Selected writings of Michael Bakunin.* (A. Lehning, Ed.; S. Cox & O. Stevens, Trans.). New York: Grove.

Baldelli, G. (1971). *Social anarchism.* Chicago: Aldine-Atherton.

Camus, A. (1991). *The rebel: An essay on man in revolt.* (A. Bower, Trans.). New York: Vintage.

Goldman, E. (1931). *Living my life.* New York: Alfred A. Knopf.

Goodman, P. (1970). *The new reformation: Notes of a neolithic conservative.* New York: Random House.

Kropotkin, P. (1987). *Mutual aid: A factor of evolution.* London: Freedom Press.

Morris, W. (2000). *News from nowhere.* New York: International Press.

Proudhon, P.-J. (1994). *What is property?* (D. R. Kelley & B. G. Smith, Eds. & Trans.). New York: Cambridge University Press.

Ruskin, J. (1985). *Unto this last and other writings.* (C. Wilmer, Ed.). Harmondsworth, UK: Penguin.

Thoreau, H. D. (1992). *Walden; and resistance to civil government.* New York: W. W. Norton.

Tolstoi, L. (1984). *The kingdom of God is within you.* (C. Garnett, Trans.). Lincoln: University of Nebraska Press.

APARTHEID

Apartheid is an Afrikaans word meaning "separation." It refers to the systematic organization of political, social, and economic life on racial grounds, designed to maintain the supremacy of the white population, which was the official policy of the South African government between 1948 and 1994. The South African apartheid system became notorious for its ruthlessness and discriminatory nature, leading to both internal resistance and international condemnation in the 1970s and 1980s. The term is often used in an informal sense to describe rigid social separation in other global contexts.

Social scientists and historians have differed in their explanations of apartheid. At one level it represented overt white racism, prevalent in South Africa where a white settler population of Dutch and British origin had colonized an indigenous black population in the course of the seventeenth through nineteenth centuries. Earlier analysts blamed this primarily on Afrikaners (descendants of Dutch settlers). But such racism was endemic in many other settler and colonial societies in the Americas, Asia, Australia, and Africa. Apartheid went further. It involved the systematic exclusion of black South Africans from citizenship and political participation, right of residence, occupation of the majority of the land, participation in the free-labor market, and many social amenities. Most analysts today believe that apartheid originated in the racial segregation practices and laws of the late nineteenth and early twentieth centuries, which in turn were part of an economic strategy to aid the growth of South Africa's capitalist economy by ensuring the availability of cheap black labor.

SEGREGATION AND THE ROOTS OF APARTHEID

The key turning point in the legalization of racial discrimination in South Africa came with the development of mining, first of diamonds in the Kimberley region from the 1870s and then, more significantly, of gold on the Witwatersrand (or Rand, the area around modern Johannesburg) from the 1890s. This "mineral revolution" ensured South Africa's transition from a diverse collection of semicommercialized rural societies to a full-fledged capitalist economy, funded by British and local capital and unified under a single settler state (formed by the Act of Union in 1910). In order to make the mines profitable, labor costs were kept artificially low through the use of black migrant labor. Single men were contracted for limited periods to work on the mines, where they were usually housed in segregated hostels, excluded from managerial or senior positions, and paid at lower rates than white workers. These discriminatory wages were justified on the grounds that the costs of maintaining families were covered by subsistence agriculture in the workers' home areas.

The migrant labor system thus favored both the mining capitalists, who lowered their wage bill, and white workers, who were protected from black competition in the better-paid jobs. Although capitalists and white workers conflicted over labor issues (notably in the Rand Revolt strike of 1922), they soon realized their common interests in maintaining migrant labor and racial discrimination. This was systematized after Union by a series of legislative acts of major significance. The Mines and Works Act (1911, amended in 1926) excluded black miners from higher-paid work defined as "skilled," a principle that was extended to all government employment in the 1920s. The Natives Land Act (1913) outlawed black land ownership in large swathes of the country and confined black cultivators to reserves, where participation in the commercial markets of the Rand region was minimized. Tax demands and, in time, overcrowding and impoverishment on the reserves ensured a ready supply of migrant labor to the mines. The Natives (Urban Areas) Act of 1923 provided for residential segregation in towns while the Native Administration Act (1927) established separate administrative structures for black Africans in the reserves, codified distinct "native law," and minimized black political participation in the rest of South Africa. By 1936, all black South Africans had also been excluded from the franchise at the national level.

South Africa before World War II was thus a highly segregated society. In this context distinct communities emerged with their own identities and experiences. In many of the rural reserves, migrant labor disrupted earlier farming and kinship patterns, placing a heavier burden of homestead production on women, youth, and older men. In reaction, some rural chiefs emphasized traditional values and norms against the threat of patriarchal breakdown caused by the absence of adult men of working age and the weakening of "traditional" values which they encountered in the cities. Organizations such as the Inkatha Zulu cultural society, the precursor to Mangosutho Buthelezi's Inkatha Freedom Party of the present day, were formed in the 1920s.

The growth of a manufacturing industry alongside mining in the 1920s and 1930s also led to urban migration for many white and black South Africans, but municipal laws in many places ensured that blacks were unable to buy property; they could only rent in separate areas known as "locations." In the 1920s, a vibrant location subculture emerged on the Rand and in the Indian Ocean port city of Durban, marked by self-help welfare organizations, independent churches, new urban language dialects, and marabi jazz music. Some working-class areas, such as Sophiatown in Johannesburg and District Six in Cape Town, were home to property owners, landlords, and tenants, and were multiracial in character.

FROM SEGREGATION TO APARTHEID

In the 1940s, this system of segregation began to weaken. During World War II, many black workers moved into the manufacturing sector and into more skilled positions in the mines, where they took the place of whites who were fighting in the armed forces. This development threatened unskilled white workers. Attempts to reverse the situation after 1945 led to conflicts, such as the 1946 black mine-worker strike. Poorer white farmers, still recovering from the long-term effects of the Great Depression of the 1930s, found it more difficult to obtain cheap farm labor.

It was in this context that the Afrikaner National Party came to prominence, under the leadership of D. F. Malan (1874–1959). The National Party drew on a revival of Afrikaner nationalist sentiment in the 1930s, stimulated largely by the economic difficulties of many poorer Afrikaners during the Depression as well as by resentment of British South African control of the most prosperous sectors of the economy and the government's unquestioning support of Britain during World War II. After 1945 Malan wedded these nationalist sentiments to fears of eroding racial segregation. The result was the policy of apartheid, by which he narrowly won the general election of 1948.

Apartheid was designed to entrench segregation, but it went much further than earlier policy to extend to all South Africans in all spheres of life. It was implemented in several stages. In the 1950s, the focus lay on rigid separation of people by race. The Population Registration Act (1950) classified all South Africans by race, and the Immorality Act (1950) prohibited sexual contact between whites and other South Africans. The Group Areas Act (1950) rigidly enforced racial segregation in all towns, street by street, as well as in the countryside. The Reservation of Separate Amenities Act (1953) extended segregation to all public amenities. School and college education was segregated under the Bantu Education Act (1953) and the extension of the University Education Act (1959). The vote was removed from those defined as "colored" (mixed race) in 1956, so that only whites retained the franchise. Black African migration to towns was strictly controlled, and all Africans had to carry pass books in which temporary work and urban residence permits were recorded. Although such measures produced strong resistance, notably in the Defiance Campaign of 1952, the Freedom Charter of 1955, and the Women's Anti-Pass Law march to Pretoria of 1956, campaigns that all included some white opponents of apartheid, the state suppressed all opposition. International awareness was increased by the massacre of anti-pass protestors at Sharpeville in 1960, an event that led to South Africa's withdrawal from the British Commonwealth in the following year after a white referendum that gave backing to the National Party government.

APARTHEID INTENSIFIED

In the 1960s, apartheid was extended still further. Partly in response to growing international and U.N. condemnation of the political exclusion of black South Africans, the government under Hendrik Verwoerd (1901–1966) and John Vorster (1915–1983) promoted the "homeland" policy. Under this policy, black South Africans were to be made citizens of quasi-autonomous homelands (or Bantustans, as they were called) formed out of the former rural reserves. This policy came to full fruition in 1976, when the Transkei homeland was granted "independence," although heavily dependent on subsidies from Pretoria and run by homeland loyalists. Similar measures followed for other homelands, such as Bophutatswana, Ciskei, and Venda. These measures were not recognized by the rest of the world, which saw them merely as a way to deprive blacks of their South African citizenship permanently.

The Bantustan policy led to massive forced removals, whereby South Africans who found themselves on the wrong side of new homeland boundaries were forcibly relocated. In particular, black urban dwellers in places such as Johannesburg, Cape Town, and Durban, many of whom had lived there all their lives, were removed to distant rural Bantustans that they had never seen before. An estimated 3.5 million black South Africans were relocated. In addition, multiracial suburbs such as Sophiatown and District Six were destroyed and their inhabitants dispersed. This destruction of communities in the 1960s and 1970s is still today one of the most bitterly remembered legacies of apartheid. Many were relocated to impoverished areas with little scope for employment or livelihood. Huge rural and urban slums resulted.

THE END OF APARTHEID

By the late 1970s and 1980s, it was becoming clear that the Bantustan strategy was not working. The desperate need for jobs led many blacks to risk arrest and deportation by living illegally in the white towns, often in squatter camps without any municipal provisions such as running water. By the 1980s, some business leaders were complaining that urban influx control, which prevented black people from moving to the cities, was making it difficult for them to recruit sufficient labor, and they called for its relaxation or removal. And massive township resistance emerged, initially in the Soweto uprising of 1976, but by the mid-1980s extending to most townships throughout the country. Although the state responded with severe repression, which included detentions without trial, the banning of anti-apartheid organizations, and the occupation of townships by armed troops, it was clear by the late 1980s that apartheid was no longer working in the economic and political interests of white, let alone black, South Africans.

The turning point came with the collapse of the Soviet Union and consequent end of the Cold War in 1989. The South African apartheid state had been consistently backed by the Western powers who, despite unease at apartheid, saw the country as an important bulwark against Communism in Africa. South African troops, armed by the United States and NATO, severely destabilized Angola and Mozambique in the 1980s. Once the Berlin Wall and the Soviet Union collapsed, U.S. and NATO support could no longer be guaranteed. Moreover, the South African government assumed that international support for its main opponents, the African National Congress (ANC) and the South African Communist Party (SACP), would be weakened. In early 1990, the National Party premier, F. W. de Klerk (b. 1936), therefore legalized the ANC and SACP, released many political prisoners—including Nelson Mandela (b. 1918), who had become a symbol of the anti-apartheid struggle—and in the subsequent year repealed key items of apartheid legislation such as the Land Act, the Population Registration Act, and the Group Areas Act.

Negotiations between 1991 and 1994 led to South

Africa's first democratic election, in which the ANC won 62.6 percent of the vote and became the dominant power in a coalition government of national unity. The new government dismantled the last legislative vestiges of apartheid, and the national constitution of 1996 outlawed discrimination on grounds of race, ethnicity, gender, religion, or sexual orientation, making it one of the most liberal constitutions in the world. However, the social and economic legacy of apartheid could not be so easily resolved. Huge disparities of wealth continue to exist largely, although no longer totally, on a racial basis. The squatter settlements that surrounded all towns and the rural slums of the former Bantustans continue to be deeply impoverished, lacking basic necessities. Unemployment rates have risen, not least because of the inflow of cheaper foreign goods, which has undercut some South African manufacturing industries, such as textiles.

In this context, the word *community* has acquired a peculiarly localized South African meaning. During the years of struggle against apartheid, it came to be associated in a general sense with the oppressed. In many townships in the mid-1980s, state structures were boycotted and replaced by unofficial people's courts, councils of "comrade youth," and community education initiatives. This usage drew on the strong sense of local community that had emerged in the locations, townships, and squatter camps of the segregation and apartheid years. Loyalty to a wider state, especially to the Bantustans, was associated with selling out to apartheid policies. In the years since 1994, the new state has had to combat this sense of alienation, which is marked, for example, by refusal to pay local taxes and municipal rates. Not only does the struggle for national unity involve attempts to produce a national identity that transcends the divided South African past (for example, in a new flag, anthem, and national education curriculum), but it also requires the harnessing of local community loyalties to the national state. Attempts to forge a sense of community that breaks from apartheid racial divisions is the main challenge facing the new South Africa.

—Nigel Worden

See also CASTE

Further Reading

Beinart, W. (2001). *Twentieth-century South Africa* (2nd ed.). Oxford, UK: Oxford University Press.

Bozzoli, B., & Nkotsoe, M. (1991). *Women of Phokeng: Consciousness, life strategy and migrancy in South Africa, 1900–1983.* Portsmouth, NH: Heinemann and Johannesburg, South Africa: Ravan Press.

Maharaj, G. (Ed.). (1999). *Between unity and diversity: Essays on nation-building in post-apartheid South Africa.* Cape Town,

Preamble to the Constitution of South Africa (Adopted: May 8, 1996 / Amended: October 11, 1996/ In Force: February 7, 1997)

Preamble

We, the people of South Africa, Recognise the injustices of our past;

Honour those who suffered for justice and freedom in our land;

Respect those who have worked to build and develop our country; and

Believe that South Africa belongs to all who live in it, united in our diversity.

We therefore, through our freely elected representatives, adopt this Constitution as the supreme law of the Republic so as to–

Heal the divisions of the past and establish a society based on democratic values, social justice and fundamental human rights;

Lay the foundations for a democratic and open society in which government is based on the will of the people and every citizen is equally protected by law;

Improve the quality of life of all citizens and free the potential of each person; and

Build a united and democratic South Africa able to take its rightful place as a sovereign state in the family of nations.

May God protect our people.

Nkosi Sikelel iAfrika. Morena boloka setjhaba sa heso.

God sen Suid-Afrika. God bless South Africa.

Mudzimu fhatutshedza Afurika. Hosi katekisa Afrika.

Source: South Africa Constitution. Retrieved on 3 January 2003 from http://www.oefre.unibe.ch/law/icl/sf00000_.html.

South Africa: IDASA and David Philip Publishers.

Maylam, P., & Edwards, I. (1996). *The people's city: African life in twentieth-century Durban*. Portsmouth, NH: Heinemann and Pietermaritzburg, South Africa: University of Natal Press.

O'Meara, D. (1996). *Forty lost years: The apartheid state and the politics of the National Party, 1948-1994*. Athens: Ohio University Press and Johannesburg, South Africa: Ravan Press.

Posel, D. (1991). *The making of apartheid, 1948–61: Conflict and compromise*. Oxford, UK: Clarendon.

Ross, R. (1999). *A concise history of South Africa*. Cambridge, UK: Cambridge University Press.

Worden, N. (2000). *The making of modern South Africa: Conquest, segregation and apartheid* (3rd ed.). Oxford, UK and Malden, MA: Blackwell.

APPALACHIA

Drawing informed conclusions about community life in Appalachia is difficult. Geographically, the region is divided into three quite different subregions that have given rise to a variety of community forms and experiences. In addition, no consensus exists on what constitutes Appalachia's boundaries. The most widely accepted view, as offered by the Appalachian Regional Commission, is a specific geographical definition of 410 counties in thirteen states extending over 995 miles from southern New York to northeastern Mississippi. This area is home to nearly 23 million people. This definition, shaped in large part by the efforts of politicians to include their jurisdictions in a specific government initiative, encompasses large cities such as Pittsburgh and Birmingham; the suburbs of Cincinnati, Memphis, and Atlanta; towns and cities dominated by coal, chemical, and textile industries; tourist and agricultural economies; and numerous small rural counties with populations of under 10,000. The Appalachian region is so diverse that government officials have divided it into northern, central, and southern subregions. Social and economic conditions vary widely between and within the subregions.

This diversity, along with a number of scholarly studies, gives lie to the popularly held notion of Appalachia as "a coherent region inhabited by an homogeneous population possessing a uniform culture" (Shapiro 1978, p. ix), which was first put forth by local color writers, missionaries, educators, social reformers, and industrialists between 1870 and 1920. But this myth, which is linked to degrading hillbilly stereotypes of Appalachians, persists today and is one of the reasons why most residents in the region do not use the term *Appalachian* to describe themselves or their communities.

THE STUDY OF COMMUNITY LIFE IN APPALACHIA

Few reputable regionwide studies of community life in Appalachia exist. Even the earliest of these studies caution against generalizations concerning residents of the region. The majority of community studies focus on a single community or county, usually in central Appalachia—the poorest and most rural section of the region—or in the more rural areas of southern Appalachia. Until the mid-1970s, with a few notable exceptions, these studies shared the assumption that the far-reaching social and economic problems prevalent in Appalachia were the result of forces unique to the Appalachian region. In particular, these studies often linked low educational achievement, dysfunctional families, violence, poverty, welfare dependency, and a host of other community problems to the existence of an Appalachian folk culture that had failed to prepare its people for the cooperative, interrelated, technical society in which they now lived. During this same period, family and community historians of Appalachia were offering a romanticized notion of a preindustrial Appalachia that closely exemplified Thomas Jefferson's democratic vision of self-sufficient communities characterized by widespread land ownership, a relatively equal distribution of resources, few class distinctions, and egalitarian cooperation.

Beginning in the late 1970s, a new generation of Appalachian scholars began to examine the devastating impact of modernization and concentrated corporate ownership and power on communities in Appalachia. Community studies now explored how the social and economic hardships faced by local residents were not a result of a defective folk culture peculiar to the region but rather were a direct consequence of corporate and government policies and actions that left people dependent upon a national and global economy. Relatedly, by locating the preindustrial history of Appalachia in the context of global capitalism, scholars are discovering the ways in which persistent poverty in Appalachian communities has been linked to the historical interaction of capitalist markets and state policies. A study by Dwight Billings and Kathleen Blee (2000) is particularly notable in this regard. This study makes clear that Appalachian communities are very much a part and product of the American mainstream and demonstrates the varied ways they survive and change in the face of economic crisis.

COMMUNITY-BASED RESISTANCE

Earlier studies of Appalachian communities frequently portrayed residents as fatalistic and quiescent people who were complicit in their own oppression. More recent studies recognize that the Appalachian region has never lacked a politics of resistance and alternative development. These studies, including works by Mary Anglin, Mary Ann Hinsdale, Helen Lewis, Maxine Waller, and Richard Couto, make major contributions to the broader activist literature on community organizing and change.

Appalachian identity and cultural and political expressions related to that identity are not naturally part of community life in Appalachia, nor do they always arise spontaneously in local struggles to challenge oppression or inequality. Rather, they are the outgrowth of political dynamics and social change that often require careful educational and political work. The seeds for such expression exist, but these seeds must be deliberately cultivated and nourished by individuals and institutions that recognize the value of such work to local resistance efforts.

Successful change efforts in the Appalachian mountains have centered more often around the concept of "community" than the centralized workplace of the mine, mill, or factory. Many of the popular struggles in the region have been fueled by historical memory and reliance on, and defense of, traditional community values—a strong commitment to land, kin, and religious beliefs, an emphasis on self-rule and social equality, and patriotism. These single-issue, community-based struggles have won important victories, but as local resources have been depleted and local economies gutted by national and global market forces, there is an increasing recognition of the need for new organizing strategies. One encouraging sign has been the establishment and success of multi-issue, membership-driven organizations such as Save Our Cumberland Mountains, Kentuckians for the Commonwealth, the Virginia Organizing Project, and the Community Farm Alliance, which connect local community issues to state, national, and global patterns and concerns.

Coal miners in Appalachia heading to the mine in 1984.
Source: David Turnley/Corbis; used with permission.

THE FUTURE

One should exercise caution in making generalizations about the Appalachian experience. But a new generation of Appalachian scholars and activists is engaged in a critical discourse and practice that are undermining long-standing myths about the region, identifying the ways in which the Appalachian experience is similar to or different from experiences elsewhere, and developing strategies and organizations to empower community residents for the long term.

—Stephen L. Fisher

Further Reading

Anglin, M. K. (2002). *Women, power, and dissent in the hills of Carolina*. Urbana: University of Illinois Press.

Billings, D. B., & Blee, K. M. (2000). *The road to poverty: The making of wealth and hardship in Appalachia*. New York: Cambridge University Press.

Couto, R. A. (1994). Appalachia. In R. A. Couto, N. L. Simpson, & G. Harris (Eds.), *Sowing seeds in the mountains: Community-based coalitions for cancer prevention and control* (pp. 14–26). Washington, DC: National Institutes of Health.

Couto, R. A. (1999). *Making democracy work better: Mediating structures, social capital, and the democratic prospect*. Chapel Hill: University of North Carolina Press.

Fisher, S. L. (1993). *Fighting back in Appalachia: Traditions of resistance and change*. Philadelphia: Temple University Press.

Halperin, R. H. (1990). *The livelihood of kin: Making ends meet the "the Kentucky way."* Austin: University of Texas Press.

Hinsdale, M. A., Lewis, H. M., & Waller, S. M. (1995). *It comes from the people: Community development and local theology*. Philadelphia: Temple University Press.

Raitz, K. B., & Ulack, R. (1984). *Appalachia, a regional geography: Land, people and development*. Boulder, CO: Westview.

Shapiro, H. D. (1978). *Appalachia on our mind: The southern mountains and mountaineers in the American consciousness, 1870–1920*. Chapel Hill: University of North Carolina Press.

Williams, J. A. (2002). *Appalachia: A history*. Chapel Hill: University of North Carolina Press.

ARCHITECTURE, VERNACULAR

See VERNACULAR ARCHITECTURE

ARCOSANTI

Located in the semiarid desert region of central Arizona in the United States, about 70 miles north of Phoenix, Arcosanti, when complete, will be a small town of around 7,000 people on about 25 acres of an approximately 4,060-acre land preserve. Since construction work began in 1970, its founder, the Italian-born architect Paolo Soleri (b. 1919), and a dedicated community of volunteers have designed, built, and inhabited Arcosanti as an urban laboratory. As the main project of the not-for-profit Cosanti Foundation, Arcosanti is devoted to research into and development of a different kind of urban environment.

In opposition to urban sprawl, Soleri has proposed highly integrated, compact, car-free cities in which walking would be the main form of transportation. He calls these environments *arcologies*, because they fuse *arc*hitecture with ec*ology*. Inspired by the point Omega hypothesis, a theory of spiritual evolution put forward by the priest and paleontologist Pierre Teilhard de Chardin (1881–1955), Soleri believes that arcologies can be instrumental in our human evolution. Within an arcology, material recycling, waste reduction, energy conservation, and the use of renewable energy sources would be the basis of sustainable urban production and consumption. The drawing together of diverse city functions into mixed-use, self-contained arcologies would encourage cultural intensification and social integration within their boundaries and would permit the surrounding hinterland to remain natural. Soleri also believes that by adopting a more frugal lifestyle inside an arcology, citizens would have the potential not only to do less harm to the planet but also to develop themselves spiritually.

Arcosanti is the name given by Soleri to the thirtieth arcology for which Soleri produced designs, published in 1969 in *Arcology: The City in the Image of Man.*

Arcosanti was designed to be an experimental complex providing a testing ground for arcological concepts. Like arcology, "Arcosanti" is a fused word of Italian origin. "Arco" refers to architecture (or the arch), "cosa" is a widely used word meaning "thing," and the annex "nti" suggests a certain permanence of timeless quality. Together the name suggests a non-material (or spiritual) process at the heart of architecture—an "architecture before things."

While following in the tradition of the 1960s counterculture communes and the more recent ecovillages movement, the community at Arcosanti is unique in that its motivation lies primarily in the production of ecological architecture. The community has focused on building the project's various concrete structures using an earth-casting construction method based on ancient techniques. These structures and spaces, many characterized by the apse form, are built into the south-facing edge of a mesa above the Agua Fria River. They now define the living, working, and learning processes of around one hundred residents. In addition to their ongoing construction work, residents are involved in such diverse tasks as project development, research activity, exhibitions, drafting and design work, conference organization, wind-bell production, and site maintenance.

Arcosanti lacks the levels of economic investment and skilled labor that would have seen it finished long ago, but the community remains intact, the work continues, and Soleri's determination to build remains undiminished. His experience as an apprentice of architect Frank Lloyd Wright (1867–1961) at Taliesin between 1947 and 1948 undoubtedly influenced his establishment of an educational program that has brought more than 3,000 volunteers from around the world to participate in construction workshops and seminars within this experimental learning-by-building laboratory at Arcosanti.

—David Grierson

Further Reading

Grierson, D. (2000). Ecology, sustainability and the city. Towards an ecological approach to environmental sustainability: With a case study on Arcosanti in Arizona. Unpublished doctoral dissertation, University of Strathclyde, Glasgow,UK.

Soleri, P. (1969). *Arcology: The city in the image of man.* Cambridge, MA: MIT Press.

Soleri, P. (1981). *The Omega seed: An eschatological hypothesis.* Garden City, NY: Anchor Press/Doubleday.

Soleri, P. (1983). *Arcosanti: An urban laboratory?* San Diego, CA: Avant Books and the Cosanti Foundation.

Teilhard de Chardin, P. (1959). *The phenomenon of man.* London: Collins.

ARISTOTLE (1909–1972)

Greek philosopher

Aristotle, student of Plato and tutor of Alexander the Great, is considered one of the greatest Western philosophers and is well known for his overwhelming influence on Western science and society. He developed a teaching about community that is still studied seriously and still has adherents, especially among those who prize a political culture focused on the cultivation of virtues and manners. Contemporary communitarians who oppose the breakdown of historic social groups and longstanding traditions by political and economic forces continue to invoke Aristotle's name as an authority in their cause.

Aristotle's idea of political community must be sharply distinguished from the modern idea of a collection of individuals united to secure their own interests, founded on contract and dedicated to the protection of individual rights. Aristotle emphasizes the organic integrity of any community worthy of the name, and understands that integrity with reference to its most fundamental purposes. Ethics, for Aristotle, is part of politics—but the point of genuine political community is an ethical purpose: the development of moral and intellectual excellence.

A FOCUSED AND NORMATIVE CONCEPT OF COMMUNITY

Aristotle's notion of community is a focused concept—what scholars call a *pros hen* equivocal. This involves a core meaning flanked by various peripheral meanings. The core is a paradigmatic case that serves as a norm from which the peripheral meanings deviate in different ways. The notion of community, therefore, has a single normative core surrounded by variants that are communities in derivative senses of the word. In this model, we do not say that a group either is or is not a community; rather, we say it is or is not a community in a particular way or in a certain respect. The standard of comparison is always the central case, against which the real or imagined communities are measured.

Aristotle is a realist about values and norms: Questions such as "What is the purpose of human life?" or "What is a genuine community?" admit of objective answers that are independent of the beliefs of individuals and societies. The norm at issue is neither the central tendency of a population's behaviors or beliefs nor a customary convention. It is a standard based on what actually satisfies human needs, supports decent relationships, and develops the human potential for moral and intellectual flourishing. This is the primary or focal sense of community, the norm with which other communities are compared.

COMMUNITY AND FRIENDSHIP

Most of Aristotle's key concepts are focused, in the sense described above. Consider friendship, a notion integral to Aristotle's normative idea of community. Human relationships motivated by pleasure or the usefulness of the other are not friendships in the full sense; the latter are motivated by and dedicated to the development of the friend's well-being. This diverges from our idea of friendship as a private association based in feeling, aiming at mutual pleasure, and legitimated by personal preference. Aristotle would deny that friendships for fun and profit are full-fledged; they are merely friendships "in a way." He argues that the focal case of friendship is a steady human relationship based on reciprocal support in developing moral and intellectual excellence.

Genuine community involves friendship in just this sense. It is an enduring social whole whose members are bound to each other by ties of true friendship. Since the forms of friendship dominant in a society can vary, the communities based on those forms will differ. But the best aim at the cultivation of moral and intellectual virtue. The normative sense of community turns on the central case of friendship.

POLITICAL COMMUNITY AND SHARED ETHOS

In a paradigmatic political community, citizens are friends; its size, therefore, must be limited. An organization of millions could be a community only in some offshoot sense. In a genuine political community, citizens share a conception of the good and share equitably in deliberation about action based on that conception. All citizens are educated by the community to participate in its cultural, political, ethical life.

These shared practices and beliefs are informed by a common ethos. Ethos consists of both shared individual habits (the affective-cognitive-behavioral dispositions that define character) and the large-scale sociocultural patterns that reflect and reinforce those habits. This reciprocal relationship mimics the organic relationships among parts in a whole: Character is shaped by community, and community is shaped by the character of its members.

This reciprocal causation among parts and wholes can yield good ethos or bad. Aristotle argues that tyrannical regimes, for instance, are communities only in a remote and derivative sense, since their members become distrustful, fathers tend to act like tyrants and oppress their spouses and children, and so forth. In a democratic regime, parents tend to treat each other and their children like equals, and try to institute something like contractual consent in home rule. (That too, according to Aristotle, is a distortion. Both domination and laxity destroy community, if in opposite ways.)

From the premise that ethos is basic, Aristotle argues the importance of education for community and virtue, the priority of custom to formalized law and political constitution, and the centrality of character in the individual. Community grows character. Good community grows good character, supports harmonious relationships, and builds a civilized common life. People and communities grow up together—develop or devolve together.

COMMUNITY "BY NATURE"

Community is inborn in humans because we are social animals "by nature." This claim has two aspects. Factually, we depend biologically and psychologically on others; we need affiliation and rely on others for support and training. Normatively, the point of our existence is to develop morally and intellectually, and that requires living with good people in a good community. We become fully human only in this way. A truly human life is always and essentially in community with others.

Aristotle's claims about nature, proper function, and specific capacity must be understood with reference to his metaphysics, his study of the first principle(s) and cause(s) of whatever exists insofar as it exists. The most fundamental way of understanding anything is by reference to a definitive purpose. This is its *final cause,* or *telos*, and understanding things in this way is called "teleological." Aristotle's approach to community is strongly teleological.

To explain by analogy, axes may be made of different materials but all are, in essence, for chopping; a house may be made of wood or stone, but its definitive function is sheltering. The definitive purpose of community is human happiness. The essence of happiness is moral and intellectual excellence (the whole of happiness includes various external goods as well). We can know this essence because we can identify those distinctively human capacities for moral and intellectual function that distinguish us among living things. Those distinctive functions define our essence, our being; their excellence defines our well-being.

ARISTOTLE AND CONTEMPORARY COMMUNITARIANISM

Many contemporary communitarians are inspired by Aristotle. Almost all reject his teleological metaphysics. Since teleological metaphysics is Aristotle's principle of unity, rejecting it leads to differing modern views. The key issues among these rival views are the role of rights (a modern notion lacking in Aristotle) and the relationship between microcommunities and the state.

Liberal communitarians assert that an Aristotelian brand of well-being can flourish in small communities united in a shared vision of excellence and a common way of life. These are sharply distinguished from the state, which is not a community but a coalition of communities constructed for common defense and social services. Rights are normative principles whose recognition opens spaces for experiments with different visions of morality and community that must agree only on minimal principles of democratic procedure. Fearing authoritarianism, liberal communitarians reject substantive moral education as a purpose of the state. Liberals hence are relativistic and accommodating where Aristotle is naturalistic and doctrinaire.

Libertarian communitarians recommend an even more minimal role for the state, and they tend to individual rather than cultural relativism. They agree with Aristotle that virtue is the point of personal development but believe that virtues are achieved in and through modern political and economic systems—especially free-market systems. They deny Aristotle's claim that *pleonexia* (the incessant calculation of personal advantage in every transaction with others) is a master vice destructive of community. Rights are conceived to be higher-order principles that are at the foundation of legal and political and economic systems.

Conservative communitarians often appeal to virtue and character and Aristotle. Most, however, are so opposed to Enlightenment rationalism (the movement launched in seventeenth and eighteenth century Europe that glorified individual experience and critical reason) that they shun all kinds of universal rules and abstract principles, even those of a sort Aristotle would endorse. Rights are regarded as elements of modern legal systems not grounded in human nature or universal truths. Rights are political precautions that make a perilous guide to ethics. (Conservative communitarians argue that relativism and typically hedonism result if ethics are based on a right to pursue any virtue one wants—or even no virtues—so long as one does not interfere with the rights of others to pursue their interests.) Neo-Aristotelian conservativism either tends to a sort of romanticism or is tempted simultaneously to economic liberalism and a credulous support of state in its moral and military functions.

Roman Catholic thinkers retain Aristotelian teleology and add St. Thomas Aquinas's theory of natural and divine law. Thomists distinguish between our natural happiness (which, they say, is as Aristotle claimed), and our supernatural happiness (a superordinate end revealed in scripture and tradition). They argue as a matter of public reason that communities should serve our natural happiness, and argue as a matter of faith that some communities, at least, should cultivate the theological virtues that prepare us for a supernatural and ultimate happiness. This division results in a cosmopolitan view of the Catholic community itself. It is a particular community able to serve as a general moral authority for the world, able to speak up for universal truths from a special and privileged place. Most Catholic communitarians acknowledge rights but believe they are means to an end in that they are preconditions of virtue (life, means of subsistence, access to political and judicial systems, etc.). Virtues, not rights, are ultimate.

—C. Wesley DeMarco

Further Reading

Arendt, H. (1958). *The human condition*. Chicago: University of Chicago Press.

Aristotle. (1989). *Nicomachean ethics* (T. Irwin, Trans.). Indianapolis, IN: Hackett.

Aristotle. (1998). *Politics* (E. Barker, Trans.). New York: Oxford University Press.

Barker, E. (1959). *The political thought of Plato and Aristotle*. New York: Dover.

Bellah, R. N., Madsen, R., Sullivan, W. M., Swider, A., & Tipton, S. M. (1991). *The good society*. New York: Knopf.

Broadie, S. (1991). *Ethics with Aristotle*. New York: Oxford University Press.

Hardie, W. F. R. (1980). *Aristotle's ethical theory* (2nd ed.). New York: Oxford University Press.

Kraut, R. (1989). *Aristotle on the human good*. Princeton, NJ: Princeton University Press.

Kraut, R. (1997). *Aristotle: Politics, Books VII and VIII*. Oxford, UK: Clarendon Press.

MacIntyre, A. (1984). *After virtue* (2nd ed.). Notre Dame, IN: University of Notre Dame Press.

MacIntyre, A. (1988). *Whose justice? Which rationality?* Notre Dame, IN: University of Notre Dame Press.

MacIntyre, A. (1999). *Dependent rational animals: Why human beings need the virtues*. Chicago: Open Court.

Nussbaum, M. (1986). *The fragility of goodness: Luck and ethics in Greek tragedy and philosophy*. New York: Cambridge University Press.

Sherman, N. (1989). *The fabric of character*. Oxford, UK: Clarendon Press.

Sim, M. (Ed.). (1995). *The crossroads of norm and nature*. Lanham, MD: Rowman and Littlefield.

Taylor, C. (1989). *Sources of the self: The making of the modern identity*. Cambridge, MA: Harvard University Press.

Taylor, C. (1992). *The ethics of authenticity*. Cambridge, MA: Harvard University Press.

Rasmussen, D. B. (1991). *Liberty and nature: An Aristotelian defense of liberal order.* Peru, IL: Open Court.

Walzer, M. (1983). *Spheres of justice: A defense of pluralism and equality*. New York: Basic Books.

ARTISTS' COLONIES

Artists' colony is a loose term that refers to a place where a group of artists congregate and work. Artists live in close proximity to one another, yet the circumstances under which they live can vary significantly. They might live communally, sharing expenses and dividing chores, or they might remain individually responsible for their personal expenses and day-to-day tasks. In some cases, artists gather and work under the auspices of a wealthy patron. Today, an artist colony can connote a greater community, in which artists and their art play a vital force in the area's economy. It can also signify a particular area of a town or city in which artists and art galleries are located.

Artists' colonies flourished in the late nineteenth century in rural areas of Europe and the United States. Originally, they were established by young painters in France to meet the growing interest in *plein air* (open-air) painting and the portrayal of peasant life. Throughout the early part of the nineteenth century, Westerners perceived Rome, with its rich history of classical and Renaissance art, as the art capital of the world. Art students were taught that historical, mythological painting was the most essential style to master, and they worked exclusively inside the studio, relying mostly on artificial light to paint the classical scenes preferred by their teachers. Gradually, however, dissatisfaction with conventional academic art training grew, and young painters rebelled against the classical tradition by painting landscapes in the open air and by portraying unknown people, often from the lower classes. As a result of this shift in aesthetic interest, Paris gradually replaced Rome as the mecca for Western artists.

As early as 1820, the first plein air painters departed Paris during the summers for the hamlet of Barbizon near the forest of Fontainebleu. Here they lived among the peasants, found cheap lodging and food, and depicted with realism the countryside and rural figures that intrigued them. Jean François Millet (1814–1875) and Charles Émile Jacque (1813–1894) were two residents who became legendary for their moving representations of peasant life. By the mid-1850s, Barbizon had developed into a colony of international renown, attracting numerous Europeans and Americans. Within two decades, similar colonies were flourishing in other parts of France and throughout Europe. These included Grèz-sur-Loing, also located near the Fontainebleau forest; Pont-Aven in Brittany; Giverny, outside Paris; Worpswede, in northern Germany; St. Ives, at the southwestern tip of Great Britain; Skagen, in northern Denmark; and Nagybánya, in central Hungary. Many American artists who had lived in European art colonies were inspired upon their return home to establish comparable communities in the United States. By the early 1900s, the United States boasted art colonies of its own, most notably Woodstock, New York; Provincetown, Massachusetts; Laguna Beach, California; and Taos, New Mexico.

By the early part of the twentieth century, critics of modern society had established numerous cooperative communities that became more far-reaching in scope, both artistically and ideologically, than the painters' settlements of France. These colonies shared the goal of incorporating nature into everyday life, thereby resurrecting a long-shunned connection between the human being and his or her natural surroundings. Disconcerted by the alienating aspects of urban modernity, inhabitants believed that through creativity, collective work, and economic self-sufficiency, one could live well and fully independent of the pressures of fast-paced industrialism. These colonies became an attractive sanctuary for poets, writers, and dancers, as well as painters, and often reflected the political and social mores of the residents. Monte Verità (1900–1920) in Ascona, Switzerland, for example, offered a vegetarian, free love, back-to-nature way of life for resident artists, while simultaneously serving as a haven for conscientious objectors during World War I.

By the middle of the twentieth century, young artists showed a declining interest in artists' colonies, mainly because the aesthetic focus of the avant-garde shifted from the concerns of rural life to those of postwar urban society. While some art colonies still exist in rural areas of Europe and the United States, they no longer carry with them the resonance of a major artistic movement. Nevertheless, the political and social ideals of these colonies remain a significant component of numerous successful alternative communities today.

—Sydney Jane Norton

Further Reading

Gomes, R. (1995). *Impressions of Giverny: A painter's paradise, 1883–1914.* San Francisco: Pomegranate Artbooks.

Jacobs, M. (1985). *The good and simple life: Artist colonies in Europe and America.* Oxford, UK: Phaidon Press.

Sellin, D. (1982). *Americans in Brittany in Normandy, 1860–1910.* Phoenix, AZ: Phoenix Art Museum.

Shipp, S. (1996). *American art colonies, 1850–1930.* Westport, CT: Greenwood Press.

ARTS

See COMMUNITY ARTS

ASHRAMS

An ashram is a distinctive form of spiritual community. It is a Hindu creation that emerged in India some twelve centuries ago. The word *ashram* derives from the Sanskrit *asram,* meaning "hard work" or "striving" or "exertion," and it has three associated meanings: (1) a place where hard work is done, (2) hard work itself, and (3) a place of rest or retreat. The work referred to is spiritual practices and disciplines. In ancient times, the ashram was a hermitage or dwelling place where a *rishi* (a sage or guru) lived along with students, or *sisyas.* The term *guru* means teacher, from *gu* ("darkness") and *ru* ("remover"), one who brings others from darkness to light.

Ashrams are to be found in every state in India, in settings as varied as forests, mountains, deserts, along rivers, by the sea, in the countryside, and in cities. They may be made up of just three or four people, or they may have several hundred residents. From their early days until the late fifteenth century, they were limited to men, but that limitation was challenged by the *bhakti,* or devotional, movements. Caitanya (1485–1533), the great reviver of Krishna devotion, opened the *samnyasin,* or renunciate path, to women. But it was the Hindu revival of the nineteenth and twentieth centuries that sparked an ashram movement that spread across the many streams of Hindu religious life.

ORIGINS

The date of the emergence of the first ashrams is not known. Some believe that an ashram-as-hermitage was originally associated with the *rishis* that composed the Upanishads (c. 800 B.C.E.), sacred writings of the Hindus. Here, an ashram is simply a hermitage or dwelling of those who are pursuing a life of spiritual discipline. Within the Hindu traditions, one finds four ways of yoga, or discipline, that lead to union with the Absolute, which is the ultimate goal of spiritual practice. Those ways are through *jnana* ("knowledge"), bhakti ("devotion"), karma ("action"), and *raj* ("spiritual exercises"). Often, particular ashrams will emphasize one of these ways more than another, but elements of all are likely to be present.

Two men meditate at the shrine of an ashram in Puri, Orissa, India.
Source: Alison Wright/Corbis, used with permission.

GURU AND *SISYA*

At the heart of the ashram lies the relationship of guru and *sisya* ("student, disciple"). This relationship is a sacred bond that is based on involvement, commitment, and obligation. The guru and *sisya* are said to be bound to each other forever. In this relationship the guru assumes responsibility for the spiritual growth of the disciple and the *sisya* listens, obeys, serves, and reveres the guru. As a spiritual guide and a teacher, the guru's task is to instruct the disciple in spiritual practice, to awaken the power of spiritual intuition, to remove the ego or "little self" by correction, and to initiate the disciple through ritual in how to attain union with the Absolute.

MODERN ASHRAMS

The nineteenth and early twentieth centuries saw a remarkable revitalization of the Hindu traditions. It is associated with Raja Roy (1772–1833) and the Brahmo Samaj movement, a reformist Hindu movement that rejected the caste system and the authority of Hinduism's Vedic scriptures. Other important figures in the revitalization movement were Vivekananda (1863–1902), Aurobindo Ghose (1872–1950), and Mohandas K. Gandhi (1869–1947), the Mahatma. Vivekananda, a disciple of the Bengali saint Ramakrishna (1836–1886), brought modern Hinduism to the West at the Parliament of the World's Religions in Chicago in 1893. He also founded the Ramakrishna Mission. Aurobindo was a remarkable figure who developed "Integral Yoga," which was pursued at the Aurobindo Ashram in Pondicherry, in southern India. By the 1960s, the Aurobindo ashram had grown to include more than 2,000 ashram members and 400 buildings throughout Pondicherry. Mahatma Gandhi was the spiritual heart of the movement that led to India's independence from Great Britain in 1947. Gandhi founded ashrams in South Africa in the 1890s and in India when he returned there in 1915.

GANDHI'S ASHRAM

Gandhi's satyagraha ("truth force") ashrams at Wardha in Maharashtra (central India) and Ahmedabad in Gujarat (western India) are noteworthy for several reasons. While they drew upon the ancient ashram tradition, they were also seen as creating a new society. Ashrams became places of social experimentation. They were "moral laboratories where [Gandhi's] experiments with truth and non-violence were conducted in the living of daily life" (Rao 1989, p. 132). Gandhi's ashrams included people from all four *varnas*, or social classes of Hinduism into which the dozens of castes fall, which was unusual because custom dictated that members of castes in the higher *varnas* not associate with members of castes in the lower *varnas*. Even more remarkable, Gandhi's ashrams included untouchables, people outside the caste system who occupied the lowest social status of all. Gandhi called them Harijans, meaning "children of God," and sought to alter their status and treatment. Gandhi's ashrams also had an interfaith aspect: Hindus, Muslims, Jains, and Christians were all welcome. The religious festivals and practices of these different traditions were respected within the ashrams. Gandhi loved Christian hymns, which were sung in the ashram, as were devotional songs of other traditions. He also read from the sacred books of different traditions. In these ways Gandhi's ashrams sought to be exemplary communities that could move India beyond the divisions that characterized the wider society.

CONTEMPORARY ASHRAMS

Contemporary India is home to a bewildering array of ashrams. One concentration of ashrams can be found at the "ashram city" of Rishikesh. Located on the banks of the Ganges where the Himalayas meet the plains of India, Rishikesh's name indicates that it is literally a "city of *rishis*." Dozens of ashrams line its banks. Among the most well known is the Shivananda Ashram, also known as the Divine Life Society, founded by Swami Shivananda (1887–1963) in the 1930s. It teaches Vedanta, one of the schools of Indian philosophy, and several forms of yoga. From its modest beginnings it has grown into a large organization with branches around the world. In Rishikesh it has become a large and extensive ashram complex with many buildings and a vibrant spiritual life. Following the death of the founder, it came under the direction of Swami Chidananda, widely recognized for his charismatic spiritual leadership. Within the Shivananda Ashram there are also many gurus having particular responsibilities and duties. Here, the ashram has become an institution. People can be part of the ashram for varying periods of time, from day visits to actual residence lasting years.

Another ashram, located in Vrindaban in northern India, is Jai Singh Ghera. It is the home of Sri Purushottam Goswami and his family, and it is a vital center for the Vaishnavite (Vishnu worship) tradition that traces its origins to Caitanya. The ashram is centered on devotion to Krishna (an incarnation of Vishnu) and his beloved Radha. The ashram is both a family dwelling and a place to which adherents of the Krishna tradition come to participate in devotional rites and rituals and for instruction and initiation by Purushottam.

NON-HINDU ASHRAMS

The twentieth century has also seen the development of non-Hindu ashrams. In Rishikesh there is a Jewish ashram. Elsewhere in India one can find ashrams that are Jain, Sikh, and Buddhist. A Christian ashram movement has also emerged. E. Stanley Jones (1887–1972), a Methodist from the United Kingdom who lived at Gandhi's satyagraha ashram at Wardha, founded the Sat Tal Ashram based on Gandhian principles of ashram life, though with mostly Christian content. This Christian ashram movement has spread worldwide. Christa Prema Seva Sangh Ashram in Pune, Maharashtra, was founded in 1927 by the British Anglican Jack Winslow. When the ashram was revived in the 1970s, Sarah Grant, a British Catholic laywoman who spent most of her life in India, served as its *acharya* ("teacher"), but the ashram insisted that the risen Christ was its guru. Residents of the Christa Prema Seva Sagh Ashram practice yoga and incorporate many Hindu elements into their liturgy and life. The Shantivanam ("Forest of Peace") Ashram, founded in the 1950s on the banks of the Cavery River in southern India, was led for years by the well-known Catholic monk Dom Bede Griffiths (1907–1993). The residents seek to live the Christian monastic life in an Indian style.

The contemporary ashram, though remarkably varied in its form, is constant in its focus on the creation of a spiritual community centered in the realization of the Absolute as its goal.

—M. Darrol Bryant

Further Reading

Abhishiktananda. (1974). *Guru and disciple.* London: S.P.C.K.

Gyan, S. C. (1980). *Sivananda and his ashram.* Madras, India: Christian Literature Society.

Minor, R. (1999). *The religious, the spiritual, and the secular: Auroville and secular India.* Albany, NY: SUNY Press.

Murray, M. (1980). *Seeking the master: A guide to the ashrams of India.* St. Helier, UK: Neville Spearman.

Olivelle, P. (1993). *Asrama system: The history and hermeneutics of a religious institution.* New York: Oxford University Press.

Ralston, H. (1987). *Christian Ashrams: A new religious movement in contemporary India.* Lewiston, NY: The Edwin Mellen Press.

Rao, K. L. S. (1989). Gandhi's experiments in interreligious dialogue. In M. D. Bryant & F. Flinn (Eds.), *Interreligious dialogue: Voices from a new frontier* (pp. 127–138). New York: Paragon House.

ASIAN AMERICAN COMMUNITIES

The Asian American community has existed in the United States for more than 150 years. It is a vastly diverse ethnic community consisting of people whose ancestors, or who themselves, were born in more than twenty Asian countries. In 2000, the Asian American population had grown to 11.9 million, up from 1.4 million in 1970, with a median age of 31.1 years, 4.2 years younger than the general U.S. population (35.3 years).

The group's sevenfold growth in the span of 30 years is primarily due to immigration. Currently, more than 60 percent (or 7.2 million) of the Asian American population are foreign born (the first generation), another 25 percent are native born with foreign-born parents (the second generation), and only 15 percent are native born with native-born parents (the third generation), with the exception of Japanese Americans, who are entering the fourth generation in America. Immigration from Asian countries has remained high since the 1970s. The share of immigrants from Asia as a proportion of U.S. total inflow grew from a tiny 5 percent in the 1950s to around 35 percent in the 1980s and 1990s. China, India, Korea, the Philippines, and Vietnam have been on the list of top ten countries of origin for immigrants to the United States since 1980. As recently as 1970, no Asian country was on this list. While most of the immigrants have come directly from their ancestral homelands, others have arrived from a different country. For example, Chinese immigrants come into the United States not only from the People's Republic of China but also from Taiwan, Vietnam, Cambodia, Malaysia, and the Americas. Similarly, some Indians have arrived from Canada, England, and Uganda, and most of the Southeast Asians settled in the United States only after stops in third countries, having fled their ancestral homelands. Among Asian immigrants, about 42 percent have arrived in the U.S. since 1990 and 47 percent are naturalized U.S. citizens.

Table 1. Asian American Population, 1970–2000

	*1970**	*%*	*1980*	*%*	*2000*	*%*
Chinese	435,062	30.2	806,040	22.7	2,734,841	23.0
Filipino	343,060	23.8	700,974	19.7	2,364,815	19.9
Asian Indian*	--	--	361,531	10.2	1,899,599	16.0
Korean*	--	--	354,593	10.0	1,228,427	10.3
Vietnamese*	--	--	261,729	7.4	1,223,736	10.3
Japanese	591,290	41.1	700,974	19.7	1,148,932	9.6
Other	70,150	4.9	364,598	10.3	1,306,330	11.0
Total	1,439,562	100.0	3,550,439	100.0	11,906,680	100.0

Source: Compiled from the 1970, 1980, and 2000 U.S. censuses.

* Asian Indian, Korean, Vietnamese, and other Asian-ancestry subgroups were not tabulated in the 1970 census.

DEMOGRAPHIC TRENDS

The term *Asian American* is a socially constructed term because the variety of ethnically distinct subgroups far exceeds the similarities that these subgroups share. Before 1970, the Asian American community was largely made up of three ancestry groups: Japanese (41.1 percent), Chinese (30.2 percent), and Filipino (23.8 percent), as shown in Table 1. The "other" category included a much smaller group of Koreans and Asian Indians and insignificant numbers of others. After 1990, in contrast, the community has expanded to include at least twenty-four national-origin groups officially tabulated into the census.

As Table 1 shows, Americans of Chinese and Filipino ancestries are the largest subgroups, at more than 2 million, followed by Asian Indians, Koreans, Vietnamese, and Japanese, all of whose numbers surpass the one-million mark. There are many other national-origin groups or ethnic groups that have become a visible presence in the United States only after the 1970s, such as Cambodians (206,052), Pakistanis (204,309), Laotians (198,203), Hmong (186,310), Taiwanese (144,795), Thai (150,283), Indonesians (63,073), and Bangladeshis (57,412).

Asian Americans are diverse not only in terms of origins but also in terms of socioeconomic status. Unlike earlier immigrants from Asia or Europe, who were mostly laborers with few skills, today's immigrants from Asia include those who fill the labor market demands for highly skilled labor. Scientists, engineers, physicians, and other skilled professionals tend to be overrepresented among Chinese, Taiwanese, Indians, and Filipinos, while less educated, lower-skilled workers tend to be overrepresented among Southeast Asians, most of whom enter the United States as refugees. Middle-class immigrants are able to start their American life with high-paying professional jobs and comfortable suburban living, while low-skilled immigrants and refugees, like immigrants in the past, have to accept low-paying menial jobs and ghettoized inner-city living. The 2000 census shows that Asian Americans have made remarkable socioeconomic strides. Their median household income is $55,525, the highest of all racial groups, and their poverty rate is 10.7 percent, the lowest of all racial groups. But internal differences in socioeconomic status continue to be significant, with Hmong and Cambodians trailing behind other Asians.

Asian Americans tend to settle in urban areas and concentrate in the West. California alone is home to 35 percent of all Asian Americans (4.3 million), and California also has the largest number of each of the six main national-origin groups. New York accounts for 10 percent (1.2 million) of all Asian Americans, second only to California. Chinese, Indians, and Koreans are heavily concentrated in New York, but Filipinos, Japanese, and Vietnamese are not. Several other states deserve special mention. Texas has the second largest Vietnamese population; Illinois has the third largest Filipino population, after California and Hawaii; Washington has the third largest Japanese population, after California and Hawaii; and New Jersey has the third largest Indian and Korean populations, after California and New York. Among cities with populations greater than 100,000, New York City, Los Angeles, and Honolulu have the largest number of Asians, while in Daly City, California, and Honolulu, Asian Americans make up an outright majority of the population. Some smaller cities in California, such as Monterey Park (which in 1990 became the first U.S. city to have an Asian American majority), also have a majority Asian American population.

Traditional urban enclaves such as Chinatown, Little Tokyo, Manilatown, Koreatown, Little Phnom Penh, and Thaitown have continued to exist or have emerged in recent years, but they no longer serve as primary centers of initial settlement because many new immigrants, especially the affluent and highly skilled, are bypassing inner cities to settle in suburbs immediately after arrival. For example, in 2000, only 8 percent of Chinese in San Francisco and 12 percent in New York lived in inner-city Chinatowns. Only 13 percent of Vietnamese in Orange County, California, lived in Little Saigon; 14 percent of Koreans in Los Angeles lived in Koreatown; and 27 percent of Cambodians in Los Angeles live in Little Phnom Penh. The majority of the Asian American population is spreading out in outer areas or suburbs in traditional gateway cities as well as in new urban centers of Asian settlement across the country.

DIVERSITY IN LANGUAGE AND RELIGION

It is almost impossible to define *the* Asian American culture, as the various cultures of origin are diverse and have been incorporated into American society in varied ways. Except for sharing the experience of having a native homeland across the Pacific Ocean, there is no single ancestral language or religion that dominates the community. Linguistically, Chinese, Japanese, Korean, and Vietnamese immigrants come from countries with a single official language. Filipino immigrants, in contrast, come from a country where Pilipino, a variation of the native language Tagalog, and English are both official languages, and most of the educated Filipino immigrants are fluent bilinguals before entering the United States. Highly educated Indian immigrants are proficient in English, as India also designates English as an official language, along with sixteen other official languages. The most common Indian languages spoken in Indian homes include Hindi and Gujarati, followed by Punjabi, Tamil, Telugu, Bengali, Urdu, and some others. Moreover, there are many local and regional dialects spoken within each group. Similarly, immigrants from China and Taiwan share the same written Chinese language but speak a variety of Sinitic languages—Yue (or Cantonese), Mandarin, Min, Chaozhounese (spoken in the Chaozhou region), and Wu (spoken in Shanghai)—that in most cases are not mutually intelligible.

In the Asian American community, although no single religion unifies the pan-ethnic group, religion serves as one of the most important ethnic institutions in the community. Chinese, Japanese, Korean, and Vietnamese come from non–Judeo-Christian backgrounds in which Confucianism, Buddhism, or both are widespread, along with their variations and many folk religions. Western colonization in the homelands and immigration to the United States have led to a trend of conversion to Christianity prior to and after arrival. For example, only 20 percent of South Korea's population is Protestant, but the majority of Koreans Americans are Protestants. Existing research suggests that Protestant Koreans are more likely than others to emigrate. In Vietnam, only 10 percent of the population is Catholic, but about a third of the Vietnamese population in the United States is Catholic. Many Vietnamese refugees converted to Catholicism after they fled Vietnam as a way to obtain U.S. sponsorship, largely due to the active role Catholic charities played in resettling Vietnamese refugees in the United States. Conversion to Christianity is also noticeable among immigrants from Taiwan; fewer from mainland China and Japan convert. The majority of Filipino Americans are Catholics, as the population in their homeland is 80 percent Catholic.

Indian Americans come from more diverse religious backgrounds, with Hindus dominating, followed by smaller numbers of Muslims, Christians, Sikhs, and Buddhists; conversion to Christianity is relatively rare in comparison with other major Asian subgroups.

In a mix of cultures and religions, the Papal motorcade passes through Koreatown in Los Angeles on September 15, 1987. Many Korean Americans are Christian, but most are Protestant rather than Catholic.

Source: Bettmann/Corbis; used with permission.

Although religious practices are organized along ethnic lines, especially among immigrants, there is a trend in the second or later generations to congregate pan-ethnically.

Despite religious diversity, some significant common patterns can be discerned. First, religion takes on a new twist when it is practiced in the United States. To varying degrees, religion responds not only to uprooted immigrants' need to reestablish a moral order, fulfill spiritual needs, and learn new ways of organizing individual and collective action, but also to their material needs of initial settlement, survival, and social mobility. For example, Korean Christian churches provide tangible resources to immigrants, such as language and job training, financial and manpower services, and counseling, while also functioning as a social-status hierarchy in which religious and nonreligious positions can be achieved. Those immigrants who experience downward mobility upon arrival in the United States can regain social status within their own cultural institution. Hindu organizations, such as Satsang ("Religious Congregation") and Bala Vihar ("Child Development Organization"), offer both spiritual and secular services to immigrants and their children.

Second, religion not only reorients old symbols and ways to the new environment but also provides a physical space in which immigrants come together to worship, and more important, to reconnect and reestablish social networks that have been disrupted through the process of migration. For example, before new immigrants are able to build their own churches, they usually congregate at suburban public high schools, rather than merge into existing American churches; in this way, they can worship and socialize among coethnics and use their own native language.

Third, cultural mixing in religious practices is common. Ethnic religious practices enable followers to selectively preserve certain elements in their ancestral culture and strengthen ethnic solidarity around a common cultural heritage. When conversions occur, there emerge visible forms of "Confucianized" or "Asianized" Christianity that sustain or reaffirm ethnic identity.

THE FAMILY

Like religion, the family is a backbone institution in the Asian American community. Variations in household structures and family patterns in the Asian American community are significant. However, most of the Asian-origin groups come from a strong tradition of extended, patriarchal family and kinship ties. These ties are disrupted during migration but are quickly rebuilt to shape family patterns in different historical periods. In the second half of the nineteenth century and the first half of the twentieth century, most immigrants from Asia were male sojourners who left their close relatives—parents, wives, and children—in the homelands and sent remittances to support them. Anti-Asian legislation, beginning with the Chinese Exclusion Act of 1882, denied entry to immigrants from Asia while also restricting the migration of women and family members of those already in the United States. The Asian American communities in urban areas became bachelors' societies. In 1900, the sex ratio for Chinese was 1,385 men per 100 women; for Japanese it was 487 men per 100 women.

The development of the Japanese American community prior to World War II was unique, even though it

Hmong in Minneapolis

The arrival of immigrants often causes concern among existing residents of the communities where the newcomers settle. The following text from a large study of rumors associated with the settlement of Hmong refugees in the Phillips and Elliot Park neighborhoods of Minneapolis indicates that such concerns are often not supported by fact.

Rumor #3

Have the Hmong been given preferential treatment in employment hiring to the detriment of the American Indians and blacks? Not many people know about overall Indochinese participation in the labor force.

Jane Kretzmann of the State Refugee Office once informed the author that probably 70 to 80 percent of the Indochinese were eligible and receiving some form of welfare. The percentage for the Hmong is slightly higher because they are the least educated minority of the four Indochinese groups. At present approximately 80 percent of the Hmong residents of the two neighborhoods qualify for welfare. However, no one knew the status of the remaining 20 percent.

Existing information suggests that the Hmong are not highly employable. The majority are at present preoccupied with learning English. However, some have attended and are attending vocational training and according to Douglas Olney, a University of Minnesota researcher, there are now approximately 40 Hmongs attending the University as opposed to 20 last year.

Source: Calderon, Eddie L. (1982). "The Impact of Indochinese Resettlement on the Phillips and Elliot Park Neighborhoods in South Minneapolis." In *The Hmong in the West: Observations and Reports*, edited by Bruce T. Downing and Douglas P. Olney. Minneapolis: University of Minnesota, pp. 377–378.

started as a bachelors' society. Because of the Gentlemen's Agreement of 1907–08 that closed entry to laborers but permitted the entry of wives and relatives, the Japanese American community gradually evolved into a family-based community, with the temporary departure of many first-generation *(issei)* men who returned to Japan permanently between 1909 and 1924. During the same period, those Japanese who decided to settle permanently in the United States sent for their wives, or for picture brides, from Japan, which gave rise to a significant cohort of second-generation *(nisei)* children before World War II. This also explains why Japanese Americans are now entering their fourth generation in the United States, while the Chinese American community, who as a group arrived in the United States much earlier, is still primarily made up of first and second generations, with a relatively small third-plus generation.

Contemporary Asian immigrants from different countries of origin come mainly with their families, thanks to the Hart-Celler Act of 1965, which aimed at family reunification. Because of the recentness of Asian immigration, the typical Asian American family consists of immigrant parents and their native-born children or foreign-born children who arrived in the United States before school age (also referred to as the 1.5 generation), with the exception of Japanese Americans. Asian American families are generally larger; 22 percent of family households consisted of five persons or more in 2000, and the proportion of families that is structured around extended kinship ties is higher in the Asian American community than in the larger American society. Marital disruption is uncommon among immigrant families from Asia, but divorce rates steadily increase with time since immigration and with each succeeding generation. In 2000, 80 percent of Asian American family households were maintained by married couples, 12 percent by women with no spouse present, and 7 percent by men with no spouse present. Interracial and interethnic marriages and dating are also high among U.S.-born Asian Americans, particularly among Japanese Americans. Of the six largest Asian subgroups, Japanese Americans were most likely to report mixed-race heritage (a combination of Japanese with one or more other races or Asian groups) in the 2000 census: Almost a third of them were offspring of intermarriages.

Common family values in the Asian American family include an emphasis on the centrality of the family; filial piety; respect for elders; reverence for tradition and education; and social order between the self, family, community, and the state, such that the self is subjected to the interest of the family, the family to the community, and the community to the state. While these traditional values offer a strong moral basis that sustains the Asian American family, they have often clashed with dominant American cultural values and have caused emotional pain and detrimental consequences in the family and community. One common cultural clash is between the strict formality and collectivist orientation of the Asian American family and the permissiveness and individualism of mainstream

American society. For example, a Vietnamese father who accepted being beaten by his father as a youth in Vietnam was jailed in the United States for beating up his sixteen-year-old daughter with an electrical cord for suspected promiscuous misconduct.

EDUCATION

Like most Americans, Asian Americans regard education as the most important means to social mobility. What is unique about the Asian American emphasis on education is the family's control over educational choices and the community's institutional support. Families have high expectations of children and instill in their children that educational achievement brings the family honor as well as securing future livelihood. The family's educational goal is reinforced by the ethnic community. In some ethnic communities, such as the Chinese and Koreans, educationally oriented private institutions have become a key sector in the ethnic economy. Various SAT cram schools, after-school tutoring, and music and art schools run by immigrant entrepreneurs, combined with similar services offered at ethnic churches, community cultural centers, and other nonprofit social service organizations based in the community, form a system of supplementary education that assists families and children.

Tremendous family and community pressure to achieve has yielded positive results. Asian American children are indeed doing exceptionally well in school. They frequently appear on the lists of high school valedictorians and in competitive academic decathlon teams, and win prestigious awards and honors at the national, state, and local level. They are also gaining admissions to the nation's Ivy League and other prestigious colleges in disproportionate numbers. In the past few years, Asian American students represented more than 20 percent of the undergraduate student population at all nine campuses of the University of California, and more than 40 percent at several of those campuses. They are also visible, at 20–30 percent of the total undergraduate student population, at Harvard, Yale, Stanford, MIT, Cal Tech, and other Ivy League or highly ranked colleges. In 2000, Asian Americans had attained the highest level of education of all racial groups in the United States: Forty-four percent of Asian American adults had earned a bachelor's degrees or higher, and the ratio for those with advanced degrees is one in seven.

There is a downside to overachievement. Because of family and community pressure to achieve and the burden of bringing the family honor, many Asian American youth have to sacrifice their personal interests to pursue what their parents think is best for them—a career in science, medicine, or technical professions. For example, one Chinese American college student gave up a promising singing career to enroll in medical school just to make his parents happy. Asian American youth also suffer from mental health problems that often go unnoticed until symptoms become chronic. For example, a Korean American high school senior made multiple suicide attempts because she was not selected the valedictorian of her graduating class and was not admitted to her parents' top-choice college.

ETHNIC ENTREPRENEURSHIP

Entrepreneurship is another effective means of social mobility in the Asian American community. Historically, Chinese and Japanese Americans have depended on ethnic businesses as a way to climb up the socioeconomic ladder, especially during the era of legal exclusion and labor market discrimination. Since the 1970s, unprecedented Asian immigration, accompanied by the tremendous influx of human and financial capital, has set off a new stage of ethnic economic development. New immigrant groups, such as Koreans, Indians, and Vietnamese, show exceptionally high rates of self-employment, ranging from 10 percent for Vietnamese to 26 percent for Korean.

Growth in business ownership among Asian Americans is the fastest of any racial group. Although the number of black- and Hispanic-owned businesses grew by 93 percent from 1977 to 1987, neither came close to matching the rapid expansion of Asian American businesses, which grew by 238 percent. From 1987 to 1997, the number of Asian-owned businesses continued to grow at a rate of 121 percent (from less than 355,331 in 1987 to 785,480 in 1997). Adding the Asian-owned "C" corporations, which were not counted in the previous surveys, Asian-owned firms in 1997 numbered 913,000, employed more than 2.2 million people, and generated $306.9 billion in revenue. Asian-owned business enterprises made up 4 percent of the total U.S. nonfarm businesses and generated 2 percent of the total nonfarm gross receipts. Forty-four percent of Asian-owned businesses are in the service sector and 21 percent are in the retail sector; this compares with 43 percent and 14 percent, respectively, for all U.S. firms when taken together. Overall, there was approximately one ethnic firm for every thirteen Asian Americans, as compared with one ethnic firm for every forty-two blacks and every twenty-nine Hispanics.

HOME OWNERSHIP

Owning a home is a big part of achieving the American dream, and it is an important measure of socioeconomic mobility. In 2000, about 60 percent of Asian American families (and 52 percent of Asian immigrant families) owned their homes. This homeownership rate is highest of all racial minority groups but substantially below that of non-Hispanic whites, among whom 82 percent own their own homes. The disparity in homeownership may be due to the fact that Asian American families are generally more likely to be headed by the foreign born, are younger, and have less accumulated wealth. Many Asian American families achieve homeownership through two typical means: the pool of family savings, including the contribution of unmarried children's incomes, and ethnic financial institutions. Through the pool of family and kin resources, many Asian American families are able to put a considerable amount (at least 25 percent of the mortgage) as a down payment in order to secure a bank loan. In some ethnic communities, such as the Chinese and Korean communities, ethnic banks and other ethnic financial institutions provide home mortgage loans, especially for immigrants who may not have the English proficiency, cultural literacy, and credit necessary to navigate the mainstream banking system.

Home ownership in the Asian American community is considered not only an end but also a means to an end. Many immigrant families use homeownership to access the best possible public education for their children. For Asian Americans, one of the most important criteria when choosing a home is whether the area has good public schools. Proximity to an ethnic community or coethnics is of secondary importance. In recent years, well-performing public schools have witnessed a rapid increase in Asian American enrollment.

CHALLENGES AND PROSPECTS

Asian Americans have made remarkable inroads into mainstream America. This progress, however, has not been easy; it has required their conscious effort and collective struggle for equality in citizenship, civil rights, and representation. The long-standing issue still relevant to the Asian American community today is racism and stereotyping. Even though Asian Americans have made extraordinary achievements and are celebrated as model minorities or "honorary whites," they are still perceived as foreigners and are targeted by such racial slurs as "chink," "geek," and "gook," or told to "go back to your own country." Moreover, Asian Americans have continued to receive unequal returns on education. They often have to score exceptionally high in order to get into a good school and work twice or many more times as hard in order to achieve occupational and earnings parity with their non-Hispanic white counterparts. They often feel that doing just as well as everybody else is not enough; they feel it is necessary to stand out, to work much harder, and to do much better. Moreover, professional Asian Americans constantly face glass-ceiling barriers. One consequence of the glass ceiling effect is their underrepresentation in the ranks of executives and managers. They are often considered hard workers, competent scientists, engineers, and technicians, but not good managers. Within the Asian American community, there is also persistent inequality between the rich and the poor. Other problems that require immediate community action include a lack of political participation, cultural conflicts, youth delinquency, mental health, elderly care, and undocumented immigration.

—Min Zhou

See also Chinatowns; Immigrant Communities

Further Reading

Chan, S. (1991). *Asian America: An interpretive history.* New York: Twayne.

Chan, S. (Ed.). (1994). *Hmong means free: Life in Laos and America.* Philadelphia: Temple University Press.

Shankar, L. Dh., & Srikanth, R. (Eds.). (1998). *A part yet apart: South Asians in Asian America.* Philadelphia: Temple University Press.

Hing, B. O. (1993). *Making and remaking Asian America through immigration policy, 1850–1990.* Stanford, CA: Stanford University Press.

Kibria, N. (1993). *Family tightrope: The changing lives of Vietnamese Americans.* Princeton, NJ: Princeton University Press.

Kitano, H. (1996). *The Japanese Americans.* New York: Chelsea House Publishers.

Maki, M. T., Kitano H., & Berthold, S. M. (1999). *Achieving the impossible dream: How Japanese Americans obtained redress.* Urbana: University of Illinois Press.

Min, P. G. (1996). *Caught in the middle: Korean communities in New York and Los Angeles.* Berkeley and Los Angeles: University of California Press.

Min, P. G. (Ed.). (1995). *Asian Americans: Contemporary trends and issues.* Thousand Oaks, CA: Sage.

Min, P. G., & Kim, J. Ha (Eds.). (2001). *Religion in Asian America:*

Building faith communities. Walnut Creek, CA: Altamira Press.
Matsumoto, V. (1993). *Farming the homeplace: A Japanese American community in California, 1919–1982.* Ithaca, NY: Cornell University Press.
Nash, J. W. (1992). *Vietnamese Catholicism.* Harvey, LA: Art Review Press.
Root, M. P. P. (Ed.). (1997). *Filipino Americans: Transformation and identity.* Thousand Oaks, CA: Sage.
Smith-Hefner, N. J. (1999). *Khmer American: Identity and moral education in a diasporic community.* Berkeley and Los Angeles: University of California Press.
Takaki, R. (1989). *Strangers from a different shore: A history of Asian Americans.* New York: Penguin Books.
Tuan, M. (1998). *Forever foreigners or honorary whites? The Asian ethnic experience today.* New Brunswick: Rutgers University Press.
Wei, W. (1993). *The Asian American movement.* Philadelphia: Temple University Press.
Wu, F. H. (2002). *Yellow: Race in America beyond back and white.* New York: Basic Books.
Zhou, M. (1992). *Chinatown: The socioeconomic potential of an urban enclave.* Philadelphia: Temple University Press.
Zhou, M., & Bankston, C. L., III. (1998). *Growing up American: How Vietnamese children adapt to life in the United States.* New York: Russell Sage Foundation.
Zhou, M., & Gatewood, J. V. (Eds.). (2000). *Contemporary Asian America: A multidisciplinary reader.* New York: New York University Press.

ASSET-BASED COMMUNITY DEVELOPMENT

Asset-Based Community Development (ABCD) refers to a set of perspectives and strategies that emphasize the importance of mapping and mobilizing the existing strengths—or assets—of struggling neighborhoods. Though developed initially through work in inner-city neighborhoods, these approaches have been successfully adapted to suburban and rural contexts as well.

Codified by John P. Kretzmann and John L. McKnight, two researchers from Northwestern University, in their 1993 book *Building Communities From the Inside Out: A Path Toward Finding and Mobilizing a Community's Assets,* this approach contrasts starkly with those that focus mainly on a community's problems, needs, and deficiencies. While the asset-based perspective acknowledges the serious challenges facing many neighborhoods, it argues that an exclusive emphasis on needs produces not development but dependency.

ABCD's proponents note that even the most devastated communities contain five basic categories of assets: the skills and capacities of the residents; the power of local voluntary associations; the resources of local public, private, and nonprofit institutions; physical resources such as land, buildings, and so forth; and local economic activity. The process of development involves discovering, or mapping, these five kinds of assets, strengthening connections among them, and mobilizing their power to achieve a community's vision.

In many cases, local community builders who have adopted the ABCD approach have improved their communities significantly. For example, "capacity inventories" of residents' skills have led in many communities to the development of micro-enterprises and small businesses. Minneapolis's successful "Mercado Central," now home to more than 50 small businesses owned by recent Hispanic immigrants, provides one instance of the power of this approach. Similarly, these skill surveys have enabled reintegration of marginalized populations, such as elders, new immigrants, or people with disabilities, into mainstream community life and institutions. In other cases, local governments and public institutions such as schools, libraries, and parks have discovered that the contributions of neighborhood residents can strengthen their own missions. In Seattle, for example, the Department of Neighborhoods' "Involving All Neighbors" initiative has successfully connected dozens of people with disabilities to community-based organizations where their talents can be productively used. Private and public funders have explored the advantages of investing in local citizens' problem-solving capacities.

The asset-based approach to development is clearly compatible with more established community organizing strategies. It provides a reminder to economic development leaders that holistic community building involves both leveraging outside resources (from government programs, banks, and funders) and rediscovering the capacities of local citizens to produce and consume. Similarly, the most powerful organizing strategies combine dual foci—one focus aims to hold outside powers (such as government and banks)

DID YOU KNOW...

Successful asset-based community development combines resources from outside the community, such as money from banks or advice from experts, with the untapped assets of the community such as local knowledge, leadership of local organizations, and unused property or buildings.

accountable; the other recognizes the capacities of local residents to solve problems and build stronger communities themselves.

Most critics of asset-based community development point out that it provides less than a complete analysis and strategy of a community's situation—that it may underemphasize the powerful systemic forces, both political and economic, that affect communities from the outside. In reply, many ABCD advocates acknowledge the point, noting that an asset-focused, inside-out approach is a necessary, but not sufficient, perspective for successful community building. A combination of strategies, designed both to mobilize internal resources and to pressure outside powers, holds the greatest promise for building stronger communities.

—John P. Kretzmann

Further Reading

Green, G. P., & Haines, A. (2002). *Asset building and community development.* Thousand Oaks, CA: Sage.

Kingsley, G. T., McNeely, J. B., & Gibson, J. O. (1997). *Community building coming of age.* Washington, DC: The Development Training Institute and the Urban Institute.

Kretzmann, J. P., & McKnight, J. L. (1993). *Building communities from the inside out: A path toward finding and mobilizing a community's assets.* Evanston, IL: ABCD Institute, Institute for Policy Research.

Kretzmann, J. P., McKnight, J. L., & Sheehan, G. (1997). *A guide to capacity inventories: Mobilizing the economic capacities of local residents.* Evanston, IL: ABCD Institute, Institute for Policy Research

Kretzmann, J. P., McKnight, J. L., & Turner, N. (1999). *A guide to mapping and mobilizing the associations in local neighborhoods.* Evanston, IL: ABCD Institute, Institute for Policy Research

Sirianni, C., & Friedland, L. (2001). *Civic innovation in America: Community empowerment, public policy, and the movement for civic renewal.* Berkeley: University of California Press.

ASSIMILATION

The concept of assimilation in the literature on immigration has usually been associated with the conversion of immigrants into citizens of the host country. But it can also be associated with a more direct encompassing of foreigners within a national culture and society. The concept has been linked to numerous debates concerning immigration, and it has changed in ideological value in recent years as well. The concept has been used in different ways by numerous authors, but the sense conveyed by the term is, of course, much older. *Assimilation* refers to the inclusive transformation of minority cultural and social practices in such a way that they become indistinguishable from those of the dominant society and culture. There are numerous takes on this transformation depending on *to what* one is said to be assimilating. For example, in the development of the French nation-state (a form of political organization under which a relatively homogeneous people inhabits a sovereign state), one witnesses the transformation of regionally quite different cultures into an increasingly homogeneous culture, a process captured by the work of Romanian-born historian Eugen Weber. The very title of his well-known book captures the process quite well: *Peasants Into Frenchmen.* The process of nationalization via a whole array of institutions to socialize a population, from schools to the production of common history, values, and so forth, is a process of primary assimilation that is instrumental in the sociocultural formation of national populations. This process includes more than mere "socialization" insofar as it is part of a more general transformation of the modern state, the disintegration of local and regional communities and political structures, large-scale displacements of population, urbanization, and individualization. These are all tendencies rather than absolute changes, and so assimilation must also be understood as a partial process that always harbors a great deal of ambivalence. The nationalization process should be understood as a historically specific phenomenon and ought not be confused with the more specific case related to the integration of foreign individuals and populations. It is, however, necessary to highlight the general characteristics of assimilatory processes so that they are not erroneously limited to the nation-state. All societies can be understood as assimilation machines insofar as they socialize individuals and groups into specific practices of social and political relations and of representation as well. Traditional societies often use rituals to socialize subjects into social roles that are sanctioned by elders, chiefs, or other social authorities. This is important to keep in mind when discussing the nature of integration within nation-states.

THE NATION-STATE AND IMMIGRATION

The issue of assimilation of immigrants within nation-states is today a major field in Western social science as well as in politics. It has become the target of a great deal of historical study in recent years when the nation-state itself has come under critical assessment. *Assimilation*

English as a Second Language

A key component of assimilation is learning the language of the new nation or society. The following study describes the various initiatives undertaken in Dade County, Florida in the 1960s to teach English to recently arrived Cuban immigrants.

Thus, the teaching of English as a Second language became top priority. But as more students entered the public schools, it was apparent that changes were needed. Special training was provided to teachers assigned to teach English as a Second Language.

Approximately 250 Cuban refugee teacher aides were employed during the 1962-1963 academic year. These aides, most of whom were former teachers, were assigned to assist the regular teacher with the special language and cultural needs of the Cuban refugee pupils. Students were divided according to their command of English into independent, intermediate, and non-independent groups. At the elementary level, independent students were offered the regular curriculum without modification. Also, as an enrichment activity, whenever possible, they received Spanish classes designed for native Spanish speakers (Spanish S). Intermediate students received content subjects as close to grade level as possible with English as a Second Language substituted for the usual English language arts program. They also received Spanish for native speakers. The non-independent students were given a special program, including English as a Second Language at least two hours daily, with one period of oral drill and another with reading and writing based on the materials practiced orally. In addition, they were offered arithmetic on their grade level, and Spanish for Spanish speakers. Secondary students classified as intermediate and non-independent were taught for two or three hours, respectively, in English as a Second Language. [. . .] Although all students were required to meet the normal subject achievement standards, the non-independent and intermediate pupils were excluded from the regular standardized testing program since its norms did not offer a valid evaluation of individuals with a language barrier.

As problems continued to arise, a group of Dade County educators formulated a plan to develop new materials and adapt the curriculum. The Ford Foundation supported the idea and provided in January 1963, a three-year grant to Dade County Public Schools for a Bilingual Education Project. [. . .] The project included the preparation of language and reading materials for non-English speakers, the revision and adaptation of the Fries American Series, into the Miami Linguistic Readers, the preparation of guides and audio-visual materials for teachers, and the establishment of a bilingual school. This last objective became the most important one since it developed a whole new concept of bilingual education. [. . .] The team included three bilingual Cuban teachers and three monolingual American teachers who were to teach first, second, and third grades at Coral Way Elementary School, located in what was later to become the heart of Little Havana. Programs from Cuba, Canada, Latin America, and Europe were evaluated. By September of 1963, when the school program had been completed and teachers trained, Coral Way opened its doors.

The success of the program created great interest in the community and the student participation grew from 761 in 1963 to 1,375 by September 1972. Coral Way Elementary became a model of a United States school where students could become completely bilingual. The model was later called a bilingual school organization (BISO). This term refers to a curriculum offered at the elementary level to Spanish language, English language, and other non-Spanish language students who also receive instruction in the regular school program. BISO consisted of four components: English for Speakers of Other Languages (ESOL), Spanish for Spanish Speakers (Spanish S), Spanish as a Second Language (Spanish SL), and Curriculum Content in Spanish (CCS). Later, Curriculum Content in English using an ESOL approach (CCE/ESOL) was added.

Source: Badia, Arnhilda. (1991). "The Impact of the Cuban Exodus on Dade County's Educational System." In *Cuban Exiles in Florida: Their Presence and Contribution*, edited by Antonio Jorge, Jaime Suchlicki, and Adolfo Leyva de Varona. Miami, FL: University of Miami, North-South Center Publications for the Research Institute for Cuban Studies, pp. 151–154.

became a term within a larger set of concepts, such as pluralism, racism, and integration, that were much debated during the first two decades of the twentieth century. This was a period of mass migration similar in some respects to today's situation. The United States, whose demographic composition became almost 15 percent first-generation immigrant during this period, hosted some hot debates concerning everything from the supposed racial characteristics of immigrants to whether the country should be divided into different political zones based on ethnic composition or should follow a soon-to-become-dominant ideology of assimilation that implied the transformation of immigrants into Americans. It is interesting to compare the concepts, words, and projects of that era with today's multiculturalist debate. Some, such as journalist Randolph Bourne in 1916, argued for a cultural pluralism and even used such currently popular terms as *transnational.* "Bourne celebrated the deprovincializing effect of immigrants on the native-born population and hailed a new 'cosmopolitan' America as superior to the more homogeneous societies left behind by the immigrants" (Hollinger 1995, p. 93).

Multiethnic and multicultural projects were by and large rejected during this period of expansion. The hierarchical and colonial ideology of the times consisted in a "civilizing" process of elevation of traditional populations to a higher level of social existence. Education for assimilation, as it became increasingly dominant, was organized around the inculcation of "American" values: explicit ways of acting, dressing, and eating, but even more important, values assumed to be typically American—liberty, equality before the law, a strong belief in economic freedom and social success. Loyalty to these American values was a crucial aspect of socialization. These were values that were thought to be provided by the United States and that accounted for much of the emigration from Europe for hundreds of years. It is interesting to consider the quite explicit assimilation policy of the United States compared to the European situation at the same period. The well-known sociologist Maurice Halbwachs, a student of French sociologist Emile Durkheim, made a trip to Chicago in the 1920s to investigate what seemed to be a growing multiethnic society, the immediate product of mass migration. On returning he wrote an article on the importance of ethnicity in Chicago, arguing even that the Chicago School of sociology was a direct product of this large-scale demographic change. Interestingly enough, France was equally a society in which immigration accounted for a large percentage of the population, but there was little interest in the issue, and one might venture to suggest that ethnicity was an insignificant social category for the French state and its cultural elites. The general awareness of ethnic difference is a product of the dominant categories of society. If ethnic difference is organized on a continuum from more to less French, for example, it is unlikely to become a category having political or intellectual import.

In European states, national identity is more complex than in immigrant societies such as the United States. Whereas for the latter, national identity is very much a political question, or an issue of explicitly stated values, for the former it is more implicit, related to language, to history, to culturally specific forms of behavior. In this context, assimilation is an issue not of conscious models but of unconscious structures of practice, of *habitus* (habit). An interesting aspect of this phenomenon is that it is unrelated to phenotypical (relating to the visible properties of an organism that are produced by the interaction of the genotype and the environment) properties of individuals and populations. In strongly centralized states, national identity was, until recently, a question of what might be called "being like," which includes "acting like" and "thinking like," at least, and especially, in the eyes of other members of society. Origins are less important in this kind of a reality than behavior itself. Assimilation in such states has been taken for granted, just as national or ethnic origins have been deemed irrelevant. This may account for the way in which Halbwachs understood the ethnic phenomenon in his day.

HISTORICAL CONFIGURATIONS

Assimilation was a major issue for the Chicago School of sociology. The model that became standard in the subject was generational. First-generation immigrants might be integrated economically but not socially or culturally. Second-generation immigrants, on the other hand, had a tendency to become strongly integrated and practiced a kind of self-assimilation, aspiring to become like the majority population in all ways. This often caused generational conflict with the first generation, which often sought to maintain "traditional" values. Finally, the third generation, a product of two generations of schooling, intermarriage, and economic integration, could be said to be culturally assimilated in a rather complete way, but often this generation became conscious of its origins and harked back to grandparents, investing in what is called "symbolic ethnicity," a kind of ritualized and objectified culture that is used in ceremonies of self-identification for people who are, in fact, more or less totally assimilated in their everyday lives. This is a powerful model of economic and social integration as well as of cultural assimilation in which numerous processes do not occur simultaneously and may even seem to contradict one another. Thus third-generation reidentification seems to occur in situations of strong cultural assimilation, and the reidentification must of necessity take on a symbolic character because those involved live the lives not of their grandparents but rather of their contemporaries in the majority of the national population.

This model of assimilation was developed in a situation of economic expansion. It predicts increasing integration of immigrants and their eventual transformation into national citizens. But such a development is not a logical necessity. On the contrary, one must investigate situations in which such developments are reversed and what effects they might have on assimilatory phenomena. This is especially important when considering the contemporary situation, in which assimilation no longer seems functional or desirable to either state elites or minorities themselves. Since the mid-1970s, a reversal of colossal proportions has occurred with respect to the politics of integration. This is a period when most Western states have entered into a series of financial crises. Assimilation is a costly process requiring funding for education of various kinds as well as a strong national ideology providing some general framework of identification for assimilation. The combination of declining state finances and a major shift in ideology provides the grounds for the decline of assimilationist politics. The decline in assimilationism is related to the decline of the structures of Western hegemony (influence over others) and the closely related decline in modernism. National identity has been imbued with modernist ideals, ideals of progress, of a sense of movement, of social evolution. The decline of hegemony has also meant the growth of a sense of diminishing returns. Downward mobility, a loss of faith in the future, and even a certain desperation or anguish have led many to seek alternative identities, often related to religion, tradition, or ethnicity, including an ethnicization of national identity.

Assimilation as a desire to be part of the larger culture is being replaced by a desire to have autonomy, at least culturally. Assimilation is no longer the official goal of immigrants and certainly not of regional and indigenous populations. Since the 1970s, there has been a massive increase in politics of self-identification, indigenous politics, regional politics, and immigrant minority politics. In the United States, the official politics of assimilation has been replaced by various programs of multiculturalism, often without a clear concern with the issue of integration as a social and cultural issue. The more extreme forms of multiculturalism are close to the older model of cultural pluralism in which the nation-state was to be replaced by or transformed into an ethnic federation in which governance was passed on to local minorities. It should be noted that this model is quite similar to the one that was developed under colonial rule. It is characterized by the presence of a colonial state, one that does not represent in any way a particular "people," and a division of the ruled into segments of ethnic or regional character where certain rights and forms of local governance are delegated to the local sphere while more general rights and forms belong to the central state. Assimilation is quite the opposite of this kind of situation. The famous French colonial consultant J. S. Furnivall compared the modern nation-state with the colony in no uncertain terms: "Like a confederation, a plural society is a business partnership rather than a family concern, and the social will linking the sections does not extend beyond their common business interests" (Furnivall 1948, p. 308).

He also contrasted the protective and closed nature of the nation-state with that of the colony: "It is significant that, in Canada and the United States, and also in Australia, when the influx of alien elements threatened national life and common social standards, barriers were raised against free immigration. In tropical dependencies there was no common social will to set a bar to immigration, which has been left to the play of the economic forces. The plural society arises where economic forces are exempt from control by social will" (Furnivall 1948, p. 306).

It is important to take note of this major ideological shift with respect to assimilation. Unlike the era of Furnivall when assimilation was a clearly dominant phenomenon, today Western elites have become increasingly antinational, seeing in the nation-state an oppressive homogenizing and/or excluding apparatus that is to be rejected. For contemporary multiculturalists, assimilation is often characterized as a kind of racism because it aims to impose conformity to the norms and values of the dominant society onto immigrant minorities. In strictly logical terms, however, this is a gross error. The very notion of assimilation implies that culture can be replaced and that individuals are not indelibly marked by their origins. Although the practice of assimilating foreign populations may well imply social oppression of a kind and even more violent acts, it is wrong to define this as simply another form of racism because assimilation is premised on the capacity to change one's culture.

THE LOCUS OF ASSIMILATION

Another interesting and important issue is that assimilation can occur at different levels of a state society, an issue that is usually ignored. It is often assumed that assimilation or even weaker forms of integration are applicable to the relation between minorities and nation-states. This assumption is a simple category error. Assimilation within the minority group itself is entirely ignored in this kind of discourse. In fact, such a group may maintain a high degree of internal integration, and assimilation to the minority may be said to vary inversely with assimilation to the national society. Many diasporas (dispersals of people) are excellent examples of this relation. Although they span a number of different state societies, they are able to maintain a high level of internal integration via the strong assimilatory practices of their leaderships, including forced endogamy (marriage within a group), strict socialization into stringent rule systems, and economic strategies of a transnational nature that ensure, where successful, the strength of the diaspora as a whole. In such situations there is a structural conflict between minority and national forces of assimilation. The native Hawaiians represent an example of this kind of conflict. Hawaiians live in minority enclaves within the larger society. They seem in one sense to be marginalized yet part of American society. But within their own villages and/or neighborhoods they practice a strong form of integration in which Hawaiianness is defined as a mode of behavior, a mode of relating to other people, in which family relations are paramount and generosity enforced. Males from outside of these enclaves who marry in soon have to learn to what extent they need to assimilate to a particular set of social rules. This kind of strong minority integration might be described as a kind of endosociality—a practice of social relations within a particular group that ignores the outside world or reduces it to an arena of secondary importance. Many diasporas function in a similar way so that what is transnational in reference to the nation-state is simultaneously a strongly bounded group. In reference to the economics and politics of such groups one might speak of "transnations."

ASSIMILATION AS A FUNCTION OF STATE STRUCTURE

Assimilation is a process that is variable in time, dependent on the historical capacity of nation-states or other collectivities to actually transform incoming as well as local subjects into a single cultural unity. During periods of strong national integration, assimilation can often be taken for granted. During periods of decline, assimilation is reversed in the form of a growing pluralism. Periods of strong national integration are usually periods of strong economic growth and even of hegemony in the larger international arena. Nation-states during periods of hegemony also have a tendency to become culturally homogeneous, but this can take different forms depending on the nature of the nation-state. It is important here to note that the homogeny of the nation-state does not imply the production of identical subjects and mind-sets. It merely refers to the production of a common public culture, and this involves a split between the public and the private. The latter is a sphere that is in principle free of the constraints of the public except with regard to basic rules of morality and legality. Here there is room for a great deal of cultural variation, with respect to both ethnic and religious difference. In nation-states such as the United States, the public sphere is very much defined in political terms, whereas in European states the same sphere is associated with an array of cultural and natural attributes. The way that a public sphere is institutionalized should not be equated with socialization into a particular lifestyle. Thus although there is surely a strong tendency to cultural assimilation in the United States in relation to shopping centers, a specific kind of consumption, and so forth, these phenomena are not part of the self-identity of the nation-state. In France, on the contrary, although there may well be a similar kind of socialization, the self-identity of the country includes a definite selection of French literature, music, and art—that is, high culture—but also images of nature, language, and history that are included in the process of education and that tend to produce a stronger cultural conformity in the population, one that is linked explicitly to national identity.

The difference among nation-states also contains another important aspect that has often been discussed as a difference in the nature of incorporation. In legal terms, this is expressed in the opposition between *jus sanguinis* (right of blood) and *jus soli* (right of the soil). The former, associated with Germany but not exclusively so, identifies citizenship on the basis of descent. Thus Germans by "blood" who live anywhere in the world are granted citizenship in the German nation-state, no matter what other affiliations they might have. *Jus soli* refers to membership by way of birthplace or a specific relation to territory. The former is an ethnic definition of citizenship, whereas the latter is strictly territorial. *Jus soli* is a relic of feudal rights over individuals attached to an estate and a means of incorporation of foreigners into a political unit irrespective of particular origins. This notion of belonging is the basis of assimilation, whereas *jus sanguinis* is closer to a notion of multiethnicity as a definition of the composition of the nation-state.

Assimilation is about the ways in which individual subjects of origins other than that of already socialized members of a particular group are incorporated into that group, irrespective of whether the latter has the form of a nation-state or some other form. The nature of assimilation depends on the nature of the group within which it occurs and the way by which such groups are transformed over time. Although the concept of assimilation has usually been associated with the nation-state, it is suggested here that it can be understood in more general terms and that this broader approach can help people understand the historical variation in the way people are or are not integrated into the larger and smaller political entities that constitute the world.

—Jonathan Friedman

See also Immigrant Communities; Latino Communities; Refugee Communities

Further Reading

Bourne, R. S. (1916, July). Trans-national America. *The Atlantic Monthly, 118*(1), 86–97.

Brubaker, R. (1992). *Citizenship and nationhood in France and Germany*. Cambridge, MA: Harvard University Press.

Ekholm Friedman, K., & Friedman, J. (1995). Global complexity and the simplicity of everyday life. In D. Miller (Ed.), *Worlds apart: Modernity through the prism of the local* (pp. 134–168). London: Routledge.

Friedman, J. (1994). *Cultural identity and global process*. London: Sage.

Friedman, J., & Randeira, S. (2003). *Worlds on the move: Migration and cultural security.* London: I. B. Tauris.

Furnivall, J. S. (1948). *Colonial practice and policy*. Cambridge, UK: Cambridge University Press.

Gans, H. (1979). Symbolic ethnicity: The future of ethnic groups and cultures in America. *Ethnic and Racial Studies, 2*(1), 1–20.

Gellner, E. (1983). *Nations and nationalism*. Ithaca, NY: Cornell University Press.

Glick Schiller, N., Basch, L., & Blanc-Szanton, C. (Eds.). (1992). *Towards a transnational perspective on migration: Race, class, ethnicity and nationalism reconsidered*. New York: New York Academy of Sciences.

Gordon, M. M. (1964). *Assimilation in American life: The role of race, religion and national origins*. New York: Oxford University Press.

Halbwachs, M. (1932, January). Chicago expérience ethnique [Chicago: The ethnic experience]. *Annales d'Histoire Economique et Sociale* [Annals of Social and Economic History], *IV*.

Hollinger, D. (1995). *Postethnic America*. New York: Basic Books.

Noiriel, G. (1996). *The French melting pot: Immigration, citizenship and national identity*. Minneapolis: University of Minnesota Press.

Portes, A., & Rumbaut, R. (1990). *Immigrant America: A portrait*. Berkeley & Los Angeles: University of California Press.

Weber, E. (1976). *Peasants into Frenchmen: The modernization of rural France 1879–1914*. Stanford, CA: Stanford University Press.

ASYLUM

Asylum was originally a Latin word adopted into that language from a cognate word in classical Greek that had the implication of inviolability. Asylum has both concrete and abstract meanings and, depending on usage, can have either positive or negative connotations.

CONCRETE AND ABSTRACT SANCTUARIES

First, an asylum may be a sanctuary or place of protection for criminals and debtors, from which their forcible removal would constitute sacrilege. Such places as churches, monasteries, and bishops' houses have had this role in the past, particularly in medieval times in parts of the continent of Europe. Second and more generally, an asylum may be simply any secure place of refuge or retreat. These first and second meanings contain or imply a circumscribed physical location or a building, which may sometimes have been made for the purpose of providing security. Third and in the abstract, asylum (without the indefinite article) can be inviolable shelter or refuge, or simply protection. Thus, the right of asylum (in this third meaning) necessarily has geographical limits to its extent (for example, the territorial borders of the nation-state granting it), but that physical aspect is not a component of the definition. A phrase such as "church asylum" combines this third meaning with one of the types of place constituting an asylum in the first meaning. In contemporary times there have been occasional attempts, without legal foundation, to resurrect the concept of church asylum, made by such people as illegal immigrants and rejected political-asylum seekers. Asylum in all these three senses was variously a feature of societies as old as those of ancient Greece and Rome, as well as of Biblical Jewish societies.

PLACES OF SUPPORT OR CONFINEMENT

Fourth, an asylum can be a building or institution for the provision of shelter and support, purportedly with benevolent intent, to those who are destitute or who are in some way disabled or impaired, especially mentally. Workhouses and lunatic or mental asylums are examples of asylums in this fourth sense. Although buildings called asylums existed in earlier centuries, the association with purportedly therapeutic mental hospitals is particularly a development of the second half of the nineteenth century, a time that saw the rise of an asylum

The Charter House

The excerpt below—from an early nineteenth-century English yearbook—describes a residence for youth and pensioners (elderly people on a fixed income) who apparently had nowhere else to live.

In the city of London, between St. John's street on the west, Goswell-street on the east, Long-lane on the south, and Wilderness-row on the north, stands the Charter-house, an edifice originally purchased for the burial of those who died of the plague in 1349. Here sir Walter Manny founded a Carthusian monastery, which, by corruption of the French term, *Chartreux*, obtained the name of the Charter-house. It shared the common fate of religious houses at the dissolution, and in 1611 was purchased by Thomas Sutton, esq., citizen and girdler, a rich old bachelor for £13,000. He fitted up the house at an expense of £7000, and endowed the hospital and school with fifteen manors and other lands, yielding £1493 19s. 10½ d. annually, as a charitable foundation, guaranteed by letters patent of James I., and confirmed by parliament. The income has since largely increased.

When Noorthouck, who may be deemed the best historian of London, wrote in 1773, the Charter-house maintained eighty pensioners. According to the founder's direction they "*ought to be* decayed gentlemen, merchants, or soldiers." The pensioners are provided with apartments, and all necessaries except clothes, instead of which, in Noorthouck's time, each was allowed a cloak, and £7 per annum. Their allowances in 1800 are stated below, from an official MS.

Besides the adult pensioners there are forty-four boys supported in the house, where they are lodged and classically instructed. Twenty-nine of these are sent as students to the Universities, with an annual allowance of £20 each, for eight years. Others are apprenticed to trades, with a fee on binding of £40 for each. Nine ecclesiastical preferments in the patronage of the governors are conferred, by the constitution of the foundation, upon those who derive education from it. Both pensioners and youths are received upon the recommendation of the governors, who appoint in rotation.

Particulars of Charter-house. Allowance to Pensioners

Summer Season

Monday	Mutton
Tuesday	Roast Veal
Wednesday	Boiled Mutton
Thursday	Roast Beef
Friday	Boiled Mutton
Saturday	Flank Beef
Sunday	Roast Beef and boiled mutton; with plumb puddings the winter six months

(Lamb at times, while in season.)

Winter Season

The same as above, excepting Tuesday; then they have roast or boiled pork.
Every Saints day in the year, plumb pudding.
Michealmas-day, roast geese.
Founder's day, fowls, bacon, wine, and strong beer.
Shrove-Sunday, calves head and bacon.
Easter Sunday, [ditto]
Christmas-day, a mince pie each man
Fresh butter, one pound and a quarter per week, each man.
Two quarts of beer per day.
Michaelmas, three sacks of coals.
Christmas, [ditto]
Candles, thirteen pounds per annum.
Allowed to go where they please two months in the year, with three shillings per week, while absent.

Source: Hone, William. (1832). *The Year Book of Daily Recreation and Information.* London: William Tegg, pp. 1463–1464.

movement in a number of countries and the building of large, often physically isolated, dedicated mental hospitals for the intended treatment, as opposed to the mere confinement, of the mentally ill or disabled. In 1837, W. A. F. Browne (1805–1885) published five lectures titled *What Asylums Were, Are, and Ought to Be*, an early example of the literature of the asylum movement.

On the other hand, such asylums were not regarded wholly in a benevolent light by the general public; their physical appearance alone encouraged them to be viewed as institutions of confinement and segregation of the mentally ill, and they often developed reputations to match. It is as a result of these connotations that asylum came to have one of its principal contemporary associations in social science, which is as a place of confinement. The author most immediately responsible for this was Erving Goffman (1922–1982), whose book *Asylums: Essays on the Social Situation of Mental Patients and Other Inmates* was published first in 1961. Interestingly, however, though *Asylum* was in the title of the book, the word apparently occurred nowhere in it, and seemed to have been chosen with a hint of irony. Goffman usually used terms such as *mental institution or mental hospital*. The book consisted of four long essays, the most influential of which has been the first, "On the Characteristics of Total Institutions," first published in a shorter version in 1957. Although Goffman did not discuss the point, it is hard to escape the inference that he was using the word *asylum* as a general synonym for the term *total institution,* and this has become an occasional social science usage. Total institutions were defined by the encompassing character of their regimes and the various barriers confining social intercourse between their residents and the outside. There were different types, and they included establishments as diverse as homes for the incapable, mental hospitals, tuberculosis sanitaria, jails, army barracks, boarding schools, and monasteries. Goffman may have chosen the term *asylum* to cover such a variety because he felt the word, with its both concrete and abstract connotations, aptly applied to all these institutions. It is unclear whether, in his choice of title, he was aware of, or influenced by, the work of the French philosopher and historian Michel Foucault (1926–1984). The latter's *Folie et déraison: Histoire de la folie à l'âge classique* (In English, *Madness and Civilization: A History of Insanity in the Age of Reason*) was first published in 1961 and included a chapter on "the birth of the asylum" that discussed the growth of the asylum movement from the eighteenth century in the critical manner far removed from the benevolence of some of the nineteenth-century literature. Foucault's book did not appear in English translation until 1967. However, it is especially Foucault to whom is owed one other sociological understanding of asylum, one with also an almost metaphorical definition as well as a physical one: Foucault describes the asylum as "a religious domain without religion, a domain of pure morality, of ethical uniformity" (Foucault 1967, p. 257).

POLITICAL ASYLUM

Within the past decade or more, asylum (in the third meaning) has become particularly associated in the public mind with asylum-seeking, that is, with requesting political asylum, generally on the grounds specified in Article 1(2) of the 1951 Geneva Convention Relating to the Status of Refugees and in its 1967 Protocol. Because of suspicions that many seeking political asylum do not merit such asylum and in fact are merely trying to better their economic position, this meaning of asylum dominates current lay usage and is responsible for the negative connotations often contemporarily associated with the word. Many countries, especially those in the European Union, have in recent years taken legal and administrative steps to make it more difficult to obtain political asylum, and asylum issues have become a significant component of international law.

—Christopher T. Husbands

Further Reading

Browne, W. A. F. (1991). What asylums were, are, and ought to be: Being the substance of five lectures delivered before the managers of the Montrose Royal Lunatic Asylum. In A. Scull (Ed.), *The asylum as utopia: W. A. F. Browne and the mid-nineteenth century consolidation of psychiatry.* London and New York: Tavistock/Routledge. (Original work published 1837)

Foucault, M. (1967). *Madness and civilization: A history of insanity in the age of reason* (R. Howard, Trans.). London: Tavistock Publications.

Goffman, E. (1961). *Asylums: Essays on the social situation of mental patients and other inmates.* Garden City, NY: Anchor Books.

Hailbronner, K. (2000). *Immigration and asylum law and policy of the European Union.* The Hague, Netherlands, and Boston, MA: Kluwer Law International.

ATTACHMENT

See COMMUNITY ATTACHMENT

AUROVILLE

Auroville, an intentional community located in India, aspires to be "a universal town where men and women of all countries are able to live in peace and progressive harmony, above all creeds, all politics, and all nationalities" (Sullivan 1994, p. 46). About 2,000 call this community home, and about 4,000 are employed in its industries and services, while the number of visitors is rising to over 10,000 annually. Together with assistance from governments and nongovernmental organizations worldwide, they are all helping to build Auroville. The purpose of Auroville is to realize human unity by supporting individual evolution.

INAUGURATION, 1968

On February 28, 1968, 5,000 people gathered for Auroville's inaugural ceremony on an eroded plateau next to a solitary banyan tree. The government of India classified this site, on the east coast of Tamil Nadu State and just north of the city of Pondicherry, as a backward area on its way to becoming a desert. M. S. Adiseshiah, at that time deputy director-general of UNESCO, was present and expressed his hope that Auroville would succeed where UNESCO had failed in bringing unity to humankind. Youth representatives ceremoniously poured handfuls of earth brought from 127 countries and all the states of India into a lotus-shaped urn. Sealed in the lotus urn with the earth is the original parchment copy of the Auroville Charter (Sullivan 1994, p. 53):

1. Auroville belongs to nobody in particular. Auroville belongs to humanity as a whole. But to live in Auroville one must be a willing servitor of the Divine Consciousness.
2. Auroville will be the place of an unending education, of constant progress, and a youth that never ages.
3. Auroville wants to be the bridge between the past and the future. Taking advantage of all discoveries from without and from within, Auroville will boldly spring towards future realizations.
4. Auroville will be a site of material and spiritual researches for a living embodiment of an actual Human Unity.

THE MOTHER AND SRI AUROBINDO

The author of the Auroville Charter and founder of Auroville was Mirra Alfassa (1876–1973), who was known simply as the Mother. Born in France, she had settled permanently in India in 1920 to work with Sri Aurobindo (1872–1950), a revolutionary architect of India's Freedom Movement. In 1910, Sri Aurobindo left politics to develop an all-inclusive system for the transformation of the human species. He created a synthesis of traditional yoga methods to verify "truth-consciousness," a state that embraces the most material of realities as well as the ultimate spiritual planes of existence—nothing was left out. The world, as he viewed it, had reached a critical condition requiring an energy beyond the mind, which he termed "supramental." Sri Aurobindo affirmed that each person now has the capacity to open to this force and participate consciously in the evolution of our species. He wrote in 1911: "The principal object of my Yoga is to remove absolutely and entirely every possible source of error and ineffectiveness . . . in order that the work of changing the world . . . may be entirely victorious and irrestible" (Sullivan 1994, pp. 37–38).

In 1968, when she was ninety-two, the Mother was asked why she started Auroville. She replied that "India is the representation of all human difficulties on earth and it is in India that there will be the cure. And it is for that, it is FOR THAT, that I had to create Auroville" (Sullivan 1994, p. 51).

GETTING AUROVILLE STARTED

In 1954, the Mother published what she called a "dream," her vision of the establishment of a place that would belong to no one nation, where "supreme truth" would have authority and where money would not have the power it does in the rest of the world. A decade later, India's prime minister Jawaharlal Nehru endorsed the Mother's vision, proposing a small international center to both U.S. president John F. Kennedy and Nikita Khrushchev, the leader of the Soviet Union, both of whom supported the idea. Then Kennedy was assassinated, Khrushchev was dismissed, and Nehru died. Still, international enthusiasm grew and Prime Minister Indira Gandhi extolled the project while UNESCO passed resolutions in its favor.

In 1967, a ballet dancer and an artist from the United States moved into the "interior" of the area designated as "Auroville." These first inhabitants aptly called their settlement "Forecomers." There was no road and no water. By 1971, there were about a hundred Aurovilians who had arrived intentionally and haphazardly from many countries including France, Africa, Holland, Brazil, Mexico, Canada, Australia, Tibet, and the states of India. Somehow they organized themselves in several settlements scattered over the approximately 12 square miles of land designated as the "City of Dawn." Adding to the challenge of restoring degraded land in a semiarid zone, the Auroville plots were interspersed with village lands, government wastelands, and private holdings that made town planning a nightmare. Marauding bands of undernourished goats and cattle would devour any plant not continually guarded. Yet by 1974, 300 people were living in thirty different settlements. Massive tree plantings, erosion control measures, and continual construction had initiated the process of regenerating a dying land, nourishing a biosphere to support a global village.

MANAGING AUROVILLE

It takes a lot of work to keep a community as diverse as Auroville together while relying on an ethic of "spiritual anarchy." Consensus is part of the labor, and all who participate in a particular work are responsible for it: Teachers are the working group for education just as the farmers are for agriculture. The more than seventy settlements within Auroville also act as an organizational focus. Settlements range in size from one to a hundred people. Pour Tous ("For All") was the first financial and food distribution service. The Pour Tous Meetings became an established tradition in 1976 as community-wide forums at which issues and policies were decided, often in response to crises.

A major crisis occurred after the Mother's passing in 1973, when the Sri Aurobindo Society, which had been entrusted with the legal and financial arrangements for Auroville, claimed the management from the residents, as well as ownership of the land. A bitter and protracted battle went all the way to India's supreme court. In 1980, the court decided in favor of the Auroville Community, and in 1988 the parliament of India passed the Auroville Act. This Act set up the Auroville Foundation to guarantee that Auroville belongs to humanity and that the ideals of its Charter are upheld. The foundation instituted the Residents' Assembly (preserving the Pour Tous Meeting tradition) as the authority in Auroville. Three other groups complete the system of governance: the "Working Committee" of Aurovilians for coordinating the work in Auroville and serving as a liaison with both the "Governing Board," a group of prominent persons from India, and the "International Advisory Council," a group of world-renowned persons.

AUROVILLE MATURES

In 1972, Auroville began building at its center what is called the "soul of the city." Named *Matrimandir* (Sanskrit for "House of the Mother"), the interior of this building is a bare white room in which the sun illumines a glass crystal. It is a place for concentration (as well as meditation) in a setting of twelve gardens in a parklike area. By 1985, Auroville was hosting and sponsoring international conferences and events. Beginning in the 1990s, students worldwide started to study in Auroville through new programs that allow for academic credit and field experience.

The second visit of the Dalai Lama in 1993 to lay the foundation stone of the Tibetan Cultural Pavilion helped inspire the construction of cultural pavilions for other countries. In 2002, Auroville opened the first phase of a model village for demonstrating within rural India how a village can be built with eco-friendly architecture in a cost-effective way. Auroville's Village Action Group has over the years evolved appropriate strategies to help the more than thirty thousand neighboring villagers raise their standards of living. Enormous challenges remain in terms of water supply, housing, cultural integration, and sustainable living.

Ram Dass on Auroville

It is clear in the excerpt below that the American spiritual teacher Ram Dass was greatly moved by his visit to Auroville.

> I was blown away by the trees—I want to honor what Auroville has done in reclaiming the land—and by the size of the experiment. It has all the levels; from the bottom up, the social, economic and political levels, and from the top down, the spiritual level.
>
> . . . It is very rare that a community that is based on so much individualism succeeds. Usually, everybody goes for the truth at first, but, after a while, everybody pulls back and only wants the truth on Saturday night.
>
> . . . In Sri Aurobindo's metaphysical dynamism you stay in the world while attempting to transform it. It's brilliant, but it's a profound and difficult path because the toxicity of the market place is very high, and it is so easy to fall asleep in the drama of life. For, to the extent to which you put each other to sleep through relationships, work, etc—you've lost it!

Source: Sullivan, W.M. (1994). *The Dawning of Auroville.* Auroville, India: Auroville Press, p. 229.

AUROVILLE IN THE YEARS AHEAD

Articles and travel literature about Auroville vary from unconditional praise and high commendations to condemnation for utopianism, elitism, or neocolonialism. This happens mostly because observers can discover in the diversity of Auroville, and from those living in Auroville, whatever their predisposition would like to find. The context of Auroville is one's own inner discovery. In the late 1970s, when Auroville was in litigation and there was a police presence, journalists predicted its demise, but in fact the community has recovered and is flourishing. In the words of Anuradha Majumdar, an Indian author and dancer who lives in Auroville (Sullivan 1994, p. 230): "Man has to surpass himself. It is no longer a question of one nation, one man—it is the question of the whole race—and it starts with you, with me—from the fire within."

—*B (W. M. Sullivan)*

Further Reading

Glenn, J. (1979). *Linking the future: Findhorn, Auroville, Arcosanti.* Boston: Center on Technology and Society.

Metcalf, B. (Ed.). (1996). *Shared visions, shared lives.* Forres, UK: Findhorn.

Sullivan, W. M. (1994). *The dawning of Auroville.* Auroville, India: Auroville Press.

Satprem. (1980). *L'agenda de Mère* [Mother's agenda] (Vols. 1–13). Paris: Institut de Recherches Evolutives.

Sri Aurobindo. (1971). *Sri Aurobindo birth centenary library* (Vols. 1–30). Pondicherry, India: Sri Aurobindo Ashram Press.

AVATAR COMMUNITIES

Avatars—online representations of people—allow millions of Internet users to represent themselves to others, experience life in virtual communities, build their dream homes on digital landscapes, and engage in a novel form of human expression.

The term *cyberspace* was coined by the novelist William Gibson in his 1984 work *Neuromancer*, and virtual worlds were colorfully described in Vernor Vinge's *True Names* in 1981 and in Neal Stephenson's *Snow Crash* in 1992. All three writers conceived of a computer network that would immerse its users in three-dimensional virtual worlds. Hollywood has given us a tantalizing view of human beings entering into digital landscapes in films such as *Tron* (Disney, 1982). In the 1970s at laboratories such as NASA Ames, MIT, and Xerox Palo Alto Research Center, researchers first created networked cyberspaces on computer workstations with graphical displays and chased each other about as cartoon eyeballs in the game *Maze War*.

In 1985 at Lucasfilm, the inventor Chip Morningstar, working with his colleague Randall Farmer, created Habitat, a virtual town with two-dimensional cartoon representations of users, all connected by dial-up connections and running on the popular Commodore 64 home computer. Chip needed a term to describe the digital personification of users in the Habitat worlds, and he chose the word *avatar,* for its meaning from Hindu theology (as defined in *Webster's Revised Unabridged Dictionary*): "the descent of a deity to earth, and his incarnation as a man or an animal." Avatar has now entered the technical lexicon as "an icon or representation of a user in a shared virtual reality" (Jargon.net 2003).

Avatars can take many forms. They may be detailed human or animal figures, such as those that were found in one of the first Internet-based virtual spaces, Worlds Chat, in 1995. There are avatar communities that allow thousands of users to work together to build structures in three dimensions, as in AlphaWorld (1995) and Adobe Atmosphere (2002). In others, participants can transmit their actual voices and share music (Traveler, 1996), or they can engage in sword-and-sorcery quests, as in Meridian 59 (1996), Ultima Online (1999), and EverQuest (2000). There are even avatar communities in which participants can design and run the lives of whole fictitious communities, as in The Sims Online (2002). The U.S. military has been using avatars in training and recruitment environments since 1983 (with SIMNET) and continues to do so today (with America's Army, 2002).

Avatars shown talking in the voices of their users in Traveler, an early avatar community.
Source: Bruce F. Damer; used with permission.

Avatars should not be confused with bots or agents, which are software-driven entities that often mimic human behavior. An avatar is always representative of a living, breathing human being. Users often take great care in designing their digital personae and the virtual worlds they live in. They often accessorize their avatars with clothing, weapons, and supplies, and they accumulate skills or "health units." Users almost never want their avatar to resemble their physical selves, preferring the liberation of expression and societal strictures that anonymity brings. Over time, users tend to treat their avatars less as string puppets and more as a direct digital costume they don when they log on.

Today, avatar communities lie at the center of a great deal of design, investment, research, and public debate on identity, challenging the norms of more conventional forms of human contact.

—Bruce F. Damer

Further Reading

Benedikt, M. (Ed.). (1991). *Cyberspace: First steps.* Cambridge, MA: MIT Press.

Damer, B. F. (1998). *Avatars! Exploring and building virtual worlds on the Internet.* Berkeley, CA: PeachPit Press.

Jargon.net. (n.d.) *Avatar.* Retrieved January 9, 2003, from http://www.jargon.net/jargonfile/a/avatar.html

Schroeder, R. (Ed.). (2002). *The social life of avatars.* New York: Springer Verlag.

Stephenson, N. (1992). *Snow crash.* New York: Bantam Spectra.

B

BANKRUPTCY

Bankruptcy—called creative destruction by the economist Joseph Alois Schumpeter (1883–1950)—is the process by which the old and inefficient give way to the new and dynamic. The fear of bankruptcy is the stick, which together with the carrot of profits, drives firms to be efficient. The occurrence of a small number of bankruptcies is a normal, healthy part of community economic life, but during recessions the number tends to increase sharply, often causing damage to communities through lost resources and human distress. Occasionally, a community itself goes bankrupt.

THE CAUSES OF CORPORATE FAILURE

Firms fail because they are in difficulty, but bankruptcy implies not only short-term problems with cash flow, but the fact that proceeds from the sale of the firm would be insufficient to meet its debt. A failure to make profits, a root cause of bankruptcy, is cyclical in nature: When the economy moves into a downturn, some firms that were previously profitable cease to be so. Most of these firms are relatively young and thus rarely large. Individually these unprofitable firms seldom make headlines, but cumulatively they represent considerable distress to their owners and perhaps also their workers. Such new firms fail because of incompetence of one form or another or because of bad luck such as an unexpected increase in interest rates, which increases loan repayments.

Firms in declining industries also experience bankruptcy. This type of bankruptcy is necessary to the progress of the economy. Such firms are not profitable because their products are not wanted at a price that covers costs. Because such firms are inefficient, their resources—labor, land, and capital (machines, trucks, and so on)—should be reallocated to other firms that can use them more efficiently. Typically these firms, although probably in the midst of a long drawn-out decline, are still large.

Not all large bankrupt firms, however, are in declining industries. A temporary shock, such as a war that drives up oil prices, can lead even firms with good long-term prospects to become bankrupt.

THE SOCIAL AND ECONOMIC COSTS OF BANKRUPTCY

When a small firm closes, it can represent significant hardship to the owner, whose life savings may be invested in the firm. Similarly, employees may suffer distress, although, possibly with some retraining, they should find other employment opportunities in the area. Thus the impact on both employees and the community at large is limited.

When a large firm goes bankrupt, particularly if the large firm is a dominant employer in the locality, the results are more drastic. Some employees may choose to remain in the area and wait for new employment opportunities to emerge. In this case, house prices fall, and social capital institutions—schools, hospitals, and roads—are underused. Apart from the social costs, there are macroeconomic costs such as reduced tax revenue for governments and higher welfare payments.

BANKRUPTCY SYSTEMS

A bankruptcy system must achieve several objectives. First, it must return assets to creditors as fully and

The Ten Largest Bankruptcies in U.S. History (as of January 1, 2003)

Company	*Date*	*Total Pre-Bankruptcy Assets*
Worldcom, Inc.	7/21/2002	$103,914,000,000
Enron Corp.	12/2/2001	63,392,000,000
Conseco, Inc.	12/18/2002	61,392,000,000
Texaco, Inc.	4/12/1987	35,892,000,000
Financial Corp. of America	9/9/1988	33,864,000,000
Global Crossing, Ltd.	1/28/2002	30,185,000,000
UAL Corp.	12/9/2002	25,197,000,000
Adelphia Communications	6/25/2002	21,499,000,000
Pacific Gas and Electric Co.	4/6/2001	21,470,000,000
MCorp.	2/31/1989	20,228,000,000

Source: BankruptcyData.com. New Generation Research, Inc. Boston, MA.

quickly as possible and identify with certainty which creditors fare best (which are paid most) in the bankruptcy procedure. Second, it must put into effect the creative-destruction role by which the old and inefficient are disposed of as quickly as possible. Third, it must ensure that potentially profitable firms survive the bankruptcy process.

Different countries have placed different emphases on these various objectives. In contrast to the socially conscious European countries, the United States, with its emphasis on the free-market economy, has emphasized keeping firms in business rather than satisfying the needs of creditors. Chapter 11 of the Bankruptcy Code of the United States contains provisions giving firms protection from creditors who may be trying to close them down, sell off assets, or both. A firm has a certain period in which to file a survival plan, which creditors can be forced to accept, although in reality this possibility is open only to large firms due to the costs of court proceedings. European countries have been moving toward a form of Chapter 11 bankruptcy procedure, but on the whole they remain more open to the needs of the creditors, particularly the banks.

Not surprisingly, Chapter 11 is a controversial piece of legislation, which economists have severely criticized. They worry that it may damage the working of credit markets and slow the process of creative destruction. Despite these valid concerns, there is little evidence that the U.S. economy is becoming less dynamic. Indeed, since 1979, when the new Bankruptcy Code was introduced, the U.S. economy has become increasingly dynamic. In particular, it has managed to escape the periodic recessions characterizing European economies during this period. Chapter 11 is certainly not the only reason for the American economy's superior performance, but it is an essential part of the policy jigsaw responsible for this performance. It remains to be seen whether Chapter 11 bankruptcies will help or hurt the U.S. economy in the years to come.

—John Hudson

Further Reading

Baird, D. G. (1993). *The elements of bankruptcy.* Westbury, NY: Foundation Press.

Bradley, M., & Rosenzweig, M. (1992). The untenable case for Chapter 11. *Yale Law Journal, 101,* 1043–1095.

Franks, J. R., Nyborg, K. G., & Torous, W. N. (1996). A comparison of US, UK and German insolvency codes. *Financial Management, 25,* 86–101.

Hudson, J. (1989). The birth and death of firms. *Quarterly Review of Economics and Finance,* 29, 68–86.

Skeel, D. A. (1998). An evolutionary theory of corporate bankruptcy law and corporate bankruptcy. *Vanderbilt Law Review, 51,* 1325–1398.

White, M. J. (1989). The corporate bankruptcy decision. *Journal of Economic Perspectives, 10,* 87–103.

BARS AND PUBS

Throughout the world, cultures that condone the consumption of alcoholic beverages have found that the places that serve them to the public become centers of community life. The most studied and reported among these are the American bar and the English pub, both of which have evolved through many stages as social, economic, and political changes served to alter their character if not their basic functions.

THE ENGLISH PUB

Whereas the Irish pub evolved out of the local grocery stores, the English version began in the living rooms of countryside homes located along the stage routes. A dead bush hanging from a pole signaled that, for a small fee, the homeowner or his wife would bring draughts from their alehouse that travelers could enjoy while seated near the fireplace. Eventually a store of ale inside the house saved steps to the back of the property. Although there is no consensus on when alehouses began to appear, a 1557 census recorded some 24,000 of them in England and Wales.

The bar counter followed, another room was opened to serve those of higher social standing, and the pub emerged (most likely during the seventeenth century). As the English middle class began to grow in the second half of the nineteenth century, several strata were recognized within it, and for some time city pubs were partitioned around an oval bar such that many segments of society could be served under the same roof but remain "protected" from one another. In time the partitioned pubs faded, but there remained two "sides" of the house. The "public" side was crudely appointed, and the floor was often a continuation of the cobblestones outside. The other side was the "saloon bar," which achieved its greatest elegance in Victorian times. "Other side!" the publican would shout at a char maid approaching the wrong door. The public side of the house was the lively side, however, and in time those from the saloon bar tended to drift over, and the pubs became more and more democratized in the early decades of the twentieth century.

The English pub is also called a "local," and everyone seems to have his or her local, which is regarded as an extension of the English person's living room. The pub promotes a civic persona duly noted:

> The pub . . . is the only kind of public building used by large numbers of ordinary people where their thoughts and actions are not in some way arranged for them. In other kinds of public buildings they are the audiences, watchers of political, religious, dramatic, cinematic, instructional or athletic spectacles. But within the pub [the customer] has entered an environment in which he is participator rather than spectator. (Mass Observation Team 1943, p. 1)

The importance of the pub is also illustrated today by those villages that have lost them. Many professionals who work in England's big cities buy homes in charming old villages within commuting distance of the city. Rural depopulation often means that these villages no longer have shops, a post office, or a local pub of their own, with the consequence that the newcomers neither work nor spend their shopping money in them. That fact contributes to ill feeling between newcomers and locals. By contrast, in villages that still have pubs, newcomers and locals meet and talk, and relations—and community atmosphere—are better.

Although there are independent pubs, the majority of Britain's pubs are affiliated with a particular brewer and feature that brewer's ales. Pub life today suffers from both the government's and the brewers' desire to have fewer but larger premises. Government wants easier supervision and the brewers want greater profit. The result is that the term *local* applies less and less, as there are fewer pubs. Pub life also suffers from the heavy

Men in a pub in Kenilworth, Warkshire, England, in 1998 enjoying a pint.

Source: Stephen G. Donaldson Photography; used with permission.

taxes on beer and ale. In the north, particularly, many have given up pub sociability because they can no longer afford it.

THE AMERICAN BAR

From the seventeenth century until the Revolutionary War, when what are now the eastern states of the United States were colonies of Great Britain, the colonial tavern—percursor of the American bar—flourished. The tavern was of great importance to town and village development. Colonial governments not only required that taverns be built, but also stipulated their locations. They were to be in close proximity to meeting halls. Because administrative funding was meager, they were also to serve as courtrooms for circuit-riding lawyers and judges who dispensed common law. In addition, they served as enlistment centers and staging areas for local militia.

Informally, taverns were news centers. Here the literate read political tracts aloud for the benefit of the illiterate, and here news from other areas was gleaned from visitors, for the taverns also served as inns. Tavern association generated social capital essential to the fledgling economy. Getting first to know and then to trust others in the convivial atmosphere of the tavern encouraged cooperative economic ventures.

The colonists were serious drinkers, exceeding twice the average per capita consumption in the United States today, yet there was no temperance movement prior to the Revolutionary War. A great many regulations and controls were eventually imposed upon the taverns, however, in part because so many colonists preferred the warmth and friendliness of the tavern to the atmosphere of the church.

Strenuous opposition to drinking did not arise until the nineteenth century. As factories grew, so did saloons and, as neither municipal governments nor the captains of industry provided more wholesome relief from the drudgery of factory labor, the saloons thrived. Later, motion-picture theaters would become a popular alternative, while for its part the saloon became an even greater target of the Prohibition movement than alcohol itself.

One of the ironies of Prohibition (which was in force from 1920 to 1933) is that the illegal speakeasies admitted women, whereas most saloons did not. With repeal of Prohibition, bars became very popular, and most alcohol consumed in the United States until the 1950s was consumed in public places. After World War II, single-use zoning, which allowed some areas to restrict development to residential construction, was pervasively adopted, with the result that the bars did not follow Americans to the suburbs. No longer did they serve as neighborhood meeting places. Today most alcohol is consumed in the home, and whiling away an hour or two in a bar is no long acceptable middle-class behavior.

The number of "drinking only" establishments in the United States decreased by over two-thirds between 1948 and 1986, but the number of licenses decreased only slightly, as places that also serve food were issued them. Because in restaurants diners confine conversation to their own party, most licensed establishments are not the social mixers they once were.

The public bar in America has often been referred to as the poor man's social club. While it is true that working-class bars are the most animated and regularly attended, there are also bars that serve as the after-work socializing stops for particular groups of workers such as lawyers, hospital employees, schoolteachers, journalists, and so forth.

American bars are presently in the process of improving their image and their décor, expanding their fare, and becoming more responsible as purveyors of adult beverages. In many states, however, they are heavily taxed and subject to a bewildering number of regulations that are constantly being changed. The future of the bar as a business is uncertain. Government agencies, research institutes, and the media have adopted what sociologist Joseph Gusfield calls the "malevolence assumption" regarding bars and drinking; that is, they assume all consequences of alcohol consumption are negative and, therefore, bars and drinking cause social problems. There is scant recognition of the community-building function of American bars.

—Ray Oldenburg

See also Third Places

Further Reading

Davis, B. (1981). *The traditional English pub: A way of drinking.* London: Architectural Press.

Gorham, M. (1949). *Back to the local.* London: Percival Marschall.

LeMasters, E. E. (1975). *Blue collar aristocrats: Life styles at a working-class tavern.* Madison: The University of Wisconsin Press.

Lender, M. E., & Martin, J. K.(1987). *Drinking in America: A history.* New York: The Free Press.

Mass Observation Team. (1943). *The pub and the people: A worktown study.* London: Victor Gollancz.

Oldenburg, R. (1989). There was a tavern in the town. *North American Culture, 5*(2), 4.

Oldenburg, R. (1999). *The great good place* (3rd ed.). New York: Marlowe and Company.

BARTER

In the modern world, most trading involves the use of money. A person sells something, is given cash in exchange, and then uses the cash to buy something else. This was not always the case, however. In the past, trading often involved some form of barter. In a barter transaction, no money is involved and the acts of buying and selling are combined: The two participants simply swap whatever they have. Barter continues to be used in certain circumstances even today (for example, in places where the money economy has been disrupted by war, or in informal situations).

COUNTERTRADE AND COMMERCIAL BARTER

The most commercially important form of barter today is countertrade, in which a seller accepts payment in goods rather than money. It is used to enable sales to be made to countries with a shortage of foreign exchange or when a purchasing government has stipulated that an overseas supplier has to offset a proportion of the price of his goods by buying local goods for export. It comprises 10 to 15 percent of world trade, and specialist firms usually handle the sale of the unwanted goods the seller acquires. Every year during the 1990s, Cuba swapped sugar for French wheat and machine parts.

The traders who received the sugar then sold it on the world market.

Strictly speaking, commercial-barter companies do not engage in barter at all because they use a notional money for accounting purposes and buying and selling are not combined. Typically, one of these firms will invite businesses to sell their surplus stock through its network of contacts. For example, a hotel might offer some of its rooms through a barter company at a slack time of year, or a manufacturer might offer a discontinued line. The sellers are not paid in regular dollars but in barter dollars, which are credited to their accounts with the barter firm and can be used only to buy goods and services offered by other companies through the barter organization. Most barter companies have a large sales staff to arrange the trades and charge a commission to both buyer and seller.

That system allows commercial barter to overcome one of the largest drawbacks of genuine barter; namely, that each side must have something the other wants that both regard as being equivalent in value. These conditions are very hard to achieve unless the quantity of at least one of the goods or services being swapped can be varied—the weight of wheat being exchanged for a house, for example—and at least one of the people involved is willing to take something he or she doesn't want, knowing that the unwanted good or service can be bartered later for something more desirable. In the past, some commodities became barter goods—items people accepted purely to be able to swap them for something else later on. Such items attain the status of currency: In Germany immediately after World War II, nonsmokers would accept cigarettes in payment for small items they had sold because they knew they could use them to buy things that they did want. Bottles of whiskey were used in the same way for larger deals.

In ancient Egypt, grain was the standard barter good. Farmers who deposited their crops in government-run warehouses were given receipts showing the amount, quality, and date. They could then pay their rent and buy goods simply by writing what was effectively a check transferring grain from their account in the store to that of someone else. People using another grain store in another part of the country could be paid with these checks. The various stores would balance out their claims against each other just as banks do with money today, and the grain itself would be moved only if there was a net flow of checks from one town to another and the grain was actually needed there for consumption.

Valuing Trade Goods

In all systems of exchange, a crucial element of the interaction is placing a value on the goods being exchanged. The following example from the Asantei of Ghana indicates that place of origin of the goods is one factor considered in setting value.

> Exposure to central place analysis had predisposed me to take note of the regional geography of trading, but the conspicuous appearance of place-names and geographical identities in Kumasi market conversations confirmed this interest early in my research. Location was treated as an important characteristic of both people and goods. When I asked traders to identify the suppliers and buyers visiting their stalls with the simple question, "Who is this?" they most often chose to mention the person's primary trading location first, "She is from Obuasi," rather than her name, ethnic group, commercial role, family, or other known identifier. This title also represented her value to the trader; those receiving the warmest welcome were the trader's link to a location especially important for her commodity as a supply or distribution area.
>
> Goods also gained in value because of their geographical identity. Retailers crying out their wares featured the name of the district of origin (Sehwi plantain, or Axim cassava) in order to attract customers. Longstanding local specializations apparently help maintain consumer acceptance through districts' reputations for consistent quality as well as reasonable price. I noticed that quieter traders often discussed the origin of their goods with customers during bargaining, but also with competitors and neighbors, suggesting that this was considered an important piece of information but no secret. I soon began consistently asking traders, "Where is this from?" and found that they readily answered and almost always knew, even when they had purchased the goods themselves from intermediaries in Kumasi.

Source: Clark, Gracia. (1994). *Onions Are My Husband: Survival and Accumulation by West African Market Women.* Chicago: University of Chicago Press, p. 36.

GIFT GIVING

It is a mistake to think that genuine barter—that is, trading without the use of barter goods or a local currency—was carried out extensively in the past before money became common. Only those trading over long distances would have used it frequently. According to the French anthropologist Marcel Mauss (1872–1950), people living in the same area usually used what he called the gift exchange, making generous gifts to each other. When someone accepted a gift, he or she was obliged to give something back at some time in the future of at least equivalent value. Meanness or the total failure to give anything in return greatly reduced the person's standing in the eyes of the community, whereas generosity increased it.

A system along these lines survived in rural Ireland until the 1950s. Called the *meitheal,* it was an arrangement whereby one family would have relationships often going back for several generations with other families in the area. If one of the families had a surplus of something, perhaps after killing a pig, for example, they would give it to the others. The families would help each other at harvest time, or if someone fell ill. No one ever checked to see if one family was giving as much as it received. It was having a reliable relationship that was important.

In his 2001 book *Soil and Soul,* the writer Alastair McIntosh describes three different exchange systems on the Scottish Isle of Lewis where he grew up in the 1960s. There was mutuality: Elderly people and others who needed help were looked after and nothing was expected in return. There was reciprocity: You gave someone the fish you caught and later they would reciprocate with a dozen eggs. And then there was barter—a regular exchange of goods on a prearranged basis. The line between giving and getting was fuzzy, and the whole arrangement formed what he calls an "alternative insurance system" for the community, where needs were met through one exchange system or another.

In a largely unconscious effort to create systems similar to the one operating on the Isle of Lewis, several thousand communities around the world have established Local Exchange Trading Systems (LETS) since they were developed by Michael Linton in British Columbia in the early 1980s. These systems are often called barter networks but, as with commercial barter, this is a misnomer as each system has its own local currency. The sellers use the local currency they receive to buy goods or services from other members. Most LETS are small and their survival rate has been poor because their rules are not usually strict enough to enforce reciprocity. With no credit controls, some members take more from the system than they give back. This upsets the more conscientious members, who leave.

THE FUTURE OF BARTER

In today's world, barter and forms of near-barter such as LETS are more frequently used whenever money becomes scarce. If an economic downturn looks likely, people become too pessimistic about the future to take out as many new loans from the banks as they did in the past. Consequently, when the old loans are repaid, the amount of money in circulation falls. This makes trading difficult and people who have goods and services they want to buy and sell but too little money to carry out the transaction will turn to barter to help them do so. For this reason, some form of barter will always be with us.

—Richard Douthwaite

Further Reading

Davis, G. (1994). *A history of money.* Cardiff, Wales: University of Wales Press.

Douthwaite, R. (1996). *Short circuit.* Dublin, Ireland: Lilliput Press.

Douthwaite, R. (1999). *The ecology of money.* Dartington, UK: Green Books.

Lietaer, B. (2001). *The future of money.* London: Century.

Mauss, M. (1950). *The gift: The form and reason for exchange in archaic societies.* London: Norton.

McIntosh, A. (2001). *Soil and soul: People versus corporate power.* London: Aurum Press.

Woodruff, D. (1999). *Money unmade: Barter and the fate of Russian capitalism.* Ithaca, NY: Cornell University Press.

BEDROOM COMMUNITIES

In its purest form, a bedroom community provides little more to its residents than a place to rest between the commutes necessary to acquire the goods, services, and employment not provided within their own community. Also referred to as sleeper towns and dormitory towns, these communities often have highly regarded public schools but few of the other business and municipal facilities found in most towns and many contemporary suburbs.

Typically, bedroom communities are found in suburban areas, often in the outer rings farthest from the central business district that earlier predicated the formation of the inner-ring suburbs. But there are also dense, inner-city areas that meet the definition; in parts of St. Louis, Missouri, and Detroit, Michigan, for example, residents gain little more from their immediate surroundings than dormitory-style services. In those sectors of St. Louis and Detroit, residents are surrounded by block upon block of housing but do not have significant local sources of food, clothing, or entertainment. Many urban areas now designated as bedroom communities were not originally developed as such but lost their diversity of shops, employment, and services through resident flight, economic problems, regional growth shifts, or other phenomena.

HISTORY OF BEDROOM COMMUNITIES

Most bedroom communities were intentionally planned, originating as outgrowths of the suburban movements of the mid-nineteenth century in the United States, Great Britain, and other industrialized countries. As parts of the industrial economy grew and many cities became increasingly dense and polluted, the middle- and upper-income classes sought to separate their work lives from their home lives. At that time, suburban areas such as Brooklyn Heights in Brooklyn, New York, provided residents with more space—and less dirt and noise—in more bucolic settings while still affording easy access to the jobs, businesses, and other amenities of the central city. As transit options progressed from horse to train to car, people could more easily live farther and farther away from the city's central core and still maintain daily connections with their inner-city centers of work, society, and commerce. Although discernable bedroom communities have existed for more than a century in many countries, the United States experienced a major boom in the phenomenon in the post–World War II years. In addition to wanting to separate themselves from city life for environmental and class reasons, some cultures, such as much of post–World War II middle-class U.S. culture, found that bedroom communities supported the societal ideal of further segregating gender roles. The wife stayed home and kept house while her husband traveled a significant distance away from home to earn the household income.

Most bedroom communities developed from land-use plans that favored the mass grouping of a more narrow range of socioeconomic status and housing choice than was usually found in urbanized areas. In many bedroom communities, a very limited style of housing is repeated over and over. However, just as is found in some contemporary suburban developments, many bedroom communities now provide more housing choices and cater to a wider socioeconomic range. There are now many bedroom communities that offer the full range of housing options, from small apartments to large single-family compounds.

PROBLEMS ASSOCIATED WITH BEDROOM COMMUNITIES

While many bedroom communities continue to crop up around the world—often where crops once were raised—zealous debates are held over whether this form of community is good for society and the environment. Some experts say it is a mistake to think of all bedroom communities as environmentally negative, but such communities do typically encourage automotive travel and help engender sprawl. Some recent bedroom communities are specifically designed to cluster housing and preserve the natural environment. Many residents, particularly teenagers and stay-at-home parents, complain bitterly of social isolation. This complaint has been voiced for much of the history of the bedroom-community phenomenon. Of course, many other types of community also engender isolation, but the tenants of bedroom communities are predominantly expatriate urbanites and not former rural residents or others who might have more experience dealing with this type of social isolation.

There are other problems associated with these communities. With few businesses to shoulder some of the tax load, residents' property taxes become the main vehicle to support local roadways, sewers, and other vital community infrastructure. And because most of the residents are transplants from more densely settled communities that included more community social infrastructure, they increasingly lobby for more communal facilities and services. In many bedroom communities, local schools were not designed to accommodate the population influx that results from rapid development. In other bedroom communities, residents are encountering the urban woes they originally sought to escape, such as crowded roadways, illegal drug use, and crime. Many residents increasingly complain about commuting time and gas prices. Andrew Hurley, a professor of history at the University of Missouri–St. Louis who specializes in urban history, says that the decline of the nuclear family has also had a negative impact on the demand for such communities. "The nuclear family drove the creation of bedroom communities," says Hurley. "In the United States, for example, that kind of family is no longer dominant. Many single parents find it very difficult to earn a living and cater to the needs of their offspring in a decentralized, drive-everywhere community."

It is still not clear whether these serious problems will cause a decline in the creation of bedroom communities. In the United States, despite anger from long-term locals and environmentalists, major bedroom community developments are being installed daily. Planners have tried to address the social, fiscal, and other issues long associated with bedroom communities by designing communities that are more environmentally friendly and socioeconomically diverse. Many communities now include more communal structures in the early planning stages, such as recreation centers. Even without planned intervention, many of the bedroom communities of the past have gradually become more diverse and more equipped with public services and spaces.

—Gabriel Shapiro

Further Reading

Clark, S. D. (1966). *The suburban society.* Toronto, Canada: University of Toronto Press.

Fishman, R. (1987). *Bourgeois utopias: The rise and fall of suburbia.* New York: Basic Books.

Goldston, R. (1970). *Suburbia: Civic denial.* New York: Macmillan.

Hurley, A. (n.d.) Personal communication.

Jackson, K. T. (1985). *Crabgrass frontier: The suburbanization of the United States.* New York: Oxford University Press.

Look magazine. (1968). *Suburbia: The good life in our exploding utopia.* New York: Cowles Education Corporation.

Muller, P. O. (1981). *Contemporary suburban America.* Englewood Cliffs, NJ: Prentice Hall.

BEGUINE COMMUNITIES

Spontaneously arising in many localities of the Low Countries of Europe in the later twelfth century, Beguine communities were religious associations that were semimonastic in nature, providing spiritual and actual homes for women of several classes. Adherents took no formal vows of celibacy, poverty, or obedience but otherwise reflected in their lives the piety and sacrificial life of cloistered nuns. They were noted for their care of the poverty-stricken and ill, and because of this benevolence were held in high esteem by their contemporaries. In the beginning, many of the Beguines were women of property. They ordinarily elected a superior to maintain order and discipline. The movement spread widely, by the fourteenth century to be found in many of the urban areas of France, Belgium, the Netherlands, and the Germanies.

There is no consensus on the origin of the term *Beguine,* but two of several possibilities are that it either derives from a corruption of the name *Albigensian* (Albigensians adhered to beliefs branded heretical by the Church and were active in this era) or that it derives from the name of a priest, Lambert le Bègue (d. 1177), who favored the gathering of female parishioners into a community in Liège, in the Brabant region of present-day southern Netherlands and northern Belgium. The male counterparts of the movement, never as numerous or as well established, were known as the *Beghards.*

Specific Beguine communes, usually called Beguinages, are identified as early as 1207 in Belgium, where they persisted in large numbers. The most populous Beguinage, that of Ghent, had several thousand members by 1300, when it was a virtual city within a city, with eighteen convents for younger sisters, one hundred houses for older sisters, two churches, an infirmary, workshops, and a brewery. The site may still be visited. The site of another often-visited community, the Begijnhof, is found in Amsterdam off the Spui; it is perhaps best known by foreign visitors for its Pilgrim or English Church, used by Puritan dissenters from England after 1585.

Beguines did not form a monastic order and were thus independent, causing many Church authorities to be suspicious of their orthodoxy. This distrust persisted, though in many cases the Beguines were provided religious services by mendicant orders, especially the Dominicans. Their piety centered on the Eucharist and the human personality of Jesus. Members of the movement considered themselves to be staunch supporters of the Church and, in fact, from time to time gained the privileges of church orders from some of the hierarchy. Nevertheless, the taint of heresy (and associated immorality) hung over them, and in 1311–1312 the Council of Vienne formally pronounced them to be heretical and hence to be suppressed. In many cases, Beguines were then forced either to marry or to enter religious orders.

Occasionally the former communities continued on as almshouses or hospitals. The impact of the sixteenth-century Reformation, followed by that of the Napoleonic Wars of the early eighteenth century, essentially finished off any communities still remaining.

—Donald F. Durnbaugh

Further Reading

Lambert, M. (1992). *Medieval heresy* (2nd. ed.). London: Blackwell.

McDowell, E. W. (1969). *The Beguines and the Beghards in Medieval culture, with special emphasis on the Belgian scene.*

New Brunswick, NJ: Rutgers University Press.
Simons, W. (2001). *Cities of ladies: Beguine communities in the medieval Low Countries, 1200–1565.* Philadelphia: University of Pennsylvania Press.

BIRTH

Every society has rituals associated with birth. The newborn is brought into society and officially becomes a member. The timing of these rituals may vary from society to society—traditional societies typically wait a period of time to be sure that the newborn lives—but in general, the rituals resemble one other.

Just as each society has rituals associated with birth, each gives birth a meaning in conformity with its material condition and ideational (relating to the forming of ideas) system. For example, in Europe and the United States during the seventeenth and eighteenth centuries, rituals acknowledged a woman's maternal role but as part of her entire role set. Her role as a wife was more important than her status as a mother. Motherhood was a rather passive state in the perception of the times, a mere working-out of nature with little room for agency (power) on the part of women. As a result, the mere prospect of birth was a terrifying one for most women. Nature—or, for Protestants, God—would take its course, and nothing that appeared magical could be done to aid the birth.

Birth has the usual three stages of any rite of passage—separation, transition, and reincorporation. In the modern United States, the social separation of the pregnant woman is the stage of the ritual most emphasized. In earlier times the final stage, reincorporation, was emphasized. In Christian countries this stage included the baptizing of the baby and the churching of the mother, or her purification. Such rituals are communal ones, emphasizing the importance of introducing the new member to society and returning the mother to her communal responsibilities.

These traditional rites emphasized the communal consequences of birth. Therefore, little preparation was made for birth itself because it was in the hands of God, and to anticipate such events was considered unlucky. The consequences of pregnancy, however, were communal, and a society could establish rituals preparing the family to unite with other family units into a community. A woman was a wife first, a companion, helper, and lover. Protestant Europe taught that she was modeled after Eve before Eve left Eden. Indeed, women were true partners in their husbands' enterprises; true economic assets for them in the community and the rituals emphasized that fact. Child care was secondary to a woman's wifely responsibilities until fairly modern times—the late nineteenth century.

MODERN RITUALS AND WOMEN

Contrary to general belief, birthing rites in the modern world are generally more elaborate than they were during earlier periods. There is a shift in rituals to focusing on the role of women from conception forward. Women's agency is a matter of prime concern. Elaborate rituals surround each step of the process, including prenatal care, the hospital process, natural childbirth, and neonatal care. The emphasis in modern female rites of passage is on the woman's identity as mother. It is an identity that society means her to value above all others—above wife, helper, and lover.

In traditional societies the midwife generally cut the umbilical cord. This cutting marked the separation of the child symbolically from the mother, bringing it into the community. Today a father typically attends the birth as a "coach" and cuts the cord. The father is symbolically noting his tie to his partner, and they jointly bring the child into the community. Typically in the past, parents would take the child to the hearth to identify it with the household and not just with the mother. In many U.S. and European communities, the child is held soon after birth by both parents—a means of identifying it with the family and stressing the parents' role in making it a member of the community. Granted, such births tend to be the fashion in middle-class families, but the media choose to present them as normal on television shows such as *Friends,* even when the parents are not married.

RITES OF INCORPORATION

Societies find ways to introduce the newborn to other members. Whether it is the act of lifting a West African child to the heavens and then carrying it throughout the village, or a Muslim naming day, or a Christian baptism, the child is presented to the community, placing it as a member of the group and making the group in some way responsible for it. Such a ritual marks a second, sociocultural birth. In Europe during the seventeenth century, a bath was absolutely essential to mark this ritual, symbolizing purity and readiness to join the community.

For the eighteenth-century English gentry, the birth

of a firstborn son was an event of great celebration. The wife presented her husband with the son. In turn, the husband presented the son to the community. There were generally a great feast, bonfires, and the distribution of presents. All this marked the continuation of communal ties and the perpetuation of the community into the future.

Traditionally, women underwent a period of reincorporation as well. This period in Europe was called "her month." The reincorporation took some time. A woman remained quietly in bed for the first week after birth. Her relatives were the first to visit, then female friends. Her husband was the first male whom society allowed to see the new mother. No sexual relations, even touching of the breast, could take place. Indeed, the breast was a thing to be feared at this time. A wife stayed in her room, lying in, until the last week of her month. Then she began to enter other rooms of the house. Churching was the last ceremony in her reincorporation, introducing her to her old life and the community. People considered an unchurched mother to be dangerous and generally avoided her.

MODELS OF BIRTH

Each society has its own model of birth. The United States tends to view birth from a technological framework. Its foundational metaphor is that of the assembly line. The hospital, therefore, is a factory that produces babies. The basic idea of this model is the separation of mind and body. The model holds that the female body is somehow defective and thus dependent on modern technology. Without technology the woman would be incapable of birth. Obstetrical procedures thus become rituals by which the culture seeks to bring women into line with its chosen role for them.

Other models prevail in other societies. Agricultural societies talk of sowing seeds and the power of male seed and the passiveness of women, who are impregnated rather passively. Models depict power relationships in the society, cultural beliefs of how children are to prosper, and basic religious and philosophical values.

In the changing cultural atmosphere of the twentieth-century United States, women saw modern science as a means to enter the community in a more equitable manner. They began to use science to control nature, enabling them to join the world outside the home and take part in work, education, and politics. Soon there was a movement away from blocking out the full experience of childbirth. Anthropologist Margaret Mead was a leader in that movement, demanding of her doctor, Benjamin Spock, that he help her achieve the greatest possible awareness during the birth of her daughter, Mary Catherine. Departing from the technological school of birth, Mead insisted on breastfeeding her daughter. Natural childbirth with its redefined image of the community soon followed.

During the 1980s and 1990s, women at a Tennessee community called "the Farm"—and especially its leader's wife, Ina May Gaskin—became influential in the movement toward natural birth, home births, and the revival of midwifery.

Modern rituals of childbirth continue the tradition established at the beginning of the modern age when women became active agents in the birth of their children. Motherhood remains an integral part of a woman's identity. There has been an elaboration of rituals surrounding birth, emphasizing the significance of family, even in an age with high divorce rates. The ideal culture continues to emphasize the importance of the family and the place of the family in the wider community.

—Frank Salamone

Further Reading

Bell, C. (1997). *Ritual: Perspectives and dimensions.* New York: Oxford University Press.

Chichester, D, Kwendo, C., Petty, R., Tobler, J., & Wratten, D. (1997). *African traditional religion in South Africa: An annotated bibliography.* Westport, CT: Greenwood Press.

Colson, E. (1960). *Social organization of the Gwembe Tongo.* Manchester, UK: Manchester University Press.

Davis-Floyd, R. E., & Walters, R. (1987). The technological model of birth. *Journal of American Folklore, 100*(398), 479–495.

Driver, T. F. (1998). *Liberating rites: Understanding the transformative power of ritual.* Boulder, CO: Westview Press.

Gaskin, I. M. (1977). *Spiritual midwifery.* Summertown, TN: Book Publishing.

Gillis, J. R. (1996). *A world of their own making: Myth, ritual, and the quest for family values.* New York: Basic Books.

Hancock, M. E. (1999). *Womanhood in the making: Domestic ritual and public culture in urban south India.* Boulder, CO: Westview Press.

Hilger, M. I. (1951). *Chippewa child life and its cultural background.* Washington, DC: U.S. Government Printing Office.

Hogbin, H. I. (1963). *Kinship and marriage in a New Guinea village.* London: University of London Press.

Hunt, N. R. (1999). *A colonial lexicon of birth ritual, medicalization, and mobility in the Congo.* Durham, NC: Duke University Press.

Kendall, L. (1987). *Shamans, housewives, and other restless spirits: Women in Korean ritual life.* Honolulu: University of Hawaii Press.

Monaghan, J., & Just, P. (2000). *Social and cultural anthropology: A very short introduction.* Oxford, UK: Oxford University Press.

Reeves, S. P., & Goodenough, R. G. (Eds.). (1990). *Beyond the second sex: New directions in the anthropology of gender.* Philadelphia: University of Pennsylvania Press.

Romanucci-Ross, L. (1991). *One hundred towers: An Italian odyssey of cultural survival.* New York: Bergin & Garvey.

Spickard, J. V. (1991). Experiencing religious rituals: A Schutzian analysis of Navajo ceremonies. *SA: Sociological Analysis, 52*(2), 191–204.

Spiro, M. E. (1977). *Kinship and marriage in Burma: A cultural and psychodynamic analysis.* Berkeley and Los Angeles: University of California Press.

Stone, L. (1997). *Kinship and gender: An introduction.* Boulder, CO: Westview Press.

Turner, V., & Abrahams, R. D. (1995). *The ritual process: Structure and anti-structure.* New York: Aldine de Gruyter.

BLACK ECONOMY

A black economy (sometimes called the black market or the shadow or parallel economy) comes into existence in any community when both legal and illegal enterprises affecting daily life avoid paying taxes. While a minority of people benefit from the illegal activity of not paying taxes, the majority are victims, and a black economy encourages scarce resources to be spent on nonessentials. The flexibility of a community's moral code determines the response to the black economy, at both individual and collective levels.

The notion of a black economy emerged in the West during World War II, in reaction to rigid controls on the distribution of goods enforced via taxes and price regulations. A black economy disappears when there is a free, unregulated flow of goods and services. Some scholars have distinguished between activities connected with formal occupations and those that are essentially black economic activities, such as moonlighting or working on the side. It is confusing, however, to use the term "informal economy" loosely in connection with "black economy." Not all informal-sector activities are illegal, but some informal activities that occur in illegal businesses generate black income.

SOURCE AND USE OF BLACK MONEY

It is difficult to assess the size of the black economy for various communities because by their very nature they remain undetected and unrecorded. It is said that black economy in India accounts for 40 to 50 percent of the gross domestic product. Black economy thrives in a variety of contexts. On the illegal front, sources of income may come through smuggling, gambling, black marketing, prostitution, or bribes made as payments for favors. In any community, individual underreporting of income or profits—even in the context of a legal transaction or business—also refers to black income. For example, a person may use cash to pay in part for a home or car, so that the purchase price reported to the government will be lower and a lower tax will be assessed. Self-employed individuals may not be reporting the exact income earned over time. At the institutional level, estimates of the current national income and output are constantly underestimated because of deliberate fuzziness in the records of wealth and falsification of taxable income and invoices, undeclared commissions, fudging of corporate accounts towards meeting private ends. The majority of the black money is spent on conspicuous consumption, namely, consumer goods, vacations, entertainment, purchase of property, assets, and so forth.

CONSEQUENCES

The black economy increases the sense of economic and social deprivation in the community, affecting its citizens not only socially and economically but also on moral and political levels.

Social and Moral Effects

The social consequences of the black economy are numerous. First, it promotes corruption, whereby illegal commissions and bribes are offered to conduct legitimate and illegitimate business. For example in some nations, even securing a death certificate requires the payment of a bribe. Providing such illegal compensation for services leads to a depletion of precious resources necessary to promote social welfare objectives for the poor in the community. Social goals such as improving education, reducing poverty, and providing health care services are compromised, and values of thrift, honesty, cooperation, and diligence in a community are bartered in favor of pursuing material wealth. Black economy therefore increases social and economic inequality and disparity in the community. The resulting increases in criminal activities divert government resources toward policing communities. A black economy also fosters low productivity, poor quality of services, and increasing inefficiency. Indeed, public morality tends to be lower where the incidence of black economy is high. Black economy has disastrous consequences for the environment, too, due to the violation of rules and regulations

The Mafia and the Black Economy

One activity of organized crime in the United States is the provision of stolen goods at low cost to members of community. The following account describes the role of the Mafia in this activity in New York City in the early twentieth century.

Another syndicate activity was the sale of merchandise stolen from trucks and warehouses (i.e., "swag") at prices that were often below wholesale. Although this was engaged in on a petty basis by truck drivers and warehousemen, any increase in scale warranted the protection and distribution networks maintained by the syndicate, largely because it was adverse to competition on its turf.

The syndicate made available regular supplies of goods to neighborhood Italians and to workers who patronized local bars and luncheonettes. Samples of stolen merchandise were cavalierly displayed on the street or inside a commercial establishment. Vendors hardly bothered to remove the items from their shipping cartons. Cigarettes, a popular bootleg item, were sold from the trunk of a parked automobile. Neighborhood shops, truck terminals and warehouses sold "hot" goods purchased in lots as a sideline. One candy store advertised appliances and men's sport shirts one week, boy's sneakers the next. Makeshift signs informed passersby of the current special, although the grapevine was a more effective manner of advertising.

Not surprisingly, the neighborhood supported this underground marketplace with enthusiasm. Highly regarded consumer goods, the conspicuous symbols of acculturation and upper class status, were made accessible to ethnic workers; there also seems to have been some satisfaction in the knowledge that upper class consumers paid more for the item and that a big company had been duped. Lamps, toasters, television sets and perfume (brands sold in uptown department stores) all made their way into the neighborhood as swag. Perhaps the only complication was when a scarce supply of stolen merchandise resulted in competition among neighbors, or when a neighbor endeavored to become a middleman and purchased caseloads to sell to friends and neighbors at a profit.

Source: Tricarico, Donald. (1984). *The Italians of Greenwich Village: The Social Structure and Transformation of an Ethnic Community.* New York: Center for Migration Studies of New York, Inc., pp. 65–66.

because of corruption and criminalization. Moral codes no longer remain constant, and democratic institutions and values are compromised.

Economy

There are serious consequences in the allocation of scarce resources with a dilution of social goals and commitments by the state. Institutionalization of corruption at the community level means illegal payments for regular public services as commissions and kickbacks. Profits and income not reported to the government result in a loss of public revenue (because taxes are not assessed accurately) and promote the black economy, as individuals and businesses come to believe that "cheating the government" is acceptable.

Political Consequences

The political consequences of the black economy relate to the unraveling of moral fabric of a community. Real economic resources are diverted to profit-seeking at every opportunity. If tax authorities, political institutions, and the police, to name but a few important elements in a community, begin to indulge in illegal dealings, these agencies lose sight of purpose and social commitment toward community interests.

Further, such dealings lead to an erosion of faith in public institutions. The existence of a black economy has also been used by some as an excuse to discredit state intervention in meeting social goals and objectives. Political philosophies that promote the "market" over the nation or state often cite mismanagement and corruption in their attacks against policies that attempt to provide relief to the poor. Monetary assistance to the developing countries by the World Bank or the IMF is made conditional on the ground that the state receiving the aid introduce measures to tighten fiscal discipline. Consequently, the black economy has not only local and regional implications for communities but global ramifications as well.

—M. Satish Kumar

Further Reading

Acharya, S. N. (1986). *Aspects of the black economy in India.* New Delhi, India: National Institute of Public Finance and Policy (Mimeo).

Baruch, B. M. (1941, Spring). Priorities: The synchronising force. *Harvard Business Review, 19*(3), 261–270.

Cowell, F. A. (1990). *Cheating the government: The economics of evasion.* Cambridge, MA: MIT Press.

Dallago, B. (1990). *The irregular economy: The underground economy and the black labour market.* Dartmouth, UK: Aldershot.
Ditton, J. (1977). *Part time crime: Ethnography of fiddling and pilferage.* London: Macmillan.
Gupta, S. B. (1992). *Black income in India.* New Delhi, India: Sage.
Harding, P., & Jenkins, R. (1989). *The myth of the hidden economy: Towards a new understanding of informal economic activity.* Buckingham, UK: Open University Press.
Heertje, A, Allen, M., & Cohn, H. (1982). *The black economy: How it works, who works for, and what it costs.* London: Pan Books.
Henry, S. (1982). The working unemployed: Perspectives on the informal economy and unemployment. *Sociological Review, 30,* 460–477
Kabra, K. N. (1982). *The black economy in India: Problems and policies.* New Delhi, India: Chanakya Publications.
Kreugar, A. O. (1974). The political economy of rent-seeking society. *American Economic Review, 64*(2), 291–303.
Kumar, A. (1999, March 20). The black economy: Missing dimension of macro policymaking in India. *Economic and Political Weekly,* 34, 681–694.
Kumar, A. (1999). *The black economy in India.* New Delhi, India: Penguin Books
Pyle, D. J. (1989). *Tax evasion and the black economy.* Hampshire, UK: Macmillan.
Roemer, M., & Jones, C. (1991). *Markets in developing countries: Parallel, fragmented and black.* San Francisco: ICS Press.
Smithies, E. (1998). *Black economy in England.* London: Gill & Macmillan.
Tanzi, V. (1982). *The underground economy in the United States and abroad.* Lexington, MA: Lexington Books.

BLOCKBUSTING

Blockbusting is a set of policies and practices used to encourage the turnover of residential properties in the United States by pandering to the racial prejudices and fears of many whites and exploiting the limited housing opportunities available to blacks. Particularly in the 1950s and 1960s, many real estate agents and their financial partners reaped substantial profits from blockbusting. By encouraging a handful of white residents to sell their homes, predicated on the fear that black families would be moving in and lowering neighborhood property values in the process, and then making those homes available to black families desperately in need of housing, a process of rapid racial transition was launched. Once under way, blockbusting made it possible for agents to purchase homes at below-market rates from panicking white households and sell them at above-market rates to black home buyers. Blockbusting was a vicious practice that exploited both whites and blacks. But to fully understand this practice, it is important to understand the larger context of the dual housing market, of which blockbusting has been just one part.

THE DUAL HOUSING MARKET

Racial segregation persists as an enduring feature of housing patterns in urban and metropolitan areas in the United States. If most measures of segregation (such as the index of dissimilarity, which is a measure of how evenly different groups are distributed, and the exposure index, which is a measure of how isolated one groups is from another) have moderated somewhat in recent years, most of that change has occurred in metropolitan areas with relatively few nonwhites. And if communities have become more diverse, segregation nevertheless remains a dominant characteristic of the demography of metropolitan regions. According to the 2000 census, whites, on average, reside in neighborhoods that are 83 percent white, blacks live in neighborhoods that are 56 percent black, and Hispanics have settled in communities that are 42 percent Hispanic.

The fact of segregation is basically uncontested. The question of why segregation persists generates heated debate. Some point to individual choice, arguing that households generally prefer to live in culturally homogeneous neighborhoods. Others point to economic disparities among racial groups that lead to spatial concentration. But the social science evidence demonstrates that historical and contemporary discrimination remains the dominant explanation. Choice and income count, but far more significant is a range of public policies and private practices that are grounded in racial prejudice, stereotypical thinking, and intentional discrimination.

Among the influential public policies were Federal Housing Administration (FHA) lending practices that virtually required segregation in order for properties to qualify for the agency's federally insured mortgages until at least the mid 1960s. As an early FHA underwriting manual stated, "If a neighborhood is to retain stability, it is necessary that properties shall continue to be occupied by the same social and racial classes" (U.S. Federal Housing Administration 1938, paragraph 937). Enforcement of racially restrictive covenants, exclusionary zoning laws, concentration of public housing in central city neighborhoods, and construction of a federal highway system that facilitated suburban development were among the public policies that created and nurtured racial segregation. Private practices included racially discriminatory redlining (refusing to lend money or insure property if the applicant is black) by mortgage lenders and property insurers, subjective and discriminatory appraisal practices, and racial steering by real estate agents.

Blockbusting fit into the picture as a particularly vicious tool that promoted neighborhood instability and turnover, appropriately defined by one observer as "the intentional action of a real estate speculator to place an African American resident in a house on a previously all-white block for the express purpose of panicking whites into selling for the profit to be gained by buying low and selling high" (Orser 1994, p. 84).

The success of blockbusting depends on old-fashioned prejudice and bigotry, fueled by the institutional racism of government policy at all levels and discriminatory practices of housing and housing-related industries. But as W. Edward Orser observed, blockbusters did fill a void created by the dual housing market. Blacks needed housing, and exploiting white racial fears enabled some real estate agents and lenders to fill it through manipulative and exploitative practices that victimized buyers and sellers. Although the practice of blockbusting has waned, its impact and the reality of dual housing markets in urban communities remain.

FEAR, FLIGHT, AND UNEQUAL OPPORTUNITY

Blockbusting took many subtle and not so subtle forms. The basic process began with a real estate agent looking for a home that was for sale in an all-white neighborhood bordering an integrated or black community. The agent, or a buyer working with the agent, would make an offer on the home, sometimes above the market price. That offer would often come with a warning that the seller had better take it because, with blacks threatening to move in, property values might well be declining. A black family would then be offered the home, frequently at a most favorable below-market price. Once the black family moved in, the real estate agent would get word out to the neighbors that the neighborhood was changing and offer to buy homes, initially at fair-market values. After a few more black households moved in, the agent would continue to buy up properties, but at quickly declining prices. The homes would then be resold, generally to black families, at substantially higher prices. Agents and their financial partners made large profits on the sale price of the homes and the fees associated with each transaction. Not only were individual buyers and sellers exploited, but entire neighborhoods experienced quick and dramatic turnover—sometimes in a matter of just a few years—leading to instability and social disorganization, all of which undercut the financial standing and quality of life of the neighborhood. For example, Edmonson Village, which had been a white middle-class neighborhood of 10,000 people in Baltimore in 1955, was an all-black neighborhood of comparable size just ten years later.

Specific tactics may have varied across communities, but most were manifested in several major cities. In some cases, real estate agents hired black women just to walk their babies in their strollers through white neighborhoods. Young black teenagers were hired simply to drive up and down the streets. Black children delivered handbills door-to-door advising homeowners that now was the time to sell their house. Sexual fears were also exploited in some cases, with the fact that a number of young black men were moving in being emphasized. White homeowners were bombarded with telephone solicitations, frequently late at night, warning them that they had better sell their homes quickly. As one Kansas City resident recalled:

> Unscrupulous realtors were trying to scare our residents with racial fear in order to buy houses cheaply and make big profits. Phone calls were often made to white home owners [who were] told that their property values were dropping and they had better move quick and get as much money as they could before "they" move in. . . . You would have people coming in saying that "your house is worth so and so, are you interested in selling? You know that black people are moving into the area, and we can't guarantee that we would be able to get you that amount of money next year or two years from now, but we could get you that amount of money now." (Gotham 2002, p. 97)

Buyers were also victimized by exploitative financing. Real estate agents and their financial partners often provided land contracts instead of conventional mortgages. Land contracts were more costly and far less secure. They involved higher fees and interest rates. More important, speculators held the deed until the entire loan was paid off. If a payment was missed, families were often evicted and the home was resold. In other cases, families were offered federally insured loans, such as FHA or Veterans Administration (VA) loans, which they often could not repay. Because these loans were guaranteed by the federal government, agents and lenders received their fees and the balance of the loans. Taxpayers picked up the cost of the unpaid federally insured loans and many families lost their homes and savings, but the blockbusters profited handsomely. This basic pattern played out in Chicago,

Detroit, Kansas City, and many other cities with large black populations.

REVULSION AND REACTION

Many residents in cities across the nation and public policy officials at all levels have taken actions to combat blockbusting. Perhaps the most significant step was enactment of the 1968 Fair Housing Act (Title VIII of the Civil Rights Act, revised in 1988), which prohibits actions "to induce or attempt to induce any person to sell or rent any dwelling by representations regarding the entry or prospective entry into the neighborhood of a person or persons of a particular race, color, religion, or national origin" (Fair Housing Act, U.S. Code. Vol. 42, sec. 3604 [1988]). Subsequent court rulings have interpreted this to constitute a ban on blockbusting.

Local communities have taken a variety of actions. "For sale" signs have been banned in some areas, and in some cases residents have put "Not for sale" signs in their front yards. In efforts to respond to fears about declining property values, some communities offer home equity insurance to guarantee homeowners a specified amount of money if in fact they cannot sell their home for that amount. A few communities, most notably Oak Park, Illinois, and Shaker Heights, Ohio, have taken much more aggressive action to combat racial fears and segregation and encourage stable integration. Steps include providing mortgage incentives to families that make a "pro-integrative" move, working with real estate agents to assure that they show families homes throughout the communities (and not just in areas where the majority of the residents are the same race as the prospective buyers), instituting rigorous building inspection programs to assure potential buyers that homes are well maintained, and providing an array of educational programs to counter racial myths and stereotypes.

Blockbusting, like other forms of overt, explicit racism, has waned substantially in recent decades. But neighborhood racial transition still occurs. Race remains a significant consideration in real estate markets. Today real estate agents often advise their black clients to remove all family photographs, artifacts of African art, or any other indicator that a black family currently resides in a home they are trying to sell. However, the systematic, blatant blockbusting of the 1950s and 1960s rarely, if ever, occurs today.

It is critical to remember that the opportunity for blockbusting was created by the pillars of the real estate establishment. Local real estate associations, following the guidance of the Federal Housing Administration, pursued their vision of neighborhood stability by making sure that neighborhoods would be occupied by members of the same racial group. In Detroit, real estate agents who failed to do so were often denied access to listings of available properties. Until passage of the Fair Housing Act, the Kansas City Real Estate Board threatened to revoke licenses of real estate agents and mortgage bankers who violated the Board's code prohibiting the sale of homes in white neighborhoods to black families. Restricting areas in which black families could shop for housing, when black demand for housing was rising, and nurturing well-established racial prejudices and stereotypes created the opportunity for blockbusting. Many "respectable" real estate agents would not be the first to sell a home in a white neighborhood to a black family, but once the panic-peddling started, they were quick to jump in and take the profits. Blockbusting was not simply the outcome of a few unethical actors on the fringes of the U.S. housing industry.

LOOKING BACK TO THE FUTURE

If blockbusting has faded, the reality of housing segregation has not, and the leading institutional actors in the public and private sectors continue to fuel that pattern. Today neighborhoods continue to experience the effects of policies and practices that were condoned just a few years ago, including blockbusting, even if they are not widespread today. Unfortunately, unlike blockbusting, many practices are not just historical artifacts. Despite real progress in recent decades, race and racial composition of neighborhoods continue to affect access to mortgage loans and other financial services. Racial steering persists. Exclusionary zoning laws are on the books in most suburbs. Many of the institutionalized forces that created the nation's dual housing markets in years past, including prejudicial attitudes on the part of home buyers and home sellers, continue to nurture those patterns today.

—Gregory D. Squires

Further Reading

Bradford, C. (1979). Financing home ownership: The federal role in neighborhood decline. *Urban Affairs Quarterly, 14*(3), 313–335.

Cose, E. (1993). *The rage of a privileged class.* New York: Harper-Collins Publishers.

Fair Housing Act, 42 U.S. C. § 3604 (1988).

Goodwin, C. (1979). *The Oak Park strategy: Community control of racial change.* Chicago: University of Chicago Press.

Gotham, K. F. (2002). Beyond invasion and succession: School segregation, real estate blockbusting, and the political economy of neighborhood racial transition. *City and Community, 1*(1), 83–112.

Helper, R. (1969). *Racial policies and practices of real estate brokers.* Minneapolis: University of Minnesota Press.

Hirsch, A. R. (1983). *Making the second ghetto: Race and housing in Chicago, 1940–1960.* Cambridge, UK: Cambridge University Press.

Jackson, K. T. (1985). *Crabgrass frontier: The suburbanization of the United States.* New York: Oxford University Press.

Keating, W. D. (1994). *The suburban racial dilemma: Housing and neighborhoods.* Philadelphia: Temple University Press.

Lewis Mumford Center. (2001). *Metropolitan racial and ethnic change: Census 2000, Washington, DC-MD-VA-WV PMSA.* Retrieved November 15, 2002, from http://www.albany.edu/mumford/census/

Massey, D. S. (2001). Residential segregation and neighborhood conditions in U.S. metropolitan areas. In N. J. Smelser, W. J. Wilson, & F. Mitchell (Eds.), *America becoming: Racial trends and their consequences* (Vol. 1, pp. 391–434). Washington, DC: National Academy Press.

Massey, D. S., & Denton, N. A. (1993). *American apartheid: Segregation and the making of the underclass.* Cambridge, MA: Harvard University Press.

Orser, W. E. (1994). *Blockbusting in Baltimore: The Edmonson Village story.* Lexington: The University Press of Kentucky.

Sugrue, T. J. (1996). *The origins of the urban crisis: Race and inequality in postwar Detroit.* Princeton, NJ: Princeton University Press.

U.S. Federal Housing Administration. (1938). *Underwriting manual.* Washington, DC: U.S. Government Printing Office.

Yinger, J. (1995). *Closed doors, opportunities lost: The continuing costs of housing discrimination.* New York: Russell Sage Foundation.

BLOGS

A blog is an online journal, or Web log (with the word *blog* taking the *b* at the end of *Web* and putting it at the front of *log*). Blogging is the process of creating, organizing, interacting with, and archiving posts to a Web environment. Blog entries focus on an individual, theme, or organization, and may be posts that explore personal thoughts, update users on a product, or organize news of the day. Most blogs are updated at least daily, functioning as a window into the author's world.

Blogging is less a private act of journaling than it is personal publishing. Every blog has an audience, intended or unintended. Most sites have comments functions built in or as add-ons that allow visitors to contribute to the discussion. Unlike other online tools that facilitate dialogue between individuals, blogs are primarily monologues, presenting the voice of the blogger(s). Blogs are conceptual tools for sharing stories and personal narrative, allowing individuals to manage an online identity. Many blogs become linked through various means. Most have a permanent link (permalink) for each post that connects to a specific archived entry, meaning that each entry can be accessed on a single page as part of a chronological list and as a discrete date-based direct entry. Constellations of narratives and community develop as blogs, and specific blog entries are linked in a dynamic hypertext of interwoven communication. Blogdex—an index of blogs produced at the Massachusetts Institute of Technology (http://blogdex.media.mit.edu)—tracks this web and make it possible to locate an individual within the hierarchy of bloggers. Position in the community is determined by who reads whom: If a blog maven links to your blog, the visits to it may rise to thousands a day.

Blogs have been traced back to 1997, according to Rebecca Blood, an early chronicler of blogging and author of *The Weblog Handbook*. They were termed "weblogs" by blogger Jorn Barger, and only twenty-three were known to exist when "Peter Merholz announced in early 1999 that he was going to pronounce it 'wee-blog' and inevitably this was shortened to 'blog'" (Blood, 2000). Blogs are children of older online technologies such as Usenet News, bulletin boards, handrolled Web pages, and even MOOs (Multi-User Object Oriented systems), but the blogging revolution comes from the ease with which one can update and maintain an online journal.

Tools for blogging can be anything that helps maintain chronological lists of entries. Originally, blogs were updated with a text editor, hand-coded HTML (hypertext markup language; the language of most documents on the Web), and FTP (file transfer protocol; a protocol that makes it possible to move files from one's computer to a remote server or vice versa). The main tools today are Blogger, LiveJournal, Moveable Type, Greymatter, Radio Userland, Bloxom, Manila, Zope, and Slash. Popular consensus is that Blogger is the easiest to use. Userland targets corporate and organizational users, and Zope and Slash are group environments.

Blogging is hyped as publishing for the masses. Children, seniors, homemakers, industry executives, programmers, and poets are all keeping online journals, but these masses are overwhelmingly English-speaking, are technologically literate, and have regular access to the Internet. As blogs are inherently about "me," they are of more interest to cultures that privilege individualism.

There are also claims that blogs are without bias and

are a location for free speech, because they are not controlled by corporations. However, corporations are starting to notice, and there is much self and community censoring. Many assume that viral marketers are targeting the community. Blogs are also criticized for clogging up the Internet with meaningless, irrelevant, and irresponsible content. Often, however, that criticism comes from professional media people who feel that content needs to be vetted, reviewed, and edited.

—Jason Nolan

Further Reading

Blood, R. (2000). *Weblogs: A history and perspective.* Retrieved October 25, 2002, from http://www.rebeccablood.net/essays/weblog_history.html

Blood, R. (2002). *The weblog handbook: Practical advice on creating and maintaining your blog.* Cambridge, MA: Perseus Publishing.

Doctorow, C., Dornfest, R., Johnson, S., Powers, S., Trott, B., & Trott, M. (2002). *Essential blogging: Selecting and using weblog tools.* Sebastopol, CA: O'Reilly.

Krol, E. (1992). *The whole Internet.* Sebastopol, CA: O'Reilly.

Nolan, J. (2002). "Ceci n'est pas un blog!" E2K: *A journal for the new literary paradigm.* Retrieved March 20, 2003, from http://netauthor.org/e2k/jan2002/features.html111

Nolan, J. (2003). *Blog links.* Retrieved January 30, 2003, from http://jasonnolan.net/eoc/links.html

BOOK CLUBS AND READING GROUPS

Book clubs, or reading groups as they are commonly called in the United Kingdom, are communities of people who come together in either a physical or virtual setting to discuss books. Perhaps the best-known book club is that of talk show host Oprah Winfrey. Although many book clubs have existed for more than twenty years and have fulfilled readers' needs for camaraderie and intellectual exchange in the perceived increasing individualization of society, Oprah's book club may have helped to make "book club" a household term and to spur new clubs to form. Over five years, Oprah's Book Club discussed forty-seven titles. The videotaped segment usually included Oprah, several pre-selected members of her 21 million-strong viewing audience, and the author of the book, in a relaxed environment such as Oprah's living room. The books selected for discussion usually included discussion guides—now commonly added by publishers to their "book club books"—for the audience to follow with the show or to use on their own.

Oprah Winfrey's original book club ended in 2002; however, major networks throughout the world immediately stepped in re-create the fervor. NBC's "Today Book Club," Good Morning America's "Read This!," and Kelly Ripa's "Reading with Ripa" on *Live With Regis and Kelly* are examples in the United States. In Canada, "Open Book" with comedienne-turned-book-club-moderator Mary Walsh airs on Canada's national broadcaster. And in 2003, Oprah Winfrey decided to bring back her book club, this time focusing on classic works from such writers as William Shakespeare and Ernest Hemingway.

Radio book clubs, such as Great Britain's BBC Radio 4's interactive book club, are another type of mediated book community. In Australia, the public broadcaster hosts "Write On," an online book club. Recently, citywide (such as "One Great Read, One Great Lafayette"), statewide (such as New Jersey's Governor McGreevey's book club for children), and even nationwide book clubs (such as "Canada Reads") have seen readers reading the same book at the same time and discussing it with one another over the airwaves, in libraries, and in their own community-level book clubs. It is in the private homes of individual members that intimate reading communities are formed. Throughout the world, thousands of clubs gather together to discuss the literary merit of a book while simultaneously interpreting the world they live in. The collective space of a reading group demonstrates how people form communities, why they form these connections, what these relationships mean, and how literature acts as the conduit for all of these events to happen.

The book club as a cultural site provides new opportunities to view literature not only as a text to be interpreted but also as a social form itself. As a social practice, book clubs provide insight into the importance that some readers place on literature and reading to enrich their lives and into the passion behind both individual and collective interpretation. Book clubs not only act as sites in which readers interpret their world through literature, but also provide space for a kind of organic (instrumental and natural) dialogic democracy in which the community members work together to create systems that work for everyone. The clubs provide a space for dissension, they nurture and embrace differences of opinions, and they encourage personal and collective growth. Not only do readers feel that there are intellectual benefits of book club membership, but also emotional bonds are formed with the other members.

The Popularity of Online Book Clubs

"I love the idea of online book clubs although I have not joined one. I think I'll look into it because it really makes so many connects possible. I read one author–I think it was Jennifer James–who called it "global intimacy"–love that concept!"

–A face-to-face book club member

A query for "book clubs" on the Internet search engine Google.com brings up 424,000 hits. Many of these sites offer opportunities for readers to join online reading communities if they do not have or do not want access to clubs that meet face-to-face. Readers can choose from different genres, or different discussion schedules and or formats, for example.

Readers who want to join face-to-face groups can also use the Internet. Search for city libraries, or universities. Often the words "book club" with the city name will result in several choices.

–DeNel Rehberg Sedo

HISTORY

Studies of the eighteenth- and nineteenth-century literary societies, precursors to contemporary book clubs, demonstrate that the members were usually women and were not only constituents of the wealthy class but also members of the increasing middle class. Under the guise of helping those in need, women overcame resistance from their spouses, society, and their emotional consciences to form benevolent societies that often branched into reading circles.

Between World War I and the late 1960s, North American literary societies faded from public psyche. They were replaced by organized, formal continuing education programs such as the Great Books Foundation, which were based on programs such as the Chautauqua reading circles or the National Home Reading Union. During the late 1960s and early 1970s, feminist consciousness-raising groups motivated women to meet in groups where subjectivity could be discussed, and there appears to have been a simultaneous resurgence of book club formation. Today it has been estimated that there are 500,000 book clubs in the United States, 50,000 in the United Kingdom, and 40,000 in Canada.

RATIONALE FOR EXISTENCE

Whatever the era or the country or the setting, readers have come together for different reasons. The only consistent rationale appears to be a love of reading. Some gather to socialize outside of the confines of their domestic spaces or daily experiences; others to learn new ideas; others to achieve self-improvement. Most often they join their group because they want intellectual stimulation. These readers say they gain great satisfaction by reading books that they would not normally read and feel connected with other book lovers. According to sociologist Elizabeth Long, an individual's participation in a book club is based on a shared need that informs the individual's sense of identity and contributes to the group's solidarity. She contends that members join a group to fill a gap that society, or the members' social situations, has failed to fill.

PROFILE OF MEMBERSHIP

Contemporary book clubs are predominantly composed of middle-class women, although there are mixed-gender groups and all-male groups. The ethnic composition of the groups is varied, and members range in age from early twenties to late eighties. Age diversity within each group can be quite marked, but many groups seem to be composed of members who are at the same life stages (all professionals with no children or all mothers with small children, for example); ethnic diversity, on the other hand, is not as common. The size of the reading club usually ranges from four to fifteen members.

Reading choices and interpretations of the books read are influenced by each member's life experiences and differ from one club to another. The clubs usually meet at a member's house once a month, and most often in the evenings. Whenever they meet, it is most likely the result of a negotiated process, and is a time that all members have prioritized. Depending on the club's rituals of discussion, preparing for a meeting may be as simple as reading the book, or at least one member of the club may do research and write a synopsis of the author, setting, or context.

Meeting in a member's living room or great room creates an intimacy in which the readers feel comfortable. Lasting from two to four hours, meetings most always include food and drink of some sort. The ritual of eating and drinking—whether it is a theme dinner and wine according to the book choice of the month or simple desserts and coffee—acts as an opportunity to enhance the experience and as a bonding process.

Book clubs are interpretive communities. Readers move from the private space and intensely personal activity of reading into a collective space that encapsulates and is influenced by the interpretations of others in the club to create a collective interpretation through dialogue. This community offers readers the opportunity to simultaneously feel part of a larger community of readers while paradoxically also providing the social space in which to differentiate their book clubs from others and themselves from the larger society through their book choices and discussion processes.

Book clubs should not be generalized as either elitist or populist; rather, they should be viewed as sites of constant struggle between the two. The complex cultural web of gender, ethnicity, power, economics, and identity influences the reasons why people join book clubs and how the texts are decoded or interpreted within the communities, and it provides a picture of book clubs' influence on readers and on society, and vice versa.

—DeNel Rehberg Sedo

Further Reading

Anderson, B. (1991). *Imagined communities: Reflections on the origin and spread of nationalism.* London: Verso.

Blair, K. (1980). *The clubwoman as feminist: True womanhood redefined, 1868–1914.* New York: Holmes & Meier.

Burns, M., & Dillon, A. (1999). *Reading group journal: Notes in the margin.* New York: Abbeville Publishing Group.

Davis, J. A. (1961). *Great books and small groups.* New York: Free Press of Glencoe.

Firor Scott, A. (1991). *Natural allies: Women's associations in American history.* Urbana: University of Illinois Press.

Flint, K. (1993). *The woman reader: 1837–1914.* Oxford, UK: Clarendon Press.

Hartley, J. (2001). *Reading groups.* Oxford, UK: Oxford University Press.

Laskin, D., & Hughes, H. (1995). *The reading group book: The complete guide to starting and sustaining a reading group, with annotated lists of 250 titles for provocative discussion.* New York: Plume.

Long, E. (1987). The book as mass commodity: The audience perspective. *Book Research Quarterly*, 3(1), 9–27.

Long, E. (1992). Textual interpretation as collective action. In B. Boyarin (Ed.), *The ethnography of reading* (pp. 180–212). Berkeley and Los Angeles: University of California Press.

McHenry, E. (1995) "Dreaded eloquence": The origins and rise of African American literary societies and libraries. *Harvard Library Review, 6*(2), 32–56.

Murray, H. (2002). *Come, bright improvement!: The literary societies of nineteenth-century Ontario.* Toronto, Canada: University of Toronto Press.

Pearlman, M. (1999). *What to read: The essential guide for reading group members and other book lovers* (2nd ed.). New York: HarperCollins.

Rehberg Sedo, D. (2003). Predications of life after Oprah: A glimpse at the power of book club readers. *Publishing Research Quarterly, 18*(3), 11–22.

Ruggles Gere, A. (1997). *Intimate practices: Literacy and cultural work in U.S. women's clubs, 1880–1920.* Chicago: University of Illinois Press.

Sicherman, B. (1989). Sense and sensibility: A case study of women's reading in late-Victorian America. In C. N. Davidson (Ed.), *Reading in America* (pp. 201–225). Baltimore: Johns Hopkins University Press.

Snape, R. (1995). *Leisure and the rise of the public library.* London: Library Association Publishing.

Stock, B. (1983). *The implications of literacy: Written language and models of interpretation in the eleventh and twelfth centuries.* Princeton, NJ: Princeton University Press.

BOOMTOWNS

Until the mid-1970s, the literature on rural industrialization generally drew on classic economic logic and emphasized the positive implications of economic and industrial development for local communities. After the 1973–1974 oil embargo, however, a series of massive energy development projects in sparsely populated regions brought extremely rapid growth to communities that came to be known as "energy boomtowns," several of which doubled in population within a period of three to four years. The rapid growth also led to a new focus on the potential drawbacks of such rapid growth. Particularly in the late 1970s, this literature tended to draw from classical sociologists such as Émile Durkheim and Ferdinand Tönnies, emphasizing the disruptive implications of rapid social change. Some of the literature was produced by human service providers whose primary focus was on helping communities and individuals cope with problems, rather than on carefully documenting those problems' occurrence.

This initial emphasis on boomtown disruptions led to reactions of its own, particularly in the influential 1982 critique by noted rural sociologist Kenneth Wilkinson and his colleagues, who questioned the validity of much of the work on this topic. Still, just as the literature on the boomtown disruption hypothesis had been too ready to accept assertions about negative consequences of rapid community growth, some literature appearing in the wake of Wilkinson's critique seemed to reflect an overreaction, with several studies apparently bent on proving that disruptive outcomes were entirely absent. From approximately the 1990s

The boomtown of Goldfield, Nevada, in 1902. The town grew rapidly after gold was discovered in the area and then declined after the mines played out.

Source: Bettmann/Corbis, used with permission.

onward, the literature has shown balance, in at least two ways.

First, closer examination has led to more nuanced understandings of the immediate boom experience. Although a sudden influx of new people into a previously stable community can indeed lead to a decline in a community's density of acquaintanceship (the proportion of people in the community who know one another), that social change was not found to lead to the kind of psychological disruption predicted by Durkheim and Tönnies. Instead, it appears to have affected mainly those social functions that depend on high levels of interpersonal acquaintanceship, such as control of deviance and socialization of the young. More broadly, researchers increasingly emphasized that rapid growth creates complex combinations of impacts—positive and negative—and that some groups adjust to disruptions far better than others.

Second, researchers have examined more than just the immediate boom period. This process may have begun when the rediscovery of a genuinely pre-boom data set in the 1980s showed that some of the most significant social impacts may have taken place during the pre-development phase, before large numbers of construction workers began moving into an area. Importantly, there has also been greater examination of longer-term impacts in the bust, or post-completion, phase. In economic terms, this research suggests that communities may find it difficult to return to pre-project conditions, not because of a failure to adapt to the boom, but because *overadaptation* leaves both individuals and institutions poorly prepared for the transition that occurs when resource-based industries begin to wane. In social terms, by contrast, longitudinal studies show that boom-period disruptions in social well-being, evidenced by such changes as increased fear of crime, declining levels of interpersonal trust, lower levels of social integration, and reduced community satisfaction, are followed by a rebound to essentially pre-boom conditions once the rapid growth phase has ended and more stable economic and demographic conditions prevail.

—William R. Freudenburg and Richard S. Krannich

Further Reading

Brown, R. B., Geertsen, H. R., & Krannich, R. S. (1989, Winter). Community satisfaction and social integration in a boomtown: A longitudinal analysis. *Rural Sociology, 54*(4), 568–586.

Cortese, C. F. (1982). The impacts of rapid growth on local organizations and community services. In B. A. Weber & R. E. Howell (Eds.), *Coping with rapid growth in rural communities* (pp. 115–135). Boulder, CO: Westview.

Finsterbusch, K. (1985, March). State of the art in social impact assessment. *Environment and Behavior, 17*(2), 193–221.

Freudenburg, W. R. (1986, July). The density of acquaintanceship: An overlooked variable in community research? *American Journal of Sociology, 92*(1), 27–63.

Gramling, R., & Freudenburg, W. R. (1992, Summer). Opportunity-threat, development, and adaptation: Toward a comprehensive framework for social impact assessment. *Rural Sociology, 57*(2), 216–234.

Hunter, L. M., Krannich, R. S., & Smith, M. D. (2002). Rural migration, Rapid growth and fear of crime. *Rural Sociology, 67*(1), 71–89.

Smith, M. D., Krannich, R. S., & Hunter, L. (2001). Growth, decline, stability and disruption: A longitudinal analysis of social well-being in four Western communities. *Rural Sociology, 66*(3), 425–450.

Summers, G. F., Evans, S. D., Clemente, F., Beck, E. M., & Minkoff, J. (1976). *Industrial invasion of nonmetropolitan America: A quarter century of experience.* New York: Praeger.

Wilkinson, K. P., Thompson, J. G., Reynolds, Jr., R.R., & Ostresh, L. M. (1982). Local social disruption and Western energy development: A critical review. *Pacific Sociological Review, 25,* 275–296.

BOOSTERISM

Boosterism refers to the efforts of individuals, business leaders, or fraternal groups to enhance a community's image and to promote its growth and development. The term can describe a booster club's efforts to raise funds to buy uniforms for the school band, or it can apply to public officials and developers who promise cleared land, highway improvements, and tax breaks to induce a corporation to locate a manufacturing plant in a particular community.

Boosterism has long been associated with the attitudes of American businessmen. After visiting the United States, the English novelist Charles Dickens (1812–1870), in *Martin Chuzzlewit* (1844), caricatured the booster as a sleazy promoter of worthless vacant lots. The American novelist Sinclair Lewis (1885–1951), in *Babbitt* (1922), saw the booster as a real estate agent whose pompous talk in praise of civic virtue masked hypocrisy and selfishness. Daniel Boorstin and other contemporary American historians, however, have written appreciatively of nineteenth-century businessmen who turned their Middle Western communities into thriving trading centers, and whose efforts in support of libraries, schools, hospitals, and parks created a vital urban culture.

TEMPLES AND HOLY RELICS

"Do you know how to play the fiddle?" the Athenian statesman Themistocles (c. 524–c. 460 BCE) was asked. "No," he said, "but I understand the art of raising a little village into a great city" (as cited in Boorstin 1995, p. 113). Ever since, boosters have been promising to do the same for their hometowns, though predicting and promoting development is a difficult task. In the Old Testament, it is the Lord who appears to make the great development decisions: Pious cities flourish; proud and profane cities are destroyed.

The origins of boosterism may date to the competitive Greek city-states such as Athens, which built magnificent temples not only to honor and propitiate the gods but also, in a boosterish sense, to glorify the city. Boosterism may also be seen at work in the medieval European town that promoted market fairs to stimulate trade or that boasted of possessing sacred relics to encourage the pilgrimages from which the town profited.

That a community might promote itself is an ancient idea, but that it should also encourage visitors to settle there is a modern notion that would have been bewildering to the majority of the world's people, who, throughout history, have lived in agricultural settlements. Because villagers resided in places where land and resources were often scarce, they feared having too many mouths to feed and were wary of strangers, settlers, and change. In contrast, the modern booster, an optimist who believed that there would always be enough food to go around, welcomed newcomers who could contribute to communal prosperity.

Boosterism in the Twenty-First Century

Once criticized and satirized, boosterism is now commonplace. The following text from the Grinnell, Iowa, Web site, is typical of Web sites for many towns and cities around the world.

> Welcome to Grinnell, a small, progressive city in Iowa's heartland! We take our living here seriously and we want you to know that you are welcome—whether for a short visit or for a lifetime. Quality of life is fantastic here—for raising a family, for obtaining higher education or for just plain living! There is opportunity here. Jobs are plentiful. Recreational and cultural opportunities abound for all age groups and abilities. There are interesting shops in our quaint downtown and there are many eating establishments—including several fine dining spots for those special times.
>
> —Gordon R. Canfield, Mayor

Source: City of Grinnell, Iowa, Web site. Retrieved January 3, 2003, from http://www.grinnelliowa.org.

AMERICAN BOOSTERISM

It is probably no accident that "booster" and the related term, "boomer" (as in boomtown) originated in the nineteenth-century United States, where land and resources were abundant and where the success of a community depended on how many people settled there. And because land (at least for white settlers) was neither sacred nor steeped in tradition, it could be bought, sold, and traded like any other commodity. Investors and land speculators were naturally on the lookout for those who promised to turn a village into a city.

The trick was to find a site worth boosting. Shortly after the Louisiana Purchase (1803), when the United States bought from France all the land from the Mississippi River to the Rocky Mountains, potential investors pored over maps of navigable rivers and the Great Lakes, trying to locate a waterfront settlement that might become the trading hub of this great agricultural hinterland. Cairo, Illinois, at the intersection of the Mississippi and Ohio Rivers, seemed a good bet, but after a promising start, this swampy village did not live up to expectations. Meanwhile, shrewd New York City investors put their money on a Lake Michigan outpost where in 1830, 50 people lived; thirty years later, 100,000 resided in what had become Chicago.

For the better part of the nineteenth century, U.S. towns competed to surpass one another in trade, industrial output, and population. To make that happen, local boosters—mostly a town's businessmen—sought to gain improved waterfront shipping facilities and, above all, good rail connections for their communities. Physician Daniel Drake (1785–1852), an early and exemplary booster, wrote *Picture of Cincinnati* (1815), touting the virtues of the Queen City while working for an improved transportation infrastructure. He also founded the city's first medical college. Similarly, William B. Ogden (1805–1877), a transplanted New York businessman, became Chicago's first mayor, built the city's first railroad (Chicago would become the nation's rail hub), designed a swing bridge over the Chicago River, and gave land for the Rush Medical College.

Even small towns with few assets promoted themselves as the next Chicago. "To 'boom' a town in Dakota," *The Century Magazine* (1882) reported, "is an art requiring a little money, a good deal of printer's ink and no end of push and cheek" (Mathews 1951, p. 162).

OTHER URBAN FRONTIERS

With their own vast frontiers, Canada, Australia, and Argentina would seem to have been ripe for boosterism. Indeed, wherever cities were highly competitive, they excelled at promoting themselves. David Hamer has suggested, however, that boosterism flourished in the United States as nowhere else because other frontier settlements were under more central government control than in the United States. Whereas American businessmen—natural promoters—moved into municipal leadership positions, businessmen in other parts of the world deferred to the leadership of well-born or well-educated civil servants who were not inclined to boosterism.

Boosterism was probably not a critical factor in determining whether a population settled in the city or countryside. The general economic conditions of a nation and the outlook of its settlers were far more important: Australia and Argentina—without much boosting—urbanized more rapidly than did the United States. Yet while boosterism may not have been the critical factor in determining overall rates of urbanization, the individual initiatives of businessmen-politicians who were instrumental in realizing such mega-projects as the Erie Canal (New York State) and Owens River Aqueduct (Los Angeles) were paramount in spurring the growth of specific cities and regions.

THE SUBURBAN AND GLOBAL TRANSFORMATION

During the 1920s, the sardonic economist Thorstein Veblen (1857–1929) and the critic H. L. Mencken (1880–1956), both Americans, joined Sinclair Lewis in depicting American boosterism as a narrow-minded, self-serving business culture centered on the local chamber of commerce and the Rotary and Kiwanis clubs.

"Old boy" boosterism now seems quaint. Today's boosters (women as well as men) focus not on the civic and commercial life downtown, but on the development of shopping malls and the building of research and office parks along suburban highways. American suburbs compete intensely for such development because it generates substantial tax revenues, which make it possible to keep local residential property taxes low. These suburbs often discourage much new housing, fearing that newcomers with children will require tax increases to pay for the construction of expensive new schools. "Come work and shop in our fine community," says the modern suburban booster, "but please look elsewhere for your housing."

Meanwhile, boosterism, once associated with small-town Middle America, has been embraced by the world. As tourism emerged as a major component of the global economy, cities moved to retain public relations and advertising firms to burnish their image and to promote their museums, opera houses, sports teams, and upscale shopping districts. From Athens to New York to Seoul, great cities now "boost themselves" to win the right to host the Olympic games and trade shows, and to become the headquarters for multinational corporations. As the medieval town once lured pilgrims to its fairs and holy shrines, so the city today promotes its attractions, seeking as always tourists and investors with deep pockets.

—James L. Wunsch

See also COMMUNITY ATTACHMENT

Further Reading

Abbott, C. (1981). *Boosters and businessmen: Popular economic thought and urban growth in antebellum Middle West.* Westport, CT: Greenwood.

Boorstin, D. (1965). *The Americans: The national experience.* New

York: Random House.
Hamer, D. A. (1990). *New towns in the new world: Images and perceptions of the nineteenth-century urban frontier.* New York: Columbia University Press.
Lewis, S. (1996). *Babbitt.* New York: Penguin . (Original work published 1922)
Mathews, M. M. (Ed.). (1951). *A Dictionary of Americanisms* (Vol. 1). Chicago: University of Chicago Press.
Weber, A. F. (1963) *The growth of cities in the nineteenth century: A study in statistics.* Ithaca, NY: Cornell University Press. (Original work published 1899)

BOUNDARIES

From a national point of view, boundaries are lines separating countries. But this conception is rather recent: It appeared at the end of the eighteenth century. It was a long process instituting such limits; the long straight line that runs along the forty-ninth parallel and marks the boundaries between the United States and Canada, for example, was not specified before 1925. Some boundaries—such as between India and China—continue to be problematic today. This new linear type of border claimed to erase all previous ones, whether cultural, linguistic, or economic. Obviously, this objective has never been achieved, and populations living near borders often remember being part of other polities and retain strong ties to kin across the border.

In Europe from the Middle Ages onwards, border areas were places with numerous and tangled feudal land divisions and with many different ethnic enclaves. Such areas were called in French *terres pesle-meslées* ("jumbled lands").

Border areas continue to be vibrant regions today. Languages are often the same on both sides of a national boundary, and people interact and marry without paying much attention to the cartographer's demarcation. In fact, peoples who straddle a boundary line are often syncretized; that is, they encompass characteristics of the cultures on either side of the boundary. In the European Union, these border regions enjoy an official recognition as a twenty-kilometer strip of land on either side of national boundaries.

Border zones are thus transition zones with unique, specific characters, resulting from a compromise between official documents and informal economic, social, and cultural local factors. But at the same time, each boundary splits its border zone into two distinct entities and represents a real divide between two types of spatial organization.

It would be wrong to limit the concept of boundaries to territorial demarcations between nations. Any institutional, economic, or social divide between distinct territories is also a boundary. According to the economist Edgar M. Hoover, any physical or legal obstacle that distorts economic and social exchanges can be called a boundary.

Nowadays, boundaries are of decreasing importance within regional organizations such as the European Union, the North Atlantic Free Trade Association (NAFTA), and the Association of Southeast Asian Nations (ASEAN). But it is highly unlikely that any region in the world will give up its centuries-old history: attitudes, behaviors, manners, suspicions, and memories of threatened interests remain. For that reason, border areas are more likely to lean toward becoming states—or at least autonomous regions—in their own right than to want to remain part of this or that polity that claims them. Further, the opening of a boundary sometimes has pernicious consequences for the border area—some regions are favored to the detriment of others.

Boundaries can also separate and distinguish different perceptions of time and space. The American western frontier and the Great Wall of China are two examples, one abstract and one concrete, of that sort of boundary. Their role is ambivalent and invasive; they are created to impose peace and order, but in fact they are immediately broken and become the basis of new conquests. This sort of boundary demarcation leads to the less powerful neighbor on the other side of the limit being stigmatized or ignored, a situation that then legitimates the seizure of its territory by the boundary creator. Any territory can become—at least partially—a pioneer front when its culture and organization is denied by a hostile national, intra-national, or supranational structure. All borders thus have the potential to advance relentlessly, even when they are physically marked.

—François Mancebo

Further Reading

Hoover, E. M. (1948). *The location of economic activity.* New York: McGraw Hill.
Mancebo, F. (1999). *La Cerdagne et ses frontières: Conflits et identités transfrontalières* [Cerdanya and its boundaries: Conflicts and cross-border identities]. Perpignan, France: Trabucaïre.
Mancebo, F. (2001, March). Discontinuités, lisières et territoires: Tentative de généralisation de la notion de frontière et de compréhension des dynamiques frontalières [Discontinuities, edges, and territories: Generalizing the notion of border and understanding border dynamics]. *Sud-Ouest Européen, 10,* 77–87. Toulouse, France: PUM.
McLean, I., & Butler, D. (1995). *Fixing the boundaries.* Dartmouth, NH: Aldershot.

Raffestin, C. (1992). Autour de la fonction sociale de la frontière [A discussion around the social function of the border]. *Espaces et Sociétés, 70–71,* 157–164.

Sahlins, P. (1986). *Between France and Spain: Boundaries of territory and identity in a Pyrenean valley, Cerdanya* (Vols. 1–2). Princeton, NJ: Princeton University Press.

BRUDERHOF

Bruderhof is the informal name of a radical Christian communitarian movement that has been known at different times as the Bruderhof Communities, Society of Brothers, and Hutterian Society of Brothers. One of the most vital communitarian societies active in modern times on several continents, the Bruderhof has in recent years also become one of the most controversial, as former members accuse it of cultlike practices.

ORIGIN OF THE BRUDERHOF MOVEMENT

The Bruderhof took form in Germany following World War I among those seeking to make sense of the bankrupt German political, religious, and social life following 1918. It formed around a dedicated couple, Eberhard Arnold (1883–1935) and his wife Emmy Arnold, née von Hollander (1884–1980). Arnold had originally studied theology, but he came to reject the state church system and was blocked from finishing his degree. He therefore switched to philosophy, receiving his doctoral degree with highest honors in 1910.

His military service in 1914 was brief because his health was poor; he had spent much of 1913–1914 in the South Tyrol to heal a case of tuberculosis. In 1915 the Arnolds moved to Berlin, where he became a leader in the Student Christian Movement, serving from 1916 to 1919 as editor of its journal. He became known as a prophetic and powerful leader, and many young adults flocked to hear him. They gathered in the Arnold home in Berlin for intense discussions on how to shape their future lives. In their disillusionment with traditional society, they were open to radical ideas, such as Christian Socialism.

THE SANNERZ COMMUNITY AND THE HUTTERIAN BRETHREN

In 1920, the Arnolds and several young colleagues decided to break with bourgeois society and make a new beginning. Leaving Berlin for the country (a reflection of the return-to-nature theme of the German youth movement), they founded a small intentional community in the small village of Sannerz, near Fulda. A crisis in 1922 over the economic basis of the community split the group, leaving Eberhard and Emmy Arnold with five others to begin again. This they did at a nearby farm, in what became the Rhönbruderhof. The major innovation was that the Arnolds and their followers now placed their communal movement squarely within the Anabaptist tradition.

A product of the Reformation tumult of the sixteenth century, the Anabaptists were radical dissenters who demanded a separation of church and state, complete religious liberty, and disciplined adherence to the demands of Christian discipleship. Because they rejected the age-old practice of infant baptism, contending that baptism was only for adults, they were called Anabaptists ("re-baptizers"). Some found a haven in Bohemia and Moravia, where under the pressure of refugee status they began communal ownership of property. They were called Hutterian Brethren after an early leader Jakob Hutter (d. 1536).

The Arnolds were convinced that communal life following Hutterian principles provided the only possible basis for Christian life with integrity. To their surprise, they learned that not all Anabaptists had been killed off as heretics in the sixteenth century; instead, many of their descendants had survived in western North America, both in the United States and Canada.

In 1930–1931, Arnold made an extended visit to the North American Hutterian Brethren. His goals were to unite the small movement he led with the much larger and older body of communitarians and to secure economic support from them for his struggling commune. He was successful in the first goal, but for the most part he failed in the second. For the Hutterites in North America, Arnold's visit was a surprising event. They found him a man of powerful intellect, deep learning, and passionate conviction, and after initial reluctance, they decided to ordain him as a Hutterian elder and to accept the Rhönbruderhof as a full-fledged Hutterite colony. When Arnold returned, he sought to conform the Rhönbruderhof to Hutterite ways by adopting their plain garb, with modest peasant dresses and headkerchiefs for the women, and dark clothes and mandatory beards for the men. The Bruderhof has largely maintained this discipline to the present.

THE NAZI ATTACK

Following the rise to power of the National Socialists (Nazis) in 1933, the Bruderhof in Germany faced a profound threat. As a communal, religious, international, and peace-loving movement, the Bruderhof stood for all that the Nazis hated. Arnold made the Bruderhof position clear in candid communications to top Nazi leadership. In the plebiscite of November 12, 1933, designed to confirm Nazi policies, Bruderhof members placed on their ballots labels that affirmed their discipleship to Jesus Christ.

Four days later, some 140 armed men from the Nazi security forces raided the Rhönbruderhof, seizing records and publications. Although local authorities protected them for a time (because of their appreciation for the Bruderhof's social programs), increasing restrictions on hosting guests and selling their publications and crafts soon throttled the economic basis of the community.

Just at this critical juncture in late 1935, Eberhard Arnold died, following an unsuccessful operation. In March 1934, facing Nazi-imposed teachers in their schools and compulsory military service for their young male members, the community set up emergency accommodations in neutral Liechtenstein. At the same time, they began to look for more secure shelter in Great Britain, which they found in the Cotswold area in 1936. On April 14, 1937, a final Gestapo raid drove the remaining members from the Rhönbruderhof; they found refuge as a group in the Netherlands.

THE BRUDERHOF IN GREAT BRITAIN AND PARAGUAY

Through the aid of Dutch Mennonites and British Quakers, Bruderhof members were able to reorganize their communal life again in Great Britain, at the Cotswold Bruderhof and a nearby farm, Oaksey. All went well until the outbreak of war in September 1939, when local opposition to the foreigners grew virulent. The British government, though otherwise supportive, informed the community in late summer 1940 that their German members would soon have to be interned as "enemy aliens."

In order to keep the community together, members decided to emigrate as a body to another country. They tried but failed to secure settlement in both Canada and the United States; the only country that would accept them was Paraguay. With the aid of the Mennonite Central Committee, they reached this refuge in late 1940 and early 1941, despite the great danger of ocean crossings in wartime. Under great privations, they established three settlements (together called Primavera) in the Paraguayan interior, enduring severe hardship and some loss of life, particularly among the children.

The Bruderhof managed to survive its very difficult resettlement in Paraguay, but by 1961 fell prey to a huge internal crisis over the direction of the movement. Although a complex situation, the crisis involved division between those of more humanistic and communal orientation (largely British) and those of religious and Hutterian orientation (largely German and North American). The leadership role of the Arnold family was also a central issue. A son of Eberhard Arnold, Johann Heinrich (Heini) Arnold (1913–1982) took decisive leadership, aided by a number of members from the United States who had recently joined. The struggle led to the mass expulsion or voluntary departure of 600 persons (those opposed to Arnold's leadership), one-third of the membership, some of whom were stranded in South America with very few resources. Although many of the expelled members were later reinstated and leaders of the continuing Arnold-led community eventually apologized for mistakes made at this time, this trauma left many long-lasting wounds.

RELOCATION IN NORTH AMERICA

In part to overcome the damage caused by the Paraguay crisis, in part to find a location more accessible to new members and increased support, Bruderhof leadership decided in 1960–1961 to concentrate their work in the United States. By 1954, they had already created a colony called Woodcrest, at Rifton, New York. In addition to closing the three Paraguayan communities, they also brought their British members to the United States. A few members had been left there in 1940 to close down the two colonies, but they remained when negotiations dragged on and permission to emigrate was delayed. In the meantime, a number of new British members joined to form the Wheathill community in Shropshire (1941–1961) and the Bulstrode community near London (1958–1966). Eventually these communities in England were also terminated, but others were later initiated there.

Soon other communities were founded in the United States. Besides Woodcrest, which retained central administration, these included New Meadow Run (originally called Oak Lake), near Farmington, Pennsylvania (founded in 1957); Deer Spring (originally called Evergreen), in Norfolk, Connecticut (1958–1998); Maple Ridge (originally called Pleasant View), in Ulster Park, New York (founded in 1985); Spring Valley, next to

New Meadow Run (founded in 1989); Catskill, in Elka Park, New York (founded in 1990); Fox Hill, in Walden, New York (founded in 2001); and Bellvale, in Chester, New York (founded in 2002).

Two new colonies were formed in Britain: Darvell, at Robertsbridge in Sussex (founded in 1971), and Beech Grove, at Nonington in Kent (founded in 1995). Although it proved impossible to recover the original colony in Germany, attempts were made to reintroduce communities on the Hohenstein, near Nürnberg (1955), the Sinntalbruderhof, near Bad Brückenau (1955–1961), and the most recent, Michaelshof, at Birnbach in the Westerwald (1988–95).

As membership continued to grow in the late 1990s, three large tracts of land were purchased in Australia, all in New South Wales, to form the basis of the Danthonia Bruderhof in Inverell, New South Wales (founded 1999). Personnel and funds were committed in 1992 and thereafter to assist a group of Nigerians in creating the Palmgrove (Palm Grove) Bruderhof in Africa, but this failed amidst acrimony (including litigation) in 1994.

LIFESTYLE

Following the Hutterite pattern, Bruderhof members are encouraged to marry and bear many children. Families are assigned their own apartments and take breakfasts and some other meals there. All adults dine communally at noon and in the evening, with women preparing the food and men doing the serving and cleaning up. Children are cared for communally from an early age, freeing both parents for assigned tasks in the colonies. When infants are born, the mother and father are given as much as six weeks to bond with the baby; if there are other children in the family, they are readily cared for in the community. Even after infants begin receiving community care, mothers are freed from their assigned jobs as needed during the day to nurse and tend to them.

Bruderhof communities emphasize education, and their children are well cared for in the colony schools from nursery age through middle school. Those of high school age attend local public schools, where their distinctive dress draws attention at first. Bruderhof teenagers usually excel in their studies. The community also sponsors many young people who wish to attend college. Another area emphasized is music, with choirs and instrumental groups both active and appreciated in the community. In general, music plays an essential role in the maintenance of community morale, with special concerts and events held often. Youth choirs often travel to give public concerts, presenting well-received programs of religious and folk music. The Plough Press publishes attractive songbooks and record albums.

RELIGIOUS FOUNDATION

Potential converts to the Bruderhof are expected to live in the community for an extended period as novices, as a time of testing for both sides to see whether full membership is appropriate and desired. Leaders make very clear to converts that to be a member is a very serious lifetime commitment; members place themselves under the discipline of the community and its designated leaders, and they are expected to submit their will and desires to those of the body.

Discipleship to Jesus Christ is the core of the faith commitment of Bruderhof members and is symbolized by baptism by immersion. Those later found to have failed to live up to this baptismal covenant are "set back" from the community for a time (i.e., barred from certain meetings). More serious offenses can be punished by expulsion. One principle held firmly from the beginning is that any differences between members must be resolved immediately. Members explain that this expectation can make community life demanding, as it is not possible simply to avoid or ignore someone found difficult or offensive.

ECONOMIC FOUNDATION

The material foundation of the Bruderhof has shifted over the years with changing circumstances. In Germany, members attempted farming with mixed success. Publishing, woodworking, and the schooling of children brought in more funds, but it usually proved difficult to raise sufficient income. Contributions by outside donors and means contributed by new members were crucial for survival. In South America, farming and ranch life, though difficult for members more accustomed to desk work, provided basic support. It was only in North America that income began to be more than adequate. Production of well-crafted and sturdy children's toys (Community Playthings) became very profitable, with large sales to public schools and Head Start programs. Later the Bruderhof branched out into the creation of equipment for the physically challenged, especially children (Rifton Equipment for people with disabilities). The Plough Publishing House developed an aggressive publishing program, although the Bruderhof considers this activity to be more of an outreach witness than a money-making venture. A recent venture creates and sells signage. The *Wall Street Journal* reported gross revenues for the American communities of $20 million for 1995, with a profit of $9 million; when living costs were deducted, the net gain approximated $2 million.

COMMUNITY OUTREACH

For many decades the Bruderhof sought to attract new members by inviting those interested to visit and live in the communities, but otherwise lived in substantial isolation. This policy changed in the early 1980s. Members became active in local community affairs and in peace demonstrations, and gave special attention to prison visitation and advocacy for those considered to be unjustly imprisoned. Members went on delegations to many other nations to visit movements they deemed progressive.

CONTROVERSIES

Although the visit by Eberhard Arnold to North America in the early 1930s led to a union of the Bruderhof with the older Hutterian Brethren, the relationship was marked from the start by tension and stress, and it continues to be difficult. The Bruderhof was disappointed that the wealthy American and Canadian colonies were laggard in sending it aid. When Hutterian elders visited Germany in the mid-1930s, they found that the conduct of Bruderhof members was not completely consistent with their own. This was also the finding in 1950, when Hutterite leaders visited Paraguay and charged the colonists there with worldliness. For their part, the Bruderhof criticized the Hutterians for loss of their original missionary zeal.

During the time of the great schism in Paraguay in the late 1950s, the Bruderhof broke with the Hutterian Brethren. One precipitant was Bruderhof recruitment into their ranks of some Hutterians from the Forest River colony in North Dakota. In 1974, under the leadership of Heini Arnold, the rupture with the Hutterians was healed. However, in the early 1990s when the Bruderhof colonies in the eastern United States sided with a leading Hutterite elder who was caught up in a great intercolony dispute, other Hutterite elders heavily criticized the Bruderhof, admonishing them for (among other things) their involvement in controversial political issues and for their mission efforts. In 1995 Johann Christoph Arnold, the Bruderhof leader after 1983 and grandson of Eberhard, published an open letter harshly critical of the western Hutterian colonies and their leadership; this made the rupture final.

Former members of the Bruderhof have also been critical of the communities. Ramon Sender, a member for a time in the late 1950s, organized a group of former members in 1989 as critics of the Bruderhof. After leaving the community, Sender's contact with his wife and daughter (who remained members) had been severely limited, to the extent that Sender was not notified when his daughter died of cancer. Sender's group of former members and families of members offer one another mutual support, seek greater contact with family members, and work to expose alleged Bruderhof misconduct. Their Peregrine Foundation funds a newsletter called *KIT* (Keep In Touch), which in 1995 was mailed to nearly 1,000 recipients. It provides an open forum for anyone aggrieved by Bruderhof experiences or policies. The foundation has also published a number of books, which contain withering criticism of the Bruderhof. Accusations of child abuse, including sexual abuse and mental and physical coercion, abound.

Although some attempts have been made by concerned third parties to reconcile the wide differences between the KIT group and the Bruderhof, nothing satisfactory has been accomplished. The KIT side has been aggressive in publicly attacking the Bruderhof as a dictatorial cult in the mass media and on the Internet; for their part, the Bruderhof has taken legal action (and evidently permitted harassing actions by some younger members) to try to silence this opposition. It seems unlikely that the two sides will soon reach resolution of this bitter dispute.

OUTLOOK

Despite recurrent crises over its eighty-plus years of existence, the Bruderhof movementit remains a vigorous entity, attractive to many highly educated professionals as well as to its own offspring. It continues to be active in its outreach witness extending worldwide. The community publishes well-received books, many by the current elder, Johann Christoph Arnold, on religious topics of interest to many. More than 2,500 men, women, and children in ten communities on three continents remain dedicated to their demanding commitment, living communally to pursue a variety of ministries.

—Donald F. Durnbaugh

Further Reading

Arnold, Eberhard. (1995). *Why we live in community* (Rev. ed.). Farmington, PA: Plough Publishing House.

Arnold, E., & Arnold E. (1974). *Seeking for the kingdom of God: Origins of the Bruderhof communities.* Rifton, NY: Plough Publishing House.

Arnold, Emmy. (1971). *Torches together: The beginning and early years of the Bruderhof communities.* Rifton, NY: Plough Publishing House.

Baum, M. (1998). *Against the wind: Eberhard Arnold and the Bruderhof.* Farmington, PA: Plough Publishing House.

Durnbaugh, D. F. (1991). Relocation of the German Bruderhof to England, South America, and North America. *Communal Societies, 11,* 62–77.

Hutterian Brethren. (Ed.). (1988). *Brothers unite: An account of the uniting of Eberhard Arnold and the Rhoen Bruderhof with the Hutterian church.* Ulster Park, NY: Plough Publishing House.

Mow, M. (1989). *Torches rekindled: The Bruderhof's struggle for renewal.* Rifton, NY: Plough Publishing House.

Oved, Y. (1996). *The witness of the brothers: A history of the Bruderhof.* New Brunswick, NJ: Transaction Publishers.

Peters, J. (1996). New Meadow Run: A Christian witness for the 21st century. In B. Metcalf (Ed.), *Shared visions, shared lives: Communal living around the globe* (pp. 177–186). Forres, UK: Findhorn Press.

Rubin, J. M. (2000). *The other side of joy: Religious melancholy among the Bruderhof.* New York: Oxford University Press.

Zablocki, B. (1980). *The joyful community: An account of the Bruderhof, a communal movement now in its third generation.* Chicago: University of Chicago Press. (Original work published 1971)

BUDDHISM

The Buddhist ideal of *sangha* ("community" in Sanskrit) is a cohesive group in harmony or in union with virtue. Usually the term *sangha* is used to refer to a community of Buddhist monks or nuns rather than to a community of lay Buddhists**.** The basic expectation of the members of a *sangha* is that they respect the law of cause and effect, or karma (a Sanskrit term for actions and, by implication, their inevitable consequences.) Although causal relationships are not easy to establish, many ancient Indian Buddhist masters, including Nagarjuna (flourished c. 150–250 CE) and Dharmakirti (flourished seventh century CE), cogently argued that the infallibility of karmic law could indeed be ascertained by relying upon *pratyaksapramana* (direct valid cognition) and *anumanapramana* (inferential valid cognition). Since nonvirtuous intents and acts will invariably bring about suffering, *sangha* members are admonished to abandon ten major nonvirtuous acts. Three pertain to the body: killing, stealing, and sexual misconduct. Four pertain to speech: divisive speech, lying, harsh speech, and senseless talk. Finally, three pertain to the mind: covetousness, harmful intent, and wrong view. The *sangha* is further encouraged to engage diligently in the practice of the virtues of generosity, discipline, patience, perseverance, meditation, and development of wisdom. The practice of these six virtues is considered to be the source of true happiness.

As mentioned earlier, the more traditional and rigorous definition of *sangha* extends only to ordained monks and nuns, thus excluding lay believers. Nonetheless, the authentic *sangha* in its most refined meaning refers to those who have realized *dharmata* (the true nature of all phenomena) through their direct experience. They are known as the *arya sangha,* the holy, sublime, spiritual community.

Alternatively, the Buddhist community can be conceptualized in accordance with the teachings of Gampopa (1079–1154), a prominent Tibetan Buddhist master of his time. In his taxonomy, the ordinary *sangha* includes those who strive for a favorable condition of rebirth in either the human realm or one of the godly realms. However, when their karmic merit for such a favorable rebirth is exhausted, they are bound for lower rebirths again. In this endless cycle of rebirths, which is known as samsara, one cannot hope to find lasting happiness, because everything is impermanent. In fact, Buddhists argue that, with enhanced perspicacity achieved through meditation (and not philosophical pessimism), one will discern the nature of samsara as one of pervasive suffering.

All Buddhists would say that those who renounce samsara and its temporary seeming pleasures are wiser than those who merely look for a comfortable rebirth. Those Buddhists who, due to their intense urge to renounce samsara, seek liberation from samsara for themselves only, are seen by those who aspire to liberate all sentient beings as less spiritually advanced than they themselves are. The latter group calls the former the *Hinayana sangha* ("community of the Small Vehicle"), because their vehicle to liberation is only large enough to accommodate themselves, and they refer to themselves as the *Mahayana sangha* ("community of the Greater Vehicle"). Surviving Buddhist traditions of the former type reject the term *Hinayana* and call their tradition *Theravada* ("the way of the elders"). However, according to what Buddha himself stated (in the Lotus Sutra and in many other instances), the Hinayana sangha will give rise to Bodhicitta—aspiring to

Punishment for Damaging the Sangha

As is evident from this extract, the importance of the sangha (community) to Buddhists is indicated by the severe punishment that awaits those who disrupt it.

> Hell is believed to have been divided into a number of classes. Those who commit the most heinous crimes, which according to the Buddhist concept consist of an intentional murder of one's own parents or an *arhat* (the enlightened one), of causing even a bruise on the body of the Buddha, and of instigating a split in a *Sangha* congregation (the Buddhist Order), will be punished in the deepest part of the underworld. This part is traditionally known to be "so deep that a new *batr* (a monk's food bowl, made of steel) would be rusted away long before reaching its very bottom." Criminals are to be punished for the longest time. They may be reborn as a human being, but they would not be able to rise into a deific class or become enlightened.

Source: Kingkeo Attagara. (1968). *The Folk Religion of Ban Nai, a Hamlet in Central Thailand.* Ann Arbor, MI: University Microfilms, p. 36.

achieve enlightenment for the sake of all sentient beings. Ultimately, then, the Hinayana sangha are not different from the Mahayana sangha.

Tibetan Buddhists see their own tradition as higher still; they term their community the *Vajrayana sangha* ("community of the Adamantine Vehicle"), and believe it to have the highest caliber of all because they not only seek to liberate all sentient beings from samsara but promise to do so comparatively quickly.

In the final analysis, all schools of Buddhism accept that all sentient beings, and not just humankind, are endowed with Buddha nature, irrespective of their religious orientation. One will not stop striving for eternal peace or happiness until it is realized. In that sense, all sentient beings are by definition members of the Buddhist community.

—Joseph Cheng and Kin Lau

Further Reading

Choedak, P. N. (1997). *The triple tantra.* Canberra, Australia: Gorum Publications.

Gyatso, T., & Hopkins, J. (1989). *Kalachakra Tantra: Rite of initiation.* London: Wisdom Publications.

Khyentse, D. (1988). *The wish-fulfilling jewel.* Delhi, India: Shechen & Shambhala.

Rinpoche, K. (1987). *The gem ornament of manifold oral instructions.* Ithaca, NY: Snow Lion Publications.

Rinpoche, T. (1988). *Buddha nature.* Kathmandu, Nepal: Rangjung Yeshe Publications.

BURGESS, ERNEST WATSON (1909–1972)

Leading U.S. sociologist of the Chicago School

Born in Ontario, Canada, Ernest Watson Burgess received his B.A. from Kingfisher College in Oklahoma in 1908 and his Ph.D. from the University of Chicago in 1913. He taught at the University of Toledo (Ohio), the University of Kansas, and Ohio State before starting a long career at the University of Chicago, where he worked from 1916 in the first department of sociology in the United States. Burgess became a professor emeritus in 1951 and continued his association with the department until his death.

In his first years at the University of Chicago, Burgess worked closely with the sociologist Robert Park. Together they edited the first major textbook of sociology, *Introduction to the Science of Sociology* (1921), as well as the pioneer text of urban sociology, *The City* (1925). In his essay "The Growth of the City," Burgess designed the famous concentric map illustrating the expansion of city space and the incorporation of ethnic communities into urban life. According to Burgess, any town or city expands radially from its business district. What triggers expansion and urban growth is the tendency of each inner zone to extend its area by invading the next outer zone. Like other works by members of the Chicago School, Burgess's conceptualization of urban communities exhibits a dynamic tension between a biological and a cultural standpoint. On the one hand, Burgess finds that the city and its communities produce several cultural manifestations. On the other hand, he claims that immigrant communities become urbanized through processes of "*urban metabolism* and mobility which are closely related to expansion" (Burgess 1925, p. 47). In this respect he is viewing the city as a physical organism whose internal laws can be explained through science and biology. Urban growth is a result "of organization and disorganization analogous to the *anabolic* and *katabolic* processes of *metabolism* in the body" (Burgess 1925, p. 53). In this process, immigrants are digested by the city, which disorganizes their communities only to create a greater urban one. Through several purgatorial stages, Burgess, like a twentieth-century Dante, moves his characters from the slum up into the area of second immigrant settlement and beyond. It is the characteristically American tale of social mobility, through which the immigrant progressively loses his or her ethnic peculiarities and becomes more cosmopolitan and thus Americanized. Yet there are passages in the essay that introduce an element of perpetual instability into Burgess's vision, as the immigrant is constantly looking to urban areas beyond the one in which he or she is living at present.

Later in his career, Burgess focused his research on other types of communities: the institution of the family and the elderly. In particular, he tried to elaborate a model to investigate marriage stability, which, he hypothesized, is reached when a steady synthesis of attitudes and social characteristics of husband and wife occurs. From his research, Burgess developed a chart to assess the possible failure or success of a marriage. His work on the elderly is concerned with the effects of retirement and the efficacy of government programs.

—Luca Prono

Further Reading

Abbott, A. (1999). *Department and discipline: Chicago sociology at one hundred.* Chicago: The University of Chicago Press.

Bulmer, M. (1986). *The Chicago School of sociology: Institutionalization, diversity, and the rise of sociological research.* Chicago: The University of Chicago Press.

Burgess, E. W. (1925). The growth of the city: An introduction to a research project. In R. E. Park, E. W. Burgess, & R. D. McKenzie (Eds.), *The city* (pp. 47–62). Chicago: The University of Chicago Press (Reprinted from *Publications of the American Sociological Society, 18,* 85–97)

Cappetti, C. (1993). *Writing Chicago: Modernism, ethnography and the novel.* New York: Columbia University Press.

BURNING MAN

Burning Man, founded by the artist and landscaper Larry Harvey (b. 1948), is an annual event held for a week culminating in Labor Day. It brings together participants through art, celebration, gifts, and the creation of community. The Burning Man Web site (www.burningman.com) describes the project as "an experiment in temporary community, and one that is radically all-inclusive."

The first Burning Man was a small bohemian gathering in 1986 on Baker Beach in San Francisco, California. Harvey and his friend Jerry James constructed an eight-foot wooden figure to burn at the beach. Accounts of the event note that, once lit, the crowd doubled and instantly created community. Since its spontaneous inception, Burning Man has grown from 20 participants to over 25,000 in 2001. In 1990, the venue changed to Black Rock Desert in Nevada. Each year, participants and project staff create a temporary city, called Black Rock City, in the desert, with infrastructure, newspapers, radio stations, and camps for the week-long event.

Burning Man community is created by and for participants (called Burners) who share a commitment to free art and expression, participation, and a spirit of giving. In a speech at the 1998 Burning Man, Harvey stated, "We've given all of you a chance to live like artists out here . . . that means you can give everything away and live on the edge of survival" (Harvey 1998). Burners come from various backgrounds and geographical regions, and membership in the community is open to anyone who can purchase a ticket and attend the event. The price of tickets (between $165 and $225 for the 2003 event) and additional costs (for food, artistic materials, and so on) of attending are potential limitations to membership. Within the larger community dedicated to free expression, participants represent a diverse group of interests and communities. They include performance artists, musicians, nudists, fire dancers, hedonists, and activists. Many Burners create elaborate costumes or new personas for the event. Media reports often describe Burning Man as an amalgam of various facets of counterculture coming together for wild celebration in the desert. While the association with counterculture is accurate, Harvey and other members of the Burning Man organization stress the importance of artistic expression, involvement, and giving as key to the creation of the Burning Man community.

Art is an essential element of community in Black Rock City. Planned and spontaneous art installations and performances occur throughout the city. At the center of the city stands the man, an enormous wooden figure ranging from forty to seventy feet. The climax of the week comes when participants gather for "the Burn," a metaphorical purification in which the wooden man is set on fire, followed by a wild citywide celebration including fire dancing performances, drumming, and burning of various art installations.

Participants are admonished to bring enough food, water, and supplies to last a week in the desert, remove everything brought in upon leaving (including trash), and observe rules of safety and well-being. Although the gradual increase in rules in Black Rock City is unpopular with some members of the community, the Burning Man organization maintains that those few rules (for example, concerning fire safety) are necessary and enhance the community. One of the few protocols guiding Burners is the no-spectator rule, which encourages participation in the community. Rather than just watching the festival, participants are expected to get involved in the creation and maintenance of community through art, free expression, volunteerism, and interaction.

The Burning Man community is sustained through a gift economy that prohibits vending, advertising, and consumerism: It depends on free gifts to the community, often with no intended recipient or expectation of reciprocity. Gifts come in many forms. Theme camps, which double as living and public spaces, are created by groups of participants and present art, performances, music, food and drink, shade from the sun, and activities at which everyone is welcome. Additionally, volunteers maintain the city's infrastructure; the Lamplighters, for example, install over a thousand oil lamps every evening. The gift economy is also manifest in individual acts, as participants are encouraged to bring small gifts to give to those they meet. Though cash and bartering are not completely absent, the gift economy differentiates Burning Man from other festivals that rely on vending. Harvey emphasizes the gift economy as essential to the creation of community at Burning Man.

Though the event lasts a week, the sense of community does not end with the deconstruction of Black Rock City. Harvey urges participants to incorporate the tenets of creative free expression and giving in their lives outside of Black Rock City. Many Burners stay connected with the community throughout the year via the Internet, newsletters, local organizations, regional events, and planning for the next year's Burning Man.

—Danielle Endres

Further Reading

Burning Man Organization. (2002). Retrieved January 21, 2003, from http://www.burningman.com

Doherty, B. (2000). Burning Man grows up: Can the nation's premier underground event survive its success? *Reason, 31*(9), 1–14.

Harvey, L. (1998). *Larry Harvey's 1998 Speech.* Retrieved January 21, 2003, from http://burningman.com/whatisburningman/1998/98_speech_1.html.

Harvey, L. (2002). *Viva las Xmas.* Retrieved January 21, 2003, from http://www.burningman.com/pdf/speeches/2002_Cooper_Union.pdf.

Kozinets, R. V. (2000). Can consumers escape the market? Emancipatory illuminations from Burning Man. *Journal of Consumer Research, 29*(1), 20–38.

Pike, S. M. (2001). Desert gods, apocalyptic art, and the making of sacred space at the Burning Man festival. In K. McCarthy & E. Mazur (Eds.), *God in the details: American religion in everyday life* (pp. 155–176). New York: Routledge.

Plunkett, J., & Wieners, B. (Eds.). (1997). *Burning Man.* San Francisco: Wired Books.

Raised Barn Press. (2002). *Drama in the desert: The sights and sounds of Burning Man.* San Francisco: Author.

CALVIN, JOHN (1509–1564)

Protestant theologian

The French Protestant reformer and humanist John Calvin (in Latin, Johannes Calvinus) developed the notion of holy community, a godly Christian society, which still exercises much influence on Protestant evangelical movements who strive to ground all spheres of life on God's word. For Calvin, the common goal of the Christian social organism, the glory of God, should be placed before the individual's interests. In this context there is a close affinity between Calvin and contemporary communitarianism, which stresses the social nature of individual rights and obligations.

LIFE AND WORKS

Calvin was born in Noyon, Picardy, in France. He studied arts in Paris from 1521 to 1526; there he was introduced to humanistic scholarship and appeals to reform the church. On his father's insistence, he transferred into the University of Orléans in 1528 to study civil law. At the University of Orléans he became more familiar with the ideas of Humanism and of the Protestant reformer Martin Luther (1483–1546). Upon the death of his father in 1531, Calvin went back to Paris and returned to his first love—classics and theology.

A Renaissance portrait of John Calvin, French reformer and founder of Calvinism.

Source: Archivo Iconografico, S.A./Corbis; used with permission.

Forced to flee France in 1535 because of his support for the ideas of the Protestant Reformation, he went to Basel, Switzerland, where he composed the *Institutes of the Christian Religion* (1536), in which he set down his reformed belief and defended the cause of the persecuted French Protestants, or Huguenots. The book provided a massive account of Protestant doctrine and soon became the most important theological text of the Protestant Reformation. It was the Reformation's only genuine systematic theology and for that reason exerted extraordinary influence on future generations of theologians.

In 1536, while passing through the city of Geneva,

Selections From the *Ecclesiastical Ordinances*, by John Calvin (1541)

First there are four orders of offices instituted by our Saviour for the government of his Church: namely, the pastors, then the doctors, next the elders nominated and appointed by the government, and fourthly the deacons. If we wish to see the Church well-ordered and maintained we ought to observe this form of government.

The duty of pastors

Pastors are sometimes named in the Bible as overseers, elders and ministers. Their work is to proclaim the Word of God, to teach, admonish, exhort and reprove publicly and privately, to administer the sacraments and, with the elders or their deputies, to issue fraternal warnings.

[. . .]

There follows the second order which we have called the doctors

The special duty of the doctors is to instruct the faithful in sound doctrine so that the purity of the gospel is not corrupted by ignorance or wrong opinion.

As things stand at present, every agent assisting in the upholding of God's teaching is included so that the Church is not in difficulties from a lack of pastors and ministers. This is in common parlance the order of school teachers. The degree nearest the minister and closely joined to the government of the Church is the lecturer in theology.

[. . .]

Here follows the third order, or elders

Their duty is to supervise every person's conduct. In friendly fashion they should warn backsliders and those of disorderly life. After that, where necessary, they should report to the Company [of pastors] who will arrange for fraternal correction...

As our Church is now arranged, it would be most suitable to have two elected from the "council of 24," four from the "council of 60" and six from the "council of 200." They should be men of good repute and conduct...They should be chosen from each quarter of the city so that they can keep an eye on the whole of it.

[. . .]

The fourth order of ecclesiastical government, namely, the deacons

There have always been two kinds of these in the early Church. One has to receive, distribute and care for the goods of the poor (i.e. daily alms as well as possessions, rents and pensions); the other has to tend and look after the sick and administer the allowances to the poor as is customary. In order to avoid confusion, since we have officials and hospital staff, one of the four officials of the said hospital should be responsible for the whole of its property and revenues and he should have an adequate salary in order to do his work properly.

Source: Bergier, J. F, & Kingdon, R. M. (1983). *John Calvin* (G. R. Potter & M. Greengrass, Trans.). London: Edward Arnold, p. 71. (Originally published 1962–1964)

Calvin was persuaded by the minister Guillaume Farel (1489–1565) to assist in organizing the reformation in that city. Strong opposition from civil authorities led to his departure in 1538. He went to Strasbourg, staying there for three years, continuously revising his *Institutes*.

In 1541, Calvin was invited back to Geneva and during the next years devoted himself to establishing a theocratic regime there. The city adopted his ecclesiastical ordinances, which dealt with the form of church government, and accepted his view that ecclesiastical discipline should be placed in the hand of a consistory. This church-run moral and religious judiciary, a type of morals court with the power to impose spiritual penalties, was established in order to control the behavior of the entire population and to see that everyone accepted the Reformed doctrine and behaved in a godly, Christian way. By these means and others, Calvin transformed Geneva into Protestant Rome. In 1559, with the founding of the Genevan Academy for the education of theologians, the city became the center of international Protestantism.

HOLY COMMUNITY

According to Calvin, life should be based on total obedience to God, whose moral order is declared in the scriptures. A well-ordered Christian community results from a synthesis of rule, cooperation, and order emanating from the divine laws of God, and it should be unified, organized, and structured in order to advance the glory of God in the world. Accepting the views of classical writers, especially Aristotle and Seneca, Calvin argued that human beings are social animals by nature, hence community is essential to human life. Calvin thought that human beings were under two kinds of government: spiritual, by which piety is formed, and political, by which they are instructed in the duties of humanities and civility. A well-ordered community is based on the concept of calling, or vocation, the notion that God calls people to serve him in their own appointed place and sphere of activity in the world. By God's own will, then, human beings are not equal; each has a calling and vocation, some lowly and some high.

A holy community is a godly society in which the secular and ecclesiastical authority's main responsibility is to glorify God by obeying and realizing his word. Church and state are but two means for ordering godly society; the magistrate ought to punish in order to clean the church of offenses, and the minister should help the magistrate in combating sin. Civil government should cherish and protect the worship of God and defend sound doctrines of piety, while the church should adjust members' lives in light of society, shape their social behavior to civil righteousness, reconcile them one with another, and promote general peace and tranquility. Calvin thus put community squarely under the sovereignty of God, believing the state should order all functions of life, from hunting heretics to closing taverns.

For Calvin, the common good of the Christian social body, the *corpus christianum,* should be placed before selfish interests. The glorification of God in action, in the world, is the community's goal. In contrast to Luther, Calvin was not interested in passively enduring and tolerating the world, but in transforming it according to the divine will and word.

CALVIN AND CONTEMPORARY COMMUNITARIANISM

While liberalism and libertarianism are committed to individualism, stressing individual self-sufficiency, for Calvin, God is the ultimate source of all rights and obligations. Yet, given that, God has ordered human existence socially so that divine rights and obligations are mediated by social institutions, and the individual's sphere is defined and shaped by the larger community in which he or she lives. Hence, Calvin anticipated contemporary communitarians, for whom individual rights and obligations derived from the social and political institutions to which individuals belong.

—Avihu Zakai

Further Reading

Battles, F. L. (1996). *Interpreting Calvin.* Grand Rapids, MI: Baker Books.

Bouwsma, W. J. (1988). *John Calvin: A sixteenth-century portrait.* New York: Oxford University Press.

Graham, W. F. (1952). *The constructive revolutionary: John Calvin and his socio-economic impact.* Richmond, VA: John Knox Press.

Höpel, H. (1982). *The Christian polity of John Calvin.* Cambridge, UK: Cambridge University Press.

McGrath, A. E. (1990). *A life of John Calvin: A study in the shaping of Western culture.* Oxford, UK: Basil Blackwell.

McNeill, J. T. (1962). *The history and character of Calvinism.* New York: Oxford University Press.

Monter, E. W. (1967). *Calvin's Geneva.* New York: John Wiley.

Muller, R. A. (2000). *The unaccommodated Calvin: Studies in the foundation of a theological tradition.* Oxford, UK: Oxford University Press.

Prestwich, M. (Ed.). (1986). *International Calvinism, 1541–1715.* Oxford, UK: Oxford University Press.

Simhoni, A., & Weinstein, D. (Eds.). (2001). *The new liberalism: Reconciling liberty and community.* Cambridge, UK: Cambridge University Press.

Stevenson, W. R. (1999). *Sovereign grace: The place and significance of Christian freedom in John Calvin's political thought.* New York: Oxford University Press.

Troeltsch, E. (1960). *The social teaching of the Christian churches* (Vols. 1–2). New York: Harper & Row. (Original work published 1911)

CASTE

The term *caste* is derived from *casta,* a word used by the Portuguese to describe the Hindu religious system. The caste system categorizes people into various hierarchical levels, which determine and define their social, religious, and hegemonic standings within the society. The caste system has also maintained a nexus and a sense of community for caste members for more than 2,000 years. A classic example of the caste system is the one found in India, which has existed there for hundreds of years.

ORIGIN AND DESCRIPTION OF THE CASTE SYSTEM IN INDIA

Hinduism has been aptly described as a way of life rather than a set of religious dogma and principles. Accordingly, there is a great deal of variation in the religious practices. Citations and references about caste in India go back to the ancient scriptures—such as the Veda, Purana, and Upanishad texts and the works of legal or religious scholars like Manu—but the caste system has evolved and changed significantly over the years, and the system often varies significantly from one region to another in India. Thus it would not be hard to discover exceptions to most of the descriptions and statements of the caste system in the literature, because of the disagreements between

An Untouchable woman cooks dinner in a hut in Chennai (Madras), India, while children look on.
Source: Bradley Smith/Corbis; used with permission.

the scriptures, regional variations, vagueness of the system, changes over time, and the divergent practices of different castes.

The traditional Hindu caste system consists of both the *varna* system, which categorizes the Hindus into four major divisions, and hundreds of subdivisions called *jatis.* The *jatis* themselves are divided into several subcategories, or local castes. The terms *jati* and *caste* are used here synonymously. Over the years, the number of subcastes has tended to grow with the division of labor.

There are four major *varnas* in Hinduism: Brahman, Kshatriya, Vaisya, and Sudra. The Brahmans are typically the priestly class, the Kshatriyas are the warriors, Vaisyas are the merchants and traders, and the Sudras are the laborers and the service class. Traditionally, the system is hereditary and hierarchical in status and prestige, with the Brahmans at the top and the Sudras at the bottom.

In addition, there is large group consisting of outcasts, or Untouchables, which is outside the boundaries of the *varna* system even though it is an integral part of the Hindu religious customs, traditions, and practices. The concepts of purity and pollution play an important role in defining a member of a caste. Large groups of people are called Untouchables because touching them or being touched by them ritually pollutes persons such as Brahman priests. The Untouchables are also called Harijans, a term coined by Gandhi that means God's people. The preferred term of self-reference is *Dalits,* which means oppressed people (based on the Marathi word for "ground or broken to pieces"). There is also a legal designation called Scheduled Castes, which is used in the literature—especially the official publications of the Indian government—to identify this group. It is a category that was introduced by the British, which was later borrowed and used in the Constitution of India. The federal government publishes this official list of the Untouchable Castes periodically.

TRADITIONAL CASTE SYSTEM

The traditional practice of the caste system as a social arrangement has the following major characteristics. A particular *varna* and *jati* are ascribed at birth to an individual. Persons born in a particular caste are expected to remain in that caste for their lifetimes, as are their offspring and their offspring's offspring. (There are a large number of gradations of the caste, with the social status being prominently affected by the *varna* to which they belong—though sometimes it is a matter of contention.) It has a fairly rigid system of hereditary occupations; for example, a son of a carpenter is expected to be a carpenter and so would his sons. It involves a hierarchical status system, with women customarily having a lower status than men in the family, and it restricts many types of social interactions. For example, the members of the upper castes are not expected to mingle socially with the lower castes nor share food prepared by them, as these activities would ritually pollute the members of the upper castes. It is also endogamous in nature; a person belonging to a caste is expected to marry someone else from that caste.

In India, caste is an all-pervasive phenomenon affecting a large number of significant areas of attitudes, beliefs, values, and behaviors of Hindu caste members. In the recent past, even among the Untouchable caste groups, there were subcastes or local castes that did not touch one another for fear of pollution. It is so entrenched that the features of the caste system can be found among members of other religious castes in India, even though Islam and Christianity are not supposed to have caste features. The caste system also exists in neighboring countries like Nepal and Bangladesh. Hindus have migrated and settled down around the world in a number of countries, including Africa, Latin America, Europe, and Asia. In these places, the caste system has been preserved in a revised form, one that is usually more flexible.

Some groups outside India have also been mentioned as having castelike features. The Wolof in Senegal and Gambia have been described as castelike based on their elaborate hierarchical occupational strata. The status of the Burakumin (Dowa) in Japan and the Rodiya in Sri Lanka was thought to be similar in some aspects to the lowest castes in India. The race relations between whites and African Americans in the United States in the past has been described as a caste system based on a rigid hereditary demarcation, prohibition of intermarriage between the two groups, and limited social mobility for the minorities.

Caste is an important topic for study because a large number of people around the world follow caste-based or castelike practices. In addition, it is crucial to discuss ways and means to redress the caste problems that have existed for more than 2,000 years and that currently affect more than 160 million caste minorities around the world, such as the Dalits, who are separate and unequal.

THEORIES OF CASTE

A number of scholars, Hindu religious leaders, and commentators have speculated about the origins of the caste system. Weber, Hocart, Dumont, Marriot, Milner, Ghurye, and Shrinivas are among the widely discussed group of caste theorists. The theories are complex and wide ranging in scope, and they are presented here in a simplified form.

The issues of ritual purity and pollution are attributed to the fact that the four different orders of the society (*varnas*) originated from different parts of the body, namely, the mouth, arms, thighs, and feet. The hierarchical status and functions of the four *varnas* have been attributed to this origin. This explanation is too biological and religious in nature to serve as a satisfactory social explanation.

Another point of view is presented to explain the definition of the term *varna,* which means color. The original settlers in India were dark. The group of people who reached India from outside and who gradually conquered the original local inhabitants proceeded to subjugate them to a lower status and to stratify the social system. This theory does not address the problem of the multiplicity of *jatis* and the absence of such a development in all the other conquered parts of the world.

Another explanation takes a conflict perspective and suggests that the system was created and sustained by the monarch of the conquering country as supreme authority. The occupational categories solidified and developed into castes. A different type of explanation posits that to maintain ritual purity, the Brahmans could not associate with unclean occupations. Though widely discussed, both these theories also fail to explain adequately why all the other agricultural nations did not develop such an elaborate caste system.

It has also been argued that the colonial rule with its divide-and-conquer policy crystallized already existing caste differences. While this criticism is valid to some extent, evidence provided by early observers, travelers, and writers indicates that many caste divisions and practices were quite inflexible prior to the British rule in India.

Another theory argues that the status of a caste conferred social power in India though it was not highly correlated with economic or political power. The status conferred on a caste was dependent on adherence to the social, religious, and cultural norms specific to that particular group. This theory does not provide an adequate explanation for this unique type of a status inconsistency, where power is independent of the usual correlates. In addition, some of the tenets about status as a zero-sum game are open to discussion.

There is generally no argument with the criticisms of feminists about patriarchal families and domination of females in the traditional caste system. However, the feminist perspectives do not adequately explain the origin, proliferation, hereditary occupations, and purification aspects of the caste phenomenon.

CASTE PRACTICES AND SOCIAL CHANGE

Actual caste practices are rarely as rigid as one would expect from the descriptions in the literature. There are always exceptions. Even the Indian epics, such as the Ramayana and the Mahabharata, contain examples of intercaste marriages and sharing of food or water with lower-caste members. Extramarital alliances, mainly of upper-caste males with women of a lower caste, is condoned in actual practice. Caste hypergamy, or marriage with someone of a higher caste, is accepted in some parts of India in the case of women marrying men of higher castes. Similarly, a few castes have attained a higher status with the accumulation of wealth by members of that group or the attainment of sainthood by someone in their caste. There are widespread disagreements among the caste and the subcastes about their status vis-à-vis other castes. The social changes in India are affecting some facets of the caste system more significantly than others, and this change is not uniform.

Social change and its impact on the Indian caste system have often been described as a result of four major trends. They are Sanskritization, Westernization, urbanization, and industrialization. Sanskritization refers to the process of closer adherence to Brahmanic practices, such as cleanliness, purity, and eating vegetarian food. This is generally considered an avenue for achieving higher status in the caste hierarchy. Westernization implies a host of changes including the adoption of Western diet, clothing, and technology; belief in an open, democratic society; proficiency in a Western language; and acceptance of intercaste marriages. These are seen to challenge the basic assumptions of the caste system. The large number of Indians studying or working abroad and preference for schools with English as a medium of instruction are other significant factors in this process.

The urbanization of India is also gradually breaking down the rigidity of the caste system, as seen, for example, in the context of public transportation and eating food at restaurants. As caste differences cannot be as easily distinguished as alleged racial differences, a person cannot be sure to what caste the person sitting next to him or her belongs, nor can one be sure who is cooking the food in a restaurant. In addition, with higher levels of education and the proliferation of new types of occupations due to technological changes, the old value systems based on inequality, ascribed stratification, and hereditary occupations are being seriously challenged. The concept of occupational mobility is gaining acceptance and is even something to aspire to. For example, a career in the military is now open to all castes. Large-scale social mobility also undermines the rigidity and inflexibility of the caste system.

Industrialization is often concomitant with urbanization and has an impact on the caste system resembling that of urbanization. Workers in a factory are not in a position to object to persons of lower castes working next to them, which helps breaks down the occupational barriers between different castes and makes occupational mobility feasible. These processes are making the caste system more flexible and susceptible to further change. It is important to note that significant changes are also taking place in the Indian villages, as many case studies have substantiated. For example, developments such as farmers' cooperatives radically alter the traditional caste-based institutional arrangements.

India gained political independence from British colonial rule in August 1947. The Constitution of India, adopted in 1949, prohibited discrimination based on caste. It is a matter of controversy as to how and to what extent the Constitution has affected the caste system and practices of the past. Generally speaking, obvious or overt discrimination has diminished. It is now uncommon, for example, to see segregation in seating arrangements based on caste in an elementary school. Even though caste members do not differ physically, many of their last names indicate to which caste they belong. This aspect of caste identification is likely to endure for some time.

There have been many efforts to challenge and change the Hindu caste system from the days of Buddha and Mahavira 2,500 years ago. Many of these challenges have come from within the religion. Many religious reform efforts were initiated in various parts of the country over the centuries. Buddha, Mahavira, Kabir, Vivekananda, Roy, Periyar, Ambedkar, and Gandhi are among the better known personages involved in such efforts, but none of these efforts has changed the caste system significantly. Ironically, because of the rigidity of the caste system, members of some religious movements ended up being given a new caste status, as in the case of Brahmo Samaj in Bengal in the nineteenth century. In the earlier cases, new religions such as Buddhism and Jainism were established. Efforts by Gandhi to educate members of the upper castes about the evils of the caste system were somewhat more successful. Mass conversion to Buddhism of millions of Dalits, led by Ambedkar, was an effort to improve the status of Dalits based on the assumption that it was impossible to change the rigidity of the caste system from within the Hindu religious framework.

In addition, there have been ongoing efforts to change the status of the Dalits through legal measures. Since the enactment of the Constitution in 1949, the Dalits were given reserved seats (similar to a quota system) to make up for the neglect and discrimination of the past and present. The Supreme Court of India has upheld this policy. In addition to the Scheduled Castes, the Scheduled Tribes and other "Backward Castes," which also hold disadvantaged positions in Indian society, though not to the extent of the Scheduled Castes, were also allotted quotas for government jobs and reserved seats for admission institutions of higher education such as medical and engineering schools. Thus, in some states, the majority of admissions in the highly competitive medical and engineering fields are filled by quotas, a process that has frustrated the upper castes. A few castes have even petitioned the government to officially change their caste status to the Scheduled Castes or other Backward Classes category in order to receive the benefits of reservations for admission to colleges, universities, and government jobs. A recent effort to allot quotas for promotion in jobs was barred by the court.

Caste in Indian Society

Although the caste system in South Asia is associated most strongly with Hinduism, it is important to remember that caste permeates social relations across India. The following text provides an example of how caste and caste-like restrictions on social contact affect social relations in Hindu and other groups in India..

> So far as Hindus are concerned, to be intimate sexually with a person of another caste is as much a crime as it is for Santals. It is not surprising therefore that many Hindus either adopt an attitude of tolerant neutrality or while disassociating themselves from the ritual they accord their approval to the custom. The Brahmans and Bhagats of Debinagar, for example, said to Mr. R. D. Pande, "Bitlaha [a purification ceremony] is a good custom. It should always be done when a Diku has relations with a Santal. It would be great cruelty to Santals to deprive them of this right."
>
> In the meeting which preceded the bitlaha of Isri Sahu the local Hindus fully cooperated and it was with their full concurrence that bitlaha was finally sanctioned.
>
> Moreover a Hindu boy who commits this offence cannot normally expect much sympathy from his caste people. He is blamed for disgracing his community. He is himself outcasted by them. "If the Santal girl is pregnant," said Hindus of Karbinda, "we will never take him back." If his casteman interfere at all it is only to ascertain that the allegation is correct, to plead that no substantial damage should be done and to see that the ritual is not misapplied for private ends.
>
> The attitude of Mohammadans [Muslims] is also not dissimilar. At Raksi the Muslims said to Mr. S.C. Hansdakm "sexual intimacy between a Muslim boy and a Santal girl is as bad as illicit intimacy between a Muslim girl and a Muslim boy. One who has illicit intercourse should be punished with eighty stripes. Mr. Burhanuddin Khan, M.L.A., with whom I discussed the attitude of Muslims also told me that to Muslims illicit intercourse is a crime, the Muslims would boycott the offender and would exact a penalty feast. If there is any difference, it is rather that Muslims are somewhat more prone to tamper with Santal girls, partly because they marry later. To both communities the act is abhorrent but individual Muslims flout their community opinion a little more than do Hindus.
>
> [. . .]
>
> "Dikus" said the Santals at Nonihat, "think themselves much higher than us. If we did not punish them for making our caste bad, they would utterly corrupt us. Then they have have spoilt our caste, our only remedy is spoil theirs back. If we did not bitlaha Dikus how would they fear us? How would they ever leave our girls alone? It is for this that we hang up bullocks's legs and pig's trotters and do stools and make water. It is because of this that our girls are safe and can go everywhere freely . . . We can not shut them in our houses. We must send them out to work. We can not tend them like cows. Only bitlaha protects us."

Source: Archer, W. G. (1984). *Tribal Law and Justice: A Report on the Santal*. New Delhi: Concept, pp. 586–587.

There is no doubt that the Dalits (along with some tribal groups) are still among the poorest people in India, with the lowest level of education and the highest percentage of unemployment, and they are still being discriminated against. They are residentially segregated in a majority of the rural areas and in some urban areas.

They are also subject to exploitation and violence. There is no doubt that there have been positive changes in education, employment, and occupational choice and mobility. For example, even in rural areas, some Untouchables have been able to move out from their segregated quarters, with the help of government loans, subsidies, and grants. However, the percentage of Dalits who have benefited by the various programs is quite small. There is a considerable amount of backlash among members of the upper castes because of the preferential treatment given to Dalits and other castes and tribes through the process of educational and employment reservations. It is generally agreed, however, that the Dalits have not attained equality with the rest of the population in spite of the efforts of the state and national governments.

CASTE, CLASS, AND COMMUNITY

It is clear that caste and class have both similarities and differences, as many scholars have pointed out. Some scholars have used caste and class as parallel categories in their analysis of minorities. However, in India, income or wealth and political power are not highly correlated with the caste hierarchy, though there is a high correlation in terms of prestige and education. For example, Brahmans, who occupy the apex of the social hierarchy, have a higher level of education and hold prestigious occupations, but in terms of income and wealth, they are clearly lower on the economic ladder compared to many other castes.

Caste is probably better understood in the context of a community rather than as a class. While the class system is typically divided into two to nine categories, there are approximately 3,000 castes and probably about 25,000 subcategories of castes or local castes. The membership in the *jatis* varies from thousands to millions, unlike the class system. Though there are only four *varnas,* there is not likely to be a high correlation between the *varnas* and social classes, except according to social status and prestige. Many of the castes have their own group of elders, consisting of a caste *panchayat,* which acts as an informal judiciary and has the influence and authority to mediate between two contesting parties in matters related to caste. In many cases, for example, members belonging to a caste or subcaste often make demands on each others' time and resources based on the fact that they are caste members. Such obligations may be fulfilled even after they migrate to other countries. Unlike classes, castes exhibit communality and commensality.

In sum, the integrity of the caste system has been challenged and is eroding, although many caste features still influence social and religious life and rituals, such as endogamous caste marriages. The caste system has proven to be pernicious in nature and is affecting the Indian society in new areas. It has, for example, infiltrated and corrupted the body politic in India. The elections have been politicized basically along caste lines, especially in local and regional politics and elections. At the local and regional levels it is often impossible to win a political election unless one belongs to a particular caste.

More than 150 million Dalits have been alienated as a result of prejudice and discrimination. Their position has not significantly improved even after Indian independence. The caste system has been credited with the management of a system-wide occupational division of labor; however, it is largely hereditary and has limited vertical occupational mobility for millions of people. On the positive side, the caste system has provided a lifelong sense of belonging in a community of caste members.

It is difficult to predict the future of the caste system because, despite recent opposition, it has demonstrated an ability to survive for a very long period of time. In the short term, at least in India, the caste system will continue to exercise its weakened hold on the life of most Indians in one form or another. In the long run, however, with the emphasis on a secular state, economic and educational improvement of the lower castes, the process of urbanization and globalization, increased opportunities for economic mobility, and commitment to a democratic form of government, the caste system will lose many of the virulent characteristics currently associated with it.

—Subhash R. Sonnad

Further Reading

Béteille, A. (1965). *Caste, class, and power: Changing patterns of stratification in a Tanjore village.* Berkeley: University of California Press.

Cameron, M. M. (1998). *On the edge of the auspicious: Gender and caste in Nepal.* Urbana: University of Illinois Press.

Dirks, N. B. (2001). *Castes of mind: Colonialism and the making of modern India.* Princeton, NJ: Princeton University Press.

Dumont, L. (1970). *Homo hierarchcus: An essay on the caste system.* (M. Sainsbury, Trans.). Chicago: University of Chicago Press.

Ghurye, G. S. (1961). *Caste, class and occupation.* Bombay, India: Popular Book Depot.

Gordon, F. L. (1995). *Caste & class: The black experience in Kansas, 1880–1920.* Athens: The University of Georgia Press.

Hocart, A. M. (1950). *Caste: A comparative study.* New York: Russell and Russell.

Human Rights Watch. (2001). *Caste discrimination: A global concern.* A Report by Human Rights Watch for the United Nations World Conference Against Racism, Racial Discrimination, Xenophobia and Related Intolerance. Durban, South Africa. Retrieved from http://www.hrw.org/reports/2001/globalcaste.

Jodhka, S. S. (2001). *Community and identities: Contemporary discourses on culture and politics in India.* New Delhi, India: Sage.

Malhotra, A. (2002). *Gender, caste and religious identities: Restructuring class in colonial Punjab.* New Delhi, India: Oxford University Press.

Mendelsohn, O., & Marika, V. (1998). *The Untouchables: Subordination, poverty and the state in modern India.* Cambridge, UK: Cambridge University Press.

Milner, M., Jr. (1994). *Status and sacredness: A general theory of status relations and an analysis of Indian culture.* New York: Oxford University Press.

Pandey, G. (1990). *The construction of colonialism in colonial north India.* Delhi, India: Oxford University Press.

Raheja, G. G. (1988). *The poison in the gift: Ritual, prestation, and the dominant caste in a north Indian village.* Chicago: The University of Chicago Press.

Selvam, S. (2000). *Caste and class in India in the late 20th century.* Lewiston, NY: Edwin Mellen.

Singer, M., & Cohn, B. S. (1968). *Structure and change in Indian society.* Chicago: Aldine.

Unnithan-Kumar, M. (1997). *Identity, gender and poverty: New perspectives on caste and tribe in Rajasthan.* Providence, RI: Berghahn.

Weber, M. (1958). *The religion of India: The sociology of Hinduism and Buddhism.* (H. Gerth & D. Martindale, Trans. & Eds.). Glencoe, IL: Free Press.

Willie, C. V. (1979). *The caste and class controversy.* New York: General Hall.

CATTLE TOWNS

Many American communities with railway connections, from New Mexico to Montana, served as sale and shipping points for free-range cattle in the Old West, but only a few such "cattle towns" (or, less respectfully, "cowboy towns" or "cowtowns") became well-known.

Such frontier settlements as Ogalalla, Nebraska, Cheyenne, Wyoming, and Miles City, Montana, achieved temporary reputations as cattle-shipping centers. The most famous, however, were those of post–Civil War Kansas, each located at a juncture of a railroad and a trail from Texas. The earliest was Abilene, which served the Texas cattle trade from 1867 through 1871, when farmers overran its outlying ranges and ended its access to the trail. Ellsworth and Wichita existed as competing cattle towns from 1872 through 1875, when surrounding settlements closed them both. Dodge City was a cattle shipping center from 1876 through 1885, and Caldwell flourished in the same capacity from 1880 through 1885. In the latter year, Kansas finally closed its borders to the direct "trailing" of southern bovines, ending the Texas cattle trade in that state.

The cattle town experience encompasses two issues of historical and sociological interest: the prevalence of gun violence and the theoretical relationship between frontier democracy and frontier social change.

GUN VIOLENCE

The legendary homicide associated with western cattle towns has been much overdrawn by journalists, novelists, screenwriters, and popular historians. In the Kansas cattle towns between 1870 and 1885 (including justifiable killings by the police), only forty-seven adults are known to have died violently—an average of about 1½ fatalities per cowboy season. Recent scholarly efforts to exaggerate this relatively low body count by transforming it into the criminologists' "per 100,000 population" ratio have proved statistically questionable due to the towns' small populations.

People did not customarily die in a Hollywood-style street duel at the Kansas cattle towns. Fewer than one-third of the victims returned fire. A number were not even armed. Four deaths were accidental shootings. Three victims were women, two of them murdered by domestic partners. Famous "bad men" (the term "gunfighter" was not invented until the 1890s) accounted for few deaths. John Wesley Hardin killed a man who was snoring too loudly in an adjoining hotel room; Wyatt Earp (or another policeman) fatally wounded a carousing cowboy; W. B. ("Bat") Masterson revenged his brother's murder; John H. ("Doc") Holliday and Ben Thompson sojourned at Dodge City without incident; J. B. ("Wild Bill") Hickok killed two men, one—a security guard—by mistake.

In large part, the low cattle town body count resulted from businesspeople's fear of violence, which would certainly deter new middle-class in-migrants. Yet local elites felt it necessary to offer facilities for drinking, gambling, and commercial sex to transient cowboys and cattlemen alike. Their solution was to maintain "good order" by means of tough gun-control laws, multiple police officers, and the (illegal) taxation of gamblers and prostitutes to pay police salaries. Also important

Dodge City, Kansas, in 1878.
Source: Bettmann/Corbis; used with permission.

was the segregation of brothels and dance halls from the towns' residential areas and main business districts.

THEORETICAL RELATIONSHIP BETWEEN FRONTIER DEMOCRACY AND FRONTIER SOCIAL CHANGE

In part, the theoretical relationship between frontier democracy and social change extends back to the famous 1896 essay by the historian Frederick Jackson Turner, who emphasized the role of the American frontier in the nation's development. More simply, it reflects the American folk belief that the typical frontier community was sociologically cohesive—a kind of ongoing husking bee or barn raising in which sturdy pioneers coped with the challenges of a hostile environment.

The cattle towns, however, did not conform to this simple model. Their citizens indeed worked together to obtain railroads, to preserve access to cattle trails, to suppress violence, to present the proper community image to outsiders, and often enough to oppose political interference in local affairs by outlying farmers. But the cattle town people also fell to quarreling among themselves as a result of fierce business rivalries and competing real estate values. For example, Wichita's businessmen collectively agreed from 1871 through 1876 to raise money to promote the town to cattlemen and cattle buyers, but at the same time they continued to be bitterly divided and mutually predatory over whether Main Street or Douglas Avenue would be the prime locus of downtown growth.

And when social reform (after 1880 including liquor prohibition) arrived at each latter-day cattle town, conflict could—and by 1885 did—turn ugly. Antiliquor extremists set Dodge City's business district afire two nights running. At Caldwell, prohibition fanatics lynched a bootlegger. At that point, community conflict was serious indeed.

Whether the cattle town inhabitants cooperated or conflicted depended simply on whether the resolution of a specific issue required them to coalesce or impelled them to divide. Thus local social change involved a combination of cooperation and conflict. It was conflict, however, rather than consensus and cooperation, that maximized local participatory democracy.

In recent decades, local studies by historians of the United States have largely tended to concern themselves with social structure. Therefore the "cattle town model"—a political rather than a structural formulation—has been rarely applied to other frontier settlements.

—Robert R. Dykstra

Further Reading

Dykstra, R. R. (1968). *The cattle towns.* New York: Knopf.

Dykstra, R. R. (1996). Overdosing on Dodge City. *Western Historical Quarterly, 27,* 505–514.

Dykstra, R. R. (1999a). To live and die in Dodge City: Body counts, law and order, and the case of *Kansas* v. *Gill.* In M. A. Bellesiles (Ed.), *Lethal imagination: Violence and brutality in American history* (pp. 210–226). New York: New York University Press.

Dykstra, R. R. (1999b). Violence, gender, and methodology in the "new" western history. *Reviews in American History, 27,* 79–86.

Dykstra, R. R., & Silag, W. (1987). Doing local history: Monographic approaches to the smaller community. In H. Gillette, Jr., & Z. L. Miller (Eds.), *American urbanism: A historiographical review* (pp. 291–305). New York: Greenwood.

Haywood, C. R. (1991). *Victorian West: Class and culture in Kansas cattle towns.* Lawrence: University Press of Kansas.

Hogan, R. (1990). *Class and community in frontier Colorado.* Lawrence: University Press of Kansas.

Mann, R. (1982). *After the Gold Rush: Society in Grass Valley and*

Nevada City, California, 1849–1870. Stanford, CA: Stanford University Press.

Miner, H. C. (1982). *Wichita: The early years, 1865–80.* Lincoln: University of Nebraska Press.

Turner, F. J. (1920). *The frontier in American history.* New York: Henry Holt.

CELEBRATION, FLORIDA

Celebration is a mixed-use community developed by the Walt Disney Company as an unincorporated part of Oscoela County in central Florida. It was founded in 1996 and constructed on land that the company had acquired in the 1960s to the west of Kissimmee and southeast of Disney World. The first large-scale community development to be built in the United States in almost three decades, it originally was projected to accommodate up to 20,000 residents upon completion, though the residential scope of the development has been scaled back in subsequent revisions to the master plan. Renters and owner-occupiers are accommodated in multifamily apartments and single-family homes. The town also boasts a corporate campus, with commercial office buildings running along a corridor that bisects the 10,000-acre site (half of which is preserved wetlands).

The design of the town identifies it as a stepchild of New Urbanism, a zealous movement in town planning that emerged in the mid-1980s and declared war on automobile-oriented suburban development. New Urbanists have pledged to forge an environmentally sustainable alternative to urban and suburban sprawl, and have vowed to reintroduce Americans to the civic virtues of an active community life as it is popularly imagined to have existed in the prewar U.S. small town. Distinguishing marks of New Urbanism in Celebration include the neotraditional style of the housing, the high density of suburban development, an interconnected grid-like street pattern (as opposed to cul-de-sacs), a mixed-income range of housing and rental prices, an active downtown center with shops and restaurants, and a strong emphasis on public space and "walkability." The town plan also includes provision for a nonprofit community foundation to seed civic organizations and sponsor community life in general.

Celebration was perceived by some as a visible counterpunch to the privatizing ethos of the high-end gated community. More skeptical commentators saw Disney's role (initially dominating the governance boards, as is typical for a community developer) as a paradigm of postmodern corporate power, extending itself from consumer packaging to all aspects of the residents' social and cultural life. For communitarians, the town was hailed as a model of high civic participation. For libertarians, the rules and standards to which residents of the community must adhere were construed as restricting the rights of a free citizenry. In practice, residents wrestled with the tension between these competing views of their town. So high were the expectations for the performance of the community that the early years of settlement were filled with frustration, contention, and turmoil, much of it covered in the national and international press and in two book-length studies of the pioneer residents. These conflicts continued to reverberate and flare up with each new revision to the town plan. Far from being the conformist automatons that some in the media predicted residents of Celebration would be, the town's citizenry were responsive and outspoken from the outset, often to the chagrin of the Disney officials who oversaw the development. Whether they prove to be as active in the county and region only time will tell.

Children on a sidewalk in Celebration, Florida, in 1996.
Source: Mark Peterson/Corbis; used with permission.

—Andrew Ross

Further Reading

Duany, A., Plater-Zyberk, E., & Speck, J. (2000). *Suburban nation: The rise of sprawl and the decline of the American dream.* New York: North Point Press.

Frantz, D., & Collins, C. (1999). *Celebration, U.S.A.: Living in Disney's brave new town.* New York: Holt.

Kunstler, J. H. (1996). *Home from nowhere: Remaking our everyday world for the twenty-first century.* New York: Simon & Schuster.

Pollan, M. (1997, December 14). Town-building is no Mickey-Mouse operation. *New York Times Magazine,* p. 56ff.

Ross, A. (1999). *The Celebration chronicles: Life, liberty, and the pursuit of property value in Disney's new town.* New York: Ballantine.

CHAIN STORES

Since the time of the Greek agora, local markets and retail stores have been at the heart of community life. They are a source of essential goods and services, as well as places to meet friends and neighbors. Retail stores are one of the few types of businesses that can be found in virtually every community. Their vitality is a good measure of the overall health of the local economy. This essay will focus on the history and growth of, as well as the controversy over, and community responses to, chain stores in the United States.

There are two types of retail stores: chain stores and independent businesses. A chain store is one of multiple retail stores under the same ownership. All stores in a chain typically share a common name, range of merchandise, visual appearance, and method of operation. Many retail chains are publicly traded companies owned by stockholders. Some chains, such as McDonald's and Dunkin' Donuts, are franchises; that is, each outlet is partly owned and managed by a local business person, who must share profits with the parent corporation and follow strict rules and uniform procedures governing every aspect of the business.

Chain stores can be contrasted with independent, locally owned retail stores. These are one-of-a-kind small businesses owned by a sole proprietor, family, or group of partners.

HISTORY

Chain stores first appeared in the late nineteenth century, but they did not become a significant force in U.S. retailing until the 1920s, when they underwent a substantial growth spurt. In 1900, chain stores accounted for only 3 percent of U.S. retail sales. By 1926, they were capturing 9 percent of sales, and by 1933, they controlled more than 25 percent of the market. The largest of these new retail companies was the Great Atlantic and Pacific Tea Company, a chain of grocery stores more commonly known as A&P. The company grew from 200 stores in 1900 to more than 15,000 outlets in 1929. Other large chains of the period included JC Penney (with 1,500 stores), Woolworth's (with 1,900 outlets), and Montgomery Ward (with 550 stores).

After this period of rapid growth, the chains' market share shrank during the 1930s and 1940s, due in part to widespread concerns about their detrimental effects on local economies, which led to boycotts and legislation to slow their growth. These concerns subsided, and the chains began to multiply again in the 1950s. Their expansion was aided by suburbanization and increased automobile ownership, which made freestanding chain stores and shopping malls accessible to larger numbers of people. This shifted economic activity away from downtown shopping districts, which housed many independent merchants and had long served as centers of commerce and shopping.

EXPLOSIVE GROWTH

Chain stores underwent an explosive period of growth during the late 1980s and 1990s. A majority (as much as 80 percent by some estimates) of new retail construction in the United States during this period was in the form of "superstores," also known as "big box" stores because of their large, square, featureless buildings. These stores range in size from 20,000 to 300,000 square feet. (By comparison, a football field is 45,000 square feet and a typical downtown store might be 3,000 square feet.) The term *superstores* encompasses general merchandise stores, such as Wal-Mart, Kmart, and Target; "category killers" that offer a broad selection in one category of goods, such as Home Depot (for home improvement supplies), Toys R Us (for toys), Office Max (for office supplies), and Sports Authority (for sporting goods); and "warehouse" stores such as Costco and Sam's Club, which offer goods at wholesale or near-wholesale prices. Smaller chains, including clothing stores such as The Gap and Banana Republic, restaurants or coffee shops such as Starbucks and The Olive Garden, and drugstores such as Walgreens, CVS, and Rite Aid, also expanded rapidly during this period.

As chain stores have multiplied, they have captured a larger share of retail sales, and tens of thousands of locally owned businesses have closed. Since 1990, the United States has lost more than 11,000 independent pharmacies; chain drugstores now account for more than half of all U.S. drugstore sales. More than 40 percent of the United States' independent bookstores failed during this decade. Barnes & Noble and Borders Books now capture half of all U.S. bookstore sales. Local hardware stores have likewise declined; Home Depot and Lowe's control nearly 40 percent of that segment in the United States. Three chains—Staples, Office Max, and Office Depot—capture 75 percent of all U.S. office supply sales. Blockbuster and Hollywood Video account for nearly half of all U.S. movie rentals. More than 40 percent of U.S. restaurant spending is captured by the top hundred chains. Perhaps most striking, a single firm, Wal-Mart, captures more than seven percent of *all* U.S. retail spending. Founded in 1962 when Sam Walton opened a single five-and-dime store in Rogers, Arkansas, Wal-Mart today is the largest corporation in the world, with $220 billion in revenue in 2001 and more than 4,400 stores worldwide.

CONTROVERSY

Chain stores are highly controversial. Although popular with many shoppers, chain stores, especially the larger ones like Wal-Mart, have faced growing opposition to their expansion plans in recent years. In hundreds of cities and towns nationwide, citizens have organized grassroots protests, boycotts, petition drives, and the like to block the arrival of a new chain store.

Chain retailers and their supporters argue that they have created an efficient and innovative method of retailing. By buying in large quantities, dealing directly with manufacturers instead of going through wholesalers, operating their own warehouses and distribution systems, adopting sophisticated information technologies, and centralizing many management and accounting functions, large retail chains have significantly reduced costs. These savings, say supporters, are passed on to consumers in the form of lower prices.

Supporters also note that chains have developed appealing store designs and offer wider selection, longer hours, and greater consistency than independent retailers. The larger superstores, such as Wal-Mart, have also provided consumers with the convenience of "one-stop" shopping. These features have made chain stores extremely popular, according to supporters, and given them a competitive edge over independent businesses. Moreover, supporters say, the arrival of a national retailer benefits the local community by creating growth, new jobs, and added tax revenue.

Critics argue that chain stores come with hidden costs that are not reflected in their price tags. Chain stores, they argue, can harm local economies. When chain stores come to town, they typically force locally owned businesses to close, thereby eliminating as many jobs and as much tax revenue as they create.

Retail Pricing Matched to Community Income

JACKSON, Miss. (ANS)—A network of 12 discount shops in Mississippi's poorest counties prices its merchandise according to the income of the town where the store is located.

"That means that a shirt that we might sell for $3.50 in one town we would sell for $1.99 in a neighboring town," explains Babs Salu, executive director of Thriftco, Inc. This custom pricing helps people in an area of proven financial need get the most for their money, Salu says.

Thriftco, Inc. opened its doors in 1981 with its Community Distribution Service Program. The organization maintains shops in low-income communities that sell groceries, essentials, and used and "irregular" clothing. They also process and recycle for sale more than 50 tons of household goods each year, says Salu.

The merchandise is made up of donated goods from individuals, manufacturers' seconds and overruns, and damaged merchandise which Thriftco repairs before selling.

"We will also sometimes give merchandise away in cases of need, but only when we are sure that the need is genuine," Salu says.

Thriftco also provides community groups with merchandise to sell in their own local stores. Proceeds of these sales are used as seed capital to open more stores.

Thriftco states as its goals: to provide at low cost essential household and clothing items to poor families in Mississippi; to develop an economic base within the poor community; to provide a source of employment and management training in the community; to allow community residents to become involved in shaping their community's social, political and economic destiny; to encourage the development of local leadership; to provide a source of income to support local Christian ministries; and to engage people, particularly those with low incomes, in the ownership of their own economic enterprise.

Source: "Thrift Chain in Poor Mississippi Region Links Prices to Shopper Income." American News Service, Article No. 335B, December 15, 1997.

The jobs gained, moreover, are not necessarily equivalent to the jobs lost. Most of the jobs at big retail chains are low-wage, part-time positions with no health care, pension, or other benefits. In the United States, critics point out, many employees of these stores must rely on food stamps and other taxpayer-funded programs to survive.

Direct job and tax losses, according to critics, are only part of the economic drain caused by chain stores. Consider what happens to a dollar spent at a locally owned business. Not only do profits stay in the community, but local retailers support a variety of other local businesses. They bank with local banks, advertise in local newspapers, and hire local accountants and printers—each of which in turn spends that revenue at still other local businesses. The result is a cascade of economic activity—called the multiplier effect—that sustains a wide variety of jobs in the local community and generates, through every transaction, new tax revenue to support schools, libraries, parks, and other public services.

In contrast, much of a dollar spent at a chain store leaves the community immediately. Because they are not locally owned, chains do not keep profits in the local economy and have little use for local goods and services. As a result, when chains displace local business, many communities experience a decline in local economic activity and overall tax revenue.

According to critics, there are also social consequences to trading locally owned businesses for national chains. Local merchants live in the community and have a vested interest in its long-term health. Many sponsor local events and take a leadership role in community affairs. A study commissioned by the U.S. Small Business Administration found that U.S. small businesses give more than twice as much per employee to charitable causes as do large companies.

Finally, critics worry that as chains open virtually identical stores nationwide and even worldwide, they are making communities homogeneous and destroying their local character. Corporate retail chains are also undermining the vitality of historic downtowns and exacerbating sprawl and traffic congestion by building massive stores on the outskirts of towns and cities. A single big box store consumes about 12 acres of land, requires more than a thousand parking spaces, and generates as many as 10,000 car trips daily.

COMMUNITY RESPONSES

The divergent opinions about the merits of chain stores have resulted in some communities actively encouraging chains to locate within their borders, while others work to restrict their proliferation. In the United States, the Constitution prohibits cities from banning or discriminating against businesses based on whether they are locally owned or part of a chain, but communities do have the authority to determine what types of development are appropriate in different areas of town and to set basic parameters on the size and characteristics of that development. These rules are written into the city's comprehensive plan and zoning code.

Some communities encourage the construction of big box stores and shopping malls by zoning much of their undeveloped land for large-scale retail development. Many of these communities also use public resources to actively recruit chain stores. For example, they may provide chains with substantial tax breaks and subsidies or use tax dollars to cover the cost of building roads, sewers, and other infrastructure to support big box stores or other chain retail growth.

Other communities have adopted planning and zoning rules that prohibit big box stores, shopping malls, and other retail development on the outskirts of town. New stores must instead be located in or near the downtown and be in keeping with the community's existing scale and character. Some cities and towns also require detailed studies of the potential environmental, economic, and community impacts of any proposed retail development and allow only those stores that bring substantial benefits and have few negative impacts. Many of these communities are also investing public resources into rehabilitating their downtowns and helping locally owned businesses survive and thrive.

—Stacy Mitchell

Further Reading

Beaumont, C. E. (1994). *How superstore sprawl can harm communities, and what citizens can do about it.* Washington, DC: National Trust for Historic Preservation.

Beaumont, C. E. (1997). *Better models for superstores: Alternatives to big-box sprawl.* Washington, DC: National Trust for Historic Preservation.

Bloom, J. (2001, August–September). Chains on main: A new look at national retailers. *Main Street News,* pp. 2–18.

Mitchell, S. (2000). *The home town advantage: How to defend your main street against chain stores and why it matters.* Minneapolis, MN: Institute for Local Self-Reliance.

Norman, A. (1999). *Slam-Dunkin'g Wal-Mart! How you can stop superstore sprawl in your hometown.* Atlantic City, NJ: Raphel Marketing.

CHARISMA

Social scientists use the term *charisma* to describe a special form of authority based on the belief that a person possesses extraordinary and perhaps divinely ordained powers. The concept is useful for understanding the relatively small, extraordinarily cohesive inner circles of sectarian communities and social movements that develop around revolutionary religious prophets, extremist political zealots, rebellious vanguard artists, radically creative entrepreneurs, and other nonconformist leaders who attract devoted, sometimes fanatical followers and disciples. In their pure form, charismatic movements, based on intense, shared experiences of rapport and rapture, are necessarily short-lived. They yield to what the German sociologist Max Weber (1864–1920) called the routinization of charisma and become reintegrated into the social structure, or they eventually disappear with the group's disenchantment with the leader or with the leader's death.

THE CONCEPT AND ITS ORIGINS

The term *charisma* (from the Greek *charisma,* favor or gift) was widely used in early Christian thought, and early twentieth-century German theologians used the word when explaining that early Christianity was transformed from an ecstatic prophetic (charismatic) sect into an institutionalized church. The term's meaning in social science was established by Max Weber, who noted that the phenomenon characterized the rise and transformation of various groups that believed that they and their leaders were charismatic and above dealing with matters of everyday life. Remarkably, until about 1950 charisma was a little known and mostly unused concept in English-language publications, while today seemingly countless articles and books in sociology, anthropology, history, political science, psychology, psychoanalysis, and economics consider charisma a powerful force.

Although each of the social sciences has adapted its own interpretation of charisma, Weber's conception is still valid: "a certain quality of an individual personality by virtue of which he is set apart from ordinary men and treated as endowed with supernatural, superhuman, or at least specifically exceptional powers or qualities. These are such as are not accessible to the ordinary person, but are regarded as of divine origin or as exemplary, and on the basis of them the individual concerned is treated as a leader" (Weber 1946, p. 329).

THE NATURE OF CHARISMA: DISTRESS, ENTHUSIASM, AND ANTINOMIANISM

The relationship between charismatic leaders and their followers leads to the formation of charismatic communities, which in their pure forms have been called bunds (communions) or fusions. In these groups, charismatics and their followers are bound together by mutually shared inspirational feelings and experiences. Charismatic movements and communities tend to arise during times that call for revolutionary or at least extraordinary behavior. Such movements generally form around "natural leaders in moments of distress—whether psychic, physical, economic, ethical, religious, or political" (Weber 1968a, p. 1112). Charismatic movements such as radical political parties, nonconforming religious sects, avant-garde artistic salons, or utopian communes always stand in opposition to the status quo. This inherently oppositional quality led Weber to see charisma, in its pure forms, as the most primal revolutionary force in social life.

Because of the revolutionary attitude associated with charismatic movements, outsiders often regard them with hostility, especially in the formative stages, when charismatic authority is purest. At these times, charismatic movements are most intense and, undiminished by routinization, most threatening to established social values. "The mere fact of recognizing the personal mission of a charismatic master establishes his power . . . this recognition derives from the surrender of the faithful to the extraordinary and unheard-of, to what is alien to all regulation and tradition and therefore is viewed as divine—surrender which arises from distress or enthusiasm" (Weber 1968, p. 1115).

That charismatic religious movements arise in distressing times has been noted in the sociological literature, but Weber's assertion that such movements are often enthusiastic in origin has largely been ignored. Enthusiasts believe that they are seized and guided in an extraordinary manner by immediate, direct, divine inspiration and revelation. In its most extreme manifestations, enthusiasm—the claim to immediate direct revelations—has often led to antinomianism (a disregard for all established social institutions) and to rebellion against both ecclesiastical and civil authorities. "The commands of the world do not hold for the man who is assured in his obsession with God" (Weber 1946a, p. 348). Following Weber, contemporary sociologists, such as Daniel Bell, Edward Shils, and S. N. Eisenstadt, have also noted the connection between charismatic movements and antinomianism.

Underscoring this enthusiastically antinomian component of charisma, Weber said that in their most extreme form, a charismatic movement overturns reason, tradition, and "all notions of sanctity. Instead of reverence for customs that are . . . sacred, it enforces the inner subjection to the unprecedented and absolutely unique and therefore Divine." In this sense "charisma is indeed the specifically creative revolutionary force of history" (Weber 1968a, p. 1117).

Antinomianism is strongest during the formative phases of charismatic movements. These early phases have been referred to as liminal, representing transitions between old and new identities for both leaders and disciples. Victor Turner, the anthropologist who first introduced the idea of liminality into the language of social theory, recognized that charismatic religious movements often arise outside normal ritual structures, and that "their liminality is not institutionalized." Instead, Turner wrote, this charismatic liminality is "spontaneously generated in a situation of radical structural change. . . . It is in this limbo of structure that religious movements, led by charismatic prophets, powerfully reassert the values of communitas, often in extreme and antinomian forms" (Turner 1974, p. 248). On the other hand, almost from the beginning, the revolutionary tide that accompanies the birth of charismatic movements begins to ebb and is routinized, transformed into an institution, such as a church, political party, or profession, with permanent structures and traditions.

DIFFUSION AND USE IN THE SOCIAL SCIENCES

Social scientists do not try to evaluate whether charismatics are actually endowed with supernatural, superhuman powers of divine origin, but only whether the followers subjecting themselves to the charismatic's authority on that basis believe in the leader's powers. The charismatic bond between leaders and followers "finds its limits at the edges of these groups" (Weber 1968a, p. 1113). Many casual observers have attributed charisma to leaders with mass appeal, such as Adolph Hitler. In fact, such leaders often do have charisma, but only in relation to those in their inner circles. When the parties or social movements headed by these leaders are successful, it is because they have been transformed into mainstream rational or traditional institutions. If pure charismatic movements do not yield to routinization, they eventually fail.

Challenges to the established ways of doing things in ongoing communities—from community units as small as families to units as large as nations—are usually first met by resistance. Charismatic movements, driven by passion and enthusiasm, can be likened to firestorms of change, sweeping across the normative social landscape. Often they burn out or are put out by the communities that they threaten to change. Sometimes, however, their challenges prevail and the communities change because of them. It is in this sense that Weber saw charisma as the most revolutionary agent in history.

—Howard G. Schneiderman

Further Reading:

Bell, D. (1971, Fall). Religion in the sixties. *Social Research, 38*(3), 447–497.

Duverger, M. (1959). *Political parties: Their organization and activity in the modern state.* New York: Wiley.

Eisenstadt, S. (1973). *Tradition, change and modernity.* New York: Wiley.

Geertz, C. (1983). Centers, kings, and charisma. In C. Geertz (Ed.), *Local knowledge* (pp. 121–146). New York: Basic Books.

Knox, R. (1950). *Enthusiasm.* Oxford, UK: Oxford University Press.

Kohut, H. (1985). Creativeness, charisma and group psychology. In H. Kohut & C. B. Strozier (Eds.), *Self psychology and the humanities.* New York: Norton.

Lindholm, C. (1990). *Charisma.* Cambridge, MA: Blackwell.

Noll, R. (1994). *The Jung cult: Origins of a charismatic movement.* Princeton, NJ: Princeton University Press.

Oakes, L. (1997). *Prophetic charisma: The psychology of religious personalities.* Syracuse, NY: Syracuse University Press.

Panebianco, A. (1988). *Political parties: Organization and power.* New York: Cambridge University Press.

Redich, F. (1998). *Hitler: Diagnosis of a destructive prophet.* New York: Oxford University Press.

Schmalenbach, H. (1977). *On society and experience.* Chicago: University of Chicago Press.

Schumpeter, J. (1989). *Essays: On entrepreneurs, innovations, business cycles, and the evolution of capitalism.* New Brunswick, NJ: Transaction Books.

Shils, E. (1965). *Center and periphery.* Chicago: University of Chicago Press.

Taylor, L. (1995). *Occasions of faith.* Philadelphia: University of Pennsylvania Press.

Turner, V. (1969). *The ritual process: Structure and anti-structure.* New York: Aldine.

Turner, V. (1974). *Dramas, fields, and metaphors.* Chicago: Aldine.

Weber, M. (1946). *From Max Weber: Essays in sociology.* New York: Oxford University Press.

Weber, M. (1968a). *Economy and society.* New York: Bedminster.

Weber, M. (1968b). *On charisma and institution building.* Chicago: University of Chicago Press.

Willner, A. (1984). *The spellbinders: Charismatic political leadership.* New Haven, CT: Yale University Press.

Wilson, B. (1975). *The noble savages.* Berkeley and Los Angeles: University of California Press.

Zablocki, B. (1980). *Alienation and charisma.* New York: Free Press.

CHAUTAUQUA

Chautauqua is a cultural and educational community in western New York State. It was founded in 1874 as a center of intellectual and moral guidance. The community, officially called the Chautauqua Institution, became famous in the nineteenth century for its cultural events, lectures, concerts, theater performances, dance shows, and summer school.

Although less well-known today, the Chautauqua Institution is still thriving along the shore of Chautauqua Lake, one of New York's Finger Lakes. During the winter, about 400 people live at Chautauqua; during the summer, the population grows to 8,000. The community members share an appreciation of artistic expression and academic pursuits. The summer school courses include foreign languages, dance, painting, sculpture, and music.

Chautauqua was born from the vision of Lewis Miller (1829–1899), an inventor from Akron, Ohio, and John H. Vincent (1832–1920), a minister in Galena, Illinois. Together they organized a nationally renowned adult educational movement, originally called the Fair Point Sunday School Assembly. Their philosophy was to create a planned community, with a Christian basis, that allowed learning to flourish in an idyllic residential setting. Vincent's credo that "every man has the right to be all that he can be" (Simpson 1999, p. 21) shaped the development of a community in which adults could pursue self-improvement. Academic subjects and art classes were added to courses for Sunday school teachers. Chautauqua was a household name until the 1920s, and it became a symbol of U.S. culture and values. During this time, the experiment also evolved into a university-style center for education.

Chautauqua has a town-like campus that covers approximately 723 acres, known as the Grounds. There is an admission charge to enter the Grounds, and nearly 150,000 visitors come from around the world each year. The property encompasses a collection of 1,200 Victorian cottages, contemporary homes, condominiums, hotels, shops, and public meeting halls. During the summer, car access is limited, so residents travel on foot to attend the programs. Events take place in the amphitheater or open pavilions. A board of trustees establishes the policies and direction of the not-for-profit organization, which has an annual budget of $15.6 million.

Summer passes, which include admission to all amphitheater events, are fairly expensive, so pass holders are generally wealthy and conservative. The summer school students tend to be younger and more diverse. Despite their differences, Chautauqua residents coexist harmoniously, mainly because of their shared interest in cultural pursuits. The community is unique in that residents can attend events such as ballet performances, symphonies, or art openings nearly every night of the week, all within walking distance.

The bell tower of the Chautauqua Institution in New York State in 1954.

Source: Bettmann/Corbis; used with permission.

In its early years, Chautauqua was a national podium, featuring prominent speakers such as Ulysses S. Grant and orator William Jennings Bryan. Chautauquans in the late nineteenth century paid less than ten dollars for a week of camping by the lakeshore and attending lessons, lectures, and performances. Members have had their own daily newspaper throughout the summer season since 1876. The first reading club in America—the Chautauqua Literary and Scientific Circle—was formed there in 1878, allowing devoted students to continue receiving enlightenment from the community during the winter months.

Under the leadership of Arthur E. Bestor (1879–1944), who became its president in 1915, Chautauqua evolved into the nation's first arts festival. In the early twentieth century, the Chautauqua movement was a social and cultural phenomenon that spread throughout the rural parts of the United States; at its peak in 1924, Chautauqua banners waved in 12,000 towns and villages across the country. Chautauqua "tent circuits" tried to reproduce the artistic and intellectual community atmosphere of the Institution in those towns and villages. The tents featured choruses, operas, orchestras, and other performers. This national movement lost popularity in the ensuing years, but the original Chautauqua maintained its prominence. A few decades of financial troubles followed the Great Depression. Chautauqua continued to hold its summer programs, but many of its public buildings decayed. In the 1970s, financial needs were addressed, and a renaissance of Chautauqua began. In 1973, the Chautauqua Grounds were officially added to the National Register of Historic Places.

Chautauqua has attracted famous authors, opera singers, composers, diplomats, aviators, and revivalists, as well as nine U.S. presidents. In 1905, President Theodore Roosevelt delivered an address on the Grounds in which he stated that Chautauqua was "typically American, in that it was typical of America at its best" (Simpson 1999, p. 18). In 1936, President Franklin Delano Roosevelt delivered his "I Hate War" speech at Chautauqua. The community was visited by President Bill Clinton and his wife during their 1992 campaign tour and continues to serve as a forum for national issues and adult education.

—Robin O'Sullivan

Further Reading

Case, V., & Case, R. O. (1948). *We called it culture: The story of Chautauqua.* Garden City, NY: Doubleday.

Gould, J. E. (1961). *The Chautauqua movement.* Albany: State University of New York Press.

Morrison, T. (1974). *Chautauqua.* Chicago: University of Chicago Press.

Orchard, H. A. (1923). *Fifty years of Chautauqua.* Cedar Rapids, IA: The Torch Press.

Simpson, J. (1999). *Chautauqua: An American utopia.* New York: Harry N. Abrams.

Vincent, J. H. (1886). *The Chautauqua movement.* Boston: Chautauqua Press.

CHERNOBYL

The 1986 Chernobyl nuclear disaster is internationally recognized as the world's worst nuclear accident, resulting in 31 initial deaths and as many as 6,000 eventual deaths due to radiation exposure and induced cancers. The Chernobyl power station in Ukraine finally was closed down on December 15, 2000; yet the "sarcophagus," or tomb, surrounding reactor No. 4 is cracked and still emitting radiation, requiring continual monitoring, maintenance, and eventual replacement. The technological, environmental, medical, psychosocial, and religious repercussions of the nuclear accident will ripple through the contaminated regions of Ukraine, Belarus, and Russia for years to come.

THE EVENT

On the banks of the Pripyat River in Ukraine, near the border of Belarus, a nuclear power plant was hastily constructed in 1983, utilizing outdated 1960s technology. On April 26, 1986, an explosion occurred, blowing the lid off the reactor and releasing seven tons of radioactive particles into the atmosphere. A mile-high nuclear cloud rained down isotopes on an unsuspecting population of several million. Because of the direction of the winds after the explosion, Belarus received 70 percent of the fallout (Ukraine received 20 percent, Russia 5 percent, and 5 percent was scattered globally).

The actual explosion was the size of a small atomic bomb. However, in actual fallout, Chernobyl produced 200 times the radioactive contamination of the atomic bombs dropped on Hiroshima and Nagasaki combined, and 6 million times the emissions of Three Mile Island in Pennsylvania. While the atmospheric radiation has returned to normal, hot particles of plutonium and cesium remain in the soil, in the water supply, and in plant and animal life. Much of the land will remain contaminated for hundreds or thousands of years.

THE LONG-TERM EFFECTS

At least 5 million people were exposed to dangerous radiation, and thousands have died or are disabled. Some 2 million "children of Chernobyl," now adolescents and young adults, remain at risk for developing thyroid cancer and other Chernobyl-related diseases. More than 10,000 square miles of farmland and forests in Ukraine, Belarus, and Russia were contaminated. Honey, milk, mushrooms, fruit, and fish are particularly absorbent and remain unsafe for consumption; children no longer pick berries or harvest mushrooms in the forest. Residents anxiously live with the fear of ingesting "hot particles" that would dramatically increase their chances of getting cancer.

An abandoned collective farm near Chernobyl, Ukraine, in the 1990s.
Source: Yann Arthus-Bertrand/Corbis; used with permission.

Approximately 230,000 residents were evacuated from the "dead zone" and resettled in relatively safer regions. The new locations lacked adequate housing, jobs, and access to medical care. Relocation also caused secondary traumatic stress and a host of other psychological difficulties. After months or years of attempted resettlement, many families returned to their ancestral homes and farms due to a variety reasons, including the belief that the contaminated regions were not unsafe; the desire to be "home"; and social fatalism ("whatever is to happen will happen"). Also, the government's playing down of the seriousness of the long-term effects of Chernobyl during the first five years subsequent to the disaster has made the Chernobyl community highly distrustful of the government. Thus, the communities in the contaminated regions of Belarus and Ukraine remain in psychological crisis and emotional despair.

In the years following the disaster, a popular antinuclear and environmental movement in Ukraine and Belarus began and brought pressure on the government until the plant was finally closed. Environmental groups and public policy advocates continue to insist that the Chernobyl nuclear power plant never be reopened, that the sarcophagus encasing reactor No. 4 be reconstructed, that all the other unsafe Chernobyl-type reactors also be closed down before their intended date of decommissioning, and that alternative sources of energy be tapped and developed.

For pessimists, Chernobyl was a harbinger of a coming apocalypse, which they claim is implicit in its prophetic name. The Slavic word *chernobyl* (literal translation: bitter existence) is the name of a bitter herb called wormwood in English. The Chernobyl disaster in most Russian and Ukrainian minds are thus associated with the apocalyptic "wormwood star" in the Bible (see Revelation 8:11) and in the writings of the sixteenth-century French prophet Nostradamus. For optimists, Chernobyl was a watershed event that marked the end of the nuclear era (and the Cold War between the Soviet Union, which collapsed in 1991, and the West), as well as the advent of new thinking about a coming age of security, peace and prosperity. At the beginning of the twenty-first century, the verdict is still out on whether Chernobyl was a warning bell that the world heeded, or the unheeded pangs of more nuclear disasters yet to come.

—Michael J. Christensen

Further Reading

Carter, M., & Christensen, M. J. (1993). *Children of Chernobyl.* Minneapolis, MN: Augsburg.

Marples, D. (1996). *Belarus: From Soviet rule to nuclear catastrophe.* New York: St. Martin's.

Medvedev, G. (1991). *The truth about Chernobyl.* New York. Basic Books.

CHILD CARE

All societies need to care for their children, and they do so in a variety of ways. Parents, paid care workers, the state, and friends and neighbors contribute to the care of children.

In familialistic countries, such as Italy, it is assumed that families are responsible for the care of their members. In comparison, de-familialized countries assume that families are not able to meet all of their own child care needs. Thus, alternatives for child care are made available. In social democratic welfare states, such as Sweden, the state provides universal child care for citizens through publicly funded day care centers and services. In liberal states, such as the United States, child care is available for purchase on the market. Parents pay day care centers, nannies, or au pairs to care for their children.

Child care also can be provided through informal community networks of family, friends, and neighbors. Illustrating the well-known proverb "It takes a village to raise a child," some African societies rely on dense informal networks to provide care for children. Studies in Uganda and Nigeria show that while biological mothers may play a prominent role in the care of a child, a number of other adult women, siblings, and other children also regularly provide care to infants, in addition to

Child Care in West Africa

The following description of the Dogon of West Africa is a good example of the major child care role played by siblings in many African societies.

In general, the natives treat small children with great gentleness, they play with them or rock them, and one often sees a baby in the arms of a very distant kinsman, who will leave the child in the care of his neighbor if a domestic task claims him; but the kindly guardian may have a moment of inattention, and this is why many babies roll into the flames which attract them or are seriously burned by water or the boiling grease that escaped from a cooking pot. A small child may also be entrusted to the supervision of an elder brother or of a sister of more advanced age, who holds it on her hip or settles it astride her back. A common sight in the villages mornings and evenings is that of boys or girls, still quite young, bent under the weight of their little brother or their little sister.

In order to quiet or put to sleep the child that cries one softly sings a lullaby to him, i somio ni, the words of which scarcely vary: baby, it is necessary to be good, your mother is gone, do not cry, she is going to come back soon: . . . that is to say: baby, come, be quiet, your mother has gone, she is going to come back, take and drink the millet porridge come, be quiet, I shall give you fish, come, be quiet, baby, your mother has gone, she is going to come back, I shall give you some meat, look.

Source: Paulme, Denise. (1940). *Organisation sociale des Dogon (Soudan francais)* [Social organization of the Dogon (French Sudan)]. Paris: Editions Domat-Montchrestien, F. Loviton et Cie, pp. 436–437. Translated from the French for the HRAF by Frieda Schutze.

cooperating in other household work. In isolated regions of Kenya, however, where cultural norms emphasize an exclusive relationship between biological mother and child, caregiving networks are less dense.

Child care through the community is also found in rural and urban communities in industrialized countries. In rural communities, informal networks of care serve to fill the gap in available formal child care services. Child care is traded between neighbors as part of an informal economy. Rural residents also describe caring for neighbors' children as an essential part of the rural way of life and local culture, which are based on close-knit ties. Nor are such communities of care limited to rural areas. "Urban villages" also exist and provide informal child care. City residents often have a number of kin within walking distance and visit regularly with neighbors. These relatives and nonrelatives play a significant child care role. As in rural communities, the exchange of care in the network can be part of an informal economy supplying affordable child care. Within ethnic communities, the sharing of care also can be culturally important and valued.

The support provided through community networks benefits children and parents. Benefits to children include improved school performance and social competency and fewer behavioral problems. The relationship between community and child outcomes is both direct and indirect, as a result of increased quality of parenting. Parental support, stimulation, coping, and effectiveness can increase in community networks.

Regardless of which strategy for child care is used—parenting, formal, or informal care—caring for children, across cultures, is principally done by women. Children are cared for by mothers, women working as paid care providers, and female friends, sisters, aunts, and grandmothers providing care in community networks.

—Carrie L. Yodanis

Further Reading

Elder, G., & Conger, R. (2000). *Children of the land: Adversity and success in rural America.* Chicago: University of Chicago Press.

Esping-Anderson, G. (1999). *Social foundations of postindustrial economies.* Oxford, UK: Oxford University Press.

Halliday, J., & Little, J. (2001). Amongst women: Exploring the reality of rural childcare. *Sociologia Ruralis, 41*(4), 423–437.

LeVine, R., Dixon, S., LeVine, S., Richman, A., Leiderman, P. H., Keefer, C., et al. (1994). *Child care and culture: Lessons from Africa.* Cambridge, UK: Cambridge University Press.

Marshall, N., Noonan, A., McCartney, K., Marx, F., & Keefe, N. (2001). It takes an urban village: Parenting networks of urban families. *Journal of Family Issues, 22*(2), 163–182.

Stack, C. (1974). *All our kin: Strategies for survival in a black community.* New York: Harper & Row.

CHILDREN

For children, community is defined as the social and physical arena in which daily life takes place. Community is the place in which children first negotiate friendships, attend school, play organized or spontaneous sports games, develop an idea of who they are outside of home, and encounter an array of adult and peer influences. Children begin the complex process of transitioning from home to neighborhood and eventually to wider community contexts early in their development. In industrialized Western nations, regular interactions with people and places outside the home are routine by eight years of age. By fifteen to sixteen years of age, people and places in the community emerge as a central focus of life. Thus community, as the "territory of childhood" (Garbarino 1982, p. 150), has important developmental implications for children.

In the 1980s and 1990s, researchers in the United States devoted increasing attention to understanding how the community, or more immediately the neighborhood, shapes the daily lives and developmental outcomes of children. That research culminated in the publication in 2001 of *Does It Take a Village? Community Effects on Children, Adolescents, and Families,* edited by Alan Booth and Ann Crouter. While presenting the definitive research to date on the topic, the authors concede that despite the reemphasis on place, a precise measure of the effect of community on human development and well-being continues to elude social scientists. Empirical associations between community and child outcomes are often weak, contradictory, or overly specific to one particular place, group, or developmental epoch. To date, although there is widespread agreement with the African proverb "It takes a village to raise a child," no specific models of how the village shapes human development or why the village appears to matter so much have successfully been generalized over place and time. Still, strong hints of the mechanisms through which community influences child development emerge from the research.

Three theoretical streams dominate the study of children and community in industrialized Western nations. The first emphasizes the importance of structural features, such as the demographic composition of community; the second underscores the significance of the social processes of place; the third focuses on family management strategies as a key factor in children's experiences in community. Each stream of research yields different insights into the intricate role the whole village can play in raising a child.

STRUCTURAL FEATURES OF COMMUNITY

The physical infrastructure, demographic composition, and institutional resources of a community shape the day-to-day reality of its residents, including children. Such factors as whether adequate housing, transportation, and utilities are available, whether health and social services are offered locally, and whether the demographic composition of the community presents a concentration of poverty or a concentration of affluence appear to have much to say about the relative capacity of a community to successfully nurture its children. Of these structural features, demographic composition has received the most research attention in reference to its role in child development. The aggregate socioeconomic status, residential stability, and child dependency ratios (the ratio of dependent children to supporting adults) of a community all emerge as structural or demographic variables important to developing children.

Socioeconomic Status

The impact of a community's aggregate socioeconomic status on children in Western industrialized nations has been studied mainly in lower-income urban contexts. Thus, there is far more known about how a concentration of poverty undermines children's development than about how a concentration of affluence might perhaps support development in these nations. Clustering together the poorest, youngest, and least educated of residents presents a troublesome developmental context for children. Concentrated poverty typically comes bundled together with an array of other social problems. Early parenthood, families headed by women, substance abuse, delinquency, crime, mental health problems, and domestic violence are prevalent in impoverished contexts within the United States. When a community has a dense concentration of social problems, the power of place to predict compromised developmental outcomes is pernicious. It is theorized that just as a child is likely to catch chicken pox from exposure to an infected individual, a child is likely to pick up troubling behaviors and beliefs by mere exposure. Further, when such behaviors and beliefs are present in concentrated levels, as they are in many impoverished neighborhoods, transmission occurs in an epidemic fashion with few left unaffected.

Residential Stability

Length of residence and homeownership typically predict individual-level social and sentimental ties to place. At the community level, residential stability is vital to a local capacity to nurture families and children. When generations of the same families live in the same place, strong attachments to place and a sense of community develop and are maintained. A shared history,

Children of various ages pose for a photograph in the village of Chaprut, Hunza Valley, Pakistan, in 1996.
Source: Stephen G. Donaldson Photography; used with permission.

culture, and tight social networks emerge among residents and support a sense of safety, consistency, mutual trust, and social order within place. Such community-level attributes can buffer children and families from volatility within the home or wider society. Thus, whether a community presents a pattern of residential stability or instability influences its child-rearing capacity.

Child Dependency Ratios

The age composition of a community, particularly the ratio of adults to children in a community, has important implications for child rearing as well. Raising children well requires a huge investment of time and attention on the part of parents. When such resources are in short supply in families, as is the case in many modern single-parent or dual-earning households, the presence of other community adults becomes even more important. Elders, extended kin, and even young-adult role models in the community can offer the extra time and attention necessary to buffer a child from the effects of family-level deficiencies. Even when appropriate adult models roles do not exist within a family or immediate neighborhood, interaction with adults at school, through religious institutions, and in the wider community through other institutions (such as sports clubs) supplies children with access to valuable, broadening social resources. Attachment to teachers, for example, serves as a significant deterrent to delinquent activity. Thus, the ratio of adults to children is another key structural factor in understanding the capacity of the village to raise a child.

Structural features of community clearly yield important clues as to the connection between context and child development. It is equally clear, however, that those features do not fully answer the question of how or why the village appears so important to child development. Structural factors do little to shed light on the within-group differences evidenced in the research. Even in the communities most at risk, not all children flounder, not all families fail to effectively nurture their children, and not all neighborhoods default in their child-rearing capacity. Thus, it is important to consider the contribution of other factors.

SOCIAL PROCESSES OF COMMUNITY

Another stream of research in the field considers the social processes of place. Whether a community develops strong social networks, how adults and children relate to each other, and whether residents develop shared social norms and act to effect social control appear related to the capacity of place help children develop successfully.

When social organization is characterized by overlapping social networks of family, kin, religious institutions, school, and community, a place can function well to collectively support, monitor, and channel children on a pathway to successful development. A high level of trust and a sense that everyone knows everyone else emerge within such social organization. These attributes of community facilitate the construction of shared norms or ideas for behavior and the communal application of sanctions against deviant or troublesome behavior. For families embedded in these social networks, children are seen as a collective responsibility or as belonging to everyone. Important shared resources, such as adults' time and attention, are readily concentrated on the socialization of children. As an example, children in such contexts often report "not being able to get away with anything," as their parents know all that happened during the day, particularly if there was a problem, well before the child arrives home. Close connections in these densely knit networks make supportive watchfulness and communication efficient.

Further, if a community shares an ideology that the children belong to everyone, it readily invests in educational and recreational opportunities important to successful child development. Children with access to supportive community institutions and opportunities are more resilient in overcoming serious family traumas than are those with access to fewer such resources. Essentially, a community characterized by cohesive social organization enhances children's access to social, educational, and other resources important to their development while at the same time protecting them from risks or behavior that might threaten their progress.

These social, educational, and other resources are often not equally available across the community. To benefit from supportive social processes, a family must be integrated into the social networks of place that offer access to such resources. Social hierarchy in a tight-knit community is strong and often rigid. Residence patterns that cluster poor families in open-country pockets, ghetto neighborhoods, rental apartments, or trailer parks create neighborhoods marked as inferior by the larger community. Families residing in such places, along with those having ne'er-do-well reputations, deserved or otherwise, struggle daily with social stigmatization. The social ramifications of being structurally or perceptually "outside" of the resourceful social networks or low in the communities' social hierarchy intensify the effects of family problems and essentially narrow the life chances of children by excluding them from educational and cultural experiences that would otherwise support successful development.

Accounting for the social processes of place appears to add much to understanding the child-community link. Yet translating social process theories into measurable constructs is tricky. In trying to make social processes measurable, there is the danger of reducing them to structural attributes and failing to acknowledge their dynamic nature as processes. Moreover, the structural features and social processes of a place even added together are not the sum total of contextual factors that explain outcomes for children. Families operate as a mitigating system between the community and the child and thus have an equal or even larger influence that must be figured into the equation of community effect.

Children at Play

Play is one of the most meaningful of all childhood activities. It provides immediate gratification, develops social and cognitive skills, and is almost always a happy experience. The following ethnographic account of children playing in the village of Ban Klang in central Thailand shows some of these positive elements of spontaneous play.

> It was a beautiful time of the day. The sun was low on the horizon in the west. The houses, high on stilts, threw cool shade over the open space in the front yards. In front of one house in the shade a few children gathered. They were soon joined by more children from the houses nearby. Before long the atmosphere vibrated with the sounds of laughter, singing, running, and shouting. A game session was on its way in a home playground in Ban Klang.
>
> The children started with the game Bagnet. One child stood in the middle of the circle, blindfolded, while the others, holding hands to form a circle, walked around, singing gaily. Half an hour passed. Another hour rolled by. The children were still playing. By then they had played another game, Store the Pork Oil, and one team was hopping around on one leg in the game One-legged Rabbits. The last game, highly strenuous, soon wore them out. The shady spot under the coconut tree provided them the coolness and peacefulness they needed for a rest. They talk amiably. Some were joking.
>
> Suddenly, Ang, a ten-year-old girl leaning against the coconut tree trunk, told her sisters, "I've thought of something new. Let's try to play at guessing. I'll close my eyes and you two change places, then I'll guess where you are."
>
> She turned to face the coconut tree trunk, her eyes closed. Her two sisters changed their standing places. They were giggling.

Source: Anderson, Wanni W. (1973). *Children's Play and Games in Rural Thailand: A Study in Enculturation and Socialization*. Ann Arbor, MI, University Microfilms, p. 72.

FAMILY MANAGEMENT STRATEGIES

Family management strategies shape how community risks and resources are perceived and experienced by children. Family management strategies—the processes by which a family manages various tasks—are essentially adaptations to contextual factors. That is, such strategies, particularly in terms of child rearing, evolve from a family's rational effort to maximize benefits and minimize perceived harm within a given context. Family strategies, intended to ameliorate the negative effects of a harmful neighborhood and to promote social mobility, are well documented for urban contexts. Using what sociologist Robin Jarrett calls "bounding" or "bridging" strategies, parents attempt to protect children from risks and to link them to vital, mobility-enhancing resources and opportunities not available in the immediate neighborhood. Ethnographic images vividly document such processes in high-risk urban contexts. Parents may restrict even older children to the home in hopes of keeping them away from the drug trade on the streets. Other parents try to integrate their children into better-off contexts by traveling long distances each day across town to school or to a special program.

Limited evidence exists for whether families outside of the urban setting adopt either bounding or bridging strategies for child rearing. The description of life within open-country pockets of poverty suggests poor rural families use bounding strategies. Such families geographically isolate themselves into a small, kin-based cluster. They then add to this isolation the distinction of the external community as a hostile "outside world." Such strategies do little to increase family access to community resources and are linked to the intergenerational perpetuation of poverty because alternative pathways or resources are unattainable. Bridging strategies are suggested in rural context through the efforts of other families to embed a child in the social networks and institutions of the wider community. Through the deliberate choice of school volunteerism, church involvement, or civic engagement, some families attempt to increase access community social resources. Children whose families are successful at these strategies exhibit high degrees of social and academic competence.

Community bounding and bridging strategies appear to hold great promise for better outcomes when they can be applied effectively. Such strategies, however, require a large investment of family time and energy, and the availability of time and energy among lower-income families in either rural or urban contexts is limited by many factors—unpredictable work schedules, lack of adequate transportation, and higher child dependency ratios, for instance. Such barriers lead researchers to conclude that successfully implementing these strategies without a supportive community requires a huge effort on the part of parents.

THE ROAD AHEAD

Clearly, much of the failure of social science to define the connection between children and community derives from the complicated nature of the problem. Disentangling the effects of community from those of family processes and individual attributes is a complicated task. As a result, current conceptualizations tend to offer only a starting point for understanding the complex connection between community and child development. Enough of an image has been revealed to make it clear that community does matter. Further, the effects of community appear to be transmitted through an array of mechanisms associated with various aspects of community. It will be for future researchers to find more of the pieces to the important puzzle of understanding precisely how and why it takes a village to raise a child.

—Katherine L. MacTavish

Further Reading

Benson, P. (1997). *All kids are our kids: What communities can do to raise caring and responsible children and adolescents.* San Francisco: Jossey-Bass.

Booth, A., & Crouter, A. (Eds.). (2000). *Does it take a village? Community effects on children, adolescents, and families.* Mahwah, NJ: Lawrence Erlbaum.

Comer, J., Haynes, N., Joyner E., & Ben-Avie, M. (1996). *Rallying the whole village: The Comer process for reforming education.* New York: Teachers College Press.

Elder, G., & Conger, R. (2000). *Children of the land: Adversity and success at century's end.* Chicago: University of Chicago Press.

Furstenberg, F., Cook, T., Eccles, J., Elder, G., & Samaroff, A. (1999). *Managing to make it: Urban families and adolescent success.* Chicago: University of Chicago Press.

Garbarino, J. (1982). *Children and families in the social environment.* New York: Adline.

Jarrett, R. (1995). Growing up poor: The family experiences of socially mobile youth in low-income African American neighborhoods. *Journal of Adolescent Research, 10,* 111–135.

Leventhal, T., & Brookes-Gunn, J. (2000). The neighborhoods they live in: The effects of neighborhood residence on child and adolescent outcomes. *Psychological Bulletin, 126*(2), 309–337.

MacTavish, K. (2001). *Going mobile in rural America: The community effect of mobile home park residence on child and youth development.* Unpublished doctoral dissertation, University of Illinois, Champaign-Urbana.

McLeod, J. (1987). *Ain't no makin' it: Aspirations and attainment in a low-income neighborhood.* Boulder, CO: Westview.

Salamon, S. (2003). *Newcomers, old towns: Community change in the rural midwest.* Chicago: University of Chicago Press.

Schorr, L. (1997). *Common purpose: Strengthening families and neighborhoods to rebuild America.* New York: Anchor Books.

Wilson, W. J. (1987). *The truly disadvantaged.* Chicago: University of Chicago Press.

CHINATOWNS

Chinatown, a term that has been used in English since 1857 to refer to the Chinese section of a city outside China, has meant different things to different people at different times and in different cities in North America. For some, Chinatown represents an enclave of vices; for others, a rundown inner-city neighborhood. For still others, Chinatown is a historic district, a cultural hearth, a suburban shopping plaza, or a tourist mecca.

The discovery of gold and demand for labor in the United States and Canada during the nineteenth century lured the rural Chinese to leave their poverty-stricken villages. After their arrival, they lived in Chinatowns, enclaves where they felt safe from the abuse and hostility of the surrounding white community. Being unable to speak in English, they felt more comfortable in Chinatown, where they could communicate with their fellow countrymen in their dialects, and where they could follow their own customs. At the same time, Chinatown functioned as their training base where they learned to master English and live in a foreign environment. Chinatown, a self-contained community, was at that time an idiosyncratic, Asian community amid a Western, urban environment. The mixture of commercial, residential, institutional, and recreational uses, and the Chinese-style decorative facades of buildings gave Chinatown a unique townscape, clearly distinguishable from other parts of the city.

After the war, Chinese immigrants no longer needed to rely on Chinatowns for security and protection, as prejudice and discrimination against them subsided, allowing them to be more easily assimilated into the host society. More and more Chinese left Chinatowns to seek better accommodation in other parts of the city or in the suburbs. Many Chinatowns in small towns and cities became defunct. However, Chinatowns in metropolitan cities remain a Chinese rendezvous spot for social gatherings and for the events of many Chinese clan associations (such as Wong's Association), county associations (associations of people from the same area in China, such as Zhongshan Association), fraternal societies (such as the Chinese Freemasons), and kung fu clubs and recreation societies. Chinese who live in other parts of the city, especially the old-timers, come to their clubs and associations to meet friends and play mah-jongg and other games. To some old-timers, Chinatown is a second home.

Many old Chinatowns in metropolitan cities have been revitalized, and the living situation has been improved. Old prewar buildings have been demolished to provide space for multistory senior citizens' homes or commercial and residential apartment buildings. This gentrification has attracted both Chinese and non-Chinese residents to some old Chinatowns, expanded their population base, and diversified their ethnic composition. Some old Chinatowns have become tourist destinations, not only because of the Chinese arches at the entrance to the neighborhood, the Chinese gardens, and other beautification projects, but also because of the unique prewar buildings.

To Help Their Children

A major reason for immigration to the United States is to provide more opportunity for one's children. The account provided by Mrs. Li of her immigration to and settlement in New York City's Chinatown shows some of the hardships parents endure in this quest.

> I decided to come mainly because that was the only way I could get my three grown children out of China. In fact, I did not benefit from immigration at all. My husband, who was a university professor, could not find a job commensurable with his education and experience because of his poor English skill and age. He ended up working for five dollars an hour in a food-manufacturing company in Chinatown. I had to work in a garment factory. I was very slow because of my poor eyesight and had little experience in operating a sewing machine. I was paid by the piece. No matter how hard I worked, twenty dollars a day [for at least eight hours] was about the most I could make. What else could we do? We had to pay the rent, the food and all the basic expenses. We could not afford just to stay home. We simply had a difficult time adjusting to the life here.
>
> I came because I wanted my children to come. Immediately after I arrived here, I filed a petition for immigrant visas for my three adult children. Shortly after they came, my husband went back to China to teach and I stayed to take care of my children. Now all my children have worked their way through college, and now they have all settled down and gotten married. I feel that I have done enough for them, and that it is now time to think about going back to China to join my husband for the rest of my life.

Source: Zhou, Min. (1992). *Chinatown: The Socioeconomic Potential of an Urban Enclave.* Philadelphia: Temple University Press, pp. 156–157.

After the 1960s, new Chinese immigrants came to North America from Hong Kong, Taiwan, China, and other parts of Asia such as Vietnam, Singapore, Malaysia, and Indonesia. They are heterogeneous, not only in terms of origin but also in terms of wealth, education, and cultural background. Many of them live in better inner-city neighborhoods or affluent suburbs of large cities. New Chinatowns, established after the war, have emerged. A new Chinatown is basically a commercial entity, characterized by a concentration of Chinese businesses along a section of a street or in one or two city blocks. Unlike an old Chinatown, a new Chinatown does not have a Chinese residential population although it is usually located close to neighborhoods with a Chinese population. A new Chinatown may be developed in a suburban shopping plaza or mall. Such malls were built not only by Chinese investors but also by non-Chinese developers. Many of these malls may not have oriental decorative motifs or a Chinese name, although most of their businesses are operated by Chinese, have Chinese store signage, and cater mainly to Chinese and other Asian people. Hence, they are commonly called Chinese malls, Asian malls, or Asian-themed malls instead of Chinatowns. More than fifty Chinese malls have been established in Richmond, a suburban municipality of metropolitan Vancouver, Canada, and there are over sixty in Richmond Hill, Markham, Scarborough, and North York, which are suburban districts of metropolitan Toronto.

The concept of Chinatown has greatly changed over time. In the twenty-first century, the businesses and residential population of old Chinatowns will be more diversified and multiethnic. New types of Chinatowns will continue to emerge, such as those developed by Chinese from Vietnam, Taiwan, or mainland China, who may call their Chinatowns "Vietnamese Chinatown," "Little Taipei," or "Little Shanghai" respectively.

—David Chuenyan Lai

Further Reading

Kinhead, G. (1992). *Chinatown: A portrait of a closed society.* New York. HarperCollins.

Lai, D. C. (1988). *Chinatowns: Towns within cities in Canada.* Vancouver, Canada: University of British Columbia Press.

Lai, D. C. (1995). Three Chinatowns. In B. Hesketh & F. Swyripa (Eds.), *Edmonton: The life of a city* (pp. 256–266). Edmonton, Canada: NeWest.

Lai, D. C. (2001). *A study of Asian-themed malls in the Aberdeen district of the city of Richmond, British Columbia.* Vancouver, Canada: Vancouver Centre of Excellence for RIIM.

Loo, C. M. (1991). *Chinatown: Most time, hard time.* New York: Praeger.

Zhou, M. (1992). *Chinatown: The socioeconomic potential of an urban enclave.* Philadelphia: Temple University Press.

CHRISTIANITY

Christianity is a religion that combines the concept of individual salvation with a strong emphasis on community. Christians believe that God calls the individual person to faith and discipleship, but the ensuing life of faith is never solitary or individualistic. Rather, Christian believers recognize each other as fellow participants in the common life of a universal community. This community is the Church (in the widest sense of the word), the entirety of all believers past, present, and future. In Christ, they are all bound together like members of one body. All those who belong to God also belong to one another. Accordingly, Christian identity is inseparable from the idea of community. This insight is expressed in the ancient saying, *unus Christianus, nullus Christianus*—"one Christian alone is not a Christian."

BIBLICAL FOUNDATIONS

The Christian concept of community is rooted in the Bible. The basic social orientation of human nature is expressed in the creation story: "It is not good that man should be alone" (Genesis 2:18). Subsequently, the Hebrew scriptures tell the story of one particular community, the nation of Israel, whom God has called to be his people.

In the New Testament, the notion of God's people is applied to the community of the followers of Jesus Christ. With God as their common Father, all Christian believers are like brothers and sisters to one another. Collectively they form "the People of God" (I Peter 2:9–10), a new Israel under the lordship of Christ. The Apostle Paul describes this community with the Greek word *ekklesia,* a term that denotes the full assembly of citizens of a city-state. According to Paul, each local group of Christian believers represents an *ekklesia* (congregation), and all groups together form the universal *ekklesia* (church) of Christ. Another important word in Paul's vocabulary for the church is *koinonia* (partnership), which characterizes the church as a community of mutuality and solidarity. The image of the church as a collective person (the "Body of Christ") further develops this understanding of community. As one body has many members with diverse functions, so all believers form one body in Christ. They are individually members of one another and serve each other with their diverse gifts and abilities. Each member stands in need of the other, and whatever affects one member affects all (see Romans 12: 4–8 and I Corinthians 12:12–27).

Altogether, the images of family, people, and collective body suggest that the fellowship ties between Christian believers are organic and fundamental rather than merely external. A particular ethos of brotherly love accompanies this sense of community. Christians are called to love each other (see John 15:12, Romans 12:10,

The Biblical Basis for Community
(From the King James Version)

Genesis 2

18 And the Lord God said, It is not good that the man should be alone; I will make him an help meet for him.

I Peter 2

9 But ye are a chosen generation, a royal priesthood, an holy nation, a peculiar people; that ye should shew forth the praises of him who hath called you out of darkness into his marvellous light:

10 Which in time past were not a people, but are now the people of God: which had not obtained mercy, but now have obtained mercy.

Romans 12

4 For as we have many members in one body, and all members have not the same office:

5 So we, being many, are one body in Christ, and every one members one of another.

6 Having then gifts differing according to the grace that is given to us, whether prophecy, let us prophesy according to the proportion of faith.

7 Or ministry, let us wait on our ministering: or he that teacheth, on teaching;

8 Or he that exhorteth, on exhortation: he that giveth, let him do it with simplicity; he that ruleth, with diligence; he that sheweth mercy, with cheerfulness.

I Corinthians 12

12 For as the body is one, and hath many members, and all the members of that one body, being many, are one body: so also is Christ.

13 For by one Spirit are we all baptized into one body, whether we be Jews or Gentiles, whether we be bond or free; and have been all made to drink into one Spirit.

14 For the body is not one member, but many.

15 If the foot shall say, Because I am not the hand, I am not of the body; is it therefore not of the body?

16 And if the ear shall say, Because I am not the eye, I am not of the body; is it therefore not of the body?

17 If the whole body were an eye, where were the hearing? If the whole were hearing, where were the smelling?

18 But now hath God set the members every one of them in the body, as it hath pleased him.

19 And if they were all one member, where were the body?

20 But now are they many members, yet but one body.

21 And the eye cannot say unto the hand, I have no need of thee: nor again the head to the feet, I have no need of you.

22 Nay, much more those members of the body, which seem to be more feeble, are necessary:

23 And those members of the body, which we think to be less honourable, upon these we bestow more abundant honour; and our uncomely parts have more abundant comeliness.

24 For our comely parts have no need: but God hath tempered the body together, having given more abundant honour to that part which lacked:

25 That there should be no schism in the body; but that the members should have the same care one for another.

26 And whether one member suffer, all the members suffer with it; or one member be honoured, all the members rejoice with it.

27 Now ye are the body of Christ, and members in particular.

and I John 4:7), to serve and help each other, and to forgive one another. The most striking expression of this ethos is the "love-communism" of the Apostolic church at Jerusalem (Acts 2:44–47 and 4:32–37). The liturgical basis is the sacraments. Baptism signifies the believer's transition from his or her natural social ties (family, class, ethnic and cultural background) to the universal community of the Christian church: "There is neither Jew nor Greek, there is neither slave nor free, there is neither male nor female; for you all are one in Christ Jesus" (Galatians 3:28). The Lord's Supper (Eucharist), in turn, functions as a unifying meal: "The bread which we break, is it not a participation in the body of Christ? Because there is one bread, we who are many are one body, for we all partake of one bread" (I Corinthians 10:16–17).

THE CONCEPT OF THE CHURCH

The basic idea of the church in the New Testament was defined more closely in the Nicene Creed (long thought

Table 1. Views of Community in Four Denominational Traditions

Approach:	*Catholic*	*Orthodox*	*Protestant Reformation*	*Believers' Church*
Community constituted by:	Sacred hierarchy of the church	Unanimity in faithful devotion to the sacred tradition	Doctrinal agreement based on Holy Scripture	Intentional covenant between committed believers
Representative churches:	Roman Catholic Church	Byzantine tradition (e.g., Greek and Russian Orthodox Churches	Lutheran tradition, Reformed tradition	Mennonites, Baptists

to have been promulgated at the Council of Nicaea in 325 CE, but now thought to have been put forward at the Council of Constantinople in 381 CE), which characterizes the church with four attributes: one, holy, catholic (meaning universal), and apostolic. Another early document, the Apostle's Creed (sixth century), refers to the church as the "Communion of Saints." In the history of Christian thought, these passages have provided the basic categories for the Christian self-understanding as a community of faith. The church is *one;* that is, the people of God cannot be conceived of as being divided or disjointed. The church is *holy;* it belongs to God and somehow shares in God's own holiness. It is *catholic;* it possesses a universal scope and thus transcends all human boundaries and differences (geographic, ethnic, social, cultural, and so forth). It is *apostolic;* it stands in unbroken and faithful continuity with the original community of the Apostles.

Needless to say, each of these affirmations about the nature of the church raises various questions and may be interpreted in a number of ways. For example, how can the idea of ecclesial unity be reconciled with Christianity's empirical plurality and division? Should the unity of the church be understood in institutional terms, as doctrinal agreement, or as an entirely spiritual or mystical reality? For these and similar issues, a central concern is the question of how the theological idea of the church relates to the church's empirical existence in visible and institutional forms. Here, various interpretations have been proposed, including the distinctions between the "visible" and the "invisible" church and between the "church of faith" and the "church of experience." There is a general agreement that the church's spiritual reality is larger than any empirical organization and that the spiritual dimension is also in some way present within the empirical structures. Still, the precise nature of this relation has been the subject of much controversy, thus contributing greatly to the development of diverse denominational traditions.

Vital to the concept of the church, finally, is the area of social organization within the church. From the beginning, the church recognized that its sense of fellowship and connection would have to find expression in specific organizational structures. Here, the most significant development has been the formation of local gatherings (congregations) with various forms of pastoral and administrative leadership as the basic institutional unit. Institutions such as synods, presbyteries, and the office of the bishop have come to provide the connection between these individual congregations. Other important organizational elements for the creation and maintenance of community are the celebration of corporate worship, the practice of charitable ministries, the design of sacred space, and catechetical instruction in matters of faith.

DENOMINATIONAL DIFFERENCES

Christianity, as a modern world religion, is composed of thousands of different groups and traditions. In the United States alone, there are currently about 170 major denominations (by which is meant autonomous ecclesiastical bodies). This diversity springs in part from historical circumstances, but it also reflects the fact that key issues in the theological concept of community have lent themselves to conflicting interpretations. For the sake of clarity, four different approaches to understanding community can be distinguished within the wide spectrum of denominational traditions (see Table 1). The Roman Catholic model sees community as being constituted by the church's sacred hierarchy with the pope as the visible representation of order and unity. The Orthodox model (churches of the Byzantine tradition) emphasizes that community arises from a spirit of unanimity in shared faithfulness to the sacred tradition. The model of the magisterial Reformation (many mainstream Protestant denominations, including the Lutheran and Reformed churches) regards the preaching of the Gospel and agreement in matters of faith as the basis of community. Finally, for the believers' church model (for example, the Baptist and Mennonite traditions), community rests on the principle of an intentional covenant between committed believers, often involving the requirement of adult baptism or a particular conversion experience, or both. While the first three models derive from the European tradition of a state-sponsored territorial church, the believers' church model shows more affinity with the modern American concept of the church as a "voluntary society."

One force that seeks to counteract the growing fragmentation of the church is the ecumenical movement. It works toward mutual understanding and cooperation between different churches and thus testifies to the experience that, ultimately, the reality of Christian community reaches across denominational boundaries.

—Peter Vogt

Further Reading

Dulles, A. (1987). *Models of the church* (Expanded ed.). New York: Doubleday.

Dulles, A., & Granfield, P. (1999). *The theology of the church: A bibliography.* New York: Paulist Press.

Durnbaugh, D. F. (1968). *The believers' church: The history and character of radical Protestantism.* New York: Macmillan.

Jay, E. G. (1980). *The church: Its changing image through twenty centuries.* Atlanta, GA: John Knox Press.

Mead, F. S., & Hill, S. S. (2001). *Handbook of denominations in the United States* (11th ed., C. D. Atwood, Ed.). Nashville, TN: Abingdon Press.

Minear, P. S. (1960). *Images of the church in the New Testament.* Philadelphia: Westminster Press.

Moltmann, J. (1976). *The church in the power of the spirit: A contribution to messianic ecclesiology* (M. Kohl, Trans.). New York: Harper & Row.

Vogt, P. (2001). *The church as community of love: A historical and theological inquiry.* Unpublished doctoral dissertation, Boston University School of Theology.

Zizioulas, J. D. (1985). *Being as communion: Studies in personhood and the church.* Crestwood, NY: St. Vladimir's Seminary Press.

CITATION COMMUNITIES

Citation communities are abstract networks that are built up as authors cite other authors in the footnotes, endnotes, and bibliographies of learned literatures, especially when citations are made repeatedly. These communities contain not only acquaintances but persons the citer has never met, dead as well as living. Their chief significance is that they are reasonably objective manifestations of key evolutionary units of science and scholarship, whether these are called invisible colleges, discourse communities, schools of thought, disciplinary specialties, theory groups, or cultural networks (Randall Collins's phrase, "coalitions of the mind," may capture them best). As such, they are of interest to historians of ideas, to sociologists who study communication patterns among scholarly elites, and to information scientists who exploit bibliographic ties among authors to improve document retrieval.

Citation occurs when the author of one document refers explicitly to another document. The intent is generally to relate some new claim to a context set by one or more precedent texts. By convention, citations identify what is being cited by means of a few standardized details. Author and title identify a work; the other details serve to identify editions of works, copies of which are the actual units of document retrieval.

NETWORKS OF NAMES

Citation relations can be represented as graphs in which the works are nodes and the citations are links that connect some nodes but not others. Citing and cited documents can thus be rendered as networks, making graph-theoretical research on networks, especially social networks, applicable to citation data. Human communities are often studied as networks of relations between pairs of persons, and citation communities can similarly be studied by examining relations between pairs of documents. Documents, after all, are in some sense surrogates for the persons who wrote them, and, just as the attributes of persons can be used in social analysis, the attributes of both citing and cited documents can be used in analyzing citation communities.

Usually, however, the term *community* refers not to a set of documents but to a group of persons with shared attributes. The term *citation community* thus implies that the linked authors are to be understood as persons, whether they appear as citers or citees. Hence, for studying community, the key attribute of documents is authors' names, with their interesting duality of meaning. Names can be shorthand for documents, but they also evoke people. An analyst can write "E. O. Wilson" or "S. J. Gould" and mean two books or two papers in a network, but she or he can also mean two famous contemporary biologists. Using the latter interpretation, the analyst can add to the study of documents any relations that might hold between their authors as persons, such as whether they knew each other or worked in the same place or exchanged e-mail. The analyst can ask such questions as "What other marks of community do these authors share?" "Does their relatedness through citation correlate with particular social ties or communication behaviors?" "Do any of these other variables cause citation?" "Does citation cause any of them?" "Is the community formed by intellectual ties or by social ties?" "Does it exhibit lines of conflict?" The answers depend on the other variables used to interpret the citation ties.

INTERCITATION AND COCITATION

One way to study citation communities is to start with authors as the unit of analysis. In practice, this means analyzing not individual documents but *collections* of authors' works (for example, any writing by Wilson or Gould). "Relatedness through citation" can then be defined in two basic ways. In a citation-network graph—a numeric matrix with identical lists of authors on the rows and in the columns—the cells can be filled with intercitation counts or cocitation counts (both are available through online searches of the Institute for Scientific Information's citation databases in academic or special libraries).

Intercitation reflects who cites whom in a closed set—for instance, does Wilson anywhere cite anything by Gould? Does Gould likewise cite anything by Wilson? Since their choices need not be the same, intercitation is an asymmetric measure. The researcher can create a binary matrix of ones and zeroes (for "cites/doesn't cite") or a valued matrix, so called because it contains the actual frequencies of intercitation in the cells (the higher the count, the more important the tie).

The same can be done with cocitation counts, except that here the valued matrix reflects the number of documents in which any two authors have been jointly cited by citers in general—for example, in how many documents have works by Wilson been cited along with works by Gould? This matrix is symmetric—the count for Wilson-Gould is the same as that for Gould-Wilson. Matrices containing either intercitation or cocitation counts yield standard network statistics (e.g., measures of which authors are most highly connected) and can be tested for correlation with other measures of community.

Intercitation is a good focal variable if the analyst has other measures of the citers as actors and wants to explore their community in terms of why they cite (or fail to cite) each other. Cocitation is good if the analyst simply wants an empirical snapshot of who goes with whom in a field, to look for explanations such as sameness of subject matter, methods, or nationality. Author cocitation has been extensively used to map authors in "intellectual space," but relatively few studies have used cocitation or intercitation counts to probe the social space of research communities. This area seems ripe for development, especially given the software now available (e.g., UCINET). Analyzing and visualizing change over time in these communities will probably be highly valued in the future.

INTELLECTUAL VERSUS SOCIAL TIES

Studies to date leave little doubt that citation communities are based primarily on intellectual ties, such as the perceived relevance and authority of the citees. Social ties, such as acquaintanceship or personal interaction, are secondary. They co-occur with citation often enough, but they are neither necessary nor sufficient to explain it. For example, intellectual ties such as perceived relevance explain the citation of authors whom the citer has never met and in many cases could never have met (as when someone today cites Aristotle).

Some scholars take a sardonic view of "authority" in citation relations, implying that citers annex whatever citees they think make their own works most persuasive, with little regard for their real relevance. Others think that citation communities are rife with self-promotion and cronyism at the expense of true merit. When hard data are examined, these darker interpretations seem unwarranted, but considerable new research is necessary to settle the matter.

—Howard D. White

Further Reading

Baldi, S. (1998). Normative versus social constructivist processes in the allocation of citations: A network-analytic model. *American Sociological Review, 63*(6), 829–846.

Borgatti, S. P., Everett, M. G., & Freeman, L. C. (2002). *UCINET for Windows: Software for social network analysis.* Harvard, MA: Analytic Technologies.

Chen, C. (2003). *Mapping scientific frontiers: The quest for knowledge visualization.* Heidelberg, Germany: Springer-Verlag.

Collins, R. (1998). *The sociology of philosophies: A global theory of intellectual change.* Cambridge, MA: Belknap Press of Harvard University Press.

Crane, D. (1972). *Invisible colleges: Diffusion of knowledge in scientific communities.* Chicago: University of Chicago Press.

Hargens, L. L. (2000). Using the literature: Reference networks, reference contexts, and the social structure of scholarship. *American Sociological Review, 65*(6), 846–865.

Latour, B. (1987). *Science in action; How to follow scientists and engineers through society.* Cambridge, MA: Harvard University Press.

Mullins, N. C. (1973). *Theories and theory groups in American sociology.* New York: Harper & Row.

Mullins, N. C., Hargens, L. L., Hecht, P. K., & Kick, E. L. (1977). Group structure of co-citation clusters: Comparative study. *American Sociological Review, 42*(4), 552–562.

Perry, C. A., & Rice, R. E. (1999). Network influences on involvement in the hybrid problem area of developmental dyslexia. *Science Communication, 21*(1), 38–74.

Stewart, J. A. (1990). *Drifting continents and colliding paradigms: Perspectives on the geoscience revolution.* Bloomington: Indiana University Press.

Van Dalen, H. P., & Henkens, K. (2001). What makes a scientific article influential? The case of demographers. *Scientometrics, 50*(3), 455–482.

White, H. D. (1990). Author cocitation analysis: Overview and defense. In C. L. Borgman (Ed.), *Scholarly communication and bibliometrics* (pp. 84–106). Newbury Park, CA: Sage.

White, H. D. (2000). Toward ego-centered citation analysis. In B. Cronin & H. B. Atkins (Eds.), *The web of knowledge: A festschrift in honor of Eugene Garfield* (pp. 475–496). Medford, NJ: Information Today (ASIS Monograph Series).

White, H. D. (2001). Authors as citers over time. *Journal of the American Society for Information Science and Technology, 52*(2), 87–108.

White, H. D., & McCain, K. W. (1997). Visualization of literatures. *Annual Review of Information Science and Technology, 32,* 99–168.

CITIES

Cities are dense congregations in areas of concentrated economic and political activity. They have existed throughout history, but in recent times, especially in the past century or so, there has been a growing movement of people from the countryside to the city across the globe. Demographers estimate that by the year 2050, more than half of the world will live in some form of urban setting.

Cities can be both liberating and confining. During the late Middle Ages in the West, one aphorism suggested that "*Stadtluft macht man frei,*" or "the atmosphere of the town makes one free." But this, of course, was in contrast to life outside towns and villages, where, especially on the estates of the nobility, life was anything but free. Most people lived life as servants or as peasants. Their conditions were destitute; they survived only to their mid-thirties, at most, if they survived infancy at all. Those for whom they toiled had an abundance of food and the privileges of space and luxury items. What the cities offered the peasants, many of whom began making their way to them, was the chance to secure a more successful life and livelihood.

At the same time, city life has its drawbacks. Since the late nineteenth century, social theorists such as Karl Marx have noted the contrasts between life in the city and life in the countryside. Some argue that life in the countryside, particularly in small rural towns and villages, furnishes a degree of social intimacy and personal security that is lacking in the city. Rural villages and towns are seen as places of permanence, sites where one's ancestors grew up and where life continues today pretty much as it has in the past. Such life, it is argued, is basically both stable and happy.

By contrast, social theorists have waged a kind of rhetorical war against the city. They argue that once people choose to live in a city, they lose the sense of serenity and stability found in the countryside. Life in the city is fast-paced. For the newcomer, it tends to be impersonal. The essence of the city, it has been written, is the marketplace. Transactions take place between people who do not know one another intimately, but only as buyer and seller.

So the city is seen on the one hand as providing freedom to do as one pleases, but on the other as being a place of loneliness and impersonality. Are such images true? Certainly they are to an extent. But like all imagery, they tend to exaggerate certain features to make their points. Nonetheless, they remain a part of what we mean today when we think about the city.

THE MODERN CITY

The modern city dates from the early eighteenth century. By that time the city was comparatively large, housing hundreds of thousands of people. Edo (modern-day Tokyo) had a population of more than a million by the mid-eighteenth century. The growth in industry and the trade in crafts had brought increasingly large numbers of people from the countryside into the city. As they entered the city, they began to populate the numerous small shops and handicraft firms that existed in the urban confines. Amsterdam, London, and Paris were among the great Western metropolises. They exercised not only economic but also political power over their environs and over other nations. London was the seat of government of the British empire and, hence, the place from which power was exercised and the site to which commodities and goods traveled.

In North America, just after the birth of the United States, there were a variety of emerging cities—Boston, Philadelphia, and New York. They numbered in the tens of thousands of people. Very different from today's cities, or even those to be found at the end of the nine-

Seattle Matches Citizen Effort With City Dollars

SEATTLE, Wash. (ANS)–Under a towering, gray bridge over Lake Washington's ship canal, there stands a huge troll with one odd lolling eye and a giant paw crushing a very real Volkswagen bug.

Families from around the city come to this little, isolated pocket where bridge meets land in the funky, artsy neighborhood of Fremont. Crowds of youngsters climb the troll's head, hang from his nose, stare eyeball to eyeball into his face.

The troll was not the creation of a city park department fed up with drug trade under the bridge or a politician with an odd sense of how he'd like to be remembered. This creature is evidence of a unique partnership that combines the resources–and imaginations–of ordinary citizens with the assets of city government.

It's a new twist on the often-hostile relationship between neighborhood residents and city hall.

"We're not telling the city, 'We have a problem, You better fix it.' It's more like, 'We have some concerns, and this is our proposed solution,'" said Ellen Stewart, who heads a local non-profit social agency.

Residents are able to act on their proposals through Seattle's Neighborhood Matching Fund. In this cooperative effort, the city sets aside money for projects–but a neighborhood has to match the funds with donated time, materials, labor or money.

After receiving a prestigious award for innovations by state and local government, the matching fund program is now being replicated by other cities around the country.

In Seattle, the fund has actually taken in more than it has given out, if you count sweat equity and out-of-pocket offerings by residents as assets for the whole city, which most people there do.

But until recently, partnership was hardly the word to describe relations between city residents and city government. Confrontation was more like it.

"The focus then was that government needs to do more," said Jim Diers, a former community activist who now works for the city.

Residents wanted more cops on the beat. They wanted government to stop the construction of high-rise apartments in their neighborhoods of one- and two-family homes.

But activists like Diers began pushing the idea, as he explains it, that "neighborhoods could do much more for themselves."

Much to Diers' surprise, people turned out by the hundreds to dig holes, paint, work side by side with kids and seniors and generally take responsibility for their neighborhoods.

The Neighborhood Matching Fund does not balk at funding such oddities as bigger-than-life trolls, murals where horses gallop off walls and into alleys, peace parks festooned with colorful paper cranes, even a neon Rapunzel perched in a turret overlooking a busy waterway.

But the fund–$1.5 million annually from city coffers–is normally tapped for less fanciful things: community policing, anti-violence programs, and neighborhood planning, to name a few.

In all, the program has funded over 700 projects–and involved thousands of city residents.

–Theresa Morrow

Source: "Seattle Matches Citizen Effort With City Dollars." American News Service, Article No. 11, n.d.

teenth century, they were relatively small and compact. Their central areas held a number of businesses and residences, and they could easily be traversed by the population at the time. Wealth coexisted with poverty in these emerging cities, but the poverty, rather than being found in the central areas, was located on the fringes of the city. There was a relatively small class of wealthy citizens; their wealth came from small businesses or new professions, such as law and medicine. Most of the population was poor, however.

As had been true throughout history, the workings of the economy played a large role in shaping the early U.S. city. The center was dynamic and lively; it was where trade occurred and merchandise was exchanged. Local government—the little that existed—also took place at the center of the city. Some cities, moreover, grew to hold great prominence in the nation. Washington, D.C., like London, grew in importance as the strength of the nation grew. New York City, perched on the Atlantic Ocean, became both a great port of trade and the location of major business strength and interest. Indeed, as had traditionally been the case with cities, many of the new U.S. cities grew up alongside water, because it was over water that most long-distance trade occurred.

THE INDUSTRIAL CITY

By the middle of the nineteenth century, the appurtenances of the Industrial Revolution—new machines, such as the steam engine, and new modes of production—had begun to reshape the character of the city. The Industrial Revolution also brought new social forms of production, in particular, the replacement of the small handicraft shops by large factories. Moreover, as jobs began to multiply the cities brought in more and more people from rural areas. In the United States, people now began to settle in the cities not only from the countryside, but also from abroad.

No force in modern history had as great an impact as the Industrial Revolution. It reshaped the economies of nations and cities alike. Some cities became functionally specialized as manufacturing cities. In Great Britain, for example, Manchester became a center of textile manufacturing, and its life and the lives of its residents revolved around the import of goods, such as lambs' wool, and the production of all manner of clothing. In the United States, similar specialization occurred; for example, Pittsburgh, Pennsylvania, became home to the steel industry and produced vast amounts of coal.

Social changes in the new industrial city were surely as significant as the economic and political changes. New wealth was created, and thus a new social class of people whose wealth and influence began to rival and then surpass that of the older mercantile class. A new class of laborers and working people also was created, one that comprised the large majority of the urban residents. The wealthier people, though originally living near their enterprises in the central areas of the city, began to move to the outskirts and to build for themselves summer residences.

The growth in the number of workers increased the density of the urban population. New buildings went up to house the growing numbers of workers. Since workers generally were paid low wages and had relatively large families, they could afford very little in the way of housing. Tenements in cities like New York soon were overflowing with people, and with that crowding came disease. Infant mortality rates were high.

The industrial city continued as the dominant form of the city from the late nineteenth century well into the twentieth century. By the middle part of the twentieth century, however, cities began a long and often tortured decline as industries began to move away. By the 1960s and 1970s, Manchester and Pittsburgh were no longer seats of booming manufacturing empires. Industry moved where it could make its greatest profit: either overseas, where wages were considerably lower, or to those regions of industrialized nations where labor was also cheaper.

THE POSTINDUSTRIAL, POSTMODERN CITY

With cities' loss of industry in last third of the twentieth century came other noticeable changes. For example, the majority of jobs now lay in the service and professional sectors. Employment opened up in restaurants and cleaning establishments on the low end and in financial, real estate, and technology sectors at the high end. Many of the new firms established themselves not in the central areas of the downtown, but rather on the fringe areas of the city, often close to expressways that made both receiving and supplying goods and services easier. In addition, more and more people moved to the outer areas of the city, in part to be closer to their places of employment but also to secure high-status homes in the suburbs.

Yet, although many young families continued to move out to the suburban areas of the city, there are two well-to-do groups that in the last decades of the twentieth century moved to the inner parts of the city: young professional couples and older people whose children had grown and left home. As a consequence of this continuing trend, many developers are focusing on downtown areas, where there is quite a variety of available spaces—small lofts in which the beams are exposed, three- or four-story townhouses that can easily accommodate not only an older couple but also grown children or visitors, and spacious condominiums, often on a single floor.

Increasingly, then, there has been a reconcentration of the population in the inner parts of cities, a conscious effort by local officials and developers to repopulate and revitalize the downtown areas. With the flush times of the 1990s, local governments also had more money to invest in the public spaces of cities. They created new parks and public spaces in an effort to bring people back into the city. In addition, even suburban or new city developments began to change in character. New Urbanists, who seek to reinvent the older American village for the twentieth-first century, employ porches, gazebos, and small streets in their model towns, such as Seaside, Florida, and Kent, Maryland. These attributes are designed to bring a greater degree of sociability among residents and to eliminate the influence of the automobile—which, according to many New Urbanists, is a major culprit for the feeling of "sameness" and "nowhere" found among many suburban developments in the latter part of the twentieth century.

Now, if industry were one of the principal forces that drove the city of the nineteenth and twentieth centuries, how are we to depict the driving forces and key features of what has been called not only the postindustrial city, but also the postmodern city? What seem to be its essential features and qualities?

THE CITY OF SYMBOLS AND SURVEILLANCE

Cities have increasingly become the sites of various symbolic constructions and manipulations. Some cities are simulacra, constructions intended to lure people from their everyday lives into a fantasy world. Orlando, Florida, near Disney World, is one such city, as is Las Vegas, the city of illusion and mirage, built from emblems of other cities, like London and Paris. Similarly, many cities now recruit high profile architects to design cultural elements that will lure people to their particular site. Frank Gehry's design of the Guggenheim art museum in Bilbao, Spain, was so successful that many other cities now seek to create such signature landmarks for themselves.

Besides the manipulation of symbolism by architects and urban planners, there is a darker side to the postmodern city. Unlike cities of the past, in which people were in daily contact with one another, the postmodern city is fragmented, without a core, and also without a heart. The epitome of such a city, which subjects both residents and outsiders to surveillance, is the gated community. Such a community is something like a fortress—designed to protect its residents, to give them a level of great comfort, but also to ensure that no outsider can intrude on their lives. Gated communities are private associations to which entrance is totally protected by guards. It is the notion of private property carried to an extreme.

THE INFORMATION CITY

One way to think about the postindustrial city is to focus on the nature of its leading forms of business and production. Sociologist Manuel Castells does so, arguing that the production and use of information are the central features of the modern age. If the commodity-producing factory was the signature feature of the industrial age, information is the signature feature of the information age. Information technology companies (computer and telecommunications companies, for example) represent the leading edge of this era. Like the capitalist class of the past, the people who run and control today's information technology companies—people such as Bill Gates of Microsoft and Michael Dell of Dell Computer Corp.—exercise a major influence over the current era.

More important, the new technology also has demonstrable impact on how people communicate, facilitating high-speed communication and thus shortening the distances that separate people. The effect, some would argue, has been to make *place* less central in people's lives. Because people can communicate across large distances with great ease, where they live and work no longer makes a great difference. In brief, then, in Castells's eyes, the postindustrial, postmodern city lacks the centrality and form of the earlier industrial city because of the production and use of information in the present era.

THE GLOBAL CITY

A complementary interpretation of the postmodern city views it as a global creation. The modern city is, in the words of sociologist Saskia Sassen, the global city. The concept of the global city has become more popular as both people and capital have come to move around the world with increasing ease. The effect of the new global economy, Sassen argues, is to create a new kind of city, one that no longer is constrained in its operations by the workings of nations, and one that becomes the central site where the leading edges of business conduct their work, and where those businesses and political officials in charge become located. Global cities, such as London, Tokyo, and New York, do more business with one another than with their national counterparts, so that these cites are effectively cut off from their nations in terms of economics.

There are certain downsides to the new global city. Sassen points out that there has been a growing bifurcation in the skills and incomes of residents of the global city. The financial and communications empires require increasing numbers of highly skilled people to run their operations; these people comprise a new kind of business or techno class. At the same time, there has been a notable increase in the service sector of the global city. Service jobs tend to require few skills and are generally low paying. The overall effect is to increase income disparities, with a very wealthy class being separated by a very poor class by an ever widening rift.

CITIES OF THE DEVELOPING WORLD

Much of this discussion and analysis has concerned the cities of Western Europe and the United States. But most cities in the developing world do not fit the

Western pattern. Many suffer because of the overwhelming poverty of their governments and their residents. Such cities may have sparkling downtown areas, but around the edges are many people residing in shantytowns. The population living on the fringes of those cities lacks adequate health, has high infant mortality rates, and suffers greatly in other respects. When cities in the developing world have been able to develop industrial and manufacturing enterprises, they are plagued by the same problems that haunted cities in nineteenth-century Europe and the United States—illness caused by crowded, unsanitary living conditions, pollution, and a degraded environment. In Africa, the health crisis is made worse by astronomical rates of HIV infection.

One initiative of the United Nations that is aimed at improving the lives of people living in shantytowns is UN-HABITAT. UN-HABITAT has sought to direct funds from the United Nations toward cities in developing countries and to help in their reconstruction. It is clear that unless the problems of Third World cities can be addressed, First World cities can have only a precarious existence themselves. In the global age, the fate of the West is inevitably tied up with the fate of the Third World.

—Anthony M. Orum

Further Reading

Castells, M. (1989). *The informational city.* Oxford, UK: Blackwell.

Castells, M. (2000). *The Information Age: Volume 3. End of millennium.* Oxford, UK: Blackwell.

Chudacoff, H. P. (1981). *The evolution of American urban society* (2nd ed.). Englewood Cliffs, NJ: Prentice Hall.

Cohen, M. A., Ruble, B. A., Tulchin, J. S., & Garland, A. M. (Eds.). (1996). *Preparing for the urban future: Global pressures and local forces.* Washington, DC: Woodrow Wilson Center Press.

Cronon, W. (1991). *Nature's metropolis: Chicago and the Great West.* New York: W. W. Norton.

Davis, M. (1990). *City of quartz: Excavating the future in Los Angeles.* London: Verso.

Foucault, M. (1979). *Discipline and punish: The birth of the prison.* (A. Sheridan, Trans.). New York: Vintage.

Gottdiener, M. (1994). *The social production of urban space.* Austin, TX: The University of Texas Press.

Gottdiener, M., Collins, C. C., & Dickens, D. R. (1999). *Las Vegas: The social production of an all-American city.* Malden, MA: Blackwell.

McKenzie, E. (1994). *Privatopia: Homeowner associations and the rise of residential private government.* New Haven, CT: Yale University Press.

Orum, A. M. (1995). *City-building in America.* Boulder, CO: Westview.

Orum, A. M., & Chen, X. (2003). *The world of cities: Comparative and historical perspectives on places.* Malden, MA: Blackwell.

Pirenne, H. (1956). *Medieval cities: Their origins and the revival of trade.* (F. D. Halsey, Trans.). Garden City, NY: Doubleday. (Original work published 1925).

Sassen, S. (2001). *The global city: New York, London, Tokyo.* Princeton, NJ: Princeton University Press.

Sjoberg, G. (1965). *The preindustrial city, past and present.* New York: Free Press.

Tilly, C., & Blockmans, W. P. (Eds.). (1994). *Cities and the rise of states in Europe, A.D. 1000 to 1800.* Boulder, CO: Westview.

Warner, S. B., Jr. (1987). *The private city: Philadelphia in three periods of its growth* (Rev. ed.). Philadelphia: University of Pennsylvania Press.

Zukin, S. (1982). *Loft living: Culture and capital in urban change.* Baltimore: Johns Hopkins University Press.

Zukin, S. (1991). *Landscapes of power: From Detroit to Disney World.* Berkeley and Los Angeles: University of California Press.

CITIES, INNER

Inner-city communities traditionally surround a city's central business district, constituting some of the city's oldest neighborhoods. They are characterized by distinctive networks of relationships, cultural traditions, and behavioral patterns. Though many of these central-city neighborhoods have become increasingly affluent in recent years as upper-income residents move back to the city, the phrase *inner-city community* is suggestive of lower-income communities of the working class, the service-dependent, bohemian youth, the recently immigrated, and the homeless. Although inner-city neighborhoods of the sort discussed here exist in large cities throughout the developed world, this article focuses on the United States. Some of the most famous U.S. inner-city communities are New York's Harlem, Chicago's Back-of-the-Yards, and San Francisco's Tenderloin. Inner-city communities are important because the issues associated with inner cities are some of the most important of the day: immigration and acculturation, poverty and homelessness, crime and disorder, unemployment and illegitimacy, artistic innovations and countercultural social developments.

THE CHICAGO SCHOOL OF COMMUNITY STUDIES

Scholarly studies of inner-city communities generally begin with the Chicago School of urban sociology, dating to the early 1900s. This turn-of-the-century period marked the United States' transition from a rural to an urban country, with traditional lifestyles and agrarian culture giving way to modern urban diversity and eclecticism. Witnessing the social upheaval associated with this urban revolution, Chicago School scholars characterized urban life as an agent of abrupt change and dislocation—especially in the dense, heterogeneous, anonymous, and transient inner city.

Using inner-city Chicago as their main object of study, scholars like Robert Park and Louis Wirth noted that inner-city communities concentrated the most challenging effects of urban life: diversity, anonymity, transience, disorder, immorality, and a loss of tradition and kinship. Whereas many areas of the city could exclude undesirable groups (such as the poor, the recently immigrated, or the homeless) and undesirable elements (such as factories), by means of policing practices, zoning codes, and expensively priced housing, the inner-city community could exclude no one. Consequently, society's least attractive elements concentrated there, with the result that these areas became crime-ridden, poor, polluted, and dangerous. In 1906 Upton Sinclair described Chicago's Back-of-the-Yards community as "the jungle" in his novel of the same name.

REDEEMING AND REDEVELOPING THE INNER CITY

From the early 1900s until the 1960s, negative public attitudes about life in the inner city led to dramatic efforts to transform, elevate, or eliminate the inner-city community. Inspired by the settlement house movement begun in Great Britain by Samuel Augustus Barnett (1844–1913) and led in the United States by Jane Addams (1860–1935), educated reformers established inner-city centers to provide education, health care, English instruction, and skills training to the immigrants and impoverished classes that were concentrated there. By the mid-1900s, these reform efforts coalesced into a growing social work profession.

While social workers sought to lift the inner-city community out of its degraded condition, the early 1900s also saw efforts to eliminate the inner city altogether. Utopian city planners such as Daniel Burnham (1846–1912), Ebenezer Howard (1850–1928), and Le Corbusier (1887–1965) created holistic plans to uproot and rebuild the inner city in ways that would prevent the return of such a concentration of diversity, poverty, and vice. Daniel Burnham's vision of a "city beautiful" inspired cities to eliminate inner-city areas in favor of well-designed districts filled with public monuments such as grand city halls, wide parkways, and landscaped central parks. Howard's suburb-inspiring plans called for the creation of "garden cities"—smaller, well-landscaped communities surrounded by greenbelts. Le Corbusier's vision of a "radiant city" called for the destruction of inner cities in favor of expanding districts of sparkling skyscrapers, linked to bedroom suburbs by a vast freeway system.

These utopian visions helped inspire urban renewal projects in the United States immediately following World War II. Urban renewal was a strategy to use state authority and financing to declare inner-city communities "blighted," to tear them down, and to subsidize their redevelopment into office-tower complexes, retail centers, universities, and more-affluent neighborhoods. From the 1950s to the 1970s, when urban renewal was at its height, authorities destroyed four low-income inner-city housing units for every one they replaced.

THE 1960S: EMERGING VOICES FROM THE INNER CITY

Threatened by urban renewal projects and indignant over stereotypes that characterized the inner city as pathological, many inner-city communities mobilized political resistance and social education efforts in the 1960s and 1970s. New studies, often written by nontraditional scholars (for example, actual inner-city residents), began to highlight positive elements of inner-city life. These studies focused on the intricate social networks, neighborhood ties, kinship connections, and unique cultural patterns of the "ghetto." *The Death and Life of Great American Cities* (1961), a ground-breaking work by the urban activist Jane Jacobs (b. 1916), expressed the United States' growing sensitivity to neighborhood traditions and inner-city social networks. As a result, urban renewal began to take a back seat to community-based development strategies.

The literature, poetry, and music of inner-city neighborhoods became more and more accepted by a mainstream audience in the 1960s. Essayists such as James Baldwin (1924–1987) asserted the beauty and vitality of inner-city Harlem, while poets such as Amiri Baraka (originally LeRoi Jones; b. 1934) and Audre Lorde (1934–1992) produced widely read poetry of the street. *The Autobiography of Malcolm X* (1965), *Down These Mean Streets* (Piri Thomas; 1967), and *Soul on Ice* (Eldridge Cleaver; 1968) introduced the social voice and political energy of the inner city to a broader U.S. audience. *On the Road* (1957), by Jack Kerouac

Financial Skills for Minority Residents

BOSTON (ANS)—Ronald Hendricks was one of the millions of inner-city residents who leaped into the ranks of homeowners during the 1990s.

But the Jamaican immigrant is still chasing his American dream. So far he has garnered little equity in life, in part because of the high-interest mortgage loan he took out without shopping around.

"To be honest, I really didn't know what I was getting into," said Hendricks. Also, as a result of loose budgeting, he said, he slipped into a hole of consumer debt.

Still, Hendricks pulled one leg out of the red muck recently. He attended a Personal Finance Fair, an educational event where local residents got the lowdown on closing costs, property insurance, retirement saving and other money matters. It was part of expanding efforts nationwide to promote what organizers term "economic literacy."

Community leaders see this particular literacy gap as grounds for optimism—a mark of progress in the urban cores. In many neighborhoods across the country, financial services have become more readily available than at any time in the past two decades, according to analysts.

In one telling statistic, Harvard University's Joint Center for Housing Studies reports that African Americans and other minorities have accounted for nearly half of the increase in the swelling rate of American homeownership in recent years.

Boston's inner-city havens offer a vivid view of these changes.

"Basically, there were no banks in black neighborhoods, or they were very, very scarce," said Tamara Olsen, vice president of the Boston-based Organization for a New Equality, a national civil rights organization with a focus on economic opportunity.

"You had a whole generation of people with no experience interacting with a financial institution," she said. "The habits of going to a bank didn't exist for a whole group of people."

The return of banks to the city's core began, symbolically, in 1994, when BankBoston opened a branch in the Roxbury section. It was celebrated as the neighborhood's first bank in 23 years.

At the same time the bank was opening, though, the Rev. Charles Stith, founder of the Organization for a New Equality, could see there was still a missing element from the financial picture.

Stith, a Methodist minister who is now U.S. ambassador to Tanzania, said it became apparent that new bank branches would yield little return if people didn't know how to open checking accounts or tap loans for mortgages and other needs.

In an interview before leaving for Africa last fall, the ambassador said: "America touts the virtues of capitalism all around the world. But in this country, we do a pretty poor job of teaching people how the system works, at a practical level."

Stith's brainchild, The Campaign for Economic Literacy, has in five years extended from Boston to Brooklyn, Cleveland, St. Louis, Kansas City, Mo., Houston and the District of Columbia, as well as Prince Georges County, Md. Banks and other lending institutions are behind the initiative.

In each of those areas, the campaign has organized workshops, usually held in African-American churches, on weeknights, Saturdays or after Sunday worship. The two-hour training includes sessions with such titles as "Credit: Burden or Blessing."

"Economic literacy" is the buzz phrase for a wide mix of measures to teach Americans, poor and middle class, about the uses of money.

[. . .]

Citizens Bank and other companies are wooing customers in the inner city partly because of public policies and partly because of the success of community pressure to brings banks back to the urban core. The federal Community Reinvestment Act, for example, obliges lending institutions to include urban zones in their residential and commercial loan programs.

But once in the inner cities, these institutions have often found that the lending also makes good business sense, said Barbara Paige, vice president of Access Capital Strategies in Cambridge, Mass.

"They're saying, 'Hey, there's a market there, and people are spending money,'" said Paige, whose investment firm helps lenders package loans to the inner city. "And people are paying them back. Just because they're poor, doesn't mean they're deadbeats."

At the same time, she pointed to the learning curve ahead for many residents who can recognize a check-cashing storefront or pawnshop more easily than the granite facade of a bank.

"These communities have been ignored in the past. And because of that legacy, there isn't a whole lot of literacy in the use of banks" and other financial services, she said.

That estrangement from the financial system suggests one obstacle to the economic literacy drive. Another, say organizers, is the common aversion to discussing the pocketbook.

"In many urban areas, people don't want to talk about their money. It's hard for folks to say, 'My credit is messed up,'" said the Rev. Joseph Washington, a New York pastor who is national chairman of the Organization for a New Equality. "But if we don't, we'll never gain any real access to productive capital in this country."

—William Bole

Source: "As Banks Return to Inner Cities, Minority Residents Acquire Financial Skills." American News Service, Article No. 769, January 28, 1999.

(1922–1969), expressed the enchantment of a rising generation of free-spirited young people with the energy and poetry of the inner city. Many young people embraced the inner city over the sterility of suburban life and the conformity of the "man in the gray flannel suit" (the title of a 1956 film about suburban life).

THE WAR ON POVERTY AND THE NEIGHBORHOOD REVOLUTION

During the 1960s, urban neighborhoods experienced a political revival. Core-city neighborhood associations emerged to mobilize the energies of low-income residents, often people of color who had been excluded from the planning phase of urban renewal projects. Community organizers such as Saul Alinsky (1909–1972), who helped form the Industrial Areas Foundation in 1940 in Chicago, adopted strategies of neighborhood mobilization and creative conflict. Many inner-city communities mobilized to claim control of their territory, their schools, and their local businesses. The Black Power movement, especially strong in the Northeast and on the West Coast, claimed the inner city as its base, and issued calls for community control of the city's social service systems and police forces. In the Southwest, Latino communities mobilized, resulting in such developments as the establishment of alternative schools governed by Latino activists and featuring a curriculum that celebrated the culture of the inner city. (Escuela Tlatelolco, in Denver, is one example that endures to this day.)

Notable scholars of inner-city communities during this time, such as C. Wright Mills, Frances Fox Piven, and Richard Cloward, began to identify the inner-city community as a base where excluded peoples could gather together and organize movements against mainstream society. In the inner city, black and Latino communities, gay and lesbian communities, socialist and anarchist communities, and all manner of other countercultural groupings could escape pressures for mainstream conformity, could find strength in numbers, and could find the territorial base from which to mobilize. What the Chicago School had seen as defects were now taken as strengths, as alternative lifestyles, nonconformity to workplace expectations, political radicalism, and even drug use were celebrated as productive alternatives to mainstream expectations. At the same time, inner-city problems such as crime, disorder, unemployment, and illegitimacy increasingly were seen as products of an exploitative and racist mainstream society rather than as products of inner-city residents' pathological behavior.

Political mobilization and neighborhood organizing in inner cities in the 1960s helped compel the government to take a new approach to inner-city communities. The federal government sponsored job programs, youth education, and other strategies to address inner-city disorder, with the caveat that these programs were to be largely controlled by activists in inner-city communities themselves. President Lyndon Johnson introduced a host of programs under the rubric of a "War on Poverty." These were meant to empower inner-city communities by giving them new resources and access to political power. The Federal Economic Opportunity Act of 1964 delivered substantial War on Poverty funds to inner-city communities, but also required cities to insure the "maximum feasible participation of residents of the areas and members of the groups served" (Piven & Cloward 1993, p. 265). As a result, the inner-city community action programs and model cities that emerged were often controlled by members of the inner-city communities they targeted. Across the nation, inner-city activists, often low-income minorities, moved into positions of influence in their cities.

In the late 1960s and early 1970s, major court decisions began to change the definition of deviancy in ways that gave panhandlers, vagrants, and the mentally ill more freedom from police harassment. The landmark Supreme Court case of *Papachristou v. City of Jacksonville* (1972) invalidated many local vagrancy laws on the grounds that they were too vague and that they made various minority groups (e.g., non-whites and the poor) vulnerable to police harassment. As a result, cities began to direct their police to downplay "victimless" crimes, such as marijuana use and prostitution. Daniel Patrick Moynihan, a U.S. senator from New York, called this a period of "defining deviancy down," meaning that Americans began to accept a broader range of typically inner-city behaviors (e.g., public drug use, punk attire, teenage pregnancy, graffiti, panhandling, and vagrancy).

1970–1990: CRISIS IN THE INNER CITY

The political agitation and violent riots in the inner cities in the late 1960s accelerated the flight of more-affluent residents from the city to the suburbs, where the racial mix, zoning codes, and cultural expectations supported a far more predictable and mainstream lifestyle. Businesses followed suit, and soon suburban edge cities were experiencing rapid growth in residents and investment capital. Inner-city communities left behind were in crisis by the mid-1970s and 1980s.

Without investment capital, and without the presence of affluent, educated, and job-holding residents, inner cities disintegrated. Poverty and welfare rates increased, as did crime rates, and inner-city communities became increasingly dangerous. Some politicians began, once again, to advance the idea of completely redeveloping inner-city communities. In New York, planning director Roger Starr floated the idea of "planned shrinkage" in 1976. His idea was to reduce public services in low-income inner cities, to close down schools and libraries, and to subsidize residents to move out. Eventually, the inner city would be so depopulated as to justify tearing it down and replacing it with office towers, urban malls, or upper-income housing.

A tendency emerged in scholarly and political discourse to describe inner-city communities as dominated by a "culture of poverty," a culture which made any uplift efforts hopeless. Influenced by such theories, city officials retreated from the empowerment-oriented War on Poverty and began to emphasize the ideas of such urban planners as Oscar Newman and James Q. Wilson. Newman and Wilson both bemoaned the loss of moral expectations in the inner cities and offered strategies to replace inner-city license with mainstream morality. Newman offered a strategy of "defensible space," which became a guiding light for planners of public housing, parks, and other public spaces. The idea was to design space in such a way that police and reputable social elements had the maximum ability to supervise behaviors and to police incivilities by means of patrolled gates, walled-off alcoves, sophisticated surveillance systems, and the absence of privacy.

In a similar vein, Wilson advanced the "broken windows" theory of community order that argued that relentless patrolling of minor inner-city offenses such as public drinking, panhandling, and graffiti was necessary to prevent more serious crimes (such as muggings or arson). In the 1980s and 1990s, Wilson's ideas were linked to growing public investment in police forces and a recriminalization of such behaviors as aggressive panhandling, vagrancy, and public inebriation.

THE 1990s: THE BACK-TO-THE-CITY MOVEMENT REDISCOVERS INNER-CITY COMMUNITIES

The 1990s witnessed affluent citizens moving back into cities, experiencing a reenchantment with inner-city architecture, diversity, and culture. A new literature emerged that was harshly critical of suburban sterility (for example, James Kunstler's *The Geography of Nowhere*). Consequently, the 1990s saw a dramatic rebirth of the inner city, as young urban professionals and elderly cosmopolitans began to move into redeveloped lofts, trendy apartment buildings, and inner-city townhouses. Even though many poor people were displaced by this process, most officials celebrated this gentrification process as necessary if inner-city decay was to be reversed. Local officials worked closely with the federal government in advancing this process through such strategies as the Department of Housing and Urban Development's HOPE VI program. HOPE VI replaced low-income housing projects with mixed-income projects catering to both moderate-income and impoverished residents in order to bring mainstream culture and income into the inner city and thereby introduce low-income residents to the values, social networks and economic opportunities of the middle-class and affluent.

In a related development, the 1980s saw the establishment of a new federal program for inner-city "enterprise zones." This policy offered substantial tax breaks to businesses that brought jobs and investment into the inner city. Such a strategy downplayed the aspirations of inner-city communities for political power and self-determination and emphasized how focusing on business investment could bring jobs, capital investment, and business opportunities into inner-city communities.

TWENTY-FIRST-CENTURY STRATEGIES

Even as affluent residents have moved back into core-city neighborhoods, low-income inner-city communities have remained. A number of strategies targeting those communities for "uplift" have emerged; these strategies generally focus either on morals and behaviors, on economic reform, or on local community development.

An Emphasis on Morals

The approach that focuses on morals traces the problems of inner-city communities to the "culture of poverty" mentioned earlier and offers solutions such as time limits attached to welfare grants (adopted in the 1996 welfare reform act) and the construction of spaces from which certain groups of people (the homeless, for example or gang youth) are excluded.

In this vein, some have linked the rise of violent inner-city criminals to what they call "moral poverty." Moral poverty, they argue, is caused by the absence of strong and loving parents (particularly by absent fathers), and by the collapse of moralizing institutions such as character-building public schools, punishing jails, and respected churches. As solutions they promote marriage, increased penalties for crime, faith-based inner-city initiatives.

Economic Reform

Another response to the economic disintegration and social disorder of the inner city since the 1970s has been to link inner-city problems with larger problems in the U.S. (and global) economy. Leading social scientists like W. J. Wilson argue that the culture of poverty is not a product of broken morals but rather of a broader pattern of global "uneven development." Such scholars note that the modern economy is built on an increasingly inegalitarian wage structure and that poorly educated inner-city residents have few opportunities to advance educationally or economically. The result is an inner city of substantial social-psychological dysfunction.

Their response to such problems is to advocate policies that will bring jobs and related resources into the inner city or that will allow inner-city residents more easy access to jobs and resources in other neighborhoods. They support public-works programs, enterprise zone programs and other tax incentive programs to bring businesses into the inner city. In addition, they support better mass transit systems to allow workers access to suburban jobs, rules requiring publicly subsidized companies to hire inner-city workers, and increased support for jobs training programs.

Community Development

A communitarian response to inner-city problems assumes that there are many productive assets within the inner city. Advocates of inner-city community development highlight the healthy social networks in the inner city and propose ways to build more such networks through small-scale community development strategies (for example, through a community gardens project, an affordable housing cooperative, or a farmers market).

A community development strategy, sometimes called an asset-based development model, relies on residents of the inner city to identify assets and networks in their community that could be used to create positive change. Social workers, neighborhood residents, and government officials help create community leadership development programs. They bring together residents to build up trust and a sense of mutual responsibility, and they organize such activities as neighborhood festivals, clean-up drives, and voter education projects. As residents come together and work collaboratively with city officials and businesses to identify and strengthen their community's assets, even while defining community deficiencies, they develop what sociologists call social capital, an intangible social analogue of financial capital. Social capital is built when a neighborhood has healthy networks of trust and cooperation and a dependable pattern of collective action to address local issues (for example, through strong neighborhood associations).

Beyond building social capital, a community development strategy also unites neighborhood residents, agencies, and small businesses so that they can actually design and deliver physical products and services in the inner city. Local residents link up with businesses, bankers, and officials in an effort to bring such resources as affordable housing, decent jobs, and social services into their neighborhood.

These programs are typically managed by a community development corporation (CDC), a nonprofit corporation governed by a board that includes area residents and nonprofit agency representatives, business executives, and government officials. CDCs date back to the War on Poverty and its community action programs, and now number in the thousands in the United States' inner cities. CDCs boast a record of actually improving conditions in the inner city. As a consequence, leading funders such as the Ford Foundation and the Enterprise Foundation invested heavily in community development efforts throughout the 1980s and 1990s.

At the government level, passage of the Community Reinvestment Act (1977) required banks to invest more resources in inner-city communities, a requirement that was often met by investing in local CDCs. In the 1990s, President Bill Clinton expanded the federal commitment to a community development model with his empowerment zone program. The empowerment zone concept added a local-participation and social-service component to the Reagan-era enterprise zone program of delivering tax breaks to companies locating in low-income inner-city communities. Under the empowerment zone program, it was no longer enough to bring jobs and investment to the inner city. City officials and businesses were now required to build partnerships with local CDCs, schools, neighborhood associations, and faith-based organizations and to include plans to improve human services and education if they were to receive federal tax breaks and grants.

THE LOS ANGELES SCHOOL OF COMMUNITY STUDIES

In spite of the various approaches taken to improving life in the inner cities, many U.S. inner cities remain dangerous, impoverished, and ungovernable. The persistence and deepening of divisions between the inner city and the suburbs, between ghetto apartments and luxury lofts, between slum and gated enclave, has led to the emergence of a new way of looking at urban life. Just as the Chicago School took its bearings from examining Chicago in the early 1900s, today a group of scholars calling themselves the Los Angeles School are using Los Angeles as the subject of their investigations in the hopes of understanding inner-city life better.

The Los Angeles School builds much of its analysis on the implications of the Los Angeles riots of 1965 and 1992. These multiethnic riots, involving dozens of deaths and vast physical damage, suggest the ultimate fragility of U.S. cities. Scholars of the Los Angeles School believe that postmodern cities are more divided, segregated, and difficult to govern than were the modern cities described by Chicago School scholars. When Los Angeles School scholars look at inner cities, they observe areas of territorial, ethnic, moral, and ideological fragmentation that are engulfed by mutual hostilities, defined by walled communities and hypersegregated ghettos, and always on the verge of violence and collapse.

Scholars of the Los Angeles School examine the increasing use of segregation strategies such as business improvement districts, which are patrolled by private police, and narcotic enforcement zones, which are sometimes segregated behind concrete barriers and police checkpoints. They point to the explosion of underground homeless communities and the dramatic rise in undocumented immigrants in the inner city, usually met with a proliferation of antivagrancy ordinances and police raids. They argue that inner cities are increasingly segregated from the mainstream. They show that gangster communities increasingly organize the social life of inner-city communities, while more affluent neighborhoods build walls and sophisticated surveillance systems to protect themselves from inner-city disorder. It is a bleak picture of a world of the excluded and repressed.

INNER-CITY CHARACTERISTICS, FROM CHICAGO TO LOS ANGELES

Inner-city communities confront daily the most difficult problems of the day. In the inner city, residents live in concentrated poverty, amid diverse cultures and with a sense of heightened disorder. Depending on the viewer, the kind of community that emerges under these conditions has been seen as pathological, exploited, romantic, culturally rich, full of untapped assets, or suggestive of a coming revolution.

—Tony Robinson

See also Alinsky, Saul; Community Development Corporations; Community Empowerment; Culture of Poverty; Ghettos; Incivilities Thesis; Jacobs, Jane; Urban Renewal

Further Reading

Abrahamson, M. (1996). *Urban enclaves: Identity and place in America.* New York: St. Martin's.

Altshuler, Alan. (1970). *Community control: The black demand for participation in large American cities.* New York: Pegasus.

Baer, W. (1976, Fall). On the death of cities. *The Public Interest, 45,* 3–19.

Baldwin, J. (1963). *The fire next time.* New York: Random House.

Banfield, E. (1974). *The unheavenly city revisited.* Boston: Little, Brown.

Bennett, W. J., DiIulio, J. J., & Walters, J. P. (1996). *Body count: Moral poverty and how to win America's war against crime and drugs.* New York: Simon & Schuster.

Bittner, E. (1967). The police on Skid-Row: A study of peace-keeping. *American Sociological Review, 32,* 699–715.

Boston, T. D. & Ross, C. L. (Eds.). (1999). *The inner city: Urban poverty and economic development in the next century.* New Brunswick, NJ: Transaction.

Bruyn, S. T., & Meehan, J. (1987). *Beyond the market and the state: New directions in community development.* Philadelphia: Temple University Press.

Castells, M. (1983). *The city and the grassroots.* Berkeley and Los Angeles: University of California Press.

Cleaver, E. (1954). *Soul on ice.* New York: Dell.

Committee for Economic Development. (1995). *Rebuilding inner-city communities: A new approach to the nation's urban crisis.* New York: Author.

Davis, M. (1991). *City of quartz: Excavating the future in Los Angeles.* New York: Verso.

Dear, M. J. (2000). *The postmodern urban condition.* Malden, MA: Blackwell.

Dear, M. J. (Ed.). (2001). *From Chicago to L. A.: Making sense of urban theory.* Thousand Oaks, CA: Sage.

Fisher, B. (1984). *Let the people decide: Neighborhood organizing in America.* Boston: G. K. Hall.

Godfrey, B. (1988). *Neighborhoods in transition.* Berkeley and Los Angeles: University of California Press.
Gratz, R. (1989). *The living city.* New York: Simon & Schuster.
Halpern, R. (1995). *Rebuilding the inner city: A history of neighborhood initiatives to address poverty in the United States.* New York: Columbia University Press.
Hampden-Turner, C. (1974). *From poverty to dignity.* New York: Pantheon.
Hoch, C., & Slayton, R. (1989). *New homeless and old: Community and the Skid Row hotel.* Philadelphia: Temple University Press.
Jacobs, J. (1961). *The death and life of great American cities.* New York: Vintage.
Katz, M. (1988). *In the shadow of the poorhouse: A social history of welfare in America.* New York: Basic Books.
Keating, W. D., Krumholz, N., & Star, P. (1996). *Revitalizing urban neighborhoods.* Lawrence: University Press of Kansas.
Keruoac, J. (1957). *On the road.* New York: Viking.
Kunstler, J. (1993). *The geography of nowhere: The rise and decline of America's man-made landscape.* New York: Touchstone.
Long, N. (1971, Fall). The city as reservation. *The Public Interest, 25,* 14–21.
Lyon, L. (1987). *The community and urban society.* Philadelphia: Temple University Press.
Malcolm, X. (1964). *The autobiography of Malcolm X (as told to Alex Haley).* New York: Random House.
Moynihan, D. P. (1969). *Maximum feasible misunderstanding.* New York: The Free Press.
Moynihan, D. P. (1993). Defining deviancy down. *American Scholar, 62*(1), 17–30.
Park, R., Burgess, E. W., & McKenzie, R. D. (1967). *The city.* Chicago: University of Chicago Press.
Piven, F. F., & Cloward, R. A. (1977). *Poor people's movements: Why they succeed, how they fail.* New York: Vintage.
Piven, F. F., & Cloward, R. A. (1993). *Regulating the poor: The functions of public welfare.* New York: Vintage.
Putnam, R. D. (1995). Bowling alone: America's declining social capital. *Journal of Democracy, 6*(1), 65–78.
Riposa, G. (1996). From enterprise zones to empowerment zones: The community context of urban economic development. *American Behavioral Scientist, 39*(5), 536–552.
Sanchez-Jankowski, M. (1992). *Islands in the street: Gangs and American urban society.* Berkeley and Los Angeles: University of California Press.
Sennett, R. (1990). *The conscience of the eye: The design and social life of cities.* New York: Alfred Knopf.
Shuman, M. (1998). *Going local: Creating self-reliant communities in a global age.* New York: Routledge.
Siegal, H. (1978). *Outposts of the forgotten.* New Brunswick, NJ: Transaction Books.
Slayton, R. (1986). *Back of the yards: The making of a local democracy.* Chicago: University of Chicago Press.
Sternleib, G. (1971, Fall). The city as sandbox. *The Public Interest, 25,* 22–38.
Suttles, G. (1968). *The social order of the slum: Ethnicity and territory in the inner city.* Chicago: University of Chicago Press.
Thomas, P. (1967). *Down these mean streets.* New York: Vintage.
Vidal, A. C. (1992). *Rebuilding communities: A national study of urban community development corporations.* New York: New School for Social Research, Community Development Research Center.
Vigil, J. D. (1988). *Barrio gangs: Street life and identity in southern California.* Austin: University of Texas Press.
Watson, S., & Gibson, K. (1995). *Postmodern cities and spaces.* Cambridge, MA: Blackwell.
Wilson, J. Q., & Kelling, G. (1988). The police and neighborhood safety: Broken windows. *Atlantic, 127,* 29–38.
Wilson, W. J. (1987). *The truly disadvantaged.* Chicago: University of Chicago Press.
Wilson, W. J. (1997). *When work disappears: The world of the new urban poor.* New York: Vintage.
Wright, T. (1997). *Out of place: Homeless mobilizations, subcities, and contested landscapes.* New York: State University of New York Press.

CITIES, MEDIEVAL

Cities in medieval Europe (400–1450 CE) served as a nexus for social, political, cultural, economic, and religious life. Within each city was a cohesive yet stratified community whose members were interdependent in commerce, government, social welfare, and defense. These communities were continually redefined by the various political instabilities, barbarian invasions, and new institutions that developed in the medieval world. Medieval European cities varied drastically in population, ethnicity, and size but shared many other characteristics that allowed for relatively contiguous development.

LATE ANTIQUITY

Medieval Europe began with the fall of the Roman Empire. In the fourth century CE, the emperor Constantine moved the capital and his court from Rome to Byzantium (later renamed Constantinople in his honor, now modern Istanbul). Many nobles and important officials followed the emperor east, resulting in a weakened infrastructure throughout the western portions of the empire (modern France, Spain, Britain, and Italy). This instability, combined with invasions of Germanic tribes from across the Rhine River, caused a depopulation of many urban centers throughout Europe. Cities, formerly centers of culture and community, often lost contact with their neighbors or were simply abandoned.

This urban degradation gradually continued as western Europe fell further outside the control of the empire. Small communities would remain, but they would not come close to their former size and prosperity for a millennium.

DEVELOPMENT OF THE MEDIEVAL CITY

Geographic location helped to determine the development of the medieval city. Originally, the cities on the Mediterranean were located farther away from the Germanic invasions and therefore were able to both internally and collectively preserve some of their cultural continuity. Many of these cities, such as Venice, Naples, and Amalfi, used their proximity to the sea to maintain connections with each other and the Byzantine east. As a result, these cities were able to prosper and even flourish.

The northern portions of the former empire suffered from their location near the German border, and many of the existing cities were sacked or destroyed. For the surviving urban areas, these invasions created a breakdown of trade structures and weakened the bonds between towns. This increased isolation, combined with a lack of incoming trade goods, made the tenuous existence of northern European cities even more fragile.

Many of the Germanic tribes gradually began to establish small, semicohesive kingdoms and communities throughout Europe. Their communities were bonded by kinship and German law, which sought common consensus when faced with factionalism, rather than Roman law, which depended on the arbitration of a powerful centralized state. Two of the most durable were the Visigothic kingdom in Spain and the Merovingian kingdom in France; however, many other tribal bands, including the Ostrogoths, Angles, and Saxons, also interwove their cultural heritage into former weakened, abandoned, or destroyed Roman communities.

Not until the reign of Charlemagne (742–814 CE) did cities begin to reacquire some of their previous significance. Charlemagne's growing empire required a large bureaucracy to sustain it, and cities gradually became administrative and cultural centers. In addition, due to the introduction of the church school, cities became centers of learning. Under Charlemagne's rule, much of the former western empire entered a peaceful, prosperous age. Cities reestablished connections, and a sense of community was restored. Europe began to return to a cultural level that had not been seen since the days of Constantine.

Upon the death of Louis the Pious, Charlemagne's heir, the empire was divided among Louis's three sons. This process was repeated by their heirs and resulted in Europe's reversion to a collection of small, petty kingdoms. In addition, Western Europe was invaded in the ninth and tenth centuries by groups of Magyars and Vikings. These incursions, combined with a lack of political unity, destroyed the fragile bonds of community and returned the function of towns to often no more than walled, isolated places of shelter. These new invasions ultimately resulted, however, in the growth of the medieval city. With the increasing need for defense, and as more people flocked to the city from the unprotected countryside, the establishment and maintenance of walled cities became extremely important.

A section of the old city wall can be seen behind the trees in Frankfurt, Germany, in 1992. The wall enclosed the city during medieval times, but now only sections of it remain, and the city has expanded well beyond its old limits.

Source: Elias Levinson; used with permission.

With the conclusion of these invasions, cities again expanded the scope of their interactions and reestablished trade networks. Recently improved methods of farming and a warmer climatic shift allowed for an agricultural revolution in the twelfth century. These factors contributed to a population explosion, which further developed the growing primacy of the city in the medieval world. Cities again began to flourish as cultural institutions.

DESIGN AND LAYOUT OF MEDIEVAL CITIES

Medieval cities were often haphazardly designed. They were frequently built over former Roman structures but without the grid plan or city design so important to Roman urban planning. Buildings were constructed of stone, wood, and earth. Streets were often tightly packed and meandering, creating a mazelike quality.

Of paramount importance to all medieval cities was the wall. As the city increasingly became a location designed for defense, the construction of walls became a necessity. Medieval walls were often large, thick, and constructed in a circular fashion.

At the heart of the medieval city was the church. By the fourth century CE, the cathedral complex had become relatively canonical and incorporated either two buildings (a cathedral and a baptistery) or three (a baptistery and a smaller and larger cathedral). The church was the hub of the medieval community and served as a house of worship, school, hospice, and in some cases, temporary royal residence.

Another feature of the medieval city was the university. While schools had existed for some time, institutions providing access to higher learning only became established in the twelfth century. They allowed scholars to abandon their traditional nomadic lifestyle and develop communities centered on teaching, research, and knowledge. Some of the most famous universities were in Cambridge and Oxford, England, and in Paris.

COMMERCE

Isolated settlements became linked through commerce. The earliest and largest commercial towns were in northern Italy, led by the Venetian merchants who traded in Constantinople, the Mediterranean, and the Near East. Flanders was the center for northern European trade and trafficked in the wool industry. Europe and the Near East formed a web of commercial trade that brought a variety of goods to the cities. William Fitz Stephen wrote of London (c. 1175): "To this city, from every nation that is under heaven, merchants rejoice to bring their trade in ships. 'Gold from Arabia, from Sabaea spice and incense; from the Scythians arms of steel well-tempered; oil from the rich groves of palm that spring from the fat lands of Babylon; fine gems from Nile, from China crimson silks; French wines; and sable, vair, and nimiver from the far lands where Russ and Norsemen dwell.'" (Fitz Stephen 1990, p. 54).

While most money was made in the long-distance trade of luxury goods, the majority of city dwellers participated in local trade or artisanry and produced utilitarian goods for daily use or for trade. With the centrality of a market economy and a growing trend toward specialization, the inhabitants became increasingly dependent on each other.

With the exception of food products, most goods were both made and sold in the same location. Similar shops were grouped together, and the names of the streets or sections where they were located often indicated their business. In Winchester, England, there was a Sildwortenstret (Shieldmakers Street) and Scowrtenestret (Shoemakers Street), and evidence of this practice remains in London today where there is a Milk Street and a Bread Street. In addition, shops were open to the street; cobblers, saddlers, and barbers all conducted their business in full view of the public.

Women often actively participated in a city's commerce, by selling produce or livestock or working as silk weavers or brewers. Since much of the activity of producing and selling was done in a space that was for both domestic living and business, women frequently worked alongside fathers or husbands, learning their skills and overseeing apprentices. Quite often, widows ran the businesses of their deceased husbands.

The centrality of commerce in the life of a city led to changes in political and social organizations. In addition to requiring a stable infrastructure, such as reliable roads to transport goods and an adequate supply of fresh water, an increasing number of town officials and literate people were needed to participate in the growing dependency on written and accounting transactions. A rise in the number of general litigation and contract suits also necessitated a larger bureaucracy in the city.

CIVIC ORGANIZATIONS AND GUILDS

In the twelfth and thirteenth centuries, a new urban class developed from the previous agrarian society. In the early stages of trade growth, the merchants allied themselves into associations so they could collectively protect themselves from the high tolls levied by the local aristocracy. These practices developed into rights, which increased over time to include the ability to own property, to make contracts, and to appeal to a town's court rather than the lord's court. The groups, in turn, developed into guilds, with charters that allowed them to become legal and political semiautonomous groups.

From these early merchant associations, the number and variety of guilds grew to incorporate occupations from tanners to innkeepers to doctors. Many developed from religious and civic fraternities that participated in the governing of their particular city. Among their various roles, guilds controlled the quality of goods, preserved traditions, held annual celebrations, organized funerals, and cared for the families of those members who had died. Guilds were hierarchical, depending on which trade was most important to an individual city. Most women's work (as domestic servants, petty retailers, midwives, and prostitutes) was considered either too low skilled or of too low a status to merit a guild.

PRIVATE LIFE/CITY LIFE

The urban living space was created not only by the sheer number of people living in a confined area but also by the interconnectedness and dependency among them. The city's population was a stratified group consisting of the new urban merchant class, wealthier peasants, artisans, and vagabonds. All aspects of people's lives were conducted in the public sphere; in addition to shops opening onto the streets, there were civic bathhouses and public ovens.

Journeymen and apprentices lived in the dwelling where they worked and became part of the household community in all aspects. They worked, ate, slept, prayed, and played together. Since homes and workshops were not well lit, people spent a large part of their time outdoors, in the streets and marketplaces.

The streets were full of activity. Market days, when local farmers came to town to sell their products, added to the already bustling atmosphere. Itinerant traders peddled what they could carry. The town crier hurried from one street corner to the next to spread news of births, deaths, bankruptcies, lost property, applications for wet nurses, and court sentences. Weddings and funerals created processions through the streets. Festivals, theaters, and tournaments set their stage in public spaces. The streets were a place for great social interaction; people converged, mingled, and exchanged bits of news and information.

The close proximity of people living together also led to increased regulation to protect the citizens. The statutes ranged from protecting the individual to defending the city as a whole. In many cities, for example, because fires were common and quickly spread among the wooden structures, all citizens were required to participate in their local fire brigade. In Cologne, France, legal statutes required that the wells of bathhouses, alehouses, and bakeries not only be made accessible to the fire brigade but also that the employees had to assist in the event of a fire. The city was also divided into military quarters for the defense of its walls. Rules were set on how wide the streets were to be, how far the upper levels of houses could project, and later, from what materials houses could be built. On a more mundane level, people were also forbidden to leave waste at the doors of their neighbors, dump liquid or garbage onto the streets from upper windows, or let their livestock and dogs run wild.

Many of the sanitation statutes were ignored, thus attracting vermin and contaminating water supplies. That, combined with population growth, led to recurring epidemics, the most virulent of which was the bubonic plague, or Black Death (1348–1352). The rapid spread through the cities of the highly contagious and deadly disease created a terrific strain on the society. Giovanni Boccaccio, in his book *The Decameron,* writes of Florence, Italy: "Tedious were it to recount, how citizen avoided citizen, how among neighbors was scarce found any that shewed fellow-feeling for another, how kinsfolk held aloof, and never met, or but rarely" (Boccaccio 1353/1930, p. 8).

MARGINALIZED GROUPS

City governments oversaw institutions and implemented practices that sought to maintain social order (sometimes exclusionary and sometimes benevolent charity) for those who were marginal. These people were excluded from the rights shared by citizens and had to depend on protection from the king or municipal lord. All over Europe, municipal authorities founded and maintained orphanages and hospitals to care for children and the sick. However, many of these same governments also regulated brothels, which employed women who were financially forced into prostitution. The authorities restricted their trade to certain streets, required the women to wear distinguishing clothing, and in some cases, prohibited the prostitutes from attending church.

Jews had been integral in the early trade that established the cities, but by the thirteenth century, they had been forced to convert or wear special badges or hats to identify themselves as Jews. In some cities, they lived in specific quarters, called ghettos, and further separated themselves from Christians by using their own butchers and bathhouses. In the thirteenth through the fifteenth centuries, Jews were expelled from England, Spain, Portugal, and parts of France. Muslims, especially after the reconquest of Spain in 1492, were geographically and culturally separated from society and lived under their own laws and tax system. Despite these restrictions, however, some Jews and Muslims actively participated in urban society and greatly added to biblical, medical, and philosophical scholarship.

IMPACT

The development of communities in medieval cities reflected the changing political, social, intellectual, religious, and economic conditions of the time. During adverse periods, the cities endured by forcing the inhabitants to maintain their sense of community in order to survive. During prosperous times, communities in medieval cities established cultural traditions and social institutions that drew upon the past and laid the foundation for the future.

—Andrew Donnelly and Beth Forrest

Further Reading

Bennett, J. M., Clark, E., O'Barr, J., Vilen, B. A., & Westphal-Whil, S. (Eds.). (1989). *Sisters and workers in the Middle Ages.* Chicago: University of Chicago Press.

Boccaccio, G. (1930). *The decameron* (J. M. Rigg, Trans.). New York: Routledge. (Original work published 1353)

Druks, H., & Lacetti, S. (1971). *Cities in civilization: The city in Western civilization.* New York: Robert Speller.

Duby, G. (1988). *A history of private life: Revelations of the medieval world.* Cambridge, MA: Belknap Press of Harvard University Press.

Fitz Stephen, W. (1990). Norse London (F. Stenton, Trans.). In F. Stenton, *Norman London: An essay* (p. 54). New York: Ithaca Press. (Original work written c. 1175)

Goetz, H.-W. (1993). *Life in the Middle Ages.* (A. Wimmer, Trans.). S. Rowan (Ed.). Notre Dame, IN: University of Notre Dame Press.

Hodges, R., & Whitehouse, D. (1983). *Mohammed, Charlemagne and the origins of Europe.* Ithaca, NY: Cornell University Press.

Hollister, C. W. (1990). *Medieval Europe: A short history.* New York: McGraw-Hill.

Holt, R., & Rosser, G. (1990). *The English medieval town: A reader in English urban history 1200–1540.* New York: Longman.

Mumford, L. (1961). *The city in history: Its origins, its transformations, and its prospects.* New York: Harcourt, Brace & World.

Nicholas, D. (1997). *The later medieval city 1300–1500.* New York: Addison Wesley Longman.

Pirenne, H. (1925). *Medieval cities: Their origins and the revival of trade.* (F. Halsey, Trans.). Princeton, NJ: Princeton University Press.

Power, E. (1963). *Medieval people.* New York: Harper & Row.

Saalman, H. (1968). *Medieval cities.* New York: George Braziller.

Thompson, J. (1988). *Towns and townspeople in the fifteenth century.* Wolfboro, NH: Alan Sutton.

CITIZEN PARTICIPATION AND TRAINING

Citizen participation is the involvement of people in the institutions and decisions that affect their lives. The process of encouraging citizen participation includes formal efforts by agencies to involve people in their proceedings, as well as informal efforts by people themselves to join together to take initiative on their own. People in both rural and urban areas, in both developing and industrialized nations, and from diverse income, racial, ethnic, and other population groups, participate in education, the environment, housing, health care, human services, and other issues.

Citizens participate in activities such as door-to-door campaigning and focus groups, town meetings and community councils, voting, and protest demonstrations. These activities can be evaluated in terms of their scope (their number, frequency, or duration) or in terms of their quality or impact on decisions. From the latter perspective, the quality of participation is considered high if it shows some effect, influences a particular decision, or produces a favorable outcome.

Training for citizen participation takes many forms. Some people learn about participation through formal educational programs managed by governments to perpetuate a given social order. Others learn from families, friends, neighbors, and informal systems that convey beliefs and behaviors through everyday life. Still others learn from the educational efforts of community organizations, civic agencies, and private institutions, including business, media, and telecommunications.

SCHOOL-BASED AND COMMUNITY-BASED TRAINING

School-based training for citizen participation is common in democratic societies. Schools in the United States, for example, offer courses such as civics or social studies that explain formal features of U.S. government, with which young people need to be familiar if they are to become active participants. These features include the rights of citizens; the branches of government and their functions; the nature of the federal system and intergovernmental relations; the importance of voting; the roles of elected officials, political parties, and interest groups; and public policy formation and legislative advocacy. Students learn that they can attend meetings, serve on councils, vote in elections, contact a public official, or run for office themselves.

Recent evidence suggests that measurable levels of formal participation in public affairs, such as membership in voluntary associations and voting in elections, are decreasing. Studies indicate that a significant proportion of the population are either uninvolved or minimally involved, that a small group of people are very active, and that those who actively participate are not representative of the overall population. Lower-income people are less likely to participate in political activities or government programs, although there is evidence of long-term increases in their political efficacy and in their use of tactics that increase their influence.

Community-based training for citizen participation is also pervasive in the United States. The number of training programs and populations they reach is large. At the local level, they operate in grassroots groups, religious institutions, labor unions, and business corporations. At the national level, they include intermediary organizations and national associations that represent diverse ideologies, such as the Center for Third World Organizing, the National Association for the Advancement of Colored People, the National Council of La Raza, the American Medical Association, the National Association of Homebuilders, Boy Scouts, and 4-H Clubs. Those organizations all provide training in citizen participation.

CORE CONCEPTS

Although participation training differs in content from one place to another, a review of practice literature and curricular content suggests that some core concepts receive repetitive emphasis.

For example, a central tenet of participation training is that participation should start with the people, that the people themselves are the best judge of their own situations. Other tenets are that developing leadership is instrumental to participation; that the process should identify individuals who are willing and able to step forward as leaders; and that agents of change, such as community organizers, can supply experience and contribute to the process over the long haul.

Other core concepts deal with collective action and political power. Those who support citizen participation point out that people joined together in solidarity can accomplish more than any single individual acting alone. When people get organized and formulate strategy, they are more effective than when they take unplanned or random actions. Participation is an empowering process that is multilevel in nature; it includes individual involvement, organizational development, and community change.

A Definition of Citizenship

In the Education for Democratic Citizenship (EDC) project of the Council of Europe's Directorate of Education, Culture and Sport (DECS), the definition proposed by scholar François Audigier provides a framework for education for democratic citizenship.

> Despite the differences within each definition and between languages, there are some common anchoring points which thus provide a sound base for pursuing our exploration of citizenship. It is always a matter of belonging to a community, which entails politics and rights, notably political rights. In this sense, the citizen is always a co-citizen, somebody who lives with others. This community is defined essentially at two levels: on the one hand the local level, the city, often in the urban sense, in which the person lives, to which he belongs, and on the other hand the state, connected to being a national which confers the full rights accorded to the members of this state. This belonging always refers to a level of political organisation, a level of authority, and to rights; in other words, citizen and citizenship always involve the delimitation of a territory and a group, a territory where the rights are applicable, a group as all the persons entitled to these rights; they are thus anchored in the first place on the political and the legal. Lastly, depending on the tradition, the accent may be more on the local as the first level of belonging and a space sufficiently limited for it to be easier for the person to be active and participate, or on the national-state level as the main level where the law is decided and where collective public identity is constructed. In no state is one level or the other exclusive; it is more a matter of priority being accorded to one or the other, a choice which has consequences for the conceptions of EDC.

Source: Audigier, François. (1999). *Basic Concepts and Core Competences of Education for Democratic Citizenship.* Second Consolidated Report. Retrieved March 4, 2003, from http://www.lend.it/documenti/audigier.htm.

STRATEGIES

Trainers recognize several strategies of participation. For example, people can mobilize around issues through public actions and mass demonstrations, or they can organize grassroots groups that gain power by building organizations for social and political action. People can involve themselves in policies and programs through formal roles in citizen committees and public hearings, or they can advocate for groups by representing those groups' interests in legislative or other established institutional arenas. People can educate themselves by raising their critical consciousness through small group discussions; they can also develop community-based programs and services of their own.

Trainers emphasize that these strategies each have their own empirical basis and pattern of practice. Mobilization is not organization and advocacy is not development; each strategy has its own roles, power orientation, and conflict style. Knowledge of several strategies strengthens the foundation for effective participation.

STEPS IN THE PARTICIPATION PROCESS

Trainers are often asked about the basic steps in the citizen participation process. Although participation is not a recipe whose ingredients must be added in prescribed amounts or in a particular order, some steps are frequently mentioned in training workshops.

For example, trainers instruct people to identify the individuals and groups who should participate, to articulate goals and objectives, to identify the techniques relevant to those objectives, to analyze the resources that are available and needed, and to fit the tools and techniques to the specific situation. People gain the skills to make contact with others, bring them together, and form core groups for action. They learn how to conduct meetings, strengthen diversity, manage conflict, and evaluate activities.

Each of the strategies mentioned above has its own techniques of fostering participation, which can be modified to suit the nature of the community and the resources that are available. Methods include interviews, surveys, committees, task forces, review boards, conferences, hearings, charettes, workshops, game simulations, referenda, interactive telecommunications, public information programs, and various forms of consultation and technical assistance.

CULTURAL FRONTIERS

It is more complex to encourage citizen participation in a society whose communities are multicultural, whose people have significant differences among them, than it is in a monocultural one, whose people have more similarities among them. Population changes will challenge communities to reconceptualize training for citizen participation. In the United States, for example, future training will be expected to recognize cultural differences between population groups and also encourage increased interaction and collaboration across cultural boundaries. New training models are arising that attempt to do that; they represent new directions for the future.

—Barry Checkoway

Further Reading

Arnstein, S. (1969). A ladder of citizen participation. *Journal of the American Institute of Planners, 35,* 216–224.

Checkoway, B. (1995). Six strategies of community change. *Community Development Journal, 30,* 2–20.

Checkoway, B. (1997). Core concepts for community change. *Journal of Community Practice, 4,* 11–29.

Checkoway, B. (1998). Involving young people in neighborhood development. *Children and Youth Services Review, 20,* 765–795.

Checkoway, B., & Van Til, J. (1978). What do we know about citizen participation? A selective review of research. In S. Langton (Ed.), *Citizen participation in America.* Lexington, MA: Lexington Books.

Gutierrez, L., et al. (1997). Multicultural community organizing: A strategy for change. *Social Work, 41,* 501–508.

Putnam, R. D. (2000). *Bowling alone: The collapse and revival of American community.* New York: Simon & Schuster.

Rivera, F. G., & Ehrlich, J. L. (Eds.). (1998). *Community organizing in a diverse society.* Boston: Allyn & Bacon.

Sanoff, H. (2000). *Community participation methods in design and planning.* New York: John Wiley.

Tropman, J., Erlich, J. L., & Rothman, J. (Eds.). (2001). *Tactics and techniques of community intervention.* Itasca, IL: F. E. Peacock.

CITIZENSHIP

Citizenship refers to the rights and responsibilities of members of a political unit. Which individuals are legally considered citizens is determined by the political leadership and varies over time. In some nations citizenship might be determined by lineage while in other countries citizenship might be determined by place of birth. What specifically constitutes those rights and responsibilities and how they are expressed also vary depending on the nature of the governmental system, the society, and the political culture. Thus, citizenship in a democracy carries with it different rights and duties than does citizenship in an authoritarian regime. Likewise, the nature of citizenship (and the people who were citizens) in the United States in the nineteenth century was quite different from citizenship today. Even within similar types of political systems, the character of citizenship varies depending on the cultural traditions and norms of the society.

CITIZENSHIP AND COMMUNITY LIFE

There are different interpretations of what community life in a democracy should be like and hence what constitutes citizenship in the community. These different perspectives derive from competing visions of democracy and civic life. They are sometimes complementary, but often contradictory about the meaning of citizenship. There are three major political traditions that each prescribe somewhat different rights and responsibilities associated with citizenship in a community: elite democracy, communitarianism, and participatory democracy.

W. E. B. Du Bois on the Town Meeting and Democracy

In his autobiography, African American scholar and civil rights pioneer W. E. B. Du Bois recounted how the Great Barrington, Massachusetts, town meetings influenced his views about democracy and civic life.

> From early years, I attended the town meeting every Spring and in the upper front room in that little red brick Town Hall, fronted by a Roman "victory" commemorating the Civil War, I listened to the citizens discuss things about which I knew and had opinions: streets and bridges and schools, and particularly the high school, an institution comparatively new. We had in the town several picturesque hermits, usually retrograde Americans of old families. There was Crosby, the gunsmith who lived in a lovely dale with brook, waterfall and water wheel. He was a frightful apparition but we boys often ventured to visit him. Particularly there was Baretown Beebe, who came from forest fastnesses which I never penetrated. He was a particularly dirty, ragged, fat old man, who used to come down regularly from his rocks and woods and denounce high school education and expense.
>
> I was 13 or 14 years of age and a student in the small high school with two teachers and perhaps 25 pupils. The high school was not too popular in this rural part of New England and received from the town a much too small appropriation. But the thing that exasperated me was that every Spring at Town Meeting, which I religiously attended, this huge, ragged old man came down from the hills and for an hour or more reviled the high school and demanded its discontinuance.
>
> I remember distinctly how furious I used to get at the stolid town folk, who sat and listened to him. He was nothing and nobody. Yet the town heard him gravely because be was a citizen and property-holder on a small scale and when he was through, they calmly voted the usual funds for the high school. Gradually as I grew up, I began to see that this was the essence of democracy: listening to the other man's opinion and then voting your own, honestly and intelligently.

Source: Du Bois, W. E. B. (1968). *The Autobiography of W. E. B. Du Bois.* New York: International Publishers, pp. 91–92.

ELITE DEMOCRACY

The dominant orientation of U.S. politics may be most accurately described as elite democracy. The focus of elite democracy is not so much on the citizenry as it is on the representatives of the citizens. Elite democracy holds that average citizens think in stereotypes and are often swayed by their passions or narrow self-interests, and so their political desires and judgments cannot be trusted. Given the opportunity, they may actually act to undermine democratic principles. Ironically, the protectors of democracy are thus the political leaders. Consequently, citizens' involvement in government should be limited primarily to the exercise of voting rights and secondarily to pursuing self-interest by joining groups (aptly called interest groups). This view of citizenship is likely to be found in large, industrialized democratic states where it is impossible for all citizens to actively participate, or even be consulted, on most decisions.

Critics of elite democracy contend that it is antithetical to the creation and maintenance of a rich vision of community. They argue that community cannot be created on the basis of individuals pursuing narrow self-interests, nor can it be created by citizens whose governmental and societal decision making is limited to the selection of representatives. Individual self-interests cannot be added up to create the common good.

COMMUNITARIAN DEMOCRACY

While elite democracy tends to emphasize citizenship rights rather than responsibilities, communitarianism places the greatest emphasis on citizenship responsibilities. Communitarianism holds that the common good of the community is achieved when virtuous citizens are united in public action. It is not enough that citizens merely vote (although they should); they should also be engaged in all facets of civic life. Similarly, the ideal citizen is not motivated by self-interest or private gain, but by a powerful feeling of public spiritedness that leads to the rooting out of corruption so that the common good may prevail. Virtue is shaped primarily in private institutions such as churches, families, and occupations, but it is the responsibility of citizens to put that virtue to use for the sake of the public life of the community. Because this form of citizenship requires intense interaction, it is possible only in small geographical areas—a neighborhood or small town. Alan Ehrenhalt (1995) describes three such neighborhood communities in the 1950s in Chicago, each was composed of no more than several thousand people.

The communitarian view has been criticized as being both dangerous and unrealistic. It is dangerous because it leads some citizens to encourage excessive conformity. This is a particular danger in small political units. Communitarianism is also criticized as being unrealistic since it requires so much of education; education is expected to instill the ethic of citizenship in the entire population.

PARTICIPATORY DEMOCRACY

A third view of citizenship derives from the tradition of participatory democracy. In participatory democracy, citizens are expected to participate in face-to-face direct governance. This model of citizenship emphasizes the importance of economic and political equality. In order for participatory governance to work, all citizens must be considered equals when approaching civic dialogue. It is the strength of arguments that should determine the decisions, not the economic or social status of the participants. But because economic distinctions tend to favor some while working to the disadvantage of others, participatory democracy supports attempts to curb economic inequalities that undermine civic participation. In particular, criticism has been leveled at monopoly capitalism. Citizens should approach civic participation from an equal footing. It is critical that citizens be able to discuss communal issues with other citizens. In the process of deliberation, citizens not only become educated about the specific issues that are being discussed but also come to understand the importance of fundamental democratic principles and practices (including tolerance, equality, and majority rule). Thus, one of the advantages of involvement in a participatory democracy is that citizens are able to exercise self-determination and grow in self-esteem while at the same time enhancing their community. Classical democratic theorists, as well as America's founding fathers, believed that participatory democracy was possible only on a small scale. However, modern participatory theorists such as Benjamin Barber (1984) believe that the participatory principle can be both nurtured locally as well as extended vertically to link citizens to large nation-states.

Critics of participatory democracy contend that it is based on questionable assumptions about human nature and that it ignores the reality of authority. Participatory democracy assumes that citizens are essentially good, motivated by a desire to do what is best for the community, or at least neutral, capable of being educated to act on behalf of the common good. Critics see this as an inaccurate portrayal of human nature. Further, this perspective has been criticized for ignoring or downplaying the role that authority plays in community. It is authority based on tradition and social position, critics argue, that keeps citizens from being swept away by their fears and passions, and therefore it is authority that guards against the possibility of oppression.

There is little agreement on the meaning of citizenship in community. The model citizen varies depending upon the model of community that one embraces. The richer the vision of community that one desires, the greater the demands are for virtuous citizens who actively participate in all aspects of civic life. Where there is less interest in community, citizenship is defined less rigorously and requires only minimal involvement.

—John F. Freie

See also COMMUNITARIANISM

Further Reading

Barber, B. (1984). *Strong democracy: Participatory politics for a new age.* Berkeley: University of California Press.

Bellah, R. N., Madsen, R., Sullivan, W. M., Swidler, A., & Tipton, S. M. (1991). *The good society.* New York: Vintage.

Berry, C. J. (1989). *The idea of a democratic community.* New York: St. Martin's.

Ehrenhalt, A. (1995). *The lost city: Discovering the forgotten virtues of community in the Chicago of the 1950s.* New York: Basic Books.

Etzioni, A. (1993). *The spirit of community.* New York: Crown.

Fowler, R. B. (1991). *The dance with community: The contemporary debate in American political thought.* Lawrence: University Press of Kansas.

Frazer, E., & Lacey, N. (1993). *The politics of community: A feminist critique of the liberal-communitarian debate.* Toronto, Canada: University of Toronto Press.

Freie, J. F. (1998). *Counterfeit community: The exploitation of our longings for connectedness.* Lanham, MD: Rowman & Littlefield.

Schudson. M. (1998). *The good citizen: A history of American civic life.* Cambridge. MA: Harvard University Press.

Thompson. D. F. (1970). *The democratic citizen.* New York: Cambridge University Press.

CIVIC AGRICULTURE

As the U.S. food and agricultural system continues to industrialize on a global scale, a countertrend toward relocalization of some agricultural and food production has emerged. The term *civic agriculture* was coined to represent the rebirth of community-based agricultural and food production. Many of the organizational manifestations of civic agriculture, such as farmers' markets, community kitchens, community gardens, and community supported agriculture (CSA), are not tracked by any federal or state data collection agencies. Consequently, finding reliable data on the number of civic agriculture enterprises is often difficult.

While civic agriculture does not currently represent an economic challenge to the conventional agricultural and food industries, it does represent a set of alternative ways to produce, process, and distribute food that at least some communities and consumers will find attractive. Civic agriculture is best understood when cast against the industrial model of agriculture and food production.

INDUSTRIAL AGRICULTURE

The industrialization of agricultural production since the 1880s has been guided by the belief that the primary objectives of farming should be to produce as much food and fiber as possible for the least cost. Industrial agriculture is driven by the twin goals of productivity and efficiency and focuses primarily on commodities such as corn, soybeans, or chickens as units of observation, analysis, experimentation, and intervention. Farmers and farms have been largely ignored by industrial agriculture. From the industrial agriculture perspective, farmers are viewed as managers whose primary task is to follow a set of best management practices. And farms are simply places where production occurs, devoid of connections to the local community or social order.

The industrialization of agriculture has proceeded relatively unabated from the 1920s through today, propelled by mechanization, the increased use of chemicals (synthetic fertilizers and pesticides), and most recently by advanced biotechnologies. Since the mid-twentieth century, farms have become larger in size and fewer in number. In 1950, there were 5.3 million farms, and the average farm size was approximately 200 acres. By 1997, the number of farms had fallen to about 1.9 million farms, with an average size of nearly 500 acres. Land is being used more intensively and yields per acre of farmland have increased dramatically. The amount of farmland has decreased from approximately 1.1 billion in 1950 to approximately 930 million acres in 1997, while capital investments on the farm have increased. At the same time, farms have been woven into ever-tighter marketing channels. Many industrial farms today produce products under contracts to large food processing companies.

THE EMERGENCE OF CIVIC AGRICULTURE

The conceptual underpinnings of civic agriculture were set forth in the literature on industrial districts. Industrial districts are regions in which a group of smaller-scale, locally oriented manufacturing and distribution enterprises are located. The success and survival of industrial districts are directly tied to the collective efforts of the local community to provide infrastructure support such as roads, sewers, and Internet access and technical expertise such as vocational training and management workshops.

Research carried out in the 1940s by anthropologist Walter Goldschmidt, as well as by sociologist C. Wright Mills and economist Melville Ulmer, has illustrated the benefits of smaller-scale, locally oriented enterprises. Their studies showed that communities in which the economic base consisted of many small, locally owned firms manifested higher levels of social, economic, and political welfare than communities where the economy was dominated by a few, large, absentee-owned firms.

Goldschmidt studied agricultural communities in the Central Valley of California. One community, Dinuba, was supported by relatively small, family-operated farms. The other community, Arvin, was surrounded by large, corporate-run enterprises. According to Goldschmidt, these communities were "selected for their divergence in scale of farm operations" while being very similar in "most fundamental economic and geographic factors, particularly richness of potential resources, agricultural production, relationship to other communities, and the more general techniques and institutional patterns of production" (Goldschmidt 1978, p. 420). Using a broad array of data collection and analysis techniques, Goldschmidt concluded that "the community surrounded by large-scale farm operations offered the poorer social environment according to every test made" (1978, p. 420).

The study by C. Wright Mills and Melville Ulmer was similar in design to the Goldschmidt study. However, Mills and Ulmer focused on manufacturing communities. They studied three matched pairs of small to medium-sized U.S. cities. Two pairs provided contrasts between big business and small business, while the third provided an intermediate case. Their findings were con-

City Farming

The following announcements in Southside Green, *the newsletter of the Community Land Trust of South Providence, Rhode Island, report on some of their activities designed to encourage sustainability, better nutrition, and a sense of community.*

City Farm Update

CSA (Community Supported Agriculture)

SCLT's Community Supported Agriculture project is going strong this summer. A total of nine families and institutions have signed up and purchased shares of the harvest. These families and institutions receive each week, for 21 weeks, huge baskets of organically grown produce, herbs and flowers for a price that is lower than the supermarket. The exciting news this summer is that we have been effectively able to make this program accessible to families and community groups with limited incomes through various financial structures. SCLT has also been allowed to use USDA Food Stamps as payment for CSA shares, becoming the second CSA in the country to be granted this capacity. This summer's CSA project is still just an experiment, but we hope to continue supporting the establishment of CSA projects in low-income communities in Providence.

Farmer's Market

Do you want fresh, locally grown organic produce? Well help support SCLT by visiting our farm stand at Providence's two farmers' markets and get fresh, locally grown organic produce, herbs, flowers, and SCLT's Urban Edibles Products: infused vinegars, dried culinary herbs and herbal tea.

Hope Street Market
Located at Hope High School
Every Saturday until October 9 a.m. to 12:30 p.m.

Parade Street Market
Located on Parade Street near the Armory
Every Thursday until October
3 p.m. to 6 p.m.

Source: *Southside Green.* (2000, Spring). South Providence, RI: Community Land Trust. Retrieved March 5, 2003, from http://users.ids.net/~sclt/newsletter.htm.

sonant with those of Goldschmidt. According to Mills and Ulmer, "(1) Small-business cities provided their residents a considerably more balanced economic life than did big-business cities; (2) The general level of civic welfare was appreciably higher in the small-business cities; (3) These differences between life in big- and small-business cities were due largely to differences in industrial organization—that is, specifically to the dominance of big business on the one hand and the prevalence of small business on the other" (Mills & Ulmer 1970, pp. 124–25).

Communities that nurture local systems of agricultural production and food marketing as one part of a broader plan of diversified economic development gain greater control over their economic destinies. They also enhance the level of social capital among their residents, contribute to rising levels of civic welfare and socioeconomic well-being, revitalize rural landscapes, improve environmental quality, and ultimately, promote long-term sustainability.

CHARACTERISTICS OF CIVIC AGRICULTURE

Communities can support civic agriculture only if they maintain a farmland base and provide the technical expertise that make it possible for farmers and processors to compete successfully against the highly industrialized producers. There are several characteristics associated with the emergence of civic agriculture in the United States. First, in places where civic agriculture emerges, farming is oriented toward local market outlets that serve local consumers rather than national or international mass markets. Second, in these places agriculture is seen as an integral part of rural communities, not merely as the production of commodities. Third, farmers are concerned more with high quality and value-added products and less with quantity (yield) and least-cost production practices. Fourth, production at the farm level is often more labor intensive and land intensive and less capital intensive and land extensive. Civic farm enterprises tend to be considerably smaller in scale and scope than industrial producers. Fifth, producers more often rely on indigenous, site-specific knowledge and less on a uniform set of best-management practices. And sixth, producers forge direct market links to consumers rather than relying on middlemen such as wholesalers, brokers, and processors.

From an organizational and institutional perspective, civic agriculture manifests itself in many ways. Farmers' markets provide immediate, low-cost, direct contact between local farmers and consumers, and are an effective first step for communities seeking to develop stronger local food systems. Farm stands and pick-your-own operations provide fresh, locally grown and seasonal products to consumers and offer an alternative to the globally sourced produce found in most large supermarkets. Community and school gardens provide fresh produce to underserved populations, teach food production skills, and increase agricultural literacy. Smaller-scale organic farmers have in many cases pioneered the development of local marketing systems and have also eschewed conventional, chemically intensive farming practices, adopting methods that are more environmentally benign. Community supported agriculture (CSA) projects are forging direct links between groups of member-consumers (often urban) and their CSA farms: The member-consumers buy "shares" in the farm that entitle them to a certain amount of produce each week at harvest time. New grower-controlled marketing cooperatives are emerging to tap regional markets more effectively. Agricultural districts organized around particular commodities (such as wine) have served to stabilize farms and farmland in many areas of the United States. Specialty producers and on-farm processors of products for which there are not well-developed mass markets (venison, goat/sheep cheese, free-range chickens, organic dairy products, and so forth) and small-scale, off-farm, local processors add value in local communities and provide markets for civic agriculture farmers. Similarly, community kitchens provide the infrastructure and technical expertise necessary to launch new food-based enterprises. What all of these efforts have in common is that they have the potential to nurture local economic development, maintain diversity and quality in products, and provide forums at which producers and consumers can come together to solidify bonds of community.

Unlike traditional or conventional agricultural enterprises, all the segments of the new civic agriculture are growing in number. Although reliable data on some types of civic agriculture enterprises are difficult to find, especially at the national level, data from the U.S. Department of Agriculture shows a dramatic increase in the number of farmers who are selling directly to the public. According to the Census of Agriculture, the number of farmers selling directly to the public increased by 7.8 percent between 1992 and 1997, from 86,432 to 93,140, while the total value of products sold to the public increased by over 36 percent during this time period. Relatedly, the number of farmers' markets increased by 63 percent between 1994 and 2000. Today there are over 2,800 farmers' markets in the United States. While not all civic agriculture producers sell directly to the public, a large proportion do, and the data from the Census suggests that the trend is for more civic agriculture in the years ahead. Other sources of data on civic agriculture enterprises include departments of agriculture at the state level, organic grower and producer organizations, and other associations that deal with agriculture and food issues.

—Thomas A. Lyson

Further Reading

Berry, W. (1996). Conserving communities. In J. Mander & E. Goldsmith (Eds.), *The case against the global economy* (pp. 407–418). San Francisco: Sierra Club Books.

Goldschmidt, W.R. (1978). *As you sow.* Montclair, NJ: Allanheld, Osmun.

Kneen, B. (1993). *From land to mouth.* Toronto, Canada: NC Press.

Mills, C. W., & Ulmer, M. (1970). Small business and civic welfare. In M. Aiken & P. Mott (Eds.), *The structure of community power* (pp. 124–154). New York: Random House.

Piore, M. J., & Sabel, C. F. (1984). *The second industrial divide.* New York: Basic Books.

Welsh, R. (1996). *The industrial reorganization of U.S. agriculture* (Policy Studies Rep. No. 6). Greenbelt, MD: Henry A. Wallace Institute for Alternative Agriculture.

CIVIC ENGAGEMENT

See COLLECTIVE ACTION; COMMUNITY BUILDING; COMMUNITY ORGANIZING; LOCAL POLITICS; SOCIAL CAPITAL; TOWN MEETINGS

CIVIC INNOVATION

Civic innovation is the process of change in civic life or civil society. Civic innovation is not restricted to civil society; it often takes place in collaboration with various market, state, and professional actors. In other words, civic innovation is defined by a capacity for civic and public problem solving, not by the specific sector from which it emerges.

Although civic innovation has been shaped by the concept of social capital—the norms and social networks through which citizens associate—these two concepts are distinct. There may be periods in which relatively high levels of social capital correspond to high levels of civic innovation, but periods in which civil society is weak may also give rise to new forms of civic innovation that address the problems created by this very weakness. On the whole, the historical relationship between civic innovation and social capital is not yet clear to scholars.

Civic innovation is sometimes linked to large-scale changes such as wars, shifts in government, urbanization, immigration, or religious revivals. But it can also be the result of citizens, governments, and organizations slowly working through problems under relatively stable social and political conditions. This entry examines the large-scale changes that have triggered civic innovation in the United States, the subject of most historical scholarship on civic innovation. Then it addresses the process of social learning that advances civic innovation today. Finally, it briefly considers civic innovation in other national contexts.

CIVIC INNOVATION IN THE UNITED STATES

There have been, broadly, five periods of civic innovation in the United States: the Revolutionary period, the first half of the nineteenth century, the period stretching from just after the Civil War through the Progressive Era, the Depression and World War II, and the 1960s to the present. Scholars differ on the degree to which each of these period were innovative, the forms of innovation, and their relative importance, but there is general agreement that important innovation did take place in each.

The Revolution and the Federal System

In the period leading up to the American Revolution of 1776, civic and public ferment took many forms. American colonists built on the English civic and political reforms growing from the Glorious Revolution of 1688, which had firmly established parliamentary rule and constitutional monarchy. In the early eighteenth century, the religious revival known as the Great Awakening created congregations throughout the colonies and led to the disestablishment of religion (that is, the separation of church and state). It also laid a critical foundation for much of the associational life that would follow in the nineteenth century. Americans formed civic associations to build schools, libraries, and hospitals; they also established volunteer fire and insurance companies and societies of artisans and tradespeople. Although dominated by local elites, Americans engaged in discussion of important public issues in local town meetings in New England and the mid-Atlantic states. Local taverns, coffeehouses, and town squares, linked by an increasing number of newspapers, comprised a vibrant, if nascent, public sphere.

These innovations in civic infrastructure created networks of horizontal association that evolved into revolutionary societies, local political associations linked from town to town. Paul Revere's ride, framed in myth as the work of a small group, was in fact an early-warning system for the colonial revolutionaries.

The revolution gave rise to the federal political structure of the United States. Even in this earliest period of national life, the newly established federal postal service and post roads were critical in linking the civic associations and local public spheres established during the revolution. The federal structure of local, state, and national organization was a lasting legacy of civic innovation that remains central to the present.

The United States From 1800 to 1850

By the early nineteenth century, the innovation of the revolutionary period had created what historian Arthur Schlesinger described as a "nation of joiners." The French political scientist and historian Alexis de Tocqueville showed how Americans formed civic associations for every social, political, and economic purpose, demonstrating how the social networks generated during the revolutionary period continued to provide a stable foundation for further, incremental innovation. A second Great Awakening (c. 1800–1830) stimulated new congregations and laid the foundation for reform societies that organized to press for national temperance, the end of slavery, and the observance of the Christian Sabbath. As voting rights were extended to most adult white males, the period from 1820 to 1840 saw the rapid expansion of democratic and civic agitation among urban artisans and working people.

Civil War to the 1920s

At the outbreak of the Civil War, both the North and the South depended on local and state civilian and elected officials to mobilize for war and to organize medical relief. The war stimulated the founding of large numbers of civic organizations. The federal model of organizing—that is, having organizations with national, state, and local branches—had grown up through fraternal and reform organizations before the war. But after the war, it spread rapidly as a model for civic life, initially in veterans' associations, but then through independent women's clubs, farmers' organizations, and moral crusades for children.

The Progressive Era (c. 1900–1915) gave birth to a great wave of national associations: There were organizations that pressed for government reform, professional organizations, women's organizations, organizations to improve schools, and organizations for youth. The Progressive Era also saw the growth of unions and settlement houses, as well as the university extension school movement, which spread the ideal of knowledge in the service of the public good throughout the states.

The Depression and World War II

The Great Depression (c. 1929–1940), while a social catastrophe, stimulated new civic innovation and public problem solving, despite a severe dip in social capital as measured by membership in civic organizations. A great wave of union organizing brought millions of working Americans into labor organizations that changed the workplace and government policy while also creating new social capital networks in local communities. The New Deal itself brought thousands of civic innovators into the federal government, where they built upon the policy experiments of the Progressive Era to create new public housing, social security, and the social safety net that would last for fifty years.

World War II (which for the United States lasted from 1941 to 1945) mobilized the entire U.S. population, stimulating a sense of common purpose and shared sacrifice through scrap drives and victory gardens. The sociologist Robert Putnam believes that the "long civic generation" that came of age in the Depression and during World War II generated a fund of social capital that made great reforms such as the civil rights movement of the 1950s and 1960s possible. He attributes much of the decline in U.S. social capital to the replacement of this civic generation by baby boomers, generation X, and generation Y.

The 1960s and Beyond

For Putnam and other theorists of social capital, the period from the 1950s through about 1970 marks a high point in modern U.S. life. The social capital that began to accumulate in the post–Civil War period and flowered during the Progressive period created a long wave of stability and strong political and civic participation that, in turn, supported the great social achievements of the United States in the post–World War II era. Communities were relatively stable, active membership in civic organizations was high, and civic capacity reached its peak

This description of the history of civic life in the United States is widely accepted by scholars and social critics. It appears that, in fact, the *kind* of social capital described by Putnam did peak and has declined since 1970. But the 1960s also saw massive social changes, spurred by the civil rights movement, the crisis in U.S. cities, severe environmental challenges, and the rising feminist movement. New forms of civic innovation emerged that addressed these new challenges. New social movements worked for expanded rights for women, ethnic and racial minorities, gays and lesbians, the disabled, and others, while at the same time challenging traditional cultural norms. Public interest groups such as the Public Interest Research Groups founded by the activist Ralph Nader and others challenged entrenched corporate power over regulatory agencies and agendas; they sought expanded rights of public participation in the decisions of those agencies and the formulation of those agendas. New forms of community-based organizing emerged from the central idea that citizens should have a voice in solving the problems that affect them.

COMMUNITY DEVELOPMENT

By the early 1960s, U.S. cities were beginning to deteriorate. Middle-class, white flight to the suburbs was well under way, which meant that a rising percentage of city populations were ethnic minorities. President Lyndon Johnson's War on Poverty, announced in 1964, aimed to mobilize public and private resources to reverse this decline. A Community Action Program (CAP) mandated "maximum feasible participation" on the part of residents of the affected communities. In response, thousands of civic organizations grew up to serve on the community action agencies that administered federal money, creating tens of thousands of new civic leaders in urban communities.

Although poverty was not ended, new community organizations did emerge to push the process of fighting poverty and development communities forward. Community organizing strategies began to shift from simply placing demands on government to taking responsibility for finding solutions themselves. By the 1970s, groups like the Industrial Areas Foundation began to shift from strategies based on confrontation to congregationally based organizing to mobilize faith communities and cooperative strategies for new housing and job partnerships. The number of community development corporations (local nonprofit organizations), which numbered a few hundred in the late 1960s, grew to more than 3,600 by the year 2000.

Local community civic innovation was directly tied to government innovation. Citizens engaged the public policy process, changing policy and civic strategies as they confronted new problems and opportunities.

CIVIC ENVIRONMENTALISM

Beginning in the mid-1960s, Americans began to realize that the quality of the environment was rapidly deteriorating. Smog in cities, polluted air and water, and the logging of forests were all recognized as problems. In the early and mid-1960s, the movement for environmental improvement worked through traditional forms of regulation, which stressed industry volunteerism and bureaucratic "command and control" regulation. But the rising public interest movement of the late 1960s stressed new forms of citizen representation, including new legal norms of participation. When the National Environmental Protection Act became law in 1970, public interest environmentalism was still combined with older command-and-control tools. But as the new laws were implemented, a new form of civic environmentalism began to emerge.

New laws, like the Clean Water Act of 1972, mandated citizen participation. As this law was implemented, thousands of citizens took part in workshops, received training, and participated in state and local water planning projects, despite some frustration with bureaucratic confusion. In one leading example, the Environmental Protection Agency (EPA) funded the Chesapeake Bay Program in the early 1980s. A broad coalition of nonprofit organizations, including conservation groups, fishing and boating organizations, farms and businesses, schools and universities, neighborhood organizations, and other civic groups formed to take responsibility for deciding how to restore the badly polluted bay bordering Maryland and Virginia, with the EPA providing the resources and expertise. New laws arose out of their collaborative planning. Other results were the creation of the Chesapeake Bay Trust, which continues to fund citizen efforts, and the Alliance for Chesapeake Bay, which trains volunteers, including home owners, service groups, schools, and families. Citizen "stream teams" and river watches have formed to provide government agencies with data on pollution.

Civic environmentalism has spread throughout the United States in other areas. New citizen land trusts conserve local green space. Watershed councils and associations restore rivers and streams in what many see as a movement for "watershed democracy." Citizens have participated in new forest management programs established by the U.S. forest service, and they have established urban forestry projects and volunteer stewardship networks. Groups also have formed to find new solutions to toxic-waste management in an environmental justice movement.

Tens of thousands of citizens participated in a complex learning process as they came together to forward environmental goals, working alongside partners in government, business, and the nonprofit sector. Through the process of solving environmental problems in the civic forum, Americans came to recognize new opportunities for collaborative problem solving. New civic capacity has been built in hundreds of communities, in states and regions, in government agencies, and among market actors.

A NATIONAL CIVIC MOVEMENT

The United States' new forms of civic innovation are the result of a process of social learning that mobilizes social capital to promote broad democratic norms, enhance responsible and inclusive citizenship, and build the capacities of communities and institutions to solve their own problems. These emerging forms of civic innovation ripple across many sectors of social and community life.

Community coalitions that address health problems by providing health education and prevention tools in conjunction with broader community development and that draw civic and religious associations into partnership with public health and medical institutions often have a strong record of health improvements. They often take on the issue of providing health care to the uninsured. The Oregon Health Plan, for example, which was launched in 1989, was the result of extensive civic deliberation in community meetings and health care parliaments. Participants at those meetings discussed not only extending coverage to the uninsured but also the problems of how to dole out health care responsibly in a high-tech medical universe of continually escalating costs.

Beginning in the late 1980s, hundreds of newspaper editors formed a public, or civic journalism movement, to challenge routines of horse-race election coverage and confrontational framing of community issues. They sought to bring citizen voices onto the news pages and create new frameworks for community deliberation. By the year 2000, more than 350 newspapers had conducted civic journalism experiments. Hundreds of research universities are reinventing their relationships with their publics, incorporating service learning to engage students with surrounding communities. And young people are taking leadership roles in local communities through youth development, environmental activism, civic communication work, and other activities.

Civic innovation today takes many forms and can proceed from various directions: sometimes from the grassroots up, sometimes from nonprofit networks or government agencies, sometimes from adversaries previously locked in combat, and often from a creative mix of complementary initiatives put forward by very diverse stakeholders seeking fresh ways to solve public problems and generate new sources of civic trust. These new forms of civic innovation are embedded in larger, global, social trends, including a rise in "postmaterialist" values that stress the importance of political participation and personal satisfaction over narrow material rewards. The new forms of civic innovation are driven by a rise in education levels, by postindustrial job skills favoring autonomy, innovation, and collaborative problem solving, and by new media of political information. The new civic innovation is more closely intertwined with government and government capacity, in distinction to older forms of organization primarily rooted in autonomous groups in civil society. It is also driven by the decline of traditional political parties, the growth of interest-group representation, and public disillusionment with expert solutions. But perhaps more than anything else, today's civic innovation is a response to the growing complexity of social, political, and economic life, in which problems require the involvement of many different kinds of actors and civic stakeholders if they are to be solved.

GLOBAL CIVIC INNOVATION

There is evidence that new forms of civic innovation are emerging in many parts of the world. The nations of Eastern Europe began transforming civil society and public life before the fall of the Soviet Union in 1989, laying the foundation for the rebirth of civic and democratic life. Unions and cultural associations, nonofficial media, and new nongovernmental organizations all played critical roles.

In Asia, as the Republic of Korea (South Korea) moved from authoritarian to democratic rule in the 1980s, citizens, frustrated by government- and corporate-controlled media, founded a new newspaper, *Hangkyorei Shimbun,* with the help of the YMCA and other organizations. *Hangkyorei Shimbun* is independently staffed and owned. By the early twenty-first century, Koreans were using the Internet as a new public forum for discussion of multiple issues of national concern, from corporate corruption to international affairs. In China, too, the Internet is being used by civic organizations to circumvent censorship and form a nascent public sphere separate from state control.

In Africa, Latin America, and Asia, nongovernmental organizations are flourishing, serving as independent watchdogs for human rights, providing health care and other vital services, and helping women and the poor found new businesses through microcredit lending. These civic innovators often address more basic needs than their Western counterparts, but what they share is a common focus on citizen-led solutions to pressing social and public problems, while recognizing the vital continuing role of governments and markets.

—Lewis A. Friedland and Carmen Sirianni

See also COMMUNITY ACTION; COMMUNITY ORGANIZING

Further Reading

Cohen, J. L., & Arato, A. (1992). *Civil society and political theory.* Cambridge, MA: MIT Press.

Fischer, D. H. (1994). *Paul Revere's ride.* New York: Oxford University Press.

John, R. R. (1998). *Spreading the news: The American postal system from Franklin to Morse.* Cambridge, MA: Harvard University Press.

Putnam, R. D. (2000). *Bowling alone: The collapse and revival of American community.* New York: Simon & Schuster.

Ryan, M. P. (1997). *Civic wars: Democracy and public life in the American city during the nineteenth century.* Berkeley and Los Angeles: University of California Press.

Schlesinger, A. M. (1944). Biography of a nation of joiners. *American Historical Review, 50*(1), 1–25.

Schudson, M. (1998). *The good citizen: A history of American civic life.* New York: Free Press.

Sirianni, C. J., & Friedland, L. A. (2001). *Civic innovation in America: Community empowerment, public policy, and the movement for civic renewal.* Berkeley and Los Angeles: University of California Press.

Skocpol, T., Ganz, M., & Munson, Z. (2000). A nation of organizers: The institutional origins of civic voluntarism in the United States. *American Political Science Review, 94*(3), 527–546.

Tocqueville, A. de (2000). *Democracy in America* (H. C. Mansfield & D. Winthrop, Trans. and Eds.). Chicago: University of Chicago Press.

Warren, M. R. (2001). *Dry bones rattling : community building to revitalize American democracy.* Princeton, NJ: Princeton University Press.

CIVIC JOURNALISM

The term *civic journalism* refers to a movement led by news professionals, scholars, and nonprofit groups that aims to reform how media define, gather, and present news. Although the movement coalesced in the late 1980s, a precise definition of the term is still debatable, but common news practices of civic journalism include sponsoring public forums, convening citizen-centered focus groups, polling to identify citizen concerns, forming panels of citizens as consultants, soliciting questions from readers and viewers to pose to candidates, devoting coverage to citizen-framed issues, and publishing information that encourages citizen involvement in the political process.

In short, advocates have said, civic journalists regard news media as conveners of communities, not just chroniclers. And, they add, the movement is more about communities and their citizens than it is about journalists and their profession.

HISTORY

Civic journalism—also known as public journalism and citizen-based journalism—got its labels after the 1988 presidential campaigns of Vice President George H. W. Bush and Massachusetts Governor Michael Dukakis had prompted widespread dissatisfaction over their superficiality. In Wichita, Kansas, the newspaper editor Davis "Buzz" Merritt Jr. (b. 1936), reviewed the election for the Knight Ridder–owned *Eagle* newspaper and concluded that the campaign's focus on Bush's "Willie Horton" ad (in which Dukakis was portrayed as soft on crime) and Dukakis's tank-driving pseudoevent (in which Dukakis appeared to be strong on national defense) had insulted the intelligence of voters and, worse, demeaned democracy. Dwindling voter participation provided evidence that traditional journalism served the public poorly by passing political superficiality along to readers and viewers without adding social value to it.

Merritt's discontent led him to Jay Rosen, a scholar whose 1986 doctoral dissertation had documented the social history of the American newspaper. Rosen had concluded that the profession of journalism developed in ways that separated citizens, newspapers, and public life. In an effort to improve newspapers' relevance, substance, and community commitments, Merritt, the journalist, and Rosen, the scholar, coined the phrase *public journalism.* (For consistency, this entry uses the term *civic journalism.*)

Merritt and Rosen defined public journalism as a reform of professional norms with the aim of reintroducing citizens to the center of political coverage, joining the politicians, their handlers, and other elites. But a broader goal of Merritt, Rosen, and other civic journalism advocates was the renewal of civic engagement in the democratic process.

Declining voter participation was only one measure of a widespread generational withdrawal of citizens from public life, according to research published during the 1990s by the Harvard University professor of public policy Robert Putnam. Demonstrating the decline in public participation in the U.S. political process since the 1970s, Putnam's findings contrasted with those that the French political writer Alexis-Charles-Henri de Tocqueville (1805–1859) had gathered while traveling in the United States for nine months in 1831–1832. According to Tocqueville, early nineteenth-century U.S. communities exhibited uncommonly vigorous civic lives, and their most active participants kept abreast of the news as it appeared in print.

Tocqueville's conclusions were no longer applicable by the 1920s, when American philosopher and educator John Dewey (1859–1952) argued that the fate of democracy in an increasingly complex world depended on greater citizen involvement in civic public affairs and that the press was vital to this goal. Dewey's ideas shaped the so-called social responsibility theory of the press, which received its widest airing in the 1947 report of the Commission on Freedom of the Press. The commission, funded by *Time* magazine publisher Henry R. Luce (1898–1967), concluded that only a socially responsible press can remain a free press. The idea of civic journalism shares the same philosophical lineage as social responsibility theory, although in practice scholars tend to consider civic journalism more activist in its emphasis on public deliberation and on community.

COMMUNITY

The concept of community is key to civic journalism. Practically, civic journalism has been most associated with the medium of the newspaper. As the vast majority of U.S. newspapers are rooted in local and regional markets, some newspaper editors and publishers have advocated the civic journalism tenet of reconnecting with community.

For example, soon after the 1988 presidential campaign, the Knight Ridder newspaper chain, one of the nation's largest (and Merritt's employer), asserted the importance of the link between newspapers and their communities and allied itself with civic journalism's practices and goals. At a germinal 1989 meeting of editors, James K. Batten, the chief executive officer of Knight Ridder, argued that a newspaper and its community are part of a single system in which neither can succeed without the other. John Gardner, a Cabinet secretary in the presidential administration of Lyndon Baines Johnson and a former head of the nonprofit lobby Common Cause (which works for campaign-finance reform), added that newspaper readership was unlikely to go up as long as a sense of community continued going down.

Concepts of community and the practice of civic journalism are also linked empirically. Putnam's research showing precipitous declines in measures of civic engagement—the "bowling alone" thesis—drew critics. But none disputed the finding that newspaper readership is a key measure of citizen interest and engagement in community affairs.

CONTROVERSY

By the early 1990s, civic journalism attracted harsh criticism from traditional press leaders. The criticism clustered around several objections—that civic journalism violated traditional norms of objectivity, that loss of objectivity amounted to boosterism, that the emphasis on citizen concerns amounted to pandering and abdicating professional responsibilities, and that civic journalism was no more than good journalism. For this reason, the phrase *civic journalism* and its synonyms became forbidden buzzwords in many newsrooms.

Advocates of civic journalism indeed acknowledged a bias—in favor of a healthy democratic process—akin to a medical reporter's bias in favor of a cure for disease. Furthermore, the movement was sustained by such nonprofit groups as the Washington, D.C.–based Pew Center for Civic Journalism, established in 1993, which promoted civic journalism, supplied grants to news organizations, and awarded annual prizes.

IMPACT OF CIVIC JOURNALISM

Estimates of the number of civic-journalism-oriented news organizations vary widely. By some accounts, perhaps six hundred U.S. newspapers have practiced civic journalism since the Pew Center opened in 1993. The center estimated that more than a thousand journalists attended its civic-journalism workshops.

For more than a decade after its start in the late 1980s, the civic journalism movement offered only anecdotal evidence that its readers and viewers were more civically engaged than they had been before the movement began, but advocates argued that overcoming entrenched journalistic norms and engaging disconnected citizens required more than a decade to achieve. By the mid-1990s, however, research confirmed that civic journalism existed as a new and distinct belief system among members of the press (Bare 1998). And in 2001, the Pew Center reported the results of a survey showing a transformation in attitudes among newspaper journalists, 90 percent of whom now stated that the future of the profession depended on more interaction with readers and viewers. Broadcast news media, however, have been much less likely to practice civic journalism, which, according to some scholars, may explain why the movement's effects on civic awareness and behavior were negligible. Internet news media have also yet to make a substantial and independent showing in civic journalism.

In late 2002, after a decade of advocacy, the Pew Center closed its doors due to a sunset provision in its original ten-year grant. Whether other nonprofit groups will adopt Pew's advocacy role and whether other news media will apply civic journalism's reforms in the new century remains to be seen.

—David O. Loomis

Further Reading

Bare, J. (1998). A new strategy. In E. B. Lambeth, P. E. Meyer, & E. Thorson (Eds.). *Assessing public journalism* (pp. 83–108). Columbia, MO: University of Missouri Press.

Black, J. (Ed.). (1997). *Mixed news: The public/civic/communitarian journalism debate.* Mahwah, NJ: Lawrence Erlbaum.

Charity, A. (1995). *Doing public journalism.* New York: Guilford.

Commission on Freedom of the Press. (1947). *A free and responsible press.* Chicago: University of Chicago Press.

Dewey, J. (1927). *The public and its problems.* New York: Henry Holt.

Eksterowicz, A. J., Roberts, R., & Clark, A. (1998). Public journalism and public knowledge. *Harvard International Journal of Press/Politics, 3*(2), 74–96.

Hoy, T. (1998). *The political philosophy of John Dewey: Toward a constructive renewal.* Westport, CT: Praeger.

Ladd, E. C. (1997). *Silent revolution: The rebirth of American civic life and what it means for all of us.* New York: Free Press.

Lambeth, E. B., Meyer, P. E., & Thorson, E. (1998). *Assessing public journalism.* Columbia: University of Missouri Press.

Loomis, D., & Meyer, P. (2000). Opinion without polls: Finding a link between corporate culture and public journalism. *International Journal of Public Opinion Research, 12*(3), 276–284.

Merrill, J. C., Gade, P. J., & Blevens, F. R. (2001). *Twilight of press freedom: The rise of people's journalism.* Mahwah, NJ: Lawrence Erlbaum.

Merritt, D., Jr. (1995). *Public journalism and public life: Why telling the news is not enough.* Hillsdale, NJ: Lawrence Erlbaum.

Putnam, R. D. (2000). *Bowling alone: The collapse and revival of American community.* New York: Simon & Schuster.

Schudson, M. (1998). *The good citizen: A history of American civic life.* New York: Free Press.

Tocqueville, A. de (1969). *Democracy in America* (J. P. Maier, Ed.; G. Lawrence, Trans.). Garden City, NY: Anchor. (Original work published 1835)

CIVIC LIFE

Although the ancient Greeks did not use the term *civic life,* they understood the notion. For the Greeks, civic life encompassed the ways that citizens banded together to rule the city. But as the term passed through history, it gained other connotations that linked it to *civil society,* which refers to that part of social life, separate from the state or government, in which all citizens come together. Civic life today can refer either to this larger concept—the lives of citizens in society as a whole—or to its original meaning, the association of citizens in their local communities.

CIVIC LIFE IN THE ANCIENT AND MEDIEVAL WORLDS

Cities emerged some 5,000 years ago in Babylonia and Egypt. But these ancient cities ruled by kings, despots, pharaohs, and emperors were built as warrior states. There were no citizens in the sense of those who participated in governing the city; there were only the rulers and the ruled.

Civic life as we understand it today began to emerge only with the rise of the Greek *polis* (city) around 600 BCE. Greek democracy was still restricted to a relatively small class of property owners, with women, slaves, and foreigners excluded from citizenship. But the Greek idea of the citizen—a member of the political community of the city with full rights to participate in its governance—was a major innovation for humankind. The ancient agora (marketplace) was where all citizens assembled to debate the important questions of governance in both the city and the state. This early Greek ideal of the public sphere, with its close ties to the city and to civic and public life, continues to influence our understanding of civic life today.

In contrast with Greece, citizenship in ancient Rome was broad: Aliens and even slaves could become citizens. However, the Roman republic was ruled by nobles in the senate, and even before the fall of the republic and rise of the empire, the mass of Roman citizens had little influence on civic life.

With the fall of the Roman empire (c. 410–440 CE), Europe as a whole began its long decline into feudalism, a system in which warrior-lords ruled over an unfree population. Feudalism entailed a tangle of obligations to a hierarchy of lords: Peasants were obligated to the lord of the manor, lesser lords were obligated to greater lords, and all lords were obligated to a king or emperor. There are no citizens in a feudal system, and without citizens, civic life is unthinkable. Although developed urban civilizations existed in China, India, Mesoamerica, and Africa, these were ruled by kings, emperors, and despots. Western feudalism was also hierarchical, but the complex set of obligations that it entailed set the stage for the emergence of relatively independent cities.

THE REEMERGENCE OF CIVIC LIFE IN LATE MEDIEVAL EUROPE

Civic life began to reemerge in late medieval Europe (c. 1300) in newly formed city-states in Germany, the Netherlands, Catalonia (in present-day Spain), Provence (in present-day France), and Italy. The city-states were founded both on the maritime trade that connected many of the cities to one another and on each city's trade with its own feudal hinterland. Trade itself was linked to the establishment of law (revived from ancient Rome), which was necessary to ensure predictability. With law came rights, which were central to the new city-states. The city-states were autonomous, free from feudal obligations, and relatively free from kings and emperors, although often remaining formally under their control.

Among the rulers of the new city-states were the great guilds, medieval associations of merchants and craftsmen formed to protect and control trade. While the guilds were by no means democratic, they did choose their own members and created rules for the trades under their control. The guilds were an early model of free association in the West, in which citizens banded together to regulate their interests.

At the same time that the cities were carving out autonomous areas of self-rule by association, peasants, serfs, and others in the feudal countryside were making their way to them, alongside journeymen fleeing their obligations to masters in other towns. The slogan *stadtluft macht frei* ("city air makes one free") circulated in city and countryside alike. The cities provided breathing space and served as incubators for the emergence of modern civic ideals.

Citizens Versus Industrial "Progress"

In the excerpt below, Wendell Berry–essayist, poet, and novelist–relates his thoughts on a community meeting about building a nuclear power plant in Indiana.

Several years ago, I attended a meeting in Madison, Indiana, that I have been unable to forget, it seems so emblematic of the fate of our country in our time. In the audience at that meeting were many citizens of local communities, my own among them, who were distrustful of the nuclear power plant then being built (but now discontinued) at Marble Hill. Seated on the stage were representatives of Public Service Indiana, the company that was building the power plant, and members of the Nuclear Regulatory Commission, whose job it presumably was to protect us from the acknowledged dangers of the use of nuclear power, as well as from the already recognized deceits and ineptitudes of Public Service Indiana.

The meeting proceeded as such meetings typically proceed. The fears, objections, questions, and complaints of the local people were met with technical jargon and with bland assurances that the chance of catastrophe was small. In such a confrontation, the official assumption apparently is that those who speak most incomprehensibly and dispassionately are right and that those who speak plainly and with feeling are wrong. Local allegiances, personal loyalties, and private fears are not scientifically respectable; they do not weight at all against "objective consideration of the facts"–even though some of the "facts" may be highly speculative or even false. Indeed, in the history of such confrontations, the victories have mainly gone to the objective considerers of the so-called facts.

Those considerers were then still winning at Marble Hill, even though the fraud and incompetence of Public Service Indiana was a matter of public record. But that meeting produced one question and one answer that tell us all we need to know about the nature of such an enterprise, and about the role of education in it. A lady rose in the audience and asked the fifteen or twenty personages on the stage to tell us how many of them lived within the fifty-mile danger zone around Marble Hill. The question proved tactically brilliant, apparently shocking the personages on the stage, who were forced to give it the shortest, plainest answer of the evening: *Not one.* Not a single one of those well-paid, well-educated, successful, important men would need to worry about his family or his property in the event of a catastrophic mistake at Marble Hill.

A powerful class of itinerant professional vandals is now pillaging the country and laying it waste. Their vandalism is not called by that name because of its enormous profitability (to some) and the grandeur of its scale. If one wrecks a private home, that is vandalism, but if, to build a nuclear power plant, one destroys good farmland, disrupts a local community, and jeopardizes lives, homes, and properties within an area of several thousand square miles, *that* is industrial progress.

Source: Berry, Wendell. (1987). "Higher Education and Home Defense." In *Home Economics*. San Francisco: North Point Press, pp. 49–50.

CITIZENSHIP IN THE EARLY MODERN ERA

The Protestant Reformation (c.1517 – 1570 CE) further advanced the framework of modern civic life in three ways. First, Reformation churches challenged not only the beliefs but also the hierarchical structure of the Catholic Church. Some Protestant churches were organized as autonomous local congregations that associated with one another in federation. This, alongside the guilds, was a major underpinning of the idea of civic association in the West. Second, by encouraging the reading of the Bible in vernacular languages rather than in Latin, the Reformation spurred the rapid growth of literacy among the lower and middle classes. This in turn spurred the printing industry (the first mass medium), whose activity was a precondition for the circulation of ideas and the development of a democratic public life. Third, the Reformation split Europe and set off a period of religious strife, persecution, and war between states. This great period of civil strife exhausted Europe and laid the foundation for the ideals of religious toleration and, more generally, for the use of rules to constrain warfare.

In early modern Europe, then, we find city governments independent of feudal lords, monarchs, and the pope; autonomous guilds, regulating trade through association; the coming together in cities of people from many places and walks of life; and the rise of a modern printing industry. We begin to see the emerging outlines of a modern civic life. The modern city and the modern citizen developed together. The cities, free spaces in the heart of medieval Europe, were the laboratories of the money economy, the Enlightenment, and the great seventeenth- and eighteenth-century revolutions that, taken together, created the framework modern civic life.

THE AGE OF REVOLUTION AND MODERN CIVIL SOCIETY

The Enlightenment was that great period from the late seventeenth century through the French Revolution of 1789 during which modern Western ideas of freedom, liberty, individual rights, and the proper relation between state and civil society emerged.

The Enlightenment begins politically with the signing of the Treaty of Utrecht in 1713, which established the principle (if not practice) of religious toleration in Europe. Toleration, in turn, planted the seed of the idea of separation of church and state, the principle that citizens should be politically free to believe as they wish and that no one church should be favored by the state.

The gradual separation of the state and civil society, along with the growth of a modern public sphere, is the pillar on which modern civic life rests. The early modern state witnessed the distancing of the household of the monarch from the government. In other words, the king or emperor no longer directly controlled the national purse or exercised direct personal power over the national military. Treasuries, taxation, law, and the maintenance of public order slowly were separated from royal whim. During the English Civil Wars (1642–1651), Charles I was executed and Parliament became the ruling power in the nation. The monarchy was restored in 1660, but in 1688, when William and Mary took the throne, they did so as constitutional monarchs, not absolute monarchs, and the principle of the separation of king and government was firmly established. In France, separate *parlements,* or courts of law, grew slowly in power from about the mid-sixteenth century through the Revolution of 1789, in which the Estates General established a constitutional monarchy (shortly thereafter overthrown by the revolutionary republic). In the New World, the Revolution of 1776 resulted in the first original constitutional government in 1787–1788. Regardless of national differences, the broad principles of the modern state were held in common: The state was separate from the personal rule of king or president; the state's powers were limited; the state was governed by laws. Henceforth the state sphere was also separate from the sphere of civil society.

CIVIL SOCIETY AND THE PUBLIC SPHERE

Civil society grew up alongside the modern state. Writing about civil society in *The Leviathan* (1651), political theorist Thomas Hobbes (1588–1679) said, in part in reaction to the English Civil Wars, that civil society created the state to protect citizens one from another, to end the war of "each against all." In Hobbes's view, the state ensured order in civil society, which resembled anarchy. By contrast, philosopher John Locke (1632–1704) wrote in his *Two Treatises on Civil Government* (1690) that civil society grew from a state of nature, but through the social contract created the state for its protection; thus, civil society could dissolve the state when it failed to serve and protect the community. German philosopher Georg Hegel (1770–1831) drew from ancient Greece, seeing civil society as a community of citizens who agreed on what it took to live the good life and created civil society to realize that vision. He saw the state as embodying and protecting both civil society and the vision of the good life. All three theorists held that civil society was a sphere apart from the state.

The modern public sphere, for its part, grew up in the eighteenth century between civil society and the state, and it mediates between them. In coffeehouses and salons, through newspapers and journals, and through associations and small assemblies, citizens came together to reason about politics, the state, literature and art, and the family. They argued about how these institutions should be constructed and what should be the proper limits of their power. Private citizens, or bourgeoisie (which originally meant simply independent city dwellers or burghers), were also property owners competing in the marketplace. But at the same time, through their discussions in the public sphere, they laid the groundwork for the most important rules and rights of a liberal society: the rights of free speech, assembly, and press, as well as the more fundamental rights of the individual that guaranteed these social rights. According to the contemporary German philosopher Jürgen Habermas, the public sphere embodied the democratic principles of modern society, protecting society both from the domination of the emerging industrial marketplace and from the power of the state.

The great revolutions at the end of the eighteenth century tied together these various ideas of the state, civil society, and the public sphere in different ways. In

France, the Revolution of 1789 overthrew the emerging constitutional regime and led to the Reign of Terror and the Napoleonic empire, neither models of open civil society and public life. In the case of France, the state overwhelmed civil society. In England, the constitutional monarchy offered one evolutionary model, but one in which the economic engine of civil society, unconstrained industrialization, seemed to overwhelm a democratic public sphere (although opposition parties continued to participate in public life). The United States was a model rife with the contradictions. Although slavery continued in the South and propertied elites existed everywhere, the nation was founded on the very ideas of civil society and civic life—that citizens could act together, blending self-interest and the common good, to regulate both society and public life. In order to provide an in-depth analysis of civic life in one country rather than an overview of civic life in many, we will focus now on the United States.

CIVIC LIFE AND THE EARLY-NINETEENTH-CENTURY UNITED STATES

The great observer and theorist of U.S. civic life in the early nineteenth century was Alexis de Tocqueville (1805–1859). He came to the United States in 1831 to observe the underlying conditions of U.S. democracy. His work, *Democracy in America,* published in two volumes in 1835 and 1840, continues to set the frame for much of the discussion of civic life in the United States even today. In contrast to those who saw a radical distinction between state and civil society in Europe, Tocqueville observed a close relation between the two in the United States. He saw democracy as governed by public opinion, arising out of the opinions of individuals freely associating with one another in civil society. Therefore, for Tocqueville, the civic life of associations was the very essence of democratic life in the United States, and, because Tocqueville saw the United States as a model of modern democracy, elsewhere as well.

In a famous passage, Tocqueville describes the civic life of the United States in all of its richness:

> Americans of all ages, all conditions, all minds constantly unite. Not only do they have commercial and industrial associations in which all take part, but they also have a thousand other kinds: religious, moral, grave, futile, very general and very particular, immense and very small; Americans use associations to give fêtes, to found seminaries, to build inns, to raise churches, to distribute books, to send missionaries to the antipodes; in this manner they create hospitals, prisons, schools. Finally, if it is a question of bringing to light a truth or developing a sentiment with the support of a great example, they associate. Everywhere that, at the head of a new undertaking you see the government in France and a great lord in England, count on it that you will perceive an association in the United States.

In short, Americans associated to *do* things: worship, celebrate, and think together; govern the town, care for the sick, and imprison the criminal. Associational life for Tocqueville was not altruistic, in the sense that voluntarism connotes today. Association was linked with self-interest and getting the real work of society *and* government done. It is a powerful notion of a civic life that has real and direct consequences in the world.

THE TOCQUEVILLIAN VIEW REASSESSED

In the 1990s, U.S. scholarship began to expand, interpret, and, in some cases, challenge the classical Tocquevillian view. There are three broad areas of reinterpretation. The first reinterprets the problem of individual and community. The second challenges the political image of harmony. The third explores whether early U.S. civil society was, in fact, as rooted in local community life as Tocqueville believed.

Scholar Robert Bellah and his coauthors of the modern sociological classic *Habits of the Heart* argue that it is particularly difficult to sustain community in the United States because individualism, "the first language in which Americans tend to think about their lives, values independence above all else" (p. viii). Individualism takes two forms. One is utilitarianism, the belief that if everyone vigorously pursues his or her own interest, the social good will automatically emerge; the other is expressive individualism, which stresses the exploration of self-identity and the search for authenticity above all else. According to Bellah, this individualism has been sustainable in the United States only because people are also guided by an ethos of commitment, community, and citizenship. In *Habits,* these principles are gathered under the rubric of "civic membership," the intersection of personal identity with social identity. Bellah and colleagues were among the first to warn that, despite Tocqueville's vision, civic membership is in crisis, reflected in "temptations and pressures to disengage from the larger society" felt by every significant social group (p. xi).

Historian Mary Ryan is among those scholars who have shown that civic and public life in nineteenth-century U.S. cities was much more fractious and chaotic

Civics "Boot Camp"

ELMHURST, Ill. (ANS)—Hoping to get suburban residents out of their sport utility vehicles and into the public debate, a citizens' action group is launching a free six-month program to teach people the basic tools of civic engagement.

Participants will learn how to write a letter to their state and national representatives, request public records under the Freedom of Information Act, look up city ordinances and case law, make a comment in a public meeting, read a government budget and effectively communicate an opinion.

This citizens' action boot camp is the idea of the five-year-old Citizen Advocacy Center, which focuses on strengthening democracy in DuPage County just west of Chicago. In addition to the Citizenship Training Corps, the center litigates cases of community-wide interest, and offers monthly speakers and programs.

The emphasis of the training corps will be on practical experience. "Our goal is to teach civics like one teaches a science class," said Terry Pastika, an attorney and community organizer with the center who will help teach the 12-class course.

"In science you have to do a lab, an experiment. If you're going to learn civics, you want the entire community to be your lab. It's a hands-on training course. We're asking people who take this course to get out and do something."

The seminars were created in part as response to a recent study that found that high school students were clueless about why they should get involved in civic affairs, Pastika said. The center also receives lots of phone calls from people frustrated by the lack of responsiveness of local government but who are uncertain how to get things moving.

"Being involved should be a habit, second nature," Pastika said, mirroring the mission of the center.

The issues of concern in the suburbs are different from those in the city, Pastika admitted. There are also greater distances between neighbors and few central gathering places. Challenging the mentality that people think they can't get involved is one of the program's goals.

Nonpartisan in nature, the center in its training corps will focus on giving people the means to solve their own problems rather than advance specific causes. "It's important for people in the class to pursue their own interests," said Pastika. "It will give the class a lot more depth."

Fifteen people have signed up for the initial series. Next summer, the center plans to offer advanced civics lessons in how to get an initiative on the ballot, how to get coverage on local-access cable television and hold a press conference.

Source: "Civics 'Boot Camp' Teaches Basics of Citizen Action." American News Service, Article No. 1263, January 13, 2000.

than the Tocquevillian image. Ryan shows that civic life in New York, New Orleans, and San Francisco grew from the mingling of many different types of people in the streets, large public ceremonies, and parades and processions, as well as the skirmishes between different ethnic and racial groups. The partisan elections of the nineteenth century, she argues, were bare-knuckle fights to the death among party machines, nothing like the image of public life offered by Tocqueville. Sociologist Michael Schudson also claims that the civic ideal of the Founding Fathers was one of elite rule—civic life consisted, in part, of accepting the decisions of one's betters. This "politics of assent" gave way to a "politics of affiliation" in which membership in a political party defined one's civic and political identity through much of the nineteenth century: Partisanship replaced hierarchy.

The third debate about the growth of civic life in the nineteenth century revolves around the question of how much civic life grew from below, grassroots-style, and how much it was founded from above by large national organizations that paralleled the federal political structure of the United States. The scholar Theda Skocpol and her colleagues, drawing from "Biography of a Nation of Joiners," the seminal article by the historian Arthur Schlesinger, claim that early U.S. civic life was more closely tied to the federal structure of U.S. government than Tocqueville implies. They point to antislavery, Christian, fraternal, and temperance associations that began as national organizations and spread to local communities. They point out that after the Civil War, this federal model was responsible for the growth of major national organizations, whether farmers' alliances and veterans' organizations, the labor and women's suffrage movements, or youth organizations and even bowling congresses. They also contest the idea that industrialization, urbanization, and immigration in the latter nineteenth century were as important in creating new associations in the cities as historians have previously believed.

But virtually all scholars agree that the second half

of the nineteenth century saw the birth of major civic organizations in the United States, many of which persisted well into the twentieth century, eventually reaching into almost every city and town in the country.

THE PROGRESSIVE ERA TO THE PRESENT

The Progressive Era (c. 1900–1915) arose in the beginning of the twentieth century in part in opposition to the tumultuous, partisan street democracy of the nineteenth century. Against the urban machine, it posed the ideal of scientific government, of rule by those capable of enlightened public opinion and scientific management. The ideal citizen was a middle-class reformer, still a member of associations, but associations of a new kind. Among the U.S. associations born out of the Progressive Era are the National Civic League, the League of Women Voters, parent-teacher associations, and organizations for youth such as the Boy Scouts and the Girl Scouts. The fraternal lodges of the nineteenth century were overshadowed (but not replaced) by new business associations such as the Rotary and Lions Clubs. The Progressive Era saw the growth of unions, settlement houses, and kindergartens, as well as the emergence of the "social congregation" in the churches. Extension schools at the University of Wisconsin and elsewhere spread the ideal of knowledge in the service of the public good throughout the states. The Progressive Era also challenged certain ideals of participation. The ideal of the "informed citizen," to use Schudson's phrase, replaced the partisan citizen, but the shift also entailed a restriction of the civic franchise.

Despite its shortcomings, sociologist and political scientist Robert Putnam sees the Progressive Era as the starting point of a great wave of civic innovation in the twentieth-century United States that began to wane only in the 1960s. His research has been at the center of the argument over the decline of U.S. civic life in the twentieth century. Putnam argues that our stocks of "social capital" (defined as the norms and networks that people can draw upon to solve common problems) have been depleted. Many measures of associational membership in the United States have been in decline since the early 1970s. Participation in religious congregations, a bedrock of association in the United States, declined by one-fifth between 1980 and 2000. Membership in parent-teacher associations and organizations has plummeted since the 1960s. Union membership has fallen by half since the 1950s. Women's organizations such as the League of Women Voters and General Federation of Women's Clubs have seen 40 to 60 percent declines. Membership in fraternal and business clubs has also dropped. More worrisome for Putnam is the decline in active participation in these organizations. He estimates that the active core of the United States' civic organizations, those who serve as officers and committee chairs, declined by 45 percent from 1985 to 1994. According to Putnam, America lost nearly half of its civic infrastructure in less than a decade.

While scholars do not agree on the reasons for this decline, there is some basic agreement on certain trends. The number of self-help groups has risen dramatically in this same period, suggesting a shift from civic concerns to personal self-fulfillment. Television watching has risen dramatically, and the Internet now plays a role in many people's lives, suggesting a shift from face-to-face participation to media consumption. Women have entered the labor force in ever growing numbers, eroding the volunteer labor that sustained school and community-based association for much of this century. Suburbanization and associated sprawl have eroded communities of place. All of these trends are combined with a huge grown in professionalized, direct-mail, national organizations with little or no active membership. Putnam also posits a major generational shift, as the "long civic generation" that grew up during the Depression and World War II is replaced by baby boomers and generation X and generation Y cohorts, with each successive generation less and less involved in civic life. The causes behind these generational declines are unclear, but the larger trend towards disengagement from civic life in the twentieth century seems indisputable.

Some scholars have questioned whether the picture is as stark as Putnam suggests, however. Americans continue to volunteer at extraordinarily high levels, and some researchers have argued that participation may actually be increasing at the local community level. Robert Wuthnow argues that the new wave of self-help groups helps form loose connections that may create new forms of social capital.

CAUSES AND COUNTERTRENDS IN THE UNITED STATES

Scholars and citizen-practitioners differ on what might be done to reverse the decline in U.S. civic life. Putnam stresses that rebuilding social capital is a difficult task, and he is modest in his suggested solutions. In the final chapter of *Bowling Alone* (2000), he suggests that finding new ways to re-engage young people is the most important starting place, including developing civic curricula in schools to show how young people can become more engaged and creating more effective programs of community service. He also calls for more family-friendly policies in the workplace to create more time for community and suggests finding ways to redirect attention from television. He hopes the Internet can be used to encourage more active forms of civic communication, including more participation in local arts, and he supports reversing sprawl and getting more Americans engaged in local politics. He also suggests a socially responsible and pluralistic "great awakening" among the United States' religious communities.

There is substantial agreement with much of this program among other critics of declining civic life, but there are differences as well. Communitarians such as Amitai Etzioni claim that a breakdown in the moral fabric of society and excessive individualism in the public sphere have led to civic decline; they call for a new social philosophy that would protect individual rights while emphasizing community responsibility. Communitarians claim to stake out a middle ground between left and right. They share some affinities with conservative critics of civic decline, who see a sharp contrast between the potentially rich civic life of "mediating institutions" in local neighborhoods and communities on the one hand and government on the other. Drawing from thinkers such as Michael Novak and Robert Nisbet, they claim that the civic functions of community have migrated to government, and that it will be necessary to reverse this trajectory both by rebuilding local civic life and by shrinking government.

On the left, Theda Skocpol and her colleagues suggest a need to revive a model of the federal organization of civic life that led to the founding of so many civic organizations in the nineteenth century. Skocpol and others argue that Washington-based interest groups have displaced the multitiered structures of the earlier period and that this trend must be reversed. Skocpol also believes that revitalizing the U.S. Democratic Party is a necessary component in renewing the nation's civic life.

Finally, scholars Carmen Sirianni, Lewis Friedland, and Harry Boyte, and leaders of various organizations such as the National Civic League and Campus Compact are endeavoring to build a broad and nonpartisan civic renewal movement on the foundations of the extensive civic innovations and community-building networks that have emerged in recent years. This approach stresses that the work of civic renewal needs to go on not just in civil society, but in government, market, educational, and professional institutions of all sorts. This requires an expansive view of the productive public work of all citizens in building the commonwealth. It stresses pragmatic problem-solving skills rather than exhortation. And it stresses reliance on a multiplicity of forms of civic partnership rather than on an ideal model from the past.

—Lewis A. Friedland and Carmen Sirianni

Further Reading

Bellah, R., Madsen, R., Sullivan, W. M., Swidler, A., & Tipton, S. M. (1996). *Habits of the heart: Individualism and commitment in American life.* Berkeley and Los Angeles: University of California Press.

Boyte, H., & Kari, N. (1997). *Building America.* Philadelphia: Temple University Press.

Cohen, J. L., & Arato, A. (1992). *Civil society and political theory.* Cambridge, MA: MIT Press.

Eberly, D. E. (2000). *The essential civil society reader: Classic essays in the American civil society debate.* Lanham, MD: Rowman & Littlefield.

Nisbet, R. A. (1969). *The quest for community.* London: Oxford University Press.

Novak, M. (1980). *Democracy and mediating structures: A theological inquiry.* Washington, DC: American Enterprise Institute for Public Policy Research.

Putnam, R. D. (1995). Bowling alone: America's declining social capital. *Journal of Democracy, 6*(1), 65–78.

Putnam, R. D. (2000). *Bowling alone: The collapse and revival of American community.* New York: Simon & Schuster.

Ryan, M. P. (1997). *Civic wars: Democracy and public life in the American city during the nineteenth century.* Berkeley and Los Angeles: University of California Press.

Schlesinger, A. M. (1944). Biography of a nation of joiners. *American Historical Review, 50*(1), 1–25.

Schudson, M. (1998). *The good citizen: A history of American civic life.* New York: Free Press.

Sirianni, C. J., & Friedland, L. A. (2001). *Civic innovation in America: Community empowerment, public policy, and the movement for civic renewal.* Berkeley and Los Angeles: University of California Press.

Skocpol, T. (2003). *Diminished democracy: From membership to management in American life.* Norman, OK: University of Oklahoma Press.

Tocqueville, A. de. (2000). *Democracy in America* (H. C. Mansfield & D. Winthrop, Trans. & Ed.) Chicago: University of Chicago Press. (Original work published 1835 and 1840)

Verba, S., Schlozman, K. L., & Brady, H. (1995). *Voice and equality: Civic voluntarism in American politics.* Cambridge, MA: Harvard University Press.

Wuthnow, R. (1998). *Loose connections: Joining together in America's fragmented communities.* Cambridge, MA: Harvard University Press.

CIVIC STRUCTURE

Civic structure, an attribute of community, is the capacity of the community to engage in dialogues and undertake activities that intentionally benefit the community. Civic structure influences how communities frame problems and make decisions about resource allocations to solve those problems. There is an assumption that high levels of trust among citizens and groups, tolerance, cooperation, and civic behavior are necessary for community problem solving. This does not imply total agreement or lack of conflict, but rather respect for and enforcement of social and legal rules that permit dissenting viewpoints and opinions to be publicly voiced.

The civic structure of a community consists of two basic components: individual actions in the public domain and complex, dynamic networks among people within the community and across communities. The concept utilizes several literatures, including those on civil society, social capital, democracy, community, and leadership development. The term *civic* is political, implying citizens' voluntary engagement in matters both public and private that have an impact on the collective community. Scholars Gabriel Almond and Sidney Verba use the term *civic culture* to describe a culture characterized by high tolerance for plurality of interests, mutual trust among citizens, and consensus on the legitimacy of political institutions. Political scientist Mark Warren refers to civic virtue in associations whose goal is societal good, created through cooperation. Robert Putnam, a sociologist and political scientist, puts social trust and civic engagement in a causal chain: Individuals interact with others (civic engagement), they learn to work together to solve problems, and thus they create social trust. This social trust leads to good public policies, better economic development, and efficient public administration.

INDIVIDUAL CITIZEN ACTIONS

The most common individual civic action in democratic society is voting in elections. The citizen also demonstrates civic involvement by signing petitions, running for public office, and participating in political actions in support of or in opposition to the existing governing structure. Political parties and referendums provide focal points for citizens to discuss and rally around. Citizens' votes for or against a particular party or persons representing economic reform, environmental protection, and various social welfare issues are individual actions that contribute to civic structure. These individual actions in aggregate provide politically appropriate and legally binding direction for governments and markets.

However, it is not possible to take the sum of all individual actions and have this equal civic structure. The acts of community leaders, who can direct how community problems are framed, how resources are allocated, what alternatives are proposed and selected, and how priorities are evaluated, have more weight than the actions of the average citizen. Further, leaders often set in motion collective activities whose outcomes are not predicted by a simple count of the number of leaders in a community and a reckoning of the strength of their personal power. An accounting of individual leader and citizen actions in the public domain alone is an insufficient representation of community civic structure. The social connections among multiple organizations and citizens also contribute to that civic structure.

NETWORKS AND CIVIC NORMS OF COMMUNITY

Communities contain multiple voluntary groups and organizations that have dynamic and complex relations with one another, with governments, and with market sectors. When the normative expectations for these relations are that groups and citizens should forgo self-interest and act in the interest of their community, civic structure increases. These civic connections and relationships can be reinforced by social rewards such as status, honor, social support, and economic gains.

The networks that people maintain, often labeled social capital, are resources that provide personal and community benefits. Scholars Pierre Bourdieu and James Coleman view these networks as the resources of individuals. Sociologist Pamela Paxton writes that "social capital is the idea that individuals and groups can gain resources from their connections to one another (and the type of these connections). These resources can be used to produce certain goods" (Paxton 1999, p. 89). When individual connections are multiplied and interwoven within a community and across communities to produce good for the public and benefit for the community, they create a community civic structure.

The structure can be described in terms of the density of groups and organizations in the community and the degree to which these groups connect with each other. The density of the structure can be measured by the numbers of houses of worship, membership groups, and voluntary organizations in the community. Community groups include temporary, ad hoc groups, grassroots organizations, and established associations with long histories and local, national, and international affiliations. Some researchers suggest that the kind of groups a community has (religious, civic, educational, political, social, and so forth) will affect the kind and quality of interactions with other groups, cooperation across groups, and the way democracy is practiced.

Community norms of civic behavior and mutual trust reflect the attitudes and values of the people in the community regarding what is important, what the community's problems are, and how they should be solved. Not all groups have missions or values that support the collective needs of their community. Some narrowly focus on their own membership and mission. Other groups make contributing to public and collectively held concerns a stated goal. This does not mean these groups all agree on the means for achieving community benefit. However, when they share norms of civic behavior and mutual trust, it is expected that they will negotiate, leverage, cajole, and cooperate with others to achieve overall community goals. Civic norms facilitate some actions and constrain other actions. Community norms that encourage social trust and cooperation reduce uncertainty and offer expectations of future cooperation.

ENABLING MECHANISMS

Four enabling mechanisms influence the direction and capacity of individual citizens' actions and groups' networks to undertake collective actions that create community benefit: legal rules and regulations, information flows, tolerance of dissent and diversity, and sense of place.

Legal Rules and Regulations

The basic tenets of democracy provide the legal foundation for citizen participation in the political, social, and economic decisions of the community. However, not all communities enforce public laws that permit citizens to speak at public meetings and have access to public records, or allow groups to meet regardless of their mission. Further, while community leaders may not disobey laws that encourage citizen involvement, they may simply discourage participation by holding meetings at inconvenient times and locations and not widely sharing information about the decision-making process. Local enforcement practices affect which rules and regulations are monitored and enforced and which are overlooked. In *Making Democracy Work Better,* sociologist Richard Couto writes that when the sheriff works for the most powerful interests in the community, there are few avenues to justice, and dissenting groups may find it very difficult to challenge dominant groups.

Information Flows

Deliberate and informal communication and information flows among citizens and groups strengthen civic structure and increase the community's capacity to resolve problems. Weekly and daily newspapers, newsletters, radio, television, and electronic mailing lists are important modes of information exchange. Margaret Wheatley, an organizational consultant, writes that if people do not have information, they will make it up (gossip and rumor). People and groups need information to solve the problems of daily living. Informal communication consists of the face-to-face and unstructured conversations people have with one another. As individual exchanges multiply and are networked across many individuals and groups, the flow of information affects the quality of the community's civic structure. Whether the community accepts the information and acts together upon it—or is divided by it—depends on the content and trustworthiness of the information.

Tolerance of Dissent and Diversity

Tolerance of diverse ideas, cultures, and perspectives is another mechanism that helps citizens and groups solve problems, whereas intolerance has the opposite effect. Even though laws may protect the rights of different groups of people to join in public debates and dialogues, communities may not have civic norms of tolerance for expressions of minority viewpoints. Suppression of divergent public opinions can lead to stagnant and closed communities. Suppressed differences may also explode into conflicts that are harmful to the community, whereas expressed differences can contribute to productive change.

Sense of Place

The last important enabling mechanism is the sense of place, the attachment groups and citizens feel for where they live. This is the feeling of belonging. Members matter to one another, are committed to helping one another, and have the capacity to influence the group. Attachment to place makes groups and citizens willing to invest resources in the local community and committed to improving its quality of life. If they lack a sense of place, local employers may move their businesses to new locations, residents may move in and out without contributing to public life, and groups and organizations will find it difficult to gather members who will voluntarily undertake community projects. Community festivals and fairs, cultural and historical celebrations, and holiday parades are activities that groups undertake to reinforce sense of place.

Watershed Communities

Civic structure is not limited to political boundaries, such as city limits or county lines. Watershed communities–groups of people bound together by the land that drains water into the physical flow of their common streams, rivers, lakes, or other bodies of water–also have a civic structure. Some watersheds have citizen watershed groups, environmental groups, farm commodity groups, local Soil and Water Conservation Districts, and businesses, which share common goals to improve the water quality and prevent flooding in their watershed. Each of these groups have leaders who provide direction and catalytic motivation for others in the watershed. Members of these groups undertake such activities as water monitoring, nature mapping, testimony at public meetings, school field trips and learning activities, data collection, and volunteer for community committees, planning and zoning boards. These groups may undertake different planning and management activities and have conflicting viewpoints on how the watershed should be managed. Some groups are challenging government decisions and business interests. Others are seeking to find mutually acceptable solutions. However, if they are working at sharing information and communicating across groups, exhibiting tolerance and respect for dissenting perspectives, and seeking common areas of cooperation, the watershed has a strong civic structure. Active formal and informal discussions and negotiations within and across these multiple groups provide innovative alternatives and commitments for solving difficult water issues.

–Lois Wright Morton

CIVIC STRUCTURE AND RURAL COMMUNITIES

Because of their low population density, rural communities find it hard to finance public services and profitable business ventures. In *Rural Communities: Legacy and Change,* the authors write that rural governments must provide "adequate levels of public services with limited resources. The problem is common to all rural communities, whether they are experiencing growth or decline" (Flora et al. 1992, p. 187). Churches, voluntary organizations, and leaders who are committed to improving their community are necessary if these rural towns are to have adequate services and facilities. Community planning and management responsibilities are often allocated to part-time elected officials and appointed staff, and citizens and groups often volunteer their time, skills, and financial resources to help solve rural problems.

For example, almost all Iowa towns with populations under 10,000 have core public services such as street maintenance, water, fire, and schools. Many also have public-private partnerships that invest in youth and senior programs, recreation programs, medical services, adequate housing stock, and child care services. These community infrastructures are made possible because of the civic relations people have with each other and those outside their community. A 2002 study of the civic structure of ninety-nine Iowa rural towns found a distinct pattern of citizen satisfaction with public services and combined public-private services and facilities. Rural places with high civic structure were more likely to perceive that they had a higher quality of services and facilities than were places with lower civic structure. This suggests a self-reinforcing cycle of norms of community involvement leading to increased satisfaction with the quality of rural services, which in turn fosters a community pride and more desire to be involved in community activities.

DIFFERENCES IN CIVIC STRUCTURE FROM COMMUNITY TO COMMUNITY

Civic structure varies from community to community, as well as over time within a community. The sources of these variations are the historical pathways within communities that reinforce or obstruct information flows, legal rules, tolerance, and sense of place. Community attitudes, beliefs, and norms offer either positive or negative social sanctions in support of or against civic behaviors in individuals and groups. The behaviors of leaders and dominant organizations are contagious and lead to imitation or social pressures, thereby creating some level of civic structure. Civic structure will be high if the dominant culture sanctions individuals and groups to act for the good of the community; it will be low if leaders and high profile groups are self-seeking, placing personal or organizational goals above the community when they are in competition. Some literatures report that individuals and groups in communities that are economically struggling find it more difficult to work together and cooperate in ways that over time build a civic structure. This suggests that a strong civic structure requires a financially secure middle class with education and time to invest in public service. The challenge for rural communities that are struggling with economic security is to invest in their people infrastructure (leadership skills, education, internal and external social networks) so that community problem solving can be effective.

While much has been written about civic behavior, the definitions and variables that compose civic structure are still emerging. Little is known about how different definitions of civic structure relate to specific community outcomes. This is because attempts to connect conceptual frameworks and empirical research are still in their infancy.

—Lois Wright Morton

See also RURAL COMMUNITY DEVELOPMENT; SOCIAL CAPITAL, TYPES OF

Further Reading

Almond, G. A., & Verba, S. (1989). *The civic culture revisited.* London: Sage.

Bourdieu, P. (1986). The forms of capital. In J. G. Richardson (Ed.), *Handbook of theory and research for the sociology of education* (pp. 241–258). New York: Greenwood.

Coleman, J. S. (1990). *Foundations of social theory.* Cambridge, MA: Belknap Press of Harvard University Press.

Couto, R., & Guthrie, C. S. (1999). *Making democracy work better.* Chapel Hill: The University of North Carolina Press.

Flora, C. B., Flora, J. L., Spears, J. D., Swanson, L. E., Lapping, M. B., & Weinberg, M. L. (1992). *Rural communities: Legacy & change.* Boulder, CO: Westview.

Mcmillan, D., & Chavis, D. (1986). Sense of community: A definition and theory. *Journal of Community Psychology, 14*(1), 6–23.

Morton, L. W. (2001). *Health care restructuring: Markets vs civil society.* Westport, CT: Auburn House, Greenwood.

Paxton, P. (1999). Is social capital declining in the United States? A multiple indicator assessment. *American Journal of Sociology, 105*(1), 88–127.

Putnam, R. D. (1993). *Making democracy work.* Princeton, NJ: Princeton University Press.

Putnam, R. D. (2000). *Bowling alone: The collapse and revival of American community.* New York: Simon & Schuster.

Smith, D. H. (2000). *Grassroots associations.* Thousand Oaks, CA: Sage.

Verba, S., Schlozman, K. L., & Brady, H. D. (1995). *Voice and equality: Civic voluntarism in American politics.* Cambridge, MA: Harvard University Press.

Warren, M. E. (2001). *Democracy and associations.* Princeton, NJ: Princeton University Press.

Wheatley, M. J. (1999). *Leadership and the new science.* San Francisco: Berrett-Koehler.

Young, F. W., & Lyson, T. A. (2001). Structural pluralism and all cause mortality. *American Journal of Public Health, 91*(1), 136–138.

CIVIL DISOBEDIENCE

Civil disobedience is a deliberate offense against authority committed openly to protest what is felt to be an unjust, arbitrary, cruel, pointless, or immoral law or government policy. It rests on the assumption that moral law should prevail over civil law, that there is a higher duty or higher cause than civil authority. Proponents of civil disobedience often state that the individual is the ultimate source of authority and is sometimes morally bound to disobey a law or policy, for not to do so would betray the dictates of conscience.

Civil disobedience, however, does not refer to just any kind of deliberate violation of valid penal law or government policy. Breaking the law is civil disobedience only when it is done from certain motives, and only in certain circumstances. Although street crimes such as robbery, burglary, murder, and rape are instances of deliberate law breaking, they are not instances of civil disobedience. These kinds of crimes are committed from motives such as personal gain and malice, without regard for the welfare of others and, in some cases, with a deliberate attempt to harm the interests of others. The person engaging in civil disobedience, on the other hand, is not interested in private or personal gain; rather, the purpose of civil disobedience is to protest an injustice or a wrong.

DEFINING ELEMENTS

Philosopher John Rawls formally defines civil disobedience as "a public, nonviolent, conscientious yet political act contrary to law usually done with the aim of bringing about a change in the law or policies of the government" (Rawls 1971, p. 368). The important defining elements of civil disobedience in this definition are that the act be public, nonviolent, deliberate unlawfulness and conscientious.

A Public Act

Civil disobedience refers to action that is of a public and political nature. In that regard, acts of disobedience to family and school do not qualify as acts of civil disobedience. Rather, in engaging in openly announced defiance of particular laws or customs, the activist is interested in demonstrating that he or she is withholding allegiance from the state until its alleged abuses are corrected. In addition, civil disobedience is often engaged in with prior notice as well as openly, since the protestor wants to attract as much publicity as possible so as to draw attention to the injustice or wrong that is the subject of the protestor's acts.

A Nonviolent Act

Civil disobedience contrasts with acts of warfare against the state, such as assassination, sabotage, terrorism, riot, insurrection, and revolution. The person engaging in civil disobedience practices a kind of resistance within the accepted political structure, a violation of the law without loss of respect for law and other basic political institutions. Civil disobedience tends to be nonviolent for the simple reason that injury to others, harm to property, and other violent acts are likely to be self-defeating. Violent acts can obscure the protestor's message and distract public attention from what is important. Civil disobedients want their acts to be nonviolent so that they can convince the majority of their fellow citizens that those acts are indeed conscientious and sincere and that the acts are intended to address a perceived injustice or wrong.

Deliberate Unlawfulness

A third characteristic of civil disobedience is deliberate unlawfulness. The civil disobedient can use one of two types of deliberate unlawfulness to protest an injustice or wrong. Direct civil disobedience is a type of deliberate unlawfulness that violates the very law that is the target of the protest. White people sitting in the black section of segregated buses in the 1950s and Vietnam War protestors burning their draft cards in the 1960s are good examples of direct civil disobedience. More characteristically, the civil disobedient uses indirect acts of civil disobedience; that is, the act of civil disobedience violates some other law whose reasonableness is not in question. For example, it is hard to protest capital punishment directly. One does not protest capital punishment by attempting to have oneself executed. Rather, one may protest such perceived wrongs by the disruption of traffic into a correctional facility where an execution is scheduled.

A Conscientious Act

Finally, acts of civil disobedience are conscientious acts. This element excludes motives of private or personal gain or malicious emotion as the primary reason for the action. For example, in the United States in the nineteenth century, abolitionists attacked the institution of slavery by refusing to uphold the Fugitive Slave Acts. In the twentieth century, Mohandas Gandhi subverted colonial rule in South Africa and India with acts of passive disobedience. This practice was later adopted by Europeans resisting Nazi occupation, by U.S. civil rights activists campaigning against segregation, and by students engaging in boycotts and sit-ins to protest the Vietnam War. Through such actions, the civil disobedient suffers inconvenience, expense, threats, real danger, and eventually punishment. His or her willingness to suffer those consequences helps to demonstrate that the purpose of the acts is to protest an injustice or a wrong.

POLITICAL AUTHORITY AND CIVIL DISOBEDIENCE

The conflict between political authority and those who engage in civil disobedience is a conflict between the needs of the state and the right of the individual to disobey the state. Political authority rests on the voluntary obedience of individuals who have presumably consented to its exercise over themselves. Political authority is essential to the preservation of the social order. Civil disobedience, in contrast, rests on the assumption that the individual is the ultimate source of authority, with an imperative to act contrary to the dictates of civil authority if not to do so would betray the dictates of conscience.

Judeo-Christian traditions and political philosophers from Socrates to Thomas Jefferson teach that there is a principle of obligation higher than that of the human authority of political communities, and that in a conflict between that higher principle and the lower one, the higher takes precedence. This obligation serves as a rationale not only for acts of civil disobedience but for

Rosa Parks sitting in the front of a bus in Montgomery, Alabama, on December 21, 1956. Just one year earlier, on December 1, 1955, Ms. Parks had also sat in the front of the bus, defying local law, an act of civil disobedience that helped begin the civil rights movement.
Source: Bettmann/Corbis; used with permission.

other political acts as well. For example, when Jesus drove the money changers from the temple, he was putting religious conscience above custom and social convenience. The American Revolution was fought on the premise that the demands of the higher moral order dissolved the obligations that rebellious colonists once owed to the British crown. Three classic statements on civil disobedience can illustrate this relationship between political authority and civil disobedience.

Henry David Thoreau (1817–1862)

Henry David Thoreau's essay "Civil Disobedience" (1849) is one of the most well-known U.S. statement on the right of the solitary individual acting alone against a government that had allegedly abused its authority. In protest against the Mexican-American War (1846–1848), which Thoreau saw as a pretext for the expansion of slavery into the Southwest, he refused to pay his taxes, a gesture that led to his spending a night in jail. The text of "Civil Disobedience," however, says little about war or the institution of slavery. Rather, Thoreau writes in universal terms about the individual's relation to political authority.

Thoreau sought to demonstrate how unimportant government really is in the history of the United States. He argued that it was individuals and not government that created the conditions for liberty, educated the people, and settled the frontier. Moreover, he wrote, societal reform does not occur through politics. The regeneration of society, Thoreau insisted, must begin with self-regeneration, not political participation. In "Civil Disobedience," Thoreau advised his fellow citizens not to look to political leadership or to rely upon the electoral process. He appealed to individuals not as political citizens but as moral agents. For Thoreau, the individual was sovereign unto himself, apart from the state and even the people who compose it.

Mohandas Gandhi (1869–1948)

Mohandas Gandhi was a Hindu religious leader and social reformer who advocated the use of noncooperation and passive resistance to achieve social and political reform. Gandhi believed that there is an objective answer to the question "Has an injustice occurred?" He advocated the pursuit of *satya* (truth). Although he recognized that humans are fallible, Gandhi also believed that we should aspire to know the truth. *Satyagraha,* the movement that he inspired, refers to the idea of holding on to truth; the term may be translated as "truth-force."

Gandhi believed that in certain conditions it is not sufficient to rely on persuasion or appeal to authorities to voluntarily change their unjust ways; some conditions require the use of passive resistance and noncooperation with the state. The condition that justifies that kind of civil disobedience is the fundamental violation of human rights. However, Gandhi thought that individuals should resort to civil disobedience only after careful consideration, and that only those who were qualified should practice it. To be qualified, a person must already have acquired the habit of willing obedience to laws; those who have not learned to obey laws for the right reason do not have the right to disobey the law.

Martin Luther King Jr. (1929–1968)

Another of the best-known statements on civil disobedience and the civil rights movement in the United States is the "Letter From the Birmingham Jail" by Martin Luther King Jr., who wrote this letter following his arrest for refusing to halt a large civil disobedience campaign. Although aware of Thoreau's writings, King was more directly influenced by Mohandas Gandhi.

While Thoreau called upon citizens to disassociate from the machine of government, King called upon them to become more involved in politics in order to secure the voting rights that had been denied to black citizens. King believed that civil disobedience presupposes recognizing political authority and its processes.

King specified steps to be taken in order to bring about social and political change: collection of facts to determine whether injustices exist, negotiation, self-purification, and direct action. King also conceived of civil disobedience as a crisis-heightening tactic that would prod government into a dialogue that would lead to a solution. What King wanted was the fulfillment of racial integration in public institutions, as promised by the United States Supreme Court in the 1954 *Brown v. Board of Education of Topeka* decision. In marching to proclaim that demand, King legitimized civil disobedience as a tactic on the part of loyal citizens excluded from the conventional channels of power and social change.

CONTEMPORARY ISSUES

The historical tradition of civil disobedience lies in the belief that the individual needs to remain true to the dictates of a "higher law." The modern discussion of this belief often occurs against a background of acknowledged just institutions, democratic parliaments, and valid laws.

The focus of the act was localized; while it may have concerned an issue of relevance to a significant minority of the population of a society, those outside that society were not connected to the disobedient act. In contrast, by the late twentieth century, civil disobedience and other forms of social protest became transnational in nature and scope, largely as a consequence of the presence of mass media. The mass media can transform a local act of civil disobedience almost immediately into an event of global significance.

Civil disobedience implies that individuals have rights that derive from conscience. Although civil disobedience originates from the inner prompting of conscience, it inevitably expresses itself in a dialogue with external authority. Therefore, civil disobedience, when properly conducted, can be a stabilizing device and can work as a safety valve in that it provides a mechanism for individuals to redress perceived injustices. Without the possibility of civil disobedience, individuals may feel compelled to resort to violent measures. Therefore, by enabling individuals to get their grievances addressed, civil disobedience can advance the goal of social cohesion.

—*Patricia E. Erickson*

Further Reading

Anderson, C. (Ed.). (1973). *Thoreau's vision: The major essays.* Englewood Cliffs, NJ: Prentice Hall.

Bass, S. J. (2001). *Blessed are the peacemakers: Martin Luther King Jr., eight white religious leaders, and the "Letter from Birmingham Jail."* Baton Rouge: Louisiana State University Press.

Bleiker, R. (2000). *Popular dissent, human agency and global politics.* Cambridge, UK: Cambridge University Press.

Brown v. Board of Education (Brown I), 347 U.S. 483 (1954).

Cohen, C. (1971). *Civil disobedience: Conscience, tactics, and the law.* New York: Columbia University Press.

Crawford, C. (Ed.). (1973). *Civil disobedience: A casebook.* New York: Thomas Y. Crowell.

Feinberg, J. (1992). *Freedom and fulfillment: Philosophical essays.* Princeton, NJ: Princeton University Press.

Fischer, L. (1983). *The essential Gandhi: His life, work, and ideas: An anthology.* New York: Vintage.

Gans, C. (1992). *Philosophical anarchism and political disobedience.* Cambridge, UK: Cambridge University Press.

Goldwin, R. (Ed.). (1970). *On civil disobedience: American essays old and new.* Chicago: Rand McNally.

Hasksar, V. (1986). *Civil disobedience, threats and offers: Gandhi and Rawls.* Delhi, India: Oxford University Press.

Luedtke, L. (Ed.). (1992). *Making America: The society and culture of the United States.* Chapel Hill: University of North Carolina Press.

Rawls, J. (1971). *A theory of justice.* Cambridge, MA: Harvard University Press.

Smith, M., & Deutsch, K. (Eds.). (1972). *Political obligation and civil disobedience: Readings.* New York: The Free Press.

Soley, L. (1999). *Free radio: Electronic civil disobedience.* Boulder, CO: Westview.

Thomas, O. (Ed.). (1966). *Walden and Civil Disobedience: Henry David Thoreau.* New York: Norton.

Tolstoy, L. (1987). *Writings on civil disobedience and nonviolence* (D. H. Albert, Ed.). Philadelphia: New Society Publishers. (Original work published 1886)

Villa-Vicencio, C. (1990). *Civil disobedience and beyond: Law, resistance and religion in South Africa.* Grand Rapids, MI: Wm. B. Eerdmans.

Weber, D. R. (1978). *Civil disobedience in America: A documentary history.* Ithaca, NY: Cornell University Press.

Zashin, E. (1972). *Civil disobedience and democracy.* New York: The Free Press.

CIVIL SOCIETY

Civil society is generally understood as the broad range of civic and voluntary organizations that serve as venues in which people discuss public issues and simply participate in social life. In one definition, it is "the population of groups formed for collective purposes primarily outside of the State and marketplace" (van Rooy 1998, p. 30). Situated outside the household, and outside government structures as well, civil society is usually seen as comprising self-selected, horizontal groups that crosscut the vertical ties of kinship and patron-clientalism (Putnam 1993). Civil society includes nongovernmental organizations (NGOs), membership and professional associations, activist networks, faith-based groups, trade unions, cultural and educational bodies, charities, and other nonstate and not-for-profit entities.

The concept of civil society has a long history stretching back several centuries, but a startling revival of interest in the idea of civil society has occurred in recent years. Since the end of the Cold War, such interest has risen among researchers and activists worldwide, in developed, transitional, and developing countries. Increasingly, too, policymakers note that civil society often strengthens community cohesion and participatory democracy.

But civil society serves varied and even paradoxical functions as neoliberal economic policy agendas gain momentum worldwide. While some NGOs and voluntary groups serve as a platform for citizens working to roll back the state and privatize service delivery systems in developed, transitional, and developing countries, others constitute a site of resistance to such policies, where citizens build alternatives through organized opposition, policy influence, or grassroots initiatives. The concept of civil society therefore serves as an important point of entry for the analysis of many social, economic, and political issues of contemporary importance—from the changing nature of social welfare policy to the international anti-globalization movement.

CIVIL SOCIETY AS CONCEPT

The complex history of the civil society concept, and the debates surrounding it, have been examined by thinkers such as John Keane (1998) and Alison van Rooy (1998). A brief summary reveals the varying approaches to the idea of civil society.

Scottish Enlightenment thinker Adam Ferguson saw civil society as both a progression from the "state of nature" and a complement to the heightened individualism of emergent capitalism (Ferguson, 1767/1995). In this view, a sense of civic virtue is required of citizens, so that while they may prosper with the growth of capitalism, they maintain an engagement with wider government and society. The German philosopher G. W. F. Hegel, on the other hand, argued that self-organized civil society nevertheless needs to be balanced and ordered by the state; otherwise it becomes self-interested and does not contribute to the common good (see Hegel, 1991). Both approaches shaped the early evolution of the civil society concept.

The French adventurer and commentator Alexis de Tocqueville narrowed his attention from the broad social and political sphere to a focus on the organizations themselves. His positive account of nineteenth-century associationalism in the United States (Tocqueville, 1835/1994) stressed volunteerism, community spirit, and independent group life as society's protections against domination by the state, and indeed as counterbalances that help keep the state accountable and effective. His work has been widely influential in current policy circles and is used to support arguments for strengthening civil society. This account—and elements of those that preceded it—depicted the role of civil society as creating a kind of equilibrium in relation to the state and the market. A neo-Tocquevillian position can now be seen in current arguments in many Western countries, linking a society's level of associationalism with positive values of trust and cooperation.

Another strand of civil society thinking has also been influential in some parts of the world. Contemporary Italian activist Antonio Gramsci has argued that civil society is the arena, separate from state and market, in which ideological hegemony is contested. This view implies that civil society contains a wide range of organizations and ideologies, both challenging and upholding the existing order (see Gramsci 1971). These ideas were influential in the movements resisting totalitarian regimes in Eastern Europe and Latin America from the 1970s onward. They can also be linked to the research on social movements that seek to challenge and transform social structures and identities (Escobar & Alvarez 1992; Howell & Pearce 2001).

Nevertheless, it has been the more organizational, Tocquevillian view of civil society that has recently served as a model for policy makers in Europe and North America and for many international development agencies (Davis & McGregor 2000). The "good governance" agenda was established by the United Kingdom and other European governments in the early 1990s and was taken up by many other development donors such as the World Bank. The agenda has championed civil society as one of the initiatives that promote more competitive market economies, build better-managed states with responsive services and just laws, and improve democratic institutions to deepen political participation. Financial and capacity building support to NGOs, often taken as a proxy for civil society, has formed a central part of the good governance agenda. (Archer 1994).

Current thinking, therefore, arguably tends to conceive of civil society as "balancing" the state. But the other theories still have their applications. For example, the Hegelian concept of civil society is useful in understanding how colonial governments restricted citizenship rights and freedom of movement (e.g., South Africa under apartheid selectively applied citizenship rights only for certain sections of the population). Gramscian ideas remain relevant to understandings of organized resistance among those marginalized or excluded by political and economic power centers.

CIVIL SOCIETY AS PRACTICE

While the idea of civil society is has deep roots in political theory, it is also a real-life arena of organized activities and approaches to societal transformation. In practice, civil society may comprise activities from community development to environmental protection, from human rights advocacy to anti-globalization efforts. On a community level, groups form both formally and informally for a variety of reasons. Citizens on many local streets in Britain have formed "neighbourhood watches" to protect their property from theft. Women on the streets of Lima, Peru, opened informal soup kitchens to serve the urban poor, whose numbers were rising under structural adjustment policies in the 1990s. At a more formal level, the civil society is often used as a synonym for what has been variously termed the voluntary, not-for profit or non-governmental sector, and it has helped to legitimize and strengthen the standing of this sector.

Central to these discussions is the perception of civil society as an essentially fragile construct. Ironically, while many policy makers are concerned with the challenge of "building" civil society in transitional and developing countries, there is a feeling in many industrialized countries that civil society has been degraded and become less a feature of everyday life. Such evidence can be found in sociologist Robert Putnam's (2000) account of the "collapse" of community in the United States. Americans no longer seem to associate as widely as they did in the 1950s, Putnam suggests—a trend typified by the fact that they now go "bowling alone" instead of in leagues or groups. This trend, he argues, has negative implications for wider societal trust and cohesion at the community level, and for the functioning of wider democratic institutions and processes.

Within international development circles, policy makers have stressed civil society's role in promoting democratic institutions and market reforms in developing countries. The so-called good governance agenda launched in the early 1990s suggested that a "virtuous circle" could be built between state, economy, and civil society to balance growth, equity, and stability (Archer 1994). The number of NGOs in development work has risen dramatically since then, in part due to this changing agenda. The good governance agenda includes both service delivery and advocacy work by NGOs, and encompasses both international organizations and the work of local NGOs in developing countries.

Civil society action is now also understood to be operating at transnational levels. Historical struggles for labor rights, the campaign against the slave trade, and the fight for women's voting rights are all examples of such transnational movements. Civil society participants and observers are often present at United Nations summit meetings, and "parallel summits" are sometimes informally organized to express alternative points of view.

But the new empowerment of civil society has its critics. Some warn that the vision of civil society can devolve into a "feel-good" concept. It is necessary, they say, to acknowledge civil society's broad range of values and intentions. Indeed, some point to "uncivil society" as a necessary counterweight to an overly optimistic vision. Feminist critics have challenged the idea that civil society exists as a purely public space for organized action, pointing out that private and informal relationships extend beyond the family and influence activity in the public sphere. Others discern a historical specificity to the civil society concept, which has clear roots in Western European experience and may therefore have limited relevance in non-Western contexts (Blaney & Pasha 1993).

CHALLENGES FOR THE FUTURE

Civil society as an idea is probably here to stay, but it is worth reviewing several problems with the concept. First, since different understandings of the term exist, its precise policy implications are debatable. Indeed, since the concept of civil society is primarily a theoretical one, it may not lend itself in any straightforward way to a practical, policy-level application. Second, if the concept of civil society is arguably historically specific to particular times and places, then it may be highly sensitive to differences of history, culture, and economy. Moreover, some criticize it as a "feel-good" concept that does not account for conservative or repressive forces within the civil society arena, or what Keane has termed "uncivil society." Finally, a key problem with the concept is the frequent lack of clarity, in both the research literature and in political discourse, as to whether a discussion of "civil society" refers to an analytical concept or to actually existing social forms.

While a range of local meanings are being created around the concept in different contexts, it is clear that "civil society" refers to increasingly universal negotiations between citizens, states, and market. The idea of civil society also draws attention to the role of "uncivil" elements at the community level in the form of antisocial action and criminal networks. A narrower focus on civil society in terms of NGOs engaged in participatory development work can bring a potentially dangerous collusion with the "mythical notion of community cohesion" (see Guijt & Shah 1998, p.1) if there is a preoccupation with simplistic ideas about homogenous communities and technical management solutions to community problems. Wider understandings of civil society which take into account power and conflict can help to refine understandings of community as multifaceted and heterogeneous, containing different levels of power and voice based on class, gender, and ethnicity.

With these uncertainties in mind, it is therefore useful to hold to van Rooy's (1998) characterization of the concept of civil society as an "analytical hat-stand" on which to hang a wide range of ideas about politics, organizations, citizenship, and activism. Perhaps the very versatility of the civil society concept partly explains its current popularity.

—David Lewis

See also Conflict Resolution; Tocqueville, Alexis de

Further Reading

Archer, R. (1994). Markets and good government. In A. Clayton (Ed.), *Governance, democracy and conditionality: What role for NGOs?* Oxford, UK: International NGO Research and Training Centre (INTRAC).

Blaney, D. L. & Pasha, M. K. (1993, Spring). Civil society and democracy in the Third World: Ambiguities and historical possibilities. *Studies in Comparative International Development, (28),* 1, 3–24.

Escobar, A., & Alvarez, S. (Eds). (1992). *The making of social movements in Latin America: Identity, strategy and democracy.* Boulder, CO: Westview.

Gramsci, A. (1971). *Selections from the prison notebooks.* London: Lawrence and Wishart.

Guijt, I., & Shah, M. K. (Eds.). (1998). General introduction: Waking up to power, process and conflict. In I. Guijt & M. K. Shah (Eds), *The myth of community.* London: Intermediate Technology Publications.

Hegel, G. W. F. (1991). *Elements of the philosophy of right* (A. D. Wood, Ed.; H. B. Nisbet, Trans.). Cambridge, UK: Cambridge University Press. (Original work published 1820)

Howell, J., & Pearce, J. (2001). *Civil society and development: A critical exploration.* London: Lynne Rienner.

Kaufman, M., & Alfonso, H. D. (Eds.). (1997). *Community power and grassroots democracy: The transformation of social life.* London: Zed.

Keane, J. (1998). *Civil society: Old images, new visions.* Cambridge, UK: Polity.

Putnam, R. D. (1993). *Making democracy work: Civic traditions in modern Italy.* Princeton, NJ: Princeton University Press.

Putnam, R. D. (2000). *Bowling alone: The collapse and revival of American community.* New York: Simon & Schuster.

Salamon, L., & Anheier, H. K. (1999). The third sector in the third world. In D. Lewis (Ed.), *International perspectives on voluntary action: Reshaping the third sector.* London: Earthscan.

Tocqueville, A. de (1994). *Democracy in America.* London: Everyman. (Original work published 1835)

Van Rooy, A. (1998). *Civil society and the aid industry.* London: Earthscan.

CIVILITY

See Incivilities Thesis

CLASS, SOCIAL

The term *social class* generally refers to a group of people who share the same socioeconomic status or who have common economic, cultural, and social characteristics. The term is popularly used to divide people into categories such as upper, lower, or working class. The category is important for understanding questions of social stratification—the structured inequality of material and symbolic rewards in a given society. Issues of social mobility, collective action, and community and group consciousness are all touched by the concept of social class. The main debate in the field of sociology about the nature of class revolves around whether *class* denotes a group of actual or potential social and political actors consciously motivated by shared inequality, or merely a category of individuals differentially ranked by status and prestige levels. Is class a political relationship that becomes, evolves, and shapes people's thoughts, actions, and ideologies, or is it merely a descriptor of different people's positions in society?

THE CHANGING MEANINGS OF SOCIAL CLASS

Since its earliest use, the meaning of *class* has fluctuated between a description of social groupings and a political relationship. The concept first appeared with the uses of the Latin word *classis,* by Roman census takers, to differentiate the population on the basis of wealth and property to determine obligations for military service. However, in the seventeenth century, the first use of the English word *class* encompassed a general classification for categories of plants, animals, objects, or people.

The usage of the term that connected economic power and social groupings, similar to the modern usage, reappeared in the nineteenth century around the time of the Industrial Revolution. *Class* began to replace words such as *rank, estates, order,* and *degree* as the primary classification of social groupings under modern capitalism. The main social divisions in capitalist society became (1) those owning the means of production (the instruments and raw materials of the productive process) and (2) the workers in the new urban factories dependent on their labor for wages.

KARL MARX

Much of the present-day understanding of the term *class* emerging in the nineteenth century came from the writings of the German sociologist Karl Marx (1818–1883). Marx was not the first theorist to analyze the concept of class; the English philosopher Thomas Hobbes (1588–1679), the French philosopher Jean-Jacques Rousseau (1712–1778), and the social reformer Claude-Henri de Saint-Simon (1760–1825) all had begun developing the idea of class divisions in society. Marx, however, is recognized as the first person to explore fully the causes and consequences of a stratified society according to class. He considered the concept of class not as a stratum or fragment of the population but as a relationship based on people's positions vis-à-vis the means of production.

Marx's analysis, adapted from his mentor Georg Hegel (1770–1831), is rooted in dialectical reasoning—a method of examining the evolution and development of society not as a series of unconnected historical events but as an interconnected process of contradictions and change. Marx believed one could uncover certain societal laws that explain the transformations of social systems from one historical epoch to the next. But unlike Hegel, who believed the transformation of ideas heralded new stages in human development, Marx saw the antagonisms between classes in the productive process or economy as the fulcrum of revolution. "The history of all hitherto existing society" wrote Marx, "is the history of class struggles" (Marx & Engels 1848). Throughout time, various modes of production (the state of technology and the division of labor) are composed of two basic classes—producers and non-producers. Producers create the goods and wealth of society. Non-producers live off the surplus of the producers' labor through the ownership of the means of production—the factories, land, property, and machinery of society.

The relationship between these two classes, therefore, is based on the exploitation of one by the other and is inherently antagonistic. While non-producers seek to control the goods and services created by the producers, the producers become alienated, or separated, from their labor and the goods they produce. Rather than getting the full value of their work, they are only partially compensated, with the rest going to the non-producers. Under modern industrial capitalism, the two great classes are represented by the proletariat/workers (producers) and the bourgeoisie/capitalists (non-producers). Antagonisms between workers and capitalists caused by the deskilling of the labor process, the relative decline in workers' standards of living compared to capitalists, the increasing concentration of workers into factories, and heightened class polarization eventually will lead to the proletarian revolution and overthrow of the capitalist order.

Some in the social sciences have dismissed Marx due to the failure of his predictive theories; the overthrow of capitalism by the proletariat has not occurred, and instead, capitalism seems to have been embraced by populations in all corners of the globe. But his concepts of class and class struggle remain an important core component of sociological analysis. Most sociological theorists since Marx have "struggled with Marx's ghost" and with his analysis of social structure and the nature of society.

MAX WEBER

Another important German sociologist—Max Weber (1864–1920)—was interested in many of the same issues as Marx but reached different conclusions about how society was divided. Weber described two major social divisions that determined people's "life chances" or future possibilities for achieving good health, education, success, and wealth. These divisions were "class" and "status." Weber's concept of class was

The Hired Help

Beeton's All About Everything *has long been a source of advice on etiquette and home life in England. The following is advice concerning housemaids provided in the 1890 edition of the manual.*

Housemaids, Upper And Under

Housemaids, in large establishments, have usually one or more assistants; in this case they are upper and under housemaids. Dividing the work between them, the upper housemaid will probably reserve for herself the task of dusting the ornaments and cleaning the furniture of the principal apartments, but it is her duty to see that every department is properly attended to. The number of assistants depends on the number in the family, as well as on the style in which the establishment is kept up. In wealthy families it is not unusual for every grown-up daughter to have her waiting-maid, whose duty it is to keep her mistress's apartment in order; thus abridging the housemaid's duties. In others, perhaps one waiting-maid attends on two or three, when the housemaid's assistance will be more requisite. In fact, every establishment has some customs peculiar to itself, on which we need not dwell; the general duties are the *same in all*, perfect cleanliness and order being the object.

"Cleanliness is next to godliness," saith the proverb, and "order" is in the next degree; the housemaid, then, may be said to be the handmaiden to two of the most prominent virtues. Her duties are very numerous, and many of the comforts of the family depend on their performance; but they are simple and easy to a person naturally clean and orderly, and desirous of giving satisfaction. In all families, whatever the habits of the master and mistress, servants will find it advantageous to rise early; their daily work will thus come easy to them. If they rise late, there is a struggle to overtake it, which throws an air of haste and hurry over the whole establishment. Where the master's time is regulated by early business or professional engagements, this will, of course, regulate the hours of the servants; but even where that is not the case, servants will find great personal convenience in rising early and getting through their work in an orderly and methodical manner. The housemaid who studies her own ease will certainly be at her work by six o'clock in the summer, and, probably, half-past six or seven in the winter months, having spent a reasonable time in her own chamber in dressing. Earlier than this would, probably, be an unnecessary waste of coals and candle in winter.

Source: *Beeton's All About Everything: Being A Dictionary Of Practical Recipes And Every-Day Information.* (1890). London: Ward, Lock And Co., pp. 162–163.

based on that of Marx, but added further conceptual clarification to the term.

Weber agreed with Marx's analysis of the fundamental division between labor and capital but believed no one factor, such as the relationship to the means of production, defined a person's location in the class structure. Weber saw multiple cleavages rooted not only in the productive process but in the market capacities of individuals as well. Among the property class, or Marx's bourgeoisie, Weber made distinctions between landowners, rentiers (people living on income from property), entrepreneurs, and business owners. Among the propertyless class (proletariat), occupational skills altered people's life-chances and therefore distinguished highly skilled workers from, for example, unskilled workers. To Weber, therefore, a "social class" became a group of people who shared the same economically determined life-chances.

While social class was an objective fact, Weber considered "status," or ranking by social prestige, a subjective phenomenon that further complicated the class picture. "Status" refers to a person's or a position's respect or regard in society. Status-groupings—communities of individuals sharing style of life and coexisting as status equals—are generally determined by economic criteria but can also be influenced by other factors such as honor and prestige.

Weber's analyses of class and divisions in society are more generally accepted in the United States than are Marx's theories of class. Weber's legacy is evident in the current understanding of social class divisions as shown in Gilbert and Kahl's typical characterization of the U.S. class structure, whereby the upper or capitalist class consists of the wealthiest and most powerful people, who own large businesses and corporations and operate on an international scale. The upper-middle class is made up of highly educated professionals such as physicians, attorneys, and top corporate managers. The middle class are white-collar workers and low-level professionals and managers; the working class are semiskilled, blue-collar workers in factories, clerks, and many service workers. The working poor are those living at or just below the poverty line who are unskilled minimum-wage workers. In this classification, poor people have little education, lack employability, and earn low wages. Their life-chances evince long-term deprivations.

CLASS AND COMMUNITY

In both Marx's and Weber's work, what makes a class a community? How does a group of people become more than just a series of individuals occupying similar positions in the social structure? How do the individuals become a conscious group exhibiting shared consciousness, solidarity, and identity?

Classes, according to Marx, are not uniformly aware of their existence as a class. At first, classes exist only "in themselves," as a group of people sharing a similarly structured relationship to the means of production. They are not necessarily conscious of their shared position, nor are they able to express solidarity. However, over time, recognition of their common economic interests, alienation, and exploitation leads to class organization; these people become a class "for themselves." Marx also offered the concept of "false" consciousness, wherein workers identify with the interests of the capitalist class rather than with their own, allowing for community to be built across class lines. However, this idea is not well developed in Marx's work and is particularly controversial.

Weber outlined a similar perspective, in which economic position does not necessarily equate with particular forms of consciousness. According to his concept of status groupings, while members of a class may exhibit no sense of shared identity, members of status groupings are more likely to think of themselves as a community with a common lifestyle and culture. This does not imply that economic position is unimportant. Class position allows the possibility of earning an income that permits a certain lifestyle in which people make friends and build relationships to create a sense of community. But in and of itself, class does not necessarily equate with shared consciousness.

E. P. Thompson (1924–1993), an English sociologist, offered a critique of stratification research and Marxist determinism, both of which unproblematically claim a link between objective class structures and people's subjective experiences of those structures. Instead, Thompson attempted to rescue human agency and the development of subjective communities by exploring the link between a class "in itself" and a class "for itself." Class, according to him, is an active, relational process that occurs "when some men, as a result of common experiences . . . feel and articulate the identity of their interests as between themselves and as against other men whose interests are different from theirs" (Thompson 1996, p. 9). While productive relations shape people's experience, class consciousness represents how these experiences are embodied in values, norms, traditions, and institutional forms. Workers' reactions to the changing structural conditions of economic development are mediated through both the workplace and the community in raising people's consciousness.

Thompson's work, therefore, inspired labor historians and sociologists to examine how consciousness developed in the community, the family, social clubs, unions, and other collective activities. In addition, Thompson helped set the stage for challenging traditional representations of workers (typically white, male wage earners), and it expanded the field of investigation to include other actors and identities in the community, such as gender, race, ethnicity, and the ways that these identities shaped class development. For example, labor historian Sonya Rose points out that the dominant portrait of the working class rests on the assumption of the "quintessential" worker as a white, male skilled worker. But this portrait incorrectly universalizes this experience as the experience of the working class as a whole, when in fact many other workers, due to their different experiences at the point of production and in their communities, experienced different paths to consciousness. Similarly, the relationship between race and class is also problematic. The experiences of working-class blacks, for example, historically have been fundamentally different from those of the white working class. Race has been used as a means of dividing working-class individuals. For instance, blacks were employed as strikebreakers or a reserve army of labor to force compliance by white workers. Such actions can create split-labor markets that can be determinative in shaping black and white working-class communities

The significance of class dynamics in the racial experience of minorities is highlighted in the work of William Julius Wilson. Wilson argues that the absence of jobs and economic opportunities for minority populations is more significant in their experience than is their racial background. While his ideas are controversial, Wilson points to the importance of understanding the intersection of race and class in shaping people's experience.

FUTURE DEBATES

The extent of class identification among both the working class and upper classes has always been questioned by U.S. scholars. While British and continental class theorists maintained a more Marxist orientation to the study of class and a recognition of class antagonisms and struggle, U.S. scholars beginning in the 1950s characterized postindustrial America as having transcended class conflict. The absence of class-based political parties such as those in Europe and elsewhere in the world has inspired debate on the "exceptionalist" nature of the American working-class. U.S. workers, so the theory goes, satisfied with high standards of living, opportunities for upward mobility, early suffrage, Western expansion, and the dominance of the two-party political system, incorporated the working class into the dominant political and social culture of the United States. Whether people accept the idea of the "bourgeois" worker, the relevance of class remains an open debate in sociological theory.

A recent example is represented by Paul W. Kingston in his *Classless Society.* He argues that "for the most part, groups of people having common economic position do not share distinct, life-defining experiences" (Kingston 2000, p. 1). Classes, he believes, are composed of people from different backgrounds, who do not necessarily associate exclusively with each other, exhibit distinct cultures, predict political orientation, or develop particular forms of consciousness. Instead, culture, gender, race, lifestyle, ethnicity, and religion are more important for defining beliefs and ideologies.

Yet other class theorists such as Rick Fantasia argue that the lack of class consciousness and identification in the United States does not reflect the absence of these traits but rather the way the subject of class is studied. A reliance on survey methodology has given the mistaken impression that class seldom forms the basis of community and solidarity. Yet when people study the action of a community of "workers," the class-based nature of their solidarity and their antagonisms with other classes is more easily grasped.

Regardless of its subjective nature, class still plays an important structuring role in modern society. Examinations of inequality throughout the Western World where capitalist class relations are most advanced consistently show that the wealthy are indeed getting richer while the poor are getting poorer. The quality of people's lives, be it their health, happiness, and lifestyle, or their opportunity for education, employment, and social mobility, is deeply shaped by their class position.

—Robert Penney

Further Reading

Fantasia, R. (1988). *Cultures of solidarity.* Berkeley and Los Angeles: University of California Press.

Gerth, H. H., & Mills, C. W. (Eds.). (1962). *From Max Weber: Essays in sociology.* New York: Oxford University Press.

Gilbert, D. (2003). *The American class structure in an age of growing inequality.* Belmont, CA: Wadsworth.

Gilbert, D., & Kahl, J. A. (1993). *The American class structure: A new synthesis* (4th ed.). Belmont, CA: Wadsworth.

Kingston, P. W. (2000). *The classless society.* Stanford, CA: Stanford University Press.

Marx, K., & Engels, F. (1848). *The communist manifesto.* Retrieved January 8, 2003, from http://www.anu.edu.au/polsci/marx/classics/manifesto.html

Rose, S. O. (1992). *Limited livelihoods: Gender and class in nineteenth-century England.* Berkeley and Los Angeles: University of California Press.

Thompson, E. P. (1966). *The making of the English working class.* New York: Vintage.

Tucker, R. (Ed.). (1978). *The Marx-Engels reader.* New York: W. W. Norton.

Wilson, W. J. (1980). *The declining significance of race.* Chicago: University of Chicago Press.

COCOONING

Cocooning is a term used in the United States to describe a retreat to the seclusion, safety, and comfort of home—the private sphere—away from the demands and risks of life outside in the public sphere or wider community. The retreat can be occasioned by a need for privacy and a desire to devote more attention to family and other intimate relationships. It can also be brought on by an intensified need for security or by fear of the outside world. Although the cocooning instinct is not unknown in other parts of the world (for example, Israelis facing the threat of terrorist attacks have been known to go through periods of withdrawing into their homes—often breaking out of this self-imposed limitation after a time), this entry focuses on cocooning in the United States.

Cocooning has been associated with a wide variety of social ills, including lack of concern about the environment, voter apathy, obesity, and a decline in community involvement. Curiously, proponents of living in intentional communities sometimes cite of the benefits of cocooning: familiarity and comfort, safety, and emotional security. Cocooning, however, is far more closely associated with life in private, single-family homes. The cocooning phenomenon ties in with consumerism as well, because the success of cocooning depends on the creation of a material world, a total environment, that allows the cocooners to live apart from the rest of the world without any loss of creature comforts.

THE GROWTH OF COCOONING

The term *cocooning* came into popular use in the United States at about the time of the publication *The Popcorn Report* (1991), a book about market trends. The term had been used during the 1980s in home design and decorating magazines as a way to describe the increasingly informal arrangement of home eating areas and the expansion of master bedrooms into "master retreats" where parents could go to escape from the rest of the household. In the United States at that time, new houses and developments were being designed to impress and protect. Gone were the welcoming porches, replaced by gates and two- or three-car garages. Faith Popcorn, author of *The Popcorn Report,* called cocooning one of the key trends of the 1990s and defined it as "the need to protect oneself from the harsh, unpredictable realities of the outside world" (Popcorn n.d.). This need on the part of consumer, she explained, provided huge opportunities to retailers in home improvement, home entertainment, and private security.

This turning to the indoor world can be seen as paralleling the turn from the activism of the 1960s and early 1970s to more materialistic and self-gratifying pursuits in the later 1970s and subsequent decades. Public life came to be seen as something to be tolerated and survived rather than as an essential source of pleasure and entertainment. That perception may also have influenced attitudes towards the natural world, which is undeniably messy and unpredictable, and therefore have influenced decisions on environment issues. Permissive fuel economy regulations for sports utility vehicles, which are notorious for their consumption of gasoline, and lack of support for public transportation can be tied to the cocooning instinct. (Cars have become what Popcorn calls a "wandering cocoon" for many Americans.)

This is not to say that cocooning is a universal phenomenon in the United States today. A visit to the café, bar, or teahouse is, even today, a regular and vital part of many people's lives. Elderly Italians still bring their chairs onto the sidewalks in New York and pass the summer evening chatting with neighbors and watching the world go by. Younger people go bar hopping and clubbing. But in many places, especially in urban areas, people feel on the defensive the moment they step out their door. The pleasures of public life are simply not available to those who are worried about its dangers, whether real or illusionary.

COCOONING, THE INTERNET, AND VICARIOUS LIVES

Until recently, people had to leave their houses, whether they wanted to or not, to work, to buy food and clothing, and even to worship. The development of the Internet and related technologies, however, has made it possible for people to stay at home for weeks on end and yet stay in touch with distant (or even nearby) family and friends, earn a living, get plenty to eat and drink, and watch the latest movies.

Home entertainment—both television and movies—plays a considerable role in cocooning. After the terrorist attacks of September 11, 2001, analysts reported changes in U.S. consumer spending, noting especially increased purchases of DVD players and increased installation of home theaters (of which there are said to be over 16 million in the United States). It is ironic that many television programs offer viewers a surrogate community, allowing them to immerse themselves in the lives of a group of characters and a particular workplace, small town, or apartment block. This vicarious sense of community is part of the comfort of cocooning.

COCOONING AND COMMUNITY

One commercial feature of cocooning is, supposedly, larger houses with larger, better-equipped kitchens. But there seems to be no evidence that Americans are entertaining at home more, or even cooking for themselves. A well-equipped kitchen has become a symbol of self-sufficiency, comfort, and caring, whether it is used to prepare meals or not. Larger homes, equipped with multiple entertainment centers, do not bring families together, and it seems to be common to find family members cocooning alone.

After the September 11 attacks, analysts pondered whether the shared grief and fear would bring people together, creating a new sense of national and global community, or whether it would intensify mutual suspicion and (among Americans) a desire to withdraw. Surveys showed little or no change in Americans' level of active community involvement or volunteering. People traveled less, stayed closer to home, and spent more time with their families, but there is little evidence that they entertained more at home. Fear of terrorism interfered with traditional neighborhood activities such as Halloween trick-or-treating.

The cocooning trend has long-term repercussions. Designers of college housing find that students want to cocoon, while housing administrators want to foster a sense of community. Some speculate that the students' cocooning instincts may have been honed during childhood years in which great emphasis was placed on continual participation in organized outside activities, generating stress from which the only relief was to be found in the cocoon of one's bedroom. Critics of overorganized childhood activities theorize that if children spent more time in informal, self-initiated play with other children, they would feel more comfortable in the community of their peers as they grew older.

Working at home, whether as a telecommuter, freelancer, or consultant, can be considered part of the cocooning trend. It can represent a desire not to deal with people face-to-face and not to face the unpleasantness of increasingly long commutes. But there is a positive community aspect to working at home as well. People who work at or near home can more easily integrate their work and family lives and be more involved in school and community activities. The desire to participate more fully in local community life can be as strong a motivation for working at or near home as the desire to avoid office interaction or long commutes.

There are many criticisms to be made of cocooning, but the concept offers a useful reminder of the importance of the private sphere and of the human need to retreat from the pressures of work and civic life. Perhaps one of the greatest challenges facing those promoting the revival of civic engagement is to acknowledge modern anxieties about the world outside and also to recognize the need for balance between people's private and public roles.

—*Karen Christensen*

See also CIVIC LIFE; NEW URBANISM; THIRD PLACES

Further Reading

Langdon, P. (1994). *A better place to live.* Amherst: University of Massachusetts Press.

Oldenburg, R. (1989). *The great good place.* New York: Paragon.

Popcorn, F. (1991) *The Popcorn report.* New York: Doubleday.

Popcorn, F. (n.d.). *Cocooning.* Retrieved February 13, 2003, from http://www.faithpopcorn.com/trends/cocooning.htm

Snider, M. (2002, January 8). Safe at home and all plugged in. *USA Today.* Retrieved March 2, 2003, from http://www.almenconi.com/news/jan02/012302.html

COHOUSING

Cohousing is a living arrangement in which multiple houses (usually twenty to thirty-five) are oriented around a common open area and a common building. Cohousing communities are custom-designed neighborhoods whose residents have decided that they do not want typical suburban, urban, or even rural neighborhoods in which neighbors don't know each other. The residents of cohousing communities work actively to create a viable and friendly neighborhood where neighbors are accustomed to cooperating and socializing.

Cohousing offers a new approach to housing rather than a new way of life. Aside from a basic adherence to democratic principles, cohousing developments espouse no ideology beyond a desire for a more practical and social home environment. A cohousing living arrangement is not a commune, nor is it an intentional community.

In addition to social advantages, cohousing offers numerous environmental benefits. Studies show that residents of cohousing communities in the United States drive about 25 percent less than other U.S. residents and that they use only about 25 percent of the energy they used in their previous living arrangements. Cohousing residences in the United States are about 60 percent of the size of average new U.S. homes, and cohousing communities occupy on average less than half as much land as the average new subdivision for the same number of households. Cohousing has taken hold in Denmark as well as the United States, and to a lesser degree in other European countries.

THE HISTORY OF COHOUSING

In 1964, Jan Gudmand-Høyer returned to Denmark from graduate school in the United States. While at Harvard, he studied U.S. "utopias" such as Shakertown, Drop City, Twin Oaks, and many more, and single-family homes. From this he developed an in-between structure, which he described in an article titled "The Missing Link Between Utopia and the Dated One-Family House." This was the start of cohousing. More than one hundred Danish families voiced an interest in the type of community Gudmand-Høyer described in the article. By 1976, there were three cohousing communities, and by 1982, twenty-two cohousing developments in Denmark were following Gudman-Høyer's ideas.

In 1984 and 1985, architects Kathryn McCamant and Charles Durrett went to Denmark to study these communities. The result of their research was *Cohousing: A Contemporary Approach to Housing Ourselves,* a book that introduced cohousing to the United States. First published in 1988, it sold almost 3,000 copies in the first month. The second edition was published in 1994 with reprints in 1996, 1998, 2000, and 2002. It remains the most comprehensive book in the United States and Denmark on cohousing. Currently, 75 cohousing projects exist in the United States, with another 20 under construction and about 150 in the planning phase.

THE SIX COMPONENTS OF COHOUSING

Cohousing takes diverse forms. Some are urban factory loft conversions, others are part of suburban neighborhoods, and a few are rural. Whatever the form, all cohousing developments share the following six components: participatory planning, designs that facilitate both community and privacy, extensive common facilities, management by residents, nonhierarchical organization, and separate sources of income.

Participatory Planning

The future residents are key participants in the planning and organization of a cohousing development. By struggling with the myriad decisions involved in building a neighborhood, they build a community even before moving in. They help design the site plan, the common house, and the private homes. They also participate in many of the organizational stages of development, including marketing, financing, and obtaining the required government approvals.

In many ways, a cohousing development is a grassroots effort. The participatory design process results not only in the best design for the people who will be living there, but also in commitment to implement that design, which is why the future residents work so hard to get the project built.

Designs That Facilitate Both Community and Privacy

What's unique about walking into a cohousing site is that you have a choice between privacy and community; ordinary neighborhoods offer only privacy. Kitchens at the front of each house, gathering areas throughout the cohousing development, peripheral parking with walkways internal to the development, and a common house for shared events offer many possible situations for interaction.

Saving Money Through Cohousing

People who choose to live in cohousing can save substantial amounts of money. The following two examples, taken from the United States, show how much can be saved in both high-end and low-end cohousing. At the high end, consider the following thirty-unit cohousing community:

> 1,250-square-foot house x $300 per square foot (sales price) = $375,000
>
> 6,000-square-foot common house x $300 per square foot (sales price) = $1.8 million.
>
> $1.8 million divided by 30 units = $60,000 for each unit's share of the common house.
>
> $60,000 + $375,000 = a total cost of $435,000.

This compares favorably to a high-end house in a conventional subdivision, in which a 2,100-square-foot house selling for $300 per square foot costs the purchaser $630,000. Each individual house saves $195,000 in cohousing.

There are savings in the low-market case as well. Consider the following low-market thirty-unit cohousing community:

> 1,250 square-foot house x $100 per square foot (sales price) = $125,000.
>
> 6,000 square-foot common house x $100 per square foot (sales price) = $600,000.
>
> $600,000 divided by 30 units = $20,000 for each unit's share in the common house.
>
> $20,000 + $125,000 = a total cost of $145,000.

By comparison, a 2,100-square-foot single-family house in a conventional subdivision, selling for $100 per square foot, would cost $210,000. Each individual house saves $65,000 in cohousing.

—Charles Durrett

Extensive Common Facilities

While each private home is a whole house, complete with kitchen, cohousing communities have common areas that supplement the private houses. Private homes can be smaller than typical houses because facilities such as guest rooms, workshops, and children's playrooms, are located in the common house. The common house is an extension of each private home, based on what the group believes will make individual lives easier and more economical. While public facilities in conventional neighborhoods often suffer because no one feels compelled to take an interest in maintaining them, common facilities work well in cohousing because those who use them feel accountable to the co-owners, their neighbors.

Management by Residents

Residents manage the development themselves, making decisions of common concern at community meetings. These meetings, usually held once a month, provide a forum for residents to discuss issues and solve problems. Consensus is usually used, with a backup system of voting when necessary. Consensus is very practical because it results in a solution that everyone agrees with and will work to achieve.

Nonhierarchical Structure

While there may be leadership roles associated with certain areas (financing, for example), the community shares responsibility for all decisions. It does not depend on any one person to set its direction. Someone with vision and inspiration may get the community off the ground, another may pull together the financing, and another may arrange the child care for every meeting. This division of labor is usually based on what each person feels he or she can contribute and what the group feels is a fair distribution of the work. No one person, however, dominates the decisions or the community process.

Separate Sources of Income

There is no shared community economy; all residents are responsible for their own finances. However, there is a common budget, financed by monthly dues, for community insurance, long- and short-term maintenance, and miscellaneous expenses such as childcare during meetings. If a community provides its residents with their primary income, then it has gone beyond the scope of cohousing.

ECONOMICS OF COHOUSING

As mentioned earlier, cohousing is an alternative to current subdivision developments, not a collective or an intentional community. Almost all cohousing residents come from or would eventually buy a single-family house or townhouse condominium rather than participate in an intentional community.

The economics of cohousing reflects this tie to conventional housing and real estate economics. Indeed, the only notable difference from conventional housing is that in addition to purchasing a house, people who choose cohousing also plan to participate in the community. As for the finances of individual households, in a survey in which one hundred U.S. cohousing residents were asked how much money they saved each month in terms of disposable income by living in cohousing, the standard answer was $100 to $200 per month. Similar figures were given in Denmark.

As for the economics of building, groups currently either develop the site themselves or codevelop it with professional developers. Even if a group can pay predevelopment costs and get construction financing on their own, they will still often join with a developer because the developer's expertise can save them more than the developer's fee costs them.

There are three ways that cohousing ownership is structured: condominiums, coooperatives, and rentals.

Condominiums

The majority of cohousing worldwide is owned as condominiums. This is the most straightforward option because banks understand this type of structure. Each unit acts like a single-family house, and ownership of the common house is divided up into individual shares and then managed by a homeowner's association. The owner gets a deed; the tax consequence are the same as when one owns a single-family home. The home can be bought and sold in the usual manner on the open market for fair market value. Potential cohousing buyers are usually asked to come to a dinner, a common meeting, and a common workday. They usually are already familiar with cohousing and are actively interested in it. Historically in the United States, cohousing units have appreciated faster than other types of housing; at the time of this writing, demand outstrips supply.

Cooperatives

In cooperatives (co-ops), a housing corporation owns the development. Each owner buys a share in the corporation and gets a proprietary lease to a certain unit rather than buying it. The co-op has a blanket mortgage on the property, which means that its members are responsible not only for paying their own mortgage but also for the nonpayment of other members. Transferability is more difficult with cooperatives because difficulty getting share financing means that the price increases. Because banks are not as familiar with cooperative financing and often require co-op members to obtain government subsidies, financing can be a long and arduous process.

Rentals

Rentals owned by nonprofit housing corporations (or in some countries, by the government) are the third ownership option. Along with co-ops, nonprofit-owned rentals are an option for developing cohousing at below-market rate prices. In this situation, a nonprofit housing corporation secures funds to subsidize construction costs and procures low-interest loans. Because of these subsidies, a specified percentage of the units are available only to those whose incomes fall below a certain level. One of the major downfalls of this system is that it is difficult to have mixed incomes in the same community. Another problem is that the process of qualifying for the rentals can make it difficult to identify prospective residents in time to participate in the design process.

Cohousing–The Ethnic Mix

Although cohousing in the United States was initially popular primarily with the educated white middle and upper-middle classes, it has come to represent a broader portion of the U.S. population. Doyle Street Cohousing in Emeryville, California, which was built in 1991, demonstrates this trend. Its residents including the following wide range of individuals:

Single white mother whose daughter had just left for college

White couple with an eight-year-old and an eleven-year-old

Single Asian American man

European (England, Norway) couple with a four-year-old and a newborn

White couple with a three-year-old and a one-year-old

Asian American and African American couple

Asian American and Mexican American couple

Asian American and white couple with a two-year-old

White couple with a ten-year-old

European couple (Italy)

Single white woman

—Charles Durrett

WHO LIVES IN COHOUSING?

Cohousing residents are looking for alternatives to the isolation associated with conventional single-family houses located in subdivisions and urban areas. They sometimes say that they are not doing anything new, but rather are simply more consciously putting together the kind of neighborhood that occurred naturally in times past.

Cohousing is on the larger communitarian continuum. A communitarian spirit is found in small towns where cooperation and community form because of economic interdependency, old family ties, and proximity. Residents have a sense of belonging, a sense of identity, and a sense of accountability. A similar conviviality can be found in extraordinary neighborhoods with single-family housing. These neighborhoods tend to have a greater number of children than other neighborhoods, more adults spending time at home during the day, and more people willing to take on the heroic effort of organizing block parties and other activities.

Cooperation seems to be the common denominator among neighbors in cohousing. People believe that their personal lives will be more economical, practical, convenient, interesting, and fun in cohousing than they would be if they chose a single-family house or other individualized arrangement.

People sometimes ask, "What if I don't want to cooperate with my neighbors?" Advocates of cohousing argue that that is what conventional housing opportunities are for—to leave people free not to cooperate except under the most tragic circumstances, when it seems that even the most individually or privately oriented people come together.

In the United States and elsewhere, the facts that more women are working outside the home and families are having fewer children are changing the nature of neighborhoods. Cohousing addresses current demographics by including the future residents of a community in the design and development process so that the resulting communities reflect their needs. One criticism of cohousing in the United States has been that it attracts mainly white, middle-class or upper-middle-class people with the income to purchase a home. Increasingly, however, cohousing has come to represent a wider cross section of U.S. population.

Cohousing projects in both the United States and

Europe usually start with a few people getting together and advertising broadly in their geographic area that they would like to start a cohousing community. After that, the group must find a site or hire someone to find one, do a feasibility study, create designs, get financing, construct the buildings, organize a cooking and work-day structure, and move in. The Cohousing Company offers a two-day workshop entitled "Getting It Built" that lays out the entire process.

THE ARCHITECTURE OF COHOUSING

A cohousing community is built in the planning phase of the project, not brick by brick, but decision by decision. The primary purpose of the architecture is to sustain relationships and a sense of community once the residents have moved in and the honeymoon has worn off. As much can depend on the physical relationships of the buildings to one another as on residents' intent to cooperate.

The site plan is crafted in such a way as to encourage community, with the parking relegated to the periphery. When residents return home from the larger world, they usually must walk past the common house and their neighbors' homes. There are generally life and activity between the houses. Twenty to thirty-five seems to be the optimum number of households in a cohousing community. This size is large enough to amortize a sizable common house and accommodate diversity, and small enough make consensus a feasible form of governance.

Homes are connected by a central path. The common house can usually be seen from most, if not all, the houses, making it possible to see from one's home whether others are in it. Often, a common terrace faces the houses and can seat everyone for a shared dinner or other activities. There are gathering nodes (consisting often of no more than a picnic table and a sandbox) along the walkway. Such nodes are associated with every five to nine houses. The houses have front porches that are at least seven feet deep and nine feet wide so people will actually use the space. The kitchen is oriented toward the common side of the house (with the sink towards the community, so someone working there can see people coming and going). The more private areas, such as the living room, face the rear or the private side of the house.

According to *E* magazine, the average house built in the United States in 2001 was 2,200 square feet. The average private house in cohousing is 1,250 square feet. The average common house for a typical thirty-unit cohousing community averages 1,650 square meters including workshops and other buildings.

THE FUTURE OF COHOUSING

In the late 1990s, *Time* magazine suggested that by the end of the first decade of the twenty-first century, there would be a cohousing community in every major U.S. metropolitan area. That would be approximately 250 to 350 communities. Today in Denmark, still less than 1 percent of the population lives in cohousing. In the end it is unlikely that the United States will even match Denmark's percentages. But, as in Denmark, the most significant legacy of cohousing in the United States is the extent to which it provides a model for other housing, including subsidized, multifamily, and even single-family houses. Almost all new houses and many old neighborhoods in Denmark have been influenced by cohousing. For example, now households along streets can elect to close part of the street to traffic.

Our society is characterized by technical advances and social changes that are often hard to deal with. Cohousing offers a refreshing and holistic approach to the problem of alienation and isolation in modern life, making it easier to accept change and grow with it.

—Charles Durrett

Further Reading

The Cohousing Journal. (2003). Retrieved February 27, 2003 from http://www.cohousing.org/services/journal

The Cohousing Network. (2003). Retrieved February 27, 2003 from http://www.cohousing.org

Gudmand-Høyer, J. (1968, June 26). "The missing link between utopia and the dated one-family house." *Information*.

McCamant, K., & Durrett, C. (2002). *Cohousing: A contemporary approach to housing ourselves.* Berkeley, CA: Ten Speed Press.

COLLECTIVE ACTION

Communities often engage in or give rise to collective action. Although the term *collective action* can refer to anything done by more than one person at a time, since the late 1960s the term has most commonly been used to refer to action oriented toward achieving a common or shared interest among a group of people. This usage derives from *The Logic of Collective Action* by the American economist Mancur Olson, especially Olson's assertion that "rational, self-interested individuals will not act to achieve their common or group interests" (Olson 1965, p. 2). Olson offers a mathematical "proof" of this assertion, along with a persuasive description of the "free rider problem." Although most researchers have moved beyond Olson's problem, it is essential to understand his contribution to appreciate subsequent work.

OLSON'S PROBLEM

Before Olson, most social scientists had assumed that the relation between individual and group interests was unproblematic, that people with shared interests acted to further them. But for several decades, economists had argued that coercive taxation systems were necessary, because rational individuals would not voluntarily contribute toward the costs of public goods such as military defense or infrastructure such as roads or other public services. Pure public goods have two characteristics. The first is nonexcludability or "impossibility of exclusion"—if the good is provided to any members of a society, everyone will have it. For example, all people in a geographic area breathe the same air, regardless of whether they pollute it or not. The second characteristic is "jointness of supply"—the cost of a good does not depend on the number of people who share it. A lighthouse has jointness of supply: The costs of building and maintaining it do not depend on the number of people who use it.

Drawing on this economic literature, Olson argued that any group goal or group interest evoked the same problem. If the benefits of collective action cannot be withheld from noncontributors, rational individuals are motivated to "free ride" on the contributions of others. Even if a group has a common interest—for instance, workers with a common interest in the wage-enhancing properties of a union contact enforced by the threat of a strike—each individual member has an individual interest in gaining the benefit of that contract without paying union dues or striking. This divergence between individual and group interest increases as the size of the group increases.

This situation is the noticeability problem—an individual cannot make a big enough difference in an outcome to compensate for the cost of making the contribution. Olson argued that collective action to provide collective goods would happen only if actors were provided with what he called selective incentives, side payments made to those who participate in the action.

Olson's theoretical argument that common or collective interests cannot logically be the motivation for collective action has aroused theoretical debates about the relation between nonexcludability and jointness of supply, as well as about the "production function" relating inputs of collective action to outputs of the collective good. In many contexts, actors can indeed make noticeable contributions to a public good, contributions that affect many more people than themselves, and in which they can rationally calculate that their own benefit from the action is worth the price. Rationally, people should not care that other people also benefit. They might engage in strategic gaming to decide whether they can expect or persuade others to contribute. Such interdependent and strategic decision making, however, yields more complex results than Olson's simple assertion that collective action is "irrational." In addition, selective incentives cannot logically solve the collective action problem: Paying the cost to use incentives to motivate others' action is, itself, a form of collective action.

BEYOND OLSON'S PROBLEM

Olson's work is nevertheless a major innovation in social science. Before Olson, social scientists generally assumed that if people had a common interest, they would act on it. The connection between interest and action was so automatically assumed that a group's refusal to act on what appeared to be a common interest was taken as proof that there was no common interest after all. If the interest was clearly manifest but no action was taken, researchers looked for a problem in the group that explained its inaction. The group might be said to lack cohesion. The concept of group cohesion confounded positive ingroup feeling and acting together to address common concerns. If a group did not act in the face of common interests, it was by definition not cohesive. There might be other communal deficits, such as a lack of education, resources, or psychological strength. In short, common action was treated as the normal response to common interests, and inaction had to be explained.

After Olson, the situation was reversed. Collective action in the face of common interests is seen as problematic, not automatic, a phenomenon that requires explanation. Resource mobilization theory in social movements (and its successor, political process theory) takes off from this point. It builds on the community organizing concept of resource mobilization and stresses that action around common problems does not automatically happen but requires resources and social networks. Instead of viewing grievances or problems as automati-

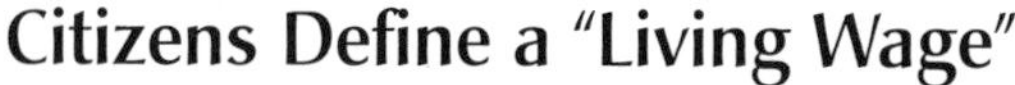

Citizens Define a "Living Wage"

(ANS)—A few years ago, the Rev. Doug Miles began to see more people lining up outside the food pantry of his downtown Baltimore church. Many were holding down full-time jobs—working for companies that do business with the city—but "they just couldn't live on what they were making."

Instead of simply enlarging the food-pantry shelves, Miles and other pastors did something radical.

Through a church-based organization called BUILD (Baltimoreans United in Leadership Development), they pushed for a new city ordinance which requires companies with city contracts to pay their workers a "living wage."

That law went into effect this summer. And now, the movement is spreading to other parts of the country, with relatively little political opposition and some surprising allies.

In cities from Baltimore to San Jose, community leaders—and workers themselves—are running with the concept of a living wage. The idea is that people who work for a living should be able to support themselves and their families.

According to backers of the concept, a true living wage is more than the current minimum wage, federally mandated at $4.25 an hour.

In Baltimore, it is now $6.10 an hour, rising to $7.70 an hour in 1999. According to city estimates, approximately 4,000 service workers will benefit from the new law. Most of them had been receiving the federal minimum wage.

In New York, the living wage would come to $12 an hour, if a community coalition has its way. The coalition—affiliated, as is Baltimore's BUILD, with the national Industrial Areas Foundation—has mustered broad support for a measure that targets companies with city contracts. Each year, the city awards contracts for an estimated $6 billion in goods and services.

In St. Paul, Minnesota, community activists rounded up twice as many signatures as needed to place a livable-wage initiative on the November ballot. Voters will decide whether firms subsidized by the city should pay workers at least $7.21 an hour. That would lift a family of four above the poverty line.

In Milwaukee, $7.70 an hour would become the living wage required of companies that want to do business with the city, under proposed legislation crafted by the community coalition Sustainable Milwaukee.

In some places, local organizations are capitalizing on the fact that many firms get direct subsidies and special tax breaks from city governments.

"A lot of the impetus for these campaigns is that people are seeing their tax dollars go to these companies, and they don't see any of the money coming back into their neighborhoods. So they're saying, 'What's going on here?'" said Jen Kern, a researcher with the Association of Community Organizations for Reform Now (ACORN) in Washington, D.C.

—William Bole

Source: "Citizens Define Their Own 'Living Wage.'" The American News Service, Article No. 1.

cally generating action, these theories stress resources, organizational capacities, and shifts in the polity as central to determining which grievances get acted on.

Olson's "selective incentives" ideas have been modified into a typology of three factors motivating individuals to participate in collective action: material incentives, solidary incentives, and purposive incentives. Common material incentives in community organizations include salaries paid workers, goods such as coffee mugs given in exchange for monetary contributions, and the possibility of putting community service on a résumé. Solidary incentives arise from social interactions, including simple sociability and the respect or esteem one receives from others. Purposive incentives are the internal psychic rewards that people experience when fulfilling their own moral or ethical standards of behavior or the intrinsic pleasures of the particular actions involved.

Empirically, attitudinal concern about the collective good is regularly found to be a major predictor of collective action. Peace activists care more about world peace than do nonactivists, environmental activists care more about the environment than do nonactivists, and neighborhood activists are more concerned about local problems than are nonactivists. This pattern is interpreted in rationalist theory by equating attitudinal concern about a collective good with a purposive incentive, for example, by assuming that those who care about the environment inherently feel better about themselves when they contribute to its improvement.

THE NOTICEABILITY OR EFFICACY PROBLEM

Olson's problem occurs when actors cannot make a big enough difference in the outcome to overcome their own cost of action. Empirically, activists tend to deny the noticeability problem, insisting to survey researchers that their own contributions make a significant difference in the collective outcome. Respondents make this claim even in circumstances in which it is manifestly implausible;

for example, when asked whether their own participation in a 100,000-person demonstration makes a difference, they say that it does. They abandon the claim only if strongly pressed by the interviewer. Psychologically, activists tend to assume that everyone else acts the same way they do; if they act, so does everyone else, but if they do not act, then no one else does. Psychologically, activists thus deny the possibility of free riding, which makes sense sociologically. Unlike isolated independent decision makers in classical economic theory, real people are embedded in social networks in which they know others are aware of their actions and are influenced by them.

Even when noticeability and free riding are overcome by social solutions, there is still an efficacy problem. Even collectively, actors seeking to provide a collective good must envision some way in which the actions produce that good. The most common source of apathy or inaction is an efficacy problem, a belief that nothing can help a situation. In practice, collective action is not abstract, but specific. A community center might be built by pooling contributions of materials and labor from among the residents or by lobbying the municipal government to build it. The two strategies require different resources and skills from community members. Often, the crucial factor for turning hopelessness into hope is a plan for achieving a goal by using the particular resources and capacities of a particular group.

The ability to make noticeable contributions to collective goods is most likely when actors work through the political system. Robert Cameron Mitchell showed that environmental activists, with relatively modest expenditures of time and effort, could get laws passed mandating that businesses spend a large amount of money in environmental cleanup efforts. Although the businesses would find it irrational to do the cleanup voluntarily, it was not irrational for environmental activists to spend their efforts in lobbying for the laws. In fact, the benefit-cost ratio for environmental activism was highly favorable. Many other groups can similarly provide themselves with collective goods through political action. Wealthy individuals and business corporations may lobby for a tax break that is beneficial enough to them to be worth their paying the entire expense of lobbying, even though many other individuals may also benefit from the tax loophole. The strategic aspects of efficacy can also be relevant, as actors may need to consider the responses of other actors. These responses may include competition for limited resources, and they may also involve concerns about violence or repression in some political contexts.

NETWORKS AND ORGANIZATIONS

Even when the illogic of collective action is overcome and actors are motivated to expend energy and resources for collective benefit, they still face the organizational problems of collective action. In some instances, one person can provide a collective good for everyone. A wealthy benefactor may build a public pool, or an energetic and talented individual single-handedly publish a community newsletter. But most often, action for collective goods must be collective; many people must combine and coordinate their actions to produce the desired outcome. This coordination is, itself, potentially costly. For this reason, organizations and social networks are critical in collective action. Empirically, the social-organizational basis for common action takes different forms in different contexts. Different organizational bases support different forms of action.

Networks of Individuals

A network-communication tie is essential for coordinated action. Individuals who have ongoing social ties to one another through relations such as kinship, co-residence, trade, or employment may be able to coordinate their actions without explicitly forming an organization. People may "pass the word" about a situation or upcoming event, in a process of information diffusion. Research on large gatherings such as protests or riots indicates that people generally attend in small groups, accompanied by people they know. Social networks are not static but grow over time in the course of action. Common problems and coming together to take action are often the basis for the formation of new ties. Organizers often specifically work to create new network ties to increase the social basis for common action. The forms of action sustained by networks of individuals typically involve either small numbers of people or the simplest forms of coordination of larger numbers, such as appearing at the same time and place for a demonstration.

Organizations as Actors

Organizations are often the basis for collective action. Organizations that already have created social connections among people and accumulated financial and other resources are much better able to provide collective goods than are disparate individuals. Organizations can provide the basis for actions involving complex divisions of labor, significant amounts of money, and continuation over a long time. In the study of social movements, there has been a debate about the relative importance and roles of preexisting organizations formed for other purposes (churches, unions, fraternal associations) versus special-purpose movement organizations, with research generally showing that preexisting organizations are more important initially but then are eclipsed by newly created movement organizations as a movement grows. The field of community organizing similarly reveals the importance of both categories of organization. The relation between both kinds of organizations and political parties varies greatly between countries, depending upon their political institutions and cultures.

Organizations as Networks

In addition to being collective actors in their own right, organizations, especially preexisting organizations, function as the site for the formation of new social ties between individuals. Research has shown that common organizational membership is the most frequent way for separate friendship and kinship groups to be linked together in networks that can support broad-based collective action. The specific patterns of organizational membership and co-membership can shape the trajectory of a collective action mobilization. Some actions stay within a network of people with a common political ideology, while others spread more broadly. When actions spread beyond a politicized core, the organizers are usually members of nonpolitical organizations that can provide the basis for their communication with a broader range of people.

Networks of Organizations

Instead of linking individuals, some social networks link organizations. These links may be explicit, as when overt coalitions are formed, but they may also be implicit or informal. In countries with large numbers of organizations, networks of organizations are an important feature of collective action. The relation between these organizational networks and political parties and networks varies between and within countries, depending on the structure of politics in a particular place. Formal coalitions are often created to link the variety of organizations concerned about a particular issue. Community organizations often form such coalitions. Even without formal coalitions, organizations often informally communicate with other organizations as a way of broadening the support for their goals.

COMMUNITY ACTION

Theories of collective action provide analytic tools for understanding the dynamics of community action. Texts and handbooks on community organizing translate these theoretical principles into practical suggestions for action. There is no automatic path from a community problem to coordinated action to address that problem. Instead, the problem of mobilization must be solved. Individuals must be motivated to act on the common problem, recognize or create a form of action that can solve the problem, and coordinate the actions of disparate individuals. The inventory of types of incentives for action—material, solidary, purposive—has often proved useful to community activists as they seek strategies for involving others. An understanding of the importance of resources and capacities has led to a recognition that there are many different ways to accomplish a particular goal, and that part of the problem of collective action is to find a strategy within the capacity of the community in question. Finally, networks and organizations provide the necessary social basis for collective action.

—Pamela E. Oliver

Further Reading

Benford, R. D., & Snow, D. A. (2000). Framing processes and social movements: An overview and assessment. *Annual Review of Sociology, 26,* 611–639.

Della Porta, D., & Diani, M. (1999). *Social movements: An introduction.* Oxford, UK: Blackwell.

Diani, M., & Eyerman, R. (Eds.). (1992). *Studying collective action* (Vol. 30). London: Sage.

Hardin, R. (1982). *Collective action.* Baltimore, MD: Published for Resources for the Future by Johns Hopkins University Press.

Jenkins, J. C. (1983). Resource mobilization theory and the study of social movements. *Annual Review of Sociology, 9,* 527–553.

Klandermans, B. (1997). *The social psychology of protest.* Oxford, UK: Blackwell.

Marwell, G., & Oliver, P. (1993). *The critical mass in collective action: A micro-social theory.* Cambridge, UK: Cambridge University Press.

Marx, G., & McAdam, D. (1994). *Collective behavior and social movements: Process and structure.* Englewood Cliffs, NJ: Prentice Hall.

Mattessich, P., & Monsey, B. (1997). *Community building: What makes it work.* Saint Paul, MN: Amherst H. Wilder Foundation.

McAdam, D. (1982). *Political process and the development of black insurgency, 1930–1970.* Chicago: University of Chicago Press.

McAdam, D., McCarthy, J. D., & Zald, M. N. (1988). Social movements and collective behavior: Building macro-micro bridges. In N. Smelser & R. Burt (Eds.), *Handbook of sociology* (pp. 695–737). Beverly Hills, CA: Sage.

McPhail, C. (1991). *The myth of the madding crowd.* New York: Aldine de Gruyter.

Mitchell, R. C. (1979). National environmental lobbies and the apparent illogic of collective action. In C. S. Russell (Ed.), *Collective decision making: applications from public choice theory* (pp. 87–123). Baltimore: Johns Hopkins University Press.

Morris, A. (1984). *The origins of the civil rights movement: Black communities organizing for change.* New York: Free Press.

Ohlemacher, T. (1996). Bridging people and protest: social relays of protest groups against low-flying military jets in West Germany. *Social Problems, 43*(2), 197–218.

Oliver, P. E. (1983). The mobilization of paid and volunteer activists in the neighborhood movement. *Research in Social Movements, Conflicts and Change, 5,* 133–170.

Oliver, P. E. (1984). If you don't do it, nobody else will—Active and token contributors to local collective action. *American Sociological Review, 49*(5), 601–610.

Oliver, P. E. (1993). Formal models of collective action. *Annual Review of Sociology,* 19, 271–300.

Olson, M. Jr. (1965). *The logic of collective action: Public goods and the theory of groups.* Cambridge, MA: Harvard University Press.

Opp, K. D. (1989). *The rationality of political protest: A comparative analysis of rational choice theory.* Boulder, CO: Westview.

Reitzes, D. C., & Reitzes, D. C. (1987). *The Alinsky legacy: Alive and kicking* (Vol. Supplement 1). Greenwich, CT: JAI .

Rubin, H. J., & Rubin, I. S. (2001). *Community organizing and development* (3rd ed.). Boston: Allyn & Bacon.

Smith, D. H., & Macaulay, J. (1980). *Participation in social and political activities: A comprehensive analysis of political involvement, expressive leisure time, and helping behavior.* San Francisco: Jossey-Bass.

Tarrow, S. (1998). *Power in movement: Social movements and contentious politics* (2nd ed.). Cambridge, UK: Cambridge University Press.

Zald, M. N., & McCarthy, J. D. (Eds.). (1987). *Social movements in an organization society: Collected essays.* New Brunswick, NJ: Transaction.

COLLECTIVE CONSUMPTION

Economists often discuss consumption as if it is necessarily an individual if not always a private activity. There is, however, as the sociologist Per Otnes has emphasized, "such a thing as public, shared, common or collective consumption" (Otnes 1988, p. 161). Collective consumption refers to the many goods and services that tend to be produced and consumed on a collective level. It includes products, services, and institutions such as roads, bridges, public transportation, schools and libraries, health care, waste disposal, public housing, welfare, fire and police protection, and parks and recreational facilities. When consumption is viewed in this way, there is an obvious connection between collective consumption and what economists call collective or public goods—those goods that are essential to consumers but which the market will not supply and which consequently government has to provide. Some of these are products that the market itself could not sensibly provide, for example, government itself, or such services as defense of the nation. Others, such as education, housing, or transportation services, are goods and services that the market could supply and usually does to some extent. The degree to which a society's goods and services are collectively consumed, that is to say, supplied by government rather than through the market, is a traditional index of how socialist the government is. For this reason, collective consumption is also sometimes called socialized consumption.

MANUEL CASTELLS AND COLLECTIVE CONSUMPTION

This link between collective consumption and government was a central feature of the neo-Marxist approach of urban sociologist Manuel Castells. His work, which came to prominence in the mid to late 1970s, set out to explain the precise location of the boundary between private and public (or collective) consumption in Western capitalist societies. He tried to understand the reasons for the limits of state or government intervention. Basically he argued that the state was forced to intervene in order to provide those goods and services "whose organisation and management cannot be other than collective" (Castells 1976, p. 45) because of the size and complexity of the problems they address. Since those services are typically located in urban areas, Castells also used the term *collective consumption* to help define the nature of the city in advanced capitalist societies, asserting that urban areas were basically organized around collective rather than individual consumption. Consequently, he defined *city* as a "unit of collective consumption corresponding more or less to the daily organisation of a section of labour power" (Castells 1976, p. 148); in other words, all of the arrangements, such as transportation, necessary for those people who work in the public sector to do their jobs. It is urbanites' shared consumption processes that create for them a common set of experiences that then lead to the development of political action. Political action follows because, although the goods and services collectively consumed are ones that the state must provide (given that capitalism cannot or will not do so), the reality is that typically the state is unable to meet their cost. Hence there is a tendency toward crisis in their provision, a crisis that precipitates urban social movements.

CRITICISM OF CASTELLS

Sociologist Ray Pahl has criticized this neo-Marxist approach for suggesting that collective consumption is a distinctive feature of monopoly capitalism when in reality it is just as apparent and significant a feature of socialist societies. In addition, Pahl finds the term itself rather misleading, given that the goods and services that are consumed are actually considered significant because they contribute to production— the production (or reproduction) of labor power. For example, a public transportation system contributes to the production of labor power by letting labor get to the site of production efficiently. In fact, partly as a consequence of these criticisms, the neo-Marxist or urban sociology approach to the study of collective consumption tended to die away in the 1990s. Indeed, apart from a 1990 study by Castells, Lee Coh, and R. Yin-Wang Kwok of its role in the economic development of modern city-states such as Singapore and Hong Kong, it was largely absorbed into a more general sociology of consumption.

AMBIGUITIES OF THE TERM

The concept of collective consumption is not without its ambiguities. For example, it is not clear if it relates to goods and services that the market is unable or simply unwilling to provide (for example, because it is not profitable enough to so). Furthermore, not all collective consumption can be understood as involving the state, either directly or indirectly. Local voluntary and charitable associations, for example, often provide services that bypass the market (especially in such fields as social work and housing) and yet operate independently of government. At the same time, no good or service can be considered to belong to either the private or collective category by virtue of any intrinsic characteristic; "correct" identification will tend to depend on a range of other variables, such as the state of current technology and prevailing market conditions. This difficulty in deciding to which category any good or service belongs has been exacerbated in recent decades by the rise of the New Right. For although their program of privatization may appear to involve a simple transfer to market provision of services previously provided by the state, such as transport, communication, and health, the reality is more complex. That nominal transfer often involves the continuation of extensive state regulation and control (frequently involving sizable subsidies) as well as a formal requirement that the private organizations continue to provide some degree of public service. At the same time, even the services that remain in public ownership are often required to meet the same standards as those prevailing in the private sector, a feat that government enterprises and public service agencies often find difficult to achieve.

COLLECTIVE PROVISION OR COLLECTIVE USE?

One of the central and unresolved difficulties presented by the concept of collective consumption concerns whether it refers to collective provision or collective use, or to both. For it is clearly the case that many of the services that are provided by the community, such as street parking and refuse collection, are nonetheless consumed individually rather than collectively. On the other hand, some provisions, such as the communal festivals and celebrations that accompanied the welcoming of the new millennium, would indeed seem to fully warrant use of the term, since in these cases the service was indeed consumed collectively, that is to say, by the community. It would seem sensible to restrict the use of the term to occasion of this kind, that is, to situations where it is clear that consumption is undertaken by a "collectivity" (such as the audience at a sporting or cultural event), rather than by a number of individuals who independently consume the same service or product.

—Colin Campbell

Further Reading

Castells, M. (1976). Theory and ideology in urban sociology. In C.G. Pickvance (Ed.), *Urban sociology: Critical essays* (pp. 60–84). London: Tavistock.

Castells, M. (1977). *The urban question: A Marxist approach* (A. Sheridan, Trans.). London: Edward Arnold.

Castells, M. (1978). *City, class and power* (E. Lebas, Supervised Trans.). London: Macmillan.

Castells, M. (1983). *The city and the grassroots: A cross-cultural theory of urban social movements.* London: Edward Arnold.

Castells, M. (1985). *The informational city.* Berkeley and Los Angeles: University of California Press.

Castells, M., Coh, L., & Kwok, R. Y. W. (1990). *The Shek Kip Mei syndrome: Economic development and public housing in Hong*

Kong and Singapore. London: Pion.
Dowding K., & Dunleavy, P. (1996). Production, disbursement and consumption: The modes and modalities of goods and services. In S. Edgell, K. Hetherington, & A. Warde (Eds.), *Consumption matters* (pp. 36–65). Oxford, UK: Blackwell.
Dunleavy, P. (1980). *Urban political analysis: The politics of collective consumption.* London: Macmillan.
Otnes, P. (1988). The sociology of consumption: "Liberate our daily lives." In P. Otnes (Ed.), *The sociology of consumption* (pp. 157–177). Oslo, Norway: Solum Forlag A/S.
Pahl, R. E. (1978). Castells and collective consumption. *Sociology, 12*(3), 309–315.
Saunders, P. (1986). *Social theory and the urban question* (2nd ed.). London: Hutchinson.

COLLECTIVE EFFICACY

Collective efficacy is a variable feature of communities that refers to the capacity of residents to achieve social control over the environment and to engage in collective action for the common good. The theory of collective efficacy was designed to go beyond the emphasis in traditional community research on compositional characteristics, such as poverty and race, and the idea that dense friendship ties are the major source of community strength. Strong ties among neighbors are no longer the norm in modern urban communities, where friends and social networks are decreasingly organized in a geographically restricted, local fashion. Weaker ties based on relatively infrequent interaction may be more efficient for securing resources because they integrate the community by bringing together otherwise disconnected subgroups.

Recent work has specifically proposed collective efficacy as a community-level concept defined by the linkage of socially cohesive relationships with shared expectations for intervention on behalf of the community. Just as an individual's self-efficacy varies with the situation (one has self-efficacy relative to a particular task; it is not an absolute quality), a neighborhood's efficacy exists relative to specific tasks, such as maintaining public order or safety for children. The term *collective efficacy* is meant to signify an emphasis on shared beliefs in a neighborhood's conjoint capability for action to achieve an intended effect, and hence an active sense of engagement and cohesion on the part of residents. The meaning of *efficacy* is thus captured in residents' expectations about the willingness and ability of their neighbors to exercise social control in achieving public goods such as a lower crime rate and better schools. Distinguishing between the resource potential represented by dense friendship ties, on the one hand, and the shared expectations for action represented by collective efficacy, on the other, clarifies how the role of communities has changed in modern society. Today, social networks foster the conditions under which collective efficacy may flourish, but they are not sufficient for the exercise of control.

Collective efficacy is typically measured in community surveys by asking residents about the willingness of their neighbors to help one another, the degree of mutual trust, and shared expectations of intervention to promote neighborhood safety and support local services. A number of recent studies have linked higher levels of collective efficacy to the general well-being of children and lower rates of crime and violence. Concentrated poverty and residential instability also predict lower levels of collective efficacy, suggesting indirect pathways through which structural community characteristics influence crime and other features of social life.

In sum, the theory of collective efficacy holds that while collective capacity for action may depend on a working trust, it does not require deep personal ties. The theory claims that we do not need communities so much to satisfy private and personal needs, which are usually met elsewhere, nor even to meet sustenance needs. (For example, we do not need to do our shopping and banking in a community context.) Rather, collective efficacy theory argues that the local community remains essential as a site for the realization of public or social goods that benefit everyone, such as public safety, clean environments, and education for children.

—Robert J. Sampson

Further Reading

Bandura, A. (1997). *Self-efficacy: The exercise of control.* New York: W. H. Freeman.
Sampson, R. J., Morenoff, J., & Earls, F. (1999). Beyond social capital: Spatial dynamics of collective efficacy for children. *American Sociological Review, 64,* 633–660.
Sampson, R. J., Raudenbush, S. W., & Earls, F. (1997). Neighborhoods and violent crime: A multilevel study of collective efficacy. *Science, 277,* 918–924.

COLLEGES

In North America, the word *college* commonly refers to an instrumental community devoted to the residentially based education of a defined cohort of young people. In that context, a college is usually either a freestanding tertiary (that is, postsecondary) institution or a

Eton College

Founded in 1440 to educate British scholars who were without the financial means to go on for advanced schooling, ironically Eton College is now an elite prep school favored by British royalty. Below is a verse about the regimented way of life at Eton in the nineteenth century.

When boys at Eton, once a year,
In military pomp appear;
He who just trembled at the rod,
Treads it a hero, talks to god,
And in an instant can create
A dozen officers of state.
His little legion all assail,
Arrest without release or bail:
Each passing traveler must halt,
Must pay the tax, and eat the Salt.
You don't love Salt, you say; and storm–
Look o' these staves, sir–and conform.

Source: Hone, William. (1832). *The Year Book of Daily Recreation and Information.* London: William Tegg, pp. 1345–1346.

residential subset of a larger institution, such as a university or an institute. In Europe, colleges are commonly secondary educational institutions, often under religious sponsorship, and they are not necessarily residential. Usage of the word for an institution elsewhere depends on the history of the institution. The remainder of this entry refers to North American (principally United States) colleges.

ORIGINS AND SPONSORSHIP OF EARLY NORTH AMERICAN COLLEGES

The North American college dates back to the seventeenth and eighteenth centuries, when British colonists, who wanted some of their young people to pursue what today would be called higher education without having to travel to England, founded Harvard College (1636), the College of William and Mary (1693), and Yale College (1701). These institutions and the handful of others established before the American Revolution largely followed the English educational model based on the medieval trivium (which focused on grammar, rhetoric, and logic) and quadrivium (which focused on arithmetic, music, geometry, and astronomy), and intended to develop in students (usually male) a broad knowledge of philosophy, rhetoric, mathematics, classical languages, history, and literature. Because of the lack of educational institutions beyond primary schools, these early colleges typically offered curricula blending secondary and tertiary education. As the most educated persons in the colonies were often Protestant ministers, they often served as teachers, ensuring a strong religious influence in most educational settings. Denominational sponsorship of colleges encouraged moral education for all students and created a supply of clergy for Protestant churches that was independent of European seminaries.

Migration to western and southern frontier regions during the nineteenth century led to the founding of hundreds of new colleges. Many were sponsored by Protestant denominations and supported by community booster groups seeking to attract colleges to their locales. Concern about the dangers of urban life often led colleges to locate far from cities. Thus, many colleges founded before the twentieth century were, of necessity, primarily self-sufficient residential communities in which young people could mature unsullied by unplanned, and unhealthy, encounters with forces beyond the community's control. These communities were often small (several hundred students), homogeneous (students were predominantly white Protestant men from nearby), with a highly prescribed curriculum (with no elective courses; all students took the same courses). Although there was socioeconomic diversity in the student body, and students displayed widely varying degrees of religious intensity, they often had similar backgrounds and collegiate experiences. Not surprisingly, strong bonds and lifetime friendships were forged in these communities among students and between students and faculty. Later in the nineteenth century, the Roman Catholic Church began to create a parallel system of colleges, usually sponsored by a religious order or a diocese (or both), and colleges for women and African Americans also arose, under varying sponsorships.

For two decades after the Civil War, enrollment at these private colleges lagged, as they faced competition from new state-supported land grant universities such as Cornell (established 1869), and early private research universities that followed the German model, such as Johns Hopkins (opened 1876). The success of the new institutions compelled many colleges to correct their dated curricula (for example, through addition of courses in the natural and social sciences and modern foreign languages) and to offer students greater freedom in choosing courses of study and out-of-class activities. Universities also were often coeducational, and a growing number of colleges began to accept women by the end of the nineteenth century, though many "elite" colleges remained closed to women until the 1970s.

THE COLLEGE COMMUNITY IN THE TWENTIETH CENTURY

The residential college model continued to develop in the twentieth century. More than 700 independent residential colleges are located across the United States in every state but Wyoming. Over 200 are liberal-arts colleges; that is, they are defined by a commitment to a version of the traditional curriculum harking back to the medieval trivium and quadrivium, with varied concessions to demands for modern subjects of study, such as business and science, to new approaches to teaching (such as internships), and to efforts to tie the college to the surrounding community through such programs as community service. A great strength of these small schools is the personalized nature of the education they offer and the opportunity to develop strong faculty-student relationships.

The individualized style of education inherent to the small residential college is relatively costly, but large lecture classes and high student-to-faculty ratios are eschewed for communitarian reasons. Additionally, residential colleges require substantial capital investments in physical plants serving relatively few students. The most successful colleges enlist former students (called "alumni" or "alumnae") in an ongoing community experience in which the former students periodically return to visit, maintain strong ties with their classmates and former professors, create alumni clubs around the country and abroad, support their colleges financially, and become involved in their colleges' management through membership in alumni associations and on boards of trustees that supervise the colleges' operation.

Over time, many colleges that had been distinctive by virtue of their denomination, the region in which they were located, or the race or gender of their students, have become demographically more similar, reflecting both U.S. social mores and the economic realities inherent in maintaining an academically selective institution with the costly social, athletic, musical, and other enrichments necessary to attract students. Colleges today face strong competition for students from a wide variety of state-supported universities (including, in recent decades, public residential colleges and honors colleges in state universities) and residential colleges in independent research universities that previously had not emphasized undergraduate education. Consequently, independent colleges, which once educated over half of U.S. baccalaureate students, now attract only 10 to 12 percent of a larger student pool comprising some two-thirds of the traditional eighteen-to-twenty-one-year-old age cohort. While a strong case is made by advocates of independent residential colleges for the superiority of their educational methods and results (demonstrated by the large percentages of their graduates that go on to distinction in various professions and leadership roles), their relatively high tuitions (even when mitigated by generous scholarship and loan programs), low public profiles, and relatively low enrollment capacities ensure that only a minority of students experience education in a traditional U.S. college.

—Richard Kneedler and David Stameshkin

Further Reading

Bullock, H. A. (1965). *A history of Negro education in the South from 1619 to the present.* Cambridge, MA: Harvard University Press.

Carnegie Foundation for the Advancement of Teaching. (1990). Campus life: *In search of community.* Princeton, NJ: Princeton University Press.

Gleason, P. (1995). *Contending with modernity: Catholic higher education in the twentieth century.* New York: Oxford University Press.

Horowitz, H. L. (1984). *Alma mater: Design and experience in the women's colleges from their nineteenth-century beginnings to the 1930s.* New York: Knopf.

Horowitz, H. L. (1987). *Campus life: Undergraduate cultures from the end of the eighteenth century to the present.* New York: Knopf.

Koblik, S., & Graubard, S. (2000). *Distinctively American: The residential liberal arts college.* New Brunswick, NJ: Transaction Publishers.

Peterson, G. E. (1964). *The New England college in the age of the university.* Amherst, MA: Amherst College Press.

Rudolph, F. (1962). The American college and university, a history. New York: Knopf.

Rudy, W., & Brubacher, J. S. (1976). *Higher education in transition: A history of American colleges and universities,* 1636–1976. New York: Harper & Row.

Rudy, W. (1984). *The universities of Europe, 1100–1914: A history.* Rutherford, NJ: Farleigh Dickinson University Press.

Veysey, L. R. (1965). *The emergence of the American university.* Chicago: University of Chicago Press.

COLONIALISM

The word *colonialism* refers to an extremely wide range of phenomena that are not always easy to compare, much less combine, under the same concept. As a product of the past centuries of European expansion, colonialism is commonly associated with empire building, especially in the nineteenth century. In the most general sense, it involves the establishment of colonial rule, a political structure in which one state controls another state or territory by forming a governing organization that is either a literal extension or a more indirect representative of the colonizing state. While colonialism refers to the formation of such systems of international rule, there is a great deal of variation in the structures of power in such systems. In this general sense, colonialism is part of imperial expansion. No empire can work without the establishment of local and regional governments. Because empires have been part of the history of civilizations for several thousand years, colonialism is certainly not a phenomenon that can be associated with Western capitalism alone.

Although colonialism occurs as a function of empire and imperial expansion, the phenomena described by words of the same family, such as *colony* and *colonization,* do not necessarily depend on the existence of imperial rule. Colonization refers to the establishing of settlements in territories beyond those of the society of origin. "Trading colonies," by contrast, have little to do with political dominance as such. Such colonies are dominated by and dependent on local elites and may pay tribute or taxes. Trading colonization may, however, be part of a process of increasing domination, especially in economic terms; for example, manufactured goods may be exchanged for raw materials or slaves. Such "unequal" exchanges are common in history, from the Anatolian colonies of ancient Assur to those of Portugal. The colonization of North America was yet another form of establishing new populations in a foreign territory as was the forced settlement of prisoners in Australia. There is an important difference between the establishment of colonies in new territories or even in other societies, and a regime of political dominance under which such colonization can, but need not always, occur. It is in conditions of political dominance that colonization can be said to be an expression of colonialism.

COLONIAL RULE

Colonial relations are relations of empire that link a center to a conquered or otherwise-dominated region or state. The notion of colonial rule is linked to the foreign nature of that rule and the control and, most often, the exploitation of indigenous inhabitants. Colonialism is in this sense more than a mere aspect of regional empire. It can as easily apply to relations within a territorial state in what is referred to as internal colonialism. This is the case in relations between a state and indigenous minorities (e.g., between the United States and North American Indians in the nineteenth century), as well as between any state in the process of expansion and the minorities that it either marginalizes or incorporates. State formation in Europe—from the end of the fifteenth century until the seventeenth century—can be understood as a kind of colonial process in which regional peoples are incorporated, often by violence, into the expanding state apparatus.

Colonialism, as previously suggested, does not necessarily imply colonization. The minimalist form of colonialism consists of an administrative center and a number of economic enterprises or concessions from the mother country. Administration varies greatly in size and elaboration depending on the function of the colony in the larger imperial arena. Colonial societies may also be host to migration or colonization from the mother country. When such colonization takes on large proportions, a colonial economic sector may become totally dominant in the colony and make use of local labor on a large scale. The large-scale plantation systems, mining enterprises, and even some forms of manufacture are common in colonial systems and are an essential element of colonialism. But settlers from the mother country can also establish private farms and enterprises of a smaller nature, becoming in this way a significant enclave within the colony. Such settlers, unlike most colonial administrators, often develop an identity with the colony as opposed to the mother country. Such settlers are historically linked with anticolonial revolts, not usually for the emancipation of native peoples, but for control over their own conditions of existence and for the establishment of local power. These revolutions are important factors in the history of Latin America, as well as in other major world regions. The United States is a quite particular example of a settler colony that sought independence in a situation where the settlers were a majority of the territorial population.

DISINTEGRATION OF LOCAL SOCIAL STRUCTURES AND CULTURES

Colonial societies in which there were considerable native populations were usually characterized by a dual organization—a central colonial sector with its own particular social organization, lifestyle, and culture; and a native sector reorganized into the colonial regime—and were usually disorganized internally as well. Colonialism itself implies a major transformation of native societies. While many changes take place because of changing structures of trade, the most devastating changes have been the result of the immediate processes of colonial rule. The African slave trade was not a result of colonialism as such. It began much earlier (in the early 1500s) and had its predecessors in Arab slave trade, which lasted much longer than the European trade. (Arab slave trade existed from the 800s into the 1800s.)

The effects of slave trading had on Central Africa were complex. European goods were pumped through royal and chiefly circuits of exchange in Africa, and slaves were sent out. This created a process by which certain chiefs increased their power through their monopoly in trade goods, and at the same time large numbers of people were sent off to the New World, ultimately depleting the population of Central Africa. The decentralization of the trade created long-term political fragmentation, with competing chiefs struggling for control over the "prestige" goods from afar. Large kingdoms such as the Congo slowly disintegrated from the early fifteenth to the eighteenth centuries. African kings whose powers had increased at the start of the trade found themselves being out-competed by former vassals who gained direct access to European slave traders. This disastrous development, however, cannot be ascribed to colonialism as such, since it occurred without any form of direct intervention in the native societies. The reorganization of Congolese societies into a large variety of smaller scale polities, with greatly transformed but related structures of political power, was the result of this global-local relationship. Related processes of fragmentation-transformation occurred in the sandalwood trade with Timor in Indonesia.

Colonial rule implies direct intervention in the lives of native societies; transformation is imposed by the regime itself, in forms such as labor conscription, schooling, and missionizing. It is a different kind of transformation since it is not one that is managed internally by native society; rather, it is orchestrated from the outside. Such transformation reorganizes people's lives in ways consistent with those of the colonial power. It is necessary to stress that this kind of change consists in both structural and physical violence. Structural violence is the result of imposing new norms, new interpretations, and new rules on a population, which is experienced as painful and dislocating. Physical violence has often been administered in the enforcement of colonial rule and some of the great massacres of history have been its result, as in the death of millions of Central Africans under the regime of King Léopold of Belgium and his introduction of the murderously exploitative system of rubber plantations near the end of the nineteenth century.

The disintegration of local political structures was usually accompanied by catastrophic social crises. The second half of the nineteenth century was a period of general political disintegration in the Congo region, accompanied by the spread of witchcraft accusations and even of cannibalism. Social crisis was translated into personal crisis. The increase in political fragmentation was also a fragmentation of the person. Witchcraft is described as the loss of the integrity of the self whose different components leave the body at night, either to "eat" others or to be captured and eaten themselves. Magical behavior increased markedly in this period as part of a defense against evil forces that seemed to be completely out of control. The control or order that previously existed was the political order, an order that was defined as a cosmic order as well, especially in societies where the two are either identical or closely related In other areas subject to colonial onslaught, there was a noticeable increase in depression and suicide. These occurrences were common in American Indian society as well as in some Polynesian societies. They were expressed in the production of an array of reactions—from a nostalgia for the past (expressed even in music, as in Hawaii), and in millenarian activities, magical cults, and various forms of what are described as insanity. Some of these activities have been associated with colonial resistance.

THE REORGANIZATION OF SOCIAL AND CULTURAL STRUCTURES IN COLONIAL SYSTEMS

Colonial rule meant a massive reorganization of the life of native populations, but quite often also the importation of large numbers of people from other parts of the larger empire or the imperial world. The European colonial system (as with other colonial systems) involved massive dislocation of millions of people and forced specialization in specific raw materials and plantation crops. The peripherality of the periphery was not a result of economic adaptation but of political power. The colony was a system of ethnic division of labor in which ethnicity was used to delegate different kinds of work and functions. Multiethnic colonial society also included the products of mixed marriage via the categorization of offspring into particular "color" classes. The most extreme form of multiethnic colonialism is perhaps South African apartheid, but there are innumerable examples of similar regimes. These were all characterized by an ethnic or color hierarchy, with white colonials at the top, and a distribution of status, wealth, and occupation according to ethnic position. Within this larger structure, new cultural and social forms emerged that are often falsely associated with traditional societies; in fact, they are the product of more complex processes of the colonial system itself. Many of the societies studied by anthropologists in this century are not relics of precolonial societies, but rather are themselves very much the product of such colonized societies. This does not mean that they bear no resemblance to previous social forms. Kinship relations may become greatly transformed without themselves disappearing and being replaced by "modern" forms. On the contrary, it is better to characterize them as contemporary forms of kinship organization. Further, there is nothing evolutionary involved in this characterization since contemporary forms need not be different in kind from previous forms.

COLONIALISM AND CLASSIFICATION

Colonialism cannot be disassociated from the cultural classifications of such social formations. The ideology of evolutionary ranking is a particular form of imperial classification that converts the spatial order of empire into a temporal order of development. "Primitivity" encountered in far-off countries is represented as the relic of a distant past. This kind of classification is not colonial as such; it is an important component of colonial discourse. Ranking in space from center to periphery is represented as an evolutionary ranking, a temporal distribution of societal types. Such classification is practiced in colonial rule in the treatment of natives and in the rationalization of such treatment. The notion of "civilizing process" is a product of this evolutionary scheme put into practice, and the classification of certain natives who are socially mobile and adopt European ways as *évolués* (evolved, developed) is a clear example of the pervasiveness of this scheme. Colonialism could be more or less assimilationist or multicultural in practice. In the former case, common to the model used in French colonies, a local ranking of native to "civilized," understood in terms of education, was an important ingredient in the colonial social order. In the latter case, pluralism was the typical organization, where difference is still ranked but not placed on a continuum in which individual mobility is common. Instead the differences are grouped into discrete populations with fixed identities.

The differences in these organizations are ideal, and in fact, there are many instances of overlap between them. Certain postcolonial phenomena can be understood as the continuation of such schemes into the present. The phenomena known in Central Africa as *la sape* (to dress up elegantly) was a migration or even pilgrimage from the Congo to Paris in pursuit of haute couture. The activity was primarily male and was based on a rank order of dress that extended outward from locally made clothing to store-bought cheap imports, and to the great names among French and Italian fashion designers. In this movement from the periphery to the center, young men aimed to travel to the temples of great clothing in Paris, where the latest fashions were available at enormous cost. This imposed tremendous pressure on these young men, and to come up with the money, they often engaged in various black market activities and illicit trades such as prostitution and drugs.

The clothes were taken back to the Congo where they were displayed publicly, with the designer labels from the acquired clothes sewn into one jacket in a kind of potlatch of prestige. The successful *sapeur* was named *un grand,* a great man or big man, and he became the center of a larger clientele. This activity has been associated with the use of chemical mixtures to lighten the skin, a practice of "whitening" also associated with high status. The French word *se jaunir* (to turn yellow) refers to the yellowish hue that results from this treatment, sometimes defined as *le maquillage à outrance* (make-up in the extreme), associated not only with color but with wealth and health, both signs of higher rank. In this phenomenon, indigenous structures of rank are mapped onto the imperial order in such a way that appearance and geography are united in a single strategy.

RESISTANCE

The formation of colonial rule implies the emergence of resistance to such rule. This resistance takes on various forms, from outright armed resistance and overt disobedience to more subtle forms of avoidance and noncompliance. The study of forms of resistance has become a popular research topic since the 1980s. One particular historical approach associated with the work of Ranajit Guha has sought to demonstrate the way in which official history has silenced the multifarious voices and historical experiences of subdued populations. The notion of "subaltern" has been used to characterize the situation of such populations within colonial and other oppressive regimes. Resistance movements are often typical of the first stages of colonial rule, and such movements are most often unsuccessful. Resistance includes armed uprisings put down with violence, along with the emergence of political leaders, of discourses of identity, and of traditions opposed to the new ways of the colonial powers.

One important aspect of the development of resistance movements is the way in which they make use of new cultural forms that emerge within the colonial sphere. Christianity, for example, is often the basis of resistance—a Christianity that is imposed from the outside but assimilated and molded to local cultural schemes. *Religious syncretism* is a term often used to refer to colonial Christianity, accentuating the fact that the colonial form combines elements of both religions. Such a vague term, however, does not capture the religion's exact nature: Christian terms and some concepts are assimilated to local meanings and religious practices in a way that reflects the native more than the Western. The church becomes a focal point in new organizations, but the church is largely assimilated in cultural terms to local practices. This complex struggle can in certain periods reflect the dominance of Western ideals, as is the case with respect to the association of certain forms of magic and especially sorcery with the devil. Even here, however, there is a tendency to incorporate the devil into the local practices and representations.

An important example of the way in which colonial categories are reversed in strategies of resistance can be found in the *kastom* movements in Melanesia. The very

Indigenous and Colonial Forms of Administration

The following description of the Tiv of Nigeria under British colonial rule indicates the problems that can result when the traditional political and social system of the colonized people is ignored or misunderstood and replaced with the hierarchical, centralized system of the colonizer.

We have seen that the largest political entity known to them before our arrival was the family-group descended from it still lower down the genealogical ladder. If therefore, we place one man over a whole clan–or worse one man over two whole clans–we cannot expect this system to work smoothly and it is asking almost the impossible of a District Head to expect him to be obeyed implicitly in areas outside his family-group areas, where the people have their own family-group chief. A straw shows which way the wind is blowing and the fact that one District Head whom I asked for his clan genealogy was totally ignorant of the most salient facts about the genealogy of a family-group area not his own but under his jurisdiction, is abundant evidence that he knew little about the area in question.

Is it therefore surprising to read the following comment by a District Officer? "The District Head is only a superior sort of family-head, who scarcely recognises himself as responsible for his district except as and when instructed by the District Officer, and in some areas where I have toured, has never been before."

This state of affairs has no doubt, arisen partly from the pre-conceived idea of the functions of a clan, such as stated by Rivers, but nothing is so dangerous as generalisations drawn from the analogy of other parts of the world. "The clan plays an important part in the political constitution of the community at large. For, throughout the world, each clan has its own council, composed of the older generation of males, which transacts all its business. The clan usually has the right to elect its own chiefs, when it has any, and depose them, without regard to the council of the larger unit of which it forms a part."

If we delete the word "Clan" in this quotation and substitute for it "Family-group," we shall obtain a true statement of the Tiv organisation, where the family-group is a kind of clan in miniature.

Another reason which has led to the creation of so-called district heads, is the European desire for centralisation and the concentration of power in the hands of one single individual with whom we can treat and whom we can hold responsible for the behavior of the population under his, shall we say, "control"? This is readily comprehensible, for it is extremely difficult to deal separately with a large number of independent chiefs. A good example of this centralisation and its bad results is to be seen in the case of German pre-war Tanganyika.

Source: Abraham, Roy C. (1933). *The Tiv People.* Lagos: The Government Printer, p. 160.

word *kastom* (pidgin English) for custom is derived from the colonial institutionalization of what was called "customary law," corpuses of traditional representations used in customary law courts and considered important for the authorities when dealing with conflicts related to land, marriage, and other issues. Such issues, pertaining to what the colonial order designated as "traditional," had to be dealt with separately from the modern legal system. Anthropologist Roger Keesing has argued that native identities are produced in the process of objectification that occurs as a result of the classification of culture by colonial authorities—a process in which colonial anthropologists play an important role. National movements then mobilize these categorizations in an act of self-identification against those very colonial powers. Whether such colonial categories are mere Western products or whether they actually contain a good deal of accurate representations of local society and culture has been much debated in recent years.

—Jonathan Friedman

See also GLOBALIZATION AND GLOBALIZATION THEORY; IMPERIALISM

Further Reading

Asad, T. (Ed.). (1973). *Anthropology and the colonial encounter.* New York: Humanities Press.

Cooper, F., & Stoler, L. (Eds.). (1997). *Tensions of empire: Colonial cultures in a bourgeois world.* Berkeley and Los Angeles: University of California Press.

Friedman, J. (1994). *Cultural identity and global process.* London: Sage.

Friedman, J. (1994). Will the real Hawaiian please stand: Anthropologists and natives in the global struggle for identity. *Bijdragen tot de Taal- Land- en Volkenkunde* [Journal of the Humanities and Social Sciences of Southeast Asia and Oceania] *47,* 137–167.

Guha, R. (Ed.). (1982–1987). *Subaltern studies, 1–5.* Oxford, UK: Oxford University Press.

Keesing, R. (Ed). (1982). Reinventing traditional culture: The politics of kastom in Island Melanesia [Special Issue]. *Mankind, 13*(4).

Larsen, M.T. (1976). *The old Assyrian city state and its colonies.* Copenhagen: Akademisk Forlag.

Memmi, A. (1990). *The colonizer and the colonized.* London: Earthscan.

COLUMBIA, MARYLAND

Planned for a population of over 100,000 on 13,838 acres, and opened in 1967, Columbia, Maryland, was famous for two contributions—the Columbia concept of racial integration and the Columbia economic model, an early financial analysis tool. The development was the pet project in the 1960s of developer James Rouse (1914–1996). Described both as a committed Christian and an unabashed liberal, Rouse had been involved with early urban renewal projects and in 1958 had built the first speculative enclosed shopping mall. He later established the Enterprise Foundation, a major organization involved with community revitalization.

By the early 1960s, Rouse had become worried about the dominant architecturally based approach to planning. In a number of venues, including a widely circulated 1963 speech delivered at the University of California at Berkeley, he proposed an alternative form of development focused on human growth, learning, participation, and social diversity. In the early 1960s, Rouse started to assemble land for a new town in Howard County, Maryland. Although employing a team of physical planners, in late 1963 and early 1964 Rouse also organized a fourteen-person social planning work group to propose ideas for this development. Although it met for only a few days a month, the group developed general recommendations about issues such as racial and economic mix, education, recreation, transportation, and the situation of youth. While not all the work group's ideas were incorporated into Columbia's planning, the group's role was widely promoted and used in marketing to attract residents interested in alternatives to generic suburban development.

Columbia had a distinctive philosophy of community and used a number of specific strategies to achieve it. Rouse was interested in racial and economic mix. The sociologist Herbert Gans, a member of the social planning work group, proposed that racial mix should be at the house level. This was a strong stand in a county that did not desegregate its schools until the mid-1960s. However, reflecting the findings of his earlier work in Levittown, Gans proposed that houses in the same cul-de-sac or small cluster should have a similar economic level because that was a likely predictor of having common interests and values and therefore the potential for friendly neighboring. Columbia has always done a better job at racial than economic mix, remaining around one-fifth to one-quarter African American since the 1970s and having a low level of racial segregation. Although Columbia has some subsidized housing, its main mechanism for promoting economic mix has been through providing a diversity of housing types and sizes.

Rouse was also attracted to the idea of re-creating

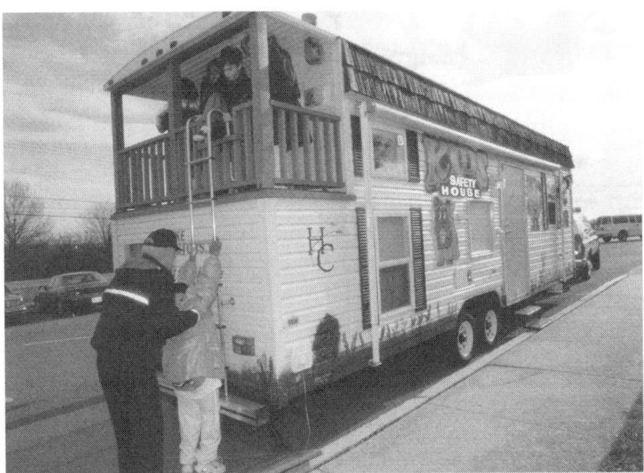

Children in Columbia, Maryland, participate in a safety house fire drill in 2001.

Source: Richard T. Nowitz/Corbis; used with permission.

small-town life. Accordingly, Columbia is organized into a series of villages of approximately 10,000 people each and made up of three or more neighborhoods. Each village has a village center that contains a mix of shops, offices, and educational, recreational, and civic facilities in a campus-style arrangement.

In the early days, Columbia attracted a unique group of pioneering residents, captivated by Rouse's vision. There has always been some tension in Columbia, with periodic accusations of racism occurring since the very start. From time to time there have also been discussions about low-income populations, in spite of their fairly low numbers—either advocating for more low-cost housing or complaining about subsidized tenants. However, Columbia stands out in terms of being a successful self-consciously heterogeneous suburb. While the early spirit of Columbia has dimmed somewhat over the years, it is still in evidence.

—Ann Forsyth

Further Reading

Bloom, N. (2001). *Suburban alchemy: 1960s new towns and the transformation of the American dream.* Columbus: Ohio University Press.

Breckenfeld, G. (1971). *Columbia and the new cities.* New York: Washburn.

Burkhardt, L. (1981). *Old values in a new town: The politics of race and class in Columbia, Maryland.* New York: Praeger.

Gans, H. (1968). *People and plans.* New York: Basic Books.

Forsyth, A. (2002). Planning lessons from three US new towns of the 1960s and 1970s: Irvine, Columbia, and The Woodlands. *Journal of the American Planning Association,* 68(4), 387–415.

Tennenbaum, R. (Ed.). (1996). *Creating a new city.* Columbia, MD: Partners in Community Building and Perry Publishing.

COMMON LAW

Laws guiding the behavior of community members are derived from three primary sources. In some instances (often called Roman, or civil, legal traditions), a legislature, monarch, or despot puts into writing the laws that will govern citizens' action and inaction. In religious and philosophical contexts, guiding laws are said to derive from, or reflect the principles of, a deity. Jewish law and Islamic law are examples of law in that tradition. The third primary source of laws is said to result from the ordinary way people in a community have handled disputes for as long as anyone can remember. The source of law in that circumstance is said to rely on custom and is referred to as common law.

It is clear that community standards have always been the initial source of norms and sanctions for maintaining social order. Whether the community operated at a familial, tribal, or village level, there were accepted standards for suitable behavior and agreed-upon consequences for misbehavior. In that sense, common law has a genesis similar to all legal traditions. However, common law is clearly different from the other forms of law in that its authority comes from custom rather than from political or religious entities. Because common law is most closely associated with English history, it is best understood in the context of that history.

The Common Law of England

Before the Norman Conquest of England (1066), disputes among community members were handled through assemblies of freemen sitting in courts associated with groups of families (hundred courts) or with people living in a particular geographic area (shire courts). Upon his arrival in England, William the Conqueror (1028?–1087) retained those traditional courts but also added courts in which manorial lords would preside over disputes between villagers. In resolving those disputes, the lord relied on the advice of the other villagers as to the traditional way of handling the quarrel. If the manor court was unavailable or inappropriate, villagers could turn to traditional shire or hundred courts, which also resolved disputes according to local custom.

Disputes among landowners were of greater interest to William, since those were the people with whom he had the most direct economic and political links. To gain knowledge about and influence over those disputes, William established a new system of royal courts that provided a base for establishing a shared system of laws throughout the realm. But full realization of laws common to all of England did not occur until the reign (1154–1189) of Henry II (1133–1189) and the recognition of custom as the key ingredient of common law.

THE IMPORTANCE OF CUSTOM

In his *Commentaries on the Laws of England* (1765–1769), Sir William Blackstone (1723–1780) characterized legal custom as ancient (no one can remember its beginning), continuous (it has never been abandoned or interrupted), peaceable (it has the common consent of those using it), reasonable (in terms of "legal" reason), certain (ascertainable), compulsory (obedience is not optional), and consistent (one custom cannot contradict another). Blackstone's definition is certainly complete, but it does not help us understand how something comes to be identified as an example of custom—especially legal custom. One way to decide if a custom met the criteria for being a good legal custom was the jury system. Presumably, if a freeman's peers settle a dispute by using principles that reflect common and immemorial custom, the decision exemplifies common law. Or, as Blackstone put it: "The only method of proving, that this or that maxim is a rule of the common law, is by showing that it hath been always the custom to observe it" (Blackstone, I, p. 68).

The medieval judge Henry de Bracton developed an effective method of determining common law in the mid-thirteenth century. Bracton saw the courts of his time as foolish and ignorant corrupters of doctrine, deciding cases by whim instead of by rule. In an attempt to return to the rule of law, Bracton reviewed the original plea rolls from the courts. He used those documents to research legal principles and then to identify cases as historical evidence of custom. In that manner Bracton showed that court decisions were governed by custom and that custom was therefore the source of law.

But even with the recognition of custom as law's key ingredient, there were problems deciding which particular customs would be applicable throughout England. Custom, after all, was not consistent across geographical regions or social classes. Local village customs settled disputes among peasants and other villagers, but occasionally those customs contradicted the habits of vassals, lords, and other freemen. For example, village customs in England frequently kept a woman's property free from her husband's control and allowed her to enter into contracts on her own. Bourgeois custom did not allow such behavior by women. As English law gradually became standardized throughout the land, the version of custom that took dominance was, not surprisingly, that of the landholders, as accepted and interpreted by the royal courts. But biased toward the customs of a specific social class or not, it was custom all the same, and those customs came to be recognized as law common to all of England.

COMMON LAW IN THE UNITED STATES

The common law of England spread as the British empire expanded during the eighteenth and nineteenth centuries. Today the United States, Australia, New Zealand, India, and other former British colonies make up the approximately thirty-five countries said to follow the common legal tradition. Even in nations where it is not the singular legal tradition, the common law has had influence. The examples of Argentina (where the legal system was affected by both common and civil legal traditions), Egypt (where common law interacts with both civil and Islamic law), and Japan (whose basic civil legal system received a strong dose of common law during the U.S. occupation following World War II) show the diverse nations in which common law is part of the country's legal system.

The common-law tradition remains strong today despite the increasing use of legislated law in common-law countries. That is because laws passed by legislators in a common-law country are not authoritatively established unless and until the courts have concurred. For example, the U.S. Congress can pass a law prohibiting the burning of the national flag, but because of the United States' common legal tradition, that law is not authoritatively established until the courts agree that it is consistent with the principles reflected in the customs of the nation in its colonial days.

THE IMPACT OF LEGAL TRADITION

Communities everywhere must deal with the broad problem of social order. As people in a society establish social norms (that is, they define behavior as either acceptable or unacceptable), they must also determine what sanctions (rewards and punishments) will be used to enforce those norms. Informal sanctions such as pats on the back by teachers or scoldings from parents are very powerful examples of how society encourages and discourages behavior. But informal sanctions are seldom sufficient, and society must turn to more formal ones. A country's legal system is a primary means of establishing formal sanctions.

—*Philip L. Reichel*

Further Reading

Blackstone, W. (1765–1769). *Commentaries on the laws of England* (4 vols.). Oxford, UK: Clarendon.

Fairchild, E., & Dammer, H. (2001). *Comparative criminal justice systems* (2nd ed.). Belmont, CA: Wadsworth.

Plucknett, T. F. T. (1956). *A concise history of the common law* (5th ed.). Boston: Little, Brown.

Reichel, P. (2002). *Comparative criminal justice systems: A topical approach* (3rd ed.). Upper Saddle River, NJ: Prentice Hall.

Sereni, A. P. (1956). The code and the case law. In B. Schwartz (Ed.), *The Code Napoleon and the common-law world* (pp. 55–79). Westport, CT: Greenwood.

COMMUNICATIONS TECHNOLOGIES

Learning from existing communications technologies, such as e-mail discussion groups and instant messaging, some researchers have attempted to combine the most useful features of such systems with theories of community and interaction. This new research includes expansions of e-mail (and the notion of the e-mail habitat), developments of virtual social spaces, and spaces that are developed to merge closely with the real world.

An online space refers to the virtual medium through which a group of people communicates, such as a newsgroup, mailing list, or discussion on a Web page. In contrast, the set of all online mailing lists is not considered a single space; the participants in each group are too disparate and are unlikely to encounter one another. A space must be bounded and must have an agreed-upon limit.

TECHNOLOGIES OF COLLABORATION

E-mail—one of the most frequently used services of the Internet—has developed far beyond a communication medium. Researchers at PARC, the Palo Alto Research Center, have convincingly argued that e-mail has become a habitat, a computer application where many people spend most of their time. They use it for a variety of activities, ranging from maintaining reminders and to-do lists to keeping contact information and calendars. Its communicative function is the glue that holds e-mail's many other functions together; yet, most e-mail clients—the programs that allow users to read their e-mail—are surprisingly limited as a way of reaching other people. Various research projects and design plans have been created in an attempt to increase the sense of interactivity in using e-mail by allowing users to understand each other's interaction histories—such as when they have sent messages, and to whom—and their activities—such as when they are available and when they can be reached.

One way of increasing e-mail users' interactivity is by giving them a sense of awareness—letting them know of the presence and activity of other users. This awareness is achieved either directly, by monitoring other users' keyboard activity, or indirectly, by building up a history of the correspondents' availability and communication patterns. These technologies are not necessarily invasive. Many awareness applications make use of the notion of mutuality—a user cannot observe another's activity without making him- or herself available for monitoring.

Awareness applications also allow collaborators on a project to work closely together. For example, one collaborator may try to complete the draft of a proposal before his or her teammates' usual times of departure from their offices. While this can be easily accomplished if all participants work in one setting, it is far more complex to achieve online, when teammates may be scattered around the globe.

Researchers have thus tried to merge the awareness information available through instant messaging into e-mail programs and to use this information to build up availability profiles—times that a partner is likely to be reachable. Such information can be displayed in a variety of ways—for example, in the Apple iMail system, a small colored dot next to each name in an e-mail inbox highlights whether a person can be reached.

Another avenue of research explores allowing e-mail users to describe their interactions with one another and to categorize their community. For instance, the ContactMap system permits users to describe the groups of people they interact with. After a list of names is compiled from an e-mail record, users can cluster the names into groups however they wish. This clustering becomes an enhanced information manager, allowing users to view contact information for each person or group and to send e-mail messages to people on the list. Future revisions may allow users to cluster and sort e-mail in its inbox by the group or to use the Map as an index of past correspondence. Further revisions may integrate the ContactMap with e-mail clients. Users will be able to view their e-mail from within the ContactMap tool, allowing them to view all messages sent back and forth within the group. Because each group represents its own projects and activities, the mail will be divided by topic and project.

PURELY VIRTUAL SPACES

Because e-mail gives users a personal view of social networks and interactions, researchers have attempted to provide similar views of history and communication to systems such as Usenet news. The Conversation Map, for example, is research software intended to help social scientists review and understand online conversations. The system allows a researcher to view newsgroups as social networks, seeing who responds to which posters and who participates in various threads. In addition, the Map uses techniques from linguistics to search for equivalent phrasing, for instance, to find similar rhetorical devices used in an advocacy group to enunciate opposing viewpoints. Because of the interlinks, a user can read one author's view, that author's arguments, arguments of other participants, and other writings of the participants.

The Netscan project is a related attempt to study newsgroups, with some differences. Netscan, a software system built by a team at Microsoft Research, was designed, among other purposes, to allow group moderators to follow conversations by means of facilities for watching what threads are the most active, who is most involved, and what topics are hottest. Netscan also allows comparisons between groups, making it easy to see which groups are most active. By interpreting the crossposts between groups—messages posted to more than one group—the system can also show relationships between closely connected groups.

The Netscan project has produced a map of the Usenet, a dynamic view of the online space, showing which newsgroups are most active and how many messages have been posted on them.

APPLIED NETWORK ANALYSIS

Social network analysis has also been used for future technology designs. The IKNOW system, for example, is a software project that helps users discover "who knows who knows what." It sorts through an organization's Web pages, looking for both links between Web pages and common information on different users' Web pages, to derive a social network and a map of different users' expertise. Users can then update their own listings by making and removing connections to other users; other members of the organization can search for people with particular information and expertise.

Social network analysis is one of a family of techniques used for "knowledge management," the workplace use of data mining and social network analysis. Knowledge management systems attempt to help businesses keep track of their implicit knowledge—ideas not explicitly part of job descriptions, but known to small groups of people in a company, who have expertise in particular topics. Users provide the system with information about their areas of knowledge, and the system attempts to connect users who need information. Social network information is valuable for knowledge management systems because it allows users to find experts whom they can contact.

While knowledge management is a way of locating the knowledge of an individual in a group, a contrasting idea is to use a group's communal understanding to help subsequent users. The study of social navigation—various techniques to interpret the movements of groups of people—originated because researchers realized that, although people can interpret subtle cues from the behavior of other people in real life, few such cues are available to people using the computer. For example, the wear on the cards in a library catalog can illustrate which books are used most frequently, but a computer-library index usually gives no such indication of frequent use.

E-commerce sites have adopted social navigation techniques to increase sales. For example, Amazon.com recommends books to online purchasers based on previous purchase records. Other systems allow users to leave "footprints" or annotations on their favorite pages, suggesting that others follow them.

In addition to leaving footprints, users want to interact with other Web travelers. Many online sites provide a number of mechanisms that allow users to see who is online, to send one another messages, or to know what activities others are engaged in. The set of things that are available in this manner is referred to as the "social affordances" of a system.

The term *social affordance* was derived from the ideas of physical and interface affordances developed by American psychologist J. J. Gibson and later by cognitive scientist Don Norman. Gibson theorized that people construct certain things to correspond to their notions of how the things should work. A chair, for example, allows for sitting, while a ladder affords sitting less well than it does climbing. Good design, Norman points out, partially entails making these affordances clear. A door with a pulling-handle that is labeled "push" is likely to be confusing; a toilet with no obvious way to flush is likely to be neglected or misused.

Social affordances are the cues and abilities for interaction in a social space. Useful social affordances include such ideas as "they are gathering there" and "this is an active area." The Babble system, developed by IBM, was built to explore the notion of social affordances. It allows users to see a representation of other users active in a conversation, but only those who participate can see the other participants. The most active users slide inward on a circular visualization; less active users slide outward. Thus, the system enforces mutuality and awareness—there can be no "lurkers" on Babble.

It is also possible to simulate certain behaviors in Babble—for instance, to generate the impression of attentiveness or activity. The converse of awareness is "social translucency"—veils of unawareness that allow users some flexibility. Translucency is the online way to seem to act, just as in a real space a person may pretend to pay attention to an uninteresting speaker. Proponents of translucency think such social "slop" should be allowed in online conversation and participation. In Babble's case, participants discover that their representations may appear active in a number of different ways; it is not always necessary to be actively typing a conversation into the Babble space.

The Babble concept is being expanded in a number of directions. Later prototypes have been used to explore larger spaces (Babble is limited to a few hundred users) and to explore forms of communication other than communal chat. For example, variants of Babble have successfully demonstrated concepts of voting results (in which different opinions drift to either side of the screen as the debate continues), auctions (in which high bidders slide away from the crowd of onlookers, "racing" toward the prize), and teaching (in which students who participate in classroom conversations become increasingly visible).

HYBRID SPACES: BRINGING TECHNOLOGY INTO THE COMMUNITY

Another trend in online community design is that of varying the degree to which interactions interpenetrate between online and offline spaces. A purely online community may be entirely divorced from its offline counterparts, with its users feeling little desire or ability to meet in the flesh. A hybrid approach uses technology to reinforce the degree or type of face-to-face involvement. Classic studies of one type of hybrid spaces (such as Hampton and Wellman's Netville and Patterson's Carlisle) have examined the changes in virtual communities that have direct physical counterparts. These studies, centered on North American villages, provided an online space to inhabitants of the villages. Physical neighbors could meet each other online; town meetings might answer online comments and be followed by more discussion in the online space. In these studies, participants in the communities had access to online systems only by living in the same place. In this way, the participants knew that behind each online persona was a real person.

Virtual participation can be brought into the real world in a different way. Personal roving presences (PRoPs) are one attempt to bring real and virtual spaces into tighter interaction. PRoPs are vehicles, both blimps and wheeled, designed with a camera, pointer, and display screen. They are set so that the display screen falls at face level, the pointer is at arm's length, and the camera looks from near where eyes might go. A visitor to a remote site—a museum, an inspection tour, or some other place where being physically present is important—can use a PRoP to participate by proxy.

Online spaces can reach more deeply into physical spaces, too. As technology has advanced from the text-based interfaces of MUDs, the multiuser dungeons that were prime hangouts for early Internet users, to the lovingly rendered massively multiplayer role playing games (MMRPGs) with their three-dimensional displays, voice connections, and complex illustrated world, users have become increasingly immersed in virtual spaces. Players in computer games can now interact by speaking to one another. Technologies such as the PHANTOM, a device that can simulate complex touch and texture, even allow systems to reproduce, with amazing accuracy, the sensation of touch within a virtual space. Online virtual spaces that incorporate technologies like the PHANTOM are being explored, in the hopes that the next generation of these online spaces might become richer experiences, allowing touch as they today allow sound and vision. For example, coworkers at a remote machining plant might use an immersive system to discuss the shape of a part with their colleagues at the main factory.

CONTINUING RESEARCH

Although the basic methods of Internet collaboration have not changed much in the last few years—e-mail and newsgroups are still commonly used—other techniques are becoming popular. These new technologies embody some developed ideas, such as awareness; other ideas, such as social translucency, are still in research.

—*Danyel Fisher*

See also INFORMATION OVERLOAD; ONLINE COMMUNITIES, COMPUTERIZED TOOLS FOR; PERSONALIZATION AND TECHNOLOGY

Further Reading

Carroll, J. M., & Rosson, M. B. (1996). Developing the Blacksburg Electronic Village. *Communications of the ACM, 39,* 69–74.

Contractor N., Zink, D., & Chan, M. (1998). IKNOW: A tool to assist and study the creation, maintenance, and dissolution of knowledge networks. In T. Ishida (Ed.), *Community computing and support systems. Lecture notes in computer science 1519* (pp. 201–217). Berlin, Germany: Springer-Verlag.

Dourish, P., & Bellotti, V. (1992, November). Awareness and coordination in shared workspaces. In *Proceedings of ACM CSCW 1992 Conference on Computer Supported Cooperative Work* (pp. 107–114). Toronto, Canada.

Ducheneaut, N., & Bellotti, V. (2001). Email as habitat: An exploration of embedded personal information management. *Interactions, 8*(5), 30–38.

Erickson, T., Smith, D. N., Kellogg, W. A., Laff, M. R., Richards, J. T., & Bradner, E. (1999). Socially translucent systems: Social proxies, persistent conversation, and the design of "Babble." In *Proceedings of CHI 1999 Conference on Human Factors in Computing Systems.* Pittsburgh, PA: ACM Press.

Harrison, S., & Dourish, P. (1996). *Re-place-ing space: The roles of place and space in collaborative systems.* Retrieved February 27, 2003, from www.ics.uci.edu/~jpd/publications/place-paper.html

Massie, T. H., & Salisbury, J. K. (1994). *The PHANTOM haptic interface: A device for probing virtual objects.* Retrieved February 27, 2003, from http://www.sensable.com/products/datafiles/phantom_ghost/ASME94.pdf

Munro, A., Höök, K., & Benyon, D. (Eds.). (1999). *Social navigation in information space.* Berlin, Germany: Springer-Verlag.

Nardi, B., Whittaker, S., Isaacs, E., Creech, M., Johnson, J., & Hainsworth, J. (2002, April). Integrating communication and information through ContactMap. *Communications of the ACM, 45*(4), 89–95.

Paulos, E., & Canny, J. (1998). PRoP: Personal roving presence. In *Proceedings of CHI 1998 Conference on Human Factors in Computing Systems* (pp. 296–303). New York: ACM Press.

Sack, W. (2000). Conversation map: A content-based Usenet newsgroup browser. In *Proceedings of the International Conference on Intelligent User Interfaces.* New Orleans, LA: Association for Computing Machinery.

Smith, M., & Fiore, A. (2001). *Visualization components for persistent conversations* (Microsoft Research Technical Report MSR-TR-2000–98). Retrieved February 27, 2003, from research.microsoft.com/research/coet/Communities/chi2001/paper.pdf

Wellman, B., & Hampton, K. (1999, November). Netville on-line and off-line: Observing and surveying a wired suburb. *American Behavioral Scientist, 43*(3), 475–492.

COMMUNISM AND SOCIALISM

Although the ideologies of Communism and socialism differ as social theories and political systems, both are now closely associated with Marxism and Leninism. (In general terms, communism refers to a political system that abolishes private property, and socialism to a system of collective ownership of the means of production and distribution.) According to Karl Marx (1818–1883) and Lenin (Vladimir Ilich Ulianov, 1870–1924), communism signifies both a form of society and a political movement aimed at bringing about that ideal form of society. Marx and Friedrich Engels (1820–1895) traced the history of human community from the primitive tribal commune through slavery, feudalism, and capitalism, finally arriving at communism, the inevitable outcome of all previous history. As an ideology, communism describes a state of human community based on common ownership and democratic control of the means of production and exchange, free of class divisions, class privileges, economic exploitation of one class by another, and political oppression. Under communism, all people work according to their capacity and are compensated according to their needs.

Although the concepts of communism and socialism are often used interchangeably, they are different in the sense that communism represents a greater degree of common life and a higher measure of equality in such matters as education, marriage, clothing, and housing. For communists, socialism is a transitional stage that ultimately develops into communism; in fact, Lenin stated that socialism is the first phase of communist society.

THE MARXIST MATERIALIST FOUNDATION

The communist concept of community is rooted in Marxist materialism, the official philosophy of communism. Marxist materialism emphasizes the determinant role of the economy in the evolution of human community, stresses social class as a potentially divisive factor in building community, and regards human community as class based (with inreconcilable conflicts among the classes). As a comprehensive account of history, Marxist materialism gives the highest priority to economic conditions and sees the progress of the human community as an outcome of the expanding forces of production and the material means of life—in other words, the development of the economy.

Selection From *The Communist Manifesto* (1848)

I. BOURGEOIS AND PROLETARIANS

The history of all hitherto existing society is the history of class struggles.

Freeman and slave, patrician and plebian, lord and serf, guild-master and journeyman, in a word, oppressor and oppressed, stood in constant opposition to one another, carried on an uninterrupted, now hidden, now open fight, a fight that each time ended, either in a revolutionary reconstitution of society at large, or in the common ruin of the contending classes.

In the earlier epochs of history, we find almost everywhere a complicated arrangement of society into various orders, a manifold gradation of social rank. In ancient Rome we have patricians, knights, plebians, slaves; in the Middle Ages, feudal lords, vassals, guild-masters, journeymen, apprentices, serfs; in almost all of these classes, again, subordinate gradations.

The modern bourgeois society that has sprouted from the ruins of feudal society has not done away with class antagonisms. It has but established new classes, new conditions of oppression, new forms of struggle in place of the old ones.

Our epoch, the epoch of the bourgeoisie, possesses, however, this distinct feature: it has simplified class antagonisms. Society as a whole is more and more splitting up into two great hostile camps, into two great classes directly facing each other–bourgeoisie and proletariat.

From the serfs of the Middle Ages sprang the chartered burghers of the earliest towns. From these burgesses the first elements of the bourgeoisie were developed.

The discovery of America, the rounding of the Cape, opened up fresh ground for the rising bourgeoisie. The East-Indian and Chinese markets, the colonisation of America, trade with the colonies, the increase in the means of exchange and in commodities generally, gave to commerce, to navigation, to industry, an impulse never before known, and thereby, to the revolutionary element in the tottering feudal society, a rapid development.

The feudal system of industry, in which industrial production was monopolized by closed guilds, now no longer suffices for the growing wants of the new markets. The manufacturing system took its place. The guild-masters were pushed aside by the manufacturing middle class; division of labor between the different corporate guilds vanished in the face of division of labor in each single workshop.

Meantime, the markets kept ever growing, the demand ever rising. Even manufacturers no longer sufficed. Thereupon, steam and machinery revolutionized industrial production. The place of manufacture was taken by the giant, MODERN INDUSTRY; the place of the industrial middle class by industrial millionaires, the leaders of the whole industrial armies, the modern bourgeois.

Source: Marx, Karl, & Engels, Frederick. (1848). *The Communist Manifesto.* Retrieved January 8, 2003, from http://www.anu.edu.au/polsci/marx/classics/manifesto.html.

According to Marxist materialism, a human community consists of an economic foundation and a political and legal superstructure. The stage of development of productive forces determines the political and ideological superstructure of human community that is crystallized into a system of social organization. The social system grows rigid, but the productive forces continue to expand, and conflict ensues between the forces of production and the social conditions of production. This conflict finally reaches a stage in which a fundamental change of the social conditions becomes necessary to bring them into harmony with the continued growth of production. This stage produces revolution, a relatively brief period in history in which outmoded social forms are discarded and new ones are created to free the shackled productive forces for a new leap forward. Marxist materialism thus considers social classes and the conflicts among them as the central features of social life throughout recorded history and as among the most important sources of social change. In *The Communist Manifesto,* Marx and Engels declared,

> The history of all hitherto existing societies is the history of class struggles. Freeman and slave, patrician and plebeian, lord and serf, guild-master and journeyman, in a word, oppressor and oppressed, stood in constant opposition to one another, carried on an uninterrupted, now hidden, now open fight, a fight that each time ended, either in a revolutionary re-constitution of society at large, or in the common ruin of the contending classes. (Marx 1977, p. 222)

According to Marxist theory, in any human community there are two basic antagonistic classes: the exploiters, the ruling class or bourgeoisie, and the exploited, the subject class or proletariat. The struggle between these two classes is the driving force transforming the human community, eventually producing the classless communist community, the highest level of human community. Communist community can settle all the questions about human community, including questions of people and nature, existence and essence, freedom and necessity, individuality and collectiveness, and ruling class and subject class.

COMMUNISM AND SOCIALISM ON CAPITALIST COMMUNITY

Communists conceived of communism as the necessary outcome of capitalism because communism is the social, political, and ideological system that breaks the fetters of the economic growth created under capitalism and opens the way to a new period of economic and social development on a large scale. Capitalist community rests on the growth of commodity production; it marks the stage at which labor itself has become a commodity. The evolution of capitalism is determined by the development of the fundamental contradiction inherent in it, between the social character of production and the private character of ownership. This contradiction manifests itself in the class struggle between the proletariat and the bourgeoisie.

Communists believed that the capitalist community was the last human community with classes and class antagonism. Because the bourgeoisie, owners of the social means of production, exploit the community's accumulated productive forces as their private property, capitalists violate the trust of the community. According to Marxist theory, there are three stages of capitalism—early, modern industrial, and monopoly capitalism or imperialism. All three stages are marked by the growth of commodity production and the intensification of antagonism between the bourgeoisie and the proletariat.

Early capitalism was characterized by simple artisan manufacturing. The common use of power-driven machinery brought about the rise of modern industrial capitalism. In this stage, based on free competition and colonial expansion, there emerged new contradictions between the big bourgeoisie and the petty bourgeoisie, urban and rural, and capitalism and colonial peoples. These conditions led to the final stage, marked by the transformation of free competition into monopoly, the export of capital, and the exploitation of colonies as sources of cheap labor and raw materials. One key aspect of this stage of capitalist community is the combination of capitalists and state power. The community is dominated by huge trusts and monopolies, and state power becomes the collective capitalist. This stage is marked by the intensification of all the major contradictions between the proletariat and the bourgeoisie, between imperialism and colonial peoples, and between rival imperialist powers; these contradictions lead to imperialist wars, until in one country after another the proletariat seizes power with the support of the masses of the peasantry and establishes itself as the ruling class. This, according to Marxist thought, is the proletarian revolution.

THE IDEAL COMMUNITY OF COMMUNISM

Considering men and women as social beings, communism values community. Communism is

> the positive abolition of private property and thus of human self-alienation and therefore the reappropriation of the human essence by and for man. This is communism as the complete and conscious return of man conserving all the riches of previous development for man himself as a social, i.e., human being. Communism as completed naturalism is humanism and as complete humanism is naturalism. It is the genuine solution of the antagonism between man and nature and between man and man. It is the true solution of the struggle between existence and essence, between objectification and self-affirmation, between freedom and necessity, between individual and species. It is the solution to the riddle of history and knows itself to be this solution. (Marx 1977, p. 89)

As a replacement of the capitalist community, the communist community is free from class antagonism and class struggle, as well as economic exploitation and class oppression. It is an association of free individuals in which all members can devote themselves to their fullest intellectual and cultural development. As Marx and Engels stated in *The Communist Manifesto,*

> Communism deprives no man of the power to appropriate the products of society; all that it does is to deprive him of the power to subjugate the labour of others by means of such appropriations. . . . When, in the course of development, class distinctions have disappeared, and all production has been concentrated in the hands of a vast association of the whole nation, the public power will lose its political character. Political power, properly so called, is merely the organized power of one class for oppressing another. If the proletariat during its contest with the bourgeoisie is compelled, by the force of circumstances, to organize itself as a class; if, by means of a revolution, it makes itself the ruling class, and, as such, sweeps away by force the old conditions of production, then it will, along with these conditions, have swept away the conditions for the existence of class antagonisms and of classes generally,

> and will thereby have abolished its own supremacy as a class. In place of the old bourgeois society, with its classes and class antagonisms, we shall have an association in which the free development of each is the condition for the free development of all. (Marx 1977, pp. 233, 237–238)

> In a communist community, where nobody has one exclusive sphere of activity but each can become accomplished in any branch he wishes, society regulates the general production and thus makes it possible for me to do one thing today and another tomorrow, to hunt in the morning, fish in the afternoon, rear cattle in the evening, criticise after dinner, just as I have a mind, without ever becoming hunter, fisherman, herdsman or critic. (Marx 1977, p. 169)

Following the cardinal principle of "From each according to his ability, to each according to his needs," an ideal communist community is "a society of billions of friends warmly joined in the rarest and most sensitive union of amity" (Strauss & Cropsy 1987, p. 822). Among such friends, not only would no individual seek advantage at the expenses of others, but the thought of doing so would never occur to him or her. In this sense, duty as duty would be transcended: What the mere sense of duty dictates to a person capable of selfishness would be the most spontaneous desire of someone as a member of the friendly society.

An ideal communist community is free of any form of coercion by the state machine. "From the moment all members of society, or at least the vast majority, have learned to administer the state themselves, have taken this work into their own hands, have organized control over the insignificant capitalist minority, over the gentry who wish to preserve their capitalist habits and over the workers who have been thoroughly corrupted by capitalism—from this moment the need for government of any kind begins to disappear altogether. The more complete the democracy, the nearer the moment when it becomes unnecessary. The more democratic the 'state' which consists of the armed workers, and which is 'no longer a state in the proper sense of the word,' the more rapidly does every form of state begin to wither away. . . . And then the door will be thrown wide open for the transition from the first phase of communist society to its higher phase, and with it to the complete withering away of the state" (Lenin 1976, pp.123–124).

COMMUNITY IN COMMUNIST REGIMES

Marx and Engels thought that people would be able to create a communist community that would eventually evolve away from capitalism, free from the prescriptions of an antiquated era and free from discrimination based on material wealth, race, color, and gender. However, they failed to describe the detailed means by which such a communist community would be created.

The ideal blueprint of a communist community outlined by Marx and Engels is a worldwide community that is based on a Communist revolution occurring simultaneously everywhere, in all civilized countries. When the October Revolution occurred in Russia in 1917, however, the proletarian revolution did not break out simultaneously in the advanced countries of the West. Instead, communist or socialist communities were established in individual countries, especially in those that were less developed than the West, such as Russia, China (1949), Cuba (1959) and Eastern Europe (during the early years after the World War II). In these countries, the growth of productive forces was slow, and the bourgeoisie, both local and foreign, had a relatively weak presence. The Communists led the workers and the peasants and successfully launched revolutions, setting up dictatorships of the working class.

In all these communist communities, however, the necessary preconditions for establishing ideal communism as described by Marx, Engels, and Lenin were never fullfilled. Although collective ownership of the means of production was established, classes and class differences still existed. More important, combining the Communist Party and the state actually strengthened the state rather than weakening it, and the party-state maintained strict control and surveillance over the entire community. Although these communist states proclaimed that they represented the interests of the working classes, the workers were not in control and had no power over the state. Because all power was instead concentrated in the Communist Party, the "vanguard" of the working class, there was little or no opposition to the outrageous use of power by the state, including such events as the Stalinist purges in Russia in the 1930s and the Cultural Revolution in China in the mid-1960s. Following classic Marxist theory, after the success of the Communist social revolutions the Communist regimes sought to eliminate private ownership on the part of the bourgeoisie by nationalizing land and the major means of production and creating two forms of public ownership: state and collective.

State ownership, also called ownership by the whole people, refers to the state or government control, on behalf of the whole people, over the means of production, such as land, natural resources, and human

Mao Zedong on Dealing With Counterrevolutionaries

In the excerpt below from a 1957 speech, Mao Zedong (1893–1976) makes it quite clear that there is no room for dissent or opposition in the People's Republic of China.

> Our state is a people's democratic dictatorship led by the working class and based on the worker-peasant alliance. What is this dictatorship for? Its first function is to suppress the reactionary classes and elements and those exploiters in our country who resist the socialist revolution, to suppress those who try to wreck our socialist construction, or in other words, to resolve the internal contradictions between ourselves and the enemy. For instance, to arrest, try and sentence certain counterrevolutionaries, and to deprive landlords and bureaucrat-capitalists of their right to vote and their freedom of speech for a specified period of time–all this comes within the scope of our dictatorship. To maintain public order and safeguard the interests of the people, it is likewise necessary to exercise dictatorship over embezzlers, swindlers, arsonists, murderers, criminal gangs and other scoundrels who seriously disrupt public order. The second function of this dictatorship is to protect our country from subversion and possible aggression by external enemies. In that event, it is the task of this dictatorship to resolve the external contradiction between the enemy and us. The aim of this dictatorship is to protect all our people so that they can devote themselves to peaceful labour and build China into a socialist country with a modern industry, agriculture, science and culture.

Source: Mao Zedong. (1957, February 27.). *On the Correct Handling of Contradictions Among the People.* Retrieved March 5, 2003, from http://www.maoism.org/msw/vol5/mswv5_58.htm.

resources. Collective ownership refers to the control by members of a collective, such as a cooperative or an urban community, over the means of production. Collective ownership is regarded as a junior level of public ownership, which will eventually develop into ownership by the whole people. Based on these two kinds of ownership, there were two kinds of enterprises in the USSR and other Communist countries. For instance, in China, public ownership of the means of production was established in the first half of the 1950s when the socialist transformation of the economy was conducted. The capital belonging to the comprador bourgeoisie was confiscated by the state and transferred directly into state ownership. The national bourgeoisie was allowed to sell their enterprises to the state at bargain prices. In the countryside, land belonging to the landlords were divided and distributed to the peasants. Then the peasants were encouraged to form mutual-aid groups. These were to develop later into agricultural co-operatives and later still into people's communes

These regimes also launched cultural revolutions to replace bourgeois ideology and promote socialist culture through the mass media, education systems, and continual agitation and propaganda. In the Soviet Union, citizens were required to be "socialist men" who exemplified the socialist principles of community, cooperation, and solidarity, people who put the common good before their own selfish interests. In China, Mao Zedong (1893–1976) launched the Cultural Revolution in 1966. For about ten years, Mao allowed groups of young adherents to apply the standards of ideological correctness to the economic, social, personal, professional, and almost every other aspect of human existence of vast numbers of people. High school and university students throughout China formed their own Red Guard group to investigate party cadres' behaviors and attitudes. Mass criticism became an everyday occurrence. Physical forces were openly used in the skirmishes between the competing factions of Red Guard groups. Party leaders were dragged out into the street and attacked by students. State and party authorities were effectively paralyzed. Finally, Mao made use of military force to end the domestic turmoil. During the Cultural Revolution, those whose behavior did not conform to revolutionary principles were guilty of political crimes and were subjected to a process of political re-education, the overt purpose of which was to root out old values and implant new ones. A large number of party members and intellectuals considered "rightest" or "counterrevolutionary" were persecuted and tortured by the Red Guards and radicals. Many people so labeled (as well as their relatives) were also punished with imprisonment or banishment to rural areas to do menial labor.

In a commuist community under the dictatorship of the proletariat, the population is divided into two categories defined by the party—people and enemies of the people. The people, mainly workers and peasants, are members of the community, while the enemies, including the former oppressors, exploiters, and capitalists, are restricted in their freedoms and excluded from the community. In Soviet Russia, in the early years of the Communist revolution, only the exploited classes—the workers, peasants, and soldiers—were members of the community. The former exploiting classes were regarded as enemies of the people and were excluded from the community. To serve the needs of class struggle, the role of the state was strengthened. In Lenin's view, the state could not wither away quickly in a socialist state; instead the state had to be strengthened because of its internal and external enemies. Joseph Stalin (1879–1953) argued that, as socialism goes from triumph to triumph, the class struggle intensifies, while the enemies become more and more desperate.

In Communist China, Mao Zedong defined the people by asking the question: Who are the people? In his early years of rule in China, the people were the working class, the peasantry, the urban petty bourgeoisie, and the national bourgeoisie. These classes, led by the working class and the Chinese Communist Party, united to form their own state and elected their own government; they enforced their dictatorship over the "running dogs" of imperialism: the landlord class and the bureaucrat-bourgeoisie, as well as the representatives of these classes, the Kuomintang (the ruling party of the Republic of China from 1927 to 1949) reactionaries, and their accomplices. Democracy was practiced within the ranks of the people, who enjoyed the rights of freedom of speech, assembly, association, and so on. The right to vote belonged only to the people, not to the reactionaries. Not only members of the exploiting classes had to go through the revolutionary transformation before being included in the community, however; members of the Communist community also received ideological education.

In the Soviet Union during Stalin's time, people were organized into different social organizations—workers in factories and farmers in collective farms. The Soviet factory, as well as the collective farm, assumed the basic functions of housing and feeding its workers. The workers, technical and managerial staff, trade-union officials, and party officials became actively engaged in forming a new urban, or rural, community and, in the process, turned the factory or farm into a "community organizer."

In Communist China during the Maoist years, people were further divided into two separate communities based on the notorious household-registration system—rural and urban residents. Horizontal movement between the rural and the urban communities was minimized. Members of the rural community were organized into thousands of people's communes, which in turn were organized into production brigades and teams. In urban areas, people were organized into various work units *(danweis),* such as factories, service-oriented units, state organs, and so on. Almost every urban resident belonged to his or her work unit. Each work unit was a closed community that served multiple functions, economic, social, and political. The work unit not only provided employment, daily necessities, and social service, but also political reward. Because it was difficult for people to survive outside their work units, people existed in a condition of organized dependence. Through the communes in the rural community and the work units in the urban community, the Chinese Communist regime exerted strict control over its people.

After the initiation of market-oriented economic reform and the open-door policy in the late 1970s, people's communes in rural China were abolished in the mid-1980s and replaced by townships and towns. With the diversification of the ownership structure and fierce competition from the nonstate sector, urban work units began to decline. Meanwhile, with the relaxation of the rigid household-registration system, rural-urban migration was allowed, and more and more peasants have made their way to the cities and towns. To reestablish its social control network, the Communist regime has begun since the mid-1980s to construct a new type of community at the grassroots level in China, especially in urban areas. This kind of community is expected to take over some functions of the old work units and to provide daily services for the residents.

IMPLICATIONS

The ideal community of communism inherits some fundamental problems, such as the tension between the democratic polity and the centralized economy and the nature of utopia. The communist communities in the former Soviet Union, Eastern Europe, and China were notorious for economic inefficiency and political coercion. The collapse of the communist regimes in the former Soviet Union and Eastern Europe in the late 1980s and the early 1990s marked a reconstruction of communities in these countries. The remnants of communist regimes in China and Vietnam have converted to the capitalism and a market economy, which is resulting in dramatic changes within these communities. All these developments imply a pessimistic future for communist communities. Nevertheless, the ideals of communism and socialism still represent the movement of human beings toward pursuing a more humane and just community.

—*Joseph Cheng and King-lun Ngok*

See also Class, Social; Collective Action; Political Economy; Rebellions and Revolutions; Social Movements

Further Reading

Heywood, A. (1994). *Political ideas and concepts: An introduction.* New York: St. Martin's.

Lenin, V. (1976). *The state and revolution.* Beijing, China: Foreign Language Press. (Originally published in 1918)

Lu, X., & Perry, E. J. (Eds.). (1997). *Danwei: The changing Chinese workplace in historical and comparative perspective.* Armonk, NY: M. E. Sharpe.

Marx, K. (1977). *Karl Marx: Selected writings* (D. McLellan, Ed.). Oxford, UK: Oxford University Press.

Selucky, R. (1979). *Marxism, socialism, freedom: Towards a general theory of labor-managed system.* London: Macmillan.

Sterba, J. P. (Ed.). (2001). *Social and political philosophy: Contemporary perspectives.* London: Routledge.

Straus, K. M. (1997). *Factory and community in Stalin's Russia: The making of an industrial working class.* Pittsburgh, PA: University of Pittsburgh Press.

Strauss, L., & Cropsy, J. (Eds.). (1987). *History of political philosophy* (3d ed.). Chicago: University of Chicago Press.

Walder, A. (1986). *Communist neo-traditionalism: Work and authority in Chinese industry,* Berkeley and Los Angeles: University of California Press.

Wang, J. C. F. (1995). *Contemporary Chinese politics: An introduction.* Englewood Cliffs, NJ: Prentice Hall.

COMMUNITARIANISM

Communitarianism is a social philosophy maintaining that society should articulate what is good—that such articulations are both needed and legitimate. Communitarianism is often contrasted with classical liberalism, a philosophical position holding that each individual should formulate the good on his or her own. Communitarians examine the ways shared conceptions of the good (or values) are formed, transmitted, justified, and enforced. Hence, their interest in communities (and moral dialogues within them), historically transmitted values and mores, and the societal units that transmit and enforce values, such as the family, schools, and voluntary associations (social clubs, churches, and so forth), which are all parts of communities.

Among early sociologists whose work is focused on communitarian issues (although they did not use the term) are Ferdinand Tönnies (1855–1936), especially his comparison of the gemeinschaft (community) and gesellschaft (association); Émile Durkheim (1858–1917), who studied the socially integrating role of values and the relations between the society and the person; and George Herbert Mead (1863–1931), who studied the self. Other early relevant sociological works are those of Robert E. Park, William Kornhauser, and Robert Nisbet.

While the term *communitarian* was coined only in the mid-nineteenth century, ideas that are communitarian in nature appear much earlier. They are found in the Old and New Testaments, Catholic theology (for example, the emphasis on the Church as community), and more recently on socialist doctrine (for example, writings about early communes and workers' solidarity) and subsidiarity—the principle that the lowest level of authority capable of addressing an issue is the one best able to handle it. In essence, moral judgments are best made at the community level rather than from the higher governing bodies.

VARIATIONS ON THE THEME OF COMMUNITARIANISM

All communitarians uphold the importance of the social realm, and in particular of community, though they differ in the extent to which their conceptions are attentive to liberty and individual rights. Early communitarians, such as Ferdinand Tönnies and Robert Nisbet, stressed the importance of closely knit social fabric and authority. Asian communitarians are especially concerned about the values of social order. They argue that to maintain social harmony, individual rights and political liberties must be curtailed. Some seek to rely heavily on the state to maintain social order (for instance, leaders and champions of the regimes in Singapore and Malaysia), and some on strong social bonds and moral culture (as Japan does). Asian communitarians also hold that the West's notion of liberty actually amounts to anarchy; that strong economic growth requires limiting freedoms; and that the West uses its idea of legal and political rights to chastise other cultures that have inherent values of their own.

In the 1980s, Charles Taylor, Michael Sandel, Michael Walzer, and Robert Bellah and his associates criticized the excessive individualism of classical liberalism as exemplified by the United States under President Ronald Reagan and Britain under Prime Minister Margaret Thatcher. In 1995, Alan Ehrenhalt's book *The Lost City: The Forgotten Virtues of Community in America* questioned the value of enhancing choice at

Democratic Communitarianism

In the excerpt below, sociologist Robert N. Bellah outlines the concept of democractic communitarianism.

I want to sketch a framework that escapes the ideological blinders of current American politics and highlights what is missing in much of our debate. As opposed to free market conservatism and welfare state liberalism, I want to describe another approach to our common problems which I will call—borrowing from Jonathan Boswell in *Community and the Economy: The Theory of Public Co-operation*—democratic communitarianism. Democratic communitarianism does not pit itself against the two reigning ideologies as a third way. It accepts the value and inevitability of both the market and the state, but it insists that the function of the market and the state is to serve us, not to dominate us. Democratic communitarianism seeks to provide a humane context within which to think about the market and the state. Its first principle is the one already enunciated in what I have said about community: it seeks to define and further the good which is the community's purpose. I want to offer four values to which democratic communitarianism is committed and which give its notion of the good somewhat more specificity:

1. Democratic communitarianism is based on the value of the sacredness of the individual, which is common to most of the great religions and philosophies of the world. (It is expressed in biblical religion through the idea that we are created in the image and likeness of God.) Anything that would oppress individuals or operate to stunt individual development would be contrary to the principles of democratic communitarianism. However, unlike its ideological rivals, democratic communitarianism does not think of individuals as existing in a vacuum or as existing in a world composed only of markets and states. Rather it believes that individuals are realized only in and through communities, and that strong, healthy, morally vigorous communities are the prerequisite for strong, healthy, morally vigorous individuals.
2. Democratic communitarianism, therefore, affirms the central value of solidarity. Solidarity points to the fact that we become who we are through our relationships; that reciprocity, loyalty, and shared commitment to the good are defining features of a fully human life.
3. Democratic communitarianism believes in what Boswell has called "complementary association." By this he means a commitment to "varied social groupings: the family, the local community, the cultural or religious group, the economic enterprise, the trade union or profession, the nation-state." Through this principle it is clear that community does not mean small-scale, all-inclusive, total groups. In our kind of society an individual will belong to many communities and ultimately the world itself can be seen as a community. Democratic communitarianism views such a multiplicity of belonging as a positive good, as potentially and in principle complementary.
4. Finally, democratic communitarianism is committed to the idea of participation as both a right and a duty. Communities become positive goods only when they provide the opportunity and support to participate in them. A corollary of this principle is the principle of subsidiarity, derived from Catholic social teaching. This idea asserts that the groups closest to a problem should attend to it, receiving support from higher level groups only if necessary. To be clear, democratic communitarianism does not adhere to Patrick Buchanan's interpretation of subsidiarity, which projects a society virtually without a state. A more legitimate understanding of subsidiarity realizes the inevitability and necessity of the state. It has the responsibility of nurturing lower-level associations wherever they are weak, as they normally are among the poor and the marginalized. Applying this perspective to current events, at a moment when powerful political forces in the United States are attempting to dismantle a weak welfare state, democratic communitarians will defend vigorous and responsible state action.

Nothing in this argument is meant to imply that face-to-face community is not a good thing. It is, and in our society it needs to be strengthened. But the argument for democratic community—rooted in the search for the common good—applies to groups of any size, and ultimately to the world as a community. It is a political argument grounded on the belief that a politics based on the summing of individual preferences is inadequate and misleading. Democratic communitarianism presumes that morality and politics cannot be separated and that moral argument, painful and difficult though it sometimes is, is fundamental to a defensible stance in today's world.

—Robert N. Bellah

Source: Bellah, Robert N. (1995/1996, Winter). "Community Properly Understood: A Defense of 'Democratic Communitarianism.'" *The Responsive Community*, *6*(1). Retrieved March 5, 2003, from http://www.gwu.edu/~icps/bellah.html.

the expense of maintaining community and authority. In his book *Bowling Alone* (2000), Robert Putnam identified what he deemed "social capital"—the element of communities that forms affective bonds among people—and stressed the importance of "bridging social capital," in which bonds of connectedness are formed across diverse social groups.

In response to the breakdown in the moral fabric of society engendered by excessive individualism, Amitai Etzioni and William A. Galston began to organize working meetings to think through communitarian approaches to key societal issues. They, along with Mary Ann Glendon, Jean Bethke Elshtain, and other figures from academia and politics, issued a platform endorsed by a wide range of leading Americans. Deeming themselves "responsive communitarians" in order to distinguish the movement from East Asian, authoritarian communitarians, Etzioni formed the Communitarian Network to study and promote communitarian approaches to social issues and began publishing a quarterly journal, *The Responsive Community.* The new communitarian movement has been credited with having influenced public leaders and elected officials of various persuasions in a number of Western countries.

CONCERNS OF COMMUNITARIANS

Communitarians also pay much attention to the relationship between the self and the community. Political theorists depict the self as "embedded," which implies that the self is constrained by the community. Responsive communitarians stress that individuals who are well-integrated into communities are better able to reason and act in responsible ways than isolated individuals, but add that if social pressure to conform rises to high levels, it will undermine the individual self.

Communitarians pay special attention to social institutions, several of which form the moral infrastructure of society: families, schools, communities, and the community of communities. Infants are born into families, whose societal role is to introduce values and begin the development of the moral self. Schools' role is to further develop the moral self and to remedy moral development if it was neglected or distorted by the family.

DEFINING COMMUNITY

Several critics have argued that the concept of community is of questionable value because it is so ill-defined. In *The Myth of Community Studies,* edited by Colin Bell and Howard Newby, Margaret Stacey argues that the solution to this problem is to avoid the term altogether. Bell and Newby argue, "There has never been a theory of community, nor even a satisfactory definition of what community is" (Bell & Newby 1974, p. xliii). In another text, Bell and Newby write, "But what is community? . . . [I]t will be seen that over ninety definitions of community have been analyzed and that the one common element in them all was man!" (Bell & Newby 1973, p. 15).

Amitai Etzioni argued that community can be defined with reasonable precision. Community has two characteristics: first, a web of affect-laden relationships among a group of individuals, relationships that often crisscross and reinforce one another (as opposed to one-on-one or chain-like individual relationships); and second, a measure of commitment to a set of shared values, norms, and meanings, and a shared history and identity—in short, a particular culture. David E. Pearson stated, "To earn the appellation 'community,' it seems to me, groups must be able to exert moral suasion and extract a measure of compliance from their members. That is, communities are necessarily, indeed, by definition, coercive as well as moral, threatening their members with the stick of sanctions if they stray, offering them the carrot of certainty and stability if they don't" (Pearson 1995, p. 47).

CRITICIZING AND DEFENDING THE CONCEPT OF COMMUNITY

Critics also suggested that those who long for community ignore the darker side of traditional communities. "In the new communitarian appeal to tradition, communities of 'mutual aid and memory,' and the Founders," writes Linda McClain in "Rights and Irresponsibility" in the *Duke Law Journal,* "there is a problematic inattention to the less attractive, unjust features of tradition" (McClain 1994, p. 1029).

Communities, critics write, use their moral voice to oppress people, are authoritarian by nature, and push people to conform. According to Will Kymlicka, this oppression can entail the community prescribing roles of subordination, roles that limit people's individual potential and threaten their psychological well-being (Kymlicka 1993, pp. 208–221). Derek Phillips adds:

> In their celebration of the ecstasy of belonging, communitarian writers exhibit a frightening forgetfulness about the past. They fail to acknowledge that the quest for community often involves domination for some and subordina-

> tion for others. In attacking post-Enlightenment liberalism and the politics of rights, communitarian theorists threaten to rob individuals of their most basic protections against abuses of power. In emphasizing the importance of community for people's everyday lives, communitarians fail to see that it is attachment rather than membership that is a general human value. (Phillips 1993, p. 195)

Amy Gutmann pointedly remarks that communitarians "want us to live in Salem" (Gutmann 1985, p. 319), a community of strong shared values that went so far as to accuse nonconformist members of witchcraft during the seventeenth century.

Communitarians counter that behind many of these criticisms lies an image of old, or total, communities, which are neither typical of modern society nor necessary for, or even compatible with, a communitarian society. Old communities (traditional villages) were geographically bounded and the only communities of which people were members. In effect, other than escaping into no-man's-land, often bandit territories, individuals had few opportunities for choosing their social attachments. In short, old communities had monopolistic power over their members.

New communities are often limited in scope and reach. Members of one residential community are often also members of other communities—for example work, ethnic, or religious ones. As a result, community members have multiple sources of attachments, and if one threatens to become overwhelming, individuals will tend to pull back and turn to another community for their attachments. Thus, for example, if a person finds herself under high moral pressure at work to contribute to the United Way, to give blood, or to serve at a soup kitchen for the homeless, and these are lines of action she is not keen to follow, she may end up investing more of her energy in other communities—her writers' group, for instance, or her church. If a person who has recently been divorced is under severe censure by his church community, on the other hand, he may well take on extra hours at work. This multi-community membership protects the individuals from both moral oppression and ostracism. However, incongruity between the values of a person's multiple communities may substantially weaken the moral voice; thus the importance of the next-level moral community.

In short, the moral voice is most powerful when people are members of only one community, but it can be overwhelming in such cases. It is more moderated when individuals are members of several communities, but it still may suffice to undergird a good part of the social order, as long as the various communities share at least some core values.

For the same reason it is a valid criticism to argue that a total and monolithic community can drive people to conformism, if this means that such a community will push people to sacrifice large parts of their individual differences in order to follow shared values. But total communities are rare in contemporary societies, while multi-community attachments are much more common. To worry, in this context, about traditionalism is like worrying about the effects of excessive savings in an economy long plagued by debts and deficits and rather reluctant to mend its ways.

Another facet of the same basic criticism is the charge that communities are authoritarian. Derek Phillips, for instance, remarks, "[C]ommunitarian thinking . . . obliterates individual autonomy entirely and dissolves the self into whatever roles are imposed by one's position in society" (Phillips 1993, p. 183). As the political scientist Robert Booth Fowler puts it, critics "see talk of community as interfering with the necessary breaking down of dominant forces and cultures" (Fowler 1991, p. 142). Some critics mean by this that communities are totalistic, a point already covered. Others mean that they are dominated by power elites or have one group that forces others to abide by the values of those in power.

Communitarians find that this criticism has merit, but it is misdirected. There are communities both past and present that have been or are authoritarian. The medieval phrase *Stadt luft macht frei* ("the air of the cities frees") captures what the farmers of traditional villages must have felt when they first moved into cities at the beginning of the industrial era. (Poor working conditions and slums aside, being away from the stricter social codes of their families and villages seems to have given them a sense of freedom, which in some cases led to anarchic behavior.) Totalitarian communities exist in contemporary societies, such as in North Korea. However, most contemporary communities, especially in communitarian societies, are not authoritarian even when they are defined by geography. Also the relative ease of mobility means that people often choose which community to join and within which to live. Agnostics will not move into a Hasidic community in Brooklyn, and prejudiced whites will not move into a neighborhood dominated by the Nation of Islam.

Dominance by power elites and other forms of authoritarianism are not basic or inherent features of community, but reflections of the way it can be distorted. To be fully or even highly communitarian, communities require authentic commitment of most—if not all—of their members to a set of core values. To attain such a commitment, the values that are being fostered need to be truly accepted by the members and responsive to their underlying needs. If some members of the society are excluded from the moral dialogue, or are manipulated into abiding by the moral voice, or if their true needs are ignored, they will eventually react to the community's lack of responsiveness in an antisocial manner. In short, communities can be distorted by those in power, but then their moral order will be diminished, and they will either have to become more responsive to their members' true needs or transform into some other, noncommunitarian, social pattern.

Still other critics have accused communitarians not merely of overlooking the less attractive features of traditional communities, but of willfully longing to revive these features. According to Michael Taves, the communitarian vision concerns itself mostly with "reclaiming a reliance on traditional values and all that entails with regard to the family, sexual relations, religion and the rejection of secularism" (Taves 1988, pp. 7–8). According to Judith Stacey, "centrists" and communitarians have enough in common with former U.S. Vice President Dan Quayle to make people on the left uncomfortable (Stacey 1994, pp. 119–22).

Early communitarians might be charged with being, in effect, social conservatives, if not authoritarians. However, many contemporary communitarians, especially those who define themselves as responsive communitarians, fully realize and often stress that they do *not* seek to return to traditional communities, with their authoritarian power structure, rigid stratification, and discriminatory practices against minorities and women. Responsive communitarians seek to build communities based on open participation, dialogue, and truly shared values. Linda McClain, a fair critic of communitarians, recognizes this feature of the responsive communitarians, writing that some communitarians do "recognize the need for careful evaluation of what was good and bad about [any specific] tradition and the possibility of severing certain features . . . from others" (McClain 1994, p. 1030). And R. Bruce Douglass writes, "Unlike conservatives, communitarians are aware that the days when the issues we face as a society could be settled on the basis of the beliefs of a privileged segment of the population have long since passed" (Douglass 1994, p. 55).

Finally, communitarians have noted that communities need to be embedded socially and morally in more encompassing entities if violent conflict among them is to be avoided. Society should not be viewed as composed of millions of individuals, but as pluralism (of communities) within unity (the society). The existence of subcultures does not undermine societal unity as long as there is a core of shared values and institutions.

—Amitai Etzioni

See also LIBERALISM; LIBERTARIANISM

Further Reading

Bell, C., & Newby, H. (1973). *Community studies: An introduction to the sociology of the local community.* New York: Praeger.

Bell, C., & Newby, H. (1974). *The sociology of community: A selection of readings.* London: Frank Cass.

Douglass, R. (1994). The renewal of democracy and the communitarian prospect. *Responsive Community, 4*(3), 55–62.

Fowler, R. B. (1991). *The dance with community.* Lawrence: University Press of Kansas.

Gutmann, A. (1985). Communitarian critics of liberalism. *Philosophy and Public Affairs, 14*(3), 308–322.

Kymlicka, W. (1993). Appendix I: Some questions about justice and community. In D. Bell (Ed.), *Communitarianism and its critics.* Oxford, UK: Clarendon.

McClain, L. C. (1994, March). Rights and irresponsibility. *Duke Law Journal, 43,* 989–1088.

Pearson, D. E. (1995). Community and sociology. *Society, 32*(5), 44–50.

Phillips, D. L. (1993). *Looking backward: A critical appraisal of communitarian thought.* Princeton, NJ: Princeton University Press.

Putnam, R. (2000). *Bowling alone: The collapse and revival of community in America.* New York: Simon & Schuster.

Stacey, J. (1994, July 25). The new family values crusaders. *Nation, 259*(4), 119–22.

Taves, M. (1988). Roundtable on communitarianism. *Telos, 76,* 7–8.

COMMUNITIES OF OPPOSITION

In every society and every social order, in every recorded epoch, a small but determined number of individuals have been dedicated to effecting social change. Given time and opportunity, these individuals seek out others of like mind, and, in the exchange of oppositional ideas, hopes, and dreams, communities of opposition—defined here as collectivities characterized by a shared ideology or theology, a sense of common destiny, and a commonly held dream for a future historical or posthistorical global order—emerge to challenge the existing temporal powers. The forms in which these communities of opposition emerge depend on historical circumstances. Most communities of resistance peacefully await a change, which they believe will be accomplished by a just God, or they withdraw into enclaves to create an ideal society. This entry, however, focuses on another type of oppositional community: revolutionary communal groups in the ancient, medieval, and modern worlds, with case studies drawn from Jewish, Christian, and Islamic societies.

EARLY REVOLUTIONARY COMMUNAL GROUPS

The most volatile oppositional communities are those characterized by a revolutionary ethos that sees the violent destruction of the existing social or political order, or both, as necessary for the emergence of a new and better world. Historically, these groups were religious in nature, and their goals were ultimately eschatological (concerned with the final events in world history); their dream was millenarian (as when Jesus Christ returns to rule for a thousand years) or messianic; and the new world they envisioned was promised in sacred text. Some of these communities tried, to the greatest degree possible, to withdraw from mainstream society. Others were driven from their societies and forced to form communal groups to survive. Most of these groups were destroyed in unequal battle with the dominant culture; a few evolved into more accommodating forms and survive to this day; even fewer triumphed, only to disband when their eschatological hopes were frustrated.

The Zealots

One of the first recorded revolutionary communal movements was that of the Zealots and the Sicarii (Greek *sikarioi,* "dagger men"), probably a radical branch of the Zealots, formed in the first century CE. One of Jesus' disciples, Simon, is identified in the Bible as a Zealot (Matthew 10:4; Mark 3:18; Luke 6:15; Acts 1:13).

The active phase of the Sicariri, named for the kind of knives that became their trademark weapon, lasted only twenty-five years, and the acute phase of Zealot activity not much longer. The Zealots arose at a time of intense eschatological excitement among the Jews, who felt for a variety of sociopolitical reasons that an imminent messianic event was about to occur. Messianic pretenders were everywhere in those years, and apocalyptic sects flourished.

For both the Zealots and the Sicarii, the aims of rebellion seem to have been religious, perhaps inspired by the Maccabean revolt (142–63 BCE) and the example of Phinehas (Num. 25). The Sicarii employed assassination as their trademark tactic, beginning with the Jewish High Priest Jonathan, and then settling on random targets of opportunity to spread terror among the populace. Soon enough, massacre was added to assassination, and the Sicarii victimized non-Jewish communities and even Jewish groups who advocated peaceful accommodation with Rome.

As their numbers grew, the Zealots grew bolder and began to oppose the Roman legions. Then the Romans added reinforcements to Jerusalem until they outnumbered the Jews, the Zealots transformed themselves into a revolutionary communal group, and in 66 CE, the Zealots led a general Jewish uprising against the Romans. In 70 CE, the Romans conquered Jerusalem, looting and destroying the Temple, crucifying many Jews, and carrying many others off to Rome as slaves. At the start of the revolt, some Zealots had seized the mountain fortress of Masada, on the shore of the Dead Sea, and after Jerusalem fell, other Jews fled to Masada to resist to the end. Masada was an ideal site for a fortress, situated as it was atop a bluff with very steep sides, and here the Zealots withstood a siege of almost two years by the Romans. Fifteen thousand strong, the Romans opposed fewer than one thousand Jews, some of whom were women and children. The Romans built a ramp up which their soldiers scrambled; the Zealots, however, chose to die rather than submit to Rome, and when in 73 CE the Romans breached the fortification wall, they found that the Zealots had committed suicide by jumping off the bluff. Two Zealot women and five children, hidden in a water conduit, lived to tell the tale. After this first recorded instance of religiously inspired mass suicide, the Jewish presence in the Holy Land was severely diminished, and the Jewish Diaspora (Greek "dispersion," begun when King Nebuchadrezzar II of Babylon conquered Jerusalem in 597 BCE and again in 586 BCE and sent many Jewish prisoners to Babylon) widened.

The Nizari Ismaili Shi'a

If the Zealots and Sicarii had been forced by unfavorable circumstances to form a revolutionary communal movement, the Nizari Ismaili Shi'a purposely withdrew in 765 CE to the periphery of the fading Abbasid empire (749/750–1258) to form a community where they could practice their form of Shi'ism (they recognized Ismail as the sixth imam or spiritual successor to Muhammad and Ismael's son Muhammad as the seventh and last Shi'ite imam, who would return as the mahdi or redeemer when the world ended). Ismailite beliefs as developed in the eighth and ninth centuries were centered on a hierarchy of wisdom headed by the imam and spread by missionaries.

As a result of a schism in the sect in 1094, the Ismailites of Iran and Syria accepted Nizar, older son of the Fatimid caliph of Egypt, and rejected the Egyptian Ismailites who recognized another son. In 1090, the Nizari group, led by Hasan-e Sabbah (d. 1124), established fortresses in the mountains of Iran and Syria, particularly at Castle Alamut in northern Persia; Hasan sent forth the *fedayeen* (dedicated ones), popularly known as the Assassins, to "purify" Islam by making terrorism a religious duty for selected sect members.

Like the Zealots and the Sicarii, the Nizari were convinced that Allah was about to send a redeemer to lead the faithful. Their lives were puritanical, and their social organization almost monastic. They preached clandestinely in urban centers and built a remarkably strong network of support that lasted almost fifty years, before the movement's own violence and the steps taken by the empires to eliminate all centers of Nizari support wiped out these cells. The Ismailis wanted to free Islam of corruption and compromise, sweep away the Islamic polities and their *ulama* (bodies of mullahs, religious leaders who supported and were supported by corrupt governments), and replace these with a single Islamic *ummah* (community), to bring peace and happiness to the Islamic realm, albeit after a reign of terror.

The revolutionary communal experiment founded by the Nizari Shi'a flourished for almost fifty years, until the Mongol invasions of the thirteenth century displaced them. Their descendants survive to this day, however, albeit in a quietist form, holding true to their Sevener Shi'ite beliefs.

The Taborites

The best documented premodern revolutionary communal group was surely the Taborites—a movement that, at the end of the fourteenth century withdrew from Prague and other Bohemian cities to create five settlements, each named Tabor. The Taborites were a radical offshoot of the reformist Hussites, followers of the Czech theologian and university professor Jan Hus. When Hus was burned at the Council of Constance in 1415, his followers responded with the Defenestration of Prague in 1419 in which the king's councilors were thrown from the window of the council chamber and impaled on pikes. Shortly thereafter, the Taborites withdrew to the South, naming their five redoubts Tabor after a passage of the Hebrew Bible (Jeremiah 46:18): "As surely as I live, declares the King, whose name is the LORD Almighty, one will come who is like Tabor among the mountains, like Carmel by the sea."

From the beginning, the Taborite experiment resonated with millenarian expectation. Reports of Jesus being seen and of Jesus' presence on earth abounded. In preparation for his coming, the Taborites sought to live according to their ideals—in this case, the example of the primitive Church as they imagined it. Based on a passage in Acts (2:44), the Taborites adopted a communalism where all possessions were held in common. In this spirit, they proclaimed in 1420:

> Henceforth, at Hradist and Tabor there is nothing which is mine or thine. Rather, all things in the community shall be held in common for all time and no one is permitted to hold private property. The one who does commits sins mortally. . . . No longer shall there be a reigning king or a ruling lord; for there shall be servitude no longer. All taxes and exactions shall cease and no one shall compel another to subjection. All shall be equal as brothers and sisters. (Taborite articles, 1420)

Education was universal, with even girls being sent for the first time to school. Indeed, when a Cardinal Pius Anneas, who later became Pope Pius II, visited the Taborite cities after successive waves of crusaders had been defeated by Taborite arms, he wrote that Christendom should be ashamed, for he found even young schoolgirls in Tabor could converse more learnedly on scripture than could most parish clergy.

Once established, the Taborites vowed to set forth from Tabor to kill the nobility and the priests—a threat Christendom could hardly ignore. Thus, over the course of Tabor's existence, no less than five great pan-European crusading armies moved against Tabor between 1419–1437, and each time the Taborites crushed the invaders. Indeed, in the 1437 crusade, so great was the reputation of the Taborites for fanatical fighting that crusaders had only to hear the Taborites battle song, "Ye Warriors of God," before fleeing without even seeing the enemy.

Ultimately however, Taborite ideals fell by the wayside, and with the offer of a doctrinal compromise by the Church, the Taborites began to filter back to the their homes, leaving a remnant of true believers who would ultimately be crushed at the Battle of Lipany in

1434. This most successful recorded example of revolutionary communalism faded into popular memory, until it was revived in polemical form by the post-1948 Communist governments of Czechoslovakia, which found in Tabor's communal experiment the roots of their own tenuous claims to legitimacy.

MODERN REVOLUTIONARY COMMUNAL GROUPS

Modern instances of revolutionary communalism bear many resemblances to the early cases just recounted. Changing times, however, had a significant impact on the opportunities available to, and ultimate fate of, these groups, particularly when confronting the primacy and power of the modern state. Because technological and bureaucratic changes have made the reach of state power far broader than had been the case earlier, a hinterland to which a revolutionary communal movement can retreat has become difficult to find in Europe, dangerous to seek in the contemporary Middle East, and difficult although hardly impossible to find in North America.

The Israeli Settlement Movement

One of the most successful revolutionary communal movements in recent years may be the Israeli settlement movement as originally spearheaded by Gush Emunim (the Bloc of the Faithful). The 1967 Arab-Israeli War, which ended in the defeat of the Arab combatant states in only six days, brought East Jerusalem and the West Bank under Israeli control and opened these areas to Jewish settlement. Beginning with the "settlement" of the Park Hotel in Hebron (in 1968), Gush Emunim and others allied with the settlement movement soon created numerous, often illegal, settlements throughout the Occupied Territories. Sometimes the settlements occurred with tacit government backing, and at other times they did not (as when the Israeli army destroyed numerous small, largely uninhabited illegal settlements in 2002). With the election of Menachem Begin and the Likud Party to power in 1977, however, settlement became an enduring facet of Israeli political life.

Communal life in the settlements varies considerably, but the primary Gush Emunim strongholds such as Kiryat Arba in Hebron emphasize Torah and land. Army service is accepted, and political parties such as the National Religious Party have among their number members of the Knesset (Israeli legislative body). Nevertheless, despite its tenuous inroads into the Israeli political mainstream, the movement remains revolutionary to the core. Its goals are messianic, its actions are militant, and the group aims at nothing less than acquiring the "full biblical patrimony" promised by God to the Jewish people. The fulfillment of this revolutionary mission is held to be the key to instigating a messianic process that will fully redeem the Jewish people.

In recent years, as the 1960s-era core activists of Gush Emunim have aged and at least some have mellowed, more radical groupings have arisen to carry further the flag of revolutionary communal settlement. Grouped under the Yesha Council, and with a radical youth branch known as the Hilltop Youth, who do not hesitate to fight the Israeli army or to beat settlement rabbis whom they deem too accommodating, the settlement movement remains very much alive amid vastly increased Palestinian resistance operations aimed at ending the occupation of their land.

The Shukri Mustafa Islamic Communal Group

In the 1970s, a bewildering series of Islamist groups and movements arose to fill the gap left by the virtual destruction of the Muslim Brotherhood as an effective force in Egyptian life. These small, highly volatile groups were characterized by a diverse set of leaders and sometimes by idiosyncratic approaches to Islamic law (*shari'a*). What unites them is a tactical approach centered on the practice of *takfir* (roughly, "excommunication"), in which the groups decide who is a true Muslim and target those whom they think to be outside the Islamic fold. Scholars therefore refer to these groups in aggregate as *takfir* movements. One of them, designed as a revolutionary communal movement, was formed by Shukri Mustafa as the Society of Muslims.

Mustafa, an agricultural student in Asyut, Egypt, was imprisoned for his Islamist activities but afterward returned to his studies while working out a new Islamist ideology. He believed that Egypt was irredeemable, and thus in the present situation true Muslims could only separate. His model was the hegira, the flight of the prophet Muhammad from Mecca to Medina in 619 until the forces of Islam were strong enough to return and conquer.

Mustafa gathered as many as 2,000 followers in the early 1970s; they formed separatist enclaves in Egypt, as well as throughout the Arab world, and branches of the society appeared in Kuwait, Jordan, and Syria, under the control of local prayer leaders. The society began to turn into a religious cult; all relationships, including marriage, could be conducted only within the group, never with outsiders. The society's main constituency were young lower-middle-class males, with secular rather than religious educational backgrounds.

Like most cults, the group was volatile and deeply suspicious of the outside world. When the Egyptian Ministry of Waqf (Islamic Endowments) issued a pamphlet denouncing the group's practices as in error, the group reacted by kidnapping and killing the person in the ministry it deemed responsible for the pamphlet. The government responded with an overwhelming show of force, arresting 600 of the group's members and killing the leadership, including Mustafa. The remnants of the society joined other, even more violent, *takfir* movements.

The Covenant, Sword, and Arm of the Lord

The Covenant, Sword, and Arm of the Lord (CSA) was an American example of a revolutionary communal group of the 1980s. The CSA was founded in 1971 under the leadership of James Ellison and Kerry Noble in a rural redoubt that hugged the border between Missouri and Arkansas, which the biblically minded founders dubbed Zarephath-Horeb. Intended as a final refuge for the Christian faithful in the oncoming apocalypse, the CSA came to fill the role of elite armorer and training ground for the most militant members of the American radical right.

Throughout the 1970s, James Ellison was a charismatic, if highly divisive, figure on the U.S. right-wing scene. He attended and addressed numerous movement gatherings, including the Aryan Nations' annual meeting in Idaho and the Christian Patriots Defense League Freedom Festivals in upstate Illinois. As a result of these appearances and of the CSA's publications, a small but steady stream of residents made their way to the Zarephath-Horeb property, often living in trailers or sharing quarters until a more permanent solution to the housing problem was found. To the frustration of the founders, who saw the CSA as a community run along military lines in preparation for the horrors of the last days, many of those attracted to the CSA's various seminars and training sessions, as well as to the community itself, were more than sixty years old and more fit for retirement than for military service. Despite these problems, the population at Zarephath-Horeb reached almost 200 at its peak.

In 1981, the CSA published a fifteen-point statement of beliefs, along with a "Declaration of Non-Surrender," in the 1981 edition of the *CSA Journal.* CSA's rhetoric became increasingly revolutionary in the early 1980s, and its side business of gunsmithing for the movement's firebrands boomed. The CSA boldly stated in its "Declaration of Non-Surrender" that it would "refuse any treaty, pact or declaration of surrender" with the hated "Babylon" government of the United States.

Beneath the surface, however, all was not well at the CSA. Disaffected adherents began to filter out of Zarephath-Horeb with lurid stories of sexual improprieties and fraudulent dealings with members' property and finances. Ellison in particular was charged with interpreting scripture to suit his whims and with forming a cult of personality, and the group was charged with such un-Christian activities as shoplifting in local stores. The charges were taken seriously by the Christian Identity community, where Ellison's constant battles with rival leaders and his polygamous lifestyle had already brought considerable suspicion. Moreover, some among the CSA faithful took Ellison's violent rhetoric more seriously than did the leader himself. A few, notably Richard Wayne Snell, became notorious in their own right for crimes up to and including murder (a charge for which Snell was executed on the very day of the Oklahoma City bombing, April 19, 1995).

As Ellison and the CSA leadership struggled to defend themselves in movement circles from the swirl of charges and countercharges, more serious problems loomed on the horizon. By 1984, the federal government began a series of prosecutions of the CSA membership, culminating in the seizure of the property itself. Ellison, Noble, and the CSA hard core, in keeping with the Declaration of Non-Surrender, vowed to defend the compound to the death. Given the large cache of armaments and supplies at their disposal, the threat was not taken lightly by the government, and in April 1985 the compound was surrounded and besieged with a force of some 300 Federal Bureau of Investigation (FBI) agents. After an initial show of bravado, Ellison meekly surrendered without a shot being fired. Some residents were allowed to remain on the property after the FBI arrests of the leadership, but the faithful soon dwindled to fewer than thirty. With the news that Ellison had betrayed the movement and would testify for the government at the 1987 Fort Smith, Arkansas, sedition trial, the dying embers of the once powerful CSA flickered and died.

FUTURE MOVEMENTS

It is clear that communities of opposition have been with us for millennia, and there is no indication that they will disappear any time soon. This, however, should not suggest that future communities of opposition will follow the model of the earlier communities detailed in this entry. Rather, as the Internet becomes more and more a part of our lives, and as wildly disparate causes and belief systems converge over issues of mutual concern—such as the diffuse antiglobalization movement and worldwide antiwar activities—the formation of "virtual" communities of opposition appears to be the direction of the future. Here, rather than intentional communities of like-minded believers, virtual communities will be formed with little or no regard to geographic proximity, and will appear, as if from nowhere, for actions or demonstrations in support of causes around whose "flag" a wildly diverse group of true believers can, at least for moment, come together.

—Jeffrey Kaplan

See also Intentional Communities in Israel—History; Islam

Further Reading

Gideon A. (1991). Jewish Zionist fundamentalism: The bloc of the faithful In Israel (Gush Emunim). In M. E. Marty & R. S. Appleby (Eds.), *Fundamentalism observed* (pp. 265–344). Chicago: University of Chicago Press.

Kaminsky, H. (1967). *A history of the Hussite revolution.* Berkeley and Los Angeles: University of California Press.

Kaplan, J. (1997). *Radical religion in America: Millenarian movements from the far right to the children of Noah.* Syracuse, NY: Syracuse University Press.

Kaplan, J. (2000). *Encyclopedia of white power: A sourcebook on the radical racist right.* Walnut Creek, CA: AltaMira.

Kaplan, J., & Lööw, H. (2002). *The cultic milieu: Oppositional subcultures in the age of globalization.* Walnut Creek, CA: AltaMira.

Lewis, B. (1968). *The assassins: A radical sect in Islam.* New York: Basic Books.

Noble, K. (1998). *Why they bombed Oklahoma City.* Prescott, Canada: Voyageur.

Rapoport, D. C. (1984, September). Fear and trembling: Terrorism in three religious traditions. *American Political Science Review, 78,* 658–677.

Sivan, E. (1985). *Radical Islam: Medieval theology and modern politics.* New Haven, CT: Yale University Press.

Sivan, E. (1994). Enclave culture. In M. E. Marty & R. S. Appleby (Eds.), *Accounting for fundamentalisms: The dynamic character of movements* (pp. 11–16). Chicago: University of Chicago Press.

Sprinzak, E. (1999). *Brother against brother: Violence and extremism in Israeli politics from Altalena to the Rabin assassination.* New York: Free Press.

COMMUNITIES OF PRACTICE

In the 1990s, the idea of a "community of practice" gained the interest of a surprising range of fields—from abstruse social theory to highly pragmatic business consulting. To some, it presented itself as an austere analytic concept. To others, it appealed through what Raymond Williams called the "warmly persuasive" attractiveness of *community,* which meant that the more complex notion of practice was often set aside. The concept has undoubtedly provoked some useful studies. Nevertheless, it remains to be seen whether its analytic usefulness is strong enough to resist the fate of most terms taken up by business consulting, which is to fade with the passing of fashion.

A THEORY OF LEARNING

The idea rose to prominence with the publication in 1991 of *Situated Learning: Legitimate Peripheral Participation,* by Jean Lave and Etienne Wenger. There were earlier uses, in particular in the work of Edward Constant, but most people rightly credit the work of Lave and Wenger as the root from which the majority of later uses grew. The concept reflects their shared interest in learning. Lave, an anthropologist, had previously challenged standard "cognitivist" accounts of how people learn, which portray learning as an event that goes on in the heads of individual humans as they absorb information. That view had proved remarkably influential among computer scientists, who tend to look at humans learning as if they were simply another type of computer processing information. Lave's resistance to this view appealed to Wenger, who, though a computer scientist himself, had questioned in his first book computational tutoring systems and the superficial, information-processing ideas of learning that lay behind most of them.

Together, Lave and Wenger propose a theory of learning that, in contrast to cognitivist and computational accounts, acknowledges its "situated" and social character. In claiming it is situated, Lave and Wenger mean that learning must be understood in the context of ongoing activity and social relations. We learn as part of everyday life. Looking, as many studies do, at individuals taken out of the ordinary situations of everyday life (and put, for example, into classrooms as so often happens in workplace training) inevitably distorts our understanding of learning. Further, Lave and Wenger insist, learning is not the acquisition of information or decontextualized knowledge. Rather, it is the development of a social identity and with it the skills that are part of that identity. Learning, they conclude, "is an integral and inseparable aspect of social practice." Leaning heavily on ideas of apprenticeship, Lave and Wenger suggest that learning takes place through the process of "legitimate, peripheral participation" in ongoing practice. People learn, that is, by being allowed to take part in an ongoing activity, beginning on its outskirts (both social and physical) and, as skills develop, participating to an increasingly greater degree.

Practice in this argument is not rote exercise, such as repeatedly playing piano scales or reciting irregular French verbs. (That is the sort of educational activity they were arguing against.) Rather, Lave and Wenger use practice in the way people do when they talk of "medical practice" or "legal practice." Increasing participation in this kind of practice brings with it the identity that other, established practitioners share. You become a lawyer not by learning about the law, but by starting to practice law itself and, as your skills grow, participating more fully with other practitioners of the law.

The community of practice is, then, the group of practitioners with whom learners must engage and in whose activities they must be able to participate in order to learn. Learning is, ultimately, the process of becoming (and becoming recognized as) a member of such a community. As such, learning involves much more than acquiring the explicit knowledge associated with a particular practice. It also requires developing the tacit understanding, inherent judgment, and shared identity that come with participation.

TENSIONS

Some have found this community-centered notion particularly comforting. Others, however, have accused it of overromanticizing relations of apprenticeship, which historically have often been thoroughly nasty. But Lave and Wenger never suggest that the community of practice was the cozy social group that many assume. Rather, they point to important tensions that emerge out of the central relationship between newcomers and oldtimers, which they describe in terms of "continuity and displacement." Communities of practice are distinguished by their ability to reproduce themselves over time through the ongoing interactions of their members. Both newcomers and oldtimers have an interest in the reproduction and so in the continuity of the community, but their perspectives are profoundly different. To oldtimers, a newcomer represents not only the future of the community but also a threat to individual oldtimers, who must ultimately be displaced for the community to survive. Similarly, newcomers see oldtimers as the means to gaining membership, expertise, and recognition, but also as a roadblock on the path to seniority. Further, oldtimers often want newcomers simply to reproduce existing community practices, whereas newcomers tend to want to transform these. Finally, oldtimers often seek to exploit the newcomers, whose need for acceptance and access make them vulnerable. Hence communities of practice are driven by fundamental tensions, tensions that give them their dynamism. (These aspects of the concept are usually missing from its more bland uses, which treat the notion as little more than another term for a transient group of coworkers.)

EXAMPLES

Empirical examples in the second half of of *Situated Learning* help leaven the austere theoretical argument presented in the first half. Lave and Wenger present studies of midwives, tailors, quartermasters, butchers, and intriguingly reforming alcoholics to show the reproduction of such expertise in social communities and to explore the related notions of situated learning, legitimate peripheral participation, and communities of practice. The examples all show how skill, practice, and identity are both manifest in and acquired from collective, situated activities of everyday life.

While such examples help clarify the concepts, they also invite the obvious criticism that this account of learning is applicable only to the "manual" skills usually associated with apprenticeship. In fact, the book rejects the conventional distinction between "mental" and "manual" labor, but in this regard the chosen examples do the richness of the concept a disservice. It would have helped to point out that even what is seen as highly "cerebral" learning—in, for example, medicine, law, or the upper reaches of any academic profession—concludes with a form of "on the job" training that is essential to understanding the practice. Comparisons between apprentices and graduate students can be traced back at least to Adam Smith's *Wealth of Nations* (1776). A later book edited by Lave and Chaiklen, *Understanding Practice,* includes accounts of psychotherapists, computer scientists, and primary medical care professionals that show that the argument is not as restricted as the examples in *Situated Learning* might suggest.

Other critics have complained that the scope of the concept is unclear. Is, for example, the community of practice that an aspiring butcher or lawyer might hope to enter a small, local community whose members a newcomer might reasonably encounter in the process of becoming a member? Or is it the extended community of all butchers or lawyers, the vast majority of whom the newcomer will never meet? Others have complained that the relationship between the community of practice and other social entities (institutions, organizations, or social classes, for example) is unclear. And yet others, that the argument tends to ignore the way individuals develop their identities around numerous practices, not all of which can be traced to a single, well-defined community and in few of which they actually become participants. (In his later book, *Communities of Practice,* Wenger addresses some of these issues by discussing "identities of non-participation" and relations of "imagination" and "alignment" as well as of participation.) Despite these criticisms, the core ideas launched by Lave and Wenger have proved both attractive and powerful in a variety of fields, from the more obvious ones, such as education and workplace training, to less obvious ones, such as artificial intelligence, information studies, social and hermeneutic psychology, social studies of technology and knowledge, activity theory, and linguistics.

INFLUENCE

It has probably been in the first two fields that the term has had most influence. Though these may seem "obvious," Lave and Wenger did little to court either directly. They sought to draw attention away from education (where most discussions of learning took place) toward learning itself, which they suggest was too often reduced to little more than a pale reflection of teaching. Legitimate peripheral participation in communities of practice, they insist, is an analytical concept, though many in the world of education still read it as simply one among many ways to learn. And though they discuss learning in the context of organizations (the butchers in relation to the supermarkets they worked for and the navigators in relation to the navy), Lave and Wenger have relatively little to say about these organizations themselves and their relations to communities of practice. Rather, organizations appear principally as éminences grises, whose main contribution seems to be to undermine what might otherwise have been a thoroughly organic process. (Indeed, though organizational learning features centrally in his more recent work, Wenger set it aside within a single footnote in *Communities of Practice* [1998].)

So for the most part, others built the bridges between the theory and these fields. Brown and Duguid, formerly colleagues of Lave and Wenger, introduced the notions to the fields of education and organizational learning, and later work by Cook and Yanow and more recently Tuomi helped further refine its usefulness there. Indeed, the concept has proved particularly attractive to organization theorists, giving new life to what one sociologist has called one of the "oldest distinctions in the literature" (Granovetter 1985, p. 502), that between the formal and the informal organization. Brown and Duguid suggest that organizational learning and knowledge can be traced neither to individuals alone, nor to an organization as a whole, but to the communities of practice that lie within it. And these communities of practice do not reflect the organizational chart. They emerge spontaneously and interstitially around ongoing organizational practices, ignoring prescribed boundaries and standard divisions, particularly those between mental and manual workers, between people paid to think and people more or less paid not to. With organizational knowledge so diffuse, it becomes clear why, as the head of Hewlett-Packard is said to have lamented in bewilderment, an organization often does not know what it knows. As it has helped explain this paradox, the notion of a community of practice has frequently been part of discussions of organizational knowledge and innovation, which became important topics for organizational theory in the late 1990s.

Entering one door of business schools in the hands of organizational theorists, the term went out another in the hands of business consultants. Inevitably the latter tried to simplify this view of organizations as a combination of formal, canonical units and interstitial, noncanonical communities of practice. Some have suggested that the organization as a whole can be defined as a community of practice, thus often replicating in community-of-practice terms much of the banal work done on organizational culture. Somehow, it is assumed, CEOs and janitors of Fortune 500 companies are members of the same community, sharing knowledge and negotiating one another's practice. Others have agreed that organizations generally comprise multiple communities of practice, but have identified these with the organization's formal divisions. Yet others have built bridges between community-of-practice theory and quasi-economic social capital theories, though the latter are generally highly individualistic and the former determinedly social. And yet others have resisted the idea that communities of practice tend to emerge spontaneously and to reproduce themselves over time and instead have suggested that, little different from other organizational "teams," they can be created deliberately for short-term tasks. Indeed, communities of practice have been presented as a form of universal panacea, both the golden egg and the goose that lays it, as one account has it.

Thus, much as the term *community* is drenched with ambiguity with regards to its scale, scope, and application, so is the term *community of practice*. It can be found applied at the level of gesellschaft and of gemeinschaft, to suburban neighborhoods, whole organizations, professions, and social networks and to transient teams and informal local groups. Moreover, much of the interest in the concept is directed toward the idea of community, while the critical notion of practice is neglected. Although applications of the community-of-practice theory proved useful to consultants, interest in the concept has faded as they turn their attention to newer fads. Nevertheless, in other fields (and particularly in other regions of the world—the idea has been adapted with great subtlety in Scandinavian countries), the notion retains its capacity to provide rich explanations of social identity, learning, organization, and innovation.

—Paul Duguid

See also Information Communities; Online Communities of Learning

Further Reading

Brown, J. S., & Duguid, P. (1991). Organizational learning and communities of practice: Towards a unified view of working, learning, and innovation. *Organization Science, 2*(1), 40–58.

Brown, J. S., & Duguid, P. (2001). Knowledge and organization: A social practice perspective. *Organization Science, 12*(2), 198–213.

Cohen, D., & Prusak, L. (2001). *In good company: How social capital makes organizations work.* Boston: Harvard Business School Press

Constant, E. W. (1987). The social locus of technological practice: Community, system, or organization. In W. Bijker, T. Hughes, & T. Pinch (Eds.), *The social construction of technological systems: New directions in the sociology and history of technology* (pp. 223–242). Cambridge, MA: MIT Press.

Constant, E. W. (1989). Science in society: Petroleum engineers and the oil fraternity in Texas, 1925–1965. *Social Studies of Science, 19,* 439–472.

Cook, S., & Yanow, D. (1993). Culture and organizational learning. *Journal of Management Inquiry, 2*(4), 373–390.

Gherardi, S. (2001). Introduction: Practice-based theorizing on learning and knowing in organizations. *Organization, 7*(2), 211–224.

Granovetter, M. (1985). Economic action and social structure: The problem of embeddedeness. *American Journal of Sociology, 91*(3), 481–510.

Lave, J. (1988). *Cognition in practice: Mind, mathematics, and culture in everyday life.* New York: Cambridge University Press.

Lave, J., & Wenger, E. (1991). *Situated learning: Legitimate peripheral participation.* New York: Cambridge University Press.

Lave, J. C., & Chaiklin, S. (Eds.). (1993). *Understanding practice: Perspectives on activity and context.* New York: Cambridge University Press.

Tsoukas, H. (2002). Introduction. *Management Learning, 33*(4), 419–426.

Tuomi, I. (1999). *Corporate knowledge: Theory and practice of intelligent organizations.* Helsinki, Finland: Metaxis.

Tuomi, I. (2003). *Networks of innovation: Change and meaning in the age of the internet.* Oxford, UK: Oxford University Press.

Wenger, E. (1987). *Artificial intelligence and tutoring systems: Computational and cognitive approaches to the communication of knowledge.* Los Altos, CA: Morgan Kaufmann.

Wenger, E. (1998). *Communities of practice.* New York: Cambridge University Press.

Wenger, E., & W. M. Snyder. (2001). Communities of practice: The organizational frontier. *Harvard Business Review, 78*(1), 139–146.

COMMUNITY

See Introduction; Civic Life; Communitarianism; Social Capital

COMMUNITY, SENSE OF

Anthropologist Anthony Cohen has said that "the concept of community has been one of the most compelling and attractive themes in modern social science, and at the same time one of the most elusive to define" (Cohen 1985, p. 7). The elasticity of the word has proved useful, allowing groups of people to use it in different ways at different times. In recent years, people—and governments—have sought to remedy the alienation of modern life by recreating or achieving a sense of community. Zygmunt Bauman's important work *Community: Seeking Safety in an Insecure World* gives us a clue as to why the idea has become more important and popular. Bauman argues that as the world becomes more complex and less secure, we seek community to make us feel safer and happier.

Bauman notes, however, that community may not always be positive. Sometimes it comes at a price—belonging to a community may risk the loss of our individuality. In seeking security in community in our globalizing world, we may also forgo personal freedom.

The Need to Keep It Small

A town needs public squares; they are the largest, most public rooms that the town has. But when they are too large, they look and feel deserted.

It is natural that every public street will swell out at those important nodes where there is the most activity. And it is only these widened, swollen, public squares which can accommodate the public gatherings, small crowds, festivities, bonfires, carnivals, speeches, dancing, shouting, mourning, which must have their place in the life of the town.

But for some reason there is a temptation to make these public squares too large. Time and again in modern cities, architects and planners build plazas that are too large. They look good on drawings; but in real life they end up desolate and dead.

Our observations suggest strongly that open places intended as public squares should be very small. As a general rule, we have found that they work best when they have a diameter of about 60 feet–at this diameter people often go to them, they become favorite places, and people feel comfortable there. When the diameter gets above 70 feet, the squares begin to seem deserted and unpleasant. The only exceptions we know are places like the Piazza San Marco and Trafalgar Square, which are great town centers, teeming with people.

Source: Alexander, Christopher, et al. (1977). *A Pattern Language.* New York: Oxford University Press, p. 311.

COMMUNITY AND GLOBALIZATION

Paradoxically, as globalization has become more prominent in the last years of the twentieth century and the early years of the twenty-first century, the idea of community has also become more relevant. "Globalization reflects a widespread perception that the world is rapidly being moulded into a shared social space by economic and technological forces . . . developments in one region of the world have profound consequences for the life chances of individuals or communities on the other side of the globe . . . the sheer scale of contemporary social and economic change appears to outstrip the capacity of national governments or citizens to control, contest or resist that change" (Held et al. 1999, p. 1). Political scientist David Held has argued that globalization does not always lead to integration or to the development of progressive, homogeneous, or unified societies. In fact, he argues, globalization may actually encourage disintegrative forces and promote fragmentation in some parts of the world. When this occurs, governments or supranational organizations (such as the European Union, the World Bank, and the United Nations) often invoke policies that they hope will strengthen local communities, particularly in less developed regions of the world. Thus, even as globalization weakens communities, global organizations sometimes seek to strengthen them. As the world has become more homogeneous and global capitalism more dominant, people have sought all the more eagerly for a sense of community, for the reestablishment of the importance of the local. Interestingly, the terrorist attack on New York City's World Trade Center on September 11, 2001, which was interpreted by some as an attack on global capitalism, spurred many Americans to increase their contribution to their local communities and their engagement, in general, with civic society. Robert Putnam, well known for his work on social capital, has shown how the stock of social capital has increased since the terrorist attack.

LOSS OF COMMUNITY

Early work on community done by pioneer sociologists such as Ferdinand Tönnies (1855–1936) stated that society had gone through a process of change because of industrialization. Relations based on personal interaction and kinship (which Tönnies linked to the concept of gemeinschaft, or community) were replaced more and more by legalistic and impersonal relationships (which Tönnies linked to the concept of gesellschaft, or association). Émile Durkheim (1858–1917) described the move as one from mechanical solidarity to organic solidarity in an increasingly complex society; he saw it as caused by industrialization, specialization of work, and the resultant changed relations between individuals. Both sociologists believed industrialization left people alienated and bereft of norms as the types of relations they had with others changed. As industrialization progressed and cities grew, there was great concern that the sense of community found in preindustrial society would disappear altogether. Academics of the Chicago school agreed, fearing loss of community would accompany urbanization.

COMMUNITY FOUND

By the late 1950s, many studies on local communities had been undertaken that questioned the idea that community was undermined by industrialization. Herbert Gans's study *The Urban Villagers* found community in Italian neighborhoods in Boston. R. E. Pahl found both gemeinschaft and gessellschaft relations in his study *Urbs in Rure* ("City in the Country"), and Ronald Frankenberg found examples of communities flourishing in rural and urban Britain. It was, however, Michael Young and Peter Wilmott's famous study of Bethnal Green in London that finally confirmed the finding of an urban village, documented in *Family and Kinship in East London.*

COMMUNITY, CULTURE, AND IDENTITY

Nevertheless, many continued to fear that with the modern age we had lost our sense of community. There was a "longing for community . . . symbolis[ing] a desire for security and certainty in our lives . . . a desire for identity and authenticity" (Lee & Newby 1983, p. 52). This interest in who we are and this concern with what our communities mean can be seen as connected to culture and to ideas on the quality of life. Sociologist Zygmunt Bauman notes that community represents that to which we aspire, our hopes for the future, because community is a "warm place, a cosy and comfortable place. . . . In a community, we all understand each other well, we may trust what we hear, we are safe most of the time. . . . Our duty . . . is to help each other, and so our right . . . is to expect that the help we will need will be forthcoming" (Bauman 2001, pp.1–2).

Community may mitigate global capitalism. It offers the possibility of something more important than money, for human loyalties, as Bauman indicates, are offered unconditionally without cost-benefit analysis. As the cultural and literary theorist Raymond Williams has noted, "The reality of community lies in its members' perception of the vitality of its culture" (Williams 1958, p. 118). Cohen suggests that community depends on consciousness and on our perceptions of boundaries between us and others. These boundaries are socially constructed and constantly renegotiated. When all is said and done, community really is culture, and recent research on the subject shows how important it is for individuals to have their own sense of community and of belonging.

—Susan L. Hodgett

Further Reading

Archibugi, D., Held, D., & Kohler, M. (1998). *Re-imagining political community.* Stanford, CA: Stanford University Press.

Bauman, Z. (2001). *Community: Seeking safety in an insecure world.* Cambridge, UK: Polity.

Bell, C., & Newby, H. (1974). *The sociology of community.* London: Frank Cass.

Cohen, A. (1985). *The symbolic construction of community.* London: Routledge.

Frankenberg, R. (1965). *Communities in Britain.* Harmondsworth, UK: Penguin.

Frazer, E. (1999). *The problems of communitarian politics.* Oxford, UK: Oxford University Press.

Gans, H. (1962) *The urban villagers.* Glencoe, IL: Free Press.

Gusfield, J. R. (1975). *Community: A critical response.* Oxford, UK: Blackwell.

Held, D. (1993). *Prospects for democracy: North, south, east, west.* Cambridge, UK: Polity.

Held, D., McGrew, A., Goldblatt, D., & perraton, J. (1999). *The global transformations reader.* Cambridge, UK: Polity Press.

Lee, D., & Newby, H. (1983). *The problem of sociology.* London: Routledge.

Pahl, R.E. (1965). *Urbs in rure.* London: Weidenfeld and Nicolson.

Putnam, R. (1995). Bowling alone: America's declining social capital. *Journal of Democracy, 6*(1), 65–78.

Putnam, R. (2002). Bowling together. *The American Prospect, 13*(3). Retrieved September 18, 2002, from http://www.prospect.org/print/V13/3/putnam-r.html

Young, M., & Wilmott, P. (1962). *Family and kinship in east London.* Harmondsworth, UK: Pelican.

Williams, R. (1958). *Culture and society.* London: Chatto and Windus.

COMMUNITY ACTION

Community action, which can be defined as collective social and political activities by people on behalf of their communities (whether geographical or more conceptual, as in, for instance, the gay community or the black community), is of great political and practical interest. Traditional analyses of why people become involved in community action typically start on the individual level. Thus, they typically revolve around individual cost-benefit analyses, individual motives, or individual dispositions. Recently, however, researchers have become increasingly interested in a collective-level analysis of these phenomena. This perspective assumes that people's willingness to engage in activities for the sake of their communities depends on whether they define themselves in terms of their collective (or social) as opposed to their individual (or personal) identity.

A River Comes Clean

GREAT BARRINGTON, Mass.(ANS)–When Rachel Fletcher and a few friends started hauling trash out of the river here, people thought she was nuts.

The waterway hadn't been used for much other than dumping ever since the Mahican Indians blazed a path for Wisconsin in 1724.

"Over there," said Fletcher, pointing across the Housatonic River to the back of an apartment house, "some guys were sitting on lawn chairs, laughing and tossing beer bottles at us."

Now, eight years later, they aren't laughing anymore.

Using their bare hands, shovels and wheelbarrows, the people of this small town in western Massachusetts have cleared over 200 tons of rubble from their stretch of the Housatonic, a notoriously polluted river. They have built a scenic "river walk" trail right behind the town's main street.

And in what national observers say is practically unheard of anywhere else, they did it by the sweat of their own brows–an all-volunteer feat. Even the beer guzzlers who heckled Fletcher cleaned up their patch of the riverbank.

"We want everyone picking up trash in the river, so the river will never be trashed again," said Fletcher, 48, who launched the citizen campaign dubbed River Walk.

The do-it-yourself thrust may be unique, but all over the country, communities are reconnecting with the rivers that run through them–though normally with the aid of paid professional cleanup crews.

One sign of this rediscovery is the explosion of walking trails that link river and town. Ed McMahon of the Conservation Fund in Arlington, Va., said his organization alone has tracked several thousand of these "greenway" projects nationwide, and there are many more.

"A lot of people are starting to realize that this is both good for business and good for the environment," he said, referring to the role of greenways in revitalizing cities and towns.

This is typically a job for professionals: planners, excavators, landscapers and others. "It's pretty unique" for regular citizens to do it all as volunteers, said McMahon.

–William Bole

Source: "A River Comes Clean–200 Tons of Rubble, 1,000 Volunteers and Eight Years Later." The American News Service, Article No. EN100, n.d. .

COLLECTIVE IDENTITY AS A COMMUNITY MEMBER

There is wide agreement in social psychology that a person's sense of who he or she is (that is, his or her sense of identity) varies with the social context. A key distinction has been made between individual identity ("I" or "me") and collective identity ("we" or "us"). Whereas a person's individual identity derives from a set of personal features that distinguish him or her from other individuals ("I am female, a New Yorker, a lesbian, a lawyer, and I like French cuisine"), a person's collective identity is based on features that he or she shares with other (but not all other) individuals in a given social context such as gender (women), city of residence (New Yorkers) or sexual orientation (lesbians). In other words, in contrast to individual identity, which is self-definition as a unique individual, collective identity represents a self-definition as an interchangeable group member.

SALIENT PRINCIPLES OF COLLECTIVE IDENTITY

A person can have many different collective identities depending on the number of communities or groups to which he or she belongs. However, not all of these collective identities are salient at the same time. Which specific collective identity moves into the psychological foreground is a joint function of personal variables and more immediate social and contextual variables. For example, depending on a person's unique prior experiences or life history, his or her membership in one specific community (the community of race or ethnicity, for example) may be more important than the membership in another community (such as city of residence). As a result, the person is more ready to define him- or herself in terms of membership in the former community than in the latter community. ("First and foremost I am black.") Collective identity salience also depends on the immediate social context because defining oneself as a member of a particular community is more meaningful or fits better in some contexts than in others. For example, categorization in terms of ethnic group membership fits better when white and black students discuss issues of white privileges than when they are discussing issues of abortion. In the former case, students are particularly likely to define themselves in terms of their collective white or black identity, and this tendency will be further intensified if students of their own race are outnumbered by students of the other race, so that their race is particularly distinctive in the immediate social context.

COLLECTIVE IDENTITY PROCESSES

Salient collective identity spurs several social-psychological processes that facilitate community action. For example, a sense of collective identity accentuates similarities between oneself and other community members with reference to experiences, needs, interests, or goals. As a result "my" and "your" experiences, needs, and so forth are transformed into "our" experiences and needs. Community members' perception that they share problems or grievances, or that their needs, goals, and interests are interchangeable is an important first step toward collective action.

Another important step toward such action entails the acceptance of and conformity to specific belief systems and community norms. For example, community members have to agree upon whom or what to blame for the community's problem (often an external opponent or enemy) and what would be the appropriate (normative) community action in the existing context (for example, whether to engage in mild or militant forms of collective protest). Collective identity fosters the acceptance of social influence from fellow community members (whereas social influence from nonmembers is rejected) and thus facilitates the development of such collective explanations and solutions.

EMPIRICAL EVIDENCE OF THE ROLE OF COLLECTIVE IDENTITY IN COMMUNITY ACTION

The role of collective identity in community action has been established in a range of empirical studies conducted in a variety of community contexts. Typically, these studies focus on one of two different types of community-serving behavior, most commonly community volunteerism or collective protest on behalf of one's community.

Community Volunteerism

Volunteerism typically involves willingly committing time and effort over an extended period for some socially desirable goal. Although volunteerism can take many different forms, individuals often choose to engage in activities that directly benefit their own community. Volunteerism for one's local community is a case in point. It has long been argued that a strong sense of "we-ness" increases citizens' willingness to engage on behalf of their local community. Recent empirical support for this hypothesis comes from a field study conducted by the scholars Stefan Stürmer, Claudia Kampmeier, and Bernd Simon in the context of two small local communities (population less than ten thousand) in Germany. This study focused on the role of identification with the local community in volunteering in the local fire brigade. Ninety-one volunteer firefighters completed a questionnaire measuring the following variables: (a) identification with the local community, (b) personal benefits of volunteerism traditionally considered in volunteerism research (for example, increased self-esteem, new learning experiences), and (c) willingness to participate in future community-serving activities provided by the local fire brigade (such as fire fighting or technical support for residents). As expected, analysis of the data corroborated that identification with the local community was a unique predictor of volunteers' willingness to participate in future community-serving activities even when the affect of the individual benefits traditionally considered in volunteerism research were taken into account. Data from an additional experimental study further substantiated the causal role of identification with the local community in volunteerism at the local level.

Further empirical evidence for the role of collective identity in community volunteerism comes from research in the context of AIDS volunteerism. In most Western countries, AIDS volunteerism started in the early 1980s as a collective response of the gay community to the AIDS crisis. Although today both homosexual and heterosexual people are engaged in AIDS volunteerism, in the West homosexual men are still the largest subgroup among people living with AIDS or HIV. It follows, then, that for homosexual AIDS volunteers, the majority of the recipients of help are members of their own community (taking sexual orientation as the defining factor in collective identity in this context). Consequently, it can be assumed that a strong sense of collective identity in terms of sexual orientation fosters gay men's willingness to volunteer in this context. A study conducted by Bernd Simon, Stefan Stürmer, and Kerstin Steffens in 2000 in the context of a German AIDS service organization provided clear support for this hypothesis. As expected, gay men were more willing to volunteer when they emphasized their collective gay identity, whereas self-definition in terms of their individual identity decreased their willingness to participate in AIDS volunteerism.

Collective Protest

While community volunteerism is typically directed towards one's own community, collective protest is directed toward antagonistic communities, political authorities, or the general public. A prominent reason why individuals engage in collective protest is to promote social change (for example, achieving equal rights or economical opportunities) on behalf of their disadvantaged community. However, the relationship between identification with the disadvantaged community and participation in collective protest is far from granted. In fact, often members of disadvantaged communities do not participate in collective action on behalf of their community, despite a strong sense of identity. Accordingly, it has been argued that collective identity has to politicize in order to foster participation in collective protest. Support for the role of politicized collective identity comes from a series of field studies conducted in several different social movement contexts such as the older people's movement in Germany, the U.S. fat acceptance movement, and the U.S. gay movement. In those studies, potential participants in the respective movements completed questionnaires measuring mainly the following variables: (a) identification with the disadvantaged community, (b) identification with the more politicized social movement or social movement organization, (c) expected costs and benefits of participation (for example, financial expenses or social recognition), a factor traditionally considered in social-movement research, and (d) indicators of collective protest (for example, participation in public campaigns, demonstrations, or sit-ins). Corroborating the relevance of "identity politicization," statistical analyses revealed that identification with the disadvantaged community increased individuals' willingness to participate in collective protest only to the extent that the sense of identification was transformed into the more politicized form of identification with the social movement. The politicized form of identification with the social movement was a strong and unique predictor of participation in collective protest even when the effects of the cost-benefit variables were taken into consideration.

IMPLICATIONS

This entry's focus on the role of collective identity in community action should not be taken to mean that other determinants of community action are unimportant. One particular important class of determinants concerns the personal benefits individuals derive from engaging in community action, benefits such as social integration, new learning experiences, or career-related benefits. It is worth noting, however, that the studies conducted by Simon, Stürmer, and colleagues established the unique role of collective identity above and beyond the effects of personal benefits. Accordingly, these researchers suggest a dual-pathway model of sociopolitical participation, with one pathway based on the calculation of costs and benefits of participation, and the other based on collective identity. Programs designed to increase participation in community action may target these two pathways.

—Stefan Stürmer

Further Reading

Haslam, S. A. (2001). *Psychology in organizations. The social identity approach.* London: Sage.

Hill, J. L. (1996). Psychological sense of community: Suggestions for future research. *Journal of Community Psychology, 24*(4), 431–438.

Klandermans, B. (1997). The social psychology of protest. Oxford, UK: Basil Blackwell.

McMillan, D. W., & Chavis, D. M. (1986). Sense of community: A definition and theory. *Journal of Community Psychology, 14*(1), 6–23.

Omoto, M. M., & Snyder, M. (in press). Considerations of community: The context and Process of volunteerism. *American Behavioral Scientist,* special issue titled Cooperation in modern society: Dilemmas and solutions.

Sarason, S. (1974). *Psychological sense of community: Prospects for a community psychology.* San Francisco: Jossey-Bass.

Schroeder, D. A., Penner, L. A., Dovidio, J. F., & Piliavin, J. A. (1995). *The psychology of helping and altruism.* New York: McGraw-Hill.

Simon, B., Stürmer, S., & Steffens, K. (2000). Helping individuals or group members? The role of individual and collective identification in AIDS volunteerism. *Personality and Social Psychology Bulletin, 26*(4), 496–506.

Simon, B., Loewy, M., Stürmer, S., Weber, U., Freytag, P., Habig,

C., et al. (1998). Collective identification and social movement participation. *Journal of Personality and Social Psychology, 74*(3), 646–658.

Simon, B., & Klandermans, B. (2001). Politicized collective identity. A social psychological analysis. *American Psychologist, 56*(4), 319–331.

Snyder, M., Clary, E. G., & Stukas, A. A. (2000). The functional approach to volunteerism. In G. R. Maio & J. M. Olson (Eds.), *Why we evaluate: Functions of attitudes* (pp. 365–393). Mahwah, NJ: Lawrence Erlbaum.

Stürmer, S., Kampmeier, C., & Simon, B. (in press). Community action at the local level: A dual-pathway model. *Psychologica Belgica,* special issue.

Stürmer, S., Simon, B., Loewy, M., & Jörger, H. (in press). The dual-pathway model of social movement participation: The case of the fat acceptance movement. *Social Psychology Quarterly.*

Turner, J. C., Hogg, M. A., Oakes, P. J., Reicher, S. D., & Wetherell, M. S. (1987). *Rediscovering the social group. A self-categorization theory.* Oxford, UK: Basil Blackwell.

COMMUNITY ARTS

Community arts include performing arts (music, theater, dance, and so forth), multimedia arts, visual arts, literary arts, culinary arts, clothing and textiles, and the multitude of other forms that people, individually and collectively, create to make the ordinary extraordinary. Community arts are first and foremost community based, community focused, and integral to the everyday life of the community. Often community art is rooted in a local culture, which may celebrate a particular regional or ethnic tradition. It may also focus on a political issue important to a neighborhood, town, or city. In that regard, community arts are often a response to the threatened erosion of cohesive, dynamic communities. Community arts can be understood in contrast to so-called fine arts, that is, art as taught in academies and institutes, which often glorifies individualism and promotes isolationist and exclusionary viewing spaces (for example, in galleries or museums).

DEFINING COMMUNITIES, DEFINING ART

Communities are often identifiable through shared purposes and history; however, it is important to recognize within any discussion of community arts that conceptions of both community and art are not static. While community used to be thought of as geographically based, community now incorporates more abstract ideas. Communities of scholars, for example, are now bound together by cyberspace. Many indigenous people feel united by common concerns of oppression and disconnection from their homeland. Talk of refugee communities must refer back to the home countries from which the refugees came. People with the same disease may never have met one another, but they may feel united by their shared trauma, as is evident with communities of cancer survivors or recovering alcoholics.

The idea of what constitutes art is also changing as the boundaries between life and that which has formally been defined as art collapse. Aestheticians and critics are proposing the idea that art is really an idea and not a thing. In this regard anything can now be called art. This makes defining community arts more difficult, especially within international contexts. Consider the community-based practices of the Lithuanian community that settled in various places in the United States in the mid-twentieth century. Their artistic practices were intended to keep a culture alive that could not be as easily saved in the homeland, where they were being oppressed. Their goal differs from that of many Dutch community arts centers, which function primarily provide a place where amateur artists can spend their leisure time. Yet another approach to community arts can be illustrated by the many Hungarian community art centers, which are houses of culture, set up to teach such diverse subjects as modern gardening and contemporary literature and to educate children about local arts as a way of preserving Hungarian heritage.

COMMUNITY ARTS PROGRAMS

Community arts are often created, taught, and exhibited within the context of community arts programs. Community arts programs encourage all members of the community to participate in the creation or enjoyment of art. They aim to work in a manner that is democratic and collaborative. Community arts programs may be associated with museums, arts councils, social service organizations, performing arts centers, local government, religious organizations, community centers, political organizations, neighborhood associations, cultural centers, businesses, and homes—and this list is not exhaustive. Funding of community arts programs comes from such varied sources as government subsidies, public and private grants, gifts, sponsorships, memberships, and fees for services.

The term "community arts" is common to such nations as the United States, Britain, Australia, and Canada. It is used to describe both government-sponsored practices and programs and independent

Arts Spark Downtown Revival

(ANS)–Hotels, office buildings, convention centers–these are the real indicators of economic progress in American cities. Or so goes conventional wisdom.

But some cities are discovering there's a softer path–that investment in the arts offers surprising economic and social benefits as well.

This realization has come full-circle in Roanoke, Va., once an important and thriving city nestled in the Blue Ridge Mountains. In the early part of this century, the heart of its cultural activity was the nearby Mill Mountain Theater.

Unfortunately, the old theater burned to the ground in the 1970s. And it wasn't much longer before Roanoke's downtown hit hard times.

During the next decade, the downtown was plagued by problems typical of many inner cities–vacant buildings, drug dealers, prostitutes. People stayed away. Businesses shut their doors.

To reverse the decline, Roanoke's business community turned to the old theater as the linchpin for economic development. A local association banded the Mill Mountain Theater together with fledgling art, science and history museums into one common Center in the Square, hoping to attract support for the downtown.

Center in the Square debuted in 1983 with the help of state, local and private funds and soon became Virginia's largest cultural center. "Center in the Square helped to spur the renaissance of the downtown area," said Jeff Walker, the center's marketing director.

Thirteen years later, Center in the Square has served over 4 million visitors, attracted more than $250 million in capital investment for Roanoke's downtown, brought over 165 new businesses to the area and created an estimated $25 million in direct and indirect annual economic benefits.

Roanoke and its cultural center are not unique. Cities large and small are discovering both the tangible and intangible benefits of the arts.

Not far away in Chattanooga, Tenn., a depressed downtown area began a turnaround in the 1980s that is still in full swing. Its rebirth sprang in part from large investments in the city's cultural renewal–including the world's largest freshwater aquarium attracting over a million visitors a year, a renovated theater involving 1,000 volunteers annually, and a new river front park.

In Chicago, the arts have given a huge economic boost to areas like the Uptown district. In the 1920's Uptown was hopping–the cultural hub and theater district for all of Chicago. By mid-century, though, the area had fallen on hard times.

Over the last few years, local arts organizations have banded together to breathe new life into Uptown.

According to a study released by the Illinois Arts Alliance Foundation in August, the arts in Uptown now employ at least 950 people and generate $4.5 million in economic impact, including indirect spending on restaurants, parking and other services.

Additionally, half of Uptown's arts organizations have made substantial renovations–an average of $143,000 per property–which have improved the community's appearance.

Nurturing the arts may even be more effective than the more familiar kinds of business and economic development, some experts believe.

"Very few industries generate that type of induced spending," said Randy Cohen, director of research and information at Americans for the Arts, a nonprofit coalition of 3,800 community-based arts agencies. He was referring to the money that museum-goers, for example, spend on parking, restaurants and shops.

–Jason Wilson

Source: "Arts Spark Downtown Revival, Just Like the Hard Stuff." American News Service, Article No. A121.

endeavors. *Animateur* (animator) is the term used in Francophone nations to describe people who facilitate (animate) the public's involvement with community arts. Radical democratic theory associates community arts with culture work (work that promotes or preserves culture). Within this perspective artists and arts facilitators are sometimes known as culture workers.

Community arts have been shaped by various academic theories, as well as by politics, economics, and the desire for social justice. Within the United States, some of the political forces that have shaped community arts are social reformism (for instance, abolitionism, utopianism, and feminism) in the mid-nineteenth century, immigration policy in the early twentieth century, the New Deal in the 1930s, the civil rights movement and the War on Poverty in the 1960s, and the environmental movement from the 1970s onward. These forces in turn encouraged such specific arts-oriented initiatives as the public works art projects of the 1930s, the first community arts councils in the late 1940s, the National Endowment for the Arts in the mid-1960s, and the so-called culture wars of the 1990s.

A wall in Riga, Latvia, built and decorated with political art in May 1990 to protect the Latvian radio station from Russian troops.
Source: Staffan Widstrand/Corbis; used with permission.

Community arts organizations have made important civic contributions. Consider, for example, the contributions made by quilting circles, hobby associations, and community arts centers. Community arts venues also function as catalysts for dialogue about individual and group identity, local and national concerns, and, potentially, the pursuit of democracy. Scholar Maryo Ewell demonstrates that historically, community arts programs in the United States have contributed to community health and vitality from the days of the American Lyceum Association (founded 1831), which sprang out of the adult-education work of Josiah Holbrook (1788–1854). Other informal and formal organizations that have brought arts and cultural activities to children, youth, and adults in the United States include those organizations associated with the San Francisco Neighborhood Arts Programs dedicated to assisting cultural development in the 1960s; Project Row Houses in Houston, Texas; Alternative Roots in Atlanta, Georgia; the Zora Neale Hurston Festival of the Arts and Humanities in Eatonville, Florida; the Koga Community Arts Program in Tokyo, Japan; and the many Houses of Culture in Hungary.

COMMUNITY ARTS AND COMMUNITY CULTURE

Community arts are closely linked to community and cultural development. When community arts programs are taken in the context of community development, they are often linked to the agendas of public and private funding sources that emphasize grassroots initiatives and community partnerships. Including community arts in community development programs recognizes the important link between the arts, economics, social justice, and lifelong learning.

Because community arts often celebrate the everyday life of everyday people, they are often aligned with folklore or folklife. Folklore comprises the traditional customs, tales, sayings, and art forms preserved among a people; folklife encompasses a people's common languages, behaviors, and ways of knowing as well. Folklorists have been developing programs that emphasize the creative processes of such contemporary community-based rituals as tattooing, tagging (making graffiti art), creating shrines and altars, and designing costumes for festival events such as Carnival (a festival that marks the start of the Roman Catholic season of Lent), and Junkanoo (a Bahamian Christmastime festival with West African roots).

ART OUTSIDE THE ACADEMY

Community art practices recognize the learning that takes place outside the academic frame of reference. Although the boundaries between what is learned in school and outside school are usually fluid, it is often said that what is central to community arts is rooted in informal interchanges, such as those between teenagers teaching one another about car culture. Sometimes aspects of a community-based aesthetic become part of a more formalized educational program, and although that process is not necessary for artistic activities to be referred to as community arts, it often is the case that community-based activities are recognized and celebrated in a formal presentation.

One such example is the exhibition coordinated by the scholars Doug Blandy and Kristin Congdon in 1987 in the Fine Art Gallery at Bowling Green State University in Ohio. Titled "Boats, Bait, and Fishing Paraphernalia" (more often called "The Fishing Show"), this exhibition relied on the expertise of local fishing experts in the northwestern Ohio community to identify, display, and educate the public about the local fishing aesthetic. The most highly publicized and attended exhibition the gallery had hosted, it brought in people who had never been to a gallery before, the first-timers mingling with professional artists, students, and regular gallery goers. Coolers were packed, a keg was tapped, and fishers-in-residence were available to explain about the fish that got away, the best lure for a certain catch, and fishing lore surrounding local spaces. Regional postcards were framed, fishing snapshots were displayed, and a taxidermist demonstrated his art. While not everyone was happy about this exhibition, it clearly celebrated local aesthetic practices.

COMMUNITY ARTS AND EDUCATION

Education, both formal and informal, is important for sustaining community arts and building appreciative audiences. The proliferation of community arts programs presents art educators with a special challenge. While research on grounding the study of visual art in its cultural context has been ubiquitous for decades, building on the scholarship of art educators such as June King McFee and F. Graeme Chalmers, less has been written about arts curriculum development within local communities. Reasons for this are plentiful: Teachers are trained in fine-art traditions; art education literature and teaching materials generally highlight famous works of art that are housed in major museums; teacher planning time does not allow for the kind of research necessary to build a curriculum that is rooted in local traditions. Nevertheless, emphasis on multicultural education in teacher-training programs helps with community-based pedagogy. Teachers become aware of differing learning styles and different cultural perspectives. Recognition of diversity helps ground teachers in community-based pedagogy, as community-based pedagogy generally recognizes that children from different ethnic backgrounds and different regions often have different learning styles, as do children with disabilities.

Bill Ivey, former chair of the National Endowment for the Arts, has declared that the members of all communities are creative and aesthetically expressive. He further states that creative expression is fundamental to humans, that aesthetic traditions are a prerequisite to social life, and that traditions thrive on creative interpretation and effort. The inclination to make and appreciate art is so ordinary that its extraordinary contribution to such commonplace activities as cooking, fishing, keeping house, gardening, computing, and the multitude of other daily endeavors is often overlooked. However, organizations such as the Center for Arts and Culture in Washington, DC, founded by a consortium of private foundations, are trying to rectify that situation. Such organizations remind people of the ways in which the arts, culture, and policy intersect in a global context.

—Kristin G. Congdon and Doug Blandy

Further Reading

Adams, D., & Goldbard, A. (2001). *Creative community: The art of cultural development.* New York: Rockefeller.

Blandy, D., & Congdon, K. G. (1988). Community based aesthetics as an exhibition catalyst and a foundation for community involvement. *Studies in Art Education, 29*(4), 243–249.

Congdon, K. G., & Blandy, D. (1999). Working with communities and folk traditions: Socially ecological and culturally democratic practices in art education. In D. Boughton & R. Mason (Eds.), *Beyond multicultural art education: International perspectives* (pp. 65–83). New York: Waxmann.

Congdon, K. G., & Blandy, D. (in press). Administering the culture of everyday life: Imaging the future of arts sector administration. In V. B. Morris & D. Pankratz (Eds.), *The arts in a new millennium: Research and the arts sector.* Westport, CT: Greenwood.

Ewell, M. (2000). Community arts councils: Historical perspective. *CultureWork,* 5(1). Retrieved December 16, 2002, from http://aad.uoregon.edu/culturework/culturework15.html

Haanstra, F., & Marjo, H. (1998). Quality assessment in Dutch community arts centers. In R. E. Stake (Series Ed.), K. G. Congdon, & D. Boughton (Vol. Eds.), *Evaluating art education programs in community centers: International perspectives on problems of conception and practice* (Vol. 4, pp. 73–87). New York: JAI Press.

Hickey, D. (1997). *Air guitar: Essays on art and democracy.* Los Angeles: Art Issues.

Ivey, B. (2000). *Cultural collision: America's creative center.* Retrieved December 16, 2002, from http://arts.endow.gov/endownews/news00/HarvardSpeech.html

Kárpáti, A. (1998). The changing nature of Eastern European art centers: Assessment issues and the clarification of goals. In R. E. Stake (Series Ed.), K. G. Congdon & D. Boughton (Vol. Eds.), *Evaluating art education programs in community centers: International perspectives on problems of conception and practice* (Vol. 4, pp. 133–149). New York: JAI.

Richardson, M. B. (2001). Elzbieta Ribokas: Lituanian-American weaver and teacher. In K. G. Congdon, D. Blandy, & P. E. Bolin (Eds.), *Histories of community-based art education* (pp. 129–140). Reston, VA: National Art Education Association.

COMMUNITY ATTACHMENT

Community attachment typically refers to two distinct things. The first is how sentimentally rooted a person is in a particular geographical community; the second is how general changes in that rootedness can be used as a measure of larger social change.

ROOTED IN PLACE

In the first use, community attachment relates to a person's sense of fit or belonging in a locality, which creates a sense of loyalty. It is only indirectly associated with the measurable characteristics of a community—characteristics such as median income of residents, availability of desirable goods and services, population stability, and so forth. These characteristics may influence one's sense of attachment to the community but often have more to do with one's level of satisfaction than one's feeling of attachment. The two—community attachment and community satisfaction—should not be automatically equated with each other. People can be very attached to their community and yet highly dissatisfied with it. The reverse is also true. Studies show, for example, that the rural South in the United States consistently scores very high on community attachment indicators and very low on objective indicators compared with other U.S. regions. Community attachment, therefore, must be viewed as a person's sentimental or subjective relationship with his or her community.

As with any subjective relationship, one's sentimental attachment to one's community will be multifaceted and somewhat idiosyncratic. Consequently, community attachment can be created and maintained in a variety of ways but will always reveal fairly consistent patterns across time periods, regions, and community types, as well as across people from similar demographic categories, in terms of how people show, express, and feel this attachment.

COMMUNITY ATTACHMENT AS AN INDICATOR OF SOCIAL CHANGE

Because of these consistent patterns, measures of community attachment have become important ways to observe and measure social changes.

It was thought that the proper way for humans to live was in small rural villages dominated by informal interaction—a belief that played a key role in the development of modern Western culture. By the late nineteenth century, during a time of phenomenal urban growth, social theorists such as Émile Durkheim, Ferdinand Tönnies, and Georg Simmel believed that as society became increasingly urban, relationships based on informal interactions would become impossible, and thus that community would be jeopardized. The argument was carried into the twentieth century by social scientists of the Chicago School, among others. These scholars believed that as population increased in size, density, and heterogeneity, people of necessity became less socially engaged and thus less attached to their community. Known as the linear development model, this theory dominated social scientists' understanding of community and social change until the 1950s, when anthropologists began documenting high levels of community attachment in urbanizing Africa. A new understanding of community and social change was needed.

John Kasarda and Morris Janowitz, two sociologists from the University of Chicago, formulated a new approach in the 1970s known as the systemic model. The systemic model emphasized that community attachment was better reflected through length of residence and other emotional elements, and was independent of urbanization. This approach recognizes that community attachment changes— as our experience of community does—over time and place. Thus larger trends in community attachment—how subjectively rooted we are to our community—over time and place, makes a good measure of social change.

—Ralph B. Brown

See also BOOSTERISM; COMMUNITY, SENSE OF; COMMUNITY OWNERSHIP; COMMUNITY SATISFACTION; PLACE IDENTITY

Further Reading

Brown, R. B., Xu, X. Barfield, M. A., & King, B. G (2000). Community experience and the conceptual distinctness of rural community attachment and satisfaction: A measurement model. *Research in Community Sociology, 10,* 425–444.

Campbell, A., Converse, P., & Rodgers, W. (1981). *The sense of well-being in America: Recent patterns and trends.* New York: McGraw-Hill.

Durkheim, É. (1964). *The division of labor in society.* (G. Simpson, Trans.). New York: The Free Press.

Goudy, W. J. (1990). Community attachment in a rural region. *Rural Sociology, 55*(2), 178–198.

Kasarda, J. D., and Janowitz, M. (1974). Community attachment in mass society. *American Sociological Review 39*(3), 328–339.

Simmel, G. (1983). The metropolis and mental life. In R. L. Warren & L. Lyon (Eds.), *New perspectives on the American community* (pp. 18–27). Homewood, IL: Dorsey.

Tönnies, F. (1963). *Community and society.* (C. F. Loomis, Ed.). New York: Harper Torchbook Edition.

Zimmerman, C. C. (1938). *The changing community.* New York: Harper & Row.

COMMUNITY BUILDING

Community building has come to refer to a variety of intentional efforts to organize and strengthen social connections or to build common values and norms that promote collective goals (or both)—that is, to build more community (an interim goal) as a way of achieving some set of desired outcomes (e.g., safer neighborhoods, healthier children and families, better-preserved cultural traditions, more profitable businesses, and so forth). While specific meanings vary widely depending on context, community building emphasizes the beneficial aspects of key processes (actions) that shape relationships, values, psychological attachment, and other aspects of community. As such, community building bears important connections to community organizing and community development.

One dominant element in community building focuses on civic action to improve quality of life or promote social justice; another focuses on the commercial use of the power of human community, as in building community around a product or market concept, often to promote customer loyalty. Both imply the use of social capital, that is, networks, trust, or other features of community life that can serve as important resources for action.

ORIGINS AND CONTEXTS

No one knows when the term *community building* was first employed or with what specific connotation. As a generic extension of *community,* the action phrase *community building* has broad origins in popular culture and public affairs; only since 1990 has it been codified to any appreciable degree—and even then primarily in professional and activist circles, not in popular use.

The Civic Context

The first and most common context in which the term is used is that of civic action to promote collective, or community, well-being. In this context, community building has at least three defining traits: problem-solving objectives that involve important public interests (as opposed to business or other private interests), an emphasis on collective action (sometimes including professionals, but emphasizing leadership by nonprofessional citizen clients), and a set of hoped-for links between the community thus created or strengthened on one hand and the target social problem on the other.

While the term *community building* has traveled across borders in this first context, it is especially popular in the United States and often includes at least an implicit critique of more traditional, expert-dominated, top-down approaches to meeting needs or solving problems. Especially in the 1990s, community building took on a second meaning, becoming a way of distinguishing creative civic action, primarily at the local level, that engaged citizen clients in key decisions and in their implementation, and that created connections—community—that lasted beyond the immediate program or project.

Consider the example of a public health program that aims to increase child immunization rates significantly in order to prevent disease and lower mortality in a particular geographic area or within a defined social group. Locals—those who live in the area or are members of the target group—may fear health professionals or be unaware of the full set of risks that childhood diseases entail; they may also favor their own, traditional remedies over vaccines. More basic still, locals may be preoccupied with a variety of other urgent concerns—meeting shelter, income, and other day-to-day needs, for example. Many social problem-solving efforts face these or similar barriers. Health professionals who seek to promote the aims of the program through informal parent networks in the area (or group) or by recruiting community insiders to validate the program's objectives may be described as building community in order to improve health outcomes.

In this case, the specified actions are motivated by social problem-solving objectives (health improvement) and not just by the strengthening of networks or mobilizing of key community members (i.e., connection making or community building as an end in itself). In addition, the effort described requires collective action, drawing on the knowledge and skills of professionals as well as non-professional community members (including the clients of immunization) to produce key results. Third, the community-building elements of the program anticipate specific, helpful links between community networks, and influence patterns (how information spreads, who listens to whom and why) and the steps, or cause-and-effect patterns on which the health improvement outcomes depend. Specifically, health professionals and their partners in the community hope that informal community networks will help diffuse reliable information about both disease and immunization, that the visible support of community insiders will help reduce fears or doubts about the immunization efforts, and so on. In effect, these are hoped-for links between particular forms of social capital, including informal networks and patterns of trust, and the larger public interest that a program aims to promote.

Fourth and finally, the key players in designing and delivering this program may believe that the new or stronger forms of social connection that the effort creates may have a value beyond the health outcomes that serve as a primary motivation for the effort. That is, the effort may represent a broader investment in the community's capacity to act on its own behalf in the future.

Note that the public health initiative outlined above might have originated outside the formal health system. It could, for instance, just as easily have originated

Characteristics of a Healthy Community

Healthy communities have some specific characteristics as well as the general ones already mentioned. Leonard J. Duh, a public health expert who has written widely on the subject of building healthy communities, suggests six characteristics that determine the health of a community. A healthy community has:

- A common sense of community, including its history and values that are strengthened by a network of leaders,
- People and community groups who feel empowered and have a sense of control,
- An absence of divided turf, conflict and polarization,
- Structures where people from diverse groups can come together to work out decisions about the community,
- Leadership that functions both from the top down and the bottom up,
- Effective channels for networking, communication and cooperation among those who live and lead there.

Source: Darling, David L., & Randel, Gayla. (1996). *Characteristics of Healthy Communities.* Manhattan, KS: Cooperative Extension Service, Kansas State University. Retrieved March 5, 2003. from http://www.oznet.ksu.edu/library/agec2/mf2064.pdf.

among concerned and activist parents or among informal community leaders—in other words, at the grassroots level. What is most important is not where the efforts originated but what logic they relied on to produce results. Community-building logic respects and develops the power of human community (variously defined) to promote some larger civic or public interest.

The Business Context

Market researchers, business strategists, and others have long recognized that intangible but powerful psychological attachments to a product (or service) and tangible relationships among those who use that product can generate powerful competitive advantages. For example, a soft-drink company may benefit if it associates itself with patriotism, a sense of adventure, attachment to family, or other important values. While feelings about these values and about how the product reflects them may be deeply personal and individual, these are fundamentally *social* values that connect us to the larger society and the judgments of others. To take another example, a bookseller may benefit by enabling fans of mystery novels (or some other genre) to exchange ideas about favorite books, characters, or story lines. Or a gourmet grocery store may organize cooking classes and cookbook lectures in order to enable lovers of good food to connect with one another. Food lovers will learn about new ingredients and so decide to purchase them; new customers may be attracted to the store if impressed by the signal that the extra activities send about the store's quality, and so on.

Stimulating the growth of these kinds of attachments (analogous to neighborhood attachments in much civic community building) may be possible only if special effort is made to understand and engage the social context in which the product is valued, used, talked about, and even transformed in people's lives. The overall logic is quite similar to that of civic community building. But in business, community building creates social and psychological connections around a product or service so as to promote customer loyalty, volume of consumption, and positive referrals (word-of-mouth advertising) for the product.

Community building has taken on new urgency and new dimensions in the age of online businesses. Consider a key strategic problem that faces many of those who sell products or services over the Internet. The Internet has created new challenges to customer loyalty, as customers have easy access to price and other information on a wider array of products and services than ever before. How should a business compete in cyberspace, which offers such low barriers to entry by new competitors? How can a business promote greater customer loyalty, attracting customers back to its site—making the Web site more "sticky," in the lingo of marketers—when so many other sites are available on the Web? Community building in business can complement price, quality, and other traditional sources of competitive advantage, and the Internet provides an almost ideal environment in which to pursue community building for business purposes.

Imagine that the bookseller mentioned earlier now has a Web site to enhance its business. The site's simplest function may be to provide customers with book information and to make possible online purchases. But its extended function may include important elements of community building on the Web. First, the bookseller can invite and share customer ratings of any and all books, with virtually no limitations on space or hours of access (two barriers that have limited physical bulletin boards, which have been used for many years). So now the customer can see what other customers think about a wide range of books, perhaps even those on highly specialized topics. Another feature, drawing on a computer database that tracks customer purchases, may tell a customer who retrieves information on one mystery novel about three other novels that buyers of that first one have also purchased. Finally, an online chat room may permit customers to communicate with fellow customers who share their interests. In those exchanges, customers can offer further reviews of books, discuss what they love about particular books or authors, and more. Particular customers may even build new relationships through these exchanges.

The extended, Web-based functions in this example add value to the services a traditional book retailer offers, all at nominal cost. The functions are thus a promising source of competitive advantage. The bookseller has invited customers not only to browse and buy but to join a community of fellow book enthusiasts.

Many such commercial communities are and probably will remain limited communities of interest, lacking the multifaceted connections of a rural village, a socially cohesive urban neighborhood, an ethnic community, or other types of communities in which deep values, shared history, ongoing face-to-face interaction, and more may play a part. Also, the boundaries and terms of these commercially constructed communities are typically set and enforced by the business and not by the customer members themselves. But limited and profit-shaped as they may be, these communities do result in durable connections and feelings of attachment among customers.

Finally, although the Web offers particularly powerful possibilities for entrepreneurial businesses, civic entrepreneurs are also creating communities of interest on the Web. The Web offers many possibilities for fluid participation and monitoring (ratings and reviews) as well as unusual, boundary-spanning connections. But it also offers new opportunities for misinformation, domination, and other abuses.

CIVIC COMMUNITY BUILDING: DILEMMAS OF REFORM AND FUTURE DIRECTIONS

Whether carried out online, face-to-face, or through broadcast or other media, the most important public interest in community building involves organizing civic action, strengthening the sense of community, and improving the delivery of social programs. Civic community building is not without distinctive challenges and dilemmas, however, and many of these relate to public policy. Three of the most important dilemmas have to do with efficiency (the scale and coordination of problem-solving efforts), power (who decides what, how the deciding gets done), and performance (how success and failure are defined and measured).

Efficiency

In the 1990s, when it became common, primarily in the United States in the fields of public health, human services, and local community development, to speak of community building, the concept was defined by the National Community Building Network and other key institutions as an alternative to well-established but often disappointing approaches toward the same ends—safer streets, children ready to learn in school, healthier families, a cleaner environment, and more. The dominant approaches emphasized large, standardized programs crafted and managed by experts in professionalized agencies. Rarely were clients and other stakeholders engaged in defining or delivering services, and the deficiencies and needs, not the special assets or strengths, of target communities (whether spatial neighborhoods or social groups) were emphasized. Advocates of community building believed that stakeholders should be engaged in decisions that matter and often in implementing the program itself (as in the immunization program example above). Formal social programs and informal civic initiatives, advocates argued, would benefit from insider knowledge not held by experts, and greater citizen trust would improve implementation as well as outcomes. A respect for local places and the assets in target communities would encourage appropriate deference on the part of the experts and a pragmatic building on strength that would replace the then-dominant needs-driven logic that reduced the beneficiaries of social programs to clients who needed "fixing."

These ideas were nothing new. They characterize a number of reform movements in modern societies' provision of social welfare, dating at least as far back as the age of industrialization, when large organizations and professions emerged to handle welfare needs. Community action in the 1960s was an earlier expression of the same frustrations in the face of similar dilemmas.

In developing more bottom-up, custom-crafted efforts, today's community builders have struggled to achieve the scale and level of coordination that large, modern bureaucracies were invented to make possible. Some of the scale problem is a function of insufficient monetary and other resources, but developing new, more user-friendly solutions to persistent, large-scale problems such as school failure, illiteracy, and pollution is inherently challenging as well.

Power

A second dilemma is how to find appropriate levels and forms of engagement for citizen clients and other stakeholders in the governance and delivery of social programs. The engagement must not lead to process paralysis (stalled progress); it must allow more than the show of participation (decisions must not have already been made); and it must promote transparency and accountability (as opposed to replacing domination from the top with domination from below, by manipulative special interests). Community-building efforts struggle with the tensions inherent in developing and effectively deploying power—tensions familiar and pervasive in democratic societies.

Performance

Third and finally, there is the challenge of trying to measure such outcomes of community building as connectedness, trust, and other features of social life, and of trying to measure success with regard to intractable problems, such as a low citywide high school graduation rate, low employment rates among disadvantaged youth, and so forth. Frontline practitioners, as well as funders, evaluators, political authorities, and others debate how quickly community-building efforts should be expected to produce the end outcomes (e.g., higher high school graduation rates, lower infant mortality, etc.) versus producing the intermediate achievements that relate to civic process and capacity (e.g., better public meetings, greater stakeholder trust in the process). And the complex (and contested) nature of cause and effect often makes tracking these efforts, not to mention the task of attributing their effects, difficult indeed.

Despite all these challenges, community building is more than a passing fad. It reflects our fascination with community and our need to make it a more central, vital force in a rapidly changing world. It also reflects deep misgivings about the impersonal, expert-led solutions to social problems that produced neither satisfactory end outcomes nor collective capacity to respond to shared problems in ways that reflect democratic values.

—Xavier de Souza Briggs

Further Reading

Chaskin, R. J., Brown, P., Venkatesh, S. A., & Vidal, A. (2001). *Building community capacity.* New York: Aldine de Gruyter.

Connell, J., Kubisch, A., & Schorr, L. (1995). *New approaches to evaluating community initiatives: Concepts, methods, and contexts.* New York: Aspen Institute.

Kim, A. J. (2000). *Community building on the web: Secret strategies for successful on-line communities.* Berkeley, CA: Peachpit.

Kingsley, G. T., McNeeley, J. B., & Gibson, J. O. (1997). *Community building: Coming of age.* Washington, DC: Urban Institute.

Marris, P., & Rein, M. (1967). *Dilemmas of social reform: Poverty and community action in the United States.* New York: Basic Books.

National Community Building Network. (2003). Retrieved December 26, 2002, from http://www.ncbn.org

Putnam, R. (2000). *Bowling alone: The collapse and revival of community in America.* New York: Simon & Schuster.

Stone, R. (1995). *Core issues in comprehensive community initiatives.* Chicago: Chapin Hall Center for Children at the University of Chicago.

Walsh, J. (1997). *Stories of renewal: Community building in America.* New York: The Rockefeller Foundation.

Winkler, M. (Ed.). (1999). *Community organizing and community building for health.* New Brunswick, NJ: Rutgers University Press.

COMMUNITY COLLEGES

Community colleges are regionally accredited postsecondary educational institutions that provide technical, vocational, and lower-division college courses. They grant associate degrees and certificates and provide the first two years of baccalaureate education. Today there are over 1,200 public and private community colleges in the United States, and there are growing numbers of community colleges in other countries. Today it is commonly accepted that education is essential not only to enhance individual opportunity, but also to preserve freedom and to improve understanding of both people's differences and their commonalities. However, education, especially beyond high school, has not always been widely available.

The first community colleges were founded over a hundred years ago as "junior college" extensions of high schools. Students who successfully completed lower-division coursework could then transfer to upper-division universities to complete their baccalaureate degrees. The idea of increased access to higher education through these junior colleges gradually spread from state to state as a grassroots movement. As the colleges added vocational education, community service, and developmental education programs to their academic curricula, they evolved into today's comprehensive community colleges. They also serve their communities by providing contract education to local businesses and by acting as cultural centers for their communities.

In some states, the colleges started as technical colleges and later added academic transfer, developmental, and community service courses. Although today's community colleges are overwhelmingly public, funded by a combination of state appropriations, local tax support, and student fees, many of the early community colleges were private. Depending upon state and local preferences the colleges are called community colleges, technical colleges, junior colleges, or some combination, although the missions are similar.

Higher education in the United States was dramatically redefined in 1947 as a result of the work of President Harry S. Truman's Commission on Higher Education. The Truman Commission report changed the course of the academy from educating only the elite to providing opportunities for every citizen to pursue higher learning. While the first junior college was founded in 1901 and other early forms of community college were founded subsequently, the Truman Commission report marked the first general use of the term *community college* and emphasized the need for colleges that would be accessible and responsive to community needs for education.

As noted by the Commission on the Future of Community Colleges in 1988, from the beginning, these "people's colleges" zealously pursued an egalitarian mission. While other institutions of higher education may define excellence in terms of exclusivity, community colleges have sought excellence in their service to the many. Community colleges are generally open to all who wish to attend, although some courses or programs may have prerequisites. Student fees are generally kept low as a means of providing access to higher education regardless of financial status. While traditional colleges and universities too often have been isolated islands that do not participate in broader community life, community colleges have built connections beyond the campus.

Providing access to affordable and high-quality higher learning is one of the most important goals of the community college movement. Students do not have to leave home to attend college because the colleges and educational centers are in their communities. The campuses and centers are located within commuting distance of over 90 percent of the population of the United States. And a growing number of community colleges are making learning even more accessible by delivering courses through distance education (for example, online courses and classes offered on television).

Community colleges have traditionally responded to local educational needs, developing important vocational programs, partnering with local institutions and agencies, and providing contract education (for example, courses for law enforcement departments or courses to train emergency service technicians) and both credit and noncredit community service programs. Some colleges provide facilities and support services to incubate new businesses; others are cultural centers for their communities. They promote appreciation for diversity and inclusion by providing diversity awareness training, foreign-language courses, and speakers' series. English as a second language and citizenship courses are offered to new immigrants. For many people, the American dream is possible only because community colleges are there.

—*George R. Boggs*

Further Reading

Baker, G. A., III. (Ed.). (1994). *Handbook on community colleges in America.* Westport, CT: Greenwood.

Commission on the Future of Community Colleges. (1988). *Building communities: A vision for a new century.* Washington, DC: American Association of Community Colleges.

Gleazer, E. J., Jr. (1980). *The community college: Values, vision, and vitality.* Washington, DC: American Association of Community Colleges.

New Expeditions Initiative (2000). *The knowledge net: Connecting communities, learners, and colleges.* Washington, DC: American Association of Community Colleges.

Vaughan, G. B. (2000). *The community college story* (2nd ed.). Washington, DC: American Association of Community Colleges.

COMMUNITY CURRENCIES

Community currencies are fast-growing money and exchange systems operating on a local level in municipalities and regions worldwide. Conventional economic theory implicitly assumes that money is a passive medium of exchange affecting neither the transactions performed nor the relationships between the people using the money. In the framework of that hypothesis, community currencies may play a role different from the national currency only because they are local, that is, exchangeable in a smaller geographic area

The Kula Ring

The Kula Ring is a system of formal, balanced ceremonial and economic exchanges among peoples of several islands in the Melanesia region of the South Pacific. The exchange of shell ornaments and trade of food maintained peaceful relations among the island communities and created intergenerational ties across traders and families. The following is the text of an invocation offered by the Trobriand Islanders to those departing on a trading expedition.

Gebobo Spell

"My father, my mother . . . Kula, mwasila.

I shall fill my canoe with bagido'u,

I shall fill my canoe with bagiriku [food stuff],

I shall fill my canoe with bagidudu, etc."

[All the specific names of the necklaces are enumerated.]

"I shall anchor in the open sea, and my renown will go to the Lagoon,

I shall anchor in the Lagoon, and my renown will go to the open sea.

My companions will be on the open sea and on the Lagoon.

My renown is like thunder, my treading is like earthquake."

Source: Malinowski, Bronislaw. (1922). *Argonauts of the Western Pacific: An Account of Native Enterprise and Adventure in the Archipelagoes of Melanesian New Guinea*. London: George Routledge and Sons, Ltd, p. 205.

than is conventional money. The logic of that argument is that such a geographical limitation provides more frequent opportunities for local interactions, which in turn promotes a sense of community.

This argument is valid, but only to the extent that frequent interactions with someone for whatever reason provide an opportunity for a relationship to grow. But if that were the whole story, then local supermarkets in downtown Manhattan or Chicago would be the most vibrant community centers on the planet. Given that this does not tend to be the case, the relevant question becomes, why do local commercial exchanges not spontaneously create a sense of community?

Research has demonstrated that the hidden hypothesis that money is value neutral is not valid. Some money systems actually tend to destroy community, while others support and help in creating it. Today's conventional currencies (such as the U.S. dollar, Euro, yen, or any other national currency) unfortunately fall in the former category.

To understand the concept of community currencies, it is necessary to consider the evidence of the linkage between community and reciprocity that occurs through gift exchanges. The reason that conventional money does not support community is that it doesn't have built-in reciprocity (reciprocity means that whatever one person does for another, he or she can expect the other to do in return for him or her) and one key characteristic of "community currencies" is that they have reciprocity built in and are therefore more compatible with community building.

The word *community* derives from two Latin roots: *cum* (with), and *munus* (gift). Hence "community" suggests people's giving to one another. Anthropologists have confirmed that community is indeed based on reciprocity, typically through gift exchanges.

The most "modern" of all communities—the scientific community worldwide—is nurtured by the unwritten rule of reciprocity. Indeed, scientists who give their ideas to the community receive recognition and status. In contrast, those who try to make money from their ideas earn little recognition; they may even be scorned. "One reason why the publication of textbooks tends to be a despised form of scientific communication [is that] the textbook author appropriates community property for his personal profit" (Hagstrom 1965, p. 22).

As another example of reciprocity, Japan is the one developed country that has been bucking the worldwide trend toward community breakdown. This is often attributed to a mysterious peculiarity in the Japanese social structure or psyche. However, here too the key of reciprocal gift exchanges is applicable. The Japanese tradition of *Butsu Butsu Kokan* (literally "object-object-exchange") refers to the reciprocal nature of gift exchanges, a key ritual in practically all aspects of Japanese life.

Thus community should be considered a process, not a state. If it is not nourished by regular reciprocal exchanges, it tends to decay or die. Therefore, a community can be defined as a group of people who honor one another's gifts and who trust that their gifts will be reciprocated someday, in some way.

A purchase, such as buying a box of nails at a hardware store, involves no expectation of future reciprocity on the part of either the buyer or the seller, and no sense of community is created by such a purchase. On the other hand, if a neighbor offers a box of nails for free, a sense of community is created, and both neighbors are more likely to help each other in future. From a purely material viewpoint, both cases are the same: A person acquires a box of nails. But an anthropologist would point out that the gift of the box of nails is a community-building transaction, and its purchase is not.

CONVENTIONAL MONEY AND COMMUNITY BREAKDOWN

A commercial transaction is a closed system, nails versus money. In contrast, a gift is an open system, which leaves an imbalance in the transaction that some possible future transaction completes. The gift process implies reciprocity, while an exchange with conventional money does not.

For this reason, monastic communities prohibit the use of money among the brethren and sisters. Each member of the group has a function to perform—abbot, doorkeeper, cheese maker, whatever—as a gift to the community. The Buddhist monastic code goes further: The monastery itself cannot trade for money with the outside world. Lay supporters provide gifts of material requisites for the monastery, while the monastery members provide supporters with the gift of teaching.

Replacing gifts with conventional monetary exchanges tends to break down the feeling of community. This is what happened, for example, in the scientific community when universities started patenting genes in order to make money from this research. According to Professor Jonathan Kind of MIT, in past decades American biomedical scientists freely exchanged materials, strains of organism, and information. In more recent years, however, genetic researchers have begun sharing less freely than they did in the past, and that corner of the scientific community has been breaking down.

For society in general, some economic theories consider the use of conventional money in all transactions as a key sign of "development," because it is only when exchanges occur using conventional money that they are measured by the national statistical system. But one of the unforeseen consequences of this process is that community decay is typically also the highest in developed countries. Fortunately, this connection between money exchanges and community breakdown is not valid for all types of money. Some currencies, so-called community currencies, encourage reciprocity and are therefore compatible with community building.

COMMUNITY CURRENCIES

Over the past few decades, there has been a remarkable development of local initiatives involving community currencies. In 1990, there were less than a hundred such systems in the world; in 2002, there were more than 4,000 in a dozen or more countries. These community currencies have various names, such as Time Dollars, Ithaca Hours (from the city of Ithaca, New York), Local Exchange Trading Systems (LETS), Tlaloc (after the Aztec rain god) in Mexico, or the Japanese Caring Relationship Tickets *(Hureai Kippu).* There is even a currency called LOVE (local value exchange), which 80,000 of the 130,000 inhabitants of Yamato City (near Tokyo, Japan) use among themselves on smartcards (smartcards look similar to plastic credit cards, but have embedded computer chips instead of a magnetic strips, enabling them to perform more sophisticated transaction processing). These new types of currencies have a wide variety of forms. A few use paper bills, but most function mainly in electronic form. They all share certain features: They operate as complements to the conventional national money and are therefore often called complementary currencies; they are created by the communities themselves for their own use; and, most important, they have reciprocity built in and therefore are compatible with community building.

Time Dollars

One such system—Time Dollars—uses as a unit one hour of time contributed to someone in the community. As an illustration, Joe is retired and lives near a high school in Brooklyn, NY. He joins the local Time Dollar system and offers to mentor two kids with their math homework for three hours per week. He obtains thereby six hour credits per week in his account, and the kids get each debited three hours. With his Time credits, Joe can pay part of his Elderplan health insurance (this Brooklyn insurance company has discovered that active elders have fewer health problems and therefore accepts up to 25 percent of its premiums in Time Dollars). The kids compensate for their debits by lawn mowing for Julia, another participating neighbor. If the kids were providing the return service to Joe, this would be barter (a bilateral exchange for a good or service for another without any currency involved). But because this transaction involves its own accounting unit (the hour) that circulates in a community, these Time credits and debits are a real currency.

What is the difference between such a Time Dollar exchange and a normal U.S. dollar exchange? First, U.S. dollars are scarce for most people, and a community or an individual cannot create them but must earn or borrow them outside the community. In contrast, Time Dollars are created automatically as a credit and a debit whenever an exchange has been agreed on, and they are therefore always available in sufficiency, even in the poorest communities. Second, there are no interest payments on Time Dollars, so reimbursements are a lot easier to achieve than when the debt automatically gets bigger over time with cumulative interest, as is the case with dollars. Interest also tends to concentrate wealth—another source of community tensions—because people with a lot of money automatically obtain more money, while money gets even scarcer for those who have to borrow with interest.

Third, reciprocity is built into the transaction: When the kids accept Joe's mentorship, they automatically also accept that they are to give something back to someone in the community. Areas where Time Dollars are used also tend to have better community relationships then do areas that lack them. Finally, the U.S. Internal Revenue Service (IRS) has ruled that income in Time Dollars is tax exempt.

Some Other Examples

Other types of community currencies have other rules and units than do Time Dollars and may not enjoy the tax exemption of the Time Dollar. For instance, in Ithaca, New York, and forty other U.S. cities, a paper currency called the Ithaca Hour has been circulating since 1995 and is denominated in time like Time Dollars. It takes the form of paper bills with the slogan "In Ithaca We Trust," with denominations of one hour, a half hour, and a quarter hour.

There are also now more than one thousand LETS in more than a dozen countries. The core idea remains fairly similar to Time Dollars, except that the unit of account is not hours of service but often is equal to the national currency. For instance, Canadian LETS systems use a "Green Dollar" whose value is the same as the Canadian dollar; in Manchester, England, a "Bobbin" with value equal to an English pound circulates. Even if these nonconventional currencies use the national currency unit as a reference, however, they are still called community currencies because they all have in common that they are created in a community; they can be made available in sufficiency; they are interest free; and they have reciprocity built in. These characteristics make them more compatible with gift exchanges and therefore with community building.

IMPLICATIONS FOR THE FUTURE

This is the first time in history—outside of wars or financial collapses—that community currencies have spontaneously appeared in such numbers and diversity worldwide. It is likely that today's systems will be looked upon in the future as early prototype tools for social engineering—a bit like we look back at Wright Brothers' aeronautics. It is a miracle that they fly, but what really matters is that they have proven that flying is possible. Community currencies indeed bear the promise to play a growing role in the future for four different reasons:

- They are a product of the information revolution, and cheap and decentralized computing possibilities will predictably further increase over time.
- It is a fact that their availability facilitates exchanges that otherwise wouldn't occur, thereby creating additional wealth and work wherever they circulate, without burdening taxpayers or needing bureaucracies to be implemented.
- They have already proven that they can contribute to solving a whole range of social problems. From fostering local employment to elderly care to youth mentoring, community currencies have helped to solve long-standing problems, and they do so on a more cost-effective basis in dollar terms than the conventional centralized solutions of yesteryear.
- Perhaps most important, they have proven that they contribute to rebuilding community, something which a majority of people in our modern society desire a lot more of.

—Bernard Lietaer

Further Reading

Douthwaite, R. (1996). *Short circuit: Strengthening local economies for security in an unstable world.* Devon, UK: Green Books.

Greco, T. (2001). *Money: Understanding and creating alternatives to legal tender.* White River Junction, VT: Chelsea Green.

Hagstrom, W. O. (1965). *The scientific community.* New York: Basic Books.

Hyde, L. (1983). *The gift: Imagination and the erotic life of property.* New York: Vintage.

Lietaer, B. (2001). *The future of money.* London: Random House.

Transaction Net. (2001). Retrieved January 8, 2003, from http://www.transaction.net/money/

COMMUNITY DEVELOPMENT CORPORATIONS

Community development corporations (CDCs), a U.S. phenomenon, are largely inner-city nonprofit businesses controlled by neighborhood residents who work to give local communities a voice in urban development strategies. CDCs vary in size and program. Noted for the production of nonprofit housing, CDCs also create social, educational, and political infrastructures that build community from the ground up. In 1999, Urban affairs and public policy experts Ross Gittell and Margaret Wilder reported that between 1991 and 1993, there were more than 2,200 CDCs, and that they existed in all fifty states. They also reported that 1,046 CDCs (77 percent) each received a $50,000 federal grant, while 150 CDCs each received $1 million in equity for housing developments. City and regional planning experts Spencer Cowen, William Rohe, and Esmail Baku reported that in 1999 the median CDC staff size was four persons, and the median budget was $134,000. Relatively small in size and impact, CDCs network local and foundation funding to provide sites of transformation, hope, and promise.

The evolutionary nature of CDCs makes it difficult to historically pinpoint its origins. The black community points to the black church as a critical originator of community development activities. In a case study that characterized the historical driving force behind black community building (1895-1910), Shirley J. Portwood found that community development activities were sustained by the strongly held and deeply rooted African American sensibility that "when the community calls you, you say yes." Other historians point to the Ford Foundation's Gray Areas Program (1960), urban redevelopment programs of the Kennedy and Johnson administration (1966) and Nixon's new federalism (1970) as critical stages in the evolution of CDCs. CDCs continue to advance integrated and democratic social and economic opportunities as part of the ongoing battle against racism. Historians such as Portwood argue that the disrupting factors of class, skin color, and gender—divisions used by black elites to undermine black community solidarity—cannot be left unexamined.

The westward expansion of the nineteenth century, the explosion of urban populations in the twentieth century, the Great Depression, and the suburban expansion of the 1940s–1960s left urban centers without middle- or upper-class support. The housing demolition of the 1960s—theoretically to make way for new, better housing that often never came—left cities with a housing crisis that continues today. In response to this situation, exacerbated by poverty and crime, The Housing and Community Development Act of 1974 created the Community Development Block Grant (CDBG) program, which financially supported CDC bottom-up development strategies. Federal funding of CDCs peaked in this decade. From their inception, CDCs faced great obstacles, as the era was one in which regulatory social institutions were being dismantled and the consequences of failing to share the benefits of the U.S. economic system with minorities was becoming painfully evident. In spite of that, substantial white resistance to minority economic development continued.

The CDCs persevered, and by the 1980s an expansive community development knowledge base was producing handbooks on community-based development and guides for obtaining technical assistance. The mid-1990s found the CDC movement with sufficient programmatic history to begin to assess its history. By 2000, those assessments, largely ethnographic in nature, found them to be effective, and they favored continuous improvement processes aimed at building capacities and at retaining skills in the community. CDCs remain popular development tools, as they are seen to correct defects in the U.S. capitalist system. International development success with economic cooperatives suggests a promising expansion of CDC activity into the international sphere.

—Victoria Lee Erickson

Further Reading

Cowen, S., Rohe W., & Baku, E. (1999). Factors influencing performance of community development corporations. *Journal of Urban Affairs, 21*(3), 325–340.

Gittell, R., & Wilder, M. (1999). Community development corporations: Critical factors that influence success. *Journal of Urban Affairs, 21*(3), 341–362.

Peirce, N, R., & Steinbach, C. F. (1986). *Corrective capitalism: The rise of America's community development corporations.* New York: The Ford Foundation.

Peirce, N. R., & Steinbach, C. (1990). *Enterprising communities: Community-based development in America, 1990.* Washington, DC: Council for Community-Based Development.

Portwood, S. J. (2000). "We lift our voices in thunder tones": African American race men and race women and community agency in southern Illinois, 1895–1910. *Journal of Urban History, 26*(6), 740–758.

Shipp, S. C. (1996, March). The road not taken: Alternative strategies for black economic development in the United States. Mondragon Cooperative Movement and black leader's economic development models. *Journal of Economic Issues, 30,* 79–95.

COMMUNITY DEVELOPMENT IN EUROPE

In Europe, the term *community* has very diverse connotations depending on the context in which it is used and on the cultural and historical background of the users. In everyday English speech in northern Europe, community connotes locality, familiarity, and common binding interests. It may refer to a specific group or place or it may be used in a vague way, based on the unarticulated values of a loosely defined group. It can be used in either of these instances to exclude people as well as to include them.

When the word *community* is used in conjunction with the term *development,* the combination has a special significance, but again, that significance varies from country to country. In northern and western European countries, it is an established term with similar resonance, while in southern Europe the term *local social development* has been used in preference to community development. In central and eastern Europe, the legacy of the social and political ideology of the Communist era is apparent. In the analysis of community published by the Hungarian Association for Community Development, Tamás A. Varga and Ilona Vercseg have described how the term had to be reinvented because in the Soviet era *community* was defined as a "quality group" that carried out the social objectives set by the political elite.

COMMUNITY DEVELOPMENT NETWORKING

The Hungarian Association for Community Development is a member of the Combined European Bureau for Social Development (CEBSD), a network of associations and organizations from across Europe that promotes community development. The interpretations of community and community development presented here are drawn from the members and associates of this network. There is increasing convergence in definitions of community as a result of exchanges of ideas and experience in the last decade.

Two CEBSD members, the Community Development Foundation (United Kingdom) and Combat Poverty Agency (Ireland), specify two main interpretations of community. One is characterized by a sense of place and usually indicates the local community or neighborhood, and the other indicates a community of interest. (Examples of the latter type of community include women, single parents, people with disabilities, students, lesbians and gay men, older people, young people, religious groups, and ethnic groups.) Landelijk Centrum Opbouwwerk in the Netherlands makes this same distinction and adds the third dimension of communities based on a shared workplace or organization, such as a locally based church or housing association.

In Italy, Spain, and in France, where the term *local social development* is used to describe what would be referred to as community development in the United Kingdom, Ireland, or the Netherlands, the perspective on development is often more directly related to international debates on development. This is evidenced in a number of fora for exchange between southern Europe and Latin America. The French member of the Combined European Bureau for Social Development (CEBSD), Le Mouvement pour un Devélopment Social Local (Movement for Local Social Development), has regular exchanges with professionals in Latin America. Similarly, Carles Riera, the director of Desenvolupament Comunitari (Community Development), based in Catalonia, Spain, represented CEBSD in a forum for cooperation among civil societies in Latin America, the Caribbean, and Europe. This forum sought to increase members' ability to influence and establish dialogue, and to develop alternatives to development models imposed from the top down. A bottom-up approach is seen to be more in keeping with the development of community and civil society. This commitment to shifting power to the local level is a common theme running through both community development and local social development.

While many northern European countries share some common concept of community, the development of a shared understanding between countries and regions has been uneven. Armin Kuphal of Paritaetisches Bildungswerk (a training and support body for small non governmental organizations) points out that the concept of community development is quite a recent one in Germany, and a new word (gemeinwesenarbeit) has been coined to distance it from the limited associations of the word gemeinschaft ("association") or the negative associations of *Volksgemeinschaft,* which was used during the Nazi era to signify the Nazi ideological definition of the community of German people (which excluded Jews, Rom Gypsies, etc.).

The professional organization of work in local communities varies considerably at every level of government. Within Belgium, the distinction between community development and local social development, described above, is reflected in the different structures in the Dutch-speaking Flanders region and the French-speaking Walloon region. VIBOSO (Vlaams Instituut ter Bevordering en Ondersteuning van deSamenlevingsopbouw; in English, "Flemish Institute for the Promotion and Support of Community Building") supports community development regional centers, community workers, and local authorities in the Flemish part of Belgium. Its activities include training, research, and publications. No similar community development body exists in the French-speaking Walloon region, where local social development is likely to be organized by local government. In those countries of the European Union with a developed social welfare system (for example, the United Kingdom, Germany, France, Sweden), "case" work rather than "community" work was the dominant mode of intervention in poorer communities in the latter half of the twentieth century. In countries with a less developed social welfare system, community activism tended to be spontaneous and voluntary.

Cross-fertilization across national boundaries has contributed to developments in the last decade, and more convergence is becoming evident. The Combined European Bureau for Social Development has close links with other European networks through its membership in the European Social Platform (an association of more than thirty-five European non-governmental organizations, federations and networks that work in the social sector and uphold the interests of a wide spectrum of European civil society). It also collaborates closely with the International Association for Community Development and supports community organizing in central and eastern Europe as a current joint priority.

COMMON PRINCIPLES

Members of the Combined European Bureau for Social Development have developed a set of shared principles appropriate to community development and local social development. These principles are outlined in a CEBSD publication, *Social Inclusion and Citizenship in Europe: The Contribution of Community Development,* by Paul Henderson, a senior manager in the Community Development Foundation. They are summarized below.

Individual and Collective

Community development is concerned with change and development of both individuals and groups. The process of change and development of a group is interconnected with individual learning. Individuals acquire skills, knowledge, and self-confidence because they are involved with a community group, or learn to value skills and knowledge that they already have. Increased individual development can enrich community development and vice versa. For this reason, provision of training and support for members of community groups and maintaining links with community and adult education programs should be integral to the process of community development.

Process and Outcomes

Linked to the above principle is a creative tension between a concern with the educational process for both individuals and groups and a desire for the achievement of concrete outcomes, such as a new community center, a local employment project, safe play areas for children, and so forth. In this sense, community development is always contestable. Some see it as being aligned closely to adult-education philosophy and methods; others are more interested in it as a means of delivering programs and services. Most community developers seek to keep a balance between process and outcome goals so as to achieve maximum effectiveness.

Focus on Disadvantage

Throughout its comparatively short history, community development has been strongly committed to working with and on behalf of disadvantaged people, whether women, members of ethnic minority groups, disabled people, or unemployed people. The commitment to equality is coupled with the understanding that the groups most at risk of poverty are those that are most likely to experience discrimination. Community development has sought to counter assumptions that poor people must depend on services from welfare agencies, that they lack the motivation and skills to do things for themselves. Community developers believe that the causes of poverty and disaffection are structural, not lodged in the pathology or supposedly inherent weaknesses of particular neighborhoods. Community developers help to build coalitions around alternatives to powerful global economic forces.

Participation

An essential principle of community development is to keep groups and organizations open. *Access* is the key word; groups that become dominated by leaders and cliques and groups that discourage new members should be challenged. A policy or strategy that does not actively involve any group affected by it is seriously flawed and likely to fail. Participation should be organized so that all affected groups and the wider constituency that they represent are included.

It is also important for public policy makers to accept and support the participation of community groups in matters that affect them. Community development leaders are very alert to the ease with which participation of local people can be reduced to a mere token gesture without commitment to change; for the participation to be genuine, policy makers must be committed to following through on proposals and decisions.

Prevention

Community development is just as concerned with enabling people to bring to fruition projects and ideas that they support as with empowering them to fight those they oppose. There are exciting examples of local people in effect becoming planners: discussing with officials how they would like to see their community develop and playing key roles in realizing the vision. The involvement and active participation of local people in finding solutions to potential problems is one means by which community development can prevent problems from materializing. Similarly, social and educational activities (for instance, the establishment of a neighborhood advice center, family center, or playground) can divert energy from potentially negative manifestation into positive channels and thus help prevent problems from arising or escalating.

Change and Influence

A commitment to bring about change, as well as to help people cope with the effects of change, is fundamental to community development. A passionate concern to question the status quo, to challenge, stimulate, and support people to organize together in order to achieve agreed-upon objectives, is central to community development.

PRINCIPLES AND PRACTICE

The above principles are the raw material that is combined with a region or nation's social, cultural, economic, political and ideological history. In the 1990s, the Swedish member of the CEBSD, Centrum För Samhällsarbete och Mobilisering (Centre for Community Work and Mobilisation, known by its Swedish acronym, CESAM) recognized that community work and community mobilization were also appropriate in Sweden. They combined theory and practice from the Anglo-Saxon model with models drawn from local experience in Sweden. Their approach did not always fit easily into the structures for care and welfare in Sweden, but it is increasingly relevant to discussion and action on democratic community organization. CESAM has developed a national database and training materials (especially on techniques for democratic meetings) for joint planning and decision making. Work on greater participation in the democratic life of the community has generated interest in neighboring Norway, where an organization called Idébanken ("Ideas Bank") is a member of the Combined European Bureau for Social Development. The Ideas Bank was set up in 1991; its main purpose is to demonstrate good practice in community development and to promote creative dialogues on local futures within a sustainable framework. Like CESAM in Sweden, the Ideas Bank works with both community groups and municipalities.

The recognition that there are multiple interpretations of community and the need to find common ground for exchange of ideas and practice has preoccupied the CEBSD for more than a decade. In 1991, Wim van Rees, a researcher in urban planning, community, and social development and director of the Combined European Bureau for Social Development from 1990 to 1995, compiled and edited a survey of community development in Europe. In his chapter titled "Neighbourhoods, the State and Collective Action," he rooted the concept of community in a multidimensional context, taking into account its social and spatial reality, the interplay of health, education, and welfare services, and ideological or political realities. He wrote, "Many of the neighbourhoods with which we are concerned are the outcome of a mix of decentralised, urban planning, infrastructural and human service factors. . . . They have little in common with romantic notions of 'community' which refer to identity, homogeneity, security and sense of place" (van Rees 1991, p. 134).

COMMON CONCERNS

Faced with these many different dimensions and interpretations, many would question whether a shared understanding of community is possible. In *Social Inclusion and Citizenship in Europe: The Contribution of Community Development,* Paul Henderson acknowledges that many would argue that inner-city neighborhoods have too little in common with, for instance, the depopulated rural villages of France to allow for a Europe-wide approach to community. Nonetheless he argues that a shared experience of social exclusion and a concomitant sense of powerlessness link those divergent environments. These common themes are then integrated into the broader picture of what is meant by an inclusive community. Tamás A. Varga and Ilona Vercseg, in their analysis of community development in the Hungarian context, question whether it is possible to speak about communality in modern societies at all, or whether communality is abstract ideal with no identifiable contemporary reality. They conclude that the concept of community is useful and emphasize that the gap between the human and humane values implicit in a sense of community and the economic and policy priorities of governments needs to be closed.

Members of the Combined European Bureau for Social Development seek to achieve interaction between social, economic, political, and cultural values and explore ways of linking the individual citizen with the different levels of government. As part of the commitment to working toward more inclusive and equal communities, community developers place a strong emphasis on the principle of participation in this process. When the word *community* is added to technical terminology, it has the effect of implying that the users of a particular service are participating in its management. Consider, for example, the terms *community audit, community business, community health,* and *community policing.* In one of the most comprehensive international studies of community development, *Community Development around the World,* Hubert Campfens, a professor of community development and social planning at Wilfred Laurier University in Ontario, Canada, advocates "a more pluralistic and participatory approach to planning in which state agencies function more in partnership with NGOs [nongovernmental

Creating Social Cohesion in Europe

The following extract is from a report prepared by the Council of Europe on the importance of creating social cohesion in the European Community.

The Importance of Social Cohesion

The need to address the issue of social cohesion is rooted in society's fragmentation. Insecurity and instability (including the impact of organised crime and corruption), alienation through poverty, the loss of confidence in democratic systems, the growth of individualism within society, competition right up to global level—all of these explain people's reluctance to participate in civil society. What is at stake in social cohesion is the need to preserve democratic society while simultaneously establishing new forms of social relationships in response to ongoing and deep-seated change. The challenge is how to live together in democratic societies.

Definitions of Social Cohesion

Social cohesion is an unlimited, multidimensional concept. It is linked to exclusion in the many fields of housing, health, social protection and education. Its aim is to mould society into a coherent—but not a homogeneous—whole. In order to achieve this, an answer must be found to the question: what is it that binds people together?

Social cohesion comprises a sense of belonging: to a family, a social group, a neighbourhood, a workplace, a country or, why not, to Europe (though care must be taken to avoid erecting a Schengen Wall to replace the Berlin Wall). Yet this sense of belonging must not be exclusive; instead, multiple identity and belonging must be encouraged. Social cohesion implies the well-being of individuals and that of the community, founded on tenets such as the quality, health and permanence of society. In addition to social ties, cohesion must be built upon social justice. Social cohesion also constitutes a process of membership of and contribution to a blueprint for society. As active citizens, individuals must be able to feel responsible and to prosper both in terms of personal development and as regards their income and living standards.

One paradox pointed out during discussion was that multinational companies have a part to play in creating shared experiences, for example through fast food chains, which are gaining ground all over the world. [the "McDonalds effect" in social cohesion]. Although social cohesion is closely linked to employment, it is nonetheless not exclusively dependent on it, because work is no guarantee in itself of social integration. Social ties are built less upon employment than upon active participation—whether paid or not.

Source: Council of Europe. (1999). *Education for Democratic Citizenship & Social Cohesion.* Retrieved March 5, 2003, from http://www.coe.int/T/e/Cultural_Co-operation/Education/E.D.C/Documents_and_publications/By_Type/Reports/edc_social.asp.

organizations] and community organisations" (Campfens 1997, p. 21). The European Union recognizes the importance of social cohesion to sustained economic growth. A Community Action Programme to Combat Social Exclusion 2002–2006 has been set up, and there is a strong commitment to an open method of coordination in the development of policy to counteract social exclusion. More information about the European Union's social inclusion process can be found at the page on employment and social affairs on the Web site of the European Commission, accessed through the European Union Web site (http://europe.eu.int/comm/employment_social/soc-prot/soc-include/index_en.htm).

THE EUROPEAN COMMUNITY

When *European* prefixes *community,* the latter term has a radically different resonance than it does when community workers use it. Both poles are nonetheless important in European networking and to those interested in international exchange of community development ideas. The European Community is an official entity formed by a contract between its fifteen member states. Its objectives are as follows:

- to promote European unity;
- to improve living and working conditions for citizens;
- to foster economic development, balanced trade and fair competition;
- to reduce economic disparities between regions;
- to help developing countries;
- to preserve peace and freedom.

(The Court of Justice of the European Communities 2002)

These objectives have resonance at both national and local levels of community and are reflective of a common consensus. However, there are underlying concerns. For example, there is concern over the limitations of representative democracy in truly representing the interests of local communities. There is further concern over those whose interests are not represented, as they are not citizens of a member state (for example, refugees). Many nongovernmental organizations are concerned that marginal communities will be even more marginalized by European centralization. Others worry that the sovereignty of each member state may be eroded by European convergence, or that more steps to "European" unity will result in increased globalization. They fear domination by larger states at the expense of small states, regional governments, and local government.

THE FUTURE OF COMMUNITY IN EUROPE

In spite of the many differences, governments, nongovernmental organizations, the European Union, European networks, and other European institutions are formulating a fragile and open set of working criteria from which a new understanding of community could develop. Common themes in the discussion of community are individual and collective interdependence, a sense of belonging, social and cultural interaction, interaction of the community with economic and political forces, and shared interests. A further addition is a commitment to equal development within and between communities. Networks at every level of operation from the most local to the European Council now face the challenge of whether a common concept of community can be sustained and developed at all levels and for all interest groups in the further enlargement of the European Union.

—Margo Gorman

Further Reading

Campfens, H. (1997). *Community development around the world.* Toronto, Canada: University of Toronto Press.

Chanan, G. (1992). *Out of the shadows: Local community action and the European community.* Dublin, Ireland: European Foundation for the Improvement of Living and Working Conditions.

Chanan, G., Garrett, C., & West, A. (2001). *The new community strategies: How to involve the local people.* London, UK: Community Development Foundation.

Combat Poverty Agency. (2000). *The role of community development in tackling poverty.* Retrieved September 20, 2002, from http://www.cebsd.org/social_14.htm

Combined European Bureau for Social Development. (2002). Retrieved August 23, 2002, from http://www.cebsd.org

Court of Justice of the European Communities. (2002). *What is the European Community?* Retrieved September 20, 2002, from http://curia.eu.int/en/pres/qce.htm

European Commission. (1996). *Community social policy: Programmes, networks and observatories.* Luxembourg City, Luxembourg: Author.

Gester, L., & Crossley, R. (2000). *Community development.* York, UK: York Publishing

Henderson, P. (2002). *Social inclusion and citizenship in Europe: The contribution of community development.* The Hague, Netherlands: Dr. Gradus Hendriks-stichting.

Partners for Livable Communities. (2000). *The livable city: Revitalizing urban communities.* Washington, DC: McGraw-Hill.

Pierson, J., & Smith, J. (Eds.). (2001). *Rebuilding community: Policy and practice in urban regeneration.* New York: Palgrave.

Russell, H. (1998). *A place for the community?* Bristol, UK: Polity.

van Rees, Wim. (1991). *Survey of CD in Europe.* The Hague, Netherlands: Dr. Gradus Hendriks-stichting.

Vercseg, I., & Varga, T. A. (1998). *Community development.* Budapest, Hungary: Hungarian Association for Community Development and Hungarian Institute for Culture.

COMMUNITY EMPOWERMENT

Empowerment refers to a process whereby a sense of powerlessness is replaced with the ability to exercise greater control over circumstances or conditions that affect a person's quality of life or life situation. Often, improving these circumstances or conditions requires overcoming obstacles that hinder access to social or economic resources, such as quality health care, job opportunities, or safe, affordable housing. Obstacles to acquiring these resources may stem from inequities in social institutions or structures, resulting in discrimination and oppression among certain populations or communities. Some organizations may stand firm in an attempt to maintain the status quo of power, refusing to relinquish their control over the decision-making process that determines the distribution of resources among communities. Obstacles can also develop when the level of social organization within a community declines, leaving residents feeling powerless and isolated from one another, resulting in a loss of social networks and neighboring relationships important to the fabric of community life. Empowerment at a community level can address these structural, political, and social obstacles.

PRINCIPLES OF COMMUNITY EMPOWERMENT

Despite the popularity of the term *community empowerment*, the concept eludes a precise definition. While some disciplines have contributed to defining aspects of community empowerment, these contributions often refer only to a particular viewpoint. For example, the field of public health often defines community empowerment in terms of "wellness" and the ability of local residents to increase health-promoting behaviors. From this definition, a campaign aimed at reducing alcohol or tobacco use would constitute one method for empowering the community through education, leading to a collective change in behavior. Therefore, community empowerment is best defined by understanding the principles that it embodies. A review of the literature in this area reveals the recurrence of three key principles: capacity building, collaboration, and community action.

The first key principle involves building the competence or capacity of local residents and groups. Robert Chaskin, a professor of sociology, and others have described community capacity as the basis of what makes a community "work." Efforts directed at building the capacity of a community focus on identifying the knowledge, talents, skills, and social networks of individuals, groups, and local organizations. Empowered communities can successfully transform these assets or capacities into sources of power to be applied to addressing community concerns. One example of such a transformation is the creation of "intergenerational childcare" programs; members of the growing aging population enhance their sense of purpose by caring for children, and children benefit from a nurturing environment provided by experienced caregivers that promotes a healthy social and emotional development. Capacity building supports a strengths-based perspective that recognizes the existing level of competence or experience of individuals, families, and groups. Empowered communities engage in capacity-building strategies as an important means of increasing the information and resources available for developing innovative partnerships that promote community well-being.

A second aspect of community empowerment is providing opportunities for residents and local organizations to collaborate as change agents in resolving problems. The aim is to reduce dependence on larger institutions and social systems, usually external to the community, that have traditionally played a major role in addressing local concerns. Instead, empowered communities can develop collaborations that harness power at the grassroots level. Partnerships that draw on the assets, skills, and resources of individuals and groups can help to construct creative solutions to community issues. Viewing collaboration as an inclusive process helps to ensure that all those with a stake in the future of the community have an opportunity to become involved in defining problems and developing solutions. University-community partnerships constitute one type of grassroots collaboration designed to bring together resident groups, neighborhood-based organizations, and local institutions such as churches and schools to assess and address community issues.

The third key principle in defining community empowerment is the use of advocacy and community or social action as change strategies to promote community well-being. Community empowerment includes the notion of developing or shifting power to those who have become marginalized and therefore have not participated in local policy- and decision-making processes. Social advocacy and social action focus on changing policies, institutions, and systems that restrict or hinder access to services and resources or that interfere with the equitable distribution of those services and resources throughout a community. Empowered communities display a sense of collective efficacy, so that the knowledge and skills of individuals and groups can be mobilized to bring about social and political change to improve the quality of life and life choices in the community. Increasing the level of power among those residing in the community is also important for sustaining change efforts. As residents and partners (such as local businesses, faith-based organizations, and voluntary associations) gain power, they are better equipped for determining what issues are important to address and how resources should be allocated. Community action programs, established under President Lyndon Johnson's 1964 Economic Opportunity Act, for example, focus on training local residents in the skills of organizing and citizen leadership to ensure a strong voice for political and social action.

PERSPECTIVES OF COMMUNITY EMPOWERMENT

Several disciplines have been instrumental in developing frameworks or perspectives for understanding the dynamics of empowered communities. The fields of public health, community psychology, and social work have studied community empowerment as a paradigm for social change. Historically, the discipline of public health has relied on the concept of community empowerment to support prevention and early intervention services in urban neighborhoods and rural towns, by involving residents in recognizing health and safety issues in the larger environment and by drawing on local assets for developing resources to change behaviors effectively. In this view, a healthy community rests on individual choices, so that empowered communities can engage in decision-making processes about new policies and behaviors that promote wellness. For instance, the Healthy City and Community Movement that was launched in Europe in 1986 (and which grew into an international program in six years), endorses a broad definition of health that encompasses social, economic, behavioral, cultural, and environmental indicators as measures of community well-being. The overarching goal of the Healthy City and Community Movement is to build stronger, healthier, and sustainable communities through citizen involvement and local asset development.

Community psychology scholars, such as Julian Rappaport, viewed community empowerment as drawing on the existing skills and knowledge of local residents, groups, and organizations, including churches, clubs, and voluntary associations, rather than relying on professionals or outside experts. Research in this area has examined the effectiveness of mutual networks of support, informal service-delivery systems, and collaborative partnerships in reversing the plight of disempowered communities. Research findings suggest that building empowered communities is directly related to feeling a greater sense of personal empowerment among community members.

The social work discipline is also concerned with using the notion of community empowerment in disadvantaged and marginalized communities. Beginning with the settlement house movement of the late 1860s, social workers such as Jane Addams (1860–1935) sought to reform social systems that contributed to discrimination and oppression among vulnerable populations, and attempts at community empowerment continued during the late 1960s and into the 1970s. Several decades later, community organizing continues to be a strategy in revitalizing urban and rural communities. From the social work perspective, community empowerment is a means of social and economic change that emphasizes citizen participation, reforming oppressive social institutions, and advocating policies that are socially and economically just.

CURRENT INFLUENCES OF COMMUNITY EMPOWERMENT

From the late 1980s on, the concept of community empowerment gained renewed interest as a social change strategy to address issues adversely affecting the quality of life in urban and rural communities. During this time, many inner-city neighborhoods were faced with rising rates of crime, unemployment, and poverty, coupled with declining economic resources and diminishing social services. Many rural communities also experienced hardships through the loss of job opportunities and declining social and economic resources. To combat these problems, Kretzman and McKnight began the assets-based community development movement through the Institute for Policy Research at Northwestern University in Evanston, Illinois. Their assets-based model embraces several principles related to community empowerment, such as the idea of creating power through the recognition and development of the assets and competencies of local individuals, groups, and organizations.

Kretzman and McKnight also emphasized "building from the inside out," stressing that leadership and responsibility begin in the community, not outside it. Drawing on local assets, those with a direct stake in the welfare of the community must begin the process of growing those assets into innovative resources that can expand the potential of the community. In this way, empowered communities can mobilize their human, social, and economic resources to address local problems or structural barriers.

The assets-based model thus calls for community development efforts to be locally driven. Resident participation is a necessary ingredient for sustainability. Although collaborative partnerships are encouraged, long-term change requires that local leaders emerge to direct community power toward resolving community issues and developing additional community resources.

Since the 1990s, many researchers and scholars interested in the study of community empowerment have expanded their focus to study how empowerment is related to the concept of social capital. Similar to the concept of community empowerment, social capital eludes a precise definition but generally refers to the bonds, networks, or relationships among individuals and between individuals and local institutions, bonds that are sustained by trust.

Two forms of social capital are bonding and bridging. Bonding refers to the ties that develop through face-to-face exchanges with community members and

Selection From *The Quest for Community*

Robert Nisbet's The Quest for Community, *originally published in 1953, is considered a classic work of political sociology. It was a powerful statement about the value of traditional small communities as well as an attack on political centralization Popular and influential with conservatives and strongly anti-Communist, it was republished in 1970 and 1990. In the excerpt below, from the 1970 edition, the author discusses the evolution of his thoughts on the "quest for community" in the years since he first wrote the book.*

I believe today, as I believed throughout the 1940's, when this book was beginning to take form in my mind, that the single most impressive fact in the twentieth century in Western society is the fateful combination of widespread quest for community—in whatever form, moral, social, political—and the apparatus of political power that has become so vast in contemporary democratic states. That combination of search for community and existing political power seems to me today, just as it did twenty years ago, a very dangerous combination. For, as I argue in this book, the expansion of power feeds on the quest for community. All too often, power comes to resemble community, especially in times of convulsive social change and of widespread preoccupation with personal identity, moral certainty, and social meaning. This is, as I try to make clear throughout the book, the essential tragedy of modern man's quest for community. Too often the quest has been through channels of power and revolution which have proved destructive of the prime sources of human community. The structure of political power which came into being three centuries ago has remained—has indeed become ever more—destructive of the contexts of new forms of community.

No, the central argument of the book would remain the same, were I writing it today instead of twenty years ago. There would be, however, some changes of emphasis, if only as a means of making clearer the central argument of the book. Let me indicate briefly what these few changes would consist of.

In the first place, I would, to the best of my ability, preclude any possible supposition on the reader's part that there is in this book any lament for the old, any nostalgia for village, parish, or other type of now largely erased form of social community of the past. Rereading the book today, I am frank in saying that I cannot find a nostalgic note in the entire book. It is not the revival of old communities that the book in a sense pleads for; *it is the establishment of new forms*: forms which are relevant to contemporary life and thought. What I have tried very hard to do, however, is to show that a structure of power capable of obliterating traditional types of community is capable of choking off new types of community. Hence the appeal, in the final pages of the book, for what I call a new *laissez-faire*, one within which groups, associations, and communities would prosper and which would be, by their very vitality, effective barriers to further spread of unitary, centralized, political power.

Source: Nisbet, Robert A. (1970). *The Quest for Community.* London: Oxford University Press, p. vii–viii. (Original work published 1953)

through interactions with local institutions. Churches, schools, and voluntary or civic associations have a role in forging such ties, which strengthen the social fabric. As individuals become more connected with the resources surrounding them, a stronger sense of collective action may emerge.

Bridging involves expanding social ties to networks and institutions external to the local community. This type of social capital allows community empowerment to transcend geographic boundaries and encourages ties with new sources of information, resources, and power.

In the still-emerging theory of social capital as an empowerment strategy, the roles of civic engagement, social networks, and building trust with local institutions are being explored as ways of creating opportunities that strengthen the connections between individuals and their surrounding community. In this regard, social capital is viewed as a vehicle for building political power through the development of social assets and ties to influential networks. Empowered communities can engage in collective efforts by harnessing internal resources from residents and local organizations as well as resources gathered through strong ties to external institutions. One such example is that of university-community partnerships, which serve to hold the institution accountable as a good neighbor by making both social and economic investments off campus that enhance the quality of life for students, employees, and local residents. This approach seems to hold particular promise for communities described as distressed or "resource poor." In such cases, building social capital can develop the capacities of local communities and encourage involvement in revitalization activities that foster political power.

—Robin L. Ersing

Further Reading

Baron, S., Field, J., & Schuller, T. (Eds.). (2000). *Social capital: Critical perspectives.* New York: Oxford University Press.

Brueggemann, W. G. (2002). *The practice of macro social work.* Belmont, CA: Brooks/Cole.

Cashman, S. B., Fulmer, H. S., & Staples, L. (1994). Community health: Beyond care for individuals. *Social Policy, 24*(4), 52–63.

Chaskin, R. J., Brown, P., Venkatesh, S., & Vidal, A. (2001). *Building community capacity.* New York: Aldine de Gruyter.

Dreier, P. (1996). Community empowerment strategies: The limits and potential of community organizing in urban neighborhoods. *Cityscape: A Journal of Policy Development and Research* 2(2), 121–159.

Fawcett, S. B., Paine-Andrews, A., Francisco, V. T., Schultz, J. A., Richter, K. P., Lewis, R. K., et al. (1995). Using empowerment theory in collaborative partnerships for community health and development. *American Journal of Community Psychology, 23*(5), 677–698.

Gutierrez, L. M. (1990). Working with women of color: An empowerment perspective. *Social Work, 35*(2), 97–192.

Hancock, T. (1997). Healthy cities and communities: Past, present, and future. *National Civic Review, 86*(1), 11–22.

Kirst-Ashman, K. K. (2000). *Human behavior, communities, organizations, & groups in the macro social environment: An empowerment approach.* Belmont, CA: Wadsworth Brooks/Cole.

Kretzmann, J. P., & McKnight, J. L. (1993). *Building communities from the inside out: A path toward finding and mobilizing a community's assets.* Chicago: ACTA.

Morrison, J. D., Howard, J., Johnson, C., Navarro, F. J., Plachetka, B., & Bell, T. (1997). Strengthening neighborhoods by developing community networks. *Social Work, 42*(5), 527–534.

Norris, T., & Pittman, M. (2000, March–June). The healthy communities movement and the coalition for healthier cities and communities. *Public Health Reports,* 118–128.

Perkins, D. D. (1995). Speaking truth to power: Empowerment ideology as social intervention and policy. *American Journal of Community Psychology, 23*(5), 765–794.

Perkins, D. D., Brown, B. B., & Taylor, R. B. (1996). The ecology of empowerment: Predicting participation in community organizations. *Journal of Social Issues, 52*(1), 85–110.

Perkins, D. D., & Zimmerman, M. A. (1995). Empowerment theory, research, and application. *American Journal of Community Psychology, 23*(5), 569–580.

Rappaport, J. (1987). Terms of empowerment/exemplars of prevention: Toward a theory for community psychology. *American Journal of Community Psychology, 15*(2), 121–148.

Saegert, S., Thompson, J. P., & Warren, M. R. (Eds.). (2001). *Social capital and poor communities.* New York: Russell Sage.

Saegert, S., & Winkel, G. (1996). Paths to community empowerment: Organizing at home. *American Journal of Community Psychology, 24*(4), 517–551.

Saleebey, D. (Ed.). (1997). *The strengths perspective in social work practice* (2nd ed.). New York: Longman.

Simon, B. L. (1994). *The empowerment tradition in American social work: A history.* New York: Columbia University Press.

Speer, P. W., & Hughey, J. (1995). Community organizing: An ecological route to empowerment and power. *American Journal of Community Psychology, 23*(5), 729–749.

COMMUNITY GARDEN MOVEMENT

Community gardens are plots of urban land on which community members can grow flowers or foodstuffs for personal or collective benefit. Community gardeners share certain resources, such as space, tools, and water. Though often facilitated by social service agencies, nonprofit organizations, park and recreation departments, housing authorities, apartment complexes, block associations, or grassroots associations, commu-

Turning Vacant Lots Into Community Gardens

CHICAGO (ANS)–The city of Chicago enlists young people to turn vacant lots into gardens and then helps the local community take ownership of the garden to ensure its upkeep.

Project Save Our Urban Land hires inner-city teen-agers to rehabilitate depleted lots and stabilize them by creating gardens and turning them over to community groups. Another program, NeighborSpace, tackles a problem faced by many urban community gardens once they've been established: securing the land they use.

Save Our Urban Land began five years ago when Ron Wolford, educator for urban gardening for the University of Illinois Cooperative Extension Service, was creating environmentally oriented projects for inner-city teen-agers. He chose Englewood, a neighborhood of some 60,000 people with the city's highest murder rate, highest high school dropout rate and lowest ACT scores.

The students, as they have done each year since then, spend their spring inventorying the trash on two or three empty lots, counting the old cars, mattresses, refrigerators and dead animals and seeing first-hand the blight of such refuse.

Once school is out for the summer, they work four days a week from 9 a.m. to 2 p.m., clearing trash, pulling weeds, building raised-bed gardens and planting the lots, which typically measure 25 by 150 feet. The fifth day is set aside for educational field trips such as touring the city's water reclamation plant, visiting environmental organizers or canoeing the Chicago River to pick up trash, Wolford said.

Each garden is built in association with a community group or nonprofit organization, so it can be tailored to those specific needs, Wolford said. So if a group of senior citizens wants a vegetable garden, the teen-agers will construct a raised bed for each one and help with the watering and weeding.

At the end of the summer, each garden presents a harvest festival and ceremony where the garden is turned over to its associated community group.

Depending on where the lot is, nonprofits like churches and schools can purchase the lot for $1 from the city with the stipulation that they keep it green for at least five years, Wolford said.

But those lots that remain city-owned are in little danger of being sold and replaced by a building, as is the case in New York City, Wolford said. "Mayor (Richard) Daly is pro-greening," he said. "Over the last few years, we've had really good support. There's never a problem here."

NeighborSpace, one of the mayor's programs, protects lots by buying them from the city for as little as $1 and providing liability insurance, said Kathy Dickhut, project director. "Our mission is to hold that property in perpetuity," she said.

About half the land NeighborSpace owns is acquired for practically nothing from the city; the rest is from the county and private individuals, she said. If the property is more expensive, her group gets additional funds from the city to buy it. "Whatever we have to do, we try to do it," she said.

The group acquires lots on behalf of neighborhood groups who usually want to create and preserve gardens, she said. "NeighborSpace allows people to have some control over the space in their neighborhood," she said.

NeighborSpace acquires lots in all areas of the city, not just the poor neighborhoods, Dickhut said. "There's not that many sites, so the few that there are, people are taking them over (for green space)," she said.

[. . .]

"Some of the kids didn't know the difference between a hoe and rake," Wolford said. "They didn't know a marigold from a zinnia, never used a hammer and never built raised beds." But they enjoyed the process of creating the gardens, he said. "They took a lot of pride and ownership in what they'd done."

Source: "Chicago Tries to Ensure Beautified Vacant Lots Stay That Way." American News Service, Article No. 965, June 10, 1999.

nity gardens nevertheless tend to remain under the control of the gardeners themselves. As such, they often provide disenfranchised individuals with opportunities to join a group effort, become active members of a community, take on leadership roles, and work toward collective goals. Accordingly, empowerment is a common benefit associated with community gardening and the other activities (such as fundraising, community cookouts, and fence building) associated with the establishment and operation of urban garden projects. Moreover, community gardens offer places where people can gather, network, and identify together as members of a community; they also provide spaces in which people of different social circles can integrate successfully. For these reasons, community gardens are good sites for community building and locality development.

Given that potential, it is not surprising that community garden movements, although varied, have aimed to effect social change from their earliest days. Beginning with the Allotment Acts of 1887 and 1890, and followed by the Local Government Act of 1894, local authorities in Great Britain provided space to urban residents for community, or allotment, gardens in an effort to address some of the public health issues associated with urban overcrowding. Many community gardens were premised on the idea that providing space in which residents could enjoy nature within their crowded urban neighborhoods would be beneficial to public health and well being. The first U.S. community gardens were established in the late 1890s in Detroit through an unemployment relief plan enacted to help those in need of social assistance and sustenance. Residents were encouraged to grow crops in "potato patches." Similar efforts, called relief gardens, provided sustenance to those affected by the Depression in the 1930s. During the early 1970s, anti-inflation gardens combated the inflation of food prices by giving land and supplies to people so that they could grow crops themselves. Community gardening spread to countries other than the United States and Great Britain, as well. In Canada, several garden movements emerged that were similar to the ones described from the United States, albeit with other names (for example, railway gardens, 1890–1930; moral gardens, early 1900s; school gardens, 1900–1913; vacant lot gardens, 1910–1920; war gardens, 1914–1947; counter-culture gardens, 1965–1979; and community open space, 1980–the present). In short, community garden movements have been established largely in response to social crises.

Patriotism and civic pride underpin other community garden movements. In the United States, liberty gardens and victory gardens emerged as ways to rally support for the war effort during World War I and World War II, respectively. In both cases, urban residents were encouraged to farm idle land to free rural farmers to ship produce to Europe and to ease the burden of food transportation domestically. In many contemporary urban neighborhoods, creating community gardens allows residents to convert dilapidated, abandoned lots into green spaces in a show of civic pride and an effort to create positive neighborhood change, address urban decay, and reclaim neighborhood spaces. In sum, community garden movements nurture collective identity and community pride.

—*Troy D. Glover*

Further Reading

Glover, T. D. (in press-a). Social capital in the lived experiences of community gardeners. *Leisure Sciences.*

Glover, T. D. (in press-b). The story of the Queen Anne Memorial Garden: Resisting a dominant cultural narrative. *Journal of Leisure Research, 25*(3).

Jamison, M. S. (1985). The joys of gardening: Collectivist and bureaucratic cultures in conflict. *The Sociological Quarterly, 26*(4), 473–490.

Linn, K. (1999). Reclaiming the sacred commons. *New Village, 1*(1), 42–49.

Pottharst, K. (1995). Urban dwellers and vacant lots: Partners in pride. *Parks and Recreation, 30*(9), 94–101.

von Baeyer, E. (1984). *Rhetoric and Roses, A History of Canadian Gardening 1900–1930.* Markham, Ontario: Fitzhenry & Whiteside.

Waliczek, T. M., Mattson, R. H., & Zajicek, J. M. (1996). Benefits of community gardening on quality-of-life issues. *Journal of Environmental Horticulture, 14*(4), 204–209.

COMMUNITY HEALTH SYSTEMS

When examining how communities across the globe meet their members' health needs, certain patterns emerge. Common traits in community health systems are based on shared ideas about what health is and, related to that, what a health system should do, what it should include, and how it should be organized.

DEFINING HEALTH

The following definition of health from the preamble to the constitution of the World Health Organization (WHO) has guided the development of the WHO's policies and programs since 1948, when it became operational:

> Health is a state of complete physical, mental and social well-being and not merely the absence of disease or infirmity. (World Health Organization 1948)

The definition is broad and multidimensional, making the point that health is not just about physical status, but mental and social condition as well. Health is equated with well-being, not with the mere absence of sickness.

TREATING ILLNESS

Trying to make this notion of health a reality has been challenging in part because many of the world's health care systems might in fact be more accurately termed illness care systems. That is, they concern themselves more with treating or preventing illness than with establishing well-being. This model of health, sometimes referred to as the medical model, aims to get patients to the point where they are not manifesting symptoms of illness, that is, they are not sick. In this view, then, one who is not sick is well. But people who are not sick may not be particularly well, either. They are simply asymptomatic—of either illness or wellness.

Medicine and the allied professions assume responsibility for treating illness. Public health has traditionally made its purview the prevention of illness, although this delimitation is changing as the profession embraces the development of what has been called the "new public health"—helping people move toward wellness. Health education as a field fully embraces the promotion of wellness, although it too has struggled in the past with self-imposed limitations, overemphasizing the role of cognition as opposed to the role of beliefs in determining—and changing—behavior.

The Peckham Experiment

In 1935, the Pioneer Health Centre was opened in Peckham, southeast London. Run as a family club, it was an experiment to discover, promote, and study the growth of positive health. Each family member was given an annual medical check-up, known as a "health overhaul," and the findings were communicated at a family consultation. It combined the medical facilities, family planning, antenatal and postnatal clinics, nurseries for babies and pre-school children, leisure activities, and a cafeteria. The building was especially designed for easy movement and visibility from one part to another. Families who lived in its catchment area were able to join this unique family club by paying a weekly fee. Members organized their own activities and had a swimming pool and gym available. It was a place where leisure activities were as important as medical overhauls. Mothers shared in the preparation of the nursery teas, and families spent many of the free hours at the Centre.

Dr. George Scott Williamson and Dr. Innes Pearse were the cofounders and directors of the Centre and described it as an experiment into the nature of health. The emphasis was on cultivating health, as well as catching disease at an early stage by regular examinations.

The Peckham Centre closed during the War but was re-opened in 1946 on public demand. The closure of the Centre in 1950 was due to financial problems and the founding the National Health Service. In social and research terms it was doing very well, with a membership of almost 900 families.

–Karen Christensen

PROMOTING WELLNESS: THE HEALTH FIELD CONCEPT

In 1974, Marc Lalonde, Canada's minister of health at the time, released a report entitled *A New Perspective on the Health of Canadians.* That report set forth the idea of health as the result of four determinants—human biology, the environment, health care, and lifestyle—that constantly interact in a person's life and within community to produce health status. This concept of health has helped people move from the medical view of health to a more systemic and ecological view and has led to the development of concepts of health promotion. Understanding the conditions producing illness and the resulting need for health care requires assessment of root causes—going upstream, as it were—to identify the factors producing the illness for which the medical care system was designed in the first place.

HEALTH AS PROCESS

Another current understanding of health views it as the process of becoming all that one can be. If one accepts this view, then the role of the health care system, in concert with other segments of the community, is to help people become as healthy as possible. That means helping them to explore and express their potential in all the multiple dimensions of health: physical, mental, emotional, social, cultural, spiritual, intellectual, economic, and so forth. In this health-as-process model, individuals assume ultimate responsibility for their own health status and look to their communities, including their families, schools, business and industry, institutions of faith, government, and the health care system, to facilitate their process of self-actualization.

REGIONAL HEALTH CARE SYSTEMS

Regional health care systems tend to fall into certain generic and universal patterns that show up almost regardless of the cultural, political, or economic systems of the countries in which they are located. For the sake of this discussion, a region is defined as an urban center surrounded by towns and communities of smaller and smaller size, down to rural areas with sparse populations and very little infrastructure. The concentration or mass of resources at the regional center has a sort of gravitational pull, attracting individuals throughout the region for commercial, political, recreational, educational, social, and health care purposes. The larger the mass of resources at the regional center, the stronger its gravitational field and the larger the region. A country may have several regions or it may have only one, often centering on the capital city.

Local or community-level health care services are offered in the context of a regional health care delivery system. These regional systems have three different levels of health services: primary, secondary, and tertiary.

Primary Health Care

Primary care is the most basic and ubiquitous type of health care offered in a regional system. When individuals seek treatment for minor illness or injury, they receive primary care services. Prenatal care and health maintenance services such as regular checkups and inoculations are also part of primary care. Primary care, which is often defined as the first point of contact one has with the health care system (excepting the case of medical emergencies), offers services mainly for the "vertical" or ambulatory patient. Typically, treatment is rendered quickly, is relatively simple and inexpensive, and is delivered by providers with less-specialized training than those at subsequent care levels.

Primary care is fundamental to the efficiency and efficacy of regional health systems. Primary care includes medical, dental, pharmaceutical, mental, developmental, and social services to treat illness and maintain wellness. Participants in the International Conference on Primary Health Care, held in 1978 in Alma-Ata, USSR (now Almaty, Kazakhstan), described primary health care as follows:

> Primary health care is essential health care based on practical, scientifically sound and socially acceptable methods and technology made universally accessible to individuals and families in the community through their full participation and at a cost that the community and country can afford to maintain at every stage of their development in the spirit of self-reliance and self-determination. It forms an integral part both of the country's health system, of which it is the central function and main focus, and of the overall social and economic development of the community. It is the first level of contact of individuals, the family and community with the national health system bringing health care as close as possible to where people live and work, and constitutes the first element of a continuing health care process. (World Health Organization 1978)

Primary care providers also evaluate the level of severity of each patient's illness or injury to develop an appropriate treatment regimen and to identify patients who cannot be adequately treated at the primary care level. These patients are referred to more specialized health care providers at the next level in the regional health system, the secondary care level. In the case of medical emergencies, primary care providers attempt to stabilize patients before referral.

Secondary Health Care

The secondary care level receives patients referred by the primary care level. Secondary care providers are medical specialists capable of treating health problems that are more serious and infrequent than those dealt with by primary care providers. Secondary care is inpatient care, dealing with "horizontal" patients; it includes such medical specialties as emergency medicine, family medicine, general surgery, anesthesiology, internal medicine, obstetrics and gynecology, ophthalmology, pathology, and radiology, as well as the typical services of a general, acute-care community hospital. These can include emergency, laboratory, pharmacy, outpatient, and nutritional services, as well as physical therapy, respiratory therapy, imaging, and often hospice and home health services.

Tertiary Health Care

The tertiary care level in a regional health system receives patients referred from the secondary level. It provides specialized medical services for extraordinarily acute and infrequent medical maladies not typically treatable at secondary-level facilities. Tertiary care providers are commonly involved in medical research and education and usually affiliated with academic medical centers. They offer specialized diagnostic and treatment services, including burn care, neonatology (work with newborns), pediatric surgery, trauma surgery, neurosurgery, cardiothoracic and vascular surgery, organ transplant, positron-emission tomography (an imaging service), radiation oncology, and other services.

CONCENTRIC SERVICE AREAS

The hierarchy of services in a regional health system from primary to tertiary care requires each level to offer all the services available at preceding levels in addition to the services it has been designed to deliver. Because secondary-level medical facilities deal with illnesses that are much more complex, expensive to treat, and infrequent than those treated in the family clinic, they must serve a larger area to generate the volume of cases necessary to make the provision of their more expensive services feasible. However, the community hospital will also provide primary care to the area immediately surrounding the hospital. The hospital is therefore at the center of two concentric circles of service delivery: a large circle for the delivery of secondary care and a smaller circle for the delivery of primary care.

Tertiary providers handle the most infrequent, complex, and expensive cases and require the largest service areas to make offering their services cost effective. The tertiary care service area typically comprises the entire region. The tertiary facility will also provide both primary and secondary care services to the population in the area surrounding it.

EMERGENCY MEDICAL SERVICES IN A REGIONAL SYSTEM

Emergency medical services represent a special case in regional and community health systems. Like primary care institutions, institutions offering emergency medical services are often a patient's first point of contact with the health system, but emergency medical services do not deal with primary health problems, nor do they always refer their patients just to the secondary level. Emergency medical personnel transport stabilized patients to the facilities deemed most appropriate for their particular medical needs, directly from the scene of an accident to a tertiary facility, bypassing a secondary facility if necessary. Emergency medical service providers handle cases of serious illness and trauma requiring immediate assessment, stabilization, and treatment. Paramedics, located strategically throughout a community and connected to a communitywide emergency call-dispatch system, routinely respond within five to eight minutes in well-equipped ambulances that are in contact with emergency physicians in hospital emergency rooms in countries across the globe.

TIME AVAILABILITY STANDARDS FOR REGIONAL HEALTH SYSTEMS

Health care may be available without necessarily being accessible. Barriers to access may be economic, cultural, social, or linguistic; physical design features such as unnecessary steps or poorly marked entrances can also render health care inaccessible, as can a lack of adequate transportation. Whether people can gain access to health care in a timely manner depends both on the mode of transportation available to them and the distance they must travel. Time availability standards are used instead of distance to service in deciding where to locate facilities because congestion and transportation systems in communities vary so widely. The trip times associated with different modes of transportation (by foot, by animal, or in a vehicle) in different communities affect decisions about where to locate health facilities.

The time it takes to access emergency medical care needs to be quite short to deal effectively with acute illnesses and trauma. Ideally, one should be able to access emergency services within five to eight minutes. Health systems planners in many countries plan for access to primary care within thirty minutes, secondary care services within one hour, and access to tertiary care within four hours.

COMMUNITY HEALTH SYSTEMS, HEALTH PROMOTION, AND COMMUNITY BUILDING

A community health system used to be simply the array of medical facilities that had developed in a community to treat the illnesses and trauma experienced by it residents. But when one adopts an expanded definition of health, a definition that views health status primarily as the result of lifestyle choices mediated by genetics and environment and only secondarily the result of medical treatment, then one's notion of a community health system expands to include all the subsystems or segments of a community that bear upon those choices. Health status is affected by education, employment, family values, faith, self-esteem, nutrition, crowding, air and water quality, health care, waste management, recreation, crime, culture, customs, and so on. To promote health, to help all their members to become all that they can be, communities are learning to build coalitions of interested individuals and organizations from many different segments of society. This pooling of resources, energy, and commitment makes possible the development of timely and flexible solutions to complex, intractable, and interwoven problems that have resisted simplistic, mechanistic intervention. The World Health Organization offers the following definition of a health system:

> A health system includes all the activities whose primary purpose is to promote, restore or maintain health. Health systems have a responsibility not just to improve people's

health but to protect them against the financial cost of illness—and to treat them with dignity. (World Health Organization 2002)

In other words, the community health system is the community itself.

—Donald A. Sweeney

Further Reading

Ashton, J., & Seymour, H. (1988). *The new public health.* Buckingham, UK: Open University Press.

Dever, A. G. E. (1991). *Community health analysis: Global awareness at the local level* (2nd ed.). Gathersburg, MD: Aspen

Glouberman, S., Kisilevsky, S., Groff, P., & Nicholson, C. (2000). *Towards a new concept of health: Three discussion papers* (CPRN Discussion Paper No. H/03). Ottawa, Canada: Canadian Policy Research Networks,.

Green, L. W., & Kreuter, M. W. (1999). *Health promotion planning: An educational and ecological approach* (3rd ed.). New York: McGraw-Hill Education.

Lalonde, M. (1974). *A new perspective on the health of Canadians.* Ottawa, Canada: Health and Welfare Canada.

Roemer, M. I. (1991–1993). *National health systems of the world* (Vols. 1–2). New York: Oxford University Press.

Texas Department of Health. (2002). *Tertiary medical care program: Frequently asked questions.* Retrieved February 27, 2003, from http://www.tdh.state.tx.us/hosprfp/TMCPFAQ.htm

Travis, J. W., & Ryan, R. S. (1988). *Wellness workbook* (2nd ed.). Berkeley, CA: Ten Speed Press.

Tsiknakis, M., & Orphanoudakis, S. C. (1997, April). An integrated architecture for the provision of health telematic services in a regional network. *ERCIM News, 29*, 30–31.

World Health Organization. (1978, September). *Declaration of Alma-Ata.* Geneva, Switzerland: Author. Retrieved February 27, 2003, from http://www.who.int/hpr/backgroundhp/almaata.htm

World Health Organization. (2002). *The world health report 2002: Reducing risks, promoting healthy life.* Geneva, Switzerland: Author. Retrieved February 27, 2002, from http://www.who.int/whr/en/ World Health Organization. (1948). *Constitution of the World Health Organization.* Geneva, Switzerland: Author.

COMMUNITY IN DISASTER

When disaster strikes, not only are individuals traumatized but the entire community context and social system are affected. Critical incidents, whether natural disasters or man-made calamities, damage more than the sum of individual psyches that compose a community. For example, technological disasters, such as the 1986 Chernobyl nuclear crisis or the 2001 terrorist attack on New York, traumatized thousands of individuals who will need psychological help to recover; but such disasters also upset the social fabric and homoeostasis of the community matrix, which will require sociological and political resources to recover. A systems approach is necessary to understand communities in disaster, and a community-based relief and development response is most appropriate for assessing community needs and resources and facilitating the process of community healing. This is especially true for man-made, terrorist, and technological disasters.

TECHNOLOGICAL DISASTERS

Kai Erikson, a Yale sociologist who has studied disasters since the mid-1970s, makes a qualitative distinction between "natural" and "technological" disasters. The latter constitutes "a new species of trouble" (the title of his book). For Erikson, there is "a profound difference between those disasters that can be understood as the work of nature and those that need to be understood as the work of humankind." Thus, such diverse disasters as the mercury spill at the Grassy Narrows Indian Reserve, and the toxic gas leak at East Swallow, Colorado, share something in common with Three Mile Island and Chernobyl. Their similarity is due not to the *extent* of the damage but to the *nature* of the crisis (Erikson 1994, pp. 19–20).

Community disaster in its technological dimension is a new species of danger that tears apart fundamental structures of human existence, Erikson argues. "Human beings are surrounded by layers of trust, radiating out in concentric circles like the ripples in a pond. The experience of (collective) trauma, at its worst, can mean not only a loss of confidence in the self, but a loss of confidence in the scaffolding of family and community, in the structures of human government, in larger logics by which humankind lives, and in the ways of nature itself" (Erikson 1994, p. 234). It is the *community* that offers persons a cushion for pain, a context for intimacy, a repository for binding traditions. When the community suffers violation, "one can speak of a damaged social organism in almost the same way that one would speak of a damaged body" (p. 242).

Erikson has studied five communities in disaster that were impacted by technological crises in the twentieth century: (1) Buffalo Creek—a West Virginia rural community devastated by a flood; (2) Grassy Narrows—an Ojibwa Indian reserve in Canada damaged by a mercury spill; (3) Immokalee—Haitian migrants in a farmworker camp in south Florida, robbed of their resources, struggle to survive American exploitation after their narrow escape by boat from their native land; (4) East Swallow—a suburban community in Colorado contaminated by toxic gas; and (5) Three Mile Island—neighborhoods exposed to radioactivity adjacent to the nuclear power plant in Pennsylvania. In his damage assessments, he identifies three diagnostic principles for understanding this new species of danger.

First, technological disasters, unlike natural disasters, are a product of human hands; there is always a moral to be drawn from them, outrage to be explored, and blame to be assigned, and retribution or repentance is required. As Erikson explains: "They provoke outrage rather than acceptance or resignation. They generate a feeling that the thing ought not to have happened, that someone is at fault, the victims deserve not only compassion and compensation but something akin to what lawyers call punitive damages" (Erikson 1994, pp. 142–143).

Admittedly, some disasters are difficult to classify as either natural or technological. When an epidemic such as AIDS spreads across Central Africa and into the United States, "it owes its virulence to both tough new strains of bacillus and stubborn old human habits" (p. 142), which spread internationally through the technology of air travel and worldwide immigration. Generally speaking, however, natural disasters are usually viewed by the community as "acts of God" or caprices of nature, while technological disasters often "visit us, as from afar." Since they are at least in principle preventable, "there is always a story to be told about them, always a moral to be drawn from them, always a share of blame to be assigned," which requires community support and response (p. 142).

Second, technological disasters often involve deadly toxins that contaminate body, soul, and spirit. "They pollute, befoul, and taint rather than just create wreckage; they penetrate human tissue indirectly rather than wound the surfaces by assaults of a more straightforward kind" (p. 144). Toxic crises scare human beings in new and special ways long after the disaster is declared over.

An investigation of Three Mile Island, for example, revealed that the nuclear disaster persisted long after the initial crisis was contained. The fallout frightened and violated the population in traumatic and uncanny ways. Toxic crisis has the capacity to induce chronic dread and primal fear. It is a "thing of darkness and foreboding" like poison gas—inherently horrific and insidious—which draws on something deeper in the human psyche that affects community structures and systems, resulting in more than individual and community despair (pp. 146–147).

A cafe stands in floodwater in the town of Xbacab, Mexico, flooded in October 1995 by Hurricane Roxanne.

Source: Danny Lehman/Corbis; used with permission.

Third, technological disasters create the kind of *community trauma* in which traditional distinctions between acute and chronic, traumatic and post-traumatic stress are blurred. Community symptoms of anxiety, fear, dread, and despair constitute a new kind of diagnosis that threatens not only the individual but the cohesive threads of society. Conventional treatment of posttraumatic stress disorder—externalizing individual traumatic stress through debriefing and retelling one's story of trauma—does not quite work, for there is no resolution to the crisis. The rules of plot are violated. The tragedy does not end but continues to traumatize the individual victim and the community network, and to poison future generations.

COMMUNITY TRAUMA

Sudden natural disasters traumatize individuals according to established rules of plot, having a beginning, a middle, and an end. An alarm signals the event, a period of destruction follows, and sooner or later the disaster comes to an end. The suffering may endure, dreams may haunt, and wounds prove difficult to heal, but the traumatic event itself is over. What follows will be described as "aftermath." Technological disasters, however, violate the established rules. Some, like Chernobyl, have a definite beginning (an accidental meltdown), and a middle (after-effects), but the trauma does not end. The fallout and contamination continue to poison generations to come. "Invisible contaminants remain a part of the surroundings, absorbed into the grain of the landscape, the tissues of the body, and worst of all, the genetic material of the survivors" (pp. 147–148). Thus, the normal medical and psychological distinctions between acute trauma and chronic stress break down. Here, Erikson identifies collective trauma as something qualitatively distinct from individual trauma:

> By *individual trauma* I mean a blow to the psyche that breaks through one's defenses so suddenly and with such brutal force that one cannot react to it effectively. . . .
>
> By *collective trauma,* on the other hand, I mean a blow to the basic issues of social life that damage the bonds attaching people together and impair the prevailing sense of community. . . ."I" continue to exist, though damaged and maybe even permanently changed. "You" continue to exist, though distant and hard to relate to. But "we" no longer exist as a connected pair or as linked cells in a larger communal body. (p. 233)

Thus, toxic disasters result in community trauma of apocalyptic proportions, characterized by a pervasive sense of the world being out of control, of a community-wide feeling of foreboding. Victims not only experience a general loss of identity, purpose, and hope for the future, they also tend to develop a passive and fatalistic outlook: a sense of being subjected to dark and uncontrollable forces and possessed by powers and principalities from beyond normal life. Toxic trauma in its social dimension creates a new ethos—a group culture—that is different from and greater than the sum of its private wounds (pp. 230–231).

Consider the case of Chernobyl as a community disaster. Widespread fear of radiation and contamination, which was dismissed by government officials and many academics as "radio-phobia," persisted in the region for over a decade. According to a 1993 national study by Belarusian scientists, for example, considerable numbers of those living in contaminated areas of Belarus (and Ukraine) manifested symptoms local psychologists called at the time "a permanent condition of socio-radiological stress (characterized by) feelings of uneasiness, a constant fear of being exposed to radiation and an awareness of the permanent threat to the health and lives of people" (p. 44). This widespread and chronic condition, according to the researchers, resulted in "somatization" (24 percent), "apathy" (22 percent), and traumatic fixation (16 percent), reaching the point of "complete obsession with doom and hopelessness" (*Main Scientific Reports* 1994, p. 45). These are symptoms that Erikson would call "a new species of danger" and others who study communities in disaster might characterize as "collective toxic trauma" or simply "community trauma." Toxic crisis points to the reality that something horrific has happened, that the world has become a place of danger and numbing uncertainty, that the very structures of existence have crumbled, and that the end of the world, as it was known, has come (Christensen 1997, p. 197).

—Michael J. Christensen

See also CHERNOBYL

Further Reading

Christensen, M. J. (1997). *Chernobyl apocalypse: A theological case study.* Doctoral dissertation, Drew University.

Erikson, K. (1994). *A new species of trouble: Explorations in disaster, trauma, and community.* New York: W.W. Norton.

Lifton, R. J. (1987). *The future of immortality and other essays for a nuclear age.* New York: Basic Books.

Main scientific reports, proceedings from the Second International Congress: The world after Chernobyl. (1994). Minsk, Belarus.

COMMUNITY INDICATORS

Community indicators are sources of quantifiable information about the state of a community. The communities in question are typically towns, cities, or regions, but sometimes they are entities as large as an entire state or province. The movement to use community indicators to evaluate communities became popular in the United States in the mid-1980s; since then, more than 200 communities have completed community indicator projects. The community indicator reports from many of these communities are posted on Web sites and are open to public review and comment. For these projects to be successful, all sectors of the community must be involved in developing and sharing a common vision of community life. Within the community, a community indicators project may be initiated by businesses, concerned citizens, the government, or action groups such as environmental groups.

GOALS AND APPROACHES

There are four different approaches to community indicators, but all share a basic set of common goals. They seek to collect quantifiable information, to make comparisons over time and across communities, to establish community plans, to use the process to build or strengthen a shared vision of community life, and to assess progress. The four major approaches to community indicators are the quality-of-life approach, the sustainability approach, the health indicators approach, and the benchmark approach.

The quality-of-life approach began with the Jacksonville, Florida, Community Council, in 1985. It focuses most heavily on indicators of economic well-being, although it has expanded over the years to incorporate other indicators as well. The sustainability approach is tied to the environmental movement and began with the Sustainable Seattle initiative in 1993. More so than other approaches, the sustainability approach focuses on environmental quality and takes an ecological perspective, with the local community seen as an organic entity that interacts with the global system. It has been influential internationally and played a role at the 1992 Earth Summit. The health indicators movement measures community well-being by examining community public health. The Association for Community Health Improvement (formerly the Coalition for Healthier Cities and Communities), a U.S. national organization, is an active supporter of the healthy-community model. The benchmark approach began in Oregon in 1991 and seeks to apply local measures of community well-being at the state level

CHOOSING INDICATORS

Regardless of approach, all community indicators projects measure community life in several domains. The most common ones are the economy, environment, government and civic life, social life, culture and recreation, health, education, mobility and transportation, and public safety. For each of these domains, information is gathered for several indicators. The information is always presented in quantitative form, most commonly as a rate or percentage (for example, population growth rate or percentage of high school graduates). The use of quantitative data allows for comparisons from year to year and with other communities. However, because the indicators used reflect local beliefs about and goals regarding quality of life, health, or sustainability, different communities use different sets of indicators. For example, a community that uses the quality-of-life approach is likely to rely heavily on economic indicators, while a community following the sustainability model will use more environmental indicators. The data come from a variety of sources, including local and regional governments and their agencies, nonprofit organizations such as chambers of commerce or branches of the League of Women Voters, interest groups, commissioned surveys, and the state and national governments.

Community indicators tell community members about the community's state of well-being in accord with community beliefs about well-being. They allow communities to gauge their progress toward targets over time and to make comparisons with other communities. The process of using community indicators brings people together to develop a shared vision of their community and to set goals for the future.

AN ALTERNATIVE APPROACH

A different approach to community indicators has recently been developed in the United Kingdom. In work carried out for the British government Home Office in 2002–2003, Gabriel Chanan of the Community Development Foundation analyzed whether the quality of communities could be systematically measured. He came to the conclusion that communities themselves could not meaningfully be measured because they are fluid and overlapping, not fixed entities, and that most of the existing "community" indicators are in fact indicators of *localities* or *local populations*. While these are highly informative on issues such as health, education, and the environment, ironically they are often lacking in measures of community life itself—that is, levels of community activity, volunteering, social capital, participation in local governance, and particularly the extent and effectiveness of the local community and voluntary sector, consisting of autonomous groups and organizations.

Chanan identifies a variety of possible and actual measures that can be used to assess these factors for a neighborhood or local population, and these are being considered for use in connection with a variety of UK government social programs that now put a high premium on community involvement. The Home Office settled on sixteen factors, grouped into five clusters:

A. Individual
1. Self determination
2. Concern with locality and/or public issues
3. Level of volunteering and community activity

B. Community Involvement—Horizontal
4. Community and voluntary organizations (quantity; range; effectiveness; connectedness)
5. Social capital / mutual aid

OFTEN USED COMMUNITY INDICATORS

The following is a partial list of the indicators typically used in the United States. The data provided for these indicators are usually in the form of a rate, percentage, or quantity.

Population

Total population
Population growth rate
Population over age sixty-five
Population under age eighteen
Number of marriages
Number of dissolutions of marriage
Live-birth rate
Net migration
Population distribution by age
Population distribution by race and ethnicity

Government/Politics/ Civic Participation

Percent of voting-age population registered to vote
Percent of registered voters who voted in last general election
Per capita charity donations
Culture and Recreation
General fund expenditures for city, parks, recreation, and public lands
Total park acres
Number of volumes in city/county library
Number of volumes and annual circulations in city/county library
Art organizations

Health

Percentage of population who use chewing tobacco
Percentage of students who smoke regularly
Dental emergencies (yearly average)
Average monthly number of Medicaid recipients
Infant mortality rate
Percentage of low-birth-weight babies
Reported sexually transmitted disease cases
Reported AIDS cases
Percentage of the population that is overweight
Alcohol consumption
Number of adult smokers
Teen substance abuse
Adult alcohol abuse
Death rate
Suicide rate
Children immunized by age two
Physicians per capita
Nursing beds per capita
Prenatal care
Health care coverage
Mammograms
Participation in regular physical activity

Social Indicators

Percentage of live births out of wedlock
Number of induced abortions
Number of low-birth-weight births
Number of youths in foster care (and other placements)
Number of child care slots available
Percentage of live births to mothers aged nineteen and under
Teen pregnancy rate
Child abuse and neglect rate
Total homeless population
Number of domestic violence crisis calls
Child care costs
Teen substance abuse

Economy

Employment rate
Employment rate by industry
Industry and occupational employment projections
Employment growth
Unemployment rate
Per capita income
Consumer price index
Price level index
Personal income
Affordable wage
Poverty rate
Median household income
Interest rates
Number of housing vacancies
Home ownership rate
Average percentage of population receiving food stamps
Average sales price of homes
Median sales price of homes
Affordable housing
Commercial real estate market
Bank deposits valuation
Number of homes sold
Number of residential building permits
Number of commercial building permits
Number of new businesses
Taxable sales
Exports
Potential tax revenues
Long-term debt
Fiscal capacity
Fiscal effort

Mobility/Transportation

Number of traffic fatalities
Number of automobile registrations
Vehicle miles traveled
Public transportation modes
Total traffic volume
Bus ridership
Paratransit
Number of buses with wheelchair lift

Environment

Sulfur dioxide data (SO_2)
Air Quality: particulate averages (UG/M3)
Water quality: Total hardness
Water quality: Lead
Water quality: Fluoride
Water quality: pH
Water quality: water turbidity
Solid waste management index
Air quality standards attainment
Toxic release
Pollutant standard index
Watershed water quality
Water imported
Water usage
Municipal land annexations
Farm and rangeland
Energy consumption
Wind energy consumption
Recycled solid waste
Business involvement in pollution reduction
Species extinct or threatened

Public Safety

Police officers per 1,000 people
Dispatched calls for fire protection
Dispatched calls for police protection
Nonviolent crime rate: burglary
Violent crime rate: homicide, rape, robbery
Nonviolent crime rate for juveniles: burglary, larceny
Violent crime rate for juveniles: robbery, assault
Partner or family member assault
Traffic accident rate
Motor vehicle theft rate
Adult driving under the influence
Juvenile driving under the influence
Percentage of drivers under twenty-one involved in alcohol-related crashes
Number of youth drug charges
Number of youth arrested for carrying a concealed weapon

Education

School enrollment
Operating expenditure per student
Student/teacher ratio
Percentage of fourth grade students in above-average range in math, science, social studies, language
Percentage of eighth grade students in above-average range in math, science, social studies, language
Percentage of eleventh grade students in above average range in math, science, social studies, language
Average ACT/ SAT scores
Public high school graduation numbers
General equivalent diplomas earned
Adult basic-education center enrollment
Percent of students receiving free/reduced lunches
Dropout rate
Adults with BA degree

C. Community Involvement—Vertical
   6. Voting turnout
   7. Responses to consultation
   8. Community representation, leadership and influence

D. Services And Economic Activity
   9. Contribution to public services
   10. Social economy and assets

E. Inclusion, Diversity And Cohesion
   11. Inclusion
   12. Diversity
   13. Cohesion

F. Provision/Support/Empowerment
   14. Community development provision
   15. Community and voluntary sector infrastructure
   16. Support from partnerships, Neighbourhood Renewal and all public services.

These two approaches (American and British) are in some ways complementary, but more importantly, they suggest somewhat different views of what "community" means in the two nations. In the United States, the emphasis is on material measures of community well-being, while in the United Kindom, the emphasis is on social cohesion. A full understanding of community indicators requires a consideration of both.

—David Levinson

Further Reading

Besleme, K., Maser, E., & Silverstein, J. (1999). *A community indicators case study: Addressing the quality of life in two communities.* San Francisco: Refining Progress. Retrieved January 27, 2003, from http://www.rprogress.org/publications/pdf/CI_CaseStudy1.pdf

Chanan, G. (2002). *Measures of community.* London: Active Community Unit, Home Office.

Chanan, G. (2003). Community indicators briefing. London: Community Development Foundation.

Hart, M. (1999). *Guide to sustainable community indicators* (2nd ed.). North Andover, MA: Hart Environmental.

Swain, D., & Hollar, D. (in press). Measuring progress: Community indicators and the quality of life. *International Journal of Public Administration.*

COMMUNITY INFORMATICS AND DEVELOPMENT

Community informatics and development (CI) can be defined as a practice associated with the use and adoption of new information and communications technologies (ICTs) such as the Internet to influence the social, cultural, and economic development of community structures and relationships. Worldwide, CI manifests itself in the huge numbers of neighborhoods, voluntary organizations, social support networks, and government agencies that are committed to exploring the potential of the new media to improve community life. The proclaimed transforming qualities of CI have led to the development of a wide range of initiatives designed, for example, to increase democratic participation, overcome geographic and social isolation, improve business opportunities, tackle poor health, raise educational standards, and regenerate deteriorating community relations.

WHAT IS COMMUNITY INFORMATICS?

The origins of the term itself can be traced to the work of the Community Informatics Research and Applications Unit (CIRA) based in Middlesbrough, United Kingdom. Here as well as in Canada the concept was initially related to the redevelopment of local communities in what had previously been heavily industrialized regions. Since then, however, CI has been adopted throughout the world by researchers, practitioners, and community activists engaged in the formation and analysis of CI projects drawn from a much broader range of situations. In this sense it is intended to capture the growing ubiquity of ICTs into everyday experience and also to study how these are both shaped by community relations and in turn influence the development of community structures. Significantly, therefore, CI attempts to avoid those overly technical approaches that often present the new media as a determining force for change and that give little opportunity for human choices, resistance, or mediation. Instead, CI emphasizes human agency as an essential component for the creative adoption, alteration, and diffusion of the new technologies into community relations. It emphasizes a grassroots perspective whereby community members are centrally involved in the application of ICTs for community development.

HISTORY AND ANTECEDENCE

While CI is a relatively new concept, it has a strong lineage arising particularly from the community networking movement in the United States as well as in the electronic village hall social experiments in Scandinavia. Many valuable lessons have been learned from these initiatives and consequently have informed the design of many CI projects. They all shared a common desire to utilize computer-based systems to support geographically based communities by augmenting and even extending existing social networks. Typically they provided free or low-cost access to computers and communication networks, provided training to use them, and were run by and for the communities themselves.

In the United States, the community networking movement began in the mid-1970s with the Community Memory project based in Berkeley, California, and begun by Ken Colstad, Lee Felsenstein, and Efrem Lipkin. The values driving the movement are reflected in the original Community Memory brochure, which argued that "strong, free, nonhierarchical channels of communication—whether by computer and modem, pen and ink, telephone, or face-to-face—are the front line of reclaiming and revitalizing our communities." The intention was to develop and distribute a technology that would enable the free exchange of information between individuals and communities around the globe. This early experiment began with a number of public computer terminals that provided unmediated two-way access to a message database. The system was financed through coin-operated terminals, which allowed users to freely access forums but charged twenty-five cents to post a message and a dollar to begin a new discussion. Such computer-mediated communication, the instigators believed, offered a tremendous opportunity as an alternative means of community publishing and thereby helped preserve the cultural, social, and political memory of the community. While Community Memory ceased operating in July 1994, perhaps in part due to its inaccessibility by modem and the Internet, its influence continued to inform later discussions around CI.

A more open model of community networking was introduced by what Thomas Grunder was to describe as "free-nets." Beginning with the Cleveland Free-Net, this movement spread across the United States and Canada and even into parts of Europe and Asia. Predating the World Wide Web, these electronic networks were text based and provided wider public access to the Internet and community-run forums. A range of question-and-answer forums on such topics as health issues, automobile repairs, and social services provided community spaces for sharing information and experiences. Although Cleveland Free-Net was closed down in 2000 (officials at Case Western Reserve University claimed that the system was not year-2000 compliant), most free-nets evolved into more general Community Network projects that utilize a wide range of new media technologies to stimulate social capital and local social cohesion.

In Europe, perhaps the most significant antecedents of CI arose from the development of electronic village halls (EVHs) in Denmark, Sweden, and Norway. These social experiments began in the 1980s as an attempt to use ICTs to overcome the cultural and economic isolation felt by many rural communities in Scandinavian countries. The activities undertaken in EVHs varied a great deal according to local circumstances and policy objectives. Typically, however, they included a mixture of introductory computer courses and distance-learning programs; business and technical advice; facilities for teleworking (telecommuting); telecommunications equipment to facilitate teleconferences; video links and access to telefax terminals; and rooms for local democratic meetings and conferences. The actual physical location could range from purpose-built amenities to the refurbishment of existing public buildings.

Once again, the values supporting these experiments in the use of ICTs for community development were strongly influenced by the democratic traditions of community autonomy and self-help associated with the folk high school and cooperative movements in nineteenth-century Denmark. In particular, the philosophy of Nikolai Grundtvig (1783–1872), who based his liberal Christian enlightenment project on the principles of active participation, collective organization, cultural pluralism, social dialogue, and popular mass education, is regarded by some to have been very influential.

By the end of the program, even if the high expectations of the original founders had not been fulfilled, a number of important lessons had been learned that helped shape future CI projects. Particularly important was the use of social spaces to incorporate the technology where community members could build their confidence through a supportive and shared environment. Similarly, success was often achieved through the adoption of more informal learning practices whereby participants would teach each other how to use the technology. This more relaxed approach also facilitated local democratic decision making and cultural interaction. More critical lessons were also provided over the clash of perspectives between the techno-enthusiasts and the technophobes as well as the difficulties of financial sustainability for such enterprises.

FORCES FOR CHANGE

The new wave of interest in CI across the world is the result of at least four major social and economic forces. First is the phenomenal explosion of innovation in new ICTs during the last decade of the twentieth century. Particularly significant has been the growing convergence between the computing and telecommunications industries, the consequences of which have yet to be fully worked out, but which has already led to ICTs becoming an increasingly pervasive aspect of our lives. The Internet, World Wide Web, digital TV, cellular telephony, and the like are becoming commonplace technologies in business, public service, and domestic environments. But it is their capacity to enable people and organizations anywhere in the world to communicate and share knowledge and experiences at any time of the day that provides the revolutionary potential for radically changing our institutions, relations, identities, and procedures. Such computer networking has led to questions about its potential influence upon community structures and relations. For some, it represents a threat to face-to-face relations and thereby contributes to the breakdown of community relations. Other commentators, such as Howard Rheingold, point to the potential it offers for stimulating virtual communities of people who may be geographically remotely distributed but exchange information and provide common support to each other. Community Informatics initiatives are often interested in the potential interaction of virtual and geographical communities and how the new media may both foster a wider range of social networking and use such community spanning to enrich local social ties and opportunities.

Second, the impressive developments in the new media have led many commentators to proclaim the emergence of a new epoch called the *information age.* Frequently associated with related terms such as the *information society,* the *knowledge economy,* the *network society,* and others, this new period is distinguished from the preceding agrarian and industrial ages. In the information age, information becomes the primary resource for economic development, with the majority of workers occupied in knowledge industries and the service sector. Consequently, governments and international organizations have exhorted their citizens to participate in the race to become information societies. Individuals and communities who remain ignorant of the new ICTs and the benefits they offer fall behind other economic and cultural competitors. It follows from this that a common concern that informs many CI initiatives around the world continues to be its potential as a means to combat the "digital divide" between those people who have access to the new media and those who are unable to share in its benefits.

Third, the new information age is also characterized by processes of globalization. Computer-mediated networks are one of the main drivers that enable increasing cross-boundary flows of finance and business transactions. Decisions made in the boardrooms of global corporations are perceived as increasingly more important for sustainability and development of local communities than those made by their own politicians and political institutions. Indeed, the competition between national governments to attract inward investment from multinational companies may lead to the weakening of employment rights, environmental protection, and the quality of life for community members. Consequently, some CI initiatives are concerned with the potential of the new ICTs to enhance the democratic voice of citizens and communities in a global context. Questions emerge about the prospect of citizens and community groups utilizing the "many-to-many" communication opportunities offered by the Internet, which enable them to become information producers as well as receivers. Government and commercial statements can be challenged, for example, by global networks of citizens and alternative messages can be produced. Communities subjected to pollution as a consequence of the manufacturing practice of a global corporation can find a platform to air their protest to the world. Communities subjected to human rights violations can also use the World Wide Web to raise awareness of their plight.

Last, there has been a growing and widespread concern in many countries that community relations and the social capital they engender are degenerating. Most famously in the United States, this deterioration of community ties and support has been documented by Robert Putnam. But the same concerns over declining social support and voluntary activity among community members are to be found elsewhere and particularly in economically and socially deprived areas. The loss of strong communities comes at a time when such intermediate spaces between the family, market, and state spheres are being recognized as important for economic, social, and cultural well-being. As the limitations of the welfare state, family structures, and commercial sectors are being identified, policy-makers are turning to the need to regenerate communities as a part of their wider economic and social objectives. Questions are consequently being raised about what community structures and relations could be like in an information age.

THE FUTURE OF COMMUNITY INFORMATICS AND DEVELOPMENT

Throughout the world, CI approaches have been used to raise awareness of the potential benefits of new ICTs to improve employment opportunities, combat educational underachievement, enhance social support networks, and improve people's quality of life. A variety of community-based projects have provided information technology training and access to ICTs through community facilities and computer networks. The fundamental emphasis in most of these CI initiatives is the attempted adoption of a grassroots approach whereby community members are responsible for the design and direction of the project themselves. This is often achieved by working in partnership with other stakeholders (for example, local government, education institutions, local media, business interests, and the like) rather than being directed by them from above.

A key factor shaping the potential success of CI programs is their ability to overcome technological phobias and fears often associated with social factors such as social class, race, gender, age, disability, nationality, and other social characteristics. A variety of innovative projects and schemes attempt to stimulate people's interest in ICTs by focusing less on the technology and more on existing social relationships between people and their everyday interests. These include efforts to help popularize folk music from Cape Breton and other towns in the maritime provinces in northeast Canada through the imaginative use of the Internet; the development of popular online quizzes between communities in the United Kingdom and elsewhere; and the development of numerous community-group Web sites devoted to hobbies, interests, and self-help sites.

Looking to the future, the likelihood of the CI movement to realize its potential of improving the quality of community life is of course difficult to predict. Many successful initiatives may simply become incorporated into the commercial mainstream or be adopted by the public sector. Kubicek and Wagner, for example, argue that this process leads to the necessity for CI activists and networkers to be constantly innovative in their approaches if they are to survive. Certainly the relationship between the new media and community development is an ambiguous one that is shaped primarily through a complex interaction of social, political, commercial, and political factors that can, and frequently do, produce a mixture of intended and unintended outcomes for their participants. Attempts to empower citizens and stimulate social capital may crucially depend upon a critical understanding of the ambiguities present in the social, cultural, commercial, and political circumstances that shape the design and implementation of CI projects. Only through a clearer understanding of often competing objectives can policy choices be made by the community members most directly affected. The choices are frequently between policies that emphasize empowerment and those that engender domination; between those that enable sustainable community development and those that result in consumerism; and between those that perceive the digital divide as socially structured and those that would electronically reinforce existing social divisions. Such debates and deliberations should be central to the CI movement and should thereby inform the design and development of future projects.

—Brian Loader

Further Reading

Gurstein, M. (Ed.). (2000). *Community informatics: Enabling communities with information and communication technologies.* Hershey, PA: Idea Group.

Keeble, L., & Loader, B. D. (Eds.). (2001). *Community informatics: Shaping computer-mediated social networks.* London: Routledge.

Kubicek, H., & Wagner, R. (2002). Community networks in a generational perspective: The change of an electronic medium within three generations. *Information, Communication, & Society,* 5(4).

Loader, B. D. (Ed.). (1998). *The cyberspace divide: Equality, agency, and policy in the information society.* London: Routledge.

Putnam, R. (2000). *Bowling alone: The collapse and revival of American community.* New York: Simon & Schuster.

Rheingold, H. (1994). *The virtual community: Finding connection in a computerised world.* London: Secker & Warburg.

Schuler, D. (1996). *New community networks: Wired for change.* Reading, MA: Addison-Wesley.

COMMUNITY JUSTICE

A few years ago, the lieutenant governor of Minnesota and her family were walking through a glass enclosure in Minneapolis leaving a basketball game to return to a parking ramp. They passed a group of young adolescents engaged in horseplay. Because of the large amounts of glass in the area and the need for other people to pass through, the lieutenant governor stopped and asked the youth to stop their activity, saying, "Now we don't want you to get hurt, and by the way, isn't it time for you to go home?" As the family turned to leave, one of the boys tugged the sleeve of the lieutenant governor and asked her, "Do you work here?"

The lieutenant governor's story is an illustration of one citizen's attempt to achieve what sociologists refer to as *informal social control* based on an accepted community norm: safety. The story also reflects two points about our society: The adolescent behavior toward the adults is a norm; the adult behavior toward the adolescents is *not* a norm. Many can recall a time when adults in their neighborhoods or small towns took responsibility for "looking after" neighborhood children other than their own. In effect, community members, with the encouragement and support of police, schools, and other institutions, often "took care of" problems that now end up in juvenile courts or diversion programs. These adults set community tolerance limits, affirmed community norms and expectations, and, through verbal or other sanctions to young people (including telling parents), often persuaded children to refrain from whatever troublemaking or annoying behavior they were involved in. By expressing disapproval of behavior they viewed as wrong—and just as often, expressing concern and support for neighborhood young people—family members, neighbors, teachers, coaches, faith community members, and others were generally able to maintain a climate of order.

When asked if adults engage in such informal sanctioning in neighborhoods today, most would have to acknowledge that they and their neighbors do not. And, as the lieutenant governor's experience indicates, today's youth expect that the only people who will speak to them about their behavior in public (or speak to them at all) are members of their immediate family and people who are paid to do so. The troubling lesson from the story is its implication for the relationship between adults and youth. When the only adults, besides family, who comment on children's public behavior are those who are paid to do so (e.g., police and teachers), children may feel that other members of the community do not care about them. This pattern of adult-child interaction discourages a sense of a common good beyond individual interests.

While there are still societies in the world today—and some communities in the United States, including some in large cities—where adults participate actively in exercising social control over neighborhood children and also in supporting them, such behavior is increasingly less common in the modern world. Interestingly, there is research on an international level that suggests that low crime societies are those in which, as John Braithwaite puts it, "community members do *not* mind their own business" (1989). This basic finding has also been replicated in a study in which researchers found that Chicago neighborhoods with the lowest crime rates—even when poverty and racial composition were controlled statistically—were those in which community members reported that they commonly intervened in response to neighborhood conflict and trouble.

Of course, the problem of the lack of community involvement in enforcing standards of behavior is not limited to the response to youth crime and trouble. Part of the motivation for community justice is the realization that criminal justice systems alone cannot prevent or control crime or ensure justice. Indeed, there is a growing realization that "it takes a village" not only to raise children but more generally to maintain safe, peaceful, and just communities through new partnerships between criminal justice systems and communities.

WHAT IS COMMUNITY JUSTICE?

Community justice, along with its close relative restorative justice, provides a new philosophy and set of practices to respond to what has become a crisis situation in some neighborhoods around the country. Essentially, community justice seeks to reestablish the role and responsibility of citizens in preventing crime and building safer communities. Community justice includes "all variants of crime prevention and justice activities that explicitly include the community in their processes. Community justice is rooted in the actions that citizens, community organizations, and the criminal justice system can take to control crime and social disorder. Its central focus is community-level outcomes, shifting the emphasis form individual incidents to systemic patterns, from individual conscience to social mores, and from individual goods to the common good" (Clear & Karp 1999, p. 25).

PHILOSOPHY AND CURRENT PRACTICE

The apparently sudden rise of interest in community justice in the United States in the 1990s can be attributed primarily to the efforts of the federal Department of Justice and supportive state and local officials to extend the concepts and practice of community policing to other components of the criminal justice system. Building on a critique of the reactive professional model of policing and the vision of community policing as a

Communities Help Determine Justice

(ANS)—When Brian George got in trouble recently, the Vermont teenager might have come up against the impersonal face of traditional American justice: a black-robed judge sternly pronouncing a sentence from a courtroom bench.

With George's troubled background, another negative brush with authority might only have propelled him toward more serious offenses, perhaps eventually resulting in a jail sentence.

But instead of facing a judge, George last month found himself sitting across a conference-room table from Don Pfister, an unemployed therapist with a ponytail and a sympathetic attitude.

"I want to compliment you on what you've done so far," said Pfister, as his fellow Community Reparative Board members—an engineer, a state employee, a restaurant manager—nodded agreement.

George, 18, had met most requirements of the agreement he had signed 90 days earlier in Barre, Vt., with the board, under an innovative concept in which local citizens volunteer to deal with non-violent offenders.

"Right now it's pretty unique," Ed Barajas, a correctional programs specialist for the Justice Department in Washington, D.C., said of Vermont's community boards.

"But it's part of a larger trend that's developing toward what we call community justice," Barajas said. "It's justice that's focused on the community rather than on the offender."

Other examples Barajas cited include the "community policing" efforts underway in many cities; a "community prosecution" effort in Portland, Ore., in which prosecutors work with neighborhood residents to target their worst crime problems; and "community courts" set up in some New York City neighborhoods that, for example, may sentence offenders to help clean up the streets in those areas.

But those courts are staffed by judges. What's apparently unique about Vermont's community boards is that they consist of citizen volunteers like Pfister, a former prison guard who thinks anything that potentially diverts young people like George from incarceration is a good thing.

That's actually a secondary goal of the program. The primary purpose, said Michael Dooley of the Vermont Department of Corrections, is to involve the community in the criminal justice system, especially crime victims, who often feel left out.

"People are better in touch with the problems in their local communities," Dooley said. "And when we asked the community to volunteer for these boards, the response was beautiful."

The program, which began this year and is still taking shape, so far involves 142 volunteers serving on 12 different boards. They undergo 15 to 20 hours of training, then meet twice a month, usually in groups of five.

Vermont judges can pass on to the boards non-violent offenders who traditionally would get probation and a fine, but not much supervision from overworked probation officers.

"They wouldn't be jumping through all the hoops" that community boards put them through, Pfister said.

Among those hoops are restitution to victims, community service work, victim-offender mediation and driver-improvement courses.

Offenders may also be required to meet with victim-empathy panels. An alcohol-related offender, for example, would meet with people victimized by drunk drivers to learn how serious such offenses are.

"I think victims are finding more satisfaction with this system," said Catherine Waltz, a victims' rights advocate at the Franklin County District Attorney's Office in St. Albans, Vt. "There is more contact with the victims, if that's what the victims desire."

[. . .]

—Mark Lewis

Source: "A New Approach to Non-Violent Crime: Communities Help Determine Justice." American News Service, Article No. 18, n.d.

proactive, problem-solving approach for involving citizens in crime prevention and control, community justice advocates initiated new experiments with community courts, community prosecution, community corrections, and public defense as distinctive alternatives to traditional ways of managing and processing criminal cases. As part of these new approaches, judges, defense attorneys, probation officers, and prosecutors left their centralized offices for neighborhood locations and sought to meet victim, community, and offender needs. "Beat probation," for example, is an almost direct application of community-based or neighborhood policing to the community corrections context. Similarly, the notion of prosecutors or community public defenders adopting a *neighborhood* rather than a *caseload* as their focus of intervention or service may be viewed as an application of community policing ideas to the prosecution and defense functions. The problem-solving emphasis of community courts is also similar to the practical problem-oriented and service-provision emphases of many community policing advocates.

More generally, evaluators and federal justice department administrators learned much from community policing experiments about how to make the community both a target of and partner in criminal justice interventions. A community justice mission for criminal justice agencies and systems is therefore grounded in a commitment to the community as primary client or customer of the justice system. Practically, this orientation requires that criminal justice agencies take seriously neighborhood concerns for disorder, fear of crime, and quality-of-life issues that may seem unrelated or only vaguely related to the crime rate or to formal criminal justice functions.

Community justice also includes many of the core principles and practices associated with restorative justice. Restorative justice is a new way of thinking about crime that emphasizes one fundamental fact: Crime is a violation of individuals, communities, and relationships. If crime is about harm, justice must therefore amount to more than punishing or treating those found guilty of lawbreaking. Because crime obligates citizens to "make things right," restorative justice is best described as including "all responses to crime aimed at doing justice by repairing the harm, or 'healing the wounds,' crime causes" (Bazemore & Walgrave 1999, p. 26). Understanding "harm" and determining what should be done to repair it requires input from crime victims, citizens, and offenders. Restorative justice advocates promote use of informal decision-making alternatives to court sentencing such as victim-offender mediation or dialogue, family group conferencing, and a range of other nonadversarial processes designed to involve victims, offenders, and their supporters to develop a reparative plan. Such a plan is essentially an agreement with the offender to "make things right" with victims and the community by completing any of a number of reparative obligations, including restitution, community service, apologies, and other informal sanctions.

THE NEED FOR COMMUNITY RESTORATIVE JUSTICE

Children grow up in communities, not social service or juvenile justice programs. Most people's obedience of the law is based not on fears that police officers are watching them, but rather on an intrinsic morality built up over time. In addition, as the lieutenant governor's story illustrates, the motivation for community and restorative justice is based on a growing realization that that there are some things justice systems do well, but many things they do not do well.

There can never be enough police officers to prevent crime if families, extended families, neighbors, and schools lose their ability to do so. No matter how effective, courts will never really solve the problems of victims and offenders. Advocates of community justice contend that there are vital resources and creativity within the community to which government does not have direct access. For example, supporting and reintegrating victims and offenders into productive social roles are tasks most effectively handled informally by community members and groups who, for example, identify mentoring adults who can help delinquent or at-risk youths develop new skills, improve school performance, and connect with other community organizations or small businesses that may provide employment opportunities. Indeed, supporters believe community justice works precisely because ordinary community members, offenders, victims and their families and supporters, and neighbors are more capable than justice professionals of solving problems they are familiar with and invested in. When a group of citizen volunteers in San Jose, California, who resolve delinquency cases locally and informally in some of the city's neighborhood accountability boards, were asked, "Why does this work?" they suggested a number of theories to explain their success that distinguished their work from that of criminal justice professionals: "We aren't getting paid to do this"; "We can exercise the authority that parents have lost"; "We live in their (offender's and victim's) community"; "We give them input into the contract"; "We are a group of adult neighbors who care about them"; "They hear about the harm from real human beings"; "We follow up."

PARTICIPATION AND COMMUNITY BUILDING

Essentially, community and restorative justice initiatives seek to address two related problems: the lack of citizen participation in the justice process, and the need to rebuild the skills of community members and groups in exercising both social control and social support. The success of community and restorative justice will depend on the ability of these approaches to increase involvement and build the community's capacity to police itself. In addition, an assumption of community justice is that many current problems of *injustice*—in particular the disproportionate confinement of minorities and discriminatory treatment of these groups and individuals—can be resolved only by providing opportunities for these communities to take ownership of their crime problems and justice processes.

PARTICIPATION DENIED

For most of the public, criminal justice intervention is largely incomprehensible. If support comes from understanding, and understanding from involvement and participation, there should be little wonder that community attitudes about criminal justice often range from apathy to hostility.

Indeed, a core tenet of democratic decision making and governance is that citizens denied opportunities for meaningful participation become apathetic. They may then become suspicious, then distrustful, and finally oppositional and cynical. When cynicism prevails, the sense of community is threatened. But these feelings of apathy, cynicism, and opposition do not develop naturally. Therefore, when criminal justice agencies involve citizens and community groups in meaningful ways, they should anticipate an increased sense of investment and ownership in the justice process. Such ownership makes it difficult to criticize the system without becoming part of the solution, and investment creates a sense of personal responsibility for the well-being of the community that neutralizes apathy and cynicism. Minority communities in particular are reclaiming justice processes at the neighborhood level, using restorative justice programs to deal with crime and conflict in ways that avoid sending more of their young people into justice systems from which many of them never seem to escape.

BUILDING COMMUNITY CAPACITY

Since the 1960s and 1970s, criminal justice agencies and systems have expanded and taken on increasing responsibility for tasks once dealt with by citizens at the neighborhood level by less formal means. As this has occurred, some have expressed concern that communities are losing their capacity to respond to many of the problems that now find their way into arrest files, court dockets, and probation caseloads. Indeed, efforts to centralize, professionalize, and generally expand the reach of criminal justice and social services seem, over time, to have sent a message to communities: "Leave crime to the experts." In doing so, some have suggested that justice agencies may have inadvertently undercut the role and responsibility of citizens, institutions, and community groups in responding to crime and disorder:

> When agents of the state become the key problem-solvers, they might be filling a void in community; but just as in interpersonal relationships, so in community functioning, once a function is being performed by one party it becomes unnecessary for another to take it on. . . . Parents expect police or schools to control their children; neighbors expect police to prevent late night noise from people on their street; and citizens expect the courts to resolve disputes. . . . Informal control systems may (therefore) atrophy like dormant muscles. (Clear & Karp 1999, p. 38)

The concern that citizens and community groups have lost their ability to resolve conflict, enforce standards of behavior, and essentially socialize young people has brought a sense of urgency. This sense of urgency appears to have increased community involvement in restorative decision-making processes as a way of regaining these skills by practicing them on a routine basis.

But community justice does not mean abandoning the criminal justice system, and it does not mean minimizing the role of justice professionals. Rather, it means a different role for professionals who no longer present themselves as crime-control specialists or expert service providers, but as facilitators of informal, community responses to crime and gatekeepers of community resources. In this new role, professionals work with, and through, community groups (families, victim advocates and support groups, and socializing institutions such as schools and workplaces), and citizens to achieve goals for offenders and victims. In essence, they help to rebuild, or build, the community's capacity to prevent and control crime while ensuring that basic, universal standards of justice are maintained in the process. Community restorative justice envisions citizens and justice professionals working together to build the capacity of communities to resolve conflict peacefully, prevent crime, and address harmful behavior at the local level by involving those most affected directly in the process.

—Gordon Bazemore

Further Reading

Barajas, E., Jr. (1995). Moving toward community justice. In *Topics in community corrections.* Washington, DC: National Institute of Corrections.

Bazemore, G. (1997). The "community" in community justice: Issues, themes and questions for the new neighborhood sanctioning models. *The Justice System Journal, 19*(2), 193–228.

Bazemore, G. (1998). Restorative justice and earned redemption: Communities, victims and offender reintegration. *American Behavioral Scientist, 41,* 768–813.

Bazemore, G. (2000). Community justice and a vision of collective efficacy: The case of restorative conferencing. In National Institute of Justice (Ed.), *Criminal justice 2000.* Washington, DC: U.S. Department of Justice.

Bazemore, G., & Umbreit, M. (2001). A comparison of four restorative conferencing models. *Juvenile Justice Bulletin.* Washington, DC: U.S. Department of Justice.

Bazemore, G., & Schiff, M. (Eds.). (2001). *Restorative and community justice cultivating common ground for victims, communities and offenders.* Cincinnati, OH: Anderson.

Bazemore, G., & Walgrave, L. (Eds.). (1999). *Restorative juvenile justice: Repairing the harm of youth crime.* Monsey, NY: Criminal Justice Press.

Boland, B. (1998). Community prosecution: Portland's experiences. In D. Karp (Ed.), *Community justice: An emerging field* (pp. 253–278). Lanham, MD: Rowman & Littlefield.

Braithwaite, J. (1998). Restorative justice. In M. Tonry (Ed.), *The handbook of crime and punishment* (pp. 323–444). New York: Oxford University Press.

Braithwaite, J., & Mugford, S. (1994). Conditions of successful reintegration ceremonies: Dealing with juvenile offenders. *British Journal of Criminology, 34*(2): 139–71.

Clear, T., & Karp, D. (1999). *The community justice ideal: Preventing crime and achieving justice.* Boulder, CO: Westview.

Dunlap, K. (Ed.). (1998). *Community justice: Concepts and strategies.* Lexington, KY: American Probation and Parole Association.

Earle, R. (1996). Community justice: The Austin experience. *Texas Probation, 11,* 6–11.

Etzioni, A. (1998). Community justice in a communitarian perspective. In D. Karp (Ed.), *Community justice: An emerging field* (pp. 373–378). Lanham, MD: Rowman & Littlefield.

Goldstein, H. (1990). *Problem-oriented policing.* New York: McGraw-Hill.

Kelling, G., & Coles, C. (1996). *Fixing broken windows.* New York: Free Press.

Pranis, K. (2001). Restorative justice, social justice, and the empowerment of marginalized populations. In G. Bazemore & M. Schiff (Eds.), *Restorative community justice: Repairing harm and transforming communities.* Cincinnati, OH: Anderson.

Retzinger, S. M., and Scheff, T. J. (1996). Strategy for community conferences: Emotions and social bonds. In B. Galaway & J. Hudson (Eds.), *Restorative justice: International perspectives.* Monsey, NY: Criminal Justice Press.

Sampson, R., Raudenbush, S., and Earls, F. (1997). Neighborhoods and violent crime: A multi-level study of collective efficacy. *Science, 277*(4), 918–24.

Sparrow, M., M. Moore, & D. Kennedy. (1990). *Beyond 911.* New York: Basic Books.

Stuart, B. (1996). Circle sentencing: Turning swords into ploughshares. In B. Galaway & J. Hudson (Eds.), *Restorative justice: International perspectives* (pp. 193–206). Monsey, NY: Criminal Justice Press.

Van Ness, D., & Strong, K. H. (1997). *Restoring justice.* Cincinnati, OH: Anderson.

COMMUNITY LAND TRUST

A community land trust (CLT) is a member-controlled, nonprofit organization that owns land in urban neighborhoods and rural areas, usually with the goal of building or preserving affordable housing. CLTs can be concentrated in one neighborhood or on contiguous parcels; they can also hold scattered properties throughout a city. CLTs were pioneered in the 1960s by the Institute for Community Economics, a Massachusetts-based organization that still supports CLTs. There are currently over 125 CLTs in the United States.

CLTS AND AFFORDABLE HOUSING

Most CLTs are designed to create owner-occupied affordable housing. Typically, a CLT acquires either vacant land or land with housing on it. It then sells the housing but retains the land underneath the buildings. This means that the buyers pay a lower price than they would if the land was included; for instance, a house that may ordinarily cost $100,000 may sell for $70,000 if the land is not included in the price. CLTs thereby allow families to buy houses that they could not otherwise afford.

In addition, the land value counts as security. To qualify for a mortgage with the lowest possible interest rate and still avoid high fees for mortgage insurance, families usually must make a down payment of at least 20 percent of the house value. Since the land represents substantially more than 20 percent of the value of the land-house package, buyers can qualify without making a down payment.

Some CLTs buy multiple-unit dwellings (apartments or duplexes, for example). In these cases, the occupants do not own their housing units; instead, they own shares in the building that function much like shares of stock in a corporation (this arrangement is known as a housing co-op). Their shares entitle them to live in their unit because they are part of the corporation that owns the building. Housing co-ops are one form of housing tenure that can be used within a CLT, but CLTs are not limited to housing co-ops; they also include free and clear title ownership of the housing atop the land.

Because CLTs are nonprofits with the goal of providing affordable housing, they usually have procedures to select families whose incomes do not surpass a specified threshold. They also have a way to ensure that the houses stay affordable even after the initial owners sell: CLTs lease the land underneath the houses to the homebuyer. The land lease costs very little (sometimes just a dollar a year), but the lease usually stipulates that the house may be resold only to another qualifying low-income family and that the price may not exceed a specified amount. Most CLTs entitle the sellers to their original purchase price plus a percentage of any increase in the house's appraised market value. The land lease also often requires that owners occupy the buildings.

BEYOND AFFORDABLE HOUSING

Although almost all CLTs have an affordable-housing mission, practically any land use can occur in a CLT. CLTs can make affordable commercial space available for such community services as food pantries and legal aid offices; for small businesses offering economic development opportunities; for firewood production in rural areas; and for community open space (parks and plazas). In all cases, community ownership of the land makes it less expensive to use the land. CLTs are related to, but not the same as, conservation land trusts. Conservation land trusts seek primarily to preserve open space for the enjoyment of future generations and to benefit ecological diversity.

WHEN CLTS ARE USEFUL

CLTs are often formed to moderate the gentrifying effects of rising land prices. In many cities, older low- and moderate-income neighborhoods become desirable for upper-income families, because they have well-built houses and because they are close to shopping and workplaces. As these families move in, land prices and rents increase, and established residents and businesses face rapidly rising costs. Because it owns the land and controls the prices of the buildings on it, the CLT can guard against displacement. For example, the Burlington (Vermont) Community Land Trust now owns over 600 units in and around Burlington, Vermont's largest city, where housing costs are high and vacancies rare because of strong competition and relatively high incomes.

The CLT serves a similar purpose when wealthy people begin buying property in rural areas whose established residents depend on farming, forestry, fishing, and mining. When urban residents "discover" these areas and begin to buy vacation property there, local residents are often priced out of home ownership, and local businesses cannot compete with expensive restaurants and boutiques for commercial space. The CLT can stabilize land values for these local residents and businesses. Examples of these CLTs include the Bahama Conch Community Land Trust of Key West (Florida) and several CLTs in rural Maine.

CLTs also can be useful in declining neighborhoods with substantial absentee ownership, in which the rent that local residents pay leaves the community entirely and sometimes goes to people who decide not to reinvest in the neighborhood. One of the best-known CLTs, Dudley Street Neighborhood Initiative (Boston, Massachusetts), began as a response to disinvestment.

HOW CLTS ACQUIRE PROPERTY

Community land trusts can proceed without government intervention or assistance, but they often acquire property by working with local governments, which can use federal, state, and local funding to support property purchases. Local governments also sometimes foreclose on property whose owners have not paid their property taxes, especially in declining neighborhoods, and can make this property available to CLTs. CLTs sometimes acquire new properties by making down-payment grants to qualifying families; in this strategy, the first family to buy the house provides the funds for the house, but the CLT buys—and keeps—the land, leasing the house back to the family. To encourage landowners to give their holdings to the community, donations of land to CLTs are tax deductible under U.S. federal tax law. The municipal government in Boston granted the Dudley Street Neighborhood Initiative (DSNI) an unusual power: the ability to initiate eminent-domain (the government's right to take over private property for public use) proceedings against absentee owners, which allowed DSNI to go to court to acquire properties at fair-market prices even from unwilling sellers.

WHO CONTROLS THE CLT?

The members of the CLT include the buyers of CLT property and other interested individuals and groups in the community. The CLT is governed by a board of directors that includes residents, other interested individuals, and people with special expertise in real estate, housing, or business development.

—Rolf Pendall

Further Reading

Geisler, C. C., & Daneker, G. (2000). *Property and values: Alternatives to public and private ownership.* Washington, DC: Island Press.

Institute for Community Economics. (1982). *The community land trust handbook.* Emmaus, PA: Rodale.

Medoff, P., & Sklar, H. (1994). *Streets of hope: The fall and rise of an urban neighborhood.* Boston: South End Press.

COMMUNITY MENTAL HEALTH CENTERS

Community mental health centers (CMHCs) are locally organized and locally funded organizations mandated through government regulation to provide a range of psychological and psychiatric services to residents of a designated geographic area (catchment area). CMHCs as described here are primarily a United States phenomenon, but similar centers exist in other countries, such as the United Kingdom, where they are known as community psychiatric services (CPS), and Italy, where they are called community mental health centers. Community services can now be found in many countries in Europe, Asia, and North America. These services include inpatient care, outpatient care, partial hospitalization, emergency services, and consultation and education to agencies and to the public regarding mental health issues and prevention of problems. Since the late 1990s, many centers decided to call themselves to behavioral health centers because their services include treatment programs for alcohol and other substance abuse. To understand the role CMHCs fulfill today, it is important to examine their origins and development in the context of the history of mental health care.

HISTORICAL ANTECEDENTS

In the eighteenth and nineteenth centuries, the mentally ill were subjected to an extraordinary variety of treatments. Exorcisms, eugenics, chains, and jails were all elements of the treatment package in the past. There were those who championed a more humane approach, including Philippe Pinel (1745–1826) in France, Dorothea Dix (1802–1887) in the United States, and William Tuke (1782–1822) in England. Despite their efforts, however, most mentally ill patients were confined to custodial care until the 1930s and 1940s.

The late eighteenth and early nineteenth centuries brought the development of the medical model in psychiatry, including the one-to-one relationship of doctor and patient. Such treatment was, however, available only to the wealthy. Care for most people included placement in a twenty-four-hour facility, a psychiatric ward typically run by poorly trained county, state, or federal government staff. By the 1930s, these institutions were bursting at the seams. Urbanization, economic depression, and the pressures of daily life contributed to increased admissions to these warehouse-style facilities, typically located in quieter rural areas whose distance from towns protected the patient from the family and community and the society from the patient. Few patients were discharged. Large sums were spent to provide care and seclusion from the world. Such treatments as electroconvulsive therapy, insulin coma therapy, lobotomies, and hydrotherapy (all pioneered in the 1930s) were of little value and did not encourage the patient's return to family and community.

A variety of new treatment approaches and medical interventions developed in the 1950s to 1960s, within and outside the hospital, encouraged the development of the CMHCs. These included group psychotherapy, family therapy, and the therapeutic social club (a precursor to the current psychosocial rehabilitation programs), all of which encouraged independence and redirection toward home and community. The therapeutic community, a term popularized by Doctor Maxwell Jones in the early 1950s, offered a group approach, redirecting patients toward the outside world, with the doctor acting as facilitator and other patients offering communal support. Former mental patient Clifford Beers pioneered the mental hygiene clinics, and some cities created child guidance clinics. However, perhaps the single most important development was the introduction in the mid-1950s to mid-1960s of medications known as phenothiazines (examples include Thorazine and Mellaril), which helped to calm the patient and to control the psychiatric symptoms. Patients and staff could be hopeful as mental illness became more controllable. Open-door policies began in hospitals, and some halfway houses were established. Mental health professionals now had some new tools for helping the patients to return home.

Sociologist and social anthropologist Erving Goffman's *Asylums* (1961) described the destructive effects of the infrastructure of the institutions that encouraged the status quo, and therefore encouraged the public to consider alternative approaches to mental illness. The mass media also helped with public perception by portraying the mentally ill as people with feelings, thoughts, and needs rather than simply as mad men and women. Mary Jane Ward's (1946) novel *The Snake Pit* and the 1948 film with the same title, Ken Kesey's novel *One Flew Over the Cuckoo's Nest* (1962), and articles in magazines and newspapers began to humanize these people.

THE BEGINNINGS

Concurrently, as the American Psychiatric Association was speaking out for changes, federal, state and local officials were exploring alternatives. In 1955, one out of every two hospital beds in the United States was occupied by a psychiatric patient. The largest economic and political boon to change was the Community Mental Health Act, passed in October 1963, resulting from *Action for Mental Health,* a report commissioned by President Kennedy, whose sister Rose was mentally retarded and mentally ill. This legislation created funds for construction of community mental health centers to serve 50,000 to 100,000 residents and provide the five levels of service described above. Funds were included for staffing the centers with psychiatrists, who oversaw treatment offered primarily by nurses, psychologists, social workers, and paraprofessional case managers. Funding would be on a descending scale for eight years, with the local governments and agencies mandated to provide matching funds from other sources, including state and local governments, insurance reimbursement, charitable contributions, foundation funds, and so forth.

The psychiatric community was optimistic that CMHCs could care for the severely mentally ill outside of the hospital. In addition, court decisions defined the right to treatment in the least restrictive environment possible and defended the patient's right to refuse treatment. These forces also paved the way for opening CMHCs and placing patients in neighborhoods, a process known as de-institutionalization. However, no provisions were made for linkages to the existing state psychiatric hospitals, nor were transitional housing or vocational training included. Clients who had been told what to do daily, even hourly, suddenly had to fend for themselves. Meanwhile, finances were limited, as were alternative services like vocational training. The money needed to fulfill the goals of de-institutionalization was never redirected from the budgets of the large institutions. As a result, the services needed were underfunded.

In 1981, the Omnibus Budget Reconciliation Act reorganized the funding to block grants to the states, which were not allocated uniformly among the states. The law also ended federal administration of CMHCs, passing regulation over to the states. The National Institute of Mental Health became a technical adviser rather than an administrator.

While the increase of local facilities diminished the use of the mental hospital, local facilities did not bring an end to the traditional mental hospital, in part because the CMHCs began to offer services to new client populations. These included young chronically ill patients, mentally ill chemical abusers, and MICA clients, families and children, as well as special populations such as rural clients and the homeless. CMHCs also instituted community support programs (CSPs), case management, and service linkage programs for the severely mentally ill client. These CSPs were generally affiliated with community-based agencies that offered transitional housing, health and dental care, and vocational training.

Statistics regarding usage and cost are somewhat difficult to cull because programs no longer necessarily use the acronym CMHC. In addition, now that programs are run by the states, frequently only state figures are accessible. Length-of-stay statistics in public mental hospitals show a decline in the patient census from 560,000 in 1955 to 60,000 in 2000. In 1955, 77 percent of psychiatric patients were treated primarily in twenty-four-hour care settings, 23 percent in outpatient care settings. In 1998, 24 percent were treated in inpatient units, 76 percent in less intensive environments—a nearly complete reversal.

OUTLOOK FOR THE FUTURE

Since 2000, state and federal legislatures have begun looking at the issue of insurance parity between mental health services and other medical care, so that insurance coverage for the treatment of mental illness will be the same as treatment for other health problems. This will likely be challenged legally over the next years. Ever growing numbers of client groups and family groups, such as the National Association for the Mentally Ill, have been strong supporters and have lobbied for expanded services. Many states have mandated the development and active participation of CMHC advisory committees composed of members of the general public.

CMHCs will continue to provide care for those in the community who cannot afford private treatment. The future of the CMHC is dependent on public policy regarding the mentally ill and on psychiatric treatment in general.

—*Judith L. Weinstein*

Further Reading

DiBella, G., Poynter-Berg, D., Weitz, W., & Yurmark, J. L. (1982) *Handbook of partial hospitalization.* New York: Brunner-Mazel.

Goffman, E. (1961). *Asylums.* Garden City, NJ: Doubleday.

Grob, G. N. (1994). *The mad among us: A history of the care of America's mentally ill.* New York: Free Press.

Isaac, R. J., & Armat, V. C. (1990). *Madness in the streets.* New York: Free Press.

Jones, M. (1952). *The therapeutic community.* New York: Basic Books.

Manderscheid, R. W., Atay, J. E., Hernandez-Cartagena, M. del R., Edmond, P. Y., Male, A., Parker, A. C. E., et al. (2000). Highlights of organized mental-health services in 1998 and major national and state trends. In R. W. Manderschein & M. J. Henderson (Eds.), *Mental health, United States, 2000* (pp. 1–9) Rockville, MD: U.S. Department of Health and Human Services, Substance Abuse and Mental Health Services Administration, Center for Mental Health Services.

Mosher,L., & Burti, L. (1994). *Community mental health.* New York: W. W. Norton.

Schwartz, A., & Schwartzburg, M. (1976). Hospital care. In B. Wolman (Ed.), *The therapist's handbook* (pp. 199–226) New York: Van Nostrand Reinhold.

Veroff, J., Kulka, R. A., & Douvan, E. (1981). *Mental health in America.* New York: Basic Books.

COMMUNITY ORGANIZING

Although not understood as a distinctive form of organizing until the 1960s, community organizing has much older antecedents. What distinguishes community organizing from other forms of organizing is the emphasis on community—or place of residence—as the locus of organizing efforts. This is in contrast to forms of organizing such as labor organizing, which emphasize activity at the place of work.

ANTECEDENTS

The precursors of community organizing can be found in concerns and activities focused on the poor in London and in the teeming urban tenements of such cities as New York City and Chicago. What later became known as social work took the form of Hull House, founded by Jane Addams (1860–1935), and the settlement house movement at the end of the nineteenth century and beginning of the twentieth century. In the United States, concern for the fate of rural communities drew agricultural extension personnel into community organizing—although their preferred terminology was "community development"—once agricultural extension became recognized and funded by federal, state, and local governments after the adoption of the Smith-Lever Act in 1914.

In the mid to late 1930s and early 1940s, as part of the movement of industrial workers into industrial unions (with the formation of the Committee of Industrial Organization, which later became the Congress of Industrial Organization), Chicago meatpacking workers began to organize. Standard union organizing activities that focused on the factory gate had only limited success, however. Saul Alinsky (1909–1972) introduced an important innovation when he helped form the Back of the Yards movement among the packinghouse workers. The innovation was to meet workers in their homes and neighborhoods rather than at the plant gate. This experience led Alinsky to form the Industrial Areas Foundation (IAF) in the 1940s as a distinctive organizing entity. IAF recruited and trained organizers who went on to organize in troubled communities when a local group requested IAF help.

Alinsky adapted the Marxist approach to conflict as an organizing tool, but without using the explicit Marxist approach to class struggle. This was accomplished by crystallizing support in minority and low-income communities by attacking the local community power structure and making demands on them for things such as jobs. Not only was this considered impertinent, but it was also usually done by explicitly making it clear who the individuals in the local power structure were. For example, instead of just picketing an important local company at its factory gates, Alinsky would organize pickets at the boss's home, embarrassing the person in his own neighborhood. Tactics such as these were considered outrageous but usually helped define a "we" (of the minority and low-income population) versus a "they" (of the local power structure). During the civil rights movements of the 1960s, Alinsky's approach to organizing was popular in Chicago; in Buffalo, Syracuse, and Rochester in New York State; in St. Louis, Missouri; and in various places in California.

CESAR CHAVEZ AND THE UNITED FARM WORKERS

The Alinsky approach had its most dramatic manifestation when the organizer Cesar Chavez (1927–1993) adopted it in organizing the United Farm Workers (UFW) union. Chavez was "found" by an Alinsky organizer, Fred Ross, and trained in an Alinsky-inspired Los Angeles Mexican group, the Community Service Organization (CSO). Rising in the CSO leadership,

Contract or Community?

Those philosophical liberals who tend to reject the term community altogether see society as based on a social contract establishing procedures of fairness, but otherwise leaving individuals free to serve their own interests. They argue that under modern conditions, if we think of community as based on shared values and shared goals, community can exist only in small groups and is not possible or desirable in large-scale societies or institutions.

A deeper analysis, however, reveals that it is possible to see this supposed contrast of contract vs. community as a continuum, or even as a necessary complementarity, rather than as an either/or proposition. Surely procedural norms of fairness are necessary in large-scale social institutions; but any group of any size, if it has a significant breadth of involvement and lasts a significant length of time, must have some shared values and goals. Consequently societies and institutions can never be based solely on contract, striving to maximize the opportunities of individuals. They must also, to some extent, be communities with shared values and goals.

But this reformulation leads to a further problem. Those who think of community as a form of *Gemeinschaft*, as well as their liberal critics, tend to think consensus about values and goals must be complete or nearly complete. Is such complete consensus realistic, or even desirable, in modern societies?

The answer, of course, is no. Yet this lack of unanimity needn't create problems for supporters of community. While community-shared values and goals do imply something more than procedural agreement—they do imply some agreements about substance—they do not require anything like total or unarguable agreement. A good community is one in which there is argument, even conflict, about the meaning of the shared values and goals, and certainly about how they will be actualized in everyday life. Community is not about silent consensus; it is a form of intelligent, reflective life, in which there is indeed consensus, but where the consensus can be challenged and changed—often gradually, sometimes radically—over time.

Thus we are led to the question of what makes any kind of group a community and not just a contractual association. The answer lies in a shared concern with the following question: "What will make this group a *good* group?" Any institution, such as a university, a city, or a society, insofar as it is or seeks to be a community, needs to ask what is a good university, city, society, and so forth. So far as it reaches agreement about the good it is supposed to realize (and that will always be contested and open to further debate), it becomes a community with some common values and some common goals. ("Goals" are particularly important, as the effort to define a good community also entails the goal of trying to create a good one—or, more modestly and realistically, a better one than the current one.)

—Robert N. Bellah

Source: Bellah, Robert N. (1995/96, Winter). "Community Properly Understood: A Defense of 'Democratic Communitarianism'" *The Responsive Community, 6*(1). Retrieved March 5, 2003, from http://www.gwu.edu/~icps/bellah.html.

Chavez wanted CSO to organize Mexican American farmworkers in California, outside the Los Angeles area. When CSO resisted, Chavez went off on his own to form what later became the UFW.

Chavez's adaptation of the Alinsky approach sought to avoid explicit class conflict while confronting day-to-day problems of Mexican American farmworkers. Rather than trying to find workers in the fields where they worked, Chavez and his group held house or neighborhood meetings. Understanding the historic power of California's agricultural employers, which had frustrated the development of farmworker unions in the past, Chavez formed service organizations that addressed specific problems of farmworkers. One organization was the death benefit society to which members contributed small sums weekly or monthly, with the collected money being used when a member or someone in a member's family died. Another organization was a Spanish-language credit union in which workers could deposit money when they were employed and from which they could borrow money when they weren't. Chavez's group also organized a gas station where workers could buy gas and find tools to repair their own cars. These organizations built confidence and solidarity between farmworkers and gave them organizational experience.

When a strike of Filipino farmworkers spread to Delano, California, where the Chavez organization was based, the emergence of a more traditional trade union got under way. However, Chavez generated a series of initiatives that varied markedly from traditional union organizing. Because, for farmworkers, there was no equivalent to the factory gate, it was essential that a neighborhood and family base be maintained; union membership was therefore by the family rather than the individual. Chavez quickly learned the importance of mobilizing urban support from religious, urban, liberal, and student organizations. While striking farmworkers could often recruit strikebreakers, winning them over to the strikers' side, agricultural employers were always able to find new replacements. This led to the formation of the boycott strategy, initially focused on table grapes.

The UFW's table grape boycott put the union and the idea of community organizing on the map for activists by the late 1960s. For example, Students for a Democratic Society (SDS) picked up the community organizing strategy and sent some of its members to Newark, New Jersey, and other northern ghettos to organize. At the same time, the burgeoning civil rights movements began to use community organizing strategies. Organizations such as the Southern Christian Leadership Conference (SCLC) and the Congress on Racial Equality (CORE), Mississippi Freedom Summer, and other civil rights groups adopted the approach in the South; in the North, racially divided cities such as Rochester, Syracuse, and others called on the IAF to provide them with organizers.

THE SPREAD OF COMMUNITY ORGANIZING

Some initiatives were successful; others had only partial successes or floundered. But community organizing as a distinctive approach had been established, and several organizations followed the IAF in offering training and help putting the approach into action. The activist Heather Booth, for example, established the Midwest Academy in Chicago as a training organization. A somewhat broader attempt was undertaken in the creation of Association of Communities Organized for Reform Now (ACORN), which not only trained organizers but actively sought to generate specific campaigns, primarily in low-income and minority communities. ACORN was eventually successful in organizing local groups and, in some cases, statewide groups in over forty states.

Similar organizations, such as Oregon and Massachusetts Fair Share and the National Welfare Rights Organization (NWRO) in New York, and neighborhood groups too numerous to mention, sprang up in the 1970s, 1980s, and 1990s in virtually every city and town in the United States. Whether focused on environmental, housing, social service, traffic, or more general planning issues of interest to the people living in the neighborhood, these groups tended to be created on an ad hoc basis around particular issues, but they often lived on to take up general concerns of neighbors. In some cases, such groups formed in opposition to local government policies, but in many cases local governments sought to incorporate such groups into their planning processes and supported their continued existence. In some cases, city governments themselves created such groups where none existed and provided them with at least limited city staff support and other resources. An extensive literature and several video documentaries now exist documenting the history of many of these community organizing efforts; there are also training manuals for those interested in learning from the organizing experiences of these early groups.

A few unions, notably the Service Employees International Union (SEIU), have used community organizing strategies to recruit members and extend union benefits to them. Probably the most successful attempt has been that of Justice for Janitors, organized by the SEIU in southern California during the 1990s, where the union has brought many of the service workers under union coverage.

Although many activists adopted the community organizing approach in the 1960s and 1970s, some criticized the approach for the limited goals that often characterized campaigns. Community organizers tended to focus on limited goals because they wanted their goals to be achievable, but since in some cases that meant working for something as small as getting a stop sign put up at a busy intersection, critics of community organizing labeled the approach "stop sign organizing." Despite this criticism, community organizing remains an important organizing strategy.

UNION ORGANIZING AND COMMUNITY ORGANIZING

Since the mid-1980s, there has been some blending of the traditional union organizing approach, which attempts to reach unorganized workers at their place of employment (the "point of production"), and community organizing strategies, which seek to organize workers or low-income or minority community members at their place of residence (the "point of consumption"). The SEIU and other unions across the U.S. have also been active in the creation of "living wage" campaigns, which seek higher minimum wages for employees of agencies contracting with local governments. Such campaigns have often been organized on a neighborhood or citywide basis. In the late 1990s, as part of a renewed attempt to revitalize the labor movement and recruit unorganized workers, the AFL-CIO developed an organizing strategy based on linking union organizing efforts with community organizing efforts in low-income and working-class neighborhoods. Seattle Unions Now (SUN) was one of the more serious attempts to actually implement the strategy and it had some limited success before it was for all practical purposes abandoned in 2000.

COMMUNITY ORGANIZING AND DEMOCRACY

Although community organizing efforts have varied in their scope and success, there is no question that they are now a well-established part of the U.S. political landscape. Experience in such movements is increasingly the gateway into politics for candidates for local governmental office. In many communities, such movements and organizations have replaced civic organizations, churches, labor unions, and political parties as the most significant locus of participatory democratic action. As the institutions affecting daily life become increasingly global in scope, many residents in the United States appear to be looking more and more to local, community organizing efforts as an opportunity to help take more control over the quality of their lives.

In industrialized countries and developing nations around the world, grassroots organizing is also a growing phenomenon. In low-income neighborhoods in European cities, urban barrios, and rural indigenous villages, there is a growing movement of ordinary people forming grassroots community organizations to make demands on governments for resources and local control over a wide variety of issues.

—*William H. Friedland and Michael Rotkin*

See also Alinsky, Saul; Collective Action; Community Action; Cooperative Extension System

Further Reading

Addams, J. (1910). *Twenty years at Hull-house.* New York: Macmillan.

Alinsky, S. (1989). *Reveille for radicals.* New York: Vintage.

Bobo, K., Kendall, J., & Max, S. (2001). *Organizing for change: Midwest Academy manual for activists.* Santa Ana, CA: Seven Locks Press.

Boyte, H. (1980). *The backyard revolution: Understanding the new citizen movement.* Philadelphia: Temple University Press.

Delgado, G. (1986). *Organizing the movement: The roots and growth of ACORN.* Philadelphia: Temple University Press.

Fisher, R. (1994). *Let the people decide: Neighborhood organizing in America.* New York: Twayne.

Gitlin, T., & Hollander, N. (1970). *Uptown: Poor whites in Chicago.* New York: Harper & Row.

Horwitt, S. D. (1989). *Let them call me rebel.* New York: Alfred A. Knopf.

Lissak, R. S. (1989). *Pluralism and progressives: Hull House and the new immigrants, 1890–1919.* Chicago: University of Chicago Press.

Majka, L. C., & Majka, T. J. (1982). *Farm workers, agribusiness, and the state.* Philadelphia: Temple University Press.

Shaw, R. (2001). *The activist's handbook.* Berkeley and Los Angeles: University of California Press.

Shockly, J. S. (1974). *Chicano revolt in a Texas town.* Notre Dame, IN: University of Notre Dame Press.

Stout, L. (1996). *Bridging the class divide and other lessons for grassroots organizing.* Boston: Beacon.

Susser, I. (1982). *Norman Street: Poverty and politics in an urban neighborhood.* New York: Oxford University Press.

COMMUNITY OWNERSHIP

Community ownership refers to property held for the long-term enjoyment and benefit of residents of a region, city, or town. While the term is broad enough to include everything from public park land to private jewelry collections, this entry focuses on productive properties such as businesses, banks, and farms. A central tenet of community economics is that local ownership of productive enterprise is critical to community well-being.

WHY OWNERSHIP MATTERS

From the perspective of community, local ownership of enterprise is beneficial for four reasons. First, a successful business anchored to the community through ownership is likely to produce income, jobs, tax receipts, and charitable donations for local residents over several generations. Whenever ownership coincides with the location of a business, these transactions reinforce one another and pump up the local economic multiplier, the basic building block for community prosperity. The term *multiplier* refers to the phenomenon that each dollar spent in an economy cascades into numerous follow-on expenditures of the same dollar, which, in the course of a year, can generate two to five dollars of additional economic activity.

Second, local ownership minimizes the incidence of calamitous departures by business. Across the United States, cities have seen their best companies sell their interests to outsiders who decide to shut down the hometown plant and move operations to jurisdictions with cheaper labor, lower taxes, or looser environmental regulations. These areas are often in southern or western states and increasingly in Mexican maquiladoras (where U.S. companies have easy access and Mexican regulation is lax) and other "offshore" sites. Tragic consequences usually follow. Taxpayers thrown out of work become tax-drainers through welfare and unemployment checks. When the tax base contracts, vital services such as education, police, and fire prevention are cut. Property values plummet, and, as in so many steel and auto towns in the 1970s and 1980s, the community can descend into a death spiral.

A third advantage of local ownership is that once a company agrees to stay indefinitely, the community can better shape its laws and regulations to serve the local quality of life. Today, most communities are held hostage to their largest companies. On the eastern shore of Maryland, for example, Tyson and Perdue, two large poultry companies, have successfully fought all legislative efforts to raise their workers' wages and to clean up the billions of pounds of chicken manure they dump into the Chesapeake Bay ecosystem. These companies deploy a powerful argument: Regulate us, and we'll move to more lax jurisdictions such as Georgia or Arkansas.

While not immune to pressing their case aggressively with local politicians, locally owned companies usually do not threaten to leave town—their roots in the community are too deep, and the costs of departing too high. A community filled primarily with locally owned businesses can set higher labor and environmental standards, confident that the enterprises are likely to adapt rather than flee.

In the National Football League, all franchises but one are owned by a single individual, and a half dozen have threatened to leave town if demands for hundreds of millions of dollars for new stadiums and salary increases are not met. When the city of Cleveland, Ohio, refused, Art Modell, the owner of the Browns, took "his" team to Baltimore, Maryland. The only community-owned team is the Green Bay Packers, a nonprofit whose shareholders are primarily the citizens of Wisconsin. Because fans of the Packers would never allow the team to leave town, the team is prevented from extorting an unfair share of the community resources.

Finally, locally owned businesses are, in fact, more likely to succeed than those with absentee shareholders. In 1975, the Sperry Rand Company decided to shut down any subsidiaries that were not achieving a 22 percent rate of return. One of its companies slated to get the axe was the Library Bureau, the principal employer in the town of Herkimer, New York. The workers, residents, and local banks decided to execute a buyout. In its first year of operation under new management, the newly independent Library Bureau earned a 17 percent rate of return—inadequate for Sperry Rand, but more than enough for Herkimer. The independent Library Bureau continued to perform profitably for more than a decade.

The Herkimer example underscores the fact that locally owned businesses have more flexibility and time to become profitable. Having locally owned businesses generate a positive rate of return is far more important to a community economy than having a smaller number of absentee-owned companies generating a maximum rate of return. This fact helps explain why college and state-government towns—anchored by institutions that cannot easily move—are among the most recession-proof.

WHAT CONSTITUTES LOCAL OWNERSHIP

Community ownership can come in many forms, as a brief review of available business structures in the United States reveals. A sole proprietorship or a small, family-owned business is unlikely to pack its operations and move to Singapore. Businesses that specialize in delivering local goods and services, such as a tractor-repair shop in rural Kansas or a small law firm with a nearby clientele in Bellingham, Massachusetts, usually harbor few global ambitions. The U.S. Small Business Administration notes that roughly half of the U.S. economy, as measured by employees and wealth production, is made up of small businesses.

Worker ownership of for-profit businesses can inhibit mobility and help to link a business to a community, especially if the workforce is small and lives nearby. More than 10,000 U.S. corporations have employee stock-ownership plans, and in roughly 2,500 of these, employees own the majority of stock shares. When employees are geographically dispersed, however, such as those who now own United Airlines, worker ownership may have only a tenuous connection with any specific community.

Cooperatives also rarely leave their home base, since the consumers or employees who control the firm are reluctant to surrender a wealth-producing asset. The U.S. National Center for Economic and Security Alternatives estimates that there are 47,000 cooperatives in the United States, including 4,000 consumer co-ops, 6,500 housing co-ops, 12,600 credit unions, 1,200 rural utilities, 115 telecommunications and cable co-ops, and more than 100 cooperative insurance companies. Again, scale matters. The widely studied cooperatives in Mondragon, Spain, and Bologna, Italy, have recently entered joint ventures with multinational corporations, which effectively dilute community control.

Nonprofit corporations, which account for more than 6 percent of the U.S. economy, are community friendly. One out of three nonprofits is a tax-exempt foundation or charity; the rest are primarily universities, hospitals, fraternal organizations, and day care centers. Several thousand nonprofit community development corporations (CDCs) are involved in starting new businesses, rehabilitating housing, developing commercial real estate, and training the underprivileged for jobs.

One type of corporate structure that stays put whatever its scale is a municipally owned enterprise. U.S. state and local governments have established more than 6,300 public authorities to build highways and bridges, run electric and water utilities, dispose of hazardous wastes, operate ports, and perform other public services. The state of North Dakota runs its own bank with checking and savings accounts.

Another intriguing option is to create a company whose stock can be owned—or traded—only within a locality. The noted ice cream company Ben & Jerry's, for example, restricted its first stock issue to residents of Vermont (though subsequent issues dropped this restriction, diluted local control, and opened the company up to a hostile takeover by Unilever).

A further example of this idea is provided by the Green Bay Packers. During the Depression, the Packers' executive committee convinced the Green Bay, Wisconsin, Association of Commerce to organize its members into neighborhood teams to sell $25 shares door to door. Today, several stock sales later, roughly 100,000 fans own shares of the team, and more than half live in Wisconsin. Shareholders can trade shares within their families or sell them back to the corporation for $25. No one can own more than twenty shares.

Because the Packers are a nonprofit corporation, shareholders receive neither annual dividends nor capital gains on resale, though they do exercise control over the franchise by voting for the forty-five-member board of directors. The team's general counsel, Lance Lopes, proudly says that the corporation's mission is "to field a competitive team and maintain the team in Green Bay in perpetuity." When the team runs a financial surplus, as it has in recent years, net revenues are reinvested in the stadium or in the players. If the team were ever to run a loss (it hasn't in forty years), the corporation could sell additional stock to members of the community to rejuvenate finances. The bylaws stipulate that in the event of dissolution, the proceeds are to be donated to the local chapter of the American Legion.

CORPORATE STRUCTURE AND QUALITY OF LIFE

Community ownership does not always confer unambiguous benefits on a community. It is valuable, therefore, to explore the relative strengths and weaknesses of each kind of community-owned corporate structure. Three criteria are particularly important: the usefulness of a firm's products; its labor and environmental standards, and its efficiency of operation.

Community Usefulness

No community-owned business can be considered truly community-friendly unless it provides something useful for the people living within its boundaries—that is, something more than just decent jobs. Is the business growing grains and vegetables to put food on residents' tables, or producing tobacco leaves that addict and slowly poison smokers?

Worker ownership does surprisingly little to change the basic corporate imperative to maximize profit without reference to what is produced. The worker-run Mondragon cooperatives in Spain rooted their businesses in manufacturing products for export, not meeting basic local needs. Among the first products were butane cookers, lawnmower parts, and food-handling equipment. By 1990, Mondragon cooperatives exported 40 percent of these capital goods outside Spain. The cooperatives in Bologna also produced machine tools, pasta and espresso makers, and trendy clothing, all for export.

The only two corporate structures that are naturally linked with community needs are nonprofits and publicly owned corporations. CDCs, for example, are formed to tackle specific local problems such as housing rehabilitation or credit shortages. Publicly owned corporations serve primarily local infrastructure needs such as maintaining roads, repairing bridges, running harbors, purifying drinking water, or distributing electricity. Even these bodies, however, lack the kind of governance that might make them truly responsive to community needs.

Almost every community has experienced pitched battles between neighborhood associations and public transportation authorities eager to bulldoze hundreds of blocks to make way for a highway or an airport. Public enterprises often wind up being run by political cronies who award contracts to local contractors, who in turn line the pockets of the appointing politicians. As the noted urban planner Jane Jacobs argued in *Systems of Survival*, the conflation of "guardian" and "commercial" roles creates dangerous conflicts for decision makers. A politician whose fortunes depend on how well public enterprises perform is inclined to use subsidies to cover for embarrassing management, to look the other way if the firm has horrendous labor and environmental practices, or to cook the books to bury a problem from public scrutiny. The more commercial activity a government undertakes, the more vulnerable its civil servants become to bribes and manipulation.

Politicians who have mastered the ideology and slogans of socialism are hardly immune to such corruption. Indeed, bribery was an essential part of getting anything done in the old Soviet Union. In Italy today, hundreds of leading politicians sit in jail for routinely accepting kickbacks for public works contracts. (The Italian communists, in contrast, who favored privately owned cooperatives like those in Bologna, emerged from these scandals relatively unscathed.) In countries as diverse as Brazil and South Africa, the managers of the "para-statal" corporations (enterprises created, supported, and regulated by governments and often given virtual monopolies over a given product such as petroleum) have regularly been implicated in scandals of kickbacks and embezzlement.

Nonprofit companies also are capable of self-serving behavior. A nonprofit's vision of the public interest, after all, is defined by its own leaders and board members, not by members of the community. For years, the National Rifle Association, with its national headquarters in Washington, DC, fought gun control across the country with remarkable success, utterly indifferent to

The Seikatsu Club Consumer's Co-operative Union

The Seikatsu Club is a consumer movement in Japan that relies on member ownership to achieve its economic, environmental, and social goals. The following extracts from the organization's Web site describe the movement and describe its unique member audit system.

Outline of the Seikatsu Club Consumer's Co-operative Union

There are approximately 600 co-operatives with 21,040,000 members in Japan (out of a total population of 127,000,000). From the Hokkaido in the north to Aichi Prefecture in the south, the Seikatsu Club Consumer's Co-operative Union, (hereafter SC or SCCU) which consists of an association of 22 consumer co-operatives active in 15 administrative divisions (prefectures) of Japan, has altogether 250,000 members, most of whom are women. In addition, there are 8 associated companies such as a milk factory.

The SCCU carries out the development, purchasing, distribution, and inspection of consumer materials (food, general daily goods, clothes, publications), operates a mutual assistance fund, and publishes PR and ordering information for pre-order collective purchase. In addition, the entire union works on problems such as GMOs and the environmental hormones issue by setting up committees and establishing projects which are run by SC members and SCCU staff.

The SC member unit is based on the nearly 200 independent branches, all of which have independent management and activities. SC funding is from the members, who make monthly contributions of 1000 yen per person. The accumulated contributions total 20,900,000,000 yen, an average investment of approximately 83,000 yen per member. These investments are the foundation of our healthy financial management.

Independent Control and Auditing System

SCCU has established safety, health, and environment principles which guide its operations. Producers ratify these SC principles in order to participate in the system and work with SC members to achieve improvements in terms of the principles. This system is characteristic in that it is different from general environment and quality control standards and certification systems. Producers make information public based on the independent standards in agriculture, fishery, stock raising and processed food. The Independent Control Committee, consisting of SC members and producers, examines the degree of attainment of standards and also revises standards to a higher level. Under the supervision of the Independent Auditing Committee, consisting of SC members, members carry out mass independent auditing. This auditing of the sites of production by members is one of the unique activities of the SC, which is based in SC history.

Source: Seikatsu Club Group Introduction. (2002). Retrieved March 5, 2003, from http://www.seikatsuclub.coop/english/top.html.

the devastating effects its "public interest work" was having in its violence-ridden home base. Nonprofits are not inherently representative of community interests for one reason: They are run by board members who often reelect themselves, their buddies, and their contributors. If broad community participation occurs, it is usually by chance, not by design.

Responsible Production Methods

A community-friendly corporation is one that treats its workforce and local ecosystems well. By this criterion, the production methods chosen by conventional corporations, whether privately or publicly held by shareholders, are unimpressive. In the absence of legally enforceable minimum standards, profit-driven firms are motivated to keep wages low and to minimize investments in environmental protection. Every wage hike, every worker benefit, every new smokestack cleaner usually weakens profitability.

Businesses that call themselves socially responsible try to attract politically correct consumers by advertising their investments in the workforce or in environmental protection. But even a company such as Dow Chemical, with embarrassing products ranging from Agent Orange to silicon breast implants, now advertises itself as socially responsible. The obvious point is that the behavior of any corporation must be judged by what it does, not what it says. In 1994, Lester Lave and H. Scott Matthews at Carnegie-Mellon University in Pittsburgh, Pennsylvania, surveyed fifty-four large U.S. corporations claiming great commitment to environmental protection. Only a third were willing to substitute more environmentally safe inputs for production when they raised costs by a mere 1 percent. With a 5 percent price hike, the number of companies willing to make the switch dropped to two.

Does worker ownership change a business's production methods? Certainly where the workers actually control the enterprise—and are not just passive owners of stock—treatment of the workforce improves. Even if wages and benefits are not higher, the shared sense that business decisions help or hurt all employee-owners, that "we're all in this together," boosts morale. Still, not all workers have equal say in management, and conflicts can erupt. The worker-owners of United Airlines, for example, have been involved in numerous legal disputes with the management over how to distribute profits in fat times and how to cut costs in lean ones.

Whether worker ownership promotes environmental protection is unclear. The Vermont Asbestos Group made a major investment in pollution-control equipment after it was bought by its employees. But workers and management also unite around a good bottom line, and too often environmental protection is perceived to reduce both outside investor and employee profit shares. This explains why relations between the labor and environmental groups remain uneasy. Unemployed loggers in the Pacific Northwest, for example, have practically declared war on forest preservationists who threaten their jobs.

Publicly owned enterprises may treat their workforces well but have an unremarkable environmental record. The American Federation of State, County, and Municipal Employees, an exceptionally powerful union, has pushed for strong laws protecting civil service employees and has ensured relatively high wages and job security for public employees. But environmental regulation of public utilities or port authorities creates the difficult dilemma for politicians noted earlier, between protecting the public and keeping the enterprises profitable. Some of the least environmentally sensitive utilities that plunged ahead with ambitious plans to build nuclear power plants in the 1970s were publicly owned. The Washington Public Power Supply System (WPPSS) earned the nickname "Whoops" for leading the region to embark on an environmentally and economically unwise scheme to build five gigantic nuclear power plants. Projected originally at a few billion dollars, the price tag ultimately escalated to more than $12 billion and resulted in a major default on bonds and a spate of expensive lawsuits. In the end, four out of five WPPSS reactors never produced a single kilowatt-hour of electricity.

Most nonprofits are service providers and therefore place few burdens on the environment. Those that do impact the environment, such as agencies like the charity CARE that work abroad to assist refugees, have developed guidelines to ensure a high level of ecological sensitivity. Nonprofits are, however, notoriously unpleasant places to work. Few are unionized, and most pay low wages with limited health care, retirement, and leave benefits. Each year's budget depends on very unpredictable flows of membership donations and foundation grants, and job security is low.

Efficiency

A community inevitably depends on the economic performance of its businesses, and the minimum expectation of a community-friendly business is that it should have a positive rate of return. No uncompetitive industry can last indefinitely. The costs to the public of propping up even one major money-losing venture, as the Pacific Northwest discovered with the WPPSS debacle, can be enormous. Efficiency is an important goal for community economics.

Efficiency is the singular strength of shareholder-owned corporations. For-profit corporations are structured to induce their managers to strive for the highest rate of return and to be attentive to every cost. To the successful manager come raises, bonuses, good press, and bargaining power for the next job. Whether a for-profit firm is worker-owned or socially responsible, efficiency is the overriding goal.

Nonprofits must operate with a positive cash flow, but any rate of return above zero will do. For-profits have increasingly complained that permitting nonprofits to deliver the same goods and services that for-profits produce puts them at a competitive disadvantage, since nonprofits have unique access to "soft money," tax-deductible contributions from individuals or foundations. A study by the Roberts Foundation, an entrepreneurial philanthropic organization based in San Francisco, however, suggests that nonprofits actually have a competitive *dis*advantage: The best performers in nonprofits often move into the private sector, which means that turnover in nonprofits tends to be higher, as are the resulting costs of training, transition, and severance. The prerogatives of business may be at odds with the mission of a nonprofit. Many nonprofits view the bonuses, major salary hikes, and perquisites the private sector uses to induce and reward exceptional performance as suspect. The boards of nonprofits are often more hands-on than those of for-profits, which forces nonprofit managers to spend more time preparing reports, answering questions, and involving their trustees—and less time running the business. Meanwhile, the Internal Revenue Service and myriad state and local agencies impose all kinds of special reporting requirements.

The economics of public enterprises is more complicated. The prevailing wisdom today is that the private sector is more efficient than the public sector, except in special circumstances. Laissez-faire economists (who advocate freedom from government interference) begrudgingly admit that the state has a role to play in overseeing natural monopolies and public goods, such as the delivery of electricity, natural gas, water, and telephone services. But technology is eliminating the natural monopoly once held by electrical utilities, and cell phones have made telephone monopolies obsolete. A century from now, many experts believe that electricity might come from rooftop solar cells and telecommunications through microwaves. Moreover, even where a natural monopoly exists, a smart local government opens up the business to competitive bids every few years.

Public goods are also best delivered by public agencies. They include products and services that benefit the community as a whole. The classic example is policing. Everyone in a community knows police are needed; if individuals had to buy security, warring armed bands would roam the countryside. How broadly a community defines public goods varies enormously. Most U.S. communities believe that every child is entitled to a decent education and that every citizen is entitled to enjoy public parks. Local governments in Western Europe also pump money into nonprofit groups and political participation.

A lively debate has ensued in recent years over whether private firms working under government control can deliver public goods more efficiently than can the government. The jury is still out. Certainly there are government functions that cannot be measured strictly by private-market efficiency considerations. Efficient schooling may produce students who perform well on standardized tests but poorly as community-minded citizens. Efficient policing may result in the abandoning of certain neighborhoods with a high density of crack houses and gangs. Yet even in these cases, there are notable success stories with privatization.

One strong argument in favor of minimizing government involvement in commercial activities and of privatizing government services is the moral hazard, discussed earlier, of mixing the functions of commercial regulation and commercial promotion. Once again, the history of nuclear power illustrates the dangers. No U.S. utility has ordered a new commercial reactor since the late 1970s, and the record elsewhere in the world is not very different. Nuclear-power expansion continues only in countries where public ownership of utilities has enabled state accountants to "excuse" gigantic debts. French politicians, for example, kept up appearances of a healthy reactor program by forgiving a debt of five billion francs in 1980. Whenever politics can trump markets, business managers are tempted to rely on the "good ole boy network" rather than on running an enterprise efficiently.

COMMUNITY CORPORATIONS

The analysis above suggests that there may be value in creating a new generation of corporations, owned by shareholders and workers alike, all of whom reside in a given community. This would blend the efficiency of private companies with the accountability and community-friendly behavior of nonprofits, cooperatives, and municipal enterprises. If the owners of an enterprise live close to the workforce, go to the same church or synagogue, send their children to the same school, have picnics in the same parks, and drink the same water, they have a greater incentive to make decisions responsive to their neighbors' needs. If the enterprise is for-profit, there remains a strong incentive for competitive, efficient management. And if all voting shareholders are neighbors, it is unlikely that they would allow the firm to move operations elsewhere—unless relocation were truly in the interest of the community.

A "community corporation" would blend the virtues of public responsibility with private profitability. The concept of place-based companies actually has deep roots in American history. William Penn's Free Society of Traders, chartered by the King of England in 1682, limited voting rights to shareholders living in Pennsylvania. Between the American Revolution in 1776 and 1801, the U.S. government chartered more than three hundred companies, and most of these limited voting rights. Today, a U.S. corporation may restrict shareholder rights of transfer through its articles of incorporation, bylaws, or an agreement with or between the shareholders. Few choose to do so, but the option remains intriguingly open.

—Michael Shuman

See also Tragedy of the Commons

Further Reading

Alesch, D. J. (1995, November). *The Green Bay Packers: America's only not-for-profit major-league sports franchise.* Milwaukee: Wisconsin Policy Research Institute.

Alperovitz, G., & Faux, J. (1984). *Rebuilding America: A blueprint for the new economy.* New York: Pantheon.

Daly, H. E., & Cobb, J. B., Jr. (1989). *For the common good: Redirecting the economy toward community, the environment, and a sustainable future.* Boston: Beacon.

Douthwaite, R. (1996). *Short circuit.* Devon, UK: Resurgence.

Emerson, J. (1996). *New social entrepreneurs: The success, challenges, and lessons of non-profit enterprise creation.* San Francisco: Roberts Foundation.

Gates, J. (1998). *The ownership solution: Toward a shared capitalism for the twenty-first century.* Reading, MA: Perseus.

Greenberg, J., & Kistler, W. (1992). *Buying America back.* Tulsa, OK: Council Oak Books.

Gunn, C., & Gunn, H. D. (1991). *Reclaiming capital: Democratic initiatives and community development.* Ithaca, NY: Cornell University Press.

Hawken, P. (1993). *The ecology of commerce.* New York: HarperCollins.

Hines, C. (2000). *Localization: A global manifesto.* London: Earthscan.

Imbroscio, D. A. (1997). *Reconstructing city politics.* Thousand Oaks, CA: Sage.

Jacobs, J. (1994). *Systems of survival.* New York: Vintage.

Korten, D. C. (1998). *The post-corporate world.* West Hartford, CT: Kumarian.

Krimerman, L., & Lindenfeld, F. (Eds.). (1992). *When workers decide.* Philadelphia: New Society Press.

Lave, L. B., & Matthews, H. S. (1996, November/December). It's easier to say green than to be green. *Technology Review*, 68–69.

Morrison, R. (1991). *We build the road as we travel.* Philadelphia: New Society.

Osborne, D., & Gaebler, T. (1992). *Reinventing government: How the entrepreneurial spirit is transforming the public sector.* New York: Plume.

Sale, K. (1980). *Human scale.* New York: Perigee.

Schumacher, E. F. (1973). *Small is beautiful: Economics as if people mattered.* New York: HarperCollins.

Shuman, M. H. (1999, Summer). Community corporations: Engines for a new place-based economics. *The Responsive Community, 9*(3), 50–57.

Shuman, M. H. (2000). *Going local: Creating self-reliant communities in a global age.* Armonk, NY: Routledge.

Vidal, A. (1992). *Rebuilding communities: A national study of urban community development corporations.* New York: New School Community Development Research Center.

Williamson, T., Alperovitz, G., Barber, B. R., & Imbroscio, D. L. (2002). *Making a place for community: Local democracy in a global era.* New York: Routledge.

COMMUNITY POLICING

The past twenty years have been witness to the evolution of modern policing from a traditional law enforcement perspective to a so-called community-policing approach. Also referred to as community-oriented policing or even community-oriented public safety, community policing embraces a new philosophy of policing in which the citizens and the police are viewed as partners in the effort to coproduce order, increase public safety, and prevent crime.

DEFINING COMMUNITY FROM A POLICING PERSPECTIVE

Some scholars view community policing as a return to policing's British origins in London in 1829, when Sir Robert Peel devised the first modern police force. Rather than viewing the police as an extension of a governing body imbued with the authority to legitimately use force to preserve order, similar to the British military, Peel hoped that the public would see police officers more simply as citizens in uniform. From Peel's perspective, the public represented a community of ordinary citizens who were bound together in a societal existence at a specific time in a specific place and needed an assurance of public safety. But does a group of people living together in a city like London in 1829 really constitute the same kind of community that we speak of today when we refer to the idea of community policing?

German sociologist Ferdinand Tönnies (1855–1936) used the term *gesellschaft* to refer to a loosely connected society at large in which people lived in close proximity to one another merely for convenience and safety. In contrast, he used *gemeinschaft* to signify a community made up of a closely knit group of people linked by ties of kinship and friendship, who live near one another and remain dependant on one another over time for a sense of belonging, safety, and economic well-being. Tönnies saw large, urbanized European cities (much like 1829 London) as examples of the former and viewed smaller medieval European towns as examples of the latter.

Auguste Comte (1798–1857), the founder of sociology, preceded Tönnies in linking the demise of European communities to increasing urbanization. Comte suggested that to the extent that society is made up of groups of closely knit people tied to one another by bonds of kinship and friendship, it can be composed of many communities, which in turn are made up of smaller, familial units. Cities, however, can suffer from a lack of community if their residents fail to seek and sustain mutually beneficial social relationships. Sociologist Émile Durkheim (1858–1917) noted that while city life held many advantages—greater individualism, for instance—over less urban environments, the tendency also existed for greater isolation, alienation, and crime.

The community of ideas proposed by Amitai Etzioni (b. 1929) probably comes closest to the type of community in which modern-day community policing might be found. In a community of ideas, groups of people are bound together by their principles and opinions regarding issues such as how best to govern and the prioritization of important social values. To this might be added the important dimension of geography. After all, "policing by its very nature assumes a community setting, or a place where community activities occur. In a nutshell, policing requires someone and somewhere to police" (Thurman, Zhao, & Giacomazzi 2001, p. 43).

Similarly, the view of community proposed by the scholars Todd Clear and David Karp is more inclusive of the concept of geography as well. They suggest that we can "think of community as a place from which we hail and the safe haven to which we owe our self-knowledge. In this sense, community is an entity—a geographic area or a group—to which we belong" (Clear & Karp 1999, p. 60). Furthermore, they note that residents in a strong community feel a sense of belonging and influence. Citizens feel part of a larger whole, believe that they can make a difference in the setting in which they live, and are confident that they will be rewarded for their involvement. Finally, they have emotional attachment to their community and the other people who live there due to shared values, bonds, and social conventions.

When comparing Peel's London and Etzioni's community of ideas, it is clear that Peel's 1829 London is closer to gesellschaft than gemeinschaft. While Peel might have been delighted to see London residents take an active role in the development of their own public safety model, all he really hoped for was public tolerance of the new police force. But community policing does not content itself with public attitudes of modest resistance, benign neglect, or dispassionate tolerance. On the contrary: A key goal of community policing is the engagement of the community in direct and active problem identification, planning, and problem solving.

A BRIEF HISTORY OF MODERN POLICING

While initially resisted in Britain, modern policing eventually took hold there and spread to large cities in the United States. By the mid-1800s, U.S. cities such as Boston (in 1837), New York (in 1844), and Philadelphia (in 1854) had paid employees whose job it was to maintain order, prevent crime through the provision of key social services, and apprehend criminal offenders. Within twenty-five years, most U.S. cities and many towns had adopted the British approach to public safety.

Unfortunately, with the transition to modern policing in the largest U.S. cities, locally responsive police services fell victim to political partisanship and machine politicians. Political patronage and corruption became hallmarks of this political era of policing. It was not until the 1920s that the progressive movement (c. 1900–1920) succeeded in demonstrating a compelling need for reform in public services, including policing. The call for more efficient government practices and social justice set the stage for government bureaucratization and the professionalization of the police.

Breaking Down Barriers Between Youth and Police

(ANS)—Imagine young people in the inner city sitting down to interview new police recruits, or having a say in whether their schools install metal detectors.

Such scenes aren't likely in cities where police view youth as simply a threat to be controlled. But when Nicholas Pastore took over in 1990 as police chief of New Haven, Connecticut, he decided that youth could also be a resource for solving problems—if they had a way to be heard.

It took seven months working with city leaders on the novel idea, but Pastore did find a way. It's called the Board of Young Adult Police Commissioners, believed to be unique in the nation.

One of the responsibilities of the now four-year-old board is to interview police recruits—including more than a quarter of the 400-member force since 1992.

"During these sessions, the young people get to ask whatever questions of the police they want," said the community-youth coordinator, Detective Tom Morrissey. The process "has fostered police and youth friendships."

These youth commissioners have direct access to the police chief and to the media. And they used that access when New Haven school officials decided to install metal detectors at the city's high schools after a series of weapons incidents.

The teenage commissioners objected to the detectors, arguing the move would create an atmosphere that wasn't conducive to learning and would unwisely concentrate security guards at entrances.

In the end, only one high school ended up with the detectors, and the board is still hoping it will go, too.

Detectors "wouldn't deter anyone who wanted to from bringing a gun to school," said Maya Castellon, 17, a board member for the past two years.

As an alternative, she said, the youth police board proposed—and the school board adopted—peer mediation process in which fellow students mediate disputes in every city high school. "It gets peers to solve their own problems," Castellon said.

Similarly, the board defeated an effort to impose a city-wide curfew on youth after a spate of shootings. The teenagers argued, successfully, that a curfew discriminated against kids with night jobs and others who were out late but weren't getting into trouble.

The board also lobbied successfully to preserve and expand treatment beds for adolescent alcohol and drug abusers, and raised $2,000 for a hospice for adolescents with AIDS.

The Board's 22 members, ranging in age from 13 to 19, are selected two ways. Students from the city's six high schools elect one member per school. Youth commissioners also recommend additional candidates who are screened and voted on by the board.

Mayor John DeStefano, Jr. then conducts the official swearing in. "Of course, their oath of office doesn't make any difference legally," acknowledged Detective Morrissey. "But it sends a signal—that even the mayor takes them seriously."

The board's membership reflects New Haven's diversity—its first president was a Jewish male, its second a Hispanic male, and the current president is an African-American female.

In part because of the board's work, the police "are actually becoming role models," said its former president, Augusto Rodriguez, 20, whose own two brothers are in jail.

—Leonard Felson

Source: "New Haven Breaks Down Barriers Between Youth and Police." American News Service, Article No. 3.

As policing sharpened its focus on crime control and efficiency, it gained stature and reliability but forfeited a certain type of responsiveness and effectiveness. It moved away from providing comprehensive social services, such as caring for society's misfits and economically marginalized, which it had done at the turn of the century when it operated soup kitchens and housed vagrants. Instead of informally maintaining order on the streets by its close familiarity with local residents and business owners, it promoted itself as a law enforcement authority that was dedicated to fighting crime. A uniformed presence meant that crime could be reacted to and efficiently recorded, but it seldom translated into the type of responsiveness that prevented a crime from occurring in the first place.

By the latter part of the professional era, police administrators and scholars began to notice that policing did not seem to be working well, at least in terms of effectively reducing crime and preventing it. In 1967, a presidential commission on the U.S. criminal justice system issued a report acknowledging that criminal activity and the fear of crime was negatively affecting the quality of life in the United States and that crime control was not the sole province of the police, the courts, and corrections. Rather, community participation was necessary to solve the crime problem. Just a few years later, the scholars A. C. Germann and John Angell used the terms *community policing* and *democratic policing* in their respective journal articles to signal the need to reexamine U.S. policing and to challenge police practitioners to respond to the commission's report. After all, the police were supposed to "protect and serve" the public, as the motto announces on the patrol car doors of the nation's most modern police force, the Los Angeles Police Department. Academicians' reconceptualization of the police challenged police leadership to rethink their mission in a changing social environment in which both citizens' rights and their expectations about public services and government accountability had grown.

DEFINING COMMUNITY POLICING

Scholars Robert Trojanowicz and Bonnie Buqueroux have defined community policing as "a new philosophy of policing, based on the concept that police officers and citizens working together in creative ways can help solve contemporary community problems related to crime, fear of crime, social and physical disorder and neighborhood decay" (Trojanowicz & Buqueroux 1990, p. 5). Former Edmonton police superintendent Chris Braiden offers a simpler definition: "Police others as you would have others police you" (Geller & Swanger 1995, p. 6).

Beyond needing a people and a place to police, public safety agents need to engage the community in identifying crime and crime-related problems, then must marshal the resources to resolve them. Community policing emphasizes a partnership between the police, the citizens, and any other public service agencies that might be called upon to help make communities safer and better places in which to live. Internally, police agencies must equip their employees at all ranks and levels to actually do community policing.

Criminologist Gary Cordner describes four identifying features of community policing. The philosophical dimension deals with the values and the mission of the organization. Police agencies committed to a community orientation will believe in the utility of engaging citizens in a broader public safety mission than law enforcement alone. The strategic dimension involves devising a plan for fulfilling the community policing philosophy. The agency must decide how best to reinvent itself to attack specific crime problems, prevent crime, and prioritize its services. The tactical dimension deals with daily operations designed to allow the agency to meet operational objectives. Finally, the organization must change its structure and management and alter the flow of information in order to optimize its responsiveness to the community it serves.

Just as communities are unique, so too are police departments. All agencies ultimately must take responsibility for law enforcement functions that are prescribed by state and federal statutes, but even traditional police organizations will vary according to their resources, experience, and capabilities, and the public safety demands of their communities. Particularly in a community era, police departments find themselves pulled in numerous directions by various constituencies who make up the communities they serve. If they choose to respond from a community policing focus, the problems, people, and solutions they select will further differentiate one agency from another.

The Police Executive Research Forum classifies agencies that practice community policing according to five approaches. Agencies who perceive the need to reduce social distance between citizens and the police may choose a deployment approach, introducing foot patrols, school resource officers, or neighborhood substations. These encourage familiarity with and trust of the police. Community revitalization is a second type of approach, in which police departments work with their communities in an effort to help restore confidence in public safety by attending to signs of neighborhood decay and disorder. This fits with the scholars George Kelling and Catherine Coles's idea that "fixing broken windows" (and so on) will signal would-be criminal offenders that area residents are keeping a watchful eye. This approach invokes citizen help in crime prevention through neighborhood patrols, better lighting, and the reporting of suspicious activities and persons.

A third approach to community policing involves a deliberate focus on problem solving. The most notable example of this approach is the criminologist Herman Goldstein's problem-oriented policing, which consists of scanning for problems, analysis, response, and assessment. As with the deployment perspective, the fourth approach—the customer approach—to community policing emphasizes citizen input and participation. Community engagement and assessment are necessary for determining priorities in this approach. Finally, the fifth community policing approach is from the perspective of legitimacy. As the scholars Quint Thurman, Jihong Zhao, and Andrew Giacomazzi write, police agencies that take this approach seek to establish "the credibility of the police as a fair and equitable public-service organization that dispenses resources evenly and effectively throughout the community" (Thurman, Zhao, & Giacomazzi 2001, p. 9). This approach is particularly concerned with being sensitive to the needs of racial and ethnic minorities who historically have been mistreated by public authorities and institutions.

POLICING THE COMMUNITY OF THE FUTURE

In the past, critics of community policing have questioned whether it represents something completely new or differs only slightly from traditional policing done well. Today, criticism has shifted to empirical evidence of its effectiveness. Resistance to community policing on the part of practitioners has mostly subsided, replaced with concerns about how best to implement it in the hypervigilant atmosphere of the United States after the September 11, 2001, terrorist attacks.

Policing will continue to evolve. It remains to be seen to what extent federal, state, and local resources can be counted on to meet an expanded public safety mission in the twenty-first century. Undoubtedly, the persistence of crime, disorder, and terrorism as notable social problems will continue to pose challenges for police personnel, who will continue to work in partnership with the people they serve to do the best they can to build and maintain safer and better communities.

—*Quint C. Thurman*

See also COMMUNITY JUSTICE; CRIME

Further Reading

Angell, J. E. (1971). Toward an alternative to the classic police organizational arrangement: A democratic model. *Criminology, 9*(2–3), 185–206.

Bayley, D. H. (1988). Community policing: A report from the devil's advocate. In J. R. Greene & S. D. Mastrofski (Eds.), *Community policing: Rhetoric or reality?* (pp. 225–238). New York: Praeger.

Clear, T. R., & Karp, D. R. (1999). *The community justice ideal: Preventing crime and achieving justice.* Boulder, CO: Westview.

Cordner, G. (1997). Community policing: Elements and effects. In R. Dunham & G. Alpert (Eds.), *Critical issues in policing: Contemporary readings* (3rd ed., pp. 451–468). Prospect Heights, IL: Waveland.

Etzioni, A. (1995). *New communitarian thinking: Persons, virtues, institutions, and communities.* Charlottesville: University Press of Virginia.

Geller, W. A., & Swanger, G. (1995). *Managing innovation in policing: The untapped potential of the middle manager.* Washington, DC: Police Executive Research Forum.

Germann, A. C. (1969). Community policing: An assessment. *Journal of Criminal Law, Criminology, and Police Science, 60*(1), 89–96.

Goldstein, H. (1990). *Problem-oriented policing.* Philadelphia, PA: Temple University Press.

Greene, J. R., & Mastrofski, S. D. (1988). *Community policing: Rhetoric or reality?* New York: Praeger.

Kelling, G. L., & Coles, C. M. (1996). *Fixing broken windows: Restoring order and reducing crime in our communities.* New York: Touchstone.

Monkkonen, E. H. (1992). History of urban police. In M. Tonry & N. Morris (Eds.), *Modern policing* (pp. 547–580). Chicago: University of Chicago Press.

Nisbet, R. A. (1966). *The sociological tradition.* New York: Basic Books.

Police Executive Research Forum. (1996). *Themes and variations in community policing.* Washington, DC: Author.

President's Commission on Law Enforcement and Administration of Justice. (1967). *The challenge of crime in a free society.* Washington, DC: U.S. Government Printing Office.

Roberg, R., Crank, J., & Kuykendall, J. (2000). *Police and society* (2nd ed.). Los Angeles: Roxbury.

Thurman, Q., Zhao, J., & Giacomazzi, A. (2001). *Community policing in a community era: An introduction and exploration.* Los Angeles: Roxbury.

Trojanowicz, R., & Bucqueroux, B. (1990). *Community policing: A contemporary perspective.* Cincinnati, OH: Anderson.

Wilson, O. W. (1950). *Police administration.* New York: McGraw-Hill.

Zhao, J., & Thurman, Q. (1997). Community policing: Where are we now? *Crime & Delinquency, 43*(3), 345–357.

COMMUNITY PSYCHOLOGY

Community psychology is a relatively young field of study, and, like many adolescents, it is still searching for a sense of its own identity. A university course in community psychology in one country or even one state, for example, would likely have a different content and emphasis than a course with the same title elsewhere. The main differences include greater or lesser emphases on mental health, social action, ecological approaches (that is, the relationship between people and their environment) and/or organizational perspectives. Chronologically speaking, a widely accepted birth date for the field is May 4, 1965, when a conference was held at Swampscott, Massachusetts, on the place of psychology in the community mental health movement. Several decades later, there are now undergraduate and postgraduate courses in community psychology, as well as such subdisciplines as community development, in several countries. Community psychology also has its own division in the American Psychological Association—the Society for Community Research and Action or SCRA (Division 27).

NATIONAL VARIATIONS

Community psychology emerged from within clinical psychology, and the emphasis on mental health is still a major strand in the countries that took it up in its early days. In addition to the United States, these countries include Australia and New Zealand. Community psychology in the United Kingdom, however, developed more recently, emerging in the 1990s, and there it departed from the mental health emphasis included elsewhere, although some universities do include the relationship between mental health and community factors in the curriculum. The main emphasis in the United Kingdom is on the social action approach, which typically takes a radical-left-wing, feminist perspective. In her opening address to the United Kingdom's 1998–1999 National Community Psychology Conference, community psychologist Carolyn Kagan began,

> It seems appropriate to hold the National Community Psychology Conference, with the theme of Collective Action and Social Change in Manchester. The city is the home of the Trades Union movement, the Co-operative movement and the Suffragette movement. These three concerns, workers conditions and rights, people's collective action for the common good in the face of rampaging capitalism and women's rights are issues that community psychology is still rightly concerned with at the end of the century. (Kagan 1999, p. 8)

In some countries, particularly Latin American countries such as Venezuela, the field is known as community social psychology. The content and emphasis there is similar to the content and emphasis in the United Kingdom.

THEMES AND TRENDS

If there is a common thread running across national boundaries, it is the idea that theory, research, and interventions involve individuals, social settings, and communities within a sociocultural context. In other words, whole communities can be both objects of study and also clients or partners. This is a departure from the norm in psychology, which typically emphasizes the individual, even within social psychology, which examines the effects of social phenomena on individuals. Popular areas of work and topics of study within community psychology include the empowerment of individuals, groups, and communities; the prevention and alleviation of psychological problems; the promotion of good health, well-being, and improved quality of life; and the elimination of the conditions that prevent these.

Community psychologists use the word *empowerment* in a particular way, which is well illustrated in a review article by David Chavis, president of the Association for the Study and Development of Community, as follows:

> The driving force for a healthy, just, and capable community is citizens that hold their institutions accountable to them. Active citizens insure that institutions meet their needs through community organization, participation in the political process, and participation in other governance structure. (Chavis 1997, p. 8)

A major area of research and action is community development, or planned social change. This very broad term encompasses such diverse activities as helping individuals communicate more effectively, tackling homelessness, implementing HIV/AIDS prevention programs, and helping community groups overcome conflicts. The aim is to enhance communities in some way, and usually active participation by the whole community is strongly encouraged and promoted. There are two broad approaches to community development. One is driven by problems or needs and aims to remove blocks to community development. The other is driven by skills or assets and aims to build on existing strengths. The latter is a more recent approach.

Researchers in community psychology also study the phenomenon of sense of community. This is the sense that people have of belonging to a community, and it is positively associated with people's sense of well-being. Research suggests that a sense of community has four components. These are membership, or a feeling of belonging to the community; influence, or the feeling that one can make a difference within the community; integration, or the feeling that one's needs may be met from within the community; and emotional connection, or the feeling that community membership is important and that community members will share time and experiences with one another.

Some clear trends in the field can be identified. For example, the number of experimental studies has declined over the years, while the number of qualitative studies has increased. This appears to reflect a similar trend in other areas of psychology. Views differ over whether or not this is a healthy trend. Studies of psychological or mental health problems or of involving mental health services have also declined, whereas studies involving gender or ethnicity have increased, as have studies in the area of social support.

WORKING WITH OTHER DISCIPLINES

Although located primarily within the discipline of psychology, community psychologists may also become involved in the areas of mental health, sociology, public health, politics, history, anthropology, archeology, and environmental psychology, among others. In addition, there are areas of study with similar names that may proceed independently of the work of community psychologists. For example, communitarianism is a field of study within sociology that was founded by U.S. sociologist Amitai Etzioni of George Washington University. Communitarianism has also developed as a way of conceptualizing politics that bypasses the traditional left wing–right wing dichotomy. Similarly, the field of communal studies, or the study of intentional communities, also exists within sociology and includes historians, social geographers, architects, and others. The main focus of communal studies is planned or intentional communities, that is, complete communities that were formed with the deliberate intention of creating a better life for their members. Increasingly, this is seen as including virtual communities or cybercommunities.

An area that overlaps with community psychology is community operations research, usually shortened to community OR. This systems approach to communities was developed in the late 1960s in the United States and has spread to other countries, including the United Kingdom. It uses the mathematical methods of operational research with community groups.

Operational research (OR) per se was developed to help improve operations in military, business and government applications through the use of scientific methods and the development of specialized mathematical or simulation techniques. OR provides a systematic approach to improving systems, products, or services.

A developing area that draws on concepts of community psychology is the study of groups in isolated, confined environments (ICEs). Examples of ICEs include prisons, transoceanic ships, logging camps, polar scientific communities, space capsules, and the locations of reality television shows. Among the issues studied are how physical space is used (especially with regard to privacy), leadership, integrating newcomers, handling conflict, interpersonal compatibility, changes in interpersonal exchanges, and gender roles.

TYPICAL CAREERS AND ACTIVITIES

Graduates in community psychology may be employed in health service organizations, community service organizations, government departments, the United Nations and its related organizations, other nongovernmental organizations, or in private practice. In countries where community psychology has been established longest, there is usually regular demand for graduates with community psychology skills, especially in such areas as health promotion, policy research and planning (at all levels of government), accident research and safety advice provision, community alcohol and drug services, psychological services within police departments, road safety coordination, and teaching and research work at the university level.

Specifically, a community psychologist might be found offering counseling at a community health center, or helping with a mental health promotion and awareness program. A community psychologist working from a social action perspective might help a neighborhood mobilize against the sale of illegal drugs in the neighborhood or in favor of facilities for children. A community psychologist working from an ecological perspective might study ways of building a sense of community within a group, or work to mitigate the effects of unemployment on a community. As support grows for involving members of communities in developing the community's strengths and addressing its problems, the sphere of activity for community psychologists should continue to broaden.

—Peter M. Forster

See also COMMUNITY ACTION; COMMUNITY MENTAL HEALTH CENTERS; SOCIAL JUSTICE

Further Reading

Chavis, D. M. (1997). *It takes a just and capable village: Prevention strategies for community justice.* Paper presented at the Research Seminar on Communities, Crime, and Justice sponsored by the National Institute of Justice, George Washington University, Washington, DC.

Duffy, K. G., & Wong, F. Y. (2000). *Community psychology.* Boston: Allyn & Bacon.

Etzioni, A. (1993). *The spirit of community.* New York: Crown.

Kagan, C. (1999). Introduction to the conference. In *Collective action and social change.* 1998–99 National Community Psychology Conference, Manchester Metropolitan University, Manchester, UK.

McMillan, D. W., & Chavis, D. M. (1986). Sense of community: A definition and theory. *Journal of Community Psychology, 14*(1), 6–23.

Midgley, G., & Ochoa-Arias, A. E. (1998). *Visions of community*

for Community OR. (Research Memorandum No. 17). Hull, UK: Centre for Systems Studies, University of Hull.
Peck, M. S. (1988). *The different drum.* London: Rider.
Rappaport, J. (1977). *Community psychology: Values, research and action.* New York: Holt, Rinehart & Winston.
Speer, P., Dey, A., Griggs, P., Gibson, C., Lubin, B. & Hughey, J. (1992). In search of community: An analysis of community psychology research from 1984 to 1988. *American Journal of Community Psychology, 20*(2), 195–209.
Suedfeld, P., & Steel, G. D. (2000). The environmental psychology of capsule habitats. *Annual Review of Psychology, 51,* 227–253.

COMMUNITY SATISFACTION

The term *community satisfaction* refers to people's subjective evaluations of their own well-being as measured by how well their local community meets their personal needs. The lives of human beings today are dominated by a mass consumer-oriented economy and its concomitant culture. Those who can actively engage in this consumer culture typically have the highest sense of general well-being, and thus they also tend to be more satisfied with their community than those who do not actively engage.

Though high levels of community satisfaction have traditionally been associated more with rural than with urban communities, the distinctions between these two have blurred as communities themselves have evolved, increasingly embracing mass consumer culture. Specifically, due to transportation improvements and the development of "edge cities" (strip malls and shopping centers at major transportation intersections), the local community has become less important to the average mobile American than was the case fifty years ago.

Whether consumer needs are met in the community of residence or elsewhere, people whose needs can be met tend to have higher levels of community satisfaction than those whose needs go unsatisfied. The community is a base of domestic operations for most, but people have a greater allegiance to the demands of a mass consumer economy than to their local community. Thus, the contemporary irony of community satisfaction is that the local community is no longer the focus of people's sense of satisfaction, but it remains the place that this satisfaction is manifested. Consequently, many of those with the highest levels of community satisfaction may paradoxically have the lowest levels of allegiance to any particular community. This complexity in the experience of community is predictable in today's modern consumer society, where mobility is often rewarded more generously than is "staying put."

CONCEPTUALIZING COMMUNITY SATISFACTION

Even the simple definition of community satisfaction as "people's subjective evaluation of their own well-being as measured by how well their local community meets their personal needs" creates at least two nagging questions for social scientists: First, what is meant by a person's being satisfied with his or her community? Second, what is the importance of this satisfaction?

Measuring Community Satisfaction

The earliest researchers of community satisfaction assumed that they were measuring the ways that residents saw the local goods and services of their community affecting their personal sense of well-being. Often, the sense of well-being associated with goods and services in the community was explicitly correlated with how economically "well off" a person was. In addition, because the measures used dealt so much with access to goods and services, this early research was often heavily weighted toward economic conditions in the community as explanations for varying levels of community satisfaction.

The inadequacy and narrowness of this approach were soon recognized. A sense of well-being is more complex than whatever is captured only through the economics of local services. New and improved measures of the concept were needed to capture as broad a range of community experience as possible.

Thus, in an attempt to be exhaustive, elaborate and often lengthy banks of questions were given to community residents to ascertain their range of satisfaction on a wide array of items. The questions were typically in a format that required answers ranging from "strongly agree" to "strongly disagree." An early example of such a study was published by Vernon Davies in 1945; Davies used a forty-item community satisfaction scale that included measures of goods and services, social ambience (such as how courteous people in the community were), physiological characteristics (climate, recreational opportunities, etc.), and demographic characteristics (age, income, education, sex, race).

In this scale, and others like it that soon followed, no attempts were made to ascertain whether the different indicators of satisfaction with various community attributes overlapped significantly with one another. Consequently, later researchers discovered that many indicators measured the same thing as other indicators in the scale, and thus the overall importance of these factors was exaggerated.

Not surprisingly, one of the most significant findings from these early many-item scales was that satisfaction with local community services was the primary factor in determining overall community satisfaction. One reason for this finding was that so many questions dealt with issues of satisfaction with services that such items were over-represented in the scale. Services were being consistently overcounted vis-à-vis the other items being measured.

Historical timing also played a role in the apparent importance of local community services. At the time these earliest scales were being used (1940s through the 1950s), there was a relative lack of mobility among the U.S. populace when compared with even twenty years later. At the time of Davies's work, people's local community in many respects represented the conceivable range of possibilities for shopping and other services, due to the relative inconvenience of going elsewhere. As more people came to own cars in the 1950s, and with the advent of the interstate-highway system in the 1960s, the typical American's practical range to access services was no longer tied to a local community.

In the United States, suburban culture took root during the 1950s. Extending into the 1960s and early 1970s, "bedroom" communities—whose primary function was to provide comfortable homes in the greenbelt for urban workers who commuted, along with good schools and other amenities of family life—began to dot the landscape with greater frequency. Consequently, it should not be surprising that up through the early to mid-1970s, coinciding with these changes in American mobility and a growing suburban culture, community satisfaction research almost exclusively concentrated on residents' satisfaction with their local community's services.

While the services approach dominated early research on community satisfaction, beginning in the late 1960s other researchers began to express concerns about the overrepresentation of multiple-item scales and began using smaller item sets or even single "global" measures to try to measure community satisfaction. Residents were asked to consider their community in its entirety by such phrases as "all things considered" or "considering your community as a whole." Residents were then asked to rate their overall satisfaction with their community. For example: "Taking all things into consideration, on a scale of one to five, with one being very unsatisfied and five being very satisfied, how satisfied are you with your community?" While these approaches eliminated the problems with overweighting of similar items, they introduced yet another problem into the community satisfaction literature—a lack of precision. There was no way to know what respondents were thinking about or referring to when they were asked to "take all things in consideration" and then rate their satisfaction level.

This simple discovery created a new focus in community satisfaction research in the mid-1970s. This focus emphasized the ultimate subjectivity of all research on community satisfaction, no matter how objective the indicators appeared or how meticulously they were devised. Such research is best exemplified by the 1975 work of Robert Marans and Willard Rodgers. They argued that although it might be thought possible to measure a variety of objective conditions across multiple communities and to draw conclusions as to the ways that these should or should not be desirable and thus how they should increase or decrease levels of community satisfaction, few results can be generalized across different communities even when they are measured in "objective" conditions. How people feel about these conditions is more important than how the researcher thinks they should feel about them. In other words, if a researcher thinks that people should like X, Y, or Z, for whatever reason, he or she will usually make up survey questions that will measure whether the respondents do or do not like X, Y, or Z. It is more important for the researcher to find out what people really think and feel, in their own words, categories, and concepts. For example, researchers used to think if a community had a certain amount of services available, then the residents should naturally be satisfied. What they found later is that this was not necessarily the case; often, people who were living in places with very few services had high levels of community satisfaction. This argument had the potential effect of transforming community satisfaction research into a tedious analysis of every resident's subjective life-world. Marans and Rogers summarized their findings: "In sum, we can see that the objective characteristics of a person's situation cannot be equated with how he feels about that situation" (Marans & Rogers 1975, p. 303).

Later researchers continued to refine the concept of community satisfaction in this new light without abandoning the idea that the concept can be used as a social indicator if measured precisely enough for observable general patterns to be identified and explicated. This conclusion was inspired by the fact that even when researchers applied Marans and Rodgers's logic, they found that most people were usually satisfied with their community. Thus, not only did objective conditions explain less than the earliest researchers had thought, but even taking into consideration the potential relativity of each individual resident's subjective interpretation of those objective conditions, there were still some broad patterns across cases.

WHY PEOPLE DISPLAY COMMUNITY SATISFACTION

Why did people living in less-than-ideal circumstances, for example, in poor housing, display high levels of community satisfaction? In 1978, Forrest Deseran, a rural sociologist, published an article that threw new light on the community satisfaction problem. Drawing from the work of the sociologist Erving Goffman, Deseran defined community satisfaction as "definition of the situation." According to Deseran's view, community satisfaction is an emergent and multidimensional phenomenon. By "emergent," he meant that community satisfaction cannot be objectively measured across all communities, places, and times. It "emerges" from the social interactions of people in a particular place and time. Community satisfaction is a natural, but varied, outcome of people interacting with one another in a specific context. Each interaction may produce a myriad of outcomes. The number of potential outcomes is as numerous as the number of potential interactions.

Thus, emergent outcomes are not entirely predictable, but some patterns can be established, because people typically act within known and accepted social rules and norms. For example, most people, most of the time, and in most places, do not conceive of their community in negative terms. Consequently, this one social norm overrides even objective conditions; thus residents, despite their living conditions, subjectively rate their community satisfaction high. Furthermore, community satisfaction is multidimensional because each individual resident, though following fairly predictable patterns of norms, still has his or her own idiosyncratic viewpoint.

By the 1980s, it had become conventional wisdom that community satisfaction dealt more with residents' subjective interpretations of their objective conditions than with the researcher's view of how those objective conditions should be perceived. This realization went a long way toward addressing the problem of what people mean by community satisfaction. Although precisely what they mean is still not known, researchers are confident that respondents are generally referring to their subjective evaluation of how well the community meets their needs. Researchers in the 1980s and 1990s began to address the observed phenomenon that most people, most of the time, and in most places, do not evaluate their communities negatively.

The Church Supper

Throughout human history, communal meals like the church supper described below have made life in communities far more satisfying.

> Autumn also means that we will soon be driving through the chill, translucent evenings to church suppers. There have been the walloping strawberries drowned in cream on buttered biscuits at the springtime socials on the church lawn, and also the sandwich- and salad-laden baskets of the church picnic in summer. And the fat, tender hot dogs dripping with sauerkraut and chopped beef sauce that the Christian Men's Club sells at the village ball games to raise money for a new altar. But none of these has the opulence of foods nor the special jocular warmth of the church supper.
>
> Perhaps it is the coming into the warm, crowded, brightly lighted church basement out of the cold evening: here is friendliness and sharing, the basement redolent of boiling coffee, the women bustling in the kitchen, the children slamming slatted chairs, the men occupied at the tables, eating largely in silence but with rapt brown smiles. In part, too, it is the sense of revelry and release from the summer's hard work; this is a harvest festival, the tables heaped with prize vegetables and scarlet woodbine running like a river of fire among them—while over our heads are the sanctity and protection of the vacant church. And, of course, it is also the wealth of food, supplied by the women in a spirit of (usually) cheerful competition.

Source: Heth, Edward Harris. (1968). *The Country Kitchen Cook Book.* New York: Simon & Schuster, pp. 168–169.

WHAT COMMUNITY SATISFACTION MEANS

By accepting the idea that community satisfaction is a definition of one's situation (i.e., residents implicitly "know" how they are to act, and they do so, but by so doing they continue to recreate the social rules they act by), more recent researchers began to see that community satisfaction was relative. It was tempered by the social rules and conditions of the larger society and the ways that people's needs were met through these rules. Consequently, our measures of community satisfaction constantly change because we are always redefining how our community life is a reflection of our social life in general. Measuring changes in community satisfaction over time creates a window into how society itself is redefined by social actors.

Researchers began to recognize that community satisfaction has both a local and a larger societal dimension. The local dimension is directly tied to the larger social context of a particular time, and this larger social context is acted out and reinforced by people in a place. Community satisfaction is a way to measure social change across time and place by recognizing that people's sense of their overall well-being is tied to their communities (a place) and their cultural expectations of their communities (a specific time). Tying the local and societal dimensions together provides a notion of what people mean when they say they are satisfied with their community.

As a definition of the situation, community satisfaction is also related to people's overall sense of their social standing—their position in the larger society. The larger societal context is perhaps less obvious than the localized community, but it is just as integral to the contemporary concept of community satisfaction. People look toward societal norms as the rule book for how needs are to be met. Are pinstripes in or out of fashion? Are rural communities an escape from the demands of an overly urban lifestyle, or are they backwaters to be avoided? The answers hinge on the social norms. Consequently, community satisfaction can be seen as a manifestation of how residents assess their situation vis-à-vis the expectations of the larger culture at a particular time as they act out those expectations, or norms, in their community.

Measuring community satisfaction remains an important activity for communities because it is a window not only into social change but also into the ways that community residents are dealing locally with this larger social change. Those people who have the highest levels of community satisfaction, ironically, are the ones who have the fewest things tying them to their community. Therefore, having high levels of community satisfaction allows a community the opportunity to constantly make adjustments to better meet its residents' expectations, even if, paradoxically, it means letting them go somewhere else to meet them.

Measuring community satisfaction has been primarily an activity of Western social scientists—in the United States in particular and, to a lesser degree, in Canada and Great Britain. However, as more social scientists from other countries have trained in Western universities, increasing numbers of them have begun to analyze community satisfaction in their own countries, modifying the indicators as needed to reflect each country's and region's own "definition of the situation."

—Ralph B. Brown

Further Reading

Brown, R. B., Xu, X., Toth, J. F., Jr., & Nylander, A. B., III. (1998). Historical decline of community satisfaction in U.S. rural communities: A multi-regional analysis of synthetic cohorts. *Research in Community Sociology, 8,* 183–199.

Campbell, A., Converse, P., & Rodgers, W. (1981). *The sense of well-being in America: Recent patterns and trends.* New York: McGraw-Hill.

Davies, V. (1945). Development of a scale to rate attitude of community satisfaction. *Rural Sociology, 10*(3), 246–255.

Deseran, F. A. (1978). Community satisfaction as definition of the situation: Some conceptual issues. *Rural Sociology, 43*(2), 235–249.

Goffman, E. (1974). *Frame analysis.* Cambridge, MA: Harvard University Press.

Goudy, W. J. (1977). Evaluations of local attributes and community satisfaction in small towns. *Rural Sociology, 42*(3), 371–382.

Ladewig, H., & McCann, G. C. (1980). Community satisfaction: Theory and measurement. *Rural Sociology, 45*(1), 110–131.

Marans, R. W., & Rodgers, W. (1975). Toward an understanding of community satisfaction. In A. H. Hawley & V. P. Rock (Eds.), *Metropolitan America in contemporary perspective* (pp. 299–352). New York: Russell Sage.

Sofranko, A. J., & Fliegel, F. C. (1984). Dissatisfaction with satisfaction. *Rural Sociology, 49*(3), 353–373.

COMMUNITY SCHOOLS

A community school is both a place and a set of partnerships between the school and other community resources, where an integrated focus on academics, services, supports, and opportunities leads to improved student learning, stronger families and healthier communities. Community schools are open to everyone—all day, every day, on evening and weekends.

Using public schools as hubs, community schools knit together inventive, enduring relationships among educators, families, volunteers, and community partners—such as health and social service agencies, family support groups, youth development organizations, institutions of higher education, community organizations, business, civic and faith-based groups. Partners agree to share their expertise and resources with school staff to create a more effective learning environment. As a result, schools and communities act in concert to transform traditional schools into permanent partnerships for excellence. Schools are centers of the community. Schools are not left to work alone.

Community schools are open to students, families, and community members before, during, and after school, throughout the year. They have high standards and expectations for students, qualified teachers, and a challenging, engaging curriculum.

Students engage in learning and service activities at a community school, and they have access to an array of personal and social supports. Community schools promote youth development activities and community-based learning, and offer preventive health and social services, before, during, and after school.

Before- and after-school programs build on classroom experiences and help students expand their horizons, contribute to their communities, and have fun. Family support centers help with parent involvement, child rearing, employment, housing, and other services. Medical, dental, and mental health services are readily available. Parents and community residents participate in adult education and job training programs, and use the school as a place for community problem solving. Volunteers come to community schools to support young people's academic, interpersonal, and career success.

Community schools use the community as a resource to engage students and help them become problem-solvers in their communities. The school also sees itself as a resource to the community sharing its facilities, equipment, and other assets to support community-building efforts. The concept of the community school is being explored in many nations, including the United Kingdom, the Netherlands, Italy, Germany, Sweden, France, and others.

HOW COMMUNITY SCHOOLS DIFFER FROM TRADITIONAL SCHOOLS

Community schools have advantages over traditional neighborhood schools in that they do more of what is needed to ensure young people's success. A good community school should, for example, organize additional resources and a variety of learning opportunities so that the five following conditions, necessities for learning at high levels, are met (Melaville, Shah, & Blank 2003):

> *Condition 1.* The school has a core instructional program with high standards and high expectations, qualified teachers, and a challenging curriculum.
>
> *Condition 2.* Students are motivated and engaged in learning—both in school and in community settings, during and after school.
>
> *Condition 3.* The basic medical, mental, and physical health needs of young people and their families are addressed.
>
> *Condition 4.* There is mutual respect and effective collaboration between parents, families, and school staff.
>
> *Condition 5.* Community engagement, together with school efforts, promotes a school climate that is safe, supportive, and respectful and connects students to a broad learning community outside the school.

Traditional schools often fulfill some, but rarely all, of those conditions.

Community schools also work to develop both academic and nonacademic competencies, a combination that improves long-range learning outcomes. They build networks and relationships—what some now call social capital—that support learning and create opportunity for young people while strengthening their communities. Research, practice, and common sense suggest that only under such circumstances will all young people succeed.

Those who support community schools view educators as major partners, but they do not require educators to carry the entire burden. A capable community organization or institution—a youth development organization, a college or university, a child and family services agency, a community development corporation, or a family support center, for example—can serve as the anchor partner for a community school. The partner organizations work with the school to mobilize and integrate the resources of community and school. This allows principals and teachers to focus on their core mission: improving student learning. This notion of making the school a locus of community care is not new. The settlement houses of the late 1800s had a similar idea, and in the 1930s, the Charles Stewart Mott Foundation brought the idea of community schools to national prominence through its work in Flint, Michigan.

In the 1990s, community school expansion has largely been in poor urban and rural settings with large minority populations. There are national approaches,

The Coalition for Community School's Key Principles of Community Schools

There are many community school models . . . but they tend to share a core set of operating principles:

- **Foster strong partnerships:** Partners share their resources and expertise and work together to design community schools and make them work.
- **Share accountability for results:** Clear, mutually agreed-upon results drive the work of community schools. Data helps partners measure progress toward results. Agreements enable them to hold each other accountable and move beyond "turf battles."
- **Set high expectations for all:** Community schools are organized to support learning. Children, youth and adults are expected to learn at high standards and be contributing members of their community.
- **Build on the community's strengths:** Community schools marshal the assets of the entire community–including the people who live and work there, local organizations, and the school.
- **Embrace diversity:** Community schools know their communities. They work to develop respect and a strong, positive identity for people of diverse backgrounds and are committed to the welfare of the whole community.
- **Avoid cookie-cutter solutions:** Building on the lessons of others, each community school defines its needs, identifies its assets and creates its own version of a community school.

Source: Alexander, Christopher, et al. (1977). *A Pattern Language.* New York: Oxford University Press, p. 311.

such as the work of Children's Aid Society and Beacon Schools, initiated in New York and now being adapted in many cities; Communities in Schools, reaching students and families in more than 2,300 schools; and the West Philadelphia Improvement Corps, started in Philadelphia, Pennsylvania, now operating in more than twenty communities. There are also many locally grown models, such as Bridges to Success in Indianapolis, Indiana, and the Community Learning Centers Initiative in Lincoln, Nebraska. In rural communities, the community school strategy emphasizes place-based education—engaging the community, the school, and its students in active learning and community problem solving.

Detractors of the community school approach may worry that addressing such important nonacademic factors as poverty, violence, and ill health in the school context may cause schools to lose their focus and to fail to raise their academic standards. But Paul Barton of the Educational Testing Service suggests that academic and broader social problems must be addressed together. In his words, "The seriousness of our purpose requires that we learn to rub our bellies and pat our heads at the same time" (Barton 2001, p. 22).

RESULTS IN COMMUNITY SCHOOLS

Proponents of community schools point to twenty studies of community schools that show a favorable impact on student learning. The data also show positive effects on families, the schools themselves, and communities—though fewer evaluations attempted to measure impacts in these areas. Taken as a group, these evaluations of community schools show that students made significant gains in both academic achievement and essential areas of nonacademic development, which include reduced behavioral or discipline problems, improved attendance, greater classroom cooperation, increased access to physical and mental health services, improvements in personal or family situation, and greater contact with supportive adults. Families whose children attended community schools showed greater stability, more involvement with the school, and a sense of responsibility for their children's learning. The schools themselves enjoyed stronger staff and parent relationships, higher levels of teacher satisfaction, a more positive school climate, and greater community support. Finally, communities reported improved utilization of school buildings, increased neighborhood safety and security, heightened community pride, and better rapport among students and residents.

CREATING A COMMUNITY SCHOOL

There are four keys to creating community schools: leadership, community voice, partnership, and financing.

Leadership provides energy and direction. Atelia Melaville, a writer on education and social issues, characterizes community-school leaders as people committed to the well-being of poor children and families. They "know where they want to go and have the position, personality, and power to make others want to come along" (Melaville 1998, p. 96).

Organized and vocal support from students, parents,

and neighborhood residents ensures that the community school is responsive to their concerns and helps to convince others in the community of the importance and effectiveness of the community school strategy. Partnerships are essential to galvanizing, mobilizing, and integrating communities' untapped resources for the purpose of improving student learning and community life. These partnerships bring together people and organizations from the public and nonprofit sectors, and from the local business community. Gradually, local institutions (for example, institutions of higher education, health and human services agencies, youth development and community development groups, and civic, business, and religious organizations) change and adapt to the needs in particular community school settings.

Financing, of course, is crucial. Government, school districts, philanthropic organizations, and other community institutions all have key roles to play. The work of the partnership at the community or school district level and the coordination of work at the school site generally require new investments or the use of existing funds in new and flexible ways.

BARRIERS TO THE COMMUNITY SCHOOLS MOVEMENT

Although many see the benefits of community schools, there are nevertheless numerous challenges to expanding the community schools approach. Practitioners in education, community development, youth development, health, mental health, family support, and related fields often have their own distinct ideas of what works best to help young people succeed. The cultural disconnect between school and community remains wide. One solution that has been suggested is interprofessional development programs, which could help educate practitioners to work across sectors and with schools and communities. (Jehl, Blank, & McCloud 2001).

Another difficulty facing the community schools movement is that leaders who can initiate and guide a partnership-driven community school strategy, especially those who can work across race and class, are still few in number. More efforts must be made to develop leaders committed to a collaborative community problem-solving approach. In the schools, superintendents and principals currently learn little about working with family and community. They are trained to manage their buildings, not to be leaders and partners in the education of children.

Financing presents difficulties, too, as narrowly crafted public funding streams separate people and organizations. They make it more difficult to integrate resources in ways that are consistent with a community school strategy. Funding is still insufficient to develop community schools that can create the conditions for all children to learn. All too often communities are faced with a zero-sum game; increases in federal funding for after-school programs, for example, will often be balanced out by cuts in state and local spending for education and other child and family services. Still, more can be done with existing resources within a community school's framework. The continuing expansion of community schools across the country in the face of these barriers demonstrates the power and potential of this idea.

ACTION STEPS

Stakeholders in many sectors must work together to create and sustain community schools. Community leaders have a particularly important role to play in connecting to educators laboring under the pressures of the No Child Left Behind legislation. The following action recommendations focus on what communities can do to create and sustain community schools:

- Develop and promote a vision for improving student learning that incorporates the critical role of families and communities, as well as schools.
- Build broad-based, local coalitions or multi-agency commissions to advance, develop and sustain community schools.
- Mobilize community resources—financial and otherwise—to support the community school strategy.
- Build schools as centers of community. Community schools should meet not only the needs of students and schools but also those of families and the community.

COMMUNITY SCHOOLS AND CHANGE

Organizational development expert Peter Senge argued in the *Community Youth Development Journal* that "until we go back to thinking about school as the totality of the environment in which a child grows up, we can expect no deep changes. Change requires a community—people living and working together, assuming some common responsibility for something that's of deep concern and interest to all of them—their children" (Senge 2001, p. 12). Advocates believe that community schools can help build caring, compassionate, responsible communities.

—Ira Harkavy and Martin Blank

Further Reading

Barton, P. (2001). *Facing the hard facts of education reform* (ETS Policy Information Report). Princeton, NJ: Educational Testing Service. Retrieved February 24, 2003, from http://www.ets.org/research/pic/facingfacts.pdf

Dryfoos, J. (2000, October). *Evaluation of community schools: An early look.* Washington, DC: Coalition for Community Schools. Retrieved February 24, 2003, from www.communityschools.org/evaluation/evalbrieffinal.html

Eccles, J., & Gootman, J. (Eds.). (2002).*Community programs to promote youth development.* Washington, DC: National Academy Press.

Forum for Youth Investment & The Council of Chief State School Officers. (2001). *Inputs for learning environments: Consistencies across the education and youth development research.* Retrieved February 24, 2003, from http://www.forumforyouthinvestment.org/010604sclrpt/keychrt.pdf

Jehl, J., Blank, M. J., & McCloud, B. (2001). *Education and community building: Connecting two worlds.* Washington, DC: Institute for Educational Leadership.

KnowledgeWorks Foundation. (2001). *Ohio's education matters: KnowledgeWorks Foundation 2001–2002 Poll.* Retrieved February 24, 2003, from www.kwfdn.org/2001_poll/index2.html

Lave, L. B., & Matthews, H. S. (1996, November/December). It's easier to say green than to be green. *Technology Review,* pp. 68–69.

Learning First Alliance. (2001). *Every child learning: Safe and supportive schools.* Washington, DC: Author. Retrieved February 24, 2003, from http://www.learningfirst.org/pdfs/safe-schools-report.pdf

Melaville, A. (1998). *Learning together: The developing field of school-community initiatives.* Flint, MI: C. S. Mott Foundation. Retrieved February 24, 2003, from http://www@mott.org/publications/pdf/SPECIALlearningtogether.pdf

Melaville, A., Shah, B. P., & Blank, M. J. (2003). Making the difference: Research and practice in community schools. Washington, DC: Coalition for Community Schools, Institute for Educational Leadership.

Senge, P. M. (2001). Rethinking and co-creating schools. *Community Youth Development Journal, 2*(3), 12.0

COMMUNITY SERVICE

See National and Community Service

COMMUNITY STUDIES

The systematic study of communities—community studies—had its origins with the massive shift from rural-agrarian societies to urban-industrial, large-scale societies. This shift was the product of the rise of capitalism and industrialism, which, by the mid-1800s, gave rise to the social sciences (previously not defined as a distinct field). Even before community studies emerged as a field of study, the undermining of rural villages in Great Britain stimulated writers mourning the change from small- to large-scale societies. Ronald Blythe's *Akenfield: Portrait of an English Village* (1969) is a good example of this genre of writing outside the social sciences, which continues to the present in the works of British and American writers.

EARLY FORAYS INTO COMMUNITY STUDIES

Social science concerns about the character of community took much longer to develop. Many early social scientists struggled to understand the evolution of new forms of social relations, distinguishing small-scale face-to-face forms of social organization from the sorts of organization that characterize larger societies, in which there is greater impersonality and social distance. The classic distinction drawn by the German sociologist Ferdinand Tönnies (1855–1936) between community (gemeinschaft) and society (gesellschaft) captures these differences.

In the United States, the report in 1911 of the Country Life Commission appointed by President Theodore Roosevelt marked the national beginning of concern about the future of rural, agriculturally based communities, and in 1915, an early sociologist made what was probably the first attempt at a systematic study of a rural community. In 1929, Helen and Robert Lynd conducted the classic sociological community study in Muncie, Indiana, attempting to understand, among other things, the character of classes in small-scale urban communities. For their part, anthropologists, who had previously focused their attention on preindustrial, small-scale, traditional societies, also began to look at more modern manifestations of community.

Similarly, although initiated as an attempt to understand why workers did not share their employers' enthusiasms for factory life, research in factories in the late 1930s and the 1940s began to reveal the nature of worker communities. This was the birth of industrial sociology. Subsequent studies of occupational communities have examined printers, longshoremen, meatpackers, and others.

WIDESPREAD ACCEPTANCE OF COMMUNITY STUDIES

Community analysis became a significant approach for social scientists in the 1950s and 1960s. The primary researchers were anthropologists and sociologists, who conducted a plethora of studies in North America and elsewhere. Anthropologists were particularly active in

Latin America, but for a number of reasons, including trends in anthropological theory that ran counter to the philosophy of community development, community study took on negative connotations within anthropology.

For the most part, sociologists have continued to take a community studies approach that, while incorporating descriptive ethnographic material, tends to focus on analyses of current theoretical and intellectual issues, particularly the issue of rural-urban differentiation. While Blythe's *Akenfield* was writerly or literary in character, more recent analyses of formerly rural villages have a distinctly social scientific flavor. A good example is sociologist Michael Bell's 1994 study of Childerly, a village near London (*Childerly: Nature and Morality in a Country Village)*.

Early studies assumed that rural communities differed markedly from urban ones. The researcher W. F. Whyte upset this assumption in the 1950s with the discovery near downtown Boston of an urban ethnic community whose residents maintained the intimate, face-to-face social relations believed to be found only in rural communities. This gave rise to a genre of urban community studies such W. H. Whyte's *Organization Man* (1956) and Herbert Gans's *Urban Villagers* (1962). A similar study by Arthur Vidich and Joseph Bensman, *Small Town in Mass Society* (1968), demonstrated how a small rural community was being penetrated by mass society.

The field of community studies has branched into a variety of different genres. Studies of declining or dying rural communities comprise one genre; studies of occupational communities represent another. During the 1960s, as the civil rights movements burgeoned in the United States, community studies that focused on ethnic or racial minorities also became prominent.

By the end of the twentieth century, community studies was well-established in sociology, but the term itself was beginning to lose much of its meaning as the social sciences shifted from a focus on geographically or occupationally defined communities to more theoretical concerns. Community studies were still being done, but they often focused on theoretical issues current in the social science disciplines.

COMMUNITY STUDIES AT THE UNIVERSITY OF CALIFORNIA AT SANTA CRUZ

While many universities in English-speaking countries have community studies programs, often in the context of public health or education, the University of California at Santa Cruz (UCSC) created a formal academic department devoted exclusively to community studies (the Department of Community Studies) in 1969. It derives its intellectual substance from the general developments in the social sciences, but the triggering factor in its creation was the opening of the UCSC campus in 1965, which took place at the same time as the onset of the student rebellion of the 1960s. UCSC students began almost immediately to move off campus to find "relevant" social activities. Seeking to ensure that those activities had a firm academic base, UCSC established a variety of field study programs that made it possible for students to do off-campus studies and research for degree credit. The Department of Community Studies involved undergraduate students in a six-month, full-time, social-change-oriented field study as part of a two-year academic program. Since its inception, the department has turned out thousands of students who have used the program primarily to participate in social change activities while gaining a firm academic base for their community-oriented field studies. The field of community studies seems quite likely to flourish well into the twenty-first century.

—William H. Friedland

Further Reading

Friedland, W. H., & Rotkin, M. (2003). Academic activists: Community studies at the University of California, Santa Cruz. In T. D. Dickinson (Ed.), *Community and the world: Participating in social change.* Hauppauge, NY: Nova Science.

Gallaher, A., Jr., & Padfield, H. (Eds.). (1980). *The dying community.* Albuquerque: University of New Mexico Press.

Lebow, E. (1967). *Tally's corner: A study of Negro streetcorner men.* Boston: Little, Brown.

Lipset, S. M., Trow, M. A., & Coleman, J. S. (1956). *Union democracy: The internal politics of the international typographical union.* Glencoe, IL: Free Press.

Lynd, Robert S., and Helen M. Lynd. 1929. *Middletown: A study in American culture.* New York: Harcourt Brace.

Mayo, E. (1949). *The social problems of an industrial civilization.* London: Routledge & Kegan Paul. (Original work published 1945)

Roethlisberger, F. J., & Dickson, W. J. (1939). *Management and the worker: An account of the research program conducted by the Western Electric Company.* Cambridge, MA: Harvard University Press.

Rubel, A. J. (1966). *Across the tracks: Mexican Americans in a Texas city.* Austin: University of Texas Press.

Stack, C. (1974). *All our kin: Strategies of survival in a black community.* New York: Harper & Row.

Whyte, W. F. (1955). *Street corner society: The social structure of an Italian slum.* Chicago: University of Chicago Press.

Whyte, W. H. (1956). *The organization man.* New York: Simon & Schuster.

COMMUNITY SUPPORTED AGRICULTURE

An impenetrable wall of plastic and petroleum separates people in modern urban society from the source of their food. In the United States in particular, most people eat mainly food that has been highly processed, packaged, and transported to be sold in supermarkets, vending machines, or fast-food restaurants. Few stores bother to label food with its point of origin. The 7 to 10 percent of the value of the raw food in processed products is buried by the 90 percent of chopping, blending, cooking, extruding, packaging, distributing, and advertising. There is no connection between the food and the land on which it grew or the people who grew it. A promising alternative to this state of affairs is community supported agriculture (CSA).

TYPES OF CSAs

The essence of CSA is a mutual commitment between a farm or group of farms and a group of consumers. The farm feeds the people, and in return, the people support the farm and share the inherent risks and potential bounty of farm production. In more traditional societies, people take these connections for granted. In an agrarian society such as the United States early in its history, where most people lived in the country and either grew their own food or purchased their food from a nearby farm, a CSA would not be needed; a connection with the land on which food is grown would be normal in such cases. In industrialized countries like the United States, however, this most basic of human situations must be reinvented.

Community Farm Type

The very first CSAs in the United States, Indian Line Farm in Massachusetts and Temple-Wilton Farm in New Hampshire, both initiated in 1986, established the model of the "community farm," which dedicates its entire production to the members, or sharers. Indian Line divided its produce so that every sharer received an equal share or half-share. There was one fee for all full shares, and a lower fee for all half shares. Temple-Wilton allowed sharers to take what they needed regardless of how much they paid; each member paid what he or she could afford.

The example of these farms gave rise to the image of the ideal CSA: a smoothly functioning organic or biodynamic farm dividing all its produce among a committed group of supporters who share the risks and benefits of farming with the farmers. With a market assured and income guaranteed, the farmers can concentrate on producing high-quality food and practicing careful stewardship of the land. The members get to eat the freshest, tastiest, most nutritious food they have ever experienced, as though they were master gardeners, but with much less work. They and their children learn about food production and by eating seasonally make a deep connection to a special piece of land. They respect and honor the farmers' skills and hard work and express their appreciation through friendship, financial support, and helping on the farm. Members and farmers converge into a vital, creative community that celebrates diversity, both social and biological, and makes food justice and security a living reality. Food justice and security means that everyone, regardless of income, has the right to an adequate amount of safe, nourishing, culturally appropriate food from non-emergency sources, at a price that he or she can afford. Local, regional, and, in time, even international networks of CSAs and other sustainable food enterprises could supply members year round with ecologically produced and fairly traded foods.

Other Types of CSAs and Member Participation

Only about a quarter of the CSA farms have emulated the community-farm model. Out of the forty CSA farms in Vermont, only one produces exclusively for sharers, while the others continue to sell to a variety of markets. The amount of member participation in either growing or distributing the food varies tremendously from farm to farm. At one extreme are CSAs like the Genesee Valley Organic in New York, which requires all sharers to do some work as part of their share payment. At the other extreme are what have come to be known as "Subscription" CSAs, where the farm crew does all the work, and members pay a fee and simply receive a box or bag of produce each week, similar to the "box schemes" that have become popular in Great Britain. Most CSAs range somewhere in between, with members volunteering for special work days on the farm, helping with distribution, or defraying part of their payment by doing "working" shares. Besides supplying food, most CSAs also publish newsletters to inform members about the farm, how the food is grown and handled, and how to make best use of the food.

INVOLVING CSA MEMBERS

Even subscription farms with no more than a month's commitment from the members provide more of a connection between the land and the eater of the food than do conventional food sources. As farms become more secure with this form of marketing, they are finding more ways to involve their members. Many subscription farms ask members to provide distribution sites on their porches or in their garages. After five years of supplying weekly boxes of produce to more than 800 families in and around Chicago, Angelic Organics took the further step of forming a core group. These active members are helping the farm raise funds to purchase more land, arranging for distribution of leftover food to low-income families, promoting the CSA through a newsletter, and organizing community events at the farm. The members of Bill Brammer's subscription CSA near San Diego have assisted the farm in finding more land to rent and have lobbied for changes in land-use zoning that make the rental terms more favorable to the farm.

CSAs IN NORTH AMERICA

The number of CSA projects in the United States or North America is unknown. The Robyn Van En Center for CSA Resources lists more than 1,000 CSAs on its Web site. In *Farms of Tomorrow Revisited,* author Steven McFadden estimated that in 1997, there were more than 1,000 CSAs feeding 100,000 households in the United States. CSAs vary in size from three shares to more than 1,000. They can be found as far north as Palmer, Alaska (and even farther north in Canada), and as far south as Gainesville, Florida, and San Diego, California. The densest clusters are in the Northeast; around the Twin Cities and Madison, Wisconsin; in the upper Midwest; and in the Bay area of California. The number of CSAs is increasing quickly in states like Iowa, where food activists have teamed up with the universities and the Cooperative Extension, which provides technical advice to farmers, as well as many other community services. Most CSAs are either organic or biodynamic in method of production. A few are in transition to organic farming or to a lower use of chemicals.

Throughout the United States, the number of CSAs continues to increase as word spreads among farmers, and as groups of farms and rural development projects realize the potential significance. Around Lawrence, Kansas, twelve farms cooperate in the Rolling Prairie CSA that makes its pickup point the delicatessen section of the local food co-op. Many of these same farmers are working together on a tomato-processing project. Near Hartford, Connecticut, the Hartford Food System, a community food-security organization, has set up a CSA that sells half its shares to suburban families and the other half to inner-city groups working with low-income and minority populations. One of these groups brings the homeless teenagers it serves to the farm to do farm work, and the young women sell some of the food at a stand they run to raise money for activities. Several food banks are running similar CSAs. In 2000, Goodwill Industries in Lancaster, Pennsylvania, launched a CSA combining food production with training for some of the developmentally challenged people whom they service.

IMPORTANCE OF CSAs IN COMMUNITY LIFE

Members of other CSAs around the country have expressed how important the farm connection, the chemical-free food, and the education about how food is grown are to their children. Many report that their children eat more vegetables after they have been to the farm and helped pick them. In their sociological study "Factors Influencing the Decision to Join a CSA Farm," Jane Kolodinsky and Leslie Pelch did telephone surveys of members and nonmembers of three Vermont CSAs and came to the puzzling conclusion that having children makes people less likely to join. These "scientific" data contradict the real-life CSAs in which members with children make up the majority, and so many parents say they have joined because of the children. A member of Harmony Valley wrote this comment, which typifies parent sentiment about CSAs: "The biggest benefit is that our kids could see where our veggies come from . . . and I believe this encouraged them to believe that veggies are a wonderful gift and therefore would eat them."

No two CSAs are alike. Each successful project reflects the needs, talents, and resources of its farm and community. The participants are creating CSAs as they go, inventing a great array of organizational solutions. Whether or not CSAs numbered 10,000 in the year 2000 as Robyn Van En predicted, the 1,000 to 1,200 that already exist are maturing, flowering, and sharing their best ideas with one another.

Invaluable as computer models and sophisticated indicators of sustainable development may be, the real story is happening on the ground in community supported farms and gardens, a living reality for thousands of people who are learning to work together to live more sustainably. In the shadow of the global supermarket, CSAs resemble 1,000 farmer-consumer-controlled experiment stations, busy researching the social and economic relations of a more just and equitable future.

—*Elizabeth Henderson*

See also CIVIC AGRICULTURE

Further Reading

Groh, T., & McFadden, S. (1997). Farms of *tomorrow revisited: Community supported farms—Farm supported communities.* Kimberton, PA: Biodynamic Farming and Gardening Association.

Henderson, E., with Van En, R. (1999). *Sharing the harvest: A guide to community supported agriculture.* White River Junction, VT: Chelsea Green.

Kolodinsky, J., & Pelch, L. (1998). *Factors influencing the decision to join a CSA farm.* Fayetteville, AR: Appropriate Technology Transfer for Rural Areas (ATTRA).

Laird, T. J. (1995). *Community supported agriculture: A study of an emerging agricultural alternative.* Unpublished master's thesis, University of Vermont, Burlington, VT.

Robyn Van En Center for CSA Resources. (2003). Listing of CSAs by state. Retrieved February 28, 2003, from http://www.csacenter. org.

Robyn Van En Center for CSA Resources. (2003). *CSA handbook: A practical guide to starting and operating a successful CSA.* Chambersburg, PA: Wilson College.

COMPUTERS AND KNOWLEDGE SHARING

Knowledge has always been associated with power. In the information age, knowledge is turning into the principal currency, making efficient access to data sources, services, and to expertise vital for survival.

TOWARD GLOBAL KNOWLEDGE REPOSITORIES

The ancient Bibliotheca Alexandria, created at the beginning of the third century BCE, was the first universal library in history. By the middle of the first century BCE, it provided access to close to half a million manuscripts classified and organized by highly sophisticated methods. The library also served as a meeting place, research institute, center of learning, and museum. It was an essential source of information and expertise for many generations of world-famous scholars and scientists until its disappearance in the third and fourth centuries CE.

In 1938, H. G. Wells described his conception of the future information center in his book *World Brain,* inspiring numerous efforts to create a global repository of knowledge. Vannevar Bush, in his seminal work "As We May Think," developed a new methodology called memex for the automatic storage and efficient access of books, records, and individual communications. Influenced by Bush's ideas, Douglas Engelbart's "A Conceptual Framework for the Augmentation of Man's Intellect" describes one of the first hypertext systems. Also in 1963, Theodor H. Nelson coined the words *hypertext* and *hypermedia* to describe his vision of worldwide hypertext—a universe of interactive literary and artistic works and personal writings "deeply intertwingled" via hyperlinks. Joseph Licklider, imagining the library of the future in 1960, invented the term "man-computer symbiosis" to refer to the close, mutually beneficial interaction that we strive for in the design of today's human-computer interfaces.

TOWARD SOCIOTECHNICAL KNOWLEDGE NETWORKS

The emerging global, sociotechnical communication network allows people to be connected not only to different data sources and services but also to one another. Digital libraries play an increasingly important role as they aim to provide site-neutral, open access to a great variety and granularity of information presented in multiple (multimedia) ways.

Visual interfaces to digital libraries apply powerful data analysis and information visualization techniques to transform data and information that are not inherently spatial into a visual form. They engage a human's visual and proprioceptive system to make judgments about data more reflexive and to ease cognitive load, and are intended to help humans mentally organize, electronically interact with, and manage large, complex information spaces. Frequently, visual interfaces exploit human beings' powerful spatial cognition and the method of loci (a mnemonic technique that originated with the ancient Greeks) to associate and attach any digital information, tool, or service to a spatial location or, using an identification tag, to other people.

The expansion of the worldwide electronic network leads to a continuous convergence of digital libraries with archives, museums, and diverse services into an integrated digital information space. Digital availability of multimedia documents and artifacts makes real artifacts and their physical locations in libraries, museums, and archives less important. The roles of contributors, librarians, archivists, visitors, users, and researchers blur.

Moreover, exchange of information needs to be understood as a social interaction rather than as a mere instance of goal-oriented information retrieval or interaction with an information system. As Caroline Haythornthwaite, Barry Wellman, and colleagues suggest, a person's "information neighborhood" is made up not only of documents, but also—and perhaps more importantly—of people, including family, friends, neighbors, coworkers, and a continuously changing network of acquaintances. Correspondingly, there is an increasing commercial interest in the design and utilization of information sharing and collaboration tools. For instance, "groupware" systems use computer technologies to facilitate informal flows of information, capture and replay of interaction experiences, storage and reuse of expertise, and discovery of expertise locations. In these systems, information is exchanged through social networks that facilitate local and distributed group collaboration in environments ranging from ad hoc meetings to virtual organizations. As an example, Robert Mack, Yael Ravin, and Roy J. Byrd (2001) describe community knowledge portals developed to help participants capture, access, and manage knowledge and expertise created during their work process; to link community members to each other and to relevant content; and to offer personalized services tailored to the individuals and communities based on collaborative filtering. Peter R. Monge and Noshir Contractor promote tools like I-KNOW that assist in the study, creation, and growth of knowledge networks.

Online "virtual communities," a term coined by Howard Rheingold, also function for their members as "information neighborhoods," contexts within which they can engage in ongoing information-sharing activities and information exchange.

Awareness tools convey information to users, ranging from cognizance of documents, projects, and tasks to knowledge of the location and activities of other community members.

Computer-mediated communication (CMC), according to Susan Herring, studies human communication and interaction via computer networks and in online environments—from the dynamics of group communication in Usenet news articles to how people use hypertext to shape meaning. Social network analysis is focused on uncovering the patterning of people's interaction.

A major shortcoming of today's digital online spaces is the scarcity of social navigation cues (e.g., who is online, what resources are accessed frequently), making it difficult to find relevant resources and expertise or to collaborate. Research on social visualizations aims to show data about a person, illuminate relationships among people, or visualize group activity to facilitate information access, collaboration, and decision-making (Donath et al. 1999).

OPPORTUNITIES AND CHALLENGES

The World Wide Web places humankind's knowledge, ideas, and achievements at one's fingertips. Recent advances in networking, computing, storage, and display technologies make possible the design of efficient communication facilities that connect us to any individual, group, or organization.

Research challenges concern the extension of physical information and workspaces via electronic means. Potential investigative areas include network technologies, electronic data storage, highly usable and sociable interfaces, and techniques for automatic reaction and adaptation to the information and social networking needs of temporary, dynamically evolving, professional networks and online communities.

Technological challenges comprise the sustainability, robustness, and support of heterogeneous hardware. The full implementation of the Semantic Web, described by Tim Berners-Lee, James Hendler, and colleagues, promises to bring structure to the meaningful content of Web pages and to provide the basis of interoperability between different data sources and Web services.

Social challenges relate to data protection, privacy concerns, social organization of work practices, trust, legitimacy via content contribution and evaluation by distributed subject and professional teams, and sustainable resource models. According to Amy Jo Kim, community building needs to be supported via private profiles and collaborative working practices.

The scale-free topology of the Web poses its own serious challenges with regard to multilingualism, preservation of diverse cultural heritages, traditions, views, and approaches, as only a minority of sources and experts is highly visible and accessible while the vast majority is too weakly connected to be seen. The exponential growth of the Web, caused by globalization, economic interdependencies, and technological development, leads to a global system of interconnected human beings and computer technology of unheard-of complexity. Consequently, according to R. Kling, research on efficient knowledge and expertise access will need to study, analyze, and support this emerging sociotechnical system as opposed to its individual parts.

—Katy Börner

Further Reading

Berners-Lee, T., Hendler, J., et al. (2001). The semantic web. *Scientific American, 284*(5), 43.

Börner, K. (2002). Twin worlds: Augmenting, evaluating, and studying three-dimensional digital cities and their evolving communities. In M. Tanabe, P. van den Besselaar, & T. Ishida, *Digital cities II: Computational and sociological approaches* (pp. 256–269). New York: Springer Verlag.

Börner, K., & Chen, C. (Eds.). (2002). *Visual interfaces to digital libraries.* Berlin: LNCS, Springer Verlag.

Burnett, G. (2000). Information exchange in virtual communities: A typology. *Information Research, 5*(4). Retrieved February 28, 2003, from http://informationr.net/ir/5-4/paper82.html

Bush, V. (1945). As we may think. *The Atlantic Monthly, 176*(1), 101–108.

Card, S., Mackinlay, J., et al. (Eds.). (1999). *Readings in information visualization: Using vision to think.* San Francisco: Morgan Kaufmann.

Donath, J. S., Karahalios, K., et al. (1999). Visualizing conversation. *Journal of Computer Mediated Communication, 4*(4). Retrieved February 28, 2003, from www.ascusc.org/jcmc/vol4/issue4/donath.html

Engelbart, D. C. (1963). A conceptual framework for the augmentation of man's intellect. In P. D. Howerton & D. C. Weeks (Eds.), *Vistas in information handling* (Vol. 1, pp. 1–29). Washington, DC: Spartan Books.

Erickson, T., Smith, D. N. , et al. (1999). Socially translucent systems: Social proxies, persistent conversation, and the design of "Babble." In *Proceeding of the CHI 99 Conference on Human Factors in Computing Systems: The CHI is the limit* (pp. 72–79). Pittsburgh, PA: ACM Press.

Fox, E. A., & Urs, S. R. (2002). Digital libraries. *Annual Review of Information Science & Technology, 36,* 503–589.

Freeman, L. C. (2000). Visualizing social networks. *Journal of Social Structure, 1*(1). Retrieved February 28, 2003, from http://zeeb.library.cmu.edu:7850/JoSS/article.html

Haythornthwaite, C., & Wellman, B. (1998). Work, friendship, and media use for information exchange in a networked organization. *Journal of the American Society for Information Science, 49*(12), 1101–1114.

Herring, S. (2002). Computer-mediated communication and the Internet. In B. Cronin, *Annual Review of Information Science and Technology* (pp. 109–168). Medford, NJ: Information Today Inc., American Society for Information Science and Technology.

Kim, A. J. (2000). *Community building on the web: Secret strategies for successful online communities.* Berkeley, CA: Peachpit.

Kling, R. (2000). Learning about information technologies and social change: The contribution of social informatics. *The Information Society, 16*(3).

Lakoff, G. (1987). *Women, fire, and dangerous things: What categories reveal about the mind.* Chicago: University of Chicago Press.

Licklider, J. C. R. (1960). Man-computer symbiosis. *IRE Transactions on Human Factors in Electronics, HFE*-1(1), 4–11.

Mack, R., Ravin, Y., & Byrd, R. J. (2001). Knowledge portals and the emerging digital knowledge workplace. *IBM Systems Journal, 40*(4), 925–955.

Monge, P. R., & Contractor, N. (2003). *Theories of communication networks.* New York: Oxford University Press.

Rheingold, H. (1993). *The virtual community: Homesteading on the electronic frontier.* New York: HarperPerennial.

Wellman, B. (2000). Computer networks as social networks. *Science, 293,* 2031–2034.

Wells, H. G. (1938). *World brain.* Garden City, NY: Doubleday, Doran.

CONDOMINIUMS

The term *condominium* is derived from a Latin phrase that means joint dominion or sovereignty. In the United States, a condominium is commonly an apartment house in which the units are owned individually rather than by a company or a cooperative. The occupant of a condominium unit has ownership over the space in the individual apartment and shares ownership of the common space, such as shared walls, the lobby, elevators, and hallways, with his or her neighbors. Through this joint ownership and shared interest, condominium owners and residents create a unique living community.

Condominium developments can include complexes with multiple buildings, apartment buildings, or single-family detached houses with shared, but privately owned, common facilities and spaces. Unlike a cooperative, in which the tenants are shareholders in the corporation with the right to lease a specific unit as long as they remain shareholders, the condominium corporation does not own all of the apartments and the common space.

Buying a condominium allowed the attainment of the post–World War II American dream—owning one's own home (a visible symbol of a family's status) and thereby achieving a better life. Nowadays, the condominium's strongest appeal probably stems from the idea that real estate prices will constantly climb, thereby building the condominium owner's equity. Also, condominiums are often cheaper and, due to the communal responsibilities, are often easier to maintain. Owning a condominium also provides substantial tax breaks, as all of the sections of the Internal Revenue Code that apply to single-family homes also apply to condominiums.

CONDOMINIUMS AND COMMUNITY

Condominium owners each purchase their unit as well as a portion of the common space, such as the hallways, roof, and heating systems. Each unit has a membership in the condominium homeowners association. This association or council governs the common elements, prepares a budget, and levies a monthly assessment on each unit to cover maintenance of the common elements and to maintain a reserve fund for repairs.

Condominium owners must collaborate on managing the building because they share walls and spaces. This joint ownership requires the development and enforcement of community standards. The homeowners association must regulate such matters as level of noise, ownership of pets, and design of common space.

Of course, problems can arise from joint ownership. The condominium community may be a mixture of resident owners, absentee owners, and renters, with occupants differing in their incomes, stages of life, or both. As a result of these and other differences, not all members of the community hold the same interest in the daily maintenance of the building and the facilities.

HISTORY

Condominiums have a long history. As early as the year 2000 BCE, the Babylonians (in southern Mesopotamia, modern Iraq) had the concept of condominiums. Documents from that era show that the owner of a two-family home sold the first floor to another family and retained ownership of the second floor. A Hebrew document dated 434 BCE was a deed for a condominium unit. During the Roman Empire, and later in the sixteenth-century Italian city-states, people understood the notion of multiunit ownership.

In the nineteenth century, laws concerning condominiums were first enacted in the Napoleonic Code (Code civil des Français) of 1804, and several other European states, including Belgium, Italy, the Netherlands, and Spain, adopted condominium regulations based on the Napoleonic Code. In the twentieth century, European emigrants spread the concept of condominiums to South America, where many nations adopted multiownership laws. In 1928, Brazil was the first in the world to ratified legislation to allow the development of these units. In many Latin American countries, even commercial properties are owned as condominiums.

CONDOMINIUMS IN THE UNITED STATES

Condominiums entered the United States through the commonwealth of Puerto Rico, which received the condominium concept from South America. In 1951 and 1958, the Puerto Rican legislature enacted laws permitting condominium ownership. In 1961, a Puerto Rican delegation lobbied the U.S. Congress to enact Section 234 of the National Housing Act to extend the Federal Housing Administration's mortgage benefits to condominiums. The Housing Act of 1961 extended mortgage insurance to condominiums, and state legislatures legally recognized the system. By 1968, all fifty states had condominium laws on their books.

Beginning in the 1970s, condominiums became extremely popular in the United States. The condominium offers the easy maintenance of apartment living and the ownership qualities of single-family homes. Living in a condominium, unlike living in a single-family home, eliminates individual responsibility for yard work and repairs because the homeowners association assumes those duties. Like single-family homeowners, however, condominium owners have the chance for equity appreciation and for tax shelters. The tax code for both condominiums and single-family housing has deductible features for interest, real estate taxes, and depreciation on leased units, and allows the deferral of capital gains on the sale and repurchase of another home. Due to these incentives, by 1974, condominiums accounted for one-fourth of all new for-sale housing. By 1980, more than 10 million people lived in some 50,000 condominium developments in the United States.

Inspired by possible profits, many owners of rental apartment buildings in the 1970s rapidly converted their buildings into condominiums, often displacing the renting population. In 1979, the Senate Subcommittee on Housing and Urban Affairs found that between 130,000 and 250,000 rental units had been taken off the market and converted into condominiums. These conversions put pressure on city dwellers, especially older and poor people, who were often unable to find adequate replacement housing in the same neighborhoods. In numerous cities, tenants created right-to-rent movements in reaction to these conversions, but meeting the housing needs of people with fixed incomes or low- to moderate-level incomes grew difficult. Faced with abuses of the conversion process, some states enacted a second set of condominium laws to offer some protection to tenants and to ease the jolt of conversion. For the most part, these laws require a longer period of notification, allowing the tenant more time to relocate. Even though the legislatures have passed laws to protect tenants, Americans will continue to buy condominiums because of condominium's relative financial accessibility and large tax incentives.

—Emily Straus

Further Reading

Heskin, D. A. (1983). *Tenants and the American dream.* New York: Praeger.

Lauber, D. (1980). Condominium conversions—The number prompts controls to protect the poor and elderly. *Journal of Housing, 37*(4), 201–209.

Lehrer, K. E. (1980). *Cooperatives and condominiums: Urban housing alternatives for the private residential sector.* Unpublished doctoral dissertation, New York University.

Silverman, C. J., & Barton, S. E. (1984, November). *Condominiums: Individualism and community in a mixed property form.* Paper presented at meeting of the Institute of Urban and Regional Development, University of California, Berkeley.

Silverman, C. J., & Barton, S. E. (1986, December). *Private property and private government: Tensions between individualism and community in condominiums.* Paper presented at the meeting of the American Sociological Association, University of California, Berkeley.

Welfeld, I. (1988). *Where we live: A social history of American housing.* New York: Simon & Schuster.

Wright, G. (1981). *Building the dream: A social history of housing in America.* New York: Pantheon.

CONFLICT RESOLUTION

Human conflict is as old and common as human interaction itself. Whenever two or more parties (whether individuals, groups, organizations or nation-states) have a disagreement over ideas, values, beliefs, relationships, or material resources, they may have a conflict, which can ripen into a dispute. Individuals can even have an intrapersonal conflict within themselves (for example, when they hold competing values or make inconsistent choices).

The field of conflict resolution seeks to study and implement different ways of handling and possibly resolving conflict. While some think that all human conflict is potentially destructive or harmful and should, therefore, be controlled or resolved, others think that some forms of conflict may be useful, both for individuals and for social institutions. This functionalist view of conflict sees the possibility of both individual and social change, brought about by conflicts over values, ideas, or resources that alter our thinking, our actions, and how we organize ourselves. Although conflict has produced horrible wars and record-setting deaths in recent human history, some social conflict has led to significant positive social change. This includes the expansion of the right to vote and democracy; civil rights, women's rights, and human rights; community, national and local self-determination; labor rights and unions; and environmental justice, to name just a few.

Thus, while the field is most often called conflict resolution or conflict management, others prefer to think of it as conflict analysis, or conflict "handling." How conflict is perceived, conceived, interpreted, and acted on is itself a variable process, depending on the environments or contexts in which the conflict is situated. Thus, we think of conflict as socially constructed because it is made, interpreted, and resolved by people and can be changed and controlled as cognitive, emotional, material, or social perceptions or conditions themselves change.

Conflict resolution also focuses on preventing conflicts and dealing with intractable or irresolvable conflicts (living with ongoing conflicts), and on ways to encourage reconciliation or facilitate effective implementation of resolution after a conflict is declared over. Thus, as a field of academic study and social practice, conflict resolution looks at the conditions that exist before, during, and after a conflict and considers the perceptions, conceptions, behaviors, and feelings of all the participants in the conflict, not just those that are adverse or hostile to one another, but also those who are potential interveners or conflict resolvers.

Given the ubiquity of human conflict at all levels of human endeavor and the increased levels of destruction that are possible when conflicts escalate in our modern world, it seems true, as the social philosopher Stuart Hampshire has recently opined, that "the skillful management of conflict is among the highest of human skills" (Hampshire 2000, p. 35).

METHODS OF CONFLICT RESOLUTION

Because there are so many different kinds of conflicts, ranging from intrapersonal conflicts (conflicts involving a single person) through two-party conflicts (dyadic or interpersonal conflicts*)* and multiparty or multigroup conflicts, to internal organizational or intragroup conflicts, and finally to conflicts among and between groups and nation-states (international conflicts), we have begun to develop a wide variety of forms of conflict resolution, dependent in part on whether the parties attempt to resolve their own conflicts or seek the assistance of a third-party intervener. Different processes of conflict resolution also have different purposes or goals. Some forms of conflict resolution, for example, address the deepest underlying differences of the parties and attempt to reorient or reconcile the parties to one another for a future relationship, and, with luck, with new understandings of one another's needs, interests, and objectives. Examples include marital counseling, international peace treaties, and truth and reconciliation commissions. Other forms of conflict resolution, such as dispute settlement, are focused more on ending a particular dispute, with a cessation of hostilities, agreement to change some behaviors, or payment of a monetary settlement or compensatory fee. Some conflict settlements are intended to be long lasting and binding on the parties, while others may be advisory, temporary, or contingent. And, some conflict resolution activities occur in very public settings, with many participants and observers, while others are conducted in private with only the disputing parties or their representatives present.

Avoidance and Self-Help

Perhaps the most common form of conflict resolution is avoidance. Most of the time, when there is the potential for conflicts to ripen into disputes, people simply ignore or choose not to pursue them; otherwise we would spend most of the day arguing or fighting with one another. Thus, one form of conflict resolution is to teach individuals how to manage their own conflict or anger productively—to learn to know "when to hold 'em and when to fold 'em" (Kenny Rogers, from the song *The Gambler,* 1979).

In many situations, however, people engage in self-help; that is, they take some action on their own, once they have determined that they have a grievance against someone else who can be held responsible in some way for whatever is wrong. Scholar William Felstiner and his colleagues call this process "naming, blaming and claiming" a dispute or grievance (Felstiner, Abel, & Sarat 1980–1981, p. 631). In extreme cases, this self-help can be physical violence, but it may simply be lodging a complaint, asking for compensation, restitution, or an apology, or taking or seizing property, whether legally justified or not.

Negotiation

Perhaps the most common form of conflict resolution is negotiation, in which two or more parties to a conflict or a dispute engage directly with one another, or through representatives, to reach some kind of consensual agreement to their conflict or problem by trading or sharing arguments, claims, material, or money. Negotiations can be highly principled (based on reasoned argument and using mutually agreed-to or "objective" principles), or they can be pragmatic trades or bargains about money or things that do not entail a more global agreement about purposes or reasons. Some people (and groups and nations) may negotiate agreements on the basis of emotions and feelings (the desire to end unproductive conflict) or moral, religious, or political beliefs (the belief that it is wrong to take advantage of a weaker party). While many people think of negotiation as a competitive process in which scarce resources must be divided between or among the parties (what game theorists call a zero-sum game or distributive bargaining), more modern negotiation theorists and practitioners have explored the possibilities of using collaborative processes to try to achieve maximum mutual and joint gain through integrative bargaining. This is often accomplished by using creative problem-solving strategies that seek to create new value for the parties and to expand or change conceptions or realities regarding the disputed resources. For example, rather than calling for division of the Sinai Peninsula, the 1978 Camp David Accords that ended hostilities between Egypt and Israel mandated that the entire peninsula be returned to Egypt (which desired sovereignty) but that it be demilitarized and policed by neutral forces to meet Israel's need for security. Thus, modern negotiation practice urges people in conflict to identify their underlying needs, interests, and objectives and to consider those of the other parties, in order to search for mutual gain or creative solutions that will deal more effectively with the underlying conflict than would a simple compromise in the middle or total victory for one party.

When the parties or their representatives are unable to negotiate agreements on their own, they may seek the assistance of a third party to facilitate communication or resolution or to decide the matter for them. Increasingly, parties in conflict use mediation, which is a form of facilitated negotiation, to help them resolve disputes. A mediator can work in several different ways. Sometimes the mediator may actually initiate the conflict resolution effort, as when, for example, the United States attempts to broker peace talks in situations in which it is not formally involved (for example, in the Israeli-Palestinian conflict). In most cases, however, the parties will ask for assistance, either from a neutral third party who is considered an expert in negotiation and conflict resolution processes and who has no prior interest in or bias regarding the matter in dispute, or from a wise person (such as a village elder or religious or community leader) who may, in fact, know the parties quite well and be embedded in the community in which the conflict is located.

Some mediators focus on facilitating better communication between the parties and encouraging them to acknowledge and respect each other. Such mediators are often called facilitative mediators; they may be seeking relationship changes, understanding and recognition of differences between the parties, and process goals relating to how the parties will deal with one another in the future. This form of mediation is also often called transformative mediation because it hopes to transform the parties' understanding of one another and to empower them with respect to one another and to the larger community in which their conflict is rooted.

Similar to this mode of mediation is conciliation, in which the third party facilitates communication with the express purpose of bringing the parties together for increased understanding and also to forge an agreement. The term *conciliation* is often associated with labor-management relations; in civil-law countries (such as much of Europe) it is often used instead of the term *mediation.* Many forms of dispute or conflict resolution associated with religions prefer the term *conciliation* because it is closer to reconciliation, which is intended to bring people together spiritually as well as materially. The key element uniting mediation and conciliation is that the third party, whether neutral or not, is not empowered to make any decisions for the parties. In mediation and conciliation, the parties decide for themselves how and if they want to resolve the conflict. The mediator may help the parties communicate or negotiate with one another, but may not impose a solution.

In a slightly different form of mediation, known as evaluative mediation, the third-party mediator may be a bit more active in evaluating the conflict or case for the parties, telling them how persuasive their claims are, offering suggestions for possible solutions or resolutions, or even engaging in some neutral fact finding, rights assessment, or legal assessment. This form of mediation is most common in complex legal disputes in which the mediator is a lawyer with expertise about what a court would do if the dispute were formally decided in the legal system. The advantage of mediation over court adjudication is that the parties can craft their own solutions to problems, rather than relying on a judge who doesn't know them or their situation. This makes it possible to make agreements or plans about the future. Court decisions are usually, but not always, focused on what happened in the past, and they can order damages or compensation, but cannot usually (unless there is an injunction) tell parties what they must do in the future.

Mediation can be carried out in different ways. In the international arena, it is not uncommon for a mediator to use shuttle diplomacy, moving back and forth between the parties in their own locations and being essentially a message and proposal carrier. This is particularly common when the conflict or tensions run especially high. In more typical one-on-one disputes, the mediator may either keep the parties together in joint sessions to facilitate their communication or separate them some or all of the time in caucuses. Separation into caucuses can prevent conflict and permits both parties to receive confidential information that they might not want to share with the other (for example, their real concerns, embarrassing facts, or trade secrets).

Arbitration and Adjudication

When the parties to a conflict require a formal decision about their relationship or who is right or wrong, they may turn to a third party to actually decide something about the dispute. Arbitration is a private form of conflict resolution in which those with the conflict pick the third-party neutral or decision maker and also select the rules by which the conflict resolution process will be conducted. Arbitration often involves one decision maker chosen by the parties, but it can also involve a panel of arbitrators. In some kinds of conflicts, such as labor or commercial disputes, or when there are two diametrically opposed sides, each side will pick one arbitrator of their choosing, commonly called a partisan or party-chosen arbitrator, and then the two party-chosen arbitrators will choose a third neutral person to act as chair of the panel. Arbitrators decide together and sometimes write formal decisions or opinions about how the dispute should be resolved. The parties voluntarily adhere to most arbitral decisions, but if not, the parties may have to go to court to enforce the decision.

When the parties prefer to be public about their dispute or conflict, or if they want a formal ruling, perhaps to set a precedent for other similar situations or to make new law, they will seek adjudication in the formal legal justice system. Only formal judges, selected according to the rules of the political system in effect, can decide matters that are formally filed in the court. In the United States, both individuals and larger groups (in class actions) can file lawsuits and seek formal legal remedies, such as monetary payments and injunctions ordering behavior changes.

Other Forms of Conflict Resolution

New forms of conflict resolution have developed as hybrids or combinations of these basic processes. In a form called med-arb, the parties seek facilitation of their negotiations first; only if that fails will they ask the third party to step in and decide the matter for them. Sometimes the same person acts as both mediator and arbitrator, while at other times these roles are separated. In mini-trials, the parties will use some of the formalities of a formal court adjudication—witnesses, lawyers, opening and closing arguments—in order to facilitate a negotiated settlement, with all the parties present, rather than depending on a judge to decide. This is, in a sense, an elaborate form of fact-finding and mediation and can even resemble the public mediation sessions that take place in villages in some cultures in Africa and the South Seas. In a reversal of the public and private dimensions of conflict resolution, many public courts are now urging parties to use mediation and various private forms of dispute resolution before they can have a formal trial.

Many large organizations, such as universities, corporations, and government agencies, now employ ombuds (a gender-neutral term; the older term is ombudsmen), who are neutrals within an organization who attempt to solve internal organizational conflicts and disputes by investigating complaints, counseling parties, or conciliating or mediating disputes, and by engaging in fact-finding, problem solving, and organizational conflict prevention. In some contexts, ombuds also deal with external conflicts—that is, claims or complaints from outsiders—either against the organization or between two parties (especially in governmental regulatory situations).

In a related development within the field, ombuds or outside consultants often help an organization, community, or other social institution design a dispute resolution system to resolve conflicts effectively internally and to deal with conflict prophylactically by analyzing sources of conflicts or complaints and dealing with them before they erupt.

In the last few decades, a new form of conflict resolution process called consensus building has been used in a variety of contexts in which the conflicts involve many different parties. Consensus building is a hybrid of negotiation, mediation, and formal hearings. In it, a skilled facilitator helps all the interested parties (stakeholders) reach a consensus agreement about a contested matter such as budget or resource allocation, environmental siting or clean-up, religious disputes, public policy matters, or ethnic, race or community disputes. The key is to enhance democratic participation of all the parties who will be affected by the decision. These processes are intended to increase public participation in situations in which governmental or political processes have become too burdensome or bureaucratic or marred by polarized conflict. The parties determine their own procedural rules and the rules of decision (how they will vote, what constitutes a consensus). Consensus building has been used effectively in a wide range of conflicts, including hotly contested community and political disputes. (A process called reg-neg, or negotiated rulemaking, has been used to negotiate administrative regulations in U.S. local, state, and federal governmental processes; previously the government simply adopted rules, which parties who felt left out of the process could then challenge.) Such participatory processes are now being used to enhance community participation in schools, policing, local government, crime control and prevention, and the development of good race relations.

Perhaps the least formal conflict resolution processes are so-called public or constructive conversations or dialogues. These are not intended to resolve conflicts or forge agreements, but to encourage understanding when the issues at hand generate deep conflict. The Public Conversations Project, for example, facilitates conversation exchanges on such issues as abortion, affirmative action, gun control, and religious, racial, and ethnic differences, with the objective of "supporting people in having constructive conversations in which experiences, convictions, uncertainties, ideas, feelings and questions are shared and people listen to one another with care and compassion even when what is said is different, surprising or upsetting" (Public Conversations Project 2002, p. 4).

At the most formal level, whole institutions have been founded to engage in conflict resolution. The United Nations is the most obvious institution, dedicated to promoting world peace and to enhancing the social welfare of the world's citizens through its formal governance structure (and international law) and through the humanitarian and other work done by its agencies and committees. At the level of the nation-state, South Africa's Truth and Reconciliation Commissions are intended to provide a safe place for the expression of pain and loss caused by past injustices, for acknowledgment of those wrongs, for apology by those who committed them, and for a healing process (and some restitution) to ease the transition to new forms of democracy and equal citizenship. In the criminal justice area, both formal and informal processes of restorative justice are intended to facilitate dialogue, reconciliation, and voluntary restitution between offenders and victims.

Many less formal nongovernmental organizations (NGOs), such as Search for Common Ground, the Consensus Building Institute, the International Conciliation Service of the Mennonites, and the Center for Dispute Resolution, work to enable individuals and groups to learn the philosophies, practices, and techniques associated with conflict resolution and facilitation. Peer mediation programs in schools teach children to deal with conflicts productively, to "use their words," not their weapons, when they have conflicts with others. Increasingly, universities and professional schools in a variety of disciplines now offer training, research, and educational opportunities in the field of conflict resolution.

CONTROVERSIES ASSOCIATED WITH CONFLICT RESOLUTION

Although there are many different ways to conceive of and practice conflict resolution processes, issues and controversies still challenge the effectiveness of and assumptions about those processes. For example, to the extent that conflict resolution relies on the ability to talk and to articulate feelings, beliefs, and principles, it may be making assumptions about the value of words and talk to heal people or change people's views. Such reliance on the sharing of feelings and needs may be culturally embedded: In many cultures, feelings and needs are very private matters that would not readily be shared, even among family members, and certainly not with strangers or perceived superiors. At the intercultural and international level, there is some concern that U.S. models of conflict resolution are being introduced and exported to other cultural settings, where the technologies of talk, interest trading, and assumptions of equality among the parties may not be accepted by all who participate.

There is much concern that dialogues, mediation, and negotiation processes cannot work well when there are gross disparities between the parties in economic, political, or social capital (inequalities of wealth, status, or along racial, ethnic, or gender hierarchies). Others protest the use of "expert" process facilitators in situations in which the stated goal is to promote democratic participation of the parties.

Some critics are concerned that too much effort to reduce societal conflict in society will pacify the disempowered to such a degree that it will become more difficult to organize and demand social change, whether through social movements and concerted group action or through individual lawsuits and legislative advocacy. A similar concern is that many of the conflict resolution processes are undertaken in secret, and the larger public may not know what agreements are being reached or why. Those who demand complete transparency in public matters or even in private disputes that affect significant numbers of people (such as environmental disputes) do not approve of the way some conflict resolution devices "privatize" policy making and governmental functions. (In this context, "privatizing" makes the resolution more private.) Even private actors, such as corporations, may be able to hide their wrongdoing with settlements that are arrived at secretly.

Even those who generally approve of conflict resolution processes are concerned that the animating principles of conflict resolution may be distorted, as when, for example, a voluntary and consensual process such as mediation or arbitration becomes mandatory. (This can happen when a contract requires people to use a particular dispute resolution process or when courts require disputants to go to mediation before getting a trial.)

An important philosophical issue in the use of conflict resolution processes is the relationship of peace to justice. At what point should the desire to achieve peace and diminish destructive conflict in the world give way to the need to fight for rights and justice, and to acknowledge situations that are not amenable to peaceful coexistence or agreement? At the same time, it is important to ask how likely it will be for people to achieve justice if conflicting parties cannot reason with one another or hear one another's claims and grievances.

At their best, conflict resolution sensibilities provide a way of approaching personal, social, and political problems in the world. They give people the means to come together to solve problems creatively, effectively, and humanely, within structures that maximize participation by those affected by the decisions made and that cause the least possible harm to those who are affected by the conflicts.

—Carrie Menkel-Meadow

See also CONFLICT THEORY

Further Reading

Avruch, K. (1998). *Culture and Conflict Resolution.* Washington, DC: United States Institute of Peace Press.

Bush, R. A. B., & Folger, J. P. (1994). *The promise of mediation: Responding to conflict through empowerment and recognition.* San Francisco: Jossey-Bass.

Deutsch, M., & Coleman, P. T. (Eds.). (2000). *The handbook of conflict resolution: Theory and practice.* San Francisco: Jossey-Bass.

Felstiner, W. L. F., Abel, R., & Sarat, A. (1980–1981). The emergence and transformation of disputes: Naming, blaming, claiming . . . *Law & Society Review, 15*(3–4), 631–654.

Fisher, R., Ury, W., & Patton, B. (1991). *Getting to yes: Negotiating agreement without giving in.* New York: Penguin Books.

Fung, A., & Wright, E. O. (2001). Deepening democracy: Innovations in empowered participatory governance. *Politics & Society, 29*(1), 5–41.

Greenberg, M. C., Barton, J. H., & McGuinness, M. E. (Eds.). (2000). *Words over war: Mediation and arbitration to prevent deadly conflict.* Lanham, MD: Rowman & Littlefield.

Hampshire, S. (2000). *Justice is conflict.* Princeton, NJ: Princeton University Press.

Lederach, J. P. (1995). *Preparing for peace: Conflict transformation across cultures.* Syracuse, NY: Syracuse University Press.

Menkel-Meadow, C. (Ed.). (2001). *Mediation: Theory policy and practice.* Aldershot, UK, and Burlington, VT: Ashgate-Dartmouth.

Minow, M. (1998). *Between vengeance and forgiveness: Facing history after genocide and mass violence.* Boston: Beacon.

Public Conversations Project. (2002). *Constructive conversations about challenging times: A guide to community dialogue.* Retrieved August 27, 2002, from http://conversations.forms.soceco.org/48/

Susskind, L., McKearnan, S., & Thomas-Larmer, J. (1999). *The consensus building handbook: A comprehensive guide to reaching agreement.* Thousand Oaks, CA: Sage.

Umbreit, M. (1994). *Victim meets offender: The impact of restorative justice and mediation.* Monsey, NY: Criminal Justice Press.

Ury, W. (2000). *The third side: Why we fight and how we can stop.* New York: Penguin Putnam.

Yarn, D. (Ed.). (1999). *Dictionary of conflict resolution.* San Francisco: Jossey-Bass.

CONFLICT THEORY

Since the beginning of time, human beings have come into conflict with one another. Disputes over scarce resources such as food, water, land, housing, shade, animals, tools, and materials have led to fights and physical violence. The larger the groups of people in conflict, the more devastating the consequences.

There are many reasons why conflicts develop, at both the individual and group levels. Some conflicts arise from belief systems or principles, some from personality differences, and others are conflicts over material goods, identity, status, or reputation. Because conflicts develop for so many different reasons and because much conflict is dangerous and unproductive, the theory of conflict attempts to understand the different sources of conflict, the dynamics of how conflict develops, escalates, or declines, and how conflict can be handled, reduced, or resolved.

At the same time, it must be recognized that conflict can have social utility as well. Many important changes in human society, many for the betterment of human life, have come from hard-fought conflicts that resulted in the change of human institutions, relationships, or ideas. The U.S. Civil War, for example, saw the death of more than a million Americans, but it eliminated slavery in the United States and marked the beginning of an ongoing period of change in U.S. race relations. Those changes in race relations have continued to be marked by conflicts, including, in recent years, conflicts over whether reparations should be paid to the descendants of slaves and whether there should be affirmative action in education and employment to compensate for the past wrongs of the society. Even small interpersonal conflicts (as between husband and wife or parent and child) can lead to important changes, not only in relationships between the people in conflict but in larger social movements, such as the feminist, peace, and children's rights movements. Conflicts with outsiders often clarify and reinforce commitments and norms of one's own group, and internal conflict within an individual can lead to changed views and intellectual and emotional growth.

Conflict theory tries to classify and describe the types of conflicts that exist (for example, in terms of whether they are productive or destructive). It then attempts to explain the ways in which conflict proceeds or is structured (both by internal and external forces) and how it can be managed or resolved.

A conflict can be experienced as a simple disagreement, a feeling of discomfort or opposition, or a perception of difference from, or competition or incompatibility with, others. Conflicts, then, can be perceptual, emotional, or behavioral. When a conflict is actually acted on, it becomes a dispute. In order for a conflict to develop fully into a dispute, people must perceive some wrong to themselves and identify someone else to blame for it, as well as some way to take action against that person or people. That process has been called "naming, blaming and claiming" (Felstiner, Abel, & Sarat 1980–1981, p. 631). How the conflict turns into a dispute and how it is labeled affect how it progresses and whether it escalates and gets worse, leading in extreme cases to war, or is handled, managed, or resolved. This process of conflict being experienced, labeled, and expressed is often called a process of social construction, as different people, groups, and cultures will vary within and among themselves about what they consider a conflict to be and whether and how they will act on their interpretations.

TYPES OF CONFLICTS

Conflict can exist on many different levels, including the intrapersonal, interpersonal, intragroup, intergroup, and international. Conflicts are located in a variety of social contexts (two old friends, family members, neighbors, strangers, consumers and merchants, distant nation-states) and time spans ("one-off" or "one-shot" encounters and conflicts, long-standing or embedded conflicts, and repeated conflicts in ongoing relationships).

Conflicts vary, even within the same social environment or subject matter, according to how the disputants treat the conflict. They may employ a wide variety of strategies, tactics, and behaviors (for example, avoidance, self-help, peaceful negotiation, argument, escalation, physical violence, peace seeking, mediation, or settlement), which will interact in various ways with those chosen by other parties to the conflict. And conflicts are often classified by how they affect the parties in the conflict (the consequences of the conflict) and those outside of the conflict (the "externalities" of the conflict; for example, the children in a marital argument or nations that border warring states).

In an effort to describe and diagnose conflicts so that we can understand and manage them better, the social theorist and psychologist Morton Deutsch has developed a useful typology of conflicts that contrasts objective conditions with parties' perceived concerns.

Veridical Conflict

A veridical conflict is a "true" conflict, with matched perceptions and realities, such as when two or more parties want to use the same scarce resource for different purposes. For example, family members may argue over how a room in a house is to be used, politicians may argue over how a nation's budget should be allocated, or several nations may argue over how the water in a river that runs through all their territories should be used.

Contingent Conflict

In a contingent conflict, perceptions do not match objective reality, and therefore a change in resources or perceptions of the conflict could readily resolve it. In the examples listed for veridical conflicts, for instance, if more rooms, money, or water were available or could be created, multiple or shared uses might be possible. Contingent conflicts are resolvable if the parties can change their perceptions, use creativity to expand resources, or seek resolution from outside their "limited-resources" frame of thinking.

Displaced Conflict

In a displaced conflict, the parties in conflict have manifest, or express, conflicts about one thing when they are really arguing or caring about something different—the underlying conflict. Parents and children may argue about the use of a car, for example, when the "real" conflict is about separation, responsibility, and growing up. Countries may have disputes about borders and land when the "real" dispute is about power, sovereignty, control, and economic well-being or identity.

Misattributed Conflict

In a misattributed conflict, parties pick the wrong people or groups with whom to conflict, or they come into conflict over the wrong issues. For example, siblings may fight with each other when they are really angry at their parents. Similarly, disempowered groups may fight with one another (for instance, conflicts between formerly colonized groups or racial minorities) rather than take on the powerful party that has dominated them. Individuals or groups may feel they are being treated differently (and less well) when the real issue might be a general lack of resources for anyone.

Latent Conflict

A latent conflict is conflict that may be just beneath the surface but is not yet expressed—and perhaps should be. In relationships people may not want to start a fight, so they may suppress things that make them angry, or an

Feuding

Feuding is a form of conflict involving a cycle of killings between men from different kinship groups. These kinship groups can be families, lineages, or clans. Cross-cultural surveys indicate that feuding takes place in about half of the world's societies. Feuds are most common in societies which lack strong, centralized political authority and are usually perceived by participants as a matter of honor–individual, family, or a female's. Not all feuds end in a cycle of violence as in many cases, the feud can be resolved by paying compensation. In 1966 anthropologist Christopher Boehm asked Montenegrins in what was then Yugoslavia to provide definitions of the word osveta, *which means vengeance, but not blood vengeance* (krvna osveta). *Feuding has a long history in the region and the definitions offered suggest that the idea of blood revenge remains a strong component of the concept.*

The late Savo Todorovi, who was well over seventy years old in 1966, explained the meaning of osveta thus: "Osveta, that means . . . a kind of spiritual fulfillment. You have killed my son, so I killed yours; I have taken revenge for that, so I now sit peacefully in my chair. There you are."

My neighbor Bozidar summed up osveta very simply: "Osveta? Osveta. If I come to blows with someone . . . or he kills me, if he deals me a mortal blow, then it is known what must be. Then, he has to die as well. Right away, two people die. Not one but two, necessarily."

The late Milan Baosi, a good friend who died far too young, was a man of few words: "Osveta by my understanding means: if you have killed my brother or father, I look to take vengeance and so I kill one of 'yours.'"

My friend Jovan also gave a very brief definition: "Osveta means . . . when you have killed my brother, then I must kill you. That is the meaning of osveta."

Anica, the wife of an excellent singer of heroic epics, gave a long response which began: "Osveta means if you strike me a blow, I do the same for you and there you are: I have taken revenge. Just like those Turks and the Montenegrins in the old days."

A more vivid description came from my landlord, who was also a major political leader of Upper Moraca tribe: "Osveta means people in some way have words with each other, or something, and seek vengeance. It comes under osveta when two men quarrel, one hits the other either with a stake or a rock or with his fist, or they shoot it out with pistols, one falls dead, and then osveta takes place if he is avenged. . . ."

A very dear friend and neighbor, a mild woman who dearly loved little animals, gave the following response, which I decided to follow up with some additional questions once I had secured her uninfluenced initial response: "Eh, osveta! Perhaps someone kills my brother, and then I kill that one. . . ."

Source: Boehm, Christopher. (1984). *Blood Revenge: The Anthropology of Feuding in Montenegro and Other Tribal Societies.* Lawrence: University Press of Kansas, pp. 54–55.

employee may be afraid to express dissatisfaction with a working condition or assignment. If the latent conflict is not expressed, the situation may actually get worse.

False Conflict

Parties may create conflicts or disputes without an objective reason for them, especially if there are generally bad relations between the parties or if one party prefers conflictual states of unrest or activity to relative peace. In situations of opposition (employer-employee, parent-child, academic or sports competition), disputes or conflicts may develop over minor or even major issues when there is no real reason to be in a dispute.

Other Systems of Classification

Conflicts have also been classified by various social scientists and conflict theorists by virtue of what is at stake in the conflict, such as resources (land, money, power, property, or natural resources such as water, oil, or minerals, among others), values or beliefs (regarding, for example, class, religion, nationality, and politics), preferences or interests (as when people have incompatible desires or incompatible objectives), relationships, and identity (concerns about recognition of and respect for individual and group reputations and memberships). The theory of such classifications is that if we can analyze different kinds of conflict, we can determine how they might unfold and whether a particular conflict is amenable to a positive outcome or not.

CONFLICT PROCESSES

Given the different types of conflicts that may occur and the different subject matter that may spark them, theorists are interested in discovering whether there are generalizable principles or patterns that may explain how conflict develops and is expressed and resolved. While some see almost universal principles developing, so that it is almost always easier to escalate than to de-escalate a conflict, others see situational, interpersonal, and cultural variations in how conflict is experienced and expressed.

Conflicts often follow a fairly predictable pattern, beginning with a precipitating event, followed by a response or reaction, then development of in-group and out-group loyalties and both offensive and defensive strategies, then escalation, impasse, or stalemate, and finally resolution, settlement, and solution seeking (or, in highly competitive or violent conflicts, victory for one party and defeat or annihilation for the other). But while many think of conflicts as necessarily competitive and antagonistic, there really are a wider range of behaviors that occur in most conflict situations, many of them dependent on the situation and social and political environment of the conflict, as well as the sophistication of the parties in using multiple strategies.

People's approaches to conflict are many and varied. The scholar Kenneth Thomas has observed that there are those who compete (or seek to maximize their own self-interest, even at the expense of others), those who cooperate (seeking to work with the other side[s] to find some middle or compromise grounds), those who accommodate (who may simply give in to the other party), those who avoid (by exiting or absenting themselves from the conflict), and those who collaborate (by seeking to work for joint and mutual gains for all parties, without unnecessary harm to others or needless compromise or giving in).

What makes conflict processes so complex are the interactions between the various strategies. The different conflict management strategies interact and can produce reactive and unhelpful responses, such as spiraling competition, with escalation of competitive behavior causing more violence, less information sharing, and an inability to seek mutual gain. This mirroring effect, when each party merely returns the behavior that is offered to it, often leads to stalemates and a failure to achieve resolution, because the parties cannot see or hear beyond the one strategy they have chosen.

Thus, much recent empirical work in conflict processes has studied the conditions under which parties in conflict can alter their behavioral or strategy choices. Among the types of conflicts that have been studied are those involving community relations, ethnic or racial relations, economic and resource competition, environmental disputes, lawsuits (both individual and class actions), and international relations. Parties in conflict are now asked to explore their underlying interests (apart from their conflict-producing positions), to consider the needs and interests of the other parties (using role-reversals and other communication techniques), and to develop strategies of collaborative and creative problem solving (by expanding and creating resources and alternatives, by trading preferences—that is, things that they value or prefer differently—or goods that are not mutually exclusive, by using contingent or trial agreements instead of permanent solutions, by developing processes and rules for respectful coexistence).

Both modern research and recent history have demonstrated the importance of third-party intervention by, for example, mediators, conciliators, fact-finders, and facilitators who can guide the structuring of conflict resolution processes. These third-party efforts have all levels of conflict in developing both interim "ceasefires" and more permanent resolutions or agreements to end conflicts and to attempt to resolve larger underlying problems and conflicts.

New generations of actors, from schoolchildren (in peer mediation programs) to neighbors (in community mediation boards) to professional mediators and political leaders, diplomats, and institutions, are studying conflict theory and conflict resolution processes to learn more effective methods of resolving and managing conflict. They are looking for creative solutions to human conflicts. As conflict resolution has become an area of research and training, we have learned that conflict is more variable and complex than just two people or nations having a dispute. There are more sophisticated ways of analyzing and diagnosing the structure and dynamics of conflict and greater possibilities for using, managing, and resolving conflicts. As a field of study and practice, conflict theory is multidisciplinary, drawing from many social sciences, including psychology, political science, economics, sociology, law, anthropology, and strategic studies, and other interdisciplinary fields, such as peace studies and communications. Its contributions to human knowledge about how conflicts occur and what can be done about them are relatively recent. The applicability of conflict theory to a wide variety of human interactions (in the family, workplace, community, and between nation-states) is now being tested.

—Carrie Menkel-Meadow

See also Conflict Resolution

Further Reading

Coser, L. (1956). *The functions of social conflict.* New York: Free Press.

Deutsch, M. (1973). *The resolution of conflict: Constructive and destructive processes.* New Haven, CT: Yale University Press.

Deutsch, M., & Coleman, P. T. (Eds.). (2000). *The handbook of conflict resolution: Theory and practice.* San Francisco: Jossey-Bass.

Felstiner, W. L. F., Abel, R., & Sarat, A. (1980–1981). The emergence and transformation of disputes: Naming, blaming, claiming. . . . *Law & Society Review, 15*(3–4), 631–654.

Pruitt D. G., & Rubin, J. Z. (1986). *Social conflict: Escalation, stalemate and settlement.* New York: Random House.

Ross, M. H. (1993). *The management of conflict: Interpretations and interests in comparative perspective.* New Haven, CT: Yale University Press.

Simmel, G. (1955). *Conflict and the web of group affiliations.* New York: Free Press.

Thomas, K. (1976). Conflict and conflict management. In M. D. Dunnette (Ed.), *Handbook of industrial and organizational psychology* (pp. 889–936). Chicago: Rand McNally.

CONFORMITY

Conformity (acting in accordance with prevailing standards or customs) involves a mental calculus by which socially supplied information is integrated with direct sensory inputs and prior experience in coming to a judgment or action. When confronted with an unfamiliar situation that requires a response, people typically consider three broad sources of information: past experience, direct perceptions of the important or relevant features of the context, and information supplied by others. The extent to which people integrate socially supplied information with more direct sensory inputs (perceptions or past experiences) establishes the extent of conformity in the particular context.

Conformity is an active, dynamic, process that is based on an analysis of the relative reliability of self- versus other-supplied data and the costs and rewards entailed in placing greater or lesser weight on information supplied by others. The greater the weight accorded socially supplied data over one's own direct perceptions, the greater the conformity. In some circumstances (e.g., those that involve little prior experience, high stakes, and high levels of ambiguity), a high degree of conformity makes sense—assuming that the individual(s) supplying the information have had prior experience in the setting or in some other ways appear expert. In other circumstances, overweighting socially supplied cues represents an attempt to ingratiate oneself with attractive or powerful others, to avoid sanction and maintain a position in a group. In this case, which involves compliance rather than conformity, the underlying cognitive dynamics are different.

COMPLIANCE VERSUS CONFORMITY

The distinction between compliance and conformity was most forcefully drawn by Festinger (1953), who defined public compliance as behavior involving acquiescence to the demands of the influence source, without any real acceptance of the source's position. Public compliance occurs because a source of influence has power or control over the fate or resources of the other and can monitor actions to ensure that the desired behavior is enacted. People are motivated to maintain consistency with the influence source (be it an individual or a group) because of the source's power to reward and punish. Public compliance, in short, involves people bringing their public behavior (but not their beliefs) in line with the demands of the influence source.

Private acceptance, or conformity, involves the internalization of the influence source's position. Conformity, or conversion, as it also is called, occurs when characteristics of the influence source suggest that its information is valid. This information about the appropriate action is accepted, or internalized, and becomes a part of the individual's behavioral repertoire. In the absence of forces to the contrary, this internalized information continues to guide actions even in the absence of the source that originally provided it. Conformity behavior is persistent and represents the individual's perception of appropriate behavior; hence, unlike compliance, conformity behavior persists even in the absence of surveillance by the original influence source.

PUBLIC COMPLIANCE VERSUS PRIVATE ACCEPTANCE

The distinction between public compliance and private acceptance is important for predicting the persistence of induced behaviors. A person who advocates a position solely in response to social pressure ceases to do so when the pressure is removed, or when the influence source is unable to monitor his or her behavior. But if people advocate a position because they believe it to be valid, they continue to advocate it even when the agent of influence is no longer present and thus has no ability to monitor the individual.

Asch (1955) provided the best-known example of laboratory-induced compliance. In his research, partici-

Adolescent Conformity

This passage comes from a young adult novel of the early twentieth century, best known for its lyrical nature writing and evocation of the delicate beauties of an endangered wetland region, Indiana's Limberlost swamp. Here we see the difficulties facing an impoverished country girl on her first day at the high school in town because she is dressed differently and doesn't know the rules of the community she is trying to join.

Elnora stood before the entrance and stared into the largest room she ever had seen. The floor sloped down to a awning stage on which a band of musicians, grouped around a grand piano, were tuning their instruments. She had two fleeting impressions. That it was all a mistake; this was no school, but a grand display of enormous ribbon bows; and the second, that she was sinking, and had forgotten how to walk. Then a burst from the orchestra nerved her while a bevy of daintily clad, sweet-smelling things that might have been birds, or flowers, or possibly gaily dressed, happy young girls pushed her forward. She found herself plodding across the back of the auditorium, praying for guidance, to an empty seat.

As the girls passed her, vacancies seemed to open to meet them. Their friends were moving over, beckoning and whispering invitations. Everyone else was seated, but no one paid any attention to the white-faced girl stumbling half-blindly down the aisle next the farthest wall. So she went on the very end facing the stage. No one moved and she could not summon courage to crowd past others to several empty seats she saw. At the end of the aisle she paused in desperation, as she stared back at the whole forest of faces most of which were now turned upon her.

In one burning flash came the full realization of her scanty dress, her pitiful little hat and ribbon, her big, heavy shoes, her ignorance of where to go or what to do; and from a sickening wave which crept over her, she felt she was going to become ill.

Source: Porter, Gene Stratton. (1991). *A Girl of the Limberlost.* New York: Gramercy Books, pp. 7–8.

pants viewed a stimulus line and a set of three comparison lines. Their job was to judge which of the three comparison lines matched the stimulus. The judgments were exceptionally easy. However, when naive participants were paired with experimental accomplices who gave an obviously wrong answer on six (of twelve) judgment trials, more than three-quarters of all participants agreed at least once with the accomplices. Put another way, about one-third of all influence attempts were successful, even though the correct answer was transparently obvious. There is good reason to believe the errant judgments did not represent participants' true perceptions. In postexperimental interviews, many admitted that they had merely gone along with the confederates to avoid conflict or in order not to appear stupid to their (supposed) peers.

Later research suggests that different processes operate in conformity. In research designed to mimic Asch's conceptually, Crano (1970) had participants make a series of difficult perceptual estimates in tandem with an experimental accomplice whose answers were consistently biased. After a series of thirty paired judgments, participants made another series of judgments, but this time their answers were made privately, in writing. If accomplices were introduced as experts who had prior success at the task, their influence was immediately apparent on the public trials, and it persisted in the private-judgment context, even though the alleged expert could not monitor the naive participant's responses. Evidently, the respondents had internalized the expert's point of view and used it even when the expert was functionally out of the picture.

Factors that appear to matter most in generating compliance or conformity are ambiguity, the importance of the judgment, and the apparent validity of the socially supplied information. Greater ambiguity regarding the proper action usually leads to greater compliance and conformity. Information perceived as valid has an immediate and continuing effect; paradoxically, the more important the judgment, the more likely people are to conform, given information deemed reliable. Whether the influence source is powerful (as in Asch) or is an underrepresented minority, unanimity of the influence source is critical in inducing compliance or conformity. Lack of unanimity destroys the effect.

CONFORMITY AND CONTEXT

Conformity is context-specific. Very little evidence suggests that individuals are consistently conformist or independent. In some circumstances, women appear more compliant than men, but in others, the opposite is the case. Differences in the perception of expertise appear to determine susceptibility or resistance. People might conform to a person deemed an authority on a topic about which they know little. Those who are well informed on an issue, however, are unlikely to take the bait. As presented here, conformity is a process, it is not a state of being.

—*William D. Crano*

Further Reading

Asch, S. E. (1955). Opinions and social pressure. *Scientific American, 193,* 31–35.

Crano, W. D. (1970). Effects of sex, response order, and expertise in conformity: A dispositional approach. *Sociometry, 33,* 239–252.

Festinger, L. (1953). An analysis of compliance behavior. In M. Sherif & M. O. Wilson (Eds.), *Group relations at the crossroads* (pp. 100–114). New York: Harper.

Moscovici, S. (1985). Innovation and minority influence. In G. Lindzey & E. Aronson (Eds.), *The handbook of social psychology* (Vol. 2, 3d ed., pp. 347–412). New York: Random House.

CONFUCIANISM

Confucius (551–479 BCE) is the sage who formulated the teachings (*jiao* in Chinese) that shaped Chinese culture and community. He is known in China as "Kung the Master." Appalled by the social disorder of his time, Confucius set out to construct a social teaching—a deliberate tradition—that would bring stability and harmony to society. He was not successful in his own lifetime, but within a century of his death his teachings had come to permeate Chinese life and culture.

At the heart of his teachings were the Five Great (or Five Constant) Relationships: the relationships between parent and child, husband and wife, elder sibling and junior sibling, elder friend and junior friend, and ruler and subject. In these relationships there is a propriety *(li)* that should be observed. The parent is to love the child, the child to revere the parent. The elder sibling should be gentle, the younger respectful. Husbands should be good, and wives should listen to them. Elder friends are to be considerate and younger friends deferential. The ruler should be benevolent and subjects loyal. If propriety was observed in these relationships, then, Confucius argued, there would be peace and harmony in the family and in the society. It was the family that was central to Confucius' vision of social harmony and community. Some have even referred to Confucianism as familialism.

For Confucians, the whole community included the dead, the living, and the yet unborn. The well-known Chinese practice of venerating ancestors was foundational for the Confucian social ethic. It linked those who had gone before to the living generation, centered in the family. Thus maintaining proper relationships among the living, all of whom were situated in families, was the way to create a harmonious society for the yet unborn. Even the relationship of the ruler and the subject was understood as a type of filial piety.

Education was also central to the Confucian vision. The Confucian ideal was the scholar. Scholars were learned; they cultivated the practices that let the fullness of their humanity unfold. Scholarship, music, and poetry were the arts of the sage.

Confucianism, developed by Confucius's successors, came to dominate Chinese culture and was adopted by other East Asian peoples. It remained central to the Chinese cultural mindset into the twentieth century, when it came under attack, especially during the Cultural Revolution (1966–1976). There is evidence of a resurgence of Confucian thought within the People's Republic of China beginning in the late 1990s. Contemporary Confucian scholars, such as Tu Wei-Ming of Harvard University, have exhibited the continuing vitality of Confucian thought.

—*M. Darrol Bryant*

Further Reading

de Bary, W. T., Bloom, I., Lufrano, R. (1999). *Sources of Chinese tradition* (Vols. 1–2, 2nd ed.). New York: Columbia University Press.

Thompson, L. G. (1996). *Chinese religion* (5th ed.). Belmont, CA: Wadsworth.

Wei-Ming, T. (1985). *Confucian thought: Selfhood as creative transformation.* Albany: State University of New York Press.

Yang, C. K. (1994). *Religion in Chinese society.* Taipei, Taiwan: SMC Publishing.

CONGREGATIONS, RELIGIOUS

A religious congregation, as a voluntary association, is an assembly of people organized together for the purpose of religious worship, religious education, and other faith-based activities. Those involved typically reside in relatively close geographic proximity and share common religious beliefs, rituals, and ideologies. The term *congregation* has been used primarily to refer to Christian religious communities, but it can be expanded to refer also to other religious traditions. It can, for instance, be interchanged with terms such as *parish, local church, mission, synagogue, mosque, reli-*

gious order community, and *religious commune.* In examining religious congregations, this entry draws on examples from the United States, but most of the observations are applicable to religious congregations in other countries as well.

The congregational approach to religion is evident both in Christian and non-Christian faith traditions. This model of religious life emphasizes voluntary membership, lay involvement in decision making, professional clergy, de-emphasis on denominationalism, financial support from members, community center development, and social service provision.

In the United States, the U.S. Census Bureau began collecting religious data in 1850 but ended the practice in 1936. Thus, no comprehensive list of congregations in the United States is currently available. However, several major studies have been conducted during the past decade using sample data of religious congregations. (These include the National Congregations Study, the Faith Communities Today Study, U.S. Congregational Life Survey, Religious Congregations Membership Study, and the *Yearbook of American and Canadian Churches.*) Our knowledge of religious congregations is based largely on such studies.

CHARACTERISTICS OF CONGREGATION MEMBERS

More Americans belong to religious congregations than to any other type of voluntary association. Women comprise a larger proportion of congregations (61 percent) than do men (39 percent). The highest percentage of congregation members is drawn from people between the ages of forty-six and sixty-four, with fifty being the average age. Over half of all participants (58 percent) are employed either full- or part-time. They are more likely to be retired than the average nonparticipant. Participants tend to be well educated, and are drawn from all income brackets. Individuals involved in congregational life are more likely to be married (66 percent) than the average American (52 percent), and half attend worship services with their spouse. Individuals with children are more likely to attend religious services.

Racial and ethnic characteristics tend to mirror the U.S. population. Congregational membership tends to reflect the demographic composition of the congregation's location. Those most committed to increasing their racial and ethnic diversity tend to be located in metropolitan areas. Commutes to one's congregational facility tend to be close. Approximately 61 percent of congregations draw at least half of their membership from within a ten-minute drive.

NUMBER, SIZE, AND LOCATION OF CONGREGATIONS

The number of congregations in the United States is estimated at between 300,000 and 350,000. Whereas the number of mainstream Protestant congregations declined during the last third of the twentieth century, the number of evangelical Protestant congregations grew. Roman Catholic congregations also experienced numeric decline, whereas the number of congregations of other faith groups, such as Latter-Day Saints (Mormons), Baha'i, and Muslims, grew dramatically.

America's congregations tend to be small, with a median of 75 regular participants. Only about 10 percent of congregations have more than 350 regular participants. However, not all congregations are small, as evidenced by the number of large Catholic parishes and the emergence of megachurches (discussed below). On average, Catholic congregations tend to be larger than Jewish, Muslim, or Protestant Christian congregations. Urban and suburban congregations tend to be larger than those in rural areas.

About 52 percent of congregations are in small towns and rural areas, 25 percent in suburbs, and 23 percent in cities. However, two-thirds of growing congregations are in suburbs with the largest amount of growth in the West and South. The fastest growing congregations are the megachurches, followed by Muslim, Latter-Day Saints, and Assemblies of God congregations. Congregations grew by stressing cultural affinity, engaging in community involvement, having an organizational focus, offering both care and moral standards for members, finding inspiration in worship, and offering promotional programs.

MEGACHURCHES

Megachurches emerged in the last two decades of the twentieth century. They are typically very large Protestant congregations, often with as many as 2,000 to 25,000 attendees. Although most of the more than 2,300 megachurches tend to hold conservative, evangelical Christian theological positions, several are from Catholic, Muslim, and other faith traditions. They employ charismatic, authoritative senior clergy, offer active programming throughout the week, are involved in a broad range of social and outreach ministries, and have a complex differentiated organizational structure. Megachurches typically are not highly liturgical, but focus on contemporary worship styles. Christian megachurches value the relevance of the Bible and put less emphasis on creeds and denominational doctrines. Nearly three-quarters of the megachurches are located in the suburbs of southern and western U.S. cities. Megachurches are an international phenomenon, located in a wide variety of places such as Canada, Latvia, the Philippines, South Africa, and South America. Half of the world's fifty largest megachurches are reported to be in South Korea, including the Yoido Full Gospel Church, which is the world's largest with 750,000 members.

Church and Friends

The excerpt below makes a compelling case for church-going as a community-building activity.

In fact, a lot of this amounts to saying that I miss church. You non-church-goers should know that Church As I Knew It, in the middle of the road, was nothing like Elmer Gantry. No one cried, and if you pushed people on what they believed, a lot of them were more vague than dogmatic—something about God existing, something about Jesus being special, something about modified altruism being better than pure selfishness. A lot of what was happening was people with lots of non-religious values in common (political conservatism, family life) getting together once a week to hang out. It was a nice place to hang out. If you didn't like grownups, you could volunteer to hang out with children without having to actually have any. If you didn't like big crowds, you could volunteer for the cleanup or preparation committee and hang out with other people who didn't like crowds and sort of liked shit work in a way, like the volunteers at the Jamboree. Also you could find out if you wanted to be friends with people without doing something artificial like going out to lunch.

What my new friends and I all have in common is that we don't have as many friends as we would if we were born sooner because we've renounced most institutions and are left with making friend at work or by inviting people we've met casually out to lunch. I find that un-ideal because it makes my stomach hurt and because if you take someone to lunch you just get each other's stories, but if you set up folding chairs together, you find out what people are really like and if you really like them.

Sixties leftovers have never really built a lowkey institution to hang out together at, and make friends at and casually bullshit about what to do next at. I think that's partly because compulsory education crippled us. We were in communities organized by grownups for so long we never learned to organize our own.

Source: Herbert, Ann. (1986). "Honest Hope." In *Ten Years of CoEvolution Quarterly, News That Stayed News, 1974–1984,* edited by Art Kleiner & Stewart Brand. San Francisco: North Point Press, pp. 138–139.

RELIGIOUS ORDERS AND COMMUNES

Religious orders and religious communes play a more all-encompassing role in the lives of their members than other religious congregations typically play in the lives of their members. Religious orders are often based on a history of monastic life and tradition. Members generally share a common life based on public vows, live in close proximity to one another, are committed for life to the order, recognize an accepted community status order, and have the power to exclude individuals from the group if they wish. Religious orders are commonly found in the Roman Catholic, Anglican, Episcopalian, and Buddhist faiths.

A religious commune, or a religious intentional community, differs from a religious order in that religious communes are more voluntaristic. Religious intentional communities also tend to base daily life more on the consensus of their members than on established traditional rules. Although some religious intentional communities were established during the communal movement of the 1960s, others are Anabaptist groups with roots in the Protestant Reformation of the 1500s. Religious intentional communities are based on ideals counter to popular culture and society and are characterized by a distinct religious style and form of expression. Examples of religious intentional communities include the Amish and Hutterites.

ACTIVITIES AND PROGRAMS

Worship is the central activity of religious congregations and is the most highly attended of all the activities they offer. Congregations offer worship services at various times throughout the week. Typical worship services of nearly all religious traditions include liturgy, scripture readings, music, a sermon or speech, and a collection of money donations. One change in Christian

St. Mark's Presbyterian Church in Kiowa, Colorado, in June 1998.
Source: Gary Goreham; used with permission.

worship predominant in the last quarter of the twentieth century has been in musical style, instrumentation, and presentation. The diversity of worship music tends to increase with the size of the congregation.

Religious congregations seek to form and nurture their members' faith by responding to spiritual and religious needs. Additionally, they attempt to meet members' physical, emotional, and social needs, and offer members a sense of belonging and identity. Congregational activities are quite similar across faith traditions and include scripture study, religious education, social events, self-help groups, sports teams, prayer and meditation groups, choral and instrumental groups, community service, discussion groups, spiritual retreats, summer camps, parent and marriage enrichment programs, youth groups, and young-adult or singles groups. The size and wealth of the congregation often affect the breadth of programs and activities offered.

Congregations use a variety of outreach approaches. They sponsor thrift shops, offer day care and health clinics, provide goods and services for families and members in an emergency or crisis, volunteer at or sponsor soup kitchens and homeless shelters, participate in humanitarian projects such as Habitat for Humanity, and support various activities promoting social justice and social ministry, often on an ecumenical basis.

Congregations are multifaceted, with varying emphases on education, evangelism, stewardship, community involvement, individual salvation, and social responsibility. Successful congregations tend to be ones that focus on the future rather than on heritage or the past; the former approach attracts teenagers and youth.

THEOLOGY

A religious congregation's theology guides and motivates its activities. Its theology is evident in its narratives, practices, and texts. Congregational narratives include church time lines, stories of significant leaders, and the congregation's history. Practices include the design of the congregation's physical space, patterns of worship and gathering, types of special occasions, and methods of outreach. The congregation's texts include scripture, mission statements, educational curricula, and promotional materials.

Theological differences within the congregation can be a significant source of conflict among congregational leaders and members and among generations. Conflict can be based on members' roles within the congregation, motivations for joining or staying in the congregation, and larger denominational and doctrinal issues. Acceptance of new forms of contemporary worship has been linked to increased vitality, growth in membership, and financial stability in the congregation. Conflict over worship tends to be compounded in congregations with reduced financial resources and is more likely to occur in inner-city congregations.

The role the congregation plays in the community results from its theology. According to research by sociologists David Roozen, William McKinney, and Jackson Carroll, congregations relate to the community in four ways. A sanctuary orientation sees the congregation as a sacred, safe haven from the world. An evangelistic orientation focuses on individual salvation and changing the world one person at a time. An activist orientation seeks to alleviate suffering and injustice in the world. Finally, a civic orientation focuses on preserving what is good and righteous in the world.

IDENTITY AND DENOMINATIONAL AFFILIATION

Religious congregations are one source of identity for their members. Catholic priest and sociologist Andrew Greeley sees denominationalism as providing its member with a sense of "who they are and where they stand in a large and complex society" (Greeley 1972, p. 108). Similarly, being a member of a religious congregation brings a sense of belonging and commitment with like-minded fellow members, as well as a sense of shared purpose.

A congregation's denomination affects both its source of authority and style of worship. Baptists and

Muslims place a high value on the authority of scripture. Orthodox Christians, Lutherans, Episcopalians, and Latter-Day Saints place a high value on creed, doctrine, and tradition. Jewish congregations and Universal Unitarians place a high value on human reason. Congregations that have a strong denominational affiliation are more likely to have stronger financial stability and place a higher value on tradition, creed, and doctrine.

A congregation is sometimes used to maintain ethnic, racial, or national identity. Immigrant congregations, in particular, help newcomers maintain their cultural identity in a new land. Immigrant congregations often become community centers for immigrant populations where individuals socialize with ethnically similar individuals and retain ethnic values and customs while learning the skills they need in their new country.

Not all congregations are denominationally affiliated; many are independent and nonaffiliated. According to a study carried out by Carl Dudley and David Roozen under the auspices of the Hartford Seminary's Hartford Institute for Religion Research, approximately 35,000 nondenominational and independent churches are located throughout the United States. The worship and musical style of nondenominational congregations tend to take on a contemporary electronic approach. They mirror denominational congregations in size, worship, and activities. Some nondenominational congregations affiliate with a larger network, fellowship, or association (for example, IFCA International, formerly Independent Fundamental Churches of America). A majority of nondenominational congregations participate with other nondenominational congregations for worship and social ministry.

GOVERNANCE

Congregations typically have at least one full- or part-time ordained professional religious leader, with a title such as rabbi, pastor, priest, imam, clergy, or reader. Religious leaders take on various roles in the congregation, including organizer, administrator, worship leader, preacher, counselor, and advocate in the local community. The religious leader's education can be formal or informal, and it often has a direct impact on the mission and function of the congregation.

The form of governance for Christian congregations varies among denominations. Episcopal governance is characterized by authority resting with the congregations' clergy and with higher-ranking clergy. Presbyterian governance is characterized by authority that rests with representative committees of clergy and church members. Congregational governance is characterized by authority that resides in local church members and with their representatives, who meet periodically at regional or national conventions or assemblies. Establishing a congregation varies among the faith traditions. Ten Jewish persons can form a congregation and call themselves a synagogue. Islamic adherents may meet informally for prayer in one of the member's homes before they rent a larger meeting place or construct a mosque.

CONGREGATIONAL FACILITIES

Most congregations hold their services in a building specially dedicated to that purpose, but others may meet in school buildings, storefronts, or community centers. Most congregations own their facilities, but some rent space or meet in free areas or buildings. Congregations typically support themselves financially through individual contributions, trust funds, bequests, investments, donations, or rental fees for use of their facility.

The facility the congregation occupies has a direct impact on its mission and ministry. While most facilities have enough space for worship, many congregations lack space for fellowship and education. Growing suburban congregations tend to have the greatest need for additional space. Rural and small-town congregations may have the space and facilities, but declining memberships and limited financial resources may lead to difficulty maintaining the facility. One solution has been to use the extra facility space to support rural health and social services.

ECUMENISM AND COOPERATION

Ecumenism, particularly among the various Christian denominations, has been an ever-increasing trend in the United States throughout the twentieth century and into the twenty-first. Many Christian congregations cross denominational boundaries to cooperate with each other for worship, activities, or social ministry. Although ecumenical social ministry is the most common form of cooperation between congregations, many congregations also cooperate for worship. Approximately 45 percent of Christian congregations participate in ecumenical worship, and 8 percent participate in interfaith worship. Ecumenism can lead to organic mergers of two or more congregations. Blending religious groups with differing histories, theologies, and social constituencies can be difficult due to conflicts over forms of congregational government, views of the ministry, and views on the nature and functions of religious rituals.

Cooperative ministry structures can take on various forms. Examples of cooperative ministry structures include the consolidated churches, federated churches, yoked parishes, larger/area parishes, multiple-charge churches, cluster groups, ecumenical shared ministry, and shared facilities. Each structure differs according to the degree of consolidation, denominational makeup, the type of congregational governance used, and the extent of shared facilities, resources, activities, and staff. Cooperative ministry structures are often established for economic reasons, declining memberships, the need to pool resources, and stronger community ministry and mission.

The Catholic Church and most mainline Protestant denominations maintain a commitment to ecumenical efforts among Christian denominations and with non-Christian faith groups. Nevertheless, although unity among people of faith in matters of social service has tremendous potential, particularly at the local congregational level through cooperative shared ministries, organizational uniting is highly unlikely for the immediate future. Even as conflict between faith groups diminishes, splintering within them seems inevitable. The future appears brightest as local congregations build meaning, belonging, and identity for their members and as they work cooperatively on community ministries with other local congregations.

—Nicole J. Meidinger and Gary A. Goreham

See also Cooperative Parish Ministries

Further Reading

Ammerman, N., Carroll, J. W.; Dudley, C. S., Eiesland, N. L., McKinney, W., Schreiter, R. L., et al. (1998). *Studying congregations: A new handbook.* Nashville, TN: Abingdon.

Dudley, C. S., & Roozen, D. A. (2000). *Faith communities today: A report on religion in the United States today.* Retrieved September 12, 2002, from http://fact.hartsem.edu/Final%20FACTrpt.pdf

Greeley, A. M. (1972). *The denominational society: A sociological approach to religion in America.* Glenview, IL: Scott, Foresman.

Hartford Institute for Religion Research. (2000). *The national congregations study.* Retrieved September 12, 2002, from http://hirr.hartsem.edu/org/faith_congregations_research_ncs.html.

Hopewell, J. (1987). *Congregation: Stories and structure.* Philadelphia: Fortress.

Lindner, E. W. (Ed.). (2002). *Yearbook of American and Canadian churches, 2002* (70th ed.). Nashville, TN: Abingdon.

Roozen, D. A., McKinney, W., & Carroll, J. W. (1984). *Varieties of religious presence.* New York: Pilgrim.

Sanchagrin, K. (2002). *Religious congregations and membership in the U.S. 2000.* Nashville, TN: Glenmary Research Center.

Woolever, C., & Bruce, D. (2002). *A field guide to U.S. congregations: Who's going where and why.* Louisville, KY: Westminster John.

CONGRÈS INTERNATIONAUX D'ARCHITECTURE MODERNE

The Congrès Internationaux d'Architecture Moderne (International Congresses of Modern Architecture, or CIAM) was an association of avant-garde architects founded in 1928 to advance an international modern architecture and urbanism. The congresses, attended by European delegates and, to a limited degree, by delegates from North and South America, met eleven times from the 1928 organizational meeting at La Sarraz, Switzerland, until CIAM disbanded at Otterlo, the Netherlands, in 1959. Each congress was planned in several meetings of the Comité International pour la Réalisation des Problemes d'Architecture Contemporaine (International Committee for the Implementation of Contemporary Architecture, or CIRPAC). Through extensive conversations held both at the preparatory meetings and at the congresses themselves, and with the help of exhibitions, publications, and news reports, CIAM's participants examined and articulated the purposes of a radical, twentieth-century architecture and urbanism.

CIAM claimed that contemporary building should be derived from industrialization, thus rational and standardized; and that it should be shaped by political and economic realities, therefore an agent of social change. The La Sarraz declaration stated, "Urbanism is the organization of all the functions of collective life" (Mumford 2000, p. 25), and advanced the notion of a functional order consisting of dwelling, production, transportation, and recreation. The 1929 congress in Frankfurt focused on the minimal housing unit (Die Wohnung für das Existenzminimum, or "minimal housing unit"); the 1930 congress in Brussels considered effective land use for housing projects (Rationelle Bebauungsweisen, or "rational development manner"); and the 1933 congress, held on board the SS *Patris II* en route between Marseilles and Athens, examined the functional city, and became more widely known through Spanish architect Jose Luis Sert's 1942 publication, *Can Our Cities Survive?* and the 1943 publication by Swiss architect Le Corbusier, *La Charte d'Athënes* (*The Athens Charter*). Though deliberations were often fraught with diverse opinions, the main lines of argument claimed that contemporary society was in flux, changing from a family-based structure to a more egalitarian one of individual citizens operating within a setting of cooperatives and communal law. Housing needs under these new conditions would be best met by high-rise slab apartment buildings, rationally arranged on large sites and acting as the central element of urban organization. Urban design on a human scale (a range of dimensions related to the proportions of the human body) was to "assure individual liberty and the benefits of collective action" (Mumford 2000, p. 87).

If the first two congresses were dominated by the attitudes of tough German realists with socialist leanings, the next two considered urban design as a set of generalized propositions. The Athens charter, developed in 1933 but not published until 1943, promoted idealistic and unrealizable functional zoning; CIAM 5 (Paris, 1937) considered historic structures and the larger regions surrounding cities.

After World War II, new sensibilities entered into CIAM deliberations, and participants became interested in creating a physical environment that would both satisfy people's emotional and material needs and also stimulate their spiritual growth. CIAM 8, which was titled "The Heart of the City," was held in 1951 in Hoddesdon, Great Britain, and was the most significant postwar meeting. It addressed the urban core on the basis of the complexities of human association and with a belief in the achievements possible through cooperative action. Building on this base for CIAM 10, which was held in 1956 in Dubrovnik, Yugoslavia, a faction of younger architects identified as "Team X" opposed the functional categories of the Athens Charter. In their place, they advanced notions of human association and spiritual growth in terms of the cluster: "The problem of cluster is one of developing a distinct total structure of each community, and not one of sub-dividing a community into parts" (Mumford 2000, p. 252). A sense of belonging, identity, and neighborliness were the critical values to be promoted. To pursue them, it was argued, would require a new way of thinking about and operating on the city. . Three years later in the meeting held in Otterlo, after extensive debate by its members about whether or not the organization had served its purposes, CIAM was formally dissolved.

—Christian F. Otto

Further Reading

Le Corbusier (1973). *The Athens Charter.* New York: HarperCollins. (Original work published 1943)

Mumford, E. (2000). *The CIAM discourse on urbanism, 1928–1960.* Cambridge, MA: MIT Press.

Sert, J. L. (1942). *Can our cities survive?* Cambridge, MA: Harvard University Press.

Steinmann, M. (Ed.). (1979). *CIAM: Dokumente 1928–1939.* Basel and Stuttgart, Germany: Birkhäuser.

CONSUMER CULTURE

The term *consumer culture* denotes the many ways in which material goods lend symbolic meaning to social arrangements. Material goods such as clothing, food and drink, movies and comic books, dwellings, and automobiles do not simply fulfill basic needs but also serve as symbolic materials through which we interpret our world and understand our lives. Symbolic materials may be the filaments of group solidarity when mutual tastes and consumption patterns form cultural common ground (as in ethnic or religious groups). Conversely, symbolic materials may serve as the currency of status competition when they are used to establish social standing ("keeping up with the Joneses"). Or individuals may use symbolic materials as resources for self-actualization and personal satisfaction (such as those who collect antiques for a hobby). In each of these instances, consumer culture shapes the values and ideals of consumers and communicates them to others.

Consumer culture has the ability to both aid and undermine the development of community. On the one hand, material goods aid in creating categorical differences, commemorating events, and establishing uniqueness, all of which are essential for producing and reproducing a sense of community. On the other hand, historically high levels of consumption are sometimes understood to be a threat to community because the more time and energy that is spent on shopping, the less that is left for noncommodified civic activities. For this reason, critics of consumer society associate rising levels of consumption with declines in civic association and religious activities.

Consumer culture has undergone momentous change since the industrial revolution. It has increasingly been dominated by the consumption of commodities, or goods produced for market, and supported by the economic structures and institutions of industrial societies including mass production techniques, improved transportation and communication infrastructures, wage labor, and increased leisure time. Karl Marx used the term *commodification* to describe a gradual change from production for individual consumption to the production of commodities for exchange in a money economy. While material culture has always been a major area of cultural activity, only within the past 200 years have the forces of industrial production made the commodity the centerpiece of consumer culture.

Three factors make the industrial revolution a watershed for consumer culture. First, it set the basic model of standardized, mass-produced, widely distributed goods that continues to dominate consumer culture today. Second, the industrial revolution made workers dependent on markets for satisfying their needs and desires. Third, the deadening routine of industrial work (as well as routine office work) causes workers to look to consumption and leisure for meaning and satisfaction. As a result, consumer culture has become both more democratic and more diverse. Qualitative evidence for such a claim can be found in a raft of products introduced over the past century, including automobiles, household appliances, and personal electronics, which have expanded the choices of consumers. Continual increases in real per-capita gross domestic product are quantitative evidence that more goods and services are being exchanged than ever before.

The thoroughgoing change set off by the industrial revolution sets the research agenda. At issue is the extent to which commodification affects symbolic communication. Top-down studies of the production of consumer culture tend to accentuate commodification, while bottom-up studies tend to focus on the power of consumers to interpret and shape the meaning of their activities. Studies of the production of consumer culture focus on how designs for products are developed and implemented, how the institutions of industrial society affect the kinds of material goods that are produced, and the part played by advertising and retail environments in the consumer experience. These studies are characterized by a top-down analytical strategy that places an emphasis on the commercial qualities of consumer culture. Other researchers concentrate on the meaning of consumer culture for individuals and groups, whether as a part of an individual lifestyle project or a full-blown subculture. This bottom-up strategy gives more credit than does a top-down strategy to the active consumer who uses consumer culture to generate meaning.

In practice, most social scientists agree that both commercial forces and consumers have a hand in shaping the meaning of consumer culture. Their relationship is commonly pictured as a circuit: Meaning produced by commercial forces is transformed by consumers, then commercial forces subsequently appropriate consumer trends for their own designs.

THE INSTITUTIONS OF CONSUMER SOCIETY

Scholars sometimes use the term *consumer society* to describe a society in which consumption displaces production as the most important activity. Flexible production techniques, advertising, the new means of consumption, and the credit card are the institutional pillars on which consumer society rests. They ensure a diversity of goods, demand for goods, nice places to consume, and the means to pay for a lifestyle.

Assembly-line techniques popularized by Henry Ford and others helped to make the mass production of consumer goods cheap and efficient. Yet such techniques are rigid; assembly lines designed for long runs of essentially identical products are subject to periodic crises when inventory exceeds demand. Recent advances in technology and theories of management have favored more flexible techniques of production that relies on easily programmed and configured machinery, high-speed communications, and quick decision-making to respond to shifting consumer demands. The term *flexible specialization* is used to refer to an economy that is subject to continual reengineering in a quest to profit from evolving market niches. Flexible technology frees companies from the constraints traditionally associated with more rigid production technology so they can innovate more easily. It also becomes easier to build customized products using mass-production techniques. Thus, flexible production increases the diversity of products available to consumers.

The new means of consumption are settings that enable us to consume. The rise of consumer society has been facilitated by the development by a whole range of settings, including shopping malls, superstores, and cruise ships in the post–World War II period. The new means of consumption are designed to handle large volumes of customers efficiently with the help of machines and closely controlled workers. They are often given a theme, such as the Old West or the final frontier, established with décor, props, and costumes. Themes take the new means of consumption from store to spectacle by transforming shopping into an experience. As a result of the expansion of the new means of consumption, shopping has become one of the most popular leisure time activities.

Advertising is the medium producers use to establish symbolic meanings for their products, whether in a television commercial, a print ad, direct mail, or a radio spot. At root, ads produce desires. They do their work by linking a product with an image, feeling, or lifestyle that resonates with consumers, turning a product with use-value such as a packet of cigarettes or a pair of sneakers into a symbol. A packet of cigarettes becomes an emblem of liberated, hip femininity through the magic of ads. A pair of sneakers signifies a commitment to a free-wheeling playing style through the magic of ads. Yet there are undeniable limits to the effectiveness of ads because consumers are quick to recast the advertised meanings of commodities with their own meanings. When a group of guys are all wearing the same model shoe, it signifies that they're teammates rather than a collection of free-wheeling players.

The modern era of consumer credit began with the formation of the Diner's Club in 1949. The Diner's Club card was the first "universal" credit card, meaning that it allowed users to make purchases at a variety of locations rather than only at a specific store, as the gas, hotel, and department-store cards that preceded it had done. Common sense suggests that the credit card would play some part in increasing consumer expenditures. Like the chips on a craps table, credit cards spend like funny money. With high credit limits, it is easy to imagine that some people would spend to their limit without thought for whether they could afford to make the payments. Yet economic research suggests that credit cards heighten spending among the young, while suppressing spending among those who are already servicing debt. Credit card ads, of course, encourage cardholders to spend to finance an expensive lifestyle for themselves and their priceless loved ones without giving a thought to the debt they will incur.

Flexible production techniques, advertising, the new means of consumption, and the credit card have set the stage for unprecedented diversity of consumer choice and high levels of consumption. The question is whether this system can distract people to the point where they neglect their social networks and forget about their values. Conversely, are people able to work through a world of goods to build a sense of community in their lives?

A World Without Money

The following extract is dialogue from Edward Bellamy's novel, Looking Backward, 2000–1887, *written in 1898. The novel sets forth Bellamy's vision of a cooperative world, free of economic competition.*

"You were surprised," he said, "at my saying that we got along without money or trade, but a moment's reflection will show that trade existed and money was needed in your day simply because the business of production was left in private hands, and that, consequently, they are superfluous now."

"I do not at once see how that follows," I replied.

"It is very simple," said Doctor Leete. "When innumerable different and independent persons produced the various things needful to life and comfort, endless exchanges between individuals were requisite in order that they might supply themselves with what they desired. These exchanges constituted trade, and money was essential as their medium. But as soon as the nation became the sole producer of all sorts of commodities, there was no need of exchanges between individuals that they might get what they required. Everything was procurable from one source, and nothing could be procured anywhere else. A system of direct distribution from the national storehouses took the place of trade, and for this money was unnecessary."

"How is the distribution managed?" I asked.

"On the simplest possible plan," replied Doctor Leete. "A credit corresponding to his share of the annual product of the nation is given to every citizen on the public books at the beginning of each year, and a credit card issued him with which he procures at the public storehouses, found in every community, what he desires whenever he desires it. This arrangement, you will see, totally obviates the necessity for business transactions of any sort between individuals and consumers. Perhaps you would like to see what our credit cards are like.

"You observe," he pursued as I was curiously examining the piece of pasteboard he gave me, "that this card is issued for a certain number of dollars. We have kept the old word, but not the substance. The term, as we use it, answers to no real thing, but merely serves as an algebraical symbol for comparing the values to products with one another. For this purpose they are all priced in dollars and cents, just as in your day. The value of what I procure on this card is checked off by the clerk, who pricks out of these tiers of squares the price of what I order."

Source: Bellamy, Edward. (2000). *Looking Backward, 2000–1887.* New York: Signet Classic, pp. 56–57. (Originally published 1898)

CONSUMER CULTURE AND COMMUNITY

Three basic theories of consumer culture have three different views of what the rise of consumer society has meant for community. First, the mass culture perspective emphasizes the ways in which consumers are manipulated by commercial interests, often at the expense of community values. Second, the class culture perspective draws attention to the ways in which material goods are used to signify membership in social groups, especially social classes. Third, the lifestyle consumption perspective characterizes consumers as pleasure-seeking dreamers who engage the products of consumer society with a spirit of play and develop community through affinities in lifestyle.

Both conservative and neo-Marxist scholars have argued that the institutions of consumer society have a tendency to thwart social interaction and stifle human creativity. These commentators see consumer culture as the destroyer of social distinctions, exchanging the quest for distinction for the common denominator of mass tastes. Theodor Adorno and Max Horkheimer coined the term "culture industry" to highlight the power of corporate interests to take the production of culture out of the hands of artists and artisans and turn it into a mass-produced commodity. Hollywood films, network television, popular music, and a bevy of mass-produced goods marginalize both high culture (such as opera) and folk culture (such as bluegrass). Compelling consumers to buy whatever is for sale, advertising is seen as a form of mass hypnosis. It is argued that the culture industry is peddling a kind of drug that threatens to destroy the social fabric by marketing a life of excess that isolates individuals in an ultimately unsatisfying cycle of desiring and spending, while neglecting the face-to-face interaction, community values, and moral order that make life meaningful.

An influential strain of scholarship understands consumer culture to be instrumental for sustaining and reproducing structures of social class, ethnicity, nationality, and gender. The term "conspicuous consumption," coined by the American economist Thorstein Veblen to describe the ostentatious display of wealth by the upper classes, forges a link between competition over social status and the consumption of luxury goods. The conspicuous display of consumer goods is a means of communicating social position and group affiliations to others. Tastes for particular recreational activities, foods and drink, clothing, music and literature, dwellings, and automobiles serve as markers of group membership. Veblen thought that upwardly mobile individuals who aspire to high status would imitate upper-class tastes, and upper-class members would, in turn, change their tastes to preserve their relative social position. Others have pointed out that class competition is not as straightforward as it appeared to Veblen and may include instances of the upper class borrowing from the lower class or stylized consumption such as the ironic inclinations of young consumers.

An alternative perspective on consumer culture focuses neither on competitive display nor on the culture industry's manipulations, but rather on the consumerist lifestyle. This perspective instead emphasizes the meaning of consumer culture for individuals. It suggests that consumer culture is best understood in reference to the desires and dreams of individual consumers. Consumers are understood not as dupes or competitors but as pleasure-seekers, hedonists who use consumer culture as a way of escape from the constraints of industrial society.

In this perspective, consumers become imaginative heroes who knit their own kingdoms from the scraps of material provided to them in the marketplace. The drivers of customized low-rider cars, for example, personalize a commodity to invest it with meaning. The work they put into the cars removes most traces of their commercial origins and makes them unique. Here the quest for satisfaction through consumption can lead to the formation of subcultural groups of individuals pursuing similar lifestyles.

—Todd Stillman

See also Collective Consumption; McDonaldization

Further Reading

Adorno, T., & Horkheimer, M. (1944). The culture industry: Enlightenment as mass deception. In T. Adorno & M. Horkheimer, *Dialectic of enlightenment* (pp. 120–167). New York: Continuum.

Featherstone, M. (1991). *Consumer culture and postmodernity.* London: Sage.

Miller, D. (1998). *A theory of shopping.* Ithaca, NY: Cornell University Press.

Slater, D. (1997). *Consumer culture and modernity.* Cambridge, UK: Polity.

Veblen, T. (1899). *The theory of the leisure class.* New York: Macmillan.

CONVIVIALITY

See Bars and Pubs; Festivals

COOPERATIVE EXTENSION SYSTEM

The cooperative extension system ("Extension") is the world's largest informal education system. It is part of the outreach mission of the U.S. Department of Agriculture, land grant universities, and twenty-nine colleges established for the education of American Indians. Extension offices are found in almost every county in the United States. This ubiquitous presence and the backing by all three levels of government give the extension system great strength.

Extension was made possible with the establishment of the first and second land grant universities, authorized by the Morrill Acts in 1862 and 1890, but not actually established until 1914, with the passage of the Smith-Lever Act. That act stated Extension's mission to aid in the diffusion "among the people of the United States useful and practical information on subjects relating to agriculture, home economics, and rural energy, and to encourage the application of the same" (Smith-Lever Act, Sec. 1). Seventy-four years later, Extension restated its mission: "The Cooperative Extension System helps people improve their lives through an educational process which uses scientific knowledge focused on issues and needs" (Rasmussen 1989, p. 4).

Although the focus of Extension was on farming and home economics, it did not stop there. From the beginning, there was a focus on rural life, including rural and community development. Indeed, it was the Country Life Commission, which President Theodore Roosevelt (1858–1919) appointed in 1908 to look into ways to improve life in the rural United States, that first proposed a national system to extend the knowledge of each state agricultural college through a department of extension. The hope was that Extension would improve not only agriculture, but also sanitation, education, home making, and country life in general.

In 1955, the Smith-Lever Act was expanded to include educational programming designed to assist local efforts to diversify the agricultural economy by the introduction of manufacturing. Off-farm jobs could create income to supplement farm income. From this modest beginning, county Extension offices became more involved in rural, community, and economic development. For example, in 2002, the Kansas State University Extension Service is organized around four core areas. They are (1) youth (4-H), family and community development, (2) agricultural industry competitiveness, (3) food, nutrition, health, and safety, and (4) natural resources and environmental management. All four areas of Extension education in Kansas are delivered in rural and urban counties. The traditional 4-H clubs are popular with urban and rural families. Also, horticultural programs are particularly popular in urban counties.

At present, Extension continues to flourish. At a national conference held in Florida in February 2002, Extension educators presented a wide array of programs whose intent was to strengthen communities. The programs focused on leadership development, local government management, economic development, e-commerce, land-use planning, and much more. All the programs are created and delivered through a system of county, area, and state Extension educators. In addition, four regional Rural Development Centers help coordinate multistate initiatives.

—David L. Darling

Further Reading

North Central Regional Center for Rural Development. (n.d.). Retrieved October 3, 2002, from http://www.ag.iastate.edu/centers/rdev/RuralDev.html

Northeast Regional Center for Rural Development. (2002). Retrieved September 10, 2002, from http://www.cas.nercrd.psu.edu

Prawl, W., Medlin, R., & Gross, J. (1984). *Adult and continuing education through the Cooperative Extension Service.* Columbia: Extension Division of the University of Missouri.

Rasmussen, W. D. (1989). *Taking the university to the people: Seventy-five years of Cooperative Extension.* Ames: Iowa University Press.

Smith-Lever Act, 7 U.S.C. § 341 *et seq.*

Southern Rural Development Center. (2002). Retrieved October 3, 2002, from http://ext.msstate.edu/srdc

U.S. Department of Agriculture. (2001). *Strengthening communities: Strategic directions for community resources and economic development programs.* Washington, DC: USDA Cooperative State Research, Education, and Extension Service and Land Grant University System.

Western Rural Development Center. (2002). Retrieved October 3, 2002, from http://extension.usu.edu/wrdc/

COOPERATIVE PARISH MINISTRIES

Cooperative parish ministry is a consolidation of the organizations, staffs, facilities, and/or activities of churches for common ministry and mission. These arrangements can be found among both Catholic and Protestant churches, particularly mainline Protestant denominations around the world.

Cooperative parish ministries vary according to the degree of organizational union, ranging from independent congregations to organically united congregations. Participating congregations may be of the same denomination or an ecumenical blend of several denominations. However, except for shared facilities and a few programs, it is rare to find cooperative parish ministries between Catholic and Protestants. Most typically, cooperative parish ministries are among mainline Protestant denominational congregations. They may share one or more clergy and staff members. They may keep their own separate facilities or consolidate into one facility. Each congregation may maintain relations with its own governing board, a parish-wide governing board, or both. The congregations may jointly plan, organize, and participate in a broad array of activities.

TYPES OF COOPERATIVE PARISH MINISTRY

Numerous structural arrangements have been explored by congregations and denominational judicatory since the early 1900s. Following are examples of cooperative parish ministry structures that emerged.

Consolidated Churches

A consolidated church consists of two or more smaller congregations of the same denomination that join to form one larger congregation. They have a common facility, which could be used by one of the congregations or an entirely new structure. The new congregations may use one of the former congregations' names, a combination of the former congregations' names, or an entirely new one.

Federated Churches

Federated churches are established when two or more congregations of different Protestant denominations form a single congregation and use the same facility. The members retain their own denominational identities; they maintain relations with their respective denominations; and they receive support from their denominations. Additionally, the members continue to make financial contributions to their respective denominations, which is often accomplished by a congregation's income being proportioned according to its denominational composition. Clergy are selected on an alternating basis from the participating denominations such that a minister of one parent denomination is replaced by a minister from the other parent denomination upon the expiration of his or her term.

Yoked Parishes

A yoked parish is two or more autonomous congregations, typically of different Protestant denominations, served by the same clergy person. The minister is selected by a committee comprised of representatives from each of the congregations. Each congregation maintains its own facilities, worship services, budget, and denominational affiliation, but cooperates on the clergy's salary and selected cooperative ministry programs. Each congregation's services, liturgy, and materials remain typical of its parent denomination.

Larger or Area Parishes

The larger, or area, parish is an arrangement of several congregations, usually (but not always) of the same Protestant denomination, who share clergy and staff, plan ministries, and coordinate church functions together. Each congregation maintains its own facility, which serves as a worship and ministry location for those who reside in that proximity. The larger parish typically uses a parish-wide governing board and establishes committees as needed.

Multiple-Church/Multiple Charge Parishes

A multiple-church, or multiple charge, parish consists of several congregations sharing one or more clergy that are intentionally organized as a group. This organizational structure differs from larger/area parish in that each congregation relates to its own governing board as well as to a parish-wide council.

Cluster Groups and Ecumenical Shared Ministries

Cluster groups are loosely knit organizations formed by individual congregations in the same geographic area. They share some resources and coordinate special events, but they maintain their own facilities and congregational identities. The multidenominational version of cluster groups is an ecumenical shared ministry. It is comprised of congregations from different denominations that share a common vision or ministry. They form an intentional covenant in order to implement a common ministry and programming plan. Examples of shared ministry include vacation Bible school, food pantry, day care, hospital visitation, and tutorial programs.

Shared Facilities

Sometimes multiple autonomous congregations or groups, Catholic or Protestant, share a common facility without having any further connection with one another. Sometimes the facility is not even a church building; newly established groups may, for instance, hold services in a school auditorium or a storefront. The congregations may be of different denominations or from different cultural or language groups. Each relates to its own governing board and clergy.

Nondenominational Community Churches

Although not specifically a form of cooperative parish ministry, nondenominational community churches are frequently included in discussion of such ministry. Nondenominational community churches can be a consolidation of several smaller congregations, which may have been independent and/or denominationally aligned, or a new church established for an entire community. The congregation may be entirely independent or may affiliate with an association of independent churches. Since the church has no denominational affiliation, lack of denominational support and resources often can be a cause of struggle.

REASONS FOR COOPERATIVE PARISH MINISTRIES

Cooperative parish ministry arrangements have been widely used by many denominations, particularly by the United Methodist Church. Judy Matheny, a church and community worker, found that among United Methodist congregations, cooperative parish ministry is found extensively in rural settings. The most prevalent forms of cooperative parish ministries are multiple charge parishes and cluster groups. Multiple charge parishes are frequently found in the northeastern United States; cluster groups are found most frequently in the northeastern and southeastern United States; federated and yoked churches are typically found in the north central United States. Shared-facility arrangements are found in highest frequency in urban centers in the western United States.

The specific form of cooperative parish ministry selected by a group of churches depends primarily on the functions it needs to perform. Small, struggling congregations may form cooperative parish ministry arrangements for survival purposes. As a congregation's membership diminishes, its ability to remain viable decreases. The small congregation may no longer be able to afford to hire clergy, maintain facilities, and perform functions. Some form of consolidation may be its best option to provide services to its members and the community. The consolidated church is in a better position to assist in community economic development, housing rehabilitation, care for the elderly, parish nursing programs, after-school tutoring, child day care, and transportation programs, which are so vital to rural communities, particularly those facing population decline.

For the Catholic bishop Howard Hubbard, although there may be pragmatic reasons for restructuring a parish, reasons of faith ought to be paramount. Restructuring the parish may allow for more effective ministry or evangelization. A study for successful cooperating congregations conducted by church historian Gilson Waldkoenig and theologian William Avery supported that idea. They found that large and healthy congregations may select cooperative parish ministry arrangements in order to provide successful ministries. The partnerships result in a greater availability of human, financial, and facilities resources, which in turn can make the religious mission more successful. Cooperative parish ministry arrangements may be able to support a broader base of participation given the larger number of people involved. Additionally, cooperation among several congregations in a geographic proximity fosters a commitment to place. Thus, the members of a cooperative parish ministry may be well positioned to engage in more effective community service and development efforts.

Cooperative parish ministry will likely continue to be an adaptive response to such community issues as population declines in rural areas, suburban sprawl, new immigrant communities, and a desire for a stronger sense of spiritual connection with other people. Clergy in the future will need the skills and attributes to lead cooperative parish ministries. Prospective congregations may likely ask them, "Will you be committed to the cooperative nature of ministry?" (Waldkoenig & Avery 2000, p. 200).

—Gary A. Goreham and Nicole J. Meidinger

Further Reading

Howes, R.G. (1998). *Bridges: Toward the inter-parish regional community—deaneries, clusters, plural parishes.* Collegeville, MN: Liturgical Press.

Hubbard, H. J. (1998). *Fulfilling the vision: Collaborative ministry in the parish.* New York: Crossroad.

Judy, M. T. (1967). *The cooperative parish in nonmetropolitan areas.* Nashville, TN: Abingdon.

Matheny, J. C. (1995). *A directory of cooperative parish ministries in the United Methodist Church.* New York: General Board of Global Ministries, United Methodist Church.

Schirer, M. E., & Forehand, M.A. (1984). *Cooperative ministry: Hope for small churches.* Valley Forge, PA: Judson.

Waldkoenig, G. A. C., & Avery, W. O. (2000). *Cooperating congregations: Profiles in mission strategies.* Bethesda, MD: Alban Institute.

COOPERATIVES

See COMMUNITY CURRENCIES; COMMUNITY OWNERSHIP; STUDENT HOUSING COOPERATIVES

CORPORATE SOCIAL RESPONSIBILITY

Corporate social responsibility (CSR) is an ethos proffered by people concerned about the huge and growing global influence exerted by business. Many of the world's largest businesses rival the nation-state, religions, and even nature itself as an agent of human change. Multinational corporations (MNCs) have become the primary force shaping material well-being. They help determine modern society's collective values, shape humankind's shared experience, and, indeed, they create society's future. Fifty-one of the world's 100 largest economies are businesses. For example, Wal-Mart Stores, number one on *Fortune* magazine's 2002 list of the "500 Largest U.S. Corporations," had sales just short of $220 billion. That same year, the combined gross national products of New Zealand, Greece, Costa Rica, and Cuba was $212 billion. To put it another way, 161 countries have smaller annual revenues than Wal-Mart does (Derber 1998, p. 3). The daily influence of business on the lives of billions of people, combined with the spread of globalization, make it a social as well as an economic force.

CSR broadens our understanding of a business's responsibility and role in society and asks that it move from exploiting resources for the sole purpose of maximizing shareholder profit to husbanding resources for the benefit of employees, society, and the future well-being of the planet. Thus, advocates of the new ethos demand that businesses be held accountable for a triple bottom line: In addition to its concern for profits, a business must also be measured based on its environmental performance and on its concern for social justice.

A VERY BRIEF HISTORY OF CSR

The corporation in western society was created for two purposes. The first reason was to enable the concentration of capital in order to serve the needs of the British Crown. Specifically, the British East India Company (1600–1858) became the basis for Britain's colonial expansion. At its height, by the time of Queen Victoria's death in 1901, the British Empire controlled about one quarter of the land and people of the world. It was the largest empire in history, even after losing the American colonies more than a century earlier. The Boston Tea Party (1773), a precursor to the American Revolution, was itself a protest against the East India Company for raising the price of tea.

The second reason corporations were created was to help finance public projects too extensive for state governments. The United States government chartered banks, and states financed public works such as roads and canals by granting charters to corporations for those purposes. Corporations served a public purpose and were dissolved upon accomplishing that purpose, or, if they did not live up to public expectations, they had their charters revoked.

Slowly, however, corporations mutated into investor vehicles detached from public service. By the time of the "robber barons" in the post–Civil War industrial boom, key Supreme Court decisions had given corporations unlimited life, limited liability that protected non-invested wealth of the shareholders, and some of the same rights as individuals, including the right to due process under the Fourteenth Amendment to the U.S. Constitution, the freedom to enter into contracts, and the freedom to own property.

THE IMPACT OF THE ROBBER BARONS

Outrage at the excesses of corporate leaders such as John D. Rockefeller (1839–1937; oil), John Jacob Astor (1763–1848; land development and fur trading), Andrew Carnegie (1835–1919; steel), Cornelius Vanderbilt (1794–1877; steamships and railroads), and John Pierpont (J. P.) Morgan (1837–1913; finance and industrial consolidation), stirred the public. Congress eventually mollified the rising voices that were calling for dramatic reform and regulation by passing the Sherman Anti-Trust Act of 1890, which aimed to break monopolies and open domestic markets to competition. In 1903, Congress established a Cabinet-level Department of Commerce and Labor (by 1913, an independent Department

Businesses Band Together to Aid in Child Care

(ANS)–Braxton Spahos began noticing that an increasing number of second-shift workers at the Foster Farms food-processing plant, where he is human resources director, were complaining of child care problems.

Foster Farms makes fast-food frozen corn dogs in the rural community of Demopolis, Ala., which has a population of about 8,000. A majority of the firm's 225 employees are women, and many are single parents.

"Most of them are second shift and have trouble finding child care," Spahos said. The plant's second shift runs from 3 p.m. to midnight. Spahos raised the issue during a town meeting held in Demopolis by U.S. Secretary of Labor Alexis Herman on March 12. Herman is a native of Mobile, 150 miles to the south.

Once he brought up the subject, Spahos found the town's other large employers were having the same child care problems. Then, within a week of Herman's visit, staff members of the Women's Bureau, an office of the Department of Labor, called Spahos about a newly launched project that promised to make it easier to find a solution.

The concept is simple: connect businesses that are running into employee child care problems for the first time with companies that have successfully dealt with similar issues. Since January, the Business-to-Business Child Care Mentoring Initiative has enrolled 200 companies as either mentors giving advice or mentees, who receive help.

The Women's Bureau linked the businesses in Demopolis with the Employers Child Care Alliance in the sister cities of Opelika and Auburn, about 180 miles away.

The alliance consists of 11 employers–ranging from Auburn University, with more than 5,000 employees, to the local branch of the Alabama Power Co., with 150 workers–who in 1996 began collectively trying to come up with child care options. Since then, the alliance has set up an after-school program for 10- to 14-year-olds, along with a program that helps local day care providers get national accreditation, as well as other child care services.

Spahos is pleased with the mentoring arrangement. Human resource managers are seldom trained in child care matters. "We'd still be scrambling for information and looking for someone who'd been through all these trials and tribulations," he said.

Child care is a significant concern for American workers. There are 29 million children under 13 who have both parents or their only parent in the workforce, according to the Bureau of Labor Statistics. Roughly half are taken care of by relatives, while others are in day care facilities or family care centers, which are run by licensed providers in their own homes.

A 1994 survey of 250,000 women workers by the Women's Bureau revealed that a majority of working women with children under 5 said finding affordable child care was difficult.

Businesses are increasingly paying attention when employees say they have trouble with child care. They have ample reason for doing so, says Yvette Lester, Communications Director for the Women's Bureau. "U.S. corporations lose $3 billion a year because of employees taking time off because of child care," Lester said. "They can improve their bottom line if their employees aren't worried about their child."

—Paul Bush

Source: American News Service, Article No. 969, June 17, 1999.

of Labor was created) to provide some regulatory oversight of industry. These efforts to rein in rampant business abuses of the time were largely ineffective.

RESPONSE OF THE MUCKRAKERS

Muckrakers were writers who exposed, excited public concern, and opened the way for a progressive movement insistent on reform. They included Upton Sinclair (1878–1968), who focused on conditions of immigrant workers and dangerous food processing at a meatpacking house; Ida Tarbell (1857–1944), who exposed the greed and corruption of Rockefeller's Standard Oil Company; and Henry Demarest Lloyd (1847–1903), who drew attention to child labor and unionism.

Perhaps the height of the outrage against business abuses during the Progressive Era occurred on March 26, 1911, a day after a fire broke out at the Triangle Shirtwaist Company in New York City. When the fire was finally extinguished, 146 immigrant women who had worked in the garment factory were dead and their bodies unceremoniously piled in the streets. The outrage was due to the fact that the fire was avoidable. Exits were blocked, there was no fire safety equipment, smoking was allowed (it was a cigarette that started the fire), and the working conditions were unsafe. Most important, it symbolized the textile industry's sweatshop environment that was rife in the United States, but has since migrated overseas.

During World War I and the Roaring Twenties, calls

Corporate Accountability as an International Issue

The issue of corporate responsibility has global implications. As the statement below—from a January 2002 press release about the World Economic Forum and the subsequent World Summit—indicates, organizations around the world have strong positions on corporate accountability.

Even as leaders of non-governmental organizations express their anger against the corporate leaders who are meeting at the World Economic Forum they say there are also reasons to be hopeful about the World Summit on Sustainable Development that will take place in Johannesburg from 26 August to 4 September.

One issue that has been high on the NGO priority list, the issue of corporate accountability, is now being talked about as a potential area for action at the Johannesburg Summit, and governments are taking notice.

"Corporate accountability is on the agenda," Daniel Mittler of Friends of the Earth, International told an NGO press conference held during the Preparatory Committee meeting for Johannesburg. "We need a convention on corporate accountability, and work toward a legally binding convention should start at Johannesburg."

The reason, Mittler said, was that during the years of trade liberalization, governments gave away their own ability to protect society and the environment. But he added that even governments have recognized the seriousness of the issue, and that "we are getting somewhere."

The case of Enron, according to Emmy Hafild, Executive Director of the Indonesian Environmental Forum, has helped raise awareness of the corporate responsibility issue. "People realize that these corporations can ruin a lot of people in seconds."

Kathleen Rogers, President of the Earth Day Network, noted that even President Bush had mentioned corporate responsibility in his State of the Union address. She said that NGOs were writing to the President, and other world leaders, to commit early to go to Johannesburg.

The NGOs also expressed deep reservations with the process of globalization. Shao Loong Yin of the Third World Network said that the unequal economic power relationships that exist around the world are the "limiting factor in letting us realize our dreams." He also stressed that Johannesburg had to revive the North-South compact from the Rio Earth Summit, which called for all countries to work toward sustainable development, but with the more developed countries helping the developing countries with assistance. "The North must take major action," he said.

Rogers said there were actually two kinds of terrorism plaguing the world right now: politically driven terrorism such as the attacks on the United States last September, and another, "quiet" form of economic terrorism. This terrorism, she said, "takes the form of a mother who wakes up every day and finds that she cannot feed her child, the man with AIDS who has no means of getting the drugs he needs, and the man who steals wood in a protected area for his livelihood."

Source: Johannesburg Summit. (2002). Retrieved March 5, 2003, from http://www.johannesburgsummit.org/html/whats_new/otherstories_ngo_3101html.htm.

for business reform and CSR were muted. However, after the stock market crash in 1929 and the Great Depression that followed, voices rose once again to question the role of business in society. With 25 percent of the workforce unemployed at the height of the Depression, U.S. capitalism was challenged as never before. For the first time, major alternative philosophies arose to question the legitimacy of the economic system. Socialists, communists, and unions (supportive of capitalism but seeking a voice for labor) all grew in popularity as they offered promising alternatives for fixing the broken system. President Franklin Roosevelt adopted a Keynesian philosophy (based on the theories of English economist John Maynard Keynes [1883–1946]) and stimulated the economy through large-scale government spending in public works and welfare. His efforts reduced unemployment, and created social security and an economic safety net of benefits, including unemployment compensation, in 1935.

During World War II, attention was focused on meeting the human and material demands of a two-front war and attention to CSR diminished. As European and Japanese industry was destroyed in the war, the United States emerged with the only capacity for turning out the goods for reconstruction and for meeting the needs of a consumer society with huge pent-up demand. The U.S. economy took off, and the 1950s and early 1960s saw industry and unions struggle through countless strikes, but emerge with the highest paid, and most productive, middle class in history.

Concern for CSR simmered in the background during the period but arose again with a series of environmental debacles. The first centered around Love Canal, New York. The Hooker Chemical Company deposited its toxic waste in the canal before it gave the land to the Niagara Falls Board of Education. Eventually a school was built on top of the filled-in toxic dump and a residential community developed adjacent to it. By 1977, seepage from the canal, and an alarming increase in health irregularities, alerted residents to the dangers of living near the canal. Finally, the school and the residential homes in the immediate vicinity were declared unsafe for human habitation. To this day, the area remains a ghost town.

Two years later, the Three Mile Island nuclear reactor in Pennsylvania experienced equipment and human error that caused the worst nuclear accident in U.S. history. Then, in 1984, the Union Carbide disaster in Bhopal, India resulted in the deaths of over 2,800 people and serious injuries to thousands more due to a toxic gas accidentally released into the atmosphere.

COALESCING OUTRAGE

These tragedies, and many others, drew the attention of activists seeking justice for the victims, as well as regulations to prevent future accidents, but they never led to a systematic campaign for the adoption of CSR standards—until the *Exxon Valdez* oil spill. The ecological catastrophe created in Prince William Sound, Alaska, resulted in the creation of the CERES (Coalition for Environmentally Responsible Economies) Principles. Modeled on the Sullivan Principles (a recommended code of behavior for U.S. companies doing business in South Africa prior to the end of apartheid in 1977), the CERES Principles were an effort to have all companies agree to be responsible for their environmental impact. "By endorsing the CERES Principles, companies not only formalize their dedication to environmental awareness and accountability, but also actively commit to an ongoing process of continuous improvement, dialogue and comprehensive, systematic public reporting" (Coalition for Environmentally Responsible Economies 2003). These principles were a precursor to the Business Charter for Sustainable Development created by the International Chamber of Commerce. Also, the late 1980s witnessed the Savings and Loan disgrace that eventually cost U.S. taxpayers over $1 trillion because of the need for a government bailout of insured deposits that evaporated in the scandal.

By the time the Enron Corporation collapsed in 2001, following the discovery that it engaged in fraudulent accounting practices to hide enormous debt while reporting inflated profits, the public was ready once again to consider CSR-related issues more seriously than ever before. Enron was just the beginning. By the end of 2002 several huge companies were in—or headed for—bankruptcy, leaving top executives unimaginably rich while workers' retirement funds were emptied and thousands were put out of work.

A NEW PHASE IN CSR

As outrage boiled over about executive compensation, platinum parachutes (enormous severance packages provided to top management that frequently exceeded several years worth of salary and bonuses), and the disappearing pension funds, the federal government seemed to do little except introduce additional Securities and Exchange Commission (SEC) regulations to protect investors and pass the Sarbannes-Oxley Act of 2002, which holds chief executive officers of publicly traded companies criminally liable for (among other things) fraudulent activity committed on behalf of the company. This marked progress on the domestic side of the issue, important in light of the reluctance of recent presidents and sessions of Congress to re-regulate industry after a twenty-year period of deregulation. Even though deregulation is considered one of the reasons for the breadth and the depth of the scandals that have occurred since the mid-1980s, a free market philosophy prevails at the national level.

On the international front, environmental deterioration due to resource depletion, global warming, air and water pollution, and waste mismanagement gave rise to a strong environmental movement globally. Allied with these activists, others working for social justice—particularly those working for justice in the workplace by fighting sweatshop conditions, the prevention of unionization, female and child abuse, substandard wages, the lack of any benefits, and inadequate safety and health measures—have joined in a generalized anti-globalization effort to slow the pace of change and the rapidly widening gap between the haves and the have-nots.

With the widespread public outrage over corporate abuses, bankruptcies due to financial manipulation and fraud, and deplorable working conditions in factories producing goods for the upscale U.S. market, nongovernmental organizations (NGOs) have filled a vacuum created by the overemphasis on the virtues of unfettered market forces and privatization of public services and natural resources. The NGOs are pressuring multinational corporations to apply home country standards abroad, support environmental sustainability, and end the various workplace abuses of their subcontractors, suppliers, and business partners.

NGOs are filling the regulatory void by organizing consumer pressure on corporations to sign agreements about aspects of CSR, such as the CERES principles, or to voluntarily be "audited" by third parties on their performance against standards created by organizations such as Social Accountability International (www.cepaa.org), Institute of Social and Ethical Accountability (www.accountability.org.uk), International Organization for Standardization (www.iso.ch), or other internationally recognized codes of practice that offer some measure of accountability.

THE FUTURE OF CSR

There have been many periods of corporate excess and abuse resulting in a public outcry for reform. But until today there has not been a consistent and sustained effort by the public to hold corporations accountable. The public has taken these matters in its own hands by supporting activists and NGOs in an unprecedented manner. This has happened because of the lack of appropriate government regulation and because of a major shift in the consciousness of the public regarding the proper role of business in society. Until the 1980s, the only acceptable model of modern corporate behavior was to maximize profits for stockholders. Milton Friedman (b. 1912), Nobel Prize–winning economist and author of *Capitalism and Freedom* (1962), legitimized the stockholder-centric view. According to Friedman, "Few trends could so thoroughly undermine the very foundations of our free society as the acceptance by corporate officials of a social responsibility other than to make as much money for their stockholders as possible" (1962, p. 133). The book still serves as the theoretical defense of the unregulated free market system.

In contrast to that view, opponents claim that, in the absence of a regulatory environment, considering the stockholder to be the sole interest of the corporation is dangerous and leads to the kinds of extremes and abuses we have recently experienced. Instead, they claim that a stakeholder view is more realistic and accounts for the expanded role of business and its enormous influence on the lives of people. With a stakeholder view, a corporation recognizes that its decisions impact the communities in which it operates, its employees, suppliers, customers, and the environment, in addition to the financial fortunes of its stockholders.

The ethos of corporate social responsibility and the rise of the many activist organizations calling for corporate accountability to internationally recognized standards are in a very real sense efforts to level the playing field, albeit with only voluntary people power, not regulatory government power—at least not yet.

—John Nirenberg

Further Reading

Coalition for Environmentally Responsible Economies. (2003). *Our work: The CERES principles.* Retrieved March 4, 2003, from http://www.ceres.org/our_work/principles.htm

Derber, C. (1998). *Corporation nation.* New York: St Martin's Press.

Elkington, J. (1998). *Cannibals with forks: The triple bottom line of 21st century business.* London: New Society Publishers.

Estes, R. (1996). *Tyranny of the bottom line.* San Francisco: Berrett-Koehler.

Fortune 500 Largest U.S. corporations. (2002, April 15). *Fortune,* p. F-1.

Friedman, M. (1962). *Capitalism and freedom.* Chicago: University of Chicago Press.

Greider, W. (1997). *One world, ready or not.* New York: Touchstone.

Hoffman, W. M., Frederick, R. E., & Schwartz, M. (Eds.). (1995). *Business ethics: Readings and cases in corporate morality.* New York: McGraw-Hill.

Kelly, M. (2001). *The divine right of capital: Dethroning the corporate aristocracy.* San Francisco: Berrett Koehler.

McIntosh, M., Leipziger, D., Jones, K., & Coleman, G. (1998). *Corporate citizenship: Successful strategies for responsible companies.* London: Financial Times.

Corporate reform after Enron. (2002, July/August). *Multinational Monitor,* p. 9.

Prokosch, M., & Raymond, L. (Eds.). (2002). *The global activists manual.* New York: Nation Books.

Waddock, S. (2002). *Leading corporate citizens: Vision, values and value added.* New York: McGraw-Hill.

Walker, S., & Marr, J. (2001) *Stakeholder power: A winning plan for building stakeholder commitment and driving corporate growth.* Boston: Perseus.

Zadek, S. (2001). *The civil corporation: The new economy of corporate citizenship.* London: Earthscan.

COUNTERFEIT COMMUNITIES

Counterfeit community is a term first used by John Freie in a 1998 book titled *Counterfeit Community: The Exploitation of Our Longings for Connectedness.*

According to Freie, counterfeit community occurs when people's natural desires to form communal bonds and to feel connected to others are exploited in order to advance self-interest goals (for example, economic profit, power) that run counter to the building of genuine community. Rather than growing as a result of the complex human interaction of people, feelings of connectedness are externally manipulated and therefore artificial, deceptive, and false. The creation of feelings of connectedness that characterize genuine community requires the hard work of building bonds of association through the honest recognition of disagreements, the resolution of those disagreements, the forging of agreements to work together, and the building of consensus about basic values and beliefs that unite people. Counterfeit community requires only that people have a desire for connectedness; it does not require the hard work of building community through human interaction.

Freie claims that counterfeit community permeates contemporary life. It appears in the housing industry with claims of community being made by the developers of gated communities, in the marketplace with the promotion of privately owned shopping malls as communal centers, in the workplace with the use of participatory management techniques, in politics with appeals to a national community, in religion with the use of marketing strategies by megachurches, and in cyberspace with the explicit attempt to create virtual communities. In all instances, the appearance of connectedness and community is presented without the presence of the underlying structure of diverse human interaction that characterizes genuine community.

Freie maintains that genuine community is organic, while counterfeit community is artificial. Counterfeit community is developed and marketed by those who wish to extend their own power or increase their own wealth. It is created and maintained in one of two ways: either by distorting some aspect commonly associated with community, or through the creation of simulacra (copies of aspects of community that never existed).

There are two major criticisms of the concept of counterfeit community. First, it has been suggested that counterfeit community differs from genuine community in degree rather than in kind. In other words, it might be possible that counterfeit community is merely an adolescent form of genuine community that could, in time, develop into genuine community. Second, while Freie correctly identifies people's longing for community as an impetus in the formation of community, he fails to acknowledge that people are influenced by other feelings as well, feelings that may not support the formation of genuine community but that might lead to the formation of counterfeit community. Selfishness, for example, inhibits genuine community, but it may well be a compelling component of counterfeit community. If that is the case, then counterfeit community is not so much a result of the manipulation of people's longing for community as it is a natural result of other, less communitarian, emotions and impulses.

—John F. Freie

Further Reading

Freie, J. F. (1998). *Counterfeit community: The exploitation of our longings for connectedness.* Lanham, MD: Rowman & Littlefield.

McKnight, J. (1995). *The careless society: Community and its counterfeits.* New York: Basic Books.

COUNTY FAIRS

County fairs are actually one variety of a larger institution: the American agricultural fair (other variants include state fairs and smaller district fairs). Competitive exhibits of farm and domestic produce are central to these annual, generally rural, celebrations. Entertainment elements are a second key component of the fair, including music and carnival rides, as well as a variety of specialized foods. County fairs provide important opportunities for association, celebration, and voluntarism, and they can be instrumental in maintaining bonds in the community. They are also recognized in their locales as important elements of local culture and tradition.

ORIGINS AND VARIATIONS

U.S. county fairs trace their origins to two distinct types of gatherings. The celebratory aspects of the fair stem from European and Western Asian market and harvest fairs (which date back at least to late Roman times). These fairs were opportunities for rural dwellers to come together for trade and entertainment. Contemporary fairs still act as important opportunities for residents of various communities in a county to renew acquaintances and to participate in often-unique local rituals (for example, the daily covered-dish luncheons in Neshoba County, Mississippi, or the annual lemon pie contest in Ventura County, California).

The competitive elements of the fair—the awarding of ribbons and cash prizes for the best pig, pumpkin, or pie—are a modern phenomenon, dating only to the

The Great Barrington, Massachusetts, Agricultural Fair in 1903

As the newspaper story below indicates, the county fair has long been a major community activity.

> The Great Barrington fair has come to be called a sort of unofficial old home week. It was probably more so this year than ever before. The number of persons from near and far who had come to Great Barrington hoping to meet old acquaintances and friends was without precedent. In the big crowd there was both advantage and disadvantage for such visitors–the advantage of there being more friends to meet if they could be found, the disadvantage of having to look pretty keenly to avoid missing some friends whom they were anxious to meet.

Source: *The Berkshire Courier.* (October 8, 1903), p. 2.

early nineteenth century. These originated as efforts to improve the quality of U.S. sheep stock and woolen goods. At the first agricultural fairs, held in Massachusetts's Berkshire region, farmers won cash prizes for exhibiting the finest animals—thus providing both an example and an incentive for those who fell short. Competitions soon expanded to include other farm produce, as well as the products of farm women (homespun materials, quilts, knit clothing, canned and preserved foods), and later even baby contests, where standards of child rearing were evaluated and rewarded in much the same way as standards of animal husbandry.

The 1862 U.S. Morrill Act made agricultural education a public enterprise, as opposed to being conducted by private agricultural associations. This created a precedent for public funding, although fairs are not federally funded and rely heavily on community support and participation for their success. Funding is often provided through state agricultural departments, reflecting the fair's status as a means of promoting agriculture and commerce, and these funds may be derived from dedicated sources such as parimutuel betting (wagering on horse racing, which historically took place on fairgrounds and provided another form of agrarian competition). Other fairs raise funds through the sale of shares in the fair organization, typically to local shareholders.

FAIR COMPETITIONS

County fairs still reward the same products they always have—pigs, pies, quilts, and such—as well as incorporating new objects into competition as tastes and technologies change. The contents of these competitions are similar across the United States, as are the mechanics of the process. Before the fair opens, members of the local community bring their entries, whether steers or strawberry preserves, to the fairgrounds. Each entry is placed in an established category of like objects and then evaluated by judges drawn from the local community or larger region. Judges are typically instructors, business owners, or professionals (e.g., a sewing teacher from a local adult education program, a bakery owner, a florist), or they may be accredited by a national organization (such as the American Rose Society). Judging may be conducted in public, so that competitors and observers can learn what the judges expect, or in private, to shield the judges from outside influence. Victors at county and district-level fairs are eligible to compete at state fairs, larger events where exemplary products from throughout the state are assembled and judged through a similar set of practices.

Young people participate in fair competitions as well as adults, and at many fairs they provide the bulk of the competitive exhibits. Youth may compete as individuals, through school groups, or through agricultural-education organizations such as 4-H, Future Farmers of America, and the Grange (which also includes adults). Fairs maintain a symbiotic relationship with groups like 4-H; the fairs provide material resources, as well as opportunities for exhibitors to gain public recognition, while the groups provide exhibits of animals and produce that educate and entertain fairgoers.

Most of the work of assembling, categorizing, and displaying exhibits is done by volunteers who often have long-term commitments to the fair (some volunteers may have thirty or more years of experience). These volunteers cite commitment to community and tradition, as well as the pleasure they receive from interacting with exhibitors and one another, among the motivations for contributing their labor. They work hard to display local products in ways that confer dignity on both the objects and their producers, elevating everyday goods to the status of artworks. The reliance on volunteer labor allows fair organizations to stage their annual shows relatively inexpensively, but also lends the event a continuity and a distinctly local feeling, because a fairly consistent group of local residents organizes the exhibits. The presence of these lively voluntary organizations may also strengthen the communities where they occur by facilitating the development of social capital.

HISTORICAL AND CONTEMPORARY TENSIONS

Fairs generally rely on horse racing and other forms of entertainment, including musical acts, rodeo, truck or oxen pulls, demolition derbies, and perhaps most commonly, carnival rides and midway games, to attract paying audiences. Admission fees charged to fairgoers drawn in by entertainment offerings subsidize the cost of staging the event and provide cash for awards for the competitions. These two elements, the entertainment offerings and the educational competitions, have maintained an uneasy coexistence through the fair's North American history. Nineteenth-century critics claimed that horse racing attracted an undesirable element and encouraged gambling. Midways were seen as traps for the unaware, incorporating deception into the so-called games of skill; carnival sideshows with their conjoined twins and tattooed ladies threatened standards of rural American morality (while still attracting rural men and their money). The vehemence and persistence of these conflicts reveal that locals understand the fair as an important representation of their community and carefully guard the image that it connotes.

Contemporary fairs face both old and new tensions. Fairs' efforts to remain relevant and solvent have turned many of these organizations toward endeavors that potentially contradict the institution's historic mission. Fairs in urbanizing areas may emphasize the event's entertainment and shopping opportunities or may seek to redevelop valuable fairground properties in ways that increase the sites' profitability (e.g., as a convention facility or sports complex). Participants and volunteers involved in the fair's traditional components, including agricultural and domestic competitions, may view these efforts as affronts to an important local tradition and a threat to the rural character of the place in which they live. Despite these pressures, fair remain lively community-based cultural institutions and will likely continue to provide opportunities for social interaction and affirmation of local productivity and identity.

—*Krista E. Paulsen*

Further Reading

Bogdan, R. (1988). *Freak show: Presenting human oddities for amusement and profit.* Chicago: University of Chicago Press.

Craycroft, R. (with Bute, L.). (1989). *The Neshoba county fair: Place and paradox in Mississippi.* Jackson: Center for Small Town Research and Design, Mississippi State University.

Jones, D. C. (1983). *Midways, judges and smooth-tongued fakirs: The illustrated story of county fairs in the prairie West.* Saskatoon, Canada: Western Producer Prairie Books.

Neely, W. C. (1935). *The agricultural fair.* New York: Columbia University Press.

Paulsen, K. E. (2000a). *Fairgrounds as battlegrounds: Rationality, community, and the reproduction of an American cultural institution.* Unpublished doctoral dissertation, University of California at Santa Barbara.

Paulsen, K. E. (2000b). Saving a place for the county fair: Institutional space and the maintenance of community. *Research in Community Sociology, 10,* 387–406.

Prosterman, L. (1995). *Ordinary life, festival days: Aesthetics in the midwestern county fair.* Washington, DC: Smithsonian Institution Press.

CRIME

When scholars, politicians, and ordinary people consider crime and the community, they ask themselves and one another what the connections are between community characteristics and crime. That fundamental question brings up three others.

First, why are rates of criminal behavior—or delinquency—higher in some places than others? Stated differently, why are there more criminals per person or delinquents per youth in some neighborhoods than others? Second, why are offense rates (rates of crime or victimization or calls for police service) higher in some places than others? That is, why are some places more dangerous than others? Third, what are the characteristics of the journey to crime? In other words, how can one describe how offenders travel from where they work or live or recreate to the sites where offenses of victimization or delinquent acts take place?

Crime is both cause and outcome. Generally, studies on communities and crime either have considered crime as a cause of other community attributes or changes, or have examined how various community conditions or changes in those conditions affect crime. The same holds true of delinquency, crime-related problems such as incivilities, and reactions to crime, such as fear. The reality is that over time crime, delinquency, and crime-related dynamics serve as both cause and effect in relation to neighborhood conditions.

Context matters. The connection between a community's characteristics and its crime rates or its offender rates is likely to be influenced by factors outside the immediate community, including features of adjoining neighborhoods, the city or suburb or town in question, and the region more generally.

The three central questions can be examined at different levels: street blocks; neighborhoods; regions of a city, such as a census tract or zip code; cities; or metropolitan areas. As one moves up and down these different levels of analysis, the connections between crime (or offending) and community features are likely to shift.

THEORETICAL PERSPECTIVES ON CRIME AND COMMUNITY

Investigations into these three questions have generally followed one of five different theoretical perspectives: socioeconomy, human ecology, behavioral geography, routine activities, and territorial functioning. Socioeconomy focuses primarily on the relevance of socioeconomic status and race as influences on crime and offending rates. Human ecology attends largely to the influence of community stability on delinquency rates. Behavioral geography addresses connections between offense location, offender spatial behavior, and physical features of the locale. Routine activities suggests property or personal crime incidents arise from the intersection of available targets, nearby offenders, and an absence of natural guardians, place managers, and intimate handlers of offenders. Territorial functioning suggests community safety depends in part on residents' and regular users' contributions to management of nearby activities, and to the image and upkeep of the locale.

Each of these five theoretical perspectives differs in its preferred level of analysis and in the processes it assumes connect community composition to crime or delinquency.

FACTORS THAT AFFECT CRIME RATES

What is known about the determinants of community crime rates? Racial composition of the neighborhood matters, although its impact appears to be substantially conditioned by socioeconomic status. Violent-offense rates are generally higher in neighborhoods with more substantial populations of color, although researchers differ on what dynamics best explain this connection.

Socioeconomic status matters; neighborhoods with lower socioeconomic status levels generally have higher violent crime rates. Questions persist about exactly how socioeconomic status is related to crime. Declining socioeconomic status is linked to increasing violent crime, but rapidly increasing socioeconomic status also may be linked to higher property crime rates. Neighborhoods that are more stable sometimes exhibit lower offense and offending rates, although stability is not as consistently linked to safety as socioeconomic status is.

Family structure has garnered increased attention in the last twenty years for its relationship to crime. Connections between family structure and crime appear, but they may be contingent and contextually dependent in ways not yet fully appreciated. For example, the impact of the proportion of single-parent, woman-headed households with children on delinquency may depend on socioeconomic status or community location or both.

Intense debates continue in several areas. The relative importance of each of these dimensions as determinants of crime rates is not clear. Different theoretical perspectives invoke different processes mediating between structure and crime. It is not known how those processes operate over time.

THE EFFECT OF CRIME ON COMMUNITY

What *is* known about the impact of crime rates on community fabric? Crime has economic costs. Higher crime rates adversely affect neighborhood house prices and reduce the attractiveness of neighborhoods to most groups of potential in-migrants. When crime persists in an area, it causes increases in vacant-housing rates, and changing crime rates are linked to changing vacant-housing rates.

Many believe that higher community crime rates directly influence out-migration. Research links higher crime with stronger intent to move, lower attachment to place, and lower residential satisfaction. But, despite one recent study that may link victimization to mobility, the bulk of work fails to connect crime with mobility. "At the aggregate and individual level, crime and perceptions of the crime problem do not translate into higher mobility or suburban flight" (Taylor 1995, p. 33). Low crime rates, however, may increase the attractiveness of an area for in-migration.

The effect of crime on neighborhood participation in local improvement efforts is as contested as the question of mobility. Crime does not appear to consistently reduce participation, and at least one study suggests higher crime may spur more extensive local participation.

Although the determinants of neighborhoods with high offender rates are often similar to those of neighborhoods with high violent crime rates, areas with high

Laws of Old

This excerpt from an 1832 yearbook describes a host of British laws going back as far as times of Elizabeth I and Henry VII.

Sir,

I am accustomed to seek for amusement in odd places. The other night I turned over some volumes which, to common readers, would not appear likely to afford recreation; viz. the "Statues at Large" and in the course of my pastime I noted down a few curious specimens of ancient laws. Which I subjoin for your use

I am, Sir
Yours Obliged
H.W. Lander.

Apparel—No servant of husbandrie, nor common laborer, shall weare in their clothing any cloth whereof the broad yard shall pass the price of two shillings; nor shall suffer their wives to weare any kercheffe whose price exceedeth twentie pence. And that no manner of person under the estate of a lord shall weare any gowne or mantel, unless it bee of such length, the hee being upright, it shall cover his buttocks, upon peine to forfeit twenty shillings.—(22 Edw. IV. cap. 1).

Archery—All sorts of men, under the age of forty years, shall have bows and arrows, and use shooting.—(3 Henry VIII. cap. 3). No bowyer shall sell any bow of yew to any person between the ages of eight and fourteen years, above the price of twelve pence.—(31 ibid. cap 9).

Fast Days—Whosever shall, by preaching, teaching, writing, or open speech, notify that eating of fish, or forbearing of flesh, is of any necessity for saving the soul of man, shall be punished, as spreaders of false news are and ought to be.—(5 Eliz. cap. 5, sec. 40).

Gipseys—All persons which shall be found in company of vagabonds calling themselves Egyptians, and so shall continue for the space of one month, shall be judged as felons, and suffer the pains of death.—(5 Eliz. cap. 20, sec. 3).

Libels—If any person speak any false and slanderous new or tales against the queen, he shall have both his ears cut off. And if any person shall print of set forth any book containing any matter to the defamation of the queen, or by prophecying, conjuration, &c., seek to know how long the queen shall live, he shall be adjudged a felon.—(23 Eliz. cap. 2).

Masks and Mummers—Mummers shall be imprisoned three months, and fined at the justice's discretion. The penalty for selling visors, or keeping them, is to forfeit twenty shillings, and to be imprisoned at the discretion of the justices.—(3 Henry VIII. cap. 9).

Pins—No person shall put to sale any pins but only such as shall be double-headed, and have the heads soldered fast to the shank and well smoothed, the shank well shaven; the point well and round filed, cauted and sharpened.—(34 and 35 Henry VIII. cap. 6).

Witchcraft, &c.—It shall be felony to practise, or cause to be practiced, conjuration, witchcraft, enchantment, or sorcery, to get money; or to consume any person in his body, members, or goods; or to provoke any person to unlawful love; or to declare where goods stolen be; or, for the despite of Christ, or lucre of money, to pull down any cross.—(33 Henry VIII. cap. 8).

Woolen Caps—All persons above the age of seven years shall wear upon Sabbaths and holidays, upon their heads, a cap of wool, knit, thicked, and dressed in England, upon pain to forfeit, for every day not wearing, three shillings and four pence.—(13 Eliz. cap. 19).

Source: Hone, William. (1832). *The Year Book of Daily Recreation and Information.* London: William Tegg, 1832, pp. 1453–1454.

offender rates and areas with high offense rates are somewhat spatially distinct. Areas with high offender or high delinquency rates may retain their elevated rates over decades or even generations. Community fabric, the actions of the criminal justice system and other public agencies, broader economic and social trends, and outside views of these areas are all determining factors in the offender and delinquency rates; understanding how these factors contribute individually and jointly to these rates is an exceedingly complex task.

Community features such as patterns of land use, traffic patterns, and location within the larger city or suburb or metropolitan area shape potential offenders' travel patterns. The journey to crime is thus influenced not only by where potential offenders live, but also by the destinations they seek, how those destinations are embedded in the urban and suburban fabric, and the routes and modes of transportation they use to get where they are going.

—Ralph B. Taylor

See also COMMUNITY JUSTICE; COMMUNITY POLICING; GANGS; SOCIAL CONTROL

Further Reading

Baldwin, J., & Bottoms, A. E. (1976). *The urban criminal.* London: Tavistock.

Bursik, R. J., Jr., & Grasmick, H. (1993). *Neighborhoods and crime.* New York: Lexington Books.

Covington, J. C., & Taylor, R. B. (1989). Gentrification and crime: Robbery and larceny changes in appreciating Baltimore neighborhoods in the 1970's. *Urban Affairs Quarterly, 25,* 142–172.

Dugan, L. (1999). The effect of criminal victimization on a household's moving decision. *Criminology, 37*(4), 903–930.

Felson, M. (1994). *Crime in everyday life.* Thousand Oaks, CA: Pine Forge.

Miethe, T. D., & Meier, R. F. (1994). *Crime and its social context.* Albany, NY: SUNY Press.

Reiss, A. J., Jr. (1986). Why are communities important in understanding crime? In A. J. Reiss, Jr., & M. Tonry (Eds.), *Communities and crime* (Vol. 8, pp. 1–34). Chicago: University of Chicago Press.

Rengert, G., & Wasilchick, J. (1985). *Suburban burglary.* Springfield, IL: Charles C Thomas.

Sampson, R. J., & Lauritsen, J. L. (1994). Violent victimization and offending: Individual, situational- and community-level risk factors. In A. J. J. Reiss, & J. A. Roth (Eds.), *Understanding and preventing violence: Vol. 3. Social influences* (pp. 1–114). Washington, DC: National Academy Press.

Shaw, M., & McKay, H. (1972). *Juvenile delinquency and urban areas* (2nd ed.). Chicago: University of Chicago Press.

Short, J. F. (1997). *Poverty, ethnicity and violent crime.* Boulder, CO: Westview.

Taylor, R. B. (1988). *Human territorial functioning.* Cambridge, UK: Cambridge University Press.

Taylor, R. B. (1995, May). Impact of crime on communities. *Annals of the American Academy of Political and Social Science, 539,* 28–45.

Taylor, R. B. (1996). Neighborhood responses to disorder and local attachments: The systemic model of attachment, and neighborhood use value. *Sociological Forum, 11*(1), 41–74.

Taylor, R. B. (2001). Understanding the connections between physical environment, crime, fear and resident-based control. In J. Q. Wilson & J. Petersilia (Eds.), *Crime: Public policies and crime control* (pp. 413–425). Oakland, CA: ICS Press.

Taylor, R. B., & Covington, J. (1988). Neighborhood changes in ecology and violence. *Criminology, 26*(4), 553–589.

Wilson, W. J. (1996). *When work disappears: The world of the new urban poor.* New York: Knopf.

CROWDS

From shopping in a supermarket to attending a city council meeting to participating in the Allied invasion of Normandy on June 6, 1944, crowds are ubiquitous, a part of life that most people take for granted. Webster defines a crowd as a large number of persons, especially when collected together. Sociologists have sought to define and explain crowd behavior for more than a hundred years, but they have yet to arrive at a widely accepted understanding of the phenomenon.

THE LE BONIAN VIEW OF CROWDS

Psychologie des foules, written by the French sociologist Gustave Le Bon (1841–1931) and published in 1895 (English translation *The Crowd: A Study of the Popular Mind,* 1960), is the most influential early statement about crowds. Le Bon saw his time as the "age of the crowd," a period in which crowds dominated political life. The crowd's destructive potential, according to Le Bon, emerged from "the law of the mental unity of the crowd": In crowds everywhere, the conscious individual personalities of its members disappear and are replaced by a collective mind composed of hereditary elements of a race, including long-dormant savage and destructive parts. These savage aspects of the collective mind, combined with the leveling of individual personalities and the group's psychological unity, accounted for the crowd's capacity for cruel and shocking acts as well as for generous and lofty behavior.

Le Bon thought that the collective mind gives the members of the crowd a feeling of invincible power and anonymity, which allows them to deny personal responsibility for their actions. Also according to Le Bon, because crowds are highly suggestible and irrational, ideas and behaviors that may be counter to a crowd's interests spread like infectious diseases.

ROBERT E. PARK

Robert E. Park (1864–1944), an American sociologist, is often credited with introducing the field of collective behavior, which includes the study of crowds and, among other things, conflict, crazes, cults, disaster, panic, rumor, and social movements. Influenced by Le Bon's ideas, Park described crowds as often forming during conditions of social unrest. At such times, one person's discontent is transmitted to another, who sends it to others, who transmit it back to the first participants, thereby eventually creating a common mood and reducing the participants' level of intelligence. This circular reaction often leads to crowd action.

Park also adopted and expanded a distinction between the crowd and the public, which had been developed by the French sociologist and criminologist Jean-Gabriel Tarde (1843–1904). In Park's view, a "public" forms when people disagree about an issue or issues by engaging in rational discussion. Members of a public are usually physically dispersed and therefore seldom engage in face-to-face interaction, but instead communicate through the media or assert their views, which they expect to have influence, through political parties and other interest groups.

Pilgrims gather on the banks of the Ganges and Yamuna Rivers in Allahabad, India, in November 2001.

Source: Gavriel Jecan/Corbis; used with permission.

HERBERT BLUMER

In 1939, the U.S. sociologist Herbert Blumer (1900–1987) published an elaboration and expansion of Park's views on collective behavior and social movements, which became the dominant sociological view. Adopting Park's distinction between routine or ordinary behavior and the social unrest and circular reactions characteristic of much collective behavior, Blumer saw social unrest as providing a setting in which new forms of collective behavior may develop.

Blumer described four primary kinds of crowds. The casual crowd has loose organization and little unity; its members come and go as they gain and lose interest in whatever caught their attention. The second type, the acting crowd, focuses on a goal and directs its action toward achieving the goal. It lacks such elements of social organization as formal divisions of labor, roles, norms, and recognized leadership, but instead is spontaneous and lives in the present. Individual members lose self-control and critical understanding as they become infected by the dominant mood through milling and social contagion. After this crowd has developed a common mood and has focused on an object of attention, it is ready to act aggressively, in a process sometimes called deindividuation.

The third type, the conventionalized crowd, has social norms or rules that guide its behavior. Examples are people who come together to watch athletic events, attend movies and plays, or to hear campaign speeches and lectures or attend other regular scheduled events that may have official government support, social approval, or both. The fourth type, the expressive or dancing crowd, resembles the acting crowd in that it is characterized by milling, collective excitement and social contagion, but it lacks a goal or specific objective. Tension is released through physical movement, which is often rhythmical, and excitement becomes an end in itself. The New Orleans Mardi Gras celebrations exemplify such crowd behavior.

THE VALUED-ADDED APPROACH

Neil J. Smelser, an American sociologist, has argued that collective behavior events develop through several stages in the so-called value-added process. As each stage passes, fewer alternatives remain, and the next stage becomes more probable.

The first stage is structural conduciveness. A particular manifestation of collective behavior cannot occur unless the social structure promotes or permits it. For example, massive vehicular traffic jams are impossible in social structures in which all travel is pedestrian. A financial panic is impossible in a social structure in which economic exchange takes place through barter and face-to-face trading of commodities. (A structure conducive to a financial panic is one in which money as the means of exchange moves instantly from place to place via the Internet.)

In the next stage, structural strain develops when various parts of a social system are in conflict with one another through stress, deprivation, threats, or other sources of ambiguity. In the United States, for example, there has been great ambiguity and conflict over the place of women in the economic system.

A further stage after that of structural strain may be that of new generalized beliefs that explain what is wrong, what needs to be done to correct the situation, and what will happen if nothing is done. These beliefs are often irrational and may resemble magical or mythical beliefs.

After the formation of new generalized beliefs, the next stage is that of precipitating factors or triggering events, which take many forms, such as rumor, accidents, and the revelation of secrets. These factors confirm and give substance to the new generalized beliefs and provide direction to collective action.

The stage of precipitating factors is followed by that of mobilization for action. During this stage, acts of collective behavior may be initiated by leaders who take the initiative and by the mass media spreading news or rumors. People take part in crowd actions, panics, collective flights based on hysterical beliefs, or hostile outbursts. Often there are demands or agitation for reforms or revolution.

In the final stage, the forces of social control that attempt to restore or preserve the threatened state of affairs begin to operate. Some social controls may also have been applied in the early stages to prevent the possible occurrence of acts of collective behavior. Others are applied only after a collective episode is underway.

THE DEPRIVATION, FRUSTRATION, AGGRESSION APPROACH

In the late 1930s, scholars developed the deprivation approach to explain acts of social aggression. From this viewpoint, people are sometimes deprived or think they are when they compare themselves with others. Deprivation, real or perceived, often leads to frustration, which can be followed by aggression. It is not unusual for people to act aggressively even though the actual conditions of their lives are improving. The J curve of rising expectations posited by James C. Davies, an American political scientist, was developed to account for the acting crowds, riots, and revolutions when conditions of life are improving. In such conditions, the expectations of a group may become greater than the capacity to fill them, which leads to an intolerable gap between what people thought they could and should have and what they actually get, often resulting in collective violence.

CONVERGENCE

Not all of the early scholars of collective behavior accepted the contagion approach to crowds described earlier. Some argued that the crowd is a gathering that is not representative of the general population. In this approach, crowds are said to be made up of lower-class members who share the same qualities and feelings. Belonging to a crowd intensifies these shared qualities and feelings, which leads to a reduction in restraint and perhaps to destructive action.

The term *convergence* in reference to crowds also signifies the movement of people toward an area that has suffered a disaster. People gather to help with rescue efforts, provide goods and services, and gain information about friends and families. This form of convergence may hinder organized rescue and relief efforts.

RECENT VIEWS OF THE CROWD

During the 1960s and 1970s, a time of intense unrest in the United States and much of the rest of the world, many social movements emerged to focus on civil rights, racism, the Vietnam War, the relationships between the universities and the military-industrial complex, women's liberation, and gay liberation. Thousands of crowds were associated with these social movements.

When collective behavior theorists applied the previously described theories to their research on the crowds of recent times, they were surprised to find little support for the Le Bonian position and its variants. Scholars were forced to reevaluate their theories, to reject older views almost completely, and to develop new ideas.

EMERGENT NORMS

According to American sociologists Ralph H. Turner and Lewis M. Killian, a normative system emerges when the social structure lacks the means needed for collective decision making. In crowds without normative standards, the norms then emerge spontaneously. Through keynoting—a gesture or symbolic utterance that provides a definition of the situation—the crowd takes on a normative character that provides a division of labor between leaders and followers. Often more than one definition of the situation, normative structure, potential leaders, and followers emerges. One of these becomes focused, drives out others, and thus creates an illusion of unanimity. Norms also often emerge after a disaster, when rescue, communication, medical, and other groups surface and create norms as they begin the restoration of the old social structure.

THE NO-DIFFERENCE APPROACH

The no-difference approach also developed in response to recent crowd research that cast doubt on the Le Bonian view. In its most extreme form, this new approach argues that there is no difference between collective behavior, including crowd behavior, and ordinary everyday behavior. Carl Couch demonstrated that ten characteristics once thought to refer uniquely to crowds were not confined to crowd behavior alone. These characteristics—suggestibility, destructiveness, irrationality, emotionality, mental disturbances, lower-class participation, spontaneity, creativity, lack of self-control, and antisocial behavior—are sometimes part of crowd behavior, but also occur in everyday noncrowd life.

THE RATIONAL-CALCULUS APPROACH

Another aspect of the revised theories for understanding crowds is the rational-calculus approach, which maintains that crowd behavior is rational rather than irrational. From this point of view, crowd participants give careful consideration to the potential costs, risks, and benefits that might result from taking part in a particular action. More recently, scholars have considered emotions to be a part of crowd activity, but they have avoided the extreme emphasis of the Le Bonian view of crowds as highly emotional, impulsive, and irrational.

In sum, recent research has shown that "first, individuals are not driven mad by crowds; they do not lose cognitive control! Second, individuals are not compelled to participate by some madness-in-common, or any other sovereign psychological attribute, cognitive style, or predisposition that distinguishes them from nonparticipants. Third, the majority of behaviors in which members of these crowds engaged are neither mutually exclusive nor extraordinary, let alone mad, and are therefore not even addressed by traditional theories" (McPhail 1991, p. xxii). Current thinking about crowds leans toward a middle position, which holds that crowds and different forms of collective behavior are characterized by both emotional and rational goal-oriented behavior.

THE POLITICAL AND SOCIAL IMPACT OF CROWDS

However crowds are defined and whatever types, processes, and stages may be identified with them, they have had enormous influence in both causing and preventing social change. Conventional crowds are among the most important sources of support for governments and other control institutions, as demonstrated by political speeches, patriotic parades, ceremonies conducted at memorials for heroes, and anthems sung at athletic and other events.

Also, crowds have gained concessions from governments and other control institutions and have promoted the creation of new social structures including political structures. In the view of many scholars, without crowd violence employed to force those in with political power to change their views, the general system of human rights prevailing in the Western world would never have come into existence.

Crowds that challenge the status quo, whether violent or not, are often met with resistance. Crowd violence is more likely when authorities are not open to dissent and challenge. When authorities in such systems use violence as a means of crowd control, the crowd often responds with violence. On the other hand, crowds sometimes initiate violence, and it is often difficult to tell whether the crowd or the authorities instigated the violence.

Violent crowds are often called riots especially by those who are the targets. Gary Marc, an American sociologist, has identified two kinds: the protest riot, which is explicitly political and goal oriented, and the issueless riot, which is not goal oriented, such as riots after athletic events. Control of a conventional crowd, such as that associated with a parade or a fair, presents little problem. Rioting crowds are much more unpredictable. Their behavior is often met with force, which ranges from mild to powerful and deadly measures. Sometimes, control forces lose control and engage in riotous action against crowds.

FUTURE IMPLICATIONS

Crowds, whether conventionalized or violent and hostile, have always been part of human life, and they are not diminishing in number or importance. In fact, because of the information revolution and other social changes, instances of crowds are often increasing, and new forms are emerging.

The conventionalized crowd involving activities such as speeches, parades, and memorial ceremonies can be brought to almost everyone on earth through electronic means, with spectacular views of these crowds being instantly transmitted. Crowds can be and frequently are created and managed in order to present a particular ideological view.

The information revolution has also led to the loss of monopoly by those traditionally in control of the production and transmission of information to those traditionally excluded from that power. According to writer Howard Rheingold, those formally in control will engage in an extensive struggle to hold and extend their control, while those participating in what he calls "smart mobs" will be able to resist by working together in ways that were impossible before the of items and theories of the information revolution. Information about activities of a protest crowd in one country spreads quickly to others, stimulating similar activities elsewhere and allowing people to learn from the successes and failures of others. Crowd activities today are often rapidly planned, organized, and managed across national boundaries. People who work together no longer need to be physically close. They may be seen as members of new communities held together by the interaction of like-minded people rather than by physical-neighborhood relationships. Protest crowds are now a permanent part of political life and are as much a part of the political process as voting, election campaigns, and other conventional politics.

—Joseph B. Perry

Further Reading

Allport, F. H. (1924). *Social psychology.* Boston: Houghton Mifflin.

Aveni, A. F. (1977). The not so lonely crowd: Friendship groups in collective behavior. *Sociometry, 40*(March*)*, 96–99.

Barkan, S. E., & Snowden, L. L. (2001). *Collective violence.* Boston: Allyn & Bacon.

Berk, R. A. (1974). A gaming approach to crowd behavior. *American Sociological Review, 39*(June), 355–373.

Blumer, H. (1951). Collective behavior. In A. M. Lee (Ed.), *Principles of sociology* (pp. 167–222). New York: Barnes & Noble.

Clark, T. (1969). *Gabriel Tarde: On communication and social influence.* Chicago: University of Chicago Press.

Coleman, J. S. (1990). *Foundations of social theory.* Cambridge, MA: Belknap Press of Harvard University Press.

Couch, C. J. (1968). Collective behavior: An examination of some stereotypes. *Social Problems, 15,* 310–322.

Davies, J. C. (1962). Toward a theory of revolution. *American Sociological Review, 27,* 5–19.

Dollard, J., Doob, L. W., Neal, E. M., Mowrer, O. H., & Sears R. R. (1939). *Frustration and aggression.* New Haven, CT: Yale University Press.

Fogelson, R. (1971). *Violence as protest: A study of riots and ghettos.* Garden City, NY: Anchor.

Goode, E. (1992). *Collective behavior.* New York: Harcourt Brace Jovanovich.

Gurr, T. R. (1970). *Why men rebel.* Princeton, NJ: Princeton University Press.

Lane, R., & Turner, J. J., Jr. (1978). *Riot, rout, and tumult.* New York: University Press of America.

Le Bon, G. (1895). *Psychologie des foules* (Psychology of crowds). Paris: Felix, Alcan.

Le Bon, G. (1960). *The crowd: A study of the popular mind.* New York: Viking.

Marx, G. T. (1972). Issueless riots. In J. F. Short & M. E. Wolfgang (Eds.), *Collective violence* (pp.11). Chicago: Aldine de Gruyter.

McPhail, C. (1991). Civil disorder participation: A critical examination of recent research. *American Sociological Review, 36,* 1058–1073.

McPhail, C. (1992). *The myth of the madding crowd.* New York: Aldine de Gruyter.

Meyer, D. S., & Tarrow, S. (Eds.). (1998). *The social movement society: Contentious politics for a new century.* Lanham, MD: Rowman & Littlefield.

Milgram, S., & Toch, H. (1969). Collective behavior: Crowds and social movements. In G. Lindzey & E. Aronson (Eds.), *Handbook of social psychology* (2d ed., pp. 107–123). Reading, MA: Addison-Wesley.

Miller, D. L. (2001). *Introduction to collective behavior.* Springfield, IL: Waveland.

Miller, N., & Dollard, J. (1941). *Social learning and imitation.* New Haven, CT: Yale University Press.

Mills, N. (1986). *The crowd in American literature.* Baton Rouge: Louisiana State University Press.

Neal, D. M. (1993). A further examination of anonymity, contagion, and deindividuation in crowd and collective behavior. *Sociological Focus, 26,* 93–107.

Park ,R. E., & Burgess, E.W.(1921). *Introduction to the science of sociology.* Chicago: University of Chicago Press.

Rheingold, H. (2002). *Smart mobs: The next social revolution.* Cambridge, MA: Perseus.

Rude, G. (1964). *The crowd in history.* New York: Wiley.

Smelser, N. J. (1962). *Theory of collective behavior.* New York: Free Press.

Stark, R. (1972). *Police riots: Collective violence and law enforcement.* Belmont, CA: Wadsworth.

Tarrow, S. (1994). *Power in movement: Social movements, collective action, and politics.* New York: Cambridge University Press.

Tilley, C. (1978). *From mobilization to revolution.* Reading, MA: Addison-Wesley.

Tilley, C., Tilley, L., & Tilley, R. (1975). *The rebellious century.* Cambridge, MA: Harvard University Press.

Turner, R. H., & Killian, L. M. (1987). *Collective behavior* (3rd ed.). Englewood Cliffs, NJ: Prentice Hall.

Wanderer, J. J. (1968). The 1968 riots: A test of the congruity of events. *Social Problems, 16,* 193–197.

Wanderer, J. J. (1969). Index of riot severity and some correlates. *American Journal of Sociology, 74,* 500–504.

Young, K. (2002). Standard deviations: An update on North American sports crowd disorder. *Sociology of Sports Journal, 17,* 237–275.

Zimbardo, P. (1969). The human choice: Individuation, reason, and order versus deindividuation, impulse, and chaos. In W. Arnold & D. Levine (Eds.), *Nebraska symposium on motivation* (pp. 237–307). Lincoln: University of Nebraska Press.

CULTS

During the 1970s and 1980s, several dozen new religious movements were singled out and widely labeled "cults," becoming the focus of significant public controversy. Prominent among these groups were the Unification Church, founded by Rev. Sun Myung Moon (b. 1920); the International Society for Krishna Consciousness—popularly known as the Hare Krishna movement—founded by A. C. Bhaktivedanta Swami Prabhupada (1896–1977); the Church Universal and Triumphant, led by Elizabeth Clare Prophet (b. 1940); the Children of God (later renamed The Family), founded by David "Moses" Berg (1919–1994); the Divine Light Mission, led by Guru Maharaj Ji; and the Church of Scientology, founded by L. Ron Hubbard (1911–1986).

In the United States, the cult controversy developed in the 1970s when a number of unfamiliar new religions took root in the baby boomer generation. During the late 1960s, this unusually large generation, born soon after World War II, came of age. American society was unprepared to receive so many young adults suddenly competing for jobs and living space. Many of them dropped out of mainstream life and began to develop alternative means of employment and living. While some in this alternative culture chose to live on the streets, others formed "hippie" communes and related groups that experimented with various forms of cooperative existence.

Simultaneously with the coming of age of the baby boomers, the United States changed its laws on immigration from Asia. Beginning in 1965, after half a century of being denied entry, tens of thousands of Asians began to move to the United States. Among them were some religious leaders who hoped to both serve the immigrant community and build a following among the larger body of American citizens.

The hippie movement made these many disconnected young adults more visible, and a variety of religious groups targeted them for conversion. Many of these groups invited converts not just into an affiliation, but into a full-time identity as a religious worker. They offered new members a place to live, regular meals, a job working for the group and its cause, and a sense of purpose. Because the ideology and practices of many groups were often at extreme odds with their new recruits' prior religious training, a period of intense indoctrination often followed. Devoting much time and energy to the group, new members were frequently cut off from former friends and their family of origin for a period of time.

In one common scenario, college students disappeared into the counterculture for the summer and, while out of touch with parents, joined a new religion. When they missed the fall quarter at school, parents became worried. When their offspring finally returned home for Thanksgiving or Christmas, parents were horrified at what they saw as an unwelcome religious transformation.

COMMUNAL PRACTICES

Adopting a form of communal existence is, of course, far from uncommon in new religious movements. Some groups do so to improve the quality and depth of relationships among its adherents. Some see communal life as the best possible manifestation of the unity of the faith. Others claim full-time vocation in a religious endeavor as the highest manifestation of dedication to God.

Most of these groups made no secret of the communal life to which members were being invited. The Hare Krishnas, for example, were a monastic group, and while recruiting widely, they gave converts a trial period to test their readiness. The Unification Church sent new members to live in communal houses as brothers and sisters for a period of preparation for later marriage and the establishment of nuclear family homes. Although the Children of God "converted" many with their personal witnessing and literature distribution, they recruited only a few into their communal life—those who wished to become full-time Christian missionaries.

Some noncommunal groups developed what amounted to an elite monastic community within a larger, more mundanely involved membership. The average active Scientologist might, for example, attend Sunday services and meet with a church counselor once or twice a month. However, among its hundreds of thousands of members, the Church of Scientology has a separate group of 5,000 to 7,000 members who are known as the Sea Organization. Members of this elite group give their lives to the spread of Scientology. They hold all policymaking positions in the church at the national and international levels, working six and a half days a week, and living in church facilities. Beginning in the late 1980s, the Church Universal and Triumphant developed a semi-monastic resident community at its headquarters in Montana. At the group's height in the early 1970s, these believers, most of whom worked for the church, were more than 700 in number.

THE CULT AWARENESS MOVEMENT

As the cult controversy developed, parents who protested their children's change of faith were joined by men and women who had left spouses behind in such groups. They were also joined by a few professionals, especially lawyers and psychologists, whose clients sought redress against the groups. Together, they founded a cult awareness movement that initially sought to persuade converts to leave, then took steps to weaken or even destroy the targeted groups. Their efforts received a significant boost in the late 1970s.

Several professionals in psychology fields—most prominently the Massachusetts psychiatrist John Clark, Jocelyn West of UCLA's Neuropsychiatric Institute, and the Berkeley psychologist Margaret Singer—spoke up. They suggested that these cults had established their intense communal practices not from any religious or spiritual motivation, but for purely expedient reasons. Such practice provided a ready-made pool of deployable agents to raise money for the group and spread its message. It also provided a context for an alleged process of brainwashing.

The concept of brainwashing (also known as coercive persuasion, mind control, or thought control) appeared to offer a scientific rationale to explain why so many young adults left college and career prospects behind to live within a new religious community. The concept had been originally introduced in the 1950s to explain two phenomena: the behavior of the few American prisoners who, during the Korean War, made anti-American statements, and the opinions expressed by people forced into China's "thought reform" camps following the Chinese revolution. The brainwashing theory suggested that the Chinese had developed psychological techniques that could, in fact, reprogram individuals to hold beliefs against their will. Research after the Korean War indicated that the actions of both the American POWs and the Chinese inmates could be best explained by more mundane factors.

The brainwashing hypothesis was revived in the 1970s as a defense for newspaper heiress Patty Hearst, who, after being kidnapping by a radical political group, the Symbionese Liberation Army, appeared to freely join them in a bank robbery. While the jury did not accept the explanation and convicted Hearst, Margaret Singer, who testified at the trial, took the lead in investigating the brainwashing potential of cult life. She suggested that the religious strictures imposed by groups on their members were stronger bindings even than the bars that held prisoners of war. Her ideas were used to justify "deprogramming," the practice of snatching cult members back and subjecting them to intense pressure to renounce their allegiance to the group.

The cult controversy might have slowly faded away in the early 1980s had it not been for the events of November 1978. The Peoples Temple, a congregation of the million-member Christian Church (Disciples of Christ), had developed an independent direction within its rather pluralistic parent body. Members became especially attached to the leadership of their minister, Jim Jones (1931–1978), who had become well known for advocating a Marxist liberation theology that called for radical social change. In the mid-1970s, Jones and other members moved to Jonestown, their experimental agricultural colony in rural Guyana. There the group lived somewhat communally, relying on the U.S. government checks of its poorer members to support itself.

Responding to accusations of irregularities, including the charge than some at the colony remained there against their will, California Congressman Leo J. Ryan led an investigative trip to Guyana in 1978. For several days he and his staff interviewed members and leaders and found what appeared to be an overwhelmingly contented group. Many of the poorest members testified that they had never had life so good. However, on the final day of their visit, as they prepared to leave the country, Ryan and his staff were murdered. Subsequently, the majority of the community committed suicide and took the remaining members with them. Only a very few witnesses survived. In the wake of the deaths, leaders in the cult awareness movement charged that all cults were potential "Jonestowns."

In the years after Jonestown, congressional hearings about cults were held. The loosely organized cult awareness movement solidified largely into two organizations, the Cult Awareness Network (CAN) and the American Family Foundation (AFF), and deprogrammings increased markedly. CAN and AFF charged that a wide variety of "high-demand" religious groups were in fact brainwashing cults.

NONCOMMUNAL AND QUASI-COMMUNAL PRACTICES

Notable among the targets of the cult awareness movement in the 1980s were a variety of noncommunal groups who nevertheless promoted close bonds among adherents. For example, the International Churches of Christ still practice "discipling": Each new member is paired with a more mature member for weekly conversation on a wide range of issues, both religious and secular, in the life of the new believer. While some converts found the attention appealing, others found it meddlesome and revolted against it, charging the church with manipulative practices.

Discipling had begun in the 1970s among Pentecostals who built several large campus-centered movements, most notably Maranatha Churches and Campus Ministries. Maranatha recruited students, placed them in separate campus residential communities, and then so rescheduled their lives that their coursework eventually suffered. Many converts dropped out of school altogether.

Other churches were not communal but developed some separatist tendencies. Believers worked at secular jobs, lived in their own homes, and established nuclear families. However, the church became the center of their social life, and they rarely socialized with nonmember neighbors and family.

The anxiety that some felt about cults was heightened in the 1990s by several violent tragedies: the U.S. government's attempted raid and resultant siege of the Mt. Carmel Community established by the Branch Davidian Adventists near Waco, Texas; the suicide-murder deaths of Solar Temple followers in Switzerland and Canada; the gassing of the Tokyo subway station by members of the Aum Shinrikyō in Japan; and the collective suicide of thirty-nine members of the UFO-oriented Heaven's Gate group in California. Of the several new religions involved in these violent incidents, the Branch Davidians and the Heaven's Gate groups both lived communally. The Aum Shinrikyō did not, although its membership, which numbered in the tens of thousands, included a dedicated monastic core of about 1,500. Many of these dedicated elite resided at the group's headquarters near Mt. Fuji. Some followers of the Solar Temple lived communally, some did not. However, all lived a somewhat separate existence marked by secret esoteric rituals, the content of which pointed to possible suicide for that minority which did indeed later take their own lives.

The choice to adopt a belief and practice that separates a group from the larger community often makes the group the target of criticism and discrimination. This problem becomes most acute when group life undermines commonly accepted social conventions that value family ties, individual accountability, participation in national life, and economic productivity.

New religious movements are the most likely to experiment in communal reorganization, based on the seeming logic of religious commitment and ideological

The Cult of the Leader

In the United States, we typically associate the word "cult" with religious cults, often started and led by a charismatic individual. In other parts of the world, cults often take a political form with worship of powerful political leaders such as Adolf Hitler in Nazi Germany, Mussolini in Italy, Stalin if Russia, and Mao in China. The following describes a "Cult of Tito" in Yugoslavia. Marshal Tito (Josip Broz, 1892–1980), was a leader of Yugoslav partisans in World War II and the first Communist prime minister and the president of Yugoslavia.

This raises one, final, point with regard to people's attitudes towards the state. I commented earlier that people particularly do not trust government. In Yugoslavia, however, particularly since Tito's death, there has grown a kind of "cult of Tito." Tito's picture is displayed in every place of business, and in many homes. Each night, when the television broadcasting ends for the day, a few lines of a song are sung: "Comrade Tito, we follow in your ways . . ." Tito's birthday is celebrated, and there are many other outward displays of patriotism. How does this fit with my analysis?

The people with whom I lived were members of the communist party, and devoted patriots. Yet they also tried to achieve a high level of self-sufficiency, they had many "connections" in town and in the villages, and generally behaved in a way consistent with what I have described so far. They were loyal to Tito and the Party. They were patriotic and proud of their country. But they did not trust the market, they did not trust the economy, they in short, did not trust the people who ran the government. People loved Tito: he was the image of the loving and protective father who took care of his children, all Yugoslavs. People however do not trust all those "strangers" who hold offices, head various bureau, and generally are out for their own interests and that of their friends and kin, according to popular belief. This fits very well with the pattern of dependency and loyalty felt towards the family, and the mistrust of all others. Tito and the state are respectively the good and the bad parent, or to be more accurate, Tito and the state are the good parent, but the people who now run the state are the bad parent and cannot be trusted. It follows from that that families must look out for themselves.

Source: Gilliland, Mary K. (1986). *The Maintenance of Family Values in a Yugoslav Town.* Ann Arbor, MI: University Microfilms International, pp. 386–387.

rhetoric. This logic might refer to the desire to manifest the unity of the body of Christ, or the urge to separate from the polluted ways of the world. Some groups appeal to people who are ready to identify themselves as one of the persecuted, one of the few who will ultimately be seem as correct. However, over time, most groups find a means of adapting their radical ideology to the conformist demands of society. Overwhelmingly, they are not drawn to violent confrontations.

Even groups that maintain a separatist communal lifestyle for more than a generation generally give up their communalism eventually. Such has been the case, for example, with the surviving nineteenth-century experiments at Amana, Iowa, and Oneida, New York. The communal element in the early Mormon movement (the United Order) has dissipated, succeeded by an emphasis on charity toward neighbors in distress. This emphasis remains notable within today's Church of Jesus Christ of Latter-Day Saints. Only a very few groups—one thinks of the Hutterites—have maintained a separatist communal life for as much as a century.

For the majority of those who wish to live in an alternative, high-demand community, some major religious institutions, such as the Roman Catholic Church and the larger Buddhist organizations, sponsor a variety of monastic communities. These operate under the aegis of the larger body and encourage various avenues of interaction with the public at large. In turn, society has found in such a model a means of accommodating those who wish to experiment with high-demand forms of religious existence. This accommodation suggests that when the novelty of a new religion wanes, its forms of high-demand religious living may also find a greater degree of acceptance.

—J. Gordon Melton

Further Reading

Bromley, D. G., & Melton, J. G., Eds. (2002). *Cults, religion and violence.* Cambridge, UK: Cambridge University Press.

Dawson, L. L. (1998). *Comprehending cults: The sociology of new religious movements.* Toronto, Ontario: Oxford University Press.

Jenkins, P. (2000). *Mystics and messiahs: Cults and new religions in American history.* Oxford, UK: Oxford University Press.

CULTURAL ECOLOGY

Cultural ecology is a subfield of cultural anthropology that is concerned with understanding the relationships between human groups and their environments. The intellectual roots of cultural ecology are usually traced to the pioneering work *Theory of Culture Change* (1955), by anthropologist Julian Steward (1902–1972), but the manner in which culture and the environment interact and how the environment may determine, influence, or circumscribe cultures has been a consistent feature of the social sciences since the days of French philosopher Montesquieu (1689–1755).

THE ROOTS OF CULTURAL ECOLOGY

In *On the Spirit of Laws* (1748), Montesquieu made some effort to explain why societies differed from one another and suggested that variables such as soils, climate, and the environment were among the many influential factors informing the constitution of a people. Ideas about the relationship between peoples' cultures and their mode of life, or how people interact with nature in procuring their livelihood, again arose in the nineteenth century. The theories presented to explain cultural differences were evolutionary and placed groups of people in categories based, in part, on the effectiveness of their technologies in extracting resources from the environment.

The linear evolutionary scheme most representative of the period was that of the ethnologist Lewis Henry Morgan (1818–1881). Morgan argued for what he called "ethical periods" through which all human societies passed in succession. These periods were the three stages of savagery (lower, middle, and upper), the three stages of barbarism (lower, middle, and upper), and the two stages of civilization (low and high). Morgan noted in *Ancient Society* that "improvement in subsistence . . . must have favored the general advancement of the family. It led to localization, to the use of additional arts, to an improvement of house architecture, and to a more intelligent life" (Morgan 1877/1978, p. 469).

Although the evolutionary doctrine outlined by Morgan has been thoroughly discredited in anthropology, the idea that the material conditions of life are primary still informs some approaches in anthropology, particularly cultural ecology. After the linear evolutionary theories were abandoned, two views about the role of the environment in human societies were distinguished in anthropology and geography through the first half of the twentieth century. These views were labeled environmental determinism (or environmentalism) and environmental possibilism.

Environmental Determinism and Environmental Possibilism

Environmental determinism held that environmental forms determined cultural forms. This school of thought was exemplified in the works of the geographer Ellsworth Huntington (1876–1947), who asserted that the temperate climates, with their shortened agricultural cycles and long winters, stimulated achievement, economic efficiency, thrift, and creativity. The bounty of the tropics negated the need for the production of surplus and therefore hampered creative and intellectual advancement. Huntington understood that there was an interaction of biological inheritance, environment, and culture in explaining human behavior, but he considered the climate the most influential variable in understanding human cultural capabilities.

Environmental possibilism stated that the environment presents certain limitations on cultures and societies and therefore permits a limited set of adaptations to it. One would be unlikely to find banana cultivation in northern Europe, for example, or extensive fishing technologies among the cultures of the Gobi Desert. Environmental possibilism allowed for a number of cultural phenomena as reasoned and adaptive responses to environmental constraints. Developments of food storage techniques or seasonal migration patterns, for example, are different, but equally reasonable, adaptations to seasonal changes in food supplies.

In anthropology, Alfred Kroeber (1876–1960) rejected the concepts of environmental determinism and stressed cultural and historical influences as determinants of behavior. He argued that the environment of the southwestern United States, for example, presented a limiting condition to the development of agriculture. More significant to the development of peoples living there than that limitation, however, was the peoples' culture and the historical relations they had with the peoples of Mexico, who had first developed maize agriculture. History and culture were the primary determinants in human-land relations for Kroeber; the environment simply determined the limits against which human actors were set.

The Culture-Area Hypothesis

One influence on Kroeber's thinking was the culture-area hypothesis of the anthropologist Clark Wissler (1870–1947). Wissler argued in *The Relation of Nature to Man in Aboriginal America* (1926) that there were certain correspondences between environmental characteristics and cultural traits. Wissler thought that finding relationships between environmental regions and cultural traits within those regions was a step toward finding causal relationships between cultural traits and environmental conditions.

Wissler presented nine North American culture areas that were closely associated with botanical and climatic characteristics. The utility of the culture-area hypothesis was limited because within any culture area there could be seen a variety of cultural forms that together could not be considered a single cultural, social, or demographic unit. The conclusions about relationships between culture and environment that could be drawn from the culture-area hypothesis were, therefore, trivial.

What was important about Wissler's idea was the recognition that specific human adaptations to specific environments provided the basis for understanding the relationships between certain environmental variables and a specific subsistence activity on which a number of important cultural traits depended. For example, maize cultivation was successful only in environments that afforded certain amounts of rainfall and frost-free periods, and in those areas where maize cultivation was successful, a whole panorama of cultural traits were enmeshed in maize production. Similarly, significant cultural practices surround yam and taro cultivation in the islands of the Pacific Ocean whose tropical environments provide the warm weather and bountiful rainfall that are required for those cultivars.

JULIAN STEWARD AND CULTURAL ECOLOGY

Julian Steward was influenced by these developments in his formulation of cultural ecology. Steward focused on cultural adaptations to specific environments and, unlike his mentor, Alfred Kroeber, was unconcerned with deterministic models. His fundamental goal was "to explain the origin of particular cultural features and patterns which characterize different areas rather than to derive general principles applicable to any culture-environment situation" (Steward 1955, p. 36). Specifically, he was concerned about explaining "whether the adjustments of human societies to their environments require particular modes of behavior or whether they permit latitude for a certain range of possible behavior patterns" (p. 36).

Steward presented three fundamental procedures of cultural ecology. These procedures were, first, the analysis of the relationship between the environment and the extractive and productive technology used to

Using the Cultural Ecology Model to Explain Cultural Change

The following extract is from a historical study of the Chipewyan of Canada. The author uses the cultural ecology approach to examine the influence of Chipewyan knowledge of caribou behavior on the relationship between the environment and changes in Chipewyan culture.

Three major historical adaptive phases may be recognized for the Chipewyan, the dates of which vary with the intensity of European contact in different zones. [. . .] The phases are:

(1) The Aboriginal-Early Contact, from the time of earliest European contact in their own lands in 1715–16 until substantial European impact and the development of a stabilized adaptation to the fur trade, which may be taken as after 1821. The latter date is that of the amalgamation of the Hudson's Bay and North West Companies, by which time many Chipewyan groups or bands had relocated in the interior forest because of the greater abundance of fur bearing animals, especially beaver. The approximate middle of this period, ca. 1780, represents the period when peace had been made between the Chipewyan and Cree, the early and vascillating movement into the full boreal forest by some bands began, and the first major, devastating smallpox epidemic struck the central Subarctic west of Hudson Bay. It also marks the approximate time of the penetration of the interior and the competition between the Hudson's Bay and North West Companies which through low, competitive prices made trade goods cheap and abundant, rapidly becoming necessities. Until this time dependency upon trapping and the fur trade was of limited importance. The major branch of the Chipewyan did not significantly trap themselves, but obtained furs from the Yellowknife division and from the Dogribs as intermediaries with the Hudson's Bay Company at Churchill. Until Hearne visited Yellowknife country in 1771 the Yellowknives had not yet seen a white (Hearne 1958:78). A few metal artifacts had begun to replace aboriginal types, but subsistence activities had not been altered, and travel to the Bay was limited. The period of competition, from 1763 to 1821, made the fur trade more significant for some Chipewyan groups. The Yellowknife participation in the trade took the form of operating as middlemen, by force, with the Dogribs; other Chipewyan were becoming permanent inhabitants of the full boreal forest, gradually abandoning the taiga-tundra adaptation. The Chipewyan remaining in their traditional lands at the edge of the forest, then becoming known as the Caribou Eaters, continued the traditional adaptation with only marginal participation in the trade.

(2) The Developed Fur Trade, after 1821, is that of a stabilized, long-term adaptation of the Chipewyan to the trade, characterized by dependence upon trade goods and exploitation of the fur bearing animals. After amalgamation of the companies in 1821, the Hudson's Bay Company held the monopoly on the trade, but only after the Yellowknives had been eliminated and the major body of Chipewyan (excepting the Caribou Eaters) enmeshed in the new economy, in new ecozones, and with different exploitative patterns adapted to the changed faunal resources of the full boreal forest and adjacent parkland regions. The phase culminated in the twentieth century in the "Contact-Traditional horizon" (Helm and Damas 1963), which did not begin to develop among the Caribou Eaters until the 1920's and later.

(3) The "Micro-urban Village," or Government-Commercial, begins with the extension of government social services and concentration in permanent villages in the decades following World War II. It began earliest in the Upper Churchill River drainage, and the areas around Lake Athabasca and Great Slave Lake; it developed among the Caribou Eater bands in the late 1950's and 1960's. It is characterized by concentration in villages, the presence of federal and provincial government institutions, personnel, policies, regulations, and economic dependence upon welfare programs; ethnic complexity that includes relationships between the dominant Euro-Canadians, the Chipewyan, Cree, and Metis, etc. Aboriginal patterns of subsistence were rapidly lost, and even post-contact trapping patterns are of rapidly diminishing importance. The diminished nomadism of the late developed fur trade period culminates in the increasingly endogamous village (Smith n.d.).

Source: Smith, James G. E. (1975). "The Ecological Basis of Chipewyan Socio-Territorial Organization." In *Athapaskan Conference, 1971* (Vol. 2), edited by A. McFadyen Clark. Ottawa: National Museum of Canada, pp. 393–395.

exploit environmental resources; second, "the behavior patterns involved in the exploitation of a particular area by means of a particular technology"; and third, "the extent to which the behavior patterns entailed in exploiting the environment affect other aspects of culture" (pp. 40–42). Steward used these procedures to examine the environmental relations of cultures as diverse as hunter-gatherers and established nation-states, but he was best known for his analysis of the Shoshone hunter-gatherers of the Great Basin region of the United States.

Steward noted that the Shoshone exploited an environment characterized by extreme aridity, dispersed water resources, widely scattered game animals, and a general scarcity of available plant foods. The Shoshone were organized into small groups that facilitated the gathering and distribution of food and the movement of the group over the large area needed to effectively hunt and gather. The limitations of the landscape and the scarce distribution of game made large groups or communal approaches to food collection impractical. Similarly, since men tended to remain in the geographical area where they were raised and with which they were most familiar, there would be a tendency for people related through male relatives (a patrilineage) to band together to protect a large territory.

Steward noted four factors that would produce the patrilineal band: (1) "a population density of one person or less . . . per square mile" (p. 135); (2) an environment in which the principle game food is nonmigratory and scattered; (3) transportation which is restricted to humans carriers without the use of draft animals or motorized vehicles; and (4) the "cultural-psychological fact . . . that groups of kin who associate together intimately tend to extend incest taboos from the biological family to the extended family" (p. 135). This last factor served to ensure marriage patterns that facilitated intergroup relations and fostered mutual dependence between widely scattered groups. All these factors were efficient adaptations to those environments whose widely distributed resources were most effectively exploited by patrilineal bands. Steward's model demonstrated clear relationships between forms of social organization and features of the environment. Steward limited his approach to dealing primarily with those aspects of a culture that "empirical evidence shows to be most closely involved in the utilization of the environment in culturally prescribed ways" (p. 37). These are the cultural features that Steward called the cultural core.

EXPANDING THE CULTURAL CORE

In *Pigs for the Ancestors* (1968), anthropologist Roy A. Rappaport tied ritual behavior to demonstrable environmental and agricultural conditions, thus expanding Steward's concept of the cultural core to include symbolic and ceremonial elements. Rappaport demonstrates that the ritual cycle of the Tsembaga of New Guinea plays a role in regulating their relationship to their natural environment, the redistribution of land, and their relations with other groups in the area. While pigs provide an important source of protein and have important symbolic value, they also pose a threat to the productivity of the yam gardens if their numbers increase beyond a reasonable point. As the pig herd grows, agricultural labor requirements increase and the yam fields must be expanded. Ritualized warfare, said to be necessary to appease the spirits of the ancestors, is closely tied to the size of pig herds, since fighting only happens when there are enough pigs for slaughter and feasting. The killing of pigs and the ceremonial uprooting of a symbolic tree mark the period of warfare and the culling of the pig herd. Thus, the maintenance of the ecosystem, the cycle of planting crops and ritualized warfare, and the ceremonial killing of pigs serve to maintain the balance of the system.

One of the fundamental features of Rappaport's form of cultural ecology is the depiction of human-environment relations as being in a state of balance (called homeostasis) maintained by ritual cycles that correct imbalances in the system. The question of whether or not such social systems remain in a harmonious relationship with the environment remained critical. As the cultural ecologist Robert Netting has stated, "The very cogency and holistic virtuosity of such a model has evoked scrutiny and criticism from others in the ecological camp who question whether energy actually flows in the quantity and qualities documented [by Rappaport] and whether it really moves in the postulated directions" (Netting 1982, p. 281). Netting questioned the homeostatic model and was concerned with understanding the limits of human exploitation of the environment.

Netting's study of the Kofyar (*Hill Farmers of Nigeria,* 1968) avoids depicting systems in homeostasis because he was not concerned with describing homeostatic energy flows through the Kofyar economic system. He was more concerned with testing the relationship the economist Ester Boserup stated in *The Conditions of Agricultural Growth* (1965) between population growth and agricultural intensification (increase or escalation), and he presented evidence of clear relationships among labor, production, and the maintenance of agricultural productive stability through intensification. His cultural ecology was not concerned with presenting explanations of adaptive behaviors or systems in harmonious balance with nature, but with demonstrating how agricultural things work, the essence of functional analysis in cultural ecology.

Regarding the cultural ecological approach, Netting states, "Ecological functionalism need not be the analysis of a closed static equilibrium—it should instead be comparative and historical" (1993, p. ix). His focus on historical factors of production first appeared in his study of the Swiss village of Torbel (*Balancing on an Alp,* 1981). In that work he included historical demographic analysis to show that the Swiss farmers' production system was enmeshed in external and internal factors of demographic change and intensified production. In his *Smallholders, Householders* (1993), Netting integrates the traditional functional concerns of cultural ecology with the contemporary ecopolitical concerns regarding the limits of modernized agriculture and the need for sustainable production.

POLITICAL ECOLOGY

Smallholders, Householders ties the cultural ecological approach to the analysis of contemporary, sustainable farming systems, documenting the agricultural efficiency and environmental conservation that typify small farmers. In it, Netting also criticizes the damaging aspects of growth-oriented agriculture and posits as an alternative the diverse forms of small-farm production finely tuned to local environmental conditions. The conservationist and writer Wendell Berry (*The Unsettling of America,* 1986) and the agronomist Wes Jackson (*Becoming Native to this Place,* 1994), among others, have made this approach popular in a movement called the new agrarianism.

While cultural ecology tried to maintain a scientific approach to the study of human social and cultural systems, political ecology advocates openness to both scientific and humanistic approaches. Political ecology integrates the functional analysis aspect of cultural ecology to determine how an agricultural system works and how resources flow though the system, and assesses what effects these productive systems have on particular landscapes over time. The introduction of indigenous knowledge and historical process into the analysis effectively prevents viewing human-environment relations as simple homeostatic systems. Political ecology expands the original formulations of cultural ecology by recognizing that human agents act with purpose in constructing their environment. In political ecology, homeostatic models can be used to explain the functioning of human-environmental systems only if maintenance of homeostasis is seen as a consequence of human design. That is, if the productive capabilities of the system are maintained and the system appears for some period of time to be sustainable, it is because knowledgeable human actors have made it so, not because the system itself has any intrinsic characteristics or singular motivations.

The findings of agroecologists such as Stephen L. Gleissman (*Agroecology: Ecological Processes in Sustainable Agriculture,* 1989) and Miguel Altieri (*Agroecology: The Science of Sustainable Agriculture,* 1987) give scientific credence to the indigenous knowledge that created remarkably sustainable agricultural systems, and they identify those aspects of agricultural systems that contribute to sustainability. Some farmers' techniques include making adjustments in crop density, times of planting, burning, limited tillage, fallowing and management of fallow land, multicropping, intercropping, mulching, controlled grazing, and green manuring to enhance the system's long-term productivity. The early concerns in cultural ecology with understanding human-environmental relations have led to a desire in political ecology to understand how certain techniques can render humanity's interaction with the environment less damaging and more sustainable.

—Charles J. Stevens

Further Reading

Alland, A., & McCay, B. (1973). The concept of adaptation in biological and cultural evolution. In J. J. Honigmann (Ed.), *Handbook of social and cultural anthropology* (pp. 143–178). Chicago: Rand McNally.

Altieri, M. A. (1987). *Agroecology: The scientific basis of alternative agriculture.* Boulder, CO: Westview.

Berry, W. (1986). *The unsettling of America: Culture and agriculture.* New York: Random House and Sierra Club Books.

Boserup, E. (1965). *The conditions of agricultural growth: The economics of agrarian change under population pressure.* New York: Aldine.

Bramwell, A. (1989). *Ecology in the twentieth century: A history.* New Haven, CT: Yale University Press.

Ellen, R. (1982). *Environment, subsistence and system: The ecology of small-scale social formations.* Cambridge, UK: Cambridge University Press.

Geertz, C. (1963). *Agricultural involution: The process of change in Indonesia.* Berkeley and Los Angeles: University of California Press.

Gleissman, S. R. (Ed.). (1989). *Agroecology: Researching the ecological basis for sustainable agriculture.* New York: Springer-Verlag.

Greenberg, J. B., & Park, T. K. (1994). Political ecology. *Journal of Political Ecology, 1*(1), 1–12.

Jackson, W. (1994). *Becoming native to this place.* Washington, DC: Counterpoint Press.

Montesquieu, C. de Secondat, Baron de. (1914). *On the spirit of laws.* London: G. Bell & Sons. (Original work published 1748)

Morgan, L. H. (1978). *Ancient society.* Cambridge, MA: The Belknap Press, Harvard University Press. (Original work published 1877)

Moran, E. F. (Ed.). (1990). *The ecosystem approach in anthropology: From concept to practice.* Ann Arbor: University of Michigan Press.

Netting, R. M. (1968). *Hill farmers of Nigeria: Cultural ecology of the Kofyar of the Jos Plateau.* Seattle: University of Washington Press.

Netting, R. M. (1974). Agrarian ecology. *Annual Reviews of Anthropology, 3,* 21–56.

Netting, R. M. (1977). *Cultural ecology.* Menlo Park, CA: Benjamin/Cummings.

Netting, R. M. (1981). *Balancing on an Alp: Ecological change and continuity in a Swiss mountain community.* New York: Cambridge University Press.

Netting, R. M., Wilk, R. R., & Arnould, E. J. (Eds.). (1984). *Households: Comparative and historical studies of the domestic group.* Berkeley and Los Angeles: University of California Press.

Netting, R. M. (1989). Smallholders, householders, freeholders: Why the small family farm works well world wide. In R. R. Wilk (Ed.), *The household economy: Reconsidering the domestic mode of production* (pp. 221–244). Boulder, CO: Westview.

Netting, R. M. (1993). *Smallholders, householders: Farm families and the ecology intensive, sustainable agriculture.* Palo Alto, CA: Stanford University Press.

Rappaport, R. A. (1968). *Pigs for the ancestors.* New Haven, CT: Yale University Press.

Sauer, J. D. (1990). *Historical geography of crop plants: A selected roster.* New York: CRC Press.

Sheridan, T. (1988). *Where the dove calls: The political ecology of a peasant corporate community in northwestern Mexico.* Tucson: University of Arizona Press.

Steward, J. (1955). *Theory of culture change: The methodology of multilinear evolution.* Urbana: University of Illinois Press.

Stonich, S. (1993). *"I am destroying the land!": The political ecology of poverty and environmental destruction in Honduras.* Boulder, CO: Westview.

Turner, B. L., & Bush, S. B. (Eds.). (1987). *Comparative farming systems.* New York: Guilford.

Vasey, D. E. (1992). *An ecological history of agriculture: 10,000 B.C–A.D. 10,000.* Ames: Iowa State University Press.

Wilk, R. R. (Ed.). (1989). *The household economy: Reconsidering the domestic mode of production.* Boulder, CO: Westview.

Wilk, R. R. (1991). *Household ecology: Economic change and domestic life among the Kerchi Maya in Belize.* Tucson: University of Arizona Press.

Wissler, C. (1926). *The relation of nature to man in Aboriginal America.* New York: Oxford University Press.

Worster, D. (1983). *The wealth of nature: Environmental history and the ecological imagination.* New York: Oxford University Press.

CULTURE OF POVERTY

Social scientists credit Oscar Lewis (1914–1970), an American anthropologist, with introducing the concept of a culture of poverty. He first suggested it in 1959 in his book, *Five Families: Mexican Case Studies in the Culture of Poverty.* The concept refers to the ideas and behavior developed by poor people in some capitalist societies as they adapt to urban circumstances. Lewis understood poverty and its related traits as a culture "with its own structure and rationale, as a way of life which is passed down from generation to generation along family lines" (Lewis 1968, p. xlii).

In Lewis's view, the culture of poverty in capitalist societies was not simply a matter of economic deprivation or the absence of something. It also represents something positive because it provides individuals a framework for interpreting their lives and the problems they encounter in their daily existence. The culture of poverty transcends regional, rural-urban, and national differences to produce remarkable similarities in family structure, interpersonal relations, and value systems in different societies.

POVERTY AND THE CULTURE OF POVERTY

Lewis recognized that there are degrees of poverty and many kinds of poor people. Not all societies have a culture of poverty. Lewis argued that a culture of poverty is more likely in societies with a certain set of conditions. First, these societies have a cash economy, wage labor, and production for profit. Second, they have a persistently high rate of unemployment and underemployment for unskilled labor. Third, there is the presence of low wages. Fourth, these societies fail to provide social, political, and economic organization either on a voluntary basis or by government imposition for the low-income population. Fifth, the society has a bilateral kinship system rather than a unilateral one. In a unilateral kinship system, one traces descent either through males or through females. In a bilateral system, one traces descent through males and females without emphasis on either line. Sixth, the values of the dominant class stress the accumulation of wealth and property, the possibility of upward mobility, and thrift, and it explains low economic status as the result of personal inadequacy or inferiority.

The way of life that develops among some of the poor under these conditions constitutes the culture of poverty. Lewis described this way of life in terms of some seventy interrelated social, economic, and psychological traits. These traits represent a reaction of the poor to their marginal position in a class-stratified, highly individuated, capitalistic society. They represent an effort by the poor to cope with feelings of hopeless-

Selection From Oscar Lewis's *La Vida* (1966)

Anthropologist Oscar Lewis's classic work La Vida *eloquently described the plight of poverty-stricken Puerto Rican families in San Juan and New York. The excerpt below describes one family's difficult life.*

I went to work in Bridgeboro picking tomatoes. Eddy worked there too and acted as my interpreter. I had to get up at six o'clock, leave the children with the woman who took care of them, and be on the job by seven. Whichever of us got home first in the evening cooked dinner. I washed our clothes at the laundry. Eddy took me there and showed me what coins to use. He never once beat me and we never had a quarrel either. I knew that he liked women but he never told me anything about his life.

There weren't many jobs in Bridgeboro, so after a month we went back to Salem. I got a job packing in a canning factory. Felicita wanted a job too, but they wouldn't hire her because she had worked there before and one day had just walked out. I made ninety to a hundred dollars a week there. *Don* Camacho was sending me about twenty-five dollars every month. I paid twenty-give each week to a lady to take care of my children and twenty dollars a week rent. Felicita had moved out and we were living in her little house.

After a while the lady couldn't come any more to look after the kids, so Felicita took over. One day she didn't feel like staying with them and just walked off and left them all alone. The neighbors must have called the cops because a detective came to get me at the factory. He even wanted to take me to court. I explained that I had left the children with my sister, so he let me off. He caught up with her at the railroad station but didn't do anything to her. She got mad at me and hardly spoke to me for a while. I got somebody else for the children but later Felicita took them back again.

Source: Lewis, Oscar. (1966). *La Vida: A Puerto Rican Family in the Culture of Poverty–San Juan and New York.* New York: Random House, p. 200.

ness and despair that develop from the recognition of the improbability of achieving success in the larger society. The number of traits and the relationship between them could vary from society to society.

Lewis recognized that since he was examining a portion of society, the term *subculture of poverty* was technically a more accurate concept, but he used the shorter form, *culture of poverty,* to describe the traits of the poor. Lewis theorized that the culture of poverty is not only a present adaptation to a set of objective conditions of the larger society. Rather, once it comes into existence, it tends to perpetuate itself from generation to generation because of its effect on children. For example, Lewis argued that by the time slum children are age six or seven years, they have usually absorbed the basic values and attitudes of this culture of poverty and are not psychologically geared to take full advantage of increased opportunities that occur in their lifetime.

TRAITS OF THE CULTURE OF POVERTY

Lewis derived the essential features or traits of the way of life he termed the culture of poverty from an extensive collection of life histories and psychological tests with families in Mexico and Puerto Rico. From these studies, he suggested that social scientists could identify and study the traits that formed the culture of poverty from a variety of points of view: (1) the relationship between the culture of poverty and the larger society; (2) the nature of the slum community; (3) the nature of the family; and (4) the attitudes, values, and character structure of the individual.

The Culture of Poverty and the Larger Society

Lewis argued that one of the crucial characteristics of the poor in a culture of poverty is their lack of effective participation and integration in the major institutions of the larger society. This characteristic results from a variety of factors, including lack of economic resources; segregation and discrimination; fear, suspicion, or apathy; and the development of local solutions for problems faced by the poor. While the poor "participate" in some of the institutions of the larger society as prison inmates, recipients of welfare, or soldiers in the armed services, participation in such institutions perpetuates the poverty and sense of hopelessness.

The low wages and chronic unemployment and underemployment of the poor lead to lack of property ownership and an absence of savings. These conditions reduce the likelihood of effective participation in the larger economic system. In addition, a constant shortage of cash and inability to obtain credit result in borrowing at high rates of interest, use of secondhand clothing and furniture, and pawning of personal goods.

Lewis also reported that people with a culture of poverty have a low level of literacy and education, are not active members of political parties, and make very little use of such community resources such as banks, hospitals, museums, or art galleries. Moreover, they have a critical attitude toward some of the basic institutions of the dominant classes. For example, they may hate the police, hold a mistrust of the government and those in high positions, and display a cynicism that extends to even to the church.

While people with a culture of poverty are aware of middle-class values, Lewis argued that they largely do not live by these values. For example, the poor typically do not marry, although they consider marriage an important ideal. Lewis thought that this was largely a consequence of their economic condition. Men with no steady jobs or other source of income want to avoid the expense and legal difficulties of marriage. Women believe that consensual unions are also better for them. They believe that marriage ties them down to men who are immature, abusive, and unreliable. In addition, by not marrying they have stronger ties to their children and exclusive rights to a house or any other property they own.

The Nature of the Slum Community

Lewis referred to the places where the poor resided as *slum communities.* Poor housing conditions, crowding, and a minimum of social organization beyond the level of the family characterize slum communities. While voluntary associations or neighborhood gangs are occasionally present in these communities, it is the low level of organization that gives the culture of poverty its marginal quality when contrasted with the complex, specialized, and organized larger society.

However, a sense of community or esprit de corps may exist even in slum communitie. The development of this sense of community depends on several factors, such as the size of the slum community, incidence of home ownership, low rents, stability of residence, ethnicity, kinship ties, and the slum's location in terms of the larger city. For example, Lewis's research indicated that when there are barriers that separate slums from the surrounding area, when rents are low and stability of residence is great, when the population constitutes a distinct ethnic or racial group, and when there are strong kinship ties, then a strong sense of community can develop. However, even when these conditions are absent, a sense of territoriality develops that demarcates the slum neighborhoods from the rest of the city.

The Nature of the Family

Lewis's studies indicated that people with a culture of poverty tend to form common-law marriages or cohabiting arrangements. Abandonment of families by fathers is common, and consequently there is a high incidence of female-centered families and strong ties with maternal relatives. Crowded living arrangements foster a lack of privacy, and scarcity of resources creates competition for limited goods. Sibling rivalry is common, as is rivalry for maternal affection.

Children in these families begin adult activities earlier in their life cycle when compared with children from middle-class families. For example, they are more likely to have early initiation into sex and are less likely to complete high school, thus entering the job market sooner than their middle-class counterparts.

Attitudes, Values, and Character Structure of the Individual

Individuals living in a culture of poverty share a set of traits that differentiates them from the rest of society. These traits are behavioral or psychological; the family perpetuates these traits as it passes them down from generation to generation through its psychological impact on children.

Lewis argued that the major individual characteristics are a strong feeling of marginality, helplessness, dependence, and inferiority. People with a culture of poverty also display a sense of resignation and fatalism, present-time orientation, lack of impulse control, weak ego structure, sexual confusion, and the inability to defer gratification. They also are provincial, locally oriented, and have very little sense of history. Typically, they are unable to see the similarities between their problems and those like them in other parts of the world.

CRITIQUE OF THE CULTURE OF POVERTY

The term *culture of poverty* became well known in the social sciences and in the political arena as well. During the 1960s, for example, Michael Harrington utilized the phrase in *The Other America* to emphasize how the economy and social structure limited the opportunities of the poor and produced a culture of poverty that the poor did not choose. However, criticisms of the concept also emerged. Two criticisms are especially important.

First, the media and politicians frequently used the concept in a manner different from Lewis's initial conceptualization. The connection between the political economy and the culture of poverty was frequently absent in their descriptions of the poor. The behavioral, psychological characteristics of poor individuals were emphasized, as well as the problems created by the family structures of the poor. The larger society often blamed the poor for their circumstances because analysis of the poor presented only the culture of poverty. The ties to the economic and structural dimensions of society theorized by Lewis were frequently forgotten. Scholars and activists attacked this "blaming the victim" for being in poverty and continued to conduct research and present policy proposals that link the behavioral outcomes of the culture of poverty to social structural factors.

Second, Lewis presented a view of urban poverty that argued that the urban poor develop their own adaptation that is fundamentally different from the culture of the rest of society. However, an alternative point of view emphasizes that the urban poor share many values of the larger society around them. This view emphasizes that the "subculture" of poverty is a part of the larger culture of the dominant society. While one may find in the poor the traits described by Lewis, one also finds that the poor may share values of the dominant society. For example, research reports individuals among the poor who possess a strong work ethic passed on through extended family networks, only to confront the structural reality of limited job opportunities in the urban ghetto.

POVERTY AND CULTURE

The culture of poverty is an important scientific idea. It refers to one way of life shared by poor people in given historical and social contexts. The concept enables us to see that many of the problems we think of as distinctively belonging to one society also exist in other societies. The concept also enables us to see that poverty can exist without the culture of poverty. Finally, Lewis argued that because the traits associated with the culture of poverty are passed on from generation to generation through the family, elimination of poverty per se may not be enough to eliminate the culture of poverty, which is a whole way of life.

—Patricia E. Erickson

Further Reading

Allen, V. L. (1970). *Psychological factors in poverty.* Chicago: Markham.

Auletta K. (1982). *The underclass.* New York: Random House.

Banfield, E. (1958). *The moral basis of a backward society.* Chicago: Free Press.

Clark, K. (1965). *Dark ghetto: Dilemmas of social power.* New York: Harper and Row.

Ellwood, D. (1988). *Poor support: Poverty in the American family.* New York: Basic Books.

Gans, H. J. (1995). *The war against the poor.* New York: Basic Books.

Harrington, M. (1962). *The other America.* New York: Macmillan.

Lewis, O. (1959). *Five families: Mexican case studies in the culture of poverty.* New York: Basic Books.

Lewis, O. (1961). *The children of Sanchez: Autobiography of a Mexican family.* New York: Random House.

Lewis, O. (1968). *La Vida: A Puerto Rican family in the culture of poverty, San Juan and New York.* New York: Random House.

McCelland, D. (1961). *The achieving society.* New York: Van Nostrand.

Moynihan, D. P. (Ed.). (1968). *On understanding poverty: Perspectives from the social sciences.* New York: Basic Books.

Murray, C. (1984). *Losing ground: American social policy: 1950–1980.* New York: Basic Books.

Myrdal, G. (1965). *Challenge to affluence.* New York: Vintage.

Newman, K. (1999). *No shame in my game: The working poor in the inner city.* New York: Knopf and the Russell Sage Foundation.

O'Connor, A. (2001). *Poverty knowledge: Social science, social policy, and the poor in twentieth-century U.S. history.* Princeton, NJ: Princeton University Press.

Schram, S. F. (1995). *Words of welfare: The poverty of social science and the social science of poverty.* Minneapolis: University of Minnesota Press.

Stack, C. B. (1974). *All our kin: Strategies for survival in a black community.* New York: Harper & Row.

Wilson, W. J. (1987). *The truly disadvantaged: The inner city, the underclass, and public policy.* Chicago: University of Chicago Press.

Wilson, W. J. (1996). *When work disappears.* New York: Knopf and the Russell Sage Foundation.

CURRENCIES

See COMMUNITY CURRENCIES

CYBERCAFES

Cybercafes are bars, coffee houses, or restaurants equipped with Internet access for customer use. The world's first cybercafe opened in Santa Monica, California, in 1984, on the occasion of the Olympic Arts Festival of Los Angeles. Others followed, and during the 1980s they offered the only affordable public access to the Internet. Over the 1990s, they strongly expanded throughout the First World. The first European cybercafe was founded in London in 1994.

Cybercafes were conceived as a short-lived phenomenon, expected to last in the marketplace just long enough to introduce people to the Internet; then private access would make them obsolete. But today the number of cybercafes continues to increase, even in places where private connections are common and free public access is available elsewhere. Victim of its own success, the word *cybercafe* has even undergone a semantic shift: Now it also refers to the Internet's virtual meeting places where people communicate using a chat program or by posting messages. In this acceptation, CAFE is the acronym for "communication access for everybody."

A PROCESS OF MULTIPLICATION AND DIVERSIFICATION

Today two types of real-world cybercafes can be found. Internet cafe chains such as Easyeverything are now spread throughout urban areas. They offer Internet browsing and mail services, often twenty-four hours a day, seven days a week, at very low connection costs.

Independently owned cybercafes, which are subject to intense competition, offer personal technical support and activities besides browsing and mail services, such as the creation of Web sites and Web pages and introductions to Web art, among others. They also tend to have a friendly atmosphere and a more generous policy on customers' clocked time. In both types of cybercafes, customers are charged by the hour for Internet access and other amenities.

Iranians surf the Net at a cafe in Tehran in May 2001. Such cafes were soon shut down by the government.
Source: AFP/Corbis; used with permission.

Cybercafes are concentrated mainly in the First World, mostly in major urban areas but with regional differences in distribution. There are some cybercafes in developing countries, but they are usually independent, rather than members of chains. In the European Union, cybercafes can be found even in small towns, while in the United States and Canada, they are most common in tourist areas and the largest cities. In those nations, the cost of a high-speed home connection is very low, and many public libraries offer free and unlimited access to the Internet.

In developing nations, cybercafes are few, but they play a dynamic role in opening up enclaved territories. When Mexican authorities decided to cover the whole country with public Internet access, they promoted cybercafes, which expanded quickly. The first one opened in 1993; today they number more than 200. Even in the suburbs of Mexico City, an Internet cafe is easily found, as are the "tienda" and the "comedor": small stalls on the street where immigrants can communicate with families or friends cheaply—for an average of $1.20 a hour. In South America, Peruvians and Ecuadorans are witnessing a similar process.

Africa lacks cybercafes: They are found only in the capital cities, and yet 70 percent of the continent's population lives rurally. In any case, connection costs are exorbitant, almost $9.00 an hour. Senegal and South Africa are two exceptions, according to a 1998 UNESCO report. The South African Universal Service Agency helps local communities create Internet cafes. Even in Khayelitsha, a slum near the Cape, a cybercafe called the Internet Shop opened recently. Senegal receives support from its countrymen in France, where two Parisian ethnic cybercafes—Vis@vis and Tatt@Guine—contributed to create several Internet cafes in Senegal: the Ambidou, the Champs-Elysées, and Metissacana.

As their numbers increase, cybercafes diversify.

Thematic Internet cafes have emerged, as have cultural cybercafes offering multimedia performances and virtual happenings. Some are oriented toward certain ethnic groups, others toward job seekers. Of course almost any store—from bookshop to shoemaker—can be coupled with public access to the Internet. (In Paris, even Eurocafard, which sells insecticide for use against cockroaches, offers Web access.) And Internet access can be found in many places, such as the growing number of European bistros and pubs with Webfinger, an Internet terminal with a touch-sensitive screen and no keyboard. But even such places are not cybercafes.

The genuine cybercafe requires a comfortable environment designed specifically for the Internet user. Beyond computer-supported social networks, it provides physical proximity to others engaging in online exchange with members of their respective virtual communities (Wellman & Gulia 1999). In such a context, people with similar interests can meet physically and perhaps have a drink or a meal together. So cybercafes spark tangible social networks that link customers to proxemic communities. What are the main characteristics of these specific communities?

CYBERCAFES, SOCIAL NETWORKS, AND TANGIBLE COMMUNITIES

A cybercafe embodies the meeting point of a physical public place and a virtual space. It serves as an interface between "here" and "elsewhere," thus simultaneously generating two types of communities: virtual communities between persons exchanging online, and tangible communities that form between customers of the cybercafe. This process is facilitated by the arrangement of the cybercafes, in which users can sit side-by-side, each in front of a different screen, but can also go to the bar to have a drink and discussion.

African cybercafes in Paris are a good example. They have developed specific services, such as sophisticated but affordable netmeeting facilities with videoconferencing. This is invaluable for migrants whose families and relations remain in Africa, and who would otherwise run up huge international telephone bills. Such cafes may develop many other functions, too, acting as letter-writing services, travel agencies, marriage bureaus, and African newspaper agencies. Finally, they are new city landmarks where isolated minorities can meet.

The cybercafe can also act as a pointer to potential communities in the local scene, and even awaken a neighborhood consiousness. In Paris, for example, the cybercafe Sputnik is attended by a tremendous number of neighbors—storekeepers, teenagers, adults, and seniors. They comprise most of the regular customers and give a spirit to the place. People who would otherwise never meet weave ties here.

The Internet cafe can also unveil solidarity networks that otherwise would stay invisible. In this sense, it can convert to a center of political protest. In Algeria, cybercafes—as well as stadiums and public libraries—became rallying points for students (Boumaiza 2001). This trend worries governments that would like to control what people read and write online. In China, authorities legally require cybercafes to install so-called spyfilters, which identify users and all their connections. This system, called "Filter King," is programmed to detect and inform police about anybody visiting censored Web sites (Thorel 2002).

Cybercafes are modeled by both their tangible and virtual environments and by their users, whom they model in return. They are hybrid scenes combining the partial privacy of the online relation with organized sociability; consequently they form new types of public places. Engraved in the territories of everyday life, they offer a setting for users to manage their numerous and peculiar identities. Cybercafes have lasted longer than expected and have broadened their own definitions. Their own identities and functions will probably continue to evolve.

—François Mancebo

Further Reading

Boumaiza, A. (2001, August). *Le cybercafé, lieu de rencontre privilégié* (The cybercafé, privileged place of meeting). Retrieved February 27, 2003, from http://www.arts.uwa.edu.au/MotsPluriels/MP1801ab.html

Castells, M. (1996). *The rise of the network society.* Oxford, UK: Blackwell.

Graham, G. (1999). *The Internet: A philosophical perspective.* London: Routledge.

Mancebo F., & Durand-Tornare, F. (2002). Développement des EPN et recompositions territoriales à Paris (Development of the EPN and territorial recombinings in Paris). *Numéro spécial Les Espaces Publics Numériques* (Special edition of Numerical Public Spaces). Paris: Géographie et Culture.

Thorel, J. (2002). *Les logiciels censeurs font leur irruption dans les cafés Internet de Chine* (Software critics erupt in Chinese Internet cafés). Retrieved February 27, 2003, from http://www.freelists.org/archives/helpc/06–2002/msg00175.html

UNESCO. (1998). *The Regional Informatics Network for Africa (RINAF): An external evaluation.* Paris: Author.

Wellman, B., & Gulia, M. (1999). Netsurfers don't ride alone: Virtual communities as communities. In P. Kollock & M. Smith (Eds.), *Communities and cyberspace.* New York: Routledge.

Wellman, B., & Haythornthwaite, C. (2002). *The Internet in everyday life.* Oxford, UK: Blackwell.

CYBERDATING

Cyberdating is the process of getting to know someone online via the Internet before transferring the relationship to offline or face-to-face interaction. A new form of initiating an intimate relationship, cyberdating can start at an Internet site designed to match partners, or it can happen when people meet as friends or acquaintances in chat rooms, instant messaging, or various types of online communities. Computer-related technologies have made cyberdating possible, as people can communicate locally and globally through text online.

WHEN AND WHERE ONLINE DATING OCCURS

Before the World Wide Web or browsers such as Mosaic and then Netscape became available in the early 1990s, people met online through bulletin boards, local discussion groups where they could post items. Later, on the Internet, they talked synchronously in real time (the actual time of an event) in chat groups, or postasynchronously in online communities or virtual communities, newsgroups, or e-mail lists. Some people met while role-playing characters in online games known as multiuser object-oriented domains (MODs) or multiuser domains/dungeons (MUDs).

Wherever people communicated online, they could connect further with a particular individual, while pursuing a topic of mutual interest. Those explicitly looking for a partner rather than a friend or acquaintance could search profiles of compatible others in online dating services and, later, in real-time messaging Web sites.

WHO MEETS PARTNERS ONLINE

People who met online before the Internet and the World Wide Web were established were those engaged in computer work or in scientific groups, mainly through universities. Their computer literacy made them familiar with how to connect to others online with a minimum of stress. As their subculture of "geeks" was already an outgroup of sorts, they did not object to the further stigma of meeting people online. As more and more people have begun to use this way of meeting people, the negative views about it have receded.

People once thought that only "losers" would date people they had met via the Internet or that Internet acquaintances who met face to face might risk injury or death. While such cases do occur, most people survive their dates from cyberspace, and many have pleasant experiences, depending on their expectations and the length of time they knew the person before encountering him or her offline.

THE PROCESS OF CYBERDATING

The process of cyberdating typically starts at a public online site such as a discussion group, virtual community, or dating service, and then moves to private e-mail when one person wants to communicate directly with another. Someone engaging in real-time synchronous communication can go from public chat or game playing to private correspondence, either in the chat room or game or outside by sending an instant message (IM). From there, the two progress to more frequent e-mailing, more instant messaging, or a combination of both.

Compatibility partly depends on the pair's finding the proper software, such as a downloaded instant-messaging client that works on the operating systems of both of their computers. As soon as desired, if the two people begin to like each other, they use the telephone to escalate the relationship another step. If they have not set seen photographs of one another at a Web site, they usually exchange them through e-mail. People can also choose to communicate simultaneously vocally and visually through Webcams or other online software and hardware. Friendship may be the initial goal of the relationship for some, while others express feelings of strong affection and move into romantic involvement while in the online phase. After a time, depending on the inclination and the geographical location of each party, the couple may plan to meet offline.

The offline meeting can determine whether the couple proceeds to develop the relationship. Even if feelings of compatibility are high, if one or the other of the two does not experience the "chemistry" offline, or for any reason does not see the meeting as confirming and supplementing the relationship built online, the pairing can die. The couple must relate well in real life or "meatspace" (cyber lingo for the physical world that plays on the homonyms *meet* and *meat*) rather than in virtual space in order to move toward living together, engagement, or marriage. Between meetings offline, they continue to communicate online and on the phone, until they either break up or move into a common living space.

POSITIVE AND NEGATIVE FEATURES OF ONLINE DATING

Advantages and disadvantages exist in online relationships. Compared with offline relationships, online dating seems to escalate faster to the stage of sharing information, interests, goals, and values. The only aspects of dating that occur more frequently and earlier in the traditional form of dating offline are introducing the partner to offline friends and family and the couple's greater exclusivity in dating only each other.

Disadvantages of online dating include the inability to spend enough face-to-face time with the partner, especially if he or she lives far away; the dependence on verbal or audio cues to communicate; and the possibility that one party is deceiving the other about appearance, age, marital status, or lifestyle. Advantages include the capacity for communicating thoughts and feelings fully, without the distraction of the usual dating activities. The dependence on "talk" takes away the emphasis on the other's appearance and possibly allows the relationship to gain a firmer foundation than one based primarily on physical attraction.

DIRECTIONS IN RESEARCH ON CYBERDATING

To supplement quantitative-survey analysis and small case studies with and without comparison data on offline couples, suggestions for future research include matched samples of offline and online relationships, analysis of various online meeting places to see how relationship trajectories are effected, and detailed comparisons of age and cross-cultural groups. As cyberdating occurs throughout the world, further investigations may identify differences among countries in how people meet online and their typical modes of communication after they find potential partners. Most important, longitudinal studies tracking online relationships could establish which factors promote longevity of relationships and which inhibit it.

—Andrea J. Baker

Further Reading

Baker, A. (1998, July). Cyberspace couples finding romance online and then meeting for the first time in real life. *Computer-Mediated Communication.* Retrieved October 28, 2002, from http://www.december.com/cmc/mag/1998/jul/baker.html

Baker, A. (2002, August). What makes an online relationship successful? Clues from couples who met in cyberspace. *CyberPsychology and Behavior, 5*(4), 363–375.

Chenault, B. (1998, May). Developing personal and emotional relationships via computer-mediated communication. *Computer-Mediated Communication.* Retrieved October 28, 2002, from http://www.december.com/cmc/mag/1998/may/chenault.html

McDowell, S. (2001). *The development of online and offline romantic relationships.* Unpublished master's thesis, University of Washington, Seattle.

Parks, M., & Floyd, K. (1996). Making friends in cyberspace. *Journal of Communication, 46*(1), 80–97.

Parks, M., & Roberts, L. (1998, August). Making MOOsic: The development of personal relationships on line and a comparison to their offline counterparts. *Journal of Social and Personal Relationships, 15*(4), 517–537.

Walther, J., & Parks, M. (2002). Cues filtered out, cues filtered in: Computer-mediated communication and relationships. In M. L. Knapp & J. A. Daly (Eds.), *The handbook of interpersonal communication* (pp. 529–563). Thousand Oaks, CA: Sage.

CYBERSOCIETIES

Cybersociety is a society in which computer-mediated communication significantly affects the organization and functioning of society. *Computer-mediated communication* (CMC) means the Internet in its many guises (e-mail, the Web), mobile phones (some Web enabled), instant messaging, groupware, enhanced pagers, wireless personal digital assistants, and the like. Especially in the developed world, people use the Internet extensively at home and even at work, for their community, informational, and leisure activities. Family members help each other to use computers, share online discoveries, and replace time spent watching television with net surfing. This pervasive, real-world Internet does not function on its own but is embedded in the real-life things that people do. Just as all-Internet commerce is being supplanted by "clicks-and-mortars" (physical stores integrated with online activity), so too is most online community becoming one of the many ways in which people are connected—through face-to-face and phone contact.

However, there is no pure "cybersociety." Few people spend most—or even much—of their time online. Yet, wired pundits, entrepreneurs, hypesters, and scholars have confused the public by myopically fixating on the rapidly developing Internet and wrongly proclaimed it a place apart. Systematic research shows that physical space and cyberspace interpenetrate as people actively surf their networks online and offline. Even DotComGuy, who resolved to live a year within a house running his life by the Internet, had to have frequent deliveries of material goods. There is no such thing as a virtual pizza. Only a small number of fervent interactive video gamers appear to spend most of their nonwork hours online, and they tend to cluster in a few East Asian and North American countries with widespread broadband connectivity.

The realization that the Internet is embedded in

larger society has been awhile in coming. A decade ago, the first age of the Internet was a bright light shining above everyday concerns. It was a technological marvel, supposedly bringing a new Enlightenment to transform the world, just as the printing press fostered the original Enlightenment a half-millennium ago in Renaissance times. In those early days, the Internet was exciting because it was new and special. All things seemed possible. Internet initiates became avant-garde elites. While they extolled the great changes in human endeavor coming from the Internet, others voiced concerns about these same changes. The very term *Internet* became a receptacle for both fame and infamy relating to any electronic activity or societal change. In the euphoria, many analysts lost their perspective. Most discussion of the Internet followed three types:

- Announcements of technological developments, coupled with breathless pronouncements about how they were going to change society
- Traveler's tales, as if from the darkest Amazon, providing anecdotes about the weird and wonderful ways of Internet life such as cybersex changes
- Cautionary tales of the evils of cybersociety, such as impersonation and cyberrape

Extolling the Internet as a transforming phenomenon, many analysts forgot to view it in perspective. For example, their enthusiasm for the Internet led them to forget that long-distance community ties had been flourishing for a generation. They disregarded the preference that many people have for in-person contact where they could see, smell, and touch each other. They assumed that only things that happened on the Internet were relevant to understanding the Internet, forgetting that it is men and women, rich and poor who go online, and not human beings in the abstract.

The rapid contraction of the dot.com economy has brought down to earth the once-euphoric belief in the infinite possibility of Internet life. It is not as if the Internet disappeared. Instead, the light that dazzled overhead has become embedded in everyday things. A reality check is now underway about where the Internet fits into the ways in which people behave offline as well as online. Society is moving from a world of Internet wizards to a world of ordinary people routinely using the Internet as an embedded part of their lives. It has become clear that the Internet is a very important thing, but not a special thing. In fact, it is being used more: by more people, in more countries, in more different ways. Moreover, white, young, North American men no longer dominate use: Access and use have diffused to the rest of the population and the rest of the world. Of these users, almost all Web surf, many e-mail, most probably chat in groups as well as individually, some shop online, and a small but visible percentage play online games.

Symptoms of Pathological Internet Use (PIU)

The excerpt below is from a report by Richard York, a psychologist who specializes in studying "Internet addiction."

> Symptoms of PIU are similar to those set out in previous research (Young, 1996), although in the cognitive-behavioral model the emphasis is on the cognitive symptoms. As such, the symptoms are obsessive thoughts about the Internet, diminished impulse control, inability to cease Internet usage, and importantly, feeling that the Internet is an individual's only friend. The person feels as thought the Internet is the only place where they feel good about themselves and the world around them. Other symptoms of PIU include thinking about the Internet while offline, anticipating future time online, and spending large of amounts of money on Internet time and other such expenses. An individual with PIU spends less time doing otherwise pleasurable activities than before the PIU began. What used to be fun for them is no longer enjoyable. A further complication arises when the person eventually isolates himself or herself from friends, in favor of friends online. This problematic behavior maintains the vicious cycle of PIU, in that the individual becomes socially isolated. Finally, individuals with PIU have a sense of guilt about their online use. They often lie to their friends about how much time they spend online, and consider their Internet use a secret to others. While they understand that what they are doing is not entirely socially acceptable, they cannot stop. This results in a diminished self worth and further symptoms of PIU.

Source: Davis, R.A. (1999). "A Cognitive-Behavioral Model for Pathological Internet Use (PIU)." *Catalyst.* Retrieved March 5, 2003, from http://www.victoriapoint.com/piu.htm.

THE SOCIAL AFFORDANCES OF COMPUTER-MEDIATED NETWORKS

Developments in computer-mediated communication are currently exciting the public, scholars, financiers, the media, and politicians. Yet, it is when technological changes become pervasive, familiar, and boring that they affect societies the most. This is an old story. Few scholars think about the telephone now, yet it has thoroughly affected the spatial and social structure of communities. This is not technological determinism, because people and institutions take over and reorient technological developments. Rather, technology has "social affordances," to use Erin Bradner's felicitous term: the possibilities and constraints facilitated by CMC for social relations and social structure. Key ones are reviewed here.

Broader Bandwidth

The number of bits that can be pushed through a computer network connection in a given hour has risen from 110 bits per second in the mid-1970s to routine home speeds ranging from 30,000 bps (with dial-up telephone modems) to 1 million bps (for cable modems and DSL [digital subscriber line] phone connections). It should continue to rise. High-capacity bandwidth is important for its speed, so that text messages and Web pages become readable without distracting delay. It affords instant messaging and feedback. It also affords the exchange of complex communication, so that large documents and drawings can be attached to e-mail messages or read on Web pages. Bandwidth affords the transmission of high-quality pictures, fostering "telepresence."

The always-available feature of broadband is as valuable as sheer speed. As high-speed connections do not block telephone calls from the family phone and cost no more for being online 24/7, 365 days a year, people get in the habit of sending e-mail or Web-surfing whenever the thought strikes them, glancing frequently at the incoming e-mail box, and frequently checking to see who is currently available for instant messages. The easily available Internet—no need to boot up or connect—makes the Web a convenient place to find quick information and makes e-mail a handy way to share quick thoughts. It also makes it easier to work from home. Just as employers complain about workers' use of the Internet for personal matters, family members complain that their loved ones are tied to their computers during their supposed leisure hours.

Wireless Portability

We are moving to a world of both ubiquitous and portable computing. Ubiquity means the widespread availability of usable computing and computer-mediated communication. Portability means that you can take it with you: you do not have to be dependent on others' equipment to connect to the Internet. Although wires still carry the most bandwidth, mobile phones are becoming integrated with the multifunctional capacity of computers. East Asia is leading the way in this.

Pedestrians, those in cars, and airplane passengers are gaining wireless connectivity with the Internet, enabling Internet, voice, and video access anywhere and Web browsing on the go. Favorite radio and television broadcasters are available worldwide, encouraging narrowcasting to small communities of shared interest. As portable devices proliferate, the norms of this inherently person-to-person system foster the intrusion of intensely involving private behavior into public space, as when people talk loudly on their mobile phones. Such people are not antisocial, but privately social with no regard for physical context.

The proliferation of portability will be both the embracing of and the negation of ubiquitous globalization. Computer-supported communication will be every*where,* but because it is independent of place, it will be situated no*where.* The importance of a communication site as a meaningful place will diminish even more. The person—not the place, household, or work group—is becoming more of an autonomous communication node. Contextual sense and lateral awareness are diminishing. For example, as Americans use the Internet or satellite radio to listen to favorite radio stations wherever they are, they become less aware of the importance of gospel music to southerners, farm news to midwesterners, and hip-hop to northeastern city dwellers.

Globalized Connectivity

Computer networks are expanding as the World Wide Web is becoming more comprehensive and worthy of its name. The "digital divide"—the income/locational/cultural gap between those comfortable with computerization and those not—is shrinking within the Western world; the gender gap has already disappeared.

Global portability will be afforded by the standardization of mobile phone specifications, the development of standards for tailored, ad hoc communication between changing sets of partners, the spread of wireless towers to physically isolated and impoverished nations, and the availability of satellite communication in remote areas. Bedouins already chat on mobile phones while herding sheep and use satellite dishes to participate in TV talk shows; Ecuadorian craftspeople market their wares directly.

Personalization

The Internet has changed the nature of the continuing tension between centralization and personalization. The Internet's original primary use, e-mail, has been a personal medium, with individuals usually managing their own address books and sending messages one-to-one. By contrast, the Web affords both personalization and centralization. Personalization tools are developing so that people should soon be able to tell their communications devices whom they wish to get messages from, about what, and when. They should soon be able to provide personalized responses on voicemail and e-mail to specific individuals. Personal software agents can scan online newsgroups, chat groups, buildings, and passersby, looking for compatible community members, and collecting and organizing desired information. Collaborative filtering is developing where people contribute to evaluations of books, restaurants, politicians, and movies People can use their filters and personal agents to find like-minded others and form communities of shared interest.

Personalization is not necessarily the same as portability. With portable computing, people take their communications devices with them. By contrast, personalized ubiquitous computing means that whenever people log on to communications devices, they know who these people are, where they are, and what their preferences are. Messages follow people. Thus, personalization need not mean individual isolation, but it also makes surveillance easier.

THE INTERNET IN EVERYDAY LIFE

The first phase of Internet studies was characterized mostly by punditry, laboratory experiments, and anecdotes. It treated the Internet as a special place. In the second phase, since the late 1990s, surveys and ethnographic studies have begun to shed light on how the majority of people actually use the Internet in the course of their everyday life.

The amount of time online varies enormously by country. To take two examples, nearly two-thirds of North American (United States and Canada) Internet users are online daily, many for several hours. Yet, Scottish analysts count two hours per week as heavy use.

The kinds of people using the Internet are starting to resemble the general population in North America. The former digital divide situation is easing, so that the North American Internet no longer consists mainly of young, white, university-educated, English-literate, professional men.

Who uses the Internet differs to some extent around the world. Analysts used to think that other countries would eventually catch up to North American Internet pioneers. That is, the users and uses of the Internet would be coming to resemble the North American situation. Yet, there is still a digital divide in other countries, with university-educated, young male professionals and students predominating. Although developed countries are closing the divide, it remains large in Third World countries.

The uses of the Internet vary internationally to some extent. Research has shown that although almost all Internet users access the Web, in Japan, Web-enabled mobile phones are heavily used to obtain information, sometimes in conjunction with personal computers (PCs) and sometimes instead of PCs. East Asians and Scandinavians use their mobile phones to send short messages, often instead of PC-based email. Catalans, living in a localistic, high-touch society, use e-mail much less to communicate although they Web-surf extensively.

Experience counts: the longer people have been online, the more time they spend online in a given day, and the more different aspects of the Internet they use: e-mail, group discussions in real time (chat boards) or asynchronously (through e-mail-based listservs), search engines, Web surfing, song swapping, online games, online shopping, and so on. Indeed, what often looks like a digital divide in how people use the Internet is often related to different lengths of experience. For example, one reason why women Internet users do not spend as much time online as men is that they are less experienced in its use. When experience is taken into account, the gender gap disappears.

Rather than weakening community, the Internet strengthens communication by supplementing other means of contact. The more people communicate via the Internet, the more they communicate by phone and in person. (Few send letters in the post anymore, except at Christmas.) Consequently, heavy Internet users have a great overall volume of contact. Of course, they use the Internet to contact physically distant friends and relatives. Yet, the Internet is also heavily used for contact with those living nearby: friends, relatives, workmates, and neighbors. The Internet, the phone, and in-person meetings are often used in conjunction to arrange meetings or nuanced phone conversations. Internet users probably have more relationships than in pre-Internet times. They also probably have more contact with community members than in pre-Internet times.

Overload may be more of a problem than isolation. In the old days, people watched television; now they socialize more on the Internet. However, domestic isolation may be a problem, if people spend more of their time interacting online and less of their time interacting with spouses and children. The Internet is a more immersive, demanding medium than television.

COMMUNITY IN CYBERSOCIETIES

Although physical place continues to be important, cyberspace has become cyberplace, affecting the ways in which people find and maintain community. In the short term, the Internet has made the household more important, as a base from which to operate one's computer-supported social network. At times, this has led to a rise in neighboring, as home-based people take more interest in their immediate surroundings and use the Internet to neighbor without physical intrusion and to arrange visits. Jointly with the mobile phone, the Internet is facilitating the prevalence of person-to-person community, contributing to the deemphasis of domestic relations. Its use has emphasized individual autonomy and agency. Each person is the operator of his or her personal community network, and these are likely to be communities of shared interest. Such communities have become more spatially dispersed and fragmented, although the Internet facilitates interconnections between such partial communities.

The ease of communication to a large number of people facilitates ties that cut across group boundaries. Online relationships and online communities have developed their own strength and dynamics. Participants in online groups have strong interpersonal feelings of belonging, being wanted, obtaining important resources, and having a shared identity. They are truly in cyberplaces, and not just cyberspaces. Often, the cyberspace–physical space comparison is a false dichotomy. Many ties operate in both cyberspace and physical space, using whatever means of communication is convenient and appropriate at the moment.

The Internet has increased the importance of network capital in the fund of desirable resources, along with financial capital, human capital, and cultural capital. Such network capital is variegated. It consists of knowing how to maintain a networked computer, search for information on the Internet and use the knowledge gained, create and sustain online relationships, and use these relationships to obtain needed resources, including indirect links to friends of friends.

—Barry Wellman

See also Digital Divide; Glocalization; Internet, Domestic Life and; Internet, Effects of; Internet in East Asia; Network Communities; Online Communities, Game-Playing; Personalization and Technology; Wired Communities

Further Reading

Bradner, E., & Kellogg, W. (1999, April). Social affordances of BABBLE. Paper presented at CHI [Computer-Human Interaction] Conference, Pittsburgh, PA.

Castells, M. (2001). The *Internet galaxy: Reflections on Internet, business, and society.* Oxford, UK: Oxford University Press.

Chayko, M. (2002). *Connecting: How we form social bonds and communities in the Internet age.* Albany: State University of New York Press.

DiMaggio, P., Hargittai, E., Neuman, W. R., & Robinson, J. (2001). Social implications of the Internet. *Annual Review of Sociology, 27,* 287–305.

Fischer, C. (1994). *America calling: A social history of the telephone to 1940.* Berkeley: University of California Press.

Katz, J. E., & Rice, R. E. (2002). Social consequences of Internet use: Access, involvement, and interaction. Cambridge, MA: MIT Press.

Keeble, L., & Loader, B. A. (Eds.). (2001). *Community informatics: Shaping computer-mediated social relations.* London: Routledge.

Kollock, P., & Smith, M. (Eds.) 1998. *Communities in cyberspace.* London: Routledge.

Kraut, R., Kiesler, S., Boneva, B., Cummings, J., Helgeson, V., & Crawford, A. (2002). Internet paradox revisited. *Journal of Social Issues, 58*(1), 49–74.

Rheingold, H. (2000). *The virtual community: Homesteading on the electronic frontier* (Rev. ed.). Cambridge, MA: MIT Press.

Wellman, B. (Ed.). (1999). *Networks in the global village.* Boulder, CO: Westview.

Wellman, B., & Haythornthwaite, C. (Eds.). (2002). *The Internet in everyday life.* Oxford, UK: Blackwell.

Woolgar, S. (Ed.). (2002). *Virtual society? Technology, cyberbole, reality.* Oxford, UK: Oxford University Press.

CYBORG COMMUNITIES

The neuroscientist Manfred Clynes described cyborgs (cybernetic organisms, or organisms whose biological functions are enhanced by electronic mechanisms; also called borgs and sometimes posthumans) as representing a synergy between the human and the machine such that operation of the machine does not require conscious thought or effort on the part of the human.

Humanistic intelligence (HI) theory has made the cyborg concept more precise. HI is defined as intelligence that arises from a human being in a feedback loop of computational processes in which a human and a computer are inextricably intertwined. This inextricability usually requires the existence of some form of body-borne computer. When a body-borne computer functions in a successful embodiment of HI, the computer uses the human's mind and body as one of its peripherals, just as the human uses the computer as a peripheral. This reciprocal relationship, where each uses the other in its feedback loop, is necessary for a successful implementation of HI. This theory is in sharp contrast to many goals of artificial intelligence research, which aims to have the computer replace or emulate human intelligence.

GLOGS

Early cyborg communities of the late 1970s and early 1980s were constructed to explore the creation of visual art within a computer-mediated reality. Then, with the advent of the World Wide Web in the 1990s, cyborg logs (known as glogs) became shared spaces. With the World Wide Web came the Wearable Wireless Webcam, which made an online video record of daily activities. Joi Ito's *Moblog* is a variation on that theme; Howard Rheingold's book *Smart Mobs* examines how computer technology enhances the power not just of the individual human but of collective groups, and how this capacity can be used for both good and ill.

Cyborg communities typically evolve around a glog and often entail several cyborgs sending live video to one another, as well as to the rest of the world, and receiving input from non-cyborg participants, in real time, as well.

Glogs take many of the concepts of the Internet beyond the confines of the desktop. Wearable computer-mediated reality (such as digital eyeglasses) also blur the boundary between cyberspace and the real world. But the most profound effect is probably that of decentralized personhood, as the site of one's persona is no longer limited to one's physical body.

DECENTRALIZED PERSONHOOD, "SOUSVEILLANCE," AND CYBORG LAW

The concept of an ambiguous and fragmented identity is not new; corporations have for many years enjoyed the rights and benefits conferred by personhood without having all the accountability associated with a single individual. Online communities now make similar constructs available to the individual. Glogs also capture the ideas of inverse surveillance (or "sousveillance," from French *sous,* meaning "from below" and *veiller,* meaning "to watch").

The ambiguous identity of the cyborg body has moved the world away from the modernist ideal of universally agreed-upon global objective reality to a postmodernist vision of fragmented, indeterminate, subjective, collective individualism. But its weakness is its reliance upon centralized wireless infrastructure, which makes it vulnerable to a postcyborg model of authoritarian, dictated, and centralized control. Only after a recent incident in which a cyborg's wearable computer was ripped from his body during an airport search (despite documentation explaining its purpose), resulting in harm both to the individual and his electronic implantations, has cyborg law started to develop. It raises many ethical issues, such as the damage (both physical and psychological, and to both human and electronic components) that may result when unplugging a cyborg, and how to bring the perpetrators of the unplugging to justice. (Is it a crime against a person or against a machine?) Other problems may arise when essential services are terminated, or threats of termination are encountered, as explored by science fiction writer John Varley (who coined the term "sidekick" to describe a wearable computing apparatus). Moreover, until most humans are cyborgs, non-cyborgs may feel threatened by both the personal capabilities of cyborgs and the privacy-threatening ability of cyborgs to transmit their sights and sounds over the Internet. The future of cyborg communities may rest upon the development of independent indestructible wireless peer-to-peer networks that have the unstoppable nature promised by the early Internet. For example, it is now possible using the Ouijava programming language to create group-created computer programs: a true collective consciousness. Such infrastructure might give rise to a past-cyborg (post-postcyborg) age.

—Steve Mann

Further Reading

Andrejevic, M. (2002). CO 342: *Technoculture and the information society.* Retrieved December 23, 2002, from http://www.faculty.fairfield.edu/mandrejevic/tech02.htm

Gray, C. H. (2000). *Cyborg citizen: Politics in the posthuman age.* New York: Routledge. Retrieved December 23, 2002, from http://www.routledge-ny.com/CyborgCitizen/index.html

Guernsey, L. (2002, March 14). At airport gate, a cyborg unplugged. *New York Times.*

Ito, J. (2002). *Moblog.* Retrieved December 23, 2002, from http://joi.ito.com/moblog/

Lightman, A. (2002). *Brave new unwired world.* New York: John Wiley.

Mann, S. (1998). Humanistic intelligence: WearComp as a new framework for intelligent signal processing. *Proceedings of the IEEE, 86*(11), 2123–2151. Retrieved December 23, 2002, from http://wearcam.org/hi.htm http://wearcam.org/hi/index.html

Mann, S. (1999, May–June). Cyborg seeks community. *Technology Review.*

Mann, S. (2002). *Intelligent image processing.* New York: John Wiley.

Mann, S., with Niedzviecki, H. (2001). *Cyborg: Digital destiny and human possibility in the age of the wearable computer.* Ontario, Canada: Random House, Doubleday.

Mann, S., Fung, J., & Manders, C. (2001). Living as cyborgs. *Proceedings of CAST01,* 99–103. Retrieved December 23, 2002, from http://wearcam.org/cast01/cast_html/

Mann, S., Nolan, J., & Wellman, B. (2002). *Sousveillance.* Retrieved December 23, 2002, from http://wearcam.org/sousveillance.htm

Rheingold, H. (1993). *The virtual community.* Cambridge, MA: MIT Press.

Varley, J. (1986). *Blue champagne.* Niles, IL: Dark Harvest.

DAMANHUR

Damanhur—officially the Federation of Damanhur—is an esoteric New Age society founded in 1976 in the Valchiusella valley, almost fifty kilometers north of Turin, in Piedmont, Italy, by Oberto Airaudi (b. 1950), a former spiritualist medium. Damanhur has it own constitution, its own government, and even a currency (largely symbolic). Damanhur's "citizens" live together on the basis of a particular religious philosophy and worldview. From the original 20 members, Damanhur has expanded to become the largest esoteric New Age communal group in the world, with some 500 members living in four communities all located in the same valley, and another 400 in communal houses nearby. Another satellite community has been founded in Berlin, Germany, and there are groups of sympathizers sharing the same worldview spread throughout Europe, the United States, Japan, and Australia. There are four levels of membership (indicated by the letters A, B, C, and D), the letters A and B indicating those living communally in the original community.

The central community in Piedmont is located in a series of highly symbolic buildings, including a large aboveground temple. The existence of the most important facility, the construction of which was started in 1978, became known to the outside world only in 1992, following the revelations of a disgruntled ex-member. It is the "Tempio dell'Uomo" ("Temple of Humankind"), a huge subterranean temple comprising a fantastic collection of richly decorated rooms and galleries. Although Italian authorities originally regarded it as having been built in breach of zoning regulations, Damanhur managed to either win or settle all the ensuing court cases, and it is now legally allowed both to operate and to expand its underground temple. For Damanhur's citizens, the temple is much more than a means of expressing their artistic creativity; it is a mystical pole at which ritual work takes place for the benefit of the whole humanity. A number of different rituals express a worldview based on the concepts of karma, reincarnation, the sanctity of nature, and the tradition of Western esotericism in general.

DAMANHUR'S SPIRITUAL SYSTEM

According to the beliefs of Damanhur's citizens, only one God exists, but it is impossible to contact him directly. God is accessible only through a group of lesser deities, the intermediate deities. Nine primeval deities are self-generated; all the other intermediate deities were created by humans but, as with Jungian archetypes, now have an existence of their own. Not to be confused with the intermediate deities are beings called entities, which include angels, nature spirits, and demons. According to Damanhur's cosmological scheme, which derives heavily from Theosophy, the first human is described as a primeval deity, who was the victim of a fall and lapsed into the present union with the body. Many deities and entities voluntarily followed the humans into their exile and now help humans who try to return to their original, "subtler" state.

Damanhur's cosmology includes the early generation of three Mother worlds—the world of human beings and animals, the world of plants, and the world of nature spirits—that are not able to communicate among one another but that generate Echo worlds, through which the Mother worlds become able to communicate. Each human, spiritual, or animal "race" has an astral tank (a repository of all knowledge accumulated by the race during the whole course of its history, a concept similar to the akashic memory of the Theosophical tradition). Human beings may get in touch, through particular techniques, with the human race mind (the astral tank of humanity), but they may find very useful information also in the race minds of animals. To be in touch with the animal race mind, each human being may enter into a special magical relation with an animal by assuming its name. In fact, all the citizens of Damanhur are identified not by their family names but by the name of an animal. The founder used to be called Hawk, but for many years has been referred to simply as Oberto. One finds names such as Elephant, Kangaroo, and so on. Today, citizens are often identified by two names, usually an animal name first and a plant name second. These names are freely chosen by whoever wants to use them. Noncitizens may also decide to pick up an animal name. Normally the names are reserved for adults. However, some children (age 7 or older) have insisted that they would like to receive their own animal names, and some of these requests have been granted.

DAMANHUR AND THE LOCAL COMMUNITY

Damanhur runs its own kindergarten, primary, and intermediate schools, which have succeeded in developing friendly relations with local school authorities. Relationships with neighbors in the Valchiusella valley have been more difficult. As has happened historically in the case of similar large communal settlements, some local residents initially welcomed Damanhur in the hope of reviving a struggling local economy. Damanhur has, in fact, become very much a tourist attraction, receiving more than 50,000 visitors in the year 2001. Other local residents, however, fear that Damanhur's citizens will quickly become the majority of the valley's voters, thus eventually controlling the city councils in several local small towns. The town closest to Damanhur, Vidracco, did elect a citizen of Damanhur as its mayor in 1999. There is also some Catholic opposition to a religious system perceived by Catholic countercultists as magical and neopagan, and also to the fact that Damanhur celebrates "temporary weddings," which are supposed to last one or two years. (These temporary weddings can be renewed an unlimited number of times, and several Damanhurian couples have actually remained together for decades.)

—Massimo Introvigne

Further Reading

Berzano, L. (1998). *Damanhur: Popolo e comunità.* [Damanhur: People and community]. Leumann, Italy: ElleDiCi.

Cardano, M. (1997). *Lo specchio, la rosa e il loto: Uno studio sulla sacralizzazione della natura.* [The mirror, the rose and the lotus: A study on sacralization of the nature]. Rome: SEAM.

Damanhur. (1999). *La Via Horusiana. Principi, concetti e tradizioni della Scuola di Pensiero di Damanhur secondo gli insegnamenti di Oberto Airaudi.* Baldissero Canavese, Italy: Author.

Introvigne, M. (1999). Children of the underground temple: Growing up in Damanhur. In S. J. Palmer & C. Hardman (Eds.), *Children in new religions* (pp. 138–149). New Brunswick, NJ, and London: Rutgers University Press.

Introvigne, M. (1999). Damanhur: A magical community in Italy. In B. Wilson & J. Cresswell (Eds.), *New religious movements: Challenge and response* (pp. 183–194). London and New York: Routledge.

Merrifield, J. (1998). *Damanhur: The real dream.* London: Thorsons.

DANCE AND DRILL

Engaging in community dance and/or military drill by moving rhythmically together for long periods of time is a very effective way of arousing excited, shared, and friendly feelings among the participants. This effect is reinforced by music and voicing, all the way from band music and choral singing to drill sergeants' shouts of "Hut, Hip, Hip, Four." Somehow moving muscles together in time, with voices backing up the rhythmic beat, makes people feel good, wipes out old grudges, and smoothes over personal rivalries. Even when the immediate excitement subsides, such exercises leave a residue of fellow-feeling and readiness to cooperate. This had important effects in times past and still exhibits itself in politics, religion, and innumerable social settings where people dance or march together.

Exactly how shared feelings are aroused when we dance or march is not accurately known. Hormones and the sympathetic nervous system are surely involved; so are parts of the brain. Suffice it to say that such behavior and their results are both unique to and universal among human beings. Only humans engage in community dancing and making music; and all known human societies do both. Only a few, however, harnessed this human response to keeping together in time for military purposes, though those that did so profited from the superior discipline and morale of soldiers who drilled regularly and for long periods of time.

When rhythmic dancing and music-making first arose among humankind is unknown, but it must have been very early. The advantage of greater cooperation arising from dancing together on festival occasions must have been enormous, since such dancing prevailed universally among bands of hunters and gatherers and peasant villagers when observers first began to take notice and write about it. Recent observations of our closest animal relatives, the chimpanzees of Africa, suggests why this was so. In 1970, the band Jane Goodall and her helpers were studying split in two rival parts, and in the next two years the smaller group of seceding males were hunted down and killed by their rivals, who thus regained their whole territory and the females who had seceded. Superior numbers (and perhaps stronger cohesion) among the core members of the old band thus prevailed. Obviously, if dancing together allowed our ancestors to overcome the sort of individual frictions that split the chimpanzee band apart in 1970, it is easy to imagine how larger numbers of more cooperative humans would prevail against neighbors who had not yet learned to dance—thus making that form of behavior universal within a few generations.

Thereafter different human groups elaborated the possibilities of rhythmic movement together in innumerable different ways. Dancing designed to consult and/or please the spirits or gods could and did become professionalized. From this, organized priesthoods and formal religions eventually emerged. Later on, in urban settings, expert exhibitions of dancing (and music) became entertainment for merely human audiences. But participatory dancing by believers remained a growing point for religions, as is clear from Biblical references to how Saul and David danced before the Lord and founded the Hebrew kingdom, largely on the strength of enthusiastic bands of young men who danced with them.

Dancing, once harnessed for military action, could also be separated from religion. This probably first happened among the Sumerians when kings organized groups of armored spearmen and, as carved steles show, made them march in step. Later, among the Greeks and Romans, military drill became thoroughly secular and allowed more or less democratic foot soldiers to oust aristocratic horsemen as the decisive element in battle and in city politics as well. When European armies revived (and modified) Roman drill in the sixteenth century, the political effect was different. Aristocratic officers discovered that enlisting the poorest of the poor and drilling them as soldiers made them reliably obedient—and cost little. This, in turn, along with naval guns, allowed European states to consolidate their power at home and expand overseas. That was how they were able to build globe-girdling colonial empires that disappeared only after 1945.

Women perform ritualized sport dancing in the Temple of Heaven Gardens in Beijing, China, in August 2002.

Source: Karen Christensen; used with permission.

In recent centuries, dancing in increasingly urbanized societies ceased to be a shared, community-wide experience. Together with congregational singing, it helped to sustain innumerable sectarian religious groups, especially among the urban poor. Psalm singing was, for example, a mainstay of early Protestant congregations in Europe; and some Muslim dervishes induced ecstasy by dance. Buddhist sects in China like the "Boxers" of the early twentieth century also practiced rhythmic exercises to express and strengthen their protests.

Among the upper classes, however, dancing became a way of showing off fine clothes and refined manners by or before the eighteenth century. Since then, social dancing has tended to divide into theatrical exhibitions of unusual skill and grace on the one hand, and a participatory accompaniment to the mating game among the young, on the other. Some remnants of older forms of community folk dancing persisted, but only marginally. A few revolutionary political movements also harnessed the power of keeping together time for their purposes. Nazi rallies and marches, complete with synchronized salutes and shouts, are the most infamous; but Communist regimes in China and North Korea continue to cultivate the emotional solidarity aroused by marching and gesturing in common.

Sporadic, apparently spontaneous resort to moving together in time may also be observed on television at athletic events, and at moments of political crisis and (more privately) among religious enthusiasts. South African crowds danced to celebrate the end of apartheid, for example; and groups of demonstrators often reinforce placards aimed at television cameras with rhythmic shouts and bodily movements, whether they are in the streets of Teheran, on American picket lines, or part of protests against globalization in any city of the world. Obviously, our capacity for arousing common feeling by dancing, shouting, and marching together is as varied and vigorous as ever. It is sure to persist and seems likely to remain politically and religiously important in times of crisis, even though older, localized community-wide dancing on festival occasions is in general decay.

—William H. McNeill

Further Reading

Blackman, E. L. (1977 [1952]). *Religious dances in the Christian Church and in popular medicine.* (E. Classen, Trans.). Westport, CT: Greenwood.

Hanna, J. L. (1977). African dance and the warrior tradition. *Journal of African Studies, 12,* 225.

Hanna, J. L. (1979). *To dance is human: A theory of non-verbal communication.* Austin: University of Texas Press.

Lange, R. (1975). *The nature of dance: An anthropological perspective.* London: Macdonald and Evans.

McNeill, W. H. (1995). *Keeping together in time: Dance and drill in human history.* Cambridge, MA: Harvard University Press.

Ranger, T. O. (1975). *Dance and society in East Africa.* London: Heinemann.

Sachs, C. (1937). *World history of the dance.* (B. Schonberg, Trans.). New York: W. W. Norton.

DEATH

Death and dying emerged as a topic of discourse in the United States with the 1969 publication of a book by Swiss-born Elisabeth Kübler-Ross (1926–1997), *On Death and Dying.* Her articulation of five phases of dying encouraged both the dying and those who care for them to celebrate life. Kübler-Ross revolutionized care for the dying, and since then ritual makers have come to address how the rest of us care for survivors. The performance of death rites and of other acts of commemoration strengthens social bonds within families and within religious, ethnic, and national communities. As ritual theorist Ronald Grimes (b. 1943) argues, death rites fulfill many functions. They are a form of mourning, but they also mark an end to the immediate mourning process, allowing survivors to move on with their own lives. Such rituals reconstruct social order after death and embrace death's finality.

More abstractly, public acts of commemoration perpetuate people's awareness of living in community with the beloved dead or the illustrious dead. In Britain, as happened with Princess Diana in September 1997, the Anglican Church excels at mounting funerals for royalty in such a way as to engage the widest possible community. Occasionally in France, state officials rebury renowned figures in the Pantheon in hopes of encouraging citizens to identify anew with chosen luminaries of French culture. Ritual making as it has developed in the United States over the past generation teaches ways to make mourning not only more meaningful but more effective in building community.

DEATH RITES IN JUDAISM AND IN EAST ASIAN RELIGIONS

Communal farewells to the dead foster a sense of community while also helping the bereaved cope with loss. Since it would be impossible in an article of this scope to address bereavement customs in all world religions, let us consider just a few: Jewish traditions and some traditions from East Asia. Jewish customs of mourning are widely acknowledged for their efficacy. Key components include promptness of burial, if possible within twenty-four hours, visible tearing of garments to signify mourning, and sitting together for seven days to share grieving. Sitting *shivah* ("seven" in Hebrew) obliges the chief mourners to focus on bereavement. The sharing of such unabashed grieving communalizes the mourners' suffering. The first seven days after burial are shared twenty-four hours a day. Thereafter follows a year of ritually mandated mourning, during which no one pretends that grieving has ceased. The privatizing of grieving is thereby ritually forbidden by a religion that celebrates above all the living of life.

In nearly all traditions of Buddhism practiced in Asia, and above all, in the countryside, a local monastic community *(sangha)* will strive to transfer its merit *(punya)* to a deceased person associated with that community. This religious practice strengthens bonding within the wider community. It exemplifies the wider Asian assumption that the deceased continue to belong to their families and need to be propitiated. Ignoring the Western distinction between the living and the dead, Asians posit an intermediate zone that hovers between the living and dead. Souls who die unappeased may yet be ritually released after death. In China, Japan, and Korea, Confucianism teaches that successful living requires cultivating in perpetuity a sound relationship with ancestors. Veneration for the dead helps to impart cohesion to an extended family. In Japan, Shinto teaches veneration of the nation's dead, centered on temples and groves where the spirits are believed to linger. Japanese go on pilgrimage to these sites as a communal way of experiencing ancestral presence. The cult of ancestors builds community within families, within monasteries, and within the nation.

HOW CEMETERIES EMBODY A COMMUNITY'S MEMORY

Cemeteries embody the capacity of death to enhance a sense of community. Until the early twentieth century, the preferred place of burial in European and U.S. rural communities was a churchyard. Thus Christians worshiped surrounded by the graves of their predecessors. Likewise, urban churches throughout Europe abound in burial monuments and memorial tablets, which envelop a visitor in monuments to former members of that parish. Certain prestigious sites, such as Westminster Abbey in London and the deconsecrated Church of the Pantheon in Paris, gather the tombs of famous individuals into a national memorial. A vivid instance of a community expressing itself through a burial place persists in Christian monasteries. Most have a cemetery on the property, and the monastics in residence know that they will be buried alongside their brethren. A monastic community extends backward and forward through time, and living in proximity to the place of burial enhances a sense of continuity.

HOW FEAR OF DEATH CEMENTS COMMUNAL BONDS

Death and dying can also build community in an entirely different manner: through the shared fear they inspire, under certain circumstances, of imminent death. Battlefield comradeship finds a civilian correlate in shared moments of danger, as in a transportation mishap, a fire, an earthquake, or other disaster. Persons who have faced together an imminent threat of dying will feel bonded for a lifetime, even if they never see one another again. By a similar logic, certain initiation rituals of adolescents induce a state akin to fear of death. A group of adolescents living apart in the wild for a few days undergo a bonding that launches them irreversibly into adult status. Temporary isolation from their birth community prepares them for reentry into it, having acquired a new status. Encounter with the "mystical danger" of imitating death cements a new identity within one's community.

Funerals and Social Status

The customary manner in which a person's body is disposed of after death is an important indicator of his or her social status in the community. The following description makes clear the social distinctions followed by the Ganda people of Uganda.

> As soon as it was ready for interment, the Queen sent her Kago to cover it with the buttered bark-cloth, and the body was then taken to its burial place. On the way the bodyguard caught as many people as they could, and they were killed at the sacrificial place near the tomb. The body was buried in an open place with a mound raised over the grave, and a house was built near it for the people who were to guard it. These caretakers were chosen from some of the maids of the late Queen, and the new Queen as heiress was responsible for the repairs to the grave. . . .
>
> When the King's Mother (Namasole) died, fear seized the people; the King's grief usually took the form of excessive anger, and people were captured and cast into the stocks upon the slightest provocation, and kept to swell the number sent to execution at the funeral. Everyone had to go into mourning during the time that the body was being prepared for interment. The first thing to be done was to appoint the successor to the Namasole. . . .
>
> Suicides were burned at cross roads, the materials from the house or the tree on which the deed was done being used as fuel. The same precautions as those just mentioned were observed by women, when passing the spot, in order to prevent the ghosts from entering into them, and being reborn.
>
> Slaves were buried on some part of their master's estate without any ceremony; people feared to throw them out on waste land for wild animals, because the medicine-men stated that sickness and death had been caused by the ghosts of slaves who had been thus neglected.

Source: Roscoe, John. (1911). *The Baganda. An Account of Their Native Customs and Beliefs.* London: Macmillan and Company, pp. 114, 127.

A Roman Catholic cemetery in New Mexico. The graves are marked by stones and decorated with plastic flowers and wreaths.
Source: David Levinson/Jo Ann Callegari; used with permission.

HOW MARTYRDOM BUILDS COMMUNITY

Recollection of the exemplary dead builds community intensely through the notion of religious martyrdom. Only a few of the world's religions have developed a cult of the martyr (which means "witness" in Greek), chief among them Christianity and Shi'ite Islam. For Christians, martyrdom means being killed by enemies of the faith because one has refused to recant the faith. Those who die in witness to the faith become guarantors of Christian community. Martyrs' shrines attract pilgrims, and holy cities like Rome and Jerusalem abound in memorials to martyrs, some of whose relics have been brought from a great distance. Even more dramatically, celebration of Shi`ite martyrdom means joining figuratively or actually in the death of Muhammad's grandson, the Imam Husayn, known as the "chief of martyrs," who died at the battle of Karbala, Iraq, in 680 CE. In Iran and Pakistan, Husayn's martyrdom is reenacted every year on the tenth day of the month of Muharram in passion plays that include public acts of self-mutilation. Veneration of martyrs solidifies religious community by instilling a sense of sharing in the martyrs' act of commitment to the faith. The dead died, it is believed, not least so that survivors may deepen their commitment to community.

CONTEMPORARY THREATS TO THE EFFICACY OF DEATH RITES

Whereas death rites necessarily call attention to the ineluctability of death, contemporary mass culture throughout the developed world seeks to avoid contemplating death. Media cults of youth, of athleticism, of sexuality, and of celebrity status may be said to deny or downplay the role of death in cementing community. Nevertheless, any culture that persists in seeking to evade encountering death—that inevitable element in the cycle of life—risks undermining a sense of solidarity. To combat a temptation to evade confronting death, Ronald Grimes suggests that people in the contemporary West need "a renewed mythologizing of death and the dead, one that does not require naïve belief but depends on dramatic storytelling and bold, performed images of Old Death" (Grimes 2000, p. 282). Death rites transform the coldness of death into the warmth of social cohesion. To seek to deny death and its rites is to begin to deny community, for to honor the dead is to honor the community that remembers them.

—William M. Johnston

See also LIMINALITY

Further Reading

Bowker, J. W. (1991). *The meanings of death.* Cambridge, UK: Cambridge University Press.

Grimes, R. (2000). *Deeply into the bone: Reinventing rites of passage.* Berkeley and Los Angeles: University of California Press.

Kastenbaum, R., & Kastenbaum, B. (Eds.). (1989). *Encyclopedia of death.* Phoenix, AZ: Oryx.

Kübler-Ross, E. (1996). *The wheel of life: A memoir of death and dying.* New York: Bantam.

Lifton, R. J. (1979). *The broken connection: On death and the continuity of life.* New York: Simon and Schuster.

Matlins, S. M., & Magida, A. J. (Eds.). (1995–1997). *How to be a perfect stranger: A guide to etiquette in other people's religious ceremonies* (Vols. 1–2). Woodstock VT: Jewish Lights Publishing.

DECENTRALIZATION

In the United States, decentralized government is a deeply held value built into the constitution and cultural traditions. The delegates to the constitutional convention of 1789 were obligated to seek ratification of the new constitution from state legislatures. To accomplish this, they granted significant autonomy to the states to make their own governing arrangements. The Tenth Amendment, added in 1791, allocated to state governments "or to the people" all legal powers not delegated to the national government or not prohibited to the states. This constitutional framework established a federal system of decentralized authority that has remained one of the most distinguishing hallmarks of the U.S. system of government. Decentralization is further accentuated by the fact that cities are not mentioned in the constitution; instead, they have direct connections to states but not to federal authority. As a result, although Americans share a strong sense of national identity, they also are fiercely loyal to their states and communities.

Since President Franklin D. Roosevelt's New Deal of the 1930s, the federal government has assumed greater powers. To fight the Great Depression (1929–1939), the federal government vastly expanded its authority to regulate the economy through such agencies as the Federal Aviation Administration and the Securities and Exchange Commission. Despite overwhelming public support for the new federal intervention, debates about the relative authority of the federal government vis-à-vis the states continued. Beginning with the 1968 presidential election and through the election of 2002, candidates have sparred on the question of federal authority. Richard Nixon won the election of 1968 on a platform that promised to return power to the states. Once elected, he pursued his vision of a "new federalism" that would redistribute authority downward. He persuaded Congress to approve revenue-sharing legislation in 1972 and several block grant programs in 1973 and 1974 that reduced federal oversight of federal funds received by states and localities.

The watershed in decentralized federalism occurred during the presidency of Ronald Reagan, 1980–1988. President Reagan's New Federalism promised a fundamental realignment between the federal government and the states. He sought not only to reduce federal oversight of federal programs, but also to cut the number of grant-in-aid programs drastically. During his administration, funding for grant-in-aid programs to states and localities fell sharply, and the states were given much greater control of most programs.

The Fourteenth Amendment

The Fourteenth Amendment to the U.S. Constitution and its later interpretation by the Supreme Court was a major force in the twentieth century for the centralization of power by the federal government.

Section 1. All persons born or naturalized in the United States, and subject to the jurisdiction thereof, are citizens of the United States and of the state wherein they reside. No state shall make or enforce any law which shall abridge the privileges or immunities of citizens of the United States; nor shall any state deprive any person of life, liberty, or property, without due process of law; nor deny to any person within its jurisdiction the equal protection of the laws.

Section 2. Representatives shall be apportioned among the several states according to their respective numbers, counting the whole number of persons in each state, excluding Indians not taxed. But when the right to vote at any election for the choice of electors for President and Vice President of the United States, Representatives in Congress, the executive and judicial officers of a state, or the members of the legislature thereof, is denied to any of the male inhabitants of such state, being twenty-one years of age, and citizens of the United States, or in any way abridged, except for participation in rebellion, or other crime, the basis of representation therein shall be reduced in the proportion which the number of such male citizens shall bear to the whole number of male citizens twenty-one years of age in such state.

Section 3. No person shall be a Senator or Representative in Congress, or elector of President and Vice President, or hold any office, civil or military, under the United States, or under any state, who, having previously taken an oath, as a member of Congress, or as an officer of the United States, or as a member of any state legislature, or as an executive or judicial officer of any state, to support the Constitution of the United States, shall have engaged in insurrection or rebellion against the same, or given aid or comfort to the enemies thereof. But Congress may by a vote of two-thirds of each House, remove such disability.

Section 4. The validity of the public debt of the United States, authorized by law, including debts incurred for payment of pensions and bounties for services in suppressing insurrection or rebellion, shall not be questioned. But neither the United States nor any state shall assume or pay any debt or obligation incurred in aid of insurrection or rebellion against the United States, or any claim for the loss or emancipation of any slave; but all such debts, obligations and claims shall be held illegal and void.

Section 5. The Congress shall have power to enforce, by appropriate legislation, the provisions of this article.

By the 1992 presidential election, the candidates of both parties had embraced the language of decentralization. Bill Clinton proclaimed himself a New Democrat who believed as fervently in decentralized, small government as did the Republicans. Many political observers credited his victory to this new image. During his years in office, Clinton frequently expressed his support for the principle of decentralized government. For example, in the welfare reform that he sponsored, which passed Congress as the Personal Responsibility Act of 1996, the states were given the responsibility of designing their own programs to help welfare recipients find work by the end of the five-year welfare cap imposed by Congress.

Throughout U.S. history, there has been overwhelming support for the ideology of decentralized government. The growth of federal powers in the twentieth century did not change this fact; indeed, it probably reinforced popular mistrust of centralized authority. In general, people today feel much closer to their local communities and to local governments than to the federal government.

—Dennis R. Judd

Further Reading

Elazar, D. J. (1962). *The American partnership: Intergovernmental cooperation in the nineteenth-century United States.* Chicago: University of Chicago Press.

Rich, M. J. (1993). *Federal policymaking and the poor: National goals, local choices, and distributional outcomes.* Princeton, NJ: Princeton University Press.

Robertson, D. B., & Judd, D. R. (1989). *The development of American public policy.* New York: Longman.

Walker, D. B. (1981). *Toward a functioning Federalism.* Cambridge, MA: Winthrop.

Wright, D. (1988). *Understanding intergovernmental relations: Public policy and participants' perspectives in local, state and national governments* (3rd ed.). Monterey, CA: Brooks/Cole.

DECLINING COMMUNITIES

Communities decline for many reasons, depending on the era and the location. This article examines declining communities in the United States, but many of its observations are generalizable to declining communities elsewhere in the world.

Throughout U.S. history, economic and technological innovation and constant immigration and mobility have meant smaller populations and physical decay in some territorially defined communities. Observers regularly, but not always accurately, label these changes as decline.

European immigration destroyed American Indian communities. By the end of the nineteenth century, Indians who had survived disease lived far from the communities of their ancestors in 1500. But new Euroamerican communities in North America soon faced competition for settlers from better endowed lands farther west. After a half century of rapid growth, Chelsea, in central Vermont, lost more than 40 percent of its population between 1840 and 1900; over a hundred of the state's 238 townships lost more than a quarter of their population during this period.

Many newer communities, however, had fleeting existences. The ideological basis of most utopian communities, such as Robert Owen's New Harmony in Indiana, was fragile. Transportation innovations undercut other communities. Within Onondaga County, New York, for example, Syracuse flourished following the construction of the adjacent Erie Canal while Manlius, 24 kilometers away along the old turnpike, declined. A boom-and-bust cycle particularly affected communities based on the extraction of natural resources. A collapse in the world price of copper led Jerome, Arizona, to lose half its population in the 1930s.

During the same decade, environmental conditions, such as the Dust Bowl of the southern Great Plains, checked overoptimistic expansion of farming communities. In the cutover region surrounding the Great Lakes, recognition of sandy soils and short growing seasons helped stop the schemes of boosters—and the dreams of poor immigrants—to build yeoman farming communities in the wake of commercial lumbering.

After 1945, public policies and world market conditions encouraged larger-scale agriculture. As farms declined in number, both open-country communities and the villages that served them lost viability. In Nebraska, population declined in sixty-nine of ninety-three counties between 1950 and 2000. With their remaining residents increasingly dependent on city work, rural communities lost their distinctiveness.

In the twentieth century, cities faced challenges as populations dispersed with the introduction of automobiles and, later, as the U.S. economy shifted away from manufacturing. In 2000, St. Louis had just 41 percent of the population it had in 1950. Unachieved redevelopment projects left large sections of once-great cities with a bombed-out appearance. In the 1990s, Trenton, the capital of New Jersey, had no hotel. Downtown Detroit had no department store. A cynic suggested cre-

The abandoned post office in Lumberton, New Mexico, in 1993.
Source: David Levinson/Jo Ann Callegari; used with permission.

ating a "ruins park" from the numerous empty buildings in Detroit.

Counterproductive redevelopment projects in twentieth-century cities particularly targeted black neighborhoods. In Miami in the 1930s, federal money razed Colored Town in anticipation of the expansion of the central business district. However, public housing projects rather than job-creating businesses filled the site, and neighborhood frustration contributed to a 1980 race riot that killed eighteen people. These inner-city communities also lost leadership as the relaxation of racial segregation after 1950 made it possible for middle-class African Americans to live elsewhere.

The ghost town, usually an abandoned mining settlement, epitomizes the consequences of community decline. But simple decline does not capture the variety of experiences in older, changing communities. In places like Chelsea, community ties become stronger among the residents who choose not to move. Migrants often maintained ties with the places they left, like the hundreds of attendees at the annual reunions of the Roberts Settlement, a rural African American community in Indiana, or replicated their communities by living among themselves within their new locations. Even when a mining settlement was abandoned, many of its residents moved to identical communities elsewhere.

Reuse and revitalization have reversed the decline of some communities. In Houston, the MacGregor neighborhood, abandoned by Jewish families moving to the suburbs, became a prestigious residential area for African American elites. Money from newly legalized gambling energized many American Indian reservations in the 1990s. Trenton gained a hotel in 2002; visitors can hear a concert at the restored 1932 civic auditorium and shop or do business in the renovated sprawling ironworks that was once the industrial heart of the city.

—Robert J. Gough

Further Reading

Barron, H. S. (1984). *Those who stayed behind: Rural society nineteenth-century New England.* Cambridge, UK: Cambridge University Press.

Clements, E. L. (1996). Bust and bust in the mining West. *Journal of the West, 35*(4), 40–53.

Fogelson, R. (2001). *Downtown: Its rise and fall, 1880–1950.* New Haven, CT: Yale University Press.

Gough, R. (1997). *Farming the cutover: A social history of northern Wisconsin, 1900–1940.* Lawrence: University Press of Kansas.

Procter, M., & Matuszeski, B. (1978). *Gritty cities.* Philadelphia: Temple University Press.

Russo, D. J. (2001). *American towns: An interpretative history.* Chicago: Ivan Dee.

Vincent, S. A. (1999). *Southern seed, Northern soil: African-American farm communities in the Midwest, 1765–1900.* Bloomington: Indiana University Press.

DEMOCRACY

In any community we will generally find shared principles, habits, and rules that govern the conduct of members. Democracy is one such collection of principles, habits, and rules of conduct. Democracy is rule of the many, in contrast to rule by the few (oligarchy, aristocracy) or the one (monarchy, dictatorship). The people govern themselves in a democracy, and they do so without resorting to deception or threats of violence. Something like this idea must surely have arisen independently several times over the course of human history, but the term itself comes to us from the ancient Greeks (*demos:* the people; *kratos:* to rule), who were the first to examine carefully the theory and practice of democratic government.

DEMOCRACY AND COMMUNITY

Democracy is a political concept, relating to the exercise of collective authority. A critical feature of such authority is the legitimate use of coercive force in pursuit of shared ends. And although the term *democracy* is used to describe specific forms of government, the concept is inherently normative: Before asking how a people *might* rule themselves, we must determine whether or not they *should* rule themselves, and if they should, how they *ought* to rule together.

What is the relationship between democracy, as a political and normative concept, and community? The term *community* generally describes a distinct group of individuals who identify themselves in terms of shared beliefs, traditions, and interests. We might, of course, refer to a community of nations, just as we might think of democracy as applying to several sovereign states (such as the United Nations or the European Union). But *community* most often refers to a group of individual persons, and the term invokes considerations of psychology and sociology: How do particular individuals come to identify themselves as members of a distinct community? What beliefs, rituals, and interests define this community? How are these ideas and practices sustained over time, despite countervailing forces? How are shared interests satisfied? How are conflicts among community members resolved? The latter sorts of questions raise distinctly political concerns, and from these we are easily moved toward normative considerations: How should members of a community resolve disputes and pursue shared ends? Are there some communities whose members should *not* rule themselves? To examine the relationship between democracy and community is, then, to explore the political and normative dimensions of community.

THE PEOPLE

If the people rule in a democracy, then we must have some account of who the people are and how they are to rule together. Democracy thus requires an account of citizenship. It is an open and important question whether *the people* can be defined in a democratic fashion, or whether democracy assumes some prior account of who belongs to the community that is to govern itself. Notice that the question "Who are the people?" cannot be answered by popular vote, for the very act of voting (often thought of as a defining feature of democracy) already supposes that we know who is allowed to vote.

Suppose we have an account of who the people are. Perhaps, like the philosopher Jean-Jacques Rousseau (1712–1778), we believe that distinct communities arise through accidents of geography and history, as circumstances bring people together within a given territory. Or we may discover that distinct peoples trace their origins back to considerably less benign patterns of deceit, theft, conquest, and settlement. Given that durable communities have in fact emerged over the course of human history, whether by accident or conquest, how are members to govern themselves? How should they resolve disputes among members, address past injustices, admit new members, maintain features of their shared identity across generations, and defend themselves against internal and external threats?

PARTICIPATION

If we answer that communities should govern themselves in a democratic fashion, then we will, at the very least, emphasize participation. The people cannot rule themselves if citizens do not take part in public activities. But what sort of participation is appropriate?

Again, voting is taken to be a central feature of democracy: Members of a community decide on collective actions through casting votes either to decide issues in referenda or to elect representatives to political offices, where they are responsible for pursuing the interests of their constituents. But voting is not the only way that citizens might govern themselves. In ancient Athens—often taken to be the earliest instance of a flourishing democracy—many offices were filled not by popular vote, but by lot. That is, citizens were chosen at random to fulfill public duties.

Why did Athenians use the lot to fill public offices? Didn't this risk putting reckless or incompetent individuals into positions of authority? A similar question has been asked with regard to voting: Should we let foolish or malicious persons vote in elections? Should such people have a say in matters of shared concern? How can we trust them to vote responsibly? The philosopher and economist John Stuart Mill (1806–1873), while no enemy of democracy, nonetheless thought that the votes of more educated citizens should be worth more than those of the less educated.

POLITICAL EQUALITY AND INCLUSION

Why not restrict citizenship in ways that prevent people with insufficient training and experience, or mistaken beliefs and undesirable habits, from having influence in politics? In ancient Athens, it was supposed that all citizens were similarly able to fulfill certain public duties. Thus it did not matter who occupied a particular office, and a fair way to allocate these responsibilities was to call upon citizens at random. Similarly, in most modern democracies all citizens are assumed to be competent to reflect on public matters

Jean-Jacques Rousseau on Democracy

He who makes the law knows better than any one else how it should be executed and interpreted. It seems then impossible to have a better constitution than that in which the executive and legislative powers are united; but this very fact renders the government in certain respects inadequate, because things which should be distinguished are confounded, and the prince and the Sovereign, being the same person, form, so to speak, no more than a government without government.

It is not good for him who makes the laws to execute them, or for the body of the people to turn its attention away from a general standpoint and devote it to particular objects. Nothing is more dangerous than the influence of private interests in public affairs, and the abuse of the laws by the government is a lesser evil than the corruption of the legislator, which is the inevitable sequel to a particular standpoint. In such a case, the State being altered in substance, all reformation becomes impossible. A people that would never misuse governmental powers would never misuse independence; a people that would always govern well would not need to be governed.

If we take the term in the strict sense, there never has been a real democracy, and there never will be. It is against the natural order for the many to govern and the few to be governed. It is unimaginable that the people should remain continually assembled to devote their time to public affairs, and it is clear that they cannot set up commissions for that purpose without the form of administration being changed.

In fact, I can confidently lay down as a principle that, when the functions of government are shared by several tribunals, the less numerous sooner or later acquire the greatest authority, if only because they are in a position to expedite affairs, and power thus naturally comes into their hands.

Besides, how many conditions that are difficult to unite does such a government presuppose! First, a very small State, where the people can readily be got together and where each citizen can with ease know all the rest; secondly, great simplicity of manners, to prevent business from multiplying and raising thorny problems; next, a large measure of equality in rank and fortune, without which equality of rights and authority cannot long subsist; lastly, little or no luxury—for luxury either comes of riches or makes them necessary; it corrupts at once rich and poor, the rich by possession and the poor by covetousness; it sells the country to softness and vanity, and takes away from the State all its citizens, to make them slaves one to another, and one and all to public opinion.

This is why a famous writer has made virtue the fundamental principle of Republics; for all these conditions could not exist without virtue. But, for want of the necessary distinctions, that great thinker was often inexact, and sometimes obscure, and did not see that, the sovereign authority being everywhere the same, the same principle should be found in every well-constituted State, in a greater or less degree, it is true, according to the form of the government.

It may be added that there is no government so subject to civil wars and intestine agitations as democratic or popular government, because there is none which has so strong and continual a tendency to change to another form, or which demands more vigilance and courage for its maintenance as it is. Under such a constitution above all, the citizen should arm himself with strength and constancy, and say, every day of his life, what a virtuous Count Palatine said in the Diet of Poland: *Malo periculosam libertatem quam quietum servitium*.

Were there a people of gods, their government would be democratic. So perfect a government is not for men.

Source: Rousseau, Jean-Jacques. (1762). *The Social Contract or Principles of Political Right.* Translated by G. D. H. Cole. Retrieved January 16, 2003, from http://www.constitution.org/jjr/socon.htm.

and to be able to make sincere and informed judgments when fulfilling public responsibilities such as voting, jury duty, and serving in political office. Democracy thus presumes some measure of equality with respect to citizens' competence and sincerity.

Democracy also demands equality in at least one of two further senses. First, citizens are to have equal opportunities to participate in deliberation and legislation on public matters. Second, the interests and opinions of citizens are generally to be given equal consideration in public affairs.

Equality of competence, equality of opportunity, and equality of consideration, taken together, amount to political equality. Citizens may be unequal in many respects: Some citizens may be stronger or more charismatic than others, and some will have had more formal education than their peers. Such inequalities are, however, taken to be largely irrelevant to the duties of democratic citizenship.

These three senses of equality easily conflict. If we suspect that most people are sufficiently competent to carry out public duties, then we may be tempted to cast the bounds of citizenship widely to include a great many people. That is, the presumption of roughly equal capabilities suggests greater inclusion as a democratic fundamental. If all citizens are basically equally competent, then citizenship should not be limited to those of noble birth, great wealth, or extraordinary erudition, but should extend to all minimally competent adults who are willing to abide by the laws and share in the responsibilities of public life. But when citizenship includes a great many people, it is extraordinarily difficult to ensure that each citizen has equal opportunities to participate in public deliberations and judgments. Furthermore, as states increase in size and complexity, the business of government requires considerable expertise and experience in many disparate fields, thus raising the effective costs of substantive participation for citizens. Greater inclusion, and associated increases in the scale and scope of government, may force us to understand equality less in terms of equal chances to participate in the actual business of government and more in terms of equal consideration of interests. Yet even if we emphasize such equal consideration, it is still the case that citizens with differing backgrounds, occupations, beliefs, and traditions are likely to have very different expectations and interests, and so they are likely to disagree about public matters. Thus a more inclusive standard of citizenship not only thwarts equal participation in the business of governance, but also may undermine at least the perception that all interests are receiving equal consideration. Diversity fosters disagreement, and citizens who find themselves persistently in the minority on a range of issues are likely to conclude that, regardless of formal equality, their interests are not really receiving equal consideration.

Ancient Athens avoided these problems by restricting citizenship in ways that offend modern sensibilities. Women were excluded from Athenian political life, as were some residents who could not trace their lineage back to Athens. Furthermore, the economy of Athens relied not only on women and immigrants from outside the city but also on slaves captured in various military conquests, who were of course also excluded from citizenship. Reliable demographic information about the ancient world is scarce, but the historian David Stockton estimates that fewer than two in five adult male residents of the city and surrounding territories were actually citizens of Athens during the fifth century BCE. These restrictions ensured that citizens could realistically expect equal opportunities to participate in public affairs and have their voices heard. Citizens were also likely to find that other citizens had similar values, interests, and expectations, thus ensuring equal consideration simply by virtue of citizens having so much in common to begin with.

Although the Athenian solution is unpalatable today, an intuition behind this approach still finds purchase in modern democratic thought. David Miller and Michael Sandel are among the contemporary political theorists who hold that citizens cannot succeed in ruling themselves if they do not already share a great deal by way of values, traditions, and interests. Furthermore, an important tradition of research in the social sciences has sought to identify the values and practices that are vital to a flourishing democracy.

In contemporary democracies, which often govern multiethnic and multicultural societies, the conflict between inclusion and equality tends to be resolved by appealing to a standard of fairness: Although some interests will inevitably lose out in democratic decisions, the requirements for equal consideration of interests and equal opportunities for participation are sufficiently satisfied so long as votes are given equal weight and all citizens are able to voice their political views, vote in elections, and pursue political offices. In this way, it is hoped that democracy can be inclusive and fair without badly violating a commitment to substantive equality of participation and consideration.

To be sure, many issues will not be examined in much depth in modern democratic politics. And participation will, for many citizens, be limited to the passive reception of political commentary in the media, punctuated by the occasional vote cast in an election or referendum. But at least in principle, all citizens have the opportunities to express their views in public, to vote in referenda and elections, and to mount campaigns for public office; furthermore, every vote is given equal weight. In this very modest sense, then, equality is respected in modern democracies, in principle if not always in practice.

Much research in the social sciences has explored how equality fails to be realized in actual democracies, particularly in the United States, presently the world's most affluent and influential democracy. In *Voice and Equality: Civic Voluntarism in American Politics,* Sidney Verba, Kay Schlozman, and Henry Brady (1995) report that more-engaged U.S. citizens tend to be more affluent and better educated, but not especially representative of the broader public. Other scholars have examined the pernicious consequences of inequalities in the United States' current method of financing electoral campaigns.

LIBERTY AND REPRESENTATION

Democracy suggests participation, equality, and inclusion, and there are tensions among these democratic commitments. Two further features are of vital importance in modern politics and are generally taken to be fundamental to the idea of democracy: liberty and representation.

Democracy today most often means liberal democracy, although this simple conflation in popular speech belies the historical tensions between classical liberalism and democracy. In a liberal democracy, certain basic rights are protected in equal measure for all citizens, regardless of what the majority of their fellow citizens might desire.

Liberal democracy is distinct from republican democracy and communitarian democracy. Communitarians and republicans both emphasize the importance of prior solidarity among citizens to the meaningful exercise of freedoms. Classical liberals (who generally were not "liberals" in the sense common in contemporary U.S. policy debates, where the term often refers to supporters of government intervention in the economy, especially to provide welfare programs) understood freedom primarily as the absence of interference by others. Communitarians suggest that liberty is valuable only against the backdrop of formative communities that give our lives meaning. Republicans (again, referring to bearers of a philosophical position, not members of a political party) understand liberty in terms of the freedom to participate in the government of one's political community. Some philosophical republicans share the communitarian emphasis on community membership, stressing a sense of civic belonging and an attendant desire among citizens to identify and pursue the common good together. Other republicans are less concerned with communitarian themes, and more concerned with freedom from domination: To rule together as free citizens requires that we be free from dependence upon the will of others.

Advocates of liberal democracy typically do not deny the importance of these distinct senses of liberty. They acknowledge the significance of prior attachments, civic solidarity, and freedom from domination, but they also value personal liberty, understood as freedom from outside interference in personal aspirations and chosen associations with others. Philosophical liberals not only worry about arbitrary coercion interfering with the populace's governing itself freely, they also worry about outside interference in people's personal affairs. Liberal democrats hope that we can successfully govern ourselves as free and equal persons while maintaining extensive personal liberties when it comes to how we live our lives, and all this in spite of deep differences on matters of culture, morality, religion, ethnicity, and class.

Liberty as noninterference is particularly important given the realities of modern democracies, which typically include large and diverse populations and span vast territories. At such scales, citizens must elect or otherwise appoint representatives to carry out much of the actual business of governance, and so the liberty to participate directly in governing one's political community is perhaps less important to many citizens than the liberty to be left alone.

Although representation is an essential feature of modern democracies, it is not a uniquely modern feature. Even the city-state of ancient Athens was too large to be governed entirely by popular assemblies. Instead, citizen assemblies met periodically to decide major issues and elect some major officials, but the everyday tasks of government (including the task of setting agendas for the assemblies) fell to bodies of representatives, elected or chosen by lot.

WHY DEMOCRACY?

The ancient Greeks gave us the term *democracy,* but the two great Greek philosophers, Plato (c. 428–c. 348 BCE) and Aristotle (384–322 BCE), were not especially fond of democratic government. Plato worried that democracies were like ships navigated not by the most competent sailors, but instead by the most charismatic passengers; rhetoric would inevitably prevail over careful reasoning and experience. He believed that the state should be led by those best suited to rule, not those best able to garner the support of their fellow citizens. Aristotle was similarly suspicious of democracy, noting the tendency of democracies of his day to ostracize exceptional individuals.

Aristotle was, however, as much a scientist as a philosopher, and he distinguished between different forms of democracy. In doing so, he arguably anticipated important modern distinctions between representative and direct democracy, on the one hand, and constitutional versus purely majoritarian democracy, on the other. While citizens themselves decide on some laws through referenda and ballot initiatives in several modern democracies, such as Switzerland and the United States, these decisions are generally bound by a constitution that limits the legislative power of majorities. And while some modern states, such as England, have no formal constitution, citizens generally do not decide on laws themselves, but instead elect representatives to a legislative assembly.

Furthermore, modern democracies use courts to scrutinize legislation in light of either a constitution (as in Canada and the United States) or precedents derived from a tradition of common law (as in England). There are no obvious historical examples of genuinely populist democracies in which the laws are determined directly by the majority of citizens, without mediation by representative institutions or judicial constraints (although some Mediterranean cities during the fifth century BCE, including Athens during part of its history, may have resembled such a regime). Nonetheless, several modern critics of democracy have assumed that something like genuine populism is the ideal form of democracy. Others have vigorously contested this assumption.

FINDING THE COMMON GOOD

Aristotle rejected democracy as an ideal form of government, but nonetheless he believed that it might be better than other regimes in practice. In his *Politics* he gives us the foundation of what has since become a powerful argument in favor of democracy. He noted that even if some citizens are not especially wise and noble, a democratic assembly can pool talents and knowledge in desirable ways. In the eighteenth century, Jean-Jacques Rousseau and Jean-Antoine-Nicolas de Caritat, Marquis de Condorcet (1743–1794), developed this idea further.

Rousseau argued that citizens of a democracy should vote only on questions involving the general will, that is, matters that are genuinely about the common interest. Rather than voting based on their particular interests and inclinations, citizens ought to reason about shared ends and make sincere judgments about what is in their common interest. Voting is for Rousseau an effort to identify correctly the public good.

Although many of his ideas conflict with Rousseau's, Condorcet is nonetheless thought by some to have buttressed Rousseau's claim about the nature of democratic participation. Condorcet noted that when a group such as a jury votes on a question of fact (for example, on whether someone is innocent or guilty) the majority tends to be correct with considerable certainty, and the likelihood of a correct decision increases with the number of voters. All that is required for Condorcet's claim to hold is that, on average, voters be slightly more rather than less likely to identify the correct answer.

This result, known as Condorcet's Jury Theorem, should appeal to democratic theorists. If there is a common good, then citizens can identify and achieve that good more effectively together than any of them could either alone or in small groups. Furthermore, the democratic values of participation, equality, and inclusion do not threaten to interfere with this process. Indeed, greater inclusion and equal participation may bring together diverse sources of information and ensure that facts and arguments are widely scrutinized, thus increasing the likelihood that democratic decisions will correctly identify the common good.

RESOLVING CONFLICTS OF INTEREST

But suppose that members of a community are not trying to identify the common good; instead, they want to find a democratic way to resolve conflicts among them. That is, they seek an authoritative procedure for collective choice that is inclusive, fair, and consistent, and that minimizes unsatisfactory outcomes. Voting, combined with majority rule, seems to be an obvious democratic solution: Everyone ranks policies, candidates, or possible outcomes according to their preferences, from most to least desirable, and then they vote together on these options. The outcome is inclusive insofar as everyone is permitted a vote, and fair insofar as votes are weighed equally. Furthermore, a majority of voters will be satisfied with specific outcomes. Condorcet showed, however, that there are plausible cases where this strategy yields absurd outcomes.

Consider the simple case of three voters who rank their preferences for choices a, b, and c from most preferable to least as follows: $a > b > c$, $c > a > b$, and $b > c > a$. In this case, a majority prefers a over b, b over c, but also c over a, resulting in a majority cycle, $a > b > c > a$. Given such potential outcomes, strategic manipulation is a troubling possibility: If a clever legislator has some sway over the agenda in her assembly and a decent sense of prevailing preferences among her colleagues, she may be able to introduce issues or amendments at critical moments so as to create such cycles, thus thwarting proposals she opposes and that would otherwise have passed with a majority of votes.

The economist Kenneth Arrow has shown that, for any procedure that aggregates individual preferences into a collective choice, the cycling problem cannot be avoided without also threatening at least one of several reasonable conditions of rational consistency and fairness, arguably including democratic commitments to inclusion and equal consideration. It has been known since the work of economists Harold Hotelling, Duncan Black, and Anthony Downs that, consistent with Arrow's result, cycling can be avoided if all voters order their preferences along a common dimension such that the resulting distributions have only one peak (or plateau, if a voter is indifferent among her most preferred options). But what conditions would favor the existence of a single underlying issue dimension?

If a society is characterized by one or several deep cleavages (along lines of class, race, religion, or ideology, for example), restrictions on community membership, public debate, campaign issues, or legislative agendas might forge a single issue dimension, or at least discourage the emergence of other issue dimensions if only one such dimension is evident. But such restrictions threaten expressive and associative liberties, as well as democratic inclusion. How and why do particular issue dimensions emerge, persist, and change in modern democratic societies? Republican and communitarian democrats might plausibly argue that durable community traditions are the primary force shaping such dimensions, and that a strong sense of community solidarity is vital to democracy precisely because it limits public opinion in predictable ways and ensures that a deep unity of values and interests prevails. Others suspect that public discussion, suitably moderated, may distinguish and select among particular issue dimensions.

If we hope to reconcile diversity, personal liberties, and democracy, as liberal democrats do, then the problems associated with majoritarian decision procedures should trouble us. After all, the more diverse a community is, the more often we may expect democratic institutions to be called upon not to find the common good but to resolve conflicts among the competing interests of free citizens. And those are just the conditions under which voting and majority rule tend to be problematic: There is little fundamental agreement on the values underlying political disputes, and a simple appeal to the wishes of the majority may not persuade other citizens to accept the outcome of an election or referendum.

But some scholars have suggested that, in practice, democracy in these settings involves complex patterns of bargaining among a variety of associations in society, from political parties to labor unions, neighborhood councils, and issue advocacy groups. Others have noted that democracies based on proportional representation and compromise among several political parties, such as those found in several European countries, tend to be more responsive to the diverse values and interests characteristic of plural societies, especially those deeply divided along lines of national and religious cultures. There are, however, concerns about the stability of such arrangements.

CURRENTS AND CONTROVERSIES

A great deal of recent work in political theory has examined the importance of cultural identity to democratic citizenship, in particular whether group-specific entitlements are justified on the grounds that cultural background is important to the meaningful exercise of personal freedoms. Some have further argued that forms of group representation, such as guaranteed seats in federal legislatures for all groups regardless of their popularity, may be justified on the basis of past injustices and resulting deficits of trust in diverse societies.

Other recent work has emphasized the importance of public deliberation to democracy, appealing to the idea that the people should rule themselves according to reason, or at least according to claims that are rationally defensible to others. Following that line of thought, scholars have explored strategies for enhancing the opportunities citizens have to become informed and to reflect and argue together about a range of public issues. Scholars have also focused on the ways in which local deliberative activities can be integrated into existing political institutions, making those institutions more responsive to a range of values and interests. Other scholars have explored whether and how enhanced citizen deliberation might mitigate some of the problems that national, cultural, and ethnic identities pose for democratic fairness and political stability in plural settings, both at national and global scales.

Democracy is, then, a complex and contested concept, both in theory and practice. Although there are limits to participation and agreement in large and diverse societies, there are also possibilities for bringing together diverse opinions and interests in creative and productive ways. It is possible to find cooperative solutions to many conflicts, to identify shared interests, and to resolve disputes in ways that, if not always mutually acceptable, are at least fair in a sense that seems reasonable to all parties involved, and that does not inspire some citizens either to leave the state or to take up arms against those with whom they disagree. The great promise of democracy is that, in spite of myriad differences, we can govern ourselves not by force or fraud, but by reason.

—*Loren A. King*

See also Citizenship; Communitarianism; Decentralization Grassroots Leadership; Pressure Groups; Social Capital; Tocqueville, Alexis de; Town Meetings

Further Reading

Almond, G., & Verba, S. (1963). *The civic culture: Political attitudes and democracy in five nations.* Princeton, NJ: Princeton University Press.

Aristotle. (1984). *The politics* (C. Lord, Trans.). Chicago: University of Chicago Press.

Arrow, K. J. (1951). *Social choice and individual values.* New Haven, CT: Yale University Press.

Barber, B. R. (1984). *Strong democracy.* Berkeley and Los Angeles: University of California Press.

Beitz, C. (1989). *Political equality.* Princeton, NJ: Princeton University Press.

Benhabib, S. (2002). *The claims of culture: Equality and diversity in the global era.* Princeton, NJ: Princeton University Press.

Black, D. (1948). On the rationale of group decisions. *Journal of Political Economy 56*(1), 23–34.

Black, D. (1958). *The theory of committees and elections.* Cambridge, UK: Cambridge University Press.

Blais, A. (2000). *To vote or not to vote?* Pittsburgh, PA: University of Pittsburgh Press.

Cohen, J. (1986). An epistemic conception of democracy. *Ethics, 97*(1), 26–38.

Cohen, J. (1989). Deliberation and democratic legitimacy. In A. Hamlin & P. Pettit (Eds.), *The good polity: Normative analysis of the state.* Oxford, UK: Basil Blackwell.

Cohen, J. (2001). Money, politics, political equality. In A. Byrne, R. Stalnaker, & R. Wedgwood (Eds.), *Fact and value.* Cambridge, MA: MIT Press.

Cohen, J., & Rogers, J. (1995). *Associations and democracy.* London: Verso.

Condorcet, J.-A.-N. (1994). Essay on the application of analysis to the probability of majority decisions. In I. McLean & F. Hewitt (Eds. & Trans.), *Condorcet: Foundations of social choice and political theory.* Brookfield, VT: Elgar. (Original work published 1785)

Dahl, R. A. (1962). *Who governs? Democracy and power in an American city.* New Haven, CT: Yale University Press.

Dahl, R. A. (1989). *Democracy and its critics.* New Haven, CT: Yale University Press.

Dahl, R. A. (1998). *On democracy.* New Haven, CT: Yale University Press.

Downs, A. (1957). *An economic theory of democracy.* New York: Harper.

Dryzek, J. S. (2000). *Deliberative democracy and beyond.* New York: Oxford University Press.

Fishkin, J. (1995). *The voice of the people.* New Haven, CT: Yale University Press.

Fung, A., & Wright, E. O. (2001). Deepening democracy: Innovations in empowered participatory governance. *Politics and Society, 29*(1), 5–42.

Grofman, B., & Feld, S. L. (1988). Rousseau's general will: A Condorcetian perspective. *American Political Science Review, 82*(2), 567–576.

Gutmann, A., & Thompson, D. (1996). *Democracy and disagreement.* Cambridge, MA: Harvard University Press.

Hardin, R. (1999). *Liberalism, constitutionalism, and democracy.* New York: Oxford University Press.

Hotelling, H. (1929). Stability in competition. *Economic Journal, 39*(153), 41–57.

Inglehart, R. (1988). The renaissance of political culture. *American Political Science Review, 82*(4), 1203–1230.

Kymlicka, W. (1995). *Multicultural citizenship.* Oxford, UK: Oxford University Press.

Lijphart, A. (1977). *Democracy in plural societies: A comparative exploration.* New Haven, CT: Yale University Press.

Lijphart, A. (1984). *Democracies: Patterns of majoritarian and consensus government in twenty-one countries.* New Haven, CT: Yale University Press.

Macpherson, C. B. (1965). *The real world of democracy.* Toronto, Canada: Canadian Broadcasting Corporation.

Mill, J. S. (1861). *Considerations on representative government.* London: Parker, Son, & Bourn.

Miller, D. (1992). Deliberative democracy and social choice. *Political Studies, 40* (special issue), 54–67.

Miller, D. (1995). *On nationality.* Oxford, UK: Clarendon Press.

Okin, S. M. (1999). Is multiculturalism bad for women? In J. Cohen, M. Howard, & M. C. Nussbaum (Eds.), *Is multiculturalism bad for women?* Princeton, NJ: Princeton University Press.

O'Neil, J. L. (1995). *The origins and development of Ancient Greek democracy.* Lanham, MD: Rowman & Littlefield.

Pateman, C. (1970). *Participation and democratic theory.* Cambridge, UK: Cambridge University Press.

Pettit, P. (1997). *Republicanism: A theory of freedom and government.* New York: Oxford University Press.

Popkin, S. (1991). *The reasoning voter: Communication and persuasion in presidential campaigns.* Chicago: University of Chicago Press.

Plato. (1968). *The republic* (A. Bloom, Trans.). New York: Basic Books.

Putnam, R. D. (2000). *Bowling alone: The collapse and revival of American community.* New York: Simon and Schuster.

Rousseau, J.-J. (1987). Discourse on the origins of inequality. In D. A. Cress (Trans.), *Jean-Jacques Rousseau: The basic political writings* (pp. 23–109). Indianapolis, IN: Hackett. (Original work published 1754)

Rousseau, J.-J. (1987). On the social contract. In D. A. Cress (Trans.), *Jean-Jacques Rousseau: The basic political writings* (pp. 139–227). Indianapolis, IN: Hackett. (Original work published 1762)

Riker, W. H. (1980). *Liberalism against populism: A confrontation between the theory of democracy and the theory of social choice.* San Francisco: Freeman.

Sandel, M. (1996). *Democracy's discontent: America in search of a public philosophy.* Cambridge, MA: Harvard University Press.

Schumpeter, J. A. (1950). *Capitalism, socialism, and democracy* (3rd. ed.). New York: Harper.

Stockton, D. (1990). *The classical Athenian democracy.* New York: Oxford University Press.

Verba, S., Schlozman, K. L., & Brady, H. E. (1995). *Voice and equality: Civic voluntarism in American politics.* Cambridge, MA: Harvard University Press.

Williams, M. S. (1998). *Voice, trust, and memory: Marginalized groups and the failings of liberal representation.* Princeton, NJ: Princeton University Press.

Young, H. P. (1988). Condorcet's theory of voting. *American Political Science Review, 82*(4), 1231–1244.

Young, I. (2000). *Democracy and inclusion.* Oxford, UK: Oxford University Press.

DEVELOPMENT

See Economic Planning; Environmental Planning; Sustainable Development

DEVIANCE

Deviance can be defined as behavior or activities that break generally shared social norms. Shouting, using a mobile phone, talking during a class, driving at high speeds, smoking tobacco, selling heroin, and tax avoidance can all be examples of deviance. They might also be examples of conformity, depending on the circumstances, the norms being applied, others' expectations, and the credibility of excuses or accounts given to explain the behavior. Some kinds of deviance are regulated by criminal law, or by social convention, morality, the expectations of specific groups or social settings, the welfare system, or the medical profession. Deviance is an everyday aspect of social life, and sociological discussions of deviance are not primarily concerned with bizarre, unusual, or weird activities but with the definition, emergence, and regulation of deviance in everyday life. There has been considerable research and theorization on the relationship between deviance and community, and their effects on each other.

A SOCIOLOGICAL APPROACH TO DEVIANCE

The simple definition of deviance given above belies a number of complexities. Is behavior still deviant if the norm breaking is not visible to anyone else, or is not sanctioned (i.e., restricted or limited) by others? Given the plurality of social mores in complex Western societies like Australia and the United States, is there widespread agreement on social norms? In reality there is more likely to be disagreement than agreement on appropriate behavior, standards, and expectations. Who has, or what groups have, the power and authority to determine and enforce social rules? For example, while there is considerable diversity on dress code and body presentation, employers have considerable power in enforcing both formal and informal norms regarding dress and presentation. Types of norms range from informal, unwritten social rules or etiquette, to mores or ethics, convention, organizational rules, and on to laws, especially criminal law.

Even though there are significant cultural differences in the determination of what constitutes deviance, the existence of activities deemed by others to be deviant is universal; all societies define some behaviors as deviance, as offensive to legal or moral norms. This is not to say that certain forms of behavior or activities are regarded as deviant in all societies or historical periods. Over the course of the past century, in Western societies there has been widespread normative change regarding alcohol use, smoking, sexuality, women in paid work, parenting, the use of violence, and gender relations.

The very fact that social groups have social norms or rules ensures the existence of deviance. Even though definitions of what constitutes deviance alter, there will always be some activities and practices that some members of a society agree are inappropriate and require eradication or control. Without deviance, conformity would be impossible, and vice versa. The benchmark of what constitutes deviance is a comparison with what constitutes conformity. Our conceptions of deviance are premised on notions of conformity, which in turn depend on views about deviance. Recognizing this, the sociologist Émile Durkheim writes, "Imagine a society of saints, a perfect cloister of exemplary individuals. Crimes, [or deviance] properly so called, will there be unknown; but faults which appear venial to the layman [sic] will create there the same scandal that the ordinary offence does in ordinary consciousness. If, then, this society has the power to judge and punish, it will define these acts as criminal [or deviant] and will treat them as such" (1938, pp. 68–69).

In this passage, Durkheim encapsulates many of the attributes of a sociological perspective on deviance: Deviance is universal yet variable; deviance is a social phenomenon; social groups make rules and enforce their definitions through judgment and social sanctions; deviance is situational; and definitions of deviance and its control involve power. A society of saints is impossible because a process of social redefinition continuously operates to ensure that all the positions on the scale from wickedness to virtue will always be filled. Consequently, some people will always be holier than others. The scale of social definitions of deviance expands and contracts, denoting an "elasticity of evil" (Cohen 1974, p. 5). This elasticity reflects the fact that individuals' identities contain moral aspects that place value on doing the right thing, which involves defining and responding to others who are not doing likewise. Some people develop such high stakes in their moral identities that they take the initiative in locating deviance and legislating new prohibitions, thus helping to maintain the supply of the deviance which reinforces their own identities. Sociologist Howard Becker calls these people "moral entrepreneurs" (1963, p. 147). The expansion of deviance accommodates those whose identities will be enhanced by new scales of virtue, by changing the saliency of existing scales, or by enlarging the moral significance of differences along those scales.

QUESTIONS AND ANSWERS REGARDING DEVIANCE

Three kinds of question can be asked about deviance: Why do some people engage in activities others define and punish as deviant? Why are some activities and individuals identified or defined as deviant? Who designates what is deviant and enforces social sanctions?

Three major sociological approaches to answering those questions are functionalism (particularly as articulated by Émile Durkheim), which assesses the implications of deviance for communities and social groups; the labeling perspective, which focuses on the implications of labeling for those successfully labeled; and critical theories, which emphasize inequality in explaining the existence and management of deviance, especially criminal deviance. Critical feminist theories, for example, underscore the gendered nature of many social norms and the assumptions about male and female deviance.

What makes these approaches sociological is their focus on social factors (opportunities, definitions, background, resources, inequalities, power) rather then individual characteristics (such as personality or genetic makeup) to explain the emergence of deviance.

Functionalist Theories

Every human community has its own special set of boundaries, its own unique identity, and thus every community also has its own characteristic styles of deviant behavior. When a community feels jeopardized by a particular form of behavior, it will impose more severe sanctions against it and devote more time and energy to rooting it out. For example, drug trafficking is viewed as a particularly heinous crime and many governments, including those in Australia and the United States, have turned their attention to fighting the "war" against drugs and the crime syndicates.

Émile Durkheim proposes that a certain amount of deviance or crime has positive functions for social solidarity. This is an unexpected conclusion, as most discussions of crime and deviance focus on the negative consequence—the harm done, the damage caused, and the suffering experienced by the victim. Durkheim argues that crime (and by extension other forms of deviance) unites people in shared indignation and outrage when valued rules of conduct are broken. "Crime . . . draws honest consciences together, concentrating them. We have only to observe what happens, particularly in a small town, when some scandal involving morality has just taken place. People stop each other in the street, call upon one another, meet in their customary places to talk about what has happened. A common indignation is expressed" (Durkheim 1984, p. 58). The common expression of anger increases social solidarity and reinforces morality. It makes people more conscious of shared interests and values, thus reaffirming agreement on standards or social norms. At the same time this collective expression of anger and reaffirmation of shared norms identifies individuals and activities that are deemed to be outside the shared boundaries and that constitute a threat to the collective interest and security.

While Durkheim observes that crime (or deviance) is universal because no social system—even a society of saints—avoids deviant behavior, he argues that the specific forms of deviance vary. Crime, then, is normal. This does not imply that any amount of crime is normal, or that someone who breaks the law is necessarily bio-

Correcting Deviant Behavior

The following extract of ethnographic text describes deviant behavior that occurred at a Chippewa dance in Wisconsin. The men at the dance took immediate actions to correct the deviant behavior in a way that clearly enforced appropriate behavior but without offending those whose behavior was judged to be deviant.

Directly after the feast certain speeches were made by some of the leading men relative to the attendance at the ceremony of certain whites. Other than this comparatively little of importance happened until about three p.m. when two young men from Round lake arrived and entered the dancing area prepared to participate in the ceremony. One of these men was naked above the waist and had his body more or less elaborately painted. The two danced the next round after their entry, this being one of the ordinary dances and in no way especially sacred. This young man had, however, by appearing in this half nude attire transgressed one of the many strict rules governing the ceremony and, although in olden times dancing in this sort of attire was considered proper, such action under the rules of the drum and in connection with the present day religious ideas was decidedly culpable.

Immediately following this round a "brave dance" was danced in which, of course, as the rules prescribe, only those men who belonged to the division known as "the braves" participated. Immediately following this dance one of the old men who was a member of "the braves" arose and spoke upon the impropriety of the participation of a person in such scanty attire in the dances held in the presence of the drum and in its honor. He went at considerable length into an explanation of the rules and regulations which govern such matters and was careful to state that it was in no way his desire to offer offense to this young man or to anyone else, but that he felt it his duty to remonstrate with the young man and to call his attention to what he was charitable enough to consider a lack of education upon the young man's part rather than a willful violation by him of any of the precepts of the faith. In concluding he outlined very positively that it was, according to the rules of the drum, absolutely necessary that the young man should be properly and completely attired and finally ended his discourse by walking over and presenting him with a shirt. His example was immediately followed by two others of the braves who had participated in the foregoing dance. These two men made no speeches since the first brave had voiced their sentiments and had spoken at sufficient length concerning the matter. Each simply walked over and made the young man a present. One gave him a shirt and the other a coat.

He was not obliged to immediately put on any of these garments which were presented to him for, as the above mentioned speaker said, the young man had come to the dance and had danced once in this half nude condition and he should therefore be permitted to continue throughout the remainder of the afternoon. He pointed out, however, that it must be distinctly understood that thereafter he was not to appear so attired in the ring.

Immediately following this were a few more rounds of dancing after which one of the more important men spoke further upon the same subject, saying that he felt sure that this young man had intended no offense and that his action was due solely to the fact that he was unaware that it was contrary to the rules of the cult to dance in the presence of the grandfather (meaning the drum) in such attire. He said that he deprecated very greatly any ill-feeling which might possibly arise from this little incident and that he hoped that all present would look upon the matter with due forbearance, and that the young man himself would not consider that he was being unduly upbraided. He then offered on his own behalf the materials for a feast, which action was hailed with much show of good will and appreciation by all present.

Source: Barrett, Samuel A. (1910). *The Dream Dance of the Chippewa and Menonimee Indians of Northern Wisconsin.* Milwaukee, WI: Public Museum of the City of Milwaukee, Bulletin, 1, art. 4., pp. 333–334.

logically or psychologically normal, though he or she may be. What is normal is the existence of criminality, so long as the rate does not go beyond a certain level. Nonetheless, Durkheim suggests that criminal motivations or tendencies are not social products but have biological and psychological causes "given the incorrigible wickedness of men [sic]" (1938, p. 67). The implication is that in any society there exists a normal distribution of individuals motivated to break the law.

An examination of three crime waves (as indicated by official records) in seventeenth-century colonial Massachusetts reveals the positive functions of deviance for the maintenance of the social group or community. In *Wayward Puritans,* Erikson (1966) argues that the Puritan community of Salem, Massachusetts, began to censure forms of behavior that previously had been present and tolerated by the group, as a way of reasserting its identity and moral boundaries. As the sense of mission and zeal began to diminish due to the growth and differentiation of this religious community, a spate of witchcraft trials occurred that had the effect of reinforcing the community's religious identity. The frantic displays of Puritan zeal and public witchcraft trials had the effect of clarifying the moral meaning of membership in the colony. The trials were not so much a response to an increase in witchcraft as to the need to provide work for God's agents in the battle against the devil.

When the community applies social control to combat deviance, it makes a statement about its boundaries. It declares how much variability and diversity can be tolerated within the group without risking its distinctive identity. A group's boundaries are elastic: At one point certain activities may fall within those boundaries, while at another they may not. In Salem, the apparent fits and odd actions of young girls in the community fell outside those boundaries, but they were not held responsible for their deviant behavior, as it was determined that witches were causing the fits. The people the girls identified as witches were already marginal members of the community—a West Indian slave, a beggar, and a woman who was lax in church attendance and lived with a man before marriage. In a sense, these individuals were the most dispensable members of the community. Interestingly, when the girls started to accuse respectable individuals, doubts about their infallible judgment began to grow, and the incidence of witchcraft declined. Erikson observes, "Deviant forms of behavior, by marking the outer edges of group life, give the inner structure its special character and thus supply the framework within which the people of the group develop an orderly sense of their own cultural identity" (1966, p. 13).

From research on campaigns against pornography, a similar observation can be made regarding the relationship between denoting some activity or behavior as deviant, the wider social processes (including identity formation) or structures (especially the class structure), and the limits of collective outrage against pornography. The overwhelming elite support for campaigns against vice in Boston, New York City, and Philadelphia during the late nineteenth century was related to three aspects of upper-class formation and reproduction. Specifically, the loss of political control to immigrants, the attempt to control upper-class children's education by sending them to elite boarding schools, and the construction of a high culture that distinguished the upper class from social inferiors were central to elite mobilization against vice. The social class of the viewer became a primary determinant of whether a painting or a photograph was deemed art or obscenity. This became apparent when the New York upper class failed to support the arrest of a leading art dealer on vice-related charges: The incident questioned their own purity, taste, and refinement.

More recently, the public discussion and outrage following the September 11, 2001, attacks on New York City's World Trade Center and the Pentagon in Washington, D.C., exemplify the emergence of a collective consciousness and shared abhorrence of acts deemed to be "'evil" and "terrorist." Collective sentiment was expressed in countless examples of generosity and volunteerism, which reinforced commonality and community. The attacks were referred to as crimes against humanity or crimes against America, and thus were portrayed by many Western leaders as threatening such core (Western liberal) values as freedom and democracy. One result was that certain people—especially Muslims and people of Middle Eastern origin—were labeled deviants, although they were not personally responsible for the attacks. Collective anger and common sentiment often emerge following particularly nasty or unusual homicides, such as school massacres, incidents in which children have committed murder, and cases of child sexual abuse perpetrated or covered up by people in power or those whom others trust, for example, priests.

The Labeling Perspective

Labeling theorists question the existence of a consensus on norms and argue that they are continually being contested. They do not accept that social control is the automatic and usual response to norm-breaking behavior. Reactions, they argue, depend not only on the violation of a rule but on who breaks the rules, the time and place, and whether she or he is visible to others who are motivated and have the authority to invoke sanctions. The definition of behavior as deviant depends on the social audience, not just on the norm-breaking activity, and therefore the behaviors themselves do not activate the processes of social reaction. Rule violation and the application of deviant labels are distinct. If two actors violate social norms, one may be labeled deviant while the other may escape the label; the consequences of being branded deviant may be severe, and only the actor so branded will have to face them, though both violated the same norm.

Howard Becker offers the most influential and oft-cited formulation of the labeling perspective: "Deviance is *not* a quality of the act the person commits, but rather a consequence of the application by others of rules and sanctions to an 'offender.' The deviant is one to whom the label has successfully been applied; deviant behavior is behavior that people so label" (1963, p. 9). The people so labeled may not accept the designation and may seek to resist or ignore that interpretation of them and their behavior (though sometimes this will be impossible, given the power and authority of such official labelers as the police and criminal courts); indeed, they may view the labelers as deviant. Becker suggests that the term deviant be reserved for those labeled as deviant by some segment of society and concludes that "whether a given act is deviant or not depends in part on the nature of the act (that is, whether or not it violates some rule) and in part on what other people do about it" (1963, p. 33).

Labeling theorists stress that becoming deviant, or acquiring a deviant self-identity, depends on a social audience's enforcement of a rule, which may entail a degradation ceremony in which a person's public identity is ritually replaced by another of lower status. For example, in a criminal trial, a person's public and personal identity may be transformed from that of ordinary citizen to accused or convicted criminal, rapist, pedophile, thief, or prisoner. From then on, others will make new assumptions about the kind of person he or she really is, which will affect that person's access to employment, housing, or insurance, even when the deviance does not affect conformity with other social norms. A final stage in the deviant career is participating in a deviant subculture that enables the formation of new identities. The subculture provides self-justifying rationales and ideologies, often rejecting legal or moral rules and institutions.

The labeling perspective has been criticized for focusing on the successfully labeled deviants rather than on social audiences; for neglecting self-labeling processes; for failing to explain why some individuals are motivated to break rules; for assuming that labeling only escalates deviance, thereby ignoring the deterrent effects of sanctioning; and for failing to give sufficient attention to questions of power and inequality.

Critical Theories

Critical theorists emphasize power and conflict in the definition, content, and application of criminal laws. Social norms are not conceptualized as deriving from general consensus; rather, their substance is intimately linked to the political economy and the interests of dominant segments. Critical theorists seek to demonstrate how the criminalization of certain types of conduct and the uneven enforcement of criminal laws reflect the interests of economically and politically powerful groups. The theories are less concerned with why individuals or groups are motivated to be criminally deviant and more concerned with why the behavior is defined as criminal and thereby subject to state control. Critical theorists note that the activities of lower-class people are disproportionately defined in law as criminal, and that lower-class people are more likely to be arrested, charged, convicted, and sentenced than are middle- and upper-class people.

Many of these theories commence with the writings of Marx and focus on the influence of an economic elite on the substance of the criminal law. They propose that the causes of crime are bound up with the kind of social arrangement existing at a particular time. For crime to be abolished, they argue, social arrangements must also be transformed. Some maintain that the state, via the legal system, protects its own interests and those of the capitalist ruling class, which are indistinguishable. Crime control represents the coercive means of checking threats to the prevailing social and economic order. The contradictions of capitalism produce poverty, inequality, and exploitation, which lead to crime as a means of survival. Burglary and drug dealing, crimes against the person, industrial sabotage, and other predatory crimes are rational responses to the inequities of capitalist society. The irony is that compared with the activities that criminal law prohibits, the capitalist class and the state are engaged in many more serious injurious practices, which are rarely prosecuted but affect large numbers of people. Even when price-fixing, discrimination, embezzlement, pollution, and economic exploitation are illegal, enforcement is rare.

Feminists argue that mainstream discussions of deviance are biased because they deal primarily with men and boys. Where research on female deviance exists, it tends to rely heavily on assumptions about women's nature and to centralize marital and reproductive roles, actual and anticipated, as explanations. Such approaches often reflect a deterministic view of women's and girls' behavior by claiming that supposedly essential or natural female qualities—emotionalism, deceit, irrationality, sexuality, and the tendency to promiscuity among single women and girls—constitute key factors in female deviance. Women and girls are depicted as engaging in such sex-specific and gender-related deviance as shoplifting, prostitution, and transgressing motherhood norms (for example, having children at an unusually young or old age).

Different norms get applied to men and women; many norms regarding the presentation of self, marriage and parenthood, sexuality, and occupational choice are applied to women but not to men. While expectations are made of men around these issues, arguably the scope for normal behavior is much narrower and more restrictive for women. The gender system makes certain kinds of deviance (for example, mental illness, prostitution, hysteria, obesity, shoplifting) more appropriate to or expected of women than men. While deviant behavior in women is often explained in terms of women's supposed nature, men's deviance is explained in terms of social, economic, and political conditions and normal learning processes.

Some contemporary feminist discussions of normativity, social control, and conformity focus on the body and the ways in which women's bodies are subject to greater surveillance than are men's bodies. The array of images and expectations regarding women's shape, size, diet, emotions, dress, and adornment tend to be very restrictive and affirm specific feminine models of appearance, attractiveness, and behavior. These models become norms against which many women constantly measure, judge, discipline, and modify their own bodies, even to the extent of undergoing elective cosmetic surgery. If a woman's body is evaluated as overweight, aged, or unattractive to heterosexual men, that fact is often taken as evidence that the woman lacks discipline and control and therefore is less morally worthy than others whose bodies indicate that they exercise restraint or "take care of themselves." It is not just the body that is being evaluated; the whole person is labeled as overweight, unattractive, or inappropriately attired and associated conclusions are drawn regarding the person's personality, reliability, credibility, and perceived authority.

SOURCES OF INFORMATION ON CRIME AND DEVIANCE

There are at least four major sources of information on crime and deviance: statistics that are collected routinely by government agencies (for example, police statistics); statistics and data compiled following independent research; personal or direct knowledge; and the mass media. All of these data sources have strengths and weaknesses. For example, statistics released by police departments or courts include only information about criminal deviance coming to the attention of those agencies, criminal deviance is defined differently in different jurisdictions, and decisions on whether to proceed with a case may be based on factors other than whether a crime actually occurred.

Periodically, media attention and government concern focus on young people and deviance (both actual and suspected or assumed). Youth offenses, especially such offenses as graffiti, motor vehicle theft, and street activities, have stimulated various moral panics, defined as "a condition, episode, person or group of persons [that] emerges to become defined as a threat to societal values and interests; its nature is presented in a stylized and stereotypical fashion by the mass media" (Cohen 1980, p. 9). The media are instrumental in portraying young offenders as "folk devils" by exaggerating and distorting the seriousness of the offenses, the numbers of people involved, and the degree of damage or violence in particular incidents and confrontations with the police. Media reports often emphasize several serious or violent offences committed by repeat offenders to justify arguments that the juvenile justice system requires reform and that young offenders should be punished more severely. There is also anxiety expressed about young people's use of public space or private spaces that other members of the public frequent, such as shopping malls.

IMPLICATIONS

As conceptions of deviance are socially constructed, no behavior is inherently deviant; its classification as deviant depends on social definitions and the application of norms. Often, conceptions of deviance are not a product of a general agreement among members of a particular community, but result from the activities of specific groups that attempt to have their conceptions of right and wrong, of appropriate and inappropriate behavior, translated into law and enforced. A significant portion of everyday social life and public policy remains concerned with conformity, control, designations of deviance (or at least attempts to designate some groups or individuals as deviant), and moral evaluations that affirm the importance of deviance as a site of analysis and research.

A central point is that deviance is situational, contested, and relative but present in all social settings and societies. Social movements, as well as other interest groups and political or legal activists, are often instrumental in changing public conceptions of a behavior's deviant status. This can involve attempts (which may or may not be successful) to criminalize or decriminalize a range of activities and behavior. Tobacco use, for example, has gradually become less acceptable, as has domestic violence, whereas homosexuality and abortion have become more acceptable.

—Sharyn L. Roach Anleu

See also Community Justice; Community Policing; Cults; Gangs; Social Control

Further Reading

Becker, H. S. (1963). *Outsiders: Studies in the sociology of deviance.* New York: Free Press.

Beisel, N. (1990). Class, culture and campaigns against vice in three American cities, 1872–1892. *American Sociological Review, 55*(1), 44–62.

Beisel, N. (1993). Censorship, the politics of interpretation, and the Victorian nude. *American Sociological Review, 58*(2), 145–162.

Bordo, S. (1993). *Unbearable weight: Feminism, Western culture, and the body.* Berkeley and Los Angeles: University of California Press.

Cohen, A. K. (1974). *The elasticity of evil: Changes in the social definition of deviance.* Oxford, UK: Basil Blackwell.

Cohen, S. (1980). *Folk devils and moral panics: The creation of the mods and rockers.* Oxford, UK: Basil Blackwell.

Durkheim, É. (1933). *The division of labour in society* (G. Simpson, Trans.). New York: The Free Press.

Durkheim, É. (1938). *The rules of sociological method.* (S. A. Solovay & J. H. Mueller, Trans.; G. E. G. Catlin, Ed.). New York: Free Press.

Durkheim, É. (1984). *The division of labour in society* (W. D. Halls, Trans.). London: Macmillan.

Erikson, K. T. (1966). *Wayward Puritans: A study in the sociology of deviance.* New York: Macmillan.

Garfinkel, H. (1956). Conditions of successful degradation ceremonies. *American Journal of Sociology, 61*(5), 420–424.

McRobbie, A. (1994). *Postmodernism and popular culture.* London: Routledge.

Naffine, N. (1987). *Female crime: The construction of women in criminology.* Sydney, Australia: Allen & Unwin.

Naffine, N. (1997). *Feminism and criminology.* Sydney, Australia: Allen & Unwin.

National Crime Prevention. (1999). *Hanging out: Negotiating young people's use of public space.* Canberra, Australia: Attorney-General's Department.

Roach Anleu, S. L. (1999). *Deviance, conformity and control* (3rd ed.) Sydney, Australia: Longman.

Smart, C. (1976). *Women, crime and criminology: A feminist critique.* London: Routledge & Kegan Paul.

Smart, C. (1989). *Feminism and the power of law.* London: Routledge.

Taylor, I, Walton, P., & Young, J. (1973). *The new criminology: For a social theory of deviance.* London: Routledge & Kegan Paul.

DIASPORAS

Traditionally, ethnopolitical communities have been defined by borders and states. The French live in France, the Welsh in Wales, and so on. Some groups, however, do not fit neatly into this paradigm, and many of them form communities that are recognized as diasporas (a dispersed community that does not become fully assimilated into its new place of settlement). Throughout history, small ethnoreligious, political, or economic communities have lived scattered beyond the confines of their home territories while maintaining close links to their natal lands. Such diasporic communities will play an increasingly important role in global politics, conflict, and trade in the twenty-first century as millions of people find themselves detached from, but still emotionally linked to, distant territories they consider their homelands.

THE ORIGINS OF THE TERM

The term *diaspora* comes from Greek *diaspeirein,* "to scatter," "to be apart." The term once applied to Greeks who sailed away from their overpopulated homeland in the classical period and colonized the Mediterranean and Black Seas from the eighth century BCE onwards. The Greek colonies maintained connections with the Greek mainland, through trade and other ties. Greeks in the Bosporan Kingdom on the northern shore of the Black Sea, for example, supplied Athens with grain grown in the Black Sea region and received Greek wine, pottery, and metalwork in return; the Greek colony of Syracuse in Sicily decided the outcome of the Peloponnesian War between Sparta and Athens by sending wealth, warriors, and ships to the Spartan side.

THE JEWISH DIASPORA

The Greek term *diaspora* eventually came to be applied almost exclusively to the Jewish community that was scattered throughout the ancient world following the destruction of the Jewish state in Palestine by the Romans in the 70s CE; these Diaspora Jews lived among Gentiles in various parts of the Roman and post-Roman world. Unlike many groups who were scattered by conquest (and unlike the Jews of the kingdom of Israel, the so-called lost tribes, whose capital city of Samaria was destroyed by the Assyrians in 722 BCE, and who disappeared from history after the Assyrians carried them off into slavery), the Jews kept their identity alive by refus-

Armenian American Political Issues and Parties

Political activity and political parties established by diaspora communities are an important source of continuing contact with and involvement in affairs in the homeland. The following text describes political activity in the Armenian American community.

Though Americans of Armenian blood are thoroughly active in the affairs of their communities, these people have kept in close touch with the problems of their homeland, and with the culture of their ancestors. It is a rare Armenian American who is not a member of some Armenian political party, association, or society of one kind or another.

Armenian political parties are primarily and finally interested with the country of Armenia and, as parties, have nothing whatsoever to do with American politics. Like the members of other minority groups in this country, the Armenian has retained a genuine love for the country of his fathers, and follows its misfortunes or good fortunes with compassion or joy, as the case may be.

Like other minority groups in the country, the Armenians are divided into several Armenian political parties each of which is interested in seeing that the land in the Old World is accorded the type of justice it believes to be proper. For instance, one party, the Armenian Revolutionary Federation, contends that the problem of Armenia will not be solved until Armenia, that is historic Armenia, is accorded the absolute independence which Armenian immigrants in this country have found to be so precious and desirable. Another party argues that Armenia's only hope for existence is for it to remain under the full control or guardianship of Soviet Russia. Several other parties, like the Ramgavar, or the Armenian Democratic Liberal Party, hold rather vague policies.

Armenian political parties wield a great influence on the lives of the Armenians in America. At present, the following parties exist:

1. The Armenian Revolutionary Federation, an international organization, is the strongest, most powerful, most popular of all the Armenian parties. It has as its platform the emancipation of Armenia. It has always been a strong advocate of democracy. The A. R. F. has existed in this country since 1895.

2. The Armenian Democratic Liberal Party (Ramgavar) is a fusion of the former Reorganized Hunchagian and Constitutional Democrat parties. Though its avowed aim is also the emancipation of Armenia, its frequently contradictory actions and oppositional tactics brings question upon the sincerity of its platform. The A. D. L. was founded in 1921.

3. The Social Democratic Hunchagian Party has today a negligible membership. It has actually recognized the Soviet Government. The party entered America in the 1890's.

4. "The Progressives" is the artful name given to the party of the Armenian Bolsheviks. It was once known as the Panvor Party. In its fear of government prosecution, it has avoided membership in the American Communist Party, but it is nonetheless Communistic in thought, action, intent, purpose, and ideology. The seemingly imposing and well publicized activities of a few Progressives lead one to believe that this party maintains many chapters all over this country with a huge membership; but in truth, few branches exist, actual membership in the party is very low, and scarcely any perceptible influence is exerted by the Progressives on American-Armenian life. In full truth, the Progressives hold no platform; in their eyes, the Armenian Question was solved with the establishment of the Soviets in Armenia. Almost everything they do, therefore, may be construed to be done in the interests of Communism, and not out of any particular zeal for the nation of their forefathers.

Source: Tashjian, James H. (1970). *The Armenians of the United States and Canada: A Brief Study.* San Francisco: R and E Research Associates, pp. 37–39.

ing to assimilate in such contexts as the Babylonian captivity (which began in the sixth century BCE).

This stubborn refusal to give up their unique religious and cultural beliefs and to blend into their host societies differentiated the Jews from other emigrant communities or refugee populations. The transgenerational passing on of traditions, language, religious beliefs, and identity symbolically and emotionally tied the Jewish exiles to their former homeland. During festive celebrations, Jews vowed to return to their homeland—"Next year may we meet in Jerusalem!" For many Jews of the Diaspora, this bond to a lost homeland kept them from accepting their lands of residence as a real home.

The Jewish attachment to the holy city of Jerusalem and a sacral homeland that most Jews never actually saw was defined in purely religious terms until the advent of nationalism. As the political theory of nationalism (which claims that all ethnic groups are nations that have a natural right to a national homeland) spread in the late nineteenth century, Jews living in the Christian nation-states of Western Europe began to call for the construction of a political Jewish fatherland or homeland for their scattered people.

Since the creation of the state of Israel in 1948, hundreds of thousands of Jews have emigrated to the new Jewish polity. Those Jews still living scattered in the Diaspora now have a political and geographic focus for their identity. Although Jews live throughout the world today, the Diaspora community plays a decisive role in supporting the state of Israel. The pro-Israel Jewish lobby in the United States, known as the American Israel Public Affairs Committee, is the second most powerful interest group in the country (after the AARP lobby) and tirelessly supports the cause of Israel in Washington, D.C., and throughout the world. While fully Americanized on many levels, American Jews exhibit diasporic tendencies. American Jewish religious extremists have played a key role in settling Palestinian lands seized from the Arabs of the West Bank in 1967; American Jews have actively lobbied for the United States to veto United Nations sanctions condemning Israeli aggression against Palestinians; young American Jews in conservative and orthodox Jewish congregations are encouraged to spend a year studying in Israel as part of their education; and hundreds of millions of dollars have flowed from American Jewish charities for the development of Israel.

Sikh taxi drivers in New York City in 1995. The Sikhs are a religious group from India.
Source: Bojan Brecelj/Corbis; used with permission.

THE ARMENIAN DIASPORA

While the term *diaspora* was traditionally applied to the transnational Jewish global community, it gradually came to apply to Armenians as well. This Caucasian Christian community was scattered throughout the Middle East and beyond during the Ottoman period. From the fourteenth to twentieth centuries, Armenians spread throughout the Ottoman empire as traders and middlemen (thus initially forming a merchant diaspora community as opposed to the forced Diaspora of the Jews), and Armenian neighborhoods existed in Iran, India, Turkey, Syria, the Balkan countries, Egypt, and southern Russia. In their places of diaspora, the Armenians tended to avoid marriage with non-Armenians, who were known as *Odars* (outsiders; like the Jews, the Armenians largely married within their culture). These Armenians sent money to their homeland for building schools and churches, and they kept the faith, language, and traditions of their homeland alive in a variety of political and geographic settings.

The spread of Armenians from their small mountainous homeland in the Transcaucasus throughout Eurasia was further accelerated following the genocidal assault on this community by the Ottoman government in 1915. In the process of annihilating the Armenians of much of eastern Anatolia, the Ottomans sent waves of Armenian refugees fleeing throughout the world, and today the Armenians are seen as a forced diaspora.

Armenian communities of the world are united by their nostalgia for their lost land in what is today eastern Turkey and in the small, newly independent state of Armenia (before 1991, part of the Soviet Union). For Armenians in such diverse locales as Los Angeles (where there is a large community), London, Australia, and the Middle East, the Armenian homeland—on which their unique Armenian Christian faith is based—has all the sacral significance that Jerusalem had for Jews of the Diaspora.

With the outbreak of conflict between the post-Soviet state of Armenia and its Muslim neighbor Azerbaijan in the early 1990s, the Armenian diaspora community translated the emotional-religious link to their former homeland into tangible terms and sent tens of millions of dollars to support the war.

DEFINING THE TERM

While the Jews, Greeks, and Armenians are seen as the three traditional diasporas, today myriad ethnic groups or communities can be defined as diasporas. However, some communities that are not diasporas have been so categorized, such as American Indians who have been referred to as a diaspora of Asia, or fully Americanized African Americans who define themselves as a diaspora despite having no political, religious, linguistic, financial, or cultural links to their natal lands in Senegal, Ivory Coast, Gambia, or elsewhere in Africa.

Many migrating or displaced groups are easily assimilated in their new host societies and make no effort to keep diasporic emotional, religious, or political links to their native hearths alive (for example, Americans of German, French, English, Scottish, Swedish, or African origin who often have little real knowledge of, or interest in, events in their former homelands) or to avoid assimilation. To preclude the loss of the term's essential meaning, it must be defined and quantified—otherwise, all of humanity can be considered a diaspora of the Rift Valley in Africa.

The American sociologist Williams Safran has quantified this overused term, defining a diaspora as a community that fulfills the following criteria:

> The members, or their ancestors, were dispersed from a specific original center to two or more peripheral regions;
>
> members retain a collective memory, vision, or myth about their original homeland—its physical location, history, and achievements;
>
> they believe they are not and perhaps cannot be fully accepted by their host society and therefore feel partly alienated and insulated from it;
>
> they regard their ancestral homeland as their true, ideal home and as the place to which they or their descendants would (or should) eventually return when conditions are appropriate;
>
> they believe that they should, collectively, be committed to the maintenance or restoration of their original homeland and to its safety and prosperity;
>
> they continue to relate, personally or vicariously, to that homeland in one way or another, and their ethnocommunal consciousness and solidarity are importantly defined by the existence of such a relationship.

A SAMPLE SURVEY OF TWO DIASPORA COMMUNITIES TODAY

Many groups today find themselves in a diasporic condition due to a variety of circumstances forced or voluntary. Among these are such groups as Cuban Americans, Southeast Asian Chinese, Palestinians, Tutsis, Afghans, Chechens, and Crimean Tatars. A sample survey of two of these groups sheds light on the ways in which diasporic groups that have experienced collective traumas or voluntary emigrations interact with their homelands and shape events on the ground in their natal territories.

The Palestinian Diaspora

The Palestinian diaspora was created in 1948, after civil war in Palestine, when Egyptian, Jordanian, Syrian, Lebanese, and Iraqi armies invaded to join the Arabs who had been fighting against Israeli settlers since 1947. After the United Nations intervened to stop the conflict, roughly three quarters of a million Palestinian Arabs were either expelled from their homes or fled from their villages fearing Israeli reprisals. Most of those who fled ended up in squalid refugee camps in Lebanon, the West Bank/Gaza Strip, or Jordan, where they and their descendents remain to this day. Palestinian refugees living in these camps, however, refused to consider their places of refuge as permanent homes and passed links to their lost lands in the new state of Israel to new generations that had never seen their former villages. Through such means as the retelling of ritualized stories of *Al Naqba* ("the disaster" of 1948) and the refusal to assimilate, the Palestinian refugees formed a classic diaspora. A visitor to a Palestinian refugee camp, for example, noticed that among displaced refugees "when I talked with other Palestinians in other camps in Jordan and Lebanon, I began to realize the depth of their sentiment for their former homes and lands. Children who had been born in camps talked of 'home' as though they know every inch of ground, every tree and bush" (Waines 1997, p. 117). Most Palestinian refugees still remain in limbo in their places of exile, and the issue of their right to return to their lost Israeli-controlled homeland remains one of the thorniest problems bedeviling the peace process in the Middle East.

The Crimean Tatars

The Crimean Tatars are a small Turkic-Muslim group whom Stalin expelled from their peninsular homeland in the Ukraine in 1944 and resettled throughout Central Asia. While the Soviet authorities' intention was that this small, distrusted ethnocommunity would gradually assimilate in their diverse places of exile, the Crimean Tatars responded to this state-sponsored attempt to eradicate their community by actively constructing a diasporic group identity. Crimean Tatars in their places of exile in Uzbekistan (a primary focus of Crimean Tatar forced settlement and dispersal) stated that they were taught as children that Uzbekistan was not and ever could be their real home. Their true homeland was the Crimean peninsula, where they expected to return one day even if they had to fight for the right. After almost half a century of exile, hundreds of thousands of Crimean Tatars in the Central Asian diaspora partook in a mass uncontrollable surge to their lost homeland when the Soviet Union collapsed in 1991, and today this community is once again rebuilding its ethnic identity in its cherished *Anavatan* (motherland).

THE FUTURE ROLE OF DIASPORAS IN GLOBAL POLITICS

With the growing ease of global travel and modern means of communications, it is increasingly easy for diaspora communities to interact with lands they define as their homeland or natal territory and to shape events in these countries. Hundreds of thousands of Indians living in Western Europe, the Americas, South Africa, and the Middle East send a portion of their salaries back to the subcontinent and return to their home villages to find Hindu brides. Cuban exiles in southern Florida increasingly dictate U.S. policy towards Castro's Communist Cuba. Chechens living in the Middle East and scattered throughout the independent states of the former Soviet Union continue to fund the conflict with Russia in their homeland. Mexican Americans play an increasingly important political role in affairs across the border in Mexico, and Afghans returning from camps in Pakistan and Iran to their homeland have begun to rebuild their land after years of dreaming of a return. Diasporas of this sort (both forced and voluntary), will have a profound impact on world policies and trends on a variety of levels in the twenty-first century and will increasingly shape the policies of governments, nongovernmental organizations, the military, scholars, and international bodies, as a great portion of humankind finds itself in a diasporic condition.

—Brian Glyn Williams

See also Chinatowns; Harlem; Immigrant Communities; Latino Communities; Little Italies; Lower East Side; Refugee Communities

Further Reading

Boyerain, J. (2002). *Powers of diaspora.* Ann Arbor: University of Michigan Press.

Diasporas of the world. (2003, January 4–10). *The Economist, 336*(8305), 41–43.

Safran, W. (1991, Spring). Diasporas in modern societies: Myths of homeland and return. *Diaspora, 1*(1).

Waines, D. (1977). *A sentence of exile: The Palestinian/Israeli conflict.* Wilmette IL: Medina Press.

Williams, B. G. (2001). *The Crimean Tatars: The diaspora experience and the forging of a nation.* Leiden, Netherlands: Brill.

DIGITAL DIVIDE

The digital divide is the gap that exists between individuals and societies that have access to the Internet and other new information and communication technologies (ICTs) and those that do not. The term became widely known through the mass media as a result of a 1995 report of the U.S. National Telecommunications and Information Administration (NTIA), *Falling Through the Net.*

The digital divide emerges along the familiar fault lines of social inequality—socioeconomic status, gender, ethnicity, age, and geographic location. In the first few years of widespread Internet diffusion in the early 1990s, cyberspace was predominantly the home of single, young, white, better-educated, English-speaking U.S. men. At present, income has been identified as the most important barrier to Internet access. For instance, 35 percent of Canadian households with an income less than CAN $20,000 have home access; that figure is more than twice as low as the figure for households with an income of CAN $100,000 or more. Young people often have the highest levels of Internet access and use: In the United States, at least 70 percent of children and youth use the Internet. Furthermore, there is a pronounced digital divide between usage rates for Asian Americans (63 percent) and white Americans (55 percent) on the one hand and usage rates for African Americans (30 percent) and Hispanics (28 percent) on the other.

THE DOUBLE DIGITAL DIVIDE

As important, inequality in Internet access and use is not solely contingent on individuals' resources and skills. Even the skilled and affluent cannot take advantage of the Internet in a region that does not yet have the necessary telecommunication infrastructure. Sociologist Barry Wellman and his colleagues coined the term "the double digital divide" to describe the gap in Internet access and use segregated by geographic loca-

The Digital Divide in the United States

The following information, collected by the National Telecommunications and Information Administration and reported in 1998, indicates just how wide the digital divide is in the United States.

Urban households with incomes of $75,000 and higher are more than *twenty times* more likely to have access to the Internet than rural households at the lowest income levels, and more than *nine times* as likely to have a computer at home.

Whites are more likely to have access to the Internet from home than Blacks or Hispanics have from *any* location.

Black and Hispanic households are approximately *one-third* as likely to have home Internet access as households of Asian/Pacific Islander descent, and roughly *two-fifths* as likely as White households.

Regardless of income level, Americans living in rural areas are lagging behind in Internet access. Indeed, at the lowest income levels, those in urban areas are more than twice as likely to have Internet access than those earning the same income in rural areas.

The gaps between White and Hispanic households, and between White and Black households, are now approximately five percentage points larger than they were in 1997.

The digital divides based on education and income level have also increased in the last year alone. Between 1997 and 1998, the divide between those at the highest and lowest education levels increased 25 percent, and the divide between those at the highest and lowest income levels grew 29 percent.

Source: National Telecommunications and Information Administration. *Americans in the Information Age: Falling Through the Net*, 1998. Retrieved February 2, 2003, from www.ntia.doc.gov/ntiahome/digitaldivide.

tion (urban versus rural) and neighborhood in combination with socioeconomic status. In 2000, Americans living in rural areas and central cities had substantially lower levels of Internet access (42 percent and 44 percent, respectively) than those living in suburbs (where Internet access stood at 55 percent).

Thanks to increased affordability, user-friendliness, and relevance, Internet use is currently spreading at unprecedented speed. The digital divide is narrowing in most developed nations. The growing prevalence of the World Wide Web, with its graphic Internet interface, has increased access to the extent that in North America, more than 60 percent of the total population had access to the Internet in 2002. Consequently, the Internet has become an integral part of everyday life. But disadvantaged groups still have relatively low involvement with the Internet. People living in rural, poor, or minority households and those with fewer years of formal education have the lowest levels of access to telephone, computer, and the Internet.

Having access to the Internet and having the ability to use the Internet effectively are two very different aspects of the digital divide. Ultimately, the digital divide is a matter of who uses the Internet, for what purposes, and under what circumstances, and how this use affects social cohesion and inclusion. What users bring to the online context has a profound impact on what they can gain from the Internet. To take just one example, the ways in which users communicate online are conditioned by gendered styles of relationship maintenance offline. Moreover, the length of Internet experience plays a critical role in users' online behavior and their evaluation of the Internet.

THE GLOBAL DIGITAL DIVIDE

About 10 percent of the world population was online in 2002. The digital divide exists at the international level as well as at the national level. The global digital divide is embedded in a center-periphery world order, with affluent nations at the core of the Internet-based global network and poorer nations that lack the resources to invest in a digital future pushed to the periphery. Dramatic inequalities in terms of physical and social access to the Internet exist between rich countries in North America, Western Europe, and East Asia, and poorer countries in Latin America, Eastern Europe, the Middle East, South Asia, and Africa.

The digital divide is deep and pervasive in developing countries, where Internet penetration often lingers well below 10 percent. In those countries, there is a stark contrast between those who live in major urban centers and have better education, higher income, and connections to developed countries and those who are peripheral even in their own country.

Overcoming inequalities of access to technological equipment only partly bridges the digital divide. Economic, institutional, and cultural factors significantly affect Internet access and use. High costs and the lack of local technological support prevent members of disadvantaged communities from using the technology effectively to their advantage. Furthermore, English dominance in cyberspace is a linguistic barrier to effective Internet use. Seventy-eight percent of all Web sites are in English only, while only approximately 37 percent of the world's population are native speakers of English. In addition, some countries block access to certain Web sites or to the Internet as a whole, and some countries are working to monitor online behavior of Internet users.

SOCIAL IMPLICATIONS OF THE INTERNET

More recently, debate has begun to move away from the question of Internet access and to an examination of the social implications of differing levels of knowledge of and experience with the Internet for communities, work, and society. Does the Internet bring enormous opportunities to disadvantaged social groups, or does it reproduce or even enhance the status quo of social inequality? On the one hand, the Internet is hailed as the agent of social development in the rising networked societies (both developed countries and developing countries that are becoming increasingly networked) in which access to knowledge has fundamental significance. Accelerating the global flow of information, the Internet has the potential to break down geographic and social boundaries. By making use of what is available over the Internet, members of traditionally disadvantaged groups can tap into previously unattainable resources. Moreover, initiatives such as e-government may promote transparency and accountability in developing countries in which incompetent bureaucracies and corruption have hitherto hindered social development.

On the other hand, most people in disadvantaged communities are denied access to the global digital network. Sociologist Manuel Castells warns that the networking logic of the Internet-based economy may reinforce the unevenness of Internet development. If preexisting inequalities deter people in developing countries from using the Internet, those inequalities may increase as the Internet becomes more central to such elements of everyday life as keeping in contact with migrant kin, acquiring information on employment, health, education, and politics, and engaging in entrepreneurial activities. Differential Internet use can increase differences in access to social capital, as less advantaged individuals and communities cannot sustain the social ties that facilitate access to information and resources.

The nature of the digital divide changes as the Internet evolves. Given the fact that half the world's population has never made a phone call, the journey to a networked society will be a long one. A telecommunications policy, basic communications infrastructure, access to education and training, and especially digital literacy are prerequisites for bringing marginalized communities into the information age. Increasing access to the Internet in public and commercial venues, such as cybercafes, schools, community telecenters, and public libraries would help those who cannot afford a computer or the Internet at home and who do not have Internet access at their workplace. Community facilities play an important role in providing technological training and mentoring that are crucial to bridging the skill divide. Bridging the digital divide, then, is a multistep project requiring cooperation between governments, the private sector, and NGOs. The task is to enable disadvantaged individuals and groups to obtain the necessary resources to cross over the divide and into a digital future.

—Wenhong Chen, Keith Hampton, and Barry Wellman

Further Reading

Boneva, B., Kraut, R., & Frohlich, D. (2001). Using e-mail for personal relationships: The difference gender makes. *American Behavioral Scientist, 45*(3), 530–549.

Castells, M. (2001). *The Internet galaxy: Reflections on Internet, business, and society.* Oxford, UK: Oxford University Press.

Chen, W., Boase, J., & Wellman, B. (2002). The global villagers: Comparing Internet users and uses around the world. In B. Wellman & C. Haythornthwaite (Eds.), *The Internet in everyday life* (pp. 74–113). Oxford, UK: Blackwell.

CNNIC (China Internet Network Information Center). (2002). *Semiannual survey report on the development of China's Internet.* Retrieved January 14, 2003, from http://www.cnnic.org.cn/

DiMaggio, P., Hargittai, E., Neuman, W. R., & Robinson, J. (2001). Social implications of the Internet. *Annual Review of Sociology, 27,* 287–305.

Fong, E., Wellman, B., Wilkes, R., & Kew, M. (2001). *The double digital divide.* Ottawa, Canada: Office of Learning Technologies, Human Resources Development Canada.

Global Reach. (2002). *Global Internet statistics (by language).* Retrieved January 14, 2003, from http://global-reach.biz/globstats/index.php3

National Telecommunications and Information Administration. (1995). *Falling through the Net: A survey of the "have nots" in rural and urban America.* Washington, DC: U.S. Department of Commerce.

National Telecommunications and Information Administration. (2002). *A nation online: How Americans are expanding their use of the Internet.* Washington, DC: U.S. Department of Commerce.

Norris, P. (2001). *Digital divide: Civic engagement, information poverty, and the Internet worldwide.* Cambridge, UK: Cambridge University Press.

Organisation for Economic Cooperation and Development (OECD). (2001). *Understanding the digital divide.* Paris: OECD Publications.

Reddick, A., & Boucher, C. (2002). *Tracking the dual digital divide.* Retrieved January 24, 2003, from http://www.ekos.com/media/files/dualdigitaldivide.pdf

Warschauer, M. (2003). *Technology and social inclusion: Rethinking the digital divide.* Cambridge, MA: MIT Press.

DISABLED IN COMMUNITIES

Disability is a universal—in all societies, through all ages, individuals have been born with or have acquired disabilities. The lives of these individuals, however, will in large measure be determined not by the fact that they have a disability but by how the society in which they live conceptualizes what it means to be "disabled." While specific physiological, psychological, intellectual, and sensory impairments can be discussed without reference to "culture," understanding what it means to *live* with a disability requires a solid understanding of the cultural context in which a person with a disability exists.

CULTURAL ASPECTS OF DISABILITY

It is important to underscore the fact that disability has a strong cultural component, because this has so often been overlooked. Whole libraries are devoted to the medical, rehabilitation, and psychological implications of disability on the individual. Discussion in these disciplines is sometimes expanded to include the psychology, education, or employment of the individual who has the disabling condition. But people who are disabled do not live in a vacuum. All individuals with disability live within a specific culture, and they share, with other members of their culture, learned behaviors, beliefs, attitudes, values and ideals that characterize their society. All individuals with disability are also members of a social network: In addition to being individuals with a disability, they are sons and daughters, fathers and mothers, husbands and wives, cousins, neighbors, and fellow citizens. For all these reasons, the extensive literature that discusses individuals with disability solely as patients in a medical or rehabilitation facility or clients who receive services misses much of the complexity of what it means to really live with a disabling condition (Kaplan 1999).

A relatively new field, cross-cultural analysis of disability, requires looking at disability as a "constant," and the cultural context in which it is found as the variable. Prior to the 1980s, some scholars assumed that there is no cultural variable—that all societies at all times have reacted in much the same way to persons with disability. Moreover, there was an assumption that if persons with disability fare badly in modern society, then their lives must be especially difficult in more traditional societies or in countries where modern medicine and rehabilitation are not widely available. While there is an enormous variation in how individuals with disability are incorporated into the social life of a community, many traditional and/or non-Western models of adaptation to disability have much to teach us about universal approaches to disability.

BACKGROUND

Discussion of disability in society, seen in the extensive professional literature, is too often mired in sweeping stereotypes that provide relatively little information about disability at the individual or the community level. In fact, disability, as a unified concept, is not universal. Indeed, many languages lack a single word for disability. Rather, societies around the world have tended to group together individuals with specific types of impairments (e.g., the blind, the deaf) and often have very different ways of responding to individuals, depending on what kind of social interpretation underlies their specific disability. Although, traditionally, there may be broad categories (i.e., the unfortunate, the infirm, the crippled), the idea of disability as a single category in which individuals with all types of physical, emotional, sensory and intellectual impairments are routinely placed has come into more prominent usage as a by-product of broad social insurance and social security schemes that have grouped previously distinct categories of individuals together to provide benefit packages within nation-states (Groce 1999).

At the outset of any discussion of the cultural context of disability, it is important to note that we still know relatively little about disability in any society. Although there is a growing literature on disability cross-culturally, the majority of research—particularly published research—is almost entirely from developed nations; and most of this work itself is based on studies of urban populations. Yet it is estimated that 80 percent of all individuals with disability today live in the devel-

Special Help for Deaf Women and Children Who Are Abused

SEATTLE (ANS)–Domestic violence and sexual assault are terrifying experiences, but victims who are deaf may face the additional nightmare of trying to tell their story to people who do not understand them.

Cases are cited of women returning to dangerous domestic situations because at home at least they were understood. Sometimes, an abusive partner is a woman's only translator to the outside world.

To help deaf women and children in crisis in the Seattle area, a coalition of deaf counselors and educators has put together a program called Abused Deaf Women's Advocacy Services.

The aim is to provide for the deaf community the kind of help generally available to the broader population such as crisis intervention, counseling and support groups, educational programs and, soon, emergency housing.

The group has begun to train interested agencies around the country in its methods and approaches, and programs for abused deaf women eventually are due to open in Boston, Denver, Detroit, Minneapolis, Rochester, N.Y., Austin, Texas, San Francisco and Sacramento, Calif., Des Moines, Iowa, Burlington, Vt., and Washington, D.C.

Advocates say a distinguishing feature of ADWAS is that it regards the deaf women and children it assists as members of a linguistic and cultural minority, rather than as people with a handicap.

Instead of referring clients to a crisis agency with a sign language translator who may not have a personal understanding of deafness, most ADWAS staff members are themselves deaf or deaf and blind, and all are fluent in American Sign Language.

"There needs to be an understanding and a respect for the cultural aspect of this minority and an ability to communicate and understand it isn't just adding an interpreter," said Carol Brown-Wollin, director of the Deaf-Blind Service Center in Seattle, who refers clients to the abused women's agency. "That's what ADWAS provides."

[. . .]

Smith says while the women's movement of the 1970s ushered in a host of crisis centers for middle-class white women, cultural minorities including 28 million deaf people were left out of the emerging social consciousness. It wasn't until the murder of a deaf woman by her husband in Seattle in 1981 that leaders in the deaf community realized the dearth of relevant services.

The rate of sexual assault among deaf women and children is no higher than among hearing women, Smith says, and the issues and needs of deaf victims are no different from those of persons who can hear. The problem lies in access to relevant information and emergency services.

[. . .]

Like the greater hearing community, the deaf community traditionally blamed the victim rather than the offender. But the shame associated with sexual assault is particularly debilitating in the deaf community because of its small size and the victim's fear of being ostracized. By sharing their stories, Smith says, deaf victims have created a strong bond that will help them reintegrate into their circle of friends.

[. . .]

"We had to challenge cultural rules, be willing to take risks. Beyond the equipment and signing, deaf women can't just move away and hide. We need to change people's attitudes."

–Mieke H. Bomann

Source: "Special Help Provided for Abused Deaf Women and Children." American News Service, Article No. 1040, August 5, 1999.

oping world, and of these, 60–70 percent live in rural areas (Helander 1993).

Since the 1980s, there has been an increasing awareness of the importance of understanding traditional beliefs, attitudes, and practices pertaining to disability—particularly with the rise of the field of disability studies and allied disciplines. Culturally imbedded conceptual frameworks of disability affect the way in which individuals with disability see themselves and the world around them. They affect the way in which people in their worlds—members of their families and their communities—interact with them, and they are the basis upon which societies implement policies and programs that directly and indirectly affect many if not most aspects of their lives. These conceptual frameworks, whether positive or negative, are important to understand in order to effect changes, either by addressing negative models or by building upon positive ones.

One of the most striking findings of this growing body of sociocultural research has been the discovery that around the world, there are few ideas about disability that are held to be true at all times and by all peoples.

In fact, there are considerable differences in the way disability is regarded from one society to the next. Even within the same society, different types of disability tend to be regarded differently; an individual who has vision impairment may be considered a full and active participant in a community, while an individual with mental health problems living next door may be shunned.

One conclusion can be drawn from this growing body of data: Around the globe, the lives of individuals with disability are usually far more limited as a result of prevailing cultural constraints—and the attendant social, cultural, and economic ramifications of these cultural constraints—than as a result of any specific physical, sensory, psychological or intellectual impairments.

DISABILITY IN HISTORY

Interestingly, every society in the world has a complex system of beliefs about disability. Universally, societies have explanations for why some individuals (and not others) are disabled, how individuals with disabilities are to be treated, what roles are appropriate (and inappropriate) for such individuals, and what rights and responsibilities individuals with disability are either entitled to or denied.

We do know that from the earliest human history, individuals with disability have been part of human society. Actually, the earliest evidence for an individual surviving with a significant disability predates modern humans. At Shanidar Cave in Iraq, a skeleton of an elderly Neanderthal shows that he survived for many years with a withered arm and blindness in one eye. Dying in his forties (elderly by Neanderthal standards), he was buried in a grave that his contemporaries covered with flowers, indicating that he was a valued member of that small social group (Solecki 1971).

Archaeologists rarely find any skeletal population that does not include remains indicating some disability. Ancient art and pottery, early myths and legends from Greece and Rome, India, China, and the Americas all show the presence of individuals with disability . From the dawn of written history—clay tablets at Ur and early Chinese and Sanskrit writings—down through modern times, all known human societies have included a significant proportion of individuals with disability.

The Concept of Stigma

The issue, though, is not whether individuals with disability and groups of disabled individuals existed, but rather how the societies in which they lived recognized and conceptualized such individuals. In all societies, it is recognized that there are some individuals with certain physical, psychological, intellectual, or sensory attributes that distinguish them from other nondisabled members of that society. In a well-known study, sociologist Erving Goffman (1963) called this response "stigma"; but stigma is a term with a great many pejorative connotations, and it presents a model where disability can only be conceptualized in a negative light. (For this reason, when discussing disability cross-culturally, it is perhaps more productive to call on an idea—formulated by scholar and disability rights advocate Hugh Gregory Gallagher—of disability being an "otherness.")

Goffman and his followers seems to have assumed that there is a universality to stigma, but a broader knowledge of disability now make us aware of the fact that "stigma" is in the eye of the beholder; what is a "deeply discrediting" attribute or set of attributes may well vary from one society to another. Goffman has had a profound effect on how inclusion and exclusion of individuals and groups in society are conceptualized. It is argued here, however, that his work lacks a cross-cultural resonance and must be used with caution. Grouping together individuals with disability, prisoners, and members of small religious communities, for example—as is done in *Stigma* (1963)—might make sense in terms of sociological models of exclusion. But such labeling and grouping says as much about the scholars framing the issue and the dominant society from which they come as it does about the groups being discussed.

SOCIAL INTERPRETATIONS OF DISABILITY

Societies do more than simply recognize disabling conditions in their members; they attach value and meaning to various types of disability. Although dozens of different examples exist, it is important to approach this body of data with some coherence. For the purposes of this discussion, these social beliefs will be grouped together in three categories that seem to regularly appear cross-culturally. Understanding these categories is important because they tend to allow one to predict how well an individual will fare in a given community and society. These beliefs can be grouped roughly as follows:

beliefs about causality: the cultural explanations for why a disability occurs;

valued and devalued attributes: specific physical or intellectual attributes that are valued or devalued in a particular society; and

anticipated role: the role an individual with a disability is expected to play as an adult in a community.

These categories seem to be used consistently cross-culturally as a basis upon which people's expectations and demands for (or avoidance of and passivity about) how individuals with disability are treated within a culture. The categories also seem to affect an individual's ability to participate in family and community and society's willingness to integrate these individuals into daily life. Although there are many variations, the following is an overview of the more salient issues involved in each of the above categorizations.

Causality

Cultural beliefs about why a disability occurs help determine how well or poorly societies treats these individuals. For example, in some cultures, the birth of a child with a disability is considered a sign of divine displeasure with the child's parents, evidence of incest or "bad blood" in a family or of martial infidelity, or the result of bad luck or fate. Disability that occurs later in life may also be considered divine punishment of the individual or of the community. Even when a disability is believed to be caused by the misdeeds of others, the disabled individual may not always be seen as an innocent victim. The individual who is disabled is often avoided for fear that close association with such a person will put others at risk.

Reincarnation, the belief that one's current physical and social state is a reflection of one's behavior in a previous life, often leaves individuals who are disabled in a particularly difficult situation. Their current status is seen as earned, and there may be less sympathy and less willingness to expend resources on their behalf. Moreover, improving their present lives, some believe, lessens the amount of suffering they must endure, thus compromising the possibility of future rebirth at a higher level of existence.

The cause of disability is not always believed to be divine or supernatural. The idea that a disability can be "caught"—transmitted either by touch or by sight—is found widely. Pregnant woman in particular are discouraged from seeing, hearing, or touching someone with a disability, for fear that they may give birth to a similarly disabled child. Examples can be found from Sri Lanka (Helander 1993) to the rural United States (Groce 1985; Newman 1969). The idea of "contagion" remains so strong that it was found that some Native American parents continue to discourage their children from even touching assistive-technology devices, such as wheelchairs, for fear that they will acquire a disability through this contact (Thomason 1994). Many societies have different explanations for why various types of disabling conditions appear. Profound deafness may be attributed to marital infidelity, whereas a spinal cord injury may be considered the result of personal "bad luck" or "fate."

Modern science has redefined disability causation-seeking explanations in the natural world: Genetic disorders, viruses, and accidents are now commonly accepted as explanations for why one is born with a disability or becomes disabled. But if modern medicine has replaced older causation concepts, it has often not done so completely. The idea of blame, inherent in most cultures for centuries, often reappears in more "scientific" forms. For example, both professionals and laypeople are quick to question whether the mother of the disabled newborn smoked, drank, or took drugs—even if there in no correlation between such behaviors and the disability of her child.

The need to identify a specific reason why a disability occurs, some have speculated, may be a psychological distancing. Individuals try to establish a logical reason why a disability has occurred to someone else, thus reassuring themselves that something similar will not happen to them. Another reason for such widespread attention to causality may be society's attempt to determine what demands the individual with a disability and that individual's family may justifiably make on existing social support networks and community resources.

However, beliefs that link disability to intentional causality are not always negative. For example, one study of parents of disabled children from northern Mexican found the belief that it is God's will that a certain number of disabled children be born. God, being kind, however, chooses parents who will be especially loving and protective to these "special" children (Madiros 1989). A similar finding is reported in Botswana, where the birth of a disabled child is viewed as evidence of God's trust in specific parents' ability (Ingstad 1988).

Cultural explanations about causality are intriguing, but they must be used with some caution. For example, in their work in Kenya, John Nkinyangi and Joseph Mbindyo (1982) found that although witchcraft was regularly offered as an explanation, only 2 percent of their informants with disabilities believed that witchcraft was the reason why they themselves were disabled.

Valued and Devalued Attributes

In predicting how well an individual with a disability will fare in a given society, perhaps even more important than beliefs about how a disability is caused are the personal attributes a society finds important. Those individuals who are able to manifest or master these attributes will be able to play a broader role in their societies those who cannot or who can do so only with difficulty (Wolfensberger 1982). This will, in turn, be reflected both in the manner in which these individuals are treated and in society's willingness (or unwillingness) to allocate resources to meet their needs.

For example, in societies where physical strength and stamina are valued, where one's status in the community depends in large measure on how well one can fish or farm, difficulty in walking or in lifting will diminish one's social status. Conversely (and increasingly), in societies where intellectual endeavors (requiring, say, the ability to work at a computer or deliver a speech) are considered important, the fact that one uses a wheelchair will be far less significant.

Some desirable attributes will vary from one society to the next. For example, in some Asian societies and many Native American groups, calling attention to oneself is considered improper. A valued attribute is to blend into the larger community rather than to stand out. Having a disability that automatically makes one stand out from one's peers is considered to be particularly undesirable.

It is also important to note that in a cultural context, disability also intersects with factors that are valued or devalued, and these attributes must be considered in combination. This is nowhere more apparent than in the case of gender. In societies where boys are preferred, the willingness of families to spend scarce resources on a girl with a disability might be substantially less than for a comparably disabled boy. In many societies, education for girls is considered far less important than education for boys, and parents may hesitate to spend money on female children's school fees and uniforms. When the rates of school attendance for disabled girls verses disabled boys are reviewed in such societies, it is not unusual for disabled boys to be educated and for disabled girls to be completely missing from the school register. Medical care for disabled children is another arena in which the intersection of disability and gender in some countries is very obvious. In Nepal, for example, where a strong preference for males exists, there are almost twice as many boys reported as disabled by polio as girls. Polio is gender-neutral; roughly the same numbers of males and females are affected. At issue is not who gets polio, but rather who survives in the years following the illness (Helander 1993). Much of this bias is probably subtle. A family may not want to lose a disabled female child. Should she become ill, however, the parents may wait a few days longer to invest in an expensive medication or to buy a bus ticket to get to a local clinic, hoping the girl will get better on her own.

Such issues as social class, economic status, family structure, and level of education also have implications for valued and devalued attributes. These variables affect what individuals and families hold to be important, enabling some individuals within any given culture to develop talents and abilities more than others. For example, in a society where education is held to be very important, a disabled child from a wealthy family may be at a significantly greater advantage than a child with a comparable disability from a poor family. Better schools, the ability to hire tutors and more attendant care, and the option to purchase more assistive equipment such as a newer computer may enable the wealthy child to excel.

Anticipated Roles in Communities as Adults

Finally, the willingness of any society to integrate individuals with disability into the surrounding society, including willingness to expend resources for education, health care, skills training for jobs, and so forth, depends in large measure on the roles individuals with disability are expected to play in the community as adults.

At one extreme, a society might anticipate no adult roles for those with disability and refuse to allocate any resources for them. In such societies, theoretically, children born with a disability might not be allowed to live. Infanticide of even severely disabled newborns, however, is exceptionally rare in the ethnographic literature (Scheer & Groce 1988). In traditional societies, only a handful of groups seem to have regularly practiced it. In more recent years, the use of amniocentesis, genetic counseling, and the withholding of medical care in the delivery room, while touted as medical advances by some, are viewed by many as a more technologically sophisticated (and more widely practiced) form of infanticide (Asch 1990).

While infanticide is rare, medical and physical neglect that results in death is common. In many countries, it is not unusual for infants and children with disabilities to be "allowed" to die for lack of food, medicines, or other types of care that would be considered neglect if they were withheld from nondisabled peers. Predictions that such children and adults will not live long or be healthy can become self-fulfilling prophecies.

Survival is not the only measure of cultural inclusion. In some societies, individuals with disability are kept alive but hardly welcomed. In such cases, it is not uncommon for individuals with significant disabilities to be hidden from public view in the backroom or inner courtyard of a family house or sent to an institution.

Some have argued that in many societies an individual's inability to have a paid job and thus contribute to their family's economic well-being is the deciding factor in what status he or she maintains in the household and in the community. However, calculating a person's economic contribution to his family or society in terms of formal employment, even marginal employment outside the home, may be misleading, and such data must be used with caution. Many individuals with a disability who do not work outside their own homes or family units make significant contributions to their family's economic well-being. All but the most significantly disabled individuals often make important contributions: They watch children, cook, clean, do housework and farm work; they help assemble piecework or do crafts that are brought to the marketplace in someone else's name.

Indeed, as adults, the disabled may be regularly assigned tasks that others do not want. Anthropologist Lawrence Greene (1977) reported that rural families in Ecuador were concerned that newly introduced iodized salt would eliminate the birth of children with iodine deficiency syndrome. These individuals, born with hearing loss and mild mental retardation, were regularly given the tasks of herding animals, collecting firewood, and drawing water. Who would do these onerous tasks, they asked, if such individuals were no longer born in their villages?

In some cases, while individuals with disability are valued within their own homes, they can anticipate no outside role in the community. They will be fed, housed, and cared for by relatives, but there is no provision made for their participation in society. Indeed, it is assumed that they will not want or be able to participate. In such instances, educating these individuals, training them to earn a living, or arranging for a marriage may be considered an unreasonable drain on a family's resources, particularly if such resources are very limited.

Individuals with disabilities are often allowed only partial inclusion in society and given limited roles and responsibilities. Traditional professions for disabled individuals are often reported. For example, in some societies, blind people become musicians, potters, or broom makers; physically disabled individuals work as market vendors.

Anticipated social roles are not confined to employment alone. In some societies, individuals with disability are given a special role. Used as symbols, they are sometimes believed to be particularly close to God, or to bring or hold good luck (Nicholls 1992). In other societies, individuals with disability are thought to be inspirational. Although ill-treated on a day-to-day basis, they become the center of attention at certain times of the year or on certain ceremonial occasions. (At Christmastime in the United States, for example, there is much emphasis on providing holiday meals and gifts to disabled individuals in the community.) A special or reserved status is not, needless to say, an equal status. This is evidenced by the fact that for those with disability, the most common role and source of income generation globally— by far—continues to be begging.

A full adult role in any community implies not simply employment but the ability to marry and have a family of one's own, to decide where one will live, with whom one will associate, and how one will participate in the civic, religious, and recreational life of the community. Although societies differ as to where, when, and how individuals carry out these roles, the issue is whether individuals with disability are participating in such activities at a rate comparable to that of their nondisabled peers. Full acceptance—that is, status and treatment comparable to one's nondisabled peers—is relatively rare, but it does exist and is important.

Indeed, communities may interpret even significantly disabling conditions in a positive light. On the island of Martha's Vineyard, off the northeast coast of the United States, a gene for profound hereditary deafness led to the birth of a number of deaf individuals from the mid-seventeenth to the late-nineteenth centuries. Because deafness was so common, it was in the best interests of the hearing islanders to learn and use sign language, and most did. With the elimination of the substantial communications barrier, it is perhaps not surprising that deaf individuals on Martha's Vineyard participated vigorously in the life of the small villages in which they lived. They were not considered to be (nor did they consider themselves to be) disabled. The fact that individuals with a disability assume roles comparable to all other members of a society is a good indication that real integration has been achieved (Groce 1985).

MODERNIZATION

As modernization comes to many parts of the world, new technologies will provide options to many individuals with disability in the workforce, and additional barriers to some. For example, wheelchair users have an increasing number of choices in urban areas where transportation, buildings, and sidewalks are increasingly accessible. On the other hand, the growing number of jobs, even very low-skill jobs, that require literacy and the ability to use computers and other complex machines may limit the employment options of those with some types of intellectual impairments. Indeed, their ability to compete in the workforce as an adult is considered so compromised that in many nations they are placed on a formal pension system at the age of eighteen—a system that will maintain them for the remainder of their life.

IMPLICATIONS

While physical, intellectual, sensory, or mental health impairments are universal, the experience of being disabled is largely shaped by the culture in which one lives. The examples provided are far from exhaustive, but it is hoped that an awareness of this cross-cultural variation in approaches to disability will interest readers enough so that they begin to investigate—and continue to watch—this rapidly expanding area of research.

—Nora Ellen Groce

See also ASYLUM; INTENTIONAL COMMUNITIES IN THEUNITED STATES AND CANADA—CURRENT MOVEMENT

Further Reading

Asch, A. (1990). Reproductive technology and disability. In S. Cohen & J. Nadine (Eds.), *Reproductive Laws for the 1990s.* Clifton, NJ: Humana Press.

Blancher, J. (2001). Transition to adulthood: Mental retardation, families, and culture. *American Journal on Mental Retardation, 106*(2), 173–188.

Borthwick, C. (2000). Idiot into ape. In B. Altman & S. Barnartt (Eds.), *Expanding the scope of social science research on disability* (Vol. 2, pp. 32–54). Stamford, CT: JAI.

Coleridge, P. (1993). *Disability, liberation and development.* Oxford, UK: Oxfam.

Cunningham, K. (1989, Winter). Cultural perceptions of disability. *Uts'itishtana'I: Newsletter of the American Indian Rehabilitation Research and Training Center.*

Das, V. (2001). Stigma, contagion, defect: *Issues in the anthropology of public health* (pp. 1–9). Bethesda, MD: National Institutes of Health.

Economic and Social Commission for Asia and the Pacific. (1995). *Hidden sisters: Women and girls with disabilities in the Asian and Pacific region.* New York: United Nations.

Edgerton, R. (1970). Mental retardation in non-Western societies: Towards a cross-cultural perspective on incompetence. In H. Haywood (Ed.), *Social-cultural aspects of mental retardation.* New York: Appleton-Century-Crofts.

Edgerton, R. (1996). A longitudinal-ethnographic research perspective on quality of life. In R. Schalock (Ed.), *Quality of life. Vol. I: Conceptualization and Measurement.* Washington DC: American Association on Mental Retardation.

Fine, M. & Asch, A. (Eds.) (1988). *Women with disability: Essays in psychology, culture and politics.* Philadelphia: Temple University Press.

Gallagher, H. (1990). *By trust betrayed: Patients, physicians, and the license to kill in the Third Reich.* New York: Henry Holt.

Gannotti, M., & Handwerker, W. P. (2002). Puerto Rican understandings of child disability: Methods for the cultural validation of standardized measure of child health. *Social Science and Medicine, 55*(12), 11–23.

Goffman, E. (1963). *Stigma: Notes on the management of a spoiled identity.* Englewood Cliffs, NJ: Prentice Hall.

Greene, L. (1977). Hyperendemic goiter, cretinism and social organization in highland Ecuador. In L. Green (Ed.), *Malnutrition, behavior and social organization.* New York: Academic Press.

Groce, N. (1985). *Everyone here spoke sign language: Hereditary deafness on Martha's Vineyard.* Cambridge, MA: Harvard University Press.

Groce, N. (1999.) Disability in a cross-cultural perspective: Rethinking disability. *The Lancet, 354,* 756–757.

Groce, N., & Zola, I. K. (1993). Multiculturalism, chronic illness and disability. *Pediatrics, 91*(5), 1048–1055.

Hahn, H. (1989). Theories and values: Ethics and contrasting perspectives on disability in ethical issues. *Ethical issues in disability and rehabilitation.* Oakland, CA: World Institute on Disability.

Helander, E. (1993). *Prejudice and dignity: An introduction to community-based rehabilitation.* New York: United Nations Development Programme.

Ingstad, B. (1988). Coping behavior of disabled persons and their families: Cross-cultural perspectives from Norway and Botswana. *International Journal of Rehabilitation Research, 11,* 351–359.

Ingstad, B. (1999). The myth of disability in developing nations. *The Lancet, 354,* 757–758.

Ingstad, B., & White, S. (1995). *Disability and culture.* Berkeley: University of California Press.

Kaplan, L. (1999). Community-based disability services in the USA; A pediatric perspective. *The Lancet, 9180*(354), 761–762.

Madiros, M. (1989). Conception of childhood disability among Mexican-American parents. *Medical Anthropology, 12,* 55–68.

Marfo, K., Walker, S., Charles, P. (Eds.), *Childhood disability in developing countries.* New York: Praeger.

Marshall, C., Largo, H. (1999). Disability and rehabilitation: A context for understanding the American Indian experiences. *The Lancet, 9180*(354), 750–760.

Newman, L. (1969). Folklore of pregnancy: Wives' tales in Contra Costa County, California. *Western Folklore, 28*(2), 112–135.

Nicholls, R. (1992). An examination of some traditional African attitudes towards disability. *Traditional and changing views of disability in developing societies.* Monograph #53. Durham, NH: National Institute of Disability and Rehabilitation Research.

Nkinyangi, J., & Mbindyo, J. (1982). *The condition of disabled persons in Kenya: Results of a national survey.* University of Nairobi, Kenya: Institute for Developmental Studies.

Scheer, J., & Groce, N. (1988). Impairment as a human constant: Cross-cultural and historical perspectives on variation. *Journal of Social Issues, 44*(1), 23–37.

Solecki, R. (1971). *Shanidar: The first flower people.* New York: Knopf.

Thomason, T. (1994). Native Americans and assistive technology. In J. H. Murphy (Ed.), *Technology and persons with disabilities.* Proceedings of the Ninth Annual Conference. California State University, Northridge.

UNICEF. (1999). *An overview of young people living with disabilities: Their needs and their rights.* New York: UNICEF Inter-Divisional Working Group on Young People, Programme Division.

United Nations. (1993, December). *Standard rules on the equalization of opportunities for persons with disabilities.* General Assembly Resolution 48/96. New York: United Nations.

Wolfenberger, W. (1983). Social role valorization: A proposed new term for the principle of normalization. *Mental Retardation, 21,* 234–239.

DISPLACED POPULATIONS

Displaced people are persons driven away or expelled from their houses and homelands. The term *displaced person* (DP) was first used at the end of World War II to refer to a person who had been liberated from an extermination camp or labor camp of Nazi Germany or other Axis powers but who had not yet been relocated to a permanent settlement. The United Nations Relief and Rehabilitation Administration (UNRRA) was created in 1943 to assist displaced people and liberated areas, especially in Europe and China. UNRRA repatriated 7 million displaced people and provided temporary shelter for about 1 million more who were unwilling to return to their countries of origin until they were resettled elsewhere. In 1949, UNRRA's functions were transferred to other UN agencies, such as the International Refugee Organization, the United Nations Children's Fund, the Food and Agriculture Organization, and later to the United Nations High Commissioner for Refugees (UNHCR).

The term *displaced person* increasingly has been replaced in usage by the term *displaced populations* to designate populations, not just individuals, that are forcibly displaced from their habitat. Population displacements are one of the major problems internationally and in many countries, particularly developing and transition countries. (The term *transition countries* refers to countries in transition from a planned to a market economy.) The concerns with international security have increased governmental attention to such displacements and their effects.

CAUSES

Population displacements result from numerous causes. They bear the imprints of those causes and unfold variously until they are resolved through relocation or absorption of the population at the arrival site. The causes of population displacements became more diverse during and after the Cold War, resulting in vastly increased numbers of displaced people. Social scientists distinguish five clusters of causes of population displacements: (1) Populations are displaced by wars, civil wars, and political turmoil; (2) populations are displaced by organized persecution—ethnic, religious, racial; (3) populations are displaced by environmental disasters—droughts, famines, floods, desertification, earthquakes, and so forth; (4) populations are displaced by development programs that change land use or water use and build major new infrastructure; and (5) populations are displaced by the disintegration and disappearance of state structures.

CONSEQUENCES

Although the causes of population displacement range along a wide spectrum, the consequences of displacement for the affected populations tend to have many commonalities: massive loss and destruction of assets, in many cases including loss of life; sudden drop in welfare and standards of living; prolonged uprooting, alienation, and unemployment; culture and identity loss; severe long-term psychological effects; and so forth. Almost all displacements involve human rights and civil rights infringements. Research has found that effects are even more severe on women than on men and on particularly vulnerable population segments such as children, the elderly, or indigenous groups.

In turn, at arrival sites displaced populations impose two sets of high risks: risks to the host population and risks to the environment. Increased population densities at arrival sites increase competition for resources and jobs; further, some relocation processes exceed the carrying capacity (the population that an area will support without deterioration) of the environment and entail unsustainable use of limited natural resources, soil erosion, deforestation, and so forth.

CONCEPTUAL DISTINCTIONS WITHIN DISPLACED POPULATIONS

The complexity and multiplicity of population displacements require conceptual distinctions for a better grasp of the conditions of various subgroups. A bewildering set of terms has emerged (e.g., *forced migrants, development refugees, evictees, spontaneous displacement, asylum seekers, ecological refugees, oustees, internally relocated people,* and so forth). Among these terms, the key notions are displaced populations (or forced migrants) and refugees.

The broadest notion is that of displaced populations. It encompasses all "forced migrants," and within it the principal distinction usually made is between refugees and internally displaced people. In common parlance or in the media, the word *refugee* is sometimes used loosely to describe all those who have been forced to abandon their place of usual residence. However, international law gives a specific meaning to this term by distinguishing between displaced people who cross a national border and those who, although displaced, remain in their country. Both groups are forced migrants, but only those in the first category are defined as "refugees," whereas those in the second category are defined as "internally displaced people." The difference in labeling these people reflects significant differences in their entitlements to international assistance and protection. As defined by the U.N. Convention Relating to the Status of Refugees, "the term refugee refers to a person who, owing to a well-founded fear of being persecuted for reasons of race, religion, nationality, or membership of a particular social group or political opinion, is outside the country of his nationality and is unable or, owing to such fear, is unwilling to avail himself of the protection of that country" (U.N. 1951, p. 1). In 1969, in response to the increasingly frequent flows and growing scale of refugees in Africa, the Organization of African Unity (OAU) adopted the Refugee Convention, which has a slightly broader definition: "The term refugee shall apply to every person who, owing to external aggression, occupation, foreign domination or events seriously disturbing public order in either part or the whole of his country of origin or nationality, is compelled to leave his place of habitual residence in order to seek refuge in another place outside his country of origin or nationality" (OAU 1969, p. 1). This definition of *refugee,* which stresses two key elements—violence and border crossing—is intentionally restrictive: It does not include either voluntary (economic) migrants to other countries or people displaced by planned development projects. This is because countries and international organizations that grant special entitlements to refugees are concerned to avoid confusing, for instance, a voluntary (economic) migrant with a genuine refugee.

REFUGEE FLOWS

During 2001, the number of refugees in the world reached 12 million. Because refugee populations result from (1) populations displaced by wars, civil wars, and political turmoil and (2) populations displaced by organized persecution—ethnic, religious, or racial—their total numbers tend to increase dramatically and suddenly with the eruption of conflicts or the onset of violence and persecution. Their total numbers decrease with cessation of conflicts and with repatriations. UNHCR data show that during the decade from 1992 to 2001, 86 percent of the world's refugees originated from developing countries and 72 percent found temporary asylum in other developing countries. The peak of refugee waves was reached around the middle of the 1990s because of events in the Great Lakes region of Africa, causing huge waves of Burundian and Rwandan refugees, and in southeastern Europe: Serbia, Bosnia, and Herzegovina. Conversely, during the second half of the decade, from 1997 to 2001, the global number of refugees fell by 24 percent compared to the first half of the decade. During 2001, the global refugee population remained roughly unchanged at 12 million people, distributed as follows: Asia, 5.8 million, the largest segment; Africa, 3.3 million; Latin America, 3.3 million; Europe, 2.2 million; and North America, 650,000. Consistent with the definitions mentioned, these numbers do not include (1) populations displaced by environmental disasters—droughts, famines, floods, desertification, earthquakes, and so forth; (2) populations displaced by development programs that change land use or water use and build major new infrastructure; and (3) populations displaced by the disintegration and disappearance of state structures. The UNHCR evaluated the decade from 1992 to 2001 as a period when "the situation of refugees has generally improved. Since 1992 global refugee figures have fallen; more refugees have repatriated than were forced to leave their country and new refugee outflow has diminished" (UNHCR 2002, 25–26). It must be noted, however, that the total number of people displaced by the same armed conflicts, persecutions, or violence is larger than the numbers given earlier because many such displacees, although forced to abandon their homes, have remained within the borders of their own country as *internally* displaced people and thus are not labeled "refugees." For them, too, as for those recognized fully as refugees, humanitarian action is needed to provide human security, assistance, and reestablishment.

DEVELOPMENT-INDUCED DISPLACEMENTS

The most important displacement-related process during the last three decades has been the huge growth of internally displaced populations (IDPs). Their growth has been termed "the global crisis of internal displacement" (Cohen & Deng 1998, p. 1). Their numbers are now surpassing by far those of refugees. Regular statistics are not available because governments do not supply such data; nor are IDPs included in UNHCR statistics. The IDP category includes people who are compelled to move as a result of environmental disasters; people who are forced to flee violence, war, persecutions, and so forth but who are unable to cross a frontier; and—most important—people who are displaced in a planned manner by public-sector development programs and by private-sector projects. Assistance to people in these categories is not included in the formal U.N. mandate to UNHCR, and no other global U.N. agency has been yet established to assist them. During the period 1999–2000, UNHCR began to keep statistics on, in addition to refugees, some segments flexibly described as *persons of concern to UNHCR.* However, even these segments do not include the bulk of IDPs, who are development-displaced people. Analysts, public advocates, social scientists, and some institutions during the 1990s initiated efforts "to establish the internally-displaced people (IDPs) as a discrete humanitarian category" (UNHCR 1999, p. 52). These efforts are increasingly gaining recognition: The U.N. has established a "representative of the U.N. secretary-general on internally displaced persons," and social science research on this category has intensified.

Displacements of people by development projects result from the need of countries to build modern industrial infrastructure and transportation networks, expand power generation, develop irrigated agriculture, implement urban renewal, and enhance social services—schools, drinking water supply systems, hospitals, and so forth. These developments require right-of-way and entail land expropriation and attendant dislocation of vast numbers of people from their lands, homes, shops, and so forth. Although these involuntary displacements are carried out in a planned manner, they nonetheless cause enduring economic, cultural, political, and psychological harm to the affected populations.

Not all development-caused displacements are unavoidable and justified for the general public interest. Some displacements are simply ill planned or could be averted or reduced by better planning. However, the continuous increase in population density decreases the amount of land available, and this type of displacement is predicted to continue as a companion of development and one of its painful social pathologies. Most governments do not disclose—or they understate—statistics on development-caused displacements. However, the number of people displaced by development tends now to exceed the number of people displaced by other causes. The World Bank concluded that during the last two decades of the twentieth century, 80–90 million people were displaced worldwide during each decade by development projects in just three economic sectors: urban, transportation, and dam construction (World Bank 1994, 1). Every year, 8 to 10 million people are involuntarily displaced by such development programs. These numbers would be larger if statistics on other development sectors were available. Compulsory displacements that occur for development reasons, although not resulting in refugees in foreign lands, enormously worsen the global problem of internal population displacements.

IMPOVERISHMENT RISKS IN DISPLACEMENT

Such population displacements embody a perverse contradiction in development because they reflect the inequitable distribution of gains and losses from development and raise major ethical problems. The worst and most widespread effect of development-induced displacements is the impoverishment of vast numbers of people. Research has identified the risks of impoverishment, destitution, and social disarticulation (the dismantling of a community's institutions and patterns of social organization due to the dispersal of its population) imposed on internally displaced people. These risks are synthesized in the "Impoverishment Risks and Reconstruction (IRR) Model for Resettling Development-Displaced Populations" (Cernea 1997, pp. 1569–1588), which highlights nine fundamental risks of impoverishment: landlessness, joblessness, homelessness, marginalization, increased mortality and morbidity, food insecurity, loss of education, loss of access to common property natural resources, and social disarticulation. The IRR model also highlights the poverty and environmental risks that displaced populations create at arrival sites. Because governments initiate the projects that entail such displacement, it is incumbent on these governments to provide full compensation and the investments necessary to ensure the sustainable resettlement and improved livelihood of the people displaced by development projects.

SOLUTIONS

Countries and the international community have evolved an array of solutions to increase the protection of displaced populations and to facilitate their reestablishment. Given the diverse causes of displacement, solutions must be tailored to the characteristics of each major category of displaced populations and further adjusted operationally to specific circumstances. For refugees, the main solutions include repatriation or absorption and integration at the arrival site. Humanitarian assistance during the refugee period is indispensable. Relocation of refugees in improvised camps or colonies is regarded not as a solution, but rather as only a temporary response to emergencies, and in the case of planned displacement it is fully unacceptable. For development-displaced people, the solutions are more exacting, and the obligations incumbent upon the displacing agent (the state or sometimes a private corporation) are higher. For instance, the impoverishment risks and reconstruction (IRR) model outlines the strategies necessary to counteract the risks of impoverishment through displacement, including land-based resettlement, employment provision, house reconstruction, and others. The processes of involuntary resettlement are complex, entail special policies and investment resources, and increasingly are becoming the subject of international and national regulations.

—*Michael M. Cernea*

See also RESETTLEMENT

Further Reading

Ager, A. (Ed.). (1999). *Refugees: Perspectives on the experience of forced migration.* London: Cassell Academic.
Black, R. (1998). *Refugees, environment and development.* London: Longman.
Cernea, M. M. (1997). The risks and reconstruction model for resettling displaced populations. *World Development, 25*(10), 1569–1588.
Cernea, M. M. (2001). Risks analysis and reduction in displacement. In V. Desai & R. B. Potter (Eds.), *The companion to development studies* (pp. 453–459). London: Arnold.
Cernea, M., & McDowell, C. (Eds.). (2000). *Risks and reconstruction: Experiences of resettlers and refugees.* Washington, DC: World Bank.
Cohen, R., & Deng, F. (1998). *Masses in flight: The global crisis of internal displacement.* Washington, DC: Brookings Institution Press.
Koenig, D. (2002). *Towards local development and mitigating impoverishment in development-induced displacement and resettlement* (RSC Working Paper Series). Oxford, UK: University of Oxford Press.
Organization of African Unity. (1969). *Convention governing the specific aspects of refugee problems in Africa: Article 1.* New York: Author.
United Nations. (1951). *Convention relating to the status of refugees.* New York: Author.
United Nations High Commissioner for Refugees. (1999). *The state of the world's refugees 1997–98: A humanitarian agenda.* London: Oxford University Press.
United Nations High Commissioner for Refugees. (2002). *Statistical yearbook 2001: Refugees, asylum-seekers and other persons of concern—trends in displacement, protection and solutions.* Geneva, Switzerland: United Nations High Commissioner for Refugees.
World Bank. (1994). *Resettlement and development* (Task Force Report on the Bank-Wide Review of Projects Involving Involuntary Resettlement). Washington, DC: World Bank.
Zetter, R. (1991). Labeling refugees: Forming and transforming an identity. *Journal of Refugee Studies, 4,* 39–62.

DURKHEIM, ÉMILE (1858–1917)

French sociologist

Émile Durkheim was born in the Alsace-Lorraine region of France, where his father was a prominent rabbi. Following his university education in Épinal and Paris, Durkheim spent his early career from 1887 to 1902 teaching philosophy in Bordeaux. In 1902 he was appointed professor of the science of education at the Sorbonne in Paris, and in 1913 he became a professor of education and sociology there.

Durkheim is considered one of the founders of modern sociology. Influenced by the social theories of Henri de Saint-Simon (1750–1825) and Auguste Comte (1798–1857), Durkheim proposed that methods of the natural sciences—hypotheses, statistics, impartial observation—be applied to the study of human society. He theorized that social relations were based on collective moral beliefs and symbolic representations, and he explored the changing relationship of the individual to the social group in modern society.

In addition to numerous essays, Durkheim published four major books in his lifetime. *The Division of Labor in Society* (1893) examined the historical development of social solidarity. In it, Durkheim proposed that occupational groups, such as professional associations and workers' unions, might serve as the means of moral integration in modern society. By affording a sense of belonging and fostering shared principles, such groups would instill a common ethic of obligation to the greater community. *The Rules of Sociological Method* (1895) outlined techniques for defining and delimiting social phenomena for purposes of scientific study. *Suicide: A Study in Sociology* (1897) explored the causes and consequences of weakened bonds between the individual and society. In *The Elementary Forms of Religious Life* (1912), Durkheim investigated the spiritual practices of native Australians in an effort to show how collective beliefs and rituals shaped and stabilized social order.

Although the late nineteenth-century positivism and evolutionary thought that shaped Durkheim's thinking no longer hold sway in sociology, a number of his concepts have had an enduring impact on the study of community life. In theorizing the historical development of society, Durkheim identified two contrasting, ideal typical categories of social solidarity. Mechanical solidarity was characteristic of what Durkheim termed simple or primitive societies, where there was a great homogeneity of moral beliefs with little social or economic differentiation. Organic solidarity, characteristic of complex or advanced societies, was the product of multivalent forms of social relationships and correspondingly diverse and protean moral standards. Durkheim held that the evolution from mechanical to organic solidarity was not complete. While the nature of mechanical solidarity, being largely a historical phenomena, could be fully described, the moral foundations and social bonds shaping organic solidarity in the modern world were still evolving. The decline of one moral universe before a subsequent constellation of beliefs and bonds was fully formed produced distinctively modern social pathologies, such as anomie, the loss of moral certainty, and the decline of collective life. Other ailments of modern life that Durkheim identified included egoism, the alienation of the individual from the social collective, which he distinguished from individualism, a potentially positive force for strengthening personal freedom and dignity and a promising foundation for the emerging collective moral order of modern society.

—Jeannette Redensek

Further Reading

Bellah, R. (Ed.). *Émile Durkheim: On morality and society, selected writings.* (M. Traugott, Trans.). Chicago: University of Chicago Press.

Durkheim, É. (1984). *The division of labour in society.* (W. D. Halls, Trans.). Basingstoke, UK: Macmillan.

Durkheim, É. (1995). *The elementary forms of religious life.* (K. E. Shields, Trans.). New York: Free Press.

Durkheim, É. (1997). *Suicide, a study in sociology.* (J. A. Spaulding & G. Simpson, Trans.). New York: Free Press.

Fenton, S., with Reiner, R., & Hamnett, I. (1984). *Durkheim and modern sociology.* Cambridge, UK: Cambridge University Press.

Giddens, A. (Ed.). (1986). *Durkheim on politics and the state.* (W. D. Halls, Trans.). Cambridge, UK: Polity.

Hamilton, P. (Ed.). (1990). *Émile Durkheim: Critical assessments* (Vols. 1–8). London and New York: Routledge.

Lukes, S. (1972). *Émile Durkheim: His life and work, a historical and critical study.* New York: Harper & Row.

Appendix 1

Resource Guides

Divided into twenty-one broad subject areas, the resource guides that follow cull relevant *Encyclopedia of Community* entries, and related books and Web sites, journals, and organizations. This material presents readers with the information and tools necessary to explore each topic in more depth and to become involved with organizations and activities that focus on building stronger communities.

CHILDHOOD AND ADOLESCENCE

The beginnings of our sense of self and our understanding of how we connect with others lie in the period between birth and adulthood. A large amount of scholarship has gone into trying to understand childhood and adolescence, much of it related to the interactions within families or between young people and other children, teachers, coaches, and people of different ages. As Katherine MacTavish, author of the *Encyclopedia of Community*'s "Children" entry, writes: "In the 1980s and 1990s, researchers in the United States devoted increasing attention to understanding how the community, or more immediately the neighborhood, shapes the daily lives and developmental outcomes of children." The following are lists of publications and organizations that address children and adolescents, the bonds they form, and their interactions with the communities around them.

Encyclopedia Entries

Adolescence
Adolescents and Landscape
Birth
Child Care
Children
Colleges
Community Colleges
Community Schools
Family and Work
Family Violence
Fraternities and Sororities
Friendship
Gangs
Home Schooling
Human Development
Initiation Rites
Intentional Communities and Children
Internet, Teen Use of
Online Communities, Game-Playing
Online Communities, Youth
School Consolidation
Schools
Student Housing Cooperatives
Theme Parks
Town and Gown
Youth Groups

Books and Web Sites

Booth, A., & Crouter, A. (Eds.). (2000). *Does it take a village? Community effects on children, adolescents, and families.* Mahwah, NJ: Lawrence Erlbaum.

Canadians Go Greek!: http://www.canadiangreeks.com

Carnegie Foundation for the Advancement of Teaching. (1990). *Campus life: In search of community.* Princeton, NJ: Princeton University Press.

Eccles, J., & Gootman, J. (Eds.). (2002). *Community programs to promote youth development.* Washington, DC: National Academy Press.

Elder, G., & Conger, R. (2000). *Children of the land: Adversity and success in rural America.* Chicago: University of Chicago Press.

Gelles, R. J. (1997). *Intimate violence in families* (3d ed.). Thousand Oaks, CA: Sage.

Greekpages.com: http://www.greekpages.com

Jehl, J., Blank, M. J., & McCloud, B. (2001). *Education and community building: Connecting two worlds.* Washington, DC: Institute for Educational Leadership.

LeVine, R., Dixon, S., LeVine, S., Richman, A., Leiderman, P. H., Keefer, C., et al. (1994). *Child care and culture: Lessons from Africa.* Cambridge, UK: Cambridge University Press.

McDonald, J. P. (1996). *Redesigning school: Lessons for the 21st century.* San Francisco: Jossey-Bass.

Mortimer, J. T., & Finch, M. D. (Eds.). (1996). *Adolescents, work, and family: An intergenerational developmental analysis.* Thousand Oaks, CA: Sage.

Valentine, G., & Skelton, T. (Eds.). (1998). *Cool places: Geographies of youth.* New York: Routledge.

Vigil, D. (2002). *A rainbow of gangs: Street cultures in the mega-city.* Austin: University of Texas Press.

Whyte, W. F. (1943). *Street corner society.* Chicago: University of Chicago.

Journals

Adolescence. Libra Publishers, Roslyn Heights, NY.

American Journal of Orthopsychiatry. American Orthopsychiatric Association, 330 Seventh Avenue, New York, NY 10001; http://www.amerortho.org

Child Development. Society for Research in Child Development, University of Michigan, 3131 South State Street, Ann Arbor, MI 48108; http://www.srcd.org/cd.html

Child & Youth Services. Haworth Press, 10 Alice Street, Binghamton, NY 13904-1580; http://www.haworthpressinc.com

Childhood: A Global Journal of Child Research. Sage Publications, 2455 Teller Road, Thousand Oaks, CA 91320; http://www.sagepub.com

Educational Leadership. Association for Supervision and Curriculum Development, 1703 North Beauregard Street, Alexandria, VA 22311-1714; http://www.ascd.org

Human Development. Karger Publishers, P.O. Box CH–4009, Basel, Switzerland; http://www.karger.com/journals

Journal of Youth and Adolescence. Kluwer Academic/Plenum Publishers, 233 Spring Street, New York 10013-1578; http://www.kluweronline.com

Merrill-Palmer Quarterly: Journal of Developmental Psychology. Wayne State University Press, 4809 Woodward Avenue, Detroit, MI 48201-1309; http://wsupress.wayne.edu/journals/merrill.htm

Monographs of the Society for Research in Child Development. Society for Research in Child Development, University of Michigan, 3131 South State Street, Ann Arbor, MI 48108; http://www.srcd.org/cdm.html

Youth & Society. Sage Publications, 2455 Teller Road, Thousand Oaks, CA 91320; http://www.sagepub.com

Organizations

Big Brothers Big Sisters of America, North 13th Street, Philadelphia, PA 19107-1538; http://www.bbbsa.org

Boys and Girls Clubs of America, 1230 W. Peachtree Street, NW, Atlanta, GA 30309; http://www.bgca.org

Boy Scouts of America, P.O. Box 152079, Irving, TX 75015-2079; http://www.scouting.org

Child Welfare League of America, 440 First Street NW, Washington, DC 20001-2085; http://www.cwla.org

Children's Defense Fund, 25 E Street NW, Washington, DC 20001; http://www.childrensdefense.org

Coalition of the Community Schools, c/o Institute for Educational Leadership, 1001 Connecticut Avenue, NW, Washington, DC 20036; http://www.communityschools.org/

Democratic Youth Community of Europe (DEMYC), Danasvej 4-6, 1910 Frederiksberg C, Denmark; http://www.demyc.org

Girl Scouts of the USA, 420 Fifth Avenue, New York, NY 10018-2798; http://www.girlscouts.org

JCC (Jewish Community Centers) Association of North America, 15 East 26th Street, New York, NY 10010-1579; http://www.jcca.org/

National Association of Police Athletic Leagues (PAL), 618 U.S. Highway 1, North Palm Beach, FL 33408-4609; http://www.nationalpal.org/

National Coalition for Alternative Community Schools, 1289 Jewett, Ann Arbor, MI 48104-6205; http://ncacs.org

National Institute on Drug Abuse, 6001 Executive Boulevard, Bethesda, MD 20892-9561; http://www.drugabuse.gov

United Nations Children's Fund (UNICEF), UNICEF House, 3 United Nations Plaza, New York, NY 10017; http://www.unicef.org

YMCA of the USA, 101 North Wacker Drive, Chicago, IL 60606; http://www.ymca.net

YWCA of the USA, 1015 18th Street, NW, Washington, DC 20036; http://www.ywca.org

COMMUNITY ECONOMICS

> Being for or against business is antithetical to creating self-reliant communities. It's better to sort out which kinds of businesses are the best partners for community self-reliance, and which kinds are the worst.
> For environmentalists, labor organizers, and other progressive activists in the United States, this means

> moving beyond crude tirades against corporations. For those Americans who are uncritically probusiness, this means carefully asking which kinds of businesses can best serve the interests of their community.
>
> —*Michael Shuman* (*Going Local 1998,* pp. 84–85)

As Michael Shuman—one of the editors of the *Encyclopedia of Community* and author of the encyclopedia's "Community Ownership" entry, among others—explains, viewing economics from a community perspective requires a different mindset. It also calls for some different resources than those traditionally used in the study of economics. The following are lists of publications and organizations that focus on the impact of economics from the daily lives of individuals to the systems that link the entire global community.

Encyclopedia Entries

Bankruptcy
Barter
Black Economy
Boomtowns
Chain Stores
Collective Consumption
Community Currencies
Community Development Corporations
Community Ownership
Consumer Culture
Culture of Poverty
Economic Planning
Entrepreneurship
Export-Led Development in Regional Economies
Free Rider
Growth Machine
Import-Replacing Development
Industrial Revolution
Informal Economy
Labor Markets
Labor Unions
Local Manufacturing
Markets, Street
Merchant Communities
Mill Towns
Mining Towns
Nonmonetary Economy
Nonprofit Organizations
Plant Closures
Plantations
Political Economy
Public Aid
Public Goods
Rural Poverty and Family Well-Being
Shopping Centers and Malls
Social Capital, Impact in Wealthy and Poor Communities
Social Capital and Economic Development
Social Capital in the Workplace
Subsidies
Tourist Communities
Tragedy of the Commons

Books and Web Sites

American News Service Archive: http://www.berkshirepublishing.com/brw/ans.asp

Baird, D. G. (1993). *The elements of bankruptcy*. Westbury, NY: Foundation Press.

Beaumont, C. E. (1997). *Better models for superstores: Alternatives to big-box sprawl*. Washington, DC: National Trust for Historic Preservation.

Blakely, E. J., & Bradshaw, T. K. (2002). *Planning local economic development: Theory and practice*. Thousand Oaks, CA: Sage.

Brotton, T. (1997). *Trading territories: Mapping the early modern world*. London: Reaklion.

Castells, M. (1978). *City, class and power* (E. Lebas, Supervised Trans.). London: Macmillan.

Cloward, R., & Piven, F. F. (1993). *Regulating the poor: The functions of public welfare*. New York: Vintage Books.

Daly, H. E., & Cobb, Jr., J. B. (1989). *For the common good: Redirecting the community, the environment, and a sustainable future*. Boston: Beacon.

Douthwaite, R. (1999). *The ecology of money*. Dartington, UK: Green.

Falk, W., Shulman, M., & Tickamyer, A. (Eds.). (2003). *Communities of work*. Athens: Ohio University Press.

Francaviglia, R. V. (1991). *Hard places: Reading the landscape of America's historic mining towns*. Iowa City: University of Iowa Press.

Frumkin, P. (2002). *On being nonprofit*. Cambridge, MA: Harvard University Press.

Fujita, M., Krugman, P., & Venables, A. J. (1999). *The spatial economy: Cities, regions, and international trade*. Cambridge, MA: MIT Press.

Goldman, M. (1998). *Privatizing nature: Political struggles for the global commons*. London: Pluto.

Grootaert, C., & van Bastelaer, T. (Eds.). (2002). *The role of social capital in development: An empirical assessment*. New York: Cambridge University Press.

Gunn, C., & Gunn, H. D. (1991). *Reclaiming capital: Democratic initiatives and community development*. Ithaca, NY: Cornell University Press.

Harrington, M. (1962). *The other America*. New York: Macmillan.

Hawken, P. (1993). *The ecology of commerce*. New York:

HarperCollins.

Heertje, A, Allen, M., & Cohn, H. (1982). *The black economy: How it works, who works for, and what it costs.* London: Pan Books.

Ironmonger, D. (1989). *Household work, productive activities: Women and income in the household economy.* Sydney, Australia: Allen & Unwin

Jonas, A. E. G., & Wilson, D. (1999). *The urban growth machine: Critical perspectives two decades later.* Albany: State University of New York Press.

Judd, D. R., & Fainstein, S. S. (Eds.). (1999). *The tourist city.* New Haven, CT: Yale University Press.

Kaul, I, Grunberg, I., & Stern, M. (Eds.). (1999). *Global public goods*, New York: United Nations Development Programme, Oxford University Press.

Lewis, O. (1959). *Five families: Mexican case studies in the culture of poverty.* New York: Basic Books.

Mauss, M. (1950). *The gift: The form and reason for exchange in archaic societies.* London: Norton.

Miller, D. (1998). *A theory of shopping.* Ithaca, NY: Cornell University Press.

Munck, R., & Waterman, P. (1999). *Labour worldwide in the era of globalization: Alternative union models in the new world order.* New York: St. Martin's.

Openair-Market Net: http://www.openair.org

O'Sullivan, A. (1999). *Urban economics* (4th ed.). New York: McGraw-Hill-Irwin.

Plattner, S. (Ed.). (1985). *Markets and marketing.* Lanham, MD: University Press of America.

Portes, A., M. Castells, & L. Benton (Eds.). (1989). *The informal economy: Studies in advanced and less developed countries.* Baltimore: Johns Hopkins University Press.

Saegert, S., Thompson, J. P., & Warren, M. R. (2001). *Social capital and poor communities.* New York: Russell Sage Foundation.

Satterthwaite, A. (2001). *Going shopping: Consumer choices and community consequences.* New Haven, CT: Yale University Press.

Shuman, M. (1998). *Going local: Creating self-reliant communities in a global age.* New York: Free Press.

Stearns, P. N. (1998). *The industrial revolution in world history* (2nd ed.). Boulder, CO: Westview.

Veblen, T. (1899). *The theory of the leisure class.* New York: Macmillan.

Wallace, A. F. C. (1978). *Rockdale: The growth of an American village in the early industrial revolution.* New York: Knopf.

Williamson, T., Imbroscio, D., & Alperovitz, G. (2002). *Making a place for community.* New York: Routledge.

Journals

Economic Development Quarterly. Sage Publications, 6 Bonhill Street, London, EC2A 4PU, UK; http://www.sagepub.co.uk/ejournals/ejournals.htm

Journal of Urban Affairs. Urban Affairs Association, College of Public Service, St. Louis University, McGannon Hall, Suite 232, 3750 Lindell Boulevard, St. Louis, MO 63108-3342; http://www.udel.edu/uaa/journal.html

Regional Studies. Regional Studies Association, P.O. Box 2058, Seaford BN25 4QU, UK; http://www.regionalstudies-assoc.ac.uk/publications/regionalstudies.html

Urban Affairs Review. Sage Publications, 6 Bonhill Street, London, EC2A 4PU, UK; http://www.sagepub.co.uk/journals/details/j0095.html

Work and Occupations. Sage Publications, 6 Bonhill Street, London, EC2A 4PU, UK; http://www.sagepub.co.uk/journals/details/j0195.html

Organizations

Time Dollar Institute, http://www.timedollar.org

Families and Work Institute, 267 Fifth Ave., Floor 2, New York, NY 10016; http://www.familiesandwork.org

Independent Sector, 1200 Eighteenth Street, NW, Suite 200, Washington, DC 20036; http://www.independentsector.org

Institute for Community Economics, 57 School Street, Springfield, MA 01105-1331; http://www.iceclt.org

Institute for Local Self-Reliance (ILSR), 2425 18th Street NW, Washington DC 20009; http://www.ilsr.org

Industrial Workers of the World (IWW); http://iww.org

Institute for Social and Economic Development, 910 23rd Avenue, Coralville, IA 52241; http://www.ised.org

International Labour Organization, 4, route des Morillons, CH-1211 Geneva 22, Switzerland; http://www.ilo.org/

International Confederation of Free Trade Unions, 5 Boulevard du Roi Albe II, Bte 1, 1210 Brussels, Belgium; http://www.icftu.org

Ithaca Hours, Box 365, Ithaca, NY 14851; http://www.ithacahours.com/

National Community Capital Association, 620 Chestnut Street, Suite 572, Philadelphia, PA 19106; http://www.communitycapital.org

Organisation for Economic Cooperation and Development, 2, rue André Pascal, F-75775 Paris Cedex 16, France; http://www.oecd.org

Urban Institute, 2100 M Street, N.W., Washington, DC 20037; http://www.urban.org

United States Census Bureau, United States Department of Commerce, Washington, DC 20233; http://www.census.gov

World Bank, 1818 H Street, N.W., Washington, DC 20433; http://www.worldbank.org

World Tourism Organization, Capitán Haya 42, 28020 Madrid, Spain; http://www.world-tourism.org

COMMUNITY HEALTH

"Health is a state of complete physical, mental and social well-being and not merely the absence of disease or infirmity," states the preamble to the 1948 constitution of the World Health Organization. It is in the best interests of any society to ensure that its members are provided with the right tools and information to live healthy lives. From hospitals caring for premature babies to facilities housing the elderly, many different institutions within a community play a role in promoting and sustaining "physical, mental, and social well-being." The following publications and organizations provide a comprehensive range of consumer, academic, and professional resources on health information and services.

Encyclopedia Entries

Community Health Systems
Community Mental Health Centers
Disabled in Communities
Elder Care and Housing
Healthy Communities
Hospices
Twelve Step Groups

Books and Web Sites

Active Living by Design: http://www.activelivingbydesign.org

Ashton, J., & Seymour, H. (1988). *The new public health.* Buckingham, UK: Open University Press.

Beresford, L. (1993). *The hospice handbook: A complete guide.* New York: Little, Brown.

Coalition for Healthier Cities and Communities and the International Healthy Cities Foundation: http://www.hospitalconnect.com

Dever, A. G. E. (1991). *Community health analysis: Global awareness at the local level* (2nd ed.). Gaithersburg, MD: Aspen.

FirstGov for Seniors: http://www.seniors.gov

Flower, J. (1996). *Healthy cities, healthy communities.* Retrieved February 12, 2003, from http://www.well.com/user/bbear/healthy_communities.html

Glouberman, S., Kisilevsky, S., Groff, P., & Nicholson, C. (2000). *Towards a new concept of health: Three discussion papers* (CPRN Discussion Paper No. H/03). Ottawa, Canada: Canadian Policy Research Networks.

Green, L. W., & Kreuter, M. W. (1999). *Health promotion planning: An educational and ecological approach* (3rd ed.). New York: McGraw-Hill Education.

HealthWeb: http://healthweb.org

Kurtz, L. F. (1997). *Self-help and support groups: A handbook for practitioners.* Thousand Oaks, CA: Sage.

MEDLINEplus: http://www.nlm.nih.gov/medlineplus/libraries.html

Mosher, L., & Burti, L. (1994). *Community mental health.* New York: W. W. Norton.

Norris, T., Ayre, D., & Clough, G. (2002). *Trendbenders: Building healthy and vital communities.* Chicago: American Hospital Association.

Surgeon General's Workshop on Self-Help and Public Health. (1990). Washington, DC: Bureau of Maternal and Child Health and Resource Development, U.S. Department of Health and Human Services.

University of Maryland Libraries. *Web resources in public and community health*: http://www.lib.umd.edu/ETC/SUBR/resources.public_community_health.html

Wacker, R. R., Roberto, K. A., & Piper, L. E. (1997). *Community resources for older adults: Programs and services in an era of change.* Thousand Oaks, CA: Pine Forge.

World Health Organization. (2002). *The world health report 2002—Reducing risks, promoting healthy life*: http://www.who.int/whr/en

Journals

Community Mental Health Journal, Kluwer Academic Publishers, 101 Philip Drive, Norwell, MA 02061; http://www.kluweronline.com

Harvard Public Health Review, Harvard School of Public Health, 677 Huntington Avenue, Boston, MA 02115; http://www.hsph.harvard.edu/review

Health and Social Care in the Community, 350 Main Street Malden, MA 02148; http://www.blackwellpublishing.com/journals/hsc

Journal of Aging and Health, Sage Publications, 2455 Teller Road, Thousand Oaks, CA 91320; http://www.sagepub.com

Journal of Community Health, Kluwer Academic Publishers, 101 Philip Drive, Norwell, MA 02061; http://www.kluweronline.com

Journal of Health Care for the Poor and Underserved, Sage Publications, 2455 Teller Road, Thousand Oaks, CA 91320; http://www.sagepub.com

Prevention, Rodale, 33 East Minor Street, Emmaus, PA 18098; http://www.rodale.com

Public Health Reports. Oxford University Press, Great Clarendon Street, Oxford, OX2 6DP, UK; http://phr.oupjournals.org

Organizations

Alcoholics Anonymous, Grand Central Station, P.O. Box 459, New York, NY 10163; http://www.aa.org

American Public Health Association, 800 I Street NW, Washington, DC 20001-3710; http://www.apha.org

American Society on Aging, 833 Market Street, Suite 511, San Francisco, CA 94103; http://www.asaging.org

FamiliesUSA, 1334 G Street NW; Washington, DC 20005 http://www.familiesusa.org

Healthy People 2010, Office of Disease Prevention and Health Promotion, Hubert H. Humphrey Building, Room

738G, 200 Independence Avenue SW, Washington, DC 20201; http://www.healthypeople.gov

National Hospice and Palliative Care Organization, 1700 Diagonal Road, Suite 625, Alexandria, VA 22314; http://www.nhpco.org

National Institute on Drug Abuse, 6001 Executive Boulevard, Bethesda, MD 20892-9561; http://www.drugabuse.gov

Partnership for Prevention, 1015 18th Street NW, Washington, DC 20036; http://www.prevent.org

President's Council on Physical Fitness and Sports, 200 Independence Avenue SW, Room 738-H, Washington, DC 20201-0004; http://fitness.gov

Robert Wood Johnson Foundation, P.O. Box 2316, College Road East and Route 1, Princeton, NJ 08543; http://www.rwjf.org

World Health Organization, Avenue Appia 20, 1211 Geneva 27, Switzerland; http://www.who.int

Women's Sports Foundation, Eisenhower Park, East Meadow, NY 11554; http://www.womenssportsfoundation.org

COMMUNITY ORGANIZING AND ACTIVISM

According to William H. Friedland and Michael Rotkin, coauthors of the *Encyclopedia of Community*'s "Community Organizing" entry, grassroots organizing is a "growing phenomenon" in both industrialized and developing nations throughout the world. From the smallest rural communities to the border-crossing expanse of the Internet, people come together to advocate or implement changes. The following publications and organizations are concerned with providing the public with the information and resources necessary to take a stand and organize on behalf of their communities.

Encyclopedia Entries

Activist Communities
Alinsky, Saul
Charisma
Civic Innovation
Civil Disobedience
Collective Action
Communities of Opposition
Community Action
Community Building
Community Empowerment
Community Garden Movement
Community Organizing
Garden Cities
Gay Communities
Grassroots Leadership
New Urbanism
Populism
Pressure Groups
Public Opinion
Smart Growth
Social Movements
Social Movements Online
Stakeholder

Books and Web Sites

Addams, J. (1910). *Twenty years at Hull-House*. New York: Macmillan.

Ainsworth, S. (2002). *Analyzing interest groups: Group influence on people and policies*. New York: W. W. Norton.

Alinsky, S. (1971). *Rules for radicals*. New York: Random House.

American News Service Archive: http://www.berkshirepublishing.com/brw/ans.asp

Askonas, P., & Stewart, A. (Eds.). (2000). *Social inclusion: Possibilities and tensions*. New York: St. Martin's.

Bleiker, R. (2000). *Popular dissent, human agency and global politics*. Cambridge, UK: Cambridge University Press.

Delgado, G. (1997). *Beyond the politics of place: New directions in community organizing in the 1990s*. Oakland, CA: Applied Research Center.

Glynn, C. J., Herbst, S., O'Keefe, G. J., & Shapiro, R. Y. (1999). *Public opinion*. Boulder, CO: Westview.

Goodwyn, L. (1976). *Democratic promise: The populist moment in America*. New York: Oxford University Press.

Kingsley, G. T., & Gibson, J. O. (1997). *Community building: Coming of age*. Washington, DC: Urban Institute.

Klandermans, B. (1997). The social psychology of protest. Oxford, UK: Basil Blackwell.

Marx, G., & McAdam, D. (1994). *Collective behavior and social movements: Process and structure*. Englewood Cliffs, NJ: Prentice Hall.

National Community Building Network: www.ncbn.org

Olson, M., Jr. (1965). *The logic of collective action: Public goods and the theory of groups*. Cambridge, MA: Harvard University Press.

Rivera, F., & Erlich, J. (1999). *Community organizing in a diverse society* (3d ed.). Boston: Allyn & Bacon.

Rubin, H., & Rubin, I. (2001). *Community organizing and development* (3d ed.). Boston: Allyn & Bacon.

Simon, B. L. (1994). *The empowerment tradition in American social work: A history*. New York: Columbia University Press.

Sirianni, C. J., & Friedland, L. A. (2001). *Civic innovation in America: Community empowerment, public policy, and the movement for civic renewal*. Berkeley and Los Angeles: University of California Press.

Weber, M. (1968). *On charisma and institution building*. Chicago: University of Chicago Press.

Journals

American Journal of Community Psychology. Kluwer Academic/Plenum Publishers, 233 Spring Street, New York, NY 10013-1578; http://www.kluweronline.com/issn/0091-0562

The Grassroots Fundraising Journal. Grassroots Fundraising, 3781 Broadway, Oakland, CA 94611; http://www.grassrootsfundraising.org

Journal of Personality and Social Psychology. American Psychological Association, 750 First Street NE, Washington, DC 20002-4242; http://www.apa.org/journals/psp.html

National Civic Review. National Civic League, 1445 Market Street, Denver, CO 80202; http://www.ncl.org/publications/ncr/

Public Opinion Quarterly. The University of Chicago Press, Journals Division, P.O. Box 37005, Chicago, IL 60637; http://www.journals.uchicago.edu/POQ/home.html

Responsive Community Quarterly. The Communitarian Network, 2130 H Street, NW, Suite 703, Washington, DC 20052; http://www.gwu.edu/~ccps/

Organizations

Association of Communities Organized for Reform Now (ACORN), 88 3rd Avenue, Brooklyn, NY 11217; http://www.acorn.org

Center for Third World Organizing, 1218 E. 21st Street, Oakland, CA 94606; http://www.ctwo.org

Civic Practices Network, Center for Human Resources, Heller School for Advanced Studies in Social Welfare, Brandeis University, 60 Turner Street, Waltham, MA 02154; http://www.cpn.org

Community Action Agencies, 1100 17th Street NW, Washington, DC 20036; http://www.communityactionpartnership.com

Community Tool Box; http://ctb.lsi.ukans.edu

Kennedy School of Government, Harvard University, 79 John F. Kennedy Street, Cambridge, MA 02138; http://www.ksg.harvard.edu

Midwest Academy (Training For Community, Citizen, and Environmental Organizing), 28 East Jackson Street, Chicago, IL 60604; http://www.midwestacademy.com

United Farm Workers, P.O. Box 62, Keene, CA 93531; http://www.ufw.org

Urban Institute, 2100 M Street NW, Washington, DC 20037; http://www.urban.org

COMMUNITY PLANNING AND DEVELOPMENT

As a town grows, both in population and in area, a number of people become responsible for measuring and directing its growth. There are ecological, economic, and other social concerns to keep in mind, and poor planning now can result in serious problems years later. This is why many scholars and policymakers are looking at what makes community development that is practical, beneficial, and sustainable. Such development "meets the needs of the present without compromising the ability of future generations to meet their own needs," according to United Nations Commission on Environment and Development (in the 1987 Brundtland Report). The following publications and organizations are concerned with understanding and ensuring appropriate and well-advised development of communities around the world.

Encyclopedia Entries

Asset-Based Community Development
Civic Innovation
Community Building
Community Development Corporations
Community Development in Europe
Community Indicators
Economic Planning
Environmental Planning
Export-Led Development in Regional Economies
Garden Cities
Import-Replacing Development
Land Use and Zoning
Model Cities
New Towns
New Urbanism
Regional Planning Association of America
Rural Community Development
Smart Growth
Social Capital and Economic Development
Sustainable Development
Urban Renewal

Books

Blakely, E. J., & Bradshaw, T. K. (2002). *Planning local economic development: Theory and practice*. Thousand Oaks, CA: Sage.

Brundtland, H. (1987). *Our common future*. Oxford, UK: Oxford University Press, for the U.N. World Commission on Environment and Development.

Burby, R., & May, P. (1997). *Making governments plan*. Baltimore: Johns Hopkins University Press.

Calthorpe, P., & Fulton, W. (2001). *The regional city: Planning for the end of sprawl*. Washington, DC: Island Press.

Fujita, M., Krugman, P, & Venables, A. J. (1999). *The spatial economy: Cities, regions, and international trade*.

Cambridge, MA: MIT Press.

Green, G. P., & Haines, A. (2001). *Asset building and community development.* Thousand Oaks, CA: Sage.

Grootaert, C., & van Bastelaer, T. (Eds.). (2002). *The role of social capital in development: An empirical assessment.* New York: Cambridge University Press.

Gunn, C., & Gunn, H. (1991). *Reclaiming capital: Democratic initiatives and community development.* Ithaca, NY: Cornell University Press.

Jacobs, J. (1961). *The death and life of great American cities.* New York: Random House.

Jacobs, J. (1984). *Cities and the wealth of nations.* New York: Vintage.

Kenny, M., & Meadowcroft, J. (Eds.). (1999). *Planning sustainability.* London and New York: Routledge.

Kretzmann, J. P., & McKnight, J. L. (1993). *Building communities from the inside out: A path toward finding and mobilizing a community's assets.* Evanston, IL: ABCD Institute, Institute for Policy Research.

Nelson, A., Duncan, J., Mullen, C., & Bishop, K. (1995). *Growth management: Principles and practices.* Chicago: Planners Press, APA.

Nivola, P. (1999). Laws of the landscape: How policies shape cities in Europe and America. Washington, DC: Brookings Institution Press.

Pierson, J., & Smith, J. (Eds.). (2001). *Rebuilding community: Policy and practice in urban regeneration.* New York: Palgrave.

Rich, M. J. (1993). *Federal policymaking and the poor: National goals, local choices, and distributional outcomes.* Princeton, NJ: Princeton University Press.

Selman, P. (2000). *Environmental planning* (2nd ed.). London: Sage.

Sirianni, C. J., & Friedland, L. A. (2001). *Civic innovation in America: Community empowerment, public policy, and the movement for civic renewal.* Berkeley and Los Angeles: University of California Press.

Williamson, T., Imbroscio, D. & Alperovitz, G. (2002). *Making a place for community: Local democracy in a global era.* New York: Routledge.

Journals

The Ecologist. Ecosystems Ltd, Unit 18 Chelsea Wharf, 15 Lots Road, London SW10 OQJ, UK; http://www.theecologist.org

Environment and Planning B: Planning and Design. Pion Ltd., 207 Brondesbury Park, London, NW2 5JN, UK; http://www.envplan.com

Environmental Building News. BuildingGreen, Inc., 122 Birge Street Suite 30, Brattleboro, VT 05301; http://www.buildinggreen.com

European Planning Studies. Carfax, 4 Park Square, Milton Park, Abingdon, Oxfordshire, OX14 4RN, UK; http://www.tandf.co.uk/journals

Growth and Change. Blackwell Publishing, 350 Main Street, Malden, MA 02148; http://www.blackwellpublishing.com/journals/GROW

International Regional Science Review. Sage Publications, 2455 Teller Road, Thousand Oaks, CA 91320; http://www.sagepub.com

Journal of Environmental Planning and Management. Taylor and Francis, 4 Park Square, Milton Park, Abingdon, Oxfordshire, OX14 4RN, UK; http://www.tandf.co.uk/journals

Journal of Planning Education and Research. Sage Publications, 2455 Teller Road, Thousand Oaks, CA 91320; http://www.sagepub.com

Journal of Planning History. Sage Publications, 2455 Teller Road, Thousand Oaks, CA 91320; http://www.sagepub.com

Journal of Planning Literature. Sage Publications, 2455 Teller Road, Thousand Oaks, CA 91320; http://www.sagepub.com

Journal of the American Planning Association. School of Urban Studies and Planning, Portland State University, P.O. Box 751, Portland, OR 97207-0751; http://www.planning.org/japa

Journal of Urban Affairs. College of Public Service, St. Louis University, 3750 Lindell Boulevard, St. Louis, MO 63108; http://www.udel.edu/uaa/journal.html

Land Economics. University of Wisconsin Press Journals Division, 1930 Monroe Street, Madison, WI 53711-2059; http://www.wisc.edu/wisconsinpress/journals/landecon.html

Places, A Forum of Environmental Design. http://www.places-journal.org

Planning. American Planning Association, 122 South Michigan Avenue, Chicago, IL 60603; http://www.planning.org/planning

Planning Perspectives. Routledge, 4 Park Square, Milton Park, Abingdon, Oxfordshire, OX14 4RN, UK; http://www.tandf.co.uk/journals

Preservation. National Trust for Historic Preservation, 1785 Massachusetts Ave., NW, Washington, DC 20036; http://www.nthp.org

Regional Science and Urban Economics. Elsevier, 360 Park Avenue South, New York, NY 10010-1710; http://www.elsevier.com/homepage/sae/econworld

Urban Affairs Review. Sage Publications, 2455 Teller Road, Thousand Oaks, CA 91320; http://www.sagepub.com

Urban Studies. Carfax, 4 Park Square, Milton Park, Abingdon, Oxfordshire, OX14 4RN, UK; http://www.tandf.co.uk/journals

Organizations

American Planning Association, 122 South Michigan Avenue, Chicago, IL 60603; http://www.planning.org

Association of Collegiate Schools of Planning, 6311 Mallard Trace, Tallahassee, FL 32312; http://www.acsp.org

Association of European Schools of Planning, School of Architecture, Planning and Landscape, University of Newcastle, Newcastle upon Tyne, NE17RU, UK; http://www.ncl.ac.uk/aesop

Canadian Institute of Planners, 116 Albert Street, Ottowa, ON, K1P 5G3 Canada; http://www.cip-icu.ca

European Council of Town Planners, 41 Botolph Lane, London, EC3R 8DL, UK; http://www.ceu-ectp.org

International Federation of Housing and Planning; http://www.ifhp.org

International Urban Planning and Environment Association; http://www.frw.rug.nl/upe/startkeuze.htm

Lincoln Institute of Land Policy, 113 Brattle Street, Cambridge, MA 02138-3400; http://www.lincolninst.edu

Metropolitan Area Research Corporation (MARC), 1313 5th Street SE, Suite 108, Minneapolis, MN 55414; http://www.metroresearch.org

Rocky Mountain Institute, 1739 Snowmass Creek Road, Snowmass, CO 81654-9199; http://www.rmi.org

Smart Growth America, 1200 18th Street NW, Washington, DC 20036; http://www.smartgrowthamerica.com

Sprawl Watch Clearinghouse, 1400 16th Street NW, Suite 225, Washington, DC 20036; http://www.sprawlwatch.org

Woodstock Institute, 407 S. Dearborn, Suite 550, Chicago, IL 60605; www.woodstockinst.org

COMMUNITY STUDIES

"The systematic study of communities," writes William H. Friedland, author of the *Encyclopedia of Community*'s "Community Studies" entry, "had its origins with the massive shift from rural-agrarian societies to urban-industrial, large-scale societies." As an academic discipline, community studies is fairly new. Even sociology, the field with which the subject is often aligned, only formally dates back to the nineteenth century. The publications and organizations below are representative of the types of research that have been conducted, as well as organizations and academic centers currently involved in the field of community studies.

Encyclopedia Entries

African American Communities
Asian American Communities
Cities, Inner
Community Organizing
Community Studies
Gangs
Gemeinschaft and Gesellschaft
Ghettos
Greenwich Village
Harlem
Hollywood
Jacobs, Jane
Latino Communities
Levittown
Lynd, Helen Merrell and Robert Staughton
Main Street
Redfield, Robert
Street Life
Tönnies, Ferdinand
Whyte, William Hollingsworth
Wirth, Louis

Books and Web Sites

Addams, J. (1910). *Twenty years at Hull-house*. New York: Macmillan.

Drake, S. C., & Cayton, H. (1993). *Black metropolis: A study of Negro life in a northern city*. Chicago: University of Chicago Press. (Original work published 1945)

DuBois, W. E. B. (1899). *The Philadelphia Negro*. New York: Lippincott.

DuBois, W. E. B. (1989). *The souls of black folk*. New York: Penguin. (Original work published 1902)

Foster, G., Colson, E., & Scudder, T. (Eds.). (1979). *Long-term field research in social anthropology*. New York: Academic Press.

Lebow, E. (1967). *Tally's corner: A study of Negro street-corner men*. Boston: Little, Brown.

Linkages Projects: http://eclectic.ss.uci.edu/~drwhite/linkages/linkages.html

Lynd, R. S., & Lynd, H. M. (1929). *Middletown: A study in contemporary American culture*. New York: Harcourt, Brace.

Lynd, R. S., & Lynd, H. M. (1937). *Middletown in transition: A study in cultural conflicts*. New York: Harcourt, Brace.

Neighborhoods Online: http://neighborhoodsonline.net

New American Studies Web: http://www.georgetown.edu/crossroads/asw

Osofsky, G. (1996). *Harlem: The making of a ghetto*. New York: Ivan R. Dee.

Redfield, R., & Rojas, V. (1934). *Chan Kom: A Maya village*. Carnegie Institution of Washington, Publication No. 448. Chicago: University of Chicago Press.

Roethlisberger, F. J., & Dickson, W. J. (1939). *Management and the worker: An account of the research program conducted by the Western Electric Company*. Cambridge, MA: Harvard University Press.

Stack, C. (1974). *All our kin: Strategies of survival in a black community*. New York: Harper & Row.

Suttles, G. (1968). *The social order of the slum: Ethnicity and territory in the inner city*. Chicago: University of Chicago Press.

Tönnies, F. (1940). *Fundamental concepts of sociology (Gemeinschaft und Gesellschaft)* (C. P. Loomis, Trans. and Supplements). New York: American Book Company. (Original work published 1887)

van Kemper, R., & Royce, A. (Eds.). (2002). *Chronicling cultures: Long-term field research in anthropology*. Walnut Creek, CA: Alta Mira.

Wirth, L. (1998). *The ghetto*. New Brunswick, NJ: Transaction. (Original work published 1928)

Whyte, W. F. (1955). *Street corner society: The social structure of an Italian slum*. Chicago: University of Chicago Press.

Zorbaugh, H. W. (1929). *Gold Coast and slum: A sociological study of Chicago's Near North Side*. Chicago: University of Chicago Press.

Journals

Cityscape: A Journal of Policy Development and Research. Office of Policy Development and Research, U.S. Department of Housing and Urban Development (HUD), 451 Seventh Street SW., Washington, DC 20410; http://www.huduser.org/periodicals/cityscape.html

Organizations

Center for Community Change; 1000 Wisconsin Avenue NW, Washington, DC 20007; http://www.communitychange.org

Centre for Urban and Community Studies, University of Toronto. 455 Spadina Ave., Toronto, ON, Canada M5S 2G8; http://www.urbancenter.utoronto.ca

European Community Studies Association; http://www.ecsanet.org

Institute for Community Studies, Montclair State University, Upper Montclair, NJ 07043; http://www.montclair.edu/Pages/ICS/ics.html

Institute for Local Self-Reliance (ILSR), 2425 18th Street NW, Washington DC 20009; http://www.ilsr.org

University of California, Santa Cruz Community Studies Department, 207 College Eight, Santa Cruz, CA 95064; http://communitystudies.ucsc.edu

CONFLICT AND JUSTICE

Whether it consists of two neighbors fighting over the building of a fence or nations fighting over a large strip of land, conflict has always played a role in shaping communities. Much effort on the part of governments and citizens has gone into resolving conflicts and suppressing crime, violence, and other forms of deviance. The publications and organizations listed below focus on conflicts within and between communities.

Encyclopedia Entries

Apartheid
Civil Disobedience
Collective Action
Common Law
Community Justice
Community Policing
Conflict Resolution
Conflict Theory
Crime
Deviance
Environmental Justice
Family Violence
Genocide
Hate
Human Rights
Luddism
Natural Law
Organized Crime
Prisons
Public Harassment
Social Control
Social Justice
Social Movements
Social Movements Online
Town and Gown
Town and Hinterland Conflicts
Vigilantism
Warsaw Ghetto

Books and Web Sites

Avruch, K. (1998). *Culture and conflict resolution*. Washington, DC: United States Institute of Peace Press.

Bazemore, G., & Walgrave, L. (Eds.). (1999). *Restorative juvenile justice: Repairing the harm of youth crime*. Monsey, NY: Criminal Justice Press.

Becker, H. S. (1963). *Outsiders: Studies in the sociology of deviance*. New York: Free Press.

Boren, M. E. (2001). *Student resistance: A history of the unruly subject*. New York: Routledge.

Brewer, M. B., & Miller, N. (1996). *Intergroup relations*. Ann Arbor, MI: Brooks/Cole.

Bursik, R. J., Jr., & Grasmick, H. (1993). *Neighborhoods and crime*. New York: Lexington Books.

Chalk, F., & Jonassohn, K. (1990). *The history and sociology of genocide*. New Haven, CT: Yale University Press.

Cohen, C. (1971). *Civil disobedience: Conscience, tactics, and the law*. New York: Columbia University Press.

Cohen, S. (1980). *Folk devils and moral panics: The creation of the Mods and Rockers*. Oxford, UK: Basil Blackwell.

Coser, L. (1956). *The functions of social conflict*. New York: Free Press.

Davis, M. (1999). *Ecology of fear.* New York: Vintage.

Deutsch, M., & Coleman, P. T. (Eds.). (2000). *The handbook of conflict resolution: Theory and practice.* San Francisco: Jossey-Bass.

Felson, M. (1994). *Crime in everyday life.* Thousand Oaks, CA: Pine Forge.

Gelles, R. J. (1997). *Intimate violence in families* (3d ed.). Thousand Oaks, CA: Sage.

Graham, H. D., & Gurr, T. R. (Eds.). (1969). *The history of violence in America: Historical and comparative perspectives*. New York: Frederick A. Praeger.

Ianni, F., & Reuss-Ianni, E. (1972). *A family business: Kinship and social control in organized crime*. New York: Russell Sage Foundation.

Ishay, M. R. (1997) *The human rights reader.* New York: Routledge.

Kanter, R. (1972). *Commitment and community*. Cambridge, MA: Harvard University Press.

Kelling, G. L., & Coles, C. M. (1996). *Fixing broken windows: Restoring order and reducing crime in our communities*. New York: Touchstone.

Lasswell, H., & Kaplan, A. (1950). *Power and society*. New Haven, CT: Yale University Press.

Levin, J., & McDevitt, J. (2002) *Hate crimes revisited: America's war on those who are different*. Boulder, CO: Westview.

Levinson, D. (Ed.). (2002). *Encyclopedia of crime and punishment*. Thousand Oaks, CA: Sage.

Morris, N., & Rothman, D. J. (Eds.). (1998). *The Oxford history of the prison: The practice of punishment in Western society*. New York: Oxford University Press.

Rawls, J. (1971). *A theory of justice*. Cambridge, MA: Harvard University Press.

Real Justice: http://www.realjustice.org

Reichel, P. (2002). *Comparative criminal justice systems: A topical approach* (3d ed.). Upper Saddle River, NJ: Prentice Hall.

Reiss, A. J., Jr. & Tonry, M. (Eds.). (1986). *Communities and crime.* Chicago: University of Chicago Press.

Rossi, A. (Ed.). (2001). *Caring and doing for others: Social responsibility in the domains of family, work, and community*. Chicago: University of Chicago Press.

Simmel, G. (1955). *Conflict and the web of group affiliation.* New York: Free Press.

Tarrow, S. (1998). *Power in movement: Social movements and contentious politics* (2nd ed.). Cambridge, UK: Cambridge University Press.

Thurman, Q., Zhao, J., & Giacomazzi, A. (2001). *Community policing in a community era: An introduction and exploration*. Los Angeles: Roxbury.

Walls, D. (1993). *Activist's almanac: The concerned citizen's guide to the leading advocacy organizations in America*. New York: Simon & Schuster.

Wilson. J. Q. (1975). *Thinking about crime*. New York: Basic Books.

Journals

British Journal of Criminology. The Centre for Crime and Justice Studies, in association with Oxford University Press, Great Clarendon Street, Oxford, OX2 6DP, UK; http://bjc.oupjournals.org

Canadian Journal of Criminology. Canadian Criminal Justice Association, 383 Parkdale, No. 207, Ottawa, ON, Canada K1Y 4R4; http://www.ccja-acjp.ca/en/cjc.html

Current Issues in Criminal Justice. Institute of Criminology, Faculty of Law, University of Sydney, 173-5 Phillip St, Sydney, NSW 2000, Australia; http://www.law.usyd.edu.au/~criminology/noframes/publicat/journal/journal.htm

European Journal of Criminology. Sage Publications, 6 Bonhill Street, London, EC2A 4PU, UK; http://www.sagepub.co.uk/journals/details/j0485.html

Law and Society Review. Law and Society Association, 205 Hampshire House, University of Massachusetts, 131 County Circle, Amherst, MA 01003-9257; http://www.lawandsociety.org/review.htm

Journal of Conflict Resolution. Sage Publications, 6 Bonhill Street, London, EC2A 4PU, UK; http://www.sagepub.co.uk/journals/details/j0058.html

Social Problems. Society for the Study of Social Problems, Department of Sociology, 901 McClung Tower, University of Tennessee, Knoxville, TN 37996-0490; http://www.sssp1.org/index.cfm?tsmi=26

Western Criminology Review. Western Society of Criminology; http://wcr.sonoma.edu/

Organizations

Academy of Criminal Justice Sciences (ACJS), 7319 Hanover Parkway, Suite C, Greenbelt, MD 20770; http://www.acjs.org

American Bar Association, 750 N Lake Shore Drive, Chicago, IL 60611; http://www.abanet.org/

American Society of Criminology (ASC), 1314 Kinnear Road, Columbus, OH 43212-1156; http://www.asc41.com

Amnesty International, 99-119 Rosebery Avenue, London, UK; http://www.amnesty.org

Association for Conflict Resolution, 1527 New Hampshire Avenue, Northwest, Washington, DC 20036; http://www.acresolution.org

Australian and New Zealand Society of Criminology, DCG Consulting Pty Ltd, C/- Belli Group, Level 3, 31 Pelham Street, Carlton, VIC 3053, Australia; http://www.law.ecel.uwa.edu.au/anzsoc/

British Society of Criminology, Room A1024a, The Law Department, University of East London, Longbridge Road, Dagenham, Essex, RM8 2AS, UK; http://www.britsoccrim.org

Canadian Bar Association (CBA), 500–865 Carling

Avenue, Ottawa, ON, Canada K1S 5S8; http://www.cba.org

Canadian Criminal Justice Association (CCJA), 383 Parkdale, No. 207, Ottawa, Ontario, Canada K1Y 4R4; http://www.ccja-acjp.ca/en/cjc.html

European Academy of Criminology, Milan, Italy; www.euroacademy.it

Human Rights Watch, 350 Fifth Avenue, 34th Floor, New York, NY 10118-3299; http://www.hrw.org

Law and Society Association, 205 Hampshire House, University of Massachusetts, 131 County Circle, Amherst, MA 01003-9257; http://www.lawandsociety.org

United Nations Office of the High Commissioner for Human Rights, 8-14 Avenue de la Paix, 1211 Geneva 10, Switzerland; http://193.194.138.190

CONNECTION TO PLACE

One of the basic questions about community is whether physical location—and face-to-face contact—matter. Many people, including historians as well as landscape planners and environmental activists, believe that connection to place is essential. Much discussion about community and social capital is related to cultivating local knowledge, local identify, and a sense of home. The following publications and organizations examine the importance of a strong connection to one's home region, as well as detailing ways in which this connection can be strengthened.

Encyclopedia Entries

Adolescents and Landscape
Appendix 3—Community in Popular Culture
Community, Sense of
Community Attachment
Community Satisfaction
Ecovillages
Place Identity
Residential Mobility
Villages

Books

Alexander, C., et al. (1977). *A pattern language: Towns, buildings, construction*. New York: Oxford University Press.

Allen, B., & Schlereth, T. (1991). *Sense of place: American regional cultures*. Lexington: University Press of Kentucky.

Altman, I., & Low, S. (Eds.). (1992). *Place attachment*. New York: Plenum.

Amato, J. A. (2002). *Rethinking home: A case for writing local history*. Berkeley: University of California Press.

Andruss, V., et al. (Eds.). (1990). *Home: A bioregional reader.* Santa Cruz, CA: New Society.

Berry, W. (1987). *Home economics*. San Francisco: North Point.

Cooper-Marcus, C. (1995). *House as a mirror of self: Exploring the deeper meaning of home*. Berkeley, CA: Conari.

Gallagher, W. (1993). The power of place: How our surroundings shape our thoughts, emotions, and actions. New York: Poseiden.

Hiss, T. (1990). *The experience of place*. New York: Knopf.

Kemmis, D. (1990). *Community and the politics of place.* Norman: University of Oklahoma Press.

Knopp, L. (2002). *The nature of home: A lexicon and essays*. Lincoln: University of Nebraska Press.

Lippard, L. R. (1997). *The lure of the local: Senses of place in a Multicentered society.* New York: New Press.

Proshansky, H. M., Ittelson, W. H., & Rivlin, L. G. (Eds.). (1976). *Environmental psychology: People and their physical settings*. New York: Holt, Rinehart & Winston.

Journals

Journal of Environmental Psychology. Academic Press / Elsevier; http://www.elsevier.com/locate/issn/0272-4944

Orion. Orion Society, 187 Main Street, Great Barrington, MA 01230; http://www.orionsociety.org

Places, A Forum of Environmental Design. http://www.places-journal.org

Preservation. National Trust for Historic Preservation, 1785 Massachusetts Ave., NW, Washington, DC 20036; http://www.nthp.org

Southern Living. P.O. Box 62376, Tampa, FL 33662; http://www.southernliving.com

Sunset Magazine. 80 Willow Road, Menlo Park, CA 94025; http://www.sunset.com

Utne Magazine. Editorial and Management Offices, 1624 Harmon Place, Minneapolis, MN 55403; http://www.utne.com

WI Home and Country. Women's Institute, 104 New King's Road, London, SW6 4LY, UK; http://www.csu.edu.au

Yankee. 1121 Main Street, P.O. Box 520, Dublin, NH 03444; http://www.yankeemagazine.com

Organizations

Common Ground, Gold Hill House, 21 High Street, Shaftesbury, Dorset, SP7 8JE, UK; http://www.commonground.org.uk

National Trust for Historic Preservation, 1785 Massachusetts Ave., NW, Washington, DC 20036; http://www.nthp.org

Orion Society, 187 Main Street, Great Barrington, MA 01230; http://www.orionsociety.org

Orton Family Foundation: Community Mapping Program, Orton Family Foundation, 128 Merchants Row, 2nd Floor, Rutland, VT 05701; http://www.communitymap.org

GLOBAL AND INTERNATIONAL

This section features publications and organizations about issues that transcend political boundaries. Some are universals—such as death—that affect communities around the world; others, such as festivals, are institutions that can be found in any number of different countries; and still others, such as colonialism, are processes that occur when groups interact. As the world becomes "smaller," such global issues are likely to have an ever-increasing effect on all communities.

Encyclopedia Entries

Apartheid
Artists' Colonies
Ashrams
Assimilation
Buddhism
Christianity
Cities
Cities, Medieval
Civil Disobedience
Colonialism
Communism and Socialism
Communities of Opposition
Community Currencies
Confucianism
Cultural Ecology
Culture of Poverty
Dance and Drill
Death
Democracy
Diasporas
Displaced Populations
Ecovillages
Environmental Justice
Ethnicity and Ethnic Relations
Fascism
Festivals
Food
Food Systems
Gay Communities
Genocide
Global Cities
Globalization and Globalization Theory
Glocalization
Hinduism
Horticultural Societies
Human Rights
Immigrant Communities
Imperialism
Internet in Developing Countries
Islam
Judaism
McDonaldization
Migrant Worker Communities
Millenarianism
Pastoral Societies
Pilgrimages
Plantations
Political Economy
Rebellions and Revolutions
Refugee Communities
Resettlement
Sikhism
Social Capital and Economic Development
State, The
Sustainable Development
Tourist Communities
Transnational Communities
Villages
World War II
Xenophobia

Books

Bauman, Z. (1998). *Globalization: The human consequences*. New York: Columbia University Press.

Barber, B. (1996). *Jihad vs. McWorld.* New York: Ballantine/Random House.

Bleiker, R. (2000). *Popular dissent, human agency and global politics.* Cambridge, UK: Cambridge University Press.

Boyerain, J. (2002). *Powers of diaspora.* Ann Arbor: University of Michigan Press.

Castells, M. (1996). *The information age: Economy, society and culture: Vol. 1. The rise of network society.* Oxford, UK: Blackwell.

Castells, M. (1997). *The information age: Economy, society and culture: Vol. 2. The power of identity.* Oxford, UK: Blackwell.

Castells, M. (1998). *The information age: Economy, society and culture: Vol. 3. End of millennium.* Oxford, UK: Blackwell.

Cernea, M., & McDowell, C. (Eds.). (2000). *Risks and reconstruction: Experiences of resettlers and refugees.* Washington, DC: World Bank.

Dowsett, G. W. (1996). *Practicing desire: Homosexual sex in the era of AIDS.* Stanford, CA: Stanford University Press.

Friedman, J. (1994). *Cultural identity and global process.* London: Sage.

Goody, J. (1982). *Cooking, cuisine, and class: A study in*

comparative sociology. Cambridge, UK: Cambridge University Press.

Grootaert, C., & van Bastelaer, T. (Eds.). (2002). *The role of social capital in development: An empirical assessment.* New York: Cambridge University Press.

Hardt, M., & Negri, A. (2002). *Empire*. Cambridge, MA: Harvard University Press.

Harvey, D. (1996). *Justice, nature and the geography of difference.* Oxford, UK: Basil Blackwell.

Ishay, M. R. (1997) *The human rights reader.* New York: Routledge.

Landes, R. A. (2000). *Encyclopedia of millennialism and millennial movements.* New York: Routledge.

Lewis, O. (1968). *La vida: A Puerto Rican family in the culture of poverty, San Juan and New York.* New York: Random House.

Lijphart, A. (1984). *Democracies: Patterns of majoritarian and consensus government in twenty-one countries*. New Haven, CT: Yale University Press.

Marcuse, P., & van Kempen, R. (2000). *Globalizing cities: A new spatial order.* New York: Blackwell.

Marx, K. (1977). *Karl Marx: Selected writings* (D. McLellan, Ed.). Oxford, UK: Oxford University Press.

Mumford, L. (1961). *The city in history: Its origins, its transformations, and its prospects*. New York: Harcourt, Brace & World.

Pirenne, H. (1925). *Medieval cities: Their origins and the revival of trade* (F. Halsey, Trans.). Princeton, NJ: Princeton University Press.

Portes, A., & Rumbaut, R. (2001). *Legacies*. Berkeley and Los Angeles: University of California Press.

Rappaport, R. A. (1968). *Pigs for the ancestors*. New Haven, CT: Yale University Press.

Ritzer, G. (2000). *The McDonaldization of society*. Thousand Oaks, CA: Pine Forge.

Sahlins, M. (1968). *Tribesmen*. Englewood Cliffs, NJ: Prentice Hall.

Shuman, M. H. (2000). *Going local: Creating self-reliant communities in a global age*. Armonk, NY: Routledge.

Skocpol, T. (1979). *States and social revolutions.* New York: Cambridge University Press.

Smith, V. L. (1989). *Hosts and guests: The anthropology of tourism.* Philadelphia: University of Pennsylvania Press.

Spencer, P. (1998). *The pastoral continuum*. London: Oxford University Press.

Sterba, J. P. (Ed.). (2001). *Social and political philosophy: Contemporary perspectives.* London: Routledge.

Suarez-Orozco, C., & Suarez-Orozco, M. (2001). *Children of immigration*. Cambridge, MA: Harvard University Press.

Tomlinson, J. (1999). *Globalization and culture*. Chicago: University of Chicago Press.

Totten, S., Parsons, W., & Charny, I. (Eds.). (1997). *Century of genocide: Eyewitness accounts and critical views* (Rev. ed.). New York: Garland.

United Nations High Commissioner for Refugees. (2000). *The state of the world's refugees: Fifty years of humanitarian action.* Oxford, UK: Oxford University Press.

Voll, J. (1994). *Islam: Continuity and change in the modern world.* Syracuse, NY: Syracuse University Press.

Wallerstein, I. (1974). *The modern world system: Capitalist agriculture and the origins of the European economy in the sixteenth century*. New York: Academic Press.

Warburton, D. (1998). *Community and sustainable development: Participation in the future*. London: Earthscan.

Organizations

International Forum on Globalization, 1009 General Kennedy Avenue #2, San Francisco, CA 94129; http://www.ifg.org

International Studies Association Network, 324 Social Sciences, Tucson, AZ 85721; http://www.isanet.org

Trade Regulation Organization (formerly World Trade Organization), rue de Lausanne 154, CH-1211 Geneva 21, Switzerland; http://www.gatt.org

United Nations, 1 UN Plaza, New York, NY 10017; http://www.un.org

World Federalist Association, 418 Seventh Street SE, Washington, DC 20003; http://www.wfa.org

World Health Organization, Avenue Appia 20; 1211 Geneva 27, Switzerland, http://www.who.int

World History Association, 2530 Dole Street, Sakamaki Hall A203, Honolulu, HI 96822; http://www.thewha.org

HOUSING AND HOMELESSNESS

A crucial consideration of any neighborhood, town, or nation is ensuring that its residents have adequate shelter. Developing and providing housing is a complex social and political issue. As R. Allen Hays, author of the *Encyclopedia of Community*'s "Housing" entry, writes: "The difficulties in creating housing policies that truly enhance the quality of individual and community life stem, in large part, from the complexity of the human needs that housing is intended to serve." The following list of publications and organizations focus on policies and approaches from around the world that address issues of housing and homelessness.

Encyclopedia Entries

Blockbusting
Cohousing
Community Land Trust
Condominiums
Homelessness

Housing
Housing, Affordable
Seasonal Homes
Student Housing Cooperatives
Urban Homesteading

Books and Web Sites

American News Service Archive: http://www.berkshirepublishing.com/brw/ans.asp

Bauman, J. F., Biles, R., & Szylvian, K. M. (Eds.). (2000). *From tenements to the Taylor homes: in search of an urban housing policy in twentieth-century America*. University Park: Pennsylvania State University Press.

Hays, R. A. (1995). *The federal government and urban housing: Ideology and change in public policy.* Albany: State University of New York Press.

Hooton, S. (1996). *A to Z of housing terminology*. Coventry, UK: Chartered Institute of Housing.

Mathey, K. (Ed.). (1990). *Housing policies in the socialist third world.* New York: Mansell.

McCamant, K., & Durrett, C. (2002). *Cohousing: A contemporary approach to housing ourselves.* Berkeley, CA: Ten Speed Press.

National Coalition for the Homeless. (1997). *Homelessness in America: Unabated and increasing*. Washington, DC: author.

Shidlo, G. (Ed.). (1990). *Housing policy in developing countries*. New York: Routledge

Stone, M. E. (1993). *Shelter poverty: New ideas on housing affordability.* Philadelphia: Temple University Press.

Van Vliet, W. (Ed.). (1998). *The encyclopedia of housing.* Thousand Oaks, CA: Sage.

Welfeld, I. (1988). *Where we live: A social history of American housing*. New York: Simon & Schuster.

Journals

Cityscape: A Journal of Policy Development and Research. United States Department of Housing and Urban Development, P.O. Box 23268, Washington, DC 20026-3268; http://www.huduser.org/periodicals/cityscape.html

Habitat International. Habitat International, Faculty of Architecture, Building and Planning, University of Mebourne, Victoria 3010, Australia.

Housing, Theory and Society. 11 New Fetter Lane, London, UK EC4P 4EE; www.tandf.co.uk/journals/titles/14036096.html

Housing and Society. American Association of Housing Educators, Illinois State University, Campus Box 5060, Normal, IL 61790-5060.

Housing Policy Debate. Fannie Mae Foundation, 4000 Wisconsin Avenue, NW, North Tower, Suite One, Washington, DC 20016-2804; http://www.fanniemaefoundation.org/programs/hpd.shtml

International Journal for Housing Science and Its Applications. International Association for Housing Science, P.O. Box 340254, Coral Gables, FL 33114; http://www.iahs30.com

Journal of Housing & Community Development. National Association of Housing and Redevelopment Officials (NAHRO), 630 Eye Street, NW, Washington, DC 20001; http://www.nahro.org

Journal of Housing Economics. Massachusetts Institute of Technology Center for Real Estate, Building W31-310, Cambridge, MA 02139-4307

Journal of Housing for the Elderly. National Council on Aging (NCOA), 300 D Street, SW, Suite 801, Washington, DC 20024; http://www.haworthpressinc.com/store/SampleText/J081.pdf

Journal of Housing Research. Fannie Mae Foundation, 4000 Wisconsin Avenue, NW, North Tower, Suite One, Washington, DC 20016-2804; http://www.fanniemaefoundation.org/programs/jhr.shtml

Journal of Real Estate Research. American Real Estate Society, University of North Dakota, P.O. Box 7120, Grand Forks, ND 58202-7120; http://www.aresnet.org

Land Use Law & Zoning Digest. American Planning Association, 1776 Massachusetts Ave., NW, Washington, DC 20036-1904; http://www.planning.org/lulzd/index.htm

New Urban News. P.O. Box 6515, Ithaca, NY 14851; http://www.newurbannews.com

Real Estate Economics. American Real Estate and Urban Economics Association, P.O. Box 1148, Portage, MI 49081-1148; http://www.areuea.org/publications/ree/

Recent Research Results. United States Department of Housing and Urban Development, P.O. Box 23268, Washington, DC 20026-3268; http://www.huduser.org/periodicals/rrr.html

Shelterforce. National Housing Institute, 460 Bloomfield Avenue, Suite 211, Montclair, NJ 07042-3552; http://www.nhi.org/online/index.html

Organizations

American Association of Housing Educators (AAHE); http://www.extension.iastate.edu/Pages/housing/aahelinks.html

Community Associations Institute, 225 Reinekers Lane, Suite 300, Alexandria, VA 22314; http://www.caionline.org/

European Network for Housing Research, Uppsala University, P.O. Box 785, SE-801 29 Gävle, Sweden; http://www.enhr.ibf.uu.se/index.html

Fellowship for Intentional Community, RR 1 Box 156-W, Rutledge, MO 63563-9720; http://www.ic.org/

Habitat for Humanity International, 121 Habitat St., Americus, GA 31709; http://www.habitat.org

Housing Information Gateway; http://www.colorado.edu/plan/housing-info/menu0.html

Housing Resource Guide; http://housinguk.org

International Federation for Housing and Planning, Wassenaarseweg 43, 2596 CG, The Hague, The Netherlands; http://www.ifhp.org

National Coalition for the Homeless, 1012 Fourteenth Street, NW, #600, Washington, DC 20005-3471; http://www.nationalhomeless.org/

National Housing Institute, 460 Bloomfield Avenue, Suite 211, Montclair, NJ 07042-3552; http://www.nhi.org/

National Low Income Housing Coalition (LIHIS), 1012 Fourteenth Street NW, Suite 610, Washington, DC 20005; http://www.nlihc.org

New Urbanism, 615 King Street, Suite 103, Alexandria, VA 22314; http://www.newurbanism.org

Rural Housing Service, U.S. Department of Agriculture, Room 5037, South Building, 14th Street and Independence Avenue, S.W., Washington, D.C. 20250; http://www.rurdev.usda.gov/rhs/index.html

United Nations Economic Commission for Europe, Palais des Nations, CH-1211 Geneva 10, Switzerland; http://www.unece.org

United Nations Human Settlements Programme (UN-HABITAT), P.O. Box 30030, Nairobi, Kenya; http://www.unchs.org

United Nations Population Information Network (POPIN), 2 United Nations Plaza, Rm. DC2-1950, New York, NY 10017; http://www.un.org/popin/

United States Department of Housing and Urban Development, 451 7th Street S.W., Washington, DC 20410; http://www.hud.gov

Urban Land Institute, 1025 Thomas Jefferson Street, NW, Suite 500 West, Washington, DC 20007; http://www.uli.org

INTENTIONAL COMMUNITIES

Bill Metcalf, one of the *Encyclopedia of Community*'s editors and coauthor of the main entry "Intentional Communities," defines the term as: "Five or more people, drawn from more than one family or kinship group, who have voluntarily come together for the purpose of ameliorating perceived social problems and inadequacies." Intentional communities have existed for thousands of years, but many people associate the term with phenomena from the past 200 years: the utopian societies of the nineteenth century and the kibbutzim and communes of the twentieth century. In the twenty-first century, intentional communities of all kinds exist in virtually every part of the world, and range from well-established spiritually oriented communities such as Findhorn in Scotland to more recent innovations such as ecovillages and cohousing. The following publications and organizations are dedicated to either the study of historic or contemporary intentional communities or the promotion of alternative ways of living in the modern world. Many will be useful to readers who are thinking about joining, or forming, an intentional community.

Encyclopedia Entries

Amana
Amish
Arcosanti
Ashrams
Auroville
Bruderhof
Community Land Trust
Damanhur
Ecovillages
Emissaries of Divine Light
Ephrata
Family, The
Farm, The
Findhorn Community Foundation
Fourierism
Hare Krishnas
Harmony Society
Hutterites
Intentional Communities
Intentional Communities and Children
Intentional Communities and Communal Economics
Intentional Communities and Daily Life
Intentional Communities and Environmental Sustainability
Intentional Communities and Governance
Intentional Communities and Mainstream Politics
Intentional Communities and New Religious Movements
Intentional Communities and Their Survival
Intentional Communities in Australia and New Zealand
Intentional Communities in Eastern Europe and Russia
Intentional Communities in France
Intentional Communities in Germany, Austria, and Switzerland
Intentional Communities in India
Intentional Communities in Israel—Current Movement
Intentional Communities in Israel—History
Intentional Communities in Italy, Spain, and Portugal
Intentional Communities in Japan
Intentional Communities in Latin America
Intentional Communities in Scandinavia and the Low Countries
Intentional Communities in the United Kingdom and Ireland

Intentional Communities in the United States and Canada—Current Movement
Intentional Communities in the United States and Canada—History
Monastic Communities
Moravians
Mormons
New Harmony
Oneida
Osho
Riverside Community
Shakers
Twin Oaks
Utopia
Zoar

Books

Bainbridge, W. S. (1997). *The sociology of religious movements*. New York: Routledge.

Bartkowski, F. (1989). *Feminist utopias*. Lincoln: University of Nebraska Press.

Bunker, S., et al. (Eds.). (2001). *Diggers & dreamers: The guide to communal living*. London: Diggers and Dreamers Publications.

Cohn, N. (1970). *The pursuit of the millennium: Revolutionary millenarians and mystical anarchists of the Middle Ages* (Rev. ed.). New York: Oxford University Press. (Original work published 1961)

Fellowship for Intentional Community. (2000). *Communities directory: A guide to intentional communities and cooperative living*. Rutledge, MO: Author.

Fogarty, R. (1990). *All things new: American communes and utopian movements, 1860–1914*. Chicago: University of Chicago Press.

Hagmaier, S., et al. (Eds.). (2000). *Eurotopia*. Poppau, Germany: Eurotopia.

Kanter, R. M. (1972). *Commitment and community: Communes and utopias in social perspective*. Cambridge, MA: Harvard University Press.

Knudson, B. (Ed.). (2000). *Eco-villages & communities in Australia and New Zealand*. Maleny, Australia: GEN.

Lloyd, P. (1998). *Spiritual Britain: A practical guide to today's spiritual communities, centres and sacred places*. Winkford Hill, UK: Pilgrims' Travel Guides.

Metcalf, B. (Ed.). (1996). *Shared visions, shared lives: Communal living around the globe*. Forres, UK: Findhorn Press.

Miller, T. (1998). *The quest for utopia in twentieth century America: Vol. 1. 1900–1960*. Syracuse, NY: Syracuse University Press.

Nordoff, C. (1875). *The communistic societies of the United States: From personal visit and observation*. New York: Harper and Bros.

Oved, Y. (1986). *Two hundred years of American communes*. New Brunswick, NJ: Transaction.

Pitzer, D. (1997). *America's communal utopias*. Chapel Hill: University of North Carolina Press.

Journals

Cohousing. Cohousing Network, 1504 Franklin Street, Suite 102 Oakland, CA 94612; http://www.cohousing.org/services/journal/

Communal Societies. Communal Studies Association, P.O. Box 122, Amana, Iowa 52203; http://www.swarthmore.edu/Library/peace/CSA/

Communes At Large Letter (CALL). International Communes Desk, Yad Tabenkin, Ramat Efal, Israel 52960; http://www.communa.org.il/e-call.htm

Communities. Fellowship for Intentional Community, RR 1 Box 156-W, Rutledge MO, 63563-9720; http://fic.ic.org/cmag/

Utopian Studies. Society for Utopian Studies, Department of Political Science, University of Missouri-St. Louis, 8001 Natural Bridge Road, St. Louis, MO 63121-4499; http://www.utoronto.ca/utopia/journal/

Organizations

Cohousing Network. Promotes and encourages cohousing communities in North America through networking, information, and publishing the quarterly magazine *Cohousing*. 1504 Franklin Street, Suite 102, Oakland, CA 94612; http://www.cohousing.org

Communal Studies Association (CSA). Scholarly organization based in the United States. The CSA holds an annual conference at a historical commune site somewhere in the United States, and publishes the journal *Communal Societies*. P.O. Box 122, Amana, IA 52203; http://www.swarthmore.edu/Library/peace/CSA/

Diggers & Dreamers. Promotes intentional communities in the United Kingdom and around the globe. Edge of Time Ltd., BCM Edge, London, WC1N 3XX, UK; http://www.diggersanddreamers.org.uk

Federation of Egalitarian Communities (FEC). A mutual support network of a dozen North American intentional communities. http://www.thefec.org

Fellowship for Intentional Community (FIC). The FIC serves communities and interested people in North America with information and networking. RR 1 Box 156-W, Rutledge, MO 63563-9720; http://www.ic.org

Global Ecovillage Network (GEN). GEN's main purpose is to support and encourage the evolution of sustainable settlements on all continents. http://gen.ecovillage.org/

International Communal Studies Association (ICSA). Headquartered in Israel, the ICSA includes people from intentional communities and those interested in studying historical and contemporary communal groups internationally. Yad Tabenkin, Ramat Efal, 52960 Israel; http://www.ic.org/icsa

Living Routes—Ecovillage Educational Consortium. This organization, based in Massachusetts, facilitates university students undertaking periods of live-in, accredited education within ecovillages in Europe, India, and the United States. 85 Baker Road, Shutesbury, MA 01072-9703; http://www.livingroutes.org

Society for Utopian Studies (SUS). The SUS is for people from around the globe who are interested in utopianism in literature and psychology, as well as how utopianism is implemented within intentional communities. Department of Political Science, University of Missouri–St. Louis, 8001 Natural Bridge Road, St. Louis, MO 63121-4499; http://www.utoronto.ca/utopia/

INTERNET AND CYBERCOMMUNITIES

The rise of the Internet and online communities has forced the world to reconsider traditional definitions of "community." The degree to which these new technologies either promote or endanger the spirit of community is a much-debated topic. The Internet provides people around the world with easier access to a vast amount of information, as well as the ability to communicate with friends, relatives, and even complete strangers, who live anywhere from the house next door to the other side of the planet. The following publications and organizations examine the development and ramifications of these new technologies.

Encyclopedia Entries

Avatar Communities
Blogs
Communications Technologies
Community Informatics and Development
Computers and Knowledge Sharing
Cybercafes
Cyberdating
Cybersocieties
Cyborg Communities
Digital Divide
Electronic Democracy
Electronic Government and Civics
E-Mail
Glocalization
Information Communities
Instant Messaging
Internet, Domestic Life and
Internet, Effects of
Internet, Social Psychology of
Internet, Survey Research About
Internet, Teen Use of
Internet, Time Use of
Internet in Developing Countries
Internet in East Asia
Internet in Europe
Newsgroups and E-Mail Lists
Online Communities, African American
Online Communities, Communication in
Online Communities, Computerized Tools for
Online Communities, Diasporic
Online Communities, Game-Playing
Online Communities, History of
Online Communities, Religious
Online Communities, Scholarly
Online Communities, Youth
Online Communities of Learning
Telecommuting
Virtual Communities
Virtual Communities, Building
Wired Communities

Books and Web Sites

Abramson, M. A., Means, G. E. (Eds.). (2001). *E-government 2001*. PricewaterhouseCoopers Endowment Series on the Business of Government. Lanham, MD: Rowman & Littlefield.

Arms, W. Y. (2000). *Digital libraries*. Cambridge, MA: MIT Press.

Blood, R. (2002) *The weblog handbook: Practical advice on creating and maintaining your blog*. Cambridge, MA: Perseus.

Brown, B., Green, N., & Harper, R. (Eds.). (2002). *Wireless world*. London: Springer-Verlag.

Brown, J. S., & Duguid, P. (2000). *The social life of information*. Boston: Harvard Business School Press.

Information Society Highway: http://europa.eu.int/information_society/eeurope/index_en.htm

Jacko, J. & A. Sears (Eds.). (2002). *The human-computer interaction handbook*. Mahwah, NJ: Lawrence Erlbaum.

Kamarck, E., & Nye, J. (Eds.). (2002). *Governance.com: Democracy in the information age*. Washington, DC: Brookings Institution Press.

Katz, J. E., & Rice, R. E. (2002). *Social consequences of Internet use: Access, involvement, and interaction*. Cambridge, MA: MIT Press.

Loader, B. D. (Ed.). (1998). *The cyberspace divide: Equality, agency, and policy in the information society*. London: Routledge.

Monge, P. R., & Contractor, N. (2003). *Theories of communication networks*. New York: Oxford University Press.

Munro, A., Höök, K., & Benyon, D. (Eds.). (1999). *Social navigation in information space.* Berlin, Germany: Springer-Verlag.

Nelson, A., & Tu, T. L. N., with Hines, A. H. (Eds.). (2001). *Technicolor: Race, technology, and everyday life.* New York: New York University Press

Norris, P. (2001). *Digital divide? Civic engagement, information poverty and the Internet in democratic societies.* Cambridge, UK: Cambridge University Press.

Online Gaming League: http://www.worldogl.com/main.php

Online Gaming Network: http://www.ogaming.com/

Rheingold, H. (2000). *The virtual community: Homesteading on the electronic frontier* (Rev. ed.). Boston: MIT Press.

Rudestan, K. E., & Schoenholtz-Read, J. (Eds.). (2002). *Handbook of online learning: Innovations in higher education and corporate training.* Thousand Oaks, CA: Sage.

Schroeder, R. (Ed.). (2002). *The social life of avatars.* New York: Springer Verlag.

Warschauer, M. (2003). *Technology and social inclusion: Rethinking the digital divide.* Cambridge, MA: MIT Press.

Wellman, B. (Ed.). (1999). *Networks in the global village.* Boulder, CO: Westview.

Wellman, B., & Haythornthwaite, C. (Eds.). (2002). *The Internet in everyday life.* Oxford, UK: Basil Blackwell.

Zukowski, A., & Babin, P. (2002). *The gospel in cyberspace: Nurturing faith in the Internet age.* Chicago: Loyola Press.

Journals

Behavior and Information Technology. Taylor and Francis Group, 11 New Fetter Lane, London, EC4P 4EE, UK; www.tandf.co.uk/journals/tf/0144929X.html

Communication Research. Sage Publications, 2455 Teller Road, Thousand Oaks, CA 91320; www.sagepub.com/journal.aspx?pid=191

Fast Company: http://www.fastcompany.com

First Monday. Peer Reviewed Journal on the Internet; www.firstmonday.dk

Human Computer Interaction. Lawrence Erlbaum Associates, 10 Industrial Avenue, Mahwah, NJ 07430–2262; http://hci-journal.com

Information, Communication and Society. Routledge, 11 New Fetter Lane, London, EC4P 4EE, UK; http://www.infosoc.co.uk

Interacting with Computers, Elsevier, P.O. Box 945, New York, NY 10159-0945; http://www.elsevier.nl/inca/publications/store/5/2/5/4/4/5/

IT & Society. Stanford Institute for the Quantitative Study of Society, Encina Hall, West, Room 104, Stanford University, Stanford, CA 94305-6048; http://www.itandsociety.org

Journal of the American Society for Information Science and Technology, 1320 Fenwick Lane, Suite 510, Silver Spring, MD 20910; http://www.asis.org/Publications/JASIS/jasis.html

Journal of Computer Mediated Communication. Annenberg School for Communication, University of Southern California, 3502 Watt Way, Los Angeles, CA 90089-0281; http://www.ascusc.org/jcmc/

Journal of Broadcasting and Electronic Media. Broadcast Education Association, 1771 N Street, N.W., Washington, DC 20036-2891; http://www.beaweb.org

New Media & Society. Sage Publications, 6 Bonhill Street, London, EC2A 4PU, UK; http://www.sagepub.co.uk/ejournals/ejournals.htm

Social Science Computer Review. Sage Publications, 6 Bonhill Street, London, EC2A 4PU, UK; http://hcl.chass.ncsu.edu/sscore/sscore.htm

Wired: http://www.wired.com

Organizations

American Sociological Association Section on Communication and Information Technologies, American Sociological Association, 1307 New York, Avenue, NW, Suite 700, Washington, DC 20005; http://www.princeton.edu/~soccomp

Association of Internet Researchers; http://aoir.org

Center for Media Education. 2120 L Street, NW, Suite 200, Washington, DC 20037; http://www.cme.org

Media Ecology Association; http://www.media-ecology.org

National Telecommunications and Information Administration, United States Department of Commerce, 1401 Constitution Ave. N.W., Washington, DC 20230; http://www.ntia.doc.gov

Pew Internet & American Life Project, 1100 Connecticut Avenue, NW, Suite 710, Washington, DC 20036; http://www.pewinternet.org

SIGCHI (Special Interest Group—Computer-Human Interaction), P.O. Box 11315, New York, NY 10286-1315; http://sigchi.org/

POLITICS AND GOVERNMENT

Political leaders and institutions can have profound effects on shaping the future of a community. The laws and other regulations issued by the government determine many aspects of community life, from the development of land to the definition and handling of deviance. The following publications and organizations examine types of government, civic participation, community organizing, and popular movements, as well as exploring the relationship between governments and citizens.

Encyclopedia Entries

Alinsky, Saul
Anarchism
Boosterism
Citizen Participation and Training
Citizenship
Civil Disobedience
Civil Society
Communism and Socialism
Decentralization
Democracy
Electronic Democracy
Electronic Government and Civics
European Community
Fascism
Grassroots Leadership
Human Rights
Imperialism
Interest Groups
Land Use and Zoning
Leadership
Liberalism
Libertarianism
Local Politics
Moses, Robert
National and Community Service
National Community
Patriotism
Polis
Political Economy
Populism
Pressure Groups
Progressive Era
Public Aid
Public Libraries
Public Opinion
Social Services
State, The
Tocqueville, Alexis de
Town Meetings
Urban Renewal

Books and Web Sites

Adorno, T. W., Frenkel-Brunswik, E. Levinson, D., & Sanford, R. N. (1950). *The authoritarian personality*. New York: Harper & Row.

Ainsworth, S. (2002). *Analyzing interest groups: Group influence on people and policies*. New York: W. W. Norton.

American News Service Archive: http://www.berkshirepublishing.com/brw/ans.asp

Anderson, C. (Ed.). (1973). *Thoreau's vision: The major essays*. Englewood Cliffs, NJ: Prentice Hall.

Anderson, D., & Cornfield, M. (2003). *The civic web.* Oxford, UK: Rowman & Littlefield.

Aristotle. (1984). *The politics* (C. Lord, Trans.). Chicago: University of Chicago Press.

Barber, B. (1984). *Strong democracy: Participatory politics for a new age.* Berkeley: University of California Press.

Bellah, R. N., Madsen, R., Sullivan, W. M., Swidler, A., & Tipton, S. M. (1991). *The good society.* New York: Vintage.

Bleiker, R. (2000). *Popular dissent, human agency and global politics.* Cambridge, UK: Cambridge University Press.

Burns, J. M. (1978). *Leadership*. New York: Harper & Row.

Caro, R. (1975). *The power broker.* New York: Random House.

Cohen, C. (1971). *Civil disobedience: Conscience, tactics, and the law*. New York: Columbia University Press.

Cohen, J., & Rogers, J. (1995). *Associations and democracy*. London: Verso.

Dahl, R. A. (1989). *Democracy and its critics*. New Haven, CT: Yale University Press.

Eisenstadt, S. (1973). *Tradition, change and modernity*. New York: John Wiley.

Eisner, M. A. (2000). *Regulatory politics in transition* (Rev. ed.). Baltimore: Johns Hopkins University Press.

Elazar, D. J. (1962). *The American partnership: Intergovernmental cooperation in the nineteenth-century United States*. Chicago: University of Chicago Press.

Etzioni, A. (1993). *The spirit of community.* New York: Touchstone.

Fischer, L. (1983). *The essential Gandhi: His life, work, and ideas: An anthology*. New York: Vintage.

Fowler, R. B. (1991). *The dance with community: The contemporary debate in American political thought.* Lawrence: University Press of Kansas.

Frazer, E., & Lacey, N. (1993). *The politics of community: A feminist critique of the liberal-communitarian debate.* Toronto, Canada: University of Toronto Press.

Gandhi, M. (1987). *The moral and political writings of Mahatma Gandhi* (R. Iyer, Ed.). Oxford, UK: Oxford University Press.

Goldman, E. (1931). *Living my life.* New York: Alfred A. Knopf.

Gutmann, A., & Thompson, D. (1996). *Democracy and disagreement*. Cambridge, MA: Harvard University Press.

Hobbes, T. (1968). *Leviathan*. Harmondsworth, UK: Penguin.

Hofstadter, R. (1962). *Anti-intellectualism in American life.* New York: Vintage.

Judd, D. R., & Swanstrom, T. (2002). *City politics: Private power and public policy* (3d ed.). New York: Longman.

Kamarck, E., & Nye, J. (Eds.). (2002). *Governance.com: Democracy in the information age.* Washington, DC: Brookings Institution Press.

Kropotkin, P. (1987). *Mutual aid: A factor of evolution.*

London: Freedom Press.
Lijphart, A. (1984). *Democracies: Patterns of majoritarian and consensus government in twenty-one countries*. New Haven, CT: Yale University Press.
Lindholm, C. (1990). *Charisma*. Cambridge, MA: Blackwell.
Locke, J. (1960). *Two treatises of government.* London: New English Library.
Margolis, M., & Resnick, D. (2000). *Politics as usual: The cyberspace "revolution."* Thousand Oaks, CA: Sage.
Marx, K. (1977). *Karl Marx: Selected writings* (D. McLellan, Ed.). Oxford, UK: Oxford University Press.
Mill, J. S. (1861). *Considerations on representative government*. London: Parker, Son, & Bourn.
Murray, C. (1997). *What it means to be a libertarian.* New York: Broadway Books.
Murray, O., & Price, S. (Eds.). (1990). *The Greek city: From Homer to Alexander.* Oxford, UK: Clarendon.
Norris, P. (2001). *Digital divide: Civic engagement, information poverty, and the Internet worldwide*. Cambridge, UK: Cambridge University Press.
Novak, M. (1978). *The spirit of democratic capitalism.* New York: Simon & Schuster.
Panebianco, A. (1988). *Political parties: Organization and power*. New York: Cambridge University Press.
Plato. (1968). *The republic* (A. Bloom, Trans.). New York: Basic Books.
Putnam, R. D. (2000). *Bowling alone: The collapse and revival of American community*. New York: Simon & Schuster.
Rawls, J. (1971). *A theory of justice*. Cambridge, MA: Harvard University Press.
Ross, B., & Levine, M. (2000). *Urban politics: Power in metropolitan America* (6th ed.). Itasca, IL: F. E. Peacock.
Rousseau, J.-J. (1968). *The social contract.* Harmondsworth, UK: Penguin. (Original work published 1762)
Shils, E. (1965). *Center and periphery*. Chicago: University of Chicago Press.
Shklar, J. N. (1998). *Political thought & political thinkers.* (S. Hoffman, Ed.). Chicago: University of Chicago Press.
Sterba, J. P. (Ed.). (2001). *Social and political philosophy: Contemporary perspectives.* London: Routledge.
Thoreau, H. D. (1992). *Walden; and resistance to civil government.* New York: W. W. Norton.
Tocqueville, A. de (1990). *Democracy in America*. New York: Vintage. (Original work published 1835 and 1840)
Tolstoi, L. (1984). *The kingdom of God is within you*. (C. Garnett, Trans.). Lincoln: University of Nebraska Press.
van Maurik, J. (2001). *Writers on leadership*. London: Penguin.
Verba, S., Schlozman, K. L., & Brady, H. E. (1995). *Voice and equality: Civic voluntarism in American politics*. Cambridge, MA: Harvard University Press.
Voltaire. (1978). *The portable Voltaire*. New York: Penguin.
Weber, M. (1946). *From Max Weber: Essays in sociology*. New York: Oxford University Press.
Willner, A. (1984). *The spellbinders: Charismatic political leadership*. New Haven, CT: Yale University Press.
Woodward, C. V. (1963). *Tom Watson: Agrarian rebel.* New York: Oxford University Press. (Original work published 1938)
Zimmerman, J. F. (1999). *The New England town meeting: Democracy in action*. Westport, CT: Praeger.

Journals

Academy of Management Review, Academy of Management, P.O. Box 3020, Briarcliff Manor, NY 10510-8020; http://www.aom.pace.edu/amr/

Administrative Science Quarterly. Graduate School of Business and Public Administration, Cornell University, Ithaca, NY 14850-1265; http://www.johnson.cornell.edu/asq/

American Review of Public Administration. Sage Publications, 6 Bonhill Street, London, EC2A 4PU, UK; http://www.sagepub.co.uk/journals/details/j0212.html

Environment and Planning C: Government and Policy. Pion Ltd., 207 Brondesbury Park, London, NW2 5JN, UK; http://www.envplan.com/epc/epc_current.html

Governing. 1100 Connecticut Ave. N.W., Suite 1300, Washington, DC 20036; http://governing.com

Journal of Policy Analysis and Management. Association for Public Policy Analysis and Management, P.O. Box 18766, Washington, DC 20036-8766; http://www.appam.org

Journal of Public Administration Research and Theory. Oxford University Press, Great Clarendon Street, Oxford, OX2 6DP, UK; http://www3.oup.co.uk/jopart

Nation's Cities Weekly. National League of Cities, 1301 Pennsylvania Avenue NW, Suite 550, Washington, DC 20004; http://www.nlc.org/nlc_org/site/newsroom/nations_cities_weekly/index.cfm

Public Administration. American Society for Public Administration, 1120 G Street, Suite 700, Washington, DC 20005; http://www.aspanet.org

Public Administration Review. American Society for Public Administration, 1120 G Street, Suite 700, Washington, DC; 20005; http://www.aspanet.org

Review of Public Personnel Administration. Sage Publications, 6 Bonhill Street, London, EC2A 4PU, UK; www.sagepub.co.uk/journals/details/j0421.html

Sage Urban Studies Abstracts. Sage Publications, 6 Bonhill Street, London, EC2A 4PU, UK; http://www.sagepub.co.uk/journals/details/j0105.html

Urban Affairs Review. Sage Publications, 6 Bonhill Street, London, EC2A 4PU, UK; http://www.sagepub.co.uk/journals/details/j0095.html

Organizations

Communitarian Network, 2130 H Street, NW, Suite 703, Washington, DC 20052; http://www.gwu.edu/~ccps

International City/County Management Association, 777 North Capitol Street, NE, Suite 500, Washington, DC 20002; http://www.icma.org

National Association of Schools of Public Affairs and Administration, 1120 G Street NW, Suite 730, Washington, DC 20005; http://www.naspaa.org

Public Administration Training Association (PATA), Birutes str. 56, Vilnius 2600, Lithuania; http://www.fmmc.lt/vala/eng

Public Management Research Association; http://bush.tamu.edu/research/cpg/pmra

Saguro Seminar, Taubman Center 364, Kennedy School of Government, Harvard University, 79 JFK Street, Cambridge, MA 02138; http://www.ksg.harvard.edu/saguaro/

RACE AND ETHNICITY

Race and ethnicity play an important role in both self-identity and community identity. Ignorance and prejudice over race and ethnicity have caused many problems throughout human history, but group identity has resulted in strong communities and the empowerment of racial and ethnic minorities. The following publications and organizations are committed to the study of identity and relations, and the promotion of cultural understanding.

Encyclopedia Entries

African American Communities
African Americans in Suburbia
Apartheid
Asian American Communities
Assimilation
Blockbusting
Chinatowns
Diasporas
Ethnicity and Ethnic Relations
Eugenics
Genocide
Ghetto
Harlem
Human Rights
Immigrant Communities
Latino Communities
Little Italies
Lower East Side
Multiculturalism
Native American Communities
Race and Racism
Shtetls
Social Darwinism
Sociolinguistics
Transnational Communities
Xenophobia

Books and Web Sites

Bannister, R. C. (1979). *Social Darwinism: Science and myth.* Philadelphia: Temple University Press.

Barth, F. (Ed.). (1969). *Ethnic groups and boundaries: The social organization of cultural difference.* Oslo: Norwegian University Press.

Basch, L., Glick-Schiller, N., & Blanc-Szanton, C. (1994). *Nations unbound: Transnational projects, postcolonial predicaments and deterritorialized nation states.* Sydney, Australia: Gordon & Breach.

Blount, B. G. (1995). *Language, culture, and society: A book of readings, second edition.* Prospect Heights, IL: Waveland.

Boyerain, J. (2002). *Powers of diaspora.* Ann Arbor: University of Michigan Press.

Champagne, D. (Ed.). (1999). *Contemporary Native American cultural issues.* Walnut Creek, CA: AltaMira.

Du Bois, W. E. B. (1899). *The Philadelphia Negro.* New York: Lippincott.

Ethnic NewsWatch: http://enw.softlineweb.com

Gans, H. (1962). *The urban villagers.* New York: Free Press.

Gellner, E. (1983). *Nations and nationalism.* Ithaca, NY: Cornell University Press.

Gordon, M. M. (1964). *Assimilation in American life: The role of race, religion and national origins.* New York: Oxford University Press.

Hall, S., & P. DuGay (Eds.). (1996). *Questions of cultural identity.* London: Sage.

Ignatieff, M. (1997). *The warrior's honor: Ethnic war and the modern conscience.* New York: Henry Holt.

Levinson, D. (Gen. Ed.). (1991–1996). *Encyclopedia of world cultures* (10 vols.). Boston and New York: G. K. Hall/Macmillan.

Levinson, D. (1998). *Ethnic groups worldwide.* Phoenix, AZ: Oryx.

Levinson, D., & Ember, M. (Eds.). (1997). *American immigrant cultures: Builders of a nation* (2 vols.). New York: Macmillan.

Lynn, R. (2001). *Eugenics: A reassessment.* Westport, CT: Praeger.

Portes, A., & Rumbaut, R. (1990). *Immigrant America: A portrait.* Berkeley and Los Angeles: University of California Press.

Pozzetta, G. (Ed.). (1991). *Emigration and immigration.* New York: Garland.

Takaki, R. (1989). *Strangers from a different shore: A history of Asian Americans.* New York: Penguin.

Worden, N. (2000). *The making of modern South Africa: Conquest, segregation and apartheid* (3d ed.). Oxford, UK, and Malden, MA: Blackwell.

WWW Virtual Library on Migration and Ethnic Relations: http://www.ercomer.org.

Journals

Canadian Ethnic Studies Journal. Canadian Ethnic Studies, c/o Department of History, University of Calgary, 2500 University Drive N.W., Calgary, AB T2N 1N4 Canada; http://www.ss.ucalgary.ca/ces/

Ethnic and Racial Studies. Taylor & Francis, 11 New Fetter Lane, London, EC4P 4EE, UK; http://www.tandf.co.uk/journals/routledge/01419870.html

Ethnicities. Sage Publications, 6 Bonhill Street, London, EC2A 4PU, UK; htttp://www.sagepub.co.uk/journals/details/j0338.html

International Migration Review. Center for Migration Studies of New York, Inc., 209 Flagg Place, Staten Island, NY 10304; http://www.jstor.org/journals/cmigrations.html

Journal of American Ethnic History. Transaction Publishers, 390 Campus Drive, Somerset, NJ 07830; http://www.transactionpub.com/cgibin/transactionpublishers.storefront

Journal on Ethnopolitics and Minority Issues in Europe (JEMIE). The European Centre for Minority Issues, Schiffbrücke 12, D, 24939 Flensburg, Germany; http://www.ecmi.de/jemie/

Multicultural Review. Greenwood Publishing Group, Inc, 88 Post Road West, Westport, CT 06881; http://www.mcreview.com

Race and Class. Sage Publications, 6 Bonhill Street, London, EC2A 4PU, UK; http://www.sagepub.co.uk/journals/details/j0320.html

STANDARDS, The International Journal of Multicultural Studies. Stanford University and the University of Colorado; http://www.colorado.edu/journals/standards/

Organizations

American Sociology Association Section on Racial and Ethnic Minorities; http://www.asanet.org/sectionrem/

Balch Institute for Ethnic Studies, The Historical Society of Pennsylvania, 1300 Locust Street, Philadelphia, PA 19107; http://www.balchinstitute.org

Centre for European Migration and Ethnic Studies; http://www.cemes.org

Centre for Research in Race and Ethnic Relations, CRER at the University of Warwick, Coventry, CV4 7AL, UK; http://www.warwick.ac.uk/fac/soc/CRER_RC/

Cultural Survival, 215 Prospect Street, Cambridge, MA 02139; http://www.culturalsurvival.org/home/index.cfm

Institute of Migration and Ethnic Studies, Universiteit van Amsterdam, Rokin 84 1012KX, Amsterdam, Netherlands; http://www.pscw.uva.nl/imes

National Association for Ethnic Studies, College of Arts and Sciences, Arizona State University, 4701 West Thunderbird Road MC3051, Glendale, AZ 85306-4908; http://www.ethnicstudies.org

RELIGION

Much like race and ethnicity, religion has traditionally played an important role both in shaping one's sense of self and in forging connections among a group of people. For many people, churches, synagogues, mosques, and other places of worship are regular gathering places, where they can find both physical and spiritual community. The following publications and organizations examine the role that religion plays in the lives of individuals and in the lives of their communities.

Encyclopedia Entries

Amana
Amish
Ashrams
Auroville
Beguine Communities
Bruderhof
Buddhism
Calvin, John
Christianity
Confucianism
Congregations, Religious
Cooperative Parish Ministries
Cults
Damanhur
Emissaries of Divine Light
Faith Communities
Hare Krishnas
Harmony Society
Hinduism
Hutterites
Initiation Rites
Intentional Communities and New Religious Movements
Islam
Jerusalem
Judaism
Millenarianism
Monastic Communities
Moravians
Mormons
Oneida
Pilgrimages
Puritans
Quakers
Religion and Civil Society
Rituals
Sacred Places
Scientology
Shakers
Shtetls
Sikhism
Zoar

Books and Web Sites

Ammerman, N., Carroll, J. W., Dudley, C. S., Eiesland, N. L., McKinney, W., Schreiter, R. L., et al. (1998). *Studying congregations: A new handbook*. Nashville, TN: Abingdon.

Becker, G. (1997). *Disrupted lives: How people create meaning in a chaotic world*. Berkeley and Los Angeles: University of California Press.

Coleman, S., & Elsner, J. (1995). *Pilgrimages, past and present: Sacred travel and sacred space in the world religions*. London: British Museum Press.

Dawson, L. L. (1998). *Comprehending cults: The sociology of new religious movements*. Toronto, Canada: Oxford University Press.

Dulles, A. (1987). *Models of the church* (Expanded ed.). New York: Doubleday.

Durkheim, É. (1965). *The elementary forms of religious life*. New York: Free Press. (Original work published 1915)

Hartford Institute for Religion Research. (2000). *The national congregations study*. Retrieved from http://hirr.hartsem.edu/org/faith_congregations_research_ncs.html

Johnston, W. M. (Ed.). (2000). *Encyclopedia of monasticism*. Chicago: Fitzroy Dearborn.

Juergensmeyer, M. (1993). *The new cold war: Religious nationalism confronts the secular state*. Berkeley and Los Angeles: University of California Press.

Landes, R. A. (2000). *Encyclopedia of millennialism and millennial movements*. New York: Routledge.

Mandaville, P. (2001). *Transnational Muslim politics: Reimagining the umma*. New York: Routledge.

Park, C. C. (1994). *Sacred worlds: An introduction to geography and religion*. New York: Routledge.

Turner, V. (1969). *The ritual process: Structure and anti-structure*. Chicago: Aldine.

Van Gennep, A. (1960). *The rites of passage*. Chicago: University of Chicago Press.

Weber, M. (1963). *Sociology of religion*. Boston: Beacon. (Original work published 1922)

Journals

Journal of the American Academy of Religion. American Academy of Religion, 825 Houston Mill Rd. NE, Suite 300, Atlanta, GA 30329-4246; http://www3.oup.co.uk/jaarel/

Journal of Applied Missiology. Missions Department, Abilene Christian University, Abilene, TX 79699; http://www.bible.acu.edu/missions/page.asp?ID=272

Journal of Religion and Society. Center for the Study of Religion & Society, Creighton University, Omaha, NE 68178; http://www.creighton.edu/JRS/

Journal for the Scientific Study of Religion. Society for Scientific Study of Religion, Alfred University, Division of Social Sciences, Saxon Drive, Alfred, NY 14802; http://las.alfred.edu/~soc/SSSR/

Public Theology. Center for Public Theology, P.O. Box 676, Gig Harbor, WA 98335; http://www.pubtheo.com/

Organizations

American Academy of Religion, 825 Houston Mill Rd. NE, Suite 300, Atlanta, GA 30329-4246; http://www.aarweb.org

American Anthropological Association, 4350 North Fairfax Drive, Suite 640, Arlington, VA 22203-1620; http://www.aaanet.org

American Sociological Association, 1307 New York Avenue, Northwest, Suite 700, Washington, DC 20005; http://www.asanet.org

Communal Studies Association, P.O. Box 122, Amana, IA 52203; http://www.swarthmore.edu/Library/peace/CSA/

Society for the Scientific Study of Religion, Alfred University, Division of Social Sciences, Saxon Drive, Alfred, NY 14802; http://las.alfred.edu/~soc/SSSR/

RURAL LIFE AND STUDIES

Rural communities face many of the same problems as their urban counterparts, but often in different degrees. In addition, there are a host of issues unique to rural life. Rural sociology and other aspects of rural studies seek to break down the stereotypes associated with rural communities and to understand the similarities and differences in the challenges they face and the strategies they use in order to be successful. The following publications and organizations are representative of the work currently being done in this field of study.

Encyclopedia Entries

Agrarian Communities
Agrarian Myth
Agricultural Scale and Community Quality
Amish
Appalachia
Cattle Towns
Civic Agriculture
County Fairs
Ecovillages
English Parishes
Homesteading
Horticultural Societies
Out-Migration of Youth
Pastoral Societies
Ranching Communities
Rural Community Development

Rural Poverty and Family Well-Being
Town and Hinterland Conflicts
Transporation, Rural

Books

Adams, J. (1994). *The transformation of rural life: Southern Illinois 1890–1990.* Chapel Hill: University of North Carolina Press.

Allen, J. C., & Dillman, D. A. (1994). *Against all odds: Rural community in the Information Age.* Boulder, CO: Westview.

Barlett, P. F. (1993). *American dreams, rural realities: Family farms in crisis.* Chapel Hill: University of North Carolina Press.

Bates, D. (2001). *Human adaptive strategies.* Boston: Allyn & Bacon.

Beaulieu, L. J., & Mulkey, D. (Eds.). (1995). *Investing in people: The human capital needs of rural America.* Boulder, CO: Westview.

Bell, M. M. (1994). *Childerley: Nature and morality in a country village.* Chicago: University of Chicago Press.

Bennett, J. W. (1969). *Northern plainsmen: Adaptive strategy and agrarian life.* Arlington Heights, IL: AHM.

Brown, D. L., & Swanson, L. E. (Eds.). (2003). *Challenges for rural America in the twenty first century.* State College: Pennsylvania State University Press.

Buttel, F. H., & Newby, H. (Eds.). (1980). *The rural sociology of advanced societies.* Montclair, NJ: Allanheld, Osmun.

Castle, E. N. (Ed.). (1995). *The changing American countryside: Rural people and places.* Lawrence: University Press of Kansas.

Cloke, P., Marsden, T., & Mooney, P. (Eds.). (2003). *Handbook of rural studies.* London: Sage.

Davidson, O. G. (1996). *Broken heartland: The rise of America's rural ghetto* (Expanded ed.). Iowa City: University of Iowa Press.

Duncan, C. M. (Ed.). (1999). *Worlds apart: Why poverty persists in rural America.* New Haven, CT: Yale University Press.

Dykstra, R. R. (1968). *The cattle towns.* New York: Knopf.

Elder, G. H., Jr., & Conger, R. D. (2000). *Children of the Land: Adversity and success in rural America.* Chicago: University of Chicago Press.

Ellis, F. (1988). *Peasant economics.* Cambridge, UK: Cambridge University Press.

Erikson, K. T. (1976). *Everything in its path: Destruction of community in the Buffalo Creek flood.* New York: Simon & Schuster.

Fitchen, J. M. (1991). *Endangered spaces, enduring places.* Boulder, CO: Westview.

Flora, C. B., Flora, J. L., Spears, J. D., & Swanson, L. E. (1992). *Rural communities: Legacy & change.* Boulder, CO: Westview.

Goldschmidt, W. R. (1978). *As you sow: Three studies in the social consequences of agribusiness.* Montclair, NJ: Allanheld, Osmun. (Original work published 1942)

Haney, W. G., & Knowles, J. B. (Eds.). (1988). *Women and farming: Changing roles, changing structures.* Boulder, CO: Westview.

Hine, R. V. (1980). *Community on the American frontier: Separate but not alone.* Norman: University of Oklahoma Press.

Hummon, D. M. (1990). *Commonplaces: Community ideology and identity in American culture.* Albany: State University of New York Press.

Lobao, L. M. (1990). *Locality and inequality: Farm and industry structure and economic conditions.* Albany: State University of New York Press.

Lyson, T. A. & Falk, W. W. (Eds.). (1993). *Forgotten places: Uneven development in rural America.* Lawrence: University Press of Kansas.

Nam, C. B., Serow, W. J., & Sly, D. F. (1990). *International handbook on internal migration.* New York: Greenwood.

Redfield, R. (1958). *The primitive world and its transformations.* Ithaca, NY: Cornell University Press.

Salamon, S. (1992). *Prairie patrimony: Family, farming, and community in the Midwest.* Chapel Hill: University of North Carolina Press.

Salamon, S. (2003). *Newcomers to old towns: Suburbanization of the heartland.* Chicago: University of Chicago Press.

Smith, P. (1966). *As a city upon a hill: The town in American history.* New York: Knopf.

Stack, C. (1996). *Call to home: African Americans reclaim the rural South.* New York: Basic Books.

Wilkinson, K. P. (1991). *The community in rural America.* New York: Greenwood.

Journals

Agricultural History. Agricultural History Society; http://www.ucpress.edu/journals/ah/index.htm

Agriculture and Human Values. Agriculture, Food, and Human Values Society, P.O. Box 14938, Gainesville, FL 32604; http://web.archive.org/web/20011201132536/http://web.clas.ufl.edu/users/rhaynes/afhvs/

Culture and Agriculture. Culture and Agriculture Section of the American Anthropological Association; http://colfa2.utsa.edu/organization/culture&agriculture/

Journal of the Community Development Society. Community Development Society, 17 S. High St., Suite 200, Columbus, OH 43215; http://comm-dev.org/

Rural Society. Centre for Rural Social Research at Charles Sturt University, School of Humanities and Social Sciences, Building 26, Wagga Wagga, 2678, NSW Australia; http://www.csu.edu.au/research/crsr/

Rural Sociology. Rural Sociological Society, 104 Gentry

Hall, University of Missouri, Columbia, MO 65211-7040; http://ruralsociology.org

WI Home and Country. Women's Institute, 104 New King's Road, London SW6 4LY, UK; http://www.csu.edu.au

Organizations

Agricultural History Society; http://www.iastate.edu/~history_info/aghissoc.htm

British Agricultural History Society (BAHS), Department of History, University of Exeter, Amory Building, Rennes Drive, Exeter EX4 4RJ, UK; http://www.bahs.org.uk

European Society for Rural Sociology, Centre for Rural Economy, Agriculture Building, University of Newcastle Upon Tyne, NE1 7RU, UK; http://www.esrs.hu

International Rural Sociology Association (IRSA); http://www.irsa-world.org

Orton Family Foundation, 128 Merchants Row, 2nd Floor, Rutland, VT 05701; www.orton.org

Rural School and Community Trust, 1825 K Street NW, Suite 703, Washington, DC 20006; www.ruralchallengepolicy.org

Rural Sociological Society, 104 Gentry Hall, University of Missouri, Columbia, MO 65211-7040; www.ruralsociology.org

SMALL TOWNS AND VILLAGE LIFE

According to Alexander Thomas, author of the *Encyclopedia of Community*'entry on "Small Towns," "There are more small towns in industrialized countries than there are cities, [but] the proportion of small-town residents is normally quite low when compared to those who live in metropolitan areas due to the relative populations of both types of settlements." Small towns are often stereotyped, either as idyllic locations that avoid the corruption of the big cities or as stagnant communities that fear change and the encroachment of the modern world. The following publications and organizations examine the role of the small town in the modern world.

Encyclopedia Entries

Agrarian Communities
Agrarian Myth
Appendix 3—Community in Popular Culture
Ecovillages
English Parishes
Main Street
Small Towns
Villages

Books

Bell, M. M. (1994). *Childerley: Nature and morality in a country village.* Chicago: University of Chicago Press.

Jackson, K. T. (1985). *Crabgrass frontier: The suburbanization of the United States.* New York: Oxford University Press.

Jones, A. (2002). *A thousand years of the English parish.* London: Weidenfeld Nicolson.

Kunstler, J. H. (1994). *The geography of nowhere.* New York: Touchstone.

Lewis, S. (1961). *Main street.* New York: New American Library.

Lingeman, R. R. (1980). *Small town America: A narrative history, 1620–the present.* New York: Putnam.

Lyson, T. A., & Falk, W. W. (Eds.). (1993). *Forgotten places: Uneven development in rural America.* Lawrence: University of Kansas Press.

McNeill, J. R., & McNeill, W. H. (2003). *The human web: A bird's eye view of world history.* New York: W. W. Norton.

Stull, D., Broadway, M. J., & Griffith, D. (Eds.). (1995). *Any way you cut it: Meat-processing and small-town America.* Lawrence: University Press of Kansas.

Toennies, F. (1957). *Community and society* (C. P. Loomis, Trans.). New York: Harper Torchbooks. (Original work published 1887)

United States Census Bureau. (2000). *County and city databook.* Washington, DC: Author.

Vidich, A. J., & Bensman, J. (1968). *Small town in mass society: Class, power, and religion in a rural community* (Rev. ed.). Princeton, NJ: Princeton University Press.

Young, F. W. (1999). *Small towns in multilevel society.* New York: University Press of America.

Journals

New Village. Architects/Designers/Planners for Social Responsibility (ADPSR), 690 5th Street, Suite 206, San Francisco, CA 94107; http://www.newvillage.net

Small Town. Small Towns Institute. No longer published, but available in many library collections.

Organizations

American Planning Association, Rural and Small Town Planning Association, 1776 Massachusetts Ave., NW, Washington, DC 20036-1904; http://aalto.arch.ksu.edu/jwkplan/star/starapa.htm

National Association of Towns and Townships, 444 N. Capitol Street, NW, Suite 397, Washington, DC 20001-1202; http://www.natat.org/natat/

National Trust for Historic Preservation, 1785 Massachusetts Ave., NW, Washington, DC 20036; http://www.nthp.org

Orton Family Foundation: Community Mapping Program, Orton Family Foundation, 128 Merchants Row, 2nd Floor, Rutland, VT 05701; http://www.communitymap.org

Rural & Small Town Programme, Mount Allison University, 144 Main Street, Sackville, NB, E4L 1A7, Canada; http://www.mta.ca/rstp/rstpmain.html

SOCIAL AND PUBLIC LIFE

As the British poet John Donne wrote in 1624, "No man is an island . . . every man is a piece of the continent, a part of the main" (*Devotions upon Emergent Occasions,* "Meditation 17"). From gathering with friends to watch a baseball game to waiting in line with strangers at a fast-food restaurant, from meeting coworkers at the local bar to offering help to a stranded motorist, interactions between people form a large component of human existence. Although new technologies and shifts in lifestyle are changing the ways in which people interact, such connections are still a vital part of a person's self-identity and understanding of the rest of the world. Conviviality is an aspect of life that is understood in every culture, and promoted today as something that builds social capital. The Italy-based Slow Food Movement has, in fact, made conviviality a core part of its mission. The following are lists of publications and organizations that focus on information public life and the personal bonds that form the basis of community.

Encyclopedia Entries

Age Integration
Age Stratification and the Elderly
Agrarian Myth
Alienation
Altruism
Bars and Pubs
Caste
Civil Society
Class, Social
Community Psychology
Conflict Resolution
Conformity
Crowds
Cybercafes
Cyberdating
Elderly in Communities
Festivals
Food
Friendship
Gated Communities
Gender Roles
Guanxi
Hate
Healing
Hierarchy of Needs
Homelessness
Household Structure
Intentional Communities and Daily Life
Internet, Domestic Life and
Kinship
Loneliness
Love
Marriage
Men's Groups
Neighborhoods
Neighboring
Peer Groups
Privacy
Public Harassment
Recreation
Secret Societies
Small World Phenomenon
Social Distance
Social Network Analysis
Sport
Street Life
Theme Parks
Third Places
Ties, Weak and Strong

Books and Web Sites

Allport, G. W. (1954). *The nature of prejudice*. Reading, MA: Addison-Wesley.

Baumohl, J. (1996). *Homelessness in America*. Phoenix, AZ: Oryx.

Bellah, R. (1985). *Habits of the heart.* Berkeley and Los Angeles: University of California Press.

Béteille, A. (1965). *Caste, class, and power: Changing patterns of stratification in a Tanjore village*. Berkeley: University of California Press.

Birren, J. E. (Ed.). (1996). *Encyclopedia of gerontology.* New York: Academic Press.

Blauner, R. (1964). *Alienation and freedom: The factory worker and his industry.* Chicago: University of Chicago Press.

Bogardus, E. S. (1959). *Social distance.* Yellow Springs, OH: Antioch.

Coakley, J. (2001). *Sport and society: Issues and controversies. New York:* McGraw-Hill.

Deutsch, M., & Coleman, P. T. (Eds.). (2000). *The handbook of conflict resolution: Theory and practice.* San Francisco: Jossey-Bass.

Duffy, K. G., & Wong, F. Y. (2000). *Community psychology.* Boston: Allyn & Bacon.

Durkheim, É. (1951). *Suicide: A study in sociology.* Glencoe, IL: Free Press. (Original work published 1897)

Erikson, E. H. (1980). *Identity and the life cycle.* New York: Norton.

Etzioni, A. (1993). *The spirit of community.* New York: Crown.

Fehr, B. (1996). *Friendship processes.* Thousand Oaks, CA: Sage.

Frayser, S. G. (1985). *Varieties of sexual experience.* New Haven, CT: HRAF.

Goffman, E. (1959). *The presentation of self in everyday life.* New York: Anchor.

Goffman, E. (1971). *Relations in public.* New York: Basic Books.

Goody, J. (1982). *Cooking, cuisine, and class: A study in comparative sociology.* Cambridge, UK: Cambridge University Press.

Huizinga, J. (1950). *Homo ludens.* New York: Roy.

International Network for Social Network Analysis: http://www.sfu.ca/~insna

Jacobs, J. (1961). *The death and life of great American cities.* New York: Vintage.

Jacobs, J. (1974). *Fun City: An ethnographic study of a retirement community.* New York: Holt, Rinehart & Winston.

Kirp, D.L. (2000). *Almost home: America's love-hate relationship with community.* Princeton, NJ: Princeton University Press.

Le Bon, G. (1895). *Psychologie des foules* [Psychology of crowds]. Paris: Felix, Alcan.

Lofland, L. H. (1998). *The public realm.* Hawthorne, NY: Aldine de Gruyter.

Manning, F. E. (1983). *The celebration of society: Perspectives on contemporary cultural performance.* Bowling Green, OH: Bowling Green University Popular Press.

Maslow, A. (1970). *Motivation and personality* (2nd ed.). New York: Harper & Row.

Massey, D. (1994). *Space, place, and gender.* Minneapolis: University of Minnesota Press.

Moody, H. R. (2002). *Aging: Concepts and controversies* (4th ed.). Thousand Oaks, CA: Pine Forge.

Murdock, G. P. (1949). *Social structure.* New York: Macmillan.

Oldenburg, R. (1999). *The great good place* (3d ed.). New York: Marlowe.

Oldenburg, R. (Ed.). (2001). *Celebrating the third place: Inspiring stories about the "great good places" at the heart of our communities.* New York: Marlowe.

Pasternak, B. (1976). *Introduction to kinship and social organization.* Englewood Cliffs, NJ: Prentice Hall.

Putnam, R. D. (2000). *Bowling alone: The collapse and revival of American community.* New York: Simon & Schuster.

Redfield, R. (1955). *The little community.* Chicago: University of Chicago Press.

Riesman, D., with Glazer, N., & Denny, R. (1961). *The lonely crowd.* New Haven, CT: Yale University Press. (Original work published 1950)

Rushton, J. P. (1980). *Altruism, socialization, and society.* Englewood Cliffs, NJ: Prentice Hall.

Schweizer, T., & White, D. (Eds.). (1998). *Kinship, networks and exchange.* New York: Cambridge University Press.

Scott, J. (2000). *Social network analysis: A handbook.* London: Sage.

Suttles, G. D. (1972). *The social construction of communities.* Chicago: University of Chicago Press.

Tönnies, F. (1963). *Community and society* (C. F. Loomis, Ed.). New York: Harper Torchbook Editions.

Veblen, T. (1967). *The theory of the leisure class.* New York: Vintage. (Original work published 1899)

Visser, M. (1991). *The rituals of dinner: The origins, evolution, eccentricities, and meaning of table manners.* New York: Grove.

Wellman, B., & Haythornthwaite, C. (2002). *The Internet in everyday life.* Oxford, UK: Basil Blackwell.

Willmott, P. (1987). *Friendship, networks and social support.* London: Policy Studies Institute.

Wirth, L. (1938). Urbanism as a way of life. *American Journal of Sociology, 44*(1), 1–24.

Zorbaugh, H. W. (1929). *Gold Coast and slum: A sociological study of Chicago's Near North Side.* Chicago: University of Chicago Press.

Journals

American Journal of Sociology. 5835 S. Kimbark Avenue, Chicago, IL 60637-1684; http://www.journals.uchicago.edu/AJS

British Journal of Sociology. London School of Economics and Political Science, Houghton Street, London, WC2A 2AE, UK; http://www.lse.ac.uk/serials/Bjs/

The Gerontologist. Gerontological Society of America, 1030 15th Street NW, Washington, DC 20005-1503; http://gerontologist.gerontologyjournals.org

Human Organization. Society for Applied Anthropology, P.O. Box 2436, Oklahoma City, OK 73101-2436; http://www.sfaa.net/ho

Human Relations. Tavistock Institute, in association with Sage, 6 Bonhill Street, London, EC2A 4PU, UK; http://www.tavinstitute.org/hrindex.htm

Journal of Community Psychology; John Wiley & Sons; 111 River Street, Hoboken, NJ 07030; http://www.interscience.wiley.com/jpages/0090-4392

Journal of Gerontology. Gerontological Society of America, 1030 15th Street NW, Suite 250, Washington, DC 20005; http://www.gerontologyjournals.org/

Journal of Health and Social Behavior. American Sociological Association, 1307 New York Avenue, NW, Suite 700, Washington, DC 20005-4701; http://www.asanet.org/

Journal of Marriage and the Family. National Council on Family Relations, 3989 Central Ave., NE, #550, Minneapolis, MN 55421; http://www.ncfr.org/authors/index.htm

Journal of Social and Personal Relationships. Sage Publications, 6 Bonhill Street, London, EC2A 4PU, UK; www.sagepub.co.uk/journals/details/j0036.html

Law and Society Review. Law Society Association, 205 Hampshire House, University of Massachusetts, 131 County Circle, Amherst, MA 01003-9257; http://www.lawandsociety.org/review.htm

Research on Aging. Sage Publications, 6 Bonhill Street, London, EC2A 4PU, UK; www.sagepub.co.uk/journals/details/j0142.html

Signs. University of Chicago, 1427 E. 60th Street, Chicago, IL 60637-2954; http://www.journals.uchicago.edu/Signs/journal/

Social Forces: International Journal of Social Research. Social Forces, 168 Hamilton Hall, University of North Carolina, Chapel Hill, NC 27599-3210; www.irss.unc.edu/sf/

Social Issues. Society for the Psychological Study of Social Issues, 1901 Pennsylvania Avenue NW, Suite 901, Washington, DC 20006-3405; http://www.spssi.org/index.html

Social Problems. Society for the Study of Social Problems, 901 McClung Tower, University of Tennessee, Knoxville, TN 37996-0490; http://www.sssp1.org/index.cfm?tsmi=26

Organizations

American Anthropological Association, 4350 North Fairfax Drive, Suite 640, Arlington, VA 22203-1620; www.aaanet.org

American Sociological Association, 1307 New York Avenue, NW, Suite 700, Washington, DC 20005; www.asanet.org

National Amusement Park Historical Association; www.napha.org

Slow Food Movement, Via Mendicità 8; 12042 Bra (CN) Italy; 434 Broadway, New York, NY 10013; http://www.slowfood.com

SOCIAL CAPITAL

"At the most general level," writes Michael Woolcock, author of the *Encyclopedia of Community*'s entry "Social Capital," the term "refers to the quality and quantity of our social connections, as captured in the popular aphorism 'It's not what you know, it's who you know.' " The concept has attracted a lot of attention (and criticism) recently, sparked largely by the publication of Robert Putnam's *Bowling Alone*. The following publications and organizations take a look at the debate over social capital and its effects on communities.

Encyclopedia Entries

Altruism
Citizen Participation and Training
Civic Agriculture
Civic Innovation
Civic Life
Civil Society
Collective Efficacy
Community Development Corporations
Community Garden Movement
Community in Disaster
Good Society
Network Communities
Nonprofit Organizations
Progressive Era
Religion and Civil Society
Service Learning
Social Capital
Social Capital, Benefits of
Social Capital, Downside of
Social Capital, Impact in Wealthy and Poor Communities
Social Capital, Trends in
Social Capital, Types of
Social Capital and Economic Development
Social Capital and Human Capital
Social Capital and Media
Social Capital in the Workplace
Social Network Analysis
Ties, Weak and Strong
Trust
Voluntary Associations
Volunteerism
World War II
Youth Groups

Books and Web Sites

Ahn, T. K., & Ostrom, E. (Eds.). (in press). *Foundations of social capital: A reader.* Cheltenham, UK: Edward Elgar.

Bellah, R., Madsen, R., Sullivan, W. M., Swidler, A., & Tipton, S. M. (1996). *Habits of the heart: Individualism and commitment in American life.* Berkeley and Los Angeles: University of California Press.

Better together, the report of the Saguaro Seminar: Civic Engagement in America (Reprint version). (2002): http://www.bettertogether.org/pdfs/bt_1_29.pdf, http://www.bettertogether.org/pdfs/bt_30_87.pdf, and http://www.bettertogether.org/pdfs/bt_88_100.pdf

Briggs, X. de Souza. (1997, Summer). Social capital and the cities: Advice to change agents. *National Civic Review, 86*(2), 111–118.

DeFilippis, J. (2001). The myth of social capital in community development. *Housing Policy Debate, 11*(4): http://www.fanniemaefoundation.org/programs/hpd/v12i4-defilippis.shtml

Edwards, B., Foley, M., & Diani, M. (Eds.). (2001). *Beyond Tocqueville: Civil society and the social capital debate in comparative perspective.* Hanover, NH: University Press of New England.

Gladwell, M. (1999, January 11). Six degrees of Lois Weisberg. *New Yorker*: http://www.gladwell.com/1999/1999_01_11_a_weisberg.htm

Lemann, N. (1996, April). Kicking in groups. *Atlantic Monthly,* pp. 22–24: http://www.theatlantic.com/issues/96apr/kicking/kicking.htm

Nisbet, R. A. (1969). *The quest for community.* London: Oxford University Press.

Portes, A., & Landolt, P. (1996, May–June). The downside of social capital. *The American Prospect, 26*, 18–21, 94: http://epn.org/prospect/26/26-cnt2.html

Putnam, R. D. (2000). *Bowling alone: The collapse and revival of American community.* New York: Simon & Schuster. See also: http://www.bowlingalone.com

Putnam, R. D. (2002). *Democracies in flux.* New York: Oxford University Press.

Ridley, M. (1997). *The origins of virtue: Human instincts and the evolution of cooperation.* New York: Penguin.

Skocpol, T. (2003). *Diminished democracy: From membership to management in American life.* Norman: University of Oklahoma Press.

Social Capital Community Benchmark Survey (SCCBS): http://www.ksg.harvard.edu/saguaro/communitysurvey

Sobel, J. (2002, March). Can we trust social capital? *Journal of Economic Literature, 40,* 139–154.

Wuthnow, R. (1998). *Loose connections: Joining together in America's fragmented communities.* Cambridge, MA: Harvard University Press.

Organizations

Civic Practices Network, Center for Human Resources, Heller School for Advanced Studies in Social Welfare, Brandeis University, 60 Turner Street, Waltham, MA 02154 http://www.cpn.org

Communitarian Network, 2130 H Street NW, Suite 703, Washington, DC 20052; http://www.gwu.edu/~ccps

Cooperative State Research, Education, and Extension Service (U.S. Department of Agriculture), 1400 Independence Avenue SW, Stop 2201, Washington, DC 20250-2201; http://www.reeusda.gov

National Civic League, 1445 Market Street, Denver, CO 80202; http://www.ncl.org

Saguro Seminar, Taubman Center 364, Kennedy School of Government, Harvard University, 79 JFK Street, Cambridge, MA 02138; http://www.ksg.harvard.edu/saguaro/

World Bank—Social Capital for Development, 1818 H Street, Northwest, Washington, DC 20433; http://www.worldbank.org

URBAN AND SUBURBAN STUDIES

The world's urban population saw a dramatic increase during the twentieth century as many towns grew into cities. With the growth of cities, new and unique issues and problems developed. The fields of urban and suburban studies are concerned with the rise of cities and suburbs, phenomena that are observable in countries around the world, as well as the lifestyles of their inhabitants. The following publications and organizations are devoted to studying the problems faced by urban populations, as well as the strategies that have evolved or have been implemented to deal with these issues.

Encyclopedia Entries

African Americans in Suburbia
Bedroom Communities
Chinatowns
Cities
Cities, Inner
Cities, Medieval
Columbia, Maryland
Edge Cities
Garden Cities
Geddes, Patrick
Gentrification
Gentrification, Stalled
Ghettos
Global Cities
Greenbelt Towns
Greenwich Village
Harlem
Jacobs, Jane
Las Vegas
Left Bank
Levittown
Little Italies
Lower East Side
Mumford, Lewis

New Towns
New Urbanism
Radburn, New Jersey
Sprawl
Suburbanization
Suburbia
Transportation, Urban
Urban Homesteading
Urban Renewal
Urbanism
Urbanization

Books and Web Sites

Ambrose, P. (1994). *Urban process and power.* London: Routledge.

Baumgartner, M. P. (1988). *The moral order of a suburb.* New York: Oxford University Press.

Bellah, R., Madsen, R., Sullivan, W., Swidler, A., & Tipton, S. (1985). *Habits of the heart: Individualism and commitment in American life.* New York: Harper & Row.

Bloom, N. (2001). *Suburban alchemy: 1960s new towns and the transformation of the American dream.* Columbus: Ohio University Press.

Caro, R. (1975). *The power broker.* New York: Random House.

Castells, M. (1989). *The informational city.* Oxford, UK: Basil Blackwell.

Childe, V. G. (1996). The urban revolution. In R. T. LeGates & F. Stout (Eds.), *The city reader* (pp. 20–30). London: Routledge. (Original work published 1951)

Cohen, M. A., Ruble, B. A., Tulchin, J. S., & Garland, A. M. (Eds.). (1996). *Preparing for the urban future: Global pressures and local forces.* Washington, DC: Woodrow Wilson Center Press.

Dahl, R. A. (1961). *Who governs? Democracy and power in an American city.* New Haven, CT: Yale University Press.

Davis, K. (1965, September). The urbanization of the human population. *Scientific American, 212*(3), 41.

Eade, J., & Mele, C. (2002). *Understanding the city: Contemporary and future perspectives.* Oxford, UK: Basil Blackwell.

Fishman, R. (1987). *Bourgeois utopias: The rise and fall of suburbia.* New York: Basic Books.

Frug, G. (1999). *City making: Building community without building walls.* Princeton, NJ: Princeton University Press.

Gans, H. J. (1962). *The urban villagers: Group and class in the life of Italian-Americans.* New York: Free Press.

Gans, H. J. (1967). *The Levittowners.* New York: Vintage.

Garreau, J. (1991). *Edge City: Life on the new frontier.* New York: Doubleday.

Geddes, P. (1915). *Cities in evolution: An introduction to the town planning movement and to the study of civics.* London: Williams and Norgate.

Gillham, O. (2002). *The limitless city: A primer on the urban sprawl debate.* Washington, DC: Island Press.

Howard, E. (1945). *Garden cities for tomorrow.* London: Faber and Faber. (Original work published 1898 by Swann Sonnenschein under the title *To-morrow: A peaceful path to real reform.*)

Index to Current Urban Documents Online: http://greenwood.scbbs.com/_icud/icud.jsp

Jackson, K. T. (1987). *Crabgrass frontier: The suburbanization of the United States.* New York: Oxford University Press.

Jacobs, J. (1992). *The death and life of great American cities.* New York: Vintage. (Original work published 1961)

Katz, P. (1993). *The new urbanism: Toward an architecture of community.* New York: McGraw-Hill.

Kelly, B. M. (1993). *Expanding the American dream: Building and rebuilding Levittown.* Albany: State University of New York Press.

Langdon, P. (1994). *A better place to live: Reshaping the American surburb,* Amherst: University of Massachusetts Press.

Marcuse, P., & van Kempen, R. (Eds.). (1999). *Globalizing cities: A new spatial order?* Oxford, UK: Basil Blackwell.

Mollenkopf, J. H. (1983). *The contested city.* Princeton, NJ: Princeton University Press.

Mumford, L. (1961). *The city in history.* New York: Harcourt, Brace & World.

National Commission on Urban Problems. (1969). *Building the American city.* New York: Praeger.

Oliver, J. E. (2001). *Democracy in suburbia.* Princeton, NJ: Princeton University Press.

Orum, A. M., & Chen, X. (2003). *The world of cities: Comparative and historical perspectives on places.* Malden, MA: Blackwell.

Pirenne, H. (1956). *Medieval cities: Their origins and the revival of trade.* (F. D. Halsey, Trans.). Garden City, NY: Doubleday. (Original work published 1925)

Popenoe, D. (1977). *The suburban environment: Sweden and the United States.* Chicago: University of Chicago Press.

Salamon, S. (2003). *Newcomers to old towns: Suburbanization of the Heartland.* Chicago: University of Chicago Press.

Sassen, S. (2001). *The global city: New York, London, Tokyo.* Princeton, NJ: Princeton University Press.

Schaffer, D. (1982). *Garden cities for America: The Radburn experience.* Philadelphia, PA: Temple University Press.

Sjoberg, G. (1965). *The preindustrial city, past and present.* New York: Free Press.

Suarez, R. (1999). *The old neighborhood: What we lost in the great suburban migration, 1966–1999.* New York: Free Press.

Tilly, C., & Blockmans, W. P. (Eds.). (1994). *Cities and the rise of states in Europe, A.D. 1000 to 1800.* Boulder, CO: Westview.

United Nations Centre for Human Settlements, Habitat I. (1996). *An urbanising world: Global report on human settlements*. New York: Oxford University Press.

Walmsley, D. J. (1988). *Urban living*. Harlow, UK: Longman Scientific & Technical.

Wilson, J. Q. (Ed.). (1966). *Urban renewal: The record and the controversy.* Cambridge, MA: MIT Press.

Wirth, L. (1998). *The ghetto*. New Brunswick, NJ: Transaction. (Original work published 1928)

Zorbaugh, H. (1929). *The Gold Coast and the slum.* Chicago: University of Chicago Press.

Zukin, S. (1991). *Landscapes of power: From Detroit to Disney World.* Berkeley and Los Angeles: University of California Press.

Journals

African Urban Quarterly. African and Afro-American Studies Department, State University of New York, Albany, 1400 Washington Avenue, Albany, NY 12222

American City and County. PRIMEDIA Business Magazines and Media, Inc., 2104 Harvell Circle, Bellevue, NE 68005; http://www.americancityandcounty.com/

American Demographics. American Demographics, Inc., P.O. Box 68, Ithaca, NY 14851

American Review of Public Administration. Sage Publications, 6 Bonhill Street, London, EC2A 4PU, UK; http://www.sagepub.co.uk/journals/details/j0212.html

Annals of the Association of American Geographers. Association of American Geographers, 1710 Sixteenth Street NW, Washington, DC 20009-3198; http://www.aag.org/Annals/intro.htm

Berkeley Planning Journal. University of California, Berkeley, CA 94720; http://dcrp.ced.berkeley.edu/bpj/

Building Journal. Building.com.hk. Hong Kong; http://www.building.com.hk/bjhk/bjindex.html

Bulletin of Science, Technology and Society. Sage Publications, 6 Bonhill Street, London, EC2A 4PU, UK; http://www.sagepub.co.uk/journals/details/j0246.html

Canadian Journal of Urban Research. University of Winnipeg, 346 Portage Avenue, Winnipeg, Manitoba, R3B 2E9, Canada; http://www.uwinnipeg.ca/%7Eius/cdn_journal.htm

Cities: The International Journal of Urban Policy and Planning. Elsevier, 360 Park Avenue South, New York, NY 10010-1710; http://www.elsevier.com/inca/publications/store/3/0/3/9/6/

Cityscape : A Journal of Policy Development and Research. U.S. Department of Housing and Urban Development (HUD), P.O. Box 23268, Washington, DC 20026-3268; http://www.huduser.org/periodicals/cityscape.html

Education and Urban Society. Sage Publications, 6 Bonhill Street, London, EC2A 4PU, UK; http://www.sagepub.co.uk/journals/details/j0134.html

Environment and Planning A: International Journal of Urban and Regional Research. Pion Ltd., 207 Brondesbury Park, London NW2 5JN UK; http://www.envplan.com/epa/epa_current.html

Environment and Planning B: Planning and Design. Pion Ltd., 207 Brondesbury Park, London, NW2 5JN, UK; http://www.envplan.com/epb/epb_current.html

Environment and Planning C: Government and Policy. Pion Ltd., 207 Brondesbury Park, London, NW2 5JN, UK; http://www.envplan.com/epc/epc_current.html

Environment and Planning D: Society and Space. Pion Ltd., 207 Brondesbury Park, London, NW2 5JN, UK; http://www.envplan.com/epd/epd_current.html

Environment and Urbanization Pages. International Institute for Environment and Development, 3 Endsleigh Street, London, WC1H 0DD, UK; http://www.iied.org/human/eandu/eandu_details.html

European Urban and Regional Studies. Sage Publications, 6 Bonhill Street, London, EC2A 4PU, UK; http://www.sagepub.co.uk/journals/details/j0133.html

Fordham Urban Law Journal. Fordham University, 140 West 62nd Street, New York, NY 10023; http://law.fordham.edu/publications/index.ihtml?pubid=400

Habitat International. Elsevier. 360 Park Avenue South, New York, NY 10010-1710; http://www.elsevier.com/locate/issn/01973975

Harvard Design Magazine. Harvard University, 48 Quincy Street, Cambridge, MA 02138; http://www.gsd.harvard.edu/research/publications/hdm/

Harvard Journal of Law and Public Policy. Harvard University, 1541 Massachusetts Avenue, Cambridge, MA 02138; http://www.law.harvard.edu/studorgs/jlpp/

The Housing Journal. New York City Housing Authority, 250 Broadway, New York, NY 10007; http://www.nyc.gov/html/nycha/html/journal.html

Housing Policy Debate. Fannie Mae Foundation, 4000 Wisconsin Avenue, Northwest, North Tower, Suite One, Washington, DC 20016-2804; http://www.fanniemaefoundation.org/programs/hpd.shtml

International Journal of Urban and Regional Research. Blackwell Publishers, 108 Cowley Road, Oxford OX4 1JF, UK; http://www.blackwellpublishing.com/journals/IJURR/descript.htm

Journal of Housing and Community Development. The National Association of Housing and Redevelopment Officials (NAHRO), 630 Eye Street, Northwest, Washington DC 20001; http://www.nahro.org/publications/johcd.html

Journal of Housing Economics. Elsevier, 360 Park Avenue South, New York, NY 10010-1710; http://www.elsevier.com/locate/issn/1051-1377

Journal of Planning Education and Research. Sage Publications, 6 Bonhill Street, London, EC2A 4PU, UK; http://www.sagepub.co.uk/journals/details/j0371.html

Journal of Planning History. Sage Publications, 6 Bonhill Street, London, EC2A 4PU, UK; http://www.sagepub.co.uk/journals/details/j0481.html

Journal of Planning Literature. Sage Publications, 6 Bonhill Street, London, EC2A 4PU, UK; http://www.sagepub.co.uk/journals/details/j0129.html

Journal of Public Policy. Cambridge University Press, 40 West 20th Street, New York, NY 10011-4211; http://uk.cambridge.org/journals/

Journal of Social Issues. Society for the Psychological Study of Social Issues (SPSSI), in association with Blackwell Publishing, Osney Mead, Oxford, OX2 OEL, UK; http://www.spssi.org/jsi.html

Journal of the American Planning Association. The American Planning Association. Portland State University, P.O. Box 751, Portland, OR 97207-0751; http://www.japa.pdx.edu/

Journal of Urban Affairs. Urban Affairs Association, College of Public Service, St. Louis University, McGannon Hall, Suite 232, 3750 Lindell Boulevard, St. Louis, MO 63108-3342; http://www.udel.edu/uaa/journal.html

Journal of Urban Economics. Elsevier, 360 Park Avenue South, New York, NY 10010-1710; http://www.elsevier.com/locate/issn/0094-1190

Journal of Urban History. Sage Publications, 6 Bonhill Street, London, EC2A 4PU, UK; http://www.sagepub.co.uk/journals/details/j0187.html

Nation's Cities Weekly. National League of Cities, 1301 Pennsylvania Avenue Northwest, Suite 550, Washington, DC 20004; http://www.nlc.org/nlc_org/site/newsroom/nations_cities_weekly/index.cfm

New Urban News. P.O. Box 6515, Ithaca, NY 14851; http://www.newurbannews.com

Planning. American Planning Association, 122 South Michigan Avenue, Suite 1600, Chicago, IL 60603; http://www.planning.org/planning/nonmember/default.htm

Planning Commissioners Journal. Champlain Planning Press, Inc., P.O. Box 4295, Burlington, VT 05406; http://www.plannersweb.com/

Planning Perspectives. Routledge, Taylor & Francis Group, 11 New Fetter Lane, London, EC4P 4EE, UK; http://www.tandf.co.uk/journals/titles/02665433.html

Public Administration. Oxford University Press, Great Clarendon Street, Oxford, OX2 6DP, UK; http://jpart.oupjournals.org/

Public Budgeting and Finance. Blackwell Publishers, 108 Cowley Road, Oxford, OX4 1JF, UK; http://www.blackwellpublishing.com/journals/PBAF/descript.htm

Public Finance, Decentralization and Poverty Reduction (PFD&PR) Newsletter. World Bank Group, MSN J4-403, 1818 H Street, Northwest, Washington, DC 20433; http://www.worldbank.org/wbi/publicfinance/newsletter/archive.html

Public Finance Review. Sage Publications, 6 Bonhill Street, London, EC2A 4PU, UK; http://www.sagepub.co.uk/journals/details/j0055.html

Public Roads Magazine. Turner-Fairbank Highway Research Center, 6300 Georgetown Pike, McLean, VA 22101; http://www.tfhrc.gov/pubrds/pubrds.htm

Radical Urban Theory. http://www.rut.com/

Real Estate Economics. American Real Estate and Urban Economics Association (AREUEA), P.O. Box 1148, Portage, MI 49081-1148; http://www.areuea.org/publications/ree/

Review of Public Personnel Administration. Sage Publications, 6 Bonhill Street, London, EC2A 4PU, UK; http://www.sagepub.co.uk/journals/details/j0421.html

Sage Urban Studies Abstracts. Sage Publications, 6 Bonhill Street, London, EC2A 4PU, UK; http://www.sagepub.co.uk/journals/details/j0105.html

Social Forces. University of North Carolina, 168 Hamilton Hall, Chapel Hill, NC 27599-3210; http://www.irss.unc.edu/sf/

Social Problems. Society for the Study of Social Problems, in association with the University of California Press, 2120 Berkeley Way, Berkeley, CA 94720; http://www.sssp1.org/index.cfm?tsmi=26

Soziale Welt. Institut für Soziologie, Universität München, Konradstr. 6, 80801 München, Germany; http://www.lrz-muenchen.de/~uf32101/www/sozialwe.htm

Urban Affairs Review. Sage Publications, 6 Bonhill Street, London, EC2A 4PU, UK; http://www.sagepub.co.uk/journals/details/j0095.html

Urban Design Quarterly. Urban Design Group, 70 Cowcross Street, London, EC1M 6DG, UK; http://www.udg.org.uk/UDQ_inter.html

Urban Education. Sage Publications, 6 Bonhill Street, London, EC2A 4PU, UK; http://www.sagepub.co.uk/journals/details/j0109.html

Urban Geography. Bellwether Publishing, Ltd. 8640 Guilford Road, Suite 200, Columbia, MD 21046-2612; http://www.bellpub.com/ug/index.html

Urban History Review. Department of History, Université de Montréal, 3150 rue Jean-Brillant, Pavillon Lionel Groulx, Montreal, QC; http://www.fas.umontreal.ca/HST/urbanhistory/urbanenglish.html

Urban Studies. University of Glasgow, Adam Smith Building, Glasgow, G12 8RT, Scotland; http://www.gla.ac.uk/urbanstudiesjournal/

Organizations

American Planning Association, 122 S. Michigan Ave., Suite 1600, Chicago, IL 60603; http://www.planning.org/

American Real Estate and Urban Economics Association, P.O. Box 1148, Portage, MI 49081-1148; http://www.areuea.org

Asian Urban Research Association (AURA), Department of

Geography & Planning, University of Akron, Akron, OH 44325-5005; http://www3.uakron.edu/geography/resources/aurban.htm

British Urban Regeneration Association (BURA), 63-66 Hatton Garden, London, EC1N 8LE, UK; http://www.bura.org.uk

Brookings Institution: Center on Urban and Metropolitan Policy, 1775 Massachusetts Ave NW, Washington, DC 20036; http://www.brookings.org/es/urban/urban.htm

Center for Urban Research Policy (CUPR), Edward J. Bloustein School of Planning and Public Policy, Rutgers, State University of New Jersey, 33 Livingston Avenue, Civic Square, Suite 400, New Brunswick, NJ 08901-1982; http://policy.rutgers.edu/cupr/

Community & Urban Sociology Section of the American Sociology Association; http://www.commurb.org

International Network for Urban Development, Nassau Dillenburgstraat, 44 NL-2596 AE, The Hague, The Netherlands; http://www.inta-aivn.org

New Urbanism, 615 King Street, Suite 103, Alexandria, VA 22314; http://www.newurbanism.org

United States Department of Housing and Urban Development (HUD), 451 7th Street Southwest, Washington, DC 20410; http://www.hud.gov

Urban Affairs Association, University of Delaware, Newark, DE 19716; www.udel.edu/uaa/

Urban and Regional Information Systems Association, 1460 Renaissance Drive, Suite 305, Park Ridge, IL 60068; http://www.urisa.org

Urban History Association, University of Nebraska, Lincoln, NE 68588; http://www.unl.edu/uha/news.html

Urban Institute, 2100 M Street, Northwest, Washington, DC 20037; http://www.urban.org

Urban Land Institute, 1025 Thomas Jefferson Street, NW, Suite 500 West, Washington, DC 20007; http://www.uli.org

Urban Libraries Council, 1603 Orrington Avenue, Suite 1080, Evanston, IL 60201; http://www.urbanlibraries.org

VOLUNTEERISM

Volunteerism is a community activity in several different ways. First, it involves performing activities that are usually intended to benefit a community in some way. Second, as John Wilson, author of the *Encyclopedia of Community*'s entry "Volunteerism," writes: "Most volunteer work takes place in connection with, or on behalf of, an organization." This means that volunteerism is often performed by a group of like-minded people working together toward a common purpose. The following publications and organizations provide information on studying, arranging, and performing volunteer work.

Encyclopedia Entries

Altruism
Boosterism
Citizen Participation and Training
Citizenship
Community Action
Faith Communities
Neighborhood Watch
Nonprofit Organizations
Social Services
Twelve Step Groups
Voluntary Associations
Volunteerism

Books and Web Sites

Campbell, K. N., & Ellis, S. J. (1995). *The (help!) I-don't-have-enough-time guide to volunteer management.* Philadelphia: Energize.

Canada's Source for Information on Volunteering: http://www.volunteer.ca

Council on Foundations. (1996). *Measuring the value of corporate citizenship.* Washington, DC: Council on Foundations.

Devney, D. C. (1992). *The volunteer's survival manual: The only practical guide to giving your time and money.* Cambridge, MA: Practical Press.

Ellis, S. J. (1995) *The board's role in effective volunteer involvement.* Washington, DC: National Center for Nonprofit Boards.

Ellis, S. J. (1996). *The volunteer recruitment book* (2nd ed.). Philadelphia: Energize.

Fisher, J. C., & Cole, K. M. (1993). *Leadership and management of volunteer programs: A guide for volunteer administrators.* San Francisco: Jossey-Bass.

Heblad, A. (Ed.). (2002). *Encyclopedia of associations: regional, state, and local organizations* (38th ed.). Farmington Hills, MI: Gale Group.

Herman, M., & Jackson, P. (2001). *No surprises: Harmonizing risk and rewards in volunteer programs* (2nd ed.). Washington, DC: Nonprofit Risk Management Center.

Independent Sector. (1999). *Giving and volunteering in the United States.* Washington, DC: Author.

Ladd, E. C. (1999). *The Ladd report: The surprising news of an explosion of voluntary groups, activities, and charitable donations that is transforming our towns and cities.* New York: Free Press.

McCurley, S., & Lynch, R. (1996). *Volunteer management: Mobilizing all the resources of the community.* Downers Grove, IL: Heritage Arts.

O'Connell, B., & O'Connell, A. B. (1989). *Volunteers in action.* New York: Foundation Center.

Pidgeon, W. P., Jr. (1998). *The universal benefits of volun-*

teering: A practical workbook for nonprofit organizations, volunteers, and corporations. New York: John Wiley.

Pitts, E. T. (1999). *People and programs that make a difference in a multicultural society: Volunteerism in America.* Lewiston, NY: Edwin Mellen.

Troy, K. (1997). *Corporate volunteerism: How families make a difference.* New York: Conference Board.

White, B. J., & Madara, E. (1995). *The self-help sourcebook: Finding and forming mutual aid self-help groups* (5th ed.). Dublin, OH: American Self-Help Clearinghouse.

World Volunteer Web: http://www.worldvolunteerweb.org

Wroblewski, C. J. (1994) *The seven Rs of volunteer development.* Chicago: YMCA of the USA.

Periodicals

Australian Journal of Volunteering. Volunteering Australia, 11 Queens Road, Melbourne 3004, Australia; http://www.volunteeringaustralia.org/publications/journal.shtml

e-Volunteerism: Online Journal of the Volunteer Community. Energize, Inc., 5450 Wissahickon Avenue, Philadelphia, PA 19144; http://www.e-volunteerism.com

International Journal of Nonprofit and Voluntary Sector Marketing. The Centre for Voluntary Sector Management, Henley Management College, Henley-on-Thames, Oxfordshire, RG9 3AU, UK; http://www.henleymc.ac.uk/General/hmcprog.nsf/pages/cvsmjournal

Journal of Volunteer Administration. Association for Volunteer Administration. P.O. Box 32092 Richmond, VA 23294; http://www.avaintl.org/product/journal.html

Nonprofit and Voluntary Sector Quarterly. Association for Research on Nonprofit Organizations and Voluntary Action. Indiana University Center on Philanthropy, 550 W. North Street, Suite 301, Indianapolis, IN 46202; http://www.evans.washington.edu/nvsq/

Nonprofit Times. 120 Littleton Road, Suite 120, Parsippany, NJ 07054-1803; http://www.nptimes.com

Philanthropy Journal. A. J. Fletcher Foundation, P.O. Box 12800, Raleigh, NC 27605; http://www.philanthropyjournal.org

Voluntas: International Journal of Voluntary and Nonprofit Organizations. International Society for Third-Sector Research, 3400 N. Charles Street, Baltimore, MD 21218-2688; http://www.jhu.edu/~istr/

Organizations

AmeriCorps, Corporation for National and Community Service, 1201 New York Avenue, NW, Washington, DC 20525; http://www.americorps.org

Association of Junior Leagues International Inc., 132 West 31st Street, 11th Floor, New York, NY 10001-3406, http://www.ajli.org

Independent Sector, 1200 Eighteenth Street, NW, Suite 200, Washington, DC 20036; http://www.jhu.edu/~istr

International Volunteer Programs Association, 71 West 23rd Street, 17th Floor, New York, NY 10010-4102; www.volunteerinternational.org

Kiwanis International, 3636 Woodview Trace, Indianapolis, IN 46268-3196; http://www.kiwanis.org

Lions Clubs International, 300 West 22nd Street, Oak Brook, IL 60523-8842; http://www.lionsclubs.org

Peace Corps, 1111 20th Street NW, Washington, DC 20526; http://www.peacecorps.gov

Points of Light Foundation, 1400 I Street, NW, Suite 800, Washington, DC 20005; http://www.pointsoflight.org

Rotary International, One Rotary Center, 1560 Sherman Avenue, Evanston, IL 60201; http://www.rotary.org

United Nations Volunteers, Postfach 260 111, D-53153, Bonn, Germany; http://www.unv.org

United Way of America, 701 North Fairfax Street, Alexandria, VA 22314; http://www.unitedway.org

Voluntary Services Overseas, 317 Putney Bridge Road, London, SW15 2PN, UK; http://www.vso.org.uk